Law for Professionals

The *Law for Professionals* book series contains publications in all fields of the law aimed at professionals and practitioners. The book series is dedicated to publish high quality books that provide in-depth insights into the workings and the practical functioning of the law, international organizations or regional legal frameworks.

The authors contributing to the book series are experienced legal professionals and practitioners whose expertise combines theory and practice.

Can Eken

Third-Party Funding in Investment Arbitration

A New Player in the System

Springer

Can Eken
Durham Law School
Durham University
Durham, UK

ISSN 2662-141X ISSN 2662-1428 (electronic)
Law for Professionals
ISBN 978-3-031-63619-6 ISBN 978-3-031-63620-2 (eBook)
https://doi.org/10.1007/978-3-031-63620-2

This Springer imprint is published by the registered company Springer Nature Switzerland AG
The registered company address is: Gewerbestrasse 11, 6330 Cham, Switzerland

Acknowledgments

This book is based on my 4-year PhD research at the Chinese University of Hong Kong. I would like to thank Professor Julien Chaisse, for meeting me countless times, answering every question I had, for being an excellent mentor to me. I would also like to extend my appreciation to the following professors for their support and encouragement: Professors Bryan Druzin and Fernando Dias Simoes for their continuous support; Professor Stephen Hall for sharing his knowledge and experience with me, enjoyable conversations and letting me to teach in his contracts class; Professor Christopher Gane, Professor Lutz-Christian Wolff, Professor Gregory Gordon, and Mr Rudi Cohrssen for their amazing conversations we had.

I also thank Professors Bryan Mercurio, Chao Xi, Anatole Boute, Rehan Abeyratne, Benoit Mayer, Chin Leng Lim, Steven Gallagher, Jyh-An LEE, Jae Woon Lee, Michael Ramsden, Ryan Mitchell, Noam Noked, Michael Lower, Eliza Mik and all the faculty, friends, students, and everybody at the institutions I spent my time during the writing of this book including Durham University, the Chinese University of Hong Kong, Max Planck Institute in Luxembourg, and Stanford Law School.

I would love to thank Professor Jan Kleinheisterkamp from London School of Economics and Political Science for making arbitration classes interesting when I was an LLM student so that I grew further interest in arbitration. I thank Professor Deborah Hensler for her excellent guidance and for sharing her knowledge and experience in empirical research. I thank both directors of Max Planck in Luxembourg, Helena Ruiz Fabri and Burkhard Hess, for their generous comments which all made this book better and better.

I would like to thank Barrister Emma Edhem for her comments on earlier drafts of my book.

I would also like to thank my parents, my partner, family, and friends for supporting me morally and spiritually during completion of my book. Lastly, I would like to thank Manuela Schwietzer, Peter Pushpanathan, and all the editorial team of Springer.

Contents

Chapter 1
The New Phenomenon in Investment Arbitration

1.1 Introduction

International arbitration has been constantly chosen as the preferred method of resolving cross-border disputes.[1] While arbitration has such popularity as a dispute settlement mechanism, the competing reality is that international arbitration has significant costs.[2] In this respect, an "average 'all in' costs of an investment treaty arbitration are just short of $ 10 million".[3] The existing fact of excessive costs in investment law is a problem as it is "potentially prohibitive for a significant number of smaller and medium sized investors".[4] However, a new development in international arbitration is affecting this potential prohibitive effect and enables a wider group of parties to access international arbitration. This book examines this new phenomenon in international arbitration, namely, Third-Party Funding (TPF).

TPF has its own history. Indeed, TPF is not an entirely new phenomenon in the context of domestic litigation, especially in common law jurisdictions.[5] However, by contrast to TPF in domestic litigation, TPF in international arbitration has much shorter history. In this connection, it has been observed in 2013 that TPF is in its infancy period.[6] TPF is a funding mechanism in exchange for the potential return of

[1] Queen Mary University and White & Case International Arbitration Survey 2021 shows that 90% of the respondents indicate international arbitration is their preference either on a stand-alone basis (31%) or in conjunction with ADR (59%) at 5. Queen Mary University and White & Case International Arbitration Survey 2018 shows 97% of the respondents indicate international arbitration is their preference either on a stand-alone basis (48%) or in conjunction with ADR (49%) at 5.

[2] CIArb Costs of International Arbitration Survey 2011 at 13 shows the average cost of international arbitration to be approximately £1,580,000 for claimants and £1,413,000 for respondents.

[3] Hodgson et al. (2015), p. 749.

[4] Possible reform of investor-State dispute settlement (ISDS) Submission from the European Union, UNCITRAL Working Group III, Thirty-fifth session New York, 23–27 April 2018 at 11.

[5] Frignati (2016), pp. 505–522.

[6] Sahani (2013), p. 452.

C. Eken, *Third-Party Funding in Investment Arbitration*, Law for Professionals,
https://doi.org/10.1007/978-3-031-63620-2_1

the case. It is similar to contingency fee agreements but the difference is that in TPF, funders are not lawyers of the funded party. Funder gives the money to the client to proceed arbitration and if the client wins the case TPF company gets its share as the return of its investment. The important feature of TPF is that it is a non-recourse investment.[7] Even though it might seem like very simple financial assistance for parties similar to, but surely different than other types of financial assistance such as loans, insurance etc. TPF has unique features and it raises some concerns in international arbitration.

As TPF is becoming a frequent practice in international arbitration, there is an increasing number of disputes which generate discussions as for the legality and conditions attached (or, which should be attached) to TPF. One decade earlier, only a few cases discussed TPF.[8] However, case law increased dramatically in recent years. Now, there are already more than thirty cases that discussed the topic in the Investor-State Dispute Settlement (hereinafter "ISDS") regime. When we think of that, "in 2016 over 40 per cent of the current investment arbitration claims have either secured or explored TPF" how big the impact of the TPF practice and how important TPF for the proceedings can be better understood.[9] While TPF is used so extensively, its implications and effect on the procedure have become important as well. Thus, in the recent case law, arbitral tribunals discussed TPF in many aspects. The most important ones; arbitrator's jurisdiction over TPF companies, the potential conflict of interest (hereinafter "CoI") issues between arbitrators and TPF companies, disclosure of TPF agreement, security for cost (hereinafter "SfC") and allocation of costs (hereinafter "AoC").[10] There are also looming issues that have not been discussed by tribunals such as the effect of the TPF on the client-lawyer relationship and privacy. Even though tribunals discussed TPF in many aspects, the general notion for the TPF is, as stated by a tribunal in an International Centre for Settlement of Investment Disputes (hereinafter "ICSID") case, "the practice is by now so well established both within many national jurisdictions and within international investment arbitration that it offers no grounds in itself for objection to the admissibility of a request to arbitrate".[11] Thus, we can see that tribunals are accepting TPF as a well-established practice and then start discussing potential implications of TPF on proceedings.

The importance of the topic of TPF can be seen from the recent increase in the case law.[12] Moreover, the increasing discussion by academics of the topic also

---

[7] More detailed explanations regarding what TPF is and different definitions are given in Chap. 2.

[8] The first investment case referred to TPF, RosInvestCo UK Ltd. v The Russian Federation, SCC Case No V079/2005, brought before the SCC tribunal in 2005. In this case, TPF was not discussed extensively. However, since then, the case law dramatically increased and the arbitral tribunal spent more time and pages on TPF related issues in its awards.

[9] Wang (2018), p. 147.

[10] See Chap. 3 for the full list of procedural issues.

[11] Giovanni Alemanni and others v Argentine Republic, ICSID Case No ARB/07/8, Decision on Jurisdiction and Admissibility (17 November 2014) para 278.

[12] For the list of investment case law related to TPF see Chap. 3.

shows growing interest in TPF.[13] In addition to the developments in academia, some jurisdictions legalised third-party funding which helped the industry to grow. As an example, Singapore and Hong Kong passed legislations specific to TPF to legalise TPF in their jurisdictions. TPF was earlier forbidden in the two jurisdictions due to the prehistoric common law principles of maintenance and champerty.[14] Bao states that in Hong Kong "The regulation will be implemented in stages".[15] So, we can expect ongoing regulations related to TPF. This is in line with other common law jurisdictions which abolished champerty and maintenance or changed their rules related to these doctrines. Moreover, arbitral institutions started passing specific rules regarding TPF.[16] All these recent and still ongoing developments prove that the increasing attention on the topic continues and it is easy to see how TPF has been an important feature of international arbitration and the investment regime itself.

TPF in international arbitration has brought a new financial tool for parties to consider and broadened the playfield of arbitration for more companies and disputants to bring or defend their legal claims. Furthermore, in some cases without the help of funder, funded-parties would otherwise have not accessed international arbitration and defended their claims before an arbitration tribunal in the first place. Thus, the clear consequence of TPF is that for parties who do not have the financial power to bring a case such as when they are insolvent and when they do not have money, TPF enables those parties to access arbitration.[17] Thus, TPF may provide an efficient solution to a major practical problem: Access to justice, which has systematic implications. Besides, preventing parties from such help might be equal to the denial of justice for parties who would have been left out of the arbitration without the help of TPF. Therefore, before criticising or even cutting a tool available to parties in judicial mechanisms, it is important to understand its role

---

[13] ICC issued a special dossier for TPF in international arbitration in 2013. Queen Mary-ICCA Report on TPF and for many other articles written on the subject; *see* Bibliography.

[14] Hong Kong Arbitration and Mediation Legislation (Third Party Funding) (Amendment) Ordinance 2017 (Amendment Ordinance) was published in the Government Gazette on 23 June 2017 and the Code of Practice for Third-party funders came into force on February 1, 2019. Singapore Civil Law (Amendment) Act 2017 was passed in Parliament on 10 January 2017 and came into force on 1 March 2017. For an article comparing the two legislations, *see* Eken (2022).

[15] Bao (2017), p. 397. Thus, more regulations in Hong Kong in the coming years are expected.

[16] CIETAC Rules on International Investment Disputes Article 27 and SIAC Article 24, 33 and 35 bring new rules specific to TPF.

[17] Access to justice is the main justification of TPF and explains why TPF is accepted widely and easily in the first place. Access to justice for parties with the help of TPF company is expressed by many high court judgements. England and Wales Court of Appeal in Arkin v. Borchard Case at p. 38 states that *"commercial funders who provide help to those seeking access to justice which they could not otherwise afford are not deterred by the fear of disproportionate costs consequences if the litigation they are supporting does not succeed"*.Again, High Court of Australia in Campbells v Fostif case at p. 145, Judge Kirby explicitly refers to the role of funders for "access to justice". Also, in the reputable and impactful work of Lord Justice Jackson's 'Review of Civil Litigation Costs at 117, Lord Justice Jackson holds the view that TPF is beneficial and should be supported on grounds of five essential reasons, the first of which is access to justice.

to make judicial mechanisms more efficient[18] and for disputants, to provide easy access to justice.

While it is widely accepted as a financial instrument, it also attracts some concerns and critics from scholars, lawyers and judges around the world, which need to be addressed. Thus, while many works have been done by academics and non-governmental organisations,[19] government bodies,[20] and articles and increasing case law[21] available on this subject, those concerns have not been addressed properly. This shows that there is still a substantial *lacuna* to develop for TPF market and theory.[22]

The entire explanations allow us to understand that the importance of the topic is increasing and some issues are left unaddressed. Thus, in this novel and important topic, additional research is required. This research will fill those gaps left unaddressed. The empirical research is going to address the important aspect of TPF practice such as the impact of TPF on settlements. On the theoretical side, the book explains how TPF improves justice from a legal theory perspective. This requires further examination in academia. Even though ethical concerns have been raised;[23] there are not many academic works for the TPF and how TPF improves justice. More importantly, a comprehensive examination of the case law will show the situation and different views on procedural challenges associated with TPF.. After analysing the case law and available rules, all procedural challenges TPF might raise are addressed. Moreover, the book proposes a best practice guideline as its result. This guideline will be the result of the 4-year research and interactions with practitioners and knowledge acquired throughout the PhD program. It will be an original guideline, which adds more knowledge and understanding of TPF. Consequently, the book leads practitioners, potential users of the TPF agreements, and lawyers. The book overall contributes to the literature by analysing TPF in ISDS holistically, gives important data on TPF with its empirical research and creates a guideline for funders to follow. The book gives academics food for further thought.

[18] How TPF contributes to the efficiency of arbitration mechanism is explained in the following chapter.

[19] One of the most recent and important works on the subject is done by International Council for Commercial Arbitration and Queen Mary University of London together and published in April 2018, *see:* International Council for Commercial Arbitration. (2018), Report for public discussion of the ICCA-Queen Mary Task Force on Third-Party Funding in International Arbitration.

[20] "The Law Reform Commission of Hong Kong, Third Party Funding for Arbitration Sub-Committee" published a consultation paper in October 2015. The consultation paper is accessible via https://www.hkreform.gov.hk/en/publications/tpf.htm.

[21] See the Bibliography and cases in Chap. 3.

[22] Such further research suggested by many scholars. As an example, ICCA- Queen Mary report suggested further work regarding the disclosure requirement of reinsurers at 95, regarding the impact of third-party funding agreements on settlements at 249. This book examines the impact of TPF on settlements in Chap. 4, where empirical research conducted to give some answers to the impact of TPF on settlements and on other further issues.

[23] Rogers (2014); Wendel, W. Bradley, Alternative Litigation Financing and Anti-Commodification Norms, Cornell Legal Studies Research Paper No. 13–91.

In short, the book analyses the advantages and disadvantages of TPF in ISDS, case law related to the presence of TPF companies, and proposes its own suggestion to the readers. In this first part, the book gives a picture of the current status of the topic, introduce its methodology and scope of inquiry. This chapter now continues with the existing literature on TPF and then the overall structure of the book is given afrerwards.

1.2 Overview of Third-Party Funding

Examining the status quo is important to understand the current position of third-party funding, discussions and main arguments around it. Only after a clear review, the book can create a guideline for funders and contribute to the existing knowledge on the topic. This section constituted both from primary sources and secondary sources. As primary sources international agreements, legislations, rules and investment arbitration awards; and as secondary sources, a broad range of journal articles, books, book chapters, commentaries and law firm notes have been referred. To have updated knowledge, recent works have been used more often and the author avoided referring heavily to articles older than 5 years. This section covers the most recent cases, legislation and important literature written in English.

Funding disputes is an evolving topic. It started in litigation first, then spread into international arbitration. The first "Litigation funding was pioneered in the last years of the Twentieth Century in Australia by the founders of IMF Bentham".[24] And with the beginning of the Twenty-first Century, funding arbitration cases developed as a practice. In a decade, TPF became a very important part of international arbitration practice. This short history of the topic shows that it is not an old subject and requires further research.

Considering the recent case law on the subject, we can easily see the increasing number of cases in the last decade. When the first ICSID case was registered in 1972,[25] there was no such phenomenon called TPF and no one could imagine any regulations for TPF agreements or any code of practice for third-party funders, while recently ICSID paid specific attention to the issue and TPF has attracted many comments.[26] Today, according to the case law, TPF is a well-established practice.[27]

[24] Gayner Khouri (2017), p. 1035.

[25] Holiday Inns S.A. and others v. Morocco (ICSID Case No. ARB/72/1).

[26] Compendium of State and Public Comments on Proposed Amendments to the ICSID Rules has been published in ICSID website on January 18, 2019. In this Compendium, third-party funding finds a great space attracted so many attentions from many participants. As a result of these works, ICSID published new rules and it came into effect by 1 July 2022. See: https://icsid.worldbank.org/rules-regulations.

[27] Giovanni Alemanni and others v Argentine Republic, ICSID Case No ARB/07/8, Decision on Jurisdiction and Admissibility (17 November 2014) para 278. This wording has been repeated or by other tribunals as well.

However, TPF also raised many issues in different tribunals.[28] Those procedural issues are on jurisdiction and admissibility, allocation of costs, security for costs, the challenge to arbitrators, discontinuation of arbitration, disclosure of the funders, the disclosure of the terms of the TPF agreement and the impact of TPF agreement on a stay of enforcement of an ICSID award. There is no consensus on any of it. One of the book goals is to clarify those procedural issues and gives explanations on how those issues can be addressed. The book aims to bring the best practice guideline by answering all these procedural issues.

With regard to the importance of the topic, apart from the ICSID Compendium and the case law, there is also a considerable amount of literature that exists on litigation funding in academia. However, most of it covers funding cases in domestic courts in common law jurisdictions,[29] while it does not touch upon TPF in international arbitration. Thus, it leaves the literature on the subject incompleted. Sahani & Nieuweveld examine TPF in international arbitration and give clear explanations regarding the TPF market in international arbitration in different jurisdictions.[30] However, the book does not address procedural issues. Two important works examine procedural issues raised by TPF. Goeler addresses the impact of TPF in international arbitration,[31] and Honlet examines all the available case law in investment arbitration until 23 June 2015, when he completed the article.[32] However, these two works were completed a considerable time ago since many more developments occurred after the completion of both works. Hong Kong and Singapore passed legislation and there are other studies on TPF.[33] Arbitration institutions passed specific rules on TPF. SIAC and CIETAC, as examples of such institutions, have

[28] A complete list of the case law and procedural issues TPF has raised discussed in Chap. 5.

[29] As an example Rowles-Davies and Cousins (2014) is an important work on Third-party litigation funding and it presents detailed explanations on litigation funding process, mechanism, funding models High Court case law and overview of international funding market in different jurisdictions. However, the book neither examines TPF in international arbitration nor the case law regarding TPF in arbitration.

[30] Nieuwveld and Sahani (2017).

[31] von Goeler (2016).

[32] Honlet (2015), pp. 699–712. There are more articles on third-party funding: Abrams and Chen (2013), pp. 1075–1109; Painter (1995), pp. 625–697; Ahn Keon-Hyung; Ahn et al. (2013), p. 55; Alrashid et al. (2012), p. 101; Andrews (2018); Baker (2013), pp. 229–241; Barker (2012), pp. 451–524; Bertrand (2011), pp. 607–615; Bogart (2013), pp. 148–149; Burch (2016), p. 889; Cameron and Kalajdzic (2013), pp. 1–16; Chan (2015), pp. 281–322; Chen (2019), pp. 21–40; Choi (2016), p. 883; Clanchy (2016), p. 222.

[33] *See* Eken (2022); Darwazeh and Leleu (2016), pp. 125–149; Daughety and Reinganum (2014), pp. 2552–2566; De Brabandere and Lepeltak (2012), pp. 379–398; DeStefano (2014), pp. 305–376. https://via.library.depaul.edu/law-review/vol63/iss2/6; Pérez-Aznar (2017), pp. 326–355 Available at: http://oxia.ouplaw.com/view/10.1093/law-iic/9780198809722.016.0009/law-iic-9780198809722-document-9; Garcia et al. (2015), pp. 861–892; Gaillard (2017), pp. 17–37.

issued specific rules on TPF. and new case law emerged.[34] The market changes rapidly and new developments require re-assessment of the topic in light of the new developments. Currently, there is no literature exists covering TPF in ISDS as this book does comprehensively and this book will fill this gap.

As an example of a procedural issue raised by TPF, one of the most important cases can be a starting point to examine the SfC orders in the presence of a TPF agreement.[35] In this case, the opinion of the three arbitrators in the tribunal and later the opinion of scholars were divided on whether to grant or not to grant a SfC order. In the case, members of the tribunal held different opinions, resulting in an arbitration award as well as assenting and dissenting opinions. Briefly, in this claim, the claimant was funded by a TPF company and the tribunal ordered the funded party to pay SfC. This decision attracted many comments by practitioners as well as scholarly articles. This is mainly because of Dr. Griffith's assenting opinion. Dr. Griffith criticised TPF harshly and addressed funders as embracing the "Gambler's Nirvana Heads I win, and Tails I do not lose".[36] He also used another term which has been popular and used by other scholars in academia, "mercantile adventurers",[37] and suggested that in the presence of a TPF company, it should be the funded party's duty to justify why SfC orders should not be made.[38] In other words, according to Dr. Griffith, in the presence of a TPF company, the default rule should be ordering SfC.[39] Instead of this strict opinion, in academia, it is generally suggested that "whether security should be ordered likely remains a case by case determination that may require consideration of a litigation funding agreement's individual terms, notably termination rights".[40] This approach seems more logical instead of creating a general rule of SfC order in the presence of TPF.

Apart from the important SfC issue in the RSM case, Joubin-Bret suggests that "The Tribunal provided further food for thought and discussion when it dismissed an argument raised by the Claimant that the Respondent had also benefitted from third-party funding".[41] Thus, even though generally claimants have the opportunity to benefit from TPF, respondents might have the same opportunity as well. There are further articles, books and book chapters on TPF,[42] as well as blog posts, reports and

[34] Examples are South American Silver v. Bolivia UNCITRAL Case, 2016, where TPF arrangements were addressed and Interocean v. Nigeria ICSID Case, 2017, where arbitrators were challenged.

[35] RSM Production Corporation v Saint Lucia, ICSID Case No ARB/12/10.

[36] Ibid., assenting reasons of Gavan Griffith (Griffith), p. 13.

[37] Griffith, p. 14. The term mercantile adventurers is used to name some articles or book chapters, for example, De Brabandere (2016), pp. 105–128).

[38] Griffith, p. 18.

[39] *Ibid.*

[40] Brekoulakis and von Goeler (2017), pp. 1–19.

[41] Joubin-Bret (2015), p. 733.

[42] Garimella (2014), p. 45; Garimella (2018), p. 1; Geisker (2018), pp. 81–83; Heidemann (2012), pp. 329–332.

consultation papers.[43] The increasing number of articles and books prove the growing importance of the topic.

There are other important cases such as Essar v. Norscot, where an arbitral tribunal ordered the losing party to pay the successful claimant's fees that have to be paid to a TPF company as a result of the TPF agreement and the English High Court saw no irregularity in this decision based on the English Arbitration Act, Section 59.[44] Scholars expressed different opinions, some disagreed[45] and others agreed[46] with the decision given in this case.

When TPF is examined it is easy to understand why it attracts so much attention, mostly in favour of it but some opponents as well. First of all, supporters state that "Third-party funding is justified in the first place by [the] access to justice".[47] Furthermore, TPF is levelling the playfield.[48] TPF gives a free assessment of its case by a potential funder and facilitates the arbitration mechanism by providing more cases chances to be heard. TPF is not only limited to impecunious litigants. TPF "may also assist in overcoming liquidity issues, or more simply, allow a litigant to diversify and share the risks attendant to any piece of litigation."[49] Thus, even financially strong companies can use TPF and manage their litigation costs. The opponents of TPF raise ethical issues regarding TPF.[50] They also suggest that TPF is "a slippery slope in opening up the floodgates of frivolous claims".[51] However, "it is hard to argue that litigation financiers are a systemic harm just because they prevent governments from getting away with unchallenged, wrongful expropriations."[52]

While these are main arguments for and against TPF, there are some concerns that have to be dealt with separately.[53] Firstly, the control exercised by TPF companies and second is the potential CoI between arbitrators and TPF companies, which may cause the disqualification of the arbitrator. Disclosure is suggested as a solution to the potential CoI issues and it seems to be the main trend so far.[54] Disclosure will

---

[43] Shirlow (2020); Kalderimis (2014); Trinidad (2017); (Donny) Trinh (2019); Biasiolo and Santin (2019); American Bar Association (2011), U.S. Chamber of Commerce Institute for Legal Reform; Law Council of Australia. (June 2011). "Regulation of Third-Party Litigation Funding in Australia" Position Paper; Marius Nicolae Iliescu. "A Trend Towards Mandatory Disclosure of Third Party Funding? Recent Developments and Positive Impact" Kluwer Arbitration Blog, May 2 2016.

[44] Essar Oilfields Services Ltd. v. Norscot Management PVT Ltd. [2016] EWHC 2361 (Comm).

[45] Kühn and Oeveren (2018), pp. 307–328.

[46] Sullivan (2018) URL: www.transnational-dispute-management.com/article.asp?key=2577.

[47] Honlet at 712.

[48] Yeoh (2016).

[49] Owczarek and Stoyanov (2015), p. 172.

[50] *See* supra note 5 (Frignati).

[51] Derric at 117. "Slippery slope" is first used in the following article: Baker (2013), pp. 229–241.

[52] McGlinchy (2018), p. 164.

[53] For further references on third-party funding, *see:* Matthews and Steinitz (2011); Menkel-Meadow (2016), pp. 207–253; Molot (2010), pp. 65–115.

[54] For the Disclosure suggestions see Trusc (2013), pp. 1649–1682; De Brabandere, supra note 37. Taylor and Francis; Shaw (2017), pp. 109–120.

also increase the transparency of the ISDS. Regarding the control of funders over the proceedings, each funder has different approaches to this issue.[55] It must also be mentioned that if TPF takes too much control of arbitration proceedings it might be a champertous according to common law: "Three important anti-champerty factors are, namely, independent advice, an absence of conflicts of interest, and no improper control".[56] The degree of control can bring "assignment of the claims and its effect on questions of jurisdiction and admissibility" to the mind as well.[57] Thus, TPF should follow a regular practice and avoid such vague areas by forming the TPF agreement properly.

In the end, it is a choice of policy either to opt for TPF and enable more disputants to access justice with the help of TPF companies, or by not allowing this capitalization, preventing them from this opportunity. Which one is better is a question that must be answered, and no consensus is reached upon. TPF is already a crucial part of the investment regime and international commercial arbitration systems. Thus, researching and improving the intellectual discussion level regarding TPF is important. As already stated, some examples, the significant number of cases proves the importance of the subject.[58] TPF, turning an inaccessible judicial mechanism into an accessible one for parties is alone an important feature, and deserves further study.[59] The next subsection will explain the contribution of the book to the literature.

1.3 Further Discussions on TPF

This book examines the topic holistically, covering all the procedural and ethical issues raised by TPF, as well as prove data from an empirical research. Reflecting funders' perspective on selected issues and addressing ethical concerns over TPF will enable the topic to be covered comprehensively. All the case law on TPF available until the date of publication of this book is a major contribution of this book to the literature. Moreover, the book also provides new insights into difficult, dynamic, and necessary questions related to justice and ethics in Chap. 5. Even though access to justice is repeated many times in academia, this term has not been examined deeply enough in terms of the legal theory of justice and TPF together. This part fills this gap in academia and provides further justifications for TPF, and shows how TPF helps to access justice, provided that the guidelines in this book is followed.

[55] For an insight of funders' control rights on cases, see Kantor (2009), p. 77.

[56] Mulheron (2014), p. 582. For the brief explanation of champerty and maintenance, *see* Chap. 2.

[57] ICCA report at footnote 18, at 215.

[58] See the case law discussed below.

[59] More explanations regarding the theory of justice and TPF interaction is discussed in Chap. 5. Ethical considerations can be found in the Chap. 4 as well.

Addressing procedural issues raised by TPF is another major feature of this book. How to address them has not reached a consensus and requires further research. Apart from addressing them, as listed in Chap. 3, also a guideline to avoid those problems in practice is given in Chap. 7 of the book. This guideline aims to represent the best practice drawn from the holistic analysis the book brings for the TPF market. The book analyses the advantages and disadvantages of each approach in the market, the case law related to the involvement of TPF companies in investment cases, and propose its own suggestion to the readers. It is hoped that the best practice created by this research will guide many TPF companies, lawyers who are seeking TPF opportunities for their clients, academics for further thought, and anyone who has interest in and wants to learn more about the subject.

A lot of international companies and hedge funds have the possibility to take part in the arbitration process as third-party funders. That is why they need to know their responsibilities and rights by doing so. Until their rights and responsibilities are clear the process of their involvement will be slower, thus, the ambiguity in the practice must be cleared. Since users of arbitration do not know their rights and obligations when a TPF company involves, they cannot use TPF efficiently. With good knowledge, it would enable a better understanding of TPF and increase its efficient use. This efficient use is going to be achieved with the best practice guideline in Chap. 7 of the book and provide the TPF agreements used in ISDS without distorting the system. Therefore, to make the involvement of third parties more effective, this book is carrying out important work.

The lack of empirical research on the topic leaves practitioners, academics and the literature unaware of the real concerns of funders. With the empirical research conducted in Chap. 4, what the concerns of the third-party funders are, how they operate, and if their concerns match with the concerns of the public or practitioners are tested. Chap. 4 allows the readers to delve into concerns of the TPF companies as well as those raised in the literature. Thus, the lack of such an empirical study is filled since such a study has not been done on the subject and what is missing in academia is filled with this research.

The possibility of funding a case in Asia is higher compared to other jurisdictions since the numbers of cases are much higher in Asia rather than other arbitration centres in other parts of the world. The number of disputes the China International Economic and Trade Arbitration Commission (CIETAC) hears alone is nearly equal to the sum of numbers of all other major arbitration centres' cases.[60] Hence, if we make an estimate based on the high number of cases in Asia, it is probable that TPF will have a bigger market share in Asia than other jurisdictions. Thus, studying TPF in Asia is particularly important because of the high potential of TPF in Asia. The literature on TPF is not enough compared to the importance of the topic and growing TPF market. By filling this gap, this book enhances the knowledge regarding the use and efficiency of TPF.

---

[60]Numbers can be checked via the link: https://www.lexology.com/library/detail.aspx?g=73afdeb0-e147-433a-9d10-4a1e4ddf73ca (The number of cases before the CIETAC is 1968 in 2015).

1.4 Methodology

The present book uses doctrinal analysis as the main legal research method. This method is used in the book to give the views of scholars and shed light on the current and past discussions in academia and case law on TPF. However, where necessary, the book benefitted from other methods as well. Especially, a historical approach is used when the background of TPF is covered in Chap. 2. Doctrinal analysis is the main method in Chap. 3 as well, where the case law in investment arbitration are examined. To determine the best practice and create a guideline for users, in the end, an empirical research is also conducted and findings of this empirical research are given in Chap. 4. The empirical research also enhances the understanding of the readers on the topic and gives a clear position of TPF practice in investment arbitration. Thus, we can also see developments in the world as a whole since these funders are based in different parts of the world.

The book aims not only to provide a theoretical discussion but also to give a practical overview of the market as well. Thus, empirical research leads Chap. 4, where the viewpoint of the funders and as funders are reflected in that part via interviews the author conducted. The author conducted interviews with funders including TPF company managers, chief executive or chief finance officers, and other officers in TPF companies. This method enabled the book not only staying as black letter law but also giving a practical dynamic as well. When the case law is analysed, chronological order is used to present how decisions by tribunals follow each other.

1.5 Scope of the Book

TPF is a broad subject. Thus, to draw the limits of the topic is important to cover all substantial parts of the topic, and while doing so to give enough space for discussions regarding the topics chosen. At the outset, it is important to note that the book does not analyze the effect of TPF on a certain group of countries (e.g. the Global South).[61] The book analyzes TPF in its current state and provides guidelines for funders with the help of doctrinal analysis of the literature, case law, and empirical research.

The main research question in this book is whether TPF is distorting the ISDS system. In addition, as a follow-up inquiry, the book creates principles for funders to follow so that their practice will not distort the system. In order to do so, the book uses doctrinal and empirical analysis throughout the book.

The book mainly focuses on TPF where a professional TPF company, not related to the dispute, funds the case in exchange for a return from the award. A short history

[61] Even though there are useful sources: *see* Chimni (2020), pp. 1211–1221https://doi.org/10.1093/ejil/chab004; Chimni (2017); Anghie (2019), pp. 68–94.

of TPF, parties to the TPF agreement and their rights and obligations, and comparative TPF practice in different jurisdictions are covered in the book. One of the major contributions of the book to the literature is to suggest solutions to procedural issues associated with TPF involvement. The significant case law discussed the topic. The book examines all the case law available and from its assessment advances its proposed solutions. To understand parties' approach, an empirical study is conducted with broad participants from TPF company top managers to the entry level officers. The lack of empirical research on TPF in literature is filled at some point with the results of the empirical study conducted in this book. The results add original views and highlight important features and considerations of the practice from the viewpoint of funders. Different theories of justice are discussed to address ethical considerations and elaborate on the contribution of the TPF to the legal justice and judicial mechanisms in general.

This book examines the case law and regulations related to TPF. To limit the topic, some topics have not been covered. For example, detailed explanations regarding some of the ancient doctrines such as maintenance and champerty are not covered in this book since TPF is already well established in practice.[62] Those doctrines are only mentioned by name and explained briefly at the outset of Chap. 2. Also, insurance, loan or other similar finance options available to the parties are not examined in detail in this book. They are only compared with TPF to understand the topic better. Similarly, contingency or conditional fee agreements are not covered as well since the financer is a lawyer who is related to the party and this is not the typical definition of TPF.

Regarding the case law examined, the book mainly covers investment arbitration cases in detail. Commercial arbitration cases—at the rate the author could access—and high court decisions are sometimes mentioned to serve as an analogy for investment arbitration cases. These commercial arbitration cases, while limited in number, may be used to illustrate issues that have yet to be addressed in investment arbitration. Thus, they are mentioned briefly.

1.6 Structure of the Book

The structure of the book is the following. Introduction of the topic, its scope and a general overview constitute this chapter. Different definitions and basic mechanisms of TPF as well as a short history are covered in Chap. 2. Procedural issues raised by TPF and case law on TPF in investment arbitration are examined in Chap. 3. All case law mentioning TPF in investment law, and some other cases, available until the

[62] As referred before, in many cases, tribunals accepted the fact that the practice is well established. As an example, Giovanni Alemanni and others v Argentine Republic, ICSID Case No ARB/07/8, Decision on Jurisdiction and Admissibility (17 November 2014) paragraph 278, the tribunal explicitly states the practice is well established.

book's submission are examined and discussed in Chap. 3. Following this chapter, an empirical research on TPF forms Chap. 4. With this empirical research, the book is not confined to black letter law which examines established case law and literature only; furhermore, it also brings important data from practitioners. Thus, Chap. 4 adds a practical approach. Following this chapter, ethical considerations and the interaction of TPF with the theory of justice are examined in Chap. 5. This section considers ethical issues TPF raises and suggests solutions to eliminate them. It also explains the access to justice rhetoric regarding how TPF is facilitating the investment arbitration mechanism. Finally, Chap. 5 is followed by the conclusion of this book. In the end, in Chap. 7, guidelines are added by the author as a model that can be followed by third-party funders operating in investment arbitration. For further considerations, it is a useful model provided for funders in ISDS and provides that their operation will not distort the investment arbitration regime.

References

Abrams DS, Chen DL (2013) A market for justice: a first empirical look at third party litigation funding. Univ Pa J Bus Law 15(4):1075–1109

Ahn K-H, Kim S-R, Joe I-H (2013) Major legal issues with third party funding in international investment arbitration. J Arbitr Stud 23(2):55

Alrashid MN, Wessel J, Laird J (2012) Impact of third party funding on privilege in litigation and international arbitration. Disp Resol Int 6(2):101

American Bar Association (2011) Issues paper concerning lawyer's involvement in alternative litigation financing

Andrews N (2018) The three paths of justice: court proceedings, arbitration, and mediation in England, vol 65. Springer, Cham

Anghie A (2019) Asia in the history and theory of international law. In: Chesterman S, Owada H, Saul B (eds) The Oxford handbook of international law in Asia and the Pacific. Oxford University Press, pp 68–94

Baker T (2013) Paying to play: inside the ethics and implications of third-party litigationfunding. Widener Law J 23(1):229–241

Bao C (2017) Third party funding in Singapore and Hong Kong: the next chapter. J Int Arbitr 34(3): 387–400. https://kluwerlawonline.com/journalarticle/Journal+of+International+Arbitration/34.3/JOIA2017020

Barker GR (2012) Third-party litigation funding in Australia and Europe. J Law Econ Policy 8(3): 451–524

Bertrand E (2011) The brave New World of arbitration: third-party funding. ASA Bull 29(3): 607–615

Biasiolo A, Santin L (2019, September 30) The Milan Chamber of Arbitration introduces new rules: Pioneering or codifying? Kluwer Arbitration Blog. http://arbitrationblog.kluwerarbitration.com/2019/09/30/the-milan-chamber-of-arbitration-introduces-new-rules-pioneering-or-codifying/

Bogart CP (2013) Dispute resolution - third-party funding: helping companies control runaway litigation costs. Bus Law Rev (UK) 34(4):148–149

Brekoulakis SL, von Goeler J (2017) The arbitration agreement and arbitrability, it's all about the money: the impact of third-party funding on costs awards and security for costs in international arbitration. In: Klausegger C, Klein P et al (eds) Austrian yearbook on international arbitration 2017. Wolters Kluwer, pp 1–19

Burch EC (2016) Financing issue classes: benefits and barriers to third-party funding. NYU J Law Bus 12(3):889
Cameron C, Kalajdzic J (2013) Commercial litigation funding: ethical, regulatory and comparative perspectives. Canadian Bus Law J (2014) 55(1):1–16
Chan E (2015) Proposed guidelines for the disclosure of third-party funding arrangements in international arbitration. Am Rev Int Arbitr 26(2):281–322
Chen T (2019) The outsider's identity in international commercial arbitration—from the group of companies doctrine and IBA guidelines on conflict of interest to adverse costs awards against third-party funders. Contemp Asia Arbitr J 12(1):21–40
Chimni BS (2017) International law and world order: a critique of contemporary approaches, 2nd edn. Cambridge University Press. https://doi.org/10.1017/9781107588196
Chimni BS (2020) The articles on state responsibility and the guiding principles of shared responsibility: a TWAIL perspective. Eur J Int Law 31(4):1211–1221. https://doi.org/10.1093/ejil/chab004
Choi M (2016) Third-party funders in international arbitration: a case for protecting communication made in order to finance arbitration. Georgetown J Legal Ethics 29(4):883
Clanchy J (2016) Navigating the waters of third-party funding in arbitration. Int J Arbitr Mediat Disp Manage 82(3):222
Darwazeh N, Leleu A (2016) Disclosure and security for costs or how to address imbalances created by third-party funding. J Int Arbitr 33(2):125–149
Daughety A, Reinganum J (2014) The effect of third-party funding of plaintiffs on settlement. Am Econ Rev 104(8):2552–2566
De Brabandere E (2016) 'Mercantile adventurers'?: The disclosure of third-party funding in investment treaty arbitration. In: Litigation, costs, funding and behaviour: implications for the law. Taylor and Francis (Brabandere), pp 105–128
De Brabandere E, Lepeltak J (2012) Third-party funding in international investment arbitration. ICSID Rev 27(2):379–398
DeStefano M (2014) Claim funders and commercial claim holders: common interest or common problem? DePaul Law Rev 63(2):305–376
Eken C (2022) A detailed comparison of third-party funding regulations in Hong Kong and Singapore. Asia Pac Law Rev 29(1):25–46. https://doi.org/10.1080/10192557.2021.1979799
Frignati V (2016) Ethical implications of third-party funding in international arbitration. Arbitr Int 32(3):505–522. https://doi.org/10.1093/arbint/aiw011
Gaillard E (2017) Abuse of process in international arbitration. Foreign Invest Law J 32(1):17–37. https://doi.org/10.1093/icsidreview/siw036
Garcia FJ, Ciko L, Gaurav A, Hough K (2015) Reforming the international investment regime: lessons from international trade law. J Int Econ Law 18(4). https://doi.org/10.1093/jiel/jgv042
Garimella SR (2014) Third party funding in international arbitration—issues and challenges in Asian jurisdictions. AALCO J Int Law 3(1):45
Garimella SR (2018) Arbitration reforms in India—the case for third party funding of arbitral claims. Transnatl Disp Manage 15(2):1
Gayner O, Khouri S (2017) Singapore and Hong Kong: international arbitration meets third party funding. Fordham Int Law J 40(3):1046
Geisker J (2018) Litigation funding in Australia: a year of review and change? LSJ. Law Soc NSW J 46:81–83
Heidemann M (2012) Review of the book *Dalhuisen on Transnational Comparative, Commercial, Financial and Trade Law*, vol. 1–3 – *Introduction – The New Lex Mercatoria and its Sources* (vol. 1); *Contract and Movable Property Law* (vol. 2); *Financial Products, Financial Services and Financial Regulation* (vol. 3), by J. Dalhuisen. Eur Bus Law Rev 23(2):329–332
Hodgson M, Kalicki J, Joubin-Bret A (2015) 32 costs in investment treaty arbitration: the case for reform. In: Kalicki JE, Joubin-Bret A (eds) Reshaping the investor-state dispute settlement system journeys for the 21st century. Brill Publishers, pp 748–759

Honlet J (2015) Recent decisions on third-party funding in investment arbitration. ICSID Rev-Foreign Invest Law J 30(3):699–712

Joubin-Bret A (2015) Spotlight on third-party funding in investor-state arbitration. J World Invest Trade 16:727

Kalderimis D (2014) Third party funding in international arbitration – lessons from litigation? Kluwer Arbitration Blog, December 15 2014. http://arbitrationblog.kluwerarbitration.com/2014/12/15/third-party-funding-in-international-arbitration-lessons-from-litigation/

Kantor M (2009) Third-party funding in international arbitration: an essay about new developments. ICSID Rev Foreign Invest Law J 24(1):65–79. https://doi.org/10.1093/icsidreview/24.1.65

Kühn W, Oeveren H (2018) The full recovery of third-party funding costs in arbitration: to be or not to be? J Int Arbitr 35(3):307–328

Matthews JM, Steinitz M (2011) TDM special issue: contingent fees and third party funding in investment arbitration disputes. TDM 4 www.transnational-dispute-management.com

McGlinchy J (2018) Champerty, sham suits and the squeeze: third party litigation finance in investor-state arbitration. Int Trade Bus Law Rev 21:151

Menkel-Meadow C (2016) Ethical ordering in transnational legal practice? Georgetown J Legal Ethics 29(1):207–253

Molot JT (2010) Litigation finance: a market solution to a procedural problem. Georgetown Law J 99(1):65–115

Mulheron R (2014) England's unique approach to the self-regulation of third-party funding: a critical analysis of recent developments. Cambridge Law J 73(3):570-597 at 582

Nieuwveld LB, Sahani VS (2017) Third-party funding in international arbitration, 2nd edn. Wolters Kluwer

Owczarek O, Stoyanov M (2015) Third-party funding in international arbitration: is it time for some soft rules? BCDR Int Arbitr Rev 2(1):171–199. https://kluwerlawonline.com/journalarticle/BCDR+International+Arbitration+Review/2.1/BCDR2015010

Painter RW (1995) Litigating on a contingency: a monopoly of champions or a market for champerty? Chicago-Kent Law Rev 71(2):625–697

Pérez-Aznar F (2017) Federal states and investment arbitration. In: Sachs LE, Johnson L (eds) Yearbook on international investment law & policy 2015–2016. Oxford University Press, pp 327–356

Rogers C (2014) Ethics in international arbitration, 1st edn. Oxford University Press

Rowles-Davies N, Cousins J (2014) Third party litigation funding. Oxford University Press

Sahani V (2013) Recent developments in third-party funding. J Int Arbitr 30(4):443–452

Shaw GJ (2017) Third-party funding in investment arbitration: how non-disclosure can cause harm for the sake of profit. Arbitr Int 33(1):109–120

Shirlow E (2020, March 23). UNCITRAL Working Group III: an introduction and update. Kluwer Arbitration Blog. http://arbitrationblog.kluwerarbitration.com/2020/03/23/uncitral-working-group-iii-an-introduction-and-update/

Sullivan J (2018) Essar v. Norscot: are the costs associated with third party funding recoverable? TDM 4, www.transnational-dispute-management.com

Trinh BD (2019, October 28). From Trinh Vinh Binh to EUVIPA: Vietnam's meritorious step towards transparency in ISDS. Kluwer Arbitration Blog, http://arbitrationblog.kluwerarbitration.com/2019/10/28/from-trinh-vinh-binh-to-euvipa-vietnams-meritorious-step-towards-transparency-in-isds/

Trinidad A (2017) Third-party funding's older sibling: legal costs insurance and the issue of regulation. Kluwer Arbitration Blog, August 31 2017, http://arbitrationblog.kluwerarbitration.com/2017/08/31/third-party-fundings-oldersibling-legal-costs-insurance-issue-regulation/

Trusc JA (2013) Full disclosure? Conflicts of interest arising from third-party funding in international commercial arbitration. Georgetown Law J 101(6):1649–1682 von Goeler J (2016) Third-party funding in international arbitration and its impact on procedure. Kluwer Law International

Wang H (2018) Third-party funding in arbitration: potential trends and implications for China. J Bus Law 2:147

Yeoh D (2016) Third party funding in international arbitration: a slippery slope or levelling the playing field? J Int Arbitr 33(1)

Chapter 2
Definition, History and Basic Mechanism of TPF

2.1 Introduction

This chapter sets a background for TPF and its impact on investment arbitration. To have more sophisticated discussions in the chapters that follow, a fundamental understanding of what TPF does is essential. There is one fact that the use of TPF is increasing. However, what constitutes TPF is not always understandable. Thus, this part analyzes and explores through doctrinal analysis the definition of TPF, the historical development of TPF, and different TPF models. With the fundamentals set out in this chapter, further analysis and discussions on each specific procedural and ethical issue will be possible. What the stages in the TPF process are, what the considerations of both sides in a TPF relationship are, and how this TPF process is positioned in the Investor-State Dispute Settlement (ISDS) regime are also explained here.

In this chapter, the stages of obtaining TPF, different types of finance methods are also discussed. What costs are covered by TPF agreements, different TPF arrangements other than TPF to cover those costs, arguments for and against TPF, and some basic terms used in TPF literature are thoroughly discussed. This approach visualizes potential problems faced during this process. The relationship between lawyer-client-funder, and control of the case are examples of some of those procedural problems. More specifically, TPF creates other procedural problems particular to investment arbitration. Funders nearly always finance claimants against states in the existing investment arbitration regime. This is because of the specific structure of ISDS as set out in this chapter and the fact that counterclaims by states are not common in ISDS. Additionally, TPF raises ethical concerns. The tension between access to justice and monetization of investment claims is the main reason for those concerns. Those procedural and ethical concerns could only be discussed after anlysing what TPF does, how the process works, and its effects in investment arbitration here substantially.

C. Eken, *Third-Party Funding in Investment Arbitration*, Law for Professionals,
https://doi.org/10.1007/978-3-031-63620-2_2

Before setting the framework for TPF in the context explained above, it is important to keep in mind that TPF is a dynamic subject. This signifies that the extent of TPF, available TPF methods, and jurisdictions open to TPF are rapidly changing. The ICCA-Queen Mary University report on TPF, accepting "how rapidly international arbitration practice and funding models are evolving" stated that their report was not "either definitive or permanent" nor "the last word" on TPF.[1] Therefore, this chapter takes TPF one step further from the existing literature and presents an extensive analysis of available TPF models.

2.2 Definition of TPF

TPF is a straight-forward procedure, and in a way, the goal of the parties in this relationship is pretty much clear. On the other hand, consensus has not yet been reached on the definition of TPF. The grounds for the aforementioned is that depending on how you define TPF, the scope of TPF can become very limited, or it can be rather broad. Similarly, agreement is lacking on the definition of other fundamental terms in the TPF relationship.

The definition is essential when attempts are made to bring in regulatory requirements for third-party funders. What constitutes TPF and what does not must be clarified and criteria must be set. For instance, Hong Kong and Singapore brought in TPF regulations.[2] Both sets of regulations defined TPF, but the definitions are different from each other. There are also other soft law such as the International Bar Association Rules (hereinafter "IBA Rules"), or some treaties or constitutional rules, which bring in some rules on TPF as well. The definition varies on those sources, too. Each definition precludes or encompasses a particular kind of TPF arrangement. Since each regulation and international rule defines TPF in its own way, TPF is treated differently in each specific regulation. As a result, what constitutes TPF in Hong Kong does not necessarily mean the same as in Singapore, or the IBA Rules. We can see two different patterns in those rules towards TPF: defining it (i) narrowly or (ii) broadly.

2.2.1 Narrow Definition of TPF

TPF, if no criteria are set and no limitation is brought, is a very broad term. However, various definitions bring different limitations and make the scope of TPF narrow to

[1] ICCA report at Chap. 1 in footnote 18, p. 13.

[2] Hong Kong Arbitration and Mediation Legislation (Third-party Funding) (Amendment) Ordinance 2017, and Singapore Civil Law (Amendment) Bill. For the difference in their definitions, see Eken (2022).

some extent. Thus, those definitions can be categorized as narrow TPF definitions. In the following paragraphs, those different definitions are identified.

In investment arbitration, there is no one general definition of TPF and what is accepted under TPF is questioned by arbitrators.[3] This inquiry shows that it is not always understandable for arbitrators what TPF is and what TPF is not. However, we can see TPF definitions in some regulations, treaties, or association guidelines, all of which try to clarify the subject. At the local scale, there are some TPF regulations in Hong Kong and Singapore as mentioned. Hong Kong's and Singapore's legislations are of course not directly applicable to investment arbitration. However, when the enforcement of a TPF agreement is sought in those jurisdictions, those regulations can be applied. Since the legislation in those two jurisdictions is exemplary, they constitute a model for defining TPF.

In Hong Kong, the TPF legislation provides:

> Third-party funding of arbitration is the provision of arbitration funding for an arbitration:
>
> (a) Under a funding agreement;
> (b) to a funded party.
> (c) by a third-party funder; and.
> (d) in return for the third-party funder receiving a financial benefit only if the arbitration is successful within the meaning of the funding agreement.[4]

The Hong Kong Ordinance also defines the meaning of a TPF agreement, a funded party and a third-party funder. Importantly, according to the Hong Kong Ordinance, a funder by no means has any interest in the claim apart from TPF, thus it excludes lawyers from being funders.[5] By limiting the scope of funders, and the eligibility of funders, the Hong Kong Ordinance narrows the scope of the TPF relationship.

In Singapore, the validity of certain contracts for the TPF of claims is defined as: "a contract under which a qualifying Third-Party Funder provides funds to any party to fund all or part of the costs of that party in prescribed dispute resolution proceedings is not contrary to public policy or otherwise illegal by reason that it is a contract for maintenance or champerty".[6] Singapore's legislation sets some criteria to define what a qualifying third-party funder is. The Association of Litigation Funders brings similar criteria for funders as well.[7] Like the Hong Kong Ordinance,

---

[3] RSM Production Corporation v. Saint Lucia, ICSID Case No. ARB/12/10, Dissenting Opinion of Edward Nottingham of 12 August 2014, para. 19.

[4] Hong Kong Arbitration and Mediation Legislation (Third-party Funding) (Amendment) Ordinance 2017, Section 98G.

[5] *Ibid.* Section 98J.

[6] Singapore Civil Law (Amendment) Bill, Section 5B.

[7] The Association of Litigation Funders (ALF) of England and Wales published a Code of Conduct. This Code is a guideline for its members. It is not mandatory for non-members. However, members of the association must abide. The Code can be accessed via their website: https://associationoflitigationfunders.com/wp-content/uploads/2018/03/Code-Of-Conduct-for-Litigation-Funders-at-Jan-2018-FINAL.pdf.

by differentiating funders as qualifying and non-qualifying funders, the Singapore legislation also selects certain types of funders and leaves others outside the scope of its legislation. Thus, it is also narrowing the TPF relationship in its jurisdiction.

Sometimes, the terms of litigation funding and TPF are used to give the same meaning.[8] Lord Justice Jackson defined TPF as "The funding of claims by commercial bodies in return for a share of the proceeds".[9] Even though this definition is very broad, it also excludes non-commercial bodies, such as TPF by non-profit organizations.[10] Thus, limiting TPF to only commercial purposes also narrows its scope.

Another TPF definition can be found in the China International Economic and Trade Arbitration Commission (CIETAC) Hong Kong Arbitration Centre (HKAC) Guidelines for TPF in Arbitration. According to these guidelines, TPF: "arises when a professional third person or entity ('Funder') contributes funds, or other material support to a party in arbitration ('Funded party') and has a direct economic interest in the award to be rendered in the arbitration".[11] Again here, the possibility of donation is excluded.

Apart from these rather narrower definitions, perhaps Yves Derains may have given the shortest and most essential definition. Derains defines TPF as "an investment per se in arbitration by a corporation specialized in this business".[12] TPF is indeed investment from the funder's perspective, and such investment is generally made by expert companies in this market. Most of the TPF companies have legal experts who can assess the cases and decide which cases are suitable for investment and which are not. Moreover, they have also other experts to manage their investments such as fund managers, or investment managers. Therefore, funders are large and they consist of various professionals who take important investment decisions collectively. This structure of funders is elaborated in the following sections. However, as explained before, this is not the only method available for TPF, and excluding other types of third-party funders, even though they might be the minority compared to professional funders in the market, equals limiting the definition of TPF.

All these different rules set standards for third-party funders and by doing so limit the definition of TPF. Their scope is not broad because the criteria for who can be funders are narrowed. In the broadest term, anyone can be a funder, and any restraint in the definition constitutes a limitation in the scope. Thus, these definitions in this section can be categorized as "narrow" definitions of TPF. The number of rules

---

[8] Lord Justice Jackson (2011).

[9] *Ibid.*

[10] A very famous example of non-profit funding example is Philip Morris v. Uruguay, ICSID Case No. ARB/10/7. In this case, the Bill & Melinda Gates Foundation financed Uruguay without any profit to contribute to the campaign for tobacco-free kids.

[11] China International Economic and Trade Arbitration Commission (CIETAC) Hong Kong Arbitration Centre (HKAC) Guidelines for Third-Party Funding in Arbitration, 2016, Section 1.2. Full text is available at https://hkarbitration.files.wordpress.com/2016/05/cietac-draft-guidelines-17-may-16.pdf.

[12] Derains (2013), p. 5.

defining TPF also shows the growing importance and impact of TPF. It also proves that TPF is accepted internationally. Apart from these narrow definitions, there are several broad definitions of TPF, too. Interestingly, in investment treaties, the preference for the definition of TPF is generally a broad one.

2.2.2 Broad Definition of TPF

As explained above, some of the definitions limit the scope of TPF. The rationale for this is to provide some regulations for a certain type of TPF but not for all TPF. However, in principle, TPF is a very broad term and it includes a different variety of TPF methods with different purposes, commercial or non-commercial. There are some definitions in various sources that do not limit TPF to commercial TPF, and instead give a very broad meaning to this term. In investment law, TPF is generally defined without limiting the subject. Here, some of those examples are stated.

Without limiting TPF, the definition gives a very broad meaning to TPF. The Investment Protection Agreement between the European Union and Vietnam sets out TPF being: "any funding provided by a natural or juridical person who is not a party to the dispute but who enters into an agreement with a disputing party to finance part or all of the cost of the proceedings in return for a remuneration dependent on the outcome of the dispute, or any funding provided by a natural or juridical person who is not a party to the dispute in the form of a donation or grant".[13]

As we can see, this definition does not exclude any person and does not exclude non-commercial purposes. Any party funding the Claimant other than the Claimant itself is a funder under this definition. Similarly, any party funding the Respondent other than the Respondent itself is also a funder under this definition. Therefore, this is a very good example of a very broad definition of TPF.

Similarly, in the Transatlantic Trade and Investment Partnership (TTIP) draft text, TPF is: "any funding provided by a natural or legal person who is not a party to the dispute but who enters into an agreement with a disputing party to finance part or all of the cost of the proceedings in return for a remuneration dependent on the outcome of the dispute or in the form of a donation or grant".[14]

Another broad definition example is the CETA definition of TPF between Canada-EU. CETA describes TPF being: "any funding provided by a natural or legal person who is not a party to the dispute but who enters into an agreement with a disputing party to finance part or all of the cost of the proceedings either through a

---

[13] Investment Protection Agreement (2019) between the European Union (hereinafter "EU") and Its Member States, of the One Part, and the Socialist Republic of Vietnam, of the Other Part, October 17, 2018. Moreover, the Vietnam Investment Protection Agreement (2019) has a separate article on TPF (Article 3.37). This article provides that third-party funding is a factor determining security for costs orders, the disclosure requirement for third-party funding, its timing and procedure.

[14] Transatlantic Trade and Investment Partnership, Commission Draft Text, Article 1/2. Article 8 of the agreement also imposes disclosure requirement for TPF arrangements.

donation or grant or in return for remuneration dependent on the outcome of the dispute".[15] These two definitions of TPF give very broad meaning to it.

Another important work on the reforms of the Investor-State Dispute Settlement (ISDS) system is done by United Nations Commission On International Trade Law (hereinafter "UNCITRAL") Working Group III and it also gives a broad definition of TPF. UNCITRAL Working Group III, by considering all the treaties referred above and others, considered TPF as:

- Funding provided by the counsel of the disputing party under a pro bono, contingency fee or conditional fee arrangement;
- Different forms of insurance policies, including after-the-event insurance;
- Equity investments by third-party funders".[16]

UNCITRAL Working Group III also adopted a broad definition of TPF by accepting a variety of TPF methods such as not only TPF from professional funders but also different insurance policies and finance provided by lawyers. All these examples show that in investment arbitration, the general tendency is towards defining TPF broadly, so every type of TPF by a third-party is considered as TPF. Therefore, whilst in some regulations and rules in different jurisdictions, TPF is defined narrowly, UNCITRAL Working group III and investment treaties in investment arbitration defines TPF broadly. Thus, as this book focuses on TPF in investment arbitration, accepting the term with its broad meaning is more suitable to the existing approach in the adjudication of investment disputes.

2.2.3 Conclusion

These explanations and examples above showed that in investment arbitration the tendency is towards accepting a broad definition of TPF. As can be seen in the Chap. 3 of this book, there are a variety of TPF methods that are already used in investment arbitration. And many more possible TPF structures are yet to be explained. Thus, excluding a certain type of TPF method is not useful for this book. Since tribunals generally do not make any differentiation between different TPF methods, accepting all methods under one broad definition is more practical. This also helps us in classifying different TPF methods under a broad definition of TPF.

However, there are indeed narrow definitions of TPF in other regulations and it is difficult to reach a unanimous definition. The TPF market in the world is developing in different jurisdictions and funders need to comply with those local regulations and

[15] Comprehensive Economic and Trade Agreement (hereinafter "CETA"), Article 8.1. Similarly, CETA has a TPF article, Article 8.26, and it provides mandatory disclosure of TPF agreement as well. Full text can be accessed via: http://trade.ec.europa.eu/doclib/docs/2014/september/tradoc_152806.pdf.

[16] A/CN.9/WG.III/WP.172, para. 12, p. 5/11.

rules in case they are operating in one of those jurisdictions. The same funder in investment arbitration is also investing in litigations and other types of arbitrations. Funders generally use the same TPF structures regardless of whatever platform through which they provide TPF. They also use the same considerations as elaborated in further sections of this chapter. Thus, it is impossible to deny other definitions. To be able to see the big picture of the TPF market and how it is affecting investment arbitration, it is necessary to refer to those regulations on TPF, to some extent. Even though the majority of TPF available is commercial TPF, there is a possibility of non-commercial funders and there are indeed examples of such TPF in investment arbitration.[17]

Another difficulty for reaching a common definition of TPF comes from the different types of TPF options that are available in the market. As explained in Sect. 3.3 of this chapter, there are several different TPF models. This fact makes it more difficult to find one regular definition for all different types of TPF arrangements. However, TPF started appearing in more regulations, institutional rules and treaties. The most important ones are referred to above. ICSID, which administers a high number of investment arbitration cases, brought new rules in 2022 covering TPF.[18] While demand for TPF is increasing, this trend in having more TPF rules will continue. Thus, it is very likely that there will be more instances where the TPF is defined differently and various rules covering it. With this growth, soon there will perhaps be a common ground on what TPF is and what it is not. For now, we can say that for investment arbitration, the tendency is a broader definition, while in other arbitrations and litigation finance, the tendency is restricting the scope of regulations to professional funders.

In conclusion, a broad definition of TPF is preferred in this book. In investment arbitration, there are examples of all types of TPF arrangements such as donations by NGOs, finance by lawyers on a contingency basis, or a sui generis TPF agreement specific to the case or a mix of the other TPF models. However, it is a fact that in investment arbitration, most of the TPF is offered by professional funders as in commercial arbitration and litigation. And, unless otherwise stated specifically, TPF must be understood as TPF offered by professional funders. Before the analysis of the TPF agreement, a brief history of TPF in general, and in ISDS in particular, is given in the following section.

2.3 History of TPF

TPF did not start in investment arbitration. It first started in litigation, then spread over to arbitration, and lastly and more specifically investment arbitration. This section explicates the historical developments of TPF. Therefore, it covers firstly

[17] *See* Chap. 3 for a full analysis of investment case law on TPF.

[18] ICSID Arbitration Rules, available at https://icsid.worldbank.org/rules-regulations/convention.

how TPF started in litigation in major jurisdictions, and then secondly, the history of TPF towards ISDS.

2.3.1 The History of TPF in the World

Historically, the involvement of third parties was not generally welcomed by any courts because of the potential threat to justice. The possibility that rich and powerful people might affect judges and this might result in unfairness in cases was the rationale behind it. Especially in the medieval period, it was more apparent.[19] This gave rise to champerty and maintenance doctrines in common law jurisdictions. These two doctrines will be explained in this chapter separately. The reason why those doctrines were developed in the first place is well summarized in the following lines: "the sword of a baron, stalking into court with a rabble of retainers at his heels, might strike terror into the eyes of a judge upon the bench".[20] However, in the same book, written two centuries ago, it is also stated that "At present, what cares an English judge for the swords of a hundred barons?".[21] Considering that the book was written in the nineteenth century, in today's twenty-first century, courts are more powerful and independent. Thus, it is not surprising that the champerty and maintenance doctrines lost their power. This development paved the way for the birth and growth of TPF market today in the world.

In the historical aspect, the maintenance and champerty doctrines are important because they were the principal obstacles before the TPF market in common law jurisdictions could develop. Once maintenance and champerty doctrines lost their status in common law jurisdictions, then the TPF practice could rather develop quickly. This is because the market demands finance for legal costs. This book focuses on TPF in investment arbitration; however, to understand the TPF market completely, its historical development should be examined in its entirety. Eventually, TPF started in courts and then spread over into arbitration and investment arbitration. Thus, it is important to show this development process. Now, nearly in every major common law jurisdiction and some civil law jurisdictionsTPF is used as an accepted and available finance method for parties. Investment arbitration is only one of the platforms through which TPF is used as a finance option. Nonetheless, TPF of investment cases raises more concerns than the TPF of litigation and other arbitration proceedings because of the specific role of investment arbitration. Moreover, TPF attracted some resistance and some states even suggested that it should be

[19] W. Holdsworth, A History of English Law (4th ed) Vol. III at 394–395 from David Neuberger, Harbour Litigation Funding First Annual Lecture 8 May 2013, available at https://adam1cor.files.wordpress.com/2013/05/lord-neuberger-harbour-litigation-lecture-8-may-2013.pdf.

[20] Bentham (1818), p. 40.

[21] *Ibid.*

completely banned in investment arbitration.[22] Together with other ongoing ISDS problems, TPF is accused of being another problem of the system. Yet, there is no champerty doctrine that prohibits TPF and there is no rule in investment arbitration rules that prevents parties from benefitting from such finance options. Therefore, TPF grew rapidly in investment arbitration.

The TPF market is very popular and successful. Even in 2017, the TPF market operating in the UK was estimated above 10 billion USD.[23] Another estimate in 2018, predicted that the size of the market was between "$50 billion to $100 billion".[24] However, these numbers are not certain. According to another study, even though the potential market size was unknown, one anecdotal estimate was showing the size of $80 billion in 2009.[25] 2009 is the year the leading funder of them all now, Burford Capital, was founded. Burford alone has $2.5 Billion assets under its investment management.[26] Considering the company was established in 2009 with a $130 million initial public offering, it is a great achievement over 10 years.[27] Another report shows that until 2014, the market for arbitration funding "has probably grown by well over 500 per cent since 2012, in terms of both the number of completed deals and the volume of active funders looking for viable opportunities".[28] All this shows how big the potential of the third-party market is and how rapidly it is growing. These figures also show how the funders themselves have grown in a short period, too.

There are different theories about why the TPF market growth has occurred so quickly. One suggestion for the growth of TPF was the 2008 economic crisis.[29] It might be true that the demand could be higher in time of crisis, however litigations and arbitrations are always costly, and an option not to spend for those costs are a constant demand even at the time when the economy is stable. The actual reason for the growth of the TPF market is clear. Legal proceedings are costly and businesses need TPF to bring their cases. Even financially strong companies might prefer to

---

[22] Some states suggested that third-party funding should be prohibited in UNCITRAL Working Group III meetings even though this suggestion was only shared by a small minority of countries. For a complete analysis of those suggestions, *See* Chaisse and Eken (2020).

[23] Financial Times, "Arbitration academics are living in the dark ages" (19 November 2017) available at https://amp.ft.com/content/926355de-c941-11e7-ab18-7a9fb7d6163e.

[24] Brian Baker, In low-yield environment, litigation finance booms (Published on August 21, 2018), available at https://www.marketwatch.com/story/in-low-yield-environment-litigation-finance-booms-2018-08-17.

[25] Hodges et al. (January 30, 2012), p. 45. Available at SSRN: https://ssrn.com/abstract=2126506 or https://doi.org/10.2139/ssrn.2126506.

[26] Burford Annual Report 2018, p. 3 available at https://www.burfordcapital.com/media/1526/bur-31172-annual-report-2018-web.pdf.

[27] About Burford, Burford Capital Website, available at https://www.burfordcapital.com/about-burford/.

[28] Delaney (2014), https://globalarbitrationreview.com/article/1033321/mistakes-to-avoid-when-approaching-third-party-funders.

[29] ICCA Queen Mary Report (n 1), p. 18.

fund their legal costs so that they can do more investments instead of using the money for their legal costs. Moreover, there is no rule anymore banning TPF as there was in the past as explained above. On this account, there is no indication that the TPF market will stop growing. In the future, we can easily predict that the TPF market will continue growing globally.

The reason the market keeps growing is because TPF can be extremely lucrative. To show how lucrative TPF can be, an example from one of Burford's funding is illuminating. Burford invested "US$5 million in exchange for 33 per cent of any settlement and 40 per cent of any judgment".[30] A US$110 million verdict was handed down for Burford's client and Burford took 44 million USD, a near 880 per cent return on its investment.[31] This shows how lucrative the TPF market is.

How and when this lucrative and massive market was created happened a few decades earlier. TPF does only have three decades of past. First, TPF started developing in the 1990s by the abolition of the two doctrines in New South Wales,[32] and became well-established in Australia with a landmark decision by the Australia's high court in *Campbells v. Fostif*.[33] Then England and Wales followed this trend as examined below. Noticeably, in England and Wales, Justice Jackson's report was considered as the largest analysis of civil procedure since the Access to Justice Report by Lord Woolf in 1996.[34] Also, the USA and other jurisdictions followed as well.[35] In some jurisdictions, TPF was considered illegal or at least the legality of it was questionable. The development of TPF is directly related to the degree of the operation of maintenance and champerty.

In Australia, TPF is very well developed. We must note that class actions constitute an important part of the TPF marke. According to a study covering the period between 2001 and 2017, 63% of class actions were supported by funders in Australia.[36] This figure alone proves how much the TPF market developed. In Australia, maintenance and champerty were put to an end by law in several states. In South Australia, both doctrines were put to an end by the Criminal Law Consolidation Act.[37] In Victoria, the Wrongs Act abolished champerty and maintenance.[38] In New South Wales, they were put to an end by the *"Maintenance, Champerty and*

---

[30] Cremades Román (2011), p. 14.

[31] *Ibid.*

[32] Maintenance, Champerty and Barratry Abolition Act 1993 No 88.

[33] Avraham and Wickelgren (2014), p. 242. The full text of the case is available at http://eresources.hcourt.gov.au/downloadPdf/2006/HCA/41. For the aforementioned case's full details, *see* Campbells Cash and Carry Pty Ltd. v. Fostif Pty Ltd. [2006] HCA 41.

[34] Chris Shilvock, UK: Jackson Cost Reforms: A Summary Of The Key Changes To Civil Litigation Costs, May 2013, available at https://www.mondaq.com/uk/Real-Estate-and-Construction/236810/Jackson-Cost-Reforms-A-Summary-Of-The-Key-Changes-To-Civil-Litigation-Costs.

[35] For developments in Australia, the UK and USA, *see* Victoria Shannon Sahani (2013), pp. 443–452.

[36] For the class actions filed in history, *see* Morabito (2017).

[37] Criminal Law Consolidation Act 1935 (SA) Sch 11 ss 1(3).

[38] Wrongs Act 1958 (Vic) s32 and Crimes Act 1958 (Vic) s322A.

Barratry Abolition Act".[39] Lastly, in the Australian Capital Territory, the Civil Law (Wrongs) Act abolished them.[40] By these rules, it was made clear that the champerty and maintenance doctrines were no longer applicable in respective Australian states. Moreover, the high court judges confirmed this situation. Justice Kirby asserted that:

"The importance of access to justice, as a fundamental human right which ought to be readily available to all, is a new consideration that stimulates fresh thinking about representative or grouped proceedings".[41]

Therefore, it is seen that access to justice is a very important argument for TPF explaining why TPF was welcomed in the first place.

Moreover, as stated before, the High Court of Australia has found that litigation funding is not "unusual",[42] that there should be "less hostility to litigation funding",[43] and that "the law looks neutrally on the prosecution of the proceedings being funded unless they are an abuse of process".[44] A more "relaxed common law attitude to litigation funding" is well accepted.[45] Furthermore, "the importance of not preventing [humble men] from receiving [contributions to meet a powerful adversary] has been long recognized".[46] Thus, we can conclude that litigation funding is presumptively valid and courts look at it favourably in Australia. Litigation funding can be illegal if it is against the public policy by abusing legal proceedings in limited situations as the individual case may describee.

In the United Kingdom (UK), a similar trend is observed. UK Criminal Law Act 1967 abolished maintenance and champerty and stated that no person shall be criminally and civilly liable unless public policy requires.[47] Moreover, the long-recognized "the importance of not preventing [humble men] from receiving [contributions to meet a powerful adversary]"; in simpler terms, access to justice considering the impecunious rule, originated in England and Wales as referred to in this case.[48] In the UK, after the 1967 Criminal Law Act, more court decisions stated the effect of champerty and maintenance. Mr. Justice Coulson brought together those rules.[49]

---

[39] Maintenance, Champerty and Barratry Abolition Act 1993 (NSW) sections 3, 4 and 6.

[40] Civil Law (Wrongs) Act 2002 (ACT) s 221.

[41] Campbells Cash and Carry Pty Ltd. v. Fostif Pty Ltd. [2006] HCA 41 at 145 citing Thai Trading Co v Taylor [1998] QB 781 at 786 per Millett LJ; cf. Aitken (2006), p. 177.

[42] Campbells Cash and Carry Pty Ltd. v. Fostif Pty Ltd. [2006] HCA 4, para. 120.

[43] *Ibid.* para. 142.

[44] *Ibid.* para. 256.

[45] *Ibid.* referring to Martell v Consett Iron Co Ltd. [1955] Ch 363 at 386 per Danckwerts J.

[46] *Ibid.*

[47] UK Criminal Law Act 1967, Section 14/2, available at http://www.legislation.gov.uk/ukpga/1967/58/section/14.

[48] *See* Chap. 1 in *Supra* note 35 (referred to, Martell v. Consett, England and Wales Case).

[49] London & Regional (St George's Court) Ltd. v Ministry of Defence [2008] EWHC 526 (TCC), 18 March 2008, para. 103 citing to Mansell v. Robinson [2007] EWHC 101 (QB).

(a) the mere fact that litigation services have been provided in return for a promise in the share of the proceeds is not by itself sufficient to justify that promise being held to be unenforceable.[50]
(b) in considering whether an agreement is unlawful on grounds of maintenance or champerty, the question is whether the agreement has a tendency to corrupt public justice and that such a question requires the closest attention to the nature and surrounding circumstance of a particular agreement.[51]
(c) the modern authorities demonstrated a flexible approach where courts have generally declined to hold that an agreement under which a party assisted with litigation in return for a share of the proceeds was unenforceable.[52]
(d) the rules against champerty, so far as they have survived, are primarily concerned with the protection of the integrity of the litigation process in this jurisdiction.[53]

After this consistent case law in England and Wales, TPF was established as a valid finance method.

In the USA, the TPF market varies depending on the states. According to Stoyanov ve Owczarek, there are four main trends regarding maintenance and champerty in the USA.[54] States have a different degree of acceptance and application of maintenance and champerty doctrines along with these four trends, starting from a complete denial of champerty and maintenance doctrines in California up to a very broad acceptance of champerty and maintenance doctrines in the District of Columbia.[55]

Before 2005, the litigation funding market was largely limited to personal injury claims. Specialized litigation funding started in 2006, e.g. Credit Suisse Securities founded a litigation risk strategies unit.[56] In the USA, two states promulgated rules on TPF. In Maine in 2007, there was a regulation on specific to legal TPF contracts.[57] In Ohio similarly, the Uniform Commercial Code provides non-recourse civil litigation advance contracts.[58] According to these regulations, now in Maine and Ohio, TPF is legal but must follow the regulatory requirements. In the USA, there are also ethical rules related to TPF. Under the ABA Rules, legal practitioners must not accept compensation for representing a client from someone other than the client unless "(i) the client gives informed consent, (ii) there is no interference with the lawyer's independence of professional judgement or with the lawyer-client relationship;" and (iii) information relating to the representation of a client remains

[50] *Ibid.* For this rule, see R (Factortame) Ltd. v Secretary of State for Transport (No.8) [2003] QB 381, para. 38.

[51] *Ibid.* For this rule, see Justice Coulson refers to Giles v Thompson [1994] 1 AC 142.

[52] *Ibid.* For this rule, Justice Coulson gives the following case as an example, citing: Papera Traders Co Ltd. v Hyundai (Merchant) Marine Co Ltd. (No.2) [2002] 2 Lloyd's Rep 692.

[53] *Ibid.*, para. 43.

[54] *See* Chap. 1 in supra note 49, p. 179.

[55] *Ibid.* p. 180.

[56] Lake Whillans, The History And Evolution Of Litigation Finance, Jan 27, 2017, https://abovethelaw.com/2017/01/the-history-and-evolution-of-litigation-finance/.

[57] Me. Rev. Stat. Ann. tit. 9-A §§ 12-104, 12-106.

[58] Ohio Rev. Code Ann. § 1349.55.

confidential.[59] Thus, in the USA we can see that some rules have already been enacted to regulate TPF.

In the USA; however, one type of TPF, contingency-fee agreements is well established, and is an important part of legal practice. Attorneys might enter into a contingent fee agreement with their clients, and this means that the attorney finances the case and gets a share from the award in return if the case results in favour of his client. Stephen S. Susman claims that his law firm is the first commercial litigation funding firm in the USA.[60] However, contingency fees are not the litigation funding method as understood today in the world, it is only one method that lawyers use to finance the case. In some jurisdictions, however, contingency fees are still not legal.[61] In the USA, contingency fees are well established in all states,[62] and TPF as a market developed in the world today does not have as long a history as contingency fees have.

In Canada, TPF started developing as well. The first third-party funder who opened a branch in Canada is IMF Bentham in 2016 and expanded to Quebec, Canada's only civil law jurisdiction, in 2018.[63] And only in 2019, IMF received over 430 applications for funding.[64] This shows how fast TPF started growing in Canada as in other jurisdictions. Champerty and maintenance were also in Canada's legislation, by the Act Respecting Champerty RSO (1897) (the Champerty Act),[65] even though they were removed for being criminal offences, but they remained as torts.[66] Regarding contingency agreements, Ontario passed a regulation in 2004 and brought specific conditions for legally accepted contingency fee arrangements.[67] Regarding TPF agreements, in Ontario, the Superior Court of Justice has held that TPF agreements are not categorically illegal on the grounds of champerty or maintenance

---

[59] American Bar Association Model Rules of Professional Conduct ("ABA Model Rules"), Rule 1.8 (f).

[60] Susman and Wilkins (2019), available at https://thepractice.law.harvard.edu/article/risky-business/. The conversation between Stephen D. Susman, a founding partner at the law firm Susman Godfrey and David B. Wilkins, faculty director of the Harvard Law School Center on the Legal Profession gives important insight on contingency fees in the US market.

[61] In Hong Kong and Singapore, third-party funding legislations specifically permit funding in arbitration proceedings as explained and lawyer-financing is not allowed in those legislations. Funding of cases in courts, as well as contingent fee agreements by lawyers, stay illegal as before.

[62] For a history of contingency fees see Landsman (1998), Available at https://via.library.depaul.edu/law-review/vol47/iss2/4.

See Chap. 1 in *supra* note 55.

[63] Hugh A Meighen, Canada *in* The Third Party Litigation Funding Law Review - Edition 3 available at https://thelawreviews.co.uk/edition/the-third-party-litigation-funding-law-review-edition-3/1212001/canada.

[64] *Ibid.*

[65] Statute of Champerty, RSO 1897, c 327.

[66] Canada's Criminal Code Consolidation in 1953, cited Chap. 1 in *supra* note 54.

[67] Contingency Fee Agreements, O Reg 195/04, available at http://canlii.ca/t/1llx.

and the court should approve the TPF agreement in class actions.[68] Thus, as we can see the market is developing in Canada and courts are not hostile against TPF agreements, even though there are some specific requirements in some provinces in Canada.

In Hong Kong and Singapore, similar to each other, there was a specific need for clarification on the situation of TPF. Both jurisdictions had supreme court case decisions creating uncertainty whether TPF is legal or illegal because of champerty and maintenance. In Hong Kong, TPF for impecunious claimants and insolvency proceedings were allowed.[69] This was because of general acceptance that access to justice is desirable.[70] However, in the same claim, the court expressly left the question unanswered regarding if maintenance and champerty pertain to TPF arrangements regarding arbitrations seated in Hong Kong.[71] In Singapore, the Supreme Court did not discern arbitration from litigation and declared that champerty equally applies to both.[72] Therefore, in both jurisdictions, the application of champerty to TPF was not clear and the legality of TPF was uncertain. This made the legislation necessary and both jurisdictions passed their legislation after a public consultation period.[73] Thus, we can clearly see that Hong Kong and Singapore also followed the global trend and welcomed TPF, albeit differently than others, they limited their TPF to arbitration alone.[74] Thus, TPF in litigation, except in limited scenarios as explained, remain illegal.

In Civil Law jurisdictions, there were similar doctrines; however, there was no direct equivalent of maintenance and champerty. Thus, technically, there was no legal obstacle in respect of TPF and thus, TPF could be developed well. Therefore, any civil law country can be the next TPF jurisdiction that can develop rapidly. The Netherlands is an example of a rapidly developing TPF jurisdiction and Germany and Spain are examples of well-developed TPF markets in Europe, and yet others are either small or even completely unfamiliar with TPF.[75] The Netherlands, however,

---

[68] Bayens v Kinross Gold Corporation, 2013 ONSC 4974 (Bayens); available at https://www.harbourlitigationfunding.com/wp-content/uploads/2015/08/final-bayens_v_kinross_funding_mtn_25july13.pdf.

[69] *See* Unruh v. Seeberger [2007] 10 HKCFAR 31, available at https://www.hklii.hk/eng/hk/cases/hkcfa/2007/10.html.

[70] *Ibid.*, para. 95–96.

[71] *Ibid.*, para. 123.

[72] Otech Pakistan Pvt. Ltd. v Clough Engineering Ltd. and Another - [2006] SGCA 46, para. 38, available at https://harbourlitigationfunding.com/wp-content/uploads/2015/08/otech_pakistan_pvt_ltd_v_clough_engineering_ltd_and_another.pdf.

[73] See Chap. 1 in *Supra note 2* and *Supra note 5*. Singapore legislation came into force in 2017. Hong Kong passed third-party funding legislation in 2017 as well; however, the important terms of Hong Kong legislation came into force on 1 February 2019 together with Code of Practice for Third-Party Funding of Arbitration.

[74] In Hong Kong, third-party funding is allowed in Arbitration, both domestic and international arbitration, while in in Singapore it is allowed only in international arbitration. For a detailed comparison, *See* Eken (2022).

[75] *See* Perrin (2019).

also hosts one of the oldest funders which was founded as early as in 1986.[76] Considering the number of countries in Europe and a limited presence of funders in certain countries, civil law countries wait as optimum TPF markets starting from Europe, without the danger posed by the ancient doctrines of maintenance and champerty.

2.3.2 The History of TPF in Investment Arbitration

After a brief description of how TPF started over the world, now we can talk about investment arbitration specifically. Without surprise, after the TPF market expanded and it became more accepted in the world, third-party funders started investing in investment arbitration cases as well. This is without surprise because investment arbitration is famous for having expensive proceedings and high returns for investors. The characteristics of the ISDS regime are reasons for funders to fund ISDS claims. Thus, there is no surprise that TPF started playing an active role in investment arbitration. The first known funded case in ISDS was in 2007. Since the disclosure of the funder is not mandatory, when the first case in ICSID was funded is difficult to accurately determine. We have only information that has been made public via either legal news, reports, court decisions, arbitration awards, or via publications by funders. Therefore, it is clearly possible that TPF started in ICSID cases before the practice was made public, which means probably earlier than 2007. Since then, the number of funded cases increased and the impacts of TPF in investment arbitration grew dramatically.

As stated above, the first known third-party funded case in ICSID is a case brought in 2007.[77] The first Arbitration Institute of the Stockholm Chamber of Commerce (hereinafter "SCC") case funded by a funder was brought in 2007 as well,[78] and lastly, the first case administered by Permanent Court of Arbitration (hereinafter "PCA") funded by a third-party funder was brought in 2011.[79] This number continues to grow.[80] As an example, anecdotal numbers suggest that in two-thirds of investment arbitration cases filed in 2013, the claimants had sought resources from a major funder.[81] However, we should state that funders show no

---

[76] Omni Bridgeway was founded in the Netherlands in 1986 and joined forces with IMF Bentham in 2020. *See* https://omnibridgeway.com/insights/blog/blog-posts/blog-details/global/2019/10/15/imf-bentham-and-omni-bridgeway-announce-plans-to-merge-to-become-a-global-leader-in-disputes-financing.

[77] Abaclat and others v. Argentine Republic (ICSID Case No. ARB/07/5).

[78] Quasar de Valores and others v The Russian Federation (Quasar v. Russia), SCC Case No 24/2007.

[79] Guaracachi America, Inc. and Rurelec plc v The Plurinational State of Bolivia, UNCITRAL, PCA Case No 2011-17.

[80] See Chap. 3 that analyzes all investment cases funded by a third-party.

[81] Park and Rogers (2014), p. 42.

additional special interest in investment arbitration. For funders, it is an investment decision just like other arbitration proceedings or litigation in courts. Whether the proceedings are in courts, in any type of arbitration, or investment arbitration does not matter. Even though it is true that one attraction for funders in investment arbitration is potential high amount of compensation as we stated, funders are considering different factors as explained in the following paragraphs in this chapter and decide whether to invest or not according to those criteria. These criteria are the same for all cases brought before funders. As long as it is a good investment option, they decide to fund the case.

In investment arbitration, tribunals discussed TPF on various grounds.[82] However, tribunals did not discuss TPF on some grounds, which have already been discussed in courts. As explained above, TPF has a playfield beyond investment arbitration and this scope of TPF created case law in nearly all major jurisdictions. In England and Wales, for example, there is an important portion of case law on TPF in the domestic context. Investment arbitration will create more cases in the coming years continuously and it is going to be interesting to see whether this case law will align with or whether it will differ from existing case law. As an example, however, it is important to mention this existing case law briefly.

The Court of Appeal in England and Wales examined that:

> a professional funder, who finances part of a claimant's costs of litigation, should be potentially liable for the costs of the opposing party to the extent of the funding provided.[83]

This is known as "Arkin Cap" and even the decision itself states that "funders are likely to cap the funds that they provide to limit their exposure to a reasonable amount".[84] In another case, the Court of Appeal differs from the Arkin Case and did not cap the responsibility of the funder, instead ordered against funders.[85] And a later case confirmed this approach and abolished Arkin Cap in England and Wales completely.[86] In later cases, such as *Chapelgate v Money*, this approach was confirmed.[87] However, large TPF firms claim that this will not affect their business.[88] Thus, there are two approaches regarding the amount of liability of funders.

[82] For a complete analysis of investment cases *see* Chap. 4.

[83] Arkin v Borchard Lines Ltd. and others [2005] EWCA Civ 655, para. 41, available at https://www.bailii.org/cgi-bin/format.cgi?doc=/ew/cases/EWCA/Civ/2005/655.html&query=(arkin)%20AND%20(borchard).

[84] *Ibid.* para. 42.

[85] Excalibur Ventures v Texas Keystone and others [2016] EWCA Civ 1144, para. 22, available at https://www.harbourlitigationfunding.com/wp-content/uploads/2016/11/EXCALIBUR-VENTURES-LLC.pdf.

[86] *See* Davey v Money [2019] EWHC 997 (Ch), cited in https://www.nortonrosefulbright.com/en-us/knowledge/publications/c015054d/developments-in-third-party-funding-in-arbitration and https://www.whitecase.com/publications/alert/high-court-heralds-end-arkin-cap.

[87] Chapelgate Credit Opportunity Master Fund Ltd-v-Money & Others [2020] EWCA Civ 246.

[88] Craif Arnott, The end of the Arkin cap is not a big story for big legal finance, available at https://www.burfordcapital.com/insights/insights-container/arkin-cap-not-big-story/.

However, in arbitration cases, including investment arbitrations, it is less likely for arbitrators to order against a third party that has not signed the arbitration agreement. Since funders are external parties and did not consent to the arbitration agreement in the first place, it is more problematic in arbitration to order against a non-signatory funder.[89] More interestingly, in England and Wales, the High Court (Commercial) decided that other costs can include the costs of obtaining litigation funding.[90] Under the English Arbitration Act (1996), section 59, costs include *"legal and other costs of the parties"* and in this case, importantly, the High Court concluded that costs of obtaining litigation funding are recoverable as *"other costs"* under section 59. Whether these issues will be discussed in investment arbitration and if they are, how arbitrators would decide them will be seen in the coming years. Surely, such case law from litigation funding present examples for arbitration funding.

In summary, international investment arbitration has seen increasing numbers of funded cases over a decade. However, TPF has not been discussed before investment arbitral tribunals in all respects. In some jurisdictions' courts, TPF has been discussed with some interesting decisions as discussed above. Thus, it is certain that the number of cases on TPF in investment arbitration and its impact will grow in the coming years. Accepting this fact UNCITRAL Working Group III and ICSID are already working on a possible code of conduct, which brings disclosure requirements for adjudicators.[91] European Parliament also recently passed a resolution with recommendations on responsible private funding of litigation.[92] These regulations and case law on TPF will certainly expand, whether arbitral tribunals will follow pre-existing case law in local courts is an exciting development to follow.

2.4 The ISDS Regime and TPF

2.4.1 Investor-State Dispute Settlement (ISDS) Regime

As stated, TPF is a new player in investment arbitration. However, investment arbitration itself has not had a very long history either. Noticeably, the ISDS mechanism started playing an active role in the late 1990s, and most of the cases were brought especially in the last 10 years.[93] Having known this fact alone, we can

[89] *See* Brekoulakis (2017), pp. 610–643; Park (2008), pp. 17–27.

[90] Essar Oilfields Services v Norscot Rig Management Pvt. [2016] EWHC 2361, para. 68, available at https://www.casemine.com/judgement/uk/5a8ff75760d03e7f57eab7c1.

[91] ICSID and UNCITRAL Draft Code of Conduct for Adjudicators, Article 5/2. The Draft is available at https://icsid.worldbank.org/en/.

[92] European Parliament, Responsible private funding of litigation European Parliament resolution of 13 September 2022 with recommendations to the Commission on Responsible private funding of litigation (2020/2130(INL)), Document 52022IP0308, (2023/C 125/01).

[93] United Nations Conference on Trade and Development (UNCTAD), Investor State Dispute Settlement: Review of Developments in 2016, at 2 (May 2017), available at https://unctad.org/en/

understand better why TPF has a short history in the ISDS system as the book explained in the previous section. Thus, before explaining. The role of TPF in investment arbitration, the basic characteristics of the ISDS mechanism itself must be addressed.

The whole idea of ISDS started with the goal to improve foreign direct investment, even in "the first Bilateral Investment Treaty (hereinafter "BIT") between Germany and Pakistan in 1959", by creating an objective dispute settlement mechanism so that it will serve the "ultimate economic development of both states".[94] Now, there are reform studies of ISDS going on,[95] and according to the European Commission, an investment court should take the place ad hoc investment arbitration.[96] Predominantly, there are four plausible reform schemes: "(i) incremental changes to the existing rules and regulations, but with no significant structural reforms, referred to as 'investment arbitration improved' (IA Improved); (ii) the introduction of an appellate mechanism to investment arbitration, referred to as 'investment arbitration + appellate mechanism' (IA + Appeal); (iii) the creation of a multilateral investment court (MIC); and (iv) the termination of ISDS altogether, referred to as No ISDS".[97] Apparently, there is dissatisfaction with the existing ISDS regime and reform studies regarding the existing ISDS regime are a result of it.

Investment arbitration has some features that distinguish it from other dispute settlement mechanisms, commercial arbitration and litigation in courts. One party is always the state and states give their consent to arbitration much longer before the investor sues them in arbitration. By entering into bilateral investment treaties (BITs), states consent to arbitrate, within the scope of BITs, any disputes that might arise in the future. Moreover, by signing the ICSID Convention they also agree that the award will be binding and not contingent on any appeal or similar remedy except laid out in the ICSID Convention.[98] Because of its power as a global dispute settlement mechanism, one author stated that investment arbitration is the "global administrative law".[99] Furthermore, states have a public interest in

PublicationsLibrary/diaepcbinf2019d4_en.pdf. More Notes are available at https://unctad.org/en/pages/publications/Intl-Investment-Agreements%2D%2D-Issues-Note.aspx.

[94] Sachs (2018), p. 196. For the BIT between Germany and Pakistan, *see* https://investmentpolicy.unctad.org/international-investment-agreements/treaty-files/1387/download.

[95] For UNCTAD, *See* https://unctad.org/en/PublicationsLibrary/diaepcbinf2019d3_en.pdf For OECD, *See* Joachim Pohl, Societal Benefits and Costs of International Investment Agreements: A Critical Review of Aspects and Available Empirical Evidence (OECD Working Papers on International Investment, 2018:1), available at https://doi.org/10.1787/e5f85c3d-en and for UNCITRAL ISDS Reform works, *See* https://uncitral.un.org/en/working_groups/3/investor-state.

[96] *See* Commission Proposes New Investment Court System for TTIP and Other EU Trade and Investment Negotiations, European Commission (Sept. 16, 2015), A Multilateral Investment Court, European Commission (Sept. 2017), http://trade.ec.europa.eu/doclib/docs/2017/september/tradoc_156042.pdf. http://europa.eu/rapid/press-release_IP-15-5651_en.htm European Commission, "The Multilateral Investment Court Project," Oct. 6, 2019.

[97] Bottini et al. (2020), p. 255.

[98] ICSID Convention, Article 53.

[99] Van Harten and Loughlin (2006), pp. 121–150.

investment arbitration,[100] as taxpayers are paying for the award. This feature calls for greater extent transparency. All these characteristics are distinctive features of investment arbitration. Because states created this global administrative law in the first place by entering into investment treaties, they now engage in ongoing works to continue to develop it. The purpose of this book is not to give detailed explanations of the problems and all features of the ISDS regime. However, giving a brief framework here is important to place TPF in this big picture, where the main goal is to support the economic developments of states by fostering foreign direct investment. This will help us to understand why some parties and scholars are not comfortable with the fact that TPF is playing an active role in the ISDS regime. Especially in the ethics section of this book, those concerns will be addressed.

In summary, there are different views on how efficient the current ISDS mechanism is and whether it should be amended or completely replaced with another mechanism. TPF entered into the scene in the middle of such controversial time. It is important to stress that because it might help us to understand why TPF raises so many concerns in investment arbitration, while it does not raise that many concerns in commercial arbitration or litigation. High expectations of states in the investment regime to solve problems and dissatisfaction with the existing system are reflected in TPF as well. Moreover, the characteristics of the investment regime require more transparency than commercial arbitration. This is another reason for the ongoing disclosure requirement for TPF arrangements. This is how TPF is situated in the existing—problematic—investment regime. Now, we can move onto specifically how TPF is playing a role in this system.

2.4.2 TPF in the Investment Regime: Overall Look and Arguments for and Against

In investment arbitration, TPF is known as an option, generally, only for claimants. This brought the notoriety of funders to the consideration of states. This is because of the mechanism of the ISDS regime. In investment arbitration, investors are the ones bringing claims against states and seeking compensation. States, on the other hand, are the parties who committed an act which is the disputed issue, and as a response, investors are the ones who sue states and seek compensation. And generally, states do not have many options to bring a counterclaim and seek compensation from the investors.[101] Even though there are some attempts to bring counterclaims by states, they have not been successful in the end and the scholars agree on the difficulty of

[100] *See* Gehring and Euler (2015), pp. 7–27.

[101] *See* Vohryzek-Griest (2009), pp. 83–123, available at http://www.scielo.org.co/pdf/ilrdi/n15/n15a04.pdf.

bringing counterclaims in ISDS.[102] Thus, the result that TPF is favouring investors against the interests of states is not a deliberate choice of funders; instead, it is a design problem of the investment arbitration system. Investors are the ones who are supposed to bring a claim in this system. Thus, in principle, investors decide to bring a case. It is not a deliberate choice of funders to fund only investors, not states. Whether it is a problem that systems are designed in this way or not is another issue to discuss. However, these explanations are true for professional funders, who are investing in claims. As stated, TPF practice can be broad and it does not only consist of professional funders. As a result, there are different examples of states received TPF for various reasons and there are even examples of state funding offered by professional funders. The practice of TPF is developing, and it is possible that soon states will have more options for different TPF models.

Even if we focus on TPF for claimants only, there are certainly good arguments in favour of it. One might very well argue that the investor-state dispute settlement mechanism is gives investors the chance to seek justice when the state's actions are unjust and violate the legal protections of the investor and this is how it is supposed to be. States are the strong parties in this equilibrium and naturally, investors will sue states when something goes wrong. States have always the power to cancel the license of investors, cancel the project the investor is working on, or change the law or increase the tax, etc. While doing so, however, states must act within the limits of the law or otherwise investors have rights to sue them according to the provisions of investment treaties or any other available laws states enacted and are bound to comply. If this argument is found sound, which is investors are the ones who should be the claimants and investors should have the capacity to sue states, TPF must be favoured. Generally, investors, after losing their investment in the state, are not always in a position to bring and continue costly and lengthy arbitration proceedings. Thus, TPF gives them a chance to initiate a claim when they are impecunious. Moreover, if they are not impecunious, it is not an easy decision to bring an investment arbitration claim either, even for well-established companies. Especially considering that the average cost is over 8 million USD per party,[103] and the average length of an investment case is 4 years,[104] it is not an easy decision to make. Thus, it

[102] *See* Spyridon Roussalis v. Romania, ICSID Case No. ARB/06/1 (7 Dec. 2011); Goetz v. Burundi, ICSID Case No. ARB/01/2 (21 June 2012). In *Urbaser* case, the tribunal accepted the jurisdiction but rejected the counter-claim; *see* Urbaser S.A. and Consorcio de Aguas Bilbao Bizkaia, Bilbao Biskaia Ur Partzuergoa v. The Argentine Republic, ICSID Case No. ARB/07/26. For a range of scholarship over counter-claims, *see* de Nanteuil (2018), pp. 374–392; Shao (2021), pp. 157–179; Boon (2022), 253–284; Ishikawa (2019), pp. 33–37; Popova and Friedman (2014), pp. 1–42; Bjorklund (2013), pp. 461–480; Kryvoi (2012), pp. 216–252.

[103] *See* http://arbitrationblog.kluwerarbitration.com/2016/02/29/how-much-does-an-icsid-arbitration-cost-a-snapshot-of-the-last-five-years/ and https://www.allenovery.com/en-gb/global/news-and-insights/publications/investment-treaty-arbitration-cost-duration-and-size-of-claims-all-show-steady-increase.

[104] *See* https://www.allenovery.com/en-gb/global/news-and-insights/publications/investment-treaty-arbitration-cost-duration-and-size-of-claims-all-show-steady-increase.

is certain that TPF is increasing access to justice for both impecunious or well-established claimants and facilitates the ISDS system by increasing its accessibility.

The main argument against TPF is that the "number of frivolous claims might increase with TPF".[105] However, as explained in the following paragraphs, TPF is a non-recourse investment and funders would not invest their money if the case does not have a substantial possibility of winning. However, even though imagining some funders would do that, this danger could easily be prevented by granting SfC orders in such cases. The only fear for states against ill-faith claims is the possibility for states not to be able to recover the expenses they spent to defend themselves against such claims. However, SfC orders would stop this danger since the money, securing the expenses of states, will be paid in advance by the party who brought such claims. Therefore, even if some funders would try to invest in weak cases, SfC order would protect states against those cases. Alternatively, sanctions against such cases might be increased so the system might eliminate such possibilities. The new ICSID rules can bring such sanctions against investors who bring frivolous claims or anyone who supports or funds such claims. However, in the new ICSID rules, there are no such provisions.[106]

Not surprisingly, this mythical "frivolous" claim was always an argument against any type of external finance of ISDS.[107] Funders generally take cases if the chance of winning is over 60%.[108] Funding cases that have at least 60% chance of winning does not seem frivolous at all. As a caveat, we must add that this percentage might change depending on the preference of a funder, but generally, a funder can be presumed not to invest in a case if there is a less than 50% chance to win. Thus, it seems difficult for funders to fund meritless cases, otherwise, they would lose their investment. Even if they do, SfC orders against such meritless cases would remove this small risk since SfC orders would secure recovering money spent by the respondent states.

There is also a negative perception of TPF. Because of the position of funders, generally funding claimants, TPF is seen as an institution against state interests, and anti-state and anti-citizens of such states, even as an exploitation of the ISDS system.[109] However, this is an unfair accusation. First of all, if states do not violate any law or any protection for investors that they promised to provide, there could be no compensation imposed on the shoulders of states nor citizens. As long as states are acting within the limits of the law, no investor can get any award against states. States must pay compensation only if they breached the law and failed to provide protection to investors, which states promised in the first place to attract those foreign investments. What TPF can achieve is that by facilitating the system, by enabling more claimants to use the system, funders can be only a deterrent for states,

[105] Tan and Bouchenaki (2015), p. 250.

[106] ICSID Arbitration Rules, available at https://icsid.worldbank.org/rules-regulations/convention.

[107] Galanter (1983), pp. 69–71.

[108] Hodges et al. (2012), p. 45.

[109] *See* Garcia (2018), pp. 2911–2934.

forcing states to act within the limits of the law, otherwise they might have to face a lawsuit launched against them. The system was designed to protect investors, and force states to act within the limits of the law. By facilitating this system, funders serve only to increase the accessibility of such a system. Therefore, we can see with the participation of funders that there is no exploitation of the system but only facilitation of the system.

In the current ICSID rules, there are two rules concerning TPF, and it is not surprising.[110] It was mentioned that the number of investment cases has increased and the ISDS system has been active recently. The fact that TPF is starting to be an important player in ISDS has been even more recent. At the time most investment treaties and the ICSID Convention came into force, there was not even a market in the world called TPF. In recent BITs, it is key to record that TPF started being at least defined.[111] Moreover, ICSID's new rules also prescribe disclosure requirements for TPF agreements.[112] The expect there will be at least some basic regulations regarding TPF in investment arbitration soon.

Finally, after the explanations of the specific role of TPF in the investment regime, and the negative perception of funders, arguments for and against TPF, it is important to understand how the TPF process starts, continues and ends. The next section explains the basic mechanism of TPF. Under this, when a party starts looking for TPF, how do funders decide whether to fund or not to fund, and if they decide to fund, how do they monitor the case, who decides case management, and the relation between the lawyers and funders, what are the entitlement and duties of both sides in a typical TPF agreement will all be explained.

2.4.3 TPF Agreements in Investment Arbitration: A Doctrinal Analysis

TPF emerged from a very basic need and demand from the market. As an example, Burford Capital CEO Christopher Bogart declared that he first started TPF as a hobby and founded his company after increasing demand from his friends.[113] With any legal proceeding, either arbitration, litigation or even negotiation and settlement proceedings, there is a cost. This cost consists of attorney fees, and court or arbitration fees.[114] Who pays those fees? Generally, the party who brings the claim. However, if the investor lacks the necessary funds to bring the case, to cover the attorney fees and other fees, then TPF can help to cover those expenses

[110] ICSID Arbitration Rules, Article 14 and 53.

[111] For example, *see* Comprehensive Economic and Trade Agreement (hereinafter "CETA"), Article 8.1; Vietnam Investment Protection Agreement (2019), Article 3.37.

[112] ICSID Arbitration Rules, Article 14. The new ICSID rules came into force by 1 July 2022.

[113] https://www.ft.com/content/17cbe4d8-baaf-11e9-96bd-8e884d3ea203.

[114] For a full list of potential costs, see the explanations under the following Sect. 2.4.3.1.

and get a share from the award in return. This is the simplest summary of why TPF is needed and how does it works, and even maybe why the market developed so fast. There are many details in this summary and this part which will explain the basic mechanism of TPF, starting from the funder's analysis of the case, to concluding a TPF agreement and the end of a TPF relationship.

TPF is a financial option available for parties. It has different purposes for different parties. The purpose of professional funders is an investment. Explanations here in this section are for professional funders,[115] and most of the explanations are true for TPF of ISDS claims in addition to TPF of cases in courts or other arbitration proceedings. Since it is an investment for professional funders, considerations are the same regardless of the TPF forum. For professional funders, like Burford Capital, TPF of a claimant, or a respondent state does not matter as long as it is a viable investment. For parties who take finance from such funders, a TPF "deal" is a strategic choice. This strategic choice relieves parties from taking the risk of the ISDS process in exchange for a portion of the award. The parties in TPF agreements are the funder who finances the case and the party who has a case against the state (hereinafter "investor") in the first place. Besides, the relationship between the investor and the funder is controlled by the terms of the TPF agreement between them. However, there are common stages before deciding on TPF and considerations for funders and investors. Those common steps and features will be analyzed here.

Overall, there are four different TPF methods in ISDS cases. The first and most common, as mentioned above, entails a professional funder funding a case in return for a share of the award.[116] Second, an entity can collect claims of a group of claimants to fund and continue proceedings on the claimants' behalf, which is different than typical TPF agreements.[117] This type of TPF arrangements might be called as "sui generis" TPF arrangements. Third, an external party who has an entitlement in the award can finance the party in the dispute.[118] Fourth, lawyers finance the case on a contingency fee.[119] Lastly, in some cases, a third-party funder finances a party without any financial expectation but for charitable purposes.[120] However, even under this classification, some of them can be divided into sub-categories, too; depending on whether the funded party is the state or claimant,

[115] *See* Explanations under Sect. 2.3.3.2 for explanations of professional funders.

[116] The case in many investment arbitrations falls under this category. For an example of such funding in investment arbitration: *See* Teinver S.A., Transportes de Cercanías S.A. and Autobuses Urbanos del Sur S.A. v. Argentine Republic (ICSID Case No. ARB/09/1).

[117] *See* Giovanni Alemanni and others v Argentine Republic, ICSID Case No ARB/07/8.

[118] *See* RSM Production Corporation v Grenada, ICSID Case No ARB/05/14.

[119] An example was reported by Luke Eric Peterson, IA Reporter, Investor and Lawyers Fall Out Over Contingency-Fee Arrangement in Aftermath of ICSID Arbitration, available at https://www.iareporter.com/articles/investor-and-lawyers-fall-out-over-contingency-fee-arrangement-in-aftermath-of-icsid-arbitration/. *See* Waguih Elie George Siag and Clorinda Vecchi v. Arab Republic of Egypt (ICSID Case No. ARB/05/15).

[120] *See* Philip Morris Brand Sàrl (Switzerland), Philip Morris Products S.A. (Switzerland); Abal Hermanos S.A. (Uruguay) v. Oriental Republic of Uruguay (ICSID Case No. ARB/10/7).

or some TPF models can be the combination of two or more. Note that there might also be after the event insurance,[121] and in the broadest term this can be within the definition of TPF as well, however insurance agreements are not considered as TPF in this book due to the lack of case law in ISDS related to insurance agreements.[122] This should show us that TPF methods are diverse and there is no one single framework we can put all types of TPF into. Nevertheless, these five categories each present distinctive features and have purposes different from each other. Before examining each in detail, the next section continues with some common features pertain to all TPF agreements.

2.4.3.1 Costs Covered in the TPF Agreements

When we talk about TPF, there are certain types of costs covered by the TPF agreement. The TPF agreement can cover all or some of those costs as agreed by the parties. Nonetheless, naming the potential types of costs is important to materialize what is the subject matter TPF companies finance. There is not a study naming those costs specific to investment arbitration, however, TPF of any case regardless of the forum, has similar types of costs that can arise in a legal proceeding. Thus, the costs named here are not specific to investment arbitration, but a rather broader representation for any type of TPF agreements.

The amount of finance the TPF agreement covers can change depending on a variety of factors. The general costs that the TPF agreement might cover depends on the TPF agreement between the parties. The share the funder will receive also depends on many components. A comprehensive list by the Hong Kong Law Reform Commission enumerates these components as follows:

> (1) the amount in dispute; (2) the fees of the solicitors and barristers whom the party instructs; (3) the length and complexity of the procedural timetable set by the Tribunal;
>
> (4) the complexity and number of the legal and factual issues in dispute, which will require commensurate work by the parties' counsel to put forward in legal submissions; (5) whether experts are required (and the fees that they charge); (6) the fees of the Tribunal (which vary either due to the set fees charged by each arbitral institution, or the fees of each arbitrator as agreed to be paid by the parties, ie, not against a set scale); (7) the administrative and registration fees of an arbitral institution if it is an institutional arbitration; (8) the amount of documentation that is required to be reviewed and produced in the arbitration, and the cost of the solicitor's fees and/or the technical tools (ie, specialised document review IT programs) to review that documentation; (9) the costs of holding a hearing, including the cost of hiring

[121] *See* Eskosol S.P.A. in Liquidazione v. Italian Republic, (ICSID Case No. ARB/15/50) Procedural Order No. 3. In this ICSID case, a claimant had purchased ATE insurance. This is not third-party funding under the definitions accepted in several investment treaties. Only, according to UNCITRAL Working Definition, it can be considered as third-party funding. For this reason, Eskosol case is surveyed under Chap. 4 of this book.

[122] Insurance agreements have not raised any concerns as TPF did. Therefore, the book does not deal with different type of insurance agreements. For explanations regarding certain types of insurance *See* Sect. 2.3.3.2.6.1.

facilities in which to hold the hearing, the cost of accommodation and transport for the Tribunal as well as counsel. A hearing is also a cost intensive phase in relation to legal representation fees incurred by the parties; and (10) the costs of enforcing an Award, or applying to a court to challenge or set aside the Award.[123]

As mentioned, those costs are not restricted to the above factors. When thinking of specific investment arbitration costs, we can easily add a few more items to this costs list. Expenses of arbitrators and lawyers, experts, and witnesses or other expenses specifc to the case that can come up can increase the overall costs more. TPF agreements will generally describe what costs the funder will cover, the limit funders will cover up to, conditions for the funding, and the decision mechanism regarding whether to pay for other costs that come up during the proceedings or not.

2.4.3.2 Analysis of Professional Funders

As mentioned, the most typical funders in the market are professional funders. Major funders all around the world such as Omni Bridgeway, Burford Capital, Harbour Litigation Funding, and Vannin Capital come to mind first when TPF is mentioned. And in ISDS, those funders have financed many cases.[124] However, no arbitral tribunal has named them as "professional funders" yet. We can see the "professional funder" term in some court decisions when such professional funders fund the cases in the same way they fund investment arbitrations. Those high court decisions generally make a differentiation between professional funders and others.[125] The reason for this is because of two long-standing common law doctrines that ban what professional funders do.[126] Professional funders are again described in some high court decisions. According to one of those decisions, "almost always the TPF arises out of a contractual obligation" and "normally such a funder exercises considerable control, management and supervision of the litigation".[127] Therefore, the professional funder has a contract with the party it funds, and monitors its investment until the proceedings are over. Even though investment arbitration tribunals did not name any of the funders as professional funders, they are known to bear this label with this name in the market and the reason for using this classification here is to stress that not all types of TPF arrangements are identical to the arrangements professional third party funders offer. Nonetheless, it is a fact that most TPF arrangements in

[123]This list is taken from The Law Reform Commission of Hong Kong, Third Party Funding for Arbitration Sub-Committee, Consultation Paper, Third Party Funding for Arbitration, October 2015, available at https://www.hkreform.gov.hk/en/publications/tpf.htm p. 27.

[124]*See, e.g.* https://www.iareporter.com/, *See* also Chap. 4 for a detailed analysis.

[125]In Ireland, professional third-party funding is banned due to the decision in Persona Digital Telephony Ltd. and another v The Minister for Public Enterprise and others [2016]. For the high court decision, *see* https://www.courts.ie/judgments.

[126]Those two doctrines, namely maintenance and champerty, are explained in Sect. 3.3.4.1.

[127]Roach v News Group Newspapers Ltd. [1998] EMLR 161, para 48, cited in Arkin v Borchard Lines Ltd. and others [2005] EWCA Civ 655, para. 31.

investment arbitration are entered into by professional funders. Moreover, this type of arrangements seems more problematic and raises more concerns because of the funders' monitoring over the case. The three-way relationship between lawyer-party-funder also raises ethical concerns, especially in investment arbitration. An external entity who is not an investor has an interest in the outcome and this raises ethical concerns in investment arbitration as explained in the fifth chapter of this book. This is the orthodox method of TPF. Thus, professional funders deserve more attention and more explanations are given under the professional funders section here than other classifications.

In general terms, TPF is made by professional funders by funding one of the party's arbitration expenses during the resolution of the dispute and getting a share from the award if the funded party prevails. Even though it seems like a simple process, it is not that simple. The TPF process involves "claim holders, funders, lawyers and, potentially, funding brokers".[128] How this financing or none-financing decision is given, what costs are covered, when parties can cancel their agreements and what are the basic rights and responsibilities of the parties are decided in the TPF agreement. Even though it depends on the terms of the TPF contract, there are characteristics and patterns or some guidelines and examples available. For example, the Association of Litigation Funders offers a guideline for its members.[129] The websites of prominent funders, articles and other literature are analyzed to create this section.

2.4.3.2.1 TPF Process

This section explains the considerations of funders before entering into a TPF agreement. For funders, deciding to fund a case is not a simple decision. Since it is a non-recourse investment, they require extensive analysis of the case before accepting to fund the case. Non-recourse means that if the funded case fails, funder loses all its investment and do not recover any money invested. There are some stages for a funder before accepting to finance the case. Those stages are (i) legal assessment of the case and (ii) investment decision by the funder. When the TPF decision is made, there is a monitoring process until the proceedings are over which will be explained separately, where funders monitor how the case is developing. First, the legal assessment of the case and investment decision are examined.

In general, third-party funders are looking for the minimum 1/10 ratio between the funding amount requested and the real value of the claim.[130] This means that the real value of the case must be ten times the amount required for the financing of the case. In this ratio, funders generally take three/four-fold return in their investment.[131]

[128] ICCA Queen Mary Report (n 1), p. 20.

[129] *See* https://associationoflitigationfunders.com/documents/

[130] ICCA Queen Mary Report (n 1), p. 25.

[131] *Ibid,.* p. 26.

One way of explaining the rationale for the 1/10 ratio is that otherwise, funders would take more than the funded party, which would create the perception of exploitation of the status of the funded party. To avoid this type of impression, funders might usually choose not to fund any case whose real value of its claim is less than 10 times the fund required for the arbitration/litigation proceedings.

Lastly, depending upon the jurisdiction where the third-party funder operates, TPF might be subject to some regulations. Hong Kong and Singapore for examples provide some guidelines and regulations for funders.[132] Similarly, in England and Wales, the Association of Litigation Funders offers some guidelines for its members.[133] At present, there is zero common regulatory scheme in investment arbitration. In investment arbitration surely there is none. However, since a funder is physically going to be located in a jurisdiction, those regulations and guidelines will be relevant to the funders in which they are operating. This book is focused on the investment arbitration regime and its regulations and cites other regulations or cases only to explain the practice better. This book does not aim to elaborate each jurisdictions' approach and rules, this would be broader than the aim of this book.[134] Now, having learned that the majority of the cases funders examine are rejected, and that there are two stages before entering into a TPF agreement, those two stages will be elaborated more below.

2.4.3.2.1.1 Legal Assessment

Request for TPF and securing that TPF are different things. The TPF request is as simple as sending an email to a third-party funder, preferably together with a legal memorandum from an arbitration practitioner.[135] This legal memorandum will help you to secure TPF if it attests that you have a strong case. Considering that funders receive many requests and that due diligence for each case can take a long time, it is not difficult to see that funders will consider a TPF request more seriously if the request is accompanied but a memorandum attesting the strength of the case from a famous practitioner. Lawyers play an active role for their clients to secure TPF. Two major funders, Burford and Juridica's investments "are referred to them by large law firms mostly".[136] This shows how lawyers are important to play a significant role as intermediaries between funders and their clients. Lawyers in today's world have a

[132] For a comparative analysis of Hong Kong and Singapore third-party funding regulations, *See* Eken (2022).

[133] Code of Conduct for Litigation Funders, Association of Litigation Funders, January 2018.

[134] For the third-party funding market in a number of jurisdictions, *see* Litigation Funding 2020, Woodsford Litigation Funding, available at https://woodsfordlitigationfunding.com/us/wp-content/uploads/sites/3/2020/01/GTDT2020.pdf.

[135] Obtaining Third-Party Funding for International Arbitration—How It Works, Aceris Law, available at https://www.acerislaw.com/obtaining-third-party-funding-international-arbitration-works/.

[136] Schaner and Appleman (2012), p. 178.

role to offer their clients the best finance options. Moreover, lawyers also play a role in assessing the case legally.

As it can easily be guessed, funders do not accept all TPF requests. In reality, rejection rates are as high as 90 per cent or even higher.[137] This means that only less than 10 per cent of TPF requests are accepted. To choose one out of ten successful cases to be funded, now, the first step is legal assessment. However, whatever the result of the TPF process is, the whole process is confidential and parties proceed with the TPF under a non-disclosure confidentiality agreement.[138] The acceptance rate of some funders is even as low as 3.5 per cent.[139] This shows how scrupulous legal assessment is and funders reject a big majority of cases while accepting a tiny portion of all requests they received. The rest of the cases which could not secured funding will either try their chances with other TPF mechanisms, or another funder who wants to take the risk or they will not be able to bring their cases at all.

2.4.3.2.1.2 Investment Decision

If the legal assessment of the case proves that it is strong, then the investment decision can be considered. After the legal assessment of a case and deciding that it is viable case with a high chance of winning, there must be another decision to make: the investment decision. The legal assessment gives only a conclusion regarding the legal strength of the case, whether the case has a strong possibility of winning or not. The investment decision is a very strategic decision for funders. Is it a good investment decision or not? And to answer this question, more than legal skills and knowledge are required.

The investment decision is generally not left to the lawyers only but also to different stakeholders. A committee needs to assess how much money they are willing to pay for the case, and how much of the award they should take as well as it can consider other human rights or other responsibilities funder should consider.[140] This process can be considered under other names as well such as final due diligence, or second stage of assessment etc. In the end, what is considered in this later stage before a final decision whether to fund or not is to discover responses to inquiries such as is it a good decision to fund the case, is it coherent with their corporate responsibility, how much money the funder is willing to spend, for how long, and as a result what is going to be their profit? As shown, this process involves more than only legal considerations. All these questions are answered by a

[137] ICCA Queen Mary Report (n 1), p. 25.

[138] Woodsford Litigaiton Funding, A practical Guide to Litigation Funding, available at https://woodsfordlitigationfunding.com/wp-content/uploads/2019/01/A-Practical-Guide-to-Litigation-Funding_ROW.pdf.

[139] *Ibid.*

[140] Burford does not finance cases if financing might result in a violation of human rights or unjust social impact. For example, "Burford refrains from financing litigation against impoverished small states, even when the underlying cases may well have merit"; *See* https://www.burfordcapital.com/shareholders/responsibility/.

committee and if the answer is positive, then the TPF agreement can be concluded. Only after passing these stages can the case be funded.

2.4.3.2.1.3 Conclusion

The TPF decision is not made easily. The ground for the aforementioned is that the TPF is typically a non-recourse litigation finance method, meaning that funders lose all their investment in case the case is not successful.[141] It requires both legal and economic evaluation of the claim and the whole process. In summary, funders take into consideration several factors before deciding, which can be subcategorized under legal and economic assessment. As a whole, those elements are summarized by Cremades together as follows: (1) value of the lawsuits; (2) amount to be advanced; (3) jurisdictional obstacles; (4) defenses; (5) nature and length of the proceeding (including whether arbitration or litigation; venue and applicable rules); (6) possibilities of settlement; (7) creditworthiness of client and the opposing party (particularly with a view to collection prospects); (8) counsel chosen and compensation structure (whether there is a contingency fee agreement in place) or (9) additional obligations of the party to be funded linked to the potential risk of recovery (such as previous funding agreements or any other alliance).[142]

Legal assessment of a case is an important process and has other benefits to the party seeking TPF. The legal assessment provides an objective assessment of the party's case. It is beneficial even though the TPF agreement is not signed at the end since the party will have an assessment of its case and see its weak and strong sides of its case. Furthermore, if the TPF agreement is signed, there are additional benefits to the funded party. A funder's acceptance proves a strong case against the opposing party. Thus, the opposing party might be more susceptible to accept a settlement agreement since the opposing party knows that: (i) The case is strong and that is why the funder decided to invest, (ii) the funded-party will have enough financial resources to continue its case so that the funded-party will not have financial distress if the case continues. Tactics to extend the arbitration or litigation period will not be successful since the funded party has strong finance in place to continue its case. Thus, these are additional benefits of the TPF process and, if concluded, the TPF agreement.

Also, the length of the legal assessment depends on many variables. If the case is brought to the funder before any legal proceedings have started, it can be quick while if the case is ongoing and there are many documents, provisional orders and decisions, witness statements etc. to analyze, then the process can take longer. A case close to trial can take as little as three weeks while an early-stage investment treaty case with limited preparation will most likely take longer.[143] Therefore, it is difficult to give an average period for how long this process can take. If the party is

[141] ICCA Queen Mary Report (n 1), p. 18.

[142] Cremades (2013), p. 153.

[143] Smith (2012), p. 20.

represented by an experienced lawyer and has presented all relevant documents in an early stage, it is more likely to conclude all the assessment process in three weeks. Anything causing more time and effort will extend these three weeks.

2.4.3.2.2 Concluding TPF Agreements

When the assessment is completed and the funder accepts the funding, a TPF agreement can be concluded. The reason for parties to get TPF can be various. Impecunious claimants, structurally impecunious corporations, to transfer risks of legal proceedings to a funder or using the money of legal proceedings for more efficient purposes, such as financing other investments or projects. When this is the case, parties look for a funder, and when the funder accepts to finance the case, the outcome is the TPF agreement.

The funder is an external party.[144] The funder in this type of TPF has no previous relationship with the party. Lawyers are not professional third-party funders and the contingent fee agreements between lawyers and clients are not a type of agreement under this category. Moreover, insurance, in general, is different than TPF. However, we must note that most professional funders offer after the event (ATE) insurance in their services,[145] but ATE insurance is not going to constitute a TPF agreement. Therefore, we are going to explain TPF agreements as when the funder finances litigation/arbitration proceedings.

There are two parties in a TPF agreement, the party who seeks finance for its claims and the funder. For an investment case, generally investor, or respondent-State and the funder. Thus, one party to the TPF agreement will be the party who has an ISDS claim. This party can technically be both the claimant and the respondent. However, because of the explanations above, since in investment arbitration investors are the ones who are bringing claims for compensation, not states, investors are generally the party to the TPF agreement. If states bring a case against the investor or have a counterclaim that the respondent-State might recover from the investor, then respondent states might also seek TPF and transfer the risk and costs of ISDS to the funder. Although, this possibility is little because of the structure and purpose of the current ISDS regime, which is to protect investors as explained above. As long as states are responsible for their acts and investors need protection, investors will bring cases against states and those investors are the ones who might need TPF.

The other party to the TPF agreements is the professional funder. Professional funders are generally corporations founded for profit. Some of the funders are even publicly held companies sold off in stock exchanges. Currently, there are two publicly-traded third-party funders. Burford Capital is sold at the London Stock Exchange and IMF Bentham, now its name after the merger is Omni Bridgeway is

---

[144] Nieuwveld & Sahani at Chap 1, footnote 29, p. 3.

[145] *See* https://harbourunderwriting.com/harbour-underwriting-partners-with-gs-group-to-provide-after-the-event-ate-insurance-to-scottish-lawyers/.

sold at the Australian Securities Exchange.[146] However, usually, when they provide finance, they create an entity for this purpose. The reasons for creating an entity are varied, such as protecting their investment. Those entities are called special purpose vehicles. Special purpose vehicles are legal entities, which are usually used because of tax reasons, created for a variety of purposes, including the purchase, funding, or both, of a business or the structure of a monetary contribution. For a model TPF agreement, an article can be referred.[147]

In summary, potentially both claimants and respondent states can be parties to a TPF agreement. However, in practice, claimants are more likely the party to the TPF agreement. And, on the other side of the agreement, there are professional funders and they might use a special purpose vehicle created for TPF purposes.

2.4.3.2.3 Ancillary Agreements

The TPF agreement is not the sole agreement funders sign with the funded party. There are other agreements to support the TPF process. One such agreement accompanies every TPF process to secure the investment return first and before anyone else gets any share of the award. Funders enter into a priority agreement apart from the TPF agreement itself. The priority agreement is called a "waterfall agreement", too.[148] While the TPF agreement is between the funded party and the funder, the priority agreement involves more than those two parties.

As the name suggests, this agreement arranges who has the priority to take its share of the award. All parties who have an entitlement in the award must join this agreement to be effective. Naturally, both parties to the TPF agreement are the funder and funded party. Besides, the funded party's lawyers are parties to this agreement as well. Therefore, there are three parties in a waterfall agreement and it shows the order of the payment among these three parties. A typical return structure is as follows:

(1) repayment to the third-party funder of its investment to date;
(2) payment to the third-party funder of its return and to the insurer of any contingent or deferred premium;
(3) to lawyers in respect of any deferred or contingent or conditional success fees; and
(4) the balance to the claimant.[149]

In summary, the funder takes its expenses and fees first, then other stakeholders take their fees and the funded party takes last. This agreement accompanies all TPF

[146] For their market prices, *see* https://www.londonstockexchange.com/exchange/prices-and-markets/stocks/summary/company-summary/GG00B4L84979GGGBXAMSM.html, and https://www.asx.com.au/asx/share-price-research/company/OBL.

[147] Steinitz and Field (2014), p. 749.

[148] ICCA Queen Mary Report (n 1), p. 27.

[149] Smith and Wesolowski (2017), p. 25.

procedures since funders want to make sure that they will get paid first. There are other ancillary agreements that accompany the TPF agreement. For example, funders might insure themselves against adverse costs with adverse cost insurance, or if the party leaves the choice of lawyers to the funder, then funders will enter into a retainer agreement with lawyers as well. However, as it can be seen, those other agreements are not always necessary, rather optional and depend on whether the funded party will retain lawyers or whether the funder will do so. Thus, other ancillary agreements are not automatically concluded in every TPF process as the priority agreement is and no further explanations regarding them are required here. This section only addresses the common features of all TPF transactions where the funder is a professional funder. Professional funders almost always require all necessary parties to sign a priority agreement in addition to the TPF agreement.

2.4.3.2.4 Monitoring the Case

As in the last step, after concluding the TPF agreement, professional funders, as expected, will monitor their investment and follow how the case is developing. It is natural because those funders are investing in a case as a non-recourse investment, meaning that if the case fails funders will lose all the money and will not be able to recover anything from the funded party.

There is an interest from the funder's side in monitoring the case. The degree of this monitoring depends on how much control funders have over the case, and the two interests are conflicting with each other. On one side, existed the control that the funded party should have and on the other side, existed the funder's interest in monitoring the case that needs to be balanced. There must be a balance between the two interests and a good TPF agreement addresses these two conflicting interests and sets clear limits on both parties' rights and obligations. The ultimate decision of who holds what rights, and which judgments the funder can make, or the funded party can have a say alone are important issues which need to be dealt.[150] For example, settlement decisions must stay with the funded party, while the budget will be decided by the funder.

A famous funder explains the monitoring stage: "As passive capital providers we monitor investments to help maximize value for our clients".[151] Thus, the goal of monitoring is to protect their investments and maximize their profit for their business. Monitoring is the last step of the TPF process. Monitoring continues until the case concludes. A case can end in two different ways, in favour of the funded-party or against it. When the funded-party wins its case, the funder gets its share according to the TPF agreement they have agreed initially. If the funded party loses, this is

[150] The degree of control possesses an important procedural issue to examine, which is analyzed in detail in Chap. 3.

[151] https://www.burfordcapital.com/how-we-work/.

naturally a very unpleasant result for the funder because this means that it lost all the money it invested in the case.

2.4.3.2.5 TPF Arrangements Third-Party Funders Offer

The section above has set out the basic mechanics of a TPF process. The main steps are shown there. Nevertheless, it is also important to show that there are different types of services a third-party funder can offer. Here, the different services a funder provides are explained. Rather than covering subjects mentioned extensively, the purpose is to inform the reader about their existence and different services available for parties. Moreover, depending on which party is funded or in what platform TPF is provided, TPF can be known under different names. Explanations here are also regarding those different types of TPF.

2.4.3.2.5.1 Portfolio Funding v. Single Case Funding

A TPF arrangement can either be for a single case or many cases as the funder can accept to provide TPF as a group or portfolio. They are both "non-recourse investment", thus, the funder needs to make a good decision. Thus, all the assessments and other mechanisms explained above are valid here, too. Portfolio funding is now engaged in international arbitration, and there is also anecdotal evidence of defence-side portfolio funding of states in investment arbitration.[152] This means in investment arbitration that if a state has several cases against itself, then a funder can offer a portfolio funding for all the cases against that state. This also proves that respondent states have chances to get TPF as portfolio funding as well. However, portfolio funding has risks of increasing frivilous cases and should not be allowed in ISDS, as this issue is addressed in the best practice guideline.

Portfolio funding is not only available as a finance option for states, or big companies that might have a large number of cases, but also for law firms. A major third-party funder divides portfolio funding as monetization portfolio, risk-share portfolio, and expense-only portfolio.[153] Therefore, we can conclude that TPF might vary and open possibilities for a limitless number of possibilities with different structures of finance. It is not possible to name every type of finance arrangement that has ever been done or that can ever be done. However, these explanations will make possible to see a pattern and general trends and structures of TPF. According to each client's need, TPF agreements can be tailored and differ from the general structure given here.

---

[152] ICCA Queen Mary Report (n 1), p. 74.

[153] Burford, Portfolio Finance, available at https://www.burfordcapital.com/how-we-work/expertise/portfolio-finance/.

2.4.3.2.5.2 Litigation Funding v. Arbitration Funding

Generally, funders advertise their services of TPF as litigation and arbitration funding. By litigation, generally, courts are meant. And by arbitration, any type of arbitration including commercial and investment arbitration, is meant. Between litigation and arbitration funding, there is no difference in terms of the decision mechanism explained above for legal assessment and the investment decision. The only difference is the platform where the claim is brought. By litigation finance generally, cases in courts are referred, and by arbitration finance, cases in arbitration are referred. Apart from this, there is no outstanding difference in terms of decision making or consideration of funders. Those considerations listed under the assessment section are the same for all TPF agreements regardless of litigation or arbitration.

2.4.3.2.5.3 Claimant Financing v. Respondent State Financing

As mentioned above, in investment arbitration, TPF is generally available for claimants, since they are the investors bringing a case against states and claiming compensation for their loss. Therefore, in investment arbitration, third-party funders are generally on the claimants' side and provide financing for claimants. This is not consistently accurate though. In some scenarios, respondent state financing is also possible. Therefore, this book can make these two definitions depending on which side is getting finance from a funder. Apart from the difference in name, there is also no structural difference between the two.

2.4.3.2.5.4 Monetization of Claims

Third-party funders do not only offer to provide finance for litigation and arbitration. One other service a funder provides is to monetize claims.

Each legal asset carries a value in the future. Since this value is not immediate, what monetization does is to predict the future award for the claim and turn into cash for immediate use. One funder explains this service as "legal claims are assets—sometimes extremely valuable ones—but they are highly illiquid and carry a huge amount of uncertainty as to timing and outcome. Legal finance enables companies and firms to unlock cash flows associated with their legal assets".[154] Thus, in short, monetization of claims turns claims into cash. This service can be used both by companies and law firms.

By mentioning some services third-party funders offer for their clients, this section is concluded. These services such as monetization are also a kind of TPF and funders offer such services. As stated above, the TPF market is an innovative market where funders develop new tools and services according to the needs of their clients. Thus, those services should be brought under the structure of the TPF

[154] Burford Capital, Monetization, available at https://www.burfordcapital.com/how-we-work/expertise/monetization/.

mechanism as explained in detail above. After mentioning some important services offered by funders, now we can mention some other types of finance available for parties other than TPF.

2.4.3.2.6 Other Types of TPF Arrangements

As explained, TPF works in a mechanical way whereby the funder takes on the risk of legal proceedings and the funded party agrees to give a certain amount of its claim to the funder. This is not the only arrangement a party can utilize to finance its legal proceedings. There are many other monetary settings for the fees and costs of a legal claim. Here, those other models are identified.

2.4.3.2.6.1 Insurance

Insurance and TPF are two different options for a party. However, they are not completely different from one another. Some insurance types are pretty similar to TPF,[155] at least to some extent. Therefore, it is important to pay attention to those similarities and differences to understand the limits of each better.

There are two types of insurances that have closeness with TPF: Before the Event (hereinafter "BTE") and After the Event (hereinafter "ATE") insurances. BTE Insurance- "is a type of legal expenses insurance whereby customers purchase insurance to cover legal costs that may arise in either a personal or business context".[156] ATE insurance "is a type of commercially available insurance policy which provides coverage for legal costs, subject to an agreed limit of indemnity".[157] The difference between the two is that before the event insurance can be obtained before a dispute has arisen, while "ATE insurance can be obtained at any time after a dispute has arisen, and even after proceedings have commenced".[158] As can be seen, there is a great similarity between TPF and those two specific types of insurances. They all cover legal costs and expenses. They all transfer the risk from the party to the insurer or funder. Moreover, ATE and BTE insurances are offered either as separate from TPF agreements or together with the TPF agreement by funders. However, there is a big distinction, of course: the main purpose of both types of insurances is insuring as in all other insurances, while in TPF the main purpose is investing in the claim. As the difference between them is generally mentioned in TPF articles, it is important to mention them and inform the reader.

[155] For an analysis of the common interest privilege for insurers and related privilege extended to third-party funders, see ICCA Queen Mary Report (n 1), Chapter 5, pp. 133–135.

[156] Narinder Hothi, What is Before the Event Insurance?, Griffin Law, available at https://www.griffin.law/understanding-before-the-event-insurance-bte/.

[157] K&L Gates, After the Event Insurance, available at http://www.klgates.com/files/Uploads/Documents/Global_Insurance/After_the_Event.pdf.

[158] *Ibid.*

There is another type of insurance to protect investors and which is offered as an alternative to TPF by those who oppose TPF, which is political risk insurance.[159] This type of insurance "is designed to mitigate against the loss of commercial assets, income or property as a result of a political risk event".[160] There are several other types of insurance to protect investors, especially foreign investors, which it can be argued, could compensate investors without the need to bring a case against the state in the first place. However, those insurances do not protect investors against all the risks an investment carries. Therefore, those types of insurances cannot eliminate the need for TPF completely but may accompany it and protect investors in certain circumstances.

Moreover, the time when an investor is seeking insurance and TPF is completely different. In most of the insurance, insurance is bought before an investment is made or after the investment is made, but before any dispute arises—except for ATE insurance-. Furthermore, when you seek insurance you do not need to start a legal proceeding. You are insured and if certain conditions in your insurance policy are met, you will be entitled to the amount that you are insured. In the case of proceeding with an investment arbitration, you claim that your rights were breached by certain actions and you seek compensation. Insurance protects you and compensates your losses without any legal action. However, if your losses are beyond the insurance, then you need to start a legal proceeding anyway. In the end, even though the goal of insurance and any legal process is to compensate your losses, they are two different routes and one does not necessarily prevent the other. Thus, here in this book, the similarities and differences of certain insurances and TPF will not be discussed any further. TPF is financial assistance to bring and continue your legal proceedings and to cover those costs in return for a share. It is not an insurance policy and, therefore, they are fundamentally different from each other.

In summary, certain types of insurance can be similar to TPF. However, they do not eliminate the need for each other or offer a complete alternative to one another. Moreover, even if the investor has certain types of insurance, the loss to investors might be greater than the coverage of the insurance, so bringing a case against the state in investment arbitration might still be necessary. Thus, TPF would still be an important solution for investors during the investment arbitration proceedings. It is therefore certain that specific types of insurances and TPF can complement each other and give investors more alternatives and protections during and after their investment, and when any disputes arise.

2.4.3.2.6.2 Loans

Loans may be considered as the most direct finance method when you do not have enough financial budget for any particular purpose. When a party does not have money, they generally obtain loans, normally from a bank and they pay it back with

[159] Also see Multilateral Investment Guarantee Agency, available at https://www.miga.org/.

[160] Moorcraft (2019).

an interest in a period. Sometimes, "litigation funding" is known as "lawsuit funding" or "lawsuit loans", which are not meant here.[161] Here, loans are meant in their traditional meaning.

The basic mechanism in loans is that you need to pay the loan back. Investors might need loans when they made an investment in a foreign state, or when they bring an investment case against that state in the litigation or arbitration proceedings. Even states might need loans for the same purposes. Thus, both parties in an investment arbitration can apply for a loan for various reasons. Also, obtaining a loan is not always possible. You need to show some collateral or convince the creditor that you can pay them back. Besides, the loan does not transfer the risk to the creditor and the creditor is not interested in the result of any case since the creditor is only interested to get its money back together with the interest agreed upon. Therefore, it is completely different from TPF on nearly every aspect including structure, purpose and whether you need to pay back or share a fee from your award. TPF is interested in the result because if you lose your claim, the funder cannot reclaim any funds from you while a creditor can reclaim funds regardless of the outcome of the claim. Thus, TPF and loan arrangements are different except for one similarity that they both can help to cover the costs of the investment arbitration.

2.4.3.2.6.3 Assignment of Claims

Firstly, TPF is not an assignment of claims. The funded party is in control of the case and party to the case. The funder is not taking the place of the funded party. The funder only finances that party and gets a share from the award. However, the award still belongs to the funded party subject to the fees that the third-party funder agreed in the TPF agreement.

Assignment of claims conveys that "the transfer of a claim for payment or for other kinds of performance by agreement between the old (assignor) and the new (assignee) creditor".[162] Whereas in TPF, only the risk of litigation or arbitration is transferred, not the claim itself. Therefore, TPF is different from the assignment of claims.

2.4.3.2.6.4 Legal Aid

Legal aid is in some way close to TPF. In legal aid, there is also a pre-assessment of the case similar to TPF in most jurisdictions and not every case has an entitlement to legal aid. The party who is applying for legal aid needs to meet certain requirements to be eligible. Moreover, legal aid does not free the party from all costs. Usually, attorney fees are covered by legal aid but court fees and taxes are not depending on the jurisdiction in which legal aid is sought. More importantly, in investment

---

[161] Shields (2015).

[162] *See* https://www.trans-lex.org/917000/_/assignment-of-claim/.

arbitration, there is no legal aid available for investors or states.[163] Legal aid is available in local courts in some form, if not all, in many jurisdictions. Their common ground is access to justice.[164] The similarity of legal aid and TPF will be elaborated more in the following section.[165]

2.4.3.3 Analysis of Other Funders

Professional funders are the ones that comes to mind when TPF is the subject of the discussion. As stated above, however, there are other types of TPF arrangements apart from TPF offered by professional funders as analyzed in detail above. Those other types of TPF arrangements generally do not pose concerns as much as professional funders do. It is important to give a summary for each though.

Maybe the most common mechanism of TPF after professional funders is finance by lawyers. Generally, lawyers sign a contract with their clients on a contingency basis. It is vital to record that contingency fees are not allowed in every jurisdiction. The USA has traditionally been famous for contingency fees for a long time. In a contingency fee arrangement, attorneys of the party finance the case instead of an external financier. This does not cause any problems in terms of funder-lawyer relationship since they are the same. In this case, there is no three-person relationship. There is still a traditional two-party relation. The lawyer and the party holding the claim on the claimant side and the same on the respondent side. Regarding how contingency fee arrangements may act as financing, there are many books and articles on the subject.[166] Moreover, similar to professional funders, lawyers might buy some insurances to manage the risks.[167] Therefore, lawyer financing is also one method of TPF in the broader sense. Lawyers assess the case and decide whether to finance or not. The only difference, lawyers have dual roles in this type of financing, as a financier and as lawyers.

TPF might happen via an entity that collects claims of a group of claimants to fund and continue proceedings on claimants' behalf.[168] The book classifies this or similar types of arrangements as "sui generis" TPF arrangements. Since in each such sui generis agreement, the conditions are specific to that TPF, we cannot simply generalize any structure for finance, nor would it be possible to lay out all possible

---

[163] There is a United Nations Secretary General's trust fund to assist states in the settlement of disputes. However, this fund is not available fort he ISDS disputes. *See* https://digitallibrary.un.org/record/778872?ln=en#record-files-collapse-header.

[164] More explanations on the access to justice point are elaborated in Chap. 5, where third-party funding is analyzed ethically. Also, the following section gives a brief introduction on access to justice and legal aid.

[165] *See* Sect. 3.3.4.2 Access to Justice and Legal Aid.

[166] *See* Nieuwveld & Sahani, at Chap. 1, footnote 29.

[167] The Judge, Damages Based Agreement DBA Insurance, available at https://www.thejudgeglobal.com/dba-insurance/.

[168] *See* Giovanni Alemanni and others v Argentine Republic, ICSID Case No ARB/07/.

ways and structures of TPF arrangements. As stated above, TPF arrangements are not limited to those stated here, and the more the market develops, the more sophisticated the TPF arrangements that will emerge. This makes it impossible to foresee and lay out every type of TPF arrangement beforehand. Therefore, any TPF arrangement, other than specific groups laid out in this book can be examined under this type and they do not necessarily have common features. They can carry similar features or can be unique or can be mixed with some TPF types. It is principal to record that the types of TPF arrangements are not limited to the ones stated here. They are rather the ones that are used in investment arbitration.

Also, in some cases, a third-party funder finances a party without any financial expectation but for charitable purposes. In this type of TPF arrangement, generally, there are no complicated assessments or agreements with the party owning the claim. This is a donation or grant. Maybe the funder in this type of TPF can agree to recover its grant if the funded party prevails in the proceedings. Apart from this, there is no technicality or complexity. The third-party funder can be a non-profit organization and finances the party because the case is directly related to its campaigns or purposes.[169] However, there are many other ways to raise funds but there is no such example in investment arbitration yet. For example, online platforms offer many TPF opportunities for everyone for different purposes.[170]

Lastly, an external party who has an entitlement in the award can finance the party in its claim.[171] In this case, generally, the funder has an interest in its favor, and this is the reason for finance. It is similar to the donation for charity purposes that will be examined last in this section. Thus, in this type of TPF, the funder might also want to secure its finance by agreeing with the funded party. However, there will also be no legal assessment or investment decision. Since the motive for the funder is the result of the case, the agreement and TPF process will not have the same complexity of the TPF process when it is funded by professional funders.

In conclusion, professional funders are the most common funders in the TPF market. Whenever TPF is used in this book, professional funders are referred to unless otherwise explicitly specified. Finally, before concluding this chapter, some basic terms in TPF must be defined for a better foundation of the subject. The next section will serve for this purpose.

[169] In this case, Uruguay was funded by a third-party funder for charity purposes; *See* Philip Morris Brand Sàrl (Switzerland), Philip Morris Products S.A. (Switzerland) and Abal Hermanos S.A. (Uruguay) v. Oriental Republic of Uruguay (ICSID Case No. ARB/10/7). It was the result of the Tobacco-Free Kids campaign supported by Bloomberg Philanthropists and Bill and Melinda Gates Foundation; *See* https://www.tobaccofreekids.org/what-we-do/global/legal/trade-litigation-fund.

[170] Online platforms make it possible to raise funds for various purposes. *See* https://www.gofundme.com/ and www.giveforward.com.

[171] *See* RSM Production Corporation v Grenada, ICSID Case No ARB/05/14.

2.4.3.4 Basic Terms in TPF

Before completing this chapter, it is essential to understand some basic terms and doctrines related to TPF. Some of those terms are used to explain TPF and are often encountered in TPF articles. All terms explained here aim to help readers understand further chapters better. In the subsequent chapters of this book, most of those terms will be either analyzed further or will be used to explain other issues. Therefore, a fundamental understanding of those terms is necessary.

2.4.3.4.1 Maintenance and Champerty

Maintenance and champerty are the two doctrines that caused the TPF industry to develop late in the world. As explained in the history section, those doctrines were the barriers before the TPF market could develop. These two common law doctrines affected the validity of TPF if they were applied traditionally. When countries started abolishing them, TPF could develop quickly. For investment arbitration, there are no such doctrines limiting TPF options. Surely, it would not be expected that TPF could develop in investment arbitration when no country allows it in its jurisdiction. Therefore, when more jurisdictions abolished those doctrines and TPF developed internationally, then it expanded to investment arbitration. What exactly those doctrines mean is explained here.

Champerty and maintenance doctrines originated in medieval England.[172] Maintenance means "an unconnected third party assisting to maintain litigation by providing financial assistance" and champerty is maintenance "in return for a share of the proceeds".[173] Those doctrines are today considered ancient doctrines. How ancient those doctrines are today can be understood better by referring again to this sentence said nearly two centuries ago: "*What cares an English Judge for the swords of a hundred barons?*" as cited above.[174] This shows that even in 1843, those doctrines were criticized and suggested to be somewhat obsolete. Today, most jurisdictions have already abolished them.[175]

Maintenance is described as:

[172] Rose (2017), available at https://www.cambridge.org/core/books/maintenance-in-medieval-england/2C715E31ADC1357A34FD1ED4225D16B7.

[173] Caroline Kenny, QC, Evolution, Adaptation of Third Party Funding of Arbitrations available at https://law.asia/evolution-adaptation-of-third-party-funding-of-arbitrations/ (this article is adapted from the author's speech at a 2017 Hong Kong Summit on Commercial Dispute Resolution in China) (Feb. 11, 2018).

[174] Bentham (1843) letter XII. Available at https://oll.libertyfund.org/titles/bentham-the-works-of-jeremy-bentham-vol-3.

[175] *See* supra Sect. 2.1.

> the giving of assistance or encouragement to one of the parties to an action by a person who has neither an interest in the action nor any other motive recognized by the law as justifying his interference.[176]

Champerty is described as: "a particular kind of maintenance, namely maintenance of an action in consideration of a promise to give to the maintainer a share of the subject matter or proceeds thereof if the action succeeds".[177] Since a third-party funder is involved with the case for a profit, this would constitute champerty. Once champerty doctrines were abolished, TPF developed quickly without being threatened by such doctrines.

2.4.3.4.2 Access to Justice

In every article written by proponents of TPF,[178] access to justice is one of the major arguments to support it. It is important to note that the role of private actors such as third-party funders to facilitate access to justice is increasing in investment arbitration.[179] Therefore, it is important to explore the notion of access to justice briefly here before we delve into it further in Chap. 5.[180]

Access to justice is the major argument for TPF. Access to justice is an important concept in every legal system. All constitutions have provisions ensuring citizens have the right to access courts and choice of lawyers. And, to secure this, every legal system takes certain measures such as legal aid. In investment arbitration, justice is ensured by access to the investment arbitration system. Now, as investment arbitration is a major dispute settlement mechanism between states and investors, such aid must be available to investors to ensure they have access to investment arbitration. TPF makes a similar contribution and enables investors to have access to justice. Anything that is facilitating rather than obstructing or abusing any process should be allowed and TPF by providing access to justice is a very good reason to be allowed according to supporters of TPF.[181] TPF, because of its similarity with legal aid, can be considered a legal aid of international arbitration There are similarities between TPF and legal aid since both promise access to justice.[182] Noticeably, there is also a big difference between legal aid and TPF. Legal aid does not get any share from any

---

[176] Massai Aviation Services v Attorney General [2007] UKPC 12, quoted in Winnie Lo v HKSAR (2012) 15 HKCFAR 16, at para 10 (per Bokhary PJ).

[177] Quoted in Winnie Lo v HKSAR (2012) 15 HKCFAR 16, at para 10 (per Bokhary PJ).

[178] For example, *see* Marciante (2023), pp. 291–320.

[179] On this note, see Fach Gómez (2021).

[180] See Sect. 5.2 Ethics of TPF and Access to Justice.

[181] *See* Lord Justice Jackson (2009), p. 41.

[182] Maurits Barendrecht, Laura Kistemaker, Henk Jan Scholten, Ruby Schrader, Marzena Wrzesinska, Legal Aid in Europe: Nine Different Ways to Guarantee Access to Justice?, 2014, available at, https://www.hiil.org/projects/legal-aid-in-europe-nine-different-ways-to-guarantee-access-to-justice/.

award, while the third-party funder is recovering an important portion of the award in return for its investment.

In conclusion, it is a fact that TPF enables access to justice and facilitates the system. Moreover, there are resemblances and contrasts between TPF and legal aid. The access to justice argument is analyzed in depth together with other ethical problems directed against TPF in the fifth chapter of this book.

2.4.3.4.3 Risk, Control, Lawyer-Funder Relationship and Other Procedural Problems

TPF process creates many procedural problems. All those potential procedural problems will be analyzed in Chap. 3 in detail. However, here, an introduction and summary are given. The purpose here is to raise attention to many potential problems arising out of TPF arrangements.

Risk is an important factor when deciding to bring a legal case. If this case is an investment case against a state, where arbitration can go on for many years and costs can increase rapidly, then this is an even a more important factor. In general, a party who brings the case carries the risk of the case.

What TPF does is to take the risk of legal proceedings and get paid for taking this risk. As a result, the risk which is normally on the shoulder of the party to the case is transferred to the funder. When this happens, the funder spends money for the case instead of the original party and in return, the funder becomes entitled to a share in the award. As is the case with any legal proceeding, investment arbitration has many uncertainties and risks.

An important decision which has to be agreed between funders and the funded parties pertains to the degree of control over the proceedings. This decision can depend on the different approaches adopted by various jurisdictions. Some jurisdictions limit control over the parties, and there is generally more flexibility in civil law countries. It depends on the jurisdiction how much control a funder can exert. Legislation, case law in that jurisdiction, and ethical rules are determinative. This also depends on the style of funders. Generally, large and professional funders have minimal or little control regarding litigation or settlement proceedings to prevent any potential problems.[183]

Some legislation on TPF in jurisdictions highlight some potential procedural issues. To this end, Singapore and Hong Kong third-party regulations provide important hints regarding what kind of procedural issues are given important consideration since they offer some guidelines for third-party funders.[184] The most

[183] J. Molot, "Theory and Practice in Litigation Risk" and "Burford has no control over litigation or settlement decisions and it does not interfere with the attorney client relationship", available at http://rippmedia.com/Molot-TheoryandPractice.pdf

[184] *See* Hong Kong Code of Practice for Third-Party Funding of Arbitration and Singapore Civil Law (Amendment) Bill.

important and noticeable ones are disclosure and CoI. However, procedural problems are not limited to them. Some other procedural problems include whether TPF agreements need to be disclosed or not, and if so, what information should be disclosed? Are those disclosure requirements mandatory for parties, lawyers, or funders? Those and many other related questions are yet to be addressed in ISDS cases. However, some proposals are discussed as stated above.

Another problem that might arise from relations between funders and lawyers. Lawyers are governed by professional rules and moral principles while funders do not have such rules. Moreover, funders are not thought to be a party when professional and ethical rules for lawyers are developed.[185] Therefore, there is no specific rule regulating the relationship between funders and lawyers even though, in some jurisdictions, ethical rules have some related rules regarding fee arrangements of lawyers.[186] The ICCA-Queen Mary Report has a chapter on industry-based best practices.[187] Those possible tensions between funders' interest in monitoring cases and professional and ethical duties of lawyers to their clients may create some tensions between funders and lawyers.

In summary, potential problems frequently arise out of TPF arrangements. The most controversial ones are mentioned here briefly and a greater discussion regarding all potential procedural problems are provided in the following chapters.

2.5 Conclusion

This chapter has given a doctrinal analysis of TPF. Different definitions of TPF as well as the historical development of TPF were presented to inform readers on the development and scope of the topic. The fundamentals of the TPF relationship and how the TPF process works were elaborated to enable a fundamental understanding of further discussions. From this background and understanding, and considering current trends, predictions regarding the future are also given. In summary, the TPF definition is becoming clearer. More funders have been entering the market and also, more jurisdictions have developed TPF rules, which help the evolution of similar regulations on TPF. Considering the history of TPF and how it has been growing, the future of the TPF market is promising. There will be more funders and the demand for TPF will continue expanding.

This chapter also helps to understand the stages before a TPF agreement is signed. The process of getting TPF from a funder involves multiple assessments by the

[185] Each jurisdiction has its own Professional rules. As an example, for California, see https://www.statebardefenseattorney.com/california-rules-of-professional-conduct.

[186] USA ABA Model Rule of Professional Responsibility, (MPR) 1.8(f), available at https://www.americanbar.org/groups/litigation/committees/commercial-business/practice/2019/when-a-third-party-pays-legal-fees/.

[187] ICCA Queen Mary Report (n 1), Chapter 7.

funder including both legal and economic analyses of a case. Thus, a very small number of cases can get TPF among many more such cases for which TPF is sought. Without knowing the basics of the TPF process and its fundamentals it is not possible to discuss issues raised by the TPF agreements further.

Furthermore, the chapter has demonstrated the enormous effect of the TPF market on the legal market. The result is that legal cases not only project themselves as a dispute between parties but also serve as a financial asset for them. Claim holders can use their claim to secure financing, trade it, or even sell it. This gives them bargaining power with the opposing party or third-party funders. Moreover, this monetization creates a lucrative business area for funders. By providing financing to claim holders, funders can make a profit and facilitate the legal system at the same time. The result is that there are more users of ISDS and a substantial increase in access to justice.

TPF is a dynamic subject and it keeps evolving. The subject started recently being addressed in investment treaties, by ICSID and UNCITRAL working groups.[188] More commonly it is discussed in investment arbitration awards as examined in the third chapter of this book. Nonetheless, it is not difficult to see that there will be more discussions, rules and awards on the subject. At this time, the definition of TPF is defined broadly in investment law. To this extent, TPF means every instance of financing provided by a person or entity other than a party itself including professional funders, lawyers and donations by third parties. Despite the short history of TPF, the development of the TPF market is fast-moving. This development, to a large extent, is due to abolishing the champerty and maintenance doctrines in many jurisdictions. After the abolishment of those doctrines, TPF developed in major jurisdictions, first in litigation, then it easily spread over to arbitration. Now, TPF plays a significant part in many cases in investment arbitration.

Moreover, different types of TPF and other financing methods available to parties such as insurance, loans, and assignment of claims, and their similarity to and differences from TPF were also explained in this chapter. Legal aid and its similarity to TPF in some respects is also important to note although both type of assistance differ from each other in important ways. The TPF methods, available TPF services and structures are developing according to the needs of clients. Therefore, it presents a difficulty for those who try to classify TPF methods and structures, as this chapter has offered. Nonetheless, existing case law in investment arbitration provides a possibility for certain classification and structures as explained. Mainly, funders can be categorized into five groups. (i) professional funders, (ii) sui generis TPF arrangements, (iii) lawyer financing, (iv) donations or grants, and (v) finance by a company or investor who has an entitlement in the outcome of the claim.

[188] *See* ICSID and UNCITRAL Draft Code of Conduct for Adjudicators, available at https://icsid.worldbank.org/en/; Transatlantic Trade and Investment Partnership, Commission Draft Text, Article 1/2; Comprehensive Economic and Trade Agreement (CETA), Article 8.1; https://icsid.worldbank.org/sites/default/files/publications/rule_amendment_proposals_convention.pdf.

Lastly, TPF presents many potential problems. Some indicated in this section are such as disclosure requirements, CoI, or the relationship between funder-lawyers. Some of those issues are discussed with reference to existing case law on TPF in investment arbitration, which is analyzed in the following chapter on case law. Nonetheless, there are many other potential procedural problems that TPF agreement might create. The importance of the TPF agreement and how its presence affects the investment arbitration in many aspects are fascinating. This new player in investment arbitration has added more problems and concerns to the existing problems of the ISDS regime. Thus, TPF affects the whole procedural aspect of investment arbitration and leads us to think about investment arbitration from a new procedural paradigm, on which the next chapter sheds light.

References

Aitken L (2006) 'Litigation Lending' after Fostif: an advance in consumer protection, or a licence to 'Bottomfeeders'? Sydney Law Rev 28:171

Avraham R, Wickelgren A (2014) Third-party litigation funding - a signaling model. DePaul Law Rev 63(2):233–264

Bentham J (1818) Defence of usury. Payne and Foss, London, p 40

Bjorklund AK (2013) The role of counterclaims in rebalancing. Lewis Clark Law Rev 17(2): 461–480

Boon K (2022) Theorizing responsibility in the investor state dispute resolution. St John's Law Rev 95(2):253–284

Bottini G, Titi C, Pérez Aznar F, Chaisse J, Jovanovic M, Puigdemont Sola O (2020) Excessive costs and recoverability of costs awards in investment arbitration. J World Investment Trade 21(2):251–299. https://doi.org/10.1163/22119000-12340173

Brekoulakis S (2017) Rethinking consent in international commercial arbitration: a general theory for non-signatories. J Int Disp Settlement 8(4):610–643

Chaisse J, Eken C (2020) The monetization of investment claims: promises and pitfalls of third-party funding. Delaware J Corp Law 44(2–3):113–166

Cremades BM (2013) Concluding remarks. In: Cremades BM, Dimolitsa A (eds) Third-party funding in international arbitration. ICC Institute of World Business Law

Cremades Román BM, Jr (2011) Third party litigation funding: investing in arbitration. Transnational Dispute Management, p 14. www.transnational-dispute-management.com/article.asp?key=1743

de Nanteuil A (2018) Counterclaims in investment arbitration: old questions, new answers? Law Pract Int Courts Tribunals 17(2):374–392

Delaney J (2014) Mistakes to avoid when approaching third party funders. Global Arb Rev (Apr. 15, 2014)

Derains Y (2013) Foreword. In: Cremades Sanz-Pastor BM, Dimolitsa A (eds) Dossier X: Third-party funding in international arbitration. ICC Institute of World Business Law, pp 5–6

Eken C (2022) A detailed comparison of third-party funding regulations in Hong Kong and Singapore. Asia Pac Law Rev 29(1). https://doi.org/10.1080/10192557.2021.1979799

Fach Gómez K (ed) (2021) European yearbook of international economic law special issue: private actors in international investment law. Springer

Galanter M (1983) Reading the landscape of disputes: what we know and don't know (and think we know) about our allegedly contentious and litigious society. UCLA Law Rev 31(4):69–71

Garcia FJ (2018) Third-party funding as exploitation of the investment treaty system. Boston Coll Law Rev 59(8):2911–2934

Gehring M, Euler D (2015) Public interest in investment arbitration. In: Wong M, Hadgett R (Authors), Euler D, Gehring M, Scherer M (eds) Transparency in international investment arbitration: a guide to the UNCITRAL rules on transparency in treaty-based investor-state arbitration. Cambridge University Press, Cambridge, pp. 7–27. https://doi.org/10.1017/CBO9781139939577.004

Hodges C, Peysner J, Nurse A (2012) Litigation funding: status and issues (January 30, 2012). Oxford Legal Studies, Research Paper No 55/2012, p 45

Ishikawa T (2019) Counterclaims and the rule of law in investment arbitration. AJIL Unbound 113: 33–37. https://doi.org/10.1017/aju.2018.96

Kryvoi Y (2012) Counterclaims in investor-state arbitration. Minn J Int Law 21(2):216–252

Landsman S (1998) The history of contingency and the contingency of history. DePaul Law Rev 47:261

Lord Justice Jackson (2009) Review of civil litigation costs: Preliminary report, Vol 1. The Stationary Office, p 41

Lord Justice Jackson (2011) "Third Party Funding or Litigation Funding" (Speech delivered at the Sixth Lecture in the Civil Litigation Costs Review Implementation Programme. The Royal Courts of Justice

Marciante M (2023) Funding of claims in investor-state dispute settlements: could third-party funding enhance access to justice? İn: Storskrubb E (ed) YSEC yearbook of socio-economic constitutions 2022 funding of justice, pp. 291–320. Springer

Moorcraft B (2019) What is Political Risk Insurance, Insurance Business American. Available at https://www.insurancebusinessmag.com/us/guides/what-is-political-risk-insurance-162502.aspx

Morabito V (2017) An empirical study of Australia's class action regimes, fifth report: The first twenty-five years of class actions in Australia. Monash University. https://doi.org/10.2139/ssrn.3005901

Park WW (2008) Non-signatories and international contracts: An arbitrator's dilemma. Boston University School of Law Public Law & Legal Theory Paper, pp 17–27. https://ssrn.com/abstract=3018722

Park WW, Rogers CA (2014) Third-party funding in international arbitration: The ICCA Queen-Mary Task Force. Penn State Law Research Paper, 42. https://ssrn.com/abstract=2507461

Perrin L (ed) (2019) The third party litigation funding law review, 3rd edn. Law Business Research Ltd

Popova IC, Friedman MW (2014) Can state counterclaims salvage investment arbitration? World Arbitr Mediat Rev 8(2):1–42

Rose J (2017) Maintenance in Medieval England (Cambridge Studies in English Legal History). Cambridge University Press, Cambridge, https://doi.org/10.1017/9781107358324

Sachs L (2018) Remarks by Lisa Sachs. American society of international law. Proc Annu Meet 112:195–198

Sahani VS (2013) Recent developments in third-party funding. J Int Arbitr (Kluwer Law International) 30(4):443–452

Schaner LS, Appleman TG (2012). Third-party litigation funding in the United States. Revista de Arbitragem e Mediação 32:175–187. https://jenner.com/system/assets/publications/9221/original/RArb32_Lawrence_S._Schaner.pdf?1336668784

Shao X (2021) Environmental and human rights counterclaims in international investment arbitration: at the crossroads of domestic and international law. J Int Econ Law 24(1):157–179. https://doi.org/10.1093/jiel/jgab001

Shields J (2015) Understanding the different types of litigation finance. Yieldstreet. https://www.yieldstreet.com/resources/article/what-is-litigation-finance

Smith M (2012) Mechanics of third-party funding agreements: a funder's perspective. In: Nieuwveld LB, Shannon V (eds) Third party funding in international arbitration. Kluwer Law, pp 19–37

Smith M, Wesolowski A (2017) Mechanics of third-party funding agreements: A funder's perspective. In: Nieuwveld LB, Sahani VS (eds) Third-party funding in international arbitration, 2nd edn. Kluwer Law International, pp 21–42

Steinitz M, Field AC (2014) A model litigation funding contract. Iowa Law Rev 99:711

Susman SD, Wilkins DB (2019) Risky business. The Practice 5(6)

Tan LY, Bouchenaki A (2015) Limiting investor access to investment arbitration: a solution without a problem? In: Kalicki JE, Joubin-Bret A (eds) Reshaping the investor-state dispute system. Brill, p 250

Van Harten G, Loughlin M (2006) Investment treaty arbitration as a species of global administrative law. Eur J Int Law 17(1):121–150. https://doi.org/10.1093/ejil/chi159

Vohryzek-Griest A (2009) State counterclaims in investor-state disputes: a history of 30 years of failure. Int Law Rev Colomb Derecho Int [Online] 15:83–123

Chapter 3
Existing and Potential Procedural Problems in TPF in Investment Arbitration: Analysis of the Case Law

Follow the Trend Lines, Not the Headlines.[1]—Bill Clinton

3.1 Introduction

As Bill Clinton said in the above quotation, one must also follow the trend lines in the law. Even though TPF does not always appear in the headlines of reports on investment cases, it is discussed many times as analysed here. In many cases, it is probable that parties used TPF even though it is not discussed in the tribunals' orders and awards. As reported, a funder voiced that: "the funder had been approached by claimants concerning two-thirds of the cases that were registered at ICSID in one particular year".[2] The report continued, "funder had rejected all but one of these cases, but the rest nonetheless ended up on the case registry", which indicates that another individual or TPF company has funded those claims, or the claimants have found other resources to fund their claims to be able to initiate ISDS proceedings.[3] This is proof that many parties have sought TPF, and tribunals did not discuss TPF in all those cases. Otherwise, the number of cases analysed here would have been much higher. Still, a substantial number of tribunals have discussed TPF in various ways. Thus, we can easily say that TPF has become a trend in investment arbitration. It has happened even though TPF is a very new industry. Not long ago, a major third-party

[1]The quote is attributed to the 42nd American President Bill Clinton. See https://herostocks.ca/follow-the-trend-lines-not-the-headlines/; http://www.usfunds.com/investor-library/frank-talk/follow-the-trend-lines-not-the-headlines/#.X7gC-dMzaEs; https://www.etftrends.com/relative-value-channel/follow-the-trend-lines-not-the-headlines/; https://www.forbes.com/sites/greatspeculations/2019/07/29/follow-the-trend-lines-not-the-headlines/?sh=279becee5848.

[2]ICCA report at footnote 18, p. 254.

[3]*Ibid.*

C. Eken, *Third-Party Funding in Investment Arbitration*, Law for Professionals,
https://doi.org/10.1007/978-3-031-63620-2_3

funder celebrated its 10th year of operation,[4] and the case law has already reached a substantial number.[5] Some of the issues analysed here are interlinked and tribunals discussed them together in some cases. Therefore, sometimes some of the issues are discussed together as well and this book does not divide them either. However, whatever issue took more attention of the tribunal, it is discussed under that issue in this chapter.

TPF-related issues have been raised before ICSID, SCC and PCA. Most of these decisions are published, and handful amount of unpublished cases are made known and available to the world by the Investment Arbitration Reporter.[6] In these cases, the respondent state challenges the claimants or arbitrators on various grounds related to TPF arrangements or TPF-related issues. This chapter analyses those challenges and the resultant decisions of arbitral tribunals as well as the dissenting opinion and assenting reason of their members. While doing so, it examines similar challenges raised by respondents. In doing so, this chapter benefits from using the structural classification of this jurisprudence as formulated by Jean Christopher Honlet: jurisdiction and admissibility, allocation of costs, security for costs, the challenge of arbitrators, discontinuation of arbitration, disclosure, and impact of TPF on a stay of enforcement of an ICSID award.[7] However, since that article has been written, many more investment arbitration tribunals have discussed TPF, in which in addition to Honlet's formulation, control of funders, the definition of TPF, whether TPF costs are recoverable, whether TPF arrangement can be considered by the tribunal to render an award on a certain time were also discussed. Moreover, in some cases, TPF was pointed out by the tribunal but not discussed substantively. Lastly, the respondent state was funded in some investment arbitration cases. Therefore, those new dimensions of the discussions on TPF by investment arbitration tribunals are added to Honlet's list. Now, first, the case law on jurisdiction and admissibility is analysed.

3.2 Jurisdiction and Admissibility

The two issues because of a third-party funder's participation have been raised in a portion of claims, in all of which tribunals rejected the respondents' arguments on this ground. The first one decided was the *Abaclat Case*, also being the first ICSID

[4]Perla, David (2019) announces its 10th anniversary in 2019: Why legal finance will become increasingly valuable to law firms & legal teams, can be reached via https://www.burfordcapital.com/insights/insights-container/why-legal-finance-will-become-increasingly-valuable-to-law-firms-legal-teams-in-2019/.

[5]As of 2 December 2020, there are 45 investment arbitration cases where TPF is discussed.

[6]Investment Arbitration Reporter is a news & analysis service tracking international arbitrations between foreign investors and sovereign governments. For more info see https://www.iareporter.com/.

[7]Honlet (2015), pp. 699–712.

case to consider the issue of mass claims.[8] The claim there revolved around the purported breach of an 'Italy–Argentina BIT', which was signed on 22 May 1990, and became effective on 14 October 1993.[9] The claims arose out of the 2001 Argentine debt crisis.[10] The number of claimants at the commencement of the proceedings, as substituted, surpassed 180,000.[11] The respondent was the Argentine Republic.[12] Claimants holding bonds issued by Argentina failed to pay. From a TPF perspective, the decision is important, as the tribunal stressed the importance of the TPF arrangements without which the claimants could not have initiated their cases against Argentina. It was the first ICSID case with claimants funded by Task Force Argentine (TFA), which was established by eight major Italian banks.[13] Argentina argued that the TFA mandate did not constitute proper consent by investors to initiate an ICSID case.[14] However, the tribunal found consent after examining the TFA mandate package and found a power of attorney executed by each bondholder expressly authorizing initiation of ICSID claims and related procedures.[15] Apart from this challenge, there was no direct challenge raised regarding the TPF arrangement. However, the tribunal implicitly accepted access to justice in this case by stating:

> Whilst the representation mechanism implemented by the TFA Mandate Package does impose certain restrictions on Claimants, it should not be forgotten that it also actually entitles Claimants to conduct ICSID arbitration, at the cost and expense of the TFA's member banks. Indeed, it is very unlikely that many of the Claimants would individually be in a position to initiate and conduct ICSID arbitration, if they had to finance the arbitration themselves.[16]

In his dissenting opinion, Georges Abi-Saab, concludes that "the basis of the mass claims before the Tribunal, because they do not constitute a covered or protected investment under the ICSID Convention and the BIT, in the absence of a territorial link with Argentina" and "that this Tribunal has no jurisdiction under the ICSID Convention and the BIT over the present collective mass claims action".[17] However, this dissenting opinion did not change the decision in the case.

---

[8] Allen & Overy Publications, 8 December 2011, Abaclat and Others v Argentine Republic (Formerly Giovanna ABeccara and Others v Argentine Republic), ICSID Case No. ARB/07/5, https://www.allenovery.com/en-gb/global/news-and-insights/publications/abaclat-and-others-v-the-argentine-republic-formerly-giovanna-a-beccara-and-others-v-the-argentine-r.

[9] https://investmentpolicy.unctad.org/international-investment-agreements/treaties/bilateral-investment-treaties/135/argentina%2D%2D-italy-bit-1990-.

[10] Van Houtte and McAsey (2012), p. 231.

[11] Abaclat v. Argentine, Decision on Jurisdiction and Admissibility (4 August 2011), paras. 1.

[12] *Ibid.* paras. 5.

[13] *Ibid.* para. 65.

[14] *Ibid.* para. 423.

[15] *Ibid.* para. 446.

[16] Ibid, para. 458.

[17] *Ibid.*, Dissenting Opinion, Professor Georges Abi-Saab, 28 Oct 2011, para. 276.

We can conclude that the *Abaclat* case was the first case discussing TPF indirectly wherein jurisdiction was challenged on the grounds that claimants' consent was invalid. The tribunal's holding that without financial help the claimants would have had no access to ICSID arbitration demonstrates the important connection between finance and access to justice.

Another case similar to *Abaclat* is the *Giovanni Alemanni* case, where the respondent was again Argentine.[18] The Italian claimants were a group of debt instrument holders, comprised of "initially 183 individuals and legal entities".[19] Only 74 remained by the time the tribunal wrote the decision on jurisdiction and admissibility.[20] They alleged Argentina was in default as to the payment of the debt instrument and in breach of its obligations under the Argentina - Italy BIT.[21]

In this case, the claimants gave their consent, with a mandate to "the North Atlantic Societe d'Administration" (hereinafter "NASAM"), to initiate an ICSID claim on their behalf.[22] Concerning the NASAM Mandate, the Counter-Memorial reports it as an agreement, a contract ('Incarico' in Italian), and continues that it is"between each individual Claimant and NASAM, governed by Italian law, under which NASAM undertakes to coordinate and finance litigation against Argentina in connection with the bonds".[23]

Argentina argued that NASAM took full control of the claimants, thus claimants did not have any control over the proceedings.[24] The tribunal rejected the respondent's arguments and accepted the claimants' consent by stating that "in signing up to the NASAM Mandate package, and contributing the cash payment required from each of them ... that is enough, in the Tribunal's considered view, to dispose of the question of the Claimants' consent to the present arbitration".[25]

Argentina did not challenge the TPF agreement itself again but challenged the general provisions in the mandate including TPF. The respondent also asserted that components in the NASAM mandate, including the TPF agreement were problematic. The respondent asserted that they were all "tainted with illegality that fatally undermine[d] the Claimants' written consent to arbitration, as required by Article 25 of the ICSID Convention".[26] The tribunal saw no irregularity in those provisions, observed that it is highly important that provisions are not tainting, explicitly accepted TPF as a well-established practice, and stated that TPF does not label

[18]Giovanni Alemanni and others v Argentine Republic, ICSID Case No ARB/07/8, (Alemanni v. Argentine).

[19]Alemanni v. Argentine Republic, Decision on Jurisdiction and Admissibility, 17 November 2014, para. 1.

[20]*Ibid.*

[21]*Ibid.*

[22]*Ibid.* para. 16.

[23]*Ibid.* para. 80.

[24]*Ibid.* para 143.

[25]*Ibid.* para 277.

[26]*Ibid.* para, 78.

claims as inadmissible. It is highly significant from the TPF perspective in this claim because the Tribunal refers to TPF in the following terms:

> Individual views may differ as to whether third-party funding is or is not desirable or beneficial, either at the national or at the international level, but the practice is by now so well established both within many national jurisdictions and within international investment arbitration that it offers no grounds in itself for objection to the admissibility of a request to arbitrate.[27]

It is important because the Tribunal accepted TPF as a well-established practice and does not argue its admissibility.

However, the tribunal expressed some concerns since claimants gave the power of attorney "to a named individual who has never appeared before the Tribunal".[28] This shows that procedural due diligence is important in TPF practice. Even though it does not affect the result, for a better procedural ethic and discipline the agreement should have included the names of lawyers who would appear before the tribunal. At least, the tribunal would be informed that claimants are aware of the procedure and aware of which lawyer is representing them before ICSID.

Another important conclusion of the Tribunal, in the present dispute, is that it did not decide on costs.[29] The reason for that decision is ICSID Convention's Article 61/2, which gives a clear duty to render an award on costs "at the moment when an arbitral proceeding is brought to a definitive end through an award", not when a discontinuing order is rendered.[30] Since the tribunal was not in such a position, the tribunal has found "that it d[id] not possess the power to make the costs orders applied for either by one side or the other in this arbitration".[31] Therefore, the orders on discontinuing the procedure can affect the decision on costs.

It is interesting to see that the tribunal stated that it had"no way of knowing whether the proceeds of any costs award would have found their way into the pockets of the Claimants themselves or the litigation funders".[32] This is interesting because the tribunal considered where the money will go, giving us an important factor to consider when drawing TPF agreements. Distribution of recovery should be stated carefully, and the recipient of the payment should be determined clearly, especially when claimants finance their claims partially. In a specific case, this confusion could be cleared by presenting a statement to the tribunal regarding where the money will go and assuring the tribunal that claimants will get paid. This allocation is important. After the funded party recovers its costs, the rest will go to the funder, who covered expenses for the benefit of the claimant. The order of the

---

[27] *Ibid.* para 278.

[28] *Ibid.* para 278.

[29] Giovanni Alemanni and others v Argentine Republic, ICSID Case No ARB/07/8, Order of the Tribunal Discontinuing the Procedure (Discontinuing the Procedure), 14 December 2015.

[30] Alemanni v. Argentine, Discontinuing the Procedure, 25.

[31] *Ibid.* para. 26.

[32] *Ibid.* para. 26.

recipients for possible payments must be stated clearly in the TPF agreement since this has been considered by at least one investment arbitration tribunal in this case.

This shows that a TPF agreement should be well structured, giving tribunals no impression that third-party funders will take all the first payment of claimants. It needs to be understandable who will get paid and the order of this payment, especially between the funded party and the funder. Considering the Tribunal's concern in this case, it seems that if the claimants will get paid first and only then will the funder recover their costs, then the Tribunal would probably award the compensation to the Claimants. However, since it was not clear the Claimants were not awarded in this particular case. To avoid such instances, the order of payment should be clear.

In a typical TPF agreement, there is one claimant and one funder, and the relation between them is clear, with the funded party staying in control of the case. However, in the Abaclat and Alemanni cases, there was a group of claimants and, even when there is no funder, it is difficult to expect that each claimant will stay in charge of its claims. In such a case, the lawyer or lawyers would take control and inform the clients where necessary. Since NASAM agreed to finance the dispute on behalf of a group of claimants, it was different from typical TPF practice. Yet, it contaminates neither arbitration proceedings nor client-lawyer relations. Provided that there is no clear evidence that claimants are no longer in control of the claim and NASAM is acting as the real party of the case, there should be no reason to decide negatively on the acceptance of the parties and admissibility of the dispute. Parties can withdraw from the Mandate anytime in the mentioned case then it is clear that the control lies with the claimants, not with NASAM. It is true because anytime during the proceedings parties can withdraw from the Mandate if parties did not have the determination to continue ICSID proceedings against Argentina. However, this shows that a TPF agreement should be well structured in terms of control of the case and the relation between the lawyer-funder and claimants. If a tribunal has a concern when rendering an award regarding costs, and whether this money will go into the pocket of the claimants or funder, the provisions of a TPF agreement on this issue are a valid concern and should be clear.

The third one on the same issue is *Quasar de Valores and others v. Russia*, which is another important award rendered by the Stockholm Chamber of Commerce.[33] The claim came to light out of a purported violation of the Spain-Russia BIT.[34] The claimants were legal entities established under Spanish law and the respondent was

---

[33] Quasar de Valores and others v the Russian Federation (Quasar v. Russia), SCC Case No 24/2007. The full title of the case is Renta 4 S.V.S.A, AhorroCorporaciónEmergentes F.I., AhorroCorporaciónEurofondo F.I., RovimeInversiones SICAV S.A., Quasar de Valores SICAV S.A., Orgor de Valores SICAV S.A., GBI 9000 SICAV S.A. v. the Russian Federation, SCC No. 24/2007.

[34] Bilateral investment treaty between the two states signed on 26 October 1990 and entered into force on 28 November 1991; see https://investmentpolicy.unctad.org/international-investment-agreements/treaties/bit/2851/russian-federation%2D%2D-spain-bit-1990-.

the Russian Federation.[35] The legal entities over which the tribunal accepted jurisdiction were *Rovime Inversions SICA V S.A., Quasar de Valores SICAV S.A., Orgor de Valores SICAV S.A.* and *OBI 9000 SICA V S.A.*[36] Claimants stated that: "Russia unlawfully dispossessed Yukos Oil Company ("Yukos") of its assets and expropriated it from its shareholders. They state[d] that they [were] owners of Yukos American Depository Receipts (ADRs) and demand compensation for their loss".[37]

Regarding the TPF issue in this case, the respondent alleged that the claimants are not real parties to the dispute and that Menatep, the TPF company, was the real party and that the claimants were engaged in an abuse of process.[38] However, the tribunal did not see any misuse of procedure and stated that

> there is no reason of principle why they were not entitled to pursue rights available to them under the BIT, and to accept the assistance of a third party, whose motives are irrelevant as between the disputants in this case.[39]

The conclusion from this case should be that, as long as parties to a dispute have a legitimate interest in pursuing their claims, getting funds or support for bringing their claims is not an abuse of process and the reasons of the supporting company for bringing claimants' claims are irrelevant. Third parties' motives are irrelevant, provided that they do not vitiate the legal procedure, there is no reason to ban the involvement of such parties if parties seek their assistance.

In the RosInvestCo UK Ltd v. the Russian Federation case, the claimant was the owner of seven million ordinary shares of the Russian-incorporated Yukos Oil Company, while the respondent was the Russian Federation. The claim came into the light out of the United Kingdom-Soviet BIT, and the claimant demanded compensation because of unlawful expropriation.[40] The issue related to TPF here is the relationship between the Elliott Group, a private investment partnership, and the claimant. Russia claimed that the participation contract between the Elliott Group and the claimant precluded the claimant from becoming an investor in the meaning of the BIT between the UK and the Soviet Union. However, the tribunal rejected that claim by stating that "Participation Agreements have no bearing with regard to the description of investor restrained in Article 1 (d)(ii)".[41] From this decision, it is explicit that having external funding to bring its case, the claimant does not lose its investor status, or by no means there is prevention for such external funding.

---

[35] Quasar de Valores and others v the Russian Federation, SCC Case No 24/2007, Award on Preliminary Objections, (Preliminary Objections) 20 March 2009, paras. 1, 2.

[36] Quasar v. Russia, Preliminary Objections, para. 155.

[37] *Ibid.* para. 3.

[38] Quasar v. Russia, Award, 2012, para. 11.

[39] *Ibid.* 2012, para. 33.

[40] RosInvestCo UK Ltd v the Russian Federation, SCC Case No V079/2005, para. 2.

[41] *Ibid.* para 323.

Another Italian-bondholders case against Argentina based on the Argentine-Italy BIT is Ambiente Ufficio v. Argentina Republic case.[42] The claimants argued that Argentina had defaulted to pay bonds and claimed compensation as a result.[43] The same funder, NASAM, as in the Giovanni Alemanni case, funded claimants in this case as well. The most important feature in this case that needs to be highlighted first is that the respondent state did not see any problem with TPF arrangements, but it contested the degree of control wielded by the funder. The respondent defined genuine TPF as "deals with the provision of funds by individuals and companies having no other connection with the litigation" and argued NASAM's control went beyond that genuine practice.[44] Argentina's main worry was not the TPF arrangement by and of itself, but "that NASAM was the driving force behind the decision to initiate the present arbitration" and that it was completely in charge of it.[45] According to Argentina: "the NASAM Mandate create[d] an impermissible barrier between Claimants and their lawyers".[46] In Argentina's mind, NASAM was the "real party in interest" in this arbitration proceedings.[47] The Tribunal's findings are important to consider the issue. The Tribunal discovered that NASAM was by no means in charge of the current proceedings, also discovers that"lawyers are not bound by NASAM mandate, which [was] a contract between NASAM and the Claimants", on the contrary, lawyers "are bound to claimants by the power of attorney".[48] Thus, the tribunal decided that NASAM was not "more than a third party" and stated that "there [were] no substantiated indications that there would be an external control of the present proceedings by an external actor".[49]

Another dispute arose between Teinver and Autobuses Urbanos collectively against Argentina under the Spain-Argentina BIT.[50] The jurisdiction of the tribunal was challenged in this case and the tribunal, found that it had jurisdiction.[51] In this dispute, the respondent asserted that the TPF company was the real claimant.[52] The Tribunal did not opine whether TPF arrangements are valid or not. However, it declined the respondent's jurisdictional challenge based on the jurisdiction is

---

[42] Ambiente Ufficio SpA and others v Argentine Republic (Ambiente Ufficio v. Argentine) ICSID Case No ARB 08/9.

[43] Ambiente Ufficio v. Argentine, Decision on Jurisdiction and Admissibility (Jurisdiction and Admissibility), (8 February 2013) para. 1.

[44] *Ibid,* para. 186.

[45] *Ibid.*

[46] *Ibid.*

[47] *Ibid.* para. 276.

[48] Ambiente Ufficio v. Argentine Republic, Jurisdiction and Admissibility, para. 277.

[49] *Ibid.* para. 278.

[50] Teinver SA, Transportes de Cercanı S.A. and Autobuses Urbanos del Sur SA v Argentine Republic, ICSID Case No ARB/09/1 (Teinver v. Argentine), Decision on Jurisdiction (Jurisdiction) (21 December 2012) para 1.

[51] *Ibid.* para. 333.

[52] *Ibid.* para. 245.

"assessed as of the date the case is filed".[53] Another important indication was that the respondent contended that the claimant conveyed its rights to the funder, Burford Capital. However, the tribunal reiterated that the jurisdictions are assessed at the time of filing the case.[54] Thus, it concluded in this case that, even though the claimant transferred its rights to another person or funder after initiating its claim, it did not affect the tribunal's jurisdiction.

In conclusion, the analysis on jurisdiction and admissibility of the cases in the existence of a TPF agreement is consistent with all tribunals. TPF arrangements influence neither cases' admissibility nor tribunal's jurisdiction. However, some factors should be respected. A common and important consideration by different tribunals is that, as long as it is clear that bringing the case is the claimant's intention and the claimant controls the case, TPF arrangements cannot substantiate a challenge on jurisdiction or admissibility of the case.

3.3 Allocation of Costs (AoC)

The existence of a TPF agreement and a third-party funder raises several issues concerning the AoC between the parties: should a funded party, which has prevailed in the arbitration, be able to reclaim costs where these costs are funded by a TPF company, or should a funded party that has prevailed in the arbitration be able to recover outcome-dependent payments made to the TPF company? The answer to those questions is the answer to the effect of TPF on the AoC. Regarding AoC, the default rule at the moment is that investment arbitration tribunals do not give any weight to TPF agreements when they are deciding on costs. So far, none of the tribunals considered the TPF agreement when deciding on the AoC, irrespective of whether the funded party was the claimant or defendant. Thus, it is quite consistent, and it can be concluded that the TPF agreement does not affect cost allocation in investment arbitration, which is different from some examples in litigation funding in some jurisdictions.[55] Now, these investment arbitration cases are analyzed in more detail in the following paragraph.

The first case relating to cost allocation is the Quasar v Russia case discussed previously. This case also highlighted important implications for TPF agreements. First of all, in terms of cost allocation, Menatep who was the funder for the claimants, did not expect any return where the funded party was successful in its claim. Thus, since Menatep funded claimants as Good Samaritan who did not expect

[53] *Ibid.* para. 255.

[54] *Ibid.* para. 256.

[55] Since this chapter examines only investment arbitration cases, court decisions on this issue in various jurisdictions have not been analyzed here. However, courts in different jurisdictions have different opinions on that. For example, the High Court in England and Wales decided that third-party funding costs are recoverable. *See* Essar v Norscot [2016] EWHC 2361 (Comm).

any exchange in return,[56] and claimants were under no legal obligation to pay back Menatep in Spain,[57] the costs are not incurred by claimants and completely funded by a third-party without any return in exchange should not be recovered by the respondent. This decision regarding costs was criticized as being less convincing compared to the decision on merits.[58] The tribunal in *Kardassopoulos v Georgia* asserted that:

> The Tribunal knows of no principle why any such third-party financing arrangement should be taken into consideration in determining the amount of recovery by the Claimants of their costs.[59]

In another case, the dispute was brought under the Energy Charter Treaty and bilateral investment treaties between Georgia (the respondent) and Greece and Israel, respectively.[60] The tribunal decided that TPF arrangements cannot make a difference in a way that the funded party's costs should not be covered.[61] Thus, the tribunal granted the claimants their costs of arbitration.[62] This decision was repeated in another case where the claimant was funded by a funder.[63] Whereas in another case, the respondent state was funded and the tribunal referred to the *Kardassopuolos* case again and ordered the applicant to pay the respondent state its costs.[64] Thus, we can conclude that the decision rendered in the Kardassopoulos case constituted a consistent practice that funded parties' costs are recoverable and it does not matter whether the funded party is claimant or respondent. RSM v. Grenada is another example where it was shown that not only claimants, but states can be funded as well. A company, which had a legitimate interest as a result of RSM losing its license since Global Petroleum awarded the license, the petroleum company funded the respondent in its case against RSM. This case showed that when a company loses its rights under investment treaties, another investor can be the beneficiary and that new beneficiary can fund the state. This is another important aspect of the TPF industry.

---

[56] Quasar v. Russia, Award, 2012, para. 224.

[57] *Ibid.*, para. 223.

[58] Marboe (2013), p. 253.

[59] Ioannis Kardassopoulos and Ron Fuchs v Georgia, ICSID Case No. ARB/05/18 and ARB/07/15, Award (3 March 2010) para 691.

[60] Ioannis Kardassopoulos and Ron Fuchs v Georgia (Kardassopoulos and Ron Fuchs v Georgia), ICSID Case No. ARB/05/18 and ARB/07/15, Award 3 March 2010 (Award), para. 1.

[61] Ibid, 691.

[62] Ibid, para. 692.

[63] ATA Construction, Industrial and Trading Company v Hashemite Kingdom of Jordan, ICSID Case No ARB/08/2, Order Taking Note of the Discontinuance of the Proceeding (11 July 2011), para. 34.

[64] RSM Production Corporation v Grenada, ICSID Case No ARB/05/14 (RSM v Grenada), Order of the Committee Discontinuing the Proceeding and Decision on Costs (28 April 2011), para. 68, 69.

In another case, claimants were the natural citizens of Italy and they brought a case against Egypt under Italy-Egypt BIT.[65] The Claimants were funded by their law firm on contingent upon claimants' recovery.[66] The respondent argued that claimants' costs were unjustified and excessive.[67] The Tribunal stated that the costs were reasonable and awarded that costs.[68] When there is such claim that costs are excessive and unjustified, such arguments must be proven by concrete evidence, or otherwise, it will not be accepted by tribunals easily.

All these cases discussed above show that, as long as costs are reasonable whether parties are funded by a funder or on a contingency basis by their lawyers or via other forms, costs will be recovered when they succeed in their cases. And this result does not switch according to whether the TPF is provided to the claimant or respondent.

3.4 Security for Costs (SfC)

SfC issues may be one of the major contentious matters regarding TPF. "Security for costs is a tool that facilitates the recovery of costs awards if the debtor is unwilling or unable to pay".[69] It is controversial in academia,[70] as well as in investment arbitration partly because of a specific case discussed further below, where all arbitrators held different opinions from each other, and those different opinions are pertinent to the effect of the TPF agreements on SfC.

In the first case, the claimants were from the US and UK respectively, the respondent was Bolivia and thus, the Bolivia-US and Bolivia-UK BITs were concerned.[71] The question of SfC in the presence of TPF in a PCA-administered Tribunal was first addressed in this case.[72] The Tribunal refused to grant SfC, stating that:

> the Respondent has not shown a sufficient causal link such that the Tribunal can infer from the mere existence of third-party funding that the Claimants will not be able to pay an eventual award of costs rendered against them, regardless of whether the funder is liable for costs or not.[73]

---

[65] WaguihElie George Siag and Clorinda Vecchi v Arab Republic of Egypt, ICSID Case No ARB/05/15, Award on June 1 (Siag&Vecchi v Egypt, Award), 2009, para. 1.

[66] Siag&Vecchi v Egypt, Award, para 604.

[67] Ibid, p. 620.

[68] Ibid, pp. 621–630.

[69] Bottini, p. 289.

[70] Khairul Islam (2024), pp. 259–278.

[71] Guaracachi America, Inc and Rurelec plc v The Plurinational State of Bolivia, UNCITRAL, PCA Case No 2011-17, Terms of Appointment and Procedural Order 1, p. 1.

[72] Honlet, p. 704.

[73] Guaracachi America, Inc and Rurelec plc v The Plurinational State of Bolivia, UNCITRAL, PCA Case No 2011-17, Procedural No 14, 11 March 2013, para. 7.

This decision clearly shows according to the tribunal, the presence of a TPF company alone is not enough to grant a SfC. This is the right decision because, as the tribunal stated other factors should be contemplated for SfC orders, beyond the mere existence of a TPF company.

RSM v. Saint Lucia Case is maybe the most important and controversial case in terms of TPF because three arbitrators held three different opinions.[74] Apart from the tribunal's decision on Saint Lucia's request for SfC,[75] assenting reasons,[76] and a dissenting opinion,[77] were also rendered. It is the earliest case "in which an ICSID tribunal has ordered a claimant to pay security for costs".[78] Because of three different opinions regarding how TPF should affect the SfC decisions in a 3-arbitrator tribunal, it is a very important case, and as can be expected, the decision of the tribunal has attracted many comments.[79]

In this dispute, the claimant was RSM Production Corporation, "a company constituted under the laws of Texas USA" and the respondent was Saint Lucia.[80] The claimant's claim was grounded on the Agreement between the two parties.[81] Respondent demanded SfC. The tribunal granted this request.[82] Because of this SfC decision, since RSM could not observe the order, the tribunal discontinued the proceedings.[83]

The main reason the tribunal ordered SfC was not owing to the existence of the TPF agreement but because of the RSM's proven history, where RSM did not fulfill other ICSID tribunal decisions on SfC.[84] However, what is important regarding TPF is that the tribunal considered the factor that RSM received TPF as an additional reason to the SfC order. This has been mentioned in two decisions of the tribunal. First, in the 2013 decision, TPF was accepted as a factor "exacerbat[ing] the concern engendered by RSM's", and the tribunal stated that TPF "places an unfunded RSM and the third party funder(s) in the inequitable position of benefiting from any award

---

[74] RSM Production Corporation v. Saint Lucia (RSM v. Saint Lucia), ICSID Case No. ARB/12/10.

[75] RSM Production Corporation v. Saint Lucia ICSID Case No. ARB/12/10, Decision on Saint Lucia's request for security for costs (RSM v. Saint Lucia, Security for Costs), (13 August 2014).

[76] RSM Production Corporation v. Saint Lucia ICSID Case No. ARB/12/10, Assenting Reasons of Gavan Griffith (RSM v. Saint Lucia, Assenting Reasons), (12 August 2014).

[77] RSM Production Corporation v. Saint Lucia ICSID Case No. ARB/12/10, Dissenting Opinion of Edward Nottingham (RSM v. Saint Lucia, Dissenting Opinion), (12 August 2014).

[78] Weeramantry and Ferrer (2015), pp. 30–34.

[79] See Uchkunova (2015) and Bogart (2014).

[80] RSM v. Saint Lucia, Security for Costs, para. 1, 2.

[81] Ibid, para. 17.

[82] *Ibid,* para 90.

[83] RSM Production Corporation v. Saint Lucia ICSID Case No. ARB/12/10, Decision on Saint Lucia's Request for Suspension or Discontinuation of Proceedings (RSM v. Saint Lucia, Discontinuation of Proceedings), (8 April 2015).

[84] RSM v. Saint Lucia, Security for Costs, para. 79, 86.

in their favour yet avoiding responsibility for a contrary award."[85] Also, in the 2014 decision, the tribunal accepted TPF as a factor supporting Tribunal's concern on whether the claimant or unknown funder would comply with a cost order against the claimant.[86] As a result, the tribunal found itself in a condition where sufficient grounds existed for such an order in favour of the respondent and against the claimant's interest to access to justice.[87]

Maybe if the award did not elaborate further, it would not have attracted that much criticism. However, Dr Griffith took a step further and criticized funders harshly in his assenting reasons. He argued that TPF should be the main reason why a SfC order is rendered.[88] According to him, In the presence of a TPF agreement, there should be a default mechanism to assume that a SfC order should be rendered and if the funded party claims otherwise, the funded party has to show reasons why the SfC order should not be made.[89] He also tainted funders as embracing the Gambler's Nirvana,[90]and mercantile adventurers,[91] which are strong and accusatory terms used by also some scholars to describe funders.[92]

The third opinion in the award was outbored by Judge Edward Nottingham in his dissenting opinion.[93] He stated that a one-sentence admission used by an advocate in a trial cannot be a ground for a SfC order without knowing either the identity of the funder or financial means of the funder, or any more information regarding the TPF agreement.[94] He is of the opinion that every case should be assessed on its own circumstances, generalization should be left to the administrative council.[95]

As a few quick comments on the decisions, Griffith's suggestion of shifting the burden of proof whenever TPF is existent is far beyond a balanced approach. Not only because apart from impecunious claimants, financially strong companies are funded too, but also because of the fact that this shift has no merit at all. The reason for giving SfC orders cannot be justified only owing to the existence of a TPF company. Moreover, the decision of dismissing the disqualification application against the arbitrator Dr Griffith is the right decision. Arbitrators, like judges, should be brave and have the freedom enough to say what they think in the case they are

---

[85] RSM Production Corporation v. Saint Lucia, ICSID Case No. ARB/12/10, Decision on Saint Lucia's Request for Provisional Measures, 12 December 2013, para. 73. This is also incorporated in RSM v. Saint Lucia, Security for Costs, para. 76.

[86] *Ibid.*, para. 83.

[87] *Ibid.*, para. 87. The Tribunal, by stating "exceptional circumstances" in the paragraph, emphasized that such orders should only be given under extraordinary conditions which they thought existed in this case.

[88] RSM v. Saint Lucia, Assenting Reasons, para. 11.

[89] Ibid, para. 18.

[90] *Ibid.* para. 13.

[91] *Ibid.* para. 14.

[92] As an example even in a book chapter title, see De Brabandere (2016), pp. 105–128.

[93] RSM v. Saint Lucia, Dissenting Opinion.

[94] *Ibid.* para. 18.

[95] *Ibid.* 19 and 20.

deciding on. Thus, disqualification of an arbitrator should not be easy just because they criticize a certain practice or business. Then, even though he used very strong language, dismissing the challenge against Dr Griffith is right.

Regarding different views in the award, assenting and dissenting reasons this book is in alignment with the dissenting opinion of Judge Edward W Nottingham. General conclusions about a certain practice should not be easily made by an individual tribunal, such complicated issues that concern many parties should be handled by the Administrative Council.[96] Especially, it is the case when the practice is well-established and used commonly by parties in investment arbitration. He asks many justified questions in his dissenting reasons regarding TPF and gives further ideas for thought. The fact cannot be disregarded that TPF indeed provides access to justice and facilitates the ISDS system by providing an additional financial option to parties to cover substantial investment arbitration costs.

In another claim, the tribunal expressed that:

> financial difficulties and third party-funding – which has become a common practice – do not necessarily constitute per se exceptional circumstances justifying that the Respondent be granted an order of security for costs.[97]

The tribunal also accepted that, in the RSM v Saint Lucia case, the reason was not only that the party was funded but also had a proven record of non-compliance.[98] Thus, as many cases state, TPF alone cannot be a ground for SfC.

In the *South American Silver Limited v Bolivia Case*, where Bolivia requested SfC from the claimant, South American Silver Company incorporated in Bermuda Islands, the tribunal unanimously rejected the SfC order.[99]

In another case, the state demanded SfC.[100] The claimant first objected to the power of the Tribunal by referring to *Invesmart v. Czech Republic* case where the Tribunal rejected that request, affirming "that it did not have authority to make the order sought in the Respondent's application".[101] The Tribunal further continued and commented that even if available SfC was unwarranted since it is only available in exceptional circumstances as in the *RSM v. Saint Lucia* case.[102] Therefore, the Claimant demanded that the Tribunal reject Canada's demand to command the Claimant to post SfC.[103]

---

[96] *Ibid.* para. 17.

[97] EuroGasInc and Belmont Resources Inc v Slovak Republic, ICSID Case No ARB/14/14, Procedural Order No 3, 23 June 2015, para. 123.

[98] Ibid, para. 122.

[99] South American Silver Limited v. Bolivia, PCA Case No. 2013-15, Procedural Order 10, 11 January 2016, para. 85.

[100] Tennant Energy, LLC v. Government of Canada, PCA Case No. 2018-54.

[101] *Ibid.*, Response to Canada's Motion for Security for Costs and Disclosure of Funding 23 September 2019, para. 23.

[102] *Ibid.* para. 50.

[103] *Ibid.* para. 65/a.

Canada requested SfC by submitting legal authorities on the issue.[104] Canada submitted that the decision in *Dirk Herzig v. Turkmenistan* "addresse[d] the very concerns that Canada highlighted in its Motion for Security for Costs and Disclosure of Third-party Funding and demonstrate[d] why this Tribunal should grant the order Canada ha[d] requested".[105] In the *Herzig* case, three key elements validated the SfC order, and without the SfC order "it would be effectively impossible for Turkmenistan to enforce and collect upon an adverse costs award".[106] The three crucial factors were: "(1) the claimant's insolvency; (2) the involvement of a third-party funder in the arbitration; and (3) the explicit non-liability of the third-party funder for a cost award adverse to its funded party".[107] Canada asserted that "these three factors ha[d] either been confirmed or [were] very likely present" in this arbitration.[108] Canada asserted that:

> Tennant has failed to produce any information or documentation to prove that it could pay an adverse costs order, or that its third-party funder would do so and thus, without more, Tennant has yet to meet its burden and security for costs must be ordered.[109]

Canada further suggested that SfC can be balanced against access to justice as in the Herzig case and argued that "this Tribunal should follow the same reasoning" in the present claim, too.[110]

The Tribunal first considered the previous claims where the SfC order granted in the presence of a TPF company. "These tribunals have exercised their authority to order SfC for various reasons, including (i) the failure of claimants to prove their solvency and the existence of a TPF agreement that did not cover the payment of an adverse award on costs, as in the García Armas v. Venezuela case; and (ii) the claimant's impecuniosity and record of non-compliance with costs orders, and the existence of a TPF agreement, as in the RSM v. Saint Lucia case governed by the ICSID Convention".[111] The tribunal stated that even though in RSM v. Saint Lucia case, there was a funder, the conclusive element for the tribunal to order the SfC was due to the fact that "the claimant had a proven history of not complying with costs awards rendered against it".[112] Moreover, it pointed out that in EuroGas v. Slovak Republic, the tribunal made it clear that:

---

[104] Tennant Energy, LLC v. Government of Canada, PCA Case No. 2018-54, Government of Canada Submission on Legal Authority Regarding Canada's Motion for Security for Costs and Disclosure of Third-Party Funding, February 17, 2020.

[105] *Ibid.* para. 1.

[106] *Ibid.* para. 3.

[107] *Ibid.*

[108] *Ibid.* para. 4.

[109] *Ibid.* para. 6.

[110] *Ibid.* para. 7.

[111] Tennant Energy, LLC v. Government of Canada, PCA Case No. 2018-54, Procedural Order No. 4, 27 February 2020, para. 117.

[112] *Ibid.* para. 175.

> financial difficulties and third-party funding – which has become a common practice – do not necessarily constitute per se exceptional circumstances justifying that the Respondent be granted an order of security for costs.[113]

For the explanations laid out in the following lines, "the Tribunal is not persuaded that the Respondent has met the burden of proving exceptional circumstances".[114] The tribunal further explained that "the Respondent has not discharged its initial burden of establishing a reasonable basis that the Claimant is impecunious such that the burden then shifts to the Claimant to produce evidence of its ability to meet a cost award".[115] Moreover, "the existence of a funding agreement alone has not been found by arbitral tribunals to be sufficient to grant security fot costs as explained in South America Silver v. Bolivia".[116] The Tribunal further stated that it "ha[d] not found anything to indicate that the Claimant [would] not comply with costs orders and the presumption must be that in the absence of evidence to the contrary, a party will act in good faith".[117] As can be seen, once again, another investment arbitration tribunal confirmed that the mere existence of a TPF arrangement does not automatically justify a SfC order as long as there is no other extraordinary conditions present. The tribunal did not find any circumstance that would justify Canada's SfC application. In consequence, the application of the Claimant was declined.[118]

As we can see, a SfC order is not granted automatically when there is a TPF company. Tribunals examined thoroughly in each application according to specifics of each case and granted such orders when there are extraordinary conditions in the case.

3.5 Challenge of Arbitrator

RSM, as the funded party, after the strong language Dr Griffith used against funders, proposed his disqualification.[119] The claimant was concerned about the impartiality of Dr Griffith since he revealed a strong bias against TPF.[120] However, this challenge was denied on the ground that Dr Griffith considers both parties and his

---

[113] *Ibid.* para. 176.

[114] *Ibid.* para. 177.

[115] *Ibid.* para. 178.

[116] *Ibid.* para. 179.

[117] *Ibid.* para. 182.

[118] *Ibid.* para. 183.

[119] RSM Production Corporation v. Saint Lucia, ICSID Case No. ARB/12/10, Decision on Claimant's Proposal for the Disqualification of Dr Gavan Griffith, QC (RSM v. Saint Lucia, Proposal for the Disqualification) (23 October 2014), para. 39.

[120] *Ibid.*, para 40, 41.

wording "do not cast reasonable doubt upon Dr Griffith's capacity to issue an independent and impartial judgment in the present arbitration".[121]

Another ICSID case arose between Nigeria and Interocean Oil Development Company and Interocean Oil Exploration Company as two Claimants, "both of which were incorporated under the laws of Delaware, USA".[122] Nigeria sought to disqualify the entire tribunal in the case. One of its grounds were Professor Park's and Professor Lew's failure to disclose their membership in a task force on TPF, in which the claimant's counsel was also a member.[123] The tribunal rejected the respondent's proposal since it had not been filed promptly and filed "377days after the Respondent became aware of the facts on which its Proposal [was] based".[124]

There was another ICSID case where the relationship linking the funder and arbitrator was challenged.[125] Mr Rees, who was appointed by the claimants had a remuneration package "as a member of the Investment Committee of the company Harbour Litigation Funding Limited ("HLF" or the "Company") and concerning the disputes funded by HLF".[126] Since February 2015, he was on the investment committee of the TPF Company and had received GBP 271,169.20 in total remuneration since then.[127] The Respondent sought the disqualification of Mr Rees on four main grounds:

> (1) repeated appointments and lack of proper disclosure; (2) past and present relationship with Claimants' counsel; (3) relationship with a litigation fund; and (4) pre-judgment of a key issue in this case concerning the Tribunal's jurisdiction over intra-EU disputes.[128]

The tribunal offered lengthy discussions on each ground in its award.

Regarding the first challenge, the tribunal held the opinion that no objective evidence hae been introduced showing the independence or impartiality of Mr Rees was affected in this dispute.[129] While reaching this conclusion, the Tribunal consulted the IBA guidelines and it noted certain provisions, even though it stated that "IBA guidelines [were] not applicable in this proceeding".[130] Concerning the

---

[121] *Ibid.*, para. 90.

[122] Interocean Oil Development Company and Interocean Oil Exploration Company v. Federal Republic of Nigeria, ICSID Case No. ARB/13/20 (Interocean v. Nigeria), Decision on Preliminary Objections, 29 October 2014, para. 1.

[123] Interocean v. Nigeria, Decision on the Proposal to Disqualify all members of the arbitral tribunal, 3 October 2017 (Proposal), para. 38.

[124] Interocean v. Nigeria, Proposal, para. 78.

[125] Canepa Green Energy Opportunities I, S.á r.l. and Canepa Green Energy Opportunities II, S.á r.l. v. Kingdom of Spain, ICSID Case No. ARB/19/4.

[126] Canepa Green Energy Opportunities I, S.á r.l. and Canepa Green Energy Opportunities II, S.á r.l. v. Kingdom of Spain, ICSID Case No. ARB/19/4, Decision on the Proposal to Disqualify Mr Peter Rees QC, 19 November 2019, para. 7/iii.

[127] *Ibid.* para. 9/iii.

[128] *Ibid.* para. 23.

[129] *Ibid.* para. 63.

[130] *Ibid.* para. 54.

relationship between Mr Rees and the HLF, the Respondent set forth that "the positions of arbitrator and advisor in a litigation fund ought to be considered incompatible due to the serious risks of bias they raise".[131] On the other hand, with respect to the role of Mr Rees on the HLF's Investment Committee, the Claimants noted first that "the Respondent ha[d] failed to substantiate its claim that providing advice to an entity that funds arbitral disputes disqualifies an arbitrator in an unrelated dispute involving different parties".[132] On top of this, Mr Rees recorded that "he was no longer a member of HLF's Investment Committee since July 2019".[133] The tribunal had found that the Respondent was right that "Mr Rees did not disclose in his Declaration and Statement dated 8 May 2019 that he had been serving since February 2015 on HLF's Investment Committee",[134] and "Mr Rees should have disclosed his connection with HLF as a part of his Declaration and Statement dated 8 May 2019".[135] Interestingly, however, the tribunal stated that "a failure to disclose a relevant fact, however, does not by itself demonstrate a manifest lack of impartiality or independence",[136] and "the initial failure to disclose such information is not of sufficient gravity to merit disqualification since Rule 6(2) of the ICSID Arbitration Rules does not expressly require disclosure of an arbitrator's connection with a third-party litigation fund".[137] Ultimately, the tribunal ruled that:

> a person's involvement in a third-party litigation fund, standing alone and in light of the current rules, does not demonstrate a manifest lack of independence or impartiality of that person as an arbitrator for all ICSID cases.[138]

Furthermore, the tribunal "recalled that, as of July 2019, Mr Rees has no never again any participation with the TPF Company".[139]

With respect to the last ground of the Respondent's challenge, the Tribunal did not find that "Mr Rees' involvement in the decision to fund the Rockhopper case in September 2016 demonstrates[d] his manifest inability to act independently or impartially in this case".[140] The tribunal mostly depended upon the fact that:

> The Respondent has[d] not identified any specific, clear opinion rendered by Mr Rees as to the validity or invalidity of a jurisdictional objection to intra-EU investment arbitration and it [was] too speculative to assume that Mr Rees must have previously considered and rejected the validity of a jurisdictional objection to intra-EU investment arbitration.[141]

---

[131] *Ibid.* para. 26.
[132] *Ibid.* para. 37.
[133] *Ibid.* para. 42.
[134] *Ibid.* para. 72.
[135] *Ibid.* para. 73.
[136] *Ibid.* para. 74.
[137] *Ibid.* para. 75.
[138] *Ibid.* para. 76.
[139] *Ibid.*
[140] *Ibid.* para. 83.
[141] *Ibid.* para. 82.

Furthermore, Mr Rees had already "referenced his prior disclosure that there was no discussion at the Investment Committee in relation to the issue of an investor from an EU country making a claim against any EU State".[142]

Regarding the Respondent's application in whole is scrupulously contemplated and the Tribunal stated that: "the unchallenged arbitrators do not view such points as establishing a particular relationship of Mr Rees to the Firm that demonstrates a manifest lack of independence, nor as establishing that Mr Rees ha[d] a particular bias or predisposition, so as to merit disqualification".[143] Nor does that kind of position examined jointly demonstrate an appearance of an obvious absence of independence or impartiality.[144] Overall, this decision is important to show that in investment arbitration, past relationships with a funder in unrelated cases does not automatically disqualify an arbitrator and the Respondent must prove substantial and concrete grounds for such challenge.

As we can see, TPF might raise potential challenges against arbitrators due to some relationship arbitrators had with funders. We also see that tribunals might consult the IBA guidelines as in the *Canepa v Spain* case. However, it seems difficult to challenge an arbitrator because of past relationships with a funder. As long as the arbitrator does not have a stake in the case, does not have a continued relationship with the funder or does not benefit if the funder profits previous relationships are not going to be a reason for the arbitrator to be disqualified. To check potential conflicts between arbitrators and funders, tribunals might consult the IBA Guidelines or similar international guidelines.

3.6 Discontinuation of Arbitration

Sometimes, the tribunal's decision is not respected, and arbitration proceedings discontinued. As an example, in the *RSM case*, "Claimant's counsel informed the Tribunal that Claimant's funding arrangement had been terminated and that Claimant would be unable to provide a USD 750,000 bank guarantee or place that amount in escrow",[145] and the tribunal discontinued the proceedings.[146] SfC orders ordered by tribunals can have a deterrent effect on funders resulting in them cancelling TPF agreements. This will stop arbitration proceedings if the claimant does not have orthodox funds to pursue its cases. This creates an access to justice problem as will be elaborated in Chap. 5, where ethical analysis of TPF is presented.

[142] *Ibid.* para. 43.

[143] *Ibid.* para. 85.

[144] *Ibid.*

[145] RSM v. Saint Lucia, Discontinuation of Proceedings, 8 April 2015, para. 3.

[146] Ibid, para. 68.

Another dispute that was funded against Romania was discontinued because of that non-payment of required advance payment.[147] This case against Romania can also be associated with the access to justice problem. Since the tribunal ordered advance payment by claimants and the funder did not agree to pay those advance payments, the claimants lost the opportunity to pursue their case. It had two results: (i) tribunals should assess carefully whether they should order the claimant to post advance payments because of possible access to justice problem that decision might create as in the *S&T Oil v Romania* case; (ii) to overcome these challenges, there might be some rules against funders. For example, if a funder agrees to fund an investment arbitration case, it must post any advance payments or SfC orders. However, again, this will deter funders from TPF of the claim and may have a negative effect on the right of parties for access to justice since it will increase the costs of funders. Chapter 5 discusses this important balance in the ISDS regime further.

In conclusion, discontinuation of arbitration is an important result of the non-compliance with the investment arbitration tribunal's order. It might be the result of the Tribunal's SfC order if the funder is the only chance for the claimants to bring their cases and funders decide to stop funding the case as a result of SfC orders.

3.7 Disclosure of the Identity of Funders and Terms of TPF Agreements

The existence of TPF elevates some questions with respect to disclosure: (i) Should or must parties disclose the presence and/or funder's identity, and if so, on which grounds and when? (ii) Should or must parties disclose the nature of the TPF arrangement, and if so, on what basis, what parts of the TPF arrangement should be disclosed and when? These questions are answered in many investment arbitrations cases as analyzed in the following paragraphs.

Disclosure is getting more common especially disclosure of the funder's identity. In the Eurogas case, the tribunal was in the notion of that the claimants "should disclose the identity of the third-party funder, and third-party funder will have the normal obligations of confidentiality".[148] This has been the usual practice when we consider the recent legislation in Singapore and Hong Kong on TPF as well as IBA guidelines. More interestingly, however, in *Muhammet Cap&Sehil Insaat Endustri ve Ticaret Ltd Sti v Turkmenistan case,*[149] where the claim was brought under the

[147] S & T Oil Equipment and Machinery Ltd. v. Romania, ICSID Case No. ARB/07/13.

[148] EuroGas Inc and Belmont Resources Inc v Slovak Republic, ICSID Case No ARB/14/14. Transcript of the First Session and Hearing on Provisional Measures (17 March 2015), p. 145.

[149] Muhammet Cap & Sehil Inssaat Endustri ve Ticaret Ltd Sti v Turkmenistan, ICSID Case No ARB/12/6.

Turkey-Turkmenistan BIT,[150] the decision was different. The claimants were Mr Muhammet Cap, a Turkish citizen and *Sehil Insaat Endustri ve Ticaret Ltd Sti*, a company incorporated under the law of Turkey,[151] and the Respondent was Turkmenistan.[152] The dispute related to allegedly unlawful expropriation of claimants' construction projects in Turkmenistan.[153]

The issue related to TPF is related to the disclosure issue. The tribunal said that in a previous procedural order, reasons for disclosure are stated as:

> in particular to avoid a conflict of interest for the arbitrator, for transparency and to identify the true party to the case, and if there is an application for security for costs.[154]

Respondent, after the second procedural order, again demanded disclosure of "the identity and nature of the involvement of third-party funders for Claimants in this proceeding".[155] The respondent further consolidated its request by stating that "to have disclosure of the funder who has a direct economic interest in a potential award in this case, in order to determine if there are any conflicts and to have full transparency of all parties in interest with respect to this case".[156] Importantly, the tribunal ruled that the claimants had to disclose both the funder's identity and the TPF arrangement's terms.[157] The tribunal explained its reasons first to ensure there is no CoI and transparency regarding the existence of the funder is an important factor in such cases.[158] Second, the respondent indicated that it is going to make an application for a SfC order. To understand on what basis it was going to be made better this disclosure is necessary.[159] Two additional reasons that Kilic Insaat did not pay the cost order even though it funded annulment proceedings and the claimants were straightforward not to hide the fact that they were funded and denying that they did not assign their rights.[160] Thus, the tribunal ordered the claimant to disclose if it was funded and further:

> if so, shall advise Respondent and the Tribunal of the name or names and details of the third-party funder(s), and the nature of the arrangements concluded with the third-party funder(s),

[150] Muhammet Cap & Sehil Inssaat Endustri ve Ticaret Ltd Sti v Turkmenistan, ICSID Case No ARB/12/6, Decision on Respondent's Objection to Jurisdiction under Article VII(2) of the Turkey-Turkmenistan Bilateral Investment Treaty, 13 February 2015 para. 1.

[151] Ibid, p. 3.

[152] Ibid, p. 4.

[153] Ibid, p. 6.

[154] Muhammet Cap & Sehil Inssaat Endustri ve Ticaret Ltd Sti v Turkmenistan, ICSID Case No ARB/12/6, Procedural Order No 3 (12 June 2015), para. 1.

[155] Ibid, p. 2.

[156] Ibid, p. 4.

[157] Ibid, p. 8.

[158] Ibid, p. 9.

[159] Ibid, p. 10.

[160] Ibid, p. 11.

> including whether and to what extent it/they will share in any successes that Claimants may achieve in this arbitration.[161]

Another aspect related to TPF raised in the RSM v Saint Lucia case, which is not as important issues previously canvassed, is that claimant argued that the respondent was funded by a TPF as well, but the claimant did not substantiate this claim and thus, the tribunal did not consider it.[162] How this situation would affect the tribunal's decision is a question left unanswered. Maybe, since the respondent state does also not incur any costs, this might affect the tribunal's decision and might not order any SfC order at all. However, the tribunal chose not to address this issue based on there was no substantial evidence on this claim. Then, for better practice, if a counsel wishes to make a point regarding TPF, this claim should be supported with substantial evidence. This can be overcome by a mandatory disclosure or a disclosure order by the tribunal.

In another dispute, the Tribunal mandated the funder's identity be revealed.[163] The respondent demanded the tribunal "to disclose the identity of the funder as well as the terms of the third party funding agreement".[164] The Respondent solicited three facts to strengthen its position. These were as follows: "Claimant is a Bermuda shell company with no economic activity or assets, which is only used by the real investor (South American Silver Corporation or SASC) to improperly attempt to obtain protection under the Treaty; (ii) SASC has publicly announced that it will run out of funds by the end of the year 2015; and (iii) the costs of the Claimant in this arbitration are being funded by a third party, which confirms SAS' inability to bear the costs of this arbitration" in its request.[165] Bolivia requested SfC by stating that "there [was] no evidence whatsoever that the third-party funder [was] obliged to reimburse Bolivia's costs and expenses of this arbitration and, therefore, it [was] necessary to obtain information as to the terms of the funding of this arbitration".[166] The respondent also referred to Dr Griffith's assenting reasons to secure the costs order.[167] The respondent to support its disclosure request argued that arbitrators should have no CoI and the tribunal should ensure its integrity.[168] To consolidate its argument, the respondent referred to the IBA guidelines.[169] The disclosure of the TPF agreement's terms will enable us to see whether the claim is assigned to a TPF company or the TPF company has to pay adverse costs according to Bolivia.[170]

---

161 Ibid, p. 13.

162 *Ibid.*, Muhammet Cap (Decision on Respondent's Objection), para. 50.

163 South American Silver Limited v. Bolivia, PCA Case No. 2013-15.

164 South American Silver Limited v. Bolivia, PCA Case No. 2013-15, Procedural Order 10, 11 January 2016, para. 13.

165 Ibid, para. 18.

166 Ibid, para. 16.

167 Ibid, para. 27.

168 Ibid, para. 28.

169 Ibid, para. 29.

170 Ibid, para. 30.

In many cases, disclosure of TPF and SfC order have been demanded by the respondent state together.[171] There are more examples where the disclosure of TPF agreements and/or funder was demanded together with SfC applications rather than the disclosure demanded on its own. In a PCA-administered case, where disclosure of TPF had been ordered by the tribunal and it was stated that as an "ongoing duty to disclose any change in the information" provided.[172] The Respondent demanded that the Tribunal command:

> the Claimants to (i) provide a USD 4 million security for its costs of arbitration, in the form of a guarantee payable on first demand or a deposit held in escrow by the PCA; and (ii) disclose whether they use third party funding to cover the costs of the arbitration, and, if so, the identity of the third-party funder and the terms of any third party funding agreement.[173]

The Respondent, relying upon García Armas v Venezuela, contended that "there [was] an actual risk that its representation and other costs [would] not be recoverable because it [was] unclear whether the Claimants [were] solvent or [were] using third party funding".[174] The Claimants' position is opposed this demand by pleading that the "Tribunal reject the Respondent's application for security for costs since it fail [ed] to meet the general standard of extreme and exceptional circumstances (A) or the specific requirements set out in Article 26 of the UNCITRAL Rules (B)".[175]

After analyzing both parties' submissions, the Tribunal observed that other elements, namely TPF or a claimant's serious and proven financial difficulties, may also illustrated the assessment of whether SfC should be ordered but also the tribunal decided that those factors should be assessed in relation to all other relevant circumstances and would typically not, in and of themselves, constitute a sufficient basis for such an order.[176] Importantly, the tribunal agreed with the tribunal in EuroGas v. Slovakia by expressing that: "financial difficulties and third party-funding . . . do not necessarily constitute per se exceptional circumstances".[177] The tribunal concluded that regardless whether one concurs with the *Manuel García* decision or not, the position, in this case, [was] distinct and so that "the Tribunal [was] therefore not persuaded that exceptional circumstances exist".[178] "Finally, the Tribunal agree[d] that the urgency of an order of security for costs is a matter to be

---

[171] As happened in Muhammet Cap & Sehil Inssaat Endustri ve Ticaret Ltd Sti v Turkmenistan, ICSID Case No ARB/12/6; and South American Silver Limited v. Bolivia, PCA Case No. 2013-15.

[172] The Estate of Julio Miguel Orlandini-Agreda and Compañía Minera Orlandini Ltda. v. Bolivia, PCA Case No. 2018-39, Procedural Order No 1, February 4, 2019, para. 11.2.

[173] The Estate of Julio Miguel Orlandini-Agreda and Compañía Minera Orlandini Ltda. v. Bolivia, PCA Case No. 2018-39, Decision on the Respondent's Application for Termination, Trifurcation and Security for Cost, July 9, 2019, para. 82.

[174] *Ibid.* para. 89.

[175] *Ibid.* para. 91.

[176] *Ibid.* para. 144.

[177] *Ibid.* para. 147.

[178] *Ibid.* para. 149.

duly taken into consideration" but "the Tribunal [was] not persuaded by the Respondent's arguments on urgency".[179] Finally, the Tribunal is not convinced that circumstances existed that warranted an order of SfC and rejected the Respondent's application for SfC.[180] This case also shows that one more time an investment arbitration tribunal accepted that the mere presence of a TPF agreement alone cannot be a reason to grant a SfC application.

A SfC order was also delivered in another ICSID case.[181] Before this case, there were only two cases where SfC orders were granted and this case has become the third known investment arbitration case where the SfC order granted. In this case, since the Claimant was insolvent. To be able to pursue this arbitration, the Claimant secured TPF and the resulting TPF agreement did "not cover any award of costs against the Claimant in favor of Turkmenistan".[182]

The Claimant claimed that the reason in RSM v. Saint Lucia for SfC order was based on "exceptional circumstances", as being "based on rather unique factors showing that the claimant repeatedly failed to respect its obligations".[183] The Claimant further contended that a command for SfC contingent upon insolvency and related to TPF "would not only allow Turkmenistan to profit from its own wrong, but also encourage host states to do the job right to better ensure the investor's insolvency and prevent any BIT claim from the outset".[184] The Claimant resorted to Eurogas. In that case, the insolvent Claimant with a funder was not granted SfC.[185]

In the Herzig case:

> in response, Turkmenistan argues that an order for security for costs will not prejudice Dr Herzig's access to justice on behalf of Unionmatex, especially at this initial stage of the arbitration where there is more incentive for La Française to fund the security to allow the case to proceed.[186]

According to Turkmenistan, "the cost of the security should be considered part of La Française's commitment to pay the costs of the arbitration itself".[187] Moreover, Turkmenistan later asserted that a command for SfC was compulsory "to protect this right because Unionmatex [was] insolvent, a third party is funding the Claimant's costs of arbitration", and the TPF agreement openly precluded "third-party liability

---

[179] *Ibid.* para. 150.

[180] *Ibid.* para. 151–152.

[181] Dirk Herzig as Insolvency Administrator over the Assets of Unionmatex Industrieanlagen GmbH v. Turkmenistan, ICSID Case No. ARB/18/35.

[182] Dirk Herzig as Insolvency Administrator over the Assets of Unionmatex Industrieanlagen GmbH v. Turkmenistan, ICSID Case No. ARB/18/35, Decision on the Respondent's Request for Security for Costs and the Claimant's Request for Security for Claim, 27 January 2020, para 3.

[183] *Ibid.* para. 19.

[184] *Ibid.* para. 37.

[185] *Ibid.* para. 24.

[186] *Ibid.* para. 38.

[187] *Ibid.*

for an adverse costs award" as its shown in the TPF agreement submitted by the Dirk Herzig to the Tribunal in his letter dated 23 July 2019.[188] Turkmenistan further identified that the TPF company was not liable in the TPF agreement to create exceptional circumstances in this claim.[189] To support its assertion, Turkmenistan referred to the *Manuel Garcia v. Venezuela* case, where the SfC order was granted by the Tribunal, "finding the determinative factor to be that the third-party funder was not obliged to pay any adverse costs award against the insolvent claimants".[190]

The tribunal analyzed those arguments and made its decision. According to the Tribunal, without any doubt, "accepts Dr Herzig's argument that his reliance on TPF is not sufficient, in and of itself, to meet the exceptional circumstances standard as supported in EuroGas v. Slovak Republic, among other cases".[191] In additional, the Tribunal also admits that "Dr Herzig's argument that a party's impecunity, in and of itself, is not sufficient to meet the exceptional circumstances standard".[192] The querty the Tribunal has to determine in this case between the parties is "the import of the third factor beyond impecunity and third-party funding – the explicit non-liability of the third-party funder for a cost award adverse to its funded party".[193] According to the Tribunal:

> this presents a more extreme situation here: Dr Herzig is (i) representing Unionmatex as a bankrupt, (ii) relying on TPF from La Française, and (iii) La Française is expressly not liable under the TPF agreement for an ultimate award of costs in Turkmenistan's favor.[194]

The Tribunal accepts in this claim that "because of the terms of the TPF contract, Turkmenistan faces not a risk but, on the basis of the factual record before it, a certainty that it could not collect a costs award".[195] Similar to the tribunal in the García Armas case, "a majority of the Tribunal finds this additional factor to be critical".[196] The Tribunal has not seen any rationale "to distinguish García Armas, as Dr Herzig asks, on grounds that it was a UNCITRAL rather than an ICSID treaty arbitration".[197] Therefore, the Tribunal ordered the SfC against the Claimant. Thus, we can conclude that in the case where (i) the claimant is insolvent, (ii) the Claimant brought its claim with a TPF arrangement, (iii) and the third-party funder explicitly exclude the possibility of paying adverse costs in the TPF arrangement, investment arbitration tribunals will likely post SfC orders against such claimants in favour of respondent states to protect states from the possibility of not recovering its costs in

[188] *Ibid.* para. 22.
[189] *Ibid.* para. 26.
[190] *Ibid.* para. 27.
[191] *Ibid.* para. 54.
[192] *Ibid.* para. 55.
[193] *Ibid.* para. 57.
[194] *Ibid.*
[195] *Ibid.* para. 59.
[196] *Ibid.* para. 60.
[197] *Ibid.*

case the Claimant is unsuccessful in its claim. This issue must be definitely considered in TPF arrangements where an investor is funded in investment arbitration and it is included in the best practice guideline for funders operating in investment arbitration.[198]

In another award published in Spanish, another SfC request, which the Respondent particularly requested because of the TPF, was again rejected by the tribunal.[199] In another case, the Respondent state Italy asked the tribunal to direct Eskosol, the Claimant, to post an irrevocable bank guarantee or analogous security in the amount of $250,000 **[the "Security Application"]**; and direct the Claimant to submit Exhibits C-005 and C-006 in their integrity to permit the Respondent and the Tribunal to get confirmation whether a TPF did commit itself to cover Eskosol['s] costs of these proceedings **[the "Disclosure Application"]**.[200] Italy relied on the decision in RSM v. Saint Lucia Case, where the tribunal ordered SfC order against the funded party.[201] Similarly, the Claimant relied on decisions where "a number of arbitral tribunals have confirmed that the presence of a third-party funder would not amount to an extraordinary circumstance requiring the imposition of security for costs".[202] Moreover, the Claimant further argues that it already has obtained the ATE insurance, which makes the risk of non-payment of an award non-existent or extremely limited since the coverage in the ATE Insurance (€1 million) significantly exceeds the amount of security sought by Italy.[203]

The tribunal concluded that "Italy ha[d] not demonstrated that it [was] either necessary or urgent that Eskosol post security of $250,000 for a potential costs award in Italy's favor", especially considering the ATE insurance "policy cover[ed] up to 1,000,000 Euro in the aggregate for Opponent's Costs, with Opponent identified as Republic of Italy" as shown in the Exhibits.[204] Regarding Italy's disclosure application the tribunal agreed with the Claimant and further concluded that the issues raised by the Disclosure Application were largely moot since Italy sought disclosure to learn that whether there is a TPF company exist in the claim and if the TPF company will reimburse the value of these proceedings.[205] Eskosol already confirmed the existence of the funder,[206] and as explained, the ATE insurance was enough to cover costs of proceedings and thus, there was no need to investigate whether the funder w also cover such costs. This decision shows that it is important

[198] See the Best Practice Guideline attached to this book.

[199] Luis García Armas v. Bolivarian Republic of Venezuela, ICSID Case No. ARB(AF)/16/1, Decision on Jurisdiction, 24 July 2020, para. 454.

[200] Eskosol S.p.A. in liquidazione v. Italian Republic, ICSID Case No. ARB/15/50, Procedural Order NO. 3 (Decision on Respondent's Request for Provisional Measures), 12 April 2017.

[201] *Ibid.* para. 14.

[202] *Ibid.* para. 30.

[203] *Ibid.* para. 26.

[204] *Ibid.* para. 37.

[205] *Ibid.* para. 44.

[206] *Ibid.* para. 3.

for the respondent state's reasoning for disclosure application. If Italy had disclosure for the motive of CoI check between arbitrators-funder, the tribunal may have accepted the disclosure demand.[207] However, since Italy did not seek disclosure for this purpose and Italy's grounds had been moot, its disclosure application had been rejected by the tribunal.

In another PCA Case, this time against Canada, SfC order and disclosure was also requested together.[208] From the tribunal Canada requested an order:

> directing Tennant to disclose the existence of any third-party funding agreement that Tennant entered into in order to finance its claim in this arbitration and sought to learn the name(s) of any such third-party funder(s) and the nature of the arrangements concluded with the third-party funder(s), including whether and to what extent they will share in any potential damages awarded, or pay an adverse cost order rendered against Tennant.[209]

Moreover, Canada referred to the *Garcia Armas* and *RSM v. Saint Lucia* cases and demanded SfC from the Tribunal.

In addition to ordering SfC, Canada claims that "it [was] necessary to order Tennant to disclose the existence and terms of any TPF agreement entered into to finance its claim in this arbitration".[210] Canada referred to the *Muhammet Cap* case declaring that the Tribunal "could order the disclosure of a third-party funding agreement to protect the integrity of the arbitral process".[211] Canada requested disclosure also for the purpose to check potential CoI between funders and arbitrators and to this end, Canada referred to Article 4.6 of the Terms of Appointment, Article 9 of the 1976 UNCITRAL Rules, the IBA Guidelines on CoI in International Arbitration, 2014, and General Standard 6(b).[212] Therefore, Canada demanded the disclosure of TPF.[213]

Tennant opposed to the disclosure request.[214] First, the Claimant declared that the origins of the Investor's funding "[was] irrelevant to the issues in dispute" and no disclosure on the source was required.[215] Also, in accordance with the Claimant, Canada's concern about "the level of financial interest a potential funder might have in the outcome of this proceeding is unwarranted because Tennant is the owner of the investment that Canada treated unlawfully" and the "level of interest a funder might

[207] For the discussion respecting disclosure *see*: PCA Case No. 2018-54; ICSID Case No ARB/14/14; PCA Case No. 2013-15; ICSID Case No ARB/12/6; ICSID Case No. ARB(AF)/14/3; PCA Case No. 2012-07.

[208] Tennant Energy, LLC v. Government of Canada, PCA Case No. 2018-54.

[209] Tennant Energy, LLC v. Government of Canada, PCA Case No. 2018-54, Government of Canada Motion for Security for Costs and Disclosure of Third-Party Funding, August 16, 2019, para. 3.

[210] *Ibid.* para. 41.

[211] *Ibid.*

[212] *Ibid.* para. 43–44.

[213] *Ibid.* para. 46.

[214] Tennant Energy, LLC v. Government of Canada, PCA Case No. 2018-54, Response to Canada's Motion for Security for Costs and Disclosure of Funding 23 September 2019.

[215] *Ibid.* para. 59.

have in the outcome of the proceeding does not alter that fact".[216] Moreover, Canada's demand that the Tribunal order "the investor to disclose the terms of any TPF agreement [was] likewise unwarranted" since TPF agreements are private and need be disclosed "only in exceptional circumstances, where the precise terms of that agreement are relevant".[217] The Claimant refers to the *South American Silver Ltd v. Bolivia* case since the Tribunal, in that claim, ordered that "the identity of the third-party funder should be disclosed for the purposes of transparency, but it refused to order the disclosure of TPF agreement's terms".[218] Lastly, the Tribunal objects to the disclosure of whether a funder would assume responsibility for a cost award against the investor since the exceptional circumstances necessary for an order for SfC does not exist in this claim.[219] However, regarding Canada's concerns about a CoI, "the Investor is willing to disclose the identity of any funder to the Tribunal, if so ordered".[220] Therefore, the Claimant demands the Tribunal reject Canada's demand that the investor discloses its TPF arrangements in this arbitration.[221]

Canada sets forth that in the *Dirk Herzig v. Turkmenistan* decision, one of the grounds the Tribunal relied on to order the SfC was the fact that third-party funder was "expressly not liable under the funding contract for an ultimate award of costs in Turkmenistan's favor" and Canada submitted to the Tribunal to consider in this case, whether the funder was absolved of such duty by the terms of the TPF agreement.[222]

Canada further requested from the Tribunal both SfC and disclosure of TPF and referred to the *Dirk Herzig v. Turkmenistan* case to support its request since in that case, the Tribunal ordered SfC against the Claimant and Canada claimed that the tribunal's reasoning and conclusion on this matter were directly relevant to Canada's motion for SfC and disclosure of TPF.[223] As a response to Canada's submission on the *Dirk Herzig v. Turkmenistan* case, the Claimant submitted that Canada must show exceptional circumstances beyond mere lack of funds to warrant further inquiry into the investor's TPF terms, much less the extraordinary remedy of SfC. The Respondent has completely "failed to do so".[224]

First, "the Tribunal considered that it has the authority to order the disclosure requested if doing so would preserve the integrity of the arbitral process" and it

[216] *Ibid.* para. 61.

[217] *Ibid.* para. 62.

[218] *Ibid.* para. 63.

[219] *Ibid.* para. 64.

[220] *Ibid.* para. 60.

[221] *Ibid.* para. 65/b.

[222] Tennant Energy, LLC v. Government of Canada, PCA Case No. 2018-54, Government of Canada Submission on Legal Authority Regarding Canada's Motion for Security for Costs and Disclosure of Third-Party Funding, February 17, 2020, para. 5.

[223] Tennant Energy, LLC v. Government of Canada, PCA Case No. 2018-54, Claimant E-mail re Decision in Dirk Herzig v. Turkmenistan, February 4, 2020.

[224] Tennant Energy, LLC v. Government of Canada, PCA Case No. 2018-54, Response to Canada's submission on Herzig v. Turkmenistan, 24 February 2020, para. 8.

seemed undisputed in this claim.[225] Furthermore, the Tribunal contemplated that "the Claimant ha[d] also stated that it is willing to disclose the identity of any third-party funder to the Tribunal to address any concerns about a conflict of interest".[226] Consequently, the Tribunal ruled that:

> the Claimant should make the following disclosures to the Tribunal and the Respondent by (a) the identity of any third-party funder; (b) any terms contained in the TPF arrangement relating to the payment of adverse costs orders against the Claimant in this arbitration. Any such terms should be quoted in full in the Claimant's disclosure; and (c) where no such terms set out at (b) above exist, the Claimant is to inform the Tribunal and the Respondent of that fact.[227]

This is a continuous duty and the Tribunal commands the Claimant that if there is any change in the information provided, the Claimant should inform "the Tribunal and the Respondent of the same within two weeks from the date of the change".[228] However, the Tribunal confirmed that these disclosures are confidential and "need not be made available to the general public".[229] The tribunal gives two reasons for the disclosure. The first reason is that the presence of TPF arrangements can be taken into account by the Tribunal for SfC applications.[230] "Secondly, and in any event, the Tribunal considers that transparency as to the existence of a third-party funder is important to determine whether any conflict of interest exists".[231] Moreover, in the hearings, SfC because of TPF together with other reasons and the disclosure TPF took place and referred many times and written submissions as explained here are elaborated further.[232]

In a case governed by UNCITRAL rules, the respondent state, Russia, applied for SfC together with the disclosure of funders.[233] In respondent's SfC application, respondent demands the tribunal to supply a command"(i) requiring the Claimant to provide SfC of USD 800,000; and (ii) requiring the Claimant to disclose the name of any third-party funders as well as the terms of any funding agreement".[234] The respondent also asserts that risk of non-enforcement of any costs award also arises from claimant's failure to comply with at least twelve orders issued by the English High Court and the tribunal's request to refrain from making public statements and

[225] Tennant Energy, LLC v. Government of Canada, PCA Case No. 2018-54, Procedural Order No. 4, 27 February 2020, para. 104.

[226] *Ibid.* para. 105.

[227] *Ibid.* para. 106.

[228] *Ibid.* para. 107.

[229] *Ibid.* para. 108.

[230] *Ibid.* para. 109.

[231] *Ibid.* para. 110.

[232] Tennant Energy, LLC v. Government of Canada, PCA Case No. 2018-54, Hearing volume 1, volume 2, Here, we are not discussing all issues in the Trial but only TPF-related issues.

[233] Sergei Viktorovich Pugachev v. The Russian Federation, UNCITRAL, Interim Award, 7 July 2017, para. 2/ii.

[234] *Ibid.* para. 147.

disclosing information and gives an example where the claimant violated the freezing order by obtaining funds for legal services without seeking the appropriate authorization from the opposing party in the proceedings or the English High Court.[235] Respondents further allege that they have demanded from claimant on several occasions to disclose the names and any TPF agreement with funders and thus demands the tribunal to order the claimant to disclose any funders.[236]

The Claimant requested the tribunal to reject the respondents' request for SfC and disclosure of any TPF agreement.[237] The claimant argues that the respondent's SfC application was a mere dilatory tactic to put undue pressure on the claimant and to prevent it from participating and defending itself in the current arbitration.[238] It also asserted that the respondent had obtained a freezing order and, thus, had already a clear vision of the claimant's assets and his current financial situation.[239] The claimant agrees with the respondent that the demanding party, in a SfC application, must demonstrate that: "(i) there is a reasonable possibility that it will succeed in its defense to the claim, and it is likely to be awarded costs; (ii) that there exist extreme and exceptional circumstances warranting a security for costs; and (iii) that granting its request would not disproportionately burden the party against whom the measure is sought and contends that none of these elements is present in Respondent's security for costs application".[240] The claimant contends that apart from the respondent failure to prove the first requirement, in ISDS, ISDS tribunals have not followed the "loser pay principle" and costs awards against unsuccessful claimants "are exceedingly rare and the standard to be met is extremely high".[241] Moreover, "Article 40(1) of the UNCITRAL Rules expressly provides that tribunals retain the discretion no to apply the "Loser Pay principle".[242] With respect to the second requirement, claimant, by referring to several ISDS awards elaborates that: "(i) financial distress of a party or the risk that an adverse costs award will go unpaid do not justify ordering security for costs; (ii) the mere existence of a third party funding agreement does not warrant security for costs; (iii) the history of unpaid adverse costs awards in similar circumstances is relevant, and (iv) claimant's timely payment of the advance on the tribunal's costs militate against an order for security for costs".[243] Furthermore, in this claim, Pugachev additionally contends that "allegations of third party funding are not exceptional circumstances in investment arbitration and, in any event, no such third-party funding agreement exists in the

[235] *Ibid.* para. 157.
[236] *Ibid.* para. 161.
[237] *Ibid.* para. 163.
[238] *Ibid.* para. 164.
[239] *Ibid.*
[240] *Ibid.* para. 165.
[241] *Ibid.* para. 167.
[242] *Ibid.*
[243] *Ibid.* para. 169.

present case and this argument is therefore moot".[244] Regarding the disclosure demand, by refferring to an ISDS arbitration award, the Claimant asserted that: "disclosure of such information may only be required in exceptional circumstances, where there exists a significant risk of disruption to the proceedings".[245]

The Tribunal held that the Claimant was unsuccessful in meeting the high threshold to accept SfC.[246] Regarding the Respondent's application for disclosure of funders, since Claimant, Pugachev, had already disclosed that no TPF company was used, and the respondent had not presented proof proposing that there was one, the tribunal did not find itself in a situation that it needs to rule on such a request.[247] Interestingly, and regarding the focus of this book, the tribunal did not consider the effect of TPF agreements in SfC or whether they should be disclosed or not since there was no funding in the case. Therefore, apart from the brilliant arguments of both sides mentioned above, this tribunal did not reach any conclusion on the effect of TPF on SfC and disclosure in this case. The difference from its case, in the *Dirk Herzig* case, the funder explicitly excluded any adverse costs payment and this provision in the TPF agreement seemed to the tribunal grant the SfC order.

In another ICSID case against the Dominican Republic, disclosure of the funder was requested, and the Tribunal granted it.[248] Disclosure and SfC were discussed in another case.[249] Disclosure has not always been granted by tribunals. In a case against Colombia, the Respondent's request for disclosure of any agreement entered into with third parties to fund the claimant's claim against Colombia was not accepted and the tribunal decided that no order was required for such disclosure.[250] As we can see, disclosure has been one of the hottest topics and generally requested together with SfC orders.

[244] *Ibid.* para. 171.

[245] *Ibid.* para. 177.

[246] *Ibid.* para. 399.

[247] *Ibid.* para. 401.

[248] Corona Materials LLC v. Dominican Republic, ICSID Case No. ARB(AF)/14/3, Award on the Respondent's Expedited Preliminary Objections in Accordance with Article 10.20.5 of the DR-CAFTA, May 31, 2016, para. 22.

[249] Stans Energy Corp. and Kutisay Mining LLC v. Kyrgyz Republic (II), PCA Case No. 2015-32, Award, 20 August 2019.

[250] Eco Oro Minerals Corp. v. Republic of Colombia, ICSID Case No. ARB/16/41, Procedural Order No. 7, 5 April 2019, Respondent's Requests for Disclosure No. 2.

3.8 Impact of TPF on a Stay of Enforcement of an ICSID Award

One case is connected to the effect of TPF on the stay of the enforcement proceeding. In the *Adem Dogan v Turkmenistan* case, the claimant was a national of Germany and the dispute is under the Germany-Turkmenistan BIT.[251] The decision was not published. As reported by the investment arbitration reporter, the tribunal in the *Adem dogan v. Turkmenistan* case, decided not to lift a stay of enforcement while annulment proceedings continue and one of the grounds for its decision was the existence of the TPF company. According to the news, the tribunal concerned that if the stay of enforcement was lifted, the funded party would share the recovery with the TPF company. In this claim, the funder was Omni Bridgeway, and this sharing would make it more complicated and difficult for Turkmenistan to recover from the claimant in case the award was annulled.[252] In conclusion, TPF can have such effects on the stay of enforcement of an ICSID award.

3.9 Control of Funders

How much control funders should exercise at the case management is a crucial issue in many jurisdictions, naturally, an inevitable question that needs to be addressed in investment arbitration as well.

In a case, a very important issue, control of funders over proceedings is discussed together with the disclosure issue among other issues.[253] The Respondent recalled that: "Claimant had agreed during the Interim Measures Hearing to disclose its third-party funding arrangements and sought an order directing Claimant to disclose (i) whether third party funding arrangements have been entered into in respect of this arbitration; (ii) the identity of the funder; (iii) the terms of the funding; (iv) whether the claims have been assigned to a third party; and (v) the terms of any assignment arrangements".[254]

The Tribunal invited the Claimant to notify it with respect to: "(i) the identity of its third-party funder; (ii) the nature or type of the third party funding; and (iii) whether the third-party funder has a charge or lien on the proceeds of this claim and/or if the third party funder in any other way exercises control over the present

---

[251] Adem Dogan v Turkmenistan, ICSID Case No ARB/09/9, Decision on Annulment, 15 January 2016, p. 3.

[252] Investor's duty to pass a portion of award-recovery to the third-party funder is cited as a reason to not lift a stay of enforcement of that award, by Luke Eric Peterson, Jan 22, 2015, *see* https://www.iareporter.com/articles/investors-duty-to-pass-a-portion-of-award-recovery-to-third-party-funder-is-cited-as-a-reason-to-not-lift-a-stay-of-enforcement-of-that-award/.

[253] Mohamed Abdel Raouf Bahgat v. Egypt, PCA Case No. 2012-07.

[254] *Ibid.*, Decision on Jurisdiction, 30 November 2017, para. 59.

arbitration".[255] The Claimant did inform the tribunal by stating that, at that moment, the claimant had no TPF in place.[256] However, this shows the considerations of the Tribunal. Apart from (i) the identity and (ii) the nature of the TPF, importantly (iii) whether the third-party funder has a charge or lien on the proceeds of this claim and/or if the third-party funder in any other way exercises control over the present arbitration. This last point is important because the control was never considered by an investment arbitration tribunal before. How the tribunal would react to the degree of control was not tested in this case, but it might have been tested and most probably it will be tested in other cases. Thus, funders should not exert too much control and funders should take the control issue into consideration. This issue is addressed by the guideline at the end of this book.[257]

In conclusion, the degree of funders' control in investment arbitration proceedings was considered by the tribunal. However, since in that specific case, there was no present funder when the tribunal enquired about the degree of control exercised by funders, how the tribunal would decide on the degree of control that funders should exercise is not answered then. Probably, this issue will be addressed by other investment arbitration tribunals in the near future.

3.10 Definition of TPF

In Chap. 2 of this book, different definitions of TPF were given. As explained, there is no unanimous definition of TPF globally. The definition has not only been discussed theoretically but it has also been considered in at least one ISDS claim where the tribunal decided the definition of TPF in that case.

In one case the definition of TPF has been discussed. Apart from the important question of SfC, another important discussion on what constitutes third-party funder took place. First, in this claim, the SfC application was denied by the Tribunal.[258] The tribunal confirmed the fact that "the Claimant does not itself have the funds to meet an adverse costs order", per se "is insufficient to justify an order of security for costs, as prior tribunals have repeatedly observed".[259] Interestingly, whether financial arrangements between the claimant and third parties constituted a TPF relationship or not was the topic of the dispute.[260] The claimant claimed that there was no TPF relationship with the third-parties and explained that Gibson Dunn has merely agreed to defer payments until the claimant had resolved its TPF arrangements and Encore Mining Ltd had advanced two loans to enable the claimant to fund its costs,

---

[255] *Ibid.* para. 63.

[256] *Ibid.* para. 64.

[257] See guideline for third-party funders funding investment arbitration cases.

[258] Ipek Investment Limited v. Republic of Turkey, ICSID Case No. ARB/18/18.

[259] *Ibid.*, Procedural Order No. 7, para. 10.

[260] *Ibid.* para. 12.

In neither which do these arrangements give the third party any stake in the success or failure of the arbitration and the claimant's obligation to pay is not contingent.[261] Importantly, "the Tribunal considers that the evidence does not establish a third-party funder of these proceedings in the sense of a person who has taken a stake in the outcome of the proceedings and who might therefore be expected to bear responsibility for any costs exposure".[262] Therefore, we can state that the tribunal considered TPF as an arrangement to have a stake in the case, which is the most straightforward TPF arrangements by funders. Thus, the first time an ICSID tribunal uttered some comments with regard to the description of TPF.

In conclusion, unless there is a unanimous accepted definition of TPF within the investment arbitration regime regarding what constitutes TPF, and what does not, each tribunal might have to consider the definition of TPF and decide whether the TPF arrangement is accepted by the tribunal as TPF. Increasingly, bilateral and multilateral investment agreements have articles on the definition of TPF, and this might help tribunals to define TPF. However, this will not create a unanimous definition of TPF since definitions vary in those investment agreements and, in each dispute, the investment agreement at stake is different. Therefore, tribunals will end up defining TPF differently and this issue might need to deal by more investment arbitration tribunals growingly.

3.11 Whether TPF Costs Are Recoverable

One of the most interesting and important topics in TPF is maybe the recoverability of TPF costs. Whether costs funders are entitled to under the TPF agreement is a very important decision tribunals need to make if they are requested to do so. Since funders have a stake in the award, if the funded party can recover these costs funders are entitled to, then impecunious parties can access justice without having to give up a sum of money to funders. Moreover, if these costs are recoverable, more parties would be willing to seek TPF and it might have an effect to encourage settlement between parties at the beginning of a dispute.

This issue has been addressed in litigation in various jurisdictions, most importantly in England and Wales.[263] Not surprisingly, and even maybe later than expected, a claimant in an investment arbitration case also tried to recover the TPF fees from the respondent.[264] The claimant counted on the fact that "without TPF, he would have been unable to bring the claim because Respondent's unlawful conduct

[261] *Ibid.* para. 14.

[262] *Ibid.* para. 15.

[263] See Essar Oilfield Services Ltd. V. Norscot Rig Management Pvt Ltd, Queen's Bench Division (Commercial Court) 15 Sept. 2016, EWHC 2361 (Comm.).

[264] Mohamed Abdel Raouf Bahgat v. Egypt, PCA Case No. 2012-07, Final Award, 23 December 2019, para. 88/h, 89 and 563.

left him impecunious".[265] The claimant turned to the "Tribunal to *Essar Oilfields v. Norscot,* a decision of the English High Court which upheld an award of an arbitrator finding a claimant entitled to the costs of its litigation funding",[266] and "also notes that 2017 SIAC investment arbitration rules recognize that arbitral tribunals may take into account third-party funding arrangements in rendering costs orders".[267] On the contrary, the respondent defines that "Claimant's costs claim, amounting to approximately EUR I0 million and up to EUR 80 million in funding costs, as utterly irresponsible and simply outrageous".[268] The respondent further maintains that even in the absence of the TPF costs, they notice that "Claimant's costs claim far exceeds average costs of claimants in UNCITRAL arbitrations and is excessive in circumstances where the case was not particularly complex".[269] Importantly, the respondent objected to the claimant's claims by stating that the success fees of a counsel and funder are not recoverable.[270]

Considering both parties' submissions, the tribunal recorded that "the costs claimed by the Claimant under Article 38(e) of the UNCITRAL Rules exceed the equivalent costs of Respondent".[271] The tribunal observed that the reason is due to two reasons (i) "the success fees claimed by Saunders and by Fietta, respectively", and (ii) the TPF "costs claimed by Buttonwood and Vannin, respectively" and the "Tribunal will deal with each of these two factors in turn".[272] Regarding the first issue, the Tribunal decides that "the success fees due to Claimant's legal representatives are reasonable legal costs according to Article 38(e) of the UNCITRAL Rules".[273] Regarding the second issue, TPF costs, the tribunal considered that "Respondent's objection raises several questions, namely, whether TPF costs are legal costs, whether they were introduced appropriately into the proceedings and whether they are reasonable".[274] However, the tribunal, without discussing those considerations used "its discretion under the UNCITRAL Rules, decides that Claimant's third party funding costs shall be borne by Claimant".[275] Here, the reasoning of the Tribunal is important because actually, the Tribunal did not decide that TPF payments are not recoverable. The Tribunal left this question open and exclude them not because they are not recoverable but because the Tribunal excludes those costs by using its discretion. Therefore, the question stays open for other tribunals and we can expect as this tribunal used its discretion and decide the TPF costs will be borne

[265] *Ibid.* para. 568.
[266] *Ibid.* para. 570.
[267] *Ibid.* para. 571.
[268] *Ibid.* para. 578.
[269] *Ibid.* para. 580.
[270] *Ibid.* para. 581.
[271] *Ibid.* para. 587.
[272] *Ibid.* para. 587.
[273] *Ibid.* para. 589.
[274] *Ibid.* para. 590.
[275] *Ibid.* para. 591.

by the Claimant, another tribunal might well find that TPF costs will be borne by the Respondent under its discretion. This is a very important decision and reasoning for the question of recoverability of TPF costs.

In conclusion, this very important issue has been brought before a UNCITRAL tribunal and the tribunal avoided directly addressing the request but simply rejected it by using its discretion. Other investment arbitration tribunals will probably be asked and sooner or later we can expect a decision on this issue.

3.12 TPF Arrangements Can Be Considered by the Tribunal to Provide an Award on a Certain Time

TPF can be considered for the timing of the award. In one PCA case, the tribunal considered TPF arrangements to render an award before a certain date.[276] In this case, the claimant repeated his concerns and stated that "as to his advanced age, the time he has already spent in the case", and more importantly, regarding TPF, "explained that the arrangement with his new funder will increase the costs entailed for him if the dispute is not resolved by 31 December 2019".[277] Importantly, the tribunal, by referring to the claimant's concerns as to its TPF arrangements, stated that "it would use every best effort to issue a final award in the eight months between the close of the merits hearing and 31 December 2019, assuming the Parties likewise adhere to scheduled dates".[278] This shows that a tribunal considers the parties demands and situation and TPF arrangements with this regard can be considered by the tribunal.

3.13 TPF Pointed Out but Not Discussed

There are other third-party funded cases but not in all those cases TPF arrangements raised issues. Those cases are also funded by a funder, but TPF was not discussed. For example, in two cases against Venezuela,[279] a case against Turkey,[280] a case

[276] Mohamed Abdel Raouf Bahgat v. Egypt, PCA Case No. 2012-07.

[277] Mohamed Abdel Raouf Bahgat v. Egypt, PCA Case No. 2012-07, Final Award, 23 December 2019, para. 48.

[278] *Ibid.* para. 50.

[279] Crystallex International Corporation v. Bolivarian Republic of Venezuela, ICSID Case No. ARB (AF)/11/2; Rusoro Mining Ltd. v. Bolivarian Republic of Venezuela, ICSID Case No. ARB(AF)/12/5.

[280] Alapli Elektrik B.V. v. Republic of Turkey, ICSID Case No. ARB/08/13.

against Italy,[281] a case against Zimbabwe,[282] and a case against the Republic of Uruguay, where the respondent state Uruguay was funded by a funder.[283] However, TPF has never been debated in these claims as an objection or as a disputed issue between the parties. In fact, in many cases, even though there was a third-party funder there was no dispute on TPF agreements or TPF association. Another such example is a case against Russia.[284]

In some cases, TPF was an undisputed fact and the tribunal stated that TPF arrangements did not affect proceedings.[285] Also, not in investment arbitration, but related to the investment arbitration, the United States District Court treated them as one party since their interests and activities are so closely aligned.[286] However, this approach would not be acceptable in an investment arbitration because a third-party funder can never be treated as a party since a third-party funder is not considered as an investor in BITs and not a real party to the dispute. The funder is merely an external entity assisting a disputing party in investment arbitration. This is important to point out the treatment of funders in courts and in investment arbitrations.

In another case, the claimant voluntarily informed the tribunal about the TPF agreement and the tribunal observed if it had any CoI and decided it had no CoI and invited the respondent to provide any observations it may have in connection with the claimant's TPF arrangement and the respondent did not provide any observations on TPF arrangement.[287] This first shows that the TPF agreement again did not create any procedural or ethical issue in this case. This secondly shows that if the claimant did not voluntarily inform the tribunal, the presence of the funder would not be known by the public. Thus, considering not all claimants are disclose their TPF arrangements voluntarily, there might be many more cases where a third-party funder took place, but the presence of the funder had never been disclosed and known by the public.

Funders might attend hearings together with the funded party and their lawyers. In one case we can see that there is not any issue regarding the TPF arrangement.

[281] Rockhopper Italia S.p.A., Rockhopper Mediterranean Ltd, and Rockhopper Exploration Plc v. Italian Republic, ICSID Case No. ARB/17/14.

[282] Bernardus Henricus Funnekotter and others v. Republic of Zimbabwe, ICSID Case No. ARB/05/6.

[283] Philip Morris Brands Sàrl, Philip Morris Products S.A. and Abal Hermanos S.A. v. Oriental Republic of Uruguay, ICSID Case No. ARB/10/7 (formerly FTR Holding SA, Philip Morris Products S.A. and Abal Hermanos S.A. v. Oriental Republic of Uruguay).

[284] Renta 4 S.V.S.A, Ahorro Corporación Emergentes F.I., Ahorro Corporación Eurofondo F.I., Rovime Inversiones SICAV S.A., Quasar de Valors SICAV S.A., Orgor de Valores SICAV S.A., GBI 9000 SICAV S.A. v. The Russian Federation, SCC No. 24/2007.

[285] Oxus Gold v. Republic of Uzbekistan, UNCITRAL, Final Award 17 December 2015, para. 127.

[286] United States District Court For The District Of Columbia, Gretton Ltd., Petitioner, v. Civil Action No. 18-1755 (JEB) Republic Of Uzbekistan, Respondent, Memorandum Opinion, 6 February 2019, p. 13.

[287] Infinito Gold Ltd. v. Costa Rica, ICSID Case No. ARB/14/5, Decision on Jurisdiction, Date of dispatch to the Parties: 4 December 2017, para. 30.

However, we can see from the procedural background in procedural order 4, that a funder is also participating in the trial.[288] In the same case, the tribunal confirmed earlier that none of their signed declarations required updating as a result of the Claimants' disclosure of their funder, Alliance 1 Pty Ltd.[289] This again raises some queries about the relationship among funder-funded party-lawyers. The best practice guideline in the annex to this book addresses the three-party relationship among the funder-funded party-lawyers.

In one instance, the Respondent argued the Claimant's funding but did not request anything based on this TPF relationship.[290]

> While the annual report indicates that Churchill may secure additional funding until 2015, the Respondent argues that the Claimants will not seek funds beyond what they need to pursue this Arbitration, thus leaving the Respondent with no recourse to recover the additional millions it will have to expend over the next year to complete the scheduled rounds of briefing, disclosure and hearings on the merits and quantum.[291]

The tribunal clearly did not consider the TPF relationship as other tribunals in other cases discussed in this section. In the final award, the tribunal ruled that "As for the direct costs of the proceedings which were funded with the advances paid to ICSID, there is no reason for an abatement and, thus, the Claimants shall bear 100% of these costs".[292] Thus, one more time an ICSID tribunal confirmed that the TPF arrangements do not effect the AoC.

Another case where TPF was pointed but did not raise any issue for any request was against Romania.[293] The respondent stated that claimants delayed the constitution of the tribunal and argued that by "not requesting the Secretary-General of ICSID to appoint a president until 5 May 2016 (apparently once they were able to arrange for the TPF of these proceedings)".[294] In the hearings, the position of Tenor Capital has been clarified. Tenor Capital has a seat on the Board of Gabriel Resources, so there is an affiliation at the Shareholder-Investor level in Gabriel and they're not a third-party funder, they're an investor and shareholder in the

[288] Cortec Mining Kenya Limited, Cortec (Pty) Limited and Stirling Capital Limited v. Republic of Kenya, ICSID Case No. ARB/15/29, Procedural Order No. 4, 18 September 2020, para. 2.

[289] Cortec Mining Kenya Limited, Cortec (Pty) Limited and Stirling Capital Limited v. Republic of Kenya, ICSID Case No. ARB/15/29, Procedural Order No. 1, 29 March 2016, para. 2.2.

[290] Churchill Mining PLC and Planet Mining Pty Ltd v. Republic of Indonesia, ICSID Case No. ARB/12/14 and 12/40.

[291] Churchill Mining PLC and Planet Mining Pty Ltd v. Republic of Indonesia, ICSID Case No. ARB/12/14 and 12/40, Procedural Order NO. 12, 27 October 2014, para. 22.

[292] Churchill Mining PLC and Planet Mining Pty Ltd v. Republic of Indonesia, ICSID Case No. ARB/12/14 and 12/40, Award, Date of dispatch to the Parties: 6 December 2016, para. 553.

[293] Gabriel Resources Ltd. and Gabriel Resources (Jersey) v. Romania, ICSID Case No. ARB/15/31.

[294] Gabriel Resources Ltd. and Gabriel Resources (Jersey) v. Romania, ICSID Case No. ARB/15/31, Respondent's Further Observations on Claimants' First Request for Provisional Measures, 31 August 2016, para. 10.

company with a seat on the Board.[295] Here, by definition, Tenor capital was not considered as a funder by the tribunal. Moreover, those TPF arrangements did not raise any objections and were not used as a ground in any challenge by the respondent except merely referring to them in its statements.

In another ICSID case against Chile, TPF was mentioned but not discussed.[296] In this case, in its memorial, the claimant referred to the IBA Rules regarding disclosure requirements and explanation of IBA Rule 7, which states that:

> The parties' duty of disclosure of any relationship, direct or indirect, between the arbitrator and the party (or another company of the same group of companies, or an individual having a controlling influence on the party in the arbitration) has been extended to relationships with persons or entities having a direct economic interest in the award to be rendered in the arbitration, such as an entity providing TPF for the arbitration, or having a duty to indemnify a party for the award.[297]

However, the tribunal did not discuss the IBA Rules in its decisions yet.

In conclusion, TPF has been discussed in a greater number of cases where the TPF arrangement has not been challenged and has not created any procedural or ethical issues over proceedings. This can be accepted as another argument for the fact that TPF arrangements are widely accepted, and they are not addressed unless there is a significant concern the tribunal or by a party.

3.14 Respondent State Is Funded and TPF Did Not Cause Any Issues

In nearly all cases we analyzed so far, the claimant is funded.[298] However, it is not always how it is. In some instances, the respondent states are funded. In all those cases where the state is funded, TPF has not caused any issues. So far, there are three instances where the respondent state was funded by a funder.

In one of the ISDS disputes, the "tribunal has addressed a situation involving a not-for-profit funder trying to set a precedent".[299] Professor Sahani observes the

---

[295] Gabriel Resources Ltd. and Gabriel Resources (Jersey) v. Romania, ICSID Case No. ARB/15/31, Hearing on the Merits, Day 2, December 3, 2019, p. 41.

[296] Victor Pey Casado and President Allende Foundation v. Republic of Chile, ICSID Case No. ARB/98/2, Memorial Concerning the Annulment of the Award of 13 September 2016, 27 April 2018, para. 226.

[297] IBA Rules, Guidelines on Conflicts of Interest in International Arbitration (2014), Explanation to General Standard 7: available at https://www.ibanet.org/Publications/publications_IBA_guides_and_free_materials.aspx.

[298] Except for the case RSM Production Corporation v Grenada, ICSID Case No ARB/05/14 (RSM v Grenada), where the Respondent State Grenada was funded.

[299] Sahani (2017). For the case, *see* Philip Morris Brands Sàrl, Philip Morris Products S.A. and Abal Hermanos S.A. v. Oriental Republic of Uruguay, ICSID Case No. ARB/10/7 (formerly FTR Holding SA, Philip Morris Products S.A. and Abal Hermanos S.A. v. Oriental Republic of

increasing trend towards funding without profit and suggests the term "not-for-profit" funders for such TPF without profit.[300] The most famous example, *Philip Morris v. Uruguay* case,[301] and second, Guatemala also secured funding in its counter-claim in ICSID.[302] The state adds that the funder has "no interest whatsoever in exploiting the mine, whatever the outcome of the dispute".[303] Also, as examined in the previous sections, in the RSM v. Grenada case, the respondent state was funded by Global Petroleum.[304] In the AoC, the tribunal did not consider the TPF arrangements. Again, respondent state's TPF arrangements did not raise any concerns.

It must be admitted that it is not as customary as claimant-funding; however, it shows that there are examples where a state can also be funded by a TPF company, with different motives together with the motive of profit. Funders might fund the respondent state for non-profit reasons as well as economic reasons against the claimant such as competing for the same investment project or secured the investment project claimant quitted or the funder's relationship with the respondent state.

3.15 Conclusion

All the cases in investment arbitration where the presence of TPF is known have been covered in this chapter. As analyzed, not all the cases have brought discussions of TPF before the tribunals for a cause for concern. Moreover, there is a significant chance that the number of cases has been understated for a variety of reasons. It is very likely that the TPF company's existence was not known to the tribunals. As a result, the public has no access to information with respect to the TPF company's identity, the relationship between the TPF company-funded party, or the extent of TPF company's control. Therefore, the real effect of TPF and the number of relevant cases in ISDS can easily be much larger than what has been explored in this chapter. Considering the importance of transparency in investment arbitration, this is not an ideal situation. In light of these inconsistencies, the new ICSID Compendium and the

Uruguay); and Quasar de Valors SICAV S.A. et al. (Formerly Renta 4 S.V.S.A et al.) v. Russian Federation, Ruling of the Stockholm District Court on Jurisdiction.

300 *Ibid.*

301 Philip Morris Brands Sàrl, Philip Morris Products S.A. and Abal Hermanos S.A. v. Oriental Republic of Uruguay, ICSID Case No. ARB/10/7.

302 Daniel W. Kappes and Kappes, Cassiday & Associates v. Republic of Guatemala (ICSID Case No. ARB/18/43); *see* Cosmo Sanderson, Guatemala launches counterclaim in mining dispute, Global Arbitration Review (GAR), 12 February 2021 available at https://globalarbitrationreview.com/guatemala-launches-counterclaim-in-mining-dispute?utm_source=Free+media+outlet+threatens+claim+against+Russia&utm_medium=email&utm_campaign=GAR+Alerts.

303 *Ibid (GAR).*

304 RSM Production Corporation v Grenada, ICSID Case No ARB/05/14 (RSM v Grenada), Award, Date of Dispatch to the Parties: December 10, 2010, para. 5.2.7.

proposed ICSID draft rules are a welcome clarification of the parties' duties in relation to disclosure.[305] When these rules come into effect, all third-party funded cases must be disclosed to the tribunals. In other words, we will be given a more accurate and comprehensive picture of the number of funded cases.

Access to such information is sorely needed given the apparent ubiquity of TPF in investment arbitration. Even though the TPF practice is still at the piloting stage, the case law on the subject already amounts to a great number of cases. Since the first reported funded case in 2007, the number of cases where TPF is discussed has grown tremendously. The trend seems to be continuing as TPF becomes better known to practitioners, accentuated by the fact that more jurisdictions are introducing regulations to make TPF legal and attract funders into their jurisdictions. Since bringing investment cases is expensive, securing TPF to sponsor a case brought by the claimant, in some circumstances, to defend the respondent, is often a major hurdle. So far, the case law has given funders and parties who are considering TPF arrangements important considerations. The most relevant aspects to consider from this case law are summarized in the following paragraphs.

In this chapter, the many problems in respect of TPF in ISDS have been categorized. The first conclusion is on jurisdiction and admissibility of cases. Jurisdiction and admissibility of cases cannot be violated merely because the parties are funded. TPF is an option for the parties, and whether such an option is exercised remains a strategic and financial choice. It is also salient to record that jurisdiction and admissibility of funded cases are discussed in earlier cases but markedly discussed less in recent cases. This shows that ISDS tribunals have largely accepted TPF as a valid financial arrangement and effectively ceased to regard it as contentions tribunals' jurisdiction or admissibility of funded cases.

As indicated in the case law, it is generally accepted that TPF cannot be the only reason for SfC orders. However, some individual arbitrators have differing opinions. Even if the arbitrator and the funder have been acquainted with each other and formed a relationship where, for example, the arbitrator was involved in a TPF academic task force and ventured to express an opinion on the funder, the relationship would not constitute grounds for disqualification of the arbitrator or the tribunal as long as it does not affect the arbitrator's independence and impartiality. If a SfC order is granted and the funded party does not pay the sum ordered by the tribunal, the arbitration proceedings will be discontinued. Moreover, if the TPF agreement does not specify whether the money will directly go to the funder's pocket, the tribunals will be reluctant to order lifting the stay of enforcement awards since it would be difficult to recover in case the award is annulled.

A very important topic discussed in many cases is the disclosure of TPF agreement and/or the TPF company. In most cases, disclosure is requested together with the SfC request. Disclosure of the TPF company, or at least TPF company's identity, is necessary for establishing a more transparent investment regime and for arbitrators

[305] ICSID Compendium of State and Public Comments on Proposed Amendment to the ICSID, Working Paper #4: Proposals for Amendment of the ICSID Rules.

to check whether they could be hindered by a CoI with the TPF company. However, ordering the terms of TPF agreements may be equally problematic since it could put the funded party into a difficult position strategically if the other party knows how much budget the funded party has.

Other important decisions made by investment arbitration tribunals are about the extent of TPF company's control on the cases and the description of TPF. Regarding the extent of TPF company's control, as long as the funded party stays as the real party, has control of the case, decides whether to continue with the claim, and withdraws the claim whenever the party wishes to withdraw, TPF arrangements do not raise any procedural concern for the tribunal. Moreover, in *Mohamed Abdel Raouf Bahgat v. Egypt* case, the Claimant was invited to update the Tribunal on whether the third-party funder has a charge or a lien on the proceeds of this claim and/or in any other way exercises control over the present arbitration. However, in that case, the Claimant declared that there was no TPF arrangement present and, consequently, there was no farther debate on TPF anymore. This shows that the level of control applied by the funder can be tested in further claims. The important consideration here is that the funded party must stay in control of all the important decisions as stated in this paragraph, and that the funder should avoid taking too much control. In litigation funding, these issues have been considered by courts extensively. The extent of control would be determined by the jurisdictions. In investment arbitration, there are no mandatory guidelines except that the conclusion must be accepted in different jurisdictions. In other words, the control should stay with the funded party. This issue has been added to the guidelines on best practices at the end of this book.

Another recurring topic is the decision on whether TPF costs are recoverable. One UNCITRAL tribunal was asked to grant such a request. The tribunal, in the end, did not decide on the recoverability of TPF costs based on legal analysis. Instead, it made a decision based on its discretion and rejected such costs. What is pertinent is that the question is open to interpretation. Unless there is a unanimous approach, different tribunals might reach different conclusions. Therefore, the reasoning of such requests and the number of TPF costs are important considerations for answering requests for TPF costs. In litigation funding, there are decisions in different jurisdictions on the recoverability of success fees of funders. However, investment arbitration leaves ample room for interpretation. There will probably be investment arbitration tribunals discussing whether TPF costs are recoverable, and those tribunals will decide on such requests in the forthcoming future.

In a great amount of ISDS disputes, the presence of a TPF company and a TPF agreement was known to the Tribunal and parties. However, they did not raise any issues. However, in at least one case, the TPF agreement was considered by the tribunal in rendering the award before the end of the year so that the funded party would not have to pay a substantial success fee to the funder under its TPF agreement. Also, at least in three investment arbitration cases, the Respondent State rather than the Claimant was funded and brought a counterclaim, which was funded by a funder. Evidently, there is a likelihood that states might be funded by funders as well. In terms of respondent states' TPF arrangements, unless it is a counterclaim funded by a funder, the purpose of TPF is generally different from the Claimant's funding. The purpose can be philanthropic reasons, which the funder does not fund with economic incentives.

The main conclusions drawn from the investment arbitration case law have been summarized above. It seems that TPF related issues and considerations over the TPF arrangements are not here to stay. More tribunals will examine similar discussions and reach their own decisions. Some of those issues have already reached unanimity such as the tribunal's jurisdiction and admissibility of cases when a case is funded. Even the most problematic issues such as SfC have reached a level of consistency if not consensus regarding when the TPF agreement can raise concerns and can be taken into account to order SfC. The prospect is that there will be increased coherence and consistency for each issue discussed in this chapter. Nevertheless, individual opinions might differ, and we can see assenting and dissenting opinions in the decisions as explained in the RSM v. Saint Lucia case as analyzed here. Lastly, as the proposed ICSID Compendium brings a mandatory disclosure regime, we can expect more decisions made by investment arbitration tribunals on these points.

References

Bogart CP (2014) RSM v. St. Lucia: why the majority got it wrong on security for costs, November 9, 2014. https://globalarbitrationreview.com/article/1033695/rsm-v-st-lucia-why-griffith-was-wrong-on-security-for-costs

De Brabandere E (2016) 'Mercantile adventurers'?: The disclosure of third-party funding in investment treaty arbitration. In: Litigation, costs, funding and behaviour: implications for the law. Taylor and Francis, pp 105–128

Honlet J (2015) Recent decisions on third-party funding in investment arbitration. ICSID Rev 30(3): 699–712

Khairul Islam MD (2024) The impacts of third-party funding on cost decisions in investment arbitration. Asia Pac Law Rev 32(1):259–278. https://doi.org/10.1080/10192557.2023.2232617

Marboe I (2013) Case Comment Quasar de Valores SICAV SA and others v The Russian Federation. ICSID Rev 28(2):247–253. https://doi.org/10.1093/icsidreview/sit016. Published Advance Access 12 July 2013

Sahani V (2017, March 1) Revealing not-for-profit third-party funders in investment arbitration. Investment Claims. https://oxia.ouplaw.com/page/565

Uchkunova I (2015) 'Security for Costs in ICSID Arbitration', Kluwer Arbitration Blog, February 10, 2015. http://arbitrationblog.kluwerarbitration.com/2015/02/10/securityfor-costs-in-icsid-arbitration/

Van Houtte H, McAsey B (2012) Case Comment Abaclat and Others v Argentine Republic ICSID, the BIT and Mass Claims. ICSID Rev 27(2):231–236. https://doi.org/10.1093/icsidreview/sis020

Weeramantry R, Ferrer M (2015) Case Comment, RSM Production Corporation v Saint Lucia: security for costs—a new frontier? ICSID Rev 30(1):30–34. https://doi.org/10.1093/icsidreview/siu034. Published Advance Access 5 Jan 2015

Chapter 4
Empirical Research in the TPF Market

4.1 Introduction

This chapter presents the results of an empirical study conducted by the author of this book as principal investigator in his own capacity as part of this book. The author has not received any funding for this empirical study apart from the financial support of the Chinese University of Hong Kong (CUHK) Graduate School Postgraduate Studentship Fund. The author thanks Professor Bryan Druzin and Professor Fernando Dias Simões, as well as Professor Julian Chaisse, for their constructive feedback. The author also thanks Professor Helena Ruiz Fabri and the community at the Max Planck Institute Luxembourg for Procedural Law for their feedback and opportunity to present his initial findings from this empirical study at a departmental meeting in December 2021. The author also thanks Professor Deborah Hensler from Stanford Law School, for her invaluable insights and support in his empirical research. Finally, the author thanks all the funders who agreed to be interviewed for the study.

The fourth chapter of this book presents findings from empirical research with third-party funders through interviews. This chapter provides notable and original empirical data on TPF, the development and application of which have not yet been thoroughly investigated. Using semi-structured interviews, the author formulated a comprehensive list of open-ended questions for the funders and presents an analysis based on the answers received. The interviews started with questions that gathered background information about the funders, followed by questions on contentious issues such as CoI, disclosure, decision-making in TPF, the ethics of funders, and the funders' views on the regulation of TPF.

The analysis sheds light on the relevance of such debates to the funders' practice, reaching beyond principles and guidelines to explore how they negotiate the issues that have faced them. The chapter is especially important for two reasons. The first reason is, as explained earlier, the lack of data on third-party funding is a fact and this empirical research fills this gap by collecting important first-hand data from funders.

C. Eken, *Third-Party Funding in Investment Arbitration*, Law for Professionals,
https://doi.org/10.1007/978-3-031-63620-2_4

The second reason is that the chapter carries significant importance in shaping the guidelines proposed in this book in Chap. 7. Only after interviewing funders, the author can propose guidelines that can be applicable to funders having considered the practice of funders and their concerns.

4.2 Descriptive Information

As part of this empirical study, 26 participants from 17 different TPF companies were interviewed.[1] Funders were based in various jurisdictions. Those interviews enabled the major funders to provide their opinions on the most controversial topics on TPF arrangements and to collect data from the market. Before interviews started, as part of CUHK's regulations, the author completed an ethical course on conducting interviews,[2] and the author followed the CUHK ethical guidelines for conducting interviews.[3] To comply with CUHK regulations, all consent forms were collected from every funder who participated in these interviews. The author has not submitted those forms to any individual or institution but kept them all in his possession.

As a general rule, the author has kept all participants' personal data and company names confidential unless a participant has given additional consent to disclose such information. If no such consent was given, the author only included the quotation without attributing it to that person in an anonymous way. The author recorded as many quotes as possible, to reflect funders' opinions in their own words. If a participant did not indicate that what they said was off the record, all information the participant gave the author during the interview is reflected in this chapter.

With the exception of one participant, all others are lawyers. Participants have different levels of experience in the TPF industry as shown in Table 4.1, ranging from less than 5 years to more than 10 years.[4] 9 of the participants are female and 17 are male. The author interviewed a wide variety of people in terms of their seniority and company size to reflect the market well. All participants are representatives of third-party funding companies since they share their experience in funding

[1]The author reached out to many major funders who funded investment arbitration and whose names are made public, as well as other big funders who are well known in the market. The author did not only contact funders who invest in cases for profit but also funders who invested for nonprofit purposes including George Soros's Open Initiative and the Bill & Melinda Gates Foundation. However, not all the people the author contacted accepted to participate in this empirical study.

[2]The Chinese University of Hong Kong, The Research Ethics Certificate on Publication Ethics, certificate no: P32203840.

[3]https://hss.cuhk.edu.cn/sites/hss.prod.dpsite03.cuhk.edu.cn/files/inlinefiles/1a_SBRE_Guidelines_V4_0.pdf.

[4]See Table 4.1.

cases in their companies. However, no company name is shared in this chapter as this information is confidential as well as the participants' names. All participants shared information regarding their TPF company unless their company keeps certain information confidential as indicated further in this chapter.

The author conducted his first interview on 19 July 2021 and his last interview on 14 January 2022. The author did follow up with some of the funders via email, if the author thought he needed to clarify some information funders provided, or if he needed additional information from funders. All the interviews were conducted via Zoom except one. Only one participant sent the answers to the questions via email. After presenting the quantitative information about these interviews, the chapter continues with the questions and answers of this empirical study.

4.3 Interviews and Questionnaire

The questionnaire was prepared by the author to ask funders about the most controversial and sensitive issues TPF agreements have raised in the investment arbitration regime. Furthermore, the questions serve the purpose of understanding the general structure of the TPF process and the considerations of funders. The author asked a total of 30 questions to each funder who participated in this study followed up by an open question if they wanted to add anything else before concluding the interviews. While interviewing participants, the author asked some follow up questions depending on the funders' answers. Then, the author made notes from funders' answers. Afterwards, the author organized his notes and reflected on the answers of funders in this chapter. The author later followed up with some funders if he thought that the topics were not clear or needed elaboration. In every case, the author did not disclose the names of the participants or their companies. The author also did not attribute any quotation to any participant or their company. All the opinions and expressions are anonymous, and all responsibility belongs to the author.

These questions are classified by the author as follows: The author started with some general questions and asked about the background information of each participant. Participants were asked about their education and work experience, their expertise, funder's budget and parameters, and also whether they have any knowledge about or experience in mainland China or Hong Kong markets. The second group of questions concerned the funders' input in cases they are funding. Crucial topics such as settlement, control of funders, funders' opinions, and disclosures are discussed. The third group of questions concern ethics. The question of whether funders weigh any ethical considerations when funding a case is explored. The fourth group of questions is about the reporting requirements of funders. The fifth group of questions is specific to the Investor-State Dispute Settlement (ISDS) market and explores important aspects of ISDS cases. After exploring the major topics stated above, the author also asked the last question about whether the funder wanted to add anything before concluding the interviews. This chapter is structured in a way that aligns with the questions.[5]

4.4 Basics: General Information

4.4.1 Who Participated in the Interviews (Background Information)

As Table 4.1 shows in the demographic information, the majority of the participants are male. While the author tried to include more female funders, the author

Table 4.1 Descriptive information about the interviewees (N = 23)

N	Position	Sex	Experience in TPF
1	Global Head	F	More than 10 years
2	Investment Manager	M	5–10 years
3	Regional Director	M	5–10 years
4	Partner	M	More than 10 years
5	Investment Manager	F	5–10 years
6	Director	M	More than 10 years
7	Managing Director	F	Less than 5 years
8	Investment Manager	M	Less than 5 years
9	Director	M	More than 10 years
10	Regional Director	M	5–10 years
11	Case Manager	M	Less than 5 years
12	Head of a Region	M	Less than 5 years
13	Chief Investment Officer	M	More than 10 years
14	Managing Director	M	5–10 years
15	Chief Executive Officer	M	More than 10 years
16	Director	M	5–10 years
17	Director	M	5–10 years
18	Chief Executive Officer	M	5–10 years
19	Managing Partner	M	5–10 years
20	Senior Legal Counsel	F	Less than 5 years
21	Director	F	5–10 years
22	Former Head of Corporate Affairs	F	5–10 years
23	Head of Litigation & Arbitration	F	More than 10 years
24	Legal Counsel	F	Less than 5 years
25	Legal Counsel	F	More than 10 years
26	Investment Manager	M	Less than 5 years

[5] The full list of questions is found at the end of this chapter.

Table 4.2 Previous occupation of funders

Previous occupation of funders	Number of funders
Lawyer in a Law Firm	15
Working for Another Funder	4
Barrister	1
Finance Manager	1
Working for an Arbitration Institution	2
Working as an In-House Counsel	2
Businessman	1

acknowledges the fact that men dominate the TPF industry. This is not surprising considering that the same gender equality problem exists in the legal world and international arbitration as well. As Table 4.1 also shows, the participants are working in various roles, from case managers to chief executive officers, with different numbers of years of experience in the sector. Most of them had experience in law firms before they joined the TPF industry.

As Table 4.2 shows, most participants was working in a law firm before joining the TPF industry. The second largest group of participants started in the TPF industry, and they were working for another funder prior to their current role as a funder. All except for two participants interviewed were working in a TPF company at the time the interviews were conducted. Two of the interviewees are former employees of a funder and they gave their opinion according to the knowledge they had when they left the industry about a year before the interviews were conducted. There were also other previous roles as Table 4.2 shows, however, the common factor is that most of the participants were former lawyers and their expertise led to their current position as funders.

We can see a trend in the funders regarding their specialties. Funders might specialize in commercial or investment arbitration, a specific sector such as energy, oil, and gas, etc. or they might specialize in specific jurisdictions geographically. The author tried to speak with people whose specialty is investment arbitration. Some answers from interviewees' specialties include "investment treaty arbitration"; "International commercial arbitration and ISDS, enforcement of arbitral awards"; "all type of cases except divorce and personal injury"; "Commercial disputes in litigation and arbitration"; "everything, all commercial litigation and arbitration and investment arbitration"; "Complex international arbitration and litigation"; "International Arbitration, both commercial and investment arbitration".

The author also asked, geographically, whether funders had any activities in or knowledge about the TPF market in Hong Kong and mainland China. This question is not the primary consideration of this book. Therefore, the results are only briefly summarized here. Most of the funders do not have activities in Hong Kong or mainland China, but they regard TPF legislation in Hong Kong as a positive development. Some funders stated that they reviewed some cases in Hong Kong but rejected them. A few funders said that they are active in the Hong Kong market, but less so in mainland China. One funder interviewed is from mainland China and has a growing number of cases there. We can conclude that Hong Kong legislation is

Table 4.3 Investment size of funders

Budget of funders	Numbers of funders
Less than–15M USD	1
15M USD–100M USD	3
More than 100M USD	9
Confidential	4

still very new, but over time the Hong Kong TPF market is going to develop. Funders have already started setting up special teams or offices for the Asia and Pacific regions, to identify the opportunities, and build relations with Hong Kong. This trend is likely only to grow.[6]

These first three questions were meant as the introduction of the funders, to understand their backgrounds and profiles and their specific knowledge about and experience in mainland China and Hong Kong TPF markets. It was common for funders to work for a law firm for several years before moving towards their career in TPF companies. However, some started their careers as third-party funders or worked only a few years before joining third-party funders. As the industry grows, it is probable that TPF companies will recruit lawyers at every stage of their careers, junior lawyers, mid-level lawyers, as well as experienced lawyers.

4.4.2 Budget and Anticipated Return of Funders

After the basic information about the participants, in order to have an idea about the size of the investment, the author asked the funders some fundamental questions regarding their budget and financial parameters.

As Table 4.3 shows, some funders did not share their budget and stated it was confidential information. However, most of the funders shared this information, and it is not surprising that most have a considerable amount to invest. Since investment arbitration requires a significant amount of investment, and the funder will probably have more than one investment, he or she should realistically have a minimum of 20 million USD. Funders interviewed who regularly invest had more than 100 million USD in their portfolios. Generally, funders have a combination of several pools of funds.

Table 4.4 shows whether funders follow the 1/10 ratio in their investment. The 1/10 is a ratio between the funders' investment and the realistic claims for the value of their investment. The author asked funders whether they were willing to provide more money than 1/10 of the realistic claim value, or whether they followed the 1/10 ratio rule. Most of the funders follow this ratio in ISDS cases. One funder stated that they are not following this ratio. Seven others stated that it depends. Funders generally confirmed the 1/10 ratio as a market standard but also added that it is not

[6] Eken (2022).

Table 4.4 Funders' parameters for investment

Whether funders follow 1/10 ratio	Number of funders
Yes	9
No	1
Yes and no/it depends	7

Table 4.5 Anticipated return of funders (average)

3 times the investment	2
2 times the investment	1
30% of the awarded amount	3
20% of the awarded amount	1
No, depends on the case	10

Table 4.6 Maximum rate funders charge

Is there a maximum cap you charge?	Number of funders
Yes. No more than 50% of the awarded amount	5
No cap in our company policy	12

always strictly followed. One funder stated, "In different areas, 1/10 ratio changes, - for example, in insolvency cases, we can go with 1/7 instead of 1/10". Thus, our study confirms the Queen Mary Study which stated that the 1/10 ratio operates as the market standard.[7] However, it is not unanimously followed in the market. Funders are flexible and some can have different ratios such as 1/8 or 1/7, and this might also depend on the sector or type of case funded. The 1/10 ratio nevertheless presents a model in the market. A funder stated: "the rule is the same for every funder I guess, 1/10 with a budget and amounted dispute, if the budget is more than 10% in dispute, it becomes difficult to arrange it". Funders also highlighted the challenge and difficulty if the client goes over the agreed amount of TPF.

Funders stated that the reason why the 1/10 ratio is important is that if the committed capital by the funder is more than 1/10 of the realistic value, it is difficult to arrange a fair distribution of the awarded amount between funders and funded parties. Funders prefer that the funded party is paid more than 50% of the awarded amount; if, however, they invest more than 1/10 of the awarded amount, it is difficult to arrange this distribution considering all the stakeholders who, at a minimum, include the funded party, its lawyers, and funders. A funder stated "Criteria is standard, we would like to have a realistic case, value, facts, and follow the 1/10 ratio. There are some circumstances where we can be more flexible, but it depends on other factors (e.g., client co-funding)".

Table 4.5 shows whether funders have an average anticipated return on their investments and Table 4.6 shows whether funders have a maximum anticipated return on their investments. Many funders stated that there is no average or

[7] ICCA report at footnote 18, p. 25.

maximum anticipated return on their investments, and it depends on the specifics of each case. However, some funders stated different average numbers in their practice, 20% or 30%, or twice or three times the amount of their investments. The average number varies amongst the funders. This average number all depends on different factors such as the expertise of funders, difficulty and timeframe of the case, and so on. One funder stated, "We typically target 20% internal rate of return, we are routinely operated around that". Funders have similar return goals but sometimes the range a funder gave might change. Some funders who gave "it depends" answers, stated a range "somewhere between 15–35% or 1.5–3.5 of what we invested". Other funders gave a bigger range from as low as 10–15% of damages, to 30–40% of damages. A few funders said, "it could be as little as two times or 5, 6, or 7 times, it depends on risk, duration, and effect".

Regarding the maximum anticipated return rate, one funder stated that "There is no express cap, but we look at the economics of each case and make sure we think each party involved will take away a sufficient return on success to warrant proceeding. Often that means in practice our return will be less than 50%". Other funders also echoed this idea that they seek to establish more than 50% of the returns for the funded party; however, there is no strict investment mandate. Another funder also supported this notion by saying "No maximum return, as a rule of thumb, we try to make sure the client will get around 50% of the ultimate recovery. We try to make sure the client will get a meaningful return. It is not a hard cap per se but that is the principle." Some funders, however, said that they have a company policy of not taking more than 50% of the awarded amount. This company policy protects funded parties for sure. However, the difficulty in ensuring this, even though desired, is accepted by other funders: "When we invest in a matter, our financial models are indeed based on the assumption that funded claimants will be walking away with at least 50% of the case proceeds (unless they are okay with receiving <50%). Of course, no one really knows how things will play out in a dispute and there may be some further negotiations between funder and funded party, especially when offers to settle are extended or received". There must be certain rules providing this protection to the funded party.[8]

Funders do set different minimum return targets. In a follow-up question, a funder revealed the funder's minimum return goals. The funder stated "Currently, the minimum target return on a single-case basis is a money multiple of 3.3 of the investment (i.e., for every $100 invested, we expect $330 back which includes the 100$ invested). This is not to say that we cap our return at a 3.3 because you always have to take into account losses in our entire case portfolio – currently at 34% - and time to the resolution which may be longer than usual -e.g., >36 months – in some cases." The author asked the same question to another funder. The funder replied, "In our business, we targeted a net return to fund investors after losses and costs of two times of the investment or 25–30% internal rate of return". The more the market

[8] See the best practice guideline in Chap. 7.

and the number of funders grow, the more competitive offers funders will be able to give to the market.

4.4.3 The Calculation of Funder's Fees

Other than the 1/10 ratio, there are other parameters funders consider when calculating their fees. Funders have a similar and somewhat distinct approach to calculating their fees. The most obvious criteria for the funder's fee is the duration of the case. The longer the case takes the higher the funder's fees are. However, some funders have a set amount of fees, and this fixed fee does not change depending on time or other factors. Therefore, every funder's TPF agreement can include its own distinctive features.

One funder stated that "Other than quantum, 2 more parameters: (i) strength of the merits (merits under applicable contract or treaty, merits and jurisdictions); and (ii) recoverability of the claim, you may be able to get a quantum award, if the defendant is the one that does not have assets anymore or it is likely that assets will dissipate in the future, or assets are in jurisdictions which may not be enforcement friendly or litigation can take longer, this is also what we consider." Another funder added to this list the budget of the case. Depending on the range of money that needs to be committed to the case, funders' fees can change. Funders calculate their fees usually as a percentage or multiple of the money they invested, depending on the case. Funders boost their "flexibility" in calculating their fees. One funder stated "we offer outstanding prices, whether we take the case on a percentage or multiple bases, or a combination of both depends on the case. We can also offer different corporate structures (e.g., invest in the company itself - we always get local advice to make sure we are complying with the local regulations)".

One funder summarized its calculation as "we calculate our fees as a multiplier of what we invest, or multiple of our investment, whichever is higher, based on duration, our fees increase". Funders have different investment pools. One funder explained "we have a number of pools - co-investor, external investors on the other hand; effectively we are asset manager[s], we manage other investors' money. It is a pool of money, investors put money into those pools, we fund the cases, we do due diligence, we present to our investment committee and our investors make a decision whether to include it into a particular pool or we go to the next pool, if we think the case is good, we can generally get approval from the investor committee one way or another. We have four pools of investors in total, we announced pool three, another one is coming up soon, it is an ongoing exercise, fundraising never stops". Therefore, funders have a responsibility to their investors and that is why they need to calculate their fees in the highest amount so that they can perform their duties to their investors.

In summary, there are two main ways to calculate funders' fees: the funder either (i) takes a percentage of the awarded amount, or (ii) takes a multiple of what they invested in. Which method a funder chooses depends on their preference, and sometimes funders might use a combination of these two methods. Generally, funders invest in big claims where the real value is a minimum of 10M USD. However, even though this is a good indicator of the market, again it is not a strict rule, and some funders might be much more flexible.

4.4.4 Due Diligence

Unsurprisingly, funders perform due diligence before they consent to fund a dispute. Funders expressed that their due diligence process does not have a set time frame, it can take from as little as one month to as long as six months or even longer. It depends on how well the funded party is prepared. If the funded party prepares all the necessary documents in order, without a missing file, then the process can speed up. However, any missing document, expert report, legal issues, estimated budget, or step prolongs this due diligence period. Due diligence is very important for funders. Some funders use external counsels to conduct due diligence. They choose different counsels according to their expertise. Thus, they stated that they do not have regular counsels and they appoint an external counsel according to the specifics of a case. They choose a lawyer who is an expert in such cases.

One funder stated "We evaluate basically first the success rate of the cases. Normally, we cannot say a certain rate, or the likelihood of success in that case. Second, we assess the time of duration, whether it can be settled or resolved with one instance, or within many stages etc. The third part is the amount of money we will be committing. We decide on these three criteria to decide for us." Process can be seen, the funders have multiple criteria and stages during the due diligence. One funder stated that it follows these stages: "there are many layers of assessment, we do a preliminary assessment, claimant's lawyer writing a legal memo for us, external counsel, due diligence, conduct due diligence, we don't have internal capacity, there is an investment committee, lawyer, finance people, tearing it apart, finding weaknesses, etc., it is a challenging process". Therefore, due diligence is not a simple process, and it has many layers as funders expressed.

Funders said that the length of due diligence is subject to the difficulty of the case. One funder stated:

> it depends on the volume and complexity of the case. A construction dispute is highly advanced, then due diligence can take long. However, a mere breach of contract case, then due diligence is relatively simple and direct. We cannot tell how long it will take. What I can tell you is during the preliminary level, in two weeks, we will be able to tell the applicant how long the due diligence will take place approximately.

Therefore, even funders cannot state how long due diligence will take. After a preliminary assessment, they might give an approximate timeline. During this preliminary assessment, if the funder finds something too risky or any red flags, it can reject the case without doing any due diligence.

Another funder stated that it follows the following criteria "four areas we focus on are, (i) merits of the claim, (ii) what budget is, (iii) what real value is and (iv) enforcement; we look at these preliminarily and then we agree on terms if we like the case, then we do due diligence after we agree on terms, opinion by lawyers on merits, in some cases we might need some preliminary expert work, budget from lawyers, enforcement prospects, an inhouse intelligence team to take a look to sweep whether it is enforceable if we win, once all criteria are satisfied, then our investment committee (generally they meet ad hoc) decides to fund the case". One funder stated that they also do the due diligence of the law firm retained by the funded party. The funder said that they want to make sure that competent lawyers will be handling the case.

What funders check during due diligence includes every aspect of the case. Therefore, funders operate very closely with the funded party. One funder explained that "During the due diligence process, we work very closely with the claimant. Then we negotiate the agreement with the funded party and once we sign the TPF agreement, we take a back seat and we do not interfere". Another funder elaborated on what they check during due diligence by stating "We assess case merits, strengths and weaknesses, budget and whether the budget is reasonable, legal theories around quantum and damages, prospects of success. We require a minimum 65% chance of success to fund the case". All these quotes show the extent and depth of the due diligence process funders undertake. Funders' considerations, how to accept or decline cases, success rates to accept a case, and other factors for due diligence are elaborated on in this section.

4.4.5 Funders' Input to the Case

The author asked questions to understand the input of funders in the funded cases. TPF creates a long-term relationship between the funded party and funder, and how much input funders have during this process is the main research question the author addressed. What impact funders have on settlement proceedings, how much control funders have, how important the possibility of security for costs (SfC) and adverse costs orders is, CoI for funders, and funders' opinion on regulation and disclosure are explored in this section.

4.4.5.1 Impact on Settlements

Funders' answers show that they have no or little impact on settlement discussions. The TPF agreement has rules determining the role of funders in the settlement discussions. All funders stated that the last say in settlement discussions does not lie with them. Also, all of them said that they have zero input in the settlement.

Regarding how much input funders have, one stated "good question, we get this question quite often. I think every funder wants to have a certain amount of influence, but cases are run by the lawyers. We manage the case, we see what is going on with the case, but we never have the same amount of control of the case as the lawyers. We always rely on the suggestion of the lawyers about how to proceed with the case. If a claimant's lawyer tells us to take it or not (if it is good or not) we go with the lawyer's suggestion. If a lawyer says it is a low amount for the settlement, we agree to move on. Certain funders do that to jump in settlement discussions, the funder will be able to say, e.g., claimant wants to take the settlement offer, but the funder wants to continue with the case". This shows that even though the funders interviewed do not have an express last say in settlement decisions, there are some who openly have the last say in settlement discussions. Therefore, it is important to have a rule in the investment arbitration regime preventing funders from jumping into settlement decisions.

Funders' input in settlement decisions is generally mere support. A second consultation is available if the funded party asks for it. Otherwise, funders do not automatically attend settlement meetings or decide on them. One funder who said that they do not get involved with settlement in any way said, "they put 100% trust in the client on that, they can go to a settlement without telling anything to us and decide to settle or decline the offer without even informing us". Another funder stated that "[We have] almost no input in settlement decisions actually; obviously, people want to hear what we have to say." Many other funders also confirmed that they don't subrogate the settlement process; parties decide how and when to settle. Another funder stated, "we can discuss the settlement offers but we have no power to affect any decision". Another funder stated, "The funder may, if the client requests, support the lawyer and the client in devising the negotiation strategy, the terms of the settlement, the funder can share intelligence, case-related intelligence, that might impact settlement, so that is the typical scope of the funder's added value into the negotiation." Those interviewed stressed that the funded party stays in control. One funder stated, "we are not in control of any of the cases we fund, the claimant remains in control".

Two funders stated that they might take more steps. One stated, "I would say that we prefer settlements given the risks unless, of course, a settlement does not make sense commercially which is why we want to ensure that we deal with commercially reasonable claimants. If the funded party wants to accept an unreasonable settlement offer, then the funder might have a say according to what is a reasonable or unreasonable offer that needs to be clarified? Otherwise, this might create confusion." The second funder stated that "as the case progresses and we deploy more capital we would have more conversation, certain entitlement, we would build that into terms entitlement settlement agreed". This also shows that the funder might want to increase the control when a case takes longer than expected. Also, some funders stated that if a realistic settlement offer is made, the client has to consider it, they do not have to accept it, but funders want the claimant to have a say about the offer. Moreover, one funder stated that "All our claims are monetary; we have a base monetary amount as a requirement for settlement. And then, above this base amount, the client is free to settle." Thus, these show that the funders should follow

Table 4.7 Funders' settlement preference

Whether funders prefer settlement	Number of funders
Yes	9
No, no involvement with settlement	3
Does not matter	14

guidelines, otherwise their degree of involvement can differ, which will not always present the best practice in the market and might potentially limit the rights of claimants.

One funder also stressed the impact of settlement for the calculation of its fees. The funder stated, "whether the case settles, how long the case takes (e.g., 6 months, 12 months step up every time it goes up), how much the funded party is awarded, how much money is invested, all factors really". Therefore, the terms of such TPF agreements can encourage funded parties to settle since the case will end more quickly, and the funders' fees will be lower. Another funder stated, "various scenarios, cost of funding, on multiple amounts we invested and there is a discount if there is a settlement". Therefore, a TPF agreement can be a tool to encourage settlement for funded parties.

Table 4.7 shows whether funders prefer settlement. More than half of funders stated that they have no preference whether the case settles or not. Nearly half of the participants stated that they prefer settlement so that they can get their return early. Among those funders who prefer settlement, some said that they have terms in their TPF agreements encouraging settlement. According to the timeline of the case, funders might offer discounts on their fees if the party settles. The author finds that funders either prefer settlement since it means that they will be remunerated early, or mostly, they are indifferent to settlement. One funder stated that "We are financially indifferent as to whether a case goes to trial or settles. But yes, settlement is usually a good thing". However, not all have such terms. Some stated that they prefer settlement, but they do not actively get involved in or encourage settlement, it is completely the funded party's decision.

It is interesting to see the opinions of funders regarding settlement. One funder stated "No preference, we look at the case to see what the potential is for the settlement. When we get to the hearing, there is an even 70% chance of success, for those cases going to trial, we have a 50-50 chance always at trial." Therefore, funders generally indicate no preference, but it depends on each case. Some funders have different protocols to decide on a settlement. According to a funder "We would only back cases we will win. The trial is a riskier process if the preference is of course towards settlement. If a settlement offer is unreasonably rejected, then we can have some contractual terms to force the funded party. We usually engage an expert determination clause - an independent Queen's Counsel (QC) would decide whether we should settle. If it is a good offer or not, then this decision by the QC will be binding." Thus, according to this funder, they cannot force the decision to settle, but they can bring the attention of an independent QC to decide on the settlement offer.

Table 4.8 shows whether funders attend settlement meetings. None of the funders stated that they attend meetings, in fact they mostly do not. However, if the client

Table 4.8 Funders' attendance in settlement meetings

Whether funders' attend settlement meetings	Number of funders
Yes	0
No	11
It depends; if the client prefers, yes	15

prefers them to attend, then they attend meetings. Their default position is, however, "no, we do not attend". One funder stated that "It depends on the agreement with the client. So, in some cases I attend. In most cases, the settlement negotiations are handled by lawyers". Many other funders confirmed this position and stated, "Only if asked and not very often." Another funder who said no, stated "No, we don't. We are being informed about the settlement meetings and about the outcome. Sometimes, we are ready to discuss, but we are not attending." Thus, the funders might want to hear the results of settlement meetings, but they do not have to attend, and they even prefer not to attend. This shows that none of the funders interviewed has a policy requiring them to attend settlement meetings, generally, but it depends on what the client wants.

The author also asked funders whether they put any pressure on funded parties to settle. All funders said that they do not put any pressure on the funded parties. One funder stated "No pressure. Sometimes attend the meeting, it is the party's call." Another funder stated, "No, settlement is ultimately the client's decision. The point is, if the interest of the funder is perfectly aligned, then there should not be a case of any party putting any pressure on the other". However, further research on this issue is needed. The way the agreement is structured is important to determine whether the funders are actually putting any pressure on the funded party or not. It might be difficult to research funders' agreements since not many funders want to share them and they prefer to keep it confidential. However, some further explanations from funders as quoted below, show that there is no reason for funders to force the party unless the party is acting unreasonably for some personal reasons.

One funder stated that "It is difficult for us, what to put. It would be unwise to put any pressure on the claimant to settle, because the lawyer better knows whether to proceed with the case or not. We don't want to disturb the balance in this partnership. We want to have a good relationship with the claimant. It is really bad for the relationship if you have a 1 billion USD case, and 950 million USD is offered in settlement; the claimant wants to go and get the remaining 50 million USD if that is very close to 100%. We would ask why you want the full amount to explain, with the additional half year we can get it then, why not, the lawyer's advice is important for us." Another funder said, "our opinion carries weight, we will back a claimant who is rational, not claimants who would have a day in court for personal reasons". The funder further continued that "there is less control in ISDS – supranational space – where no rules necessarily bind other than professional conduct". Thus, funders operating in ISDS do not have any regulations and according to these answers will only disagree with the funded party if the claimants act very unreasonably.

Table 4.9 Control of funders

Funders that control the case	Number of funders
Yes	1
No, we use a hands-off approach	19
It depends on the case	6

Nevertheless, since the definition of what is unreasonable can differ from funder to funder, this should be clarified with a guideline.[9] This book offers the best practice guidelines for funders operating in the investment arbitration regime after all these considerations.

4.4.5.2 Control of the Case

The author also asked funders whether they apply control and if they do, how much control they have during the life of a case in which they are invested (Table 4.9). Funders mostly said that they do not apply any control in the cases they funded. Many funders use a hands-off approach with the cases they invested in. However, some funders stated that in some situations, they can have a degree of control in the case they invested in. Again, there is no globally uniform practice that every funder follows. It all depends on jurisdictions and domestic regulations. And again, since investment arbitration is not subject to any domestic regulation, it is supranational, and a network of treaties contains the rules, there is no specific rule for funders operating in this system. Thus, funders are not subject to any regulations in the investment arbitration business. A guideline is required for funders to operate without distorting the investment arbitration. Therefore, this book proposes a best practice guideline for funders to operate in the best standard in the investment arbitration regime.

Funders operating in very different jurisdictions all stated that they do not apply control to the funded party. However, they all pointed out that some funders in the market do apply control. They said that control of the case stays with the funded party and their lawyers together, they decide on every strategic matter and the funder does not get involved with such decisions. However, funders' opinions might be sought by the funded party and then funders are happy to provide them. A funder stated "We have no direct input. We are often asked our opinion for strategic decisions, then we provide our opinion, but it is not binding." Another funder echoed this "The funder does not control the case. If the client requests, the funder may provide support with case management, settlement or case strategy research and intelligence, etc." Nevertheless, some funders have a say in critical decisions. A funder stated that "the day-to-day management is left to the client and law firm. We are only involved in major decisions; whether to appeal, whether to settle. We have a say in these critical decisions". Again, more research on the extent of funders'

[9] For the the best practice guideline for funders operating in investment arbitration, see Chap. 7.

control is necessary. The TPF agreements must be examined in order to see the extent of funders' control. One funder gave some insights about their TPF arrangements: "We don't control the case, it is very clear in our TPF arrangement, a lawyer owes a duty to the applicant, all instructions from the applicant go to the lawyer". More funders provided insights regarding how their TPF arrangements prevent them from applying control. A funder stated, "We are not controlling, it is clearly contractually also written, only the claimant instructs the lawyers, the main part of the job we do before the signature on the TPF agreement is determine what is the strategy for the lawyers, what is the position of TPF". Other funders interviewed confirmed this position and this empirical study concludes that this is a dominant position, but not unanimous.

Based on the information provided by the funders, this empirical study concludes that the control of funders is not compelling, but rather collaborating is what is important. One funder explained "I can't quantify the control, there is no control. When we do the due diligence of a case, we do not only do the due diligence of the case itself but of the legal team, too. We need to know we can work with the legal team. It is not a question of pressuring or controlling but collaborating". This shows the importance of a collaborative approach. However, there might be some occasions when the funder-funded party relationship can stop being collaborative. This happens especially when the case takes longer than anticipated and the funder's budget is exhausted. Then, the funder's decision about whether to continue funding the case or not will be forced on the funded party.

Another important consideration about funders' control is time. Funders stated that they have a close relationship with the funded party and its lawyers until they decide to fund the case. However, once they decide to fund it, they stop getting involved with the case. A funder explained "We do something called monitoring, after deployment of the funds and executing the TPF agreement. We want to follow up on the case. However, we do not control the case". Another funder stated "None whatsoever. We are a European funder, and the law prohibits us third parties from exercising pressure or control of the case, management of the case; we would be acting illegally if we did that".

In summary, funders generally have a hands-off approach. However, to ensure the consistency of this hands-off approach, there must be a rule for funders operating in the investment arbitration business. Thus, this is added as a rule to the guidelines for funders proposed in Chap. 7.[10]

4.4.6 Security for Costs (SfC) and Adverse Costs

The author also investigated the impact of possible SfC and adverse cost orders on funders. Most funders do not see SfC as a constraint. They see it as a factor in the

[10]The guideline is attached in Chap. 7.

Table 4.10 Risk of adverse costs for funders

Whether this risk is a major or minor constraint	Numbers of funders
Major one	3
Minor one	3
It depends	8
It is not a constraint	12

Table 4.11 How do funders deal with adverse costs?

How do funders deal with adverse costs?	Number of funders
Insurance	9
Increase in returns	1
Depends on what the client wants (Negotiation)	7

calculation of their fees. One funder explained, "Not a constraint, but it is an added cost, and affects the costs a lot. Then, TPF costs more for the claimant." The funders further said that SfC does not pose any constraint on them because if they decide to fund a case, this means that they believe in the case and they would be ready to cover any such costs, buy insurance, or make other necessary arrangements. Funders also said that when there is a SfC order or adverse costs risk, they need to cover it, since the money committed to the case will increase, they increase their fees return.

Tables 4.10 and 4.11 show the risk of adverse costs and how funders deal with adverse cost risks. 9 funders voiced that they buy insurance for their clients, mostly After-the-Event (ATE) insurance. 12 funders said they do not see adverse costs as a constraint. Some funders said that they have internal insurance they offer to cover adverse cost risks, but the applicants do not have to buy their internal insurance. The advantage of internal insurers that some funders offer is that the funded parties can be sure that they will be insured. If they go to the insurance market, some insurers might not underwrite the insurance. However, since this is good for the client, they almost always decide to purchase funders' insurance if funders offer it. Even if funders do not have internal insurance, they might have insurance companies they have a relationship with and they can advise the applicants to get insurance from those companies. Some other funders do not have internal insurance and they direct applicants to the insurance market. A funder stated "Insurance, they get it from the market. We don't ourselves provide insurance to claim holders." Some funders interviewed explicitly said that they help or assist the clients in getting insurance.

A few funders stated that it is a minor constraint in their general practice, but specifically added that it is not minor in ISDS. The funder stated "Minor for us; for a lot of jurisdictions, adverse costs do not come into play, and a lot of clients bear the risk. With ISDS, it depends. The big difference, is there are a lot more impecunious claimants, because of claimed action, it is less likely the claimant will be able to bear the adverse costs risk." Therefore, even funders who said it is a minor risk, do not think it is minor in investment arbitration. Some other funders stated that it is a major concern. One said "yes, it is, of course, we know worst cost orders could be issued.

We need to take this into consideration. We need to have the budget. An additional hurdle between the budget and the amount in dispute is not a healthy one if the case is so expensive that ATE can be a deal breaker". However, whatever way funders view adverse costs risks, minor or major, they take them into consideration and negotiate with the applicants.

As said above, the majority does not see adverse cost risks as a constraint. A funder said, "it is not a constraint, it is a factor that goes into the calculation, the amount of risk and potential return". Another funder repeated that adverse costs are one of the parameters by saying "It is a parameter for assessing the investment, it is, of course, one of the parameters that needs to be looked at, depending on the jurisdiction. In court litigation, it is not a constraint, in complex arbitrations, definitely, in investment arbitration, cost award can be significant." Another funder stated that it is getting more important by saying "it is a big issue, it is increasingly being sought and increasingly awarded. Insurance is very costly also". Another fact is that ATE insurance is expensive. The premiums are not cheap and can vary between 20 and 40% of the risk according to funders interviewed. From my interviews, this study can conclude that insurance, especially ATE insurance and TPF are definitely very close, and sometimes ATE insurance is included in the TPF agreements. When the funder pays for the insurance, TPF becomes more expensive, naturally.

With adverse costs issues, funders are flexible. If the client wants to pay SfC orders or take the risk of any potential adverse cost orders, the funder lets the client do it. In the opposite case, the client wants the funder to deal with such risks, then the funders add it to the TPF agreement. Also, if the applicant asks for help, funders are happy to help in any way they can. A funder states "we know insurers that provide ATE insurance, not many in the market at all". A funder also stated that sophisticated applicants generally do not need help in reaching out to insurers. One funder answers the question by saying "It depends on what the client wants to do, how to deal with it". Another funder also brings up the effect of regulations in the jurisdiction in which they operate. The funder said, "If there were a regulation or rule that required us to have such insurance, then we would. However, in the market where we operate, we are not subject to any regulation to obtain such insurance when we fund a case". In investment arbitration, surely, there is no such regulation forcing funders to obtain ATE insurance. The arbitration tribunal might order SfC in investment arbitration, which has raised many concerns and discussions in recent years.[11] Again, the impact of the regulations where the funder operates might restrict the funder from giving insurance advice, as well. A funder said that they do not advise getting insurance because they do not offer advice for any regulated services. The funder continued "If the client wants the insurance, they can do so or they can find an insurance policy and tell us, we can cover the costs and include this in our agreement".

[11] See Chap. 3, explanations under 3.3 for SfC applications due to TPF arrangements in investment arbitration cases.

In conclusion, adverse cost risks depend on the jurisdiction and funders think differently about whether they are a major, minor, or a non-constraint. However, the majority thinks it is not a constraint and sees it as a factor in the calculation of funders' fees. In investment arbitration specifically, none of the funders said that it is a minor constraint. For investment arbitration, SfC orders and adverse costs risk is either a major constraint for funders, or they do not see it as a constraint but as a factor they take into consideration in the calculation of their fees. To deal with this risk, insurance, especially ATE, is used both by funders and funded parties. Funders might also have internal insurance, or they can provide it from the insurance market.

4.4.7 Conflict of Interest (CoI)

CoI takes a large space in academic papers and discussions. However, interviews showed that funders take CoI issues very seriously, so it leaves very little space for this issue to be a problem in practice. Funders expressed their unwillingness to fund a case where the award might be set aside due to a CoI problem. Therefore, they reduce any small chance of CoI at the beginning of the case. If there is a slight chance of CoI, funders do not fund the claim.

Some likely CoI matters funders might face are analyzed here. One funder stated two potential conflicts: "The most obvious, when we do claimant and respondent side funding, the potential conflict is when we are asked by both sides of the case which we do not do. Beyond that, the issue only arises if we come into possession of confidential information in one case that is relevant to another case. We have a conflict guideline we follow. Conflict of the funder-arbitrator is not a real conflict in my view. Why would a funder choose an arbitrator they have conflicts with? This would hurt the investment". Therefore, there are two potential conflicts: (i) if the same funder is asked for funding by both claimant and respondent of the same case, and (ii) when a funder has confidential information from another case which might be useful. The most controversial academic discussions on CoI concern those between arbitrators and funders, which is not seen as a big problem by many funders. Funders do not appoint any arbitrator with whom they have previous relationships that could raise any CoI issues.

Potential CoI issues might come to light between the funder and other parties. These other parties might include arbitrators, experts, parties of the dispute, their lawyers, and any other involved party. One funder elaborated on those two potential CoI issues by stating:

> Maybe 2 to mention: (i) CoI with the parties involved in a dispute, including tribunal members; (ii) you could also consider some funders take caution so that they ensure the client gets a meaningful return from the case. That is what differentiates a professional litigation funder from a more aggressive opportunistic funder.

The funders generally think that disclosure is a good way to resolve the potential CoI issues. A funder stated that:

> "We have to be disclosed for the CoI. The question is to disclose the presence of TPF but not the TPF agreement because that is our business interest and is a business secret, only matters known between parties to the TPF agreement. In ISDS cases we funded, none of them is public, we only disclosed to the tribunal". One funder stated, "We nearly always disclose".

Thus, it is clear that funders generally disclose their names, but not necessarily always. However, even if their name is not made public, they might still sometimes disclose their names to the non-funded party or, when ordered to do so, to the arbitration tribunal.

As stated, funders have a CoI checklist. One funder explained in detail how they prevent a potential conflict: "First of all, we list all the entities which are involved in a state case, including the legal team, existing or potential arbitrators, and we share with the lawyers when we have lawyers consult about whether Mr X, same Mr X is expected to be an arbitrator, immediately we share this information with the lawyer counsel, when we have this list we share it internally with the team, in order to know if we have such conflicts with the team, we also check the past cases, in order to check, this is the process which is a procedure, also we check that we do the same checking in order to have a second layer of control, also we check with the identity of the investors, in order to prevent conflicts with our investors, and they make sure we have no conflict." Thus, we can see that funders have a database and update it regularly to prevent any potential CoI in the cases they fund.

Another important CoI that has been raised during the interviews has not yet been discussed in academia thoroughly. There is a potential CoI between the funded parties and their lawyers if the same lawyer who acts in the case also advises the funded party during the negotiation of the TPF agreement with the funder. This is problematic because both the lawyer and the funded party will be paid by the funder. The order of payment, the amount of payment, the relationship between the funder and lawyer, might all raise concerns and problems. Indeed, there is a case brought by a Dutch national against the funder and his lawyers because of this type of conflict.[12] The number of such cases will increase if the same lawyer advises on the TPF agreement and acts in the case. Therefore, the healthiest solution should be that the lawyer who is advising on the TPF agreement should not also act on the merits of the case. In this way, the lawyer who is advising on a TPF agreement will not have a continuing financial relationship with the funder.

Funders also do not fund claims where there is a CoI between their investors, auditors, and funded parties. One funder stated that "we won't find against our investors and auditors". Another funder stated:

> CoI is shooting a bullet in your shoes, if you fund a case in which you have conflict. CoI is checked at a natural level, there is no temptation to play with them. It is an important matter, structurally, I think no third-party funders would have an interest in playing around with them, it is a very good discipline to check and avoid any CoI.

One funder stated that there is a CoI issue specific to investment arbitration. The funder stated, "well, the biggest CoI in ISDS would be if you have multiple cases

[12] See: https://globalarbitrationreview.com/king-spalding-sued-client-in-funded-bit-case.

involving a single sovereign who is a debtor, that is problematic". This is correct, if a funder is targeting a specific sovereign, this might raise concerns, especially if the state is small, or a state that has difficulty affording to defend itself in investment arbitration.

Many funders stated that they did not face any CoI issues. The reason is that they follow strict CoI guidelines. Funders either have these guidelines as a company policy, or they look at International Bar Association (IBA) guidelines or similar ones to prevent any potential CoI. One funder also stated:

> we avoid CoI issues by doing background checks properly and by doing the necessary research. Most of the funders have worked as litigators, they understand what causes potential conflict and do not fund such claims if there is any potential of CoI.

Therefore, funders avert potential CoI issues. They do not face them because they eliminate any possible CoI issues at the beginning of the TPF process. Nevertheless, the author asked them if they faced any extraordinary CoI issues and here are their answers.

Funders gave different answers, but the conclusion was unanimous: funders do not fund cases if there is even a slight possibility of conflict. Some funders did not want to share any examples, some funders stated that they did not come across or cannot remember any CoI. Some other funders shared some information off the record, so the author cannot include it in this book. However, this empirical study summarizes that all funders are taking this seriously. They either make sure that there is no CoI or when they see something fishy, it is a red flag for them, and they stay away from funding such cases. This empirical study can conclude this was the unanimous summary of all the interviews.

One funder stated "confidential, cannot talk". This shows that some funders actually faced some CoI issues but do not want to talk about them. Some funders also mentioned some examples off the record, so the author cannot mention them here. However, the author can summarize that potential CoI issues are highly probable to feature on shady deals, corruption embedded in the case, or a secret relationship between an arbitrator and a party. Funders repeatedly told me that it is "ridiculous", or "nonsense" to think that they would fund cases where they have CoI. Funders eliminate any small possibility if that possibility can harm their investment. Therefore, they are checking for any conflict seriously and thoroughly.

One funder elaborated on a potential CoI they faced and how they managed it. The funder stated "we used to have one, with an arbitrator we used, at that time when we decided to fund the case, the arbitration tribunal had not been constituted. When it was constituted, we found out that the arbitration tribunal would consist of three arbitrators, one selected by each party, then the presiding arbitrator was appointed by the institution. The presiding arbitrator helped us to assess some cases a year before and we gave him compensation. We decided not to fund the claim because of CoI with the arbitrator. We avoid these potential conflicts. There might be conflicts that cause us to terminate the contract. If there is a conflict we will withdraw. As conflict happens, if the funder cannot change the arbitrator, funders need to withdraw." This shows how strictly funders are monitoring any potential

Table 4.12 Funders' opinion regarding regulations

Funders who think regulation is necessary?	Number of funders
Yes	4
No, self-regulation is satisfactory	13

CoI. They try to prevent it, if they cannot prevent it, they withdraw from funding. Arbitration institutions should be careful in their appointments and should appoint another presiding arbitrator if they are informed that there is a conflict between the funder and an arbitrator they appointed. Again, timely disclosure will prevent any issues. Other funders provided similar examples, as well. Thus, this section shows how funders carefully assess any potential CoI issues and prevent them before they materialize.

4.4.8 Funders' Opinion on Regulation

The author also asked funders about their opinion on regulation, i.e. whether they like the current state of the TPF market, where there is no specific regulation on how TPF practice should be conducted in investment arbitration and in many jurisdictions, or whether they would want to see some forms of regulation. The majority of funders stated that they think the current state of the TPF market is working well and no additional regulation is required. However, a few funders stated a strong preference for regulation for some reasons. Now, their reasoning on whether they prefer regulation or not will be further explained (Table 4.12).

First, most funders expressed that they do not see any reason why there should be regulation on TPF. One funder stated that "I think the question here is what do they worry about? Using TPF, three concerns might arise (i) does the funder have enough money to fund a case, (ii) are they committing that money to more than one case, (iii) how much control funders are taking in the case? If these concerns need to be addressed, then regulation can be an option, but the market is already addressing these questions well". Another funder said "I think TPF should be self-regulated, and institutions should lead the way. No domestic regulation is needed". This idea is echoed by the majority of funders who think TPF should not be regulated.

One funder also stated that the industry is already regulated in different ways. The funder stated "Most countries require privately held funds to be regulated. In that sense, the industry is already regulated. Other than that, this is a private contract and private contracts do not need to be regulated from a legal perspective, and looking at legal disputes as an asset, as opposed to justice, I think that it makes sense that it is not regulated. It is another way to make money, similar to how the legal profession started. It is common sense for funders to act with integrity, otherwise, the market will fall apart". Another funder offered similar ideas and said that judges and arbitrators are the best regulators. The funder stated "I think self-regulation is adequate, but also judges and arbitration panels are the ultimate regulators. What regulation is designed to do is to protect claimants, the judicial system; judges and arbitrators are sitting there to provide this. Litigation funders have a business - so everyone is aligned to make sure only meritorious cases get a pass, lawyers on each side; a lot of responsible people are involved, litigation funders are also there – independent. What more regulators can do. . .I do not see any point there. There is no interest, people who follow these rules have a benefit, otherwise if it is challenged, in my view judges and arbitrators are the best regulators." Therefore, funders think that instead of regulators, actors in judicial systems are already regulating the practice to protect the system and claimants.

Another funder questioned the urgency to regulate TPF; "Should commercial litigation finance be regulated? No, there is no distinction in my mind. Commercial aviation finance or litigation finance, jurisdictions are free, but I don't think there is any necessity to regulate litigation finance providers more or differently, consumer funding can be a different matter, we don't do this." Another funder echoed no regulation by stating "I am not aware of any funder who does bad business in international standards, they all play clean. If they don't, they will lose everything, it is all relationships and trust". A third funder said "Being aware of what is happening now is the golden rule. What the International Chamber of Commerce (hereinafter "ICC") has now in its rules, disclosing the fact that the case is funded and disclosing who is funding are sufficient rules. Anything else would be opening a Pandora's Box, which could go into a different way".

One funder stated that people place so much importance on regulation. He continued "All that means, is you need to tick boxes. Some other funders may not, we already do, so if there is regulation, from a business point of view it is good for us". A funder said "It varies by jurisdiction. In jurisdictions where it is self-regulatory, it works well, but they are not averse to actual regulation, as well. And it is better than having nothing. People can also easily adapt to regulation". A funder who stated that no regulation is needed, added that "No one would want a regulated market. There is nobody capable, there is no need. Courts are very good at imposing their own rules to ensure the process is respected. Arbitration tribunals are the same. Recently established, the Association of Litigation Funders (ALFA) is meant to be an international standard setter".

In short, no regulation or a light-touch approach such as those in Hong Kong and Singapore, seem to be commonly accepted by the funders. Some of the funders expressed their support and positive views on Hong Kong's and Singapore's regulations. One funder stated that "the light-touch approach, for Hong Kong and Singapore, is not a high level of regulation. We consider it to be reasonable". It is not surprising that most funders do not prefer regulation and find self-regulation satisfactory. Nobody wants to be regulated. However, there are funders who prefer regulation. The main reason is that they want every funder to operate at the same high level, following the best practice is important to them. With the same reasoning, this book proposes the best practice guideline for funders operating in the investment arbitration regime, so that they can operate without causing any procedural or ethical issues.[13]

Generally, funders liked this question and talking about it. However, one funder found the question to be biased against funders in the way it is structured. He gave further comments and detailed answers after the author explained that, sometimes, questions are deliberately structured provocatively. He stated that "TPF is not different than any other. It is a capital mortgage. You go to the bank. If your security is receivable, you go to a funder if you cannot go to a bank or do not want to go to the bank. The question of financing is a specific asset, whether that asset is a house or a claim, is not bad, nor requires a regulation. Regulation is intended to ensure that there are no practices that can harm users. Regulation of TPF is used to minimize or label companies that come in with financing claims. I have not seen any single regulator propose that they are there to help claimants. Every regulation is to call out the fact that there is a TPF, not to protect the claimant. I am a fan of no regulation, why should TPF be different? If my aunt gives me money for free, do I need to report this? What is the difference? If arbitrators care where the money comes from, if that is the case, I am okay. However, states are doing it with the purpose of trying to cast TPF in a bad light". Therefore, the funder stated that the purpose of the regulation, which is generally talked about, is to point out the funder rather than protect the funded party.

After summarizing those opinions that support the self-regulated or unregulated market, there were also some funders who strongly support regulation. A funder stated "that's a good question. I can't speak for others. When I look at how we fund cases, we are careful to include and make sure opposing costs are paid if the case is lost. We make sure to disclose the presence of the TPF, not exert any influence. The way we do business does not require any additional regulation," but he can't speak for others. "If you look at the *Herzig v Turkmenistan* case, the funder did not provide ATE insurance. Now, it creates a problem, because the claimant is funded. If he wins, everybody is happy, but, if he loses, *Turkmenistan* will have a cost award against the insolvent company which will not be able to pay. It will be just another claim added to the insolvency claims. Does that mean third-party markets should be regulated? Potentially. Does it mean arbitrators should use their discretion and order SfC? Maybe there is another solution. Without regulation to root out the problems, it is worrisome for the ISDS market. Is regulation the answer? The way we do business, it would never have happened. If others don't comply, then it has to be regulated". Therefore, the funder believes that it would be good to have some sort of regulation so other funders all come up to the same level.

One other funder who supports regulation says "You have in certain countries, especially in the UK, self-regulation. Funders have an association and have guidelines, etc. We are very strongly against self-promotion or regulation because even if this works very properly, from the outside it is always questionable. I prefer a

[13]See Chap. 7: The Best Practice Guideline for Third-Party Funders Operating in Investment Arbitration Regime.

regulated market; I consider it necessary if we want to avoid any type of suspicion or questions about TPF practice. It is important to show the outside world that this is not something we are deciding together in a corporation, manipulating the answer we bring. It is something under control and the responsibility and supervision to fund anybody can be done by a minister of justice or board of law professors. I do not know but at least a mutual competent body should be regulating". Thus, this funder thinks that a regulatory body will change the way the outside world perceives TPF practice. Another funder explains the reason why regulation is needed by complaining about self-regulation. The funder says, "It is pretty poor—self-regulation does not provide everyone comfort".

Two other participants echoed the need for regulation. The second participant interviewed from the same TPF company repeated this idea. "Regulation is good, but should not be too detailed, just enough to cover the weak points of TPF arrangements." Therefore, funders who support regulation also do not want it to be too detailed. Another funder stated that "because TPF is very new in the legal industry, if it is self-regulated it is not going far enough. Maybe some funders (bad funders) may use the parties' lack of money and expertise to take a very large amount of recovery revenue. They might make a lot more money than they are supposed to make."

These concerns are valid. Since the market is growing and there are no supervising bodies, some people might exploit others to profit more, and this would damage the claim holders as well as TPF practice. Therefore, some funders believe that a certain type of regulation in which minimum standards are established should be provided to protect the claim holders.

4.4.9 Disclosure

The author asked the funders the following question: "Do you prefer it when the interests of the funder are disclosed, or do you prefer it to stay unknown?". Here is a table is drawn from funders' answers and my further analysis (Table 4.13).

This table shows the funder's preference about being disclosed or not. The majority of funders do not have a problem with the disclosure, they either stated that identity disclosure is okay, or they do not have any preference, but they are okay to disclose if they have to. A high number of funders also stated that the disclosure depends on relevant factors. Now, we will look closely at why they gave these answers.

Some funders stated that the identity disclosure is okay, have no issue with the disclosure at all and even think it is good and necessary. One funder expressed that

Table 4.13 Disclosure

Identity disclosure is OK	12
No preference-no matter	5
It depends on the situation	8
Disclosure is not required	1

the disclosure is necessary for a transparent investment arbitration process. Another funder expressed "I have nothing against disclosure, who is the funder and there is a funder. It should be an important solution for the funder. They have important information to check with the disclosure". Another funder who supported the disclosure of identity stated: "Identity disclosure is okay. I have never heard a funder who said that I will not disclose. I can also accept if the tribunal wants to see special parts of the agreement, but sharing terms and conditions, especially economic conditions--that should not happen. If that happens, anywhere in the world, prompted by a regulator, arbitrator, or judge they are just killing the market then. You are disclosing the Coca-Cola formula. It is a private contract between the parties." Therefore, the funders are okay with the disclosure of their presence or identity. However, they are not okay with disclosing specific terms of their financial interests. Anything going beyond the identity is a huge question mark and a red flag for funders.

Some funders stated that they have no preference about disclosing or not. Therefore, some are neutral to disclosing. One funder stated, "it is totally up to the claimant, if they want to disclose, they can, if they do not want to, we do not force them to disclose". Another funder stated that "I do not have any fundamental issues with our name being disclosed. In a commercial context, it is good. Typically, the funded party and its lawyers work with this". Another funder stated that "We don't really have a preference. We follow the requirements of the arbitration rules and local legislation". One funder also elaborated "I do not mind; I have no position about them asking for the disclosure. It can help in many ways, or it can prejudice the case."

A great number of funders also stated that disclosure depends on the circumstances. A funder stated that "in investor-state arbitration cases, there can be issues with disclosure, SfC issues particularly within ISDS cases; if funding is known to the tribunal, SfC is more of an issue in ISDS cases". Another funder stated "Case by case. I think generally, the respondents like to create satellite correspondence, and take the fight to funders to oppose the case. A respondent can make the funders back up; whether a funder is involved can be a distraction." Another funder echoed the same concern by saying. "It is a—context of what happened to the disclosure - by disregarding that, the respondent wants disclosure to divert the attention of the arbitrators and delay the proceedings. So, collateral issues are permitted to disrupt the case and increase costs. If that is the goal, then disclosure is bad." In short, funders have raised concerns due to the increasing number of SfC applications by respondent states in cases where a third-party funder is present.

Except for one, none of the funders interviewed was against disclosure. However, the funder who was against disclosure had a specific reason and thought arbitrators are not educated enough to make a judgment on TPF arrangements. In his own words: "I think the tribunals, ICSID, ICC and all the different organizations who run the industry do not have good financial economic understanding. These are very academic people with traditional old school views. It does not match up with the real global financial market; they must become better educated on how finance works. If that happens, we can disclose our interests. It should not matter who owns that

Table 4.14 Ethical and PR considerations

Yes	24
No	2

interest. The international arbitration community is way behind in understanding this. So, it should not be disclosed now". The same funder stated that "arbitrators have more negative views of funders than they would love to admit because of historical champerty".

In conclusion, nearly all funders interviewed are not against disclosure. 12 of the participants interviewed stated that the disclosure of presence and identity of the funder is no problem at all, but anything else would be problematic. They further explained that the question is to disclose the presence of the TPF but not the TPF agreement because that is their business interest and business secret. This should only matter between parties to the TPF agreement and not others. Therefore, in summary, the disclosure of the funder's identity seems to be the common ground, but funders put a caveat on the fact that the existence of the funder might raise concerns for some arbitrators, a potential bias, or a funded party might be forced to pay SfC in investment arbitration.

4.4.10 Funders' Ethical and Public Relations (PR) Considerations

The author also asked whether funders weigh any ethical or PR considerations in their investments. There are such considerations funders apply, but not all funders are cautious about PR. Here, the answers of funders are presented about ethical or PR considerations (Table 4.14).

We can conclude that many funders care about their reputation and how they look when they fund a case. They want to be on the right side of the dispute. However, some funders do not have any ethical considerations and they just look at the investment from a profitable and meritorious point of view, which also brings a certain ethical standard.

Many funders stressed that they follow ESG guidelines for their investors. "Environmental, social, and governance (ESG) criteria are a set of standards for a company's operations that socially conscious investors use to screen potential investments".[14] One funder stated that "We are avoiding funding cases that go against ESG guidelines and cases in the tobacco industry. I am not convinced that if they are truly ethical. We generally avoid these, and rather prefer not to get involved." Other funders also stated that they follow ESG guidelines. Some funders observe ethical considerations as part of their due diligence process. One funder explained "I think, as part of our due diligence process, we do look at what impact

[14] https://www.investopedia.com/terms/e/environmental-social-and-governance-esg-criteria.asp.

the funded case would have in the public domain, whether positive or not". Considering there is already negative criticism against funders, funders seem to be more careful not to portray a bad image in the media.

Funders also have fiduciary duties towards their investors. One funder explained "We have a tremendous number of ethical considerations. It could be anything. We have fiduciary duties to our investors. I have worked with private equity funds, we reported fiduciary obligations, our investors could sue us [if we don't]. We could not lie to them; we are managing their money." Funders do not fund any party that their investors are against TPF. Another funder stated that they are staying away if a case involves bribery, corruption, or similar problems. The funder stated "ethical considerations are ultimately about whether an entity is involved with bribery, corruption etc., these kinds of things. We wouldn't want to be associated with that party. We will be cautious about investing". Another funder pointed out that it is the choice of their investors. The funder said "our investors might have a particular interest, an investor might say 'you can't ever use my money to sue X, Y Z, etc.' It is very specific to the fund." Therefore, investors' choices are important for funders as they determine the scope of targeted potential cases to fund. If an investor does not want its money to be used for the tobacco industry, alcohol or gambling industry or whatever choice an investor makes, this will bind the investment decisions of third-party funders. Therefore, the ethics of investors shape the ethics of third-party funders, and they are strictly related to each other.

One funder explained ethical considerations in detail. The funder stated, "There are two before you go into individual jurisdictions, two sets of ethics you need to be aware of. Part 1: general business ethics - we conduct ethical business, we don't say things that are not true, we do not cheat, we use an appropriate manner, business ethics rules apply to us as they should apply to other businesses. Part 2: in addition to that, our people are almost all lawyers, we work in admitted jurisdictions all over the world, individual and collectively they are subject to ethical rules. On top of that, we are the fiduciary of capital, there are very stringent ethical rules imposed by the US Securities and Exchange Commission (SEC) that we need to follow". So, these three layers of ethical considerations, all funders need to follow. However, how much they apply can change, and since investment arbitration is operating at the supranational level, a guideline is needed, as this book proposes.

Some funders also stated that they would avoid funding small states. The funder stated "For us, we would try not to fund cases which may have a large impact on society or government. When we evaluate the case, we not only evaluate the percentage chance of winning, but we also have different considerations. We would not support the bigger party to deprive the other party's rights. Another part is that we would evaluate right or wrong in the ethical way. Whether we help the party with less strength, or whether we help some party who is big in resources, they use litigation and arbitration to deprive arbitration rights of the other party, or squeezing the other party's rights, and if so we do not fund such cases". This shows some funders evaluate many considerations. The same funder continued with an example: "In 2017, we helped some consumers, some buyers of certain real estate, houses, some houses had quality issues, we helped to sue the real estate company, on a pro bono basis. We do that as pro bono. We just get back what we invested. We did not collect an additional bonus on that. We give our investors instructions before doing that". This shows that funders can act on a pro bono basis if investors agree with such a cause.

One funder stated "Yes, we have quite strict ones, because we have regulated funds, a number of environment and social government clauses – we cannot invest in arms dealing, gambling, pornography, etc. Our investors have guidelines, through Europe and North America it is becoming more and more important. What we are able to invest is restricted." Therefore, even though TPF is not specifically regulated, funders control funds, and those funds are regulated differently in every jurisdiction. Depending on the jurisdiction, the funds are subject to different rules. Ethics is part of due diligence for some funders. One funder stated that "we do due diligence, if there is anything that smells unkosher, anything with corruption, illegality, obscurity, we do not want to get involved with such things. And otherwise, in terms of ethics, we are qualified members of various bars, we have special ethical rules that we need to adhere to. We ensure that they comply with such rules". Therefore, funders take ethical considerations into account as part of due diligence, and lawyers working for funders have their own ethical and professional rules to follow. Another funder also said that they fund only meritorious cases. The funder stated that she sees that as an ethical duty, not to fund a case where the applicant does not have a meritorious case.

Funders, not surprisingly, care about PR considerations. Since there is a huge amount of criticism against funders, they do not want to project a bad image. One funder elaborated that "When we finance investment arbitration claims, we avoid poor states because they could potentially be difficult PR. Other than that, if you believe in justice, it is tricky. You wouldn't want to look like that with negative publicity at the end, we see claims involving children that can make you start to feel uncomfortable, they are very rare though, but they do happen, and you avoid them" Another funder pointed out the reputation of their clients. The funder said "Clients' reputation is important. The funder goes into a partnership with the case, we would not want to start a partnership with the wrong sort of clients. Also, cases with political elements could fall under question." Thus, we can see that the political element is an important concern for many funders.

Funders generally want to be on the right side of dispute. A funder stated this: "We actually care about being on the right side of the case. Frontpage newspaper test - if we are in the newspaper, would we feel embarrassed, looked too opportunistic, etc? Some of the issues in ISDS cases in investment arbitration against tiny nations, winning when a tiny island state would have perished is not a good look. Or against universities, etc. Anything that would be sensitive - this is from public information. In ISDS, we generally stay away from any murky cases". Therefore, including ISDS cases, funders want to be on the right side of the dispute, right both on merits and on ethics. However, not all funders are worried about bad PR. A funder stated, "Not driven by PR, we are prepared to take on what I call noisy cases in the interest of justice. The problem of being the funder is that we do not talk about ongoing cases to the media, the other party does, so the funder does not talk.

But we don't shy away; it is not anxiety or PR, it is more a question of business ethics. We look at cases through the ethical lens before we take them on. There are probably cases we wouldn't take because claimants' motives are improper or because of who the opponent is".

Another funder elaborated on ethics, "Yes, sure. Innumerable. I would never fund a case or circumstance in which I would be on the wrong side of the dispute, I would not fund someone, an oil drilling company in the Antarctic. It goes back to ethical and moral questions. I would not fund a situation that I do not believe in. Anyone on the bad side of the dispute, or overly controversial issues. I wouldn't get involved with one side of the Palestinian and Israeli conflict, for example. Certain things, I would not fund, I would use my common sense". Generally, funders care about public appearances. A funder said "Absolutely, we always consider whether the claim is public or not, we always assume it will be public. We consider previous criminal convictions, if there is any negative association, we stay away". Another funder echoed "If it is like, the defendant is being corrupt, plaintiff suffered losses as a result, that goes to merits of their case, too, if that really affects the plaintiff we don't fund, if they are victim, it wouldn't be an issue for us then". Another funder also stated that they check the criminal history of the person who applied for TPF. "If it is an individual, we do some searches and if that individual has a criminal record in the last 10 years, especially crimes such as fraud, we check past convictions and take them into account, too." One funder stated that since there is no regulation specific to TPF, the funder sees ethics as crucial. The funder stated "we as a business need to be completely clean and transparent. We need to follow very high standards. TPF as a business is not regulated except for a few regulations. We are self-regulated only in a few jurisdictions. We are self-regulated, that's why I see ethics as one of the crucial elements". This shows that ethics are important and especially since there is no specific regulation on how to fund, whether part of due diligence or not, the funders should have certain ethical standards.

Another funder stated "we would not want to be involved with political cases. We would not fund someone on an economic sanction who draws a lot of political eyes and battles with politicians, and so on. This is something we look at very carefully because, we don't want to be in the public eye really. We don't want to be dragged into the press. That is it." Another funder stated that before they decide to fund someone, they would consider if the matter went to the public how they would be seen in the eyes of the public. Therefore, the funder stated that they would always think as if it will be public, and they would only fund a case if they would be seen as being on the right side of the dispute.

In conclusion, the negative connotation of an applicant with corruption, bribery, past criminal convictions, or similar concerns is problematic for funders and they want to stay away. Some funders are also politically neutral, and they do not want to get involved with cases heavily involved with certain political figures. Their investors' choice is another important and binding decision for funders. Ethics are very important for many funders since they do not have any specific TPF regulation, they believe that they should follow high standards so that they can be seen as doing the right thing in the market. However, not all funders see ethics in this way, and it differs from funder to funder. Certain binding ethical standards are necessary for the market.[15]

4.4.11 *Funders' Reporting Requirements*

Here, the reporting requirements of funders are elaborated on. There are two main reporting requirements: Reporting from (i) lawyers to funders and (ii) from funders to investors.

If there are no specific TPF regulations and reporting requirements, then it does not mean that funders do not have any reporting requirements to regulators. There are still regulatory requirements since funders control a large amount of money in funds, and they are subject to various monetary regulations depending on jurisdictions in which they operate, such as Financial Conduct Authority (FCA) authorization in the UK. These reporting requirements are important examples funders mentioned when interviewed. US funders have reporting requirements to the SEC as well. Funders stated that they want to ensure they are aware of all regulatory requirements in a jurisdiction before they invest in it. Even the International Centre for Settlement of Investment Disputes (ICSID) has some draft rules, which we will see them soon came to force.[16] Apart from this brief information, now we will look at reporting requirements of clients to funders.

4.4.11.1 From Lawyers to Funders

All funders stated that they have reporting requirements. However, the frequency of the reporting differs from funder to funder. Most funders prefer receiving monthly reports. Generally, funders require "Monthly reporting from lawyers, what is going on about the case." One funder explains this: "Yes, internal reporting requirements, the lawyers basically update us monthly on what is going on with the case". Another funder stated, "Yes, during the whole procedure, we ask, we are expecting to receive drafts of the writings, and regular reports of each event, each submission, the reaction of the respondent, we want to have it timely, what has happened, what is in preparation, and if necessary, provide advice. The idea is that we will provide the funded party and its lawyers with free advice. We may have information or experience useful to them, suggestions they are free to take into account or not". Therefore, funders can be provide additional help in the case if it is wanted (Table 4.15).

---

[15] See ethical suggestions in the best practice guideline.

[16] The new ICSID rules institute rules on third-party funding; *see* https://icsid.worldbank.org/sites/default/files/publications/rule-amendment_proposals_additional-facility.pdf. The New ICSID rules came into force on 1 July 2022.

Table 4.15 Reporting requirements to funders

Whether clients have reporting requirements to funders	Number of funders
Yes	17
No	0

Not all funders require monthly reports: they might be bimonthly. Some funders also stated they require reports quarterly, tri-annual reports, half-year reports, or annual reports. One funder stated, "Clients give a regular update of the case, high level of importance; monthly or bimonthly usually, the frequency differs". What they want in these reports includes "Typically, reports on a monthly basis from lawyers about case development, how much budget they have spent up to certain points, whether they are concerned about anything else, etc., if case prospects are altered, whether they expect settlement negotiations or go to trial, etc." Funders, naturally want to know any material changes in the case and any important developments throughout the case.

Reporting requirements to the funders is the funded party's duty since the funded party's lawyers do not sign the TPF agreement. The TPF contract is between funder-funded party. However, since lawyers are following the case, this reporting requirement is undertaken by the lawyers upon the instructions of the funded party. One funder explains, "Lawyers are not a party to the TPF agreement, we can't tell lawyers what to do. The claimant is under the requirement to provide information during the conduct of the case, just to inform us. The claimant tells the lawyers please provide the information, if anything goes on the case (we would want to know)".

There is no surprise in these results either. Funders want to follow the case they invest in, and they want to know what is going on with the case. Therefore, every funder has reporting requirements for the funded party, so they let them know how the case is going. These reporting requirements are generally fulfilled by the funded party's lawyers. This is generally a monthly report to funders. However, some funders adopt different practices such as wanting to know only important developments in the case, such as a settlement offer, or any important evidence coming in or any other developments.

4.4.11.2 From Funders to Investors

As funders require funded parties to report any important developments, investors require funders to report to them regularly as well, they too have reporting requirements. A funder stated that "we have extensive reporting requirements. We report to our investors". The frequency of those reports also changes. One funder stated that "yes, we make quarterly updates through our investors". Another funder stated "We certainly report to our investors, the frequency depends, periodically, sometimes monthly, sometimes circumstantially. Regarding reports to investors, the most important information we report is how the case is developing." As these answers

Table 4.16 Funders' investment of ISDS cases

Whether invested in an investment arbitration	Numbers of funders
Yes	13
No, but considered	4

show, investors want to know how the case is developing and want timely updates from funders.

4.4.12 Investment Arbitration Specific Questions

The information above was collected from funders with questions about their practice in general. This is because their practice and criteria do not differ from litigation to arbitration, or from commercial arbitration to investment arbitration. They apply the same standards and models in every investment they make. Therefore, most of the questions above do not specify any specific area of arbitration or any specific type of case. If funders' practice changes in investment arbitration or there are specific risks or concerns, funders specified their answers, and this chapter is reflected in the relevant sections. To collect data specific to investment arbitration, the author asked the interviewees some questions and analyzed their answers in the following paragraphs.

4.4.12.1 The Number of ISDS Cases

Funders invested in some cases that were not always made public/disclosed. Sometimes those TPF agreements are disclosed to the tribunal but not to the public. Some of them are made public. From the publicly available awards, I have written a case law chapter.[17] After talking to funders in this empirical study, my impression is that only a small number of cases are made public. Most of the funded cases are not in the public domain. A funder, for example, invested in 5 ISDS cases, only one of which is public. Some other funders said that none of their cases is public, but some of them are disclosed to the tribunal only for the tribunal's examination. Therefore, in reality, the number of cases funded in investment arbitration is much higher than the number of cases publicly available.

Table 4.16 shows whether funders interviewed invested in investment arbitration cases or not. Table 4.17 shows the number of cases the funders invested in. Those numbers reflect the total numbers of the TPF company, not personal numbers. The author also asked how many investment arbitration cases they have reviewed. One funder stated, "No idea how many I reviewed. We get so many inquiries and the

[17] See Chap. 3.

Table 4.17 Number of funded investment arbitration cases

Number of cases	Number of funders
0	4
1	1
2–5	2
More than 5	7
Confidential	3

majority is eradicated very quickly". Another funder stated that it has invested in 13 ISDS cases in total and received hundreds of ISDS applications. This funder explained that they have accepted around 5% of the ISDS applications so far. Another funder who said that they did not invest in any ISDS cases, stated that they have reviewed 45 ISDS cases in total. These numbers show how low the acceptance rate of funders is in ISDS cases. The funder further elaborated that "out of 45 cases, the majority is instantly rejected. There would have been roughly 10 cases we entertained with a proper diligence".

ISDS cases are generally a handful compared to litigation or commercial arbitration cases, a funder stated. When asked its success rate, a funder stated, "several won, several ongoing". The funder also stated that not all funders are successful in investment arbitration and some funders they know stopped investing in ISDS cases. Another funder stated that the considerations and parameters they apply to ISDS cases are the same as for litigation or commercial arbitration cases. Another funder specifically stated "We have invested in 3 ISDS cases since their inception, out of 252 cases we have funded". Therefore, investment arbitration does not present a major part of many funders' investments. Some of the funders did not give the number of ISDS cases they invested in, as Table 4.17 shows. One funder who spoke confidentially added, "This will be historic, and we don't talk – even if it were in the public domain, arguably, it's a breach of agreement if I talk". One funder stated that their success rate is around 85 in ISDS cases. Another funder, however, said they lost all ISDS cases they invested in.

In summary, ISDS cases are funded, not every funder but a small number of funders funds ISDS cases. Considering that in the world there are hundreds of third-party funders, investing in domestic or international arbitration as well as domestic litigation cases, a very small number of funders invest in ISDS cases and not all of them are successful. The acceptance rate is also very low in ISDS cases.

4.4.12.2 TPF Models and TPF Models for the Respondent States

The author also asked funders about the different TPF models they offer and whether they have any specific TPF models for respondent states. Different models in the market include single case funding, portfolio funding, and enforcement funding. They stated that in investment arbitration, portfolio funding is not common, though. It is very difficult to offer portfolio funding because the costs of ISDS cases are very high, and not suitable for portfolio funding. Therefore, we can say that the ISDS cases are funded on a single assessment basis.

It is no surprise that in investment arbitration, most of the time, if not always, claimants are funded. The author asked funders whether they have any TPF tools for respondent states. They generally did not want to say no but, due to the structure of investment arbitration, it is improbable that funders can fund the respondent states. Funders have no preference whether to fund claimants or respondents. However, it is difficult to fund respondent states. Claimants bring claims against the states and the states do not have counterclaims. Therefore, respondent states do not have as much opportunity as investors to be funded.

A funder stated that "It is not that we do not want to fund states, it is that it is not easy to develop a structure that is suitable for respondent states. It is generally possible to fund claimants or respondents who have counterclaims. Respondent states do not normally have counterclaims". Therefore, it is not possible to fund the respondent states. However, funders try to develop tools for the respondent states, but it seems difficult. A funder said: "Not really, it seems to be a theoretical exercise, politically difficult for them to pay fees on success. I can come up with a structure, how are they are going to pay you, that's the question". Another funder stated that one possibility for TPF of a Respondent state is when they try to recover a costs award. The funder stated "Respondent States in ISDS, they do not have counterclaims generally. One potential scenario, when respondent states can recover, it is when the respondent state wins, and the funder helps to recover the cost award." A funder suggested another possibility by saying "it is difficult as a tool for states to say that if we successfully defend our case, we will pay the funder." However, none of the funders stated that they could fund a respondent state. Moreover, apart from all the interviewees never funded a state, they also never heard of any other TPF company funded a state.[18] So, these are all theories at the moment. Another funder stated that "we certainly can fund respondent states. We looked at that, but I am not aware if we invested in a respondent state. The problem of TPF of defense, we generally require some security, we need to be careful what success is in terms of defense, defining terms, these are difficulties".

In summary, funders do not have anything against TPF of respondent states and in theory, they have TPF tools for states. However, in practice, none of the funders interviewed funded a respondent state in an ISDS case. A funder stated, "I would not say we have tools that are specific to the respondent states. It's more challenging for states to get approval, the sunshine requirements, that may raise some challenges for them". Otherwise, funders do not have any intention against TPF of a state, if the states have cases with merit funders can fund states by using the same criteria they use when they fund claimants. However, the structure of ISDS does not allow states to be funded much.[19] A funder stated that "we can do it in theory but in practice, we

[18]The author did also not come across any example in the literatüre or case law where a TPF company funded a State.

[19]This whole point comes to the structure, function and purpose of ISDS, and this has been discussed in the ethical chapter of this book, see Chap. 5.

Table 4.18 Recoverability of TPF costs in ISDS

Whether funders think it is possible	Number of funders
Yes	5
No	11
Maybe, one third or part of it	1

haven't done it yet. TPF of defense side – Respondent State – if there is a counter-claim it is much easier to fund the respondent state".

4.4.12.3 Funders' Opinion on Recoverability of TPF Costs

As Table 4.18 shows, most funders consider it tremendously implausible that TPF costs can be recovered from respondent states in ISDS. This question is inspired by the famous *Essar v. Norscot* decision in the UK.[20] In *Essar*, the TPF costs were recovered from the respondent. In ISDS, however, it seems more difficult according to the funders.

Funders generally think of this question as an interesting one. A funder stated that "I think it is a very interesting question. How will this idea develop? The question is whether the access to justice we are giving to claimants can be understood as a litigation/arbitration cost. If TPF costs are recoverable from the losing party, it can be a good sign for the funders". Another funder stated that "the claimant's inability to fund the case without TPF, if there is no chance of bringing a case without TPF, then this option should be available". One funder explained: "Why not – If the respondent state behavior is so outrageous, and the claimant had no choice but a funder, then they are rather agreeing with the procedure, then why not". Some other funders also supported this idea.

Most funders, however, do not think it is possible. A funder stated "No, I do not think that. Attacks against TPF grow up, it is hard to imagine that the tribunals will do such a thing. Also, it is really complicated. If a funder receives three times its investment, a funder spent 15M USD. The tribunal would then need to order 45M USD as a ballpark figure. The tribunal will not give back this amount to the claimant. A law firm could go on contingency, but there are too many variables". Funders generally think that it is very difficult.

Another small group of funders stated that they do not have an opinion. A funder stated "it does not depend on my view, it depends on legal rules. This is not a question for me, it's the discretion of the tribunal, and the tribunal will follow the case law, no opinion on this." Another funder said similar things, "specific wording of the arbitration act, arbitrators have discretion - broad enough to cover TPF costs - I don't know, that would depend on the rules of the treaty-we need to look at the wording". One funder said that "Some part of it" can be recoverable.

[20] Essar Oilfields Services Limited v Norscot Rig Management Pvt Ltd [2016] EWHC 2361 (Comm).

Table 4.19 Frivolous claim criticism against funders

Do funders invest in frivolous claims?	Number of funders
Yes	0
No	26

I must say that the result from this question surprised me because the answer "yes" would be beneficial and in favor of funders. Nevertheless, most funders said no, it should not be recoverable. It showed how realistic funders are and they know it is very difficult for tribunals to order such costs in ISDS.

4.4.12.4 Frivolous Claim Argument Against Funders

Table 4.19 shows that all funders said no to the question of whether they invest in weak claims. Funders are surprised that opponents think funders might invest large sums in a dispute where there is no chance to win, or probably where they will lose. One funder stated that if she was TPF of frivolous cases, she would be already out of a job, she was a housewife with no job. Another funder stated that it would be extremely improbable that they would fund such claims since it would be unethical.

All funders unanimously replied "No" to this question and there is no reason to doubt the truth of their answers. Funders have no interest in investing in weak cases. One funder stated "Why would we, we only fund meritorious cases, and they still lose". Moreover, both the success rate of funders and the rejection rate of funders are proving this. One funder shared both data. According to the funder "This is proven by two data. We accept less than 5% of TPF applications and our success rate is above 80%, close to 85%. So, we do not fund unmeritorious claims". Another funder's rate is higher. A funder stated that its rejection to be less than 4% and their success rate is around 90%. Other funders shared similar numbers. These numbers do not suggest that the funders fund unmeritorious cases. Another funder echoed this "if the claim does not make sense, it does not make sense investing. A financial decision is made carefully, investment does not make sense otherwise".

Funders do not think that their involvement causes floodgates to open as proposed in academia. A funder said "I disagree with the proposition that funders will cause floodgates, this is an out of the pocket investment. The minimum amount we need to put in is millions, if we support weak cases, we will lose everything, our clients will lose everything". Another funder stated:

> I will tell you this. That is not true in international arbitration and investment arbitration. In US commercial litigation, I have seen this, not on a standalone basis, but in portfolio funding. International arbitration is difficult to hedge. As a standalone, it is still the riskiest and therefore the most expensive. It is not possible to open floodgates in investment arbitration.

However, in some jurisdictions, where funders invest in a portfolio in litigation, then this proposition can be true. To ensure the best practice in investment arbitration, no case should be funded as part of a portfolio.

In conclusion, the frivolous claim argument against funders is not true in investment arbitration. However, in some jurisdictions, if cases are part of a portfolio, it is correct that with part of that portfolio, some weak cases can be supported. Even ISDS cases are not suitable to be part of the portfolio, to remove even the slightest possibility there must be a rule ensuring no ISDS cases can be part of portfolio funding, and there must be sanctions for funders who breach this rule. The best practice guideline this book proposes a rule to regulate this situation.

4.4.12.5 TPF of ISDS Cases

I asked every participant what is their general view on TPF of investment arbitration matters. I wanted to see how the funders look at investing in investment arbitration cases, whether they think they are extremely profitable or risky, expensive, and lengthy. It seems the latter is reflected in the answers more often.

One funder stated: "I think, certain investor-state arbitrations take longer and are more complex, the budget is also higher". Another funder stated that "the preference is TPF diverse types of claims. Investment arbitration is a relatively higher risk among other claims. The basic reason is, of course, costs are higher, and disputes are more complex. They concern the interpretation of treaties, and they generally go back in time when past events, alleged violations happened. There are many facts and documents held by the respondent state, which might create information asymmetry. Similarly, the cost and adverse cost risk is higher, these generally make investment arbitration on the riskier side of the portfolio, ISDS cases are important ways for funders to provide access to justice for investors, most of the time, the investor would be severely impacted by the state's infringement, and not able to bring the case if there is no external funding, so it is important to bring access to justice." Thus, we can summarize that it is riskier but provides access to justice most of the time.

Another funder stated that "There are potentially good cases to fund, we are worried (long historical tails, there are a lot of factual disputes on this type of case, the credibility of a witness) that the risk is sometimes hard to underline. In investment claims, where damages arise because of, single regulatory changes, those types of cases are clearer, they are more attractive." This shows certain types of investment arbitration cases might be more attractive for funders. Another funder stated that "I think it is becoming unattractive, primarily because states lobbied hard against TPF to separate claimants from finance. A lot of these claimants, with good claims, are often coming and seeking finance because the State either expropriated all of their assets. Sometimes, it is repulsive and or acted out in a discriminatory manner in the ISDS system." One more funder echoed that it is "very difficult, certain expertise required, we do not have success, lack of ability to appeal creates more difficulty. Leading firms are acting, very expensive, and those leading firms are overseen by other leading firms, and still we lose, so ISDS cases are very difficult investments".

One funder stressed the similarities between the assessment of ISDS cases and commercial arbitration cases. The funder stated that "consideration is the same, enforcement strategy, number of damages, etc. is the same as general commercial litigation and arbitration. However, different rules are embedded, different legal issues compared to general commercial disputes. We proceed the same way in ISDS and commercial arbitration". Despite this similarity in the assessment process, it is a fact that ISDS cases are more complex. An average ISDS case takes a longer time than an average commercial arbitration case, and the risk is more difficult to assess. Therefore, not all funders are investing in investment arbitration cases. And some already abandoned the idea of investing in investment arbitration cases.

4.4.12.6 Funder's Opinion on Specific Regulation in ISDS

The author also asked if the funders would like to see any specific regulation in ISDS, and if yes, what rules they would love to see.

The funders generally stated that tribunals already have tools to issue necessary rules regarding TPF. One funder stated that "tribunals are already directing disclosure. Tribunals are already directing SfC etc." Another funder stated that "I think because ISDS is not only between two equal parties, but between an investor and state, disclosure would be much stricter, for them to be more transparent. It requires confidentiality in commercial arbitration, ISDS requires more transparency, for the adverse costs or security, it may be stricter as well, that would lower the risk of frivolous claims, a lack of money to do so for investors".

There are already rules in investment arbitration.[21] One funder, by pointing out those rules, said "there are some rules, you will see published rules in United Nations Commission On International Trade Law (UNCITRAL) arbitrations, identity and fact funding has to be disclosed, there is a white paper of ICSID about disclosure identity and the fact that there is a TPF, to prevent double-hatting arbitrators (arbitrator and counsel). These are not necessary in my opinion. The notion of arbitrator double hatting, in one sense, is necessary. You need counsel experience to be a better arbitrator, TPF funders are not subrogating claims and not giving instructions etc.; their financial arrangement should not be disclosed, it is an absurdity." Another funder opposed the idea of any regulation by saying "I am not sure, if there is any reason for a TPF regulation for ISDS, you have to start with the question of why you are regulating, what you need to achieve? If what you are trying to get at is arbitrator conflict, you can write a set of rules designed to prevent arbitrator conflict. However, rules specific to TPF for that are inappropriate, me TPF of a case, and a law firm taking a case in full contingency, there is no difference". One other funder also stated, "In terms of regulation, no rule particularly came to my mind".

As can be summarized, funders do not see any reason to have any specific regulation for third-party funders. The dominant opinion is that there are already tools for arbitrators to prevent any possible issues related to TPF arrangements.

[21] See the draft UNCITRAL Rules: https://uncitral.un.org/en/thirdpartyfunding.

Funders think that there are no grounds to add on any more rules particular to TPF. The draft rules prepared by UNCITRAL and ICSID do not seem particularly attractive for funders.

4.4.13 Other Issues

After the author concluded each interview, if funders still had time, they were asked if they wanted to add anything else or stress any point we discussed. Funders generally enjoyed the interview and liked the questions. Some funders stressed various issues such as the difficulty in investing in investment arbitration cases, the increasing use of algorithms using data analysis in TPF, and even the use of artificial intelligence (AI).

The funder who stressed the difficulty investing in investment arbitration cases stated that "Some funders stopped investing in investment arbitration cases. This shows that it is not a good investment," the funder added. Another funder stated they invested in more than five ISDS cases and they all failed. These anecdotes prove that investment arbitration is a difficult area and not all the funders are in it, and not always successful. It requires more money, more patience and has more risks. Therefore, some funders do not invest in ISDS cases anymore. This is more proof that investing in ISDS cases is not particularly easy, and not everyone is successful and continuing in this area of TPF. We can also see more data usage and AI in the TPF businesses. However, the funder stated that "algorithms tell which case to fund, we are however never going to get there in ISDS, cases are too complicated for algorithms." Despite this belief, this might change, and the use of algorithms and AI might be used in ISDS cases as well.

4.5 Conclusion

This chapter provided some insights into the TPF market. The funders interviewed are not only operating in investment arbitration. They also invest in commercial arbitration and litigation cases before domestic courts. However, there are some funders in the market investing only in arbitration cases or only in litigation. The reason is simple: compared to litigation and commercial arbitration cases, the number of investment arbitration cases is much more limited. Moreover, the size of the costs in investment arbitration is generally much larger than in domestic litigation or commercial arbitration cases. Therefore, not every funder is attracted to ISDS claims or funders do not have enough financial capacity to invest in them. However, most of the funders interviewed have funded, and a few did not fund but reviewed, ISDS claims. Some of them have even funded more than ten ISDS cases. Thus, the data in this section can be used in TPF of investment arbitration as well as in the TPF market in general. TPF of ISDS is not different from TPF of commercial arbitration and litigation. Nevertheless, the most controversial issues discussed in investment arbitration are addressed to the funders and their responses, opinions, and considerations are extremely important for such issues. Now, the key points from this empirical study and insights of the funders are summarized here.

The first striking conclusion from this empirical chapter is that CoIs are not as problematic in practice as it is presented in academia. This is striking because the CoIs have been discussed in academia thoroughly.[22] Not only in academia though, but a small number of ISDS cases also discussed potential CoIs between funders and arbitrators. However, in all these investment arbitration cases, the tribunals rejected the CoI argument of the respondent state.[23] Understandably, it is not a big problem in practice, because funders try to avoid CoIs. Otherwise, the award the funded party received might be challenged and even set aside. Since funders would not want this, without exception, all funders interviewed said that conflicts check is either part of their due diligence process or something they check at the very beginning of the case to prevent any potential conflict once they are asked to fund the case. Therefore, my conclusion is that CoI is an important issue. However, because of its importance funders take it very seriously and this leaves very small space for any real problems related to the CoI issue in practice.

Another important conclusion is that TPF can have a positive effect on settlement discussions. Funders would like to get their returns as soon as possible. Surely, funders will get their return early if the funded case settles. Therefore, many funders interviewed stated that they prefer settlements. Some even stated that they have some terms in the TPF agreement to encourage settlements. Apart from that, funders do not have to attend settlement meetings, and all stated that they would not attend these meetings. Unless the funded party wanted them to be present in settlement meetings.

The third important conclusion is that funders stated that they weigh ethical and PR considerations. They want to fund the right side of the dispute. The most common considerations funders have is that they do not wish to be involved with political cases, cases where there is corruption or bribery involved, or any bad connotations. Funders also do not want to fund someone who has a bad reputation in the market, or an individual who has past criminal convictions. However, not all funders have such considerations. One funder stated that they would not be driven by PR considerations, if they find a case strong on the merits, they will not stay away from the case just because there are a lot of bad allegations against that party in the media. The same funder stated that access to justice is required for every party, regardless of whether they have a bad reputation or not.

The fourth important conclusion is specific to investment arbitration. Funders interviewed commonly stated that there are specific risks in investment arbitration, such as enforcement against a Sovereign, which has certain difficulties. Funders do not think there should be any specific rule for TPF in investment arbitration. They are

---

[22] There are many articles on this subject. *See, e.g.*, Trusc (2013), pp. 1649–1682; Osmanoglu (2015), p. 325; Melchionda and Crivellaro (2018), pp. 281–306.

[23] For a detailed discussion of those cases, see Chap. 3.

also not against disclosure; however, some funders stated that there are many arbitrators who have negative views on TPF, and they expressed their concerns that if their interests are disclosed, those arbitrators might have a bias against funded parties. These funders proposed that arbitrators should be educated about TPF arrangements. Additionally, funders' involvement does not bring frivolous claims to investment arbitration, but they provide access to justice for many investors. Lastly, it is a fact that TPF is not available for respondent states due to the structure of investment arbitration. Funders do have some TPF models for the states, however, none of them have funded any states in practice yet.

This research sheds new light on the law and practice of TPF which is an ever-increasing business. As long as funders do their due diligence and follow the high standards as the majority of funders interviewed follow, this practice will not distort the investment arbitration system. The most important conclusions are summarized at the end of this chapter. The more detailed considerations and quotes are directly driven from conversations with the funders and are in the relevant parts of this chapter to reflect funders' opinions better. This chapter concludes that there are foremost matters that need to be dealt with and these interviews gave the author more realistic considerations to draw up the best practice guideline for funders, which is appended to this book. A certain standard needs to be fulfilled and this best practice guideline serves this purpose.

Appendix Interview Questions for Third-Party Funders[24]

Introductory Questions

1. Please tell me a little about your background and education?
2. What is your area of expertise concerning TPF?
3. What is your involvement/exposure/knowledge of TPF in mainland China and HK?

[24] Appendix shows the questions I asked every participant in this empirical chapter. Those questions are constituted by the author. The author created the questionnaire during his PhD studies at the Chinese University of Hong Kong and when he was a visiting student researcher at Stanford University during the 2019–20 academic year and sponsored by Professor Deborah Hensler. The author thanks Professor Hensler for this opportunity as well as her support to improve the author's knowledge of empirical studies. The author also thanks Professor Chaisse, who gave his comments on the questionnaire to the author in the author's first year. The author lastly, of course, thanks Professor Bryan Druzin and Fernando Dias Simoes for their immense and continuing support.

Budget

4. What are your parameters for investment, particularly regarding quantum/ damages?
5. Do you have any criteria for the minimum anticipated return on your investment?
6. What is the amount currently committed across your portfolio?

Funders' Input to the Case and Settlement

7. How much input do you have in settlement discussions?
8. Do you put pressure on the funded party to settle? Are you, as a funder, attending the settlement meetings?

Control of the Case

9. How much control do you apply during the life of a case in which you are invested?
10. Do you have any reporting requirements?

Security for Costs-Adverse Costs

11. How do the funder and the claimant deal with the prospects of a costs award against the claimant?
12. Does the risk of adverse costs represent a major or minor constraint when considering TPF?
13. Do you offer advice or assistance in obtaining any adverse costs insurance?
14. How do you internally adjust to address this constraint?

Conflict of Interests

15. What are potential conflict-of-interest issues? What do you consider?
16. Can you give me some extraordinary examples you faced in the past?
17. What are the considerations you apply to prevent possible CoI issues?

Ethics

18. What are the ethical considerations that funders have to deal with? Are there, in fact, any? Where the money comes from for investment?
19. Does the current system of self-regulation go far enough? If there was a regulation in ISDS, what rule would you want to see?
20. How is the relationship between the funder and the funded party's lawyer?
21. How is the general relationship between the funded party and the funder during the TPF process?

Regulation

22. To what extent do you consider there should be a regulation of TPF?
23. Are there any controversial areas or potential PR considerations that you believe would damage your business and so lead to your refusal to fund?
24. Do you prefer when the interests of the funder are disclosed, or do you prefer to stay unknown? What is your general view on TPF of investment arbitration matters?

ISDS Specific Questions and Others

25. How many investment arbitration cases have you funded? Are there any that you can disclose i.e., your interest has been made public?
26. What are the main TPF vehicles you use (Are there any TPF purposes/models you fund other than taking a share); can you share your basic TPF agreement with me?
27. Do you have any TPF tools for the Respondent States in Investor-State Arbitration?
28. What do you think about the recoverability of TPF costs in Investor-State Arbitration?
29. How much is your percentage of success and how do you calculate it?
30. Do you invest in weak claims-related to frivolous claim arguments?

Is there anything else you want to add before concluding the interview?

References

Eken C (2022) A detailed comparison of third-party funding regulations in Hong Kong and Singapore. Asia Pac Law Rev 29(1). https://doi.org/10.1080/10192557.2021.1979799

Melchionda L, Crivellaro A (2018) Disclosure and conflicts of interest in relation to third-party funding. BCDR Int Arbitr Rev 5(2):281–306

Osmanoglu B (2015) Third-party funding in international commercial arbitration and arbitrator conflict of interest. J Int Arbitr 32(3):325

Trusc JA (2013) Full disclosure? Conflicts of interest arising from third-party funding in international commercial arbitration. Georgetown Law J 101(6):1649–1682

Chapter 5
Third-Party Funding: Threat or Facilitator of the System: An Ethical Dilemma

In investment arbitration cases, tribunals discuss TPF in various aspects as explained in Chap. 3 of this book.[1] Ethical considerations are a very important part of the analysis when TPF of ISDS is at hand. Nevertheless, ethics were not part of the discussions in those cases. In the literature, not only ethical issues related to TPF but also ethics of counsels,[2] and ethics of arbitrators are discussed.[3] However, the ethical aspects of TPF have neither been discussed in the case law nor received enough attention in the literature. Some have discussed the ethicality of TPF, but this chapter, apart from analyzing those scholars' ideas, adds to the literature by presenting a more detailed and comprehensive ethical analysis of TPF.

5.1 Introduction

Every century has its own problems and its own solutions to ethical problems. In the past, there was a strong possibility that powerful people could influence a judge and the justice system, thus; the maintenance and champerty doctrines were established to ensure that the legal procedures could continue without any external influence or oppression, and that a judge could decide objectively and naturally according to the law. By cutting the interference of unrelated third parties in the judicial system, this goal was achieved. However, today the judiciary is strong, judges are independent and not easy to influence. Thus, there is no requirement for such doctrines. There-

[1] *See* Chap. 3 of this book.

[2] *See* Ng (2019).

[3] *See* Brauch (2019); Orsi (2013), pp. 92–114.

C. Eken, *Third-Party Funding in Investment Arbitration*, Law for Professionals,
https://doi.org/10.1007/978-3-031-63620-2_5

fore, over time they were abolished.[4] In this century, there is another problem though. By becoming the main dispute resolution system, arbitration has brought its own problems, high costs in international arbitration, especially in investment arbitration. To solve this problem, TPF has grown tremendously in recent years. Now, studies are analyzing this new feature and deciding whether TPF causes problems as opposed to solving them. This chapter analyses the ethics of TPF to reach an answer to this question.

In previous chapters, an overview, general description, and important information about TPF, case law on procedural issues was discussed thoroughly. This chapter approaches TPF from a purely ethical perspective. TPF has not only raised procedural issues but also some important ethical discussions. We can break down the ethical discussions and divide them into several sections. The first and foremost is the "access to justice" argument in favour of funders. Second, historical discussions around the TPF which are champerty and maintenance doctrines, usury, and battery.[5] Third, the chapter continues by explaining specific issues regarding TPF, such as investment arbitration as well as the effect of TPF on lawyer-client relationships. This section contains various scenarios and analyzes how TPF can affect them and what its use should be. Lastly, the fourth and fifth sections analyze the role of regulation in investment arbitration and why the guidelines this book proposes are needed.

There is scholarly literature claiming the ethicality of TPF. This book advocates the position that, generally, TPF "as it is commonly employed is ethical".[6] TPF companies "do not, by their ordinary practices, create serious professional responsibility problems for attorneys. Any potential professional responsibility traps that litigation funding creates can be easily avoided by carefully drafting the funding agreement".[7] However, to ensure that all funders are operating ethically, certain guidelines specific to the investment arbitration are necessary. This book proposes such guidelines.[8] The opposing views in the literature suggest that TPF is unethical, it is speculative, and exploits the system.[9] This book shows that no problems can be attributed to TPF. TPF does no more than facilitate the ISDS regime. The problem existed in the investment arbitration regime before TPF, and resulted because of the structure of the resolution of investment disputes, not because of TPF practice.

---

[4]England and Wales abolished these doctrines in 1967 with the Criminal Law Act; in Australia New South Wales Maintenance, Champerty and Barratry Abolition Act 1993 abolished those doctrines. Most recently, Hong Kong and Singapore passed relative legislation in 2017 and abolished champerty and maintenance. See: Eken (2022).

[5]Chaisse and Eken (2020), pp. 113–166. The article rightly asks whether "TPF is an abuse of the system?" and analyzes it.

[6]Douglas (2005), p. 652.

[7]*Ibid.*

[8]See the best practice guideline in Chap. 7.

[9]*See* Chap. 2 in supra note 108 (Garcia); Santosuosso and Scarlett (2019), p. I.-8; Rogers (2014), Chapter 5, 5: Gamblers, Loan Sharks & Third-Party Funders.

5.2 A Two-Folded Ethical Dilemma

The ethical considerations analyzed in this chapter are twofold. On one side, the behavior of funders in their relationships with the parties and their lawyers is explained, should funders be subject to any ethical guidelines or not? On the other hand, does TPF practice, as a business, pose a threat to the consistency of the ISDS regime? Both aspects are important. However, the second question is a more serious and direct allegation against TPF. Nevertheless, some states asserted that TPF must be banned until regulated.[10] Not only in practice with the parties of the ISDS system, but also in academia there are some serious accusations against TPF.[11] Thus, maybe it is more important to analyze the criticism against the TPF business. Before these two issues are addressed, the definition of justice and the effect of TPF on access to justice are discussed.

5.3 Ethics of TPF and Access to Justice

The proponents of TPF support TPF arrangements because TPF enables claimants access to justice.[12] This one simple but very strong argument alone seems to be enough to alleviate any ethical concerns that TPF might raise. The use and rapid growth of TPF practices in the world are proving the need for such practice, and providing tools for parties to be able to access justice.[13] TPF arrangements "are supported by some legal ethics because they level the playing field by providing resources for claimants to prosecute 'bet the company' type claims against governments or major multinational companies, which only wealthy individuals are able to afford".[14] There is, however, strong resistance and hostility against TPF as well.

[10] Possible reform of Investor-State dispute settlement (ISDS), Submission from the Government of Morocco, Note by The Secretariat, UNCITRAL Working Group III (ISDS Reform), Thirty-seventh session, (New York, Apr. 1–5, 2019), V 30, U.N. Doc. A/CN.9/WG.III/WP.161 (Mar. 4, 2019).

[11] Rogers (2014); Garcia (2018, July 30).

[12] *See* Lord Justice Jackson (2009), Saadani and Joseph-Louisia (2017); this is stated in UNCITRAL working group discussions and various court decisions as well; see Possible Reform of Investor-State Dispute settlement (ISDS), Third-party funding, Note by the Secretariat, UNCITRAL Working Group III (Investor-State Dispute Settlement Reform), Thirty-seventh session, (Apr. 15, 2019), U.N. Doc. A/CN.9/WG.III/WP.157 (Jan. 24, 2019); Doc. A/CN.9/WG.III/WP.172, https://undocs.org/en/A/CN.9/WG.III/WP.172; Arkin v Borchard Lines Ltd. and others [2005] EWCA Civ 655, p. 38; Campbells Cash and Carry Pty Ltd. v. Fostif Pty Ltd. [2006] HCA 41, p.145; Price Waterhouse Coopers Inc. and Others v National Potato Cooperative Ltd. (448/2003) [2004] ZASCA 64; [2004] 3 All SA 20 (SCA) (1 June 2004), p. 43.

[13] https://www.globenewswire.com/news-release/2021/02/04/2169925/0/en/Global-Litigation-Funding-Investment-Market-to-Cross-USD-13-Billion-in-2021-Rise-in-Pending-Claims-Insolvency-and-Bankruptcy-Due-to-COVID-19-and-Interest-in-ROI-Among-Investors-to-.html.

[14] Chaisse and Eken (2020), p. 119; Steinitz (2011), pp. 1268, 1303–1313.

Some scholars say that third-party funders are loan sharks,[15] or cause exploitation of the system.[16] These two opposite ideas about TPF call for ethical research on the subject.

Undoubtedly, some cases could not be commenced or progress since TPF could not be secured.[17] This is not a desirable legal world. If people cannot bring their cases just because they lack money, or they must discontinue their cases for the same reason, that is a real ethical issue. How can those people try their cases and see whether or not they are right in their claims? If you do not have money, the system is automatically closed to you. There is not even a system for exploitation or swimming as loan sharks. There are many other examples such as the cited news story showing the case could not be brought because TPF could not be secured, and such stories can be seen on a regular basis. This shows that there are cases that could not be initiated because of financial reasons.[18] So, TPF might provide an additional tool for people who want their cases to be heard. However, if TPF is not secured, unfortunately it is the end of the story for those parties who do not have any other financial capacity to bring their cases.

Zoe and Florence state, "while proponents of TPF certainly frame the practice as a response to AtJ [access to justice] concerns, this can only explain one part of the 'demand' side of the TPF story".[19] It is true that funders are not in the business to provide access to justice. Funders are in the business to profit. However, as a side effect of funders' involvement, access to justice is provided to some investors who would otherwise become powerless to initiate their cases. "One of the most important benefits of TPF in international arbitration is that it allows for increased access to justice".[20] Therefore, regardless of the purpose or motive of funders, TPF brings certain access to justice to the system by enabling some additional parties' cases to be heard.

In investment arbitration, one party is always the State, which means the ISDS regime inextricably involves public law elements. The State's loss in an investment case creates a burden on the shoulders of taxpayers. Moreover, funders normally fund claimants against states. Therefore, one question that comes to mind is whether third-party funders who are funding claimants against states bring imbalance to the system? Also, it is principal to scrutinize the results. Let's imagine a state loses and pays a certain award to the investor. The investor is backed by a funder. In that case, a certain amount of that award will go to the funder. So, the result is the transfer of taxpayers' money to funders, who are also investors but are different from the State to investor, because they invested in that dispute to profit from it. Thus, those

[15] *See* Chap. 1 in supra note 23 (Rogers).

[16] *See* Chap. 1 in supra note 33 (Garcia).

[17] Hepburn (2018), https://www-iareporter-com.easyaccess2.lib.cuhk.edu.hk/articles/an-update-on-investment-treaty-disputes-involving-the-government-of-india/.

[18] Regarding the high costs of investment arbitration system, *see* Bottini at Chap. 2 in footnote 94.

[19] Dafe and Williams (2021), pp. 1362–1384.

[20] Massini (2015), p. 325.

wealthy investors who created TPF companies get richer. The second question inquires whether the transfer of taxpayers' money to third-party funders, who are wealthy investors unrelated to the dispute, is ethical or not? The third question is whether the idea that the ISDS regime is corrupted and not efficient anymore because of the involvement of third-party funders? Those questions are concerns in ISDS, but not necessarily in other types of arbitration. Now, we will analyze these issues and try to reach a conclusion in this chapter. First, it is key, to have a healthier apprehension of the theory of justice.

5.3.1 What Is Justice?

To provide a better theoretical framework under this chapter, we first analyze what justice means and how it can be distorted. So, the question here is what is justice? Justice can be defined in various ways. According to remarks of the Hon. Marilyn Warren AC, "there are layers of concepts within the concept of justice".[21] She defines justice according to who you are asking, and everyone defines it differently.[22] According to a lawyer, justice means the application of the rule of law.[23] Or, justice can be defined as simply as "-fairness- which is not at all obscure and is readily grasped even by young children".[24] However, if you go into details and try to search for more specific answers, there are many definitions depending on the type of justice you are looking for such as economic justice, political justice, procedural justice, etc. We do not need to go into that detail and define different types of justice.

To be able to address whether TPF distorts the justice in the ISDS regime, we need to understand the concept of justice and its relationship to "fairness". According to one definition, in all languages, justice "means and denotes the doing of the right thing and refraining from doing the wrong thing".[25] Third-party funders, while granting some parties access to justice, should also act "fairly". Then, we need to balance our arguments around these terms and try to answer whether the actions of third-party funders are fair, what litigation or arbitration is aiming to achieve in the end, and by their involvement, how third-party funders are affecting justice in investment arbitration? Simply, "is it the right thing to do, or is it not" should be the criteria we examine to say whether TPF is ethical or not.

---

[21] What is justice?, Remarks of the Hon. Marilyn Warren AC Chief Justice of Victoria, 2014 Newman Lecture Mannix College, 20 August 2014, available at http://classic.austlii.edu.au/au/journals/VicJSchol/2014/12.pdf. There are more resources on justice, as an example, *see*: Stauffer (2009).

[22] *Ibid.*

[23] *Ibid.*

[24] Raphael (2001), p. 1.

[25] Pikes, Georgios., Geōrgios. Pikēs, Geōrgios. Pikēs, and Ebrary, Inc. Justice and the Judiciary [electronic Resource] (2012), p.7.

Fundamentally, considering what funders are doing is not unfair or wrong. Funders are giving out their money as an investment, and according to their TPF contract with the funded party, when the claim is victorious, they are paid. If one sees this as problematic, one should surely see the problem in the real world, which is that parties do not have equal financial capacity. While one party can afford an army of lawyers with multiple law firms and experts, the other party might not even be able to afford one lawyer in investment arbitration. Having more money increases your chance to present or defend your case better. Therefore, asking for money from third-party funders or investing your money for profit by taking the risk of arbitration or litigation is normal. This is a private contract between funder-funded party. However, what can be problematic is the way in which funders are conducting their business. The conduct of funders can be problematic. As a matter of fact, there are no conduct rules for funders. Not only in investment arbitration, but many jurisdictions also lack conduct rules for third-party funders.[26] Therefore, a practice guideline for funders to set standards is necessary and is spelled out in this book.

Access to justice is a real problem. Not every investor can afford expensive investment arbitration. TPF is not the only way to bring a claim, the investor-state dispute settlement system (ISDS) should offer more options for impecunious investors who wish to bring claims against states, instead of taking the TPF option out of the hands of investors. Some authors attack TPF by stating that "TPF proponents have manipulated the ATJ rationale to their purposes, distorting its traditional applications to fit questionable ends".[27] These arguments seem to forget one indispensable fact about investment arbitration, which is that states failed to honor their responsibilities, mostly under Bilateral Investment Treaties (BIT). Thus, the investor suffered damages and has a claim to bring. If states do not breach BITs, there is no claim to fund. Only after such a breach do investors have the right to get compensation. Funders, by giving money, are assisting investors in getting their legal rights.

Access to justice is a very important ethical reason to support TPF. Having a chance to be able to bring a case, which otherwise might not be possible through the ISDS system alone is a very important reason to support TPF. Many high courts around the world have confirmed this important role of TPF.[28] However, there are some criticisms against TPF in academia. Santosuosso and Scarlett state, "Proponents of TPF in the ISDS context have hijacked this rhetoric to justify speculation on investment claims with far-reaching financial implications for disadvantaged and developing states".[29] Even though they criticize TPF in the ISDS context for hijacking access to justice rhetoric, their reason does not eliminate the fact that TPF gives the *only opportunity* for some investors to bring an ISDS claim.

---

[26] Hong Kong is one of the few examples. See Hong Kong Code of Practice, for TPF of Arbitration.

[27] Santosuosso and Scarlett (2019), p. I.-10.

[28] *See* Price Waterhouse Coopers Inc. and Others v National Potato Co-operative Ltd. (448/2003) [2004] ZASCA 64; [2004] 3 All SA 20 (SCA) (1 Haziran 2004), p. 43; [2006] HCA 41, p. 145; [2005] EWCA Civ 655, p. 38.

[29] Santosuosso and Scarlett (2019), p. I.-10.

Moreover, the financial implications of TPF are not far-reaching. TPF is not a threat for states. TPF is a tool for investors who have been treated illegally by states to bring their cases. If states want to be on the safe side of the ISDS system, they simply follow the rule of law and that way should not breach the rights of investors.

The criticism against TPF continues; "the funder would necessarily factor this correlation into its risk analysis when selecting claims to fund, resulting in non-merit-based factors driving claim selection and more claims being directed at the least-developed countries ("LDCs")".[30] How this conclusion can be reached is not clear to the author of this book. Funders invest in cases, and they want their cases to win so that they can get a share from the award. If they invest in cases that they are likely to lose, then this would mean they are wasting their money. Therefore, this argument does not make sense.

Access to justice is one of the common benefits of TPF. "Some of the most commonly cited benefits of TPF are an increased access to justice, financial management, and efficiency".[31] There are risks to TPF, too. "The most commonly cited risks are the increase in frivolous claims, conflicts of interest, inability to finance adverse costs, and waiving privilege".[32] However, as stated, frivolous claims are not possible effects of TPF in ISDS cases. Funders have a strict merit assessment of cases and therefore have high rejection rates as elaborated in other parts of this book.[33]

5.3.2 Weeding Mechanism

TPF creates another important natural result. Funders ultimately decide which case to fund, and which case not to fund, meaning that they decide which case will have access to justice and which case will not. This book defends the idea that, if there is an ethical problem for TPF, this role is played out by funders deciding which cases are passing through this "weeding mechanism" and which do not. Considering that funders reject more than 90–95% of the cases they are presented with, what happens to those rejected cases needs to be studied further.

Third-party funders are providing access to justice. However, the question here is: Who can access it? Naturally, third-party funders act as a gateway between access to justice and potential access to justice seekers, merely funded parties. Funders accept very few cases among many applications. The majority still cannot get funds, they must finance their cases in other ways, or they cannot bring their cases. Is this a desirable situation? No. However, it is still better than having no option. Otherwise, maybe those who sought and succeeded in getting TPF, less than 5–10% of the total

[30] Santosuosso and Scarlett (2019), p. I.-13.

[31] Massini (2015), p. 324.

[32] Massini (2015), p. 324.

[33] See Chaps. 2 and 4.

applications, would not have a chance to bring their cases and be heard by arbitration tribunals. The cases rejected by funders would not necessarily lose if they were heard. Therefore, in an ideal world, all cases should be heard. However, now funders have the key to access ISDS for parties who do not otherwise have the financial capacity to bring their cases, and funders decide who will have access to justice and who will not.

In conclusion, because of this role played by funders, TPF "is rightly considered as a weeding mechanism which eliminates weaker claims".[34] It is a fact that funders invest in cases and therefore they are choosing very carefully which case to invest in. Naturally, a very small number of cases can get funded. As a result, funders are becoming a gateway to the ISDS system for those who want to bring their cases with the help of TPF. Which case will be initiated, and which case will not be initiated is eventually decided by funders. Is it good that funders decide this? This can be argued, but for now this is the reality. Funders are private actors in this relationship, and they are operating for profit. No authority can force a funder to fund a case if they do not think it is a good investment. If this weeding mechanism is not a desirable situation, then alternative TPF options should be made available for both investors and respondent states.

5.3.3 Structural Imbalance: Is It a Reason to Abandon TPF?

Another consideration on whether access to justice is or is not a good thing in investment arbitration is the structural imbalance between the respondent states and investors. Investors are normally the funded parties in ISDS. This is not a deliberate choice by funders. However, due to the structure, since funders generally fund claimants and claimants are always investors, then as a natural consequence investors are the funded parties in investment arbitration.[35]

The question here is should this be a reason to deny access to justice to investors just because states cannot get TPF in this process? The answer in the opinion of the author of this book is no. This is because first, investors do not bring a case without a reason. Respondent states breached their rights and as a result, a claim was raised by investors. And second, not having the opportunity to defend a case does not justify removing such a tool from the other party who can use it. If states need such TPF, alternative TPF should be created for them, rather than removing the existing ones. Therefore, the author concludes that no one should escape from liability for their illegal actions, including the respondent states. And, not having a finance tool for states that is similar to TPF does not justify depriving investors of such TPF.

[34] *See* Chap. 1 in supra note 5 (Frignati), p. 509.

[35] None of the funders I interviewed in Chap. 4 stated that they but funded a respondent state. Some even stated that they have financial tools for the respondent states, in practice, they all funded only Claimant investors.

States, like any other party, should bear the consequences of their actions if they breached the law or their responsibilities to investors. Just because the states cannot get TPF, should not make TPF unavailable to investors. States usually are the superior parties in investment arbitration. They have the resources to cover their own expenses in investment arbitration unless they are, small island-states with very limited resources. Investors, on the other hand, are generally unable to bring a case since they might be bankrupted if they lost all their investments in the respondent state. Therefore, investors are the party that needs TPF the most in investment arbitration.[36] And the fact that investors are always or almost always funded by funders ought not to be a reason to ban TPF and abolish this financial tool for investors. This would only prove how much investors need such TPF, and more alternative TPF should be made available to them.

In short, there is a structural problem in the ISDS regime not affiliated with TPF, and therefore there is a counterblast against ISDS.[37] Frignati states that:

"TPF provides a remedy to this problem, by ensuring equal access to arbitration for parties that wish to avail themselves of it, by levelling the playing field, and thus removing "the risk of a world where only rich claimants are entitled to justice".[38]

Whether or not this is the best option can be argued, but this is one of the few options available on the market and it is a necessary tool to increase the use of investment arbitration mechanisms. Otherwise, states might easily breach their obligations under BITs. The more funders on the market, the more chances for cases to be heard. TPF increases accessibility but still, considering the high rejection rates, most cases do not pass the funders' threshold. What must be done is that all cases must be heard. Therefore, financial options must be increased not only for investors but should also be available for states.

5.3.4 More Money, More Power

It is true that "a wealthy litigant, who can outspend a poorer litigant, is generally at an advantage and may be able to obtain a favorable settlement through attrition".[39] Therefore, someone who can barely afford investment arbitration might not have a good chance even if that investor has a meritorious case. If the investors' funds are exhausted before the case ends, the investor might need to settle at a much lower amount than it would recover if they could continue with its case. Therefore, it is a fact that the more money one can spend on their cases, the more chance they have to prove or defend their cases. And, if one starts their case with limited funds and the

[36] In a small number of cases, respondent states were funded. See more explanations in Chap. 3.

[37] Waibel et al. (2010): Wolters Kluwer Law & Business; Sold and Distributed in North, Central and South America by Aspen, 2010; Berge and St John (2021), pp. 584–610.

[38] *See* Chap. 1 in supra note 5 (Frignati), p. 507.

[39] Douglas (2005), p. 649.

case continues longer than expected, it is possible the funds will be exhausted, and the claim holder will have to find alternative funding or settle with the respondent State. Considering this, it is true that funders offer the opportunity to defend one's case better and longer by providing financial support. Thus, if one is not able to fund the whole case, funding the case after one's own funds are exhausted is also possible.

What is interesting is that TPF brings equality to the party that does not have enough money and in its circumstance normally is not equal to the party that has money. Equality in the judicial process means access to lawyers, legal advice, and being able to continue its judicial process without any financial concern. Enabling access to justice is accepted by many scholars and judges cited in this chapter. What TPF provides is added flexibility for even large and financially strong companies.[40] If a financially capable company wants to invest in another project rather than paying legal fees, it can use TPF for more flexibility to pay the legal costs for such proceedings. Therefore, TPF is not only used by penniless investors but also by large corporations that do not have any financial difficulty.

TPF turns this inaccessible judicial mechanism into a possible and accessible system and thus it enables access to justice.[41] However, as stated above, not everyone is happy with this. Some suggestions are to ban TPF completely. "At a minimum, however, UNCITRAL must take immediate steps to prevent exploitative speculation by funders given the implications for developing and less-developed states".[42] Why is bringing a rightful claim seen as exploitation? It is not a matter of funders robbing states. Funders help investors who have been treated illegally by states and post their investment to get compensation from that state. If what is wanted from the ISDS system is creating a mechanism where investors cannot easily access, and states can only be sued when the claimant has the financial ability to bring a case, it is obvious that respondent states will prefer that, then TPF is not necessary. However, if what is wanted is a mechanism where investors have more options to access more easily, they can access the system and have the opportunity for their cases to be heard. The first scenario would create an idle system, whereas the second one would create a more effective system. Therefore, the second scenario better serves the purpose of having an efficient judicial mechanism.

Another criticism against TPF is that it "is more focused on large, well-resourced claimants and creative accounting that allows corporations to keep the costs of litigation off-balance sheet".[43] Is that a bad thing? Why is it presented as a bad thing? There are examples of access to justice, but if large companies are using TPF more often it is not necessarily wrong, it is just a reflection of what is occuring in the market. Funders do not offer to fund impecunious investors or any specific group,

---

[40] TPF is not used only by small investors but large companies who as well want to transfer the risk of litigation/arbitration to funders for various reasons.

[41] More explanations regarding the theory of justice and TPF interaction are discussed in Chap. 5. Ethical considerations can be found in the Chap. 4 as well.

[42] Santosuosso and Scarlett (2019), p. I.-16.

[43] Santosuosso and Scarlett (2019), p. I.-16.

they offer their service to profit. As a result, some parties who are otherwise unable to bring a case benefit from this service. However, not only those, but financially sound investors might also use this service. Whomever is using the service is the result of it being available. If there is an available option helping investors to manage their arbitration/litigation costs, then it is reasonable for them to use such options. Judging who uses TPF cannot be an argument against TPF.

5.3.5 The Purpose of the ISDS Regime and TPF's Role

TPF has raised more concerns in investment arbitration. There are some articles that accuse TPF of exploiting the investment arbitration regime.[44] Garcia suggests that "TPF in investment arbitration could in fact be working as an exploitation of the investment law system, respondent states, and their citizens".[45] He further suggests that TPF exploits the ISDS system "for the benefit of speculative financiers".[46] However, Garcia fundamentally does not blame TPF, he blames the BIT/ISDS regime by stating that the "BIT/ISDS system today is fundamentally flawed".[47] The reason he gives is unfair advantage-taking.[48] Another paper points out that it is the exploitation of funded parties in litigation funding, not states. Its counterpart would be exploitation of investors,[49] not exploitation of states that have no contracts or transactions with funders.[50] It is true as Garcia states that the BIT system is flawed and imperfect. However, this book does not agree that funders take unfair advantage of states. If a State breached the law and illegally expropriated investors' assets or harmed investors in other illegal ways, states should be responsible, and giving money to such parties is not exploitation of law-breaking states. States are not usual parties to TPF agreements and supporting only one party cannot be unfair. It is an unfair advantage against the funded parties only if funders take large percentages of the award, and this is addressed in the best practice guideline.[51]

The ISDS regime serves to ensure that investors will be compensated if the State takes an unlawful action against the investor. Investment arbitration stays within public law domains because of its sensitive function. When the states lose against investors, this means transferring the wealth of its citizens to investors for

[44] *See* Chap. 2 in supra note 108 (Garcia), p. 2911.

[45] *Ibid,* 2914.

[46] *Ibid.* 2919.

[47] *Ibid.*

[48] *Ibid.* 2919–2920.

[49] Investors here refer to investors in ISDS, who invested in a State and are now initiating a claim against that State for compensation, the party to the investment claim.

[50] Attrill (2019), p. 3 Available at https://portal.omnibridgeway.com/docs/default-source/site-documents/ethical-issues-paper-imf09%2D%2D-globalaw-conference.pdf.

[51] See the best practice guideline.

compensation. If it is for a justified purpose, there is no objection to that. However, when the investor is funded by a funder, then the situation is not that straightforward and can be more problematic by some viewpoints. Here, a third-party funder invests in a case to profit. Then when the funded party prevails, the funder gets an important portion of the award for profit, which is paid by the taxpayers' money. The question here is whether it is ethical to let funders profit from a system that was initially designed to protect and remedy investors? This is our starting point but there are many layers to discuss in the ethical consideration of TPF.

TPF has not only been blamed in the ISDS regime. There are other examples where TPF was blamed as a weapon against the media,[52] as a threat against companies,[53] and even against auditors.[54] Garcia says that TPF "is explicitly designed to take advantage of the asymmetric structure of the investment regime today for the benefit of speculative finance".[55] This is not true. Funders operate more often in litigation and commercial arbitration. This is because of the natural result of the fact that the number of disputes in courts and commercial arbitration is higher than the number of disputes in ISDS. No funder in the market solely invests in investment arbitration cases.[56] To have a better analysis, one needs to look at the underlying reasons for those accusations. Maybe the arguments from the states are the easiest to understand. TPF generally, if not always, funds claimants in ISDS cases, so funders are increasing their chances of states launching cases against them. Thus, it is not difficult to understand why states are against TPF. Maybe some scholars criticize TPF more objectively, and their arguments can give us better directions for analysis.

The development of the TPF industry is highly related to the reality of litigation and arbitration finance. "The legal ethics paradigm, while superficially very attractive given certain similarities between contingency attorneys and funders, proves, upon closer consideration, to fall woefully short in explaining and addressing the economic reality of litigation finance".[57] Some authors suggest that the legal ethics paradigm is not enough. This section has not discussed legal ethics to explain the funder's point of view, rather demonstrated and critically analyzed the discussions on ethical aspects of TPF and concluded that those criticisms against TPF are not

[52] Levi (2017), p. 761.

[53] Anon, 2017. Allianz Head of Management Liability: Companies Face Growing Threat from Litigation Funding. A.M. Best Newswire, pp. A.M. Best Newswire, 2017–02-24; Green (2017), p. 73.

[54] Anon, 2007. Litigation funding poses threat to auditors, p. 9.

[55] *See* Chap. 2 in supra note 108 (Garcia).

[56] Chapter 4, empirical research conducted with funders present this result. On the contrary, many funders do not invest in investment arbitration and a small pool of investors, compared to a large number of total third-party funding companies, which is over 800 funders in the world, invest in ISDS cases. However, again, this is just additional to TPF of other cases in commercial arbitration and litigation. Thus, what Garcia suggests does not reflect reality.

[57] Steinitz (2015), p. 1209.

right. Moreover, TPF of litigation and commercial arbitration has not attracted as many concerns as TPF of ISDS claims. Therefore, the unique criticism against TPF of ISDS makes this chapter another important part of this book, which is specifically focused on the following paragraphs.

5.3.5.1 Does TPF Pose Ethical Threats to the Investment Arbitration Regime

Whether TPF poses an ethical threat to the ISDS regime or not depends on how one interprets the function of ISDS. There are two main views on ISDS; one sees it as a mechanism that "facilitates sustainable development" and the other sees ISDS as a mechanism "providing recourse for foreign investors when governments act in ways that violate applicable treaty-based protections for their investments".[58] "Debates over third-party funding in the field of investment arbitration, in particular, are closely linked to the different views about the overarching purpose of the investment itself and the role of investment treaty arbitration".[59] As can be easily seen, according to the first view, TPF has no place since it does not contribute to sustainable development in any way. The only motive of funders, at least commercial funders, is to make a profit out of their investment. According to the second view, however, TPF is useful since it facilitates the investor by providing an alternative financing option to bring its investment cases. When one considers the role of ISDS by considering these two views, then TPF has a good place since it facilitates the system by increasing accessibility of the ISDS regime.

5.3.5.2 When Are Funders Involved?

Funders are not the ones creating disputes, funders get involved when the dispute has already arisen. This should not be forgotten. It is as simple as the fact that if states do not breach BITs there will be no cases to fund. So, the starting point of investment disputes is the breach of BITs by the respondent states.[60] Now the second step is after the dispute has arisen. At this point, investors have two options: to bring the case, or not to bring the case. What do we want to achieve with the investment arbitration? That is the question. Do we want a system, which is virtually there, but not accessible to all investors or even accessible to the potential users of the system in which investors are not willing because investment arbitration is too risky? Or do we want a system where there are additional financial tools to make the use of the

[58] Brekoulakis and Rogers (2019), p. 1.

[59] *Ibid.*

[60] For a detailed analysis of third-party funded cases, see Chap. 3.

system easier and more accessible? This book supports that the second idea should be the purpose.

Now, to start with the first step, funders are not making money out of anything; the prerequisite of ISDS is the unlawful action of a state. Thus, funders are not exploiting states when they did nothing wrong; however, they are helping to initiate arbitration cases against those states who have committed unlawful actions against investors. In this way, the third-party funder is not doing anything other than helping justice be served by facilitating the ISDS regime. With this set out, of course, the number of cases will increase when there is an additional financial tool for investors to bring their cases. Moreover, funders do not deliberately choose to fund only investors and not fund states. The structure of ISDS creates the result that investors are always claimants and states are respondents. Although nearly all arbitration rules provide for the right to assert counterclaims in investor-state disputes, many tribunals are reluctant to allow such counterclaims.[61] Investment arbitration tribunals do not commonly award damages in favor of investors to pay a monetary sum to states.[62] Moreover, some tribunals expressly voiced that they do not have an *ipso facto* consent to be sufficient to conclude that an investor's consent to ICSID counterclaims is automatic. And they found that the tribunal does not have jurisdiction over the State's counterclaims.[63] Therefore, as a result, counterclaims are difficult, if not impossible, to bring by the states in investment arbitration.

Since there is a scarcity of counterclaims and as the structure of ISDS and BITs, investors are the claimants who are demanding money from states. As a result, funders fund investors rather than respondent states. Realistically, investors are generally the party that is also in a difficult position due to obvious reasons such that if the investment failes, they might be in bankruptcy or not in a financially sound position to bear the high costs of investment arbitration. If investors cannot bring cases, then there is a real access to justice problem. TPF solves this problem to some extent. Then, what is the problem here? Technically, we can mention two problems. One is that states do not have access to this financial tool. And the second is that the motive of funders is not to provide access to justice but to profit. The first issue can be addressed by giving the opportunity to states, which is included in the best practice guideline proposed in this book.[64]

The second is related to the motives of funders. Now, we will turn to this subject that has not been sufficiently discussed. Even though there are some papers on the

---

[61] Kryvoi (2012) available at https://scholarship.law.umn.edu/mjil/321.

[62] Except for the costs of the arbitration if the investor loses the investment arbitration.

[63] Karkey Karadeniz Elektrik Uretim A.S. v. Islamic Republic of Pakistan, ICSID Case No. ARB/13/1, Award, para. 1015–1016. The award cites other investment arbitration awards where similar judgments are given: *See* CA-314, Roussalis v. Romania, ¶¶ 868-77 (analyzing the language of the BIT and denying jurisdiction over the Respondent's counterclaims); CA-321, Saluka Investments BV v. Czech Republic, UNCITRAL, Decision on Jurisdiction over the Czech Republic's Counterclaim, 7 May 2004; CA-124, Sergei Paushok et al. v. Mongolia, UNCITRAL, Award on Jurisdiction and Liability, 28 April 2011.

[64] See the best practice guideline in Chap. 7.

ethical issues TPF raises, those have not been discussed with as much detail and as deserved. Here is an ethical analysis of the monetization of investment claims.

5.3.5.3 Monetization of Legal Claims

The main criticism against TPF is around the idea of monetization of legal claims. The first question is whether it is ethical to monetize disputes? The second question, related to the first, is whether it is ethical to profit from those disputes? The third question is whether monetization is going to increase the number of disputes? The fourth question is, would that increase the number of meritless cases? Those ethical questions can be raised against TPF both in litigation finance, and arbitration finance. This book is focused on these questions in the context of investment arbitration.

ISDS is a specific procedure designed to resolve claims of investors against states. It is "a procedural mechanism that allows an investor from one country to bring arbitral proceedings directly against the country in which it has invested".[65] This type of arbitration differs from commercial arbitration because the public interest is at a much higher stake. The confidentiality that is important for both parties in commercial arbitration and a very important feature of the international arbitration system, is focused on transparency when it comes to investment arbitration. This is because ISDS relates to the public interest. In commercial arbitration, when parties lose, the losing party pays by using its own money since both parties in commercial arbitration are private parties; however, in investment arbitration, when state loses, state pays with the taxpayers' money, which means by collecting taxes from the citizens of that state. Thus, it has a high public profile and arbitration proceedings in investment disputes are much more transparent than commercial arbitration disputes. Therefore, the parties who get involved with the case become more important. This public nature of ISDS creates specific ethical concerns over TPF that are only applicable to investment arbitration but not to commercial arbitration or litigation.

First, the discussion should be focused on whether is it ethical to monetize disputes? There are articles taking this problem into account for tribunals and policymakers.[66] This book defends the idea that funders are not funding cases for no good reason. There is an underlying reason to be able to initiate an investment arbitration case and it is ethical to fund such legal cases. The fact that the funders will be paid by the taxpayers' money cannot be a reason to stop TPF. Around the world, all governments use the money of taxpayers. Some use this money reasonably and some waste taxpayers' money. This is the reality of the situation. With the presence of TPF, hopefully, governments will better realize that if they breach the rights of foreign investors, those investors have the chance to bring a case against them. And one hopes this will lead the governments to act lawfully. Arbitration is a risky

---

[65] https://uk.practicallaw.thomsonreuters.com/0-624-6147?transitionType=Default&contextData=(sc.Default)&firstPage=true.

[66] Chaisse and Eken (2020), pp. 113–166.

process and funders take it on by paying all legal costs. Without TPF, not every investor would want to take such a high risk. Therefore, every claim holder considers the matter carefully before initiating legal mechanisms whether to take the risks of arbitration or try to settle the claim.

5.3.6 Conclusion

It is true that the world is changing as have legal rules. Now that champerty and maintenance rules have been abolished in the world, financing tools are developing more flexibly. In the past, it was not possible for lawyers to take a stake in a case, but now "financial assistance and acquisition of interests rules ought to be abolished or substantially amended".[67] TPF is now a reality and operates as an accepted practice in many jurisdictions. Rules providing a better operating system for TPF will also develop.

No matter how one addresses TPF, whether as a loan shark or exploiter, if one party cannot bring their case without the help of such TPF, then it is a fact that TPF provides access to justice for those parties. We do not need to provide numbers regarding investment arbitration to show how expensive it is. It is notoriously expensive and the epitome of the high cost dispute settlement mechanism. One does not need to be an oracle to see that not everyone can afford it. Then, the ordinary inquiry would be, how we can make ISDS more accessible? TPF is one answer to this question, and it seems to be working well. However, of course, it is not free of problems. The lack of code of conduct rules is an obvious one. Therefore, the best practice guideline provided by this book offers an important solution to this problem. This guideline is provided through a doctrinal and empirical analysis of the topic and covers a great number of potential problems TPF arrangements might raise. Also, this guideline is the first comprehensive guideline analyzing TPF practice in ISDS from both ethical and procedural aspects.

How does TPF improve or obstruct the (notion of) justice in arbitration? TPF makes it easier for investors to access the ISDS system. It is not harming the justice system to have funders operating in the high market standards. As long as funders operate according to those high standards, TPF provides access to justice and poses no real risk to the integrity of the ISDS system.

---

[67] Moliterno (2003), p. 256.

5.4 Ethical Considerations: General Concerns Over TPF

There are some concerns over TPF that evolved from history and are rooted in some of the national systems around the world. These concerns are usually not relevant to investment arbitration. However, they are related to ethical considerations and thus, it is important to mention them here briefly.

5.4.1 Champerty and Maintenance Doctrines

Champerty and maintenance are ancient doctrines, developed in common law jurisdictions to protect the integrity of the judicial system from external involvements. Historically, there were champerty and maintenance doctrines that were designed to prevent such intermeddling for reasons explained previously.[68] The elements of champerty are: "(1) a party undertakes; (2) to further another's interest in a suit; (3) in exchange for a part of any favorable litigation result".[69] As can be seen, champerty is the definition of TPF. If champerty were still in effect, TPF would not be possible. Maintenance is described as:

"the ... encouragement to one of the parties to an action by a person who has neither an interest in the action nor any other motive recognized by the law as justifying his interference".[70] TPF is more than encouragement; it is monetary support for the party. The question here in this chapter is: is it ethical? Is it ethical to borrow money from someone, is it ethical for someone to make a profit from a case and what is the relationship between champerty and maintenance? The reasons why these doctrines were developed will answer this question.

Champerty was an embodiment of ethics. Steinitz said, "the outdated ethics regulation, predominantly in the form of the doctrine of champerty".[71] However, as Steinitz stated, champerty is an "outdated" regulation and has been abolished in many jurisdictions. It is a fact in today's world that financing one's case is an essential consideration that every claim holder must decide. If one does not have money to bring their case, would that be ethical? Considering today's investment arbitration regime, one cannot deny that there are positive and negative developments. Before the ISDS system, diplomatic relations were often used option if there was an international trade dispute which could result in war.[72] Now there is an investment arbitration mechanism, which is governed by rules, which constitutes a

[68] See Chap. 2.

[69] McLaughlin (2007), p. 639; see also Martin (1999), p. 58; Martin (1992), pp. 485–511.

[70] EWLC, Proposals for the Reform of the Law relating to Maintenance and Champerty (Rep. 7, 1966), at para. [3], see: https://www.lawcom.gov.uk/project/proposals-for-reform-of-the-law-relating-to-maintenance-and-champerty/.

[71] Steinitz (2011), p. 1271.

[72] Gertz et al. (2018), pp. 239–252.

huge step for the resolution of investment disputes. However, there is also a downside, which is the cost of this system. Therefore, high costs are barriers for investors who do not have the financial capacity to cover these high costs. Since there is no champerty doctrine applicable in investment arbitration, there is no obstacle to covering the costs of arbitration with TPF agreements.

There is also another doctrine called "usury" in common law jurisdictions. "Usury" refers to the "exacting, taking, or receiving of a greater rate of interest than is allowed by law for the use or loan of money".[73]

Without going into the details of usury, which may vary depending on the jurisdiction, we can conclude that since the funder's return is contingent upon the success of the funded party; a typical TPF agreement does not constitute usury. If the funder loses the case, the funder does not charge any interest and moreover, the funder loses all of his/her investment. Therefore, a TPF arrangement is highly unlikely to be tainted by usury laws, even when such laws are applicable.[74] However, the question here again relates to the ethics. Usury is closely related to ethics. If someone is exploiting a party due to their financial circumstances, lends money with higher rates, and takes more than they deserve, then this is not an ethical arrangement. Similarly, if, in investment arbitration, a third-party funder charges a party more than market rates, because no other funder would fund that case, then this arrangement would not be ethical either. Funders should not exploit and charge more than what is allowed by the market standards. In the best practice guideline in Chap. 7 in this book provides a rule on this issue.

In civil law jurisdictions, there were prohibitions similar to common law champerty and maintenance doctrines. Like champerty in common law, civil law had also a rule called the "Quota Litis Pact". "The purpose of the Roman-Dutch rule pactum de quota litis was to deter attorneys and advocates from speculating in litigation".[75] Therefore, we would conclude that similar rules were applied throughout history in civil law, common law, or Sharia law jurisdictions to protect the integrity of the judicial system and to prevent any external interference. However, through the strengthening of the judiciary, those doctrines were abolished, and today they are no longer effective, or effective only in very limited situations.

Investment arbitration operates at the supranational level. However, the lawyers operating in this system are educated in different jurisdictions. There are no maintenance and champerty doctrines operating in investment arbitration. Nevertheless, in arbitration, there are general legal principles protecting the integrity of the investment arbitration tribunals and investment arbitration process such as fair play and natural justice. Moreover, many arbitrators are educated in common law jurisdictions. They are educated about these doctrines in different degrees. Since

[73] Seaton v. City of Lexington, 97 S.W.3d 72, 76 (Mo. Ct. App. 2002).

[74] Even in Sharia Law, there are similar probations, *see* Eken (2021), www.transnational-dispute-management.com.

[75] Khoza (2018), pp. 1–22, 4 citing to Hollard v Zietsman 1885 6 NLR 93; also see Price Waterhouse Coopers 76.

they have this education in their roots and their way of thinking, they might have negative connotations about TPF or third-party funders. Arbitrators must ensure that these negative connotations will not affect their decision in favor of or against any party.

These doctrines, however, are no longer applicable in many jurisdictions and have not been for a long time. Jeremy Bentham mentioned these doctrines, and how they were no longer applicable when he wrote in the nineteenth century:

> the sword of a baron, stalking into court with a rabble of retainers at his heels, might strike terror into the eyes of a judge upon the bench. At present, what cares an English judge for the swords of an hundred barons?.[76]

A few centuries ago then, if we were discussing TPF, it would probably have been unethical. Now, the doctrines are no longer effective and have been abolished. In today's world, it is clear it is no longer unethical due to the abolition of the champerty and maintenance doctrines. Therefore, we can conclude that champerty, maintenance, usury, or battery do not pose the ethical dangers they posed centuries ago. These doctrines alone do not raise any ethical concerns in investment arbitration. However, the way funders operate might create some concerns. Now, funders' conduct and their relations with other investment arbitration actors will be discussed in more detail.

There are many concerns that are specific to investment arbitration and they will be expanded on below.

5.5 Ethical Considerations: Specific Concerns over TPF in the Investment Arbitration Regime

Problems and ethical concerns are not specific to TPF. "Modern investment treaties and treaty models increasingly include stricter ethical standards" and "Furthermore, in its new agreements the EU has replaced traditional ISDS with an Investment Court System (ICS)".[77] Thus even now the current ISDS regime is under the threat of being replaced by a court system. However, there are views that the ICSID will stay as is because "the emergence of institutional competition from other regions of the world is constrained by network effects".[78] Whether it is an investment arbitration platform resolving investment disputes, or it is another platform would not change the fact that TPF is widely used. This is because it is well established in many jurisdictions, and TPF will continue being used in the ISDS regime, whether by arbitration or in courts. Thus, this chapter, without elaborating on whether investment arbitration is

[76] Bentham, Jeremy. Defence of Usury, Payne and Foss, London, 1818, s.40.

[77] Brauch (2019). The European Commission suggests that the existing arbitration system should be replaced with an investment court and promotes the establishment of a Multilateral Investment Court.

[78] Bjorklund and Druzin (2018), p. 707.

the best way for resolving investment disputes, or should be replaced with a court system, analyzes whether TPF distorts justice in the ISDS regime somehow, as is claimed by its opponents.

Some concerns specific to litigation funding are not mirrored in TPF in investment arbitration. For example, in some cases third-party funders take so much money in consumer litigation cases that "even when the consumer wins or settles the case, they often recover no money, because the entire award or settlement goes to pay the plaintiff's attorneys or to repay the lawsuit lender".[79] In investment arbitration however, the money at stake is high so there is no such fear, and as a result there have been no such concerns expressed in the literature. Steinitz presents the incorporation paradigm in her article and addresses these problems, namely, (1) extreme conflicts of interests; (2) extreme information asymmetries; (3) extreme uncertainty; and (4) inappropriate commodification".[80] This section follows a different structure.

In this section, first, general ideas about the ethicality and legality of TPF agreements are considered. Other ethical issues might arise because of TPF arrangements. Garcia argues that "allowing speculative finance a stake in the outcome of ISDS claims, a voice in the determination of which cases to bring, which arbitrators to choose, and which cases to settle amounts to nothing less than a deliberate exploitation of the flaws in the BIT system for the benefit of speculators and at the cost of already-burdened respondent states, their taxpayers, and citizens".[81] This should be addressed. If funders are appointing arbitrators who work together behind the scenes, and those arbitrators are always voting for the funded parties, these are serious threats to the legal system. However, thinking that this concern is only specific to funders, and not to law firms or individual parties themselves would be a huge oversight. How can one be sure that big law firms, boutique arbitration firms acting in investment arbitration cases regularly, or parties who are regular users of arbitration do not have such connections with arbitrators? This is the system-wide problem of arbitration and is not specific to TPF. Therefore, TPF does not cause any additional threat to the system other than those that already exist.

TPF arrangements might create ethical problems for several parties. Ethics in arbitration is important not only for third-party funders; but for all other participants of the system, especially for arbitrators, experts, and lawyers.[82] As Frignati correctly brings up "menages a trois . . . have never enjoyed a good reputation; on the contrary, they have tended to provoke suspicion".[83] The tangled relationships between arbitrators-lawyers-parties can become even more tangled by the participation of the funder. Frignati continues:

[79] Justin Hakes is quoted in Merzer (2013, April 19).

[80] Steinitz (2015), p. 1209.

[81] *See* Chap. 2 in supra note 108 (Garcia), p. 2923.

[82] For arbitrators' ethics; *See* Brower, Charles. *'The Ethics of Arbitration: Perspectives from a Practicing International Arbitrator': Keynote Address at the Riesenfeld Symposium, University of California (2010)* available at https://bjil.typepad.com/brower_final.pdf.

[83] *See* Chap. 1 in supra note 5 (Frignati), p. 510.

> The involvement of a third-party funder in arbitration poses complex ethical issues because of the fact that it may create conflicts of interest for attorneys and arbitrators.[84]

These problems can increase throughout the case with the continuous relationship between the client-lawyer-funder. Frignati rightly concludes:

> Indeed, the influence and control exercised by funders may affect the attorney-client (the funded party) relationship, as well as the independence of arbitrators. Confidentiality, evidentiary privileges, and professional independence are the key ethical concerns that TPF puts in question.[85]

5.5.1 Confidentiality

The first ethical concern regarding the effect of TPF on the client-attorney relationship is confidentiality. It is a right concern to have that "attorneys or clients could share confidential information with the third party", which is elevating both moral and actual disturbance.[86] Therefore, client confidentiality might be affected by funders' involvement. Attorney-client privilege does not cover the funder-client relationship. Therefore, documents given to funders are not privileged. Also, while lawyers have professional duties to keep those documents confidential, funders are under no such obligation.

Therefore, "litigation funding raises concerns about client confidentiality, regardless of whether the TPF is sought by the client or by the attorney. For instance, a litigation funding company may require a client who applies for TPF to have his attorney provide the company with otherwise confidential information that will allow the company to decide whether it should fund the case".[87]

This constitutes an additional reason why the lawyers acting in the dispute should not be advising on TPF agreements. Furthermore, funders collect all the documents from parties resulting in a huge amount of data in their hands. How funders might use these documents in other cases against the same party is a big concern. This type of concern about confidentiality and privilege needs to be addressed in a guideline.[88]

Some Bar Associations have considered these issues. The Philadelphia Committee was asked about this issue and answered: "The importance of consultation with the client about the possible risk of loss of not only client confidentiality but also of the attorney-client privilege because of supplying [case] assessment-type information to the potential lender cannot be underestimated. The [attorney] is well advised to document carefully the client's assent to the disclosure and, even then, to make it clear to the lender that the disclosures will be restricted as much as possible-perhaps

---

[84] *Ibid.*

[85] *Ibid.*

[86] *Ibid.* page. 1299.

[87] Douglas (2005), p. 674.

[88] See Best Practice Guideline in Chap. 7.

even limited to only that information which would be discoverable without intrusion upon the privilege".[89] Thus, we can see that some bar associations agree about the concerns on the effect of TPF on privilege. However, in investment arbitration, this issue has not been considered yet, apart from draft disclosure rules regarding TPF.[90]

Not only bar associations but also some scholars have expressed concerns on confidentiality.

> In summation, due to the existence of TPF, confidentiality as a duty towards the client during the due diligence process, and conflicts of interest during the arbitral proceedings may well become problematic from a counsel's perspective. Given the absence of a precise ethical system all the potential ethical issues faced by an attorney in international arbitration involving TPF, the best solution may be to expressly regulate them in the TPF agreement.[91]

These types of questions will create more questions, one of which is that should there be any privilege for the documents and emails exchanged between funders and funded parties like the privilege between attorney and clients? And the answer is probably going to be "yes". Having a privilege for the communication between the funder and client will ensure that the relationship is safe and free from external intervention.[92]

As stated, funders do not have professional bodies to regulate their relationship with their clients. However, lawyers do have such professional rules. And in some jurisdictions, there are rules about the relationship between the lawyer and funder when a third-party funder pays lawyers' fees. As an example, the American Bar Association (ABA) Model rules provide certain conditions for third party payment of the legal fees of lawyers.[93] Lawyers who are subject to such rules need to follow them. Still, having a specific regulation for funders is needed, too. This is because first, not all lawyers have such rules in their jurisdictions to ensure their independence when they receive money from third parties. Second, it is because having no rules to follow, there is no mechanism ensuring that funders are operating in compliance with the best practices. Thus, professional conduct rules for funders are needed.

[89] Philadelphia Bar Ass'n, Profl Guidance Comm., Op. No. 99-8, at 1 (Feb. 2000) from Douglas (2005), p. 675.

[90] For the draft disclosure and security for costs rules regarding TPF, *see* https://icsid.worldbank.org/sites/default/files/documents/ICSID_WP_Six.pdf However, the practice guideline this book proposes brings rules on confidentiality.

[91] *See* Chap. 1 in supra note 5 (Frignati), p. 512.

[92] *See* the practice guideline this book; which proposes bringing rules on privilege.

[93] *See* https://www.americanbar.org/groups/litigation/committees/commercial-business/practice/2019/when-a-third-party-pays-legal-fees/.

5.5.2 Disclosure and Transparency

Disclosure is important, as explained in Chap. 3, in which existing and potential procedural problems raised in the present case law on TPF in investment arbitration are analyzed.[94] However, disclosure is also important for ethical reasons, especially the transparency of the ISDS system.

International arbitration has already received many criticisms; one of which is the lack of transparency.[95] The unique feature of ISDS is that it requires utmost transparency.[96] In ISDS, transparency is very important and the involvement of funders, if unknown, increases issues of transparency. Therefore, disclosure is not only procedural but also an ethical concern. To have a more transparent system, disclosure is needed. ICSID has drafted rules on disclosure.[97] On the other hand, we already see an increasing number of disclosure rules in international commercial arbitration. Some institutions have their own disclosure rules. For example, the ICC 2021 rules require disclosure by funders.[98] However, many other arbitration institutions lack specific rules on TPF.

> In fact, according to a recent chart prepared by Baker & McKenzie, the rules of ICSID, the Stockholm Chamber of Commerce, the United Nations Commission on International Trade Law, and the Permanent Court of Arbitration all lack specific provisions for third-party funding.[99]

With the increasing use of TPF and concerns over CoI and transparency, we can say that the number of disclosure rules in the world will increase.

The ISDS regime is not automatically transparent. It depends on the rules governing the arbitration procedures. However, there are ongoing and completed works toward a more transparent ISDS regime.[100] The main reason for a call for a

---

[94] See Chap. 3 of this book.

[95] Moul (2015), p. 905.

[96] For the importance of transparency, *See* UNCITRAL Rules on Transparency in Treaty-based Investor-State Arbitration: https://www.uncitral.org/pdf/english/texts/arbitration/rules-on-transparency/Rules-on-Transparency-E.pdf; Saravanan and Subramanian (2018), pp. 114–138; Kawharu (2007), pp. 159–172; Ribeiro and Sato (2017), pp. 27–51; Euler, Dimitrij, Markus Gehring, and Maxi Scherer. Transparency in International Investment Arbitration [electronic Resource]: A Guide to the UNCITRAL Rules on Transparency in Treaty-Based Investor-State Arbitration (2015).

[97] ICSID, Working Paper 6, Proposals for Amendment of the ICSID Rules, available at https://icsid.worldbank.org/sites/default/files/documents/ICSID_WP_Six.pdf.

[98] Bhushan and Thakur (2020). Other institutions are also bringing disclosure rules. For one example, *see* https://www.hkiac.org/arbitration/rules-practice-notes/hkiac-administered-2018. IBA RULES.

[99] Simson (2017), Available at https://www.law360.com/internationalarbitration/articles/880838/funders-fret-over-singapore-s-3rd-party-disclosure-measures.

[100] See UNCITRAL Working Group II, https://uncitral.un.org/en/working_groups/2/arbitration. The United Nations Convention on Transparency in Treaty-based Investor–State Arbitration (Mauritius Convention) came into force to this end, available at https://www.iisd.org/projects/transparency-and-uncitral-arbitration-rules.

transparent ISDS regime is the public interest in the disputes. The money awarded against states in ISDS is paid by the money of taxpayers. Naturally, there is a public interest in the outcome of the dispute and therefore it is inevitable that the public has a right to learn about the disputes that affect the money they pay as tax. In this way, ISDS is different from commercial arbitration since in commercial arbitration the dispute is between two private companies and the money of taxpayers is not at stake. Therefore, transparency is important in ISDS.

The International Bar Association (IBA), as a trusted source of soft law in international arbitration, in time has prescribed some rules related to funders. These do not directly refer to funders. However, from their wording, funders need to be careful with any CoI of IBA rules are applicable. Adopted by the IBA Council on 23 October 2014, The IBA Guidelines on Conflicts of Interest in International Arbitration General Standard 6 states that:

> [i]f one of the parties is a legal entity, any legal or physical person having a controlling influence on the legal entity, or a direct economic interest in, or a duty to indemnify a party for, the award to be rendered in the arbitration, may be considered to bear the identity of such party.[101]

The commentary to this general standard 6 describes that:

"Third-party funders and insurers in relation to the dispute may have a direct economic interest in the award, and as such may be considered to be the equivalent of the party".[102] Therefore, any CoI between one party with the funders will amount to a CoI with the funded party.

The risk of CoI is much higher once a funder is involved. This is because funders employ lawyers who worked as arbitration practitioners, or even sometimes served as arbitrators. Therefore, the funder is bringing in a very complex network. Thus, parties must not only check the CoI for themselves, but funders must also check to see whether they have any conflict with the other parties as well. There are various situations in which TPF can create a CoI. Frignati raises the problems in three categories:

> TPF may cause a conflict of interest with an appointed arbitrator when: (i) the arbitrator holds shares in a third-party funding corporation, (ii) there is a relationship between the funder and the arbitrator's law firm, or (iii) the same third-party funder has indirectly made multiple appointments.[103]

Third-party funders should be careful in their practice and the guideline offered in this book addresses such practices.

There are suggestions in the scholarly literature that disclosure should be necessary and taken into consideration in the decision whether to order SfC. Those suggestions state:

---

[101] *See* International Bar Association. (2015, August 10). IBA Guidelines on Conflicts of Interest in International Arbitration. https://www.ibanet.org/MediaHandler?id=e2fe5e72-eb14-4bba-b10d-d33dafee8918.

[102] *Ibid.*

[103] *See* Chap. 1 in supra note 5 (Frignati), p. 515.

> international arbitral institutions should adopt new rules requiring the disclosure of TPF agreements and allow tribunals to use the existence of such agreements as one of the factors to be weighed when determining whether or not to order security for costs.[104]

The relationship between TPF and SfC and how it is handled by investment arbitration tribunals are analyzed in the third chapter of this book.[105] In the literature, the need for guidelines is stated: "international arbitral tribunals must continue to create guidelines to deal with the potential risks related with third party funding".[106]

The question here is whether arbitrators should know the identity or even the presence of a TPF agreement? This is important because arbitrators may exercise their authority to command parties to comply with certain conditions. This book also supports the idea that disclosure might prevent concerns. There are considerable worries such as what if the same funder is funding both parties of the same dispute. There is a risk if the same funder is used by both parties of the same dispute, and the participation of the funder is not disclosed to the tribunal and to the other party, then the funder would be the only one who knows about this situation. Is it okay to allow this of the mercy of funders operating for profit? This book believes that this discretion should not be left to funders, but arbitration tribunals must decide any issues related to TPF. This is a dangerous risk, and a simple disclosure can prevent it. Therefore, with the disclosure, these and similar risks would be eliminated.

5.5.3 *Relations of Funders: Professional Independence of Lawyers*

TPF adds another party to the traditional lawyer-client relationship. In this lawyer-client relationship, lawyers are subject to ethical guidelines; however, funders mostly operate in unregulated markets.[107] Therefore, the funder's operation is not regulated and can potentially cause problems for lawyers who are subject to a number of ethical and professional rules. This section explores the potential ethical problems arising under or out of TPF in investment arbitration. Is it ethically problematic for those who claim that TPF should be banned, or is TPF not as problematic as others suggest? Maybe the answer lies between the two opinions and there might be some potential deontological considerations that can distort justice in investment arbitration. However, with better structured TPF agreements, and taking some measures those potential problems might be prevented. In this

---

[104] Massini (2015), p. 337.

[105] See Chap. 3.

[106] Massini (2015), p. 338.

[107] There is no specific rules applicable to the funders in investment arbitration. UNCITRAL has an initial draft on the regulation of third-party funding, see https://uncitral.un.org/en/thirdpartyfunding. ICSID also has draft rules on third-party funding, see https://icsid.worldbank.org/resources/rules-amendments. The new ICSID rules are in effect by 1 July 2022.

section, those problems and how they can be overcome are discussed by particularly focusing on the relationships between the lawyer-funder-funded parties.

Funders are only one of the players. There are also lawyers and arbitrators. All relations between these actors must be professional and ethical. When we think of TPF agreements, we understand that as a contractual relationship between parties. In this relationship, one party—the party to the dispute—needs money, and the other party—the funder—gives the money in return for remuneration. Both parties have consideration in this relationship and both parties benefit from it. So, one can easily see the ethical problem here. It is a straightforward contractual relationship, and you can find examples in everyday transactions. However, others see things differently. Since TPF of a dispute means that funders meddle with a dispute in which they are not a party, there might be some concerns about this relationship.

An article proposes "harmonizing the regulatory framework for third-party litigation funding in the United States by identifying the three categories of interactions— transactional, procedural, and ethical—that make up third-party litigation funding, and suggesting avenues for regulation within those three categories".[108] Ethics is surely an important aspect of this regulation as well as the guideline this book proposes.

Guven and Johnson discuss how ethical standards of lawyers prevent lawyers from exploitative behavior, how a lawyer-funding arrangement on a contingency basis is subject to ethical standards because lawyers are regulated by the bar associations and their primary loyalty is to their clients, while funders are not subject to such ethical regulations and they are loyal and answerable to the shareholders rather than the funded party.[109] However, because funders have no ethical obligations to the funded party, only to their shareholders, they face no ethical or regulatory hurdles in managing a claim.[110]

The question then comes to whether the ethical and professional rules lawyers who are working for funders, and lawyers acting for the funded parties are subject to, are enough to provide ethical standards for the business of funders, or are separate rules for third-party funders necessary? This book proposes that certain rules for funders are necessary since lawyers working for funders are not practicing law anymore. They are only providing legal expertise. However, their thinking and their alliances are different from when they were acting as lawyers. Therefore, certain guidelines for funders are necessary to provide a certain threshold of standards for their conduct. Otherwise, third-party funders might have ultimate flexibility in every decision, and this will naturally lead them to choose the best decision for themselves and their shareholders, not for the lawyers or funded parties. To ensure that third party involvement does not distort the relationship between lawyers and

[108] Sahani (2015), p. 861.

[109] Guven and Johnson (2019), p. 41, available at https://scholarship.law.columbia.edu/cgi/viewcontent.cgi?article=1007&context=sustainable_investment_staffpubs.

[110] Steinitz (2011), pp. 1268, 1319.

funded parties and the integrity of the ISDS system, setting a certain threshold is a must.

Another consideration regarding the ethical aspect of TPF business might be drawn upon the motive of third-party funders. Does it matter what motives a third-party funder is acting on? Maybe if they have a stake against the opposite side of the dispute, they do it for humanitarian purposes, or they simply do it for profit. This does not seem to the author the right way to assess the ethicality of TPF because the same analysis can apply to lawyers, arbitrators, experts, and every other participant in the ISDS system. It does not matter whether a lawyer or an arbitrator is doing his/her job for money, or they are doing it to serve justice, it should not matter what the funder's motive is. Note that if there is a funder that is bankrolling investors regularly against a certain state or certain group of states with a particular agenda and this can be proven, this cannot be allowed and there must be serious sanctions against such funders.

The question then comes down to whether profiting is allowed? Lawyers, arbitrators, experts, all actors are profiting from their expertise and TPF is no different. These are all economic sectors, and nobody can deny them. The legal profession has developed and grown throughout history because there has been a demand for it. TPF is also in demand today, and it will only grow. While growing, as in any other sector, there might be some new actors who do not know how to play and want to make easy money. To protect the potential users of TPF, the integrity of the system and the relationship between every actor, a certain guideline is required. The legal profession and arbitration did not have any regulations in the past. In time, they all developed rules. Thus, TPF will be the same. The practice is now evolving, and regulation will follow. If a new player falls below a certain threshold of standards, they might be put out of business.

5.5.4 *Various Scenarios*

Maybe the best way to explain what problems for lawyers might arise is to provide potential scenarios and specifically explain them. In this section, we will ask and answer some ethical questions. We will set some factual scenarios, which are happening in the real world, and try to analyze each situation. Some of these scenarios are hypothetical and if so it will be stated, however, most of these scenarios are the analysis of existing and developing problems.

5.5.4.1 Lawyers Advising on TPF Agreements Should Not Act on the Merits of the Case

This is a common scenario in practice. Generally, lawyers acting on the dispute are also advising on the TPF agreements. This is wrong. There is one case related to this issue and it is likely that the number of such cases will increase if it continues. An investor sued his/her lawyers and the funder. "A Dutch national who won a US$45 million investment treaty award against Vietnam sued his arbitration counsel King & Spalding, accusing the firm of colluding with third-party funder Burford Capital to cheat him out of his due share of the proceeds".[111] The plaintiff alleges that "This case illustrates what happens when attorneys, retained by a client to represent that client in arbitration, decide instead to represent their own pecuniary interests and those of a third-party funder and to make a mockery of the fiduciary obligations an attorney owes to their clients".[112] There will be more such cases if the same lawyers are advising funded parties and acting on the dispute. Lawyers who advise on the TPF agreement should be different from the lawyers who are acting on the dispute. Because the lawyers acting on the merits get paid by the funder, therefore, it would not be ethical for the same lawyers to advise on the TPF agreement in which the lawyers themselves have a stake.

5.5.4.2 Are Lawyers' Professional Rules Sufficient to Protect the Integrity of ISDS?

TPF arrangements, if not carefully constructed, might create some problems for lawyers whose allegiance is with their clients, who are not necessarily the party paying the bills. An article "examines the possible implications that TPF may have on both the attorney-client relationship and the independence and impartiality of the arbitral tribunal".[113] Furthermore, "to the extent an attorney permits a third-party financier to 'direct or regulate' the attorney's 'professional judgment,' the attorney may violate rules of professional conduct.".[114] These are not all of the potential implications, there are still issues with control of funders, funders' conduct, and other matters that will be discussed below.

TPF is a development in every legal platform including arbitration and litigation. "The ethical category has traditionally been addressed either through regulating the professional conduct of attorneys or through funders self-regulating through a voluntary code of conduct or best practices".[115] Who pays the fees, what does it matter? It does not. When it might matter is when the funder tries to impose strategies or affect the decision of the party. Therefore, in this book, existing regulatory frameworks on TPF are analyzed; concerns of states and scholars are explored, and the best practice for funders is based on those analyses. After reaching

---

[111] https://globalarbitrationreview.com/king-spalding-sued-client-in-funded-bit-case.

[112] https://www.law.com/texaslawyer/2021/06/14/alleging-gross-overpayment-of-fees-ex-client-sues-king-spalding-2-partners-over-successful-arbitration/?slreturn=20220022133401.

[113] *See* Chap. 1 in supra note 5 (Frignati), p. 505.

[114] Beisner et al. (2009), pp. 4–11, available at https://legaltimes.typepad.com/files/thirdpartylitigationfinancing.pdf, pp. 5–6.

[115] Shannon (2015), p. 861.

decisions on what best practice means for certain scenarios, the best practice guideline is attached at the end of this book.

Are lawyers' professional rules sufficient to protect the integrity of the system, or should third-party funders be subject to some standards as well? "Attorneys are ethically bound to honor their contracts",[116] funders are not. This book defends the idea that the rules are not enough, and third-party funders should be subject to certain standards as well.[117] First of all, the lawyer who is going to advise on the merits and get paid by the funder cannot and must not advise on the terms of the TPF agreements. This lawyer is going to expect to get paid during and at the end of the case by the funder. How can these lawyers independently advise their clients? They cannot. Even though they can do that in theory, on the surface it does not seem right. Thus, there should be two different lawyers, (i) one who is advising the TPF agreement and (ii) the second who is acting on the dispute. (i) and (ii) cannot and must not be the same lawyer.

TPF might raise some moral problems for lawyers. In a blog post, those problems are labelled as "unexpected ethical problems".[118] Whether it is unexpected or not depends on your expectations. Maybe those problems are not unexpected at all. The person who pays the money becomes important in service agreements. Lawyers provide legal service for their clients, and in a standard relationship, the client as the service user pays for the service. However, in the situation of funded clients, a funder pays the lawyer. Then the lawyer needs to have certain safeguards to ensure that his/her alliance is with the client, not with the funder. The lawyer represents the funded client, not the funder. In different jurisdictions, there are certain rules addressing this issue and ensuring that the lawyer-client relationship is protected and sustained in the way it should be. And in arbitration, when lawyers serve as counsels, they are still bound by their professional rules. However, those issues might be addressed more often in arbitration, especially in investment arbitration. It is added as a suggested guideline.[119]

The participation of a funder risks the ethical duties of the lawyers. Lawyers must be more careful in their dealings with funders and must ensure that their loyalty lies with their clients, and that they do not violate any professional and ethical rules in their conduct. Thus, "in addition, obtaining funds from a third party to finance a case may also create conflicts of interest for the plaintiff's attorney, particularly the attorney's duty of loyalty owed to the client".[120] Every professional has ethical and other duties that must be complied with, and funders are not bound by them, lawyers are bound. Each jurisdiction has different professional rules. And some of

[116]Douglas (2005), p. 682.

[117]See the best practice guideline in Chap. 7.

[118]*See* https://leidenlawblog.nl/articles/third-party-litigations-funds-and-the-lawyers-ethics.

[119]See guideline, annex I to this book. The best practice guideline.

[120]Beisner et al. (2009), pp. 4–11, available at https://legaltimes.typepad.com/files/thirdpartylitigationfinancing.pdf, p. 6.

those rules have specific provisions. As an example, from the United States, the ABA Model Rule of Professional Conduct states:

> A lawyer shall not accept compensation for representing a client from one other than the client unless:
>
> (1) the client gives informed consent;
> (2) there is no interference with the lawyer's independence of professional judgment or with the client-lawyer relationship; and.
> (3) information relating to representation of a client is protected as required by Rule 1.6 [confidentiality].[121]

As we can see, the ABA rules impose three conditions for a third party to pay attorney fees regarding, compensation. Each jurisdiction has different rules regarding lawyers' professional conduct.[122]

An important condition here is that a third-party funder must not interfere with the lawyer's independence of professional judgment or with the client-lawyer relationship. This is a key standard, and this book has addressed it in the best practice guideline.[123] Other jurisdictions might have similar rules. As an example, for French lawyers, their loyalty must lie with clients as reported by Global Arbitration Review (GAR).[124] More examples can be seen in other jurisdictions.[125] Across the world, bar associations are preparing ethical guidelines on this issue stressing the fact that the loyalty of a lawyer must be to the client.[126] However, in investment arbitration, there is no guideline yet. Therefore, it is important to create one in this book.

Third-party funders should never make transactions that cause other professionals such as the funded party's lawyers to be in a position that is ethically problematic for them. "Counsel's ethical obligations to clients may never be infringed based on divergent financial interests triggered by third party funding" and funders should respect that.[127] This is important and must be respected. However, this cannot be ensured without forcing funders to follow some guidelines or rules since "funders' primary ethical and regulatory obligations are to their shareholders, not to the funded party, so they may push settlement decisions or outcome demands that are different from those preferred by the local enterprise whose investment underlies the ISDS

[121] ABA Model Rules of Professional Conduct, Rule 1.8(f), available at https://www.americanbar.org/groups/professional_responsibility/publications/model_rules_of_professional_conduct/model_rules_of_professional_conduct_table_of_contents/.

[122] IBA rules are available as soft law while Professional conduct rules are mandatory for lawyers in the jurisdiction they operate.

[123] See the best practice guideline.

[124] Global Arbitration Review, Third-party funding: snapshots from around the globe, https://globalarbitrationreview.com/third-party-funding-snapshots-around-the-globe (See also HK Reform paper, https://www.hkreform.gov.hk/en/docs/tpf_e.pdf.

[125] *See Ibid.*, Hong Kong reform paper, pp-49–112.

[126] *See, e.g.*, the State Bar of California; https://www.calbar.ca.gov/Portals/0/documents/ethics/Opinions/Formal-Opinion-No-2020-204-Litigation-Funding.pdf.

[127] Miller (2017, March), p. 20.

case".[128] Thus, the importance of guidelines in investment arbitration is again repeated.

TPF, as described in this book, has not only funded parties in ISDS but also parties in litigations and other types of arbitrations around the world. Thus, many international commissions started working on TPF because of ethical issues raised in its TPF relations. As an example, "The American Bar Association Commission on Ethics 20/20, therefore, formed a Working Group on Alternative Litigation Finance to study the impact of these emerging transactional structures on the client-lawyer relationship and the professional responsibilities of lawyers".[129] This report concluded that "A lawyer must always exercise independent professional judgment on behalf of a client, and not be influenced by financial or other considerations".[130] The report shows that "the interference with independent professional judgment is one of the principal perceived risks associated with alternative litigation finance".[131] "Moreover, a lawyer must not permit a third party to interfere with the exercise of independent professional judgment".[132] In the ABA Ethical Commission report, there are various scenarios for lawyers and answers to questions about how lawyers should act in those scenarios. This book looked at those guidelines in the creation of the ethical guideline for funders operating in the investment arbitration regime.

American Bar Association (ABA) also issued a best practice guideline for third-party litigation funding.[133] In this best practice guideline, ABA has defined different types of funding available in the market.[134] The main purpose of this best practice guideline is "to educate and guide lawyers".[135] Therefore, it is different from the best practice guideline proposed by this book as its purpose is to guide the funders operating in an investment arbitration regime. Nevertheless, ABA's guideline is an important source for lawyers, especially those practising in the USA, to navigate their relationship with funders in their practice.

One of the most concerning issues is lawyers' ethical obligations and how TPF affects them.[136] Lawyers' ethical obligations and the impact of TPF can be problematic. Lawyers are bound by ethical and professional rules in their practices. Lawyers' ethical duties should not be breached by TPF arrangements. TPF

---

[128] Güven and Johnson (2019) available at https://www.iisd.org/itn/en/2019/06/27/third-party-funding-and-the-objectives-of-investment-treaties-friends-or-foes-brooke-guven-lise-johnson/#_ftnref14.

[129] American Bar Association Commission On Ethics 20/20 Informational Report To The House Of Delegates, p. 2.

[130] *Ibid.*

[131] *Ibid.* p. 25.

[132] *Ibid.*

[133] American Bar Association, American Bar Association Best Practices for Third-Party Litigation Funding, adopted by the house of delegates on August 3–4, 2020 available at https://www.americanbar.org/content/dam/aba/directories/policy/annual-2020/111a-annual-2020.pdf.

[134] *Ibid,* Part III, types pp. 4–10.

[135] *Ibid,* p. 22.

[136] Glickman (2016), p. 1061.

arrangements "can create ethical concerns related to an attorney's duty to maintain financial independence from a client".[137] It is suggested that "Collaborations with TPLF [third party litigation funding] providers should not be treated any differently than discussions about a defendant's case with its insurer".[138] Lawyers must never forget that the funded party is their client, not the funder. In practice, since funders have the money and the same lawyer might work with the same funder in future cases, the lawyers might find themselves confused in terms of to whom they owe their loyalty. "Nonetheless, it is not obvious that, without subrogation, a funder and a plaintiff can be combined as the attorney's co-clients, particularly since the review of existing litigation funding contracts reveals that, at times, parties actually disclaim co-client status. The analogy is also weakened by conflicts of interest between the funder and plaintiff that could make it ethically impossible for an attorney to represent both".[139] This relationship must be clear between lawyer-funded party-funder. Otherwise, loyalty and CoI issues might arise.

5.5.4.3 Should Funders Profit from Cases?

How should we approach legal cases? Are they divine and sacred disputes that should not be part of any commercial deal, or are they commercial assets that can be part of a bargain like any other commercial commodity? The second is a more realistic approach today for commercial and investment disputes. Funders are accused of transferring wealth 'in the form of TPF-funded settlements or arbitral awards which represent unjustifiable transfers from target states and their citizens'.[140] Is it correct to blame funders? The underlying fact is that states acted illegally and damaged the investors by breaching the investment protection rules the state agreed to attract that investment in the first place, which is totally overlooked. Later, the investors whose rights were breached by states enter a TPF agreement, either they do not have another choice to bring a claim, or they do not want to bear the risks of such proceedings. Whatever the reason, this decision lies with the investors whose rights were breached by states that should pay for their damages.

Companies or individual investors have legal cases. These cases can produce some returns depending on the judgment. At the same time, if the judgment is negative, this case can result in high legal costs including lawyer fees, expert fees, tribunal fees, etc. When considered every case is an investment. In bringing a case the company decides whether to invest in a new project, which can result in profits or if it is a failure, it needs to bear the costs. This example helps us to see the reality in the legal world. Unfortunately, justice is not a part of considerations in many firms. The important thing you see on legal pages is how many disputes a law firm has and

[137] McLaughlin (2007), p. 660.

[138] Glickman (2016), p. 1062.

[139] Steinitz and Field (2014), p. 733.

[140] *See* Chap. 2 in supra note 108 (Garcia), p. 2920.

how much is at stake in total.[141] Law firms are competing to get those cases and it does not matter whether they are defending investors or states. Law firms are competing to be counsel in an investment arbitration case because it is prestigious, reputable, and a lot of money for the lawyers who are acting on the case. The same is true for most arbitrators, who are also competing to get more cases. There is no pro bono work in investment arbitration. We do not see any news stories about a law firm deciding to defend a case just because it believes it is right and it will do it for free. Arbitrators, lawyers, experts are all in this business to profit. In such a system, blaming funders because they are in this business for profit is a ridiculous accusation. They are all in it for money at the end. There are articles in the literature blaming law firms and arbitrators.[142] In this study, one chapter is about funders.[143] Therefore, if there is a problem, it is systematic, not because of funders.

5.5.4.4 Is the Source of the Money Ethically Problematic?

Yes, it can be problematic. ISDS is a mechanism between investors and states. If any state, or political party is using this system to increase the pressure against another state, then this would constitute abuse and exploitation of the system. Here, a specific issue must be addressed regarding who gives the money to funders and for what purposes. As discussed earlier, the motive of funders is profit and it is fine, that keeps them operating. However, if investors in TPF, meaning people and institutions who give the money to funders, have different and specific agendas other than making a profit, then this should be addressed.

This can be explained with an example. The listed funders have extensive reporting requirements since their stocks are sold in stock markets. Thus, their operation is more transparent than non-listed funders. One of the largest TPF companies, listed in both London and New York Stock Exchange markets, Burford Capital, reported that 667 million USD of 1 billion USD of its strategic capital comes from a sovereign wealth fund.[144] This can be ethically concerning if the sovereign wealth fund is using its assets to initiate or back up cases against other states. This can be called a "secret war" between states. If a certain state wants to pressure another state economically, and investment arbitration is used for this purpose, this is wrong and unethical. Therefore, states should never be able to invest in TPF of ISDS claims. Commercial arbitration or litigation is separate and is possible. However, in ISDS, a state should never have the role of an investor. This would be an abuse of the

---

[141] *See* https://globalarbitrationreview.com/survey/gar-100/2021.

[142] Eberhardt and Olivet (2015), p. 27 available at https://www.tni.org/files/download/profitingfrominjustice.pdf; Brower and Blanchard (2014), available at https://harvardilj.org/wp-content/uploads/sites/15/2014/01/Brower_Blanchard_to_Publish.pdf.

[143] *See the empirical research in* Chap. 4.

[144] *See* Burford Capital 2020 Annual Report, p. viii, available at https://www.burfordcapital.com/media/2080/fy-2020-report.pdf.

system and change the position this book holds. The guideline this book offers will cover this issue as well.

In conclusion, ISDS must not be a tool of other states to back up cases against other states. Even the slightest possibility of this must be eliminated.

5.5.4.5 Do Cases with TPF Take Longer?

Funders invest in cases to profit. The more quickly they profit from a case the better and if the case does not go anywhere, there is no point in spending money on a case that they will lose at the end or that continues indefinitely. Thus, there is no point in extending the time or prolonging a case from the point of view of funders. Therefore, TPF would logically not extend the case, funders would be happy to get the case resolved as soon as possible and get their money back. The way that TPF affects the timeline of a case should be specifically researched to have more answers. However, initial thought suggests that funders would shorten this process instead of extending it. This issue is also added to the best practice guideline.

5.5.4.6 A Hypothetical Scenario: Is There an Alternative to TPF?

No TPF, no access to justice. Or if there is a limited budget of claimants, they cannot hire the best lawyers and are at a disadvantage against states. What is the purpose of the ISDS system? To protect states even when they illegally harm investors, or to provide a secure investment regime in which whenever a state breaches its obligations, investors can force their rights against states? TPF does not contradict this purpose and facilitates the use of ISDS. The easier the access to the ISDS system, the more efficient and accessible the ISDS regime is. Cutting off a financial option for investors to bring their cases is tantamount to sending the message that states can do whatever they want, and that the dispute resolution mechanism, available in theory for all investors, can be used only by financially strong investors. Other investors cannot bring their cases if they do not have enough capital. The only option for those investors is to settle with the respondent State or abandon their cases. This is not the purpose of the ISDS system, to protect only financially sound and risk-taking companies, rather it should protect all investors and make itself accessible to all by providing financial options to cover their costs. TPF provides the latter purpose, which serves justice. Therefore, in this hypothetical scenario, having TPF is much better than not having the TPF. In conclusion, this book does not see any problem for funders investing in legal claims.

5.5.4.7 Is TPF Going to Increase the Number of ISDS Cases?

Yes, it naturally will increase the number of cases. The question here is, is that is it bad? Justice is served to broader investors if this is what ISDS is for. Ideally, all investors who think their rights have been breached should have the opportunity to be heard. However, this is not an option. To be heard in investment arbitration is expensive, not every investor has the financial ability, especially after their investment soured, and even if they have the financial capacity, not every investor wants to take the risks of such expensive proceedings. Therefore, there should be additional mechanisms to further increase the accessibility of investment arbitration.

Richmond rightfully points out the expensive feature of court proceedings.[145] It is truer for investment arbitration. According to a 2016 study of 2011–2015 awards, average claimant costs were USD 5,619,261.74, average respondent costs were USD 4,954,461.27,15 and average ICSID tribunal costs were USD 882,668.19[146] So, this expensive mechanism is not accessible to everyone, not every investor would want to take the risks of arbitration if it were. Thus, transferring this risk to a third-party funder will increase the accessibility of the ISDS mechanism and therefore the number of cases will naturally increase. However, is it going to also increase the number of frivolous cases? This book does not see any reason that it will.

5.5.4.8 Possibility of Unmeritorious Cases

Whether TPF might increase the number of unmeritorious cases is a question to discuss here. A short answer to this question is: no. To prevent this possibility portfolio funding in investment arbitration is excluded in the best practice guideline.[147] As Lemos stated, "in short, a system in which private actors controlled all the levers of litigation would likely produce too little deterrence, and too much waste".[148] Portfolio funding has the danger of funding weak cases in the portfolio, and this should not be allowed in investment arbitration. Portfolio funding should also not be allowed in general. However, in this book, we are providing opinions only for investment arbitration. Even the slightest possibility of bringing meritless cases as part of a portfolio should be eliminated. If a funder is backing a case that has no obvious legal basis, then that funder should face sanctions.

There are allegations against TPF that it increases the number of cases, including frivolous cases.[149] It has been suggested that practices like TPF contribute to "the number of non-meritorious cases filed, and thus effectively reduce (not increase) the level of justice in the litigation system".[150] This is a very general judgment against the whole industry without understanding how TPF works. In investment arbitration, it is not a concern because investors choose their cases carefully after analyzing a

---

[145] Douglas (2005), p. 649.

[146] Bottini, 255.

[147] See the best practice guideline in Chap. 7.

[148] Lemos (2016), p. 526.

[149] *See* Chap. 1 in supra note 49, p. 175.

[150] Beisner et al. (2009), pp. 4–11, Available at https://legaltimes.typepad.com/files/thirdpartylitigationfinancing.pdf, p. 4.

few TPF arrangements. Is it true? We will not repeat the high costs of investment arbitration. Funders would not risk their money for a frivolous case. The success rate of funders proves that this allegation is wrong.[151]

The attorney should warn clients in the US if they are bringing a frivolous case, this duty can be placed on the funders in investment arbitration. This would increase the trust in funders because there is strong criticism against TPF, stating, "Litigation financing is a sophisticated scheme for gambling on litigation, and its impact on American companies is unambiguous: more lawsuits, more litigation uncertainty, higher settlement payoffs to satisfy cash-hungry funders, and in some instances, even corruption".[152] The increase of frivolous claims is a common denunciation against TPF. However, this is not true for investment arbitration. This might be true in some litigation cases where portfolio funding is agreed upon. However, in investment arbitration there are no such risks. No funder is funding ISDS on a portfolio basis as far as the author is aware. However, to eliminate even the slightest chance, a guideline provision on that is added to this book.[153]

It is no surprise that funders do not accept every case that has applied. It is a known fact that funders do not easily accept cases. For example, a funder states that "funders, like good business contingency firms, typically reject upwards of 90% of the investment opportunities presented to them, seeking only cases with a strong chance of success".[154] This number is not specific to one funder. In interviews conducted by the author, high rejection rates were confirmed by many funders.[155] Concerns that TPF will increase the number of unmeritorious cases dropped significantly according to a recent survey.[156] This must be because the market is more educated and understands how TPF works better than before. The TPF business model would otherwise not be able to afford funding to frivolous cases since funders would lose their investment and run out of money in the end.

In conclusion, adding third-party funders to the system is likely to multiply the number of ISDS claims. Nevertheless, it would be inappropriate to assert that it will increase frivolous cases. The number of meritorious cases will likely increase.

---

[151] *See* some of the rates in the empirical research chapter, Chap. 4.

[152] Lisa A Rickard, President of the U.S. Chamber Institute for Legal Reform 22, and Executive Vice President of the US Chamber of Commerce, states: See www.instituteforlegalreform.com.

[153] *See* best practice guideline in Chap. 7.

[154] See Bentham IMF Litigation Funding Roundtable: Key Issues and Best Practices, January 2014 Report, at page 6.

[155] *See* Chap. 4.

[156] Burford Capital, Ethical worries over third-party funding "evaporating", 07 Sep 2017, available at https://www.burfordcapital.com/media-room/media-room-container/ethical-worries-over-third-party-funding-evaporating/.

5.5.4.9 Settlement and Its Relationship with the Number of Cases

TPF will not increase unmeritorious claims but is more likely to increase the number of cases overall. Arguably, it can increase the number of settlements as well. According to Veljanovski:

"All other things being equal, the presence of a TPLF investor may result in a higher settlement rate, as defendants realize that the claimant can fully finance the costs of taking the case to court. This decreases the litigation rate, and conserves both legal and other related costs".[157] Thus, the impact of TPF on settlements might be positive. More research on this effect is needed. "A factor missed by most commentators is that TPLF may deter some claims which may otherwise have been pursued. Claimants seeking funds must first persuade a TPLF investor to fund their claim.".[158] Thus, it is true that not all claims asking for TPF will be brought up. Thus, if anyone has a case but fails to convince a funder of its value, that case will not be brought. A funder's rejection might be a wake-up call for claim holders who do not have as strong a case as they thought they had. In conclusion, cases rejected by funders might deter claimants from bringing cases and decrease the number of total cases. Such cases might deter defendants and encourage them to settle with claimants.

5.5.4.10 Is TPF Exploitation of the Funded Party?

Should there be better alternative finance? Yes. Is there a better option? No. The problem with international arbitration and investment arbitration is that there is no legal aid mechanism that can support parties who need such financial assistance. Indeed, in national courts, there are different legal aid mechanisms in different jurisdictions.[159] However a main dispute settlement mechanism for investment and cross border disputes in international arbitration, does not exist. TPF is now filling this gap in ISDS and commercial arbitration. This not only gives an opportunity to access justice for investors otherwise unable to access the ISDS mechanism but also gives additional financing options to multinational companies. The question here is while giving this opportunity to the parties, do funders exploit the parties?

Exploitation would occur if the funder were abusing his/her position and putting extra burdens and unacceptable terms in the TPF agreement. What is unacceptable should be defined and the market standards can be an indicator for this. "The compensation the funder will receive in the case of success (which varies between 15 percent and 50 percent of the amount awarded)".[160] The funder's "share is calculated from several factors, including the amount of money advanced, the length of time until recovery, the potential value of the plaintiff's case, and whether the case

[157] Veljanovski (2012), pp. 405, 439.

[158] *Ibid.*

[159] *See* Barendrecht et al. (2014).

[160] *See* Chap. 1 in supra note 5 (Frignati), p. 509.

settles or goes to trial".[161] What if funders are taking a greater percentage than the claimant? How can one ensure that such a position is not abused? Taking 80-90% of the awarded amount would be ethically wrong. How can one then ensure that funders are not abusing their position? The best way is to ensure that there is a regulation, and that noncompliance will have consequences. However, in investment arbitration there is no such regulation. At the least, there should be a guideline for funders to set a standard as is presented in this book.[162]

5.5.4.11 TPF Relationship: Potential Control Over the Funded Party

There are two different approaches of third-party funders: price the risk, or merit-based.[163] The merit-based approach seems to be a better fit for investment arbitration. However, looking at funders of the solely economically driven actors does not reflect the reality well. "Further, the claim that TPLF providers are solely driven by the profit motive while lawyers and commercial claimants are not, is far-fetched. At issue is the alignment of funder and lawyers' interests to that of the claimant(s) in a meritorious case; that is, arrangements that better resolve the inherent principal-agent problem seen when a professional lawyer, acting as an agent, represents the interests of a claimant. It is not self-evident that this alignment is achieved by banning risk-sharing arrangements with TPLF investors".[164] An important possible ethical concern is exploitation of the funded party during the TPF process. The guideline attached to this book addresses this issue.[165] Funders should not abuse, or take excessive control, or become dominant over the funded parties.

TPF raises ethical concerns, one of which is that it "can create confusion concerning the party who controls the lawsuit and concerning the attorney-client relationship".[166] There are rising concerns over some jurisdictions due to the increased number of funders.[167] In ICSID or PCA administered arbitrations do not have any specific rule regarding TPF and the control issue. There are some draft rules on both regarding disclosure, but nothing on control rule now.[168] Undue control over the funded party is a very important ethical issue.[169] Control is critical. If the funder

[161] Beisner et al. (2009), pp. 4–11, available at https://legaltimes.typepad.com/files/thirdpartylitigationfinancing.pdf, p. 2.

[162] The best practice guideline in Chap. 7.

[163] A new "fully regulated" third-party funder opens in Paris, Global Arbitration Review, 2 November 2018.

[164] Veljanovski, p. 447.

[165] See the best practice guideline.

[166] De Morpurgo (2011), p. 367.

[167] https://www.abajournal.com/magazine/article/litigation_finance_legal_ethical_concerns/P2.

[168] *See* ICSID Draft Rules, new ICSID rules and UNCITRAL Working Group III discussions.

[169] https://www.mondaq.com/unitedstates/trials-appeals-compensation/811510/third-party-litigation-funders-the-party-you-didn39t-know-was-exercising-control-over-your-litigation-and-what-you-can-do-about-it.

takes full control so that he/she acts as the party itself in the dispute, can the arbitration tribunal hold that funder as a party to the dispute? This is a jurisdiction issue related to a procedural issue that was discussed in the relevant case law, as explained in this book.[170]

This control concern is not a hypothetical one but rather a real concern. "Gary Chodes, the founder of litigation-financing company Oasis Legal Finance, has said that "clients may have to relinquish some decision-making authority to the funder" and that "the client's interests may diverge from the funder in that other business reasons may suggest that they might settle a claim for less than the funder has targeted".[171] When the control passes to the funder, "the power to make strategic decisions about the case in the hands of the funder, whose duties are to its investors, instead of in the hands of the attorney, whose duties are to the client".[172] This would create a system where a third party, instead of the investor whose rights were breached, would be in charge of the case. There is no rule in investment arbitration preventing it. However, to have a natural legal system, the claim holder should stay in control of the case and make the decisions together with their lawyers, not with the party who pays the bills.

One important consideration is that the funded party stays in control of the case. There are other interesting suggestions in the literature. One suggests that "the control over the litigation has an economic value that should be given a price".[173] This is an interesting suggestion because it is true that not all, but some funders, do give insights and input on the strategy of the case and this can be very valuable. Since lawyers are working for funders and they had several years of experience in practice before joining funders, they bring additional expertise to the case they are funding. This surely increases the likelihood of a case succeeding and this can be given a price.

Litigation and arbitration can be financed in various ways. Morpurgo stated six different methods to finance litigation, which can be applied to arbitration as well. These methods are "self-funding, lawyer funding, TPF, insurance-based solutions, assignment of claims, litigation loans".[174] Apart from self-funding, which means financing the costs of the case by the party bringing the case, all other finance options involve an external party, a third-party, and in a broad sense, they are all TPF. However, as explained earlier, most of the funders are professionals and they are established with the sole purpose of finding and funding cases.[175]

---

[170] *See* Chap. 3 of this book.

[171] Beisner et al. (2009), pp. 4–11, available at https://legaltimes.typepad.com/files/thirdpartylitigationfinancing.pdf, p. 5–6.

[172] Beisner et al. (2009), pp. 4–11, available at https://legaltimes.typepad.com/files/thirdpartylitigationfinancing.pdf, pp. 5–6.

[173] De Morpurgo (2011), p. 411.

[174] De Morpurgo (2011), p. 343.

[175] *See* Chap. 2.

Control of funders is an understandable desire but there must be a limit to that. "Litigation-financing arrangements undercut the plaintiff's control over his or her own claim because investors inherently desire to protect their investment and will therefore seek to exert control over strategic decisions in the lawsuit".[176] The desire to follow and protect their investment, which is the funded case, is very clear. However, there must be a limit and the funded party should stay in control of the case. Thus, the best practice guideline proposes a rule on this issue.[177] Allianz Prozess Finanz's managing director Arndt Eversberg "has touted plaintiffs' ability to draw on the company's legal knowledge and experience as an added benefit of obtaining litigation financing from it".[178] Therefore, instead of taking control, the funder's involvement might bring additional expertise to the case. However, the control must stay with the funded party.

Lawyers are working for the TPF companies, and they can naturally suggest arbitrators for a case they funded, this is the natural system because each party appoints one arbitrator. "ISDS gives claimants a direct voice in the selection of adjudicators and arbitration rules, allowing TPF funders a degree of influence over the tribunal that is unthinkable in domestic civil litigation".[179] However, arbitration is different from litigation. Therefore, parties have a say in the constitution of the tribunal. Whether the suggestion of arbitrator comes from the party itself, a lawyer, or funder does not change the result. The important thing is that arbitrators stay independent and impartial. This must be ensured.

5.5.5 *Evidentiary Privilege*

As a definition, "an evidentiary privilege is a rule of evidence that allows the holder of the privilege to refuse to provide evidence about a certain subject or to bar such evidence from being disclosed or used in judicial or similar proceedings".[180] When investment arbitration awards are reviewed, it shows that "issues relating to evidentiary privileges do arise regularly in investment treaty arbitrations".[181] There are different privileges for different reasons with a common power granting the party the right to resist disclosure. Nevertheless, there is no funder-funded party privilege and the question here is, should there be one? This book answers as yes.

---

[176] Beisner et al. (2009), pp. 4–11, available at https://legaltimes.typepad.com/files/thirdpartylitigationfinancing.pdf, p. 5.

[177] See Chap. 7, the best practice guideline.

[178] Beisner et al. (2009), pp. 4–11, available at https://legaltimes.typepad.com/files/thirdpartylitigationfinancing.pdf, p. 5–6.

[179] *See* Chap. 2 in supra note 108 (Garcia), p. 2920.

[180] Sheppard (2016), p. 670.

[181] *Ibid.*

There must be a privilege for the exchanges between the parties to the TPF agreement. Just as a lawyer-client privilege protects the defense of one's case, should the funder-funded party privilege be protected in the same way? There is no example of a state requesting communication between funders and funded parties. However, we might see one, and ensuring that it is given protection will give confidence to parties seeking TPF. To make this search safer, a privilege must be provided to funders.

5.5.6 Conclusion

In conclusion, Is TPF perfect? No, it is not. Funders are already operating in this system, and they do not have rules governing their relationship with other actors, or about who can be their investors. This book suggests that there must be rules. The guideline provided by this book will address many problems and prevent many from arising. Thus, a guideline is needed, and TPF should operate with a guideline. Abolishing TPF would not be the end of problems that exist within ISDS. TPF facilitates and makes access to this expensive mechanism easier. What is the other option? Not to access the ISDS system at all or have only limited access? If we really want to increase its accessibility of the investment arbitration system. Then we should do so by increasing the financial options of the users, not by limiting them. The problems that exist within the ISDS must be fixed. TPF will not make ISDS better or worse, it will only increase the accessibility. By doing that, and not adding another problem to the existing ones, the guideline provided by this book will ensure a certain level of security to the system and a certain threshold level to the operation of funders.

This book is not the first literature suggesting that TPF can operate without distorting the system. However, this book is the first to bring a comprehensive analysis and guideline for TPF in investment arbitration. DeStefano "contends that claim funding's benefits outweigh the risks, that the risks of outside influence are not uncharted or unmanageable, and that refusing to manage the transition and further allow claim funding could make the U.S. legal market even more isolated and irrelevant".[182] He further states that "with the right structures in place, claim funding can provide benefits to lawyers, claim holders, and the legal marketplace generally".[183] This book agrees with this proposition and brings a more comprehensive analysis of ethical issues regarding TPF.

---

[182] DeStefano (2012), p. 2828.

[183] *Ibid.*

5.6 The Purpose of Regulation of TPF

Investment arbitration is a special system created to resolve disputes between investors and states. "Due to the public character of investment arbitration, proceedings are evaluated under a global microscope. Because TPF introduces a host of ethical complications, it could conceivably disrupt the international investment arbitration system".[184] The question here is whether these complications can be removed, and whether TPF can resume with certain standards. This book proposes that if the guideline is followed then TPF can operate without any ethical complications.

There is less control in the supranational space. In international arbitration, a specific professional regulation is absent.[185] According to Moseley: "the safeguards that typically protect litigation from ethical concerns are weakened in the international arbitration setting".[186] This is because investment arbitration is operating in a supranational space where there is not as much regulation as in national judicial systems. Ethical standards, which should be even higher than those in national systems, are not clear. Thus, there must be clear guidelines for every actor in the ISDS system and this book provides a guideline for third-party funders operating in the investment arbitration regime, as needed..[187] This book deals with the TPF arrangements and funders and only provides a guideline for funders. However, the author believes there must be specific guidelines for every actor including arbitrators, lawyers, experts, etc.

It can be argued that professional rules of lawyers are still applicable to those lawyers acting in investment arbitration. However, this is not always true. Furthermore, counsels from different jurisdictions are subject to different ethical and professional rules that do not necessarily match each other can even create imbalance and injustice.[188] Thus, having a common ethical and professional system that every lawyer unanimously follows would remove such possibilities and provide a better and clearer regime. However, since this book proposes the best practice guideline for funders, it will not go further and suggest a guideline for lawyers. Further research and work should be done to provide such guidelines for lawyers, arbitrators and experts operating in investment arbitration and noncompliance with the guideline should attract serious sanctions so that that everyone follows the guideline.

The reason for regulation or a guideline is simple: to bring every funder to the same high-level standards. According to an author, "legislative action is necessary, given the public interest in maintaining the legitimacy of the legal justice system,

---

[184] Moseley (2019), pp. 1181–1203. https://heinonline.org/HOL/P?h=hein.journals/tlr97&i=1247, pp. 1185–1186.

[185] *See* Chap. 1 in supra note 5 (Frignati), p. 511.

[186] Moseley, p. 1194.

[187] *See* Chap. 7.

[188] A US lawyer can have more flexibility in terms of preparing a witness for a trial compared to English-qualified lawyers due to different professional rules.

implementing cost savings, promoting settlement, and affording to individuals fair hearings". Compared to individual claims, this public interest is even higher in investment arbitration since state and taxpayer money is at stake. Therefore, without regulation or any specific rules, funders operating in the system might raise some concerns since not all of them can operate in the highest standards.

Another important accusation against third-party funders is that they fund cases and merely do a "hit and run" if they are not required to pay adverse costs when the case fails. Is there a risk for a funder to hit and run? The author does not think there is such a risk. The reason is simple. Funders do not throw their money out only to hit and run. They put their money where it will hit the right case and win, not to run. If every funder is made to pay SfC, this will decrease the number of cases funded, or at least the terms of TPF agreements would be more burdensome for investors. This would not be the desired result because access to a dispute settlement mechanism must be easy for investors, not difficult or too burdensome. If it is too hard, then states would easily discriminate against foreign investors since not many of them would want to spend the money and take the risk of arbitration. In fact the opposite is true, the access should be easier so that the rule of law can be effective in the ISDS regime.

While considering whether third-party should be regulated, it is also important to note that it is not the only unregulated area in ISDS. In general, there is no ethical guideline to apply to counsels or arbitrators in international arbitration either; in other words, international arbitration "dwells in an ethical no-man's land".[189] Not surprisingly, in this no-man's land, there is no ethical guideline applicable to funders either. Thus, at the beginning of this chapter, noting this fact is important not only to TPF, but also to other actors in arbitration. Therefore, the more actors involved with the arbitration, the more complex relationships will exist between them which will increase the risk of conflicts between the parties, their lawyers, arbitrators, and now funders.

5.7 How to Bring Ethical Standards: Ethical Guidelines for Funders

In the last section of this book, the justification for an ethical (and procedural) guideline for funders operating in the investment arbitration regime is briefly explained.

Overall, as explained in each section, there are potentially worrisome issues. This book does not suggest that funders are operating in an unethical way, nor that their operation distorts the procedural fairness in the investment arbitration regime. This book, in contrast, defends funders for operating in good high standards. However,

[189] Doak Bishop (2011), p. 383; (For speech version online *See* https://www.arbitration-icca.org/media/0/12763302233510/icca_rio_keynote_speech.pdf.

there is a reality that the TPF market is growing, and as it does there will be more actors in investment arbitration cases. This book defends the idea that in order to maintain the good standards operating in the market, and to bring new funders to the same high levels, a guideline for all funders must be introduced. This is necessary to draw a line for a certain threshold. If a funder operates well above this threshold, takes additional steps to provide even higher ethical and procedural standards, there is no problem, but they should not go below these standards.

All these explanations in the relevant sections of this book are brought together and the comprehensive ethical and procedural guideline is prepared for the funders, which can be found in Chap. 7.

5.8 Conclusion

There are ethical concerns surrounding TPF. These concerns increase, especially in investment arbitration. Especially some states, since they do not derive any benefit from TPF, strongly oppose and even suggest that TPF should be banned. However, TPF increases the accessibility of the ISDS regime. The best and wisest way would not be cutting choices a party has to bring a case, it would be increasing such choices. And now, TPF is offering a good choice for funders, that is why many claimants are using it and the industry is growing. If we want an investment arbitration regime that is efficient and accessible, then TPF should remain, and other financial options for both investors and states should be developed in the market. However, to ensure that TPF arrangements do not distort the integrity of the ISDS regime and funders do not act unethically, and do not put lawyers or any other actors in a difficult position to comply with their ethical and professional rules, certain standards are necessary. This book provides such standards in the best practice guideline.

TPF is not the only option for investors to initiate their claims. It might not even be the best option for investors. However, it is an option, and it is there. There is certainly room in investment arbitration for development. There should be a legal aid mechanism for investment arbitration. The structural problems of ISDS should be removed and the ISDS itself should be improved. If investment arbitration is the primary, and sometimes only, effective mechanism to settle investment disputes, then it should be accessible. Whether we adore it or not, TPF is making ISDS more accessible. Thus, TPF is a useful financial tool to have. Nobody forces parties to use such tools. However, it is there as an additional option to parties. And to operate without any distortion in the ISDS system, this book proposes the best practice guideline for funders operating the ISDS system.

References

Attrill W (2019) Ethical issues in litigation funding. IMF (Australia) Ltd., 16 February 2019, p. 3
Barendrecht M et al (2014) Legal aid in Europe: nine different ways to guarantee access to justice? Dutch Ministry of Security and Justice (WODC)
Beisner J et al (2009) Selling lawsuits, buying trouble: third-party litigation funding in the United States. U.S. Chamber for Legal Reform, pp 4–11
Berge TL, St John T (2021) Asymmetric diffusion: World Bank 'best Practice' and the spread of arbitration in national investment laws. Rev Int Polit Econ: RIPE 28(3):584–610
Bhushan A, Thakur S (2020) Nothing changes if nothing changes: an introduction to the 2021 ICC rules of arbitration. Kluwer Arbitration Blog, October 27 2020, http://arbitrationblog.kluwerarbitration.com/2020/10/27/nothing-changes-if-nothing-changes-an-introduction-to-the-2021-icc-rules-of-arbitration/
Bjorklund AK, Druzin BH (2018) Institutional Lock-in within the field of investment arbitration. Univ Pa J Int Law 39:707
Brauch MD (2019, September 19) Toward a code of conduct for investment adjudicators: Can ethical standards salvage ISDS? Investment Treaty News. https://www.iisd.org/itn/en/2019/09/19/toward-a-code-of-conduct-for-investment-adjudicators-can-ethical-standards-salvage-isds-martin-dietrich-brauch/
Brekoulakis S, Rogers C (2019) Third-party financing in ISDS: a framework for understanding practice and policy. Academic Forum on ISDS Concept Paper 2019/13. p. 1. https://www.jus.uio.no/pluricourts/english/projects/leginvest/academic-forum/papers/papers/13-rogers-brekoulakis-tpf-isds-af-13-2019-version-2.pdf
Brower CN, Blanchard S (2014) From "Dealing in Virtue" to "Profiting from Injustice": The Case Against "Re-Statification" of Investment Dispute Settlement. Harv Int Law J 55, Feature Online January 2014
Chaisse J, Eken C (2020) The monetization of investment claims: promises and pitfalls of third-party funding in investor-state arbitration. Del J Corp Law 44(2–3):113–166. https://www.proquest.com/scholarly-journals/monetization-investment-claims-promises-pitfalls/docview/2466062187/se-2?accountid=13042
Dafe F, Williams Z (2021) Florence. "Banking on Courts: Financialization and the Rise of Third-party Funding in Investment Arbitration.". Rev Int Polit Econ 28(5):1362–1384. https://doi.org/10.1080/09692290.2020.1764378
De Morpurgo M (2011) A comparative legal and economic approach to third-party litigation funding. New Europe Law Rev 19(2):343
DeStefano MM (2012) Nonlawyers influencing lawyers: too many cooks in the kitchen or stone soup? Fordham Law Rev 80(6):2791
Doak Bishop R (2011) Advocacy and ethics in international arbitration: ethics in international arbitration. In: van den Berg AJ (ed) Arbitration advocacy in changing times, ICCA Congress Series, 2010 Rio, vol 15. Kluwer Law International, pp 383–390
Douglas RR (2005) Other people's money: the ethics of litigation funding. Mercer Law Rev 56:674
Eberhardt P, Olivet C (2015) Profiting from injustice: how law firms and arbitrators fuel the investment arbitration boom. CCPA Monitor 22(2):27
Eken C (2021) Analysis of third-party funding within the Islamic framework (TDM, ISSN 1875-4120) May 2021
Eken C (2022) A detailed comparison of third-party funding regulations in Hong Kong and Singapore. Asia Pac Law Rev 29(1). https://doi.org/10.1080/10192557.2021.1979799
Garcia FJ (2018, July 30) The case against third-party funding in investment arbitration. Investment Treaty News. https://www.iisd.org/itn/en/2018/07/30/the-case-against-third-party-funding-in-investment-arbitration-frank-garcia/
Gertz G, Jandhyala S, Skovgaard Poulsen LN (2018) Legalization, diplomacy, and development: do investment treaties de-politicize investment disputes? World Dev 107:239–252
Glickman DR (2016) Embracing third-party litigation finance. Fla State Univ Law Rev 43(3):1043

Green M (2017) The rise of funders: Allianz executive says companies face a growing threat from litigation funding—but not in the United States, yet. Best's Review (Oldwick, NJ: 2000), 117(12):73
Guven B, Johnson L (2019) The policy implications of third-party funding in investor-state dispute settlement. Columbia Law School, Columbia Centre on Sustainable Investment Staff Publications, May 2019, p 41
Güven B, Johnson L (2019, June 27) Third-party funding and the objectives of investment treaties: friends or foes? Investment Treaty News
Hepburn J (2018) An update on investment treaty disputes involving the government of India. Investment Arbitration Reporter
Kawharu A (2007) Public participation and transparency in international investment arbitration: Suez v Argentina. New Zealand Yearb Int Law 4(4):159–172
Khoza MJ (2018) Formal regulation of third party litigation funding agreements? A South African perspective. Potchefstroom Electr Law J 21(1):1–22
Kryvoi Y (2012) Counterclaims in investor-state arbitration. Minn J Int Law 321
Lemos MH (2016) Privatizing public litigation. Georgetown Law J 104(3):515
Levi L (2017) The weaponized lawsuit against the media: litigation funding as a new threat to journalism. Am Univ Law Rev 66(3):761
Lord Justice Jackson (2009) Review of civil litigation costs: preliminary report, vol 1. The Stationery Office
Martin SL (1992) Syndicated lawsuits: illegal Champerty or new business opportunity? Am Bus Law J 30(3):485–511
Martin SL (1999) Financing plaintiff's lawsuits: an increasingly popular business. Univ Mich J Law Reform 33(1–2):57
Massini K (2015) Risk versus reward: the increasing use of third funders in international arbitration and the awarding security for costs. Arbitr Law Rev 7:323, 325
McLaughlin JH (2007) Litigation funding: charting a legal and ethical course. Vermont Law Rev 31(3):615
Merzer M (2013, April 19) Cash-now promise of lawsuit loans under fire. Fox Business
Miller L (2017, March) Perils of third-party funding. Los Angeles Lawyer, pp 19–25
Moliterno JT (2003) Broad prohibition, thin rationale: the "Acquisition of an Interest and Financial Assistance in Litigation" rules. Geo J Leg Ethics 16:223
Moseley SE (2019) Disclosing third-party funding in international investment arbitration. Texas Law Rev 97(6):1181–1203
Moul E (2015) The international centre for the settlement of investment disputes and the developing world: creating a mutual investment regime. Santa Clara Law Rev 55(4):881
Ng I (2019) Rethinking counsel ethics in international arbitration. Kluwer Arbitration Blog, December 12 2019. http://arbitrationblog.kluwerarbitration.com/2019/12/12/rethinking-counsel-ethics-in-international-arbitration/
Orsi SD (2013) Ethics in international arbitration: new considerations for arbitrators and counsel. Arbitr Brief 3(1):92–114
Raphael DD (2001) Concepts of Justice [electronic resource]. Clarendon; Oxford University Press, Oxford: New York, p 1
Ribeiro J, Sato S (2017) Transparency in investment arbitration: its importance for Japan. Asian Int Arbitr J 13(1):27–51
Rogers CA (2014) Ethics in international arbitration, 1st edn. Oxford University Press, Oxford
Saadani O, Joseph-Louisia J (2017) Old İssues, new horizons: third-party funding in Morocco. Kluwer Arbitration Blog, December 3, 2017, http://arbitrationblog.kluwerarbitration.com/2017/12/03/old-issues-new-horizons-third-party-funding-morocco/?print=print
Sahani V (2015) Harmonizing third-party litigation funding regulation. Cardozo Law Rev 36(3):861

Santosuosso T, Scarlett R (2019) Third-party funding in investment arbitration: misappropriation of access to Justice Rhetoric by global speculative finance. Bost Coll Law Rev 60:I.-8. https://lawdigitalcommons.bc.edu/bclr/vol60/iss9/5

Saravanan APP, Subramanian SR (2018) Transparency and confidentiality requirements in investment treaty arbitration. Bricks Law J 5(4):114–138

Shannon V (2015) Harmonizing third-party litigation funding regulation. Cardozo Law Rev 36(3): 861

Sheppard A (2016) The approach of investment treaty tribunals to evidentiary privileges. ICSID Rev 31(3):670–689

Simson C (2017) Funders fret over Singapore's 3rd-party disclosure measures. Law360, Jan 13

Stauffer D (2009) The unity of Plato's 'Gorgias': Rhetoric, justice, and the philosophic life. Cambridge University Press

Steinitz M (2011) Whose claim is this anyway? Third-party litigation funding. Minn Law Rev 95(4):1268–1338

Steinitz M (2015) Incorporating legal claims. Notre Dame Law Rev 90(3):1155–1210

Steinitz M, Field AC (2014) A model litigation finance contract. Iowa Law Rev 99(2):711–772

Veljanovski C (2012) Third-party litigation funding in Europe. J Law Econ Policy 8(3):405

Waibel M, Kaushal A, Chung K-H, Balchin C (2010) The backlash against investment arbitration: perceptions and reality. Kluwer Law International, Frederick

Chapter 6
Conclusion

The interviews the author conducted with funders suggest that the number of publicly known funded cases is a sample of a much larger number of funded cases unknown to the public. It is likely that the increasing use of TPF in investment arbitration will persist until major changes to the practice are brought into effect. It is not only because investors lack the financial means to bring a claim against States. Even if they do have the financial resources to bring such claims, they simply do not wish to bear the risk of investment arbitration. Investment arbitration is lengthy and full of uncertainties in terms of the result of the case and the recoverability of the award. Disputant parties therefore find TPF particularly appealing where the financial risk is shouldered by funders, though the extent of the transfer of such risks is contingent upon the arrangement between the funder and funded party. In the future, new funding models might develop further to enable States to benefit from TPF, too.

It is undeniable that TPF has demonstrated considerable merit, the most significant of which is increased access to justice. It is the rhetoric of TPF practice as well as the expected outcome of every TPF case. Even if the funders' motive is to profit from their investment and not necessarily to provide access to justice, it is the ends that are of importance. The availability of TPF contributes to a more accessible investment arbitration system for investors who are either bankrupted or simply do not have the financial capacity to bring an expensive investment arbitration case otherwise. TPF facilitates the ISDS regime and allows more cases to be heard.

Granted, there is an imbalance in the system. States have no access to TPF, which is perhaps attributable to the fact that States generally possess substantially more resources than investors investing in their territories. This does not undermine the benefits of TPF, but it does highlight an area for improvement in the realm of TPF. States should be able to benefit from TPF, especially given that smaller States may have a greater need for finance compared to large corporations which are placed as Claimants in the ISDS regime.

The lack of options for States is only one of the many limitations of current TPF practice. While the demand for and the use of TPF have been increasing, questions have been raised (and remained to be addressed) in ISDS cases. Those questions

C. Eken, *Third-Party Funding in Investment Arbitration*, Law for Professionals,
https://doi.org/10.1007/978-3-031-63620-2_6

such as the recoverability of TPF fees should be discussed soon. Who is funding the case? If a state is funding cases against another state continuously, this might raise ethical problems for example. Also, are the funders controlling the case or just financing the case? Any potential conflict of interest, the conduct of the funders during the TPF relationship and many other questions are yet to answer before investment arbitration tribunals.

ICSID has since brought a disclosure rule on TPF. However, this does not seem sufficient for mitigating the potential negative effects of TPF agreements in investment arbitration cases. A comprehensive guideline, which addresses procedural and ethical concerns of the investment arbitration system, is a necessary complement that helps practitioners navigate the changing landscapes. This book has provided one such guideline. Without a prescribed model or pattern for funders to follow, which has been the case until now, the practice is essentially at the discretion of the funders. This entails great power indeed, and it is up to the funders to determine how they would like to impose such power on the proceedings. For example, lawyers who are remunerated by funders cannot be trusted advisors if they are receiving money from funders. A separate counsel advising the terms of TPF agreements would be prudent.

Of course, funders are generally against regulatory measures as they pose constraints on their flexibility. Even if funders claim that they are already following what is suggested in the guideline, this cannot be guaranteed unless their compliance is confirmed in writing. Therefore, the guidelines suggested in the book should be followed by funders. ICSID and other arbitration centres should refer to and potentially adopt these guidelines to address the concerns raised in each rule in the guideline. Arbitration is supposedly autonomous in that the procedures are developed by the conduct of its users. As a new development in investment arbitration, TPF practice will be developed by the conduct of funders, lawyers, and funded parties. How the community, including the States in investment arbitration, wants this practice to develop, and whether these guidelines should be adopted or ignored, will be at the discretion of its users.

This book contends that the use of TPF in investment arbitration should continue. However, extensive guidelines are needed to ensure the involvement of funders does not distort the investment arbitration regime. The new disclosure rules in ICSID will yield a much larger number of funded cases being public, though many other concerns are left unaddressed. The guideline attached to this book provides such confidence to the parties. This guideline is scalable, which is intended to facilitate TPF practice that is effective and calibratable to the purpose of the ISDS system such as fair use. As consistently reiterated in this book, the purpose of establishing guidelines is and should always be to protect the integrity of the system while ensuring that the flexibility of the mechanism is not stifled.

Chapter 7
The Best Practice Guideline for Funders Operating in Investment Arbitration

This best practice guideline is prepared by the author to set the minimum standards for funders operating in the investment arbitration regime to ensure that their operation does not distort the ISDS regime. If a funder operates well above the threshold set in this guideline and takes additional steps to provide even higher ethical and procedural standards, this is even better, but it must not go below these standards. The reason for such guideline is that TPF is a common practice in the ISDS regime now and their operation should be ensured that they do not distort the ISDS regime. The guideline provides principles funders should follow and a brief explanation regarding why such principles are needed.

This guideline has two parts. Part 1 suggests the minimum threshold all funders must adhere to operate in the investment arbitration regime without distorting the system. Second, further study is needed to develop it further. This is also important, and this guideline suggests a possible first step. However, a more inclusive study is needed to determine rules satisfying every stakeholder including the funded parties, investors and states and their lawyers. For this, institutions such as ICSID, SCC and other arbitration centres that administer investment arbitration cases need to collaborate or take the unilateral initiative to develop further guidelines.

First, the principles are set out and they are followed by brief explanations regarding why such principles are needed.

C. Eken, *Third-Party Funding in Investment Arbitration*, Law for Professionals,
https://doi.org/10.1007/978-3-031-63620-2_7

7.1 Guideline-1st Part: Minimum Threshold Every Funder Investing in Investment Arbitration Cases Must Observe[1]

7.1.1 Principles

1. Access to Justice
Third-party funding has been facilitating the ISDS regime, increasing its accessibility and providing access to justice for some investors who would otherwise be unable to bring such claims against states.

2. The Scope of the Principles
Third-party funding is a funding arrangement between the funded party and a third party other than the lawyer of the funded party, to fund the case partially or wholly, regardless of their motives. Their motive can be either to profit, or charitable purposes.

3. Funders' Capital
Funders' capital cannot be collected from a State, state-enterprise, sovereign wealth funds, or any private investor who is active in politics or holding any official role in a State such as president, minister, or parliament member.

4. Instructions Regarding the Use of Capital
An investor who gives the capital to the funder cannot instruct that its money must be used against a specific state and must not exclude a specific state. It can, however, exclude "specific sectors" such as the tobacco or alcohol industry.

5. Underlying Motive of Funders
(1) Funders' motives are irrelevant to the principles in this guide. However, funders cannot have an unethical purpose when they fund a Claimant in the ISDS regime. If a funder is found to have another motive against the state, they are funding the case, then the funder must face serious sanctions such as banning from investing in ISDS cases again. These sanctions must cover all directors and people involved in the decision to fund the case, those who gave money to the funder and everyone who knows that such an underlying motive exists.

(2) If it is understood that the funder or people or institutions who provided the capital to funders invested in a case that is clearly against a State with unethical motives other than stated in the scope of the principles in principle 2, then the funder shall be responsible for the claimant's costs even if the funder is not responsible for such costs in its agreement.

6. Disclosure
(1) Funders must disclose themselves in every ISDS case. The funded parties, their lawyers, and funder all have the duty of disclosure, and they must disclose the

[1] Explanations to the principles continue following to the guideline.

existence of the funder and the identity of the funder to the tribunal and the other party in every investment arbitration case.

(2) If it is a concern of the tribunal or to the other party, the disclosure must further include (i) whether the funder will pay any cost order against the funded party according to the TPF agreement, (ii) any specific details of any potential conflict between the funder and funded party. Any such disclosure should refer to the full details of (i) TPF agreement terms or (ii) past or present relationship details with an arbitrator.

(3) If a funder is requested to fund their cases by both parties (claimant and respondent) in the same dispute, the funder will automatically reject the second party (either claimant or respondent whoever is the second in order) and cannot even receive any documents or information from the second party.

7. Relationship Between Funder-Lawyer

The funder must not obstruct the lawyer's autonomy and professional decisions or the client-lawyer relationship.

8. Different Lawyer Advising on TPF Agreements

Lawyers advising on TPF agreements should not act on the merits of the case.

9. Portfolio Funding and Frivolous Claims

Funders cannot fund a case in ISDS as part of a portfolio. Only merit-based assessment is allowed. If a funder cannot show such assessment, that funder will face sanctions.

10. Conflict of Interest (Challenge to Arbitrator)

Funders cannot appoint the same arbitrators in their cases. If such conduct occurs, funders and arbitrators must face serious consequences such as being banned from ISDS forever.

11. Ethics

Funders must adhere to the ethical conduct in their business. No unethical conduct of funders shall be allowed or tolerated in the ISDS system.

12. State Funding

A funder has to offer financial tools for the respondent states, even though states don't use it.

13. Security for Costs

Third-party funding cannot be the main reason for granting security for costs applications. Each case must be considered on its own merits and in light of its specific facts.

14. Efficiency of Arbitration Proceedings

TPF terms can encourage arbitrators to render an award at an earlier date.

15. Attending Hearings

Each arbitration tribunal will decide whether the funder can attend the hearings if there is a request to do so.

16. Other Matters
Each tribunal can have any other necessary orders to provide when necessary.

7.1.2 Explanations of Principles

Principle 1
Regardless of funder's motive, TPF is giving more chances to bring a case, making it financially easy for funded parties to bring a claim. This provides access to justice, and it is now a well-established practice, which has been recognized by investment arbitration tribunals (e.g. Abaclat and Others v. the Argentine Republic, ICSID Case No. ARB/07/5; Giovanni Alemanni and others v Argentine Republic, ICSID Case No ARB/07/8). Therefore, this fact must first be acknowledged at the beginning of principles.

Principle 2
It is important to define the scope of these principles. Lawyer financing is excluded from the definition of TPF because lawyers are out of the ISDS system, they have already a role and therefore, they are not technically a "third-party" out of the dispute resolution process. Lawyers already have a client-lawyer relationship with the funded party, and they have the freedom to arrange their fees and determine the method and time of payment. Also, lawyers are not behind the doors that need to be disclosed or need to be known. One reason to inform the TPF relationship is to increase transparency in the ISDS system and ensure that there is nobody behind the doors backing a dispute against a particular state. Moreover, lawyer-finance is not bringing a complicated relationship since there are still two parties in the lawyer-client relationship and lawyers are not receiving money from any third party that can complicate the client-lawyer relationship. This exclusion is also in compliance with the Tribunal's decision in Ipek Investment Limited v. Republic of Turkey, ICSID Case No. ARB/18/18.

Principle 3
States are parties in the investment arbitration regime and cannot fund a case against another state in the ISDS regime. Political actors, politically affiliated organizations or individuals, or states, state-owned or controlled enterprises must never be able to invest in TPF in investment arbitration. They can invest in TPF for disputes in commercial arbitration or courts. However, their money should never be used in investment arbitration. This has ethical consequences, as explained in Chap. 5 of this book. Briefly, ISDS must not be a tool of a state to back cases against other states.

Principle 4
ISDS regime must never be a tool for pressuring certain states. If capital is provided to bring cases against certain countries and exclude others, this cannot be tolerated and must be strictly banned. However, investors who provide capital to the funders can have certain preferences, and ethical or religious choices not to fund certain

companies who are dealing with certain industries. Therefore, a Muslim investor, for example, can instruct the funder not to use his money in a company that is dealing with the tobacco industry or casinos etc. Similarly, an investor who cares for the environment can opt-out of funding oil and gas companies, etc.

Principle 5

This rule is further to ensure that cases are not brought against states with a secret agenda to attack the economy of a certain state or to increase pressure against certain states. To ensure that such sanctions against funders are realistic, the Association of Litigation Funders and similar associations should embrace those principles. Furthermore, ICSID and other arbitration centres should adopt those principles and empower their arbitration tribunals and centres to grant such orders.

Principle 6

Disclosure of the identity of the funder will ensure that states and the tribunal can check whether they have any confict of interest. Further disclosure is required only if there is a speicific concern. And disclosing the full details will ensure parties and the tribunal that nothing stayed hidden from them. This is important for the arbitration tribunal to decide fully on the issues. It is also in compliance with the decisions of tribunals in investment arbitration cases such as Tennant Energy, LLC v. Government of Canada, PCA Case No. 2018-54.

There is a risk if the same funder is used by both parties to the same dispute, and the participation of the funder is not disclosed to the tribunal and the other party. Then, the funder would be the only one who knows about this situation. This is a dangerous risk, and a simple disclosure can prevent it. Therefore, with the disclosure, these and similar risks would be eliminated.

Principle 7

This rule ensures that the funder does not interfere with the integrity of the lawyer-client relationship as well as the integrity of the system.

Principle 8

Lawyers advising on TPF agreement terms must be different than lawyers acting in the dispute itself. Otherwise, this can lead to a conflict of interest for the lawyer. As a recent case brought by a funded party in investment arbitration against its funder and lawyers suggests that if such a rule is not established, similar cases might increase.[2] Without waiting for the case law, it is not right for a lawyer to advise on terms of a TPF agreement where the lawyer also has an interest in the TPF relationship since the funder pays the lawyer eventually.

Principle 9

No portfolio funding is allowed in investment arbitration because otherwise portfolio funding might increase the chance of funding frivolous cases.

[2] Cosmo Sanderson, King & Spalding sued by client in funded BIT case, 15 June 2021 https://globalarbitrationreview.com/king-spalding-sued-client-in-funded-bit-case.

Portfolio funding contains risks of funding unmeritorious cases. Portfolio funding is a type of TPF where several cases are funded as a group. Cases in the portfolio are not assessed individually. As a result, there is a chance of funding cases that are not strong and will most likely fail. Since funding frivolous cases is neither an ethical nor desired result in the ISDS system, even a small possibility of funding a weak case must be eliminated by not allowing portfolio funding. Similar to explanations under principle 5, these principles must be adopted by various institutions to make such sanctions realistic and possible.

Principle 10
The funder-arbitrator relationship should be more transparent. If a funder continuously appointed the same arbitrator, it would raise red flags. Any ongoing appointment relationship between a funder and an arbitrator cannot be allowed; if such matter occurs, both the funder and arbitrator must be disqualified. This is both the duty of arbitrators and funders to disclose without being requested to do so.

Principle 11
The ethics of funders are crucial to having an efficient judicial mechanism in investment arbitration. Similar to lawyers, arbitrators, experts, and any other parties participating in this judicial mechanism, the funders must also comply with the highest ethical standards and deviating from such standards must not be tolerated.

Principle 12
This is to address concerns relating to some criticism against funders in investment arbitration where TPF is provided only to investors. Funders must provide similar tools to states even though states do not use them.

Principle 13
Tribunals should weigh the two decisions; ordering security for costs (SfC) and rejecting such applications. While weighting these two, each tribunal must assess potential consequences such as the funded party's right to access to justice and potential discontinuation of arbitration consequence if the funder does not provide security. If funders have an obligation to pay adverse costs, relevant disclosures should be made by the funder/funded party to prevent unnecessary SfC orders. The funder can instead show adverse cost insurance or relevant security they put in place to satisfy the arbitration tribunal.

Principle 14
In the *Mohamed Abdel Raouf Bahgat v. Egypt, PCA Case No. 2012-07* case, the tribunal rendered the award before a certain date considering the TPF arrangements because if the award is rendered beyond that certain date, the funding costs would increase according to the TPF arrangements. Thus, TPF arrangements can have a positive effect in speeding of the arbitration proceedings and render the award as early as possible.

Principle 15
Tribunals will eventually decide who can and should attend the hearings. This will be an issue only if a funder wishes to attend a hearing or the State calls the funder to

the hearing for a specific purpose. In any case, the tribunal will order according to their decisions.

Principle 16
This principle is to ensure that any other requests or issues related to third-party funding that has not been envisaged in these guidelines but come to the attention of the tribunal, the tribunals will decide.

7.2 Guideline-2nd Part: Conduct of Funders During the Proceedings and Details of the TPF Agreement

Control of Funders
1. The funded party stays in control of the case unless the funded party assigned the case completely.

1.1. Funders can suggest arbitrators or lawyers to the funded party to choose but have no power to make the final decision. This decision stays with the funded party and its lawyers.

Settlement
2. The funder cannot decide on behalf of the funded party; it is the funder who should decide whether the settlement offer satisfies it and whether to accept or reject it. This is the client's right. The funder doing investment must not affect the rights of the client.

2.1. To ensure that the settlement decision stays with the funder, the return of funders must be adjusted. The order should be: (i) funder receives its investment in full at a reasonable interest rate on the date of payment; (ii) funded party receives a return equal to the funder's payment; (iii) funder and funded party share equally until the funder is fully paid; (iii) funded party receives the rest. This order will ensure when and how the funder and funded party will get paid.[3]

Prohibited Conduct of Funders
3. Funders cannot apply any tactics or strategy with the purpose of delaying the case, preventing the settlement of the dispute, increasing the costs of the case, or any other tactic that results in delaying the resolution of the claim or increasing the costs of the case.

Recoverability of Funding Costs
4. If third-party funding is the only option for the investor and it is proven and the investor prevails in its claim against the State, then capped TPF fees can be recovered from the State as part of the legal costs of investor.

[3]The order of lawyers' fees is not shown in this because the purpose of this guideline is to clarify the conduct and contract of funders. If a lawyer's conduct in international arbitration in question, which may well be, a separate work should be done.

4.1 However, only reasonable market rate funding costs can be recoverable in the situation described at paragraph 4 above. If a funder exploits the funded party and takes most of the percentage of the award, the State cannot be ordered to recover such costs beyond a reasonable amount.

Discontinuation from Funding the Case
5. When the funder can cease funding the case must be clearly determined under the TPF agreement.

Criminal or Otherwise Illegal Conduct of Funders
6. Funders' any unethical conduct is strictly not tolerated. If a funder engages in a criminal or otherwise illegal conduct, aside from criminal consequences they've committed, the arbitration tribunal might sanction the party and the funder in the case severely depending on the circumstances.

Confidentiality
7. Funders' involvement must not affect the confidentiality of the process. Communication between funders and clients is privileged as well as all documents shared with the funder. If any of the documents are leaked by the funder or used against the funded party in another case, then the funder and all affiliated people lose their rights to invest in investment arbitration cases and further sanctions can be imposed against the funder and all affiliated people.

7.2.1 Explanations

Principle 1
Contractually, there should be a mechanism ensuring that the funded party is in charge.

It is understood that the desire to follow and protect their investment is very clear. However, there must be a limit and the funded party should stay in control of the case. Otherwise, it is more than mere funding. If the funder wants to assign the case, then the assignment should finalize, and it can no longer be third-party funding. Thus, the best practice guideline is to offer a rule on this issue

Principle 9.1 must also be addressed. If funders are appointing the arbitrators, they have arbitrators whom they work together behind the curtains, and those arbitrators are always voting for the funded parties, these are serious threats to the system.

Principle 2
Third-party funding should not affect the settlement of disputes in ISDS negatively. This is because ISDS seeks to settle disputes, if possible, amicably before arbitration starts or if possible, settling during the arbitration proceedings.

The funder cannot have weight in settlement, pure funded party's decision, must be

EXPLANATION: ISDS—less control supra national space, where no rules necessarily bind other than professional conducts (ethical standards-ethics chapter, why it is important-because there is no regulation supra national space)

Principle 3
Delaying is not allowed in ISDS. Fastening resolution of the dispute is appropriate. This principle does not mean that funders cannot take their time to approve funding the case. Approving to fund can take time and it is understandable. However, after the case is initiated, any dilatory tactics or tactics to increase the costs of the dispute are not allowed. States should not bear any additional risks with the involvement of funders. If a funder engages in such conduct, it should face serious sanctions including paying to the states penalties for their conduct.

Principle 4
Similar decisions are seen in litigation funding. Since in this scenario, third-party funding provides access to justice, the investor should get the whole claim amount without any deduction as much as possible. This would only be possible through TPF fees.

The funder must not use any special situation the funded party is to extort extra money for the best practice. The funder should assess the merits of cases meticulously to make its decisions based on the merits of cases.

Principle 5
Ceasing the funding is an important issue. When the funder can stop funding the case must be clearly determined in the TPF agreement. As key principles, the funder must not be able to stop funding the case of its own discretion and without any reason. Stopping to fund the case must depend on objective standards such that a certain document or fact was not disclosed to the funder.

Principle 6
Any unethical, criminal or illegal conduct is strictly prohibited and must be declared with a rule and clear sanctions must be determined to bring these high ethical standards into force, not only parties and their lawyers but now also for funders.

Principle 7
All the documents funders collect from parties create a huge amount of data in the hands of funders. How funders can use these documents in other cases against the same party is a big concern. These types of confidentiality and privilege concerns need to be addressed in a guideline. The further guideline should be developed by asking all stakeholders, lawyers, states, and investors their opinion and any problem or issues they faced.

Appendix: Investment Arbitration Cases

No	Name of the case	Case type	State	Name of the funder	Issue discussed	The decision of the tribunal
1	Abaclat and Others v. Argentine Republic, ICSID Case No. ARB/07/5	ICSID	Argentina	Task Force Argentine, established by eight major Italian banks	Consent was not properly given	It is proper and TPF provides access to justice. Georges Abi-Saab, in his dissenting opinion, states that the Tribunal does not have jurisdiction over the mass claims
2	Giovanni Alemanni and others v Argentine Republic, ICSID Case No ARB/07/8	ICSID	Argentina	NASAM Mandate	NASAM takes full control	TPF well-established practice; no irregularity in control but due diligence concerns
3	Quasar de Valores and others v the Russian Federation (Quasar v. Russia), SCC Case No 24/2007	Stockholm Chamber of Commerce	Russia	Group Menatep (Majority Yukos shareholder)	Funder is the real party	No abuse of process; parties can get help from third parties
4	RosInvestCo UK Ltd v the Russian Federation, SCC Case No V079/2005	Stockholm Chamber of Commerce	Russia	Elliott Group	Claimant lost its investor status	Having external funding does not mean that the investor loses its investor status
5	Ambiente Ufficio S.p.A. and others v. Argentine Republic, ICSID Case No. ARB/08/9	ICSID	Argentina	NASAM Mandate	The degree of control, funder is the real party	Rejected; the party holds the control of the case

(continued)

C. Eken, *Third-Party Funding in Investment Arbitration*, Law for Professionals,
https://doi.org/10.1007/978-3-031-63620-2

No	Name of the case	Case type	State	Name of the funder	Issue discussed	The decision of the tribunal
6	Teinver SA, Transportes de Cercanıias S.A. and Autobuses Urbanos del Sur S.A. v. Argentine Republic, ICSID Case No ARB/09/1	ICSID	Argentina	Burford Capital	Jurisdiction of the tribunal (Respondent argued that the funder was the real party, not the claimant)	The Tribunal had jurisdiction after the case was initiated; the party can transfer its rights to a funder
7	Ioannis Kardassopoulos and Ron Fuchs v Georgia, ICSID Case No. ARB/05/18	ICSID	Georgia	Alianz Litigation Funding	AoC (claimant claimed costs of TPF arrangement)	The Tribunal did not take TPF arrangements into account
8	ATA Construction, Industrial and Trading Company v Hashemite Kingdom of Jordan, ICSID Case No ARB/08/2	ICSID	Jordan	Former state entity, APC, was funding Jordan	AoC (Respondent argued that funded party's costs should not be covered)	TPF made no difference (The tribunal awarded the claimants their costs of arbitration)
9	RSM Production Corporation v Grenada, ICSID Case No ARB/05/14	ICSID	Grenada	Global Petroleum	AoC (the Respondent State was funded)	The Tribunal did not take TPF arrangements into account
10	WaguihElie George Siag and Clorinda Vecchi v Arab Republic of Egypt, ICSID Case No ARB/05/15	ICSID	Egypt	Contingency fee arrangements by lawyers	The Respondent argued claimants' costs were unjustified and excessive	The Tribunal stated that the costs were reasonable and awarded the costs
11	Guaracachi America, Inc and Rurelec plc v The Plurinational State of Bolivia, UNCITRAL, PCA Case No 2011-17	Permanent Court of Arbitration	Bolivia	Burford Capital	Security for costs (SfC) in the presence of TPF arrangements	The Tribunal refused to grant SfC
12	RSM Production Corporation v. Saint Lucia, ICSID Case No. ARB/12/10	ICSID	Saint Lucia	Undisclosed	Saint Lucia requested SfC	The tribunal ordered SfC mainly because of RSM's proven non-compliance history
13	EuroGasInc and Belmont Resources Inc v Slovak Republic, ICSID Case No ARB/14/14	ICSID	Slovakia	La Française	Disclosure and Confidentiality & SfC	TPF does not necessarily constitute per se granting SfC; the disclosure of the funder's identity was required

(continued)

No	Name of the case	Case type	State	Name of the funder	Issue discussed	The decision of the tribunal
14	South American Silver Limited v. Bolivia, PCA Case No. 2013-15	Permanent Court of Arbitration	Bolivia	Undisclosed	Disclosure of the identity of the funder and terms of the TPF agreement	The Tribunal ordered that the identity of the funder be disclosed for the purposes of transparency but refused to order the disclosure of the terms of the TPF agreement
15	Tennant Energy, LLC v. Government of Canada, PCA Case No. 2018-54	Permanent Court of Arbitration	Canada	Undisclosed/ Confidential	Security for costs	Rejected; the mere presence of the TPF agreement does not automatically grant a SfC order
16	Interocean Oil Development Company and Interocean Oil Exploration Company v. Federal Republic of Nigeria, ICSID Case No. ARB/13/20	ICSID	Nigeria	Undisclosed	Challenge of arbitration tribunal because of their involvement in a TPF task force, of which the claimant's counsel is also a member	The tribunal rejected the application since it had not been filed promptly because the Respondent filed 377 days after the it was aware of the facts
17	Canepa Green Energy Opportunities I, S.á r.l. and Canepa Green Energy Opportunities II, S.á r.l. v. Kingdom of Spain, ICSID Case No. ARB/19/4	ICSID	Spain	Harbour Litigation Funding	Challenge of arbitrator- because of an arbitrator's past relationship with a funder	Rejected; independence and impartiality of the arbitrator are not affected
18	S & T Oil Equipment and Machinery Ltd. v. Romania, ICSID Case No. ARB/07/13	ICSID	Romania	Juridica	Discontinuation of Arbitration	The Tribunal ordered discontinuation of arbitration because advance payments were not paid
19	Muhammet Cap & Sehil Inssaat Endustri ve Ticaret Ltd Sti v Turkmenistan, ICSID Case No ARB/12/6	ICSID	Turkmenistan	La Française	Disclosure	The tribunal ordered claimants to disclose both the identity of the funder and the terms of the TPF arrangement

(continued)

No	Name of the case	Case type	State	Name of the funder	Issue discussed	The decision of the tribunal
20	The Estate of Julio Miguel Orlandini-Agreda and Compañía Minera Orlandini Ltda. v. Bolivia, PCA Case No. 2018-39	Permanent Court of Arbitration	Bolivia	Undisclosed	Security for costs	Rejected; the Tribunal was not persuaded that the circum-stances warranted an order of SfC
21	Dirk Herzig as Insolvency Administrator over the Assets of Unionmatex Industrieanlagen GmbH v. Turkmenistan, ICSID Case No. ARB/18/35	ICSID	Turkmenistan	La Française	Security for costs	Granted; TPF arrangements explicitly excluded liabil-ity of the third-party funder for a costs award adverse to the funded party and this presented a more extreme situation
22	Luis García Armas v. Bolivarian Republic of Vene-zuela, ICSID Case No. ARB(AF)/16/1	ICSID	Venezuela	Calunius	Security for costs	Rejected
23	Eskosol S.p.A. in liquidazione v. Italian Repub-lic, ICSID Case No. ARB/15/50	ICSID	Italy	Undisclosed	SfC order and Disclosure for SfC purpose	Rejected since there was no exceptional cir-cumstances to grant security, and disclosure was moot because of this
24	Sergei Viktorovich Pugachev v. The Russian Federa-tion, UNCITRAL	Permanent Court of Arbitration	Russia	Undisclosed	Security for costs	Rejected; the Claimant failed to overcome the high threshold for granting SfC
25	Corona Materials LLC v. Dominican Republic, ICSID Case No. ARB (AF)/14/3	ICSID	Dominican Republic	Undisclosed	Disclosure of the funder	Granted
26	Stans Energy Corp. and Kutisay Mining LLC v. Kyrgyz Repub-lic (II), PCA Case No. 2015-32	Permanent Court of Arbitration	Kyrgyzstan	Undisclosed	Security for costs	Rejected
27	Eco Oro Minerals Corp. v. Republic of Colombia, ICSID Case No. ARB/16/41	ICSID	Colombia	Tenor Capital	Disclosure	No order was required by the Tribunal

(continued)

No	Name of the case	Case type	State	Name of the funder	Issue discussed	The decision of the tribunal
28	Mohamed Abdel Raouf Bahgat v. Egypt, PCA Case No. 2012-07	Permanent Court of Arbitration	Egypt	Buttonwood Legal Capital & Vannin Capital	Whether TPF costs were recoverable, Control, and Disclosure & Tribunal's rendering award date (TPF costs would increase if the dispute was not resolved by 31 December 2019)	TPF costs were not awarded. Disclosure was granted; the Tribunal considered the terms of the TPF agreement as stated by the Claimant to render the award before the end of the year, within eight months
29	Ipek Investment Limited v. Republic of Turkey, ICSID Case No. ARB/18/18	ICSID	Turkey	Undisclosed	The Definition of Third-Party Funder & SfC	SfC rejected; the mere presence of TPF is not sufficient; the relationship between the Claimant and third parties did not constitute TPF
30	Crystallex International Corporation v. Bolivarian Republic of Venezuela, ICSID Case No. ARB(AF)/11/2	ICSID	Venezuela	Tenor Capital Management & Calunius Capital	No issues discussed	Funder is present but no issues discussed
31	Alapli Elektrik B.V. v. Republic of Turkey, ICSID Case No. ARB/08/13	ICSID	Turkey	Undisclosed	No issues discussed	Funder is present but no issues discussed
32	Rockhopper Italia S.p.A., Rockhopper Mediterranean Ltd, and Rockhopper Exploration Plc v. Italian Republic, ICSID Case No. ARB/17/14	ICSID	Italy	Harbour Litigation Funding	No issues discussed	Funder is present but no issues discussed
33	Bernardus Henricus Funnekotter and others v. Republic of Zimbabwe, ICSID Case No. ARB/05/6	ICSID	Zimbabwe	Partially funded by George Soros's Open Society Initiative	No issues discussed	Funder is present but no issues discussed

(continued)

No	Name of the case	Case type	State	Name of the funder	Issue discussed	The decision of the tribunal
34	Philip Morris Brands Sàrl, Philip Morris Products S.A. and Abal Hermanos S.A. v. Oriental Republic of Uruguay, ICSID Case No. ARB/10/7	ICSID	Uruguay	Tobacco Free Kids Campaign funded Uruguay	No issues discussed (Respondent state was funded)	Funder is present but no issues discussed
35	Renta 4 S.V.S.A, Ahorro Corporación Emergentes F.I., Ahorro Corporación Eurofondo F.I., Rovime Inversiones SICAV S.A., Quasar de Valors SICAV S.A., Orgor de Valores SICAV S.A., GBI 9000 SICAV S.A. v. The Russian Federation, SCC No. 24/2007	Stockholm Chamber of Commerce	Russia	Undisclosed	No issues discussed	Funder is present but no issues discussed
36	Oxus Gold v. Republic of Uzbekistan, UNCITRAL	Permanent Court of Arbitration	Uzbekistan	Calunius	No issues discussed	Funder is present but no issues discussed; tribunal stated that TPF arrangements had no effect on proceedings
37	Infinito Gold Ltd. v. Costa Rica, ICSID Case No. ARB/14/5	ICSID	Costa Rica	Vannin Capital	No issues discussed	Funder is present but no issues discussed; the Tribunal invited the Respondent for commenting on TPF arrangements and respondent state did not provide any observations
38	Cortec Mining Kenya Limited, Cortec (Pty) Limited and Stirling Capital Limited v. Republic of Kenya, ICSID Case No. ARB/15/29	ICSID	Kenya	Alliance 1 Pty Ltd.	No issues discussed	Funder was present but no issues discussed; funder attended hearings

(continued)

No	Name of the case	Case type	State	Name of the funder	Issue discussed	The decision of the tribunal
39	Churchill Mining PLC and Planet Mining Pty Ltd v. Republic of Indonesia, ICSID Case No. ARB/12/14 and 12/40	ICSID	Indonesia	Claimant's largest shareholder	No issues discussed	Funder was present but no issues discussed
40	Gabriel Resources Ltd. and Gabriel Resources (Jersey) v. Romania, ICSID Case No. ARB/15/31	ICSID	Romania	Undisclosed	No issues Raised-Tenor Capital had a seat on the Board of the claimant	Funder was present but no issues discussed
41	Victor Pey Casado and President Allende Foundation v. Republic of Chile, ICSID Case No. ARB/98/2	ICSID	Chile	Undisclosed	No issues raised	Funder was present but no issues discussed
42	Adem Dogan v Turkmenistan, ICSID Case No ARB/09/9	ICSID	Turkmenistan	Omni Bridgeway & Contingency Arrangements	The impact of TPF on a stay of enforcement	The tribunal ordered to continue the stay of enforcement; one of the reasons for this decision was the presence of the third party funder
43	Rusoro Mining Ltd. v. Bolivarian Republic of Venezuela, ICSID Case No. ARB(AF)/12/5	ICSID	Venezuela	Undisclosed	No issues raised	TPF was present but no issues discussed
44	Daniel W. Kappes and Kappes, Cassiday & Associates v. Republic of Guatemala (ICSID Case No. ARB/18/43)	ICSID	Guatemala	Undisclosed	The respondent state was funded	Funder was present but no issues discussed

Cases

ICSID Cases

Abaclat and others v Argentine Republic, ICSID Case No ARB 07/5
Adem Dogan v Turkmenistan, ICSID Case No ARB/09/9
Alapli Elektrik B.V. v. Republic of Turkey, ICSID Case No. ARB/08/13
Ambiente Ufficio SpA and others v Argentine Republic (Ambiente Ufficio v. Argentine) ICSID Case No ARB 08/9
ATA Construction, Industrial and Trading Company v Hashemite Kingdom of Jordan, ICSID Case No ARB/08/2
Bernardus Henricus Funnekotter and others v. Republic of Zimbabwe, ICSID Case No. ARB/05/6
Canepa Green Energy Opportunities I, S.á r.l. and Canepa Green Energy Opportunities II, S.á r.l. v. Kingdom of Spain, ICSID Case No. ARB/19/4
Churchill Mining PLC and Planet Mining Pty Ltd v. Republic of Indonesia, ICSID Case No. ARB/12/14 and 12/40
Corona Materials LLC v. Dominican Republic, ICSID Case No. ARB(AF)/14/3
Cortec Mining Kenya Limited, Cortec (Pty) Limited and Stirling Capital Limited v. Republic of Kenya, ICSID Case No. ARB/15/29
Crystallex International Corporation v. Bolivarian Republic of Venezuela, ICSID Case No. ARB(AF)/11/2
Daniel W. Kappes and Kappes, Cassiday & Associates v. Republic of Guatemala (ICSID Case No. ARB/18/43)
Dirk Herzig as Insolvency Administrator over the Assets of Unionmatex Industrieanlagen GmbH v. Turkmenistan, ICSID Case No. ARB/18/35
Eco Oro Minerals Corp. v. Republic of Colombia, ICSID Case No. ARB/16/41
Eskosol S.P.A. in Liquidazione v. Italian Republic, (ICSID Case No. ARB/15/50)
EuroGasInc and Belmont Resources Inc v Slovak Republic, ICSID Case No ARB/14/14

C. Eken, *Third-Party Funding in Investment Arbitration*, Law for Professionals,
https://doi.org/10.1007/978-3-031-63620-2

Gabriel Resources Ltd. and Gabriel Resources (Jersey) v. Romania, ICSID Case No. ARB/15/31

Giovanni Alemanni and others v Argentine Republic, ICSID Case No ARB/07/8

Holiday Inns S.A. and others v. Morocco (ICSID Case No. ARB/72/1)

Infinito Gold Ltd. v. Costa Rica, ICSID Case No. ARB/14/5

Interocean Oil Development Company and Interocean Oil Exploration Company v. Federal Republic of Nigeria, ICSID Case No. ARB/13/20

Ioannis Kardassopoulos and Ron Fuchs v Georgia, ICSID Case Nos ARB/05/18 and ARB/07/15

Ipek Investment Limited v. Republic of Turkey, ICSID Case No. ARB/18/18

Karkey Karadeniz Elektrik Uretim A.S. v. Islamic Republic of Pakistan, ICSID Case No. ARB/13/1

Luis García Armas v. Bolivarian Republic of Venezuela, ICSID Case No. ARB(AF)/16/1

Muhammet Cap & Sehil Inssaat Endustri ve Ticaret Ltd Sti v Turkmenistan, ICSID Case No ARB/12/6

Philip Morris Brands Sàrl, Philip Morris Products S.A. and AbalHermanos S.A. v. Oriental Republic of Uruguay, ICSID Case No.ARB/10/7 (formerly FTR Holding SA, Philip Morris Products S.A. and AbalHermanos S.A. v. Oriental Republic of Uruguay)

Rockhopper Italia S.p.A., Rockhopper Mediterranean Ltd, and Rockhopper Exploration Plc v. Italian Republic, ICSID Case No. ARB/17/14

RSM Production Corporation v Grenada, ICSID Case No ARB/05/14

RSM Production Corporation v. Saint Lucia, ICSID Case No ARB/12/10

Rusoro Mining Ltd. v. Bolivarian Republic of Venezuela, ICSID Case No. ARB (AF)/12/5

S & T Oil Equipment and Machinery Ltd. v. Romania, ICSID Case No. ARB/07/13

Teinver SA, Transportes de Cercanías SA and Autobuses Urbanos del Sur SA v Argentine Republic, ICSID Case No ARB/09/1

Victor Pey Casado and President Allende Foundation v. Republic of Chile, ICSID Case No. ARB/98/2

WaguihElie George Siag and Clorinda Vecchi v Arab Republic of Egypt, ICSID Case No ARB/05/15

SCC Cases

Quasar de Valores and others v The Russian Federation (Quasar v. Russia), SCC Case No 24/2007

Renta 4 S.V.S.A, Ahorro Corporación Emergentes F.I., Ahorro Corporación Eurofondo F.I., Rovime Inversiones SICAV S.A., Quasar de Valors SICAV S. A., Orgor de Valores SICAV S.A., GBI 9000 SICAV S.A. v. The Russian Federation, SCC No. 24/2007

RosInvestCo UK Ltd v The Russian Federation, SCC Case No V079/2005

UNCITRAL-PCA Cases

Guaracachi America, Inc and Rurelec plc v The Plurinational State of Bolivia, UNCITRAL, PCA Case No 2011-17
Mohamed Abdel Raouf Bahgat v. Egypt, PCA Case No. 2012-07
Oxus Gold v. Republic of Uzbekistan, UNCITRAL
Saluka Investments B.V. v. The Czech Republic, UNCITRAL
Sergei Viktorovich Pugachev v. The Russian Federation, UNCITRAL
South American Silver Limited v. Bolivia, PCA Case No. 2013-15
Stans Energy Corp. and Kutisay Mining LLC v. Kyrgyz Republic (II), PCA Case No. 2015-32
Tennant Energy, LLC v. Government of Canada, PCA Case No. 2018-54
The Estate of Julio Miguel Orlandini-Agreda and Compañía Minera Orlandini Ltda. v. Bolivia, PCA Case No. 2018-39

Various High Court Cases

Arkin v Borchard Lines Ltd and others [2005] EWCA Civ 655
Bayens v Kinross Gold Corporation, 2013 ONSC 4974 (Bayens)
Campbells Cash and Carry Pty Ltd. v. Fostif Pty Ltd. [2006] HCA 41
Chapelgate Credit Opportunity Master Fund Ltd-v-Money & Others [2020] EWCA Civ 246
Davey v Money [2019] EWHC 997 (Ch)
Essar Oilfields Services v Norscot Rig Management Pvt [2016] EWHC 2361
Excalibur Ventures v Texas Keystone and others, [2016] EWCA Civ 1144
Giles v Thompson [1994] 1 AC
Giovanni Alemanni and others v. Argentine Republic, ICSID Case No ARB/07/8, Decision on Jurisdiction and Admissibility (17 November 2014)
Hollard v Zietsman 1885 6 NLR 93
London & Regional (St George's Court) Ltd v Ministry of Defence [2008] EWHC 526 (TCC), 18 March 2008
Mansell v. Robinson [2007] EWHC 101 (QB)
Martell v Consett Iron Co Ltd [1955] Ch 363
Massai Aviation Services v Attorney General [2007] UKPC 12
Otech Pakistan Pvt Ltd v Clough Engineering Ltd and Another - [2006] SGCA 46
Papera Traders Co Ltd v Hyundai (Merchant) Marine Co Ltd (No.2) [2002] 2 Lloyd's Rep 692
Price Waterhouse Coopers Inc and Others v National Potato Cooperative Ltd (448/2003) [2004] ZASCA 64; [2004] 3 All SA 20 (SCA) (1 June 2004)
R (Factortame) Ltd v Secretary of State for Transport (No.8) [2003] QB 381
Roach v News Group Newspapers Ltd [1998] EMLR 161
Seaton v. City of Lexington, 97 S.W.3d 72, 76 (Mo. Ct. App. 2002)

United States District Court For The District Of Columbia, Gretton Ltd., Petitioner, v. Civil Action No. 18-1755 (JEB) REPUBLIC OF UZBEKISTAN, Respondent, Memorandum Opinion, 6 February 2019
Unruh v Seeberger (2007) 10 HKCFAR 31
Winnie Lo v HKSAR (2012) 15 HKCFAR 16

Reports, Consultation Papers and Notes

American Bar Association. (2011). *Issues Paper Concerning Lawyer's Involvement in Alternative Litigation Financing*

American Bar Association. (2012). *Commission on Ethics 20/20 Informational Report to the House of Delegates*

American Bar Association (2020). American Bar Association Best Practices for Third-Party Litigation Funding, adopted by the house of delegates on August 3-4, 2020 available at https://www.americanbar.org/content/dam/aba/directories/policy/annual-2020/111a-annual-2020.pdf

Barendrecht, M., Kistemaker, L., Jan Scholten, H., Schrader, R., & Wrzesinska, M. (2014). *Legal aid in Europe: Nine different ways to guarantee access to justice?* The Hague Institute for Innovation of Law. https://www.hiil.org/wp-content/uploads/2018/09/Legal-Aid-in-Europe-Full-Report.pdf

Beisner, J., Miller, J., & Rubin, G. (2009). *Selling lawsuits, buying trouble: Third-party litigation funding in the United States*. U.S. Chamber Institute for Legal Reform. https://legaltimes.typepad.com/files/thirdpartylitigationfinancing.pdf

Burford. (2019). *Annual Report 2018*. https://www.burfordcapital.com/media/1526/bur-31172-annual-report-2018-web.pdf

Burford. (2021). *Annual Report 2020*. https://www.burfordcapital.com/media/2080/fy-2020-report.pdf

Chartered Institute of Arbitrators. (2011). *CIArb Costs of International Arbitration Survey 2011*. https://www.yumpu.com/en/document/read/4008900/ciarb-costs-of-international-arbitration-survey-2011/9

China International Economic and Trade Arbitration Commission (CIETAC) Hong Kong Arbitration Centre (HKAC). (2016). *Guidelines for third-party funding in arbitration*. https://hkarbitration.files.wordpress.com/2016/05/cietac-draft-guidelines-17-may-16.pdf

Eberhardt, P., & Olivet, C. (2015). *Profiting from injustice: How law firms and arbitrators fuel the investment arbitration boom*. Corporate Europe Observatory

C. Eken, *Third-Party Funding in Investment Arbitration*, Law for Professionals,
https://doi.org/10.1007/978-3-031-63620-2

and the Transnational Institute. https://www.tni.org/files/download/profitingfrominjustice.pdf

European Parliament, Responsible private funding of litigation European Parliament resolution of 13 September 2022 with recommendations to the Commission on Responsible private funding of litigation (2020/2130(INL)), Document 52022IP0308, (2023/C 125/01)

Guven, B., & Johnson, L. (2019). *The policy implications of third-party funding in investor-state dispute settlement*. Columbia Center on Sustainable Investment Staff Publications. https://scholarship.law.columbia.edu/cgi/viewcontent.cgi?article=1007&context=sustainable_investment_staffpubs

IMF Bentham. (2014). *Litigation Funding Roundtable: Key Issues and Best Practices*

International Council for Commercial Arbitration. (2018). *Report for public discussion of the ICCA-Queen Mary Task Force on Third-Party Funding in International Arbitration*

Jackson, R. (2009). *Review of Civil Litigation Costs*. The Stationery Office, The United Kingdom

Lord Justice Jackson. (2009). *Review of civil litigation costs: Preliminary report, Volume One*. The Stationary Office. https://www.judiciary.uk/wp-content/uploads/JCO/Documents/Guidance/jackson-vol1-low.pdf

Molot, J. T. (2012). *Theory and practice in litigation risk*. Burford. http://rippmedia.com/Molot-TheoryandPractice.pdf

Morabito, V. (2017). *An empirical study of Australia's class action regimes, fifth report: The first twenty-five years of class actions in Australia*. Monash University. https://doi.org/10.2139/ssrn.3005901

Queen Mary University, & White & Case. (2018). *2018 international arbitration survey: The evolution of international arbitration*. https://www.whitecase.com/publications/insight/2018-international-arbitration-survey-evolution-international-arbitration

Rickard, L. A. (2014). *The real and ugly facts of litigation funding*. The U.-S. Chamber of Commerce Institute for Legal Reform

The Law Commission, England and Wales. (1966). *Proposals for the Reform of the Law relating to Maintenance and Champerty*. https://www.lawcom.gov.uk/project/proposals-for-reform-of-the-law-relating-to-maintenance-and-champerty/

The Law Reform Commission of Hong Kong. (2015). *Consultation paper: Third party funding for arbitration*. https://www.hkreform.gov.hk/en/publications/tpf.htm

United Nations Commission on International Trade Law. (2017). *Report of Working Group III (Investor-State Dispute Settlement Reform) on the work of its thirty-fourth session (Vienna, 27 November–1 December 2017): Part I*

United Nations Commission on International Trade Law. (2019). *Possible reform of investor-State dispute settlement (ISDS): Third-party funding – Possible solutions*

United Nations Commission on International Trade Law. (2019). *Possible reform of investor-State dispute settlement (ISDS): Submission from the European Union and its Member States*

United Nations Commission on International Trade Law. (2019). *Possible reform of investor-State dispute settlement (ISDS) Third-party funding – Possible solutions: Note by the Secretariat.* https://undocs.org/en/A/CN.9/WG.III/WP.172

United Nations Commission on International Trade Law. (2019). *Report of Working Group III (Investor-State Dispute Settlement Reform) on the work of its thirty-seventh session (New York, 1–5 April 2019)*

United Nations Conference on Trade and Development. (2017). *Investor state dispute settlement: Review of developments in 2016.* https://unctad.org/en/PublicationsLibrary/diaepcbinf2019d4_en.pdf

Legislation and Rules

American Bar Association Model Rules of Professional Conduct ("ABA Model Rules")
CIETAC Rules on International Investment Disputes
Civil Law (Wrongs) Act 2002 (ACT)
Code of Conduct for Litigation Funders, Association of Litigation Funders, January 2018
Contingency Fee Agreements, O Reg 195/04, available at http://canlii.ca/t/1llx
Criminal Law Act 1967 (UK)
Criminal Law Consolidation Act 1935 (SA)
Draft Code of Conduct for Adjudicators in Investor-State Dispute Settlement, the Secretariats of the International Centre for Settlement of Investment Disputes (ICSID) and the United Nations Commission on International Trade Law (UNCITRAL) available at https://icsid.worldbank.org/en/Pages/News.aspx?CID=365
Hong Kong Arbitration and Mediation Legislation (Third-party Funding) (Amendment) Ordinance 2017
Hong Kong Code of Practice for Third-Party Funding of Arbitration
IBA Rules. (2014) "Guidelines on Conflicts of Interest in International Arbitration" available at https://www.ibanet.org/Publications/publications_IBA_guides_and_free_materials.aspx
ICSID Compendium of State and Public Comments on Proposed Amendment to the ICSID, Working Paper #4: Proposals for Amendment of the ICSID Rules. https://icsid.worldbank.org/sites/default/files/amendments/WP4__Compilation_9.17.2020.pdf
ICSID, Proposed Amendments To The Regulations And Rules For Icsid Additional Facility Proceedings, 20 January 2022, available at https://icsid.worldbank.org/sites/default/files/publications/rule-amendment_proposals_additional-facility.pdf
ICSID and UNCITRAL Draft Code of Conduct for Adjudicators, available at https://icsid.worldbank.org/en/
Maintenance, Champerty and Barratry Abolition Act 1993 No 88 (NSW)

C. Eken, *Third-Party Funding in Investment Arbitration*, Law for Professionals,
https://doi.org/10.1007/978-3-031-63620-2

Me. Rev. Stat. Ann. tit. 9-A §§ 12-104, 12-106, available at https://legislature.maine.gov/statutes/9-A/title9-Asec12-104.html

Ohio Rev. Code Ann. § 1349.55, available at http://codes.ohio.gov/orc/1349

Hong Kong Arbitration and Mediation Legislation (Third Party Funding) (Amendment) Ordinance 2017 (Amendment Ordinance)

Singapore Civil Law (Amendment) Bill

Singapore Legal Profession Act (Chapter 161)

Statute of Champerty, RSO 1897, c 327, available at: https://digitalcommons.osgoode.yorku.ca/rso/vol1970/iss6/5

USA ABA Model Rule of Professional Responsibility, (MPR) 1.8(f), available at https://www.americanbar.org/groups/litigation/committees/commercial-business/practice/2019/when-a-third-party-pays-legal-fees/

UNCIRAL, Initial draft on the regulation of third-party funding, available at https://uncitral.un.org/en/thirdpartyfunding

Wrongs Act 1958 (Vic)

International Agreements

Comprehensive Economic and Trade Agreement (CETA), September 26, 2014, http://trade.ec.europa.eu/doclib/docs/2014/september/tradoc_152806.pdf

ICSID Convention, March 18, 1965, https://icsid.worldbank.org/sites/default/files/documents/ICSID%20Convention%20English.pdf

Investment Protection Agreement between the European Union and Its Member States, of the One Part, and the Socialist Republic of Vietnam, of the Other Part, October 17, 2018, https://investmentpolicy.unctad.org/international-investment-agreements/treaty-files/5868/download

Transatlantic Trade and Investment Partnership, Commission draft text TTIP – investment, July 8, 2015, https://trade.ec.europa.eu/doclib/docs/2015/september/tradoc_153807.pdf

C. Eken, *Third-Party Funding in Investment Arbitration*, Law for Professionals,
https://doi.org/10.1007/978-3-031-63620-2

Various Other Sources

Attrill, W. (2019, February 16). *Ethical issues in litigation funding*. IMF (Australia) Ltd. https://portal.omnibridgeway.com/docs/default-source/site-documents/ethical-issues-paper-imf09%2D%2D-globalaw-conference.pdf

Baker, B. (2018, August 21). *In low-yield environment, litigation finance booms*. MarketWatch. https://www.marketwatch.com/story/in-low-yield-environment-litigation-finance-booms-2018-08-17

Banzaca, J. (2009, June 24). *In turbulent markets, hedge fund managers turn to litigation funding for absolute, uncorrelated returns*. Hedge Fund Law Report. https://www.hflawreport.com/2538426/in-turbulent-markets-hedge-fund-managers-turn-to-litigation-funding-for-absolute-uncorrelated-returns.thtml

Bentham, J. (n.d.). *The works of Jeremy Bentham, vol. 3. William Tait, 1843*. The Online Library of Liberty. https://oll.libertyfund.org/titles/bentham-the-works-of-jeremy-bentham-vol-3

Burford Capital. (2017, September 7). *Ethical worries over third-party funding "evaporating"* [Press release]. https://www.burfordcapital.com/media-room/media-room-container/ethical-worries-over-third-party-funding-evaporating/

European Commission. (2019). *Multilateral Investment Court project*

Garber, S. (2020). *Alternative litigation financing in the United States: Issues, knowns, and unknowns*. RAND Corporation

Hepburn, J. (2018, August 23). An update on investment treaty disputes involving the government of India. *Investment Arbitration Reporter*. https://www.iareporter.com/articles/an-update-on-investment-treaty-disputes-involving-the-government-of-india/

ICSID. (2020). *Compendium of state and public comments on proposed amendments to the ICSID rules*

Jackson, R. (2011, November 23). *Third party funding or litigation funding: Sixth lecture in the civil litigation costs review implementation*. The Royal Courts of Justice

C. Eken, *Third-Party Funding in Investment Arbitration*, Law for Professionals,
https://doi.org/10.1007/978-3-031-63620-2

K&L Gates. *After the Event Insurance*. http://www.klgates.com/files/Uploads/Documents/Global_Insurance/After_the_Event.pdf

Law Council of Australia. (2011, June 1). *Position paper - Regulation of third party litigation funding in Australia*

Merzer, M. (2013, April 19). *Cash-now promise of lawsuit loans under fire*. Fox Business

Miller, L. (2017, March). Perils of third-party funding. *Los Angeles Lawyer*, 19–25

Neuberger, D. (2013, May 8). *From barratry, maintenance and champerty to litigation funding: Harbour Litigation Funding first annual lecture*. https://adam1cor.files.wordpress.com/2013/05/lord-neuberger-harbour-litigation-lecture-8-may-2013.pdf

Peterson, L. E. (2005, January 22). Investor's duty to pass a portion of award-recovery to the third-party funder is cited as a reason to not lift a stay of enforcement of that award. *Investment Arbitration Reporter*. https://www.iareporter.com/articles/investors-duty-to-pass-a-portion-of-award-recovery-to-third-party-funder-is-cited-as-a-reason-to-not-lift-a-stay-of-enforcement-of-that-award/

Peterson, L. E. (2010, May 7). Investor and lawyers fall out over contingency-fee arrangement in aftermath of ICSID arbitration. *Investment Arbitration Reporter*. https://www.iareporter.com/articles/investor-and-lawyers-fall-out-over-contingency-fee-arrangement-in-aftermath-of-icsid-arbitration/

Sanderson, C. (2021, February 12). *Guatemala launches counterclaim in mining dispute*. Global Arbitration Review. https://globalarbitrationreview.com/article/guatemala-launches-counterclaim-in-mining-dispute

Sanderson, C. (2021, June 15). *King & Spalding sued by client in funded BIT case*. Global Arbitration Review. https://globalarbitrationreview.com/king-spalding-sued-client-in-funded-bit-case

Sebok, A. (2016, May 27). *Third-party litigation finance promotes justice and deters wrongdoing*. The New York Times. https://www.nytimes.com/roomfordebate/2016/05/27/the-ethics-of-investing-in-anothers-lawsuit/third-party-litigation-finance-promotes-justice-and-deters-wrongdoing

Simson, C. (2017, January 13). *Funders fret over Singapore's 3rd-party disclosure measures*. Law360. https://www.law360.com/internationalarbitration/articles/880838/funders-fret-over-singapore-s-3rd-party-disclosure-measures

The Association of Litigation Funders of England and Wales. (2018). *Code of conduct for litigation funders*. https://associationoflitigationfunders.com/wp-content/uploads/2018/03/Code-Of-Conduct-for-Litigation-Funders-at-Jan-2018-FINAL.pdf

Warren, M. (2014, August 20). *What is justice? Remarks of the Hon. Marilyn Warren AC Chief Justice of Victoria*. Mannix College. http://classic.austlii.edu.au/au/journals/VicJSchol/2014/12.pdf

Woodsford Litigaiton Funding. (2021). *A practical guide to litigation funding*. https://woodsford.com/wp-content/uploads/2021/01/Woodford-White-Paper-A-Practical-Guide-Lit-Fund-NLogo.pdf

Websites

ABA Journal. *Other people's money: Rise of litigation finance companies raises legal and ethical concerns.* https://www.abajournal.com/magazine/article/litigation_finance_legal_ethical_concerns/P2

Aceris Law LLC. (2018, January 2). *Obtaining third-party funding for international arbitration – How it works*. https://www.acerislaw.com/obtaining-third-party-funding-international-arbitration-works/

Association of Litigation Funders of England and Wales. *Doucments*. https://associationoflitigationfunders.com/documents/

Australian Securities Exchange Ltd. *Omni Bridgeway Limited*. https://www.asx.com.au/asx/share-price-research/company/OBL

Bishop, D. (2010, May 23). Ethics in international arbitration. *ICCA*. https://cdn.arbitration-icca.org/s3fs-public/document/media_document/icca_rio_keynote_speech.pdf

Burford Capital. (2021, December 15). *Burford Insights: What's ahead in legal finance in 2022?* https://www.burfordcapital.com/insights/insights-container/why-legal-finance-will-become-increasingly-valuable-to-law-firms-legal-teams-in-2019/

Burford Capital. *Monetization*. https://www.burfordcapital.com/how-we-work/expertise/monetization/

Burford Capital. *Responsibility*. https://www.burfordcapital.com/shareholders/responsibility/

Campaign for Tobacco-Free Kids. *International legal consortium: The anti-tobacco trade litigation fund*. https://www.tobaccofreekids.org/what-we-do/global/legal/trade-litigation-fund

European Commission. (2017, September). *State of the Union 2017: A multilateral investment report*. http://arbitrationblog.kluwerarbitration.com/2016/02/29/how-much-does-an-icsid-arbitration-cost-a-snapshot-of-the-last-five-years/

C. Eken, *Third-Party Funding in Investment Arbitration*, Law for Professionals,
https://doi.org/10.1007/978-3-031-63620-2

Financial Times. (2019, August 9). *Behind Burford Capital: The litigation funder under siege*. https://www.ft.com/content/17cbe4d8-baaf-11e9-96bd-8e884d3ea203

Global Arbitration Review. *GAR 100 - 14th Edition*. https://globalarbitrationreview.com/survey/gar-100/2021

Global Arbitration Review. (2012, March 5). *Third-party funding: Snapshots from around the globe*. https://globalarbitrationreview.com/third-party-funding-snapshots-around-the-globe

Harbour Underwriting. (2021, October 4). *Harbour Underwriting partners with GS Group to provide After the Event (ATE) insurance to Scottish lawyers*. https://harbourunderwriting.com/harbour-underwriting-partners-with-gs-group-to-provide-after-the-event-ate-insurance-to-scottish-lawyers/

Hodgson, M. (2017, December 14). Investment treaty arbitration: Cost, duration and size of claims all show steady increase. *Allen & Overy*. https://www.allenovery.com/en-gb/global/news-and-insights/publications/investment-treaty-arbitration-cost-duration-and-size-of-claims-all-show-steady-increase

ICSID. (2021, November). *Working paper #6: Proposals for amendment of the ICSID rules*. https://icsid.worldbank.org/sites/default/files/documents/ICSID_WP_Six.pdf

ICSID. *Amendments*. https://icsid.worldbank.org/en/amendments

International Bar Association. (2015, August 10). *IBA Guidelines on Conflicts of Interest in International Arbitration*. https://www.ibanet.org/MediaHandler?id=e2fe5e72-eb14-4bba-b10d-d33dafee8918

Investopedia. (2022, May 18). *Environmental, social, and governance (ESG) criteria*. https://www.investopedia.com/terms/e/environmental-social-and-governance-esg-criteria.asp

Jeffreys, B. S. (2021, June 14). Alleging 'gross overpayment' of fees, ex-client sues King & Spalding, 2 partners over successful arbitration. *Law.com*. https://www.law.com/texaslawyer/2021/06/14/alleging-gross-overpayment-of-fees-ex-client-sues-king-spalding-2-partners-over-successful-arbitration/?slreturn=20220022133401

Kiella, M. C. (2019, June 4). United States: Third-party litigation funders: The "party" you didn't know was exercising control over your litigation and what you can do about it. *Mondaq*. https://www.mondaq.com/unitedstates/trials-appeals-compensation/811510/third-party-litigation-funders-the-party-you-didn39t-know-was-exercising-control-over-your-litigation-and-what-you-can-do-about-it

London Stock Exchange. *Burford Capital Limited*. https://www.londonstockexchange.com/exchange/prices-and-markets/stocks/summary/company-summary/GG00B4L84979GGGBXAMSM.html

Practical Law. *Investor-State Dispute Settlement (ISDS)*. https://uk.practicallaw.thomsonreuters.com/0-624-6147?transitionType=Default&contextData=(sc.Default)&firstPage=true

Research Nester. (2021, February 4). *Global litigation funding investment market to cross USD 13 billion in 2021.* https://www.globenewswire.com/news-release/2021/02/04/2169925/0/en/Global-Litigation-Funding-Investment-Market-to-Cross-USD-13-Billion-in-2021-Rise-in-Pending-Claims-Insolvency-and-Bankruptcy-Due-to-COVID-19-and-Interest-in-ROI-Among-Investors-to-.html

The Courts Service of Ireland. *Judgments.* https://www.courts.ie/judgments

The Judge. *Contingency fee insurance.* https://www.thejudgeglobal.com/dba-insurance/

The State Bar of California. *Committee on Professional Responsibility and Conduct formal opinion no. 2020-204.* https://www.calbar.ca.gov/Portals/0/documents/ethics/Opinions/Formal-Opinion-No-2020-204-Litigation-Funding.pdf

TransLex. *The Lex Mercatoria (Old and New) and the TransLex-Principles.* https://www.trans-lex.org/917000/_/assignment-of-claim/

UNCITRAL. *Rules on transparency.* https://www.uncitral.org/pdf/english/texts/arbitration/rules-on-transparency/Rules-on-Transparency-E.pdf

UNCITRAL. *Working Group III: Investor-state dispute settlement reform.* https://uncitral.un.org/en/working_groups/3/investor-state

UNCTAD Investment Policy Hub. (2011, March). *Latest developments in investor – state dispute settlement.* https://unctad.org/en/pages/publications/Intl-Investment-Agreements%2D%2D-Issues-Note.aspx

UNCTAD Investment Policy Hub. (2016, March). *Argentina - Italy BIT (1990).* https://investmentpolicy.unctad.org/international-investment-agreements/treaties/bilateral-investment-treaties/135/argentina%2D%2D-italy-bit-1990-

UNCTAD. (2019, March). *Reforming investment dispute settlement: A stocktaking.* https://unctad.org/en/PublicationsLibrary/diaepcbinf2019d3_en.pdf

The manufacturer's authorised representative in the EU is Springer
Nature Customer Service Centre GmbH, Europaplatz 3, 69115 Heidelberg,
Germany. If you have any concerns regarding our products, please
contact ProductSafety@springernature.com

Printed and bound by CPI Group (UK) Ltd, Croydon, CR0 4YY
01/10/2026
02225897-0005

The “Proceedings of the International Neural Networks Society INNS” publishes research contributions on fundamental principles and applications related to neural networks and modeling behavioral and brain processes. Topics of interest include new developments, state-of-art theories, methods and practical applications, covering all aspects of neural networks and neuromorphic technologies for (artificially; replace with anthropomorphic) intelligent (designs; replace with systems). This series covers high quality books that contribute to the full range of neural networks research, from computational neuroscience, cognitive science, behavioral and brain modeling, (add machine) learning algorithms, mathematical theories, to technological applications of systems that significantly use neural network concepts and techniques.

The series publishes monographs, contributed volumes, lecture notes, edited volumes, and conference proceedings in neural networks spanning theoretical, experimental, computational, and engineering aspects. Submissions of highly innovative cutting-edge contributions are encouraged, which extend our understanding at the forefront of science going beyond mainstream approaches. Of particular value to both the contributors and the readership are the short publication timeframe and the world-wide distribution, which enable both wide and rapid dissemination of research output in this rapidly developing research field.

More information about this series at http://www.springer.com/series/16268

Lazaros Iliadis · Plamen Parvanov Angelov ·
Chrisina Jayne · Elias Pimenidis
Editors

Proceedings of the 21st EANN (Engineering Applications of Neural Networks) 2020 Conference

Proceedings of the EANN 2020

Springer

Editors
Lazaros Iliadis
School of Engineering,
Department of Civil Engineering
Democritus University of Thrace
Xanthi, Greece

Chrisina Jayne
School of Computing
and Digital Technologies
Teesside University
Middlesbrough, UK

Plamen Parvanov Angelov
Lancaster University
Lancaster, UK

Elias Pimenidis
University of the West of England
Bristol, UK

ISSN 2661-8141 ISSN 2661-815X (electronic)
Proceedings of the International Neural Networks Society
ISBN 978-3-030-48790-4 ISBN 978-3-030-48791-1 (eBook)
https://doi.org/10.1007/978-3-030-48791-1

This Springer imprint is published by the registered company Springer Nature Switzerland AG
The registered company address is: Gewerbestrasse 11, 6330 Cham, Switzerland

EANN 2020 Preface

Artificial neural networks (ANN) are a typical case of machine learning, which mimics the physical learning process of the human brain. More than 60 years have passed from the introduction of the first perceptron. Since then, numerous types of ANN architectures have been developed. Among them are recurrent ANN, whose nodes' connections are forming a directed graph along a temporal sequence. More recently, generative adversarial neural networks are trying to fuse "imagination" to artificial intelligence (AI) and convolutional neural networks (CNN) are significantly contributing to the enhancement of pattern recognition, machine translation, anomaly detection, and machine vision. Neural networks have a significant contribution in natural language, and they are widely employed for text classification by search engines in the web. In this domain, CNN are successfully applied by the word2vec method, in recommendation systems–sentiment analysis for movies, customer reviews, and so on. Also, they are used in text-to-speech conversion and semantic parsing plus question answering systems.

The engineering applications of neural networks conference aim to bring together scientists from all AI domains and to give them the chance to exchange ideas and to announce their achievements. Since the first conference in 1995, EANN has provided a great discussion forum on engineering applications of all artificial intelligence technologies, focusing on artificial neural networks. More specifically, EANN promotes the use of modeling techniques from all subdomains of AI in diverse application areas, where significant benefits can be derived. The conference is also reporting advances in theoretical AI aspects. Thus, both innovative applications and methods are particularly appreciated. EANN is a mature and well-established international scientific conference held in Europe. Its history is long and very successful, following and spreading the evolution of intelligent systems.

The 21st EANN 2020 was collocated with the 16th EANN 2020 conference.

The first EANN event was organized in Otaniemi, Finland, in 1995. Since then, it has a continuous and dynamic presence as a major global, but mainly European scientific event. More specifically, it has been organized in Finland, UK (England), Sweden, Gibraltar, Poland, Italy, Spain, France, Bulgaria, UK (Scotland), UK

(Bristol), and Greece. It has been technically supported by the International Neural Networks Society (INNS) and more specifically by the EANN Special Interest Group.

This proceedings volume belongs to International Neural Networks (INNS) Springer Series, and it contains the papers that were accepted to be presented orally at the 21st EANN 2020 conference. The diverse nature of papers presented demonstrates the vitality of artificial intelligence algorithms and approaches. It is not only related to neural networks, but it certainly provides a very wide forum for AI applications as well.

The event was held from June 5 to 7, 2020, and it was broadcasted live through web, to all conference participants. There was no potential for physical attendance due to the global problem with CONVI-19 virus.

Regardless of the extremely difficult pandemic conditions, the response of the international scientific community to the EANN 2020 call for papers was more than satisfactory, with 89 papers initially submitted. All papers were peer reviewed by at least two independent academic referees. When needed, a third referee was consulted to resolve any potential conflicts. A total of 47% of the submitted manuscripts (42 papers) have been accepted to be published as full papers (12 pages long) in the Springer proceedings. Due to the high quality of the submissions, the Program Committee has decided that it should accept additionally six more papers to be published as short ones (ten pages long).

Four Keynote speakers gave state-of-the-art lectures (after invitation) in the timely aspects applications of artificial intelligence.

Dr. Pierre Philippe Mathieu

European Space Agency (ESA) Head of the Philab (Φ Lab) Explore Office at the European Space Agency in ESRIN (Frascati, Italy).

Pierre-Philippe is passionate about innovation and our planet: its beauty, fragility and complex dynamics as part of an integrated Earth System. His current role at ESA is to help scientists, innovators and citizens to use high-tech (such as satellite data) to better monitor, understand and preserve our home planet, by making sustainable use of its limited natural resources.

PP's background is in Earth Sciences. He has a degree in engineering and M.Sc from the University of Liege (Belgium), a Ph.D. in climate science from the University of Louvain (Belgium), and a Management degree from the University of Reading Business School (Uk). Over the last 20 years, he has been working in environmental monitoring and modelling, across disciplines from remote sensing, modelling up to weather risk management.

Currently, PP is trying to connect the global picture we get from space with world challenges in daily life, fostering the use of our Earth Observation (EO) missions to support science, innovation and development in partnership with user communities, industry and businesses.

Professor Leontios Hadjileontiadis, Department of Electrical and Computer Engineering, Aristotle University of Thessaloniki, Greece, and Coordinator of i-PROGNOSIS, gave a speech on the subject of "**Smartphone, Parkinson's and Depression: A new AI-based prognostic perspective**".

Professor Hadjileontiadis has been awarded among other awards, as innovative researcher and champion faculty from Microsoft, USA (2012), the Silver Award in Teaching Delivery at the Reimagine Education Awards (2017–2018) and the Healthcare Research Award by the Dubai Healthcare City Authority Excellence Awards (2019). He is a senior member of IEEE.

Professor Nikola Kasabov, FIEEE, FRSNZ, Fellow INNS College of Fellows, DVF RAE, UK, Director, Knowledge Engineering and Discovery Research Institute, Auckland University of Technology, Auckland, New Zealand, Advisory/Visiting Professor SJTU and CASIA China, RGU, UK, gave a speech on the subject of "**Deep Learning, Knowledge Representation and Transfer with Brain-Inspired Spiking Neural Network Architectures**".

Professor Kasabov has received a number of awards, among them: Doctor Honoris Causa from Obuda University, Budapest; INNS Ada Lovelace Meritorious Service Award; NN Best Paper Award for 2016; APNNA "Outstanding Achievements Award"; INNS Gabor Award for "Outstanding contributions to engineering applications of neural networks"; EU Marie Curie Fellowship; Bayer Science Innovation Award; APNNA Excellent Service Award; RSNZ Science and Technology Medal; 2015 AUT Medal; Honorable Member of the Bulgarian and the Greek Societies for Computer Science.

Professor Xiao-Jun Wu Department of Computer Science and Technology, Jiangnan University, China, gave a speech on the subject of "**Image Fusion Based on Deep Learning**".

Professor Xiao-Jun Wu has won the most outstanding postgraduate award by Nanjing University of Science and Technology. He has won different national and international awards, for his research achievements. He was a visiting postdoctoral researcher in the Center for Vision, Speech, and Signal Processing (CVSSP), University of Surrey, UK, from 2003 to 2004.

Tutorials

Prof. John Macintyre

Dean of the Faculty of Applied Sciences, Pro Vice Chancellor at the University of Sunderland, UK. During the 1990s, he established the Center for Adaptive Systems—at the University, which became recognized by the UK government as a center of excellence for applied research in adaptive computing and artificial intelligence. The center undertook many projects working with and for external organizations in industry, science, and academia, and for three years ran the Smart Software for Decision Makers program on behalf of the Department of Trade and Industry.

Professor Macintyre will give a plenary talk on the following subject: "**AI Applications during the COVID-19 Pandemic - A Double Edged Sword?**"

Dr. Kostas Karpouzis

Associate Researcher, Institute of Communication and Computer Systems (ICCS) of the National Technical University of Athens, Greece. Tutorial Subject: "**AI/ML for games for AI/ML**".

Digital games have recently emerged as a very powerful research instrument for a number of reasons: They involve a wide variety of computing disciplines, from databases and networking to hardware and devices, and they are very attractive to users regardless of age or cultural background, making them popular and easy to evaluate with actual players. In the fields of artificial intelligence and machine learning, games are used in a twofold manner: to collect information about the players' individual characteristics (player modeling), expressivity (affective computing), and playing style (adaptivity) and also to develop AI-based player bots to assist and face the human players and as a test bed for contemporary AI algorithms.

This tutorial discusses both approaches that relate AI/ML to games: Starting from a theoretical review of user/player modeling concepts, it discusses how we can collect data from the users during gameplay and use them to adapt the player experience or model the players themselves. Following that, it presents AI/ML algorithms used to train computer-based players and how these can be used in contexts outside gaming. Finally, it introduces player modeling in contexts related to serious gaming, such as health and education.

Intended audience: researchers in the fields of machine learning and human–computer interaction, game developers and designers, health and education practitioners.

The accepted papers of the 21st EANN conference are related to the following thematic topics:

- Classification Machine Learning
- Convolutional Neural Networks in Robotics/Machine Vision
- Deep Learning Applications in Engineering
- Deep Learning LSTM in Environmental Cases
- Deep Learning in Engineering
- Deep Learning/Image Processing
- Deep Learning and Medical Systems
- Fuzzy Logic Modeling
- Unsupervised Machine Learning/Clustering
- Fuzzy Modeling
- Machine Learning and Neuro/Biological Modeling
- Meta-Learning/Nonlinear Modeling
- Algorithmic Foundations of Neural Networks
- Neural Networks in Engineering
- Optimization and Machine Learning
- Hybrid Machine Learning Systems

The authors of submitted papers came from 18 different countries from all over the globe, namely Bulgaria, Czech Republic, Germany, Greece, France, Hong Kong, Hungary, India, Italy, Japan, Norway, Poland, Romania, Russia, Spain, Turkey, UK, and Vietnam.

June 2020 EANN 2020 Chairs

Organization

General Co-chairs

Chrisina Jayne	Teesside University, UK
Vera Kurkova	Czech Academy of Sciences, Czech Republic
Plamen Angelov	Lancaster University, Fellow of the IEEE, of the IET and of the HEA, Vice President of the International Neural Networks Society (INNS) for Conference and Governor of the Systems, Man and Cybernetics Society of the IEEE
John Macintyre	University of Sunderland, UK

Program Co-chairs

Lazaros Iliadis	School of Engineering, Democritus University of Thrace, Greece
Ilias Maglogiannis	University of Piraeus, Greece
Elias Pimenidis	University of the West of England, UK

Honorary Co-chairs

Nikola Kasabov	Auckland University of Technology, New Zealand
Marios Polycarpou	University of Cyprus, Cyprus

Liaison Chair

Ioannis Kompatsiaris	IPTIL Research Institute, Thessaloniki, Greece

Advisory Co-chairs

Andreas Stafylopatis	Technical University of Athens, Greece
Vincenzo Piuri	University of Milan, Italy, IEEE Fellow (2001), IEEE Society/Council Active Memberships/Services: CIS, ComSoc, CS, CSS, EMBS, IMS, PES, PHOS, RAS, SMCS, SPS, BIOMC, SYSC, WIE
Petia Koprinkova	Bulgarian Academy of Sciences, Bulgaria

Workshops Co-chairs

Spyros Sioutas	University of Patras, Greece
Christos Makris	University of Patras, Greece
Phivos Mylonas	Ionio University, Greece
Katia Kermanidis	Ionio University, Greece

Publication and Publicity Co-chairs

Antonis Papaleonidas	Democritus University of Thrace, Greece
Konstantinos Demertzis	Democritus University of Thrace, Greece
George Tsekouras	University of the Aegean, Greece

Special Sessions

Tutorials on Emerging AI Research (Projects and Applications)

Panagiotis Papapetrou	Stockholm University, Sweden
Vangelis Karkaletsis	National Center for Scientific Research, NSCR "Demokritos", Greece

Steering Committee

Chrisina Jayne	Dean of the School of Computing and Digital Technologies Teesside University, UK
Lazaros Iliadis	School of Engineering, Department of Civil Engineering, Head of the Sector of Mathematics, Programming and GC, Democritus University of Thrace, Greece
Elias Pimenidis	Program Leader Computer Science, Department FET-Computer Science and Creative Technologies, University of the West of England, Bristol, UK

Program Committee

Michel Aldanondo	Toulouse University—IMT Mines Albi, France
Georgios Alexandridis	University of the Aegean, Greece
Serafín Alonso Castro	University of Leon, Spain
Ioannis Anagnostopoulos	University of Thessaly, Greece
Costin Badica	University of Craiova, Romania
Giacomo Boracchi	Politecnico di Milano, Italy
Ivo Bukovsky	Czech Technical University in Prague, Czech Republic
George Caridakis	University of the Aegean, Greece
Francisco Carvalho	Polytechnic Institute of Tomar, Portugal
Ioannis Chamodrakas	National and Kapodistrian University of Athens, Greece
Adriana Coroiu	Babeş-Bolyai University, Romania
Kostantinos Delibasis	University Of Thessaly, Greece
Konstantinos Demertzis	Democritus University of Thrace, Greece
Sergey Dolenko	Lomonosov Moscow State University, Russia
Georgios Drakopoulos	Ionian University, Greece
Mauro Gaggero	National Research Council of Italy
Ignazio Gallo	University of Insubria, Italy
Angelo Genovese	Università degli Studi di Milano, Italy
Spiros Georgakopoulos	University of Thessaly, Greece
Eleonora Giunchiglia	Oxford University, UK
Foteini Grivokostopoulou	University of Patras, Greece
Peter Hajek	University of Pardubice Czech Republic
Giannis Haralabopoulos	University of Nottingham, UK
Ioannis Hatzilygeroudis	University of Patras, Greece
Nantia Iakovidou	King's College London, UK
Lazaros Iliadis	Democritus University of Thrace, Greece
Zhu Jin	University of Cambridge, UK
Jacek Kabziński	Lodz University of Technology, Poland
Andreas Kanavos	University of Patras, Greece
Stelios Kapetanakis	The University of Brighton, UK
Petros Kefalas	University of Sheffield International Faculty CITY College, Greece
Katia Kermanidis	Ionio University, Greece
Niki Kiriakidou	University of Patras, Greece
Giannis Kokkinos	University of Makedonia, Greece
Petia Koprinkova-Hristova	Bulgarian Academy of Sciences
Athanasios Koutras	Technical Educational Institute of Western Greece
Paul Krause	University of Surrey, UK
Florin Leon	Technical University of Iasi, Romania
Aristidis Likas	University of Ioannina, Greece

Ioannis Livieris	University of Patras, Greece
Doina Logofătu	Frankfurt University of Applied Sciences, Frankfurt am Main, Germany
Ilias Maglogiannis	University of Piraeus, Greece
Goerge Magoulas	Birkbeck College, University of London, UK
Christos Makris	University of Patras, Greece
Mario Malcangi	University of Milan, Italy
Francesco Marceloni	University of Pisa, Italy
Giovanna Maria Dimitri	University of Cambridge, UK, and University of Siena, Italy
Nikolaos Mitianoudis	Democritus University of Thrace, Greece
Antonio Moran	University of Leon, Spain
Konstantinos Moutselos	University of Piraeus, Greece
Phivos Mylonas	Ionio University, Greece
Stefanos Nikiforos	Ionio University, Greece
Stavros Ntalampiras	University of Milan, Italy
Mihaela Oprea	University Petroleum-Gas of Ploiesti Romania
Ioannis P. Chochliouros	Hellenic Telecommunications Organization, Greece
Basil Papadopoulos	Democritus University of Thrace
Vaios Papaioannou	University of Patras, Greece
Antonis Papaleonidas	Democritus University of Thrace, Greece
Daniel Pérez López	University of Leon, Spain
Isidoros Perikos	University of Patras, Greece
Elias Pimenidis	University of the West of England, Bristol, UK
Panagiotis Pintelas	University of Patras, Greece
Nikolaos Polatidis	University of Brighton, UK
Bernardete Ribeiro	University of Coimbra, Portugal
Leonardo Rundo	University of Cambridge, UK
Alexander Ryjov	Lomonosov Moscow State University, Russia
Simone Scardapane	Sapienza University (Rome), Italy
Evaggelos Spyrou	National Center for Scientific Research—Demokritos, Greece
Antonio Staiano	University of Naples Parthenope, Italy
Andrea Tangherloni	University of Cambridge, UK
Azevedo Tiago	University of Cambridge, UK
Francesco Trovò	Polytecnico di Milano, Italy
Nicolas Tsapatsoulis	Cyprus University of Technology
Petra Vidnerová	The Czech Academy of Sciences, Czech Republic
Paulo Vitor de Campos Souza	CEFET-MG, Brazil
Gerasimos Vonitsanos	University of Patras, Greece

Abstracts of Invited Talks

The Rise of Artificial Intelligence for Earth Observation (AI4EO)

Pierre Philippe Mathieu

European Space Agency (ESA) Head of the Philab (Φ Lab) Explore Office at the European Space Agency in ESRIN (Frascati, Italy)
Pierre.Philippe.Mathieu@esa.int

Abstract. The world of Earth Observation (EO) is rapidly changing as a result of exponential advances in sensor and digital technologies. The speed of change has no historical precedent. Recent decades have witnessed extraordinary developments in ICT, including the Internet, cloud computing and storage, which have all led to radically new ways to collect, distribute and analyse data about our planet. This digital revolution is also accompanied by a sensing revolution that provides an unprecedented amount of data on the state of our planet and its changes.

Europe leads this sensing revolution in space through the Copernicus initiative and the corresponding development of a family of Sentinel missions. This has enabled the global monitoring of our planet across the whole electromagnetic spectrum on an operational and sustained basis. In addition, a new trend, referred to as "New Space", is now rapidly emerging through the increasing commoditization and commercialization of space.

These new global data sets from space lead to a far more comprehensive picture of our planet. This picture is now even more refined via data from billions of smart and inter-connected sensors referred to as the Internet of Things. Such streams of dynamic data on our planet offer new possibilities for scientists to advance our understanding of how the ocean, atmosphere, land and cryosphere operate and interact as part on an integrated Earth System. It also represents new opportunities for entrepreneurs to turn big data into new types of information services.

However, the emergence of big data creates new opportunities but also new challenges for scientists, business, data and software providers to make sense of the vast and diverse amount of data by capitalizing on powerful techniques such as Artificial Intelligence (AI). Until recently AI was mainly a restricted field occupied by experts and scientists, but today it is routinely used in everyday life without us even noticing it, in applications ranging from recommendation engines, language services, face recognition and autonomous vehicles.

The application of AI to EO data is just at its infancy, remaining mainly concentrated on computer vision applications with Very High-Resolution satellite imagery, while there are certainly many areas of Earth Science and big data mining / fusion, which could increasingly benefit from AI, leading to entire new types of value chain, scientific knowledge and innovative EO services.

This talk will present some of the ESA research / application activities and partnerships in the AI4EO field, inviting you to stimulate new ideas and collaboration to make the most of the big data and AI revolutions.

Smartphone, Parkinson's, and Depression: A New AI-Based Prognostic Perspective

Leontios Hadjileontiadis[1,2]

[1] Department of Electrical and Computer Engineering, Khalifa University of Science and Technology, Technology and Research, Abu Dhabi, United Arab Emirates
[2] Department of Electrical and Computer Engineering, Aristotle University of Thessaloniki, Thessaloniki, Greece
leontios@auth.gr

Abstract. Machine learning (ML) is a branch of artificial intelligence (AI) based on the idea that systems can learn from data, identify patterns, and make decisions with minimal human intervention. While many ML algorithms have been around for a long time, the ability to automatically apply complex mathematical calculations to big data—over and over, faster and faster, deeper and deeper—is a recent development, leading to the realization of the so-called deep learning (DL). The latter has an intuitive capability that is similar to biological brains. It is able to handle the inherent unpredictability and fuzziness of the natural world. In this keynote, the main aspects of ML and DL will be presented, and the focus will be placed in the way they are used to shed light upon the human behavioral modeling. In this vein, AI-based approaches will be presented for identifying fine motor skills deterioration due to early Parkinson's and depression symptoms reflected in the keystroke dynamics, while interacting with a smartphone. These approaches provide a new and unobtrusive way for gathering and analyzing dense sampled big data, contributing to further understanding disease symptoms at a very early stage, guiding personalized and targeted interventions that sustain the patient's quality of life.

Deep Learning, Knowledge Representation, and Transfer with Brain-Inspired Spiking Neural Network Architectures

Nikola Kasabov

Auckland University of Technology, Knowledge Engineering and Discovery Research Institute, Auckland, New Zealand
nkasabov@aut.ac.nz

Abstract. The talk argues and demonstrates that the third generation of artificial neural networks, the spiking neural networks (SNN), can be used to design brain-inspired architectures that are not only capable of deep learning of temporal or spatiotemporal data, but also enabling the extraction of deep knowledge representation from the learned data. Similarly to how the brain learns time space data, these SNN models do not need to be restricted in number of layers, neurons in each layer, etc. When a SNN model is designed to follow a brain template, knowledge transfer between humans and machines in both directions becomes possible through the creation of brain-inspired brain–computer interfaces (BCI). The presented approach is illustrated on an exemplar SNN architecture NeuCube (free software and open source available from www.kedri.aut.ac.nz/neucube) and case studies of brain and environmental data modeling and knowledge representation using incremental and transfer learning algorithms. These include predictive modeling of EEG and fMRI data measuring cognitive processes and response to treatment, AD prediction, BCI for neuro-rehabilitation, human–human and human-VR communication, hyper-scanning, and other.

Image Fusion Based on Deep Learning

Xiao-Jun Wu

Department of Computer Science and Technology, School of IoT Engineering, Jiangnan University, China
wu_xiaojun@jiangnan.edu.cn

Abstract. Deep learning (DL) has found very successful applications in numerous different domains with impressive results. Image fusion (IMF) algorithms based on DL and their applications will be presented thoroughly in this keynote lecture. Initially, a brief introductory overview of both concepts will be given. Then, IMF employing DL will be presented in terms of pixel, feature, and decision level, respectively. Furthermore, a DL-inspired approach called MDLatLRR which is a general approach to image decomposition will be introduced for IMF. A comprehensive analysis of DL models will be offered, and their typical applications will be discussed, including **I**mage **Q**uality **E**nhancement, **F**acial **L**andmark **D**etection, **O**bject **T**racking, Multi-**M**odal **I**mage **F**usion, **V**ideo **S**tyle **T**ransformation, and **D**eep **F**ake of **F**acial **I**mages, respectively.

Contents

Deep Learning/Image Processing-Classification

Classification/Machine Learning

A Compact Sequence Encoding Scheme for Online Human Activity Recognition in HRI Applications

Georgios Tsatiris[1(✉)], Kostas Karpouzis[1], and Stefanos Kollias[1,2]

[1] Artificial Intelligence and Learning Systems Laboratory, School of Electrical and Computer Engineering, National Technical University of Athens, 9 Heroon Politechniou Street, 15780 Athens, Greece
gtsatiris@image.ntua.gr, {kkarpou,stefanos}@cs.ntua.gr

[2] School of Computer Science, University of Lincoln, Brayford Pool, Lincoln, Lincolnshire, UK

Abstract. Human activity recognition and analysis has always been one of the most active areas of pattern recognition and machine intelligence, with applications in various fields, including but not limited to exertion games, surveillance, sports analytics and healthcare. Especially in Human-Robot Interaction, human activity understanding plays a crucial role as household robotic assistants are a trend of the near future. However, state-of-the-art infrastructures that can support complex machine intelligence tasks are not always available, and may not be for the average consumer, as robotic hardware is expensive. In this paper we propose a novel action sequence encoding scheme which efficiently transforms spatio-temporal action sequences into compact representations, using Mahalanobis distance-based shape features and the Radon transform. This representation can be used as input for a lightweight convolutional neural network. Experiments show that the proposed pipeline, when based on state-of-the-art human pose estimation techniques, can provide a robust end-to-end online action recognition scheme, deployable on hardware lacking extreme computing capabilities.

Keywords: Action recognition · Deep neural networks · Human-Robot Interaction · Radon transform

1 Introduction

Human activity recognition is a very important field of study inside the broad domain of pattern recognition, with many everyday life applications. High level human actions are an important information modality for social interaction and they play a critical role in Human-Robot Interaction (HRI) [12]. Human poses, hand gestures and overall body motion are also important for human-focused HRI, especially in applications with robots interacting with humans daily

L. Iliadis et al. (Eds.): EANN 2020, INNS 2, pp. 3–14, 2020.
https://doi.org/10.1007/978-3-030-48791-1_1

(e.g. [1,18,20]). Robotic assistants are required to understand and analyse human activity at all levels of interpretation, as well as have the ability to predict intentions and to imitate human actions when forming responses. Social robots and applications aimed at such environments will need to be employed in human-centric contexts, build trust and effectively assist humans beings [6]. In this paper, we focus on online human activity recognition pipelines with the aim to provide solutions on the inherent problems of such endeavours.

1.1 Related Work

Various works on activity analysis and understanding deal with real application scenarios. In the field of preventing unintentional falls in elderly care and assistive environments, the work presented in [29] is one of the most typical attempts for applying convolutional neural networks in a fall detection application. A dataset of daily activities recorded from many people is used as classification is performed on single frames containing human postures. This method performs well on posture classification and can detect falls with a low false alarm rate. In an earlier work [16], an efficient algorithm is proposed to identify temporal patterns in actions. It further utilizes these patterns to construct activity representations for automated recognition.

There is an extensive literature of studies focused on HRI, a comprehensive presentation of which can be found in [12]. In a typical example of such works, authors in [22] propose that state-of-the-art approaches from automatic speech and visual action recognition, fused with multiple modalities, can construct multimodal recognition pipelines focused on assistive robots for elderly environments. An end-to-end approach shown in [3] deals with dynamic gestures using a Dynamic Time Warping approach, based on features extracted from depth data, in a complete HRI scenario.

1.2 Real World Challenges

As stated in [25], applied human activity recognition pipelines are demanding in terms of hardware and general infrastructure. Most action recognition systems, especially smart-home or assistive living applications, depend on network infrastructures for easy data fusion and integration of different sensing modalities. HRI environments are no different, in the sense that they may need computing capabilities similar to common workstations, as well as networking. Especially when dealing with deep learning-based pipelines, we are used to having hardware acceleration (i.e. massive parallel computing, GPU acceleration etc.) at our disposal. This study aims to provide a lightweight pipeline with limited need for high-end infrastructures.

2 Theoretical Primer

In the following section, we attempt a brief documentation of the theoretical background on which the proposed scheme is built upon. This primer emphasizes on the statistical nature of spatio-temporal data, the use of the Radon Transform for feature encoding, as well as the necessary tools to encode the necessary information into a compact pipeline.

2.1 Variance-Based Features

As mentioned in [24], high level human pose and activity descriptors, such as spatio-temporal interest points [14] or human joints, can be treated as probabilistic distributions. Joints detected in a video frame or still image, e.g. using pipelines such as OpenPose [4], can be considered distributed in space, whereas spatio-temporal interest points are distributed both in space and time. Action recognition techniques benefit from accurately modeling these relationships between the salient features describing an action sequence.

Particularly in [24], a method to distinguish between experienced tennis players and amateurs is shown, which employees feature vectors constructed by calculating the per frame variance of interest points. Variance, as the second central moment, is an effective shape descriptor [17]. Interest points and joint locations form a 3D volumes in space and time. In that context, we extend the idea demonstrated in [24], by incorporating the use of Mahalanobis distances.

Mahalanobis Distance. Given a sample vector $\boldsymbol{x}$ from a distribution D with mean $\boldsymbol{\mu}$ and covariance matrix S, the Mahalanobis distance between $\boldsymbol{x}$ and D is given by Eq. 1.

$$mahal(\boldsymbol{x}, \boldsymbol{\mu}, S) = \sqrt{(\boldsymbol{x} - \boldsymbol{\mu})^T S^{-1} (\boldsymbol{x} - \boldsymbol{\mu})} \tag{1}$$

In this work, we are focusing on detected human joints in 3D space, like the ones extracted using depth sensors (e.g. Intel RealSense[1] or Microsoft Azure Kinect[2]) and by pipelines such as the one presented in [19], which extends common 2D heatmap-based pose detection techniques such as [4] without utilizing costly volumetric operations. There is a good indication that skeletal joints can be considered valid spatio-temporal interest points when it comes to human action analysis and, with them being a more refined and targeted source of human posture information, can lead to better results [27].

As the relative position of a joint and the human body is crucial in the definition of human motion, we believe that a compact and robust way to model these individual relations should be central to any action recognition pipeline. The Mahalanobis distance, as an established metric for point-to-distribution distances, is more suitable in this task, instead of more intuitive metrics, such the Euclidean distance between a point and the distribution centroid. Its place in this pipeline will be explained in detail in Subsect. 3.1.

---

[1] https://www.intelrealsense.com/.

[2] https://azure.microsoft.com/en-us/services/kinect-dk/.

2.2 Use of the Radon Transform

The Radon transform is effectively used as a reconstruction and feature extraction tool for several decades [2]. It has found applications in earlier human activity recognition pipelines based on hand-crafted features [7] and in novel techniques, alongside its generalization, the Trace transform [13], in offline pipelines [9,10]. Another application of the Radon transform in this field leverages the transform's ability to create translation and scale invariant features to use as input for a Recurrent Neural Network (RNN) [26]. However, for reasons which will be demonstrated in the next section, this paper avoids the use of RNN and draws inspiration from such studies as the one in [11], where source images and their Conic Radon transforms are fed into a deep convolutional neural network for fingerprint classification.

Given a 2D function $f(x,y)$ with $x, y \in \mathbb{R}$, its Radon transform R_f is equal to the integral of all values of f under all lines L, defined by parameters $\rho, \theta \in \mathbb{R}$, where ρ is each line's distance from the origin and θ is the angle formed between the line and the horizontal axis:

$$R_f(\rho,\theta) = \int_L f(x,y)dL \tag{2}$$

If we substitute the parametrical ρ, θ line equation in Eq. 2, we have the following:

$$R_f(\rho,\theta) = \int_{-\infty}^{\infty}\int_{-\infty}^{\infty} f(x,y)\delta(x\cos\theta + y\sin\theta - \rho)dxdy \tag{3}$$

where δ the Dirac delta function, ensuring that only the values of f under line ρ, θ will be integrated over.

3 The Proposed Pipeline

At this point, we have documented the theoretical tools to give spatio-temporal prominence to raw joint information using variance-based shape features and, particularly, the Mahalanobis distance. We have also seen how the Radon transform and other relevant transforms can create robust features out of otherwise non-salient 2D and 3D functions. This section will clarify how the aforementioned theoretical tools will be used in a unified and compact pipeline action encoding pipeline.

3.1 Spatio-Temporal Radon Footprints

As we have established, the relationship between the position of one joint and the rest of the body parts of a subject, at a particular point in time, can be encoded by treating the set of joints as a distribution and calculating the Mahalanobis distance (given by Eq. 1) between it and that particular joint. In our context, a point in time is a frame in an action sequence or video. So, if we extend the above claim to all the joints of a subject and across all frames of an action sequence, we can formulate a Mahalanobis matrix M, whose values for joint j and frame f can be calculated using the following equation:

$$M(j,f) = mahal(\boldsymbol{x}_f^j, \boldsymbol{\mu}_f, S_f) \tag{4}$$

where $\boldsymbol{x}_f^j$ is the coordinate vector of joint j in frame f, defined in $\mathbb{R}^2$ or $\mathbb{R}^3$, $\boldsymbol{\mu}_f$ is the mean of all joint coordinate vectors in frame f (essentially the centroid) and S_f is the covariance matrix of the joint distribution at frame f.

In essence, the Mahalanobis matrix formulated in Eq. 4 is a complete 2D representation of the action sequence in space and time. With $J \times t$ resolution, where J is the total number of joints and t is the point in time (number of frames passed) since the beginning of the sequence, each line of the matrix has the Mahalanobis distances of every joint at the corresponding frame.

What this representation lacks, however, is a way to correlate the individual frame information into a compact robust feature which will describe the action sequence from its start up to point t. For this reason, we calculate the Radon transform of the 2D function M by substituting the representation $M(j,f)$ into Eq. 3. This gives as a 2D spatio-temporal feature describing the action sequence up to point t in time. This feature will, for the rest of this paper, be called the Spatio-temporal Radon Footprint of the action up to point t, will be denoted as SRF_t and is calculated as follows:

$$SRF_t(\rho,\theta) = \int_0^{t-1}\int_0^{J-1} M(j,f)\delta(j\cos\theta + f\sin\theta - \rho)\,dj\,df \tag{5}$$

In the above equation, it must hold that $t \geqslant 2$, both for M to be a 2D function of j and f and for the representation to encode a minimum of temporal information. In practice, depending on the action itself, more frames may need to pass before starting to calculate SRFs. Naturally, it should also hold that $F > 2$, which is obvious, both for the aforementioned reason as well as because it is impossible to ascertain the nature of an activity with insufficient joint information.

The process of calculating a SRF at a point in time, from a sequence of frames containing joint information, is depicted in Fig. 1. The frames shown

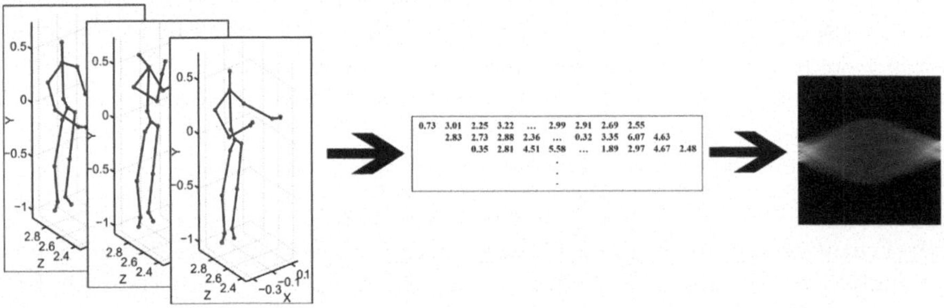

Fig. 1. Calculating SRF_t: the Mahalanobis matrix is calculated from the action sequence at point t and the Radon transform of the matrix gives the final result.

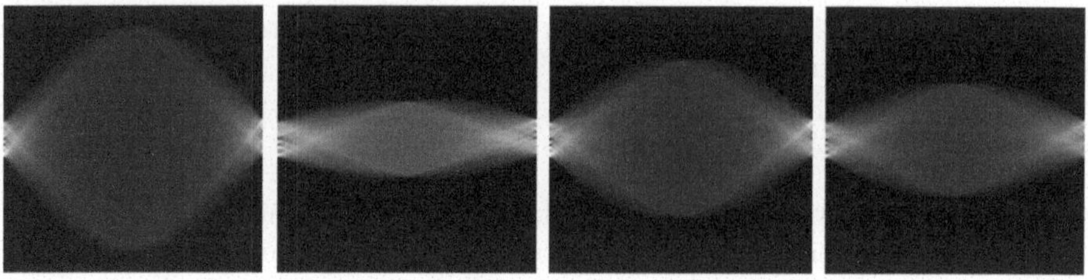

Fig. 2. *SRF* samples from various action sequences of the UTD-MHAD dataset, at varying points in time.

are samples from the UTD-MHAD dataset [5], which will be documented in Subsect. 4.1. Figure 2 shows sample *SRF*s taken from this dataset, from different sequences and at different timestamps.

3.2 A VGG CNN-Based Pipeline

In previous works such as the ones in [10] and [9], the Radon transform and its derivatives were intermediate features, used to produce the final feature vector describing the action sequence, which in turn was used as input for established machine learning techniques, such as SVMs. In this work, however, much like in [11], instead of hand-crafting features based on the transform's result, a convolutional neural network will learn those features directly from the *SRF*s. Particularly, we opted for a VGG-based architecture [23], because of the simplicity, the ease to train and deploy and the ability to adapt to complex pattern recognition problems that this family of convolutional neural networks demonstrates. The network used in our pipeline is shown in Fig. 3.

Preference over RNN-LSTM Architectures. It is customary to use Recurrent Neural Network (RNN, LSTM) architectures for online pattern recognition tasks involving temporal sequences [15], due to their ability to learn and encode temporal information. However, known issues come with the use of such networks, including the need for large training datasets in most cases, the vanishing and exploding gradient problems, as well their high demands in computational resources [8]. By encoding online spatio-temporal information in *SRF*s and using robust object detection architectures, we aim to eliminate the need for such networks and provide an online and compact action recognition pipeline which would not depend on extremely sophisticated hardware.

Per-Frame and Cumulative Classification. Human activity recognition is a temporally sensitive task. Offline techniques need to observe the complete action sequence before performing classification. In an online pipeline aiming towards real-time action recognition, per-frame classification is central. Previous studies, such as the one in [29], perform classification between unintentional falls

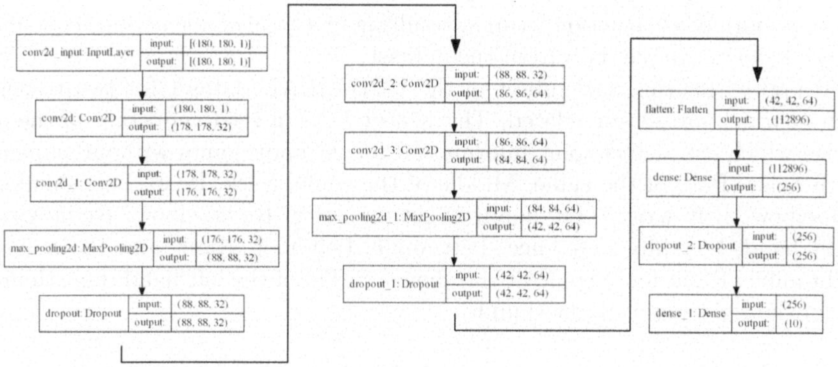

Fig. 3. The VGG-based architecture used in our experiments.

and other activities on single postures/frames, rather than complete sequences. The methodology presented in this paper performs online action analysis, while taking into account the history of every previous per-frame classification task.

In a specific frame f of the sequence, the SRF_f is calculated and fed in the aforementioned network. The network then determines the class of the action at that frame. However, the final decision is made by counting the number each action class was deemed the correct class of the sequence, divided by the number of frames which have passed up until the moment of classification. In a sense, for each action class and in every frame, we calculate a confidence that this action belongs to that class. This confidence is updated per-frame, with the ultimate goal of determining the correct class as early in the sequence as possible. This way, we eliminate the possibility of outliers (frames being classified in the wrong class) among a number of correct classifications.

4 Experimental Evaluation

In this section, we will discuss the experimental setup and the data used in the evaluation of the aforementioned methodology. The choice of the validation protocol will also become apparent, as well as the efficiency of the proposed technique.

4.1 Dataset

In our experiments, we used the UTD-MHAD dataset [5]. In particular, we used a more recent subset of this dataset, which contains data captured using the Kinect v2 depth sensor. It includes 10 actions, namely "Right hand high wave", "Right hand catch", "Right hand high throw", "Right hand draw X", "Right hand draw tick", "Right hand draw circle", "Right hand horizontal wave", "Right hand forward punch", "Right hand hammer" and "Hand clap (two hands)". These actions were performed by 6 subjects (3 female and 3 male), each one of whom performed each action 5 times, resulting in a total of 300 action sequences. Figure 4 shows sample data from the dataset.

We opted for this new subset of the UTD-MHAD dataset for two reasons, both of which are sensor related. The Kinect V2 is a relatively state of the art device which can detect joint information for 25 body joints without inducing much noise (Base of the spine, Middle of the spine, Neck, Head, Left shoulder, Left elbow, Left wrist, Left hand, Right shoulder, Right elbow, Right wrist, Right hand, Left hip, Left knee, Left ankle, Left foot, Right hip, Right knee, Right ankle, Right foot, Spine at the shoulder, Tip of the left hand, Left thumb, Tip of the right hand, Right thumb).

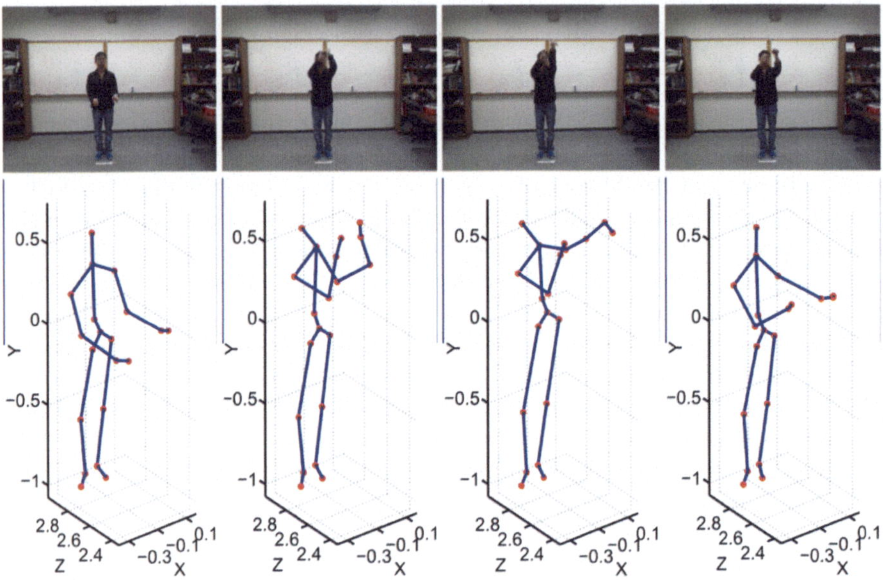

Fig. 4. Samples from the UTD-MHAD dataset.

4.2 Leave-One-Person-Out Cross-Validation

Validating a human activity recognition pipeline entails an inherent complexity which is not found in other classification tasks. In a typical scenario, we would have partitioned the dataset into a training and a testing set. Our dataset, as many other action datasets, is already partitioned by the subjects executing the actions. Simply leaving a person out for validation and training with the rest would not, however, produce reliable results.

Every person performs an action in a unique to every other person's way. For that matter, we perform the Leave-one-person-out cross-validation protocol (LOPO or LOO) across all individuals in our dataset. Essentially, we are training with the actions performed by 5 subjects and test with the actions performed by the one we left out. We repeat this process for all subjects in the dataset. The final reported accuracy would be the mean of the individual accuracies of each training-testing scenario.

4.3 Results

One of the first findings that we should report is that our pipeline achieved high training accuracy across all individual subject training tasks, with the mean training accuracy reaching **99.15%**. The highest achieved training accuracy was as high as **99.25%**, when training with all subjects except for subject #3, which was used for testing.

An expected discrepancy was noticed across the validation tasks. Notably, when testing with subject #6, the pipeline achieved validation accuracy equal to **90.08%**, whereas the worst performance was reported when testing with subject #3 (**66.02%**), on the same task that achieved the highest training accuracy. This hints towards possible issues of overfitting which may need to be dealt with in future works. The mean validation accuracy achieved after performing the complete LOPO protocol across all subjects was equal to **81.06%**. Table 1 shows the confusion matrix of the proposed pipeline after the validation process.

Figure 5 shows a characteristic sample of the evolution of class confidences according to our proposed pipeline. In this figure we observe how action class 4 ("Right hand draw X") emerges as the most possible to be the correct one with the passage of time. More extensive experimentation may lead to more robust findings concerning the similarity and relationship between classes.

Table 1. Confusion matrix of the proposed pipeline.

Truth											
Predicted	a1	a2	a3	a4	a5	a6	a7	a8	a9	a10	Total
a1	**20**	0	0	0	0	0	2	0	1	0	23
a2	0	**10**	1	0	0	0	0	0	0	0	11
a3	0	12	**26**	0	0	0	0	1	0	0	39
a4	0	0	3	**23**	0	6	1	0	0	0	33
a5	0	0	0	5	**30**	0	0	1	0	0	36
a6	4	0	0	2	0	**24**	2	0	0	0	32
a7	0	0	0	0	0	0	**14**	1	0	0	15
a8	0	7	0	0	0	0	6	**27**	0	0	40
a9	6	1	0	0	0	0	5	0	**29**	0	41
a10	0	0	0	0	0	0	0	0	0	**30**	30

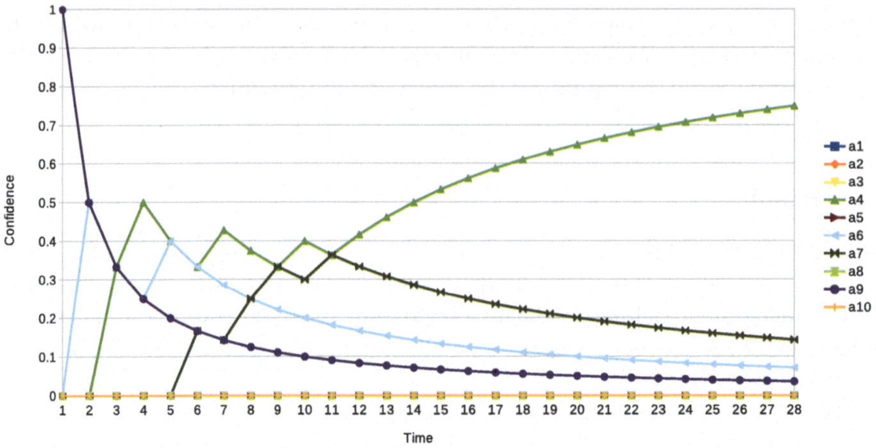

Fig. 5. Evolution of class confidences for action #4, performed by subject #6. After a certain point in time, the correct class (4, Right hand draw X) emerges as the most prevalent class.

5 Conclusion

This paper presented a compact online action recognition methodology, based on a novel sequence encoding scheme and a lightweight convolutional neural network. It is suitable for deployment on hardware with limited capabilities, which can be found even in household robotic systems. Experimentation and cross validation showed this pipeline can be used with state-of-the-art human pose estimation techniques to form efficient end-to-end activity recognition techniques.

Discrepancies in the testing data pointed out that there may be room for improvement, as more novel convolutional neural network architectures emerge. Furthermore, there may be hints of overfitting, as stated in the previous section, which may need to be dealt with.

In our future work, we will include attention models [21,28] in the CNN architecture to further improve the performance of the presented approach. Another direction could also be to focus on decrypting the inherent relationships and similarities between actions as encoded by *SRF*s, in order to evaluate the proposed scheme's performance as an action analysis and assessment tool.

References

1. Bevacqua, E., Raouzaiou, A., Peters, C., Caridakis, G., Karpouzis, K., Pelachaud, C., Mancini, M.: Multimodal sensing, interpretation and copying of movements by a virtual agent. In: André, E., Dybkjær, L., Minker, W., Neumann, H., Weber, M. (eds.) Perception and Interactive Technologies, pp. 164–174. Springer, Berlin Heidelberg (2006)

2. Beylkin, G.: Discrete radon transform. IEEE Trans. Acoust. Speech Signal Process. **35**(2), 162–172 (1987). https://doi.org/10.1109/TASSP.1987.1165108
3. Canal, G., Escalera, S., Angulo, C.: A real-time human-robot interaction system based on gestures for assistive scenarios. Comput. Vis. Image Underst. **149**, 65–77 (2016). https://doi.org/10.1016/j.cviu.2016.03.004. Special issue on Assistive Computer Vision and Robotics - Assistive Solutions for Mobility, Communication and HMI
4. Cao, Z., Hidalgo, G., Simon, T., Wei, S., Sheikh, Y.: OpenPose: realtime multi-person 2D pose estimation using part affinity fields (2018). CoRR abs/1812.08008. http://arxiv.org/abs/1812.08008
5. Chen, C., Jafari, R., Kehtarnavaz, N.: UTD-MHAD: a multimodal dataset for human action recognition utilizing a depth camera and a wearable inertial sensor. In: 2015 IEEE International Conference on Image Processing (ICIP), pp. 168–172, September 2015. https://doi.org/10.1109/ICIP.2015.7350781
6. Chen, M., Nikolaidis, S., Soh, H., Hsu, D., Srinivasa, S.: Planning with trust for human-robot collaboration. In: Proceedings of the 2018 ACM/IEEE International Conference on Human-Robot Interaction HRI 2018, pp. 307–315. Association for Computing Machinery, New York (2018). https://doi.org/10.1145/3171221.3171264
7. Chen, Y., Wu, Q., He, X.: Human action recognition by radon transform. In: 2008 IEEE International Conference on Data Mining Workshops, pp. 862–868, December 2008. https://doi.org/10.1109/ICDMW.2008.26
8. Gehring, J., Auli, M., Grangier, D., Yarats, D., Dauphin, Y.N.: Convolutional sequence to sequence learning. In: Proceedings of the 34th International Conference on Machine Learning ICML 2017, vol. 70, pp. 1243–1252. JMLR.org (2017)
9. Goudelis, G., Tsatiris, G., Karpouzis, K., Kollias, S.: 3D cylindrical trace transform based feature extraction for effective human action classification. In: 2017 IEEE Conference on Computational Intelligence and Games (CIG), pp. 96–103, August 2017. https://doi.org/10.1109/CIG.2017.8080421
10. Goudelis, G., Karpouzis, K., Kollias, S.: Exploring trace transform for robust human action recognition. Pattern Recogn. **46**(12), 3238–3248 (2013). https://doi.org/10.1016/j.patcog.2013.06.006
11. Hamdi, D.E., Elouedi, I., Fathallah, A., Nguyuen, M.K., Hamouda, A.: Combining fingerprints and their radon transform as input to deep learning for a fingerprint classification task. In: 2018 15th International Conference on Control, Automation, Robotics and Vision (ICARCV), pp. 1448–1453, November 2018. https://doi.org/10.1109/ICARCV.2018.8581072
12. Ji, Y., Yang, Y., Shen, F., Shen, H.T., Li, X.: A survey of human action analysis in HRI applications. IEEE Trans. Circuits Syst. Video Technol., 1 (2019). https://doi.org/10.1109/TCSVT.2019.2912988
13. Kadyrov, A., Petrou, M.: The trace transform and its applications. IEEE Trans. Pattern Anal. Mach. Intell. **23**(8), 811–828 (2001). https://doi.org/10.1109/34.946986
14. Laptev, I.: On space-time interest points. Int. J. Comput. Vis. **64**(2–3), 107–123 (2005)
15. Liu, J., Wang, G., Duan, L., Abdiyeva, K., Kot, A.C.: Skeleton-based human action recognition with global context-aware attention lstm networks. IEEE Trans. Image Process. **27**(4), 1586–1599 (2018). https://doi.org/10.1109/TIP.2017.2785279
16. Liu, Y., Nie, L., Liu, L., Rosenblum, D.S.: From action to activity: sensor-based activity recognition. Neurocomputing **181**, 108–115 (2016). https://doi.org/10.1016/j.neucom.2015.08.096. Big Data Driven Intelligent Transportation Systems

17. Loncaric, S.: A survey of shape analysis techniques. Pattern Recogn. **31**(8), 983–1001 (1998). https://doi.org/10.1016/S0031-2023(97)00122-2
18. Malatesta, L., Murray, J., Raouzaiou, A., Hiolle, A., Cañamero, L., Karpouzis, K.: Emotion modelling and facial affect recognition in human-computer and human-robot interaction. In: Murguía, M.I.C. (ed.) State of the Art in Face Recognition. IntechOpen, Rijeka (2009). https://doi.org/10.5772/6648
19. Nibali, A., He, Z., Morgan, S., Prendergast, L.: 3D human pose estimation with 2D marginal heatmaps. In: 2019 IEEE Winter Conference on Applications of Computer Vision (WACV), pp. 1477–1485, January 2019. https://doi.org/10.1109/WACV.2019.00162
20. Peters, C., Castellano, C., Rehm, M., André, E., Raouzaiou, A., Rapantzikos, K., Karpouzis, K., Volpe, G., Camurri, A., Vasalou, A.: Fundamentals of Agent Perception and Attention Modelling, pp. 293–319. Springer, Berlin, Heidelberg (2011)
21. Rapantzikos, K., Tsapatsoulis, N., Avrithis, Y., Kollias, S.: Bottom-up spatiotemporal visual attention model for video analysis. IET Image Process. **1**(11), 237–248 (2007)
22. Rodomagoulakis, I., Kardaris, N., Pitsikalis, V., Mavroudi, E., Katsamanis, A., Tsiami, A., Maragos, P.: Multimodal human action recognition in assistive human-robot interaction. In: 2016 IEEE International Conference on Acoustics, Speech and Signal Processing (ICASSP), pp. 2702–2706, March 2016. https://doi.org/10.1109/ICASSP.2016.7472168
23. Simonyan, K., Zisserman, A.: Very deep convolutional networks for large-scale image recognition. In: Bengio, Y., LeCun, Y. (eds.) 3rd International Conference on Learning Representations, ICLR 2015, San Diego, CA, USA, 7–9 May 2015, Conference Track Proceedings (2015). http://arxiv.org/abs/1409.1556
24. Tsatiris, G., Karpouzis, K., Kollias, S.: Variance-based shape descriptors for determining the level of expertise of tennis players. In: 2017 9th International Conference on Virtual Worlds and Games for Serious Applications (VS-Games), pp. 169–172, September 2017. https://doi.org/10.1109/VS-GAMES.2017.8056591
25. Tsatiris, G., Karpouzis, K., Kollias, S.: Applications of human action analysis and recognition on wireless network infrastructures: state of the art and real world challenges. In: 2018 Innovations in Intelligent Systems and Applications (INISTA). pp. 1–6, July 2018. https://doi.org/10.1109/INISTA.2018.8466317
26. Uddin, M.Z., Khaksar, W., Torresen, J.: Activity recognition using deep recurrent neural network on translation and scale-invariant features. In: 2018 25th IEEE International Conference on Image Processing (ICIP), pp. 475–479, October 2018. https://doi.org/10.1109/ICIP.2018.8451319
27. Varia, C., Tsatiris, G., Karpouzis, K., Kollias, S.: A refined 3D dataset for the analysis of player actions in exertion games. In: 2018 IEEE Conference on Computational Intelligence and Games (CIG), pp. 1–4, August 2018. https://doi.org/10.1109/CIG.2018.8490458
28. Wang, F., Jiang, M., Qian, C., Yang, S., Li, C., Zhang, H., Wang, X., Tang, X.: Residual attention network for image classification. In: The IEEE Conference on Computer Vision and Pattern Recognition (CVPR), July 2017
29. Yu, M., Gong, L., Kollias, S.: Computer vision based fall detection by a convolutional neural network. In: Proceedings of the 19th ACM International Conference on Multimodal Interaction ICMI 2017, pp. 416–420. Association for Computing Machinery, New York (2017). https://doi.org/10.1145/3136755.3136802

Classification of Coseismic Landslides Using Fuzzy and Machine Learning Techniques

Anastasios Panagiotis Psathas[1(✉)], Antonios Papaleonidas[1], George Papathanassiou[1], Sotiris Valkaniotis[2], and Lazaros Iliadis[1]

[1] Department of Civil Engineering, School of Engineering, Democritus University of Thrace, University Campus, PC 67100 Xanthi, Greece
{anpsatha, papaleon, gpapatha, liliadis}@civil.duth.gr
[2] Koronidos Street 9, 42131 Trikala, Greece

Abstract. Seismically generated landslides represent one of the most damaging hazards associated with earthquakes in countries with high seismicity. The delineation of prone to coseismic landsliding areas is crucial in order to predict the occurrence of earthquake-induced landslides and consequently reduce the relevant risk. The goal of this study is to investigate the correlation of the pattern of coseismic landslides with geological and topographical variables i.e. lithology, slope angle and slope aspect with the volume of landslides based on fuzzy logic and machine learning techniques. For this task, a real dataset of 421 and 767 instances for years 2003 and 2015 respectively from the island of Lefkada was used. A new approach based on *Fuzzy C-Means Algorithm* and *Ensemble Subspace k-Nearest-Neighbors (Ensemble Subspace k-NN)* is proposed. Landslides were classified according to their severity with a success rate of 99.5% and 98.7% for 2003 and 2015 respectively. The performance of the proposed approach was evaluated using "One Versus All" Strategy, calculating Accuracy, Sensitivity, Specificity, Precision and F-1 Score for each cluster.

Keywords: Landslides · Lefkada · Fuzzy C-Means · S-Nome · k-Nearest-Neighbors · Ensemble Subspace k-NN · Clustering · Classification

1 Introduction

It is well known that landslide can be triggered by rainfall, earthquakes, volcanic eruption and man-made activities. Experience has shown that seismically induced landslides represent one of the most damaging hazards associated with earthquakes in countries with high seismicity [1]. According to Jibson et al. [18], the effect of seismically-induced landslides on human lives and facilities may exceed in some cases the damage directly connected to the shaking. The correlation of coseismic landslides with the seismic and morphological parameters has been investigated by several researchers, mainly after the devastating 2008 Wenchuan, China earthquake. The outcome arisen by this correlation is that both the volume and number of landsliding phenomena are relevant to earthquake magnitude. In particular, it was shown that

L. Iliadis et al. (Eds.): EANN 2020, INNS 2, pp. 15–31, 2020.
https://doi.org/10.1007/978-3-030-48791-1_2

landslide frequencies are higher in areas of highest peak ground acceleration (PGA) and that landslide density decays with the epicentral or fault distance [2, 20, 25, 31].

The delineation of prone to coseismic landsliding areas is crucial in order to predict the occurrence of earthquake-induced landslides and consequently reduce the relevant risk. Nowadays, satellite imagery and GIS technology are considered as basic tools that are used by earth scientist for evaluating the hazard and the risk within an area, initially by the introduction and statistical analyses of geo-environmental and seismologic factors into GIS software [29]. In particular, the characteristics of the landsliding area is statistically related to control factors such as topographic, geologic and seismic parameters e.g. slope angle, slope aspect, curvature, lithology, Peak Ground Acceleration (PGA) and seismic intensity distribution, and distance from the seismic fault or epicenter [27, 39]. These correlations can provide crucial information that can be used for seismic landslide hazard analysis and planning mitigation measures for prone earthquake-induced landslides regions [6, 7, 18, 30].

Frequently, the statistical analysis is based on bivariate and multivariate approaches. The goal of this study is to investigate the correlation of the pattern of coseismic landslides with geological and topographical variables i.e. lithology, slope angle and slope aspect with the volume of landslides based on fuzzy logic and machine learning techniques. In particular, *Fuzzy C-Means Algorithm* [3, 12] was used for data clustering and Ensemble Subspace k-Nearest-Neighbors (Ensemble Subspace k-NN) was used for the classification [10, 15, 37]. Existing bibliography like [23] and [33] does not exploit the combination of the above algorithms.

The motivation for the development of this research was the need for a more flexible model. More specifically, the existing approaches (e.g. the bivariate analysis) are using crisp values for the determination of slope angle or slope aspect classes. Thus, borderline values can be easily misclassified.

2 Area of Research

The geology of the Lefkada island, comprises: (1) a carbonate sequence of the Ionian zone, (2) limestone of Paxos (Apulia) zone restricted in the SW peninsula of the island, (3) few outcrops of ionian flysch (turbidites) and Miocene marls-sandstones mainly in the northern part of the island [9, 34]. The boundary between the two different geological zones – Ionian and Paxos, runs in an approximate NW- SE direction through this region and outcrops onshore south-central Lefkada Island near Hortata village, in the form of a buried thrust fault by scree and late Quaternary deposits [28]. Pleistocene and especially Holocene coastal deposits are extended in the northern edge of Lefkada, where the homonym capital town is founded, in the valley of Vassiliki and in the coast Nydri.

Regarding the seismicity, it is pointed out that the island of Lefkada is considered as one of the most tectonically active areas in Europe being part of the high seismicity Ionian Sea area, and particularly due to the complex crustal deformation resulting from the subduction of the African plate towards NE and the Apulian platform continental collision further to the northwest [14, 16]. The main active tectonic structure, is the 140 km long dextral strike-slip Cephalonia-Lefkada Transform fault (Fig. 1) (CTF;

[24, 36, 38]), which has a GPS slip-rate bracketed between 10 and 25 mm/yr. The steep morphology on the western part of the island, where most of slope failure cases are reported is due to this offshore CTF and its onshore sub-parallel fault; the Athani-Dragano fault [9, 35]. The latter one is a NNE-SSW striking fault forming a narrow elongated continental basin, very well expressed in the region's morphology and marked on satellite images and aerial photos.

There is reliable detailed information for at least 23 events, since 1612 which induced ground failures at the island of Lefkada [26]. A first conclusion arising from the list of historical events is that earthquakes appear in couples (twin or cluster events) with time period of occurrence ranging between 2 months and 5 years e.g. 1612–1613 (16 months); 1625–1630 (5 years); 1722–1723 (10 months); 1767–1769 (2 years); 1783–1783 (2 months, possible aftershock); 1867–1869 (2 years); 1914–1915 (2 months); 1948–1948 (2 months). Thus, it is crucial to determine the location of coseismic landslides since it will be beneficial for reducing the risk and increasing the resilience at the island.

Fig. 1. Map of the island of Lefkada showing the Cephalonia-Lefkada Transform Fault CTF

2.1 Coseismic Landslides at the Island of Lefkada

The most recently occurred and well-studied earthquakes are the ones of 2003 and 2015. The penultimate event triggered extensive slope failures at the western part of the island. The volume of the debris material that moved downwards was larger than the one of the 2015 earthquake. Rock falls were widespread on the whole island and especially in the northwestern and central area, on both natural and cut slopes, as well as, on downstream road embankment slopes. The most characteristic rock falls, with diameters up to 4 m, were observed along the 6 km long road of Tsoukalades-Agios Nikitas, which is within the epicentral area, and are accompanied by gravel, small rock and soil slides [26]. The massive occurrence of these failures is the reason for the closure of the road network at this area of the island for more than 2 years. The reported rock falls followed the trace of a 300 m high morphological scarp, and especially a 10–40 m high artificial slope [26].

Regarding the 2015 earthquake, the dominant geological effects were related to slope failures i.e. rock falls and slides, and shallow and deep-seated landslides on both natural and cut slopes [28]. These failures were documented on the western part of the island, while the most densely concentration of these phenomena was reported on the coastal zone from Porto Katsiki to Egremnoi-Gialos beach and along the 6 km long coastal road of Tsoukalades - Agios Nikitas [28]. Shallow landslides and rock slides were mainly generated in areas where the clastic material covered the bedrock, and particularly in places where the rock mass was heavily jointed. Deep-seated landslides were mainly documented at the area of Egremnoi [29]. At this area, deep-seated landslides were reported, and large amount of debris material moved downslope inducing severe damages to the road network and to residential houses. The debris consists of coarse-grained size material with significant amount of large-diameter gravels and few boulders.

In order to investigate the earthquake-induced landslide density, event-based inventories were developed by taking into account aerial and satellite imagery in Google Earth in order to enrich and update existing landslide datasets, previously compiled for the two earthquakes [27]. In particular, Google Earth imagery of June 12, 2003 and December 19, 2005 was used for mapping 2003 earthquake landslides, and November 15, 2013 and April 15, 2016 for 2015 earthquake, respectively. Landslide activity along the western part of Lefkada is considered as minimal between major earthquakes, as observed on multi-date satellite imagery and confirmed by local residents. Considering this, the short period between each satellite imagery pair (2–3 years) is believed to include only the coseismic landslides, with very few if any at all landslides triggered by other factors. In total, 301 and 596 coseismic landslides were mapped for the 2003 and 2015 earthquakes, respectively. For the extraction of morphological and terrain parameters of the compiled landslide datasets, a detailed digital elevation model (DEM) with spatial resolution of 5 m was used. The 5 m DEM was obtained from Hellenic Cadastre and it was extracted from aerial imagery stereo-pairs, having a vertical accuracy of 4 m [29].

Having completed the polygon-based inventories, a statistical analysis of landslide distribution took place. In total, 596 and 301 landslides were identified covering (planar area) 1.29 km^2 and 1.6 km^2 for the 2015 and 2003 events, respectively. It is pointed out that these planar-oriented areas are obtained as projected measurements. The minimum and maximum landslide area were evaluated as 40.4 m^2 and 42940 m^2 for the 2015 earthquake, while for the penultimate event the relevant values are 129.8 m^2 and 98300 m^2, respectively [29]. The relevant values of minimum and maximum landslide area for the 2015 event, which were evaluated by taking into account the digital elevation model for the delineation of the landslide area, are 1.78 km^2 total area, 51.30 m^2 minimum and 58330 m^2 maximum area, while for the 2003 earthquake the total landsliding area covered 2.28 km^2 with minimum area of 140.9 m^2 and maximum 148469 m^2 [29].

3 Description of Dataset Pre-processing

The initial datasets (*.xlsx files) consist of 6 columns, 4 of which are numeric (Perimeter, Average Slope, Surface, Id) and 2 are nominal (Average Aspect and Geological Form). The 5th column is used only for data processing to determine the distinct incidents. Each vector represents a landslide with a specific Geological Form on the island of Lefkada. As it is already mentioned, 301 and 596 landslides were identified for years 2003 and 2015 respectively. However, numerous landslides are related to more than one types of geological forms. Taking into account this fact, the landsliding areas have been reassigned based on the geological form upon which they were delineated, resulting in 421 and 767 observations for years 2003 and 2015, respectively. The same data pre-processing approach was used for both datasets. However, data handling for each year was applied independently from the other, given that 2003 observations have been mapped on two additional geological forms compared to the case of 2015. Therefore, evaluation of the proposed approach per year has proven its efficiency and consistency. Data processing was performed in three steps. In particular, the first step was applied manually using both *.xlsx files, while second and third steps was achieved by developing code in *Matlab R2019a.*

3.1 Labeling of Nominal Values

Initially, Average Aspect was transformed from nominal to numeric in a scale from one to eight. Geological Form was similarly transformed to a scale from one to twenty for year 2003 and from one to eighteen for year 2015. The transformations can be seen in Tables 1 and 2.

Table 1. Average aspect with the corresponding label for 2003 and 2015.

Average aspect	North	North-East	East	South-East	South	South-West	West	North-West
Average aspect label	1	2	3	4	5	6	7	8

Table 2. Geological form type with the corresponding label for 2003.

Geological form	al	C	Ci	Cs	Csd	E	J1	J1d	Jar	Jc
Geological form label	1	2	3	4	5	6	7	8	9	10
Geological form	Jm	Js	M	Mb	Pc	Qc	Qp	Qt	Tc	Tg
Geological form label	11	12	13	14	15	16	17	18	19	20

Table 3. Geological form type with the corresponding label for 2015.

Geological form	al	C	Ci	Cs	E	J1	J1d	Jar	Jc
Geological form label	1	2	3	4	5	6	7	8	9
Geological form	Jm	Js	M	Mb	Pc	Qc	Qp	Qt	Tg
Geological form label	10	11	12	13	14	15	16	17	18

where al: alluvial; C, Jm, Jc, Jar, J1: limestones of Ionian; Ci, Cs: limestones of Paxos; Csd limestones; E: limestones Eocene; Js: limestone of Paxos; J1d: dolomites; M, Mb: Miocene sandstones; Pc: Pliocene conglomerate; Qc, Qp, Qt: Quaternary sediments; Tc: limestones and dolomites of Triassic; Tg: evaporites.

3.2 Landslides Fuzzy C-Means Clustering

After a statistical pre-processing of data, authors noticed that there were few high values causing a high standard deviation. Therefore, clustering of landslides is deterrent with conventional methods. To overcome this hardship, Fuzzy C-Means Clustering was employed to classify landslides according to their severity. Fuzzy C-Means was used because it offers a very flexible methodology, as each data point can be assigned to more than one clusters with different degrees of membership. This task was performed in order to develop the labeled dataset required for the deployment of the machine-learning model. A subset of available data, perimeter and surface, was used in order to apply the Clustering.

Fuzzy clustering (a well-known soft computing method [4]) is an approach in which each data point can belong to more than one cluster. One of the most widely used fuzzy clustering algorithms is the Fuzzy C-means clustering (FCM) Algorithm. This method, developed by Dunn in 1973 [12] and improved by Bezdek [3], is frequently used in pattern recognition. It is based on minimization of the following objective function:

$$J_m = \sum_{i=1}^{N} \sum_{j=1}^{C} u_{ij}^m \left\| x_i - c_j \right\|^2, \ 1 \leq m < \infty \tag{1}$$

Where m is the fuzzifier (the fuzzifier m determines the level of cluster fuzziness), u_{ij} is the degree of membership of x_i in the cluster j, x_i is the ith of d-dimensional measured data, c_j is the d-dimension center of the cluster, and $\|*\|$ is any norm expressing the similarity between any measured data and the center. Fuzzy partitioning is carried out through an iterative optimization of the objective function shown above, with the update of membership u_{ij} and the cluster centers c_j by:

$$u_{ij} = \frac{1}{\sum_{k=1}^{C} \left(\frac{\|x_i - c_j\|}{\|x_i - c_k\|} \right)^{\frac{2}{m-1}}}, \quad c_j = \frac{\sum_{i=1}^{N} u_{ij}^m \cdot x_i}{\sum_{i=1}^{N} u_{ij}^m} \tag{2}$$

This iteration will stop when $\max_{ij}\left\{ \left| u_{ij}^{(k+1)} - u_{ij}^{k} \right| \right\} < \varepsilon$, where ε is a termination criterion between 0 and 1, whereas k are the iteration steps. This procedure converges to a local minimum or a saddle point of J_m.

Parameters used for the FCM algorithm are presented in Table 4 while columns Perimeter and Surface, from source data set, were chosen as input parameters. Exponent (*m fuzzier*) controls the degree of fuzzy overlap between clusters. A large *m* results in smaller membership values, u_{ij}, and hence, fuzzier clusters. In the limit $m = 1$, the memberships, u_{ij}, converge to 0 or 1, which implies a crisp partitioning. maxIterations is the maximum number of optimization iterations and minImprovement is the minimum improvement in the objective function between successive iterations When the objective function improves by a value below this threshold, the optimization stops. A smaller value produces more accurate clustering results, but the clustering can take longer to converge. For parameters' values, the ones most used in the relevant literature were selected [21, 22].

Table 4. Options for FCM algorithm

Exponent (*m fuzzier*)	2
maxIterations	100
minImprovement	0.00001

A script *FCM.m* was developed in Matlab, aiming the transformation of *.xlsx file in Matlab tables. It has already been mentioned that the goal of this step is to create clusters for the severity of lansdlides. The chosen number of clusters is 6 (calculated as the existing combinations of 2 parameters with 3 states each). Clusters with their labels and their names are presented in Table 5. The first part of the name corresponds to Perimeter and the Second to Surface

Table 5. Cluster with the corresponding labels and names

Cluster	Name of cluster
1	Low Low
2	Low Medium
3	Medium Medium
4	Medium High
5	High High
6	Extreme Extreme

The *FCM.m* Script is presented in the form of natural language, in Algorithm 1.

Algorithm 1. *The FCM.m Matlab Script*

Script 1: *FCM.m*

Inputs: 421 incidents of 2003 and 767 incidents of 2015 exported from *.xlsx files.

Part 1:

Step 1: Read and convert each *.xlsx file to a Matlab table.

Step 2: For each Table the column Id Numbers was used to retrieve distinct Landslides. 2 new Matlab tables are constructed with the unique values

Step 3: For each new table Perimeter and Surface column is chosen

Part 2:

Step 1: FCM algorithm was applied with options described in Table 4 and clusters described in Table 5. Centers of clusters and membership degrees of each observation were calculated.

Step 2: Each instance was classified in the cluster on which the membership degree was the highest.

Part 3:

Step 1: Clusters pass to the original data

Step 2: Original data with theirs clusters are plotted in Figures 1a and 1b for 2003 and 2015 respectively.

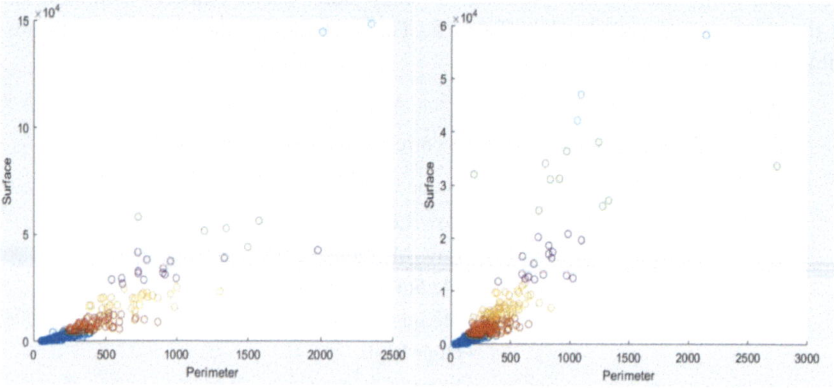

(a) (b)

Fig. 2. Clusters for original data for 2003 (1a) and 2015 (1b) respectively.

Total landslides for each cluster for the years 2003 and 2015 are presented in Table 6.

Table 6. Total landslides of each cluster for 2003 and 2015

Clusters	1	2	3	4	5	6	Total instances
2015	448	183	74	35	22	5	767
2003	238	100	44	27	7	5	421

3.3 Fuzzy Clustering with FCM Algorithm and S-Norm

After creating the clusters it was observed that some instances do not belong exclusively to a cluster (e.g. point (1981, $4.2 \cdot 10^4$) presented in Fig. 2a or point (2744, $3.3678 \cdot 10^4$) presented in Fig. 2b), as well as some instances in between 2 clusters with similar membership values for both. Considering the above observation, the re-creation of clusters for all instances is essential. Consequently, we decided that landslides, which have degree of membership, for their dominant class, below a certain threshold will be re-sorted. In order to perform this, it is necessary to use weights on each factor [5, 41].

Equation (3) implements a fuzzy coupling between many fuzzy sets, using a function $f(\mu_i, w_i)$ which assigns the weight w_i to the membership degree μ_i.

$$\mu_{\tilde{S}}(x_i) = Agg\left(f\left(\mu_{\tilde{A}}(x_i), w_1\right), f\left(\mu_{\tilde{A}}(x_i), w_2\right), \ldots, f\left(\mu_{\tilde{A}}(x_i), w_n\right)\right) \quad (3)$$

Where i = 1, 2,…, k and k the number of instances examined and n factors' number [13]. The function f used in the coupling function (Eq. (3)) can be defined as:

$$f(a, w) = a^{\frac{1}{w}} \quad (4)$$

where a is the membership degree and w is the corresponding weight.

For the Aggregation function was used Hamacher aggregation as S-Norm operator [40].

$$\widetilde{A} \cap \widetilde{B} = \frac{\mu_{\tilde{A}}(x) + \mu_{\tilde{B}}(x) - 2\mu_{\tilde{A}}(x)\mu_{\tilde{B}}(x)}{[1 - \mu_{\tilde{A}}(x) + \mu_{\tilde{B}}(x)]} \quad (5)$$

Another script *S-Norm_Clustering.m* was developed in Matlab. The second script is presented in the form of natural language, in Algorithm 2.

Algorithm 2. *The S-Norm_Clustering.m Matlab Script*

Script 2: *S-Norm_Clustering.m*

Inputs: All membership degrees of each observation for 2003 and 2015.

Part 1:

Step 1: Threshold is defined at 0.7

Step 2: Weights are defined. The highest membership's degree weight is 4, the second highest is 2, and for the others 0.

Part 2:

Step 1: If a membership degree for a cluster is higher than 0.7 the incident belong to this cluster.

Step 2: Else if the membership degree is under 0.7 the incident belongs to a new cluster, for with the membership degree is calculated through Eq. (3),(4) and (5).

After applied *S-Norm_Clustering.m,* 4 more clusters were created for landslides of 2003 and 5 more for 2015. New clusters were created between the already existing clusters. Therefore, they took their label depending the clusters that are between. For example, cluster between cluster 1 and 2 is labeled as cluster 1.5. Clusters are presented in Fig. 3a, b, and incidents for each cluster in Table 7. It is obvious that new clustering classifies observations more effectively according to severity.

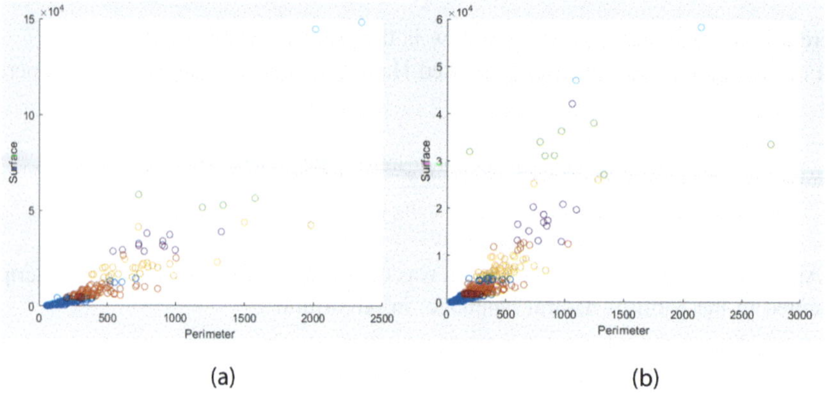

Fig. 3. Clusters for original data for 2003 (2a) and 2015 (2b) respectively after S-Norm

Table 7. Total landslides of each cluster for 2003 and 2015 after S-Norm

Clusters	1	1.5	2	2.5	3	3.5	4	4.5	5	5.5	6	Total instances
2015	417	52	145	27	56	25	18	7	15	2	3	767
2003	222	27	84	9	37	5	22	4	6	0	5	421

4 Classification Methodology

After having clustering done, we used classification algorithms to ascertain coseismic landslides' proper classification. The independent variables used for the classification are Perimeter, Average Slope, Surface, Average Aspect and Geological Form of landslides. Average Slope and Average Aspect were labeled as indicated in Tables 1, 2 and 3. The dependable value is the cluster derived from clustering with S-Norm.

A total of 23 classification algorithms have been employed namely: *Fine Tree, Medium Tree, Coarse Tree, Linear Discriminant, Quadratic Discriminant, Linear SVM, Quadratic SVM, Cubic SVM, Fine Gaussian SVM, Medium Gaussian SVM, Coarse Gaussian SVM, Cosine KNN, Cubic KNN, Weighted KNN, Fine KNN, Medium KNN, Gaussian Naive Bayes, Kernel Naïve Bayes, Boosted Trees, Bagged Trees, Subspace Discriminant, Subspace KNN, RUSBoost Trees.*

However, only the one with the highest values of performance indices will be described herein.

4.1 Ensemble Subspace k-Nearest-Neighbors (Ensemble Subspace k-NN)

Classifying query points based on their distance to specific points (or neighbors) can be a simple but yet effective process. The k-nearest neighbors (k-NN) is a lazy and non-parametric Learning algorithm [8]. It is widely used as a predictive performance benchmark, when we are trying to develop more sophisticated models. Given a set X of n points and a distance function, k-NN search finds the k closest points to a query point or set of them [17]. Dunami [11] first introduced a weighted voting method, called the *distance-weighted (DW) k-nearest neighbor rule* (Wk-NN). According to this approach, the closer neighbors are weighted more heavily than the farther ones, using the DW function. The weight w_i for the *i*-th nearest neighbor of the query x' is defined following function 1:

$$w_i' = \begin{cases} \frac{d(x' x_k^{NN}) - d(x' x_i^{NN})}{d(x' x_k^{NN}) - d(x' x_1^{NN})} & , \quad if \quad d(x' x_k^{NN}) \neq d(x' x_1^{NN}) \\ 1 & , \quad if \quad d(x' x_k^{NN}) = d(x' x_1^{NN}) \end{cases} \tag{6}$$

Finally, the classification result of the query is determined by the majority weighted voting as in function 2:

$$y' = \arg\max_{y} \sum_{(x_i^{NN}, y_i^{NN}) \in T'} w_i' \times \delta(y = y_i^{NN}). \tag{7}$$

Based on Eq. (7), a neighbor with smaller distance is weighted more heavily than one with greater distance: the nearest neighbor is assigned a weight equal to 1, whereas the furthest one a weight of 0 and the weights of the others are scaled linearly to the interval in between.

Despite its simplicity, k-NN gives competitive results and in some cases even outperforms other complex learning algorithms. However, k-NN is affected by non-informative features in the data, which is something rather common with high dimensional data. Several attempts have been made to improve the performance of nearest neighbors' classifiers by ensemble techniques. Some related work on ensemble of k-NN classifiers can be found in [10, 15, 17].

Subspace ensembles have the advantage of using less memory than ensembles with all predictors, and can handle missing values (NaNs).

The basic random subspace algorithm uses these parameters.

- m is the number of dimensions (variables) to sample in each learner.
- d is the number of dimensions in the data, which is the number of columns (predictors) in the data matrix X.
- n is the number of learners in the ensemble. Set n using the NLearn input.

The basic random subspace algorithm performs the following steps:

1. Choose without replacement a random set of m predictors from the d possible values.
2. Train a weak learner using just the m chosen predictors.
3. Repeat steps 1 and 2 until there are n weak learners.
4. Predict by taking an average of the score prediction of the weak learners, and classify the category with the highest average score.

4.2 Evaluation of the Activity Model Classifiers

Accuracy is the overall index that has been used in evaluation of the developed Machine Learning models. However, additional indices have been used to estimate the efficiency of the algorithms. Given the fact that we are dealing with a multi-class classification problem, the "One Versus All" Strategy [19, 32] was used. The calculated validation indices that have been considered are presented in the following Table 8.

Table 8. Calculated indices for the evaluation of the multi-class classification approach

Index	Abbreviation	Calculation
Sensitivity (also known as True Positive Rate or Recall)	SNS	SNS = TP/(TP + FN)
Specificity, (also known as True Negative Rate)	SPC	SPC = TN/(TN + FP)
Accuracy	ACC	ACC = (TP + TN)/ (TP + FP + FN + TN)
F1 Score	F1	F1 = 2*TP/(2*TP + FP + FN)
Precision (also known as Positive predictive value	PREC	PREC = TP/(TP + FP)

Precision (PREC) is the measure of the correctly identified positive cases from all the predicted positive cases. Thus, it is useful when the cost of False Positives is high.

On the other hand, ***Sensitivity*** (also known as Recall) is the measure of the correctly identified positive cases from all the actual positive cases. It is important when the cost of False Negatives is high. ***Specificity*** (SPC) is the true negative rate or the proportion of negatives that are correctly identified. ***Accuracy*** (ACC) is the measure of all correctly identified from the predicted cases. It represents the closeness of the measurements to a specific value. The ***F1*** score can be interpreted as the harmonic mean (weighted average) of the Precision and Recall. As it is known from the literature, ***Accuracy*** can be seriously considered when the class distribution is balanced while F1 score is a better metric when there are imbalanced classes as in the above case. Using it as a metric, we are sure that if its value is high, both precision and recall of the classifier indicate good results. In our case the F1 score is the final overall criterion of good performance evaluation.

5 Experimental Results

The experiments were performed with the use of Matlab R2019a software. The options and hyperparameters set for Ensemble Subspace k-NN are presented in Table 9 below:

Table 9. Tuning algorithm's hyperparameters

Algorithm	Hyperparameters	Optimal values-functions
Ensemble subspace k-NN	Maximum number of splits	20
	Number of learners	30
	Learning rate	0.1
	Subspace dimension	3

The Ensemble Subspace k-NN achieved an accuracy equal to 99.5% and 98.7% for 2003 and 2015 respectively. The Confusion Matrix for each year is presented in the following Figs. 4 and 5.

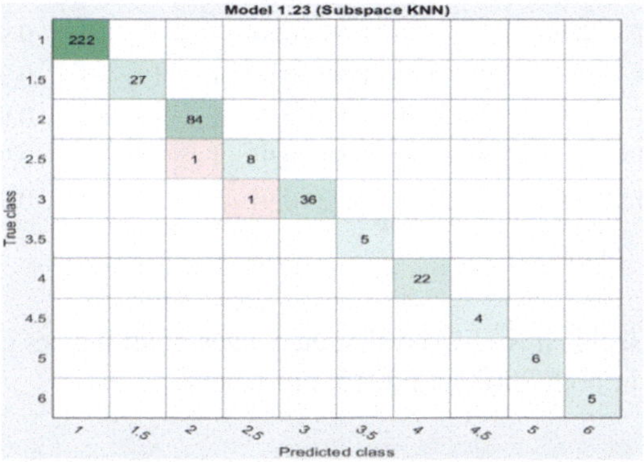

Fig. 4. Confusion matrix of the ensemble subspace k-NN algorithm for 2003

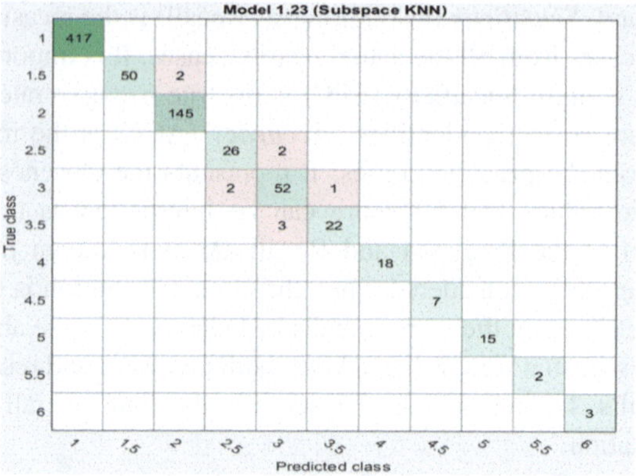

Fig. 5. Confusion matrix of the ensemble subspace k-NN algorithm for 2015

The following two Tables (10, 11), present the values of the performance indices for the above optimal algorithm.

Table 10. Cluster (Cl) classification performance indices for the Ensemble Subspace k-NN Algorithm (2003)

Index	Cl_1	$Cl_{1.5}$	Cl_2	$Cl_{2.5}$	Cl_3	$Cl_{3.5}$	Cl_4	$Cl_{4.5}$	Cl_5	Cl_6
SNS	1	1	1	0.88	0.97	1	1	1	1	0.98
SPC	1	1	0.99	0.99	1	1	1	1	1	0.99
ACC	1	1	0.99	0.99	0.99	1	1	1	1	0.99
PREC	1	1	0.98	0.88	1	1	1	1	1	0.98
F1	1	1	0.99	0.88	0.98	1	1	1	1	0.98

Table 11. Cluster (Cl) classification performance indices for the Ensemble Subspace k-NN Algorithm (2015)

Index	Cl_1	$Cl_{1.5}$	Cl_2	$Cl_{2.5}$	Cl_3	$Cl_{3.5}$	Cl_4	$Cl_{4.5}$	Cl_5	$Cl_{5.5}$	Cl_6
SNS	1	0.96	1	0.93	0.95	0.88	1	1	1	0.97	1
SPC	1	1	0.99	0.99	0.99	0.99	1	1	1	0.99	1
ACC	1	0.99	0.99	0.99	0.98	0.99	1	1	1	0.99	1
PREC	1	1	0.98	0.92	0.91	0.95	1	1	1	0.97	1
F1	1	0.98	0.99	0.92	0.92	0.91	1	1	1	0.97	1

From Tables (10, 11) it is obvious that the values of all indices clearly show a very good performance in both 2003 and 2015's instances.

6 Discussion and Conclusion

Classification of coseismic landslides according to their severity is a really interesting, important and challenging task. In this paper an approach based on *Fuzzy C-Means Algorithm* and *Ensemble Subspace k-Nearest-Neighbors (Ensemble Subspace k-NN) Algorithm* is proposed and tested. The combination of *Fuzzy C-Means* and Hamacher aggregation as S-Norm operator, sorted the data to 10 clusters for year 2003 and 11 clusters for 2015. Thereafter, *Ensemble Subspace k-NN,* using Average Aspect, Average Slope, Geological Form, Perimeter and Surface as independent input variables, managed to achieve high success rates. The overall accuracy is 99.5% and 98.7% for 2003 and 2015 respectively.

The efficiency of the model is also perceivable from Tables 10 and 11, where indices Accuracy, Sensitivity, Specificity, Perception and F1-score range at high levels. However, some ostensibly inaccurate classifications like in $Cl_{2.5}$ of 2003 or $Cl_{3.5}$ of 2015 do not affect the overall performance of the model as all indicators range from 0.88 to 1.

Concluding, the research described herein managed to correctly classify coseismic landslides according to their severity to the island of Lefkada. Future work will focus on the development of hybrid and ensembles' approaches for the forecasting of landslides' severity or even for forecasting the exact area of a landslide.

References

1. Dunn, J.C.: A fuzzy relative of the ISODATA process and its use in detecting compact well-separated clusters (1973)
2. Bezdek, J.C.: Pattern Recognition with Fuzzy Objective Function Algorithms. Springer, New York (2013)
3. Calvo, T., Mayor, G., Mesiar, R. (eds.): Aggregation Operators: New Trends and Applications, vol. 97. Physica, New York (2012)
4. Yager, R.R., Kacprzyk, J.: The Ordered Weighted Averaging Operators. Theory and Applications. Springer, New York (1997)
5. Fan, Z.P., Ma, J., Zhang, Q.: An approach to multiple attribute decision making based on fuzzy preference information on alternatives. Fuzzy Sets Syst. **131**(1), 101–106 (2002)
6. Wei, G., Lu, M.A.O.: Dual hesitant pythagorean fuzzy Hamacher aggregation operators in multiple attribute decision making. Arch. Control Sci. **27**(3), 365–395 (2017)
7. Cover, T., Hart, P.: Nearest neighbor pattern classification. IEEE Trans. Inf. Theory **13**(1), 21–27 (1967)
8. Hechenbichler, K., Schliep, K.: Weighted k-nearest-neighbor techniques and ordinal classification (2004)
9. Dudani, S.A.: The distance-weighted k-nearest neighbor rule. IEEE Trans. Syst. Man Cybern. **8**(4), 311–313 (1978)
10. Grabowski, S.: Voting over multiple k-nn classifiers. In: Modern Problems of Radio Engineering, Telecommunications and Computer Science (IEEE Cat. No. 02EX542), pp. 223–225. IEEE, February 2002

11. Domeniconi, C., Yan, B.: Nearest neighbor ensemble. In: Proceedings of the 17th International Conference on Pattern Recognition, 2004. ICPR 2004, vol. 1, pp. 228–231. IEEE, August 2004
12. Samworth, R.J.: Optimal weighted nearest neighbour classifiers. Ann. Stat. **40**(5), 2733–2763 (2012)
13. Joutsijoki, H., Juhola, M.: Comparing the one-vs-one and one-vs-all methods in benthic macroinvertebrate image classification. In: International Workshop on Machine Learning and Data Mining in Pattern Recognition, pp. 399–413. Springer, Berlin/Heidelberg, August 2011
14. Rifkin, R., Klautau, A.: In defense of one-vs-all classification. J. Mach. Learn. Res. **5**(2), 101–141 (2004)
15. Khalilia, M., Popescu, M.: Fuzzy relational self-organizing maps. In: 2012 IEEE International Conference on Fuzzy Systems, pp. 1–6. IEEE, June 2012
16. Khalilia, M.A., Bezdek, J., Popescu, M., Keller, J.M.: Improvements to the relational fuzzy c-means clustering algorithm. Pattern Recognit. **47**(12), 3920–3930 (2014)
17. Bora, D.J., Gupta, D., Kumar, A.: A comparative study between fuzzy clustering algorithm and hard clustering algorithm. arXiv preprint arXiv:1404.6059 (2014)
18. Robinson, T.R., Rosser, N.J., Densmore, A.L., Williams, J.G., Kincey, M.E., Benjamin, J., Bell, H.J.: Rapid post-earthquake modelling of coseismic landslide magnitude and distribution for emergency response decision support. Nat. Hazards Earth Syst. Sci. Discuss. **17**, 1521–1540 (2017)
19. Kritikos, T., Robinson, T.R., Davies, T.R.: Regional coseismic landslide hazard assessment without historical landslide inventories: a new approach. J. Geophys. Res.: Earth Surf. **120** (4), 711–729 (2015)
20. Ayalew, L., Kasahara, M., Yamagishi, H.: The spatial correlation between earthquakes and landslides in Hokkaido (Japan), a GIS-based analysis of the past and the future. Landslides **8**, 443–448 (2011)
21. Barlow, J., Barisin, I., Rosser, N., Petley, D., Densmore, A., Wrigth, T.: Seismically-induced mass movements and volumetric fluxes resulting from the 2010 Mw = 7.2 earthquake in the Sierra Cucapah, Mexico. Geomorphology **230**, 138–145 (2015)
22. Chang, K.T., Chiang, S.H., Hsu, M.L.: Modeling typhoon- and earthquake induced landslides in a mountainous watershed using logistic regression. Geomorphology **89**(3–4), 335–347 (2006)
23. Collins, B.D., Kayen, R., Tanaka, Y.: Spatial distribution of landslides triggered from the 2007 Niigata Chuetsu-Oki Japan Earthquake. Eng. Geol. **127**, 14–26 (2012)
24. Cushing, M.: Evoluation structurale de la marge nord-ouest hellenique dans l'ile de Lefkada et ses environs (Greece nord-occidentale). Ph.D. Thesis, University de Paris-Sud (XI), Centre d' Orsay, France (1985)
25. Ganas, A., Marinou, A., Anastasiou, D., Paradissis, D., Papazissi, K., Tzavaras, P., Drakatos, G.: GPS-derived estimates of crustal deformation in the central and north Ionian Sea, Greece: 3-yr results from NOANET continuous network data. J. Geod. **6**, 62–71 (2013)
26. Hatzfeld, D., Kassaras, I., Panagiotopoulos, D., Amorese, D., Makropoulos, K., Karakaisis, G., Coutant, O.: Microseismicity and strain pattern in northwestern Greece. Tectonics **14**(4), 773–785 (1995)
27. Jibson, R.W., Harp, E.L., Michael, J.A.: A method for producing digital probabilistic seismic landslide hazard maps. Eng. Geol. **58**, 271–289 (2000)
28. Keefer, D.K.: Landslides caused by earthquakes. Geol. Soc. Am. Bull. **95**(4), 406–421 (1984)
29. Louvari, E., Kiratzi, A.A., Papazachos, B.C.: The CTF and its extension to western Lefkada Island. Tectonophysics **308**, 223–236 (1999)

30. Meunier, P., Hovius, N., Haines, A.J.: Regional patterns of earthquake-triggered landslides and their relation to ground motion. Geophys. Res. Lett. **34**(20), L20408 (2007)
31. Papathanassiou, G., Pavlides, S., Ganas, A.: The 2003 Lefkada earthquake: field observation and preliminary microzonation map based on liquefaction potential index for the town of Lefkada. Eng. Geol. **82**, 12–31 (2005)
32. Papathanassiou, G., Valkaniotis, S., Ganas, A., Pavlides, S.: GIS-based statistical analysis of the spatial distribution of earthquake-induced landslides in the island of Lefkada, Ionian Islands. Greece. Landslides **10**(6), 771–783 (2013)
33. Papathanassiou, G., Valkaniotis, S., Ganas, A., Grendas, N., Kollia, E.: The November 17th, 2015 Lefkada (Greece) strike-slip earthquake: field mapping of generated failures and assessment of macroseismic intensity ESI-07. Eng. Geol. **220**, 13–30 (2017)
34. Papathanassiou G., Valkaniotis S., Ganas, A.: Spatial patterns, controlling factors and characteristics of landslides triggered by strike-slip faulting earthquakes; case study of Lefkada island, Greece. Bull. Eng. Geol. Environ. (Submitted, 2020)
35. Parise, M., Jibson, R.W.: A seismic landslide susceptibility rating of geologic units based on analysis of characteristics of landslides triggered by the 17 January, 1994 Northridge, California earthquake. Eng. Geol. **58**(3–4), 251–270 (2000)
36. Parker, R.N., Densmore, A.L., Rosser, N.J., de Michele, M., Li, Y., Huang, R.Q., Whadcoat, S., Petley, D.N.: Mass wasting triggered by 2008 Wenchuan earthquake is greater than orogenic growth. Nat. Geosci. **4**(7), 449–452 (2011)
37. Rondoyanni-Tsiambaou, Th.: Les seismes et l'environnement géologique de l'île de Lefkade, Grèce: Passe et Futur. In: Marinos, P., et al. (eds.) Engineering Geology and the Environment, Balkema, pp. 1469–1474 (1997)
38. Rondoyianni, Th., Mettos, A., Paschos, P., Georgiou, Ch.: Neotectonic Map of Greece, scale1:100.000, Lefkada Sheet. I.G.M.E., Athens (2007)
39. Sachpazi, M., Hirn, A., Clement, C., Haslinger, F., Laigle Kissling, E., Charvis, P., Hello, Y., Lepine, J.C., Sapin, M., Ansorge, J.: Western Hellenic subduction and Cephalonia transform: local earthquakes and plate transport and strain. Tectonophysics **319**, 301–319 (2000)
40. Scordilis, E.M., Karakaisis, G.F., Karacostas, B.G., Panagiotopoulos, D.G., Comninakis, P. E., Papazachos, B.C.: Evidence from transform faulting in the Ionian Sea: the Cephalonia island earthquake sequence of 1983. PAGEOPH **123**, 387–397 (1985)
41. Tian, Y., Xu, C., Chen, J., Zhou, Q., Shen, L.: Geometrical characteristics of earthquake-induced landslides and correlations with control factors: a case study of the 2013 Minxian, Gansu, China, Mw 5.9 event. Landslides **14**, 1915–1927 (2017)

Evaluating the Transferability of Personalised Exercise Recognition Models

Anjana Wijekoon(✉) and Nirmalie Wiratunga

Robert Gordon University, Aberdeen AB10 7GJ, Scotland, UK
{a.wijekoon,n.wiratunga}@rgu.ac.uk

Abstract. Exercise Recognition (ExR) is relevant in many high impact domains, from healthcare to recreational activities to sports sciences. Like Human Activity Recognition (HAR), ExR faces many challenges when deployed in the real-world. For instance, typical lab performances of Machine Learning (ML) models, are hard to replicate, due to differences in personal nuances, traits and ambulatory rhythms. Thus effective transferability of a trained ExR model, depends on its ability to adapt and personalise to a new user or a user group. This calls for new experimental design strategies that are person-aware, and able to organise train and test data differently from standard ML practice. Specifically, we look at person-agnostic and person-aware methods of train-test data creation, and compare them to identify best practices on a comparative study of personalised ExR model transfer. Our findings show that ExR when compared to results with other HAR tasks, to be a far more challenging personalisation problem and also confirms the utility of metric learning algorithms for personalised model transfer.

Keywords: Exercise Recognition · Transferability · Personalisation · Performance evaluation

1 Introduction

Exercise Recognition (ExR) is an ongoing Machine Learning (ML) research challenge with many practical applications such as self-management of musculoskeletal pain, weight training, orthopaedic rehabilitation and strength and balance improvement of pre-frail adults. Research in ExR falls under Human Activity Recognition (HAR) research, which has broader applications in gait recognition, fall detection and activity recognition for fitness applications, to name a few.

Fitness applications that adopt ExR as an integral component, face many challenges at deployment, compared with other conventional ML or Deep Learning (DL) applications such as image recognition or text classification. For instance

This work is part funded by SELFBACK which has received funding from the European Union's Horizon 2020 research and innovation programme under grant agreement No. 689043.

L. Iliadis et al. (Eds.): EANN 2020, INNS 2, pp. 32–44, 2020.
https://doi.org/10.1007/978-3-030-48791-1_3

lack of transferability of learned ML models is one of the main challenges that is present in many forms such as; the transferability to new sensor modalities, to new activities or to new user groups. With new sensor modalities, both heterogeneity of sensor data and differences in sensor configurations must be addressed. Transferability to new activity classes is generally addressed as open-ended HAR, where either a knowledge-intensive method is used with a corpus to learn heuristics that can cover all possible activities classes to be expected in the future [5] or; in contrast a knowledge-light method learns a feature space that is expected to adapt to new activity classes [13]. Lastly, when deploying a generic fitness application, developers are unaware of the target user group. Here transferability to a new user group, must also consider common factors applicable to the group needs.

In this paper, we focus on ExR applications; their transferability to different user groups and importantly how to design comparative studies that are informed by the ownership of data (i.e. data that is generated by a specific person). Naturally, people incorporate many personal nuances when performing exercises and in practice, these personal traits are captured by the sensors. If the ExR algorithm is unaware of the specific person it may find it challenging to map sensor readings to a specific exercise. In this paper we show that adopting the correct evaluation method is crucial to understanding the capabilities of an ExR algorithm amongst a diverse group of users.

We explore person-aware evaluation methods using the HAR personalisation algorithm MN^p [13] that was inspired by Metric-Learning and Meta-Learning ideas in the HAR (physical activity) domain. MN^p achieves personalisation without requiring test user data and learns a feature space that is transferable to a wider range of users. We expect ExR to be a harder personalisation challenge, compared personalisation of HAR models. Lets consider a typical ambulatory physical activity such as walking, where personal gait rhythm easily influences walking cycles but is consistent; contrast that to an exercise, such as a pelvic tilt or a knee roll (see Fig. 4a) where its harder to isolate and capture personal nuances and may vary over the time-period. Our evaluation shows that MN^p can be applied to ExR and is transferable to new users not seen during training.

Rest of the paper is organised as follows. In Sect. 2 we explore related literature in HAR and ExR domains. Next in Sect. 3, we present methods that are explored in this paper; followed by an analysis of results with alternative evaluation strategies in Sect. 4. Finally conclusions and future directions appear in Sect. 5.

2 Related Work

Research in ExR covers a wide variety of application areas such as weight training [6,10], rehabilitation [2] and callisthenics and gym exercises [8,15]. ExR like HAR, is a multi-class classification problem where classes are unique exercises that are captured by a stream of sensor data. Many algorithms have been explored in literature such as k-NN [8,14], Decision Trees and Random Forest [10,15] and CNN and LSTM [2,12].

Personalising such algorithms is intuitively desirable for ExR as personal nuances such as gait, posture and rhythm are known factors that are used by human experts when analysing exercise performance and adherence in the real-world. Although this remains largely unexplored for ExR; there is useful work in HAR, where early research has looked at user-dependent modelling with access to large quantities of labelled end-user data [1,7,9]. Follow on work attempts to reduce this human burden, by adopting semi-supervised learning methods [3,4] that require some model re-training after deployment.

Recent advances in few-shot learning and meta-learning with Matching Networks (MN) [11] and Personalised MN (MN^p) for HAR [13] has addressed the short comings of previous methods by only using few data instances from end-user as well as learning embeddings that are largely transferable to new activities without needing model re-training after deployment. It has also outperformed its non-personalised counterpart in the tasks of pose detection and HAR [13]. Importantly in this paper we investigate, if MN^p is transferable to ExR, which is arguably a more challenging personalised learning problem.

3 Methods

Given sensor data streams recorded while performing exercises, for supervised ExR, data instances are extracted using the sliding window method applied to each of the streams. Typical sensors include inertial sensors, depth cameras and pressure mats. More formally, given a set of data instances, $\mathcal{X}$, ExR involves learning a feature space where the mapping from each instance, x, to an exercise class, y, where y is from the set of exercise classes, $\mathcal{L}$. Accordingly, each sensor-based data instance is a data and class label pair, (x, y), where $y \in \mathcal{L}$.

$$\mathcal{X} = \{(x, y) \mid y \in \mathcal{L}\} \tag{1}$$

In comparison to computer vision or text datasets, each data instance in $\mathcal{X}$ belongs to a person, p. Given the set of data instances obtained from person p is $\mathcal{X}^p$, relationship of $\mathcal{X}^p$ and $\mathcal{X}$ formalised as in Eq. 2. As before all data instances in $\mathcal{X}^p$ will belong to a class in $\mathcal{L}$ except special instances like open-ended HAR where the class set is not fully specified at training time.

$$\mathcal{X} = \{\mathcal{X}^p \mid p \in \mathcal{P}\} \text{ where } \mathcal{X}^p = \{(x, y) \mid y \in \mathcal{L}\} \tag{2}$$

Training and testing methodologies can adopt one of two approaches; *person-agnostic* where an algorithm is trained and tested with the same user group; and *person-aware*, where an algorithm is trained and tested on different user groups. Both maintain disjointed sets of data instances in train and test; but the latter also preserves disjoint persons by preserving the person-to-data relationship during model training and testing.

3.1 Person-Agnostic Evaluation

Person agnostic evaluations can be applied as a repeated hold-out (R-HO) or a cross-fold (CF) validation methodologies. In either case, the person parameter of each data instance is discarded when creating hold-out sets, or folds. This means that a person's data can be split between train and test sets. A percentage, λ, of all data instance in $\mathcal{X}$, is used as the set of test data instances, $\mathcal{X}_{test}$, and the rest as the set of train data instances $\mathcal{X}_{train}$.

$$\begin{aligned} \mathcal{X} &= \{\mathcal{X}_{train}, \mathcal{X}_{test}\} \\ |\mathcal{X}_{train}| &\approx (1 - \lambda) \times |\mathcal{X}| \text{ and } |\mathcal{X}_{test}| \approx \lambda \times |\mathcal{X}| \end{aligned} \tag{3}$$

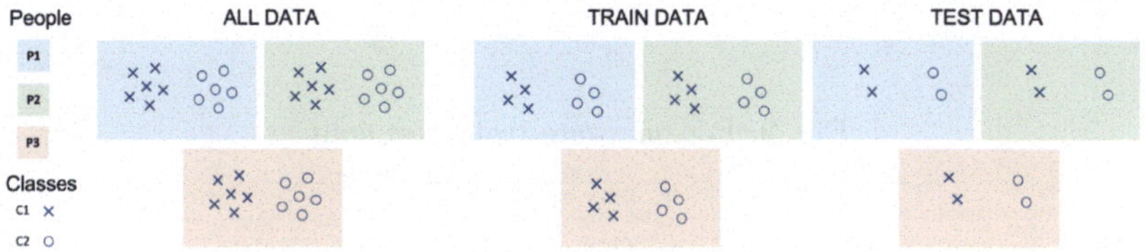

Fig. 1. Person-agnostic train/test split

With R-HO, a λ percentage of the data instances are randomly selected (without replacement) to form the test set and the remainder forming the train set. This is repeated for multiple iterations. With CF, first, the dataset is divided into a number of folds where each fold contains λ percentage of data, and at each iteration, one fold is selected as the test set and the rest of the folds as the training set. Both methods create train and test sets that share the same population $\mathcal{P}$ (see Fig. 1). Unlike with R-HO method, CF guarantees that each data instance appears once in the test set.

A person-agnostic methodology for evaluation, trains and tests on the same population. Accordingly, these methodologies are not designed to evaluate the robustness of an algorithm on a different population following typical deployment. However they provide an "upper-bound" performance of a ML algorithm.

3.2 Person-Aware Evaluation

A Person-aware evaluation can be performed as a repeated Persons-Hold-Out (R-PHO) or a Leave-One-Person-Out (LOPO) methodology. With R-PHO, a percentage, μ, of the user population is selected as the test user set, rest forming the train user set; and this is repeated for multiple iterations. With LOPO methodology, instances from a single user is put aside, to form a singleton test user group, and the rest of the users form the training user group. The train and test set formation with the test user group, $\mathcal{P}_{test}$, and the train user group, $\mathcal{P}_{train}$ can be formalised as follows:

$$\begin{gathered}\mathcal{X} = \{\mathcal{X}_{train}, \mathcal{X}_{test}\} \\ \mathcal{X}_{test} = \{\mathcal{X}^p \mid p \in \mathcal{P}_{test}\} \text{ and } \mathcal{X}_{train} = \{\mathcal{X}^p \mid p \in \mathcal{P}_{train}\} \\ \mathcal{P} = \{\mathcal{P}_{train}, \mathcal{P}_{test}\}\end{gathered} \tag{4}$$

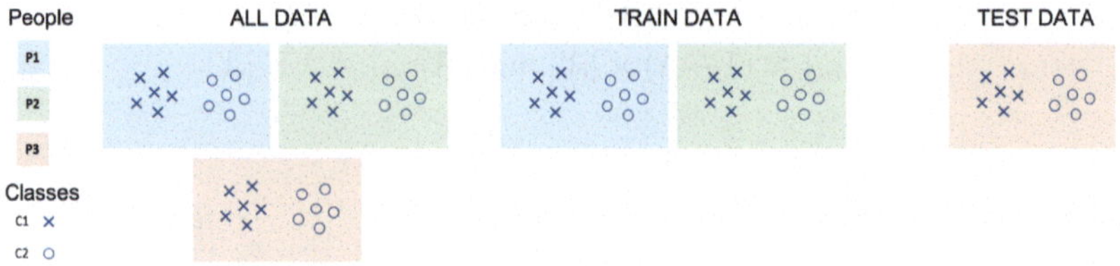

Fig. 2. Person-aware train/test split

LOPO ensures that each user in the population $\mathcal{P}$ is included in the test set in one of the trials (similar to the person-agnostic CF method), but LOPO also ensures disjointedness in selected persons (see Fig. 2). We propose that performance measures obtained with a person-aware methodology should be used as the "lower-bound", likely performance of a ML algorithm after deployment.

3.3 Personalised Matching Networks

The goal of personalisation is to learn a feature space that can dynamically adapt to different test user groups. With reference to Sects. 3.1 and 3.2, the aim here is to find algorithms that outperform the "lower-bound" set by a non-personalised algorithm when evaluated by a person-aware methodology. For this purpose we explore the Personalised Matching Networks (MN^p), which has been successfully used for personalising HAR algorithms.

MN^p is inspired by Metric Learning and Meta-Learning paradigms where the classification task is learning to match a test instance, x, to one instance from a set of representatives. The set of representative instances, S is chosen from the same user (i.e. from. $\mathcal{X}^p$) ensuring all classes are represented. An instance in, S, is a data instance, (x, y), and for each class up to, k, representatives are selected from, $\mathcal{X}^p$, as in Eq. 5.

$$S = \{(x, y) | x \in \mathcal{X}^p, y \in \mathcal{L}\} \text{ where } |S| = k \times |\mathcal{L}| \tag{5}$$

We denote the training data set obtained for person, p's data as $\mathcal{X}^p_{tr}$. An instance in, $\mathcal{X}^p_{tr}$, consists of a query and support set pairs, (q_i, S_i), where, q_i, is a sensor data and class label pair, (x_i, y_i), (similar to a conventional supervised learning training data instance). The complete training data set, $\mathcal{X}_{tr}$, is the collection of all, $\mathcal{X}^p_{tr}$, for the train user group $\mathcal{P}_{tr}$.

$$\mathcal{X}^p_{tr} = \{(q, S) \mid x \in \mathcal{X}^p, y \in \mathcal{L}\} \text{ where } q = (x, y), y \in \mathcal{L}$$
$$\mathcal{X}_{tr} = \{\mathcal{X}^p_{tr} \mid p \in \mathcal{P}_{tr}\} \quad (6)$$

During MN^p training, a parametric model learns a feature space where data instances from different users are successfully transformed and mapped to class labels. Here training can be viewed as a parameterised (Θ) end-to-end learning of a distance/similarity function, using a non-parametric attention-based kernel to compute the objective matching function (see architecture in Fig. 3). At testing, the MN^p algorithm predicts the label $\hat{y}$ for a query instance $\hat{x}$ with respect to its support set $\hat{S}$ from the same user.

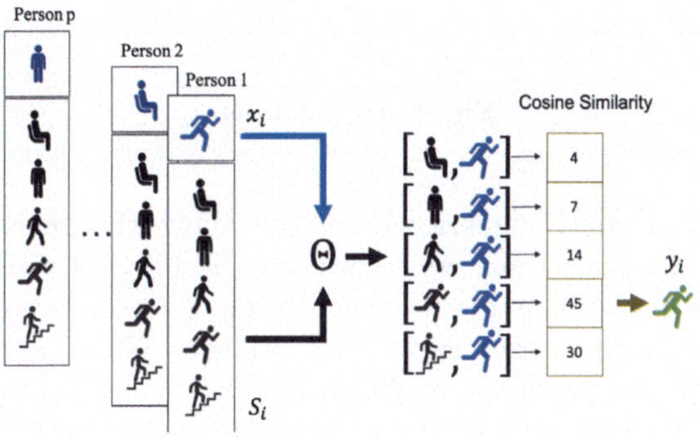

Fig. 3. Training MN^p for HAR; adapted from [13]

4 Evaluation and Results

Aim of the evaluation is two fold; firstly we analyse lower and upper bound performances of ExR algorithms using the 2 alternative methods of evaluation: person-agnostic versus person-aware, secondly we explore the transferability of personalised models for ExR from HAR. All experimental results calculate the mean F1-score and any significance is reported at the 95% level.

4.1 MEx Dataset

MEx is a sensor-rich dataset collected for 7 exercises with four sensors, publicly available at the UCI Machine Learning Repository[1]. Seven exercise classes are included in this data collection; 1-Knee Rolling, 2-Bridging, 3-Pelvic Tilt, 4-Bilateral Clam, 5-Repeated Extension in Lying, 6-Prone Punch and 7-Superman (Fig. 4a). These exercises are frequently used for prevention or self-management of LBP.

There are four sensor modalities; two accelerometers placed on the wrist and the thigh of the person; a pressure mat was where the person lays on to perform

[1] https://archive.ics.uci.edu/ml/datasets/MEx.

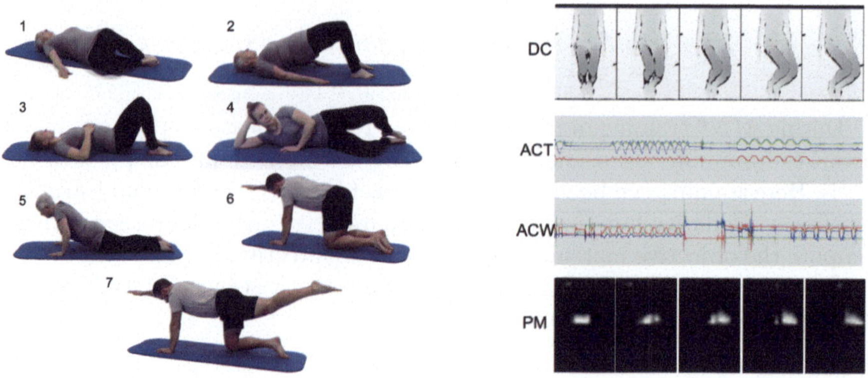

[Exercises] [Raw sensor data]

Fig. 4. MEx dataset

the exercises and a depth camera was placed above the person facing downwords. The tri-axial accelerometers record data at 100 Hz frequency within the range of ±8g. The pressure mat and the depth camera record gray scale frames at 15 Hz frequency and frame sizes are 32×16 and 240×320 respectively. Figure 4b shows a visualisation of each sensor data type.

In this study we focus on ExR with a single modality. Accordingly we create four datasets with the four modalities available on MEx; the thigh accelerometer, the wrist accelerometer, the pressure mat and the depth camera respectively referred to as ACT, ACW, PM and DC in the rest of this paper.

4.2 Pre-processing

The sliding window method is applied on each individual sensor data stream to create data instances; where the window size is 5 s with 3 s overlap. Each resulting window forms a data instance and is labelled with the exercise class. This process yields datasets of 6240 instances ($|\mathcal{X}| = 6240$), with 208 data instance per user in average ($|\mathcal{X}_p| \approx 208$). We apply a set of pre-processing steps for each sensor modality as recommended by the authors of [12]. A reduced frame rate of 1 frame/second is applied for DC and PM data and the DC data frames are compressed from 240×320 to 12×16. The inertial sensor data from ACW and ACT are pre-processed using the Discrete Cosine Transformation (DCT) according to [12].

4.3 Comparison of Person-Agnostic and Person-Aware Settings

In order to demonstrate the effect of different evaluation methods on ExR, we evaluate ExR algorithms using the two person-agnostic evaluation methodologies; R-HO and CF (Sect. 3.1) and the person-aware methodology LOPO. We choose the best performing algorithms for each sensor dataset from [12] for our comparative study. We discard the user parameter on the data instances to obtain the person-agnostic datasets, and use 1/30 as the λ parameter to split a dataset for training and testing or to create folds. Accordingly we repeat the R-HO experiments for 30 iterations and perform 30 CF experiments. These are compared with results from person-aware LOPO from [12].

Table 1. Mean F1-score results: person-agnostic vs. person-aware settings

Methodology		Algorithm	ACT	ACW	DC	PM
Person-agnostic	R-HO	From [12]	0.9807	0.9163	0.9953	0.9905
	CF		0.9798	0.9260	0.9960	0.9880
Person-aware	LOPO	From [12]	0.9015	0.6335	0.8720	0.7408

In Table 1, there is a significant difference between the performance measures obtained with person-agnostic and person-aware methods. Inevitably when there is no person-wise disjoint train and test splits, algorithms have the opportunity to configure its parameters to better fit the expected user population at test time, resulting in significantly improved performance. It is noteworthy that both person-agnostic methods achieve similar mean F1-scores consistently with all four datasets. We highlight that person-aware LOPO performance measures set the "lower-bound" and person-agnostic performance measures set the "upper-bound" for the ExR task with each sensor modality.

4.4 Comparative Study of Non-personalised vs. Personalised Algorithms for ExR

Performance of non-personalised algorithms (from [12]) is compared with the personalised algorithm MN^p (from Sect. 3.3) for ExR. We evaluate with two person-aware evaluation methodologies; R-PHO and LOPO from Sect. 3.2. With R-PHO experiments a test set is formed with randomly selected instances from 1/3 of persons forming the set of test users (μ), and the train instances selected from the other 2/3 of train users. This is repeated for 10 test-train trials. In LOPO experiments, we select the set of data instances from one user as the test set and the rest forming the train set, and this is repeated 30 times but each time with a different test user. While R-PHO helps to evaluate transferability of the algorithms with multiple users at a time, LOPO evaluates the transfer to a single user at a time, both are valid scenarios for ExR and HAR in general. For comparative purposes, we also included results obtained by authors of [13] for general HAR tasks, pose detection tasks and Activities of Daily Living (ADL) classification task.

In Table 2 results are grouped under each task and the difference between the personalised algorithm and the best non-personalised algorithm is presented in the last column. Here the best non-personalised algorithm for the first three tasks is the non-personalised Matching Networks introduced in [11] and for the MEx exercises domain they are the best performing algorithms found by the authors of [12] for each sensor modality. Person-aware evaluation methodologies require a non-parametric statistical significance test as they produce results that are not normally distributed. We use the Wilcoxon signed-rank test for paired samples to evaluate the statistical significance at 95% confidence and highlight the significantly improved performances in bold.

Table 2. Mean F1-score results for the comparison of non-personalised algorithm vs. personalised algorithm for ExR

Problem domain	Evaluation methodology	Dataset	Algorithm		Difference
			Non-personalised	MN^p	
Pose Detection	R-PHO	HDPoseDS_{17}	0.7678	**0.9837**	+21.68%
		HDPoseDS_{6}	0.4292	**0.9186**	+48.94%
General HAR	R-PHO	$\text{SELFBACK}_{W,T}$	0.7340	**0.9169**	+18.29%
		SELFBACK_{W}	0.6320	**0.8563**	+22.44%
ADL	R-PHO	PAMAP2	0.8715	0.8690	−0.25%
MEx	R-PHO	ACT	0.9064	**0.9424**	+3.60%
		ACW	0.6352	**0.6845**	+4.93%
		DC	0.8741	**0.9186**	+4.45%
		PM	0.6977	**0.8538**	+15.61%
MEx	LOPO	ACT	0.9015	**0.9155**	+1.40%
		ACW	0.6335	**0.6663**	+3.28%
		DC	0.8720	**0.9342**	+6.22%
		PM	0.7408	**0.8205**	+7.97%

The personalised algorithm, MN^p, has significantly outperformed the best non-personalised algorithm on both evaluation methodologies. Overall similar performance measures are observed across both methodologies, with the exception of the PM dataset, where there is a $\sim$+5% difference when using LOPO compared to R-PHO with the non-personalised algorithm.

We observe that personalisation has the greatest benefit for Pose detection, followed by general HAR tasks which feature both ambulatory and stationary activities; and thereafter on the ExR task. The exception here was ADL tasks, where personalisation neither improved nor degraded performance. Close examination of the activity duration of each domain suggests that pose and ambulatory activities are highly repetitive, or are performed in short repetitive time spans, which minimises the capturing of personal rhythmic nuances. In comparison, a single repetition of an exercise takes a longer time and consists of multiple sub steps making it harder to model due to potential variation opportunities

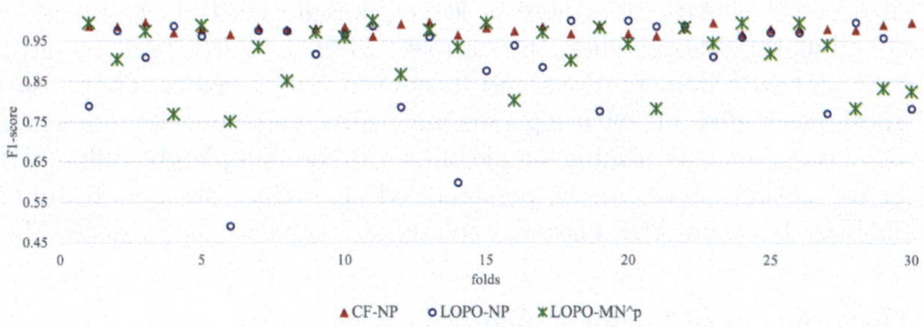

(a) ACT

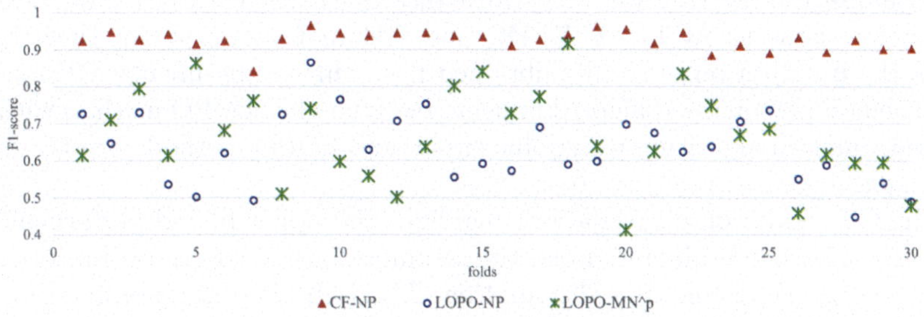

(b) ACW

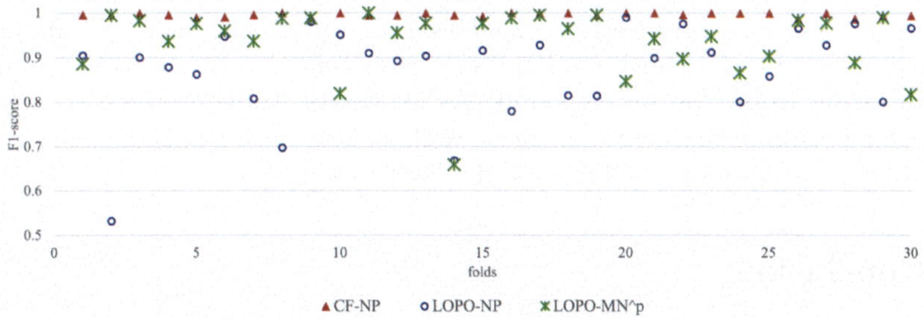

(c) DC

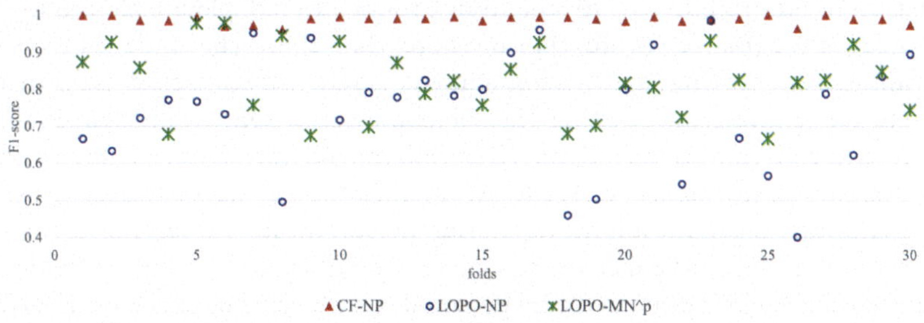

(d) PM

Fig. 5. Distribution of F1-score over the folds

between persons. Essentially MN^p is capable of finding some commonalities between exercise classes, but there is less opportunities than compared with pose or ambulatory movements. In contrast, ADL activities tend to have less clear start and stop demarcations and have even longer spans. They also have the highest possibility of featuring personal traits and nuances. For example, an ADL classes such as ironing or cleaning can be completely different from one user to another. Accordingly, personalised algorithms struggle to find such commonalities between ADL classes; explaining results we had observed here.

4.5 Distribution of Performance Measures

We visualise the distribution of performance measures with different methodologies for datasets ACT, ACW, DC and PM in Figs. 5a to 5d. Each figure shows the distribution of results obtained from three experiments; CF method with the non-personalised algorithm using red triangles, LOPO method with the non-personalised algorithm using blue circles and LOPO method with the MN^p personalised algorithm using green stars.

The CF results on every dataset highlight the upper-bound performance of the ExR task when evaluated under the assumption that the algorithm is trained and tested on the same user distribution. The LOPO results obtained for the non-personalised algorithm sets the lower-bound for the ExR task and highlights how non-personalised algorithms struggle when tested on a person that was not part of the training user group. Personalised algorithm such as MN^p, minimise the gap between the upper-bound and the lower-bound with a majority of users by improving upon the lower-bound. As shown in Table 2, MN^p, is a good choice for personalising across all tasks with significant advantages shown with pose detection and fewest gains with the ExR task.

5 Conclusion

This paper presents a comprehensive study of Exercise Recognition (ExR) model evaluation of adaptability to diverse user groups after deployment. Mainly two approaches are explored; evaluation methods that share the same user set during training and testing (i.e. person-agnostic) and methods that keep disjoint user sets for training and testing (i.e. person-aware). Our evaluation highlight that the prior method sets the upper-bound and the latter sets the lower-bound for the model performance in ExR. We highlight how person-agnostic evaluation results are normally distributed, but person-aware evaluation results are not, thus calling for non-parametric statistical significance testing methods. The paper presents the adaptation of the personalised algorithm, MN^p for ExR, that is capable of learning a feature space that is transferable to unseen users and user groups and show how it outperforms the lower-bound while using the evaluation criteria suitable for model deployment (i.e. person-aware ExR). Improving performance with personalised algorithms in the person-aware setting is a significant step towards deploying user-friendly, unobtrusive ExR algorithms with fitness applications. Finally, we highlight the need to further improve personalised algorithms to better suit the ExR domain.

References

1. Berchtold, M., Budde, M., Gordon, D., Schmidtke, H.R., Beigl, M.: ActiServ: activity recognition service for mobile phones. In: International Symposium on Wearable Computers (ISWC) 2010, pp. 1–8. IEEE (2010)
2. Burns, D.M., Leung, N., Hardisty, M., Whyne, C.M., Henry, P., McLachlin, S.: Shoulder physiotherapy exercise recognition: ML the inertial signals from a smartwatch. Physiol. Measur. **39**(7), 075007 (2018)
3. Longstaff, B., Reddy, S., Estrin, D.: Improving activity classification for health applications on mobile devices using active and semi-supervised learning. In: 2010 4th International Conference on Pervasive Computing Technologies for Healthcare, pp. 1–7. IEEE (2010)
4. Miu, T., Missier, P., Plötz, T.: Bootstrapping personalised human activity recognition models using online active learning. In: 2015 IEEE International Conference on Computer and Information Technology; Ubiquitous Computing and Communications; Dependable, Autonomic and Secure Computing; Pervasive Intelligence and Computing, pp. 1138–1147. IEEE (2015)
5. Ohashi, H., Al-Naser, M., Ahmed, S., Nakamura, K., Sato, T., Dengel, A.: Attributes' importance for zero-shot pose-classification based on wearable sensors. Sensors **18**(8), 2485 (2018)
6. Qi, J., Yang, P., Hanneghan, M., Waraich, A., Tang, S.: A hybrid hierarchical framework for free weight exercise recognition and intensity measurement with accelerometer and ECG data fusion. In: 2018 40th Annual International Conference of the IEEE Engineering in Medicine and Biology Society (EMBC), pp. 3800–3804. IEEE (2018)
7. Sun, X., Kashima, H., Ueda, N.: Large-scale personalized human activity recognition using online multitask learning. IEEE Trans. Knowl. Data Eng. **25**(11), 2551–2563 (2013)
8. Sundholm, M., Cheng, J., Zhou, B., Sethi, A., Lukowicz, P.: Smart-mat: recognizing and counting gym exercises with low-cost resistive pressure sensing matrix. In: Proceedings of the 2014 ACM UbiComp, pp. 373–382. ACM (2014)
9. Tapia, E.M., Intille, S.S., Haskell, W., Larson, K., Wright, J., King, A., Friedman, R.: Real-time recognition of physical activities and their intensities using wireless accelerometers and a heart rate monitor. In: 2007 11th IEEE International Symposium on Wearable Computers, pp. 37–40. IEEE (2007)
10. Velloso, E., Bulling, A., Gellersen, H., Ugulino, W., Fuks, H.: Qualitative activity recognition of weight lifting exercises. In: Proceedings of the 4th Augmented Human International Conference, pp. 116–123. ACM (2013)
11. Vinyals, O., Blundell, C., Lillicrap, T., Wierstra, D., et al.: Matching networks for one shot learning. In: Advances in Neural Information Processing Systems, pp. 3630–3638 (2016)
12. Wijekoon, A., Wiratunga, N., Cooper, K.: MEx: multi-modal exercises dataset for human activity recognition. arXiv preprint arXiv:1908.08992 (2019)
13. Wijekoon, A., Wiratunga, N., Sani, S., Cooper, K.: A knowledge-light approach to personalised and open-ended human activity recognition. Knowl.-Based Syst. **192**, 105651 (2020)

14. Xiao, F., Chen, J., Xie, X.H., Gui, L., Sun, J.L., none Ruchuan, W.N.: SEARE: A system for exercise activity recognition and quality evaluation based on green sensing. IEEE Trans. Emerg. Topics Comput. 1 (2018). https://doi.org/10.1109/TETC.2018.2790080
15. Zhou, B., Sundholm, M., Cheng, J., Cruz, H., Lukowicz, P.: Never skip leg day: a novel wearable approach to monitoring gym leg exercises. In: IEEE International Conference on Pervasive Computing and Communications, pp. 1–9. IEEE (2016)

Convolutional Neural Networks in Robotics/Computer Vision

Deep Learning-Based Computer Vision Application with Multiple Built-In Data Science-Oriented Capabilities

Sorin Liviu Jurj(✉), Flavius Opritoiu, and Mircea Vladutiu

Advanced Computing Systems and Architectures (ACSA) Laboratory, Computers and Information Technology Department, "Politehnica", University of Timisoara, Timisoara, Romania
jurjsorinliviu@yahoo.de,
{flavius.opritoiu,mircea.vladutiu}@cs.upt.ro

Abstract. This paper presents a Data Science-oriented application for image classification tasks that is able to automatically: a) gather images needed for training Deep Learning (DL) models with a built-in search engine crawler; b) remove duplicate images; c) sort images using built-in pre-trained DL models or user's own trained DL model; d) apply data augmentation; e) train a DL classification model; f) evaluate the performance of a DL model and system by using an accuracy calculator as well as the Accuracy Per Consumption (APC), Accuracy Per Energy Cost (APEC), Time to closest APC (TTCAPC) and Time to closest APEC (TTCAPEC) metrics calculators. Experimental results show that the proposed Computer Vision application has several unique features and advantages, proving to be efficient regarding execution time and much easier to use when compared to similar applications.

Keywords: Deep learning · Computer vision · Data collection

1 Introduction

Data is at the core of every DL application. Because the Machine Learning lifecycle consists of four stages such as data management, model learning, model verification and model deployment [1], in order to collect, analyze, interpret and make use of this data, e.g. training accurate models for real-life scenarios, in recent years, new specializations were introduced in Universities around the world such as Machine Learning and Data Science, to name only a few. Additionally, also new career positions were created recently such as Machine Learning Engineer and Data Scientist, being some of the top paid positions in the industry [2].

Regarding Computer Vision applications for image classification tasks, a major bottleneck before training the necessary DL models is considered to be the data collection which consists mainly of data acquisition, data labeling and improvement of the existing data in order to train very accurate DL models [3]. Another bottleneck is that, because the amount of data needed to train a DL model is usually required to be very large in size and because most of this important data is not released to the general

L. Iliadis et al. (Eds.): EANN 2020, INNS 2, pp. 47–69, 2020.
https://doi.org/10.1007/978-3-030-48791-1_4

public but is instead proprietary, the need of an original dataset for a particular DL project can be very crucial. In general, data can be acquired either by a) buying it from marketplaces or companies such as Quandl [4] and URSA [5]; b) searching it for free on platforms like Kaggle [6]; c) crawling it from internet resources with the help of search engine crawlers [7]; d) paying to a 24 × 7 workforce on Amazon Mechanical Turk [8] like the creators of the ImageNet dataset did to have all of their images labeled [9]; e) creating it manually for free (e.g. when the user takes all the photos and labels them himself), which can be impossible most of the time because of a low-budget, a low-quality camera or time constraints. The importance of image deduplication can be seen in the fields of Computer Vision and DL where a high number of duplicates can create biases in the evaluation of a DL model, such as in the case of CIFAR-10 and CIFAR-100 datasets [10]. It is recommended that before training a DL classification model, one should always check and make sure that there are no duplicate images found in the dataset. Finding duplicate images manually can be very hard for a human user and a time-consuming process, this being the reason why a software solution to execute such a task is crucial. Some of the drawbacks of existent solutions are that they usually require the user to buy the image deduplication software or pay monthly for a cloud solution, they are big in size or are hard to install and use.

Despite all of these options, especially in the case of scraping the images from the internet, once stored they can still be unorganized or of a lower quality than expected, with images needed to be sorted out each in their respective class folder in order for the user (e.g. data scientist) to be able later to analyze and use this data for training a performant DL model. This kind of sorting task can take a tremendous amount of time even for a team, from several days or weeks to even months [11]. Another difficult task is that once the data is cleaned, organized and ready to be trained from scratch or using transfer learning, because of the variety of DL architectures, each with different sizes and training time needed until reaching convergence [12], it can be very difficult to know from the beginning which DL architecture fits the best a given dataset and will, at the end of the training, result in a DL model that has high accuracy. Because energy consumption in DL started to become a very debated aspect in recent months, especially regarding climate change [13–17], the necessity of evaluating the performance of DL models also by their energy consumption and cost is very crucial.

Considering these aspects, our work introduces a DL-based Computer Vision application that has multiple unique built-in Data Science-oriented capabilities which give the user the ability to train a DL image classification model without any programming skills. It also automatically searches for images on the internet, sort these images each in their individual class folder and is able to remove duplicate images as well as to apply data augmentation in a very intuitive and user-friendly way. Additionally, it gives the user an option to evaluate the performance of a DL model and hardware platform not only by considering its accuracy but also its power consumption and cost by using the environmentally-friendly metrics APC, APEC, TTCAPC and TTCAPEC [16].

The paper is organized as follows. In Sect. 2 we present the related work. Section 3 describes the proposed DL-based Computer Vision application. Section 4 presents the experimental setup and results. Finally, Sect. 5 concludes this paper.

2 Related Work

Considering the advancements of DL in recent years, there is a growing interest in computer vision applications in the literature, such as regarding the automatic sorting of images, as shown by the authors in [18]. The authors propose a solution called ImageX for sorting large amounts of unorganized images found in one or multiple folders with the help of a dynamic image graph and which successfully groups together these images based on their visual similarity. They also created many similar applications, e.g. ImageSorter [19], which besides sorting images based on their color similarity, is also able to search, download and sort images from the internet with a built-in Google Image Search option. A drawback of their applications is that the user is able to only visualize similar images, without also having these images automatically cleaned and sorted in their respective class folder with high accuracy. Also, the authors in [20] created an application called Sharkzor that combines user interaction with DL in order to sort large amounts of images that are similar. By comparison, regarding sorting, their solutions only sort images by grouping them based on how similar they are to each other after a human interacted and sorted these images initially, whereas our application sorts them automatically by using in-built pre-trained DL models or gives the user an option to use his own trained DL models. An on-device option that uses DL capabilities and helps users find similar photos (e.g. finding photos that contain certain objects such as flowers, trees, food, to name only a few) is presented also by Apple in their newest version of Photos app [21].

Regarding the detection of duplicate images, this technique has practical applications in many domains such as social media analysis, web-scale retrieval as well as digital image forensics [22, 23], with several works in the literature applying it for the detection of copyright infringements [24] and fraud detection [25]. Recently, a python package that makes use of hashing algorithms and Convolution Neural Networks (CNNs) that finds exact or near-duplicates in an image collection called Image Deduplicator (Imagededup) was released in [26]. In our Computer Vision application, we make use of this package in order to offer a user the option to remove duplicate images from the images dataset (e.g. right before training a DL model).

When training DL models from scratch or by using transfer learning, usually frameworks such as Tensorflow and PyTorch are used [27], either locally (e.g. on a personal laptop or Desktop PC that contains a powerful GPU) or in cloud services such as Cloud AutoML [28, 29], Amazon AWS [30] or Microsoft Azure [31], with the work in [32] even assessing the feasibility and usefulness of automated DL in medical imaging classification, where physicians with no programming experience can still complete such tasks successfully. The problem when training locally is that the user still has to research on his own which size the images should have for a given DL architecture, which DL architecture to choose for his dataset and if it is necessary to apply fine-tuning and image augmentation. Regarding using the cloud services for training a DL model, even though these may solve most of the problems mentioned above, they still have some drawbacks such as that they can be affected by latency, can be difficult to manage (not user-friendly) and most importantly, they can be very expensive when training for several hours (e.g. Cloud AutoML from Google costs around $20 per hour when used for Computer Vision tasks [27]).

Similar work to ours is presented by the authors in [33] where they created the Image ATM (Automated Tagging Machine) tool that automatizes the pipeline of training an image classification model (preprocessing, training with model tweaking, evaluation, and deployment). Regarding preprocessing, the Image ATM tool just resizes the images to fit the model input shape. For training, it uses transfer learning with pre-trained CNNs from Keras by firstly training the last Dense layer followed by the whole network. For evaluation, it calculates the confusion matrix and other metrics. A few disadvantages of Image ATM: the tool is aimed at people with programming knowledge (developers) and is focused mainly on the training function. Also, in order to use the Image ATM tool, the user must take the work of preparing the data in a specific folder structure, e.g. the user must create a .yml file with some of the parameters desired, path to images and destination path. The user must also create a . json file containing the classification of each image. Some advantages of the Image ATM are that the tool offers the possibility for cloud training, has access to more models (although all are trained with the same dataset) and that the evaluation errors can be visualized. When compared to Image ATM, our Computer Vision application has several advantages such as that it is accessible to more kinds of people and offers more functionalities such as image web scraping and sorting, deduplication, calculators for accuracy as well as for the APC, APEC, TTCAPC and TTCAPEC metrics, all in a user-friendly Graphical User Interface (GUI).

3 The Proposed Deep Learning-Based Computer Vision Application

The proposed DL-based Computer Vision application is summarized in Fig. 1 and is built using the Python programming language. It is composed of the most common features needed in the Computer Vision field and facilitate them in the form of a GUI, without requiring the user to have any knowledge about coding or DL in order to be able to fully use it.

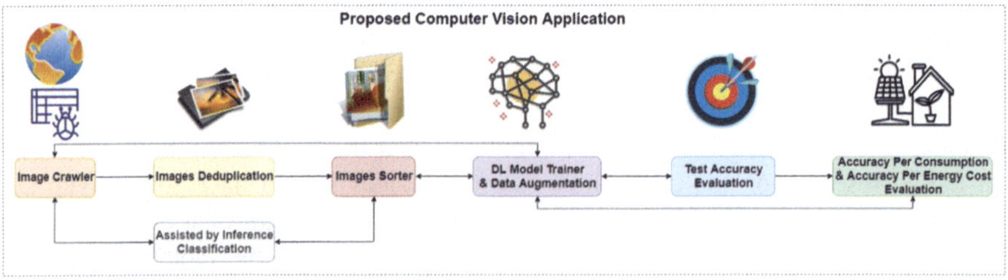

Fig. 1. Summarized view of the proposed Computer Vision application that incorporates features such as an automatic Image Crawler and Image Sorter assisted by inference classification, an Image Deduplicator, a DL Model Trainer with Data Augmentation capabilities as well as calculators regarding Accuracy, APC, APEC, TTCAPC, and TTCAPEC.

Regarding the system, the compilation dependencies and installation requirements of the proposed application are Python 3, Windows 10 (or later version) or Linux (Ubuntu 12 or later version). Regarding the Python libraries, we use PyQt5 for creating the GUI, HDF5 for loading DL model files, Tensorflow for training and inference, OpenCV for image processing, Numpy for data processing, Shutil for copying images in the system, TQDM for showing the terminal progress bar, Imagededup [26] for deduplication of images, Icrawler for crawling the images and fman build system (fbs) for creating installers.

There are certain conventions that are common in all the features of the proposed application:

1. Model files: These are .h5 files that contain the architecture of a Keras model and the weights of its parameters. These are used to load (and save) a previously trained model in order to be able to use it.
2. Model class files: These are extensionless files that contain the labels of each of the classes of a DL model. It contains *n* lines, where *n* is the number of classes in the model, and the line *i* contains the label corresponding to the *ith* element of the output of the DL model.
3. Preprocessing function: In this convention, a preprocessing function is a function that takes as input the path to an image and a shape, loads the image from the input path, converts the image to an array and fits it to the input of the model.

Images folders structures: We use two different folders structures: unclassified structures and classified structures. The unclassified images folders structure is the simplest one, consisting of just one folder containing images, presumably to be classified or deduplicated. The classified images folders structure consists of a folder which in turn contains subfolders. Each subfolder represents a class of images, is named the same as the label for that class, and contains images tagged or classified belonging to that class.

Following, we will present all the built-in features: Automatic web crawler assisted by inference classification, Images deduplication, Images Sorter assisted by inference classification, DL Model Trainer with Data Augmentation capabilities, Accuracy calculator as well as the APC and APEC [16] calculators.

3.1 Image Crawler Assisted by Inference Classification

The purpose of this feature is to collect images related to a keyword (representing a class) from the web and by using a classification algorithm, to make sure that the images are indeed belonging to this class. During the inference process needed for cleaning the images, a preprocessing is happening in the background, which, depending on the pretrained or custom DL model that is chosen, will resize the images, making them have the correct input shape (e.g. $28 \times 28 \times 1$ for MNIST and $224 \times 224 \times 3$ for ImageNet) for the DL model.

A summarized view of the implemented Image Crawler feature can be seen in Fig. 2 and is composed of the following elements: ‘Model’ - a combo box containing all the existent pretrained in-built DL models such as “mnist” or “resnet50” as well as the ‘Custom’ option which gives the user the possibility to load his own previously trained

DL model; Confidence Slider ('Confidence required') - a slider to select the minimum accuracy value to be used when classifying the images and which ranges from 0 to 99; Image Class Selector ('Select a class of images') - a combo box containing the labels of all the classes from the pretrained built-in selected DL model (e.g. 10 classes for when the "mnist" model is selected and 1000 classes when the "resnet50" model is selected). Additionally, the box contains an autocomplete search function as well; Images Amount ('Max amount to get') - a slider to select the number of images that should be crawled from the internet and which ranges from 1 to 999 and 'Destination Folder' - a browser to select the path for the final location of the obtained images.

The options under 'Custom Model Configuration' only apply when the DL model selected is "Custom" and is not built-in in the proposed Computer Vision application, e.g. when it was trained by the user itself. These options are: 'Model File' - a browser to select the .h5 file the user wishes to use for inference and Model Classes - a browser to select the extensionless file containing the name of each output class on which the selected DL model (.h5 file) was trained on. Finally, this feature's GUI interface has a button ('Add Images!') that begins the web crawling process.

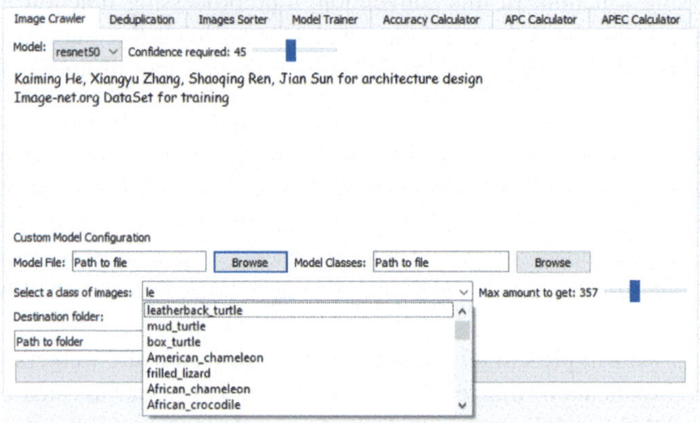

Fig. 2. Summarized view of the proposed Image Crawler feature assisted by inference classification.

With the help of this feature, images are automatically crawled by the crawler and downloaded to a temporal folder location. After that, each image is classified with the selected DL model, and if the classification coincides with the selected class and the confidence is higher than the selected threshold, the image is moved to the 'Destination folder', where each image will be saved in its own class folder.

This feature automatizes the population of image classification datasets by providing a reliable way of confirming that the downloaded images are clean and correctly organized.

3.2 Images Deduplication

The purpose of this feature is to remove duplicate images found in a certain folder. For this, we incorporated the Imagededup techniques found in [26]. A summarized view of the implemented Images Deduplication feature can be seen in Fig. 3 and is composed of the following elements: 'Images folder' - a browser to select the location of the folder containing the images that need to be analyzed for duplicate images; 'Destination folder' - a browser to select the location of the folder where the deduplicated images will be stored; 'Duplicates Folder' - a browser to select the location of the folder where the found duplicate images will be stored.

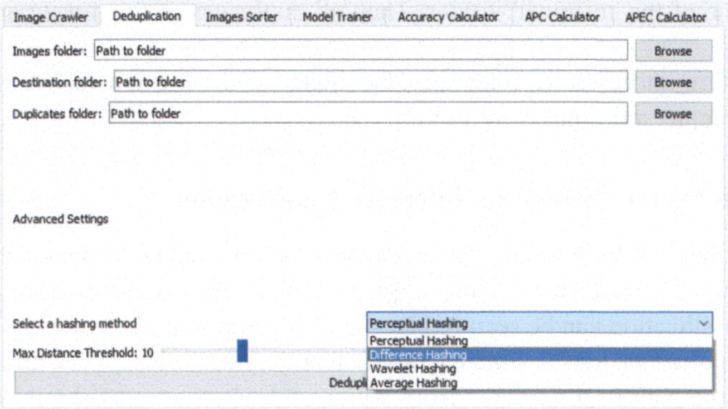

Fig. 3. Summarized view of the proposed Image Deduplication feature.

Each duplicate image found will be stored in a subfolder. Regarding advanced settings, it is composed of: Hashing method selector ('Select a hashing method') - a combo box containing 4 hashing methods that can be used for deduplication (Perceptual Hashing (default), Difference Hashing, Wavelet Hashing, and Average Hashing) as well as a 'Max Distance Threshold' - the maximum distance by which two images will be considered to be the same (default value is 10). Finally, this interface has a button ('Deduplicate!') that begins the deduplication process according to the selected parameters.

Following, we will shortly describe the types of hashes we are using in the images deduplication feature: a) **Average Hash:** the Average Hash algorithm first converts the input image to grayscale and then scales it down. In our case, as we want to generate a 64-bit hash, the image is scaled down. Next, the average of all gray values of the image is calculated and then the pixels are examined one by one from left to right. If the gray value is larger than the average, a 1 value is added to the hash, otherwise a 0 value; b) **Difference Hash:** Similar to the Average Hash algorithm, the Difference Hash algorithm initially generates a grayscale image from the input image. Here, from each row, the pixels are examined serially from left to right and compared to their neighbor to the right, resulting in a hash; c) **Perceptual Hash:** After gray scaling, it applies the discrete cosine transform to rows and as well as to columns. Next, we calculate the median of the gray values in this image and generate, analogous to the Median Hash algorithm, a hash value from the image; d) **Wavelet Hash:** Analogous to the Average Hash algorithm, the Wavelet Hash algorithm also generates a gray value image. Next, a two-dimensional wavelet transform is applied to the image. In our case, we use the default wavelet function called the Haar Wavelet. Next, each pixel is compared to the median and the hash is calculated.

Regarding this deduplication feature, first, the hasher generates hashes for each of the images found in the images folder. With these hashes, the distances between hashes (images) are then calculated and if they are lower than the maximum distance threshold (e.g. 10), then they are considered duplicates. Secondly, for each group of duplicates, the first image is selected as "original" and a folder is created in the duplicates folder with the name of the "original" folder. Then all duplicates of this image are stored on that folder.

This feature successfully integrates the image deduplication technique [26] and provides a simple and quick way to utilize it.

3.3 Images Sorter Assisted by Inference Classification

This feature helps a user to sort an unsorted array of images by making use of DL models. A summarized view of the implemented Images Sorter feature assisted by inference classification can be seen in Fig. 4 and is composed of elements similar to the ones presented earlier for the Image Crawler feature, but in this case with the function of selecting the path to the folders from which and where images should be sorted.

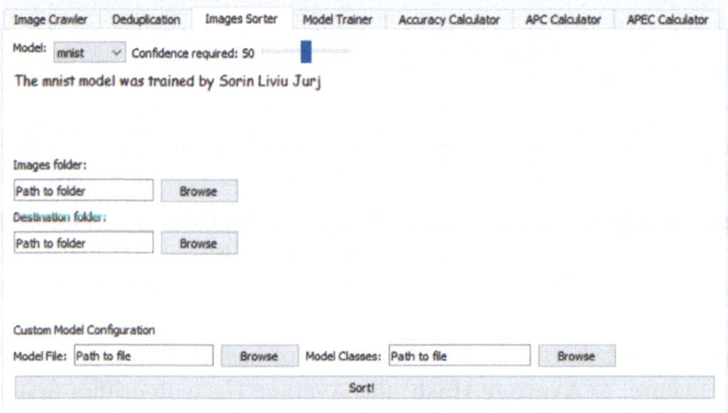

Fig. 4. Summarized view of the proposed Image Sorter feature assisted by inference classification.

In the destination folder, a new folder is created for each possible class, with the name extracted from the extensionless file that contains all the names of the classes, plus a folder named 'Undetermined'. Then, each image from the 'Images Folder' is automatically preprocessed, feed as input to the selected DL model and saved in the corresponding class folder. The highest value from the output determines the predicted class of the image: if this value is less than the minimum ‘Confidence required’, value, then the image will be copied and placed in the ‘Undetermined’ folder, otherwise, the image will be copied to the folder corresponding to the class of the highest value from the output. We took the decision of copying the files instead of moving them, for data security and backup reasons.

This feature heavily reduces the amount of time required to sort through an unclassified dataset of images by not only doing it automatically but also removing the need to set up coding environments or even write a single line of code.

3.4 Model Trainer with Data Augmentation Capabilities

This feature gives the user a simple GUI to select different parameters in order to train and save a DL image classifier model. A summarized view of the implemented DL Model Trainer feature assisted by inference classification can be seen in Fig. 5 and is composed of the following elements: ‘Model’ – as described earlier for the Image Crawler feature; ‘Sorted images folder’ - a browser to select the folder that contains the classified folder structure with the images to be trained on; ‘Number of training batches’ - an integer input, to specify the number of batches to train and ‘Size of batches’ - an integer input, to specify the number of images per batch. Regarding the custom options, they are the same as mentioned earlier regarding the Image Crawler feature.

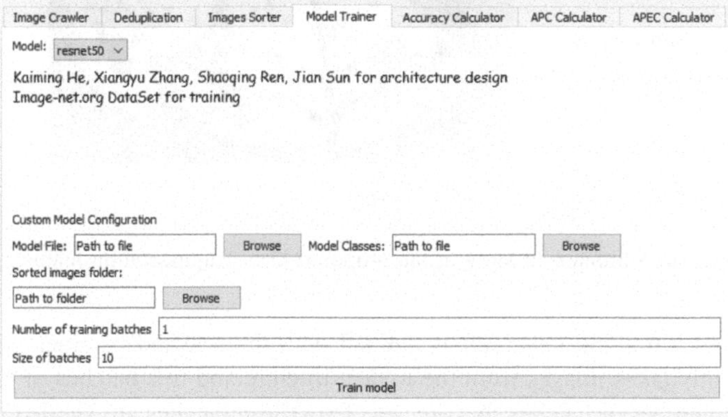

Fig. 5. Summarized view of the proposed DL Model Trainer feature.

Next, this interface has a button (‘Train model’) that, when clicked on, prompts a new window for the user to be able to visualize in a very user-friendly way all the image transformations that can be applied to the training dataset in a random way during training. More exactly, as can be seen in Fig. 6, the user can input the following parameters for data augmentation: Horizontal Flip - if checked the augmentation will randomly flip or not images horizontally; Vertical Flip - if checked the augmentation will randomly flip or not images horizontally; Max Width Shift - Slider (%), maximum percentage (value between 0 and 100) of the image width that it can be shifted left or right; Max Height Shift - Slider (%), maximum percentage (value between 0 and 100) of the image height that it can be shifted up or down; Max Angle Shift - Slider (degrees °), the maximum amount of degrees (value between 0 and 90) that an image might be rotated and Max Shear Shift - Slider (%), maximum shear value (value between 0 and 100) for image shearing. The data augmentation feature allows the user to visualize the maximum possible changes that can be made to an image in real-time, without the need of guessing the right parameters.

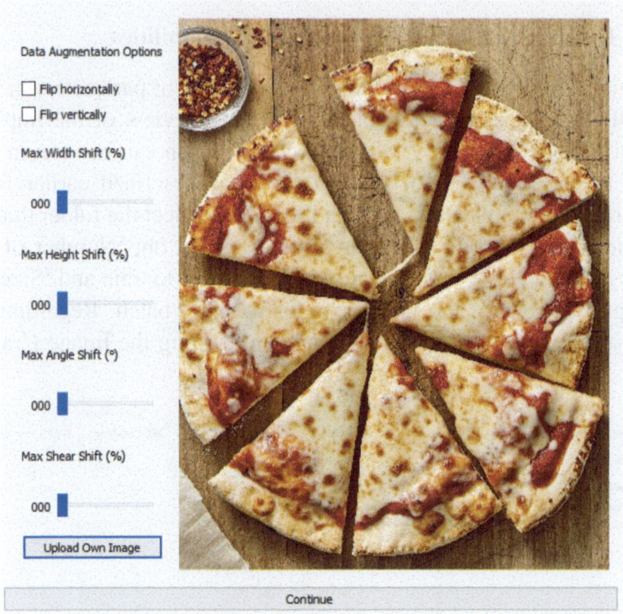

Fig. 6. Summarized view of the proposed Data Augmentation feature.

Following, a training generator is defined with the selected parameters; The generator randomly takes images from the folder structure and fills batches of the selected size, for the number of batches that are selected. These batches are yielded as they are being generated.

Regarding the training, first, the selected DL model is loaded, its output layer is removed, the previous layers are frozen and a new output layer with the size of the number of classes in the folder structure is added. The model is then compiled with the Adam optimizer and the categorical cross-entropy as the loss function. Finally, the generator is fed to the model to be fitted. Once the training is done, the total training time is shown to the user and a model file (.h5) is created on a prompted input location.

This feature achieves the possibility of training a custom DL model on custom classes just by separating images in different folders. There is no knowledge needed about DL and this feature can later also be easily used by the Image Sorting feature described earlier in order to sort future new unsorted images.

3.5 Accuracy Calculator

This section of the application GUI gives a user the option to compute the accuracy of a DL model on the given dataset in the classified images folder structure. A summarized view of the implemented Accuracy Calculator feature can be seen in Fig. 7 and is composed of the following elements: 'Model' - as described earlier for the Image Crawler feature; 'Test images folder' - a browser to select the folder that contains the classified folder structure to measure the accuracy of a DL classification model; 'Size of batches' - an integer input, to specify the number of images per batch. The custom options are the same as mentioned earlier regarding the Image Crawler feature. Finally, this interface has a button ('Calculate Accuracy') that starts the accuracy evaluation process.

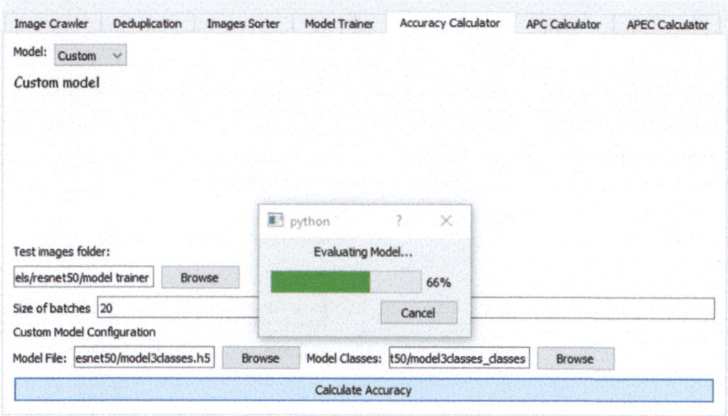

Fig. 7. Summarized view of the proposed Accuracy Calculator feature.

After loading the DL model and the list of classes, it searches for the classes as subfolders names in the classified images folder structure. Then, for each class (or subfolder) it creates batches of the selected batch size, feeds them to the DL model and counts the number of accurate results as well as the number of images. With these results, it calculates the total accuracy of the DL model and shows it to the user directly in the application GUI. This feature provides a simple and intuitive GUI to measure the accuracy of any DL image classification model.

3.6 Accuracy Per Consumption (APC) Calculator

This GUI feature makes use of our APC metric [16] and which is a function that takes into account not only the accuracy of a system (*acc*) but also the energy consumption of the system (*c*). The APC metric can be seen in Eq. (1) below:

$$APC_{\alpha,\beta}(c, acc) = \frac{acc}{\beta.WC_{\alpha}(c, acc) + 1} \quad (1)$$

where *c* stands from energy consumption of the system and it's measured in Watt/hour (Wh) and *acc* stands for accuracy; α is the parameter for the WC_{α} function, the default value is 0.1; β is a parameter (ranges from 0 to infinity) that controls the influence of the consumption in the final result: higher values will lower more heavily the value of the metric regarding the consumption. The default value is 1.

The application GUI gives a user the option to define the values for α and β as well as to specify and calculate the accuracy and energy consumption of a DL model using the above APC metric equation.

A summarized view of the implemented APC Calculator feature can be seen in Fig. 8 and is composed of the following elements: 'Model test accuracy (%)' - this widget gives a user the option to input the accuracy or use the previously described Accuracy Calculator feature to measure the accuracy of a DL model and 'Energy Consumption (Wh)' - float input to specify the power consumption of a user's DL model.

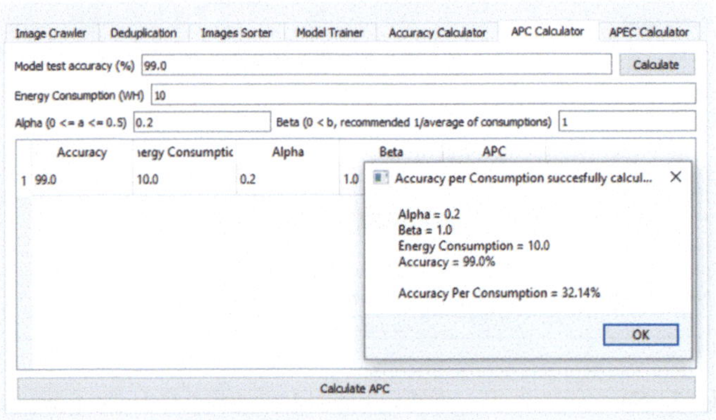

Fig. 8. Summarized view of the proposed APC Calculator feature.

Regarding the advanced options, it has: Alpha (α) - float input to specify the desired value of α (default 0.2) and Beta (β) - float input to specify the desired value of β (default 1). For simplicity, a table is shown with the following columns: Accuracy, Energy Consumption, Alpha, Beta, and APC. Whenever a value is changed, the table is automatically updated as well. Finally, the application GUI has a button ('Calculate APC') to begin the calculation of the APC metric. The function itself is a Numpy implementation of our previously defined APC metric [16] seen in Eq. (1) and takes as input parameters the values defined in the application GUI.

The implemented feature brings this new APC metric to any user by allowing them to easily calculate the accuracy per consumption and know the performance of their DL model with regards to not only the accuracy but also to the impact it has on the environment (higher energy consumption = higher negative impact on nature). However, the drawback of the current version of this APC calculator feature in the proposed application GUI is that the user has to measure the energy consumption of the system manually. We plan to implement automatic readings of the power consumption in future updates (e.g. by using the Standard Performance Evaluation Corporation (SPEC)

PTDaemon tool [34, 35], which is also planned to be used for power measurements by the MLPerf Benchmark in their upcoming mid-2020 update).

3.7 Accuracy Per Energy Cost (APEC) Calculator

This metric is a function that takes into account not only the accuracy of a system (*acc*) but also the energy cost of the system (*c*). The APEC metric can be seen in Eq. (2) below:

$$APEC_{\alpha,\beta}(c, acc) = \frac{acc}{\beta.WC_{\alpha}(c, acc) + 1} \tag{2}$$

where *c* stands for the energy cost of the system and it's measured in EUR cents per inference and *acc* stands for accuracy.

α is the parameter for the WC_{α} function, the default value is 0.1; β is a parameter (ranges from 0 to infinity) that controls the influence of the cost in the final result: higher values will lower more heavily the value of the metric regarding the cost. The default value is 1.

The APEC feature is presented in Fig. 9 and lets a user define the values for α and β, specify or calculate the accuracy of a DL model, specify the energy consumption and the cost of Wh of the DL as well as calculate the APEC using the formula seen earlier in (2).

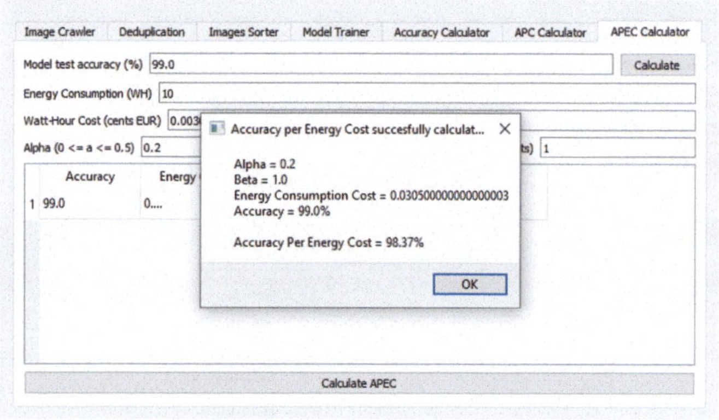

Fig. 9. Summarized view of the proposed APEC Calculator feature.

The APEC feature of the proposed Computer Vision application is composed of the following elements: 'Model test accuracy (%)' – works similar to the APC widget described earlier; 'Energy Consumption (Wh)' - works also similar to the APC widget described earlier and Watt-Hour Cost - float input to specify the cost in EUR cents of a Wh. Regarding the advanced options, we have: Alpha (α) - float input to specify the desired value of α(default 0.2) and Beta β - float input to specify the desired value of β(default 1). A similar table like the one for APC Calculator is shown also here, with the following columns: Accuracy, Energy Cost, Alpha, Beta, and APEC. Whenever a value is changed, the table is automatically updated here as well.

Finally, the application GUI has a button ('Calculate APEC') to begin the calculation of the APEC metric.

The function itself is an implementation on Numpy of our previously defined APEC metric [16] seen in Eq. (2) and takes as input parameters the values defined in the application GUI. The implemented feature brings this new APEC metric to any user by allowing them to easily calculate the accuracy per energy cost and evaluate the performance of their DL model with regards to the impact it has on the environment (higher energy consumption = higher cost = negative impact on nature). However, the drawback of the current version of this APEC calculator feature is that the user has to measure the energy consumption of the system and calculate its Wh cost manually.

3.8 Time to Closest APC (TTCAPC) Calculator

The objective of the TTAPC metric [16] is to combine training time and the APC inference metric in an intuitive way. The TTCAPC feature is presented in Fig. 10 and is composed of the following elements: 'Model test accuracy (%)' and 'Energy Consumption (Wh)', both working similar to the APEC widget described earlier; 'Accuracy Delta' – float input to specify the granularity of the accuracy axis; 'Energy Delta' – float to specify the granularity of the energy axis. Regarding the advanced options, they are the same as the ones presented earlier regarding the APEC feature.

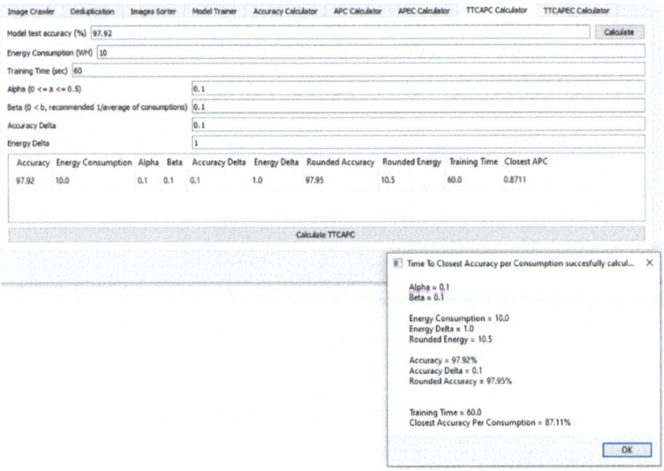

Fig. 10. Summarized view of the proposed TTCAPC Calculator feature.

A similar table like the one for APEC Calculator is shown also here, with the following columns: Accuracy, Energy Consumption, Alpha, Beta, Accuracy Delta, Energy Delta, Rounded Accuracy, Rounded Energy, Training Time and Closest APC. Whenever a value is changed, the table is automatically updated here as well.

Finally, the application GUI has a button ('Calculate TTCAPC') to begin the calculation of the TTCAPC metric.

3.9 Time to Closest APEC (TTCAPEC) Calculator

The objective of the TTCAPEC metric [16] is to combine training time and the APEC inference metric. The TTCAPEC feature is presented in Fig. 11 and is composed of the same elements like the TTCAPC feature presented earlier and one additional element called 'Energy Cost (EUR cents per Wh)' which is similar to the one presented earlier regarding the APEC metric calculator and where the user can specify the cost in EUR cents of a Wh.

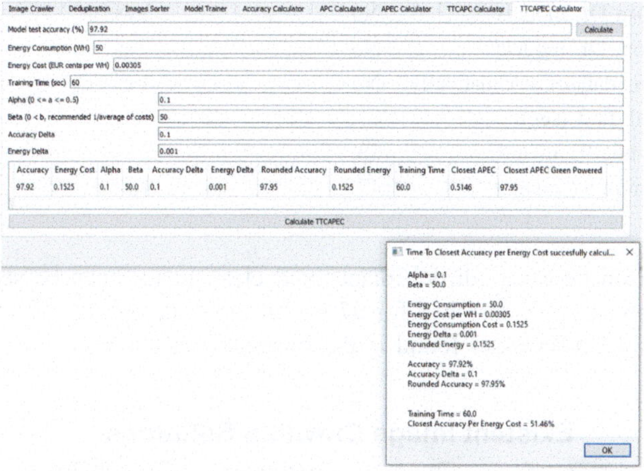

Fig. 11. Summarized view of the proposed TTCAPEC Calculator feature.

A similar table like the one for TTCAPC Calculator is shown also here, with the following columns: Accuracy, Energy Cost, Alpha, Beta, Accuracy Delta, Energy Delta, Rounded Accuracy, Rounded Energy, Training Time and Closest APEC. Finally, the application GUI has a button ('Calculate TTCAPEC') to begin the calculation of the TTCAPEC metric.

4 Experimental Setup and Results

Following, we will show the experimental results regarding all the implemented features in comparison with existing alternatives found in the literature and industry.

We run our experiments on a Desktop PC with the following configuration: on the hardware side we use an Intel(R) Core(TM) i7-7800X CPU @ 3.50 GHz, 6 Core(s), 12 Logical Processor(s) with 32 GB RAM and an Nvidia GTX 1080 Ti as the GPU; on the software side we use Microsoft Windows 10 Pro as the operating system with CUDA 9.0, CuDNN 7.6.0 and Tensorflow 1.10.0 using the Keras 2.2.4 framework.

4.1 Image Crawler

As can be seen in Table 1, our proposed Image Crawler feature outperforms existent solutions and improves upon them. Even though the crawling took the same amount of time, this is not the case regarding the cleaning part, where, because this feature is not available in any of the existent solutions, this needed to be done manually and took 47 s for a folder containing 97 images as compared to only 10 s for our proposed solution which executed the task automatically.

Table 1. Comparison between existent and the proposed Image Crawling solution.

Features	Existent solutions [7]	Proposed solution
Image crawler	Yes	Yes
Built-in DL models	No	Yes
Custom DL models	No	Yes
Cleans dataset automatically?	No	Yes
Speed Test (sec)		
Crawling 97 images	23	23
Cleaning 97 images	47	10

A comparison between "dirty" images and clean images can be seen in Fig. 12 where, for simplicity, we searched for 97 pictures of "cucumber", which is one class from the total of 1000 classes found in the ImageNet dataset [9].

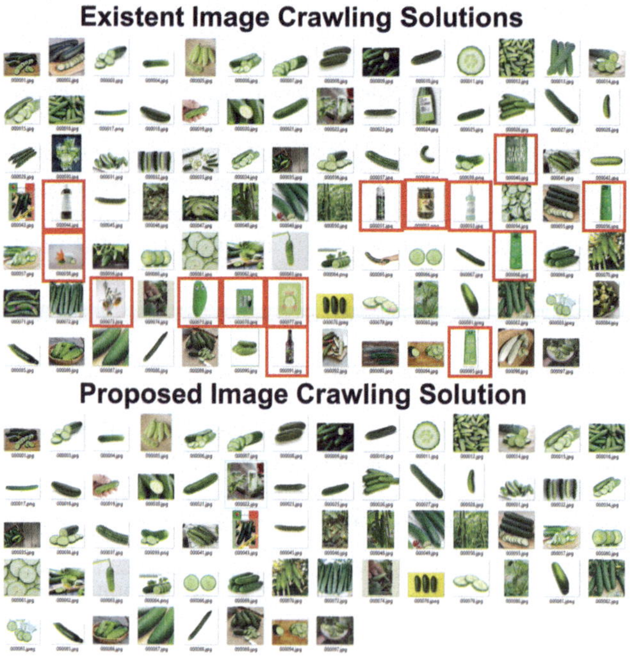

Fig. 12. Summarized view of existent and the proposed image crawling solution. The pictures marked with a red rectangle are examples of "dirty" images found when crawling with existent solutions. By comparison, the proposed image crawling feature assisted by DL inference contains only clean images.

It can be easily observed how the existent solutions provide images that don't represent an actual cucumber, but products (e.g. shampoos) that are made of it. After automatically cleaning these images with a confidence rate of 50% with the proposed feature, only 64 clean images remained in the folder.

4.2 Deduplication

For the experiments seen in Table 2, we tested the speed time of the proposed built-in image deduplication feature that uses the Imagededup python package [26]. We run these experiments on finding only exact duplicates on the same number of images with a maximum distance threshold of 10 for all four hashing methods.

Table 2. Speed Results for the 4 hashing methods of the proposed Image Deduplication feature.

Nr. of images	Hashing method	Speed time (sec)
1.226	Perceptual Hashing	16
	Difference Hashing	15
	Wavelet Hashing	17
	Average Hashing	16

As can be seen, the average speed is about 16 s for finding duplicates in a folder containing 1.226 images, with Difference Hashing being the fastest hashing method from all four.

4.3 Images Sorter

For our experiments regarding the sorting of images with the proposed images sorter feature, we used both the MNIST as well as the ImageNet pre-trained models with a confidence rate of 50% and presented the results in Table 3.

Table 3. Speed Time for the proposed Images Sorting feature.

DL model	Nr. of classes	Nr. of images	Undetermined images	Speed time (sec)
MNIST	10	70.000	69	307
ImageNet [9]	1000	456.567	135.789	40.817
Custom [37]	34	2.380	34	223

Regarding MNIST experiments, we converted the MNIST dataset consisting of 70.000 images of 28 × 28 pixels to PNG format by using the script in [36] and mixed all these images in a folder. After that, we run our image sorter feature on them and succeeded to have only 0.09% of undetermined images, with a total speed time of around 6 min. Regarding ImageNet, we used the ImageNet Large Scale Visual Recognition Challenge 2013 (ILSVRC2013) dataset containing 456.567 images belonging to 1000 classes with a confidence rate of 50%. Here we successfully sorted all images in around 11 h and 20 min, more exactly in 40.817 s, with 29.74% (135.789) undetermined images.

Regarding the custom model, we used one of our previously trained DL models (ResNet-50) that can classify 34 animal classes [37] on a number of 2.380 images of 256 × Ratio pixels (70 images for each of the 34 animal classes) with a confidence rate of 50%. Here we succeeded to have 1.42% undetermined images, with a total speed time of almost 4 min. The percentage of the undetermined images for all cases can be improved by modifying the confidence rate, but it is out of this paper's scope to experiment with different confidence values.

The time that a DL prediction task takes depends on a few variables, mainly the processing power of the machine used to run the model, the framework used to call the inference of the model and the model itself. Since processing power keeps changing and varies greatly over different machines, and all the frameworks are optimized complexity wise and keep evolving, we find that among these three the most important to measure is, therefore, the model itself used in the prediction. Models vary greatly in their architecture, but all DL models can be mostly decomposed as a series of floating points operations (FLOPs). Because, generally, more FLOPs equal more processing needed and therefore more time spent in the whole operation, we measured the time complexity of the built-in ImageNet and MNIST models in FLOPS and presented the results in Table 4.

Table 4. The time complexity of the built-in DL models measured in the number of FLOPS.

DL model	Dataset	MFLOPS	GFLOPS
ResNet-50	ImageNet	3.800	3.8
MNIST	MNIST	9	0.009

4.4 Model Trainer

For the experiments regarding the DL model training feature, because we want to evaluate the application on a real-world problem, we will attempt to show that this feature could be very useful for doctors or medical professionals in the aid of detecting diseases from imaging data (e.g. respiratory diseases detection with x-ray images). In order to prove this, we will attempt to automatically sort between the images of sick patients versus healthy patients regarding, firstly, pneumonia [38], and secondly, COVID-19 [39], all within our application and doing it only with the training feature that the application provides.

For this, first, in order to classify between x-ray images of patients with pneumonia versus x-ray images of healthy patients, we made use of transfer learning and trained a 'resnet50' architecture for around 2 h without data augmentation on pneumonia [38] dataset containing 6.200 train images by selecting 10 as the value for the number of training batches and 10 as the value for the size of batches (amount of images per batch) and achieved 98.54% train accuracy after 10 epochs. Secondly, in order to classify between x-ray images of patients with COVID-19 versus x-ray images of negative patients, we again made use of transfer learning and trained a 'resnet50' architecture for around 1 h without data augmentation on the COVID-19 [39] dataset containing 107 train images by selecting the same values for the number and size of training batches as the pneumonia model mentioned above and achieved 100% train accuracy after 100 epochs.

4.5 Accuracy Calculator

For the experiments regarding the accuracy calculator feature, we used the two custom DL models trained earlier to classify x-ray images of patients with pneumonia versus x-ray images of healthy patients and between x-ray images of patients with COVID-19 versus x-ray images of negative patients, with 20 as the size of batches (20 images per batch).

The evaluation took in both cases around 50 s with a test accuracy of 93.75% regarding the pneumonia model on 620 test images and 91% regarding the COVID-19 model on 11 test images, proving that the proposed Computer Vision application can easily be used by any medical personal with very basic computer knowledge in order to train and test a DL classification model for medical work purposes.

4.6 APC and APEC Calculators

Regarding the experiments with the proposed APC [16] calculator feature, we presented the simulated results for different model test accuracy (%) and energy consumption (Wh) values in Table 5. We run all the experiments with 0.2 as the alpha value and with 1.0 as the beta value.

Table 5. Summarized Results of the proposed APC Calculator feature.

Energy consumption [Wh]	DL model test accuracy [%]	APC [%]
10	99.0	32.14
2	99.0	69.91
1	99.7	82.91
10	99.7	32.96
50	99.7	8.96
10	94.5	27.47
50	50.0	1.61
1	50.0	31.25
10	50.0	7.14
10	40.0	5.12
1	40.0	23.8
1	100	83.33

It is important to mention that our recommendation for a correct comparison between two DL models, is that it is always necessary that they are both tested with the same alpha and beta values. As can be seen in Table 5 where we experimented with random energy consumption and test accuracy values, our APC Calculator feature is evaluating the performance of a DL model by considering not only the accuracy but also the power consumption. Therefore, DL models that consume around 50 Wh (e.g. when running inference on a laptop) instead of 10 Wh (e.g. when running inference on a low-cost embedded platform such as the Nvidia Jetson TX2) [15], are penalized more severely by the APC metric.

Regarding the experiments with the proposed APEC [16] calculator feature, we presented the simulated results for different model test accuracy (%) and energy cost in Table 6. We run all the experiments with 0.2 as the alpha value and with 1.0 as the beta value.

Table 6. Summarized Results of the proposed APEC Calculator feature.

Energy consumption [Wh]	Power cost [cents EUR]	DL model test accuracy [%]	APEC [%]	APEC green energy [%]
10	0.03050	99.0	98.37	99.0
2	0.0061	99.0	98.87	99.0
1	0.00305	99.7	99.63	99.7
10	0.03050	99.7	99.08	99.7
50	0.1525	99.7	96.71	99.7
10	0.03050	94.5	93.8	94.5
50	0.1525	50.0	45.8	50.0
1	0.00305	50.0	49.9	50.0
10	0.03050	50.0	49.1	50.0
10	0.03050	40.0	39.18	40.0
1	0.00305	40.0	39.91	40.0
1	0.00305	100	99.93	100

For simplicity, regarding electricity costs, we took Germany as an example. According to "Strom Report" (based on Eurostat data) [40], German retail consumers paid 0.00305 Euro cents for a Wh of electricity in 2017. We used this value to calculate the cost of energy by plugging it in the equation presented in (2)", where "*c*" in this case stands for the energy cost. As can be seen, the APEC metric favors lower power consumption and cost, favoring the use of green energy (free and clean energy).

4.7 TTCAPC and TTCAPEC Calculators

Regarding the experiments with the proposed TTCAPC [16] calculator feature, we simulated a custom DL model on two platforms and presented the results in Table 7.

Table 7. TTCAPC with Accuracy delta = 0.1, Energy delta = 1, beta = 0.1, alpha = 0.1.

	Desktop PC	Nvidia Jetson TX2
Accuracy [%]	97.92	
Energy Consumption [Wh]	50	10
Rounded Accuracy [%]	97.95	
Rounded Energy Consumption [Wh]	50.5	10.5
Closest APC [%]	61.28	87.11
Train seconds	60	

As can be seen, even though the accuracy and training time is the same for both platforms, the TTCAPC feature favors the platform which has less power consumption.

Regarding the experiments with the proposed TTCAPEC [16] calculator feature, we simulated with the same DL model values used also in the experiments regarding the TTCAPC calculator earlier and presented the results in Table 8.

Table 8. TTCAPEC with Accuracy delta = 0.1, Energy delta = 1, beta = 0.1, alpha = 0.1.

	Desktop PC	Nvidia Jetson TX2
Accuracy [%]	97.92	
Energy Cost (cents)	0.1525	0.0305
Rounded Energy Cost (cents)	0.1525	0.0305
Rounded Accuracy [%]	97.95	
Closest APEC [%]	51.46	82.96
Closest APEC Green (Solar) Powered [%]	97.95	
Train seconds	60	

As can be also seen in this case, the TTCAPEC feature favors the lower power consumption of a system because it results in a lower cost. Additionally and more importantly, it favors DL-based systems that are powered by green energy, because they have 0 electricity costs and no negative impact on our environment.

5 Conclusions

In this paper, we present a Computer Vision application that succeeds in bringing common DL features needed by a user (e.g. data scientist) when performing image classification related tasks into one easy to use and user-friendly GUI.

From automatically gathering images and classifying them each in their respective class folder in a matter of minutes, to removing duplicates, sorting images, training and evaluating a DL model in a matter of minutes, all these features are integrated in a sensible and intuitive manner that requires no knowledge of programming and DL. Experimental results show that the proposed application has many unique advantages and also outperforms similar existent solutions. Additionally, this is the first Computer

Vision application that incorporates the APC, APEC, TTCAPC and TTCAPEC metrics [16], which can be easily used to calculate and evaluate the performance of DL models and systems based not only on their accuracy but also on their energy consumption and cost, encouraging new generations of researchers to make use only of green energy when powering their DL-based systems [15].

References

1. Ashmore, R., Calinescu, R., Paterson, C.: Assuring the machine learning lifecycle: desiderata, methods, and challenges. arXiv:1905.04223, May 2019
2. Soni, N., et al.: Impact of artificial intelligence on businesses: from research, innovation, market deployment to future shifts in business models. arXiv:1905.02092v1, May 2019
3. Roh, Y., Heo, G., Whang, S.E.: A survey on data collection for machine learning: a big data – AI integration perspective. arXiv:1811.03402v2, August 2019
4. Quandl. https://www.quandl.com/. Accessed 29 Feb 2020
5. URSA. https://www.ursaspace.com/. Accessed 29 Feb 2020
6. Kaggle. https://www.kaggle.com/datasets. Accessed 29 Feb 2020
7. Icrawler. https://pypi.org/project/icrawler/. Accessed 29 Feb 2020
8. Amazon Mechanical Turk. https://www.mturk.com/. Accessed 29 Feb 2020
9. Deng, J., et al.: ImageNet: a large-scale hierarchical image database. In: 2009 IEEE Conference on Computer Vision and Pattern Recognition, Miami, FL, USA (2009)
10. Barz, B., Denzler, J.: Do we train on test data? Purging CIFAR of near-duplicates. arXiv: 1902.00423, February 2019
11. Swanson, A., et al.: Snapshot Serengeti, high-frequency annotated camera trap images of 40 mammalian species in an African savanna. Sci Data **2**, 150026 (2015). https://doi.org/10.1038/sdata.2015.26
12. Nakkiran, P., et al.: Deep double descent: where bigger models and more data hurt. arXiv: 1912.02292, December 2019
13. Schwartz, R., Dodge, J., Smith, N.A., Etzioni, O.: Green AI. arXiv:1907.10597v3. August 2019
14. Strubell, E., Ganesh, A., McCallum, A.: Energy and policy considerations for deep learning in NLP. arXiv:1906.02243, June 2019
15. Jurj, S.L., Rotar, R., Opritoiu, F., Vladutiu, M.: Efficient Implementation of a Self-Sufficient Solar-Powered Real-Time Deep Learning-Based System, to appear
16. Jurj, S.L., Opritoiu, F., Vladutiu, M.: Environmentally-Friendly Metrics for Evaluating the Performance of Deep Learning Models and Systems, to appear
17. Rolnick, D., et al.: Tackling climate change with machine learning. arXiv:1906.05433v2. November 2019
18. Nico, H., Kai-Uwe, B.: Dynamic construction and manipulation of hierarchical quartic image graphs. In: ICMR 2018 Proceedings of the 2018 ACM on International Conference on Multimedia Retrieval, New York, pp. 513–516 (2018)
19. Image Sorter. https://visual-computing.com/project/imagesorter/. Accessed 29 Feb 2020
20. Pirrung, M., et al.: Sharkzor: interactive deep learning for image triage, sort, and summary. arXiv:1802.05316 (2018)
21. Apple Photos. https://www.apple.com/ios/photos/pdf/Photos_Tech_Brief_Sept_2019.pdf. Accessed 29 Feb 2020
22. Morra, L., Lamberti, F.: Benchmarking unsupervised near-duplicate image detection. arXiv: 1907.02821, July 2019

23. Zhou, W., et al.: Recent advance in content-based image retrieval: a literature survey. arXiv: 1706.06064v2, September 2017
24. Zhou, Z., et al.: Effective and efficient global context verification for image copy detection. IEEE Trans. Inf. Forens. Secur. **12**(1), 48–63 (2017)
25. Cicconet, M., et al.: Image Forensics: detecting duplication of scientific images with manipulation-invariant image similarity. arXiv:1802.06515v2, August 2018
26. Jain, T., et al.: Image Deduplicator (Imagededup). https://idealo.github.io/imagededup/. Accessed 29 Feb 2020
27. Florencio, F., et al.: Performance analysis of deep learning libraries: TensorFlow and PyTorch. J. Comput. Sci. **15**(6), 785–799 (2019)
28. Cloud AutoML. https://cloud.google.com/automl/. Accessed 29 Feb 2020
29. He, X., et al.: AutoML: A Survey of the State-of-the-Art. arXiv:1908.00709v2, August 2019
30. PyTorch on AWS. https://aws.amazon.com/pytorch/. Accessed 29 Feb 2020
31. Microsoft Azure. https://azure.microsoft.com/. Accessed 29 Feb 2020
32. Faes, L., et al.: Automated deep learning design for medical image classification by healthcare professionals with no coding experience: a feasibility study. Lancet Dig. Health **1**(5), e232–e242 (2019)
33. Lennan, C., et al.: Image ATM. https://github.com/idealo/imageatm/. Accessed 29 Feb 2020
34. von Kistowski, J., et al.: Measuring and benchmarking power consumption and energy efficiency. In: Companion of the 2018 ACM/SPEC International Conference on Performance Engineering (ICPE 2018), pp. 57–65. ACM, New York (2018). https://doi.org/10.1145/3185768.3185775
35. Standard Performance Evaluation Corporation (SPEC) Power. https://www.spec.org/power_ssj2008/. Accessed 29 Feb 2020
36. MNIST converted to PNG format. https://github.com/myleott/mnist_png. Accessed 29 Feb 2020
37. Jurj, S.L., Opritoiu, F., Vladutiu, M.: Real-time identification of animals found in domestic areas of Europe. In: Proceedings SPIE 11433, Twelfth International Conference on Machine Vision (ICMV 2019), 1143313, 31 January (2020). https://doi.org/10.1117/12.2556376
38. Chest X-Ray Images (Pneumonia). https://www.kaggle.com/paultimothymooney/chest-xray-pneumonia/. Accessed 01 Apr 2020
39. Cohen, J.P., Morrison, P., Dao, L.: COVID-19 image data collection. arXiv:2003.11597 (2020). https://github.com/ieee8023/covid-chestxray-dataset. Accessed 01 Apr 2020
40. Strom-Report. https://1-stromvergleich.com/electricity-prices-europe/. Accessed 29 Feb 2020

Visual Movement Prediction for Stable Grasp Point Detection

Constanze Schwan(✉) and Wolfram Schenck

Center for Applied Data Science (CfADS), Faculty of Engineering and Mathematics, Bielefeld University of Applied Sciences, Gütersloh, Germany
{constanze.schwan,wolfram.schenck}@fh-bielefeld.de

Abstract. Robotic grasping of unknown objects in cluttered scenes is already well established, mainly based on advances in Deep Learning methods. A major drawback is the need for a big amount of real-world training data. Furthermore these networks are not interpretable in a sense that it is not clear why certain grasp attempts fail. To make the process of robotic grasping traceable and simplify the overall model we suggest to divide the complex task of robotic grasping into three simpler tasks to find stable grasp points. The first task is to find all grasp points where the gripper can be lowered onto the table without colliding with the object. The second task is to determine for the grasp points and gripper parameters from the first step how the object moves while the gripper is closed. Finally in the third step for all grasp points from the second step it is predicted whether the object slips out of the gripper during lifting. By this simplification it is possible to understand for each grasp point why it is stable and - just as important - why others are unstable or not feasible. In this study we focus on the second task, the prediction of the physical interaction between gripper and object while the gripper is closed. We investigate different Convolutional Neural Network (CNN) architectures and identify the architecture(s) that predict the physical interactions in image space best. We perform the experiments for training data generation in the robot and physics simulator V-REP.

Keywords: Robotic grasping · Convolutional Neural Network · Simulation · Physical interaction

1 Introduction

Grasping and manipulating objects are tasks humans carry out effortlessly on an everyday basis. Due to the high object variety and variability of the environment, the same tasks are hard to learn for robots. Two main approaches are distinguished in robot grasping [1]: The first approach determines from the sensory image(s) the optimal grasp pose of the robot arm. A grasp planner determines subsequently the motor commands to drive the robot arm into the optimal

L. Iliadis et al. (Eds.): EANN 2020, INNS 2, pp. 70–81, 2020.
https://doi.org/10.1007/978-3-030-48791-1_5

grasp configuration. The optimal grasp configuration is determined either analytically with force- and form-closure objectives [9] or is data-driven. In the second approach, the visuomotor controller is directly learned from the sensory image(s). State-of-the-art grasping methods involve deep learning [2–4,6] and focus on training a visuomotor controller. These aforementioned methods have in common that they learn a mapping from image pixels or regions and robot (joint-)parameters to a grasp success probability. An optimization algorithm aids to find the robot parameters that maximize the grasp probability. However it is not possible to evaluate these models such that it is traceable why a certain grasp candidate succeeded or failed. Especially in industrial applications this lack of interpretability prevents the algorithms from being applied. In this study the idea is that vision-based robotic grasping is achieved by finding robot parameters that lead to a collision free path of the robot arm to the object (selected on the image), where closing and lifting the manipulator leads to a stable grasp. We make two contributions: Our first contribution is to divide the complex task of robotic grasping into three simpler tasks that can effectively be learned by simple CNNs. In a first step all grasp points are determined where the gripper can be lowered on the table, while enclosing an object part (Lowering Model). In the second step a Convolutional Neural Network (CNN) is trained that predicts the physical interaction between the gripper and the object visually (Closing Model). Finally a model is learned that predicts the grasp points where the object is liftable (Lifting Model). This model is a simple CNN that classifies the images predicted from the Closing Model into liftable when the object remains between the gripper and not liftable when the object slips out of the gripper during lifting. Our second contribution and focus of this study is the construction of a CNN for learning the Closing Model that predicts the physical interaction between object and gripper in the image domain when the gripper is closed. To the best of our knowledge there are no grasping models where the object movement due to the closing movement of the gripper is directly predicted. There is research on predicting object movements in pushing tasks [5,7] but not in the realm of grasping. In [12,13] the effect of an force acting on an object in an image is predicted in terms of a vector field but without the prediction in the image domain. Oh et al. [10] trained CNNs to predict from an action and frames of an Atari game the next frames driven by the action. We adapt one architecture from [10] and make a thorough parameter analysis to identify the architecture that best suits our data for the Closing Model. To understand the context of the presented Closing Model, the concept of all three models is briefly described as well as the object database and the physics simulation V-REP which is used to generate the training data for each step.

2 Grasp Definition and Object Database

In our study, we use prismatic object shapes which are generated from binary (household) item images, by triangulating the boundaries of the edge filtered images and extruding the resulting faces in 3D. By this simplification the objects

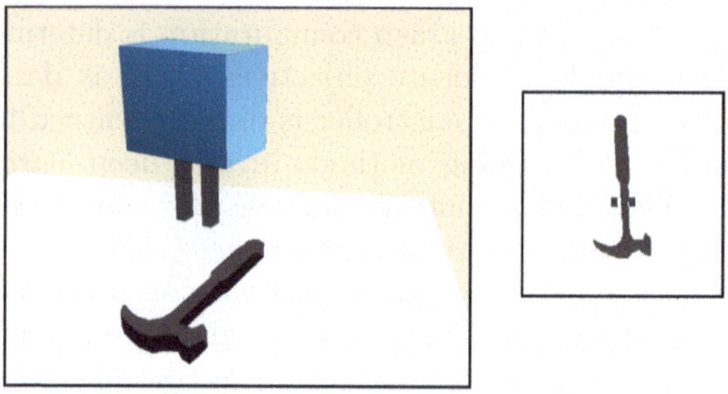

Fig. 1. Left: V-REP simulation of the gripper in pre-grasp position. Right: Image from the orthographic camera between the gripper tips in the pre-grasp position.

considered here all have the same height at each location. To increase the variability of the object shapes, 10 000 objects were created from bitmap images of household items and artificial random polygon shapes in three different sizes. On the left image of Fig. 1 a hammer that was build this way is positioned on a table. The gripper is a parallel-jaw gripper with a maximal opening width of 5 cm. In Fig. 1 the design of the simulation in V-REP [15] is shown. The prismatic objects are placed on a table, one object at a time. Since the objects by design have the same height, we use only four parameters to describe the gripper posture: (x, y, α, s), where x and y are the planar coordinates measured in the world coordinate system, α is the rotation of the gripper around the positive z-axis of the world coordinate system, and s the gripper opening width measured between the inner side of the tips. As input for the Lowering Model, a greyscale snapshot from an orthographic camera that is centred above the table is taken, with a resolution of 512×512 pixels. On this image, pixels are randomly chosen on the object shapes; these pixels are called grasp candidates from now on. The gripper with the maximal opening width of 5 cm spans 51 pixels on this image. The right image of Fig. 1 shows an example of the image obtained by a second orthographic camera which is placed between the gripper tips.

3 Three-Step Model for Stable Grasp Point Detection

The first step of grasp point detection is to determine from all randomly chosen grasp candidates on an orthographic image from the camera centred above the table those where the gripper can be lowered on the table without colliding with the object. For this purpose a two-phase model is applied. In phase I, a forward model (FM) is trained which predicts for an arbitrary gripper configuration tuple $(\alpha_i,\ s_i)$ the image of the gripper tip projections. In phase II Differential Evolution [8] is used as optimization algorithm to predict the gripper tuple $(\alpha_i,\ s_i)$ that minimizes the intersection between the gripper tip projections and the image patch for a given grasp candidate. The left column of Fig. 2 shows the randomly chosen grasp candidates (red dots) on pliers and a cup shape. The second column of Fig. 2 shows the grasp candidates (green dots) where a gripper

Fig. 2. Examples of the grasp candidates for the orthographic projection of pliers and a cup. Left column: randomly chosen grasp candidates (red dots). Center column: true positive grasp candidates (green dots) where a gripper tuple was found. Right column: false negative grasp candidates (yellow dots) where Differential Evolution was not able to find an existing solution, true negative grasp candidates (blue and pink dots).

tuple $(\alpha_i,\, s_i)$ was found such that the intersection between the object and the gripper tip projections is zero, i.e. the gripper can be lowered without collision. The third column of Fig. 2 shows the grasp candidates where no gripper tuple was found.

The second step (Closing Model) is the prediction of the physical interaction between gripper and object for the true positive grasp candidates from the Lowering Model while closing the gripper. The third step is to predict for the grasp candidates where the object remained between the gripper tips after closing if the object remains between the gripper tips when the manipulator is lifted (Lifting Model). Therefore there are three possible causes why a chosen grasp candidate does not lead to a stable grasp. The first reason is that there is no gripper parameter configuration where the gripper can be lowered onto the table without colliding with the object. This possibly means that the object is too big for the used gripper. The second reason is that for the given grasp candidate the object was pushed out of the gripper during closing due to the local shape of the object. Finally, the last reason for a failed grasp is that the object falls out of the gripper during lifting, because of the distance between the grasp point and the centre of mass of the object. The evaluation of these three steps increases the interpretability of the whole grasping procedure. In the following the Closing Model is presented in-depth together with a thorough analysis of different CNN architectures.

4 The Closing Model

Goal of the Closing Model is to predict the physical interaction between object and gripper in the image domain. More precisely: given the image of the object and gripper before closing, the Closing Model should predict the resulting image after closing the gripper and determine the gripper opening width s. If the resulting s is greater than 0, the object remained between the gripper tips, otherwise the object was pushed out. In the following a thorough analysis of different CNN architectures for the Closing Model is presented. To determine the quality

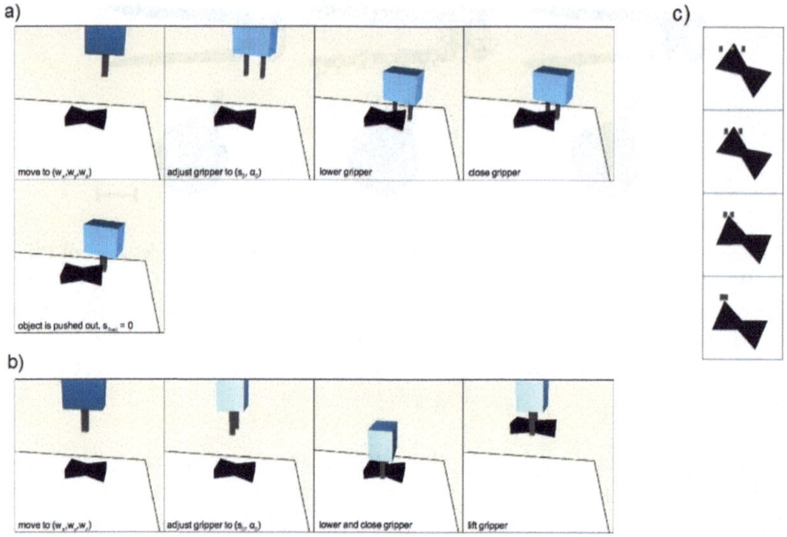

Fig. 3. a) Example of a grasp sequence in V-REP for a negative grasp candidate. b) Example of a grasp sequence in V-REP for a positive grasp candidate. c) Example of an image sequence obtained in simulation.

of the CNNs two measures are evaluated. The Intersection over Union (IOU) measure quantifies the quality of the predicted object and gripper movement. The IOU between two shapes is defined as the fraction of "intersection of the two shapes" / "union of the two shapes". When two shapes are identical in form, position and orientation in an image the IOU value is 1. The confusion matrix for the predicted gripper opening width (classes: "gripper closed" vs. "gripper not closed") is the second measure that is applied for evaluating the networks.

4.1 Training Data Generation for the Closing Model

The resulting true-positive grasp candidates from the Lowering Model are used to create the training data for the Closing Model and Lifting Model. Therefore a grasp trial is initiated for every true-positive grasp candidate and an image sequence recorded during the closing movement of the gripper in the V-REP-simulation. The grasp candidate is transformed to the world coordinate system. The orthographic camera used in this simulation is fixed to the gripper. Therefore the gripper has the 0-orientation in all image sequences. The resolution of the camera is 1024×1024. To reduce the image size, we crop a region of 250×250 pixels and rescale the images to 64×64. When the object is pushed out and the gripper opening width is 0 after the closing movement, the grasp candidate is said to be negative otherwise positive. An example for a negative and positive grasp trial is shown in Fig. 3a) and b). Figure 3c) shows an example of an image sequence obtained by this method. The images are inverted and normalized,

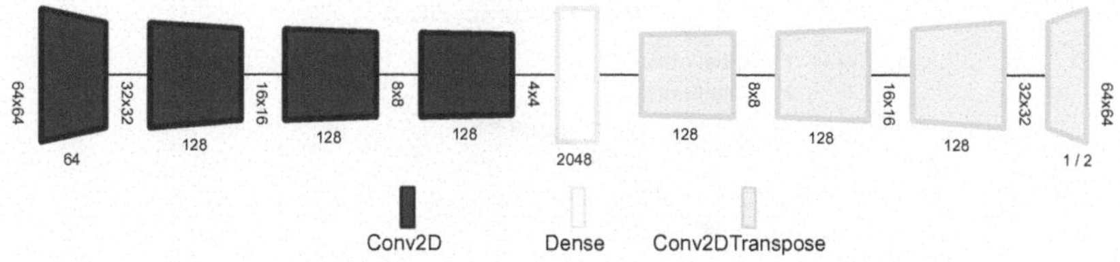

Fig. 4. CNN architecture for 1-channel and 2-channel prediction, adapted from [10]. Net2Vis was used for visualization [11].

such that the pixels of the image that represent the gripper have a value of 0.7, the pixels that represent the object have a value of 1.0 and the background is 0. The different pixel intensities are also used for separating the images into two channels one for the object and one for the gripper as is explained in the following section. All models described in this study are trained with 15 000 positive and 15 000 negative image pairs and evaluated on 2500 positive and 2500 negative image pairs.

4.2 1-Channel Vs. 2-Channel Prediction

The initial design of the CNN architecture presented here is adapted from [10]. In [10] the goal was to predict from an rgb Atari game frame and an action the next frames. The authors no-action feedforward architecture from [10] consisted of four convolutional layers, two dense layers and four deconvolutional layers. In this study this architecture is modified to incorporate only on dense layer as shown in Fig. 4. Since the gripper is closed in an uniform motion and the gripper orientation is the same for each image sequence the gripper parameters are not added as an additional input to the network structure. The kernel-sizes are chosen as (8×8), (6×6), (6×6), (4×4) and in reverse order for the deconvolutional part with a stride of 2 as in [10]. Each convolutional layer is followed by a RELU-layer. Training is done with the Adam-optimizer with the standard values. Goal of this section is to find the optimal architecture for the Closing Model through variation of the number of input and output channels. In the following the 1-channel and 2-channel predictions are compared.

The input of the CNN for the 1-channel prediction is the image of the object and gripper together in 1 channel, the output is a 1-channel image. The training data for the 1-channel network consists of the normalized first and last image of the image sequences obtained from the grasp trials in VREP, where the background is 0, the pixels of gripper tip projection are set to 0.7 and the object pixels to 1.0. The same network is also trained and evaluated with 2-channel images, where the first channel contains the object and the second channel the gripper. Both channels are again greyscale with 0 for the background, 0.7 for the gripper and 1.0 for the object pixels. For computing the IOU value for the 1-channel and 2-channel prediction, the predicted image channels of the network are thresholded such that the background is 0 and the object and gripper pixels 1.

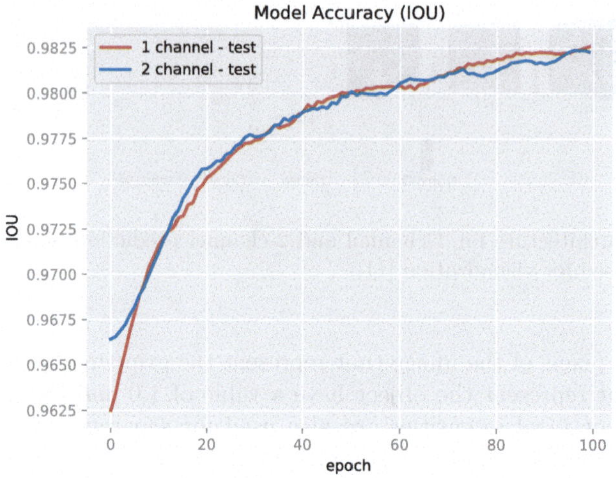

Fig. 5. IOU of the 1-channel prediction and 2-channel prediction on 2500 test data.

The training data are thresholded the same way. Figure 5 shows the improvement of the IOU over 100 epochs for both the 1-channel prediction and 2 channel-prediction. The deviation of both accuracy curves is minimal. Figure 6 shows an example for the 1-channel and 2-channel prediction on unknown objects. The first and second row show the 2-channel and 1-channel prediction respectively. Both models predict that the object is pushed downwards out of the gripper due to the closing movement of the tips. Also the gripper opening width of 0 is predicted correctly by both of the models. The third and fourth row of Fig. 6 illustrate the problem that occurs when using only one channel in contrast to two channels. Separating gripper and object pixels unambiguously is not possible for the 1-channel prediction. In the predicted 2-channel result, the gripper opening width can easily be evaluated by checking for black pixels in the centre region of the gripper channel image. The evaluation with respect to the gripper opening width after closing proves to be difficult for the 1-channel prediction. Since this is a big issue for the evaluation of the model and also for the prediction of the Lifting Model, from now on the 2-channel presentation is chosen.

4.3 CNN-Architectures

Goal of this section is to determine the optimal network architecture through a thorough parameter analysis. The results are compared with respect to two measures. The first measure is the IOU value for determining how well the object and gripper movements are learned. The second measure is the predicted gripper opening width in terms of a confusion matrix: if the gripper was not closed in prediction and physics simulation the result is true positive, if the gripper was closed in prediction and physics simulation the result is true negative. False positive and false negative are analogously defined. This measure determines

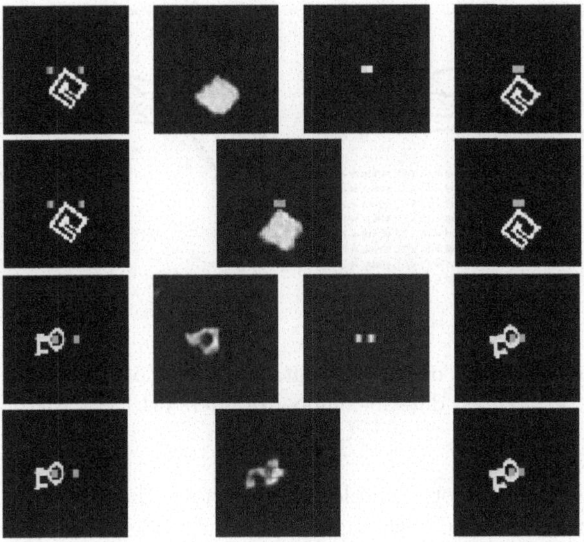

Fig. 6. Examples for 1-/ 2-channel prediction. First column: pre-close image. Second/Third column: prediction results. Fourth column: post-close image (ground truth).

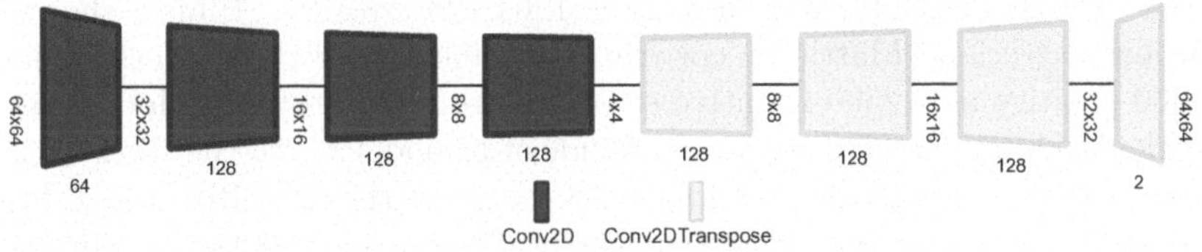

Fig. 7. CNN architectures for evaluating the influence of kernel size and stride. Net2Vis was used for visualization [11].

how good the grasp candidates are classified. However, since the resulting image of the Closing Model is a necessary input for the Lifting Model the IOU values are more important in this analysis. In order to find the optimal architecture, the effect of the kernel size in the convolutional and deconvolutional layers, the stride and the number of filters on the prediction quality for 2 channels is evaluated. Furthermore the number of dense layers that is needed is investigated. The architecture used for the comparisons is the same as in the previous section but without the fully connected layer to additionally investigate if the dense layer is really necessary for successful learning of the Closing Model (see Fig. 7). The kernel sizes for the 4 convolutional layers are varied as I:[(8×8), (6×6), (6×6), (4×4)], II:[(7×7), (5×5), (5×5), (3×3)], III:[(5×5), (4×4), (4×4), (3×3)] and IV:[(3×3), (3×3), (3×3), (3×3)], for the deconvolutional layers in reversed order. The stride is varied in [1,2] and the number of filters is set to I:[64,128,128,128] and II:[32,64,64,64]. Figure 8 shows the IOU-curves obtained

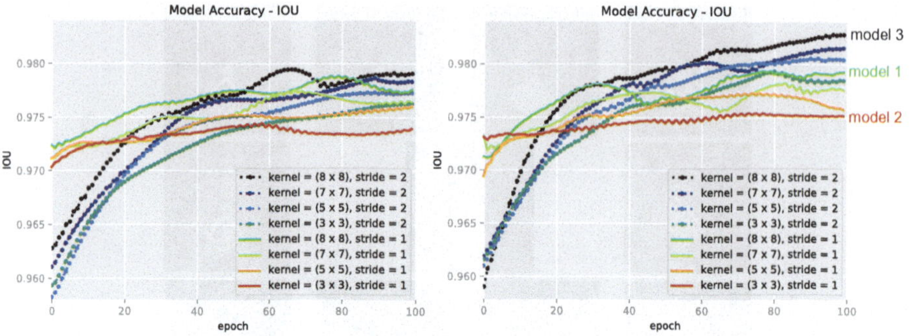

Fig. 8. Left: Model accuracy of 2500 test data for number of filters [32,64,64,64]. Right: Model accuracy of 2500 test data for number of filters [64,128,128,128].

from varying the parameters. The left image shows the model accuracy for the number of filters [32,64,64,64], the right image the model accuracy for the number of filters [64,128,128,128]. As can be seen a bigger number of filters leads to better IOU-values. Increasing the stride from 1 to 2 also increases the IOU-values. Furthermore changing the kernel sizes from bigger (I) to smaller (IV) sizes impair the results. The best IOU-curve is obtained for kernel sizes I:[(8×8), (6×6), (6×6), (4×4)] with stride 2 and filter I:[64,128,128,128]. Table 1 shows the confusion matrix and Matthews correlation coefficient for three selected models for 2500 positive and 2500 negative examples from the test set. Model 1 is the network with filter sizes I, filter I and a stride of 1, model 2 is the network with the filter sizes IV, filter I, stride 1 and model 3 the network with filter sizes I, filter I and stride 2. Matthews correlation coefficient (MCC) suggests that model 2 with the filter sizes 3×3 and stride 1 is the best model. Figure 9 shows an example for the prediction results of the three models line by line. The first column shows the pre-close image, column two and three show the prediction results for the object and gripper channel. The fourth column is the post-close ground truth. The result for model 1 (first row) reproduces a fuzzy image of the object but does not predict any object movement. The predicted gripper image is also not sharp. The predicted gripper opening width is too big compared to the ground truth. Model 2, the second row, produces visually the best result for the object shape. But like model 1 it does not predict the rotation. The gripper tips cannot be clearly seen. Model 3, the last row of Fig. 9, yields a less detailed prediction of the object but it captures the rotation correctly. Furthermore the resulting gripper tip projections and the gripper opening width are well reproduced. The reason for the smaller IOU values of the architectures with smaller filters is that they are not able to capture the movements of the objects when they remain between the gripper tips. But they are able to predict if an object is pushed out or not as the confusion matrix shows. For comparison the confusion matrix and MCC is also determined for the architecture with the fully connected layer (see Table 1 column FC). Even though the MCC is smaller than for the models without a fully connected layer the performance with respect to the IOU-curves is the same

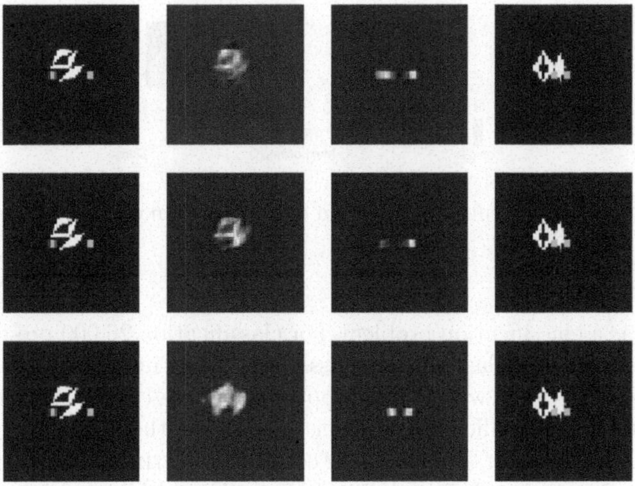

Fig. 9. Example of the influence of kernel size and stride. First column: pre-close image, second column: object channel prediction, third column: gripper channel prediction, fourth column: post-close, ground truth image. First row: result of model 1 (kernel sizes I, filters I, stride 1), second row: result of model 2 (kernel sizes IV, filters I, stride 1), third row: result of model 3 (kernel sizes I, filters I, stride 2).

Table 1. Confusion matrix, Matthews correlation coefficient and IOU after 100 epochs on test data of the described models. For details see text.

Confusion matrix				
	Model 1	Model 2	Model 3	FC
True positive	2394	2435	2375	2334
True negative	2464	2438	2475	2474
False positive	34	60	23	24
False negative	105	64	124	165
MCC	0.9447	0.9504	0.9419	0.9258
IOU	0.979	0.975	0.982	0.982

as for model 3. In summary the optimal architecture in terms of performance and network size is model 3 with kernel sizes $[(8 \times 8), (6 \times 6), (6 \times 6), (4 \times 4)]$ and stride 2. This corresponds also to the model which has the largest receptive field size in the innermost layer. This large receptive fields seems to be necessary to predict the object movement.

4.4 Classification

In order to check if the classification performance of the Closing Model is at a competitive level with classical CNNs used for classification the Closing Model is

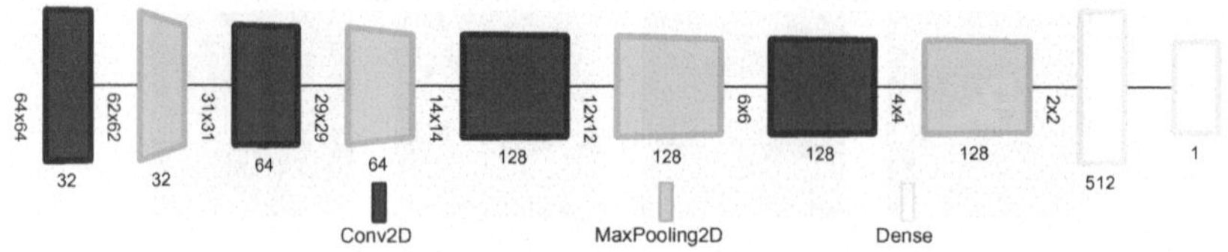

Fig. 10. CNN architecture for classification of pre-grasp images. Net2Vis was used for visualization [11].

also trained as a classification problem. For classification 26 000 pre-close images are separated into two classes. One class contains all images where the gripper can be closed, the other where the gripper cannot be closed. A standard CNN (Fig. 10) is used for classification in order to predict if the object is pushed out of the gripper during closing. The resulting confusion matrix values are true positive = 2428, true negative = 2474, false positive = 72 and false negative = 26. The MCC for the classification network is with a value of 0.9610 only slightly better in the classification task than the previously compared architectures. Therefore it can be concluded that also in this respect the optimal architecture that is chosen for the Closing Model is well appropriate.

5 Conclusion and Future Work

We have proposed to divide the task of robotic grasping into three simpler tasks that allow the interpretation of failed grasp attempts. The models that have to be learned to accomplish these three tasks are the Lowering Model, the Closing Model and the Lifting Model. In this study we have focused on the Closing Model. The task of this model is to predict from a pre-grasp image the object and gripper movement. Therefore image sequences of grasp trials on artificially generated prismatic objects were executed in a simulation. The first and last image of the recorded image sequences were used to train a variety of CNNs to find an optimal architecture. The results show that the movement of the object and gripper can be predicted successfully with high IOU values with a CNN consisting of 4 convolutional and 4 deconvolutional layer with kernel sizes $[(8 \times 8), (6 \times 6), (6 \times 6), (4 \times 4)]$, filter sizes [64,128,128,128] and stride 2. Inserting a dense layer between the convolution and deconvolution part does not increase the model accuracy. The computational complexity of the proposed Closing Model is basically determined by the complexity of the used CNNs. A thorough analysis of the complexity of convolutional layers can be found in [14].

We plan to adapt the three steps and especially the Closing Model to depth images on a real-world setup to extend the physical movement prediction into 3D. Using depth images instead of binary orthographic object images allows the model to be applied to different view angles on an object and loosens the restriction on prismatic objects with a fixed object height. Furthermore we will implement our Closing Model on a real-world robot setup to evaluate the qualitative results of the predicted object movement in the real-world physics for approximately prismatic objects like boxes, pens, pliers and other tools.

Acknowledgements. This work was supported by the EFRE-NRW funding programme "Forschungsinfrastrukturen" (grant no. 34.EFRE-0300119).

References

1. Caldera, S., Rassau, A., Chai, D.: Review of deep learning methods in robotic grasp detection. Multimodal Technol. Inter. **2**(3), 57 (2018)
2. Lenz, I., Lee, H., Saxena, A.: Deep learning for detecting robotic grasps. Int. J. Robot. Res. **34**(4–5), 705–724 (2015)
3. Redmon, J., Angelova, A.: Real-time grasp detection using convolutional neural networks. In: IEEE International Conference on Robotics and Automation (2015)
4. Levine, S., et al.: Learning hand-eye coordination for robotic grasping with deep learning and large-scale data collection. Int. J. Robot. Res. **37**(4–5), 421–436 (2017)
5. Finn, C., Goodfellow, I., Levine, S.: Unsupervised learning for physical interaction through video prediction. In: Proceedings of the 30th International Conference on Neural Information Processing Systems, pp. 64–72 (2016)
6. Morrison, D., Corke, P., Leitner, J.: Closing the loop for robotic grasping: a real-time, generative grasp synthesis approach. CoRR arXiv:1804.05172 (2018)
7. Schenck, W., Hasenbein, H., Möller, R.: Detecting affordances by mental imagery. In: Proceedings of the SAB Workshop on Artificial Mental Imagery, pp. 15–18 (2012)
8. Price, K.V., Storn, R.M., Lampinen, J.A.: Differential Evolution - A Practical Approach to Global Optimization, 2nd edn, p. 110. Springer, Heidelberg (2005)
9. Bicchi, A., Kumar, V.: Robotic grasping and contact: A review. In: IEEE International Conference on Robotics and Automation, vol. 5499, pp. 348–353 (2000)
10. Oh, J., et al.: Action-conditional video prediction using deep networks in Atari games. In: Advances in Neural Information Processing Systems, pp. 2863–2871 (2015)
11. Bäuerle, A., Ropinski, T.: Net2Vis: transforming deep convolutional networks into publication-ready visualizations. CoRR arXiv:1902.04394 (2019)
12. Mottaghi, R., et al.: Newtonian image understanding: unfolding the dynamics of objects in static images. CoRR arXiv:1511.04048 (2015)
13. Mottaghi, R., et al.: "What happens if..." learning to predict the effect of forces in images. CoRR arXiv:1603.05600 (2016)
14. He, K., Sun, J.: Convolutional neural networks at constrained time cost. CoRR arXiv:1412.1710 (2014)
15. Copellia Robotics Homepage. http://www.coppeliarobotics.com. Accessed 26 Feb 2020

Machine Learning in Engineering and Environment

Accomplished Reliability Level for Seismic Structural Damage Prediction Using Artificial Neural Networks

Magdalini Tyrtaiou(✉), Antonios Papaleonidas, Anaxagoras Elenas, and Lazaros Iliadis

Department of Civil Engineering, Institute of Structural Statics and Dynamics, Democritus University of Thrace, 67100 Xanthi, Greece
{mtyrtaio, papaleon, elenas, liliadis}@civil.duth.gr

Abstract. This research aims to determine the optimal Multi-Layer Feed-Forward Artificial Neural Network (MLFF) capable of accurately estimating the level of seismic damage on buildings, by considering a set of Seismic Intensity Parameters (SIP). Twenty SIP (well established and highly correlated to the structural damage) were utilized. Their corresponding values were calculated for a set of seismic signals. Various combinations of at least five seismic features were performed for the development of the input dataset. A vast number of Artificial Neural Networks (ANNs) were developed and tested. Their output was the level of earthquake Damage on a Reinforced Concrete Frame construction (DRCF) as it is expressed by the Park and Ang overall damage index. The potential contribution of nine distinct Machine Learning functions towards the development of the most robust ANN was also investigated. The results confirm that MLFF networks can provide an accurate estimation of the structural damage caused by an earthquake excitation. Hence, they can be considered as a reliable Computational Intelligence approach for the determination of structures' seismic vulnerability.

Keywords: Seismic intensity parameters · Multiple feedforward perceptron artificial neural network · ANN · Park and Ang damage index

1 Introduction

Earthquake structural damage detection is considered one of the core subjects of civil engineering. Numerous methods have been developed and employed for the determination of structures' post-seismic damage status. Several of them are connected with the Seismic Intensity (SIN), which is utilized as a metric of the power and the effect of seismic damage potential. Therefore, in earthquake engineering and engineering seismology, a large number of SIN parameters are considered and interrelated with the structural damage, as it is described by various indices [1–3, 7, 9–12, 24, 34].

In this research, the problem of structural damage state prediction is confronted by the use of Artificial Neural Networks. ANNs have an inherent ability to deploy prediction results for problems where the input data is known. Twenty, well established, seismic intensity parameters are utilized as input to the ANNs, aiming to predict the

L. Iliadis et al. (Eds.): EANN 2020, INNS 2, pp. 85–98, 2020.
https://doi.org/10.1007/978-3-030-48791-1_6

DRCF after the application of ninety-two seismic signals. ANNs have the ability to consider any number and combination of seismic parameters for the determination of the optimal correlation between them and the damage state, as it is expressed by the global Park and Ang damage index $DI_{PA,global}$.

This research aims to prove that the accurate estimation of the $DI_{PA,global}$ index, can be accomplished with a high degree of conformity to the actual damage state, by the employment of ANNs that consider related SIP. A large number of ANNs employing various architectures and seven different Transfer functions were developed. Regarding the development of the training set, we have tried all potential combinations of the available input parameters. Thus, the complexity of the experiments was immense.

It has finally been revealed that a large number of ANNs can be considered as reliable models capable of perfectly serving towards the assessment of the seismic vulnerability of constructions. Consequently, we have developed a very promising approach in the area of seismic earthquake engineering.

2 Literature Review - Introduction of the Novel Contribution

Artificial Neural Networks have been utilized in the field of civil engineering, and many researchers [1, 2, 31, 35, 36] have investigated the advantages of using them in the field of structural engineering. They are related to complex algorithms capable of imitating behaviors of biological neural systems. Like human brains, they have the capability to learn applied knowledge from experience in solving new problems under new environments. This task is accomplished through a Supervised Learning process, where a volume of data vectors is used as input in order to obtain the optimal combination of neurons' connection weights. The ultimate target if the estimation of a set of predefined target outputs. Once the network has fit the data, it forms a generalization of the input-output relationship, and it can be used to generate output for input it was not trained on.

There are past publications in the literature that discuss the development of ANN capable of modeling the ability of certain SIP, towards the estimation of the structures' damage potential after an earthquake [1, 2, 19, 23, 31, 35, 36]. In each of them, a limited number of neural networks has been deployed. They have considered all available SIP together, and they were trained with one or two algorithms at a time. Then they were retrained following a specific number of repetitions of the whole process. In the end, the best-retrained network was selected to export the final results. The employment of retrained models has a high probability to cause over-training. This fact means that such models are prone to memorization, and they have extremely limited Generalization ability. Generalization is the ultimate target in the development of reliable computational intelligence models. Moreover, the consideration of all features for the development of the training set does not lead to optimal models. The solution to this problem is Feature Extraction. However, this process requires a big dataset with numerous values if the dependent variable. In this case, this is quite difficult since one has to travel all over the globe where earthquakes incidents occur, and he/she has to be given access to the respective local records. Thus, we have decided to follow the trial and error approach since the availability of modern computational resources makes this process feasible.

3 Established Seismic Intensity Parameters

As aforementioned, many intensity seismic parameters in earthquake engineering literature play a significant role in the assessment of structural damage potential. Twenty of the most recognized seismic parameters in earthquake engineering, which already have been connected with the structural damage [9–11], are selected to be evaluated for a set of examined seismic excitations. These seismic parameters are presented below, in Table 1.

Table 1. Employed seismic intensity parameters

Symbol	Description	Reference
PGA	Peak ground acceleration	[22]
PGV	Peak ground velocity	[22]
PGD	Peak ground displacement	[22]
PGA/PGV	The ratio PGA/PGV	[21]
CP	Central period	[33]
I_{Arias}	Arias intensity	[5]
SMD_{TB}	Strong motion duration of Trifunac-Brady	[30]
$P_{0.90}$	Seismic power	[17]
RMS_a	Root mean square acceleration	[22]
I_{FVF}	Seismic intensity of Fajfar-Vidic-Fischinger	[15]
CAV	Cumulative absolute velocity	[7]
DP_{AS}	Seismic destructiveness potential of Araya-Saragoni	[4]
SD	Spectral displacement	[8]
SV	Spectral velocity	[8]
SA	Spectral acceleration	[8]
E_{inp}	Seismic absolute input energy	[32]
SI_K	Kappos spectrum intensity	[18]
SI_{MR}	Spectrum intensity of Martinez-Rueda	[20]
EPA	Effective peak acceleration	[6]
EPA_{max}	Maximum effective peak acceleration	[6]

4 Park and Ang Structural Damage Index

The damage index (DI) is a quantity that lumps the structural damage status in a single numerical value and can be easily handled. In earthquake engineering, damage indices can quantify the induced damage locally or globally.

Park and Ang damage index ($DI_{PA,global}$) [25, 26] is an index defined as the ratio between the initial and the reduced resistance capacity of a structure during a seismic excitation evaluated by nonlinear dynamic analysis. The classification of the structural damage status, according to $DI_{PA,global}$ values are presented in the table below.

Table 2. Structural damage classification, according to $DI_{PA,global}$.

Structural damage	Structural damage degree			
	Low	Medium	Great	Total
$DI_{PA,global}$	$DI_{PA,global} \leq 0.3$	$0.3 < DI_{PA,global} \leq 0.6$	$0.6 < DI_{PA,global} \leq 0.8$	$DI_{PA,global} > 0.80$

The value of $DI_{PA,global}$ is equal to zero under elastic response, the structural damage located in the "Great" level is non-repairable while $DI_{PA,global} > 0.80$ signifies complete collapse or total damage of the structure.

5 Calculation of Seismic Intensity Parameters and $DI_{PA,Global}$

A total number of ninety accelerograms have been applied to a reinforced concrete (RC) frame structure with a total height of 22 m. The examined structure is designed in agreement with the rules of the recent *Eurocodes* EC2 [13] and EC8 [14], for structural concrete and aseismic structures and shown in Fig. 1. The cross-section of the beams are T-shapes with 30 cm width, 20 cm plate thickness, 60 cm total beam height. The effective plate width is 1.15 m at the end-bays and 1.80 m at the middle-bay. The distance between frames in the three-dimensional structure has been chosen to be 6 m. The building has been considered as an "importance class II", "ductility class Medium", and "subsoil of type B".

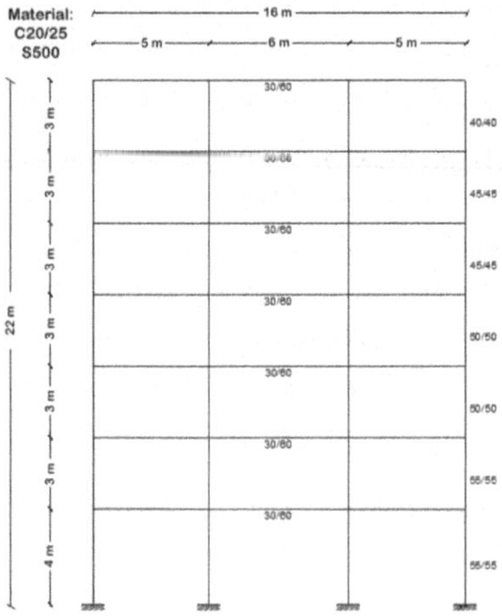

Fig. 1. Reinforced concrete frame.

Additionally, to the dead weight and the seismic loading, snow, wind, and live loads have been taken into account. The fundamental period of the frame is 0.95 s. After the design procedure of the RC frame structure, a nonlinear dynamic analysis has occurred for the evaluation of the structural seismic response for every seismic excitation utilized in the present study. For this purpose, the computer program IDARC version 7 [27] has been used. The hysteretic behavior of beams and columns has been specified at both ends of each member using a three-parameter Park model. This hysteretic model incorporates stiffness degradation, strength deterioration, non-symmetric response, slip-lock, and a trilinear monotonic envelope. The parameter values, which specify the above degrading parameters, have been chosen from experimental results of cyclic force-deformation characteristics of typical components of the studied structure. Thus, the nominal parameter for stiffness degradation and strength deterioration has been chosen. On the other hand, no pinching has been taken into account. Among the several response parameters, the focus is on the overall structural damage index of Park and Ang. From the nonlinear dynamic analysis, the overall damage indices of Park and Ang are derived, as presented in Table 3.

Table 3. The number of excitations employed per $DI_{PA,global}$ range.

$DI_{PA,global}$	Number of accelerograms
0.01–0.1	15
0.1–0.2	18
0.2–0.3	9
0.3–0.4	11
0.4–0.5	2
0.5–0.6	8
0.6–0.7	10
0.7–0.8	6
0.8–0.9	3
>0.9	8

The utilized accelerograms generate a broad spectrum of damage (low, medium, large, and total) for statistical reasons. After the selection of the ninety-two earthquake excitations, all the employed seismic intensity parameters are evaluated for every accelerogram, and their statistical values are presented in Table 4.

Table 4. Statistical values of the seismic intensity parameters.

Seismic parameter	Statistics			
	Min value	Max value	Average	Standard deviation
PGA (m/s^2)	0.304	13.615	4.804	3.343
PGV (m/s)	0.030	1.212	0.386	0.263
PGD (m)	0.003	0.950	0.149	0.146
PGA/PGV($g \cdot s/m$)	0.314	3.248	1.375	0.643
CP (s)	0.052	0.802	0.218	0.110
I_{ARIAS} (m/s)	0.015	28.274	3.728	5.081
SMD_{TB} (s)	2.080	89.100	18.250	18.949
$P_{0.90}$ (m^2/s^4)	0.005	7.442	1.823	2.033
RMS_a (m/s^2)	0.038	1.636	0.569	0.399
I_{FVF} ($m \cdot s^{3/4}$)	0.041	2.428	0.724	0.504
CAV ($g \cdot s$)	0.058	8.469	1.557	1.525
DP_{AS} ($m \cdot s$)	0.000	0.258	0.038	0.050
SD (m)	0.006	0.369	0.092	0.074
SV (m/s)	0.051	2.408	0.660	0.503
SA (m/s^2)	0.058	1.975	0.700	0.469
E_{inp}(m^2/s^2)	0.001	6.175	0.823	1.185
SI_K (m)	0.016	1.024	0.294	0.226
SI_{MR} (m/s)	0.042	1.391	0.493	0.339
EPA (g)	0.018	1.001	0.382	0.247
EPA_{max} (g)	0.030	1.035	0.413	0.264

6 Configuration of ANNs and Datasets

The development of the ANNs based on the universal approximation of MLFF networks requires the determination of the input and the output datasets, the choice of the optimal Learning algorithm, and the determination of the number of hidden layers/neurons. In this research, several Learning Algorithms were employed in order to choose the one that produces the best convergence. Back Propagation (Trainlm) has been proven to be optimal as the optimization algorithm. The obtained data set had been preprocessed in a previous research effort, so no such action was required [9–11].

The available data vectors comprise of twenty seismic intensity parameters that have already been discussed. As mentioned in Chap. 2, due to the nature of the case, it is difficult to obtain a number of $DI_{PA,global}$ data vectors, in order to perform a reliable Principal Component Analysis between those twenty seismic intensity parameters and the overall damage indices $DI_{PA,global}$.

Thus, we have followed a trial and error approach by testing a huge number of potential Input Datasets (IDS) that have emerged by combinations of the available features. Each combination comprised of at least 5 parameters. The maximum number of features was twenty. At the same time, nine different transfer functions were applied for each one of the emerged potential IDS. Every single developed dataset was utilized as Input to a different ANN in order to model the degree of the seismic parameters' influence on the value of the structural damage index. Thus, a total number of the 1,042,380 distinct input tables have been developed and used as input to the ANNs before the determination of the winner (the optimal one).

As the target output parameter of the examined ANNs for the function fitting problem in this study, we used the overall damage indices $DI_{PA,global}$ that derived from nonlinear dynamic analysis after the application of the seismic accelerograms on the structure in study. Therefore, all developed ANNs have one neuron that represents the $DI_{PA,global}$.

All networks that have been developed in this research for the prediction of the $DI_{PA,global}$ had one hidden layer in an effort to keep their architecture as simple as possible. This choice was based on the fact that the single-layered feedforward perceptron networks are able to precisely approach functions f(x): Rm → R1 [19], as well as on the fact that their efficiency has already been proved in numerous relevant investigations [19, 23]. The number of neurons in the hidden layer was also investigated. Several models with 7 to 10 hidden neurons were tried. This range was chosen after several trial and error tests and based on the small number of available vectors (92) in the source training dataset. As a result of that, four additional networks were developed for every produced ANN by the combination of the seismic parameters.

Totally, nine different training algorithms were utilized for every potential dataset, namely [16, 28]: Trainlm (Levenberg-Marquardt BP), Trainbfg (BFGS quasi-Newton BP), Trainrp (Resilient backpropagation), Trainscg (Scaled conjugate gradient BP), Traincgb (Powell-Beale conjugate gradient BP), Traincgf (Fletcher-Powell conjugate gradient BP), Traincgp (Polak-Ribiere conjugate gradient BP), Trainoss (One step secant BP) and Traingdx (Gradient descent with momentum and adaptive linear BP).

Moreover, the Sigmoid, TanH (Tangent Hyperbolic) Transfer function was employed.

7 Experiments - Evaluation and Results

Totally, 37,525,680 ANNs were developed and tested. This procedure was the result of the combination of 5 to 20 seismic parameters and the employment of 7 to 10 hidden neurons and nine training algorithms (one for each network).

For the development of the developed ANNs, MATLAB 2019 a [29] was used. Due to the vast number of different networks and the fact that most of the specific training algorithms are not GPU capable, a private distributed – parallelized environment of 10 virtual instances of Matlab was employed. Each instance had access to eight i9-9900k threads and 12 GB of memory. It was also equipped with two Matlab workers, which means that a total amount of 20 workers were available.

A proper Matlab script was developed, which was able to: a) to develop all ANNs b) to manage the fastest possible training of the total amount of networks based on the distribution and use of the available resources. From the total ninety-two employed seismic excitations, a percentage of 70% comprised the training set. From the rest of the vectors, a percentage of 15% was used as a testing set and 15% as the validation set.

For the comparison of the obtained ANNs, the "R" statistics, the "R^2", and the "Mean Squared Error (MSE)" were employed.

In statistics, R is the "correlation coefficient" between two variables, which reflects the strength and direction of a linear relationship and has a value between –1 (total negative linear correlation and +1 (total positive linear correlation). As R^2 is denoted the "coefficient of determination" with a value that ranges from zero to one and represents the proportion of variance in the dependent variable $DI_{PA,global}$, which may be predicted from the seismic intensity parameters for every investigated ANN. An R^2 value above 0.80 indicates a strong effect of the independent variables on the explanation of $DI_{PA,global}$.

The MSE is an average of the absolute difference between the true values of $DI_{PA,global}$, which considered the calculated ones by nonlinear dynamic analysis and the corresponding ones evaluated by the constructed ANNs.

In Tables (5 and 6), the basic statistics of the R and MSE calculated values are presented respectively for every training algorithm and every investigated number of neurons in the hidden layer of ANNs.

Table 5. Statistics of "R coefficient" values.

R Statistics								
Training algorithm	7 Neurons-hidden layer				8 Neurons-hidden layer			
	Min	Max	Mean	St.dev.	Min	Max	Mean	St.dev.
trainlm	−0.6646	0.9859	0.9271	0.0317	−0.7224	0.9872	0.9268	0.0327
trainbfg	−0.7377	0.9686	0.9073	0.0424	−0.6849	0.9686	0.9072	0.0414
trainrp	−0.6006	0.9647	0.8974	0.0481	−0.7622	0.9731	0.8959	0.0500
trainscg	−0.7175	0.9673	0.9060	0.0458	−0.8070	0.9681	0.9052	0.0451
traincgb	−0.7500	0.9691	0.9115	0.0401	−0.8231	0.9735	0.9110	0.0396
traincgf	−0.6974	0.9677	0.9084	0.0440	−0.6713	0.9690	0.9083	0.0434
traincgp	−0.7708	0.9671	0.9070	0.0437	−0.7407	0.9675	0.9062	0.0431
trainoss	0.7502	0.9626	0.9025	0.0454	−0.7274	0.9596	0.9022	0.0439
traingdx	−0.9015	0.9569	0.7467	0.3111	−0.9133	0.9563	0.7412	0.3142
	9 Neurons-hidden layer				10 Neurons-hidden layer			
	Min	Max	Mean	St.dev.	Min	Max	Mean	St.dev.
trainlm	−0.6030	0.9883	0.9266	0.0332	−0.6084	0.9866	0.9262	0.0345
trainbfg	−0.6751	0.9669	0.9072	0.0404	−0.5839	0.9665	0.9071	0.0402
trainrp	−0.7957	0.9680	0.8945	0.0519	−0.6713	0.9722	0.8930	0.0539
trainscg	−0.8060	0.9667	0.9044	0.0451	−0.7004	0.9681	0.9036	0.0454
traincgb	−0.6972	0.9702	0.9104	0.0399	−0.6432	0.9746	0.9098	0.0401
traincgf	−0.6994	0.9696	0.9078	0.0429	−0.7446	0.9689	0.9074	0.0434
traincgp	−0.7269	0.9708	0.9053	0.0434	−0.7446	0.9709	0.9045	0.0436
trainoss	−0.7408	0.9633	0.9017	0.0431	−0.7446	0.9636	0.9011	0.0430
traingdx	−0.8928	0.9591	0.7325	0.3211	−0.9106	0.9599	0.7222	0.3287

Table 6. Statistics of MSE values.

MSE Statistics								
Training algorithm	7 Neurons-hidden layer				8 Neurons-hidden layer			
	Min	Max	Mean	St.dev.	Min	Max	Mean	St.dev.
trainlm	0.0026	0.3825	0.0143	0.0073	0.0024	0.2789	0.0144	0.0076
trainbfg	0.0058	0.4192	0.0167	0.0074	0.0057	0.4137	0.0167	0.0074
trainrp	0.0065	0.3490	0.0187	0.0090	0.0049	0.3871	0.0190	0.0096
trainscg	0.0059	0.2861	0.0167	0.0074	0.0057	0.3347	0.0169	0.0076
traincgb	0.0056	0.3650	0.0158	0.0066	0.0049	0.3575	0.0159	0.0068
traincgf	0.0059	0.2805	0.0163	0.0072	0.0056	0.4478	0.0163	0.0073
traincgp	0.0060	0.3707	0.0166	0.0072	0.0059	0.6212	0.0167	0.0073
trainoss	0.0067	0.9041	0.0176	0.0078	0.0073	0.4138	0.0177	0.0078
traingdx	0.0077	0.9163	0.0397	0.0440	0.0079	1.2957	0.0418	0.0476
	9 Neurons-hidden layer				10 Neurons-hidden layer			
	Min	Max	Mean	St.dev.	Min	Max	Mean	St.dev.
trainlm	0.0023	0.4237	0.0145	0.0079	0.0024	0.2804	0.0147	0.0081
trainbfg	0.0060	0.3058	0.0167	0.0073	0.0061	0.4611	0.0168	0.0075
trainrp	0.0058	0.3779	0.0193	0.0102	0.0050	0.5197	0.0197	0.0108
trainscg	0.0061	0.3406	0.0171	0.0077	0.0058	0.3619	0.0172	0.0080
traincgb	0.0054	0.3423	0.0160	0.0069	0.0046	0.4284	0.0161	0.0071
traincgf	0.0056	0.4743	0.0164	0.0074	0.0056	0.6029	0.0165	0.0076
traincgp	0.0053	0.5510	0.0169	0.0075	0.0053	0.6029	0.0171	0.0077
trainoss	0.0066	0.4743	0.0178	0.0078	0.0066	0.4259	0.0179	0.0079
traingdx	0.0075	1.0538	0.0445	0.0520	0.0072	1.1863	0.0478	0.0567

The best results for every performance coefficient in study are described in Table 7 and Table 8. Table 7 presents the quantities (qty.), as a percentage of the results, in regard to the R^2 coefficient with values that range from 0.80 to 1, considering the number of neurons in the hidden layer and the training algorithm. These results are also distributed in three classes.

Table 7. Percentage of ANNs with R^2 values over 0.80.

Classification of R^2 values										
Classes of R^2	Qty. of ANNs	Trainlm	Trainbfg	Trainrp	Trainscg	Traincgb	Traincgf	Traincgp	Trainoss	Traingdx
		7 Neurons-hidden layer								
$R^2 > 0.90$	(%)	11.86	0.14	0.17	0.12	0.30	0.23	0.16	0.03	0.01
$0.85 < R^2 \leq 0.90$	(%)	63.48	46.95	33.18	45.78	54.19	50.36	47.46	38.49	29.21
$0.80 < R^2 \leq 0.85$	(%)	16.90	35.06	39.09	35.50	31.05	32.50	34.32	40.06	21.12
		8 Neurons-hidden layer								
$R^2 > 0.90$	(%)	12.53	0.17	0.22	0.14	0.36	0.29	0.19	0.04	0.02
$0.85 < R^2 \leq 0.90$	(%)	62.35	46.50	32.57	44.29	53.05	49.67	45.95	37.47	28.62
$0.80 < R^2 \leq 0.85$	(%)	16.86	35.08	38.21	35.94	31.42	32.59	34.78	40.29	20.88
		9 Neurons-hidden layer								
$R^2 > 0.90$	(%)	13.14	0.21	0.26	0.16	0.43	0.34	0.22	0.05	0.02
$0.85 < R^2 \leq 0.90$	(%)	61.26	46.01	31.79	42.91	51.88	48.66	44.47	36.50	27.83
$0.80 < R^2 \leq 0.85$	(%)	16.82	35.19	37.57	36.31	31.85	32.91	35.20	40.48	20.50
		10 Neurons-hidden layer								
$R^2 > 0.90$	(%)	13.64	0.26	0.33	0.20	0.50	0.42	0.24	0.07	0.03
$0.85 < R^2 \leq 0.90$	(%)	60.34	45.58	31.20	41.62	50.69	47.83	43.09	35.55	26.87
$0.80 < R^2 \leq 0.85$	(%)	16.75	35.27	36.77	36.69	32.22	33.10	35.66	40.61	20.20

In a correspondent way, the best results for the MSE, which range from 0.05 to 0.02, considering the number of neurons in the hidden layer and the training algorithm, are presented in Table 8.

Investigating the above Tables, the maximum R^2 coefficient, which is 0.9767, and the minimum MSE, which is 0.0023 have been obtained by the ANN, which was trained by the "Trainlm" (Back Propagation) algorithm, with nine neurons in the hidden layer, using the TanH transfer function. It is also obvious that the "Trainlm" algorithm presents the most significant percentage of the highest R^2 values and the lowest MSE values derived from all utilized algorithms.

Table 8. Percentage of ANNs regard to MSE values.

Classification of MSE										
Classes of MSE	Qty. of ANNs	Trainlm	Trainbfg	Trainrp	Trainscg	Traincgb	Traincgf	Traincgp	Trainoss	Traingdx
		7 Neurons-hidden layer								
MSE < 0.02	(%)	87.56	82.31	72.55	82.19	86.31	83.89	82.76	78.70	51.90
0.02 ≤ MSE < 0.05	(%)	11.84	16.96	26.11	17.06	13.16	15.46	16.57	20.42	23.02
MSE ≥ 0.05	(%)	0.59	0.73	1.33	0.76	0.53	0.65	0.67	0.89	25.08
		8 Neurons-hidden layer								
MSE < 0.02	(%)	86.79	81.88	71.18	81.25	85.61	83.45	81.78	77.94	50.99
0.02 ≤ MSE < 0.05	(%)	12.55	17.42	27.23	18.00	13.85	15.90	17.54	21.20	22.70
MSE ≥ 0.05	(%)	0.66	0.70	1.58	0.75	0.54	0.66	0.68	0.87	26.31
		9 Neurons-hidden layer								
MSE < 0.02	(%)	86.06	81.54	69.82	80.35	84.98	82.85	80.77	77.20	49.76
0.02 ≤ MSE < 0.05	(%)	13.21	17.77	28.34	18.85	14.44	16.47	18.51	21.92	22.30
MSE ≥ 0.05	(%)	0.72	0.69	1.83	0.80	0.58	0.68	0.72	0.88	27.95
		10 Neurons-hidden layer								
MSE < 0.02	(%)	85.40	81.18	68.54	79.51	84.25	82.30	79.83	76.35	48.38
0.02 ≤ MSE < 0.05	(%)	13.79	18.12	29.34	19.62	15.14	16.97	19.38	22.75	21.76
MSE ≥ 0.05	(%)	0.81	0.70	2.12	0.87	0.61	0.73	0.78	0.90	29.86

For the "Trainlm" function the percent of ANN cases with $R^2 > 0.80$ depending on the number of neurons in the hidden layer, ranges from 90.73% to 92.24% while the percentage of ANNs that achieved values of MSE < 0.05, ranges from 99.19% to 99.40% of the total number of ANN models that estimate the seismic damage that is expressed by the $DI_{PA.global}$ index (see Table 9). It means that at least 90.73% of the developed ANNs have shown excellent predictive accuracy with $R^2 > 0.80$ και MSE < 0.05 simultaneously. At least 85.40% of the ANNs had a performance with $R^2 > 0.80$ and MSE < 0.02 simultaneously.

Table 9. Results of ANNs with "Trainlm" algorithm

Number of neurons in the hidden layer	Percentage of evaluated MFPs		
	$R^2 > 0.80$ (%)	MSE < 0.05 (%)	MSE < 0.02 (%)
7	92.24	99.40	87.56
8	91.74	99.34	86.79
9	91.22	99.27	86.06
10	90.73	99.19	85.40

8 Conclusions and Further Work

This research designates the grade of the ability of Artificial Neural Networks to predict seismic damage from twenty well-established seismic parameters, taking into consideration the already proven in earthquake engineering strong interrelation between the structural damage and the seismic intensity parameters.

The overall damage index of Park and Ang is used to describe the damage of a reinforced concrete frame structure under a number of ninety-two seismic excitations, and the evaluated by nonlinear dynamic analyses indices are utilized as the target values of the examined ANNs. The architecture of the constructed ANNs is the Multiple Feedforward Perceptron (MFP) network with five to twenty seismic parameters as inputs, one hidden layer of seven to ten neurons, trained with nine different backpropagation algorithms. Hence, a number of 37,525,680 ANNs are calculated, and two of their statistical parameters, the "R coefficient" and the "Mean Squared Error (MSE)" of the total data, are investigated.

All the utilized training algorithms led to a significant percentage of ANNs with a high coefficient of determination ($R^2 > 0.80$) and low MSE (MSE < 0.05). The most efficient of them turned out to be the "Trainlm" algorithm. In particular, a number of 1,024,380 ANNs configured with the "Trainlm" algorithm conducted to a percentage of over 90.73% of a high explanation of variance of $DI_{PA,global}$ (with $R^2 > 0.80$) with very low MSE (MSE < 0.05) simultaneously. It is also observed that the best performance of all the investigated statistical coefficients is displayed among the ANNs with the nine neurons in the hidden layer, which use the "Trainlm" algorithm. In particular, from Table 5, the highest obtained R^2 coefficient presented to be equal to 0.9767 (R = 0.9883), while in Table 6, the lowest displayed MSE is equal to 0.0023. Furthermore, according to Table 2, it is obvious that the values of MSE under the value of 0.05 cause no substantial changes to the estimated level of $DI_{PA,global}$, and, thus, to the decisions for the repair interventions.

All the above results confirm that the use of ANNs can be considered a very reliable method for a high accuracy prediction of the post-seismic damage in existing or future structures and a powerful tool for the scientific community in order crucial decisions to be made before and after an earthquake.

In future work, this research could be extended, investigating more seismic intensity parameters with a larger sample of seismic excitations. Following this process, the most efficient parameters and the best combination of them could be obtained and utilized directly for the determination of earthquake vulnerability of the structures.

References

1. Alvanitopoulos, P.F., Andreadis, I., Elenas, A.: A genetic algorithm for the classification of earthquake damages in buildings. In: Proceedings of 5th IFIP Conference on Artificial Intelligence Applications and Innovations, Thessaloniki, pp. 341–346 (2009). https://doi.org/10.1007/978-1-4419-0221-4_40
2. Alvanitopoulos, P.F., Andreadis, I., Elenas, A.: A new algorithm for the classification of earthquake damages in structures. In: Proceedings of the 5th IASTED Conference on Signal Processing, Pattern Recognition and Applications, Innsbruck, pp. 151–156 (2008)
3. Alvanitopoulos, P.F., Andreadis, I., Elenas, A.: Neuro-fuzzy techniques for the classification of earthquake damages in buildings. Measurement **43**(6), 797–809 (2010)
4. Araya, R., Saragoni, G.R.: Earthquake accelerogram destructiveness potential factor. In: Proceedings of the 8th World Conference on Earthquake Engineering, pp. 835–842. EERI, El Cerrito (1984)

5. Arias, A.: A measure of earthquake intensity. In: Hansen, R.J. (ed.) Seismic Design for Nuclear Power Plants, pp. 438–483. MIT Press, Cambridge (1970)
6. ATC 3–06 Publication: Tentative Provisions for the Development of Seismic Regulations for Buildings. US Government Printing Office, Washington, DC (1978)
7. Cabãnas, L., Benito, B., Herráiz, M.: An approach to the measurement of the potential structural damage of earthquake ground motions. Earthq. Eng. Struct. Dyn. **26**(1), 79–92 (1997)
8. Chopra, A.K.: Dynamics of Structures. Prentice-Hall, Englewood Cliffs (1995)
9. Elenas, A., Meskouris, K.: Correlation study between seismic acceleration parameters and damage indices of structures. Eng. Struct. **23**(6), 698–704 (2001)
10. Elenas, A.: Correlation between seismic acceleration parameters and overall structural damage indices of buildings. Soil Dyn. Earthq. Eng. **20**(1), 93–100 (2000)
11. Elenas, A.: Interdependency between seismic acceleration parameters and the behavior of structures. Soil Dyn. Earthq. Eng. **16**(5), 317–322 (1997)
12. Elenas, A.: Seismic-parameter-based statistical procedure for the approximate assessment of structural damage. Math. Probl. Eng. **2014**, 1–22 (2014). Article Id 916820
13. Eurocode 2: Design of Concrete Structures—Part 1: General Rules and Rules for Buildings. European Committee for Standardization, Brussels, Belgium (2000)
14. Eurocode 8: Design of Structures for Earthquake Resistance—Part 1: General Rules, Seismic Actions, and Rules for Buildings. European Committee for Standardization, Brussels, Belgium (2004)
15. Fajfar, P., Vidic, T., Fischinger, M.: A measure of earthquake motion capacity to damage medium-period structures. Soil Dyn. Earthq. Eng. **9**(5), 236–242 (1990)
16. Haykin, S.: Neural Netw, 2nd edn. Prentice Hall, Upper Saddle River (1999)
17. Jennings, P.C.: Engineering seismology. In: Kanamori, H., Boschi, E. (eds.) Earthquakes: Observation, Theory and Interpretation, pp. 138–173. Italian Physical Society, Varenna (1982)
18. Kappos, A.J.: Sensitivity of calculated inelastic seismic response to input motion characteristics. In: Proceedings of the 4th U.S. National Conference on Earthquake Engineering, pp. 25–34. EERI, Oakland (1990)
19. Lautour, O.R., Omenzetter, P.: Prediction of seismic-induced structural damage using artificial neural networks. Eng. Struct. **31**(2), 600–606 (2009)
20. Martinez-Rueda, J.E.: Scaling procedure for natural accelerograms based on a system of spectrum intensity scales. Earthq. Spectra **14**(1), 135–152 (1998)
21. Meskouris, K., Krätzig, W.B., Hanskötter, U.: Nonlinear computer simulations of seismically excited wall-stiffened reinforced concrete buildings. In: Proceedings of the 2nd International Conference on Structural Dynamics (EURODYN'93), Balkema, Lisse, pp. 49–54 (1993)
22. Meskouris, K.: Structural Dynamics: Models, Methods. Examples. Ernst & Sohn, Berlin (2000)
23. Morfidis, K., Kostinakis, K.: Approaches to the rapid seismic damage prediction of r/c buildings using artificial neural networks. Eng. Struct. **165**, 120–141 (2018)
24. Nanos, N., Elenas, A., Ponterosso, P.: Correlation of different strong motion duration parameters and damage indicators of reinforced concrete structures. In: Proceedings of the 14th World Conference on Earthquake Engineering (2008)
25. Park, Y.J., Ang, A.H.-S., Wen, Y.K.: Damage-limiting aseismic design of buildings. Earthq. Spectra **3**(1), 1–26 (1987)
26. Ang, A.H.-S., Park, Y.J., Ang, A.H.-S.: Mechanistic seismic damage model for reinforced concrete. J. Struct. Eng. **111**(4), 722–739 (1985)

27. Reinhorn, A.M., Roh, H., Sivaselvan, M., et al.: IDARC2D version 7.0: a program for the inelastic damage analysis of structures. Technical report MCEER-09-0006, MCEER, State University of New York, Buffalo, NY, USA (2009)
28. Singh, A., Saxena, P., Lalwani, S.: A study of various training algorithms on neural network for angle based triangular problem. Int. J. Comput. Appl. **71**(13), 0975–8887 (2013)
29. The Math Works Inc.: MATLAB and Statistics Toolbox Release 2016b. Natick, Massachusetts, USA (2016)
30. Trifunac, M.D., Brady, A.G.: A study on the duration of strong earthquake ground motion. Bull. Seismol. Soc. Am. **65**(3), 581–626 (1975)
31. Tsou, P., Shen, M.H.: Structural damage detection and identification using neural network. In: Proceedings of the 34thAIAA/ASME/ASCEAHS/ASC, Structural, Structural Dynamics and Materials Conference, AIAA/ASME Adaptive Structural Forum, pt. 5 (1993)
32. Uang, C.M., Bertero, V.V.: Evaluation of seismic energy in structures. Earthq. Eng. Struct. Dynam. **19**(1), 77–90 (1990)
33. Vanmarcke, E.H., Lai, S.S.P.: Strong-motion duration and RMS amplitude of earthquake records. Bull. Seismol. Soc. Am. **70**(4), 1293–1307 (1980)
34. Vui, V.C., Hamid, R.R.: Correlation between seismic parameters of far-fault motions and damage indices of low-rise reinforced concrete frames. Soil Dyn. Earthq. Eng. **66**(11), 102–112 (2014)
35. Wu, X., Ghaboussi, J., Garrett, J.: Use of neural network in detection of structural damage. Comput. Struct. **42**(4), 649–659 (1992)
36. Zhao, J., Ivan, J.N., DeWold, J.T.: Structural damage detection using artificial neural networks. J. Infrastructural Syst. **13**(3), 182–189 (1998)

Efficient Implementation of a Self-sufficient Solar-Powered Real-Time Deep Learning-Based System

Sorin Liviu Jurj(✉), Raul Rotar, Flavius Opritoiu, and Mircea Vladutiu

Advanced Computing Systems and Architectures (ACSA) Laboratory, Computers and Information Technology Department, "Politehnica" University of Timisoara, Timisoara, Romania
jurjsorinliviu@yahoo.de, raul.rotar@student.upt.ro, {flavius.opritoiu,mircea.vladutiu}@cs.upt.ro

Abstract. This paper presents a self-sufficient solar-powered real-time Deep Learning (DL) based system that runs inference 100% on solar energy and which is composed of an Nvidia Jetson TX2 board and a dual-axis solar tracker based on the cast-shadow principle. In order to have a higher energy being generated by the solar tracker as well as a lower energy consumption by the real-time DL-based system, we have: a) updated our solar tracker's panel with a higher number of polycrystalline photovoltaic (PV) cells and connected it to a chain of two inverters, one accumulator and one solar charge controller; b) implemented a motion detection method that triggers the inference process only when there is substantial movement in webcam frame. Experimental results show that our solar tracker generates sufficient and constant solar energy for all the 4 DL models (VGG-19, InceptionV3, ResNet-50 and MobileNetV2) that are running in real-time on the Nvidia Jetson TX2 platform and which requires more than 5 times less energy when compared to a laptop having a Nvidia GTX 1060 GPU, proving that real-time DL-based systems can be powered by solar trackers without the need of traditional power plugs or need to pay for electricity bills.

Keywords: Deep learning · Real-Time · Solar energy

1 Introduction

Recent advancements in the field of Artificial Intelligence (AI), especially DL, are happening especially thanks to the availability of huge amounts of data and powerful hardware. During training and inference of a Deep Neural Network (DNN), usually expensive and power-hungry GPUs are used, resulting in a proportional growth of computational and environmental costs, with some Natural Language Processing (NLP) models even increasing the carbon footprint nearly five times the lifetime emissions of a car [1].

Because climate change is a very relevant problem in our society [2] and considering goal number 7 (affordable and clean energy) and goal number 13 (climate action) of UN's Sustainable Development Goals [3], efforts to develop and use low-power

L. Iliadis et al. (Eds.): EANN 2020, INNS 2, pp. 99–118, 2020.
https://doi.org/10.1007/978-3-030-48791-1_7

embedded devices are made by many companies, an example, in this case, being Nvidia's Jetson TX2 embedded platform [4]. Consequently, in order to reduce the carbon footprint and the electricity bills, efforts towards renewable energy are made [5], with many researchers building solar tracking systems [6, 7] in order to capture sun's energy with maximum efficiency.

Considering that the two domains of AI and renewable energy are of major importance for the development of our society, our work introduces a self-sufficient solar-powered real-time DL-based system that makes use of solar energy from the sun with the help of an updated version of our solar tracker based on the cast-shadow principle [6] and an Nvidia Jetson TX2 board that runs our real-time animal class identification model [8] on videos or using a webcam and also generates additional datasets containing images and textual information about the animals present in front of the frame, in real-time. In order to justify our decision for choosing an embedded platform instead of a laptop, in our experimental results, we present a comparison between the two platforms, mainly in terms of power consumption. Additionally, we also improve the energy efficiency of the proposed real-time DL-based system by implementing a motion detection method based on background subtraction with the help of Python and OpenCV [9].

Concerning the structure of the paper, in Sect. 2, we present an overview of the related work. Section 3 describes the proposed efficient real-time DL-based system. Section 4 presents the experimental setup and results. Finally, Sect. 5 concludes this paper.

2 Related Work

To the best of our knowledge, there is no work in the literature that makes use of a solar tracking device in order to generate solar energy for a real-time DL-based system.

Nevertheless, similar work that evaluates the power efficiency of DL inference for image recognition on embedded GPU systems is presented in [10] where the authors compare different platforms like Nvidia Jetson TX1 and TX2 as well as a Tesla P40 and show that the Nvidia Jetson TX2 board is able to achieve the highest accuracy with the lowest power consumption. The authors in [11] make use of an Nvidia Jetson TX2 to test a fully Convolutional Neural Network (CNN) for detecting traffic lights and employ a power supply unit (12 V) with stabilizer in order to increase the stability of the system, mentioning that the Nvidia Jetson TX2 has a low power consumption of around 10 Watts, which is also confirmed by our experimental results using different CNN architectures. The authors in [12] train and test two CNNs for classifying skin cancer images as Benign or Malignant on the Nvidia Jetson TX2, proving that this embedded platform is capable of handling DL computations even for training CNN models, not only for inference. The authors in [13] propose an object detection implementation using MobileNet as the backbone network on an Nvidia Jetson TX2 board, showing a higher frames-per-second (fps) and reduced model size when compared to other networks. Nvidia Jetson TX2 is used also in [14] where the authors propose a CNN based application that can run onboard a satellite in order to detect and classify boats on the open ocean from satellite imagery. Experimental results show that the Nvidia Jetson TX2 has almost half the power consumption when compared with standard systems designed for a satellite onboard processing. The authors in [15] use Nvidia Jetson TX2 for their proposed methodology regarding a faster and more accurate object detection in unmanned aerial vehicle (UAV) imagery. The work in [16] proposes a vehicle and pedestrian detection system that uses CNNs in order to evaluate traffic violations and which is implemented on an Nvidia Jetson TX2 board. Other related works that use Nvidia Jetson TX2 are regarding real-time ear detection [17], when developing embedded online fish detection and tracking system for ocean observatory network [18], real-time multiple face recognition [19], a streaming cloud platform for real-time video processing [20] and detecting diabetic foot ulcer in real-time [21]. A comparison between different computing platforms is made also by the authors in [22] which show that the Nvidia Jetson TX2 is a reliable and efficient embedded platform for the underwater robotics domain.

Regarding motion detection, the authors in [23] present a comparative analysis of motion-based and feature-based algorithms for object detection and tracking and show that Adaptive Gaussian Mixture Model (AGMM) [24] is faster and more robust to illumination (shadows) than Grimson Gaussian Mixture Models (GGMM) [25] when performing on real-time videos. Also, the authors in [26] present a study on preprocessing methods for tracking objects in soccer videos, showing that background subtraction and edge detection are advantageous for detecting moving objects. OpenCV [9] is also using AGMM together with other several algorithms for background subtraction such as BackgroundSubtractorGMG, BackgroundSubstractorMOG, and BackgroundSubstractor MOG2, which are presented in the works of [27] and [28] but, in comparison with OpenCV [9], the algorithms in OpenCV are more modern, accurate and faster (a reason for this is because they are continuously developed by the OpenCV community).

In this work, we make use of OpenCV in order to implement a motion-based Gaussian algorithm that makes use of pixel's intensity values over a period of time. We decided to implement it in order to trigger the inference process only when there is movement in the frame, thus lowering the energy consumption of the entire real-time DL-based system, as seen in our experimental results presented in Sect. 4.

3 Proposed Solar-Powered Real-Time Deep Learning-Based System

A summarized view of the proposed solar-powered DL-based system can be seen in Fig. 1. It consists of our dual-axis solar tracker based on the cast-shadow principle [6], a solar charge controller, an Ultra Cell accumulator with 12 V 9 Ah acid plumb battery, two DC-to-DC inverters (first DC-to-DC inverter converts 12 V to around 5 V necessary for the solar tracker to become autonomous regarding energy needs and the second DC-to-DC inverter converts 12 V to around 19 V necessary for the Nvidia Jetson TX2 to run only on solar energy) and an Nvidia Jetson TX2 embedded platform that uses and powers an external Logitech C920 HD Pro webcam in order to identify animal classes in real-time [8].

Fig. 1. Summarized view of the proposed solar-powered real-time DL-based system.

3.1 Dual-Axis Solar Tracker Using the Cast-Shadow Principle

Our old dual-axis solar tracker based on the cast-shadow principle [6] used a solar panel with 40 PV monocrystalline cells instead of Light Diode Resistors (LDRs) which are usually found in the literature. Twelve of these PV cells are used to control 4 low-cost circuits, namely 1 × Optocoupler LTV 847, 1 × Arduino328 Microcontroller, 2 × L298N Dual-H Bridge circuits and 2 × stepper motors which are used for the dual-axis positioning of the solar tracker. Our solar panel makes use of 3 PV cells from each corner to analyze light distribution, 2 bypass diodes (D2) to protect PV cells in case of a sudden increase or decrease in voltage that may occur due to variable light and 2 blocking diodes (D1) to protect solar panel's PV cells from reverse current (i.e. voltage from the load such as the Optocoupler or Arduino UNO).

In order for the real-time DL-based system to run inference completely on solar energy, we considered using an updated version of our earlier proposed dual-axis solar tracker that uses the cast-shadow principle [6] in order to optimize its position for a more efficient solar energy gain, without the need of sensors. The important changes that we made to update our solar tracker in order to use it for the experimental results in this paper are:

1) The effective surface area of the panel used in the above described solar tracker was increased from $L_1 \times l_1 = 36 \times 35 = 1260\ \text{cm}^2$ to an area of $L_2 \times l_2 = 43 \times 36 = 1548\ \text{cm}^2$ to accommodate 60 polycrystalline PV cells.

2) The method used to produce silicon polycrystalline solar cells is easier to implement and less expensive as compared to monocrystalline counterparts, resulting in a more cost-effective investment. Additionally, polycrystalline solar panels tend to be somewhat less tolerant of heat than monocrystalline solar panels [29]. Due to their higher temperature coefficient, the overall heat output will be less significant compared to monocrystalline solar modules. As a consequence, our old monocrystalline PV solar cells were replaced by PV polycrystalline cells that generate a maximum voltage of 0.55 V and a maximum current of 0.60 A per unit, resulting in a total voltage of 17 V and 1.5 A generated by the improved solar panel.

3.2 Deep Learning Models Used for Inference

In order to prove the efficiency of our solar-powered real-time DL-based system, we decided to use our earlier proposed implementation regarding real-time identification of animals found in domestic areas of Europe [8] which can also generate 2 new datasets in real-time, one dataset containing textual information (i.e. animal class name, date and time interval when animal was present in the frame) and one dataset containing images of the animal classes present and identified in videos or in front of a webcam. These newly generated datasets are very useful, as they can provide in-sights about what animal classes are present at a given date and time in a certain area and how they look like.

Our original DL models presented in [8] were trained and tested on a home-made dataset with a total size of 4.06 GB consisting of 90.249 animal images (72.469 images for training, 8.994 images for validation and 8.786 images for testing) belonging to 34 classes on 4 state-of-the-art modified CNN architectures (VGG-19 [30], InceptionV3 [31], ResNet-50 [32] and MobileNetV2 [33]) using Keras with Tensorflow backend, achieving high overall test accuracy (90.56% for the proposed VGG-19 model, 93.41% for the proposed InceptionV3 model, 93.49% for the proposed ResNet-50 model and 94.54% for the proposed MobileNetV2 model).

In order to successfully implement and test our Python implementation on the Nvidia Jetson TX2 board, we needed to make some adjustments and improvements in our initial code from [8] as follows:

1) First, because Keras saves its weights in a hierarchical data format (.hdf5) file which slows the loading of the model on the Nvidia Jetson TX2, we have created an optimized (converted it to a frozen graph base model; here the value of all variables are embedded in the graph itself thus the protocol buffers (.pb) file cannot be retrained) frozen file of our Keras model based on Tensorflow. Keras does not include by itself any means to export a TensorFlow graph as a .pb file, but we could do it using regular Tensorflow utilities.
2) Second, because by default Tensorflow pre-allocates the whole GPU memory [34] (which can cause "out of memory" errors) and because the Nvidia Jetson TX2 GPU doesn't have dedicated RAM and cannot use its full 8 GB processing RAM (the reason for this is because Linux and other processes are using most of the available RAM), we implemented a code to control the GPU memory allocation and to define (choose a GPU memory ratio allocation from 0 to 1) the processing memory

percentage usage of the GPU at running time. By doing this, we can now control how much data we want to transfer to the GPU that processes it and avoid any possible "out of memory" kind of problems which otherwise would appear on the Nvidia Jetson TX2 due to its lack of dedicated GPU memory. We can now choose a ratio from 0 to 1 to decide the GPU usage from low to high by passing the arguments in the command line.

3) Third, we implemented a code for testing a certain number of batch frames in one shot. For this, we make use of a Numpy array. Numpy array is a fast method for data manipulation that saves a matrix of numbers in stacks (e.g. we can observe that when we read a frame in OpenCV it becomes numbers in the Numpy array, meaning that if we have 900 frames, Numpy array size will be 900, 224, 224). Then, we transferred that batch of frames to our model for prediction by changing the number of frames (e.g. we can send 30 frames one time like this: 30, 224, 224, so we have a remaining 870, 224, 224 arrays). We have tested it on the frozen graph. The frames are passed from 1 to 60. Fps batch testing is very useful in our tests because it helps us find the optimal number of fps our model can efficiently run inference on, e.g. when all 900 frames from a 31 s video are predicted in 31 s or less than that, it means that we can run it in real-time (when the identified class name is predicted and shown on the webcam frame without being affected by latency).
4) Forth, because we wanted to increase the security of animals and humans in domestic areas, we also implemented an automated SMS alert system based on Twilio API [35]. This is very helpful, especially in the cases when a wild animal is detected on a private property such as a house or a farming area (e.g. when, because of hunger, a bear is coming near a flock of sheep or a fox is coming near a chicken coop) because it generates and sends an SMS alert to the phone number of the owner, informing him what animal class is detected in real-time trough the webcam and thus helping him to take the necessary actions to maintain security. In order to save the SMS costs and not send an SMS alert every time (e.g. every second) a wild animal is detected in the webcam frame, we wrote a function that sends the SMS only if the wild animal is present in front of the frame for at least 3 s (to make sure that there are no SMS alerts sent by mistake due to some 1 s short animal class misdetections in the webcam frame). Additionally, in case the same wild animal class was detected multiple times in the last 5 min, this SMS alert is sent only one time every 5 min (e.g. if a Bear is detected continuously in the front of the webcam for 10 min, the SMS alert will be sent to owner's phone only two times).

3.3 Motion Detection

Because we wanted to lower the power consumption on both platforms when running the DL models as much as possible, instead of buying a costly motion detection sensor, we implemented a software motion detection method based on the difference between pixel intensity of the frames.

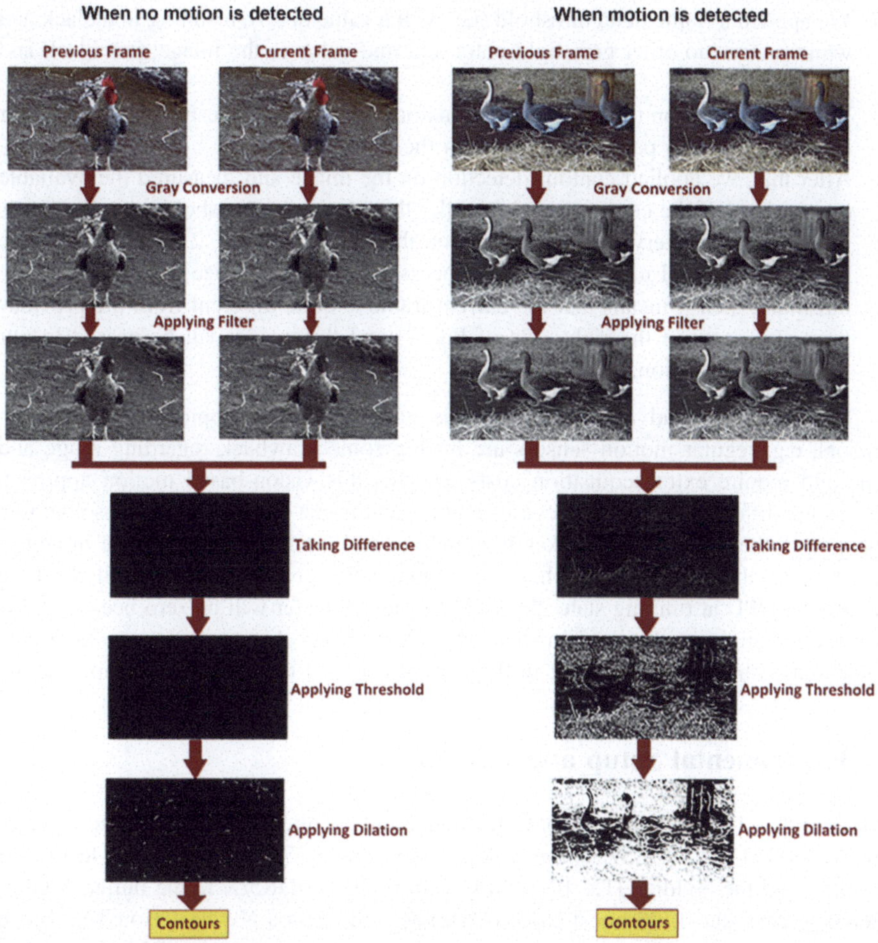

Fig. 2. Summarized view of the proposed motion detection.

For our motion detection method seen in Fig. 2, in order to speed-up the inference processing time of a video or webcam frame, we reduced its size to 224 × 244 pixels and used several computer vision techniques using OpenCV as follows:

1) We converted the frame color image to grayscale so that we can avoid some effects of illumines. This also results in faster processing.
2) We applied the Gaussian Blur filter to remove any possible noise in the frame image.
3) We computed the absolute difference (subtraction) between the current frame (foreground) and the first frame (modeled background) in order to calculate if their pixel values were close to zero, meaning that motion was not detected, otherwise when pixel values are higher, motion is detected.

4) We applied a frame delta threshold (i.e. with a value of 25), resulting in a black and white image (no other gray light color and mid-value in the image; just black and white).
5) We applied dilation (morphological transformation) to the threshold frame in order to join the broken parts of an object in the image.
6) After that, we applied contour detection on the image and measured the available contour size. If the contour size is smaller then the given threshold, then the pixels in the frame are very similar (as seen on the left side of Fig. 2) and frame image will not be passed to the inference process. If the contour size is higher than the threshold, then it means that the current frame is quite different from the previous frame (as seen on the right side of Fig. 2) and the image will be passed to our model for prediction.

There are some advantages of this vision-based motion approach over motion sensors, e.g. regular motion sensors are having some drawback regarding range and time and require extra acquisition costs whereas this vision-based motion approach checks the difference between previous and present frame in software and if something changed in the image, then it takes it as motion and sends the frame to the inference process. Another advantage is that, even though the program will run all the time having the GPU at running state, the GPU memory transfer will be zero because GPU is not computing anything when there is no significant change in the present frame compared with the previous one; in this way we protect the GPU to heat-up as well.

4 Experimental Setup and Results

We considered implementing the 4 DL model architectures both on an Acer Predator Helios 300 PH317-51-78SZ laptop with an Intel Core i7-7700HQ, 16 GB DDR4 RAM memory and the Nvidia GTX 1060 GPU with 6 GB GDDR5/X frame buffer, 8 Gbps memory speed and 1708 boost clock (MHz) as well as on a Nvidia Jetson TX2 board [4] having the following configuration on the hardware side: CPU: ARM Cortex-A57 (quad-core) @ 2 GHz + Nvidia Denver2 (dual-core) @ 2 GHz, GPU: 256-core Pascal @ 1300 MHz, Memory: 8 GB 128-bit LPDDR4 @ 1866 MHz | 59.7 GB/s, and Storage: 32 GB eMMC 5.1. On the software side, on the Nvidia Jetson TX2 board, we used Nvidia JetPack SDK [36] with Linux Ubuntu18.04 LTS and Tensorflow 1.14.0 (Keras is used from within the tensorflow.keras) for both platforms. For the experimental results using webcam and motion detection, in the case of the laptop, we use its internal webcam, whereas, in the case of the Nvidia Jetson TX2 board, we used an external Logitech C920 HD Pro webcam. It is important to mention that with the help of the command line interface nvpmodel tool, we run all our Nvidia Jetson TX2 tests on the Max-P Core-All mode.

4.1 Nvidia GTX 1060 GPU and Nvidia Jetson TX2 Inference Comparison Regarding Speed Test and Power Consumption

Following, we will show a comparison between the laptop containing the Nvidia GTX 1060 GPU and Nvidia Jetson TX2 regarding inference speed testing and also explain why frames batch testing is important when trying to run a DL model in real-time on both platforms. Finally, we will present a power usage comparison with and without the proposed motion detection on both platforms and motivate our decision for why the Nvidia Jetson TX2 is our platform of choice when designing the solar-powered real-time DL-based system.

The inference speed testing results for the Nvidia GTX 1060 GPU and Nvidia Jetson TX2 are presented in Table 1 where different number of frames were tested on both platforms in order to evaluate the time it takes for each of the 4 DL models to classify a certain number of frames in under a second, both on a video as well as using a webcam.

Table 1. Inference Speed Testing between Nvidia GTX 1060 GPU and Nvidia Jetson TX2 on a video as well as using a webcam for VGG-19 (V), InceptionV3 (I), ResNet-50 (R) and MobileNetV2 (M) model architectures.

Number of frames	Nvidia GTX 1060 GPU inference time (Seconds)				Nvidia Jetson TX2 inference time (Seconds)			
	V	I	R	M	V	I	R	M
1	0.020	0.033	0.027	0.021	0.135	0.114	0.083	0.047
2	0.029	0.030	0.066	0.021	0.223	0.145	0.115	0.062
4	0.054	0.043	0.056	0.044	0.368	0.190	0.187	0.305
8	0.106	0.065	0.080	0.056	0.503	0.289	0.332	0.385
16	0.190	0.106	0.142	0.109	0.682	0.478	0.599	0.525
24	0.304	0.158	0.227	0.177	1.107	0.682	0.898	1.059

Because the results were similar, we presented their average values only once. As can be noticed in Table 1, the inference time of the Nvidia GTX 1060 GPU is always under 1 s for all 4 DL model architectures, even with 24 fps (we also tested the GTX 1060 GPU on up to 60 fps, but it is out of scope to present these results). In comparison, when running the VGG-19 and MobileNetV2 DL models on the Nvidia Jetson TX2 platform with 24 fps, we discovered that the inference time takes more than 1 s, so we decided to run all of our Nvidia Jetson TX2 experiments presented in this paper with 16 fps for all DL architectures.

Regarding frames batch testing, we tested the effect of batch size on computing time by forwarding not just one frame but an n number of frame batches to our model for prediction. The frames batch testing is very important because it helps us choose the fps parameter that finishes the task in the shortest amount of time with the highest number of frames (the higher the number of frames, the better the prediction) and lowest energy consumption without worries of service interruption when deploying later in a real-life scenario. Because of its 6 GB dedicated RAM, we found out that the Nvidia GTX 1060 GPU can make use of 100% GPU memory utilization when running the InceptionV3 and ResNet-50 model architectures but only of 80% GPU memory utilization (a higher value than this resulted in "out of memory" errors) when running the VGG-19 and MobileNetV2 model architectures in real-time. Nevertheless, the laptop containing the Nvidia GTX 1060 GPU can help all DL model architectures run the fastest prediction (when there is no latency between present frame and predicted animal class name on the frame) at different (higher) fps and faster time values (less seconds) as compared with the Nvidia Jetson TX2 which uses more than half of its memory for running the Linux framework, and which is able to run the fps batch testing at only maximum 30% of its memory utilization. The reason for this limitation is because with other ratio values it resulted in "out of memory" related errors.

In order to show the power usage comparison between the two platforms by maintaining a high inference accuracy (more fps = better accuracy), we decided to run all the experimental results presented in this paper with 30 fps and GPU memory ratio = 1 (for the InceptionV3 and ResNet-50) and 0.8 (for the VGG-19 and MobileNetV2) on the laptop containing the Nvidia GTX 1060 GPU and with 16 fps and GPU memory ratio = 0.3 for all 4 DL model architectures on the Nvidia Jetson TX2. Because the final goal is to run the inference in real-time on real-life scenarios, we decided to run the experiments regarding power usage only using the webcam and not also on a video like in the previously described experiments.

We calculated the power consumption for the Nvidia GTX 1060 GPU on our Linux laptop by running the command "sudo powerstat" and for the Nvidia Jetson TX2 board by using a convenient power measurement script [37] and also by using the command e.g. "sudo./tegrastats". We run the experimental results for 5 h (30 samples/values taken every 10 min) for each of the 4 DL models, both with and without motion detection for both platforms and presented the results in Table 2 and Table 3.

Table 2. Power usage comparison on the laptop (GTX 1060 GPU) running the proposed real-time animal class identification implementation during a 5 h test using the webcam without and with motion detection method for VGG-19 (V), InceptionV3 (I), ResNet-50 (R) and MobileNetV2 (M) model architectures. The y-axis represents the Watts value and the x-axis represents the total number of sample values taken every 10 min.

GTX 1060 GPU Idle (Watts)	GTX 1060 GPU without motion detection (Watts)				GTX 1060 GPU with motion detection (Watts)			
V, I, R, M	V	I	R	M	V	I	R	M
15.13	53.04	50.92	53.96	49.77	49.85	50.03	53.9	50.07
15.08	52.78	50.25	54.31	50.83	49.1	52.16	54.35	50.51
15.07	53.79	51.91	54.42	54.15	49.5	52.91	52.1	47.16
14.98	52.68	50.18	53.67	52.61	51.49	53.4	53.24	49.11
14.98	53.07	50.56	54.16	51.43	50.73	53.62	50.04	49.6
14.98	51.95	51.93	55.36	49.48	49.56	52.32	49.44	49.12
14.98	52.64	52.95	54.32	48.19	50.51	54.65	49.6	49.15

(continued)

Table 2. (*continued*)

GTX 1060 GPU Idle (Watts)	GTX 1060 GPU without motion detection (Watts)				GTX 1060 GPU with motion detection (Watts)			
V, I, R, M	V	I	R	M	V	I	R	M
14.91	52.3	54.74	53.54	49.57	49.8	55.06	48.89	48.51
14.9	52.76	54.67	53.51	50.21	52.28	54.47	48.18	47.9
14.79	51.98	54.24	53.62	50.52	50.38	53.38	48.58	47.03
14.89	51.89	52.43	53.63	50.03	50.07	53.39	48.41	48.15
15.43	51.76	54.67	53.91	48.75	46.16	52.49	48.14	46.01
15.16	51.53	54.99	53.99	49.34	47.56	51.8	48.56	47.54
15.09	51.98	55.17	53.37	50.31	48.39	52.59	48.12	48.23
14.91	51.91	54.67	53.28	49.53	48.84	51.59	48.61	47.35
14.77	52.04	54.48	54.26	47.62	49.52	54.31	48.2	48.19
14.8	51.87	55.17	53.84	46.91	45.83	54.95	48.26	46.24
14.83	52.09	54.6	52.6	46.77	47.53	54.5	47.32	46.97
15.07	52.02	54.95	52.28	46.46	48.33	54.31	47.01	45.28
21.87	52.18	54.9	53.22	45.72	48.91	53.98	46.92	45.89
18.49	52.19	54.31	51.23	45.23	49.51	54.38	45.07	45.02
22.44	52.31	55.59	53.26	47.62	46.95	53.84	44.75	44.47
23.74	51.97	54.45	53.99	49.43	48.24	52.23	43.26	43.19
24.79	52.5	55.81	53.35	50.23	48.97	53.46	43.47	43.25
21.46	52.36	54.72	53.51	50.32	49.43	53.03	48.91	45.87
21.83	52.48	54.24	52.01	48.26	49.43	52.72	49.14	46.83
17.77	52.4	55.88	52.12	49.52	46.91	53.91	48.64	45.34
15.15	52.21	55.72	51.69	49.77	48.62	54.3	53.9	44.53
14.22	52.22	54.96	51.42	50.83	49.2	53.57	54.35	45.23
14.01	52.05	55.85	51.44	54.15	49.52	53.51	52.1	46.91
Avg. 16.67	**Avg. 52.29**	**Avg. 53.99**	**Avg. 53.30**	**Avg. 49.21**	**Avg. 49.03**	**Avg. 53.36**	**Avg. 48.55**	**Avg. 46.95**
Max. 24.79	**Max. 53.79**	**Max. 55.88**	**Max. 55.36**	**Max. 54.15**	**Max. 52.28**	**Max. 55.06**	**Max. 54.35**	**Max. 50.51**

Without using the proposed motion detection method, the maximum power consumption of the laptop (Nvidia GTX 1060 GPU) was 24.79 W when in idle state, 53.79 W when running the VGG-19 model, 55.88 W when running the InceptionV3 model, 55.36 W when running the ResNet-50 model and 54.15 W when running the MobileNetV2 model. With the proposed motion detection method, the power consumption is lower for both platforms, justifying our decision to implement it. More exactly, the maximum power consumption of the laptop (Nvidia GTX 1060 GPU) when using the proposed motion detection method was 52.58 W when running the VGG-19 model, 55.06 W when running the InceptionV3 model, 54.35 W when running the ResNet-50 model and 50.51 W when running the MobileNetV2 model.

The maximum power consumption of the Nvidia Jetson TX2 without using the proposed motion detection method was 4.11 W when in idle state, 14.77 W when running the VGG-19 model, 12.87 W when running the InceptionV3 model, 11.74 W when running the ResNet-50 model and 10.47 W when running the MobileNetV2 model.

Table 3. Power usage comparison on the Nvidia Jetson TX2 board running the proposed real-time animal class identification implementation during a 5 h test using the webcam without and with motion detection method for VGG-19 (V), InceptionV3 (I), ResNet-50 (R) and MobileNetV2 (M) model architectures. The y-axis represents the Watts value and the x-axis represents the total number of sample values taken every 10 min.

Nvidia Jetson TX2 Idle (Watts)	Nvidia Jetson TX2 without motion detection (Watts)				Nvidia Jetson TX2 with motion detection (Watts)			
V, I, R, M	V	I	R	M	V	I	R	M
2.51	9.99	8.7	9.62	9.61	9.91	8.86	8.9	8.85
2.5	10.87	8.6	9.92	9.33	10.82	9.31	8.93	9.01
2.5	10.14	9.47	10.68	9.61	8.16	10	9.19	9.01
2.49	9.92	8.69	10.49	9.06	7.4	9.2	9.27	9.07
2.48	12.48	9.29	10.36	8.63	12.69	9.71	9.34	6.94
2.47	13.03	10.05	10.07	9.66	12.57	10.35	9.37	8.96
2.48	12.41	10.04	9.9	9.94	12.46	10.07	9.69	9.19
2.47	11.8	11.69	10.88	10.29	12.01	11.53	10.66	9.11
2.47	12.82	11.21	10.52	9.78	12.88	10.7	10.34	9.23
2.45	13.75	10.84	10.99	9.47	13.22	9.82	10.62	9.05
2.47	13.01	11.19	10.98	9.89	13.11	11.11	10.6	9.15
2.56	14.77	12.75	11.28	10.29	12.84	12.03	11.43	9.3
2.52	12.94	12.63	11.51	9.81	12.91	11.65	11.39	8.92
2.5	10.74	11.82	11.74	9.3	9.34	10.3	11.38	9.26
2.47	10.83	12.55	11.56	9.86	10.45	11.66	11.34	9.15
2.45	11.4	11.69	11.1	9.52	12.99	10.88	11.12	9.19
2.46	13.3	12.53	10.94	9.34	12.76	12.16	11.26	9.15
2.46	12.47	12.04	10.91	9.86	11.24	11.27	11.18	9.19
2.5	12.56	11.93	10.84	9.68	12.99	10.81	11.24	9.49
3.63	12.96	12.27	10.66	9.97	12.8	11.27	11.28	9.01
3.07	13.17	12.31	10.55	10.18	12.08	11.2	11.37	9.19
3.72	12.34	12.82	11.11	9.94	10.14	11.56	11.15	9.15
3.94	12.46	12.87	11.54	9.89	12.72	11.3	11.27	9.27
4.11	13.2	12.8	11.72	9.64	12.95	11.86	11.01	9.07
3.56	12.35	11.63	11.73	10.01	12.65	10.78	10.89	9.49
3.62	12.37	11.71	11.26	9.98	12.57	10.62	11.43	9.07
2.95	13.75	12.02	11.55	10.47	12.65	10.99	11.07	9.19
2.51	12.95	12.18	9.62	9.21	12.69	11.1	8.9	9.23

(*continued*)

Table 3. (*continued*)

Nvidia Jetson TX2 Idle (Watts)	Nvidia Jetson TX2 without motion detection (Watts)				Nvidia Jetson TX2 with motion detection (Watts)			
V, I, R, M	V	I	R	M	V	I	R	M
2.36	13.68	12.46	9.92	9.45	13.07	11.68	8.93	9.19
2.33	12.87	11.92	10.68	9.08	12.84	10.52	9.19	7.89
Avg. 2.76	**Avg. 12.37**	**Avg. 11.42**	**Avg. 10.90**	**Avg. 9.69**	**Avg. 11.93**	**Avg. 10.81**	**Avg. 10.61**	**Avg. 9.03**
Max. 4.11	**Max. 14.77**	**Max. 12.87**	**Max. 11.74**	**Max. 10.47**	**Max. 13.22**	**Max. 12.16**	**Max. 11.43**	**Max. 9.49**

The maximum power consumption of the Nvidia Jetson TX2 when using the proposed motion detection method was 13.22 W when running the VGG-19 model, 12.16 W when running the InceptionV3 model, 11.43 W when running the ResNet-50 model and 9.49 W when running the MobileNetV2 model. It is important to mention that in the case of the laptop we used the existent internal webcam, whereas for the Nvidia Jetson TX2 we used the Logitech C920 HD Pro webcam having an input voltage range from +9 V to +15 V DC and which was powered directly from the embedded board itself. Also, it can be observed that for both platforms, the motion detection method reduces the energy consumption by around 5%.

Considering the experimental results from Table 2 and Table 3, which show that the laptop containing the Nvidia GTX 1060 GPU consumes around 5 times more energy than the Nvidia Jetson TX2 and because we wanted to minimize the investment in the improvement of our solar tracker (which otherwise, in the case of laptop would have required a 5× increase in the number of solar cells and solar panel size, as well as updating the entire circuitry), we decided to make the Nvidia Jetson TX2 as the platform of choice for our solar-powered real-time DL-based system.

One of the main reasons for implementing an efficient solar-powered real-time DL-based system is the consideration of recent efforts regarding climate change [1, 3, 38] as well to bring awareness to future researchers about the possibility and necessity to use alternative sources of renewable and green energy such as that from the sun when designing real-time DL-based systems.

4.2 Self-sufficient Solar-Powered Real-Time Deep Learning-Based System

As seen previously in Table 2 and Table 3, the maximum power consumed by the Nvidia Jetson TX2 was that of 14.77 W without using motion detection and 13.22 W when using motion detection for the VGG-19 model architecture during a 5 h test. The architecture that had the lowest power consumption during the 5-h test was the MobileNetV2 model architecture, with 9.69 W when not using motion detection and 9.03 W when using motion detection.

In order to make our Nvidia Jetson TX2 board also autonomous from the energy needs point of view when running inference using the 4 DL model architectures [8] in real-time, instead of using a traditional power plug, we decided to connect it to our previous proposed solar tracking device that uses the cast-shadow principle [6] which we updated and described in Sect. 3.1 of this paper. A diagram block of the summarized solar-powered real-time DL-based system can be seen in Fig. 3. Our improved solar panel comes equipped with 60 polycrystalline cells that are able to provide a maximum output voltage of around 17 V as can be seen in Table 4. The increase from 40 to 60 in the number of PV solar cells is justified by the fact that it reduces the risk of voltage drops below 12 V in order to keep the battery charged continuously even under extreme weather conditions (e.g. cloudy days).

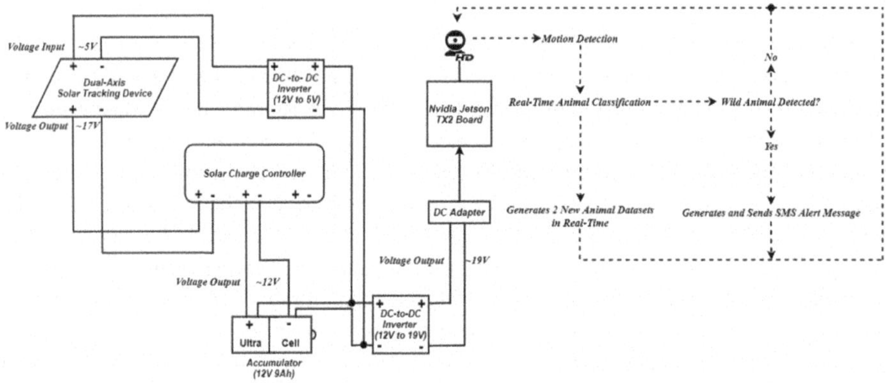

Fig. 3. Connection diagram of the proposed autonomous solar-powered real-time DL-based system.

Table 4. Experimental results regarding the energy generated by our solar tracker, the energy stored by the accumulator and the energy requirements of the Nvidia Jetson TX2 when running the VGG-19 (V), InceptionV3 (I), ResNet-50 (R) and MobileNetV2 (M) model architectures in real-time using the external webcam with motion detection during a 5 h test time.

Energy generation of our solar tracker					Energy storage of our solar tracker			
Test time (Hour)	V	I	R	M	V	I	R	M
	Voltage gain [V]				Voltage [V]			
9:00	17.3	16.98	16.67	16.35	12.8	12.74	12.7	12.66
10:00	16.03	16.3	16.59	17.06	12.6	12.66	12.71	12.75
11:00	17.14	17.06	16.99	16.91	12.8	12.8	12.79	12.78
12:00	16.83	16.64	16.46	16.29	12.78	12.76	12.75	12.74
13:00	16.1	16.08	16.07	16.05	12.73	12.76	12.8	12.87
Avg. value	**16.68**	**16.61**	**16.55**	**16.53**	**12.74**	**12.74**	**12.75**	**12.76**

(*continued*)

Table 4. (*continued*)

	Current gain [A]				Charging current [A]			
9:00	1.34	1.36	1.37	1.39	0.84	0.87	0.89	0.92
10:00	1.4	1.22	1.04	0.86	0.94	0.86	0.78	0.65
11:00	0.67	0.67	0.66	0.66	0.9	0.87	0.84	0.82
12:00	0.66	0.64	0.64	0.75	0.92	0.85	0.8	0.79
13:00	0.66	0.65	0.65	0.69	0.88	0.83	0.81	0.8
Avg. value	**0.94**	**0.90**	**0.87**	**0.87**	**0.89**	**0.85**	**0.82**	**0.79**
	Power gain [W]				Power [W]			
9:00	23.18	23.09	22.83	22.72	10.75	11.08	11.30	11.64
10:00	22.44	19.88	17.25	14.67	11.84	10.88	9.91	8.28
11:00	11.48	11.43	11.21	11.16	11.52	11.13	10.74	10.47
12:00	11.10	10.64	10.53	12.21	11.75	10.84	10.2	10.06
13:00	10.62	10.45	10.44	11.07	11.20	10.59	10.36	10.29
Avg. value	**15.76**	**15.09**	**14.45**	**14.36**	**11.41**	**10.90**	**10.50**	**10.14**

Voltage readings for DC-to-DC Inverter (12 V to 19 V)

	Voltage output [V]			
9:00	19.20	19.15	19.16	19.18
10:00	19.17	19.14	19.12	19.10
11:00	19.09	19.10	19.11	19.05
12:00	19.02	19.04	19.05	19.06
13:00	19.03	19.02	19.07	19.00
Avg. value	**19.10**	**19.09**	**19.10**	**19.07**

Energy requirement of the Nvidia Jetson TX2 with external webcam and using motion detection

	Voltage draw [V]			
9:00	19.1	19.1	19.1	19.09
10:00	19.08	19.08	19.08	19.07
11:00	19.07	19.07	19.07	19.06
12:00	19.07	19.08	19.07	19.08
13:00	19.07	19.07	19.06	19.05
Avg. value	**19.07**	**19.07**	**19.07**	**19.07**
	Current draw [A]			
9:00	0.58	0.55	0.51	0.46
10:00	0.52	0.51	0.49	0.46
11:00	0.56	0.62	0.52	0.47
12:00	0.42	0.56	0.53	0.47
13:00	0.66	0.54	0.52	0.47
Avg. value	**0.54**	**0.55**	**0.51**	**0.46**
	Power consumption [W]			
9:00	11.07	10.50	9.74	8.78
10:00	9.92	9.73	9.34	8.77
11:00	10.67	11.82	9.91	8.95
12:00	8	10.68	10.1	8.96
13:00	12.58	10.29	9.91	8.95
Avg. value	**10.44**	**10.60**	**9.8**	**8.88**

The solar charge controller is a robust all-in-one control system that provides three input-output ports: one dedicated to solar modules, one dedicated to feeding the battery from the PV panel with collected voltage, and one output module for connecting a current load. Since our main objective is to store solar energy in the accumulator, we only use two of the available ports.

A few notable features of the solar charge controller are microcontroller unit control, built-in timer, settable voltage and full protection from overvoltage and overcurrent. The Ultra Cell accumulator is a 12 V, 9 Ah acid-plumb battery that is generally used nowadays in UPS systems to provide energy for desktop systems in case of local power outages. Due to its chemical composition and charging current of around 1 A, the charging and discharging time can be analyzed both theoretically as well as in real-time scenarios. The main formula that is generally used in charging time calculus is given by the following equation:

$$T = Ah/A \tag{1}$$

where T represents the charging time, Ah depicts the Ampere hour rating of the battery and A denotes the charging current in Amperes. In our experimental results, first, we calculated the charging current for the 9 Ah battery in theory as well as in practice:

1) As we know, in theory, the charging current should be 10% of the battery's Ah rating. Therefore, charging current for a 9 Ah Battery = 9 Ah × (10/100) = 0.9 A. However, due to some possible current losses that can appear on the battery, instead of exactly 0.9 A, we consider only a value between 0.9 and 1.1 A for the charging purpose. Supposing we take 1 A for charging purposes, so charging current for 9 Ah Battery = 9/1 = 9 h (Hrs), a situation that usually occurs only in theory.
2) As we know, in practice, it has been noted that 40% of losses occur in the case of battery charging. Consequently, the formula will be: 9 × (40/100) = 3.6 resulting in 9 Ah × 40% of losses. Therefore, 9 + 3.6 = 12.6 Ah resulting in 9 Ah + Losses. According to formula (1), we will now substitute the new values and obtain:

$$12.6/1 = 12.6\,\text{h} \tag{2}$$

Therefore, because the accumulator requires 1 A charging current, its 9 Ah capacity takes almost 13 h to fully charge with solar energy from the solar tracker. However, because our solar-powered real-time DL-based system does not drain any solar energy during the night time, this does not influence our experimental outcomes. Consequently, the total discharging time of the accumulator can be determined by applying the following formula:

$$9\text{Ah}/0.6 = 15\,\text{h} \tag{3}$$

Since our accumulator is limited to a 12 V storage capacity, as can be seen in Fig. 3, we used two voltage inverters. The first DC-to-DC inverter was interconnected in parallel so that the battery's output voltage would be increased to around 19 V as can be seen in Table 4, in order to satisfy the Nvidia Jetson TX2 board's (consumer) supply voltage requirements in a real-life scenario. The second DC-to-DC inverter was connected between the energy storage element and the back of our solar panel in order to power the automation equipment (1 × Arduino UNO, 1 × Optocoupler, 2 × L298N, 2 × stepper motors) directly from the accumulator. Due to the implemented mechanical blocking elements, when in idle state, our solar tracking device consumes less energy (0.32 W) with the Arduino UNO and L298N integrated circuits and reaches 2 W power consumption [6] when it updates its position to optimize sun ray exposure (a process which usually takes up to 5 s).

This 2 W power consumption can be successfully covered by the accumulator's solar energy provision, proving that our entire solar-powered real-time DL-based system can run 100% using renewable and green energy from the sun. Finally, we linked the output of the first DC-to-DC inverter to the input of the Nvidia Jetson TX2 board with the help of a dedicated DC adapter, as seen in Fig. 3 as well.

The experimental cases were carried out with our previously described setup over a 5 h time span for each of our previously trained architectures (VGG-19, InceptionV3, ResNet-50, and MobileNetV2) [8] during 4 days test time. Our results show that the output voltage and current values of our solar panel are always maintained at an optimum level despite changing weather conditions (e.g. partial clouds in the afternoon).

Also, regarding the energy requirement of the Nvidia Jetson TX2 with the external webcam using the implemented motion detection method during a 5 h test, we present the results in Table 4. These results prove that a real-time DL-based system can easily take advantage of renewable and green energy sources such as solar energy from a solar tracking device in order to become self-sustaining from the energy needs point of view. More exactly, we can observe that the improved solar tracker generates in average around 15 Wh, the accumulator stores around 11 Wh and the Nvidia Jetson TX2 board consumes not more than around 10 Wh when running all 4 DL models with the motion detection method in real-time.

The experimental cases were considered relevant for our work due to the fact that the DL-based system can run autonomously using free energy from the portable solar tracker, thus eliminating the need of connecting it to an AC network. In order to check the working conditions and take full control of the Nvidia Jetson TX2 board when connected to our solar tracker, we made use of a 7 inch portable monitor that was connected with the help of a HDMI as well as a micro-to-USB cable to the Nvidia Jetson TX2 board, as can be seen on the right side of Fig. 1.

5 Conclusions and Future Work

This paper presents, to the best of our knowledge, the first solar-powered real-time DL-based system in the literature that is self-sustaining from the energy point of view, can run inference using 100% solar energy and which is composed of a dual-axis solar tracking device based on cast-shadow principle [6] and a low-power embedded platform called Nvidia Jetson TX2. In order to justify the choice of this platform, experimental results, especially regarding the energy consumption while running 4 DL model architectures (VGG-19, InceptionV3, ResNet-50 and MobileNetV2) in real-time [8] are made also on a laptop containing the Nvidia GTX 1060 (6 GB) GPU. Additionally, in order to reduce the power consumption of the entire solar-powered real-time DL-based system, we also implemented a motion detection method that triggers the inference process only when there is movement in the frame. Details about the construction of the entire solar-powered real-time DL-based system as well as calculations regarding the time needed for the accumulator to be charged with solar energy as well as discharged by the Nvidia Jetson TX2 when running the 4 DL models are also taken into consideration. Experimental results show that the Nvidia Jetson TX2 platform is a very good choice when designing an efficient solar-powered real-time DL-based system, consuming only around 10 Wh of power as compared to around 50 Wh consumed by a laptop.

As future work, we plan to run similar experiments also on other low-power platforms such as the Nvidia Jetson Nano Developer Kit, Google Coral, Raspberry Pi 4 Model B (4 GB) and also on FPGAs, in order to show that real-time DL-based systems can run inference 100% on solar energy using even less energy than we demonstrated, to the best of our knowledge, for the first time in literature, in this paper. Additionally to inference, we also want to train a few other state-of-the-art DL model architectures using 100% solar energy from our solar tracker on the above-mentioned platforms, with the intent to encourage new researchers to investigate the combination of green energy and AI, eventually proposing new green energy-based DL metrics. We believe that a "green" approach can lead researchers to a better understanding of how to evaluate the performance of DL-based systems and will also result in a more friendly and respectful attitude towards nature and life on this planet.

References

1. Strubell, E., Ganesh, A., McCallum, A.: Energy and policy considerations for deep learning in NLP. arXiv:1906.02243 (2019)
2. Schmidt, V., Luccioni, A., Mukkavilli, S.K., Balasooriya, N., Sankaran, K., Chayes, J., Bengio, Y.: Visualizing the consequences of climate change using cycle-consistent adversarial networks. arXiv:1905.03709 (2019)
3. UN Sustainable Development Goals. https://www.un.org/sustainabledevelopment/sustainable-development-goals/. Accessed 01 Dec 2019
4. Nvidia Jetson TX2. https://www.nvidia.com/en-us/autonomous-machines/embedded-systems/jetson-tx2/. Accessed 01 Dec 2019
5. Yan, J., Yang, Y., Elia Campana, P., He, J.: City-level analysis of subsidy-free solar photovoltaic electricity price, profits and grid parity in China. Nat. Energy **4**, 709–717 (2019)
6. Rotar, R., Jurj, S.L., Opritoiu, F., Vladutiu, M.: Position optimization method for a solar tracking device using the cast-shadow principle. In: IEEE 24th International Symposium for Design and Technology in Electronic Packaging (SIITME), Iasi, Romania, pp. 61–70. IEEE (2018)

7. Carballo, J.A., Bonilla, J., Berenguel, M., Fernandez-Reche, J., García, G.: New approach for solar tracking systems based on computer vision, low cost hardware and deep learning. arXiv:1809.07048v1 (2018)
8. Jurj, S.L., Opritoiu, F., Vladutiu, M.: Real-time identification of animals found in domestic areas of Europe. In: Proceedings of the SPIE 11433, Twelfth International Conference on Machine Vision (ICMV 2019), 1143313, 31 January 2020. https://doi.org/10.1117/12.2556376
9. Bradski, G.: The openCV library. Dr. Dobb's J. Softw. Tools **120**, 122–125 (2000)
10. Rungsuptaweekoon, K., Visoottiviseth, V., Takano, R.: Evaluating the power efficiency of deep learning inference on embedded GPU systems. In: 2nd International Conference on Information Technology (INCIT), Nakhonpathom, Thailand, pp. 1–5. IEEE (2017)
11. Yudin, D., Slavioglo, D.: Usage of fully convolutional network with clustering for traffic light detection. In: 7th Mediterranean Conference on Embedded Computing (MECO), Budva, Montenegro, pp. 1–6. IEEE (2018)
12. Shihadeh, J., Ansari, A., Ozunfunmi, T.: Deep learning based image classification for remote medical diagnosis. In: IEEE Global Humanitarian Technology Conference (GHTC), San Jose, CA, USA, pp. 1–8. IEEE (2018)
13. Yin, X., Chen, L., Zhang, X., Gao, Z.: Object detection implementation and optimization on embedded GPU system. In: IEEE International Symposium on Broadband Multimedia Systems and Broadcasting (BMSB), Valencia, Spain, pp. 1–5. IEEE (2018)
14. Arechiga, A.P., Michaels, A.J., Black, J.T.: Onboard image processing for small satellites. In: NAECON 2018 - IEEE National Aerospace and Electronics Conference, Dayton, OH, USA, pp. 234–240. IEEE (2018)
15. Vandersteegen, M., Van Beeck, K., Goedemé, T.: Super accurate low latency object detection on a surveillance UAV. arXiv:1904.02024v1 (2019)
16. Špaňhel, J., Sochor, J., Makarov, A.: Detection of traffic violations of road users based on convolutional neural networks. In: 14th Symposium on Neural Networks and Applications (NEUREL), Belgrade, Serbia, pp. 1–6. IEEE (2018)
17. Yuan, L., Lu, F.: Real-time ear detection based on embedded systems. In: International Conference on Machine Learning and Cybernetics (ICMLC), Chengdu, China, pp. 115–120. IEEE (2018)
18. Liu, S., Li, X., Gao, M., Cai, Y., Nian, R., Li, P., Yan, T., Lendasse, A.: Embedded online fish detection and tracking system via YOLOv3 and parallel correlation filter. In: OCEANS 2018 MTS/IEEE Charleston, Charleston, SC, USA, pp. 1–6. IEEE (2018)
19. Saypadith, S., Aramvith, S.: Real-time multiple face recognition using deep learning on embedded GPU system. In: Asia-Pacific Signal and Information Processing Association Annual Summit and Conference (APSIPA ASC), Honolulu, HI, USA, pp. 1318–1324. IEEE (2018)
20. Zhang, W., Sun, H., Zhao, D., Xu, L., Liu, X., Zhou, J., Ning, H., Guo, Y., Yang, S.: A streaming cloud platform for real-time video processing on embedded devices. IEEE Trans. Cloud Comput. **13**, 1 (2019)
21. Goyal, M., Reeves, N.D., Rajbhandari, S., Yap, M.H.: Robust methods for real-time diabetic foot ulcer detection and localization on mobile devices. IEEE J. Biomed. Health Inf. **23**, 1730–1741 (2019)
22. Modasshir, M., Li, A.Q., Rekleitis, I.: Deep neural networks: a comparison on different computing platforms. In: 15th Conference on Computer and Robot Vision (CRV), Toronto, ON, Canada, pp. 383–389. IEEE (2018)
23. Vaidya, B., Paunwala, C.: Comparative analysis of motion based and feature based algorithms for object detection and tracking. In: International Conference on Soft Computing and its Engineering Applications (icSoftComp), Changa, India. pp. 1–7. IEEE (2017)

24. Zivkovic, Z.: Improved adaptive Gaussian mixture model for background subtraction. In: Proceedings of the 17th International Conference on Pattern Recognition (ICPR), Cambridge, UK, pp. 28–31. IEEE (2004)
25. Stauffer, C., Grimson, W.E.L.: Adaptive background mixture models for real-time tracking. In: Proceedings 1999 IEEE Computer Society Conference on Computer Vision and Pattern Recognition (Cat. No PR00149), Fort Collins, CO, USA, pp. 246–252. IEEE (1999)
26. Moon, S., Lee, J., Nam, D., Yoo, W., Kim, W.: A comparative study on preprocessing methods for object tracking in sports events. In: 20th International Conference on Advanced Communication Technology (ICACT), Chuncheon-si Gangwon-do, Korea (South), pp. 460–462. IEEE (2018)
27. Godbehere, A.B., Matsukawa, A., Goldberg, K.: Visual tracking of human visitors under variable-lighting conditions for a responsive audio art installation. In: 2012 American Control Conference (ACC), Montreal, QC, Canada, pp. 4305–4312. IEEE (2012)
28. Kaewtrakulpong, P., Bowden, R.: An improved adaptive background mixture model for realtime tracking with shadow detection. In: Remagnino, P., Jones, G.A., Paragios, N., Regazzoni, C.S. (eds.) Video-Based Surveillance Systems, pp. 135–144. Springer, Boston (2002)
29. Berthod, C., Kristensen, S.T., Strandberg, R., Odden, J.O., Nie, S., Hameiri, Z., Sætre, T.O.: Temperature sensitivity of multicrystalline silicon solar cells. IEEE J. Photovolt. **9**, 957–964 (2019)
30. Simonyan, K., Zisserman, A.: Very deep convolutional networks for large-scale image recognition. arXiv:1409.1556v6 (2015)
31. Szegedy, C., Liu, W., Jia, Y., Sermanet, P., Reed, S., Anguelov, D., Erhan, D., Vanhoucke, V., Rabinovich, A.: Going deeper with convolutions. arXiv:1409.4842v1 (2014)
32. He, K., et al.: Deep residual learning for image recognition. arXiv preprint arXiv:1512.03385 . (2015)
33. Sandler, M., Howard, A., Zhu, M., Zhmoginov, A., Chen, L.C.: MobileNetV2: inverted residuals and linear bottlenecks. arXiv:1801.04381v4 (2019)
34. TensorflowProtobuf. https://github.com/tensorflow/tensorflow/blob/master/tensorflow/core/protobuf/config.proto/. Accessed 01 Dec 2019
35. Twilio Programmable SMS. https://www.twilio.com/docs/sms/send-messages. Accessed 01 Dec 2019
36. JetPack. https://developer.nvidia.com/embedded/jetpack/. Accessed 01 Dec 2019
37. Convenient Power Measurement Script on the Jetson TX2/Tegra X2. https://embeddeddl.wordpress.com/2018/04/25/convenient-power-measurements-on-the-jetson-tx2-tegra-x2-board/. Accessed 01 Dec 2019
38. Schwartz, R., Dodge, J., Smith, N.A., Etzioni, O.: Green AI. arXiv:1907.10597v3 (2019)

Leveraging Radar Features to Improve Point Clouds Segmentation with Neural Networks

Alessandro Cennamo[1,2(✉)], Florian Kaestner[1], and Anton Kummert[2]

[1] Aptiv Services Deutschland GmbH, 42199 Wuppertal, Germany
{alessandro.cennamo,florian.kaestner}@aptiv.com
[2] University of Wuppertal (BUW), 42199 Wuppertal, Germany
kummert@uni-wuppertal.de

Abstract. Radar sensors, unlike lidars or cameras, can measure objects' instantaneous velocity and composition. However, the ability to process and retrieve spatial information from radar point clouds has not yet been fully established. In this work, we propose a key technique for improving the performance of standard machine learning point-wise processing methods on radar point clouds. We show that a network can learn to extract object-related signatures for every point using automotive radar measurements. In addition, we propose RadarPCNN, a novel architecture for performing semantic segmentation, specifically designed for radar point clouds. RadarPCNN uses PointNet++, aided with mean shift as feature extractor module and an attention mechanism to fuse information from different neighborhood levels. We show that our model outperforms state-of-the-art solutions on our dataset.

Keywords: Radar point clouds · Neural network · Segmentation

1 Introduction

During the last years, vehicles have been equipped with sensors such as camera, radar and lidar to achieve autonomous driving capabilities [3]. While cameras produce data in the form of images – that are efficiently consumed by Convolutional Neural Networks (CNNs) [17,18] –, radars and lidars data are often processed as point clouds (PCs): 3D points representing reflections of the surrounding objects. However, CNNs do not scale well to such unstructured data-format [21], therefore new Machine Learning (ML) techniques have been devised.

The most simple method consists of structuring the data – by voxel/pixel encoding of the input PC –, thus enabling the application of 3D CNNs [4,22]. Similarly, multi-view representation techniques take several snapshots of the input and process each image with a different CNN: the features computed for every view are then fused to perform 3D shape recognition or semantic segmentation [7,20]. Despite such approaches have achieved dominating performance

L. Iliadis et al. (Eds.): EANN 2020, INNS 2, pp. 119–131, 2020.
https://doi.org/10.1007/978-3-030-48791-1_8

on a variety of tasks, they either significantly increase the input size, thus raising the computational demands, or exhibit loss of input information. In order to overcome these limitations, other approaches use order-invariant networks to consume raw PCs. Although this constraint hardens the task of extracting information of spatial correlation between points, several researchers have succeeded in the design of architectures capable to achieve state-of-the-art performance [11,14,15]. These approaches possess the advantage of maintaining low computational/memory demands while retaining all the input information.

Over the last decades, radar has been extensively used in the automotive industry [1,5], yet object recognition/classification in urban scenes remains an open challenge. Unfortunately, though extremely low-cost, automotive radars are different than other sensors. For instance, radar PCs are the result of a thresholding process and come with much lower density than lidar PCs. Hence any grid-based approach would result in either sparse cells and/or resolution degradation [8]. On the other hand, radars can capture intrinsic object-related properties. Therefore, we think that the ability of point-wise processing methods to exploit all the information present in the input plays a major role when consuming radar PCs.

We believe that addressing/exploiting intrinsic characteristics of this specific sensor is of paramount importance to efficiently process radar data. In this work, we propose to build informative point signatures by leveraging radar object features. We use a shared fully connected (FC) network to design a pre-processing module that can compute new per-point features, facilitating the final segmentation task. The output of this module can then be used as an input to any existent point-wise approach. We show that the proposed pre-processing module improves the semantic segmentation performance of PointNet++ [16] on our radar dataset. In addition, we develop RadarPCNN, a novel architecture for performing semantic segmentation on raw PCs, specifically designed for radar. We use the pre-processing module proposed in this work and the mean shift clustering algorithm [9] to improve usage of spatial relationship in such sparse data. We also use an attention mechanism to let the network learn the features of major interest. Our scheme uses PointNet++ [14] as a feature extractor module to directly consume point clouds. Finally, we show that RadarPCNN is able to achieve state-of-the-art semantic segmentation performance on radar data, outperforming PointNet++.

2 Related Works

Recently, point clouds have played a paramount role in a broad variety of applications by enabling detailed understanding of complex 3D structures/objects. Formally, a point cloud is defined as an unordered collection of $N \in \mathbb{N}$ individual points $x_i \in \mathbb{R}^m$, $i = 1, \ldots, N$ whose elements are the 2D/3D spatial coordinates. In addition, each point could possess supplementary features like color (RGBD sensor) or reflection intensity (lidar). The semantic segmentation task on such inputs consists in the estimation of a function $f : \mathbb{R}^{N \times m} \to \mathbb{R}^{N \times d}$

such that every point gets a score of the probability to belong to every one of d semantic classes. In this work we focus on point-wise processing – rather than grid-based – methods, because of their ability to exploit all the information in the input.

2.1 Deep Learning on Point Clouds

Despite DL has proven to be an effective tool for extracting information from low level data, the unordered nature of PCs precludes the direct application of standard techniques like CNNs, Recurrent Neural Networks (RNNs) or FC nets.

PointNet [15] represents a milestone for point-wise processing approaches. The authors focused on the development of a network which is invariant to point-order. They achieved this by the joint deployment of two elements: shared FC networks – to compute point-related features – and max-pooling – for global features aggregation. Furthermore, they devised T-Net – a transformation network resembling PointNet – to achieve invariance under different viewpoints. In spite of the network's good performance on a broad variety of tasks, it fails to capture the local structure induced by the input space geometry.

The authors of PointNet observed that a key factor for the success of CNNs has been their ability to hierarchically abstract local low-level structures into high-level descriptive patterns. Based on this observation, Qi et al. devised PointNet++ [14], a hierarchical architecture capable of extracting geometric information from overlapping sub-regions of the input. The network follows an encoder-decoder structure: set-abstraction (SA) layers abstract groups of points into local region descriptors, while feature-propagation (FP) layers serve to propagate high-level features back into low-level points. Skip connections are used to enrich single-point signatures and PointNet is selected as the local feature extractor module in SA layers. PointNet++ is currently considered the benchmark for point-wise processing architectures.

Further, Li et al. noticed that, provided some ordering, classical convolution could be directly applied to point clouds. Therefore, they proposed to weight and permute the input by means of a learned $\mathcal{X}$ matrix to achieve order equivariance. The resulting $\mathcal{X}$-Conv layer performs a $\mathcal{X}$-transformation on local neighborhood of points and then applies standard convolution. Finally, the authors developed PointCNN [11], a hierarchical encoder-decoder network using $\mathcal{X}$-Conv as feature extractor module. The work shows that the architecture achieves state-of-the-art results on a broad variety of tasks, thus proving the effectiveness of the $\mathcal{X}$-transformation.

2.2 Deep Learning on Radar Point Clouds

Radar has the advantage of being more reliable under various weather conditions, e.g. rain/fog. This aspect, along with the ability to measure instantaneous velocity, makes them particularly well-suited for automotive applications.

The lack of pubic radar datasets hardens the development of new ML techniques, therefore, during the last years, researchers resorted to conventional methods (described in the previous section) to process private radar data. Schumann et al. addressed the classification problem of radar reflections between 6 classes: car, pedestrian, pedestrian group, bike, truck and static targets [16]. They equipped two vehicles with several sensors and collected training and test data. Then, they trained a PointNet++ [14] to perform semantic segmentation. The authors proved that point-wise techniques designed to process dense PCs can effectively process radar data. In addition, they showed how the network can benefit from the introduction of radar-specific features (such as Doppler and RCS) as supplementary dimensions. Feng et al. wanted to classify radar reflections as vehicle or guardrail [8]. They resorted again to the PointNet++ architecture, with few minor tweaks: hand-crafted statistics of the area around the representative points (such as density, points number and covariance) were collected and appended to the neighborhood tensors. The authors showed how these features contribute to enhance the network performance.

A different approach consists of clustering together points and then deploy a ML technique to classify the whole cluster. In this direction, Wöhler et al. used DBSCAN [6] to group together reflections belonging to the same object [19]. Lately, they calculated clusters statistics from radar measurements – i.e. x, y, Doppler and RCS – and performed multi-class classification using a long-short term memory (LSTM) network [10]. The authors proved that the LSTM classifier outperforms the random forest algorithm [2]. Moreover, they ranked the cluster features according to their importance for the classification task and showed that spatial and Doppler-related features dominate the ranking.

3 Our Method

Unlike lidar, radar reflections contain valuable information about the object generating them. Classical radar processing methods generally exploit this property in a two-stage process: first, reflections from the same object are clustered together, then, they manually extract statistics from radar measurements to build cluster signatures [13]. Unfortunately, these approaches strongly rely on clustering algorithms to group measurements of the same instance. However, each single reflection contains object-related information.

Considering a ML framework, we believe that a network can learn to encode radar features into point-signatures useful for further point-wise processing. In this way we overcome the limitations of clustering algorithms. Herein, we propose to use a data-learned pre-processing module for generating new PC features, uniquely based on single-reflection measurements. Specifically, we deploy a shared FC network to produce a deeper version of the input: for each point, our module derives new features by combining together x, y, Doppler and RCS. Therefore, the new input will have the same spatial point locations, but features abstracting the radar perception of the object. In this way, we assume that the network would learn to cast the input into a representation that facilitates the classification task, by providing better separations between reflections from objects with different radar properties. Finally, due to the simplicity of the process, we think that our approach can be easily extended to any other architecture consuming raw PCs.

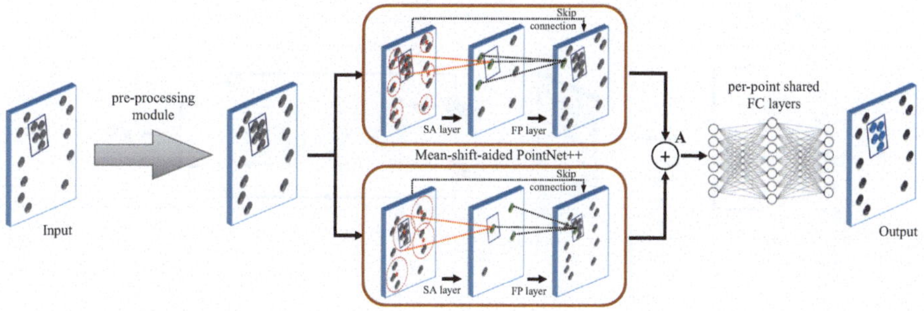

Fig. 1. RadarPCNN architecture. Our pre-processing module computes (32) new features for each reflection. Two single-layer PointNet++ extract per-point neighborhood-dependent features. FPS is substituted by mean shift to select the representative points (red stars). Per-point features are finally fused using an attention mechanism and processed with two shared fully-connected layers to produce the class scores.

PointNet++ [14] is a benchmarking architecture in the point-wise processing field. It is notoriously good at fusing information of point proximity to build useful object-part signatures. However, radar is extremely poor at providing this information. Therefore, despite this architecture has proven to perform well on radar PCs [8,16], we think that it does not represent the optimal solution for consuming such particular data. We believe that tailoring the network to operate at object level and improving the usage of spatial relationship would result in a more efficient processing. To this end, we develop RadarPCNN, a point-wise processing technique for performing semantic segmentation on radar PCs.

Figure 1 shows the architecture. Our network uses the proposed pre-processing module to build a deeper input for the remaining part. Here, meaningful classification features must be computed for every point. We decide to use PointNet++ as feature extractor module because of its ability to abstract information from local neighborhoods. However, we alter the architecture by replacing the farthest point sampling (FPS) method with mean shift (MS), to enhance usage of the scarce spatial proximity information. Specifically, we sum up Gaussian kernels (with given bandwidth) centered at each point location and use local maxima of the resulting distribution as representative points in the SA layer. Notice how we do not rely on mean shift at the grouping stage, but only to sample more meaningful representative points. In this way, MS helps the network to optimize the sampling process, obeying to the high-level input shape. Furthermore, we decide to discard the hierarchical PointNet++ structure in favor of several independent object-focused ones. More precisely, in this work we use two single-layer PointNet++. One seeking for small objects such as pedestrians, using dense representative points (MS with bandwidth 2.0) and neighborhood areas below 2 m. The other focuses on larger targets like cars/trucks, using representative points with bandwidth 8.0 and neighborhood areas from 4 to 8 m.

The two mini-PointNet++ output the input point locations, with different neighborhoods-dependent features. Since every point has two feature vectors,

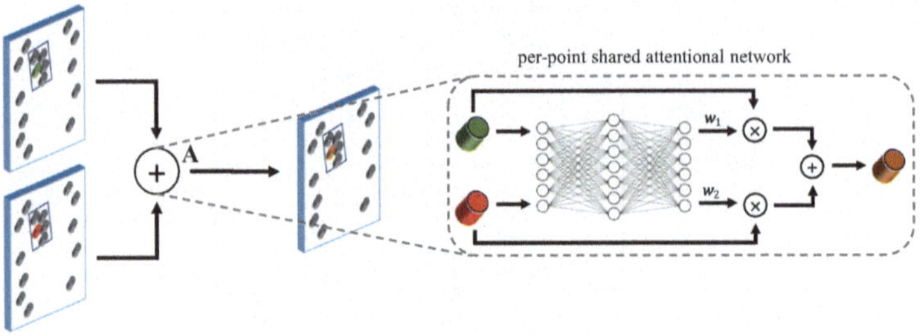

Fig. 2. Attention mechanism. For each point, the features produced by the top and bottom branches (see Fig. 1) are used as input of a FC regression network. The output of the network is used to perform a weighted combination of the input features.

similarly to [20], we let the network decide the best way to combine them. In particular, we design the attention mechanism showed in Fig. 2. Given a point location, the features computed from top (green point) and bottom (red point) PointNet++ are used as input to a shared FC network which regresses two scalars (w_1 and w_2). These scalars are then used to perform a weighted combination of the two vectors and build the classification features (orange point). In this way the network would learn to weight the features vectors based on its importance to the final task. Finally, the classification features are processed with a shared FC network to produce the output semantic segmentation score.

As every layer entails a differentiable operation, the whole network can be trained in an end-to-end fashion, using the output segmentation loss.

4 Experiments

In this section, we provide the results achieved on a 2-semantic-classes segmentation task: moving pedestrian and moving vehicle. We report precision, recall and F_1 score on the two positive classes along with the macro-average version of them (where each class contributes equally). We also show confusion matrices of the three total classes (pedestrian, vehicle, other).

4.1 Dataset

We conduct experiments on our dataset, composed of real-world radar reflections in urban scenes under different weather conditions. The data were collected by a fleet of vehicles equipped with six 77 GHz radars (sides, front and back corners), recording targets up to ±90 m, with a field-of-view of ±75°. In total, our dataset counts 84 video sequences and more than 40 million points annotated accordingly to two classes: pedestrian and vehicle. Any other point is labeled as other/clutter. In this work, we focus on moving objects because automotive radars provide low information about stationary ones: indeed, they share the same Doppler of other still instances (e.g. buildings), therefore only RCS can be used for classification purposes. A crucial decision in our evaluation is the definition of a moving object. We consider a pedestrian/vehicle to be moving if its ground-truth velocity is above 0.5/2.5 m/s. It is worth noting that high threshold values would make the problem trivial, while low ones might confuse the network. However, we find out that these parameters mostly impact the numerical results: the network would still be able to classify points slightly below the thresholds as moving. Therefore, we force reflections below these values to be transparent during training and evaluation. Yet, points from parked vehicles (which do not move at all) are present in the other/clutter class. Table 1 contains the points distribution in the dataset configuration described. We create the train/test sets to contain the same distribution of rainy/cloudy/clear scenes.

4.2 Settings

Each video sequence in our dataset is divided into frames containing a few hundreds of points. Similarly to [16], we aggregate reflections from adjacent frames (200 ms) and compensate the point locations to the ego-vehicle position at the last frame. Moreover, we fix the input size to 1200 points and use the ego-compensated Doppler feature to sample with importance. In more detail, if the input has more than 1200 points, we give higher sampling probability to reflections with large absolute Doppler value. If it has less than 1200 points, we duplicate reflections in the same fashion. Bearing in mind that Doppler is only a radial velocity measure, in this way we decrease the probability of discarding moving objects reflections or duplicating static ones, thus increasing the positive class populations. Furthermore, since our radar sensors have a low elevation resolution, we decide to discard this information and use the Doppler value as z-coordinate. RCS is used as points feature. Regarding the representative points, we set a fixed number of 500/150 positions for the top/bottom branch of Fig. 1. Therefore, if MS outputs more than the necessary number of points, we perform FPS among them. If less, we fill the gaps by FPS from the input locations.

During training, we use focal loss [12] to deal with the extreme class imbalance. Moreover, we decide to address two binary tasks (pedestrian vs non-pedestrian, vehicle vs non-vehicle) and exclude the negative class to avoid biasing the network too much. Sigmoid is used as the output activation function. The final prediction would be the class achieving the highest score. If none of the positive classes scores exceed the threshold of 0.5 the negative class is predicted. Finally, we split the train-set into sub-sets and perform five-fold cross validation to tune the hyper-parameters. The pedestrian/vehicle loss weighting factor (α in [12]) is set to 0.9/0.85 for all the networks to enable fair comparison. For evaluation, we train the models for 20 epochs on the whole train-set. Then, we select the best performing configuration and test it 10 times to average random effects. Mean values are reported, while standard deviations (<0.1%) are omitted.

Table 1. Data distribution. Percentages and total number of points are reported.

Set	Moving pedestrian	Moving vehicle	Other & clutter
Train	2.26% (721 865)	6.12% (1 955 937)	91.62% (29 282 877)
Test	1.40% (142 647)	5.63% (574 321)	92.98% (9 493 667)

4.3 Results

One could think that detecting moving objects with radar is a trivial task. To prove that it is not the case, we train a random forest model [2] to perform semantic segmentation on our dataset. Random forests use an ensemble of decision-trees to infer the classification output. Decision-trees, in turn, make predictions by comparing the input's features with a set of learned thresholds. Table 2 shows that this advanced thresholding algorithm achieves much poorer performance than our model, hence proving the non-triviality of the problem.

We decide to conduct experiments with PointNet++ as, to the best of our knowledge, it represents the best architecture tested on radar PCs. In particular, we slightly modify the implementation of [16] to account for the lower number of input-points/output-classes of our framework: both the number of samples in each SA layer and the number of nodes in the output FC network have been halved. However, we notice that the model have a much higher capacity than ours. We therefore design a shallow version of PointNet++ to enable fair comparison: the number of SA/FP layers has been reduced to two and set similarly to our architecture. Finally, we equip this shallow version of PointNet++ with the proposed pre-processing module to investigate its impact on the performance.

Table 2 contains the results. Despite the higher number of parameters/FLOPs, PointNet++ exhibits considerably poorer performance than RadarPCNN. As expected, the shallow PointNet++ experiences slight performance degradation. Interestingly, however, when equipped with our pre-processing module, it can achieve comparable results with RadarPCNN. This shows that our module can be successfully used on other point-wise processing architecture, helping the network to craft meaningful features for radar reflections. Moreover, it suggests that the proposed layer plays a major role

Table 2. Semantic segmentation results on our dataset (%).

Method	Moving pedestrian			Moving vehicle			Average			Param.	FLOPs
	Prec.	Recall	F_1	Prec.	Recall	F_1	Prec.	Recall	F_1		
Random forest	16.92	70.43	27.29	54.49	84.09	66.13	35.71	77.26	46.71	–	–
PointNet++ [16]	46.10	75.77	57.33	72.77	82.89	77.50	59.44	79.33	67.41	418.6K	1.55G
PointNet++ (shallow)	43.82	75.31	55.40	71.18	84.01	77.06	57.50	79.66	66.23	191.2K	**0.95G**
PointNet++ (sh. + our mod.)	47.70	**76.77**	58.84	73.16	**93.24**	81.99	60.43	**85.01**	70.42	198.8K	1.02G
RadarPCNN (ours)	**48.64**	75.82	**59.27**	**75.78**	91.44	**82.88**	**62.21**	83.63	**71.07**	**175.3K**	1.02G

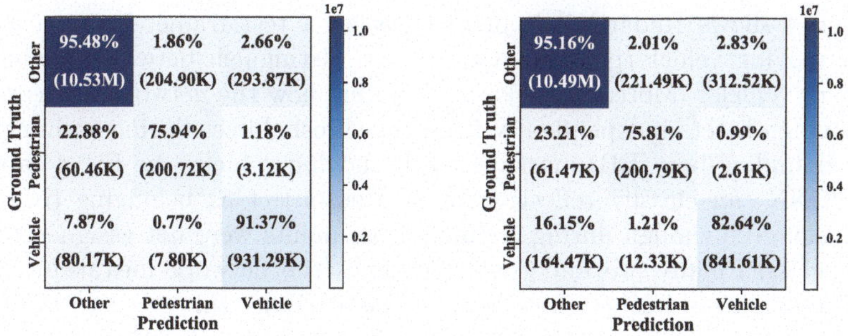

Fig. 3. Confusion matrices of RadarPCNN (left) and PointNet++ [16] (right). The color-map shows the points count: the darker the color, the higher the points number.

in the enhanced performance of our method w.r.t. PointNet++ [16]. Finally, it is worth noting that the improved shallow Pointnet++ still cannot outperform RadarPCNN, despite having nearly 15% more parameters. This suggests that our architecture has a better number-of-parameters/performance trade-off, resulting in a more efficient processing.

Figure 3 shows the confusion matrices of RadarPCNN (left) and PointNet++ [16] (right). It confirms the observation drawn from Table 2. Moreover, it is interesting to see how most of the errors come from negative predictions of positive class samples: only less than 2% of them are, indeed, mistakenly predicted as the wrong positive class. This effect is strongly due to the class imbalance in our dataset, which unfortunately makes the network marginally biased towards the negative class, despite all the precautions taken during training.

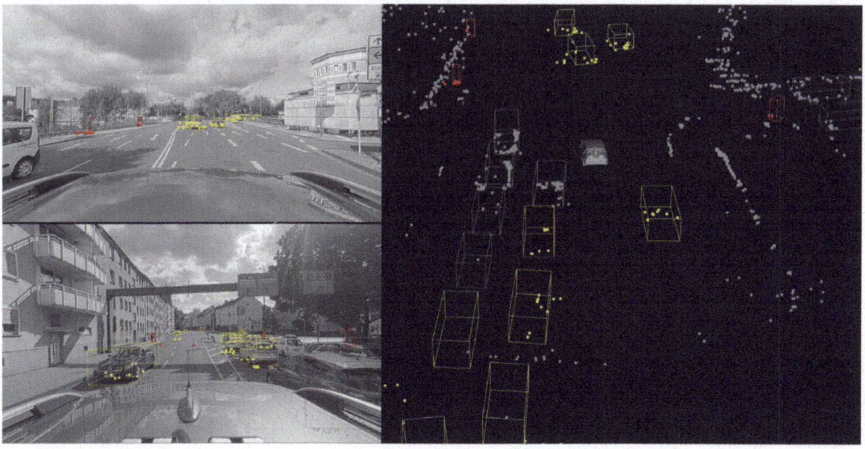

Fig. 4. RadarPCNN predictions. Yellow/red points are moving vehicle/pedestrian predictions. Ground truth BBs follow the same color-map. Gray BBs belong to stationary vehicles, while orange BBs marks vehicles with absolute speed between 1 and 2.5 m/s. Left. Front/rear camera view. Right. 3D visualization. Best viewed in color.

Figure 4 shows RadarPCNN predictions on a test frame. It can correctly classify moving vehicle/pedestrian as well as distinguish between moving and stationary vehicles. Moreover, it is worth noting how the network learns to predict moving objects independently from the threshold set during training. The orange bounding-box (BB) marks a slowly moving vehicle (see Fig. 4 caption): RadarPCNN can classify reflections from this object as belonging to a moving vehicle, even though during training these points were not assigned to that specific class. Finally, we find that sometimes the network mistakenly classifies reflections from bushes as pedestrian: we attribute this effect to the strong similarity between these two instances from the radar perspective.

4.4 Ablation Studies

Fusion Method. In this section we compare our attention mechanism with two fusion techniques: addition and concatenation. Table 3 shows that our attention mechanism represents the best solution, achieving the best F_1 scores with a reasonable number of parameters. The concatenation approach achieves comparable performance with ours, but involves ~30K more parameters. Finally, notice how all the tested methods are well-suited for fusing multiple vectors.

Mean Shift vs FPS. Herein, we assess the impact of mean shift compared with the traditional farthest point sampling method. Figure 5 plots RadarPCNN F_1 scores while changing the number of representative points in the top/bottom branches of Fig. 1. We compute MS with different bandwidth values to account for the different number of representative points. Regarding FPS, we sample the necessary number of points directly from the input. We notice that, in the best configuration (leftmost), MS brings minor improvements over FPS. This is not a surprise: indeed, as the number of representative points increases, MS and FPS will tend to be similar, achieving the very same output when we sample all the input points (MS with infinitesimal bandwidth). Interestingly, however, as the number of representative points decreases, the impact of MS increases. This suggests that, focusing on high density locations, MS optimizes the usage of spatial relationship in such sparse data. Conversely, as the number of sampled points decreases, FPS cannot significantly cover the whole input space, thus failing to generate representative points for object of interest. The different behavior of the vehicle and pedestrian classes further confirms our observations. Since pedestrians have smaller sizes than vehicles, they produce lesser radar reflections. Therefore, a decrement in the number of representative points, dramatically decreases their likelihood of being sampled by FPS. Finally, it is worth stressing that the number of representative points strongly affects the amount of FLOPs demanded by the network. Since MS proved much more robust than FPS, it represents a promising solution for trading-off performance with computation, a very crucial resource in embedded, real-time systems.

Table 3. RadarPCNN performance using different fusion methods (%).

Method	Moving pedestrian			Moving vehicle			Average			Param.
	Prec.	Recall	F_1	Prec.	Recall	F_1	Prec.	Recall	F_1	
Conc	48.27	**76.50**	**59.19**	74.98	91.78	82.54	61.63	**84.14**	70.87	206.9K
Add	47.11	75.87	58.88	74.07	**92.13**	82.12	61.09	84.00	70.50	**174.1K**
Att (ours)	**48.64**	75.82	**59.27**	**75.78**	91.44	**82.88**	**62.21**	83.63	**71.07**	175.3K

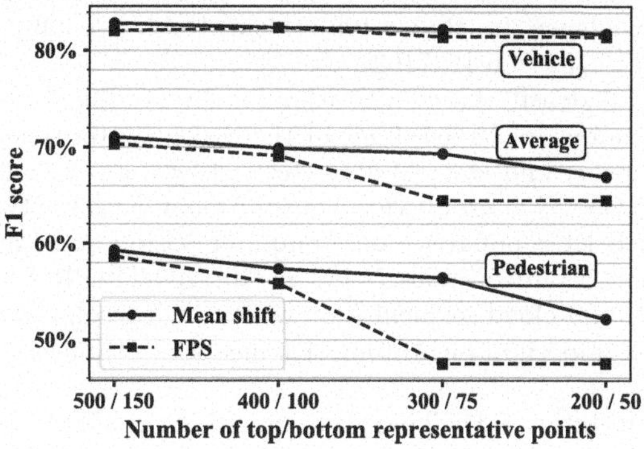

Fig. 5. MS vs FPS under various configuration of the number of representative points.

5 Conclusions

Despite PointNet++ being a milestone in raw PCs processing, radar data requires further tweaks in order to be efficiently processed. In this work, we show that the performance of PointNet++ – and presumably other methods – on radar PCs can be drastically improved by using radar information to learn new point features. In addition, we show that it is possible to further improve semantic segmentation performance by taking into account the intrinsic properties of radar while designing the architecture. Indeed, RadarPCNN is capable to achieve state-of-the-art results, using less memory than previous ML approaches.

About promising future directions, it would be interesting to see how the pre-processing module proposed in this work would suit other point-wise processing architectures. Finally, we notice from visualization analyses that most of the errors performed by our architecture are present only for few frames, therefore we believe that the network performance can be further improved by the use of temporal information. To this end, we strongly believe that MS could represent a key element for the deployment of RNNs in point-wise techniques for radar.

References

1. Alessandretti, G., et al.: Vehicle and guard rail detection using radar and vision data fusion. IEEE Trans. Intell. Transp. Syst. **8**(1), 95–105 (2007). https://doi.org/10.1109/TITS.2006.888597

2. Breiman, L.: Random forests. Mach. Learn **45**(1), 5–32 (2001). https://doi.org/10.1023/A:1010933404324
3. Caesar, H., et al.: nuScenes: a multimodal dataset for autonomous driving. CoRR **abs/1903.11027** (2019)
4. Engelcke, M., et al.: Vote3Deep: fast object detection in 3D point clouds using efficient convolutional neural networks. In: IEEE International Conference on Robotics and Automation, ICRA, pp. 1355–1361 (2017). https://doi.org/10.1109/ICRA.2017.7989161
5. Eriksson, L.H., As, B..: Automotive radar for adaptive cruise control and collision warning/avoidance.. In: Radar 1997 (Conf. Publ. No. 449), pp. 16–20 (1997). https://doi.org/10.1049/cp:19971623
6. Ester, M., et al.: A density-based algorithm for discovering clusters in large spatial databases with noise. In: Proceedings of the Second International Conference on Knowledge Discovery and Data Mining (KDD-1996), pp. 226–231 (1996)
7. Feng, Y., et al.: GVCNN: group-view convolutional neural networks for 3D shape recognition. In: IEEE Conference on Computer Vision and Pattern Recognition, CVPR, pp. 264–272 (2018). https://doi.org/10.1109/CVPR.2018.00035
8. Feng, Z., et al.: Point cloud segmentation with a high-resolution automotive radar. In: 10th GMM-Symposium on Automotive meets Electronics, AmE 2019, pp. 1–5 (2019)
9. Fukunaga, K., Hostetler, L.D.: The estimation of the gradient of a density function, with applications in pattern recognition. IEEE Trans. Inf. Theory **21**(1), 32–40 (1975). https://doi.org/10.1109/TIT.1975.1055330
10. Hochreiter, S., Schmidhuber, J.: Long short-term memory. Neural Comput. **9**(8), 1735–1780 (1997). https://doi.org/10.1162/neco.1997.9.8.1735
11. Li, Y., et al.: PointCNN: convolution on x-transformed points. In: Advances in Neural Information Processing Systems 31: Annual Conference on Neural Information Processing Systems, NeurIPS, pp. 828–838 (2018)
12. Lin, T., et al.: Focal loss for dense object detection. In: IEEE International Conference on Computer Vision, ICCV, pp. 2999–3007 (2017). https://doi.org/10.1109/ICCV.2017.324
13. Prophet, R., et al.: Pedestrian classification for 79 GHz automotive radar systems. In: IEEE Intelligent Vehicles Symposium IV, pp. 1265–1270 (2018). https://doi.org/10.1109/IVS.2018.8500554
14. Qi, C.R., et al.: PointNet++: deep hierarchical feature learning on point sets in a metric space. In: Advances in Neural Information Processing Systems 30: Annual Conference on Neural Information Processing Systems, pp. 5099–5108 (2017)
15. Qi, C.R., et al.: PointNet: deep learning on point sets for 3D classification and segmentation. In: IEEE Conference on Computer Vision and Pattern Recognition, CVPR, pp. 77–85 (2017). https://doi.org/10.1109/CVPR.2017.16
16. Schumann, O., et al.: Semantic segmentation on radar point clouds. In: 21st International Conference on Information Fusion, FUSION, pp. 2179–2186 (2018). https://doi.org/10.23919/ICIF.2018.8455344
17. Shelhamer, E., et al.: Fully convolutional networks for semantic segmentation. CoRR **abs/1605.06211** (2016)
18. Sultana, F., et al.: Advancements in image classification using convolutional neural network. CoRR **abs/1905.03288** (2019)
19. Wöhler, C., et al.: Comparison of random forest and long short-term memory network performances in classification tasks using radar. In: Sensor Data Fusion: Trends, Solutions, Applications, SDF, pp. 1–6 (2017). https://doi.org/10.1109/SDF.2017.8126350

20. Yang, B., et al.: Attentional aggregation of deep feature sets for multi-view 3D reconstruction. CoRR **abs/1808.00758** (2018)
21. Zaheer, M., et al.: Deep sets. In: Advances in Neural Information Processing Systems 30: Annual Conference on Neural Information Processing Systems, pp. 3391–3401 (2017)
22. Zhou, Y., Tuzel, O.: VoxelNet: end-to-end learning for point cloud based 3D object detection. In: IEEE Conference on Computer Vision and Pattern Recognition, CVPR, pp. 4490–4499 (2018). https://doi.org/10.1109/CVPR.2018.00472

LSTM Neural Network for Fine-Granularity Estimation on Baseline Load of Fast Demand Response

Shun Matsukawa[1(✉)], Keita Suzuki[1], Chuzo Ninagawa[1], Junji Morikawa[2], and Seiji Kondo[2]

[1] Smart Grid Power Control Engineering Joint Laboratory, Gifu University, Gifu, Japan
s_matsu@gifu-u.ac.jp
[2] Mitsubishi Heavy Industries Thermal Systems, Ltd., Kiyosu, Japan

Abstract. In the future power system called Smart Grid, power generators using renewable energies will be widely introduced to the power grid and required to balance supply and demand on the grid quickly. Therefore, fast automated demand response (FastADR) that contributes to balance the power grid from demand side through electrical facilities like building air conditioner are focused recently. When electric grid operator will pay incentive to aggregators of the demand side, it is important to estimate accurate baseline load. However, the FastADR must returns quick response by unit of seconds or minute (fine-granularity), therefore it is difficult to estimate baseline load accurately using conventional method. In this research, the baseline load estimation model for air-con time-series data is constructed using long short-term memory (LSTM) neural network, and compared with multilayer perceptron (MLP) neural network model for baseline load estimation. The training and evaluating time-series data is generated by air-con simulator (AE) carried out on the virtual building. In the estimation results using data that were simulated for a month, the average estimation error of the LSTM model is 2.7% and of the MLP model is 5.3%. Therefore, the LSTM model is more effective for baseline estimation than the MLP model. However, data in various situations are required.

Keywords: Smart Grid · FastADR · Baseline estimation · Neural networks · LSTM

1 Introduction

In the future power system, called Smart Grid, photovoltaics and other power generators using renewable energies will be widely introduced to the power grid. These generators may face difficult supply and demand balancing on the grid because these renewable supplies are depending on the environmental condition such as weather [1]. To solve this problem, it is effective to control electrical load quickly from demand side, that is, so-called demand response (DR). The quick and automatic responses of the demand side, discharge from storage batteries or power limitation of electrical

L. Iliadis et al. (Eds.): EANN 2020, INNS 2, pp. 132–142, 2020.
https://doi.org/10.1007/978-3-030-48791-1_9

facilities for example, help the grid effectively. The system for it is called fast automated demand response (FastADR) [2].

As regards target electrical facilities for FastADR, building air-conditioners (ACs) are to be promising. The power consumption of ACs accounts for about 40% of the building power consumption, and more, it can be controlled flexible [3]. These large capacity and control flexibility are advantages for the target of the FastADR. When the electrical demand is high, an aggregator receives an order of power suppression from the electric grid operator. The aggregator sends power consumption limitation commands to the ACs, and ACs suppress the power consumptions. The suppressed powers will be aggregated from many ACs in many buildings. The electric grid operator will pay incentive to the aggregator.

Here, the price of the incentive depends on the amount of the power suppressed during the DR period. Therefore, estimating the power consumption when the DR is not occurred is required. This amount of the power consumption is called baseline load. Conventional DR is a slow demand response that responds through over 30 min, and is kept for a long period of time. Therefore, a baseline load estimation method that averages past data, such as the XofY method [4], has been applied.

However, the FastADR is required to response quickly through unit of seconds or minute [5]. Therefore it is not appropriate to estimate baseline load using conventional method. The AC operation data acquired during FastADR has 2 features, 1) the data highly depends on short-term (fine-granularity) time-series, 2) only a few valuable data can be acquired from ACs on actual building. Considering these features, the regression method [4, 6] is the most appropriate for AC's baseline estimation in FastADR between some method studied previously [7].

In previous studies, the multilayer perceptron (MLP) model is adopted to estimate electrical load of many facilities [8]. Time-series data is required to input into the model parallelly. On the other hand, the long short-term memory (LSTM) neural networks [9, 10] is used as models represented AC protecting operation [11, 12]. However, the baseline estimation research work using LSTM is not very targeted.

In this research, baseline estimation model using LSTM neural networks is constructed. The model is trained and evaluated with AE [13], an air-con simulation model. In comparison, a MLP model is constructed, trained and evaluated simultaneously.

2 Simulation Environments

2.1 Baseline Load of AC Operation on FastADR

In this research, the FastADR occurs in 4 time periods, from 9:00 to 10:00, from 11:00 to 12:00, from 14:00 to 15:00 and from 16:00 to 17:00. Power limitation command is send to AC for every 10 min. The limitation command is determined by Real-Time Pricing (RTP) optimizing algorithm [12, 15].

Figure 1 shows the concept of the FastADR operation. Bold black line indicates the power limitation command and circle marker indicates the power consumption P [kW] in a minute. The baseline load [kWh] is indicated by gray area, it is integral value between dotted line (Ps when the FastADR does not occurred) and x axis line ($P = 0.0$). The dotted line does not be estimated in this research because the baseline load is estimated directly. Since the power limitation command determines the upper limit of the power consumption, power consumption does not always follow the power limitation command.

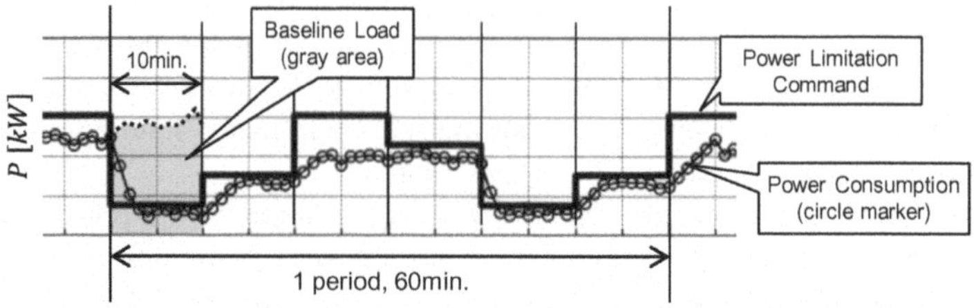

Fig. 1. Concept diagram of the power limitation command and baseline load

2.2 Construction of Virtual Building

The construction of a virtual building using in this research is shown in Fig. 2. The building has 10 floors, and all floors are separated into 2 areas, called blocks. Each block is installed 6 numbers of indoor units, and these indoor units are controlled by 20 outdoor units. Total cooling area is 6000 [m^2], separated into 20 blocks, installed 120 indoor units. This building does not exist, but assumed general office building.

The outdoor units in blocks are grouped in 3 types of rated power. The rated power of type 1 is 45 [kWh], and type 2 is 32 [kWh]. These are determined from actual units installed in office room on actual building. And the rated power of type 3 is 68 [kWh], this unit is installed in rooms that is required high air-con load like server room or ceiling floor. The AE is simulated these units by changing its parameter, therefore the power consumption and room temperature are follow to common dynamic characteristics.

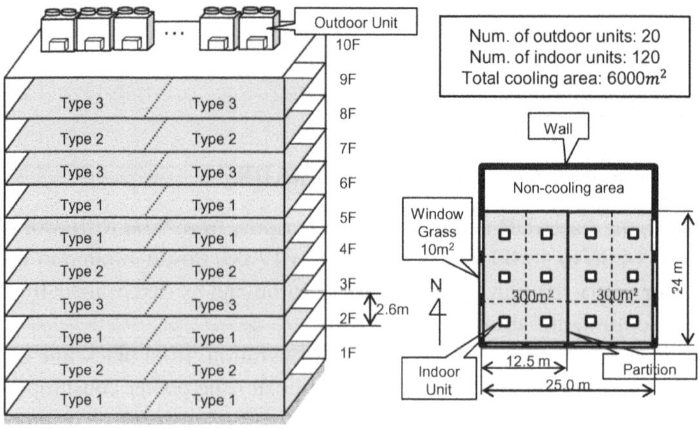

Fig. 2. Construction of the virtual building

2.3 Construction of Air-Con Simulation Model

In AE, the power consumption and room temperature is simulated according to the following formula based on the recurrence formula developed in the previous study [13]:

$$p(t+\Delta t) = p(t) + D(t)\Delta t \tag{1}$$

$$T_{Ai}(t+\Delta t) = T_{Ai}(t) + \frac{1}{C_{Hi}}(Q_{Li}(t) - Q_{ACi}(\mathrm{t}))\Delta t \tag{2}$$

Here, $P(t)$ indicates power consumption [kW] for each discrete time t [sec], and $D(t)$ indicates power change rate [kW/s]. Δt indicates a time step and 10 [sec] is assigned to it in this research. T_{Ai} indicates room temperature measured by inner unit i, C_{Hi} is heat capacity of inner unit i, $Q_{Li}(t)$ and $Q_{ACi}(\mathrm{t})$ are inner heat load and air-con cooling capacity of inner unit i, respectively. $D(t)$ is described as following formula:

$$D(t) = S_{OV}^{PL} D_{DWN} + \left(1 - S_{OV}^{PL}\right)\left\{S_{OV}^{P^*} D_{DWN} + \left(1 - S_{OV}^{P^*}\right) S_{FR}^{PL} S_{FR}^{P^*} D_{UP}\right\} \tag{3}$$

D_{UP} is the power rise rate [kW/s], and D_{DWN} is the power fall rate [kW/s]. S_{OV}^{PL} and S_{FR}^{PL} represent the current power consumption tracking state (0 or 1) with respect to the power limitation command value P_L [kW], and $S_{OV}^{P^*}$ and $S_{FR}^{P^*}$ are the target power indicates the tracking state (0 or 1) for $P^*(t)$ [kW]. $P^*(t)$ is determined from multiple linear regression model [7] with outdoor temperature and thermo-on capacity (total cooling capacity of operating indoor unit) as input variables. Since it is difficult to construct the fine vibration of P model analytically, a stochastic model is constructed from the acquired data.

Figure 3 indicates power consumption acquired from actual building on a day in August, 2018 (Fig. 3 top) and simulated power consumption on same day (Fig. 3 bottom). Some parameters like inner head load cannot acquire accurately, therefore it is impossible simulate actual consumption completely from the outset. However, AE simulates power consumption and room temperature sequentially, then the time dependency of the simulated data is plausible.

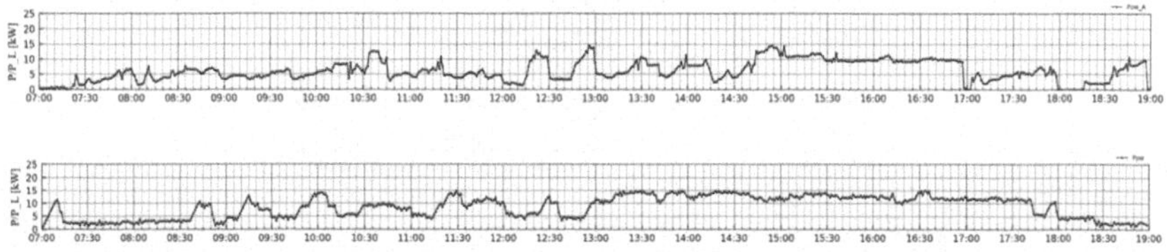

Fig. 3. Acquired power consumption (top) and simulated power consumption (bottom). The data were acquired from 7:00 to 19:00. Data is plotted on 1 min interval.

3 Long Short-Term Memory Model for Baseline Estimation

The LSTM neural network [9, 10] is a kind of recurrent neural network (RNN) used in computational neuroscience and machine learning applications widely. In LSTM, nodes in the hidden layer are replaced with complicated units called memory units, so it is possible to overcome the vanishing gradient problem and hold long time-series input data information compared with the normal RNN.

The memory unit has input/forget/output gates and a memory cell in addition to a normal input receiving node. By forgetting unnecessary information with a forget gate while recursively referring to the memory cell holding its own state, it can be expected to keep long-term characteristics of time-series into the unit. The three gates and the input receiving node are represented following formula:

$$g(\boldsymbol{x}) = f\left(\sum_i \boldsymbol{u}_{in}\boldsymbol{x}_i(t) + \boldsymbol{u}_{re} z_i(t-1)\right) \tag{4}$$

Here, u_{in} is the weight of an input variable x_i, and u_{re} is the weight of output value from the memory cell z_i. f indicates an activation function.

The LSTM model constructed in this research is shown in Fig. 4. The minimum unit of time is 5 min, called frame m. The representation value of a frame is an average value during 5 min. Moreover, q indicates the 10 min separation. A time point when estimate baseline is represented as (q, m), it means the last minute of the last frame m of the separation q. Dimension of input vector $\boldsymbol{x}(q, m)$ is 10, and dimension of output vector $\boldsymbol{y}(q+1)$ is 2.

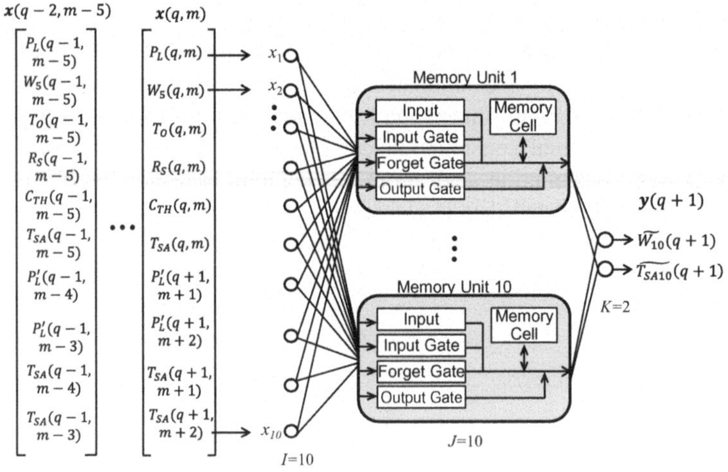

Fig. 4. LSTM model for baseline estimation

In this research, a input time-series is consisted from 6 frames data. The length of the time-series is determined from covariance of the input variables. The covariance between power consumption at time t [min.] and room temperature is maximized at $t = -15$ and others are $t = 0$, then we determined the time-series length to 30 min, in other words, 6 frames. Then a time-series contains $\boldsymbol{x}(q-2, m-5)$ to $\boldsymbol{x}(q, m)$.

The following variables were used for $\boldsymbol{x}(q, m)$; $P_L(q, m)$ is the "acquired" power limitation command [kW], $W_5(q, m)$ is the "acquired" amount of power consumption for frame m [kWh]. $T_O(q, m)$ is the outdoor temperature [°C], and $R_S(q, m)$ is the solar radiation [kWh]. T_O and R_S are acquired at Nagoya, Japan by Japan Meteorological Agency. $T_{SA}(q, m)$ is the average difference between set temperature T_{Si} and room temperature T_{Ai} of indoor unit i. $P'_L(q+1, m+1)$ and $P'_L(q+1, m+2)$ are power limitation command [kW] of "next" 10 min. While baseline estimation, these variables will be assigned a "limitation released" value. $T_{SA}(q+1, m+1)$ and $T_{SA}(q+1, m+2)$ are the "acquired" temperature difference of next 10 min. These variables have highly relation to power consumption [7].

The model outputs the power consumption and average difference between set room temperature and observed room temperature for next 2 frames.

The size of the hidden layer is 10. In our previous studies, this size effects to learning time but not accuracy, then it was determined empirically considering learning rate and learning epoch. Activation function of the hidden layer is sigmoid, and optimization algorithm is Adam [14].

4 Examination and Results

4.1 Data Processing and Model Training

The LSTM models are trained for each block. To train the LSTM models, it is necessary to observe the data simultaneously that FastADR was occurred data and was not occurred. However, these data can be acquired in an either-or situation. Therefore, in this research, the LSTM models were trained using the data simulated by the AE. The data simulated by the AE is slightly different for each block of the same type because the AE operates stochastically.

The AE simulated 5 patterns of the FastADR occurrence, 1) not occurred, 2) occurred in period 1, 3) occurred in period 1 and 2, 4) occurred in period 1-3 and 5) occurred in all periods. 17 days in August were assumed as the simulation situation. Training data was constructed based on the pattern 5. The training answer of the power consumption during 10 min W_{10} for each period was merged from each pattern data. For example, a $W_{10}(q, m)$ during a period was calculated from pattern 1 data, and it was used as one element of the $\boldsymbol{y}(q+1)$ in pattern 5. This preprocess is possible because of simulation.

After that, these frame data were scaled by max/min constant value respectively. The data per a day were acquired every minute for 10 h, therefore frame data $\{\boldsymbol{x}(1, 1), \ldots, \boldsymbol{x}(q, m), \ldots, \boldsymbol{x}(59, 119)\}$ were acquired per a day in a block.

Training time-series is constructed from them. The n-th training time-series X_n is represented as below:

$$\boldsymbol{X}_n = \{\boldsymbol{x}(\left\lfloor \frac{n}{10} \right\rfloor, n - m + 6) \mid m = 0, \ldots, 6\} \tag{5}$$

The X_n is a time-series obtained by shifting X_{n-1} forward by a frame.

All weights of the LSTM models were initialized randomly by uniform distribution between 0.0 and 0.001. The gradients of the weights were calculated by Back Propagation Through Time (BPTT) method [16] and new weights were calculated from these gradients. The training data batch size is 1 (same as online learning). The learning rate was optimized by the Adam algorithm. In this research, the training was repeated for 100 epochs.

For comparing, the MLP models were trained simultaneously. The structure of the MLP model was same as the LSTM model without inputting time-series parallelly into MLP model.

4.2 Evaluation on Performance of the Model

The models were evaluated using 2 days in August, 2018 that were not used to train. One day is the hottest day in the month, and another is the generally day in the month.

The estimation errors were defined as relative rate of difference between total estimated baseline load and total actual baseline load during FastADR periods. Represent the k-th estimated baseline load for $\boldsymbol{X}_k$ at period Pr on block b as $\widetilde{\mathrm{W}_{10}}_k^{\mathrm{Pr,b}}$. The index k is assigned from 1 to 12, it means the frame number during a period. The total estimated baseline load at period Pr is represented as follows:

$$\widetilde{\mathrm{W}_{60}}^{\mathrm{Pr}} = \sum_b^{20} \sum_k^{12} \widetilde{\mathrm{W}_{10}}_k^{\mathrm{Pr,b}} \tag{6}$$

The total actual baseline load $\mathrm{W}_{60}{}^{\mathrm{Pr}}$ is calculated in the same way. The estimation error at period Pr is represented as:

$$\varepsilon^{Pr} = \frac{\left(\widetilde{\mathrm{W}_{60}}^{\mathrm{Pr}} - \mathrm{W}_{60}{}^{\mathrm{Pr}}\right)}{\mathrm{W}_{60}{}^{\mathrm{Pr}}} \times 100[\%] \tag{7}$$

ε^{Pr} indicates the errors in a period on the entire building. The aggregator will estimate the baseline load for each entire building, therefore evaluating ε^{Pr} is considered appropriate in practice.

Estimation results are shown in Fig. 5. Black bar indicates the $\mathrm{W}_{60}{}^{\mathrm{Pr}}$, gray bar indicates the $\widetilde{\mathrm{W}_{60}}^{\mathrm{Pr}}$ estimated by the LSTM model, dotted bar indicates the $\widetilde{\mathrm{W}_{60}}^{\mathrm{Pr}}$ estimated by the MLP model. Bar with horizontal line indicates the observed power consumption, $\mathrm{W}_{60}{}^{\mathrm{Pr}'}$. ε^{Pr} is shown as difference between the black bar and the gray bar compared to the black bars and dotted bars.

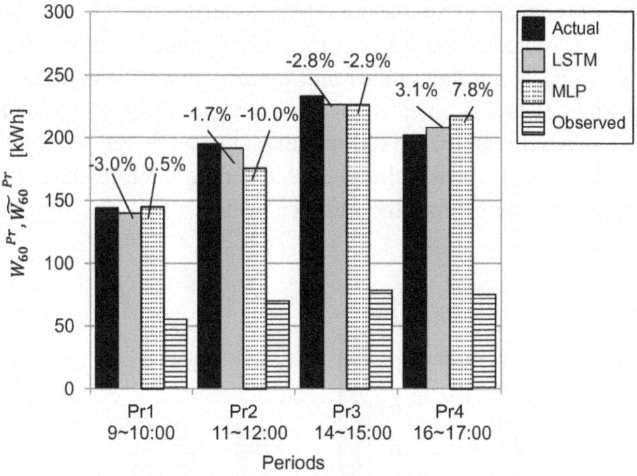

Fig. 5. Comparison of the estimation results

Calculated errors of the LSTM model are, $\varepsilon^1 = -3.0[\%]$, $\varepsilon^2 = -1.7[\%]$, $\varepsilon^3 = -2.8[\%]$ and $\varepsilon^4 = 3.1[\%]$. Calculated errors of the MLP model are, $\varepsilon^1 = -0.5[\%]$, $\varepsilon^2 = -10.0[\%]$, $\varepsilon^3 = -2.9[\%]$ and $\varepsilon^4 = 7.8[\%]$. The estimation results of the LSTM model are better than the MLP model except for period 1. In particular, the error is smaller than 8.3% in period 2.

Comparing the average $\varepsilon^{avg} = \frac{1}{4}\sum_{Pr=1}^{4}|\varepsilon^{Pr}|$ between the LSTM and the MLP model, the ε^{avg} of LSTM model is 2.7[%], and the ε^{avg} of the MLP model is 5.3[%]. Therefore, it can be said the LSTM model is more effective than the MLP model for the baseline load estimation.

4.3 Study on a Few Training Data

To train the LSTM model, large amount of data (over 1000 time series) is used in general [9]. In this research, the models were trained using data acquired in a month similarly. However, in application, there may be cases where only a small number of data can be acquired in a few days. It is necessary to examine how many and various data are required to train the LSTM model effectively.

In this study, three kinds of data sets are used. First is a data set acquired in one day, 120 time-series, from august, 2018 (set A). Second is a data set acquired in one week (5 days), 600 time-series, from august, 2018 (set B). Third, sampled 10% from data acquired in a month, 273 time-series (set C). The set A and B reproduce the situation where the number of obtainable data is small. The set C reproduces the situation where the wide variety of the few data can be acquired. The estimation results are evaluated using data that were not used to train. Kullback–Leibler divergence (KLD) [17] between the all-time actual baseline load and the all-time estimated baseline load is calculated.

Figure 6 shows the results. Sparse dotted bar indicates the KLD of the MLP model, and dense dotted bar indicates the KLD of the LSTM model. Vertical axis indicates the KLD, the lower value is similar (good) and upper value is dissimilar (poor). In this result, the MLP model is less affected by data set, but the LSTM model is affected. The MLP model is better than the LSTM model on the set A, but in the set C, that result has been reversed. It is considered that the LSTM model learns data trends through a variety of training data rather than the number of data.

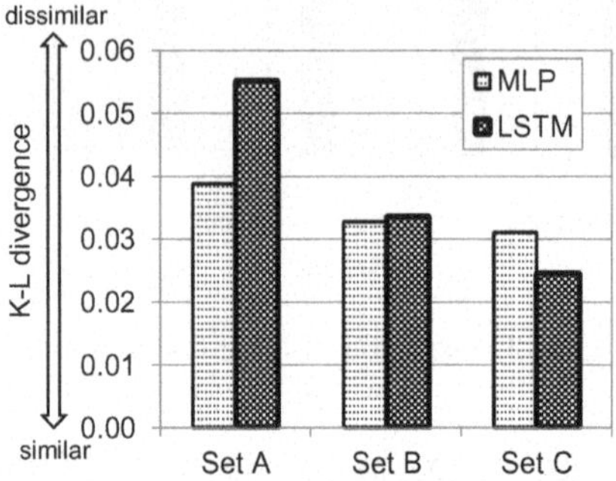

Fig. 6. Comparison between MLP model and LSTM model trained using 3 data sets

5 Conclusion

It is required to estimate baseline load in short-term (fine-granularity) time-series for FastADR in the future Smart Grid. In this research, a LSTM model was constructed to estimate baseline load under the assumed FastADR situation. The FastADR was assumed to last 1 h and send a power limitation command every 10 min.

The LSTM model was trained using time-series generated by an air-con simulator, AE. The virtual building for the AE simulation is constructed from 20 blocks on 10 floors and set upped 6 air-con inner units controlled by 1 outdoor unit for each block. AE simulated each outdoor unit on different situation. The power limitation commands were sent 4 times for a day, and the simulator generates data for a month. The estimation errors were calculated for each power limitation.

Comparison with the MLP model inputted time-series data parallelly, the average estimation error of the LSTM model is 2.7% and of the MLP model is 5.3%. Therefore, the LSTM model is more effective for baseline estimation than the MLP model. However, when trained the models using few data, the estimation error of the LSTM model was increased compared with the MLP models. On the other hand, when trained using the data set that contains various but small amounts of data, the result has been reversed. Therefore, it is more important for the LSTM model to training using various data than the amount of the data.

References

1. California ISO: What the duck curve tells us about managing a green grid. https://www.caiso.com/Documents/FlexibleResourcesHelpRenewables_FastFacts.pdf. Accessed 28 Feb 2020
2. Nakamura, T., Morikawa, J., Ninagawa, C.: Prediction model on room temperature side effect due to FastADR aggregation for a cluster of building air-conditioning facilities. Electr. Eng. Jpn. **199**(3), 17–25 (2017)
3. Ma, O., Alkadi, N., Cappers, P., Denholm, P., Dudley, J., Goli, S., Hummon, M., Kiliccote, S., MacDonald, J., Matson, N., Olsen, D., Rose, C., Sohn, M.D., Starke, M., Kirby, B., O'Malley, M.: Demand response for ancillary services. IEEE Trans. Smart Grid **4**(4), 1988–1995 (2013)
4. Wijaya, T.K., Vasirani, M., Aberer, K.: When bias matters: an economic assessment of demand response baseline for residential customers. IEEE Trans. Smart Grid **5**(4), 1755–1763 (2014)
5. PJM: PJM Empirical Analysis of Demand Response Baseline Methods Results. https://www.pjm.com/-/media/markets-ops/demand-response/pjm-empirical-analysis-of-dr-baseline-methods-results.ashx?la=en. Accessed 28 Feb 2020
6. Wang, F., Li, K., Liu, C., Mi, Z., Shafie-Khah, M., Catalão, J.P.S.: Synchronous pattern matching principle-based residential demand response baseline estimation: mechanism analysis and approach description. IEEE Trans. Smart Grid **9**(6), 6972–6985 (2018)
7. Matsukawa, S., Ninagawa, C., Morikawa, J., Inaba, T., Kondo, S.: Stable segment method for multiple linear regression on baseline estimation for smart grid fast automated demand response. In: Proceedings of 9th IEEE PES ISGT Asia 2019, pp. 2571–2576. IEEE, Chengdu (2019)
8. Debnath, K.B., Mourshed, M.: Forecasting methods in energy planning models. Renew. Sustain. Energy Rev. **88**, 297–325 (2018)
9. Hochreiter, S., Schmidhuber, J.: Long short-term memory. Neural Comput. **9**(8), 1735–1780 (1997)
10. Gers, F.A., Schmidhuber, J., Cummins, F.: Learning to forget: continual prediction with LSTM. Neural Comput. **12**(10), 2451–2471 (2000)
11. Matsukawa, S., Ninagawa, C., Morikawa, J., Inaba, T., Kondo, S.: LSTM prediction on sudden occurrence of maintenance operation of air-conditioners in real-time pricing adaptive control. In: ICANN 2019. Lecture Notes in Computer Science, vol. 11730, pp. 426–435 (2019)
12. Matsukawa, S., Takehara, M., Otsu, H., Morikawa, J., Inaba, T., Kondo, S., Ninagawa, C.: Prediction model on disturbance of maintenance operation during real-time pricing adaptive control for building air-conditioners. IEEJ Trans. Electr. Electron. Eng. **14**, 1219–1225 (2019)
13. Aoki, Y., Ninagawa, C., Morikawa, J., Kasai, T., Kondo, S.: A building multi-type air-conditioner emulator for development of machine learning algorithm on electric energy services. In: The papers of Technical Meeting on Smart Facilities. IEE Japan, Tokyo, pp. 61–66 (2019). (in Japanese)
14. Kingma, D.P., Ba, J.L.: Adam: a method for stochastic optimization. In: 3rd International Conference for Learning Representations, San Diego. arXiv:1412.6980 (2017)
15. Morikawa, J., Yamaguchi, T., Ninagawa, C.: Smart grid real-time pricing optimization management on power consumption of building multi-type air-conditioners. IEEJ Trans. Electr. Electron. Eng. **11**, 823–825 (2016)

16. Ismail, S., Ahmad, A.M.B.: Recurrent neural network with backpropagation through time algorithm for arabic recognition. In: Proceedings of 18th European Simulation Multiconference, Magdeburg. SCS Publishing House (2004)
17. Kullback, S., Leibler, R.A.: On information and sufficiency. Ann. Math. Stat. **22**(1), 79–86 (1951)

Predicting Permeability Based on Core Analysis

Harry Kontopoulos[1(✉)], Hatem Ahriz[1], Eyad Elyan[1], and Richard Arnold[2]

[1] School of Computer Science and Digital Media, The Robert Gordon University, Garthdee Rd., Aberdeen AB10 7QB, UK
h.kontopoulos1@rgu.ac.uk

[2] Corex (UK) Ltd., Units B1 - B3, Airport Industrial Park, Howe Moss Drive, Dyce, Aberdeen AB21 0GL, UK

Abstract. Knowledge of permeability, a measure of the ability of rocks to allow fluids to flow through them, is essential for building accurate models of oil and gas reservoirs. Permeability is best measured in the laboratory using special core analysis (SCAL), but this is expensive and time-consuming. This is the first major work on predicting permeability in the in the UK Continental Shelf (UKCS) based only on routine core analysis (RCA) data and a machine-learning approach. We present a comparative analysis of the various machine learning algorithms and validate the results, using permeability measured on 273 core samples from 104 wells. Results suggest that machine learning can predict permeability with relatively high accuracy. This opens new research directions in particular in the oil and gas sector.

Keywords: Machine learning · Support vector regression · Core analysis · Permeability prediction

1 Introduction

A range of different data is generated during the life-cycle of oil and gas fields, from exploration to abandonment. This data include regional geology, seismic reports, sedimentological models, drilling data, fluid and rock properties [16]. Geologists, reservoir engineers and other scientists combine this data and use their expertise to construct models of the reservoir, evaluate the volume of available hydrocarbons and engineer the most efficient and profitable way to extract them from the reservoir [18]. The most direct type of geological data about the formation come from core analysis, the laboratory examination of well core samples extracted during the drilling. It is the only time scientists can see and physically examine material from within the reservoir.

This work is part of a Knowledge Transfer Partnership (KTP) programme, funded by Corex UK Ltd. and Innovate UK.

L. Iliadis et al. (Eds.): EANN 2020, INNS 2, pp. 143–154, 2020.
https://doi.org/10.1007/978-3-030-48791-1_10

Core analysis is usually divided into two stages. The first stage is called Routine Core Analysis (RCA) and the second stage is called Special Core Analysis (SCAL) [16]. RCA usually includes tests such as fluid saturations, porosity and permeability measurements. Those measurements are taken on plugs or core samples. A SCAL programme might include the measurement of relative permeabilities, capillary pressures and wettability among others. Furthermore, the effect of coring and other fluids on the SCAL parameters could be used to evaluate the damage they cause to the formation [23].

Core analysis data are usually expensive and time consuming (several weeks) to obtain [27]. However, they are deemed to be the most accurate source of information for reservoir characterisation and a thoroughly designed core analysis programme can result in a more productive reservoir later in their lifetime [18].

2 Related Work

Machine learning techniques have been used in the past in the context of core analysis mainly to extrapolate rarely available core analysis data to other more available types of data such as well log data [27]. Examples include prediction of permeability of gas reservoirs using well logs and core data [9,22], identifying drilling sweet-spots for gas hydrate reservoirs without pre-existing well logs [10,15], rock texture image classification using support vector machines [21], predicting permeability during acidizing [11] and predicting the optimal rate of penetration during drilling [12]. The work closest to ours is the study by Erofeev et al. [5] on the Chayandinskoye oil and gas condensate field in Russia. However, that study was limited to a single field and used desalination instead of drilling mud application during core analysis.

In contrast, this work relies on high quality data of actual permeability measurements obtained in the laboratory from a substantial number of core samples across a large number of wells across multiple fields of the UKCS and the north sea. Oil and Gas operators value the core analysis derived data as indispensable. However, budget constraints often limit the number of tests included in core analysis projects. A reliable and effective predictive method could be used alongside traditional routine core analysis techniques to fill the gap. The aim is to be able to provide the next best estimate when there is not enough funding for extensive laboratory measurements. As a proof of concept, the permeability is predicted after drilling mud application has been performed to the samples.

3 Methods

3.1 Dataset

The private dataset used here is part of the historical archive of Corex UK Ltd. It covers a significant part of the offshore area of the UK Continental Shelf (UKCS) and the north sea.

Table 1. Table showing the variables used, their corresponded type in R and their units

Feature	Type	Units
Top depth	Numeric	m
Pore volume	Numeric	cc
Porosity	Numeric	rate
Grain density	Numeric	gcc
Gas permeability	Numeric	mD
Initial permeability	Numeric	mD
Final permeability	Numeric	mD
Brine concentration	Numeric	ppm
Mud weight	Numeric	ppg
Mud type	Character	NA
Reservoir temperature	Numeric	C
Pore pressure	Numeric	atm
Overburden pressure	Numeric	psi

After data cleaning and preparation, the final dataset contained 273 observations and 13 features (Table 1). The number of samples might look small but core analysis is a laborious process with relatively small pace of generating data. The features include the pore volume, porosity, grain density, the top depth of the core, gas permeability, initial permeability, final permeability (output), brine concentration, mud weight, mud type, reservoir temperature, pore pressure, overburden pressure. Mud type is a categorical feature and it is encoded into three dummy variables, with LTOBM (Low Toxicity OBM) the reference level.

Initial permeability is the permeability measurement before drilling mud application while final permeability is the permeability measured after drilling mud application. Drilling mud application for the context of this research means the laboratory simulation of the drilling procedure in the field using a specific drilling mud system. Drilling mud systems are expected to interact with the rock formation and potentially reduce its permeability (Fig. 1). When centering or scaling of the input data is performed it is explicitly mentioned at the relevant model subsection otherwise the original values were used.

3.2 Prediction Models

A range of well established machine and statistical learning algorithms were applied to the given dataset. The main research question was whether the final permeability, after drilling mud application, can be predicted using the results of routine core analysis (RCA) tests as input. Therefore, the final permeability

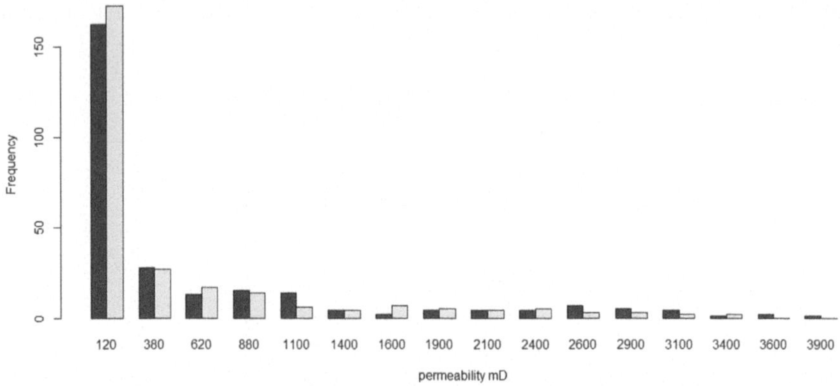

Fig. 1. The distribution of permeabilities before (dark grey) and after drilling mud application (light grey).

was selected as the output of the models. All the variables in Table 1 were used as input parameters.

Least Squares Linear Regression. The starting point of this research was to try and fit a linear model, represented by the formula:

$$Y = \beta_0 + \beta_1 X_1 + ... + \beta_p X_p + \epsilon \tag{1}$$

Least squares estimates the coefficients that minimise the following:

$$RSS = \sum_{i=1}^{n} \left(y_i - \beta_0 - \sum_{j=1}^{p} \beta j x_{ij} \right)^2 \tag{2}$$

The linear model was fitted using the **lm()** function from the R stats package [19]. The QR decomposition of the input matrix is used to estimate the coefficients [6].

Ridge Regression. Ridge regression adds a penalty to the loss function of least squares (Eq. 2). The penalty has the form $\lambda \sum_{j=1}^{p} \beta_j^2$ [13]. The penalty is controlled by the hyper-parameter λ, which is usually selected with grid search and cross validation. Ridge was fitted using the glmnet package in R [7].

Lasso Regression. This model is similar to Ridge except it applies an ℓ_1 penalty to minimise the RSS subject to the constraint $\lambda \sum_{j=1}^{p} |\beta j|$ [24]. Lasso tries to address some of the problems arising in Ridge regression. The ℓ_2 penalty used in Ridge minimises the coefficients towards zero but it does not turn any of them to exactly zero. Lasso instead can set a coefficient to zero and effectively perform feature selection. Lasso was fitted using the glmnet package in R [7].

Partial Least Squares (PLS). PLS identifies a set of components $Z_1, ...Z_M$ that are a linear combination of the original features [25]. The new components are fitted so they explain most of the variance in the predictors [14]. The idea behind this approach is that there are latent variables affecting the output that are not necessarily measured or captured in the dataset [26].

Support Vector Regression (SVR). Support Vector Regression estimates the weights of a hyperplane such that the RSS of the support vectors is minimised [4]. The support vectors are the only part of the dataset that participate in the estimation of the hyperplane equation and the minimization of the loss function. The input space was transformed into a higher dimension feature space using the radial basis function [3]. The SVR model was fitted using the e1071 R package [17]. The variables were scaled for zero mean and unit variance. The cost and gamma hyper-parameters were estimated by 10-fold cross validation, using the tune.svm() function.

Artificial Neural Networks (ANNs). A multi-layer perceptron [20] was used consisting of a feed-forward neural network with 13 neurons at the input layer, two hidden layers with five and three neurons respectively and an output layer with a single neuron for the final permeability. The model was trained using resilient back-propagation (RPROP) with weight backtracking [20] and the neuralnet R package [8]. The input was scaled with mean 0 and unit variance. The learning rate was set to 100 and the maximum number of allowed steps to 1e+05. The sum of square errors was the loss function.

Decision Trees and Random Forests. Regression Trees [1] predict the value of a continuous variable by dividing the input space into j distinct and not overlapping areas. For every new observation that falls into this area the average of the values of the training observations is returned. The regression tree was fitted with the tree package in R [2]. Random Forests build a number of trees in a bootstrapped version of the training samples. In each split step it only considers a random sample of m predictors from the total available ones. This number is typically $\sqrt{p}$, where p is the total number of features [14]. It then uses averaging across the trained trees to produce a final prediction.

4 Results and Discussion

A summary of the results for predicting the final permeability, after drilling mud application, using the various algorithms is presented in (Table 2). The dataset was divided into a training set (67%) and a test set (33%). The R^2, given by $1 - \frac{RSS}{TSS}$ with $TSS = \sum_i^n (y_i - \bar{y})$, on the training set and the MSE, given by $\frac{1}{n} \sum_i^n (\hat{y}_i - \bar{y})$, on the test set will be used to evaluate the models on the training and test set respectively.

Table 2. Table showing the R^2 on the training set and the MSE on the test set.

Algorithm name	R^2	MSE
Least Squares	0.916	50,020.24
Linear Lasso	0.725	50,927.96
Linear Ridge	0.881	51,251.47
PLS	0.894	50,150.91
SVR	0.900	44,135
ANN	0.997	323,477.3
Decision Tree	0.937	108,424.7
Random Forest	0.925	57,202.81

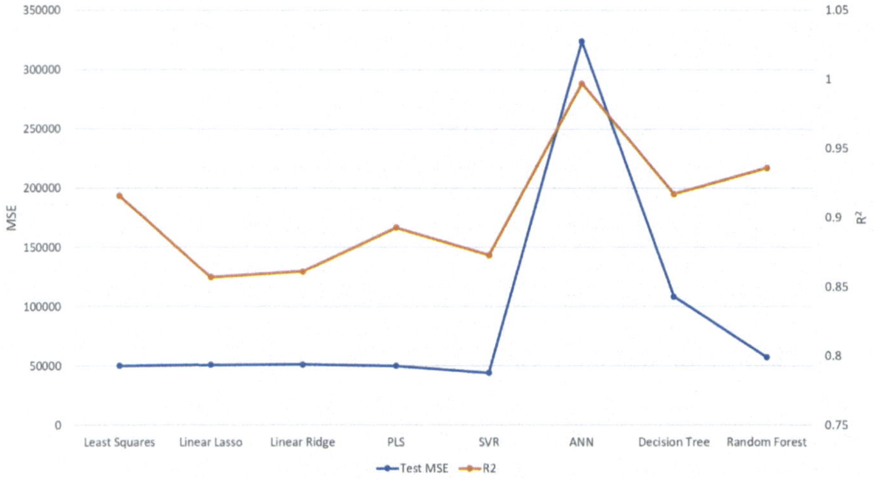

Fig. 2. Compare the models using R^2 on the training set (orange) and MSE on the test set (blue).

R^2 scores show that many algorithms fit the training data well. SVR, Least Squares and PLS having the lowest MSE (Fig. 2) on the test set. PLS and Lasso can give us great insight on the predictors affecting the response variable. According to the Least Squares model initial permeability, gas permeability and pore volume are the most significant features. (Fig. 3).

Lasso produced a sparse model only assigning the pore volume, initial permeability and mud type (WBM) non zero coefficients. PLS also produced a sparse model. The first six components are linear combinations of the top depth, gas permeability, initial permeability, brine concentration, pore pressure and overburden pressure.

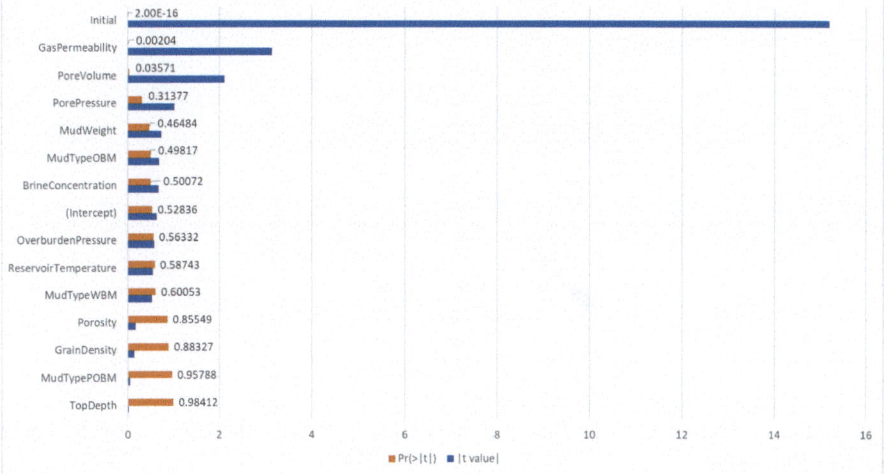

Fig. 3. The t value and the associated p value of the features for the least squares model.

Linear Regression Least Squares. The linear regression model has a R^2 on the training set of 0.916 and test set MSE 50020.24 (Fig. 4). R^2 suggests that the model fits the data relatively well but the MSE on the test set indicates that the predictive power requires further improvement.

Linear Lasso. The best lambda for the Lasso model was estimated by 10-fold cross validation at 12.429. The non zero coefficients for the best λ are pore volume, gas permeability, initial permeability, and mud type (WBM). Lasso has a test MSE of 50927.96 (Fig. 5). The model does not fit the training data as well as the Least Squares but it still manages to generalise well on the test set according to the MSE figure.

Linear Ridge. Ridge regression λ parameter was estimated similarly to Lasso using 10-fold cross validation. The value that resulted in the lowest cross validation error was 89.749. Ridge regression performance on the training dataset was estimated by means of R^2 at 0.881 (Fig. 5).

Partial Least Squares. PLS fit the data on par with the regularised linear models and SVR. R^2 is estimated at 0.894 (Fig. 6) on the training set and the MSE at 50150.91 on the test set. The number of components of the final model was estimated by 10-fold cross validation. The number of components with the lowest CV error was 5 components and it was the one used to generate the model PLS R^2 and MSE values.

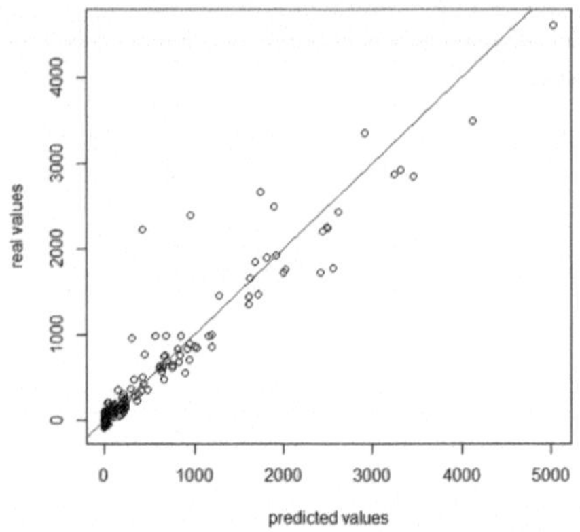

Fig. 4. The real against the predicted permeability values on the training set by Least Squares Regression.

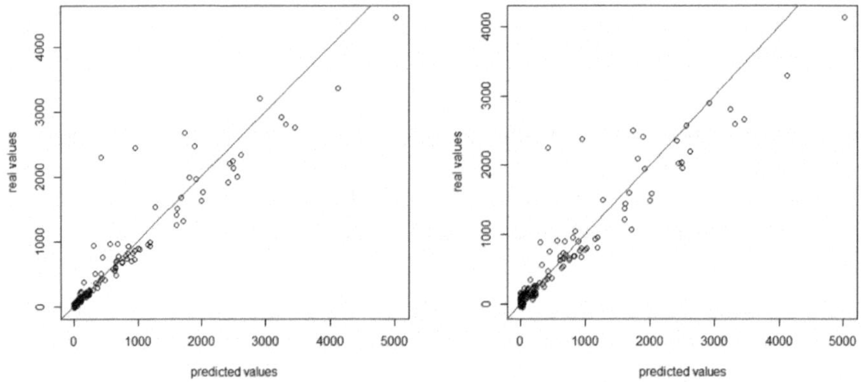

Fig. 5. The real against the predicted permeability values on the training set for the Lasso (left) and the Ridge model (right).

Support Vector Regression. SVR gave the most promising results so far. The SVR hyper-parameters were estimated by grid search at $\gamma = 0.01$ and cost = 10. The model fit the training data with a R^2 value of 0.9. Its MSE on the test set was estimated at 44135 (Fig. 6). SVR performs much better than Least Squares in the test set.

Artificial Neural Network. The Artificial Neural Network was the model that followed the closest the training data with an R^2 value of 0.997. However, it performed very poorly on the test set with an MSE of 323477.3 (Fig. 7). The high R^2 indicates that the model over-fits the training data while the very high test set MSE suggests that it fails to predict the permeability on unseen core samples.

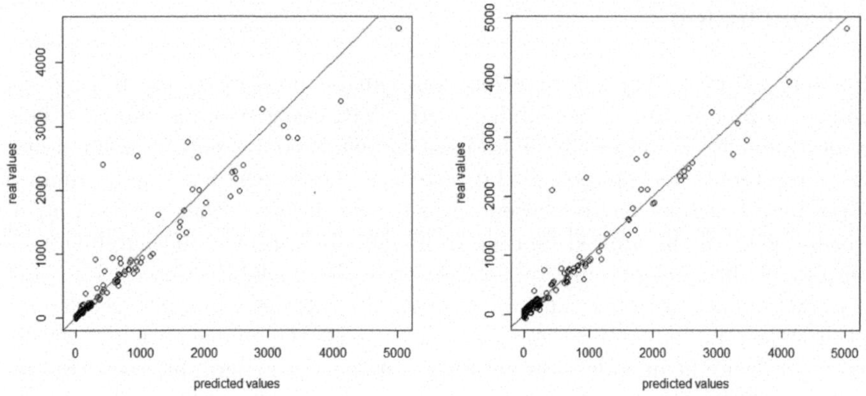

Fig. 6. The real against the predicted permeability values on the training set for the PLS (left) and the SVR model (right).

Decision Tree. The Decision tree model appeared to slightly over-fit the training data. Its R^2 was estimated at 0.937 and generalised poorly with MSE on test set at 57202.81. The decision tree model performs better on the test set than the neural network but not as good as the SVR model.

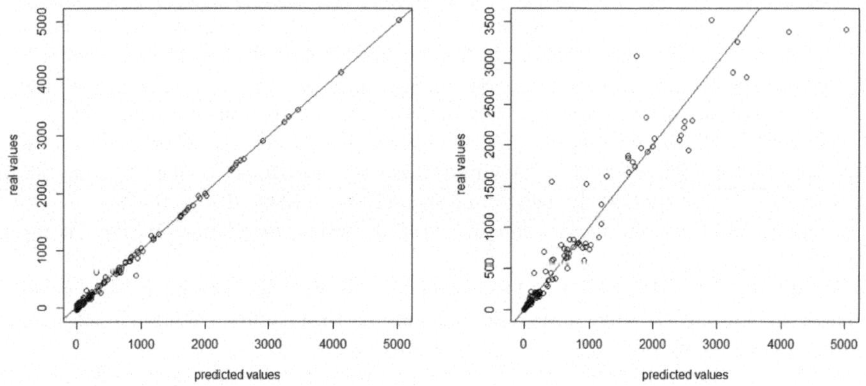

Fig. 7. The real against the predicted permeability values on the training set for the ANN (left) and the Random Forest model (right).

Random Forest. The mtry hyperparameter, that controls the number of variables randomly sampled as candidates at each split, was estimated at 11 using 10-fold cross validation, repeated three times. The R^2 value on the training set was 0.925. The Random Forest model was an improvement compare to the decision tree model and generalised relatively well on the test set with an MSE of 57202.81 (Fig. 7), albeit not as good as SVR.

5 Conclusion

This work showed that machine learning can be used alongside routine core analysis to predict final permeability, with SVR, Least Squares and PLS being the best models. Traditionally oil and gas companies only contract a small number of representative samples to be tested in the laboratory, due to financial constraints. Learning models based on historical data together with laboratory measurements of the limited number of financially approved measurements can alternatively provide a prediction for the rest of the available samples. This could be a new source of revenue for core analysis laboratories and a new service that can provide valuable information to operators to better manage their reservoirs. Future work might include more input features e.g. stratigraphic data that will improve the algorithm's performance in unseen cases or predict different types of output that can be of value for the oil and gas sector.

References

1. Breiman, L., Friedman, J., Stone, C.J., Olshen, R.A.: Classification and Regression Trees. Taylor & Francis, Monterey (1984)
2. Brian Ripley: tree: Classification and Regression Trees (2019). https://CRAN.R-project.org/package=tree. r package version 1.0-40
3. Burges, C.J.: A tutorial on support vector machines for pattern recognition. Data Min. Knowl. Disc. **2**(2), 121–167 (1998). https://doi.org/10.1023/A:1009715923555
4. Drucker, H., Burges, C.J.C., Kaufman, L., Smola, A.J., Vapnik, V.: Support vector regression machines. In: Mozer, M.C., Jordan, M.I., Petsche, T. (eds.) Advances in Neural Information Processing Systems, vol. 9, pp. 155–161. MIT Press (1997). http://papers.nips.cc/paper/1238-support-vector-regression-machines.pdf
5. Erofeev, A., Orlov, D., Ryzhov, A., Koroteev, D.: Prediction of porosity and permeability alteration based on machine learning algorithms. Transp. Porous Media **128**(2), 677–700 (2019). https://doi.org/10.1007/s11242-019-01265-3
6. Francis, J.G.F.: Comput. J., 265–271 (1961). https://academic.oup.com/comjnl/article/4/3/265/380632
7. Friedman, J.H., Hastie, T., Tibshirani, R.: Regularization paths for generalized linear models via coordinate descent. J. Stat. Softw. **33**(1), 1–22 (2010). https://www.jstatsoft.org/index.php/jss/article/view/v033i01
8. Fritsch, S., Guenther, F., Wright, M.N.: neuralnet: Training of neural networks (2019). https://CRAN.R-project.org/package=neuralnet
9. Gholami, R., Shahraki, A.R., Jamali Paghaleh, M.: Prediction of hydrocarbon reservoirs permeability using support vector machine (2012). https://www.hindawi.com/journals/mpe/2012/670723/
10. Gholami, R., Moradzadeh, A., Maleki, S., Amiri, S., Hanachi, J.: Applications of artificial intelligence methods in prediction of permeability in hydrocarbon reservoirs. J. Petrol. Sci. Eng. **122**(C), 643–656 (2014). https://doi.org/10.1016/j.petrol.2014.09.007
11. Gümrah, F., Sarkar, S., Tasti, Y.A., Erbas, D.: Genetic algorithm for predicting permeability during production enhancement by acidizing. Energy Sources **23**(3), 245–256 (2001). https://doi.org/10.1080/00908310151133942

12. Hegde, C., Gray, K.E.: Use of machine learning and data analytics to increase drilling efficiency for nearby wells. J. Nat. Gas Sci. Eng. **40**, 327–335 (2017). https://doi.org/10.1016/j.jngse.2017.02.019
13. Hoerl, A.E., Kennard, R.W.: Ridge regression: biased estimation for nonorthogonal problems. Technometrics **42**(1), 80–86 (2000). http://www.tandfonline.com/doi/abs/10.1080/00401706.2000.10485983
14. James, G., Witten, D., Hastie, T., Tibshirani, R.: An Introduction to Statistical Learning: with Applications in R. Springer Texts in Statistics. Springer-Verlag, New York (2013). https://doi.org/10.1007/978-1-4614-7138-7. https://www.springer.com/gp/book/9781461471370
15. Lee, J., Byun, J., Kim, B., Yoo, D.G.: Delineation of gas hydrate reservoirs in the Ulleung Basin using unsupervised multi-attribute clustering without well log data. J. Nat. Gas Sci. Eng. **46**, 326–337 (2017). https://doi.org/10.1016/j.jngse.2017.08.007. http://www.sciencedirect.com/science/article/pii/S1875510017303104
16. McPhee, C., Reed, J., Zubizarreta, I.: Core Analysis: A Best Practice Guide. Developments in Petroleum Science, vol. 64. Elsevier, Amsterdam (2015)
17. Meyer, D., Dimitriadou, E., Hornik, K., Weingessel, A., Leisch, F.: e1071: Misc Functions of the Department of Statistics, Probability Theory Group (Formerly: E1071), TU Wien (2019). https://CRAN.R-project.org/package=e1071. r package version 1.7-3
18. Ottesen, B., Hjelmeland, O.: The Value Added from Proper Core Analysis, p. 12 (2008)
19. R Core Team: R: A language and environment for statistical computing (ISBN 3-900051-07-0). R Foundation for Statistical Computing (2019). https://www.R-project.org/
20. Riedmiller, M.: Advanced supervised learning in multi-layer perceptrons-from backpropagation to adaptive learning algorithms. Comput. Stan. Interfaces **16**(3), 265–278 (1994). https://doi.org/10.1016/0920-5489(94)90017-5. https://linkinghub.elsevier.com/retrieve/pii/0920548994900175
21. Shang, C., Barnes, D.: Support vector machine-based classification of rock texture images aided by efficient feature selection. In: The 2012 International Joint Conference on Neural Networks (IJCNN), pp. 1–8, June 2012. https://doi.org/10.1109/IJCNN.2012.6252634
22. Singh, S.: Permeability Prediction Using Artificial Neural Network (ANN): A Case Study of Uinta Basin. Society of Petroleum Engineers (2005). https://doi.org/10.2118/99286-STU. https://www-onepetro-org.ezproxy.rgu.ac.uk/conference-paper/SPE-99286-STU
23. Stiles, J.J., Hutfilz, J.: The use of routine and special core analysis in characterizing Brent Group reservoirs, U.K. North Sea. J. Petrol. Technol. (U.S.) **44**(6) (1992). https://doi.org/10.2118/18386-PA
24. Tibshirani, R.: Regression shrinkage and selection via the Lasso. J. Roy. Stat. Soc. B **58**, 267–288 (1994)
25. Wold, H.: 11 - Path Models with Latent Variables: The NIPALS Approach**NIPALS = Nonlinear Iterative PArtial Least Squares. In: Blalock, H.M., Aganbegian, A., Borodkin, F.M., Boudon, R., Capecchi, V. (eds.) Quantitative Sociology: International Perspectives on Mathematical and Statistical Modeling, pp. 307–357. Academic Press, January 1975. https://doi.org/10.1016/B978-0-12-103950-9.50017-4. http://www.sciencedirect.com/science/article/pii/B9780121039509500174

26. Wold, S.: Personal memories of the early PLS development. Chemometrics and Intelligent Laboratory Systems **58**(2), 83–84 (2001). https://doi.org/10.1016/S0169-7439(01)00152-6. http://www.sciencedirect.com/science/article/pii/S0169S0169743901001526
27. Wong, K.W., Fung, C.C., Ong, Y.S., Gedeon, T.D.: Reservoir characterization using support vector machines. In: International Conference on Computational Intelligence for Modelling, Control and Automation and International Conference on Intelligent Agents, Web Technologies and Internet Commerce (CIMCA-IAWTIC 2006), vol. 2, pp. 354–359, November 2005. https://doi.org/10.1109/CIMCA.2005.1631494

Probabilistic Estimation of Evaporated Water in Cooling Towers Using a Generative Adversarial Network

Serafín Alonso(✉), Antonio Morán, Daniel Pérez, Miguel A. Prada, Juan J. Fuertes, and Manuel Domínguez

Grupo de investigación en Supervisión, Control y Automatización de Procesos Industriales (SUPPRESS), Esc. de Ing. Industrial e Informática, Universidad de León, Campus de Vegazana s/n, 24007 León, Spain
{saloc,a.moran,dperl,ma.prada,jjfuem,manuel.dominguez}@unileon.es
http://suppress.unileon.es

Abstract. Water is a critical resource for life on the earth but it is becoming increasingly scarce. Therefore, water use should be sustainable and properly managed. The problem of water scarcity is still more stressed in cities, where buildings consume more and more water, especially commercial and institutional ones. In those buildings, HVAC (*Heating, Ventilating and Air Conditioning*) systems make an intensive use of water, especially the water-based cooling systems such as cooling towers, where a large amount of water is evaporated. In this paper, a method is proposed in order to estimate the evaporated water in cooling towers, considering the variations of environmental and operating conditions. We propose the use of a generative model which is able to generalize the estimation of the evaporated water, even in situations not included in the training data. A generative adversarial network (GAN) is used for training a deep learning-based generative model. The proposed method is tested using real data from a cooling tower located at the Hospital of León. Results show the probability distribution within which the estimation of evaporated water can be found, given the environmental and operating conditions.

Keywords: HVAC systems · Cooling tower · Evaporated water · Probabilistic estimation · Generative adversarial network

1 Introduction

Water is an increasingly scarce resource on the earth due to population growth, water contamination and droughts provoked by climate changes [18]. All of the above entails the depletion of aquifers and changes of groundwater recharge [14]. Water is a critical resource for life, so it should not be wasted and water supplies should attract sufficient attention. However, groundwater is unmonitored and mismanaged in many places in the world [5]. Due to its global importance, the use of water should be sustainable and properly managed.

L. Iliadis et al. (Eds.): EANN 2020, INNS 2, pp. 155–166, 2020.
https://doi.org/10.1007/978-3-030-48791-1_11

In cities, proliferation of urbanization areas, deficient maintenance of water infrastructures and poor waste management stress the problem of water scarcity [13]. The public water supply represents 21% in European Union [1], including buildings which account for the major use, in particular commercial and institutional ones [19,21]. One of the facilities which make an intensive use of water (around 48%) in those buildings are HVAC (*Heating, Ventilating and Air Conditioning*) systems [3,21], specially the water-based cooling systems such as cooling towers [9]. These systems can benefit from water efficiency measures, saving water and energy [4,9]. Some reports state that up to 30% of the volume of water consumed in buildings could be saved [1]. Therefore, sustainable water management should be adopted in order to reduce water use in buildings and protect the global water resources [19].

In large buildings, water for cooling towers accounts for almost all of the HVAC system's water consumption [21]. Moreover, the performance of the cooling towers depends mainly on ambient conditions, given a fixed quantity of heat to reject. Thus, the use of water for cooling towers should be analyzed in detail, previously to establish management strategies and plan its operation.

In the literature, authors focus on the use of differential equations solved with numerical methods for predicting the water loss in cooling towers [17]. In this case, many simulations with different data are required in order to cover all scenarios. However, artificial intelligence techniques are rarely applied for that purpose. On the other hand, artificial neural networks are used for predicting the performance of cooling towers, under a range of operating and ambient conditions [6,10]. However, traditional neural networks are not able to generate a trustworthy output if the surrounding conditions are not considered in the training data. The operating and environmental conditions in a cooling tower could vary, so the method should be able to generate a likely output, given the new conditions. Generative Adversarial Networks (GAN) [7] can engender a likely output, just from noise. In the literature, GANs have been mainly used for image processing and computer vision [15,20]. Apart from that, GANs have been applied recently for time series prediction, for instance, forecasting sensory data [12], predicting stock market [23] and generating melodies from lyrics [22]. Other applications of GANs include natural language, speech, voice and data augmentation [8].

In this paper, a method is proposed in order to estimate the evaporated water in cooling towers, considering the variations of environmental and operating conditions. Our method is able to provide a probabilistic distribution of the evaporated water, considering new and varying conditions. It relies on a generative model based on real past data. On the contrary, the state-of-the-art methods predict the water loss, given known conditions. These models are based on mathematical equations or artificial neural networks. The main contributions of this paper are:

- The development of a methodology to implement a virtual sensor able to estimate the evaporated water in cooling towers in different scenarios.

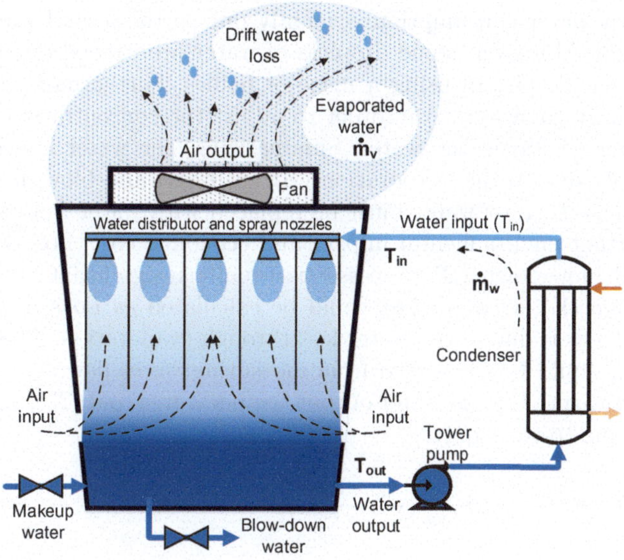

Fig. 1. Cooling tower scheme.

- The application of a generative model in a different research field, far away from well-known image generation.
- The test of the method using real data from a cooling tower located in a hospital building.

This paper is organized as follows: Sect. 2 defines the problem. In Sect. 3, the proposed methodology is presented. Here, the generative model is explained in detail. Section 4 describes the real cooling tower and the dataset used in the experiment. In Sect. 5, the experiment and results are presented and discussed. Finally, conclusions and future work are drawn in Sect. 6.

2 Problem Definition

A cooling tower is a system used to cool water by exchanging heat with the atmosphere, i.e. a water-air heat exchanger (see Fig. 1). The hot water (input) is passed through some nozzles located on the top which spray the water to increase contact surface with the air in order to improve the evaporation. Small droplets of water fall down on the fill in the tower. A fan usually induces an air draft in the opposite direction to falling droplets [11]. The water changes its phase from liquid to vapor, transferring the latent heat to the air. The air carries the heat from evaporating water in the cooling tower to the atmosphere. Therefore, atmospheric conditions influence directly on the evaporation process.

Cooling towers are commonly used by equipment in industries and buildings in order to dissipate heat. For example, water-cooled chillers make use of cooling towers to condense the refrigeration gas [10].

Their great water consumption is mainly due to the loss of water which is evaporated [10]. Moreover, some droplets of water are carried out through the air draft (drift), despite of using a maze of baffles. Furthermore, the water is drained regularly (blow-down) in order to adjust the concentration of the total dissolved solids (TDS) in the water. Summarizing, the water loss in a cooling tower is mainly due to the evaporation (E), drift (D) and blow-down (B), i.e., $Loss = E + D + B$. Lost water must be replaced with water from supply what has an important environmental impact and economic cost. Lost water due to drift (D) and blow-down (B) processes is usually insignificant with regard to the evaporation (E), so water loss could be calculated as $Loss = E$, assuming that the total loss is due to the water loss through evaporation. The evaporated water flow $\dot{m}_v$ could be calculated from measuring water flow $\dot{m}_w$, water input temperature (warm) T_{in} and water output temperature (cold) T_{out} in the cooling tower, according to the Eq. 1.

$$\dot{m}_v = \frac{\dot{m}_w * c_w * (T_{in} - T_{out})}{H_v} \tag{1}$$

c_w is the specific heat of water and H_v is the latent heat of vaporization necessary for water changes from liquid to vapor. Thus, a flow meter connected in the input of the cooling tower could provide the lost water.

On the other hand, several factors influence on the evaporation process and define the performance of the cooling tower, so they should be considered. For example, the air flow (natural or forced by the fan), the input and output water temperatures and the environmental conditions (outdoor temperature and humidity) determine the operation of the cooling tower. Moreover, these factors could vary slightly, modifying the surrounding conditions which affect the evaporation and consequently, the operation and performance of the cooling tower.

Therefore, the estimation of the evaporated water in a cooling tower, considering the environmental and operating conditions, could be useful to plan the operation of a cooling tower and save water and improve its performance. Note that, that estimation is affected by the environmental and operating conditions and therefore the quantity of evaporated water may be estimated with a certain confidence interval since those conditions could change. For that task, a method to implement a virtual sensor could be developed so that it is able to estimate the probability distribution of the evaporated water in a cooling tower, given the surrounding conditions.

3 Methodology

In this paper, we propose the development of a methodology to implement a virtual sensor able to estimate the probability distribution of the evaporated water in a cooling tower, given any potential environmental and operating conditions. Once the virtual sensor is built, it should be able to estimate the evaporated water even under abnormal conditions (not only normal ones). For example, the outdoor temperature could increase above normal values during a heat wave or

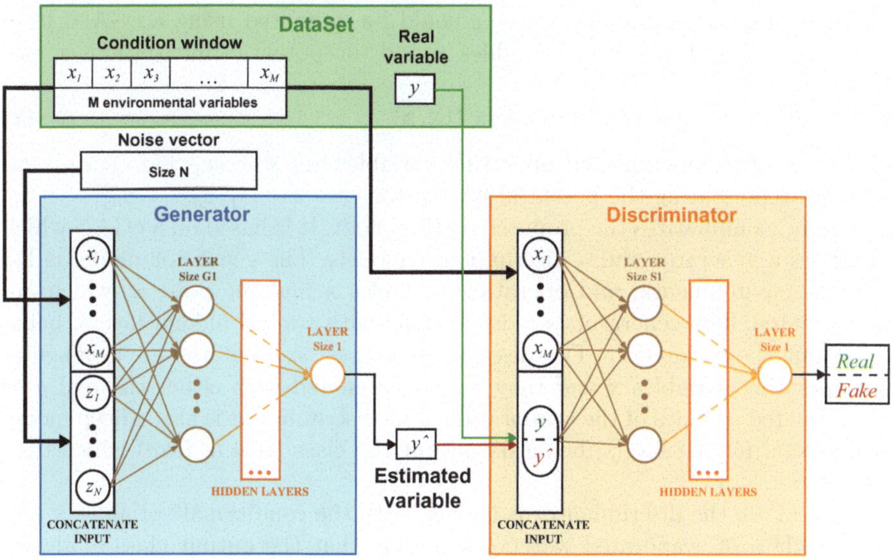

Fig. 2. Proposed methodology based on cGAN.

the relative humidity could increase because of fog banks, affecting the evaporation process in a cooling tower. These abnormal situations should be considered by the method in order to estimate a range within which the evaporated water value is very likely to be found.

In order to tackle that problem, we propose the use of a generative model which is able to generalize the estimation of the evaporated water, even in situations not included in training data. A generative adversarial network (GAN) is used for training a deep learning-based generative model. GAN is a framework for building generative models via an adversarial process, which uses two models simultaneously: a generator model that captures the data distribution and a discriminator model that estimates the probability that a sample is from the training data rather than the generator [7]. The generator is in charge of providing new plausible data that are similar to real data. The function of the discriminator is to classify data as either real (from the input dataset) or fake (from the generator). To sump up, the generator tries to fool the discriminator by generating real-looking data.

In our case, the evaporated water (estimation) is influenced by the environmental and operating conditions, so the generative model is conditioned on some auxiliary variables (outdoor temperature, humidity and air flow). Thus, an extension of GAN, called conditioned generative adversarial network (cGAN) [16], is required. A model based on cGAN is able to consider contextual information with slight variations.

Therefore, the evaporated water $\hat{y}$ could be estimated using a cGAN, from environmental and operating variables $\mathbf{x}$ and the potential fluctuations $\mathbf{z}$ (see Eq. 2)

$$\hat{y} = f(\mathbf{x}, \mathbf{z}), \tag{2}$$

where the environmental and operating variables are $\mathbf{x} = [x_1, x_2, \ldots, x_m]$ and the noise representing the potential fluctuations are $\mathbf{z} = [z_1, z_2, \ldots, z_n]$.

Figure 2 summarizes the proposed methodology. It is based on a cGAN which comprises a generator and a discriminator models. The generator model is fed with the environmental and operating variables $\mathbf{x}$ and the noise $\mathbf{z}$, which are concatenated. The generator is a deep model with several hidden layers, being its output the estimation. The discriminator uses as input the environmental and operating variables $\mathbf{x}$ and they are concatenated with either the real y or the estimated $\hat{y}$ values of the evaporation. The discriminator is also a deep model with several hidden layers, being its output the class (real of fake) which they belong to.

First of all, the discriminator is trained with the conditional variables $\mathbf{x}$ and the real data of evaporated water y assuming that the output class is always real, updating the discriminator model. Then, the combined model, i.e. both the generator and the discriminator are trained with the conditional variables $\mathbf{x}$, the noise $\mathbf{z}$ and the estimated data of evaporated water $\hat{y}$ assuming that the output class is always fake, updating only the generator model.

4 Real System and Dataset

Data from a mechanical draft cooling tower located at the Hospital of León are used in the experiment. That cooling tower by Baltimore Aircoil, model S-3654-NM (see Fig. 3), cools water from a chiller by Trane, model CVGF650 (cooling capacity of 650 tons). An axial fan, driven by a three-phase induction motor (18.5 KW) and managed by a variable speed drive (Moeller DF6-340-22K), forces the air through the cooling tower. Two pumps NK 150-315/307/BAQE by Grundfos driven by three-phase induction motors (30 KW) are used, one to propel water to the cooling tower and the other to maintain a water flow through the condenser. Moreover, the temperatures of input and output water are measured using sensors by Johnson Controls, model TS-9101-8224. It also incorporates three resistors of 5 KW to avoid water freezing.

BMS (*Building Management System*) acquires and stores data from the operation of the cooling tower (input and output water temperatures and fan speed) and also from the ambient (dry-bulb temperature and relative humidity). The water flow through the condenser ($\dot{m}_w$) has been measured by an ultrasonic portable meter (Fluxus F601 by Flexim), due to the lack of permanent flow meter in the chiller. Note that, the water flow is required to calculate the evaporated water $\dot{m}_v$ using Eq. 1. Table 1 lists the variables involved in the experiment.

According to Eq. 2, the estimation of evaporated water $\hat{\dot{m}}_v$ is

$$\hat{\dot{m}}_v = f\big([Ta, Hr, Dt, Fs], \mathbf{z}\big) \tag{3}$$

Fig. 3. Photo of cooling tower at the Hospital of León.

Table 1. Variables used in the experiment.

Symbol	Variable name	Unit
Ta	Dry-bulb temperature	°C
Hr	Relative humidity	%
Dt	Input-Output water temperature difference $(T_{in} - T_{out})$	°C
Fs	Fan speed	%
$\dot{m}_v$	Evaporated water flow	m^3/h

where the conditional variables are $\mathbf{x} = [Ta, Hr, Dt, Fs]$, and noisy variables introduced to the model are $\mathbf{z}$. The noisy variables are generated using a normal distribution centered at 0 and within 1 standard deviation.

Data from these variables are collected for 40 days. The sampling rate is 1 min, but then data are resampled, averaging values each hour. Therefore, the total number of samples is 960. The evaporated water flow $\dot{m}_v$ is computed from measured water flow $\dot{m}_w$, specific heat c_w, difference of input and output water temperatures $(T_{in} - T_{out})$ and latent heat of vaporization H_v.

Data are scaled in range $[-1, 1]$ and split into training and test datasets. 75% of total samples are used for training (30 days) and the remaining for testing (10 days).

5 Experiment and Results

Figure 4 shows the architecture of the cGAN developed to estimate the evaporated water. Several configurations were tested but a simple network with only

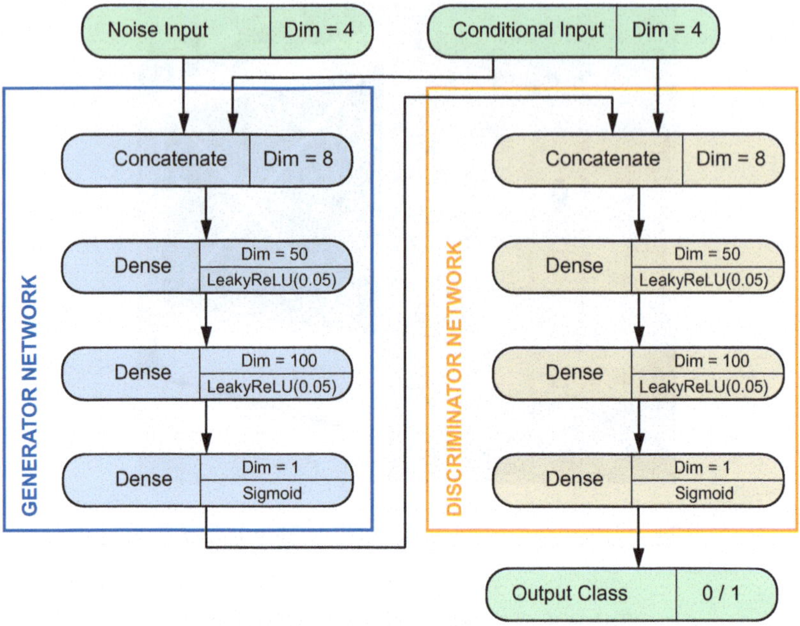

Fig. 4. Architecture of cGAN model implemented.

dense layers for both generator and discriminator is used since it gave the most accurate results. The dense layers are trained using a *LeakyRelu* activation since this function introduces non-linearity in the model without the *Dying ReLU problem* where some neurons remain inactive. The last layer of each network, since they are composed of only one neuron, uses a sigmoid function since the output of the generator is a regressor, and the output of the discriminator is a classification.

The input of the model are two concatenated vectors since we are working with a conditional GAN. One vector is composed of the variables related to the cooling tower which define the working state $\mathbf{x}$ and a noise vector $\mathbf{z}$ that is used to create the generative model. The size of the noise vector is tunable and is another parameter of the model. In our case, the size of the noise is set to 4 (equal to variables) since it provides the best results.

The MAPE index (see Eq. 4) is used as metrics to evaluate the model since the values are easily understood by any engineer providing a direct measurement of the accuracy of the evaporated water and delimits the error in the cooling production estimation [2].

$$MAPE = \frac{100\%}{n} \sum_{i=1}^{n} \left| \frac{y_i - \hat{y}_i}{y_i} \right| \tag{4}$$

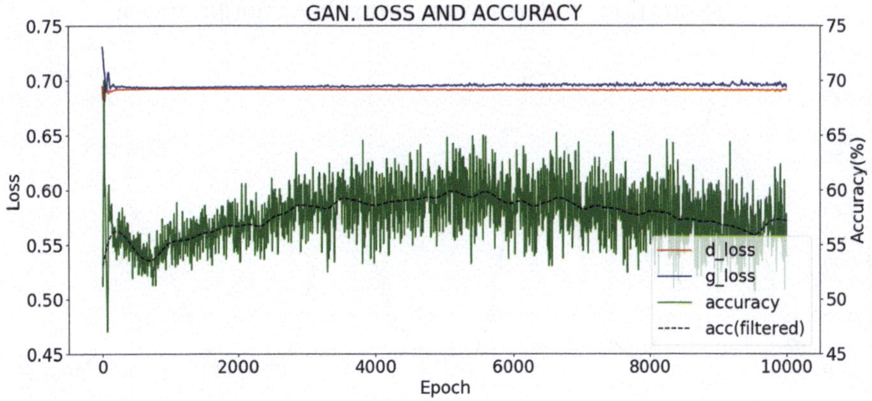

Fig. 5. Loss and accuracy for both generator and discriminator.

Since the cGAN provides a probabilistic estimation of the calculated variable, to test the performance of the algorithm, once the model is trained, several values of the evaporated water are calculated for the same timestep. The mean value is calculated for this probability distribution and this mean is used as value in the MAPE index. So the model is tuned to minimize the error of the mean value of the calculated variable, the accuracy of the distribution is not taken into account.

The model is trained using the training dataset (75% of total). Cross validation is applied for selecting the parameters which provide the lowest MAPE value. Figure 5 shows the loss results for both the generator and the discriminator and the accuracy of the model. The accuracy variability denotes that there is no convergence error so the model is not always generating false data. Since the accuracy fluctuates, the filtered value is shown. The maximum accuracy is achieved around 5000 epochs. Also, since the loss of both networks are not zero and the values are stable through the epochs, the model does not collapse.

Once the model is trained, the evaporated water of the test dataset (remaining 25% of total) is calculated. Since we want to obtain a distribution, each sample is calculated several times changing the noise values which are generated randomly. In order to obtain a detailed distribution, 5000 values are calculated for each sample. Figure 6 shows the results of applying the resulting cGAN model to the test dataset. The MAPE error for this dataset is 1.54%. Figure 6a shows the results of the mean estimated value of water evaporation (blue points) and the real one (cyan stars) and the areas are the results of the confidence interval for the distribution of each sample.

Figure 6b shows in detail the probability distribution for three different working points of the cooling tower that are considered as representative. The left one corresponds to a high cooling demand. This distribution has a high variance so the results are less accurate, also it shows a bit of asymmetry. The right one corresponds to a low cooling demand where the tower is more stable so the

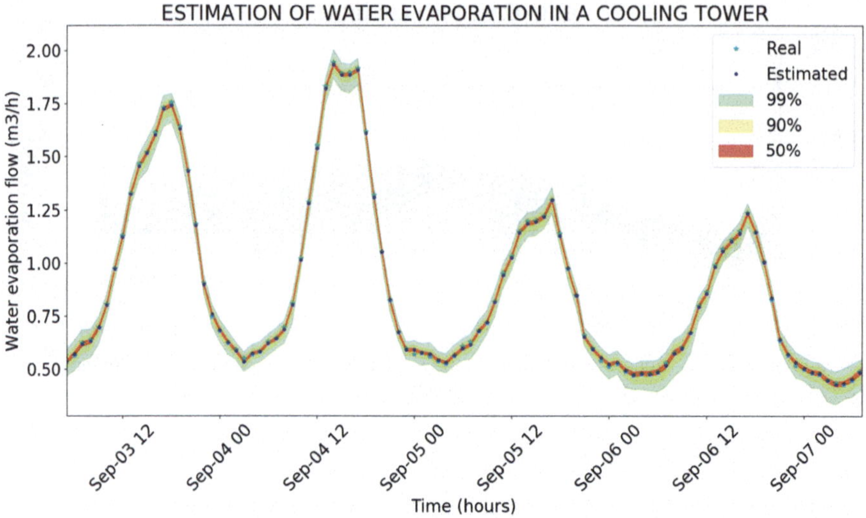

(a) Estimation of evaporated water and the confidence interval for the test dataset.

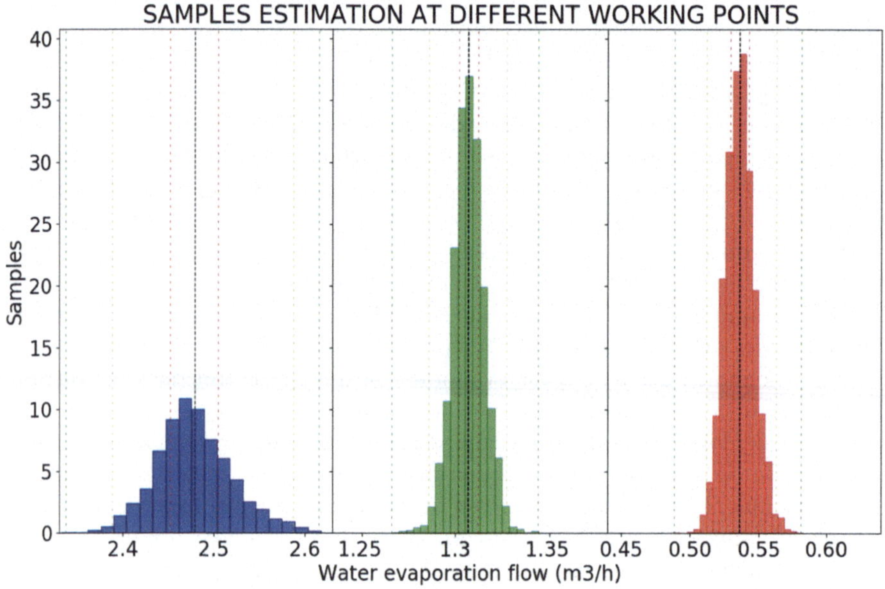

(b) Histograms of evaporated water in different working points of the cooling tower.

Fig. 6. Estimation of evaporated water.

variance is less and the forecasting is more accurate. Lastly, the central one is a transient point between two states and it also has a low variance.

6 Conclusions

This paper proposes the use of a Generative Adversarial Network (GAN) to estimate a variable that is not measured directly so it can be seen as a virtual sensor. Since the evaporated water is highly dependable of varying environmental variables, it is difficult to estimate the real value so the use of this kind of neural networks let us estimate a probabilistic distribution of the real value.

GAN, which has been widely use in image generation so far, has proven to estimate analog values taking into account external variables that provide a working condition and noise that alter the working point introducing several disturbances. The output of the model provides a probabilistic estimation of the value of the evaporated water so instead of using a unique value we can use the confidence interval to estimate the extreme values that the evaporation can have.

Although the cGAN model provides good results, only the static information has been considered, the actual sample of evaporated water is estimated using only the actual values of the conditional variables. As future work, it should be used past information of the variables with temporal layers such as LSTM to improve the results. Moreover, the proposed methodology should be compared with other probabilistic methods.

References

1. BIO Intelligence Service: Water performance of buildings. Tech. rep. Final report prepared for European Commission, DG Environment (2012)
2. Bowerman, B., O'Connell, R., Koehler, A.: Forecasting, Time Series, and Regression: An Applied Approach. Duxbury Advanced Series in Statistics and Decision Sciences. Thomson Brooks/Cole, Belmont (2005)
3. Dziegielewski, B., Kiefer, J.C., Opitz, E.M., Porter, G.A., Lantz, G.L.: Commercial and Institutional End Uses of Water. American Water Works Association Research Foundation (2000)
4. Eades, W.G.: Energy and water recovery using air-handling unit condensate from laboratory HVAC systems. Sustain. Cities Soc. **42**, 162–175 (2018). https://doi.org/10.1016/j.scs.2018.07.006
5. Famiglietti, J.S.: The global groundwater crisis. Nat. Clim. Change **4**(11), 945–948 (2014). https://doi.org/10.1038/nclimate2425
6. Gao, M., Sun, F.Z., Zhou, S.J., Shi, Y.T., Zhao, Y.B., Wang, N.H.: Performance prediction of wet cooling tower using artificial neural network under cross-wind conditions. Int. J. Therm. Sci. **48**(3), 583–589 (2009). https://doi.org/10.1016/j.ijthermalsci.2008.03.012
7. Goodfellow, I., Pouget-Abadie, J., Mirza, M., Xu, B., Warde-Farley, D., Ozair, S., Courville, A., Bengio, Y.: Generative adversarial nets. In: Ghahramani, Z., Welling, M., Cortes, C., Lawrence, N.D., Weinberger, K.Q. (eds.) Advances in Neural Information Processing Systems, vol. 27, pp. 2672–2680. Curran Associates, Inc. (2014)

8. Gui, J., Sun, Z., Wen, Y., Tao, D., Ye, J.: A review on generative adversarial networks: Algorithms, theory, and applications. CoRR abs/2001.06937 (2020). https://arxiv.org/abs/2001.06937
9. Hawit, O., Jaffe, T.: Water-energy nexus: heat rejection systems. ASHRAE J. **59**(9), 28–39 (2017)
10. Hosoz, M., Ertunc, H., Bulgurcu, H.: Performance prediction of a cooling tower using artificial neural network. Energy Convers. Manage. **48**(4), 1349–1359 (2007). https://doi.org/10.1016/j.enconman.2006.06.024
11. Jin, G.Y., Cai, W.J., Lu, L., Lee, E.L., Chiang, A.: A simplified modeling of mechanical cooling tower for control and optimization of HVAC systems. Energy Convers. Manage. **48**(2), 355–365 (2007). https://doi.org/10.1016/j.enconman.2006.07.010
12. Koochali, A., Schichtel, P., Ahmed, S., Dengel, A.: Probabilistic forecasting of sensory data with generative adversarial networks - ForGAN. CoRR abs/1903.12549 (2019). http://arxiv.org/abs/1903.12549
13. Koop, S.H.A., van Leeuwen, C.J.: The challenges of water, waste and climate change in cities. Environ. Dev. Sustain. **19**, 385–418 (2017). https://doi.org/10.1007/s10668-016-9760-4
14. Kundzewicz, Z.W., Döll, P.: Will groundwater ease freshwater stress under climate change? Hydrol. Sci. J. **54**(4), 665–675 (2009). https://doi.org/10.1623/hysj.54.4.665
15. Ledig, C., Theis, L., Huszar, F., Caballero, J., Aitken, A.P., Tejani, A., Totz, J., Wang, Z., Shi, W.: Photo-realistic single image super-resolution using a generative adversarial network. CoRR abs/1609.04802 (2016). http://arxiv.org/abs/1609.04802
16. Mirza, M., Osindero, S.: Conditional generative adversarial nets. CoRR abs/1411.1784 (2014). http://arxiv.org/abs/1411.1784
17. Qureshi, B.A., Zubair, S.M.: A unified approach to predict evaporation losses in evaporative heat exchangers. Int. J. Refrig. **34**(8), 1866–1876 (2011). https://doi.org/10.1016/j.ijrefrig.2011.06.008
18. Richey, A.S., Thomas, B.F., Lo, M.H., Reager, J.T., Famiglietti, J.S., Voss, K., Swenson, S., Rodell, M.: Quantifying renewable groundwater stress with GRACE. Water Resour. Res. **51**(7), 5217–5238 (2015). https://doi.org/10.1002/2015WR017349
19. Stec, A.: Sustainable Water Management in Buildings, Water Science and Technology Library, vol. 90. Springer International Publishing, Cham (2020). https://doi.org/10.1007/978-3-030-35959-1
20. Tran, L., Yin, X., Liu, X.: Disentangled representation learning GAN for pose-invariant face recognition. In: 2017 IEEE Conference on Computer Vision and Pattern Recognition (CVPR). pp. 1283–1292, July 2017. https://doi.org/10.1109/CVPR.2017.141
21. Weimar, D., Browning, A.: Reducing water costs in building HVAC systems. Facilities Engineering Journal **37**(3), 24–26 (2010)
22. Yu, Y.B., Canales, S.: Conditional LSTM-GAN for melody generation from lyrics. ArXiv abs/1908.05551 (2019)
23. Zhang, K., Zhong, G., Dong, J., Wang, S., Wang, Y.: Stock market prediction based on generative adversarial network. Procedia Comput. Sci. **147**, 400–406 (2019). https://doi.org/10.1016/j.procs.2019.01.256

Reconstructing Environmental Variables with Missing Field Data via End-to-End Machine Learning

Matteo Sangiorgio[1], Stefano Barindelli[2](✉), Valerio Guglieri[2], Giovanna Venuti[2], and Giorgio Guariso[1]

[1] Department of Electronics, Information, and Bioengineering, Politecnico di Milano, Milan, Italy

[2] Department of Civil and Environmental Engineering, Politecnico di Milano, Milan, Italy

stefano.barindelli@polimi.it

Abstract. Real-world time series often present missing values due to sensor malfunctions or human errors. Traditionally, missing values are simply omitted or reconstructed through imputation or interpolation methods. Omitting missing values may cause temporal discontinuity. Reconstruction methods, on the other hand, alter in some way the original time series. In this paper, we consider an application in the field of meteorological variables that exploits end-to-end machine learning. The idea is to entrust the task of dealing with missing values to a suitably trained recurrent neural network that completely by-passes the phase of reconstruction of missing values. A difficult case of reproduction of a rainfall field from five rain gauges in Northern Italy is used as an example, and the results are compared to those computed by more traditional methods. The proposed methodology is general-purpose and can be easily applied to every kind of spatial time series prediction problem, quite common in many environmental studies.

Keywords: Time series · Rainfall field · Data augmentation · Artificial neural networks · LSTM cell

1 Introduction

A frequent issue encountered while working on environmental problems, such as weather forecasting or air pollution, that exploit data recorded with ground sensors, is the presence of missing values. This may be due to human errors, but more frequently depends on the failure of the sensors or the transmission network, particularly in severe weather conditions. The most common methods to deal with missing values are imputation or interpolation [1–3]. Since both operations present critical aspects, the approach investigated in this work aims at training a Long Short-Term Memory (LSTM) Neural Network (NN) bypassing this step.

The presence of missing data can be tackled with a variety of methods, depending on the dimension of the dataset, the choice of the prediction task, and the nature of data

L. Iliadis et al. (Eds.): EANN 2020, INNS 2, pp. 167–178, 2020.
https://doi.org/10.1007/978-3-030-48791-1_12

themselves. A classical approach is to fill the gaps with the mean of the data (mean imputation) or with the closest known value (i.e., nearest-neighbour substitution). More sophisticated techniques fit a function to the known data and then evaluate it in the unknown spots to fill the gaps. The fitted function is usually a polynomial or, in case of spline interpolation, a combination of polynomials. Other techniques to perform this task investigate the statistical behavior of the dataset: one of them is the kriging method, which relies on the computation of the empirical variogram of the considered data [4, 5].

When the problem deals with both spatial and temporal distribution of different variables, the number of interpolation possibilities increases, as spatial cross-correlations and temporal autocorrelation can be taken into account. Another approach that considers both time and space relations is using an (often very complex) physically-based model which assimilates the current available data [6–9]. However, real-time assimilation is mostly computationally prohibitive and requires data about other variables that may also be missing.

Regardless of the algorithm being used to obtain the cleansed input data, this procedure introduces a reconstruction error that will propagate in the subsequent phases necessary to compute the desired output.

In this paper, we propose an end-to-end machine learning approach [10, 11] able to autonomously deal with missing input values, completely bypassing the phase of reconstruction. Our idea consists of training a Recurrent Neural Network (RNN), specifically an LSTM net, using the raw dataset with missing data, letting the RNN itself compensate for the lack of information by exploiting the spatial and temporal correlations in the dataset.

The dataset considered in this contribution consists of five time-series of rain rate, collected by a network of gauges located in Northern Italy. Artificial failures are introduced in the data series to test the capacity of an LSTM architecture to overcome the problem of missing input values. The ability to compute a nonlinear analytical function of the measurement values is used as a performance indicator.

2 Materials and Methods

2.1 The Measurement Network

The study area (Fig. 1) is located in the North of Italy and is delimited by the watersheds of the Olona, Lambro, and Seveso rivers, covering a surface of about 1400 km^2. This is an almost completely flat area, except for the northern boundary where the Alpine mountain chain begins. The region is well known to be subject to very intense and localized convective storms [12–15] that lead to severe damages, especially in Milan municipality.

The input dataset consists of 4 complete years (2015 to 2018) of rainfall values collected by five rain gauges, namely s_1, s_2, s_3, s_4, and s_5, with a temporal resolution of

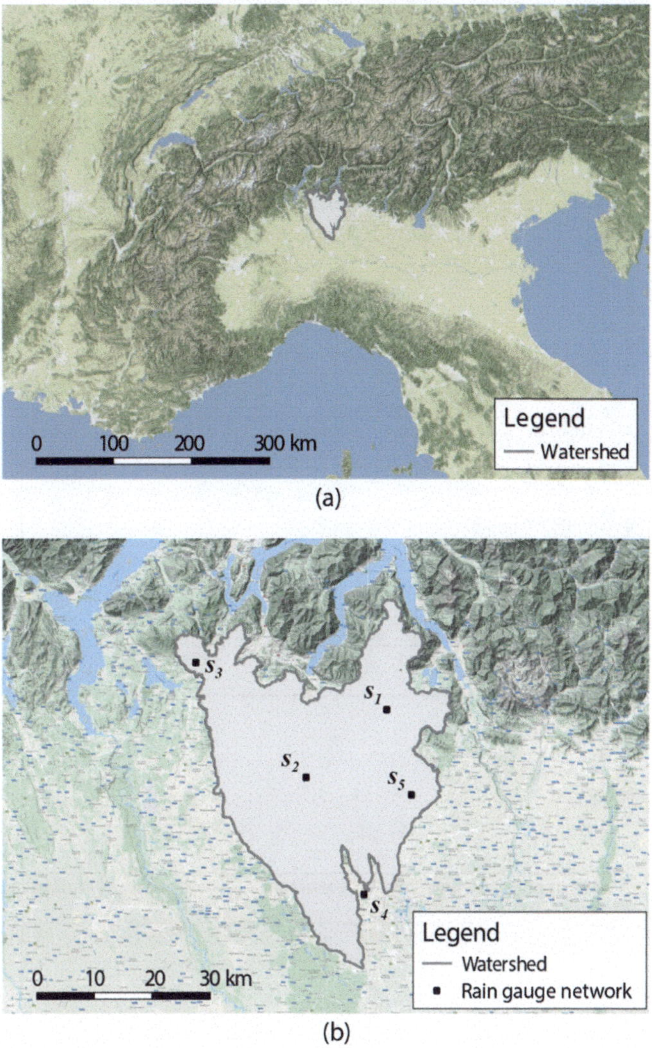

Fig. 1. Panel (a) shows a geographical overview of the study area. Panel (b) shows the position of the considered rain gauge network in the Seveso, Olona and Lambro hydrological basins

5 min (Fig. 2). These rain gauges belong to the network managed by ARPA Lombardia, the environmental protection agency of the Lombardy region.

Pearson's and Spearman's correlation coefficients have been computed to quantify the spatial correlation and the results are reported in Table 1 and Table 2. These values have been calculated for every couple of rain gauges only when they were recording at

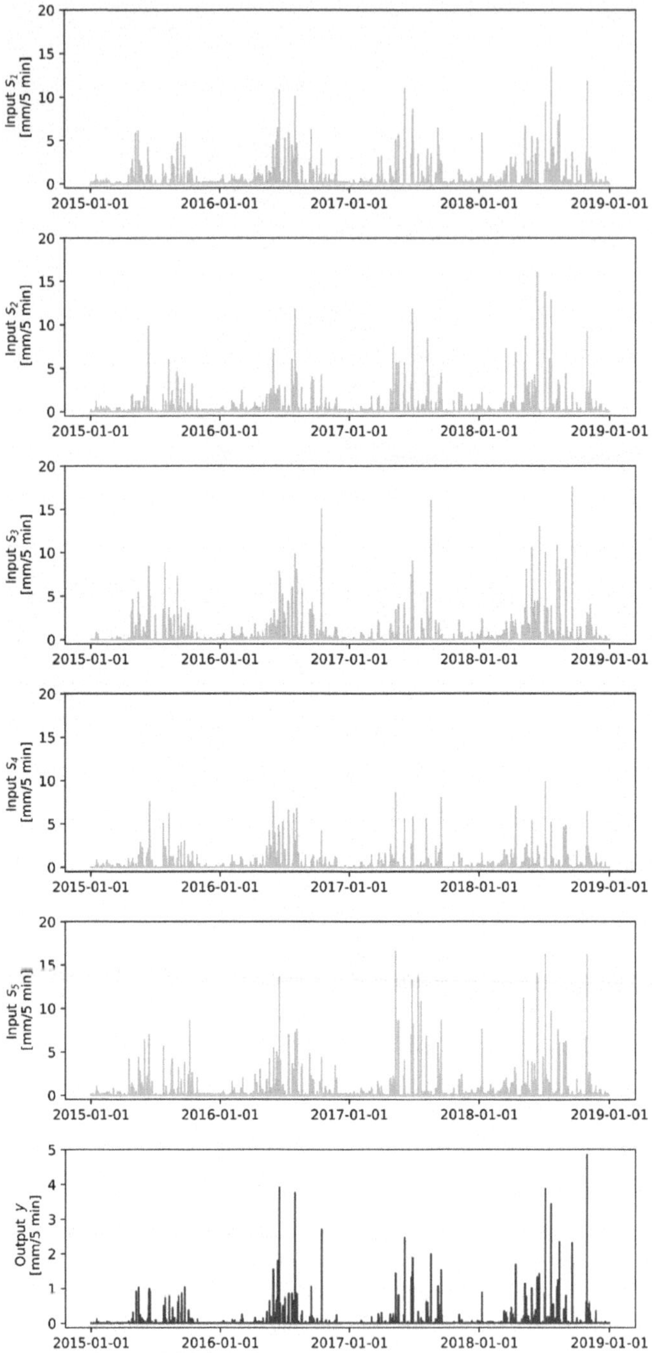

Fig. 2. Temporal series of the five inputs (light grey), i.e., the rainfall rate measured by s_1, s_2, s_3, s_4, s_5 rain gauges, and the corresponding output y (dark grey), computed as a non linear function of the inputs.

the same time an amount of rain different from zero. In this way, we investigate the correlation only during rain periods.

The spatial correlation between the measurement stations is not high, despite the relatively small dimension of the basin. This makes the reconstruction of the rainfall field particularly difficult.

Table 1. Pearson's correlation coefficients.

Stations	s_1	s_2	s_3	s_4	s_5
s_1	–	0.25	0.14	0.21	0.36
s_2	0.25	–	0.25	0.31	0.24
s_3	0.14	0.25	–	0.13	0.12
s_4	0.21	0.31	0.13	–	0.23
s_5	0.36	0.24	0.12	0.23	–

Table 2. Spearman's correlation coefficients.

Stations	s_1	s_2	s_3	s_4	s_5
s_1	–	0.30	0.20	0.30	0.37
s_2	0.30	–	0.26	0.34	0.30
s_3	0.20	0.26	–	0.23	0.20
s_4	0.30	0.34	0.23	–	0.34
s_5	0.37	0.30	0.20	0.34	–

For each time step, the five values recorded by the rain gauges are combined into a nonlinear analytical function to obtain the correspondent output:

$$s_{tot}(t) = (p_1 \cdot s_1(t) + p_2 \cdot s_2(t) + p_3 \cdot s_3(t) + p_4 \cdot s_4(t) + p_5 \cdot s_5(t)) / \sum\nolimits_i p_i \quad (1)$$

$$y(t) = f(s_{tot}(t)) \cdot s_{tot}(t) = \left(1 - e^{-s_{tot}(t)}\right) \cdot s_{tot}(t) \quad (2)$$

where $s_{tot}(t)$ is a normalized weighted linear combination of the inputs; $s_1(t)$, $s_2(t)$, $s_3(t)$, $s_4(t)$, $s_5(t)$ are the rainfall rates at each rain gauge measured at each time step (5 min); $y(t)$ is the output of the nonlinear function considered (bottom panel of Fig. 2). The weights and the function have been chosen in order to simulate the computation of the effective runoff in the catchment. This is usually computed using, as weights p_i, the areas of the Thiessen polygons represented by each sensor, or some spatial interpolation method. The exponential factor $f(s_{tot}(t))$ represents the effect of soil saturation for which runoff is small when the total precipitation is limited and becomes almost equal to the total rainfall when it is abundant. The full dynamic of the soil water content is not taken into account by this formulation.

Note that the definition of a known analytical function, instead of using the actual runoff of the river system, is necessary to detect the NN performances in solving the missing value issue alone. When using real runoff data, the overall performance of the

NN would be due both to the ability to interpret missing data and to replicate the actual rainfall-runoff process. For the same reason, using other, more complex, analytical formulations of the target set y, does not change the general conclusions we reach.

The characteristic of this dataset is the absence of missing data along the considered time horizon: this allows the computation of the output at each time step.

2.2 Machine Learning Training Dataset

Since rain gauges require careful maintenance, it is not always possible to avoid the onset of technical problems, external damages, or failures that compromise the continuity of the collected temporal series. The characterization of the missing data is performed investigating the time to failure (TTF) and the time to restore (TTR) of the entire regional rain gauge dataset managed by ARPA Lombardia, consisting of the data collected by 19 sensors for about 20 years (they were activated at different dates). The TTF is defined as the length of the time interval between two consecutive failures, i.e., the period of correct functioning of the sensor. On the other hand, the TTR is defined as the length of the time interval required to fix a malfunctioning sensor, i.e., the period in which the instrument collects no data. For both TTF and TTR histograms, an exponential distribution [16] has been fitted with $\text{mean}_{\text{TTF}} = 442.00$ and $\text{mean}_{\text{TTR}} = 10.79$ time steps, respectively. These two values also represent the exponential rate of the distributions. Thus their values strongly affect the shape of such distributions: the lower the mean value, the more the probability density function is stretched to the left. This is due to the presence of many short duration values and fewer long duration values. By sampling these two estimated distributions iteratively, it is possible to generate any number of synthetic time series of missing data within the complete input dataset of the five rain gauges. Missing values of these synthetic time series are filled with a marker constituted by an out-of-range value: in this case, -1. The obtained input sequences with out-of-range values are used to train an LSTM model together with the known output of the complete time series.

It must be noted that, despite the training set being constituted by more than a million values for each sensor, the number of rainfall episodes is much more limited: recorded values differ from zero only 3% of the time. Failures are distributed on the time series according to actual statistics, and thus cases, when a simulated failure occurs during a rainfall event, are also rare.

2.3 The Training Procedure

The proposed procedure, hereafter called end-to-end machine learning, differs from the traditional pipeline: the data filling step, with its related critical aspects, is avoided, and the LSTM model directly manages missing values (Fig. 3). Note that Fig. 3 describes the use of the model in inference mode, i.e., it shows the forward pass only, without representing the backward pass.

Starting from the four years without missing values, we generated an arbitrary number (5 in this case) of repetitions of the entire dataset with missing values extracted from the distribution of TTF and TTR. All the repetitions of 2015 (a year with low precipitation) and 2018 (with high rainfall) composed the training set. The validation

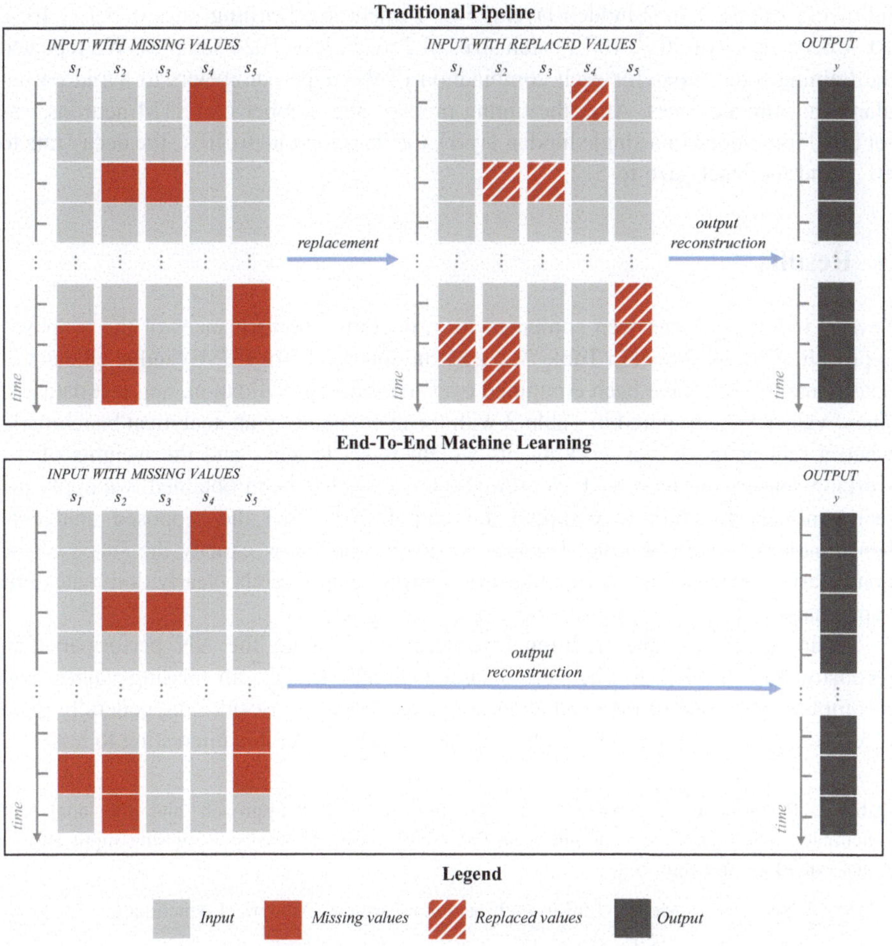

Fig. 3. Comparison between the Traditional Pipeline for managing missing data and the End-to-End Machine Learning used in this work.

set, used to determine the NN architecture and hyperparameters, is made by the five synthetic repetitions of the year 2016. Finally, the repetitions of the year 2017 have not been involved in the NN identification and are used to evaluate the network performances fairly. Performance metrics are thus computed as averages of five synthetic repetitions.

The neural structure adopted in this work is an LSTM net. Each LSTM cell has three gates (input, output, and forget gate), a cell state, and a hidden state [17, 18]. The hidden and cell states are responsible for keeping track of the relevant information provided by the input. The input and forget gates define how much a new input and the current state respectively affect the new state of the cell. The output gate determines how much the current state affects the output. The best combination of the hyperparameters has been selected using a traditional grid search approach. We evaluated the following values: 1 or 2 hidden layers; 5 or 10 neurons; learning rates of 10^{-1}, 10^{-2}, 10^{-3}; decay rates of 10^{-3}, 10^{-4}; batch sizes of 256, 512, or 1024 samples. We repeated the training three times for each combination of the hyperparameters to avoid particularly unfortunate cases. After the tuning process, the number of LSTM neurons was set to 10 (organized in a single hidden layer), the learning rate to 10^{-2}, the decay rate to 10^{-3}, and the batch size to 512.

3 Results

Several indicators have been computed to evaluate the performances of the proposed approach. First, as shown in Table 3, the Mean Squared Error (MSE) and coefficient of determination (R^2) have been computed over the training, validation, and test datasets. These values are compared in Table 3 with those obtained by an analytical benchmark: when a rain gauge is not working, its weight is set to zero, and the weights of the working sensors are increased accordingly. Once s_{tot} has been obtained, we apply the real nonlinear function to compute the output. Note that the proposed analytical benchmark is somehow unfair because we assume to know exactly the shape of the nonlinearity, which is generally unknown. Despite that, the NN clearly dominates this benchmark, with a 22% improvement of R^2 in the test set.

Figure 4 presents the traditional scatterplots showing the NN performance in reconstructing the output when the dataset is complete, i.e., no missing values, and incomplete, as in one of the synthetic sequences generated. Besides the generally good agreement between the actual output and the computed one, it is interesting to note that

Table 3. Performance comparison between the end-to-end approach and the analytical benchmark. The metrics are computed on the samples with at least one missing input and an actual output greater than 0.

Set	Metric	End-to-end machine learning	Analytical benchmark
Training	MSE	$0.83 \cdot 10^{-3}$	$1.52 \cdot 10^{-3}$
Training	R^2	0.94	0.89
Validation	MSE	$1.14 \cdot 10^{-3}$	$2.10 \cdot 10^{-3}$
Validation	R^2	0.91	0.84
Test	MSE	$1.86 \cdot 10^{-3}$	$4.81 \cdot 10^{-3}$
Test	R^2	0.86	0.64

the NN misses some episodes for which it definitely underestimated the output values. There are points in training, validation, and test datasets where the modeled output is very low, while the correct value should have been much higher. They represent the cases when the missing values were exactly related to the rain gauge where the peak precipitation was taking place.

One such episode is illustrated in column (a) of Fig. 5 (note that the input hyetographs go to −1 when the value is missing). The values recorded at s_4 are high and missing for the whole episode. Since the blackout started when it was not raining, nothing can be gained from the time profile. The rainfall episode partly interested also

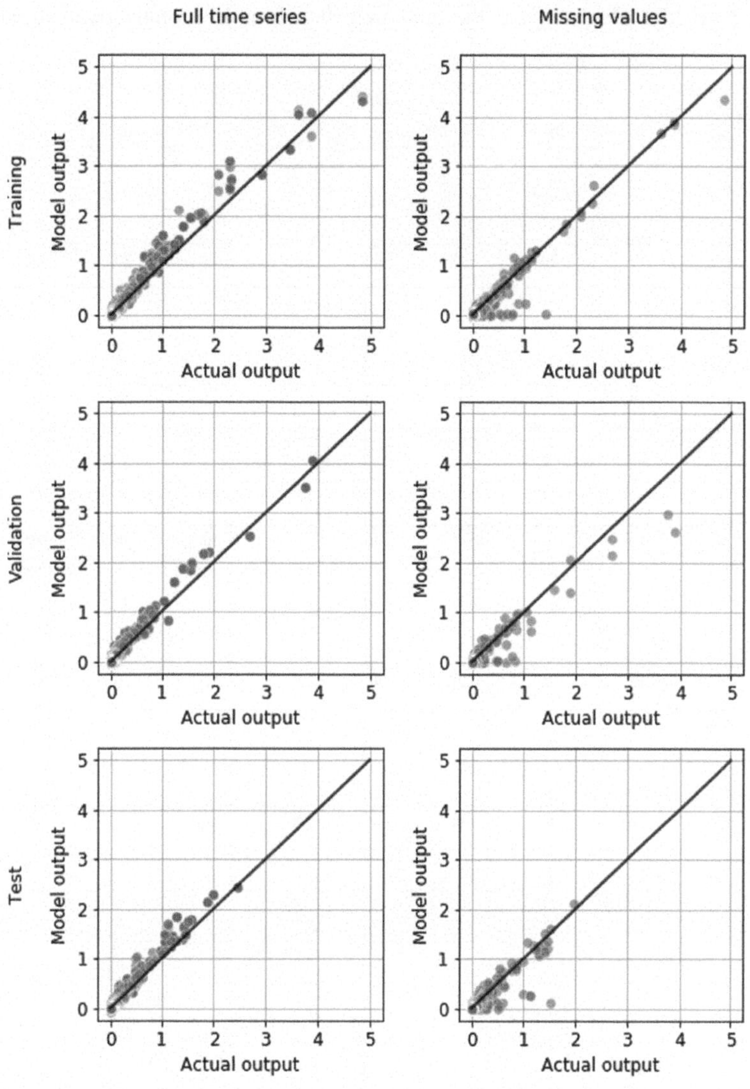

Fig. 4. Scatterplots showing the LSTM performances in the output reconstruction with a complete input dataset (left column) and with a dataset with missing values (right column). Performances are computed over train, validation, and test sets.

station 5, which however has a limited area and thus the output, particularly the second peak, is substantially missed. Things are different for the second episode in column (b). Again, station 4 is out-of-service, but the rainfall episode is more relevant on the other stations, and thus, peak values are almost perfectly fitted.

The NN performance in Fig. 5 (b), demonstrates that the information provided by the out-of-service station is not necessary to predict the output in the considered episode correctly. Despite that, the analytical benchmark strongly overestimates the peaks.

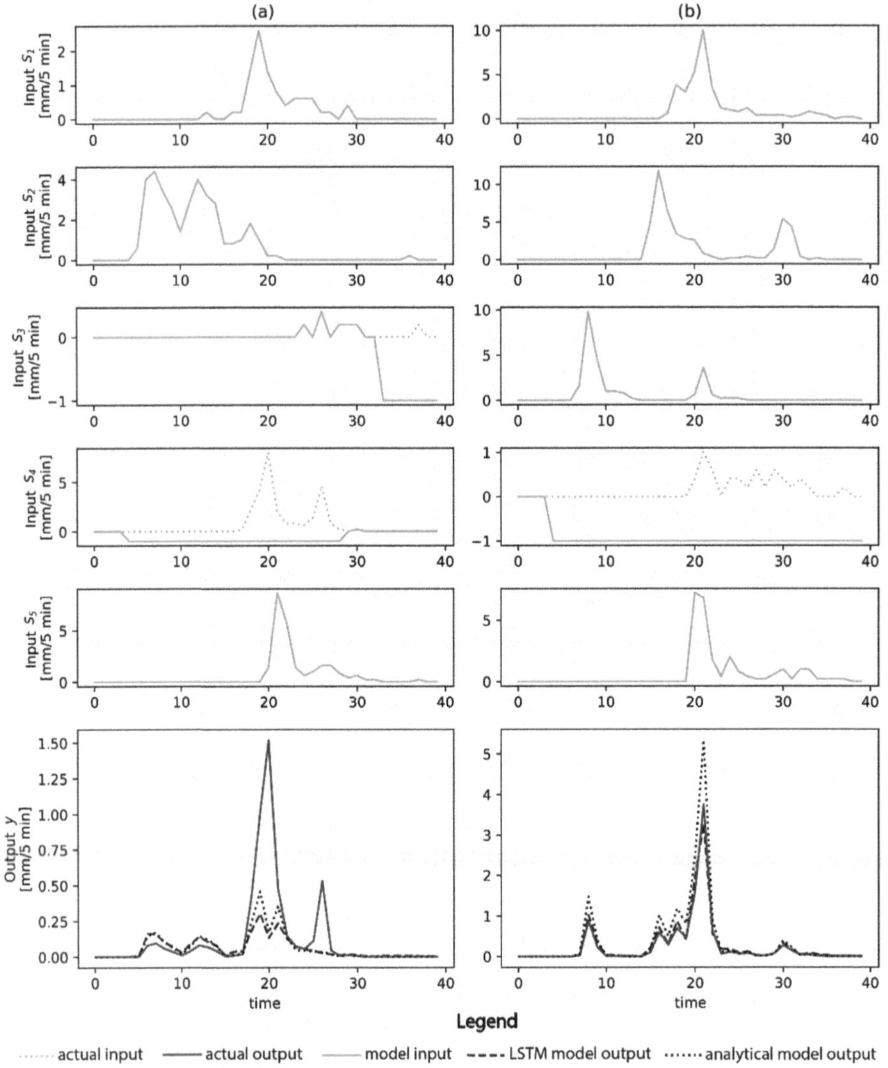

Fig. 5. Two rain episodes, (a) and (b), showing the 5 input hyetographs and the actual output compared with the LSTM model and the analytical model output.

4 Conclusion

The problem of missing data in a spatial time series set of environmental variables is addressed in this study using an LSTM neural network that directly operates between input (the time series with missing values) and output (the computed environmental variable). This means the NN operates end-to-end. The proposed approach completely by-pass the traditional phase of replacing the missing values with some external operation (some statistics, replacement with other sensor's values, omission) that, in one way or the other, alters the original information content. The NN must be suitably trained to learn how to deal with missing values, and, to do so, it is necessary to start from a complete dataset on which "artificial" failures are produced with the same statistical distribution of the real downtimes. Once this is accomplished, the NN is ready to enter operation and can immediately compute a real-time output, that inherently considers both time (on the same sensor) and space (between sensors) relations. This makes the approach much quicker than other methods, such as model assimilation that requires much more runtime power, and more precise than classical interpolation or imputation methods that simplify the time and/or space dependencies.

The proposed approach has been tested on a quite difficult case study of rainfall field reconstruction in Northern Italy, where episodes are rare, intense, and concentrated. This means that both temporal and spatial correlations are low, and when some critical sensors are not working, an accurate reconstruction of the rain field is definitely impossible. Nevertheless, even in this challenging case, the end-to-end neural approach outperforms the analytical benchmark competitor.

In this work, the gauge malfunctioning refers to a complete breakdown of a sensor, as in the actual dataset. In general, other situations may occur, leading to corrupted values (e.g., outliers). The proposed end-to-end approach can be specifically trained to compensate also for these faulty values.

When dealing with a more complex task, such as the forecasting of the actual runoff in the example considered here, the NN architecture may need to be enriched, but the results shown above suggest that the traditional "art" of filling field data gaps may progressively become obsolete.

Acknowledgements. We would like to thank ARPA Lombardia for providing the rainfall dataset. Valerio Guglieri is supported by Fondazione Cariplo (2017-0725), project: Lombardy-based Advanced Meteorological Predictions and Observations (LAMPO). The authors would like to thank all the administrative, management and scientific partners of the project.

References

1. Radi, N.F.A., Zakaria, R., Azman, M.A.Z.: Estimation of missing rainfall data using spatial interpolation and imputation methods. In: AIP Conference Proceedings, vol. 1643, no. 1, pp. 42–48. American Institute of Physics (2015)
2. Dhevi, A.S.: Imputing missing values using inverse distance weighted interpolation for time series data. In: 2014 Sixth International Conference on Advanced Computing (ICoAC), pp. 255–259. IEEE (2014)

3. Teegavarapu, R.S.: Missing precipitation data estimation using optimal proximity metric-based imputation, nearest-neighbour classification and cluster-based interpolation methods. Hydrol. Sci. J. **59**(11), 2009–2026 (2014)
4. Cressie, N.: The origins of kriging. Math. Geol. **22**(3), 239–252 (1990)
5. Stein, M.L.: Interpolation of Spatial Data: Some Theory for Kriging. Springer Science & Business Media, New York (2012)
6. Liu, Y., Weerts, A., Clark, M., Hendricks Franssen, H.J., Kumar, S., Moradkhani, H., Seo, D.J., Schwanenberg, D., Smith, P., Van Dijk, A.I.J.M., Van Velzen, N.: Advancing data assimilation in operational hydrologic forecasting: progresses, challenges, and emerging opportunities. Hydrol. Earth Syst. Sci. **16**, 3863–3887 (2012)
7. Weerts, A.H., Seo, D.J., Werner, M., Schaake, J.: Operational hydrologic ensemble forecasting. In: Applied Uncertainty Analysis for Flood Risk Management, pp. 387–406 (2014)
8. Pezij, M., Augustijn, D.C., Hendriks, D.M., Hulscher, S.J.: The role of evidence-based information in regional operational water management in the Netherlands. Environ. Sci. Policy **93**, 75–82 (2019)
9. Lagasio, M., Parodi, A., Pulvirenti, L., Meroni, A.N., Boni, G., Pierdicca, N., Marzano, F.S., Luini, L., Venuti, G., Realini, E., Gatti, A., Tagliaferro, G., Barindelli, S., Monti Guarnieri, A., Goga, K., Terzo, O., Rucci, A., Passera, E., Kranzlmueller, D., Rommen, B.: A synergistic use of a high-resolution numerical weather prediction model and high-resolution earth observation products to improve precipitation forecast. Remote Sensing **11**, 2387 (2019)
10. Xingjian, S.H.I., Chen, Z., Wang, H., Yeung, D.Y., Wong, W.K., Woo, W.C.: Convolutional LSTM network: a machine learning approach for precipitation nowcasting. In: Advances in Neural Information Processing Systems, pp. 802–810 (2015)
11. Ng, A.: Machine learning yearning, p. 96 (2017). http://www.mlyearning.org/
12. Sangiorgio, M., Barindelli, S.: Spatio-temporal analysis of intense convective storms tracks in a densely urbanized Italian basin. ISPRS Int. J. Geo-Inf. **9**, 183 (2020)
13. Sangiorgio, M., Barindelli, S., Biondi, R., Solazzo, E., Realini, E., Venuti, G., Guariso, G.: Improved extreme rainfall events forecasting using neural networks and water vapor measures. In: Proceedings of the 6th International Conference on Time Series and Forecasting (ITISE), Granada, Spain, vol. 2, pp. 820–826 (2019)
14. Sangiorgio, M., Barindelli, S., Biondi, R., Solazzo, E., Realini, E., Venuti, G., Guariso, G.: A comparative study on machine learning techniques for intense convective rainfall events forecasting. In: Advances in Time Series and Forecasting (Contributions to Statistics) stage of publication (under review)
15. Foresti, L., Sideris, I.V., Panziera, L., Beusch, L., Nerini, D., Germann, U.: Nowcasting orographic precipitation growth and decay using machine learning algorithms on a 10-year radar archive in the Swiss Alps. In: EGU General Assembly Conference Abstracts, vol. 20, p. 6361 (2018)
16. Meeker, W.Q., Escobar, L.A.: Statistical Methods for Reliability Data. Wiley, New York (2014)
17. Hochreiter, S., Schmidhuber, J.: Long short-term memory. Neural Comput. **9**(8), 1735–1780 (1997)
18. Goodfellow, I., Bengio, Y., Courville, A.: Deep learning. MIT Press, Cambridge (2016)

Semantic Segmentation Based on Convolution Neural Network for Steel Strip Position Estimation

Aline de Faria Lemos(✉) and Bálazs Vince Nagy

Department of Mechatronics, Optics and Mechanical Engineering Informatics, Budapest University of Technology and Economics, Budapest, Hungary
{alinefaria,nagyb}@mogi.bme.hu

Abstract. In this paper, a method to access the location of a steel strip in the rolling process was developed. The method consists of a hybrid system composed of a CNN-based semantic segmentation followed by morphological operation and outlier removal. The proposed method was capable of estimating the position of the strip with high precision and low computational burden, making it suitable for the application. The implementation of automatic estimation for the steel strip positioning, replacing the current human operation, can yield substantial costs saving. Future work will be carried out for the and integration of automatic control in the process.

Keywords: Steckell mill · Semantic segmentation · Convolution neural network · Hot strips

1 Introduction

Steel strips are manufactured from slabs, which undergo several times between a pair of work rolls until the obtention of the intended thickness reduction [15, 16, 31, 32]. During the rolling process in Steckell mill lines, the strips are moved in the rolling direction by the roller table. However, the strips could also be driven perpendicularly to this direction by the rolling procedure, which causes a misalignment of the strip. Consequently, the unaligned strips are prone to collide with the mill structure. As the 20 *ton* strips are rolled at 10 m/s, the collisions are an impairment for the production lines, causing material losses and severe damage to the mill structure and equipment. Annually, the material loss due to collisions and equipment failure expenses are about one million euros [9].

Most of the Steckell lines apply a semi-manual procedure to correct the aforementioned strips unalignment. In this procedure, a human operator has access to real-time process images acquired from analog cameras settled over the mill

Supported by Budapest University of Technology and Economics.

L. Iliadis et al. (Eds.): EANN 2020, INNS 2, pp. 179–189, 2020.
https://doi.org/10.1007/978-3-030-48791-1_13

structure. From the content of the images, the operator evaluates the strip position and judges whether it displays misalignment. Based on this information the operator will attempt to manually correct the strip position through an encoder, which creates a gap difference between the extremities of the work rolls pair and steers the strip on the direction of the major gap. The alignment correction procedure is susceptible to failure due to the high longitudinal speed of the strips, which requires a reaction time that might exceed the human capability. Besides, a manual encoder is not a precise tool and can lead to inadequate control [7,9].

Automate the alignment of the strips in a Steckell mill line could reduce the damage to the plant, maintenance costs, and prevent material losses [9]. The start point through the automated process is to determine the strip position, which could be accessed by detecting the strip portion on process images. Nowadays, semantic segmentation based on the convolution neural network is largely used in object detection and classification. However, from the best of the authors' knowledge, there is no work on the available literature that employes such an approach to strip detection in a rolling mill process. On the other hand, there are a considerable number of studies that apply convolution neural networks in metalworking. Some examples are the detection of defects in metal casting [3,8], recognition of slab identification numbers [17], mechanical properties predicting [30], bearing fault diagnosis [12,14,24,28,33], steel defect identification [20,26], and crystallographic defects in structural alloys [23]. This work presents a method that employs the process images to estimate the strip position. The system extracts the strip portion of the image via semantic segmentation based on convolution neural network (CNN) and infers the strip position in relation to the image bottom edge.

2 Methodology

This work presents a method that employs supervised learning to estimate the position of steel strips in a Steckell Mill line. The method consists of a system that applies semantic segmentation based on a convolution neural network to extract the strip portion from process digital images and estimate its position in relation to the image bottom edge. The flowchart presented in Fig. 1 illustrates a summary of the system steps for obtaining the position of the strips.

The dataset is composed of 704 × 480 px RGB images, which were acquired by an analog camera installed over the mill structure with a frame rate of 30 fps. The acquired images are selected by the algorithm according to the activation command signal of the descaler and the strip tracking signal. During the descaler period, the images will present excessive noise content, due to the dense steam on the region between strip and camera. Also, the images acquired in the instants that the strip is not positioned under the camera are not relevant to the analysis. Therefore, in both circumstances, the acquired images will not be processed for position estimation.

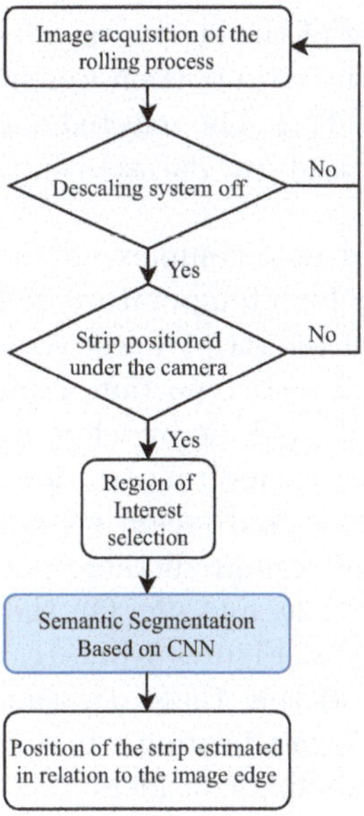

Fig. 1. System flow chart.

2.1 Regions of Interest and Labeling

The images contain a portion of the strip, horizontally aligned to the image bottom edge, and parts of the mill structure, which are irrelevant to the task in hand. Thus, a selection of a region of interest that lowers the number of mill components present on the image reduced its complexity. The elected region of interest (ROI) is highlighted in Fig. 2 over an example of the process images used as the system input.

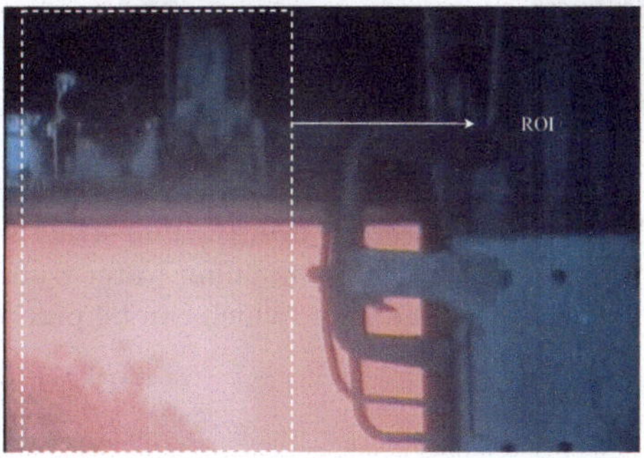

Fig. 2. Elected region of interest (ROI) over an example of the process images used as the system input.

The ground truth labeling of the strips was created by manual annotation, in which pixels belonging to the strip portion were assigned with intensity 1 and to the background with intensity 2. The selected dataset comprises 1390 images, which were split into training and test datasets on the proportion of 1112 to 278 images, respectively.

The images were acquired in a complex environment. The strip incandescence, resulting from the strip high temperature, reflects over the mill structures present in the surroundings of the strip. These structures mirror the strip color and could be easily mistaken as a strip portion. Examples of these reflections are indicated in Figs. 3-1*b*, -2*a*, -2*b*, and -2*c* by white arrows. Another complication is the presence of remaining elements from the descaler process. These elements are usually water over the strip and steam content on the strip location and surroundings. The water creates unpredictable patterns over the strip, as can be perceived in Figs. 3-1*b*, -1*c*, -2*b*, and -2*c*. On the other hand, the steam content blurry the acquired images. Figures 3-1*a*, -1*c*, and -2*a* show some of these blurring particularities. Considering these occasions, the labeling process was handled carefully to avoid misclassifications. In cases that portions of the strip were covered by steam, the labeling considers that the strip location is parallel to the image bottom.

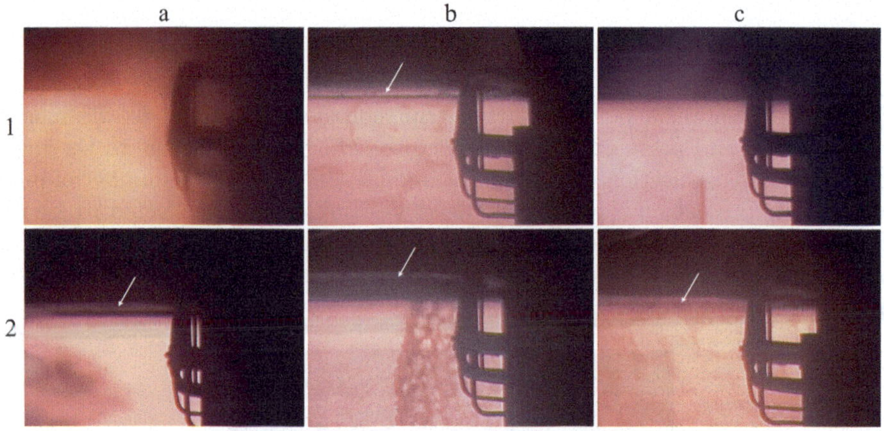

Fig. 3. Example of images acquired in a complex environment. The white arrows indicate the reflection of the strip incandescence over the mill structure. Images 1*a*, 1*c*, and 2*a* are blurred due to the steam content. Remaining water from the descaler process creates unpredictable patterns over the strip, which can be perceived in images 1*b*, 1*c*, 2*b*, and 2*c*.

2.2 Semantic Segmentation CNN Architecture

Semantic segmentation is a pixel-wise classification, which gathers pixels belonging to the same category [19,23,25]. This kind of network is widely used in autonomous driving [4,6,10,27], medical applications [1,21,22,34], object detection [11,29], automatic localization of defects in steel [8,23] to name a few. The architecture of a semantic segmentation network usually consists of an encoder-decoder task [2,13,18]. In the present work, the first part is composed of one or more convolution and max pooling operations, that extract high-level features by mapping the input to a lower dimension representation [18]. In contrast, the decoder architecture, commonly composed of transposed convolutions and up-pooling layers, expands the high-level features to recover the feature map size compatible with the input layer size [23], followed by another convolution layer and a softmax layer, enabling pixel-level classification.

In this study, 3 architecture configurations were investigated. They differ among each other by the number of encoder/decoder, varying between 1, 2, or 3 pairs. Figure 4 illustrates the largest network in terms of the number of layers (three encoders and three decoders). The influence of the number of filters in each operation was also ascertained, the number of filters could hold values from the set {2, 4, 8, 16, 32, 64}. Hence, eighteen architectures were explored altogether. Moreover, the Rectified Linear Unit (ReLU) activation function was applied after the convolution layers. As optimization parameters were selected Adam optimizer with a learning rate of 0.001.

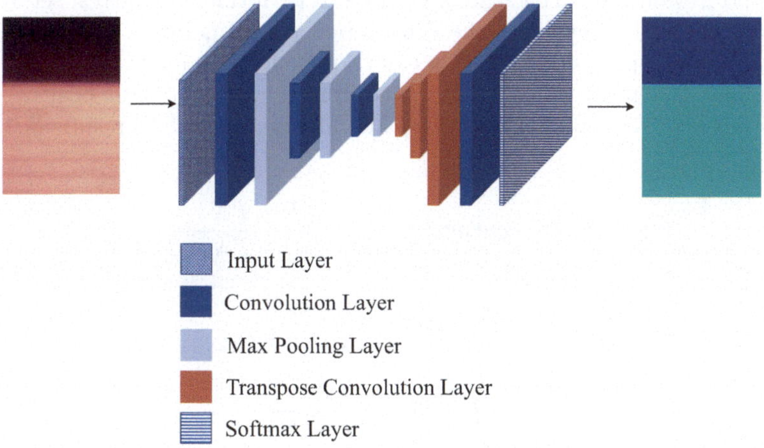

Fig. 4. Schematic illustration of one of the semantic segmentation architectures designed for strip detection.

2.3 Position Estimation

Morphological operations and outliers exclusion were employed to refine the semantic segmentation predictions. The strip portions predicted by CNN were extracted into a binary image, from which the largest connected component was kept and the smaller components were deleted. Afterward, a flood-fill was applied to fill possible holes in the strip area. Out of the resulting binary image, the strip position was estimated from the pixel locations of the top edge. As some of the predictions could present an irregular edge, an outlier removal with a threshold between 40 and 60% was applied and the position was calculated from the average of the remaining values.

2.4 Representation of the Strip Position in Physical Units

The frame size for the sampled pictures is 704×480 px. When the strip is not located under the camera it is possible to identify the presence of two rolls of the roller table arranged vertically in the image. The diameter of the rollers is equal to 400 mm and they comprehend 140 px of the image. Therefore, the images resolution is equal to 2.9 mm/px and the total area of the sampled images is 2011×1371 mm. From this information, the strip position could be estimated in millimeters.

2.5 Performance Evaluation

The proposed method is evaluated by comparing the estimated strip position to the expected values, calculated from the ground truth, by the Mean Absolute Error (MAE) and the Standard Deviation (STD). The execution time was also analyzed in order to access if the solution is fit for a real-time application. Additionally, the evaluation of each architecture was performed on the test set by common metrics used to evaluate the convolution neural network, which are pixel accuracy (Eq. 1), precision (Eq. 2), recall (Eq. 3), Jaccard index (Eq. 4), F1 score (Eq. 5), and specificity (Eq. 6) determined from the values of true positive (TP), true negative (TN), false positive (FP) and false negative (FN) results [5,19,23].

- Pixel accuracy

$$Pixel\ accuracy = \frac{TP + TN}{TP + FP + TN + FN} \tag{1}$$

- Precision

$$Precision = \frac{TP}{TP + FP} \tag{2}$$

- Recall

$$Recall = \frac{TP}{TP + FN} \tag{3}$$

- Jaccard index or Intersection-over-Union (IoU)

$$IoU = \frac{TP}{TP + FP + FN} \tag{4}$$

- F1 score (F1)

$$F1 = \frac{2 \times (Recall \times Precision)}{Recall + Precision} \tag{5}$$

- Specificity or true negative rate (TNR)

$$Specificity = \frac{TN}{TN + FP} \tag{6}$$

3 Results and Discussion

The present work aims to effectively localize steel strips in a Steckell mill line. This section presents the results achieved by the proposed methodology. All results and discussion are referring to the test set and were obtained with an Intel Core i7-8750H CPU, 2.20 GHz, processor and installed memory (RAM) of 16.0 Gb. The results of the semantic segmentation step from each network can be observed in Table 1. Concerning pixel accuracy, precision, recall, IoU, F1 score, and specificity, the models present similar performance with a maximum divergence between the best and worse results of $[0.2, 0.3, 0.2, 0.4, 0.2, 0.5]$, respectively. Considering the execution time, the results confirm the intuition that the lesser the numbers of layers and filters, the higher the processing frame rate.

Table 1. Semantic segmentation performance evaluation and position estimation metrics.

Model ID	Architecture	Number of filters	Pixel accuracy [%]	Precision [%]	Recall [%]	IoU [%]	F1 [%]	TNR [%]	Frame rate [fps]	MAE [mm]	STD [mm]
1	1	2	99.5	99.4	99.7	99.1	99.6	99.0	53.7	5.0	5.2
2		4	99.5	99.4	99.8	99.2	99.6	99.0	51.1	4.3	4.8
3		8	99.6	99.6	99.8	99.4	99.7	99.3	40.8	3.4	4.0
4		16	99.6	99.5	99.9	99.3	99.7	99.1	26.1	3.7	4.3
5		32	99.6	99.6	99.8	99.4	99.7	99.3	7.8	3.7	4.1
6		64	99.6	99.5	99.8	99.3	99.7	99.2	1.6	3.6	4.2
7	2	2	99.4	99.3	99.8	99.1	99.6	98.8	42.5	4.8	4.9
8		4	99.6	99.5	99.8	99.3	99.7	99.1	52.5	3.8	4.7
9		8	99.6	99.5	99.8	99.4	99.7	99.2	40.0	3.7	3.8
10		16	99.5	99.4	99.9	99.3	99.6	98.9	24.5	4.3	4.4
11		32	99.6	99.5	99.9	99.3	99.7	99.1	6.1	3.7	3.9
12		64	99.6	99.5	99.9	99.4	99.7	99.1	1.6	3.4	3.9
13	3	2	99.5	99.4	99.8	99.2	99.6	99.0	41.2	5.2	4.6
14		4	99.6	99.6	99.8	99.4	99.7	99.3	47.1	3.7	4.2
15		8	99.6	99.5	99.9	99.4	99.7	99.1	38.5	3.9	3.6
16		16	99.6	99.4	99.9	99.4	99.7	99.0	23.9	4.2	3.4
17		32	99.6	99.5	99.9	99.4	99.7	99.2	5.4	3.8	3.3
18		64	99.7	99.6	99.9	99.5	99.7	99.3	1.6	3.4	3.3

However, the segmentation process is only an intermediate step of the process. The actual output of the system is the strip position estimation and the system performance regarding this value is evaluated from the Mean Absolute Error and the Standard Deviation metrics, which are also presented in Table 1. Even though all the models presented satisfactory results, under 5.2 mm, a sensible differentiation can be drawn among the results.

The model configuration with architecture 1 (one encoder and one decoder set) and 8 convolution filters in each layer (Model ID 3) was elected the best model by the authors. This model achieved the best combination of Mean Absolute Error and frame rate, 3.4($\pm$4.0) mm, and 40.8 fps, respectively. Even though another two models (Model ID 12 and 18) achieved a comparable degree of precision, their frame rate is lesser than 30 fps (frame rate of the video-camera), which is non-desirable for a real-time application.

Moreover, Fig. 5 shows the evolution of the estimated and expected position through time for model 3. The graphical representation reiterates the numerical results showing that the proposed methodology can estimate successfully the strip position.

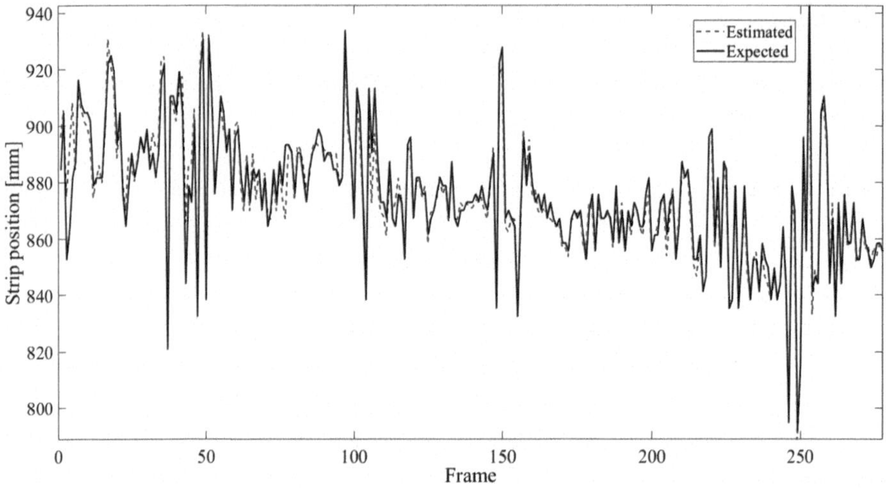

Fig. 5. Estimated strip position in relation to the expected values of model ID 3.

Lastly, Fig. 6 exemplifies the whole process, showing six samples. For each pair, it can be observed the input on the left and the output on the right. The output image consists of the image overlaid by the segmentation classification in pink and a black line showing the estimated position given by the morphological operations and outliers exclusion. It is worth mentioning the robustness of the system, correctly placing the black line even when the segmentation step provides insufficient results. The proposed methodology can estimate the strip position even in a complex environment, such as the steam presence (pairs 1*c* and 2*b*), mill structures reflecting the strip incandescence (pairs 1*b* and 2*a*) and water presence over the strip (pairs 1*a*, 1*b* and 2*c*).

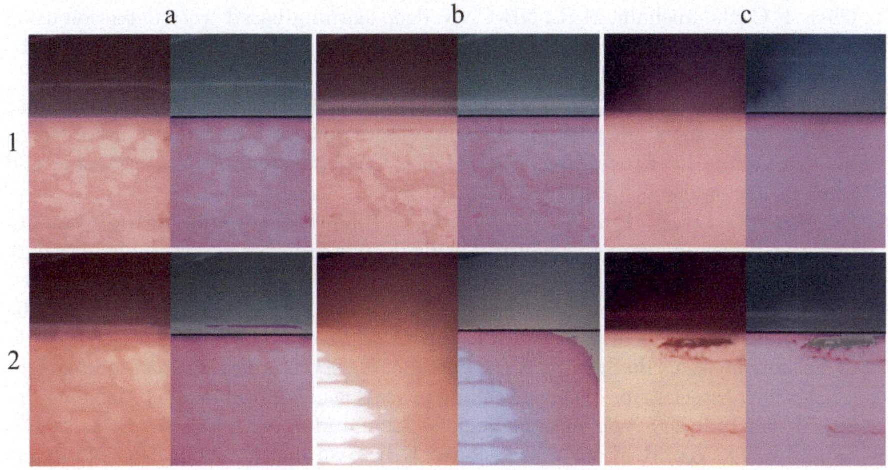

Fig. 6. Pairs of regions of interest containing the acquired image, on the left, and the semantic segmentation prediction, on the right. The black line over the labeled image indicates the position of the strip estimated by the system.

4 Conclusion

In this paper, a method to access the location of a steel strip in the rolling process was developed. The method consists of a hybrid system composed of a CNN-based semantic segmentation followed by morphological operation and outlier removal. The proposed method was capable of estimating the position of the strip with high precision and low computational burden, making it suitable for the application. The implementation of automatic estimation and control for the steel strip positioning, replacing the current human operation, can yield substantial costs saving. Future work will be carried out for the and integration of automatic control in the process.

Acknowledgment. The research reported in this paper was supported by the Higher Education Excellence Program of the Ministry of Human Capacities in the frame of Artificial Intelligence research area of Budapest University of Technology and Economics (BME FIKP-MI/FM); by the National Research, Development and Innovation Fund (TUDFO/51757/2019-ITM, Thematic Excellence Program); by the János Bolyai Scholarship of the Hungarian Academy of Sciences to BVN; and by the Stipendium Hungaricum Scholarship Programme.

References

1. Almotairi, S., Kareem, G., Aouf, M., Almutairi, B., Salem, M.A.M.: Liver tumor segmentation in CT scans using modified segnet. Sensors **20**(5), 1516 (2020)
2. Badrinarayanan, V., Kendall, A., Cipolla, R.: SegNet: a deep convolutional encoder-decoder architecture for image segmentation. IEEE Trans. Pattern Anal. Mach. Intell. **39**(12), 2481–2495 (2017)

3. Chen, F.C., Jahanshahi, M.R.: NB-CNN: deep learning-based crack detection using convolutional neural network and naïve bayes data fusion. IEEE Trans. Industr. Electron. **65**(5), 4392–4400 (2017)
4. Cordts, M., Omran, M., Ramos, S., Rehfeld, T., Enzweiler, M., Benenson, R., Franke, U., Roth, S., Schiele, B.: The cityscapes dataset for semantic urban scene understanding. In: Proceedings of the IEEE Conference on Computer Vision and Pattern Recognition, pp. 3213–3223 (2016)
5. DeCost, B.L., Lei, B., Francis, T., Holm, E.A.: High throughput quantitative metallography for complex microstructures using deep learning: a case study in ultrahigh carbon steel. Microsc. Microanal. **25**(1), 21–29 (2019)
6. Ess, A., Müller, T., Grabner, H., Van Gool, L.J.: Segmentation-based urban traffic scene understanding. In: BMVC, vol. 1, p. 2. Citeseer (2009)
7. de Faria Lemos, A., da Silva, L.A.R., Furtado, E.C., de Paula, H.: Positioning error estimation of steel strips in steckel rolling process using digital image processing. In: 2017 IEEE Industry Applications Society Annual Meeting, pp. 1–8. IEEE (2017)
8. Ferguson, M., Ak, R., Lee, Y.T.T., Law, K.H.: Automatic localization of casting defects with convolutional neural networks. In: 2017 IEEE International Conference on Big Data (Big Data), pp. 1726–1735. IEEE (2017)
9. Ferreira, A.B.S.: Adaptive fuzzy logic steering controller for a Steckel mill. Ph.D. thesis, University of Johannesburg (2005)
10. Geiger, A., Lenz, P., Urtasun, R.: Are we ready for autonomous driving? the kitti vision benchmark suite. In: 2012 IEEE Conference on Computer Vision and Pattern Recognition, pp. 3354–3361. IEEE (2012)
11. Girshick, R., Donahue, J., Darrell, T., Malik, J.: Rich feature hierarchies for accurate object detection and semantic segmentation. In: Proceedings of the IEEE Conference on Computer Vision and Pattern Recognition, pp. 580–587 (2014)
12. Hoang, D.T., Kang, H.J.: Rolling element bearing fault diagnosis using convolutional neural network and vibration image. Cogn. Syst. Res. **53**, 42–50 (2019)
13. Hong, S., Oh, J., Lee, H., Han, B.: Learning transferrable knowledge for semantic segmentation with deep convolutional neural network. In: Proceedings of the IEEE Conference on Computer Vision and Pattern Recognition, pp. 3204–3212 (2016)
14. Janssens, O., Slavkovikj, V., Vervisch, B., Stockman, K., Loccufier, M., Verstockt, S., Van de Walle, R., Van Hoecke, S.: Convolutional neural network based fault detection for rotating machinery. J. Sound Vib. **377**, 331–345 (2016)
15. Konovalov, Y.V., Khokhlov, A.: Benefits of steckel mills in rolling. Steel Transl. **43**(4), 206–211 (2013)
16. Kwon, W., Kim, S., Won, S.: Active disturbance rejection control for strip steering control in hot strip finishing mill. IFAC-PapersOnLine **48**(17), 42–47 (2015)
17. Lee, S.J., Yun, J.P., Koo, G., Kim, S.W.: End-to-end recognition of slab identification numbers using a deep convolutional neural network. Knowl.-Based Syst. **132**, 1–10 (2017)
18. Lin, G., Milan, A., Shen, C., Reid, I.: RefineNet: Multi-path refinement networks for high-resolution semantic segmentation. In: Proceedings of the IEEE Conference on Computer Vision and Pattern Recognition, pp. 1925–1934 (2017)
19. Long, J., Shelhamer, E., Darrell, T.: Fully convolutional networks for semantic segmentation. In: Proceedings of the IEEE Conference on Computer Vision and Pattern Recognition, pp. 3431–3440 (2015)
20. Masci, J., Meier, U., Ciresan, D., Schmidhuber, J., Fricout, G.: Steel defect classification with max-pooling convolutional neural networks. In: The 2012 International Joint Conference on Neural Networks (IJCNN), pp. 1–6. IEEE (2012)

21. Pham, D.L., Xu, C., Prince, J.L.: Current methods in medical image segmentation. Annu. Rev. Biomed. Eng. **2**(1), 315–337 (2000)
22. Rashed, E.A., Gomez-Tames, J., Hirata, A.: End-to-end semantic segmentation of personalized deep brain structures for non-invasive brain stimulation. Neural Netw. **125**, 233–245 (2020)
23. Roberts, G., Haile, S.Y., Sainju, R., Edwards, D.J., Hutchinson, B., Zhu, Y.: Deep learning for semantic segmentation of defects in advanced stem images of steels. Sci. Rep. **9**(1), 1–12 (2019)
24. Sadoughi, M., Hu, C.: Physics-based convolutional neural network for fault diagnosis of rolling element bearings. IEEE Sens. J. **19**(11), 4181–4192 (2019)
25. Sevak, J.S., Kapadia, A.D., Chavda, J.B., Shah, A., Rahevar, M.: Survey on semantic image segmentation techniques. In: 2017 International Conference on Intelligent Sustainable Systems (ICISS), pp. 306–313. IEEE (2017)
26. Soukup, D., Huber-Mörk, R.: Convolutional neural networks for steel surface defect detection from photometric stereo images. In: International Symposium on Visual Computing, pp. 668–677. Springer (2014)
27. Treml, M., Arjona-Medina, J., Unterthiner, T., Durgesh, R., Friedmann, F., Schuberth, P., Mayr, A., Heusel, M., Hofmarcher, M., Widrich, M., et al.: Speeding up semantic segmentation for autonomous driving. In: MLITS, NIPS Workshop, vol. 2, p. 7 (2016)
28. Wei, Y., Chang-Qing, S., Xiao-Jie, G., Zhong-Kui, Z.: Bearing fault diagnosis using convolution neural network and support vector regression. In: DEStech Transactions on Engineering and Technology Research (ICMECA) (2017)
29. Xie, C., Wang, J., Zhang, Z., Zhou, Y., Xie, L., Yuille, A.: Adversarial examples for semantic segmentation and object detection. In: Proceedings of the IEEE International Conference on Computer Vision, pp. 1369–1378 (2017)
30. Xu, Z.W., Liu, X.M., Zhang, K.: Mechanical properties prediction for hot rolled alloy steel using convolutional neural network. IEEE Access **7**, 47068–47078 (2019)
31. Yang, S.S., He, Y.H., Wang, Z.L., Zhao, W.S.: A method of steel strip image segmentation based on local gray information. In: 2008 IEEE International Conference on Industrial Technology, pp. 1–4. IEEE (2008)
32. Youkachen, S., Ruchanurucks, M., Phatrapomnant, T., Kaneko, H.: Defect segmentation of hot-rolled steel strip surface by using convolutional auto-encoder and conventional image processing. In: 2019 10th International Conference of Information and Communication Technology for Embedded Systems (IC-ICTES), pp. 1–5. IEEE (2019)
33. Zhang, W., Li, C., Peng, G., Chen, Y., Zhang, Z.: A deep convolutional neural network with new training methods for bearing fault diagnosis under noisy environment and different working load. Mech. Syst. Signal Process. **100**, 439–453 (2018)
34. Zhang, Z., Wu, C., Coleman, S., Kerr, D.: DENSE-inception U-net for medical image segmentation. Comput. Methods Programs Biomed. **192**, 105395 (2020)

Towards a Digital Twin with Generative Adversarial Network Modelling of Machining Vibration

Evgeny Zotov(✉), Ashutosh Tiwari, and Visakan Kadirkamanathan

Department of Automatic Control and Systems Engineering, University of Sheffield, Sheffield, UK
{ezotov1,a.tiwari,visakan}@sheffield.ac.uk

Abstract. Transition towards Industry 4.0 relies heavily on manufacturing digitalisation. Digital twin plays a significant role among the pool of relevant technologies as a powerful tool that is expected provide digital access to detailed real-time monitoring of the physical processes and enable significant optimisation due to utilisation of big data acquired from them. Over the past years a significant number of works produced conceptual frameworks of digital twins and discussed their requirements and benefits. The research literature demonstrates application examples and proofs of concepts, although the content is less rich. This paper presents a generative model based on generative adversarial networks (GAN) for machining vibration data, discusses its performance and analyses the drawbacks. The proposed model includes process parameter inputs used to condition the features of generated signals. The control over the generator and a neural network architecture utilising techniques from style-transfer research provide the means to analyse the signal building blocks learned by the model and explore their relationship. The quality of the learned process representation is demonstrated using a dataset obtained from a machining time-domain simulation. The novel results constitute a critical component of a machining digital twin and open new research directions towards development of comprehensive manufacturing digital twins.

Keywords: Generative adversarial network · Digital twin · Machining

1 Introduction

The 4th industrial revolution, i.e. the strategic vision of transition to Industry 4.0, draws a path to a totally customisable production with viable single-item batch production, just-in-time execution and high resource-efficiency. Advances along this path are believed to be feasible as a result of pervasive digitalisation throughout the industry, spanning from the shop-floor to the whole supply chain and to the users of the end-products [7]. Total factory digitalisation is being

L. Iliadis et al. (Eds.): EANN 2020, INNS 2, pp. 190–201, 2020.
https://doi.org/10.1007/978-3-030-48791-1_14

made possible by the technologies emerging from the research fields of big data, cyber-physical systems (CPS) and industrial internet of things (IIoT). Digital twin is a precise representation of a physical object or process in the digital realm. Development of digital twins is an important step of the digitalisation process, as the unification of digital and physical data within a single virtual object enables significant efficiency improvements across multiple stages of the object's life cycle [17].

Expert-based analytics models tend to achieve high accuracy rates, but have several drawbacks that can become blocking factors for implementation of a digital twin. On one hand, in an interconnected CPS environment interactions between the components introduce very high complexity of the modelled phenomena. On the other hand, the incremental character of module development and the fluid module composition cause an almost constant stream of changes in the system [12]. Data-driven modelling addresses these issues by making use of big data produced by the various manufacturer's CPS and automating the modelling process, thus aligning the digital twin state with the evolutionary changes in the modelled systems.

Development of efficient and flexible generative data-driven models of physical manufacturing processes is an important step towards CPS digitalisation in general, and particularly to wide adoption of digital twins throughout the industry. Artificial neural networks (ANN) have shown increasingly impressive state-of-art results on many data-driven problems during the past decades. Generative adversarial network (GAN) is a type of ANN architecture based on a minimax game between two ANN: the generator that learns to produce artificial data samples and the discriminator that learns to identify fake data samples [5]. Recently GANs found various uses, most notable in generation of realistic images of human faces [10].

GAN is a suitable candidate for digital twin development due to its efficiency at inference time and the generative nature of the model, in addition to the flexibility of a data-driven method. This paper proposes a GAN-based digital twin model that captures the conditional distribution of a signal, conditioned on the controlled parameters of the underlying process. Vibration is selected as the analysed signal type based on the low expected cost of its acquisition and potential usefulness in analysis of the process.

2 Methodology

2.1 Dataset: Machining Tool Vibration

The proposed model is tested on a simulated dataset representing the displacement (vibration) of a cutting tool along the x direction originating from the interactions between the tool and a workpiece. The operation considered is a linear non-slotting milling cut performed with a straight-teeth cutting tool on a metal workpiece. The dataset is produced using a physics-based time domain simulation model described in [15]. The model tracks the position of each cutting tooth and the workpiece geometry produced by previous cuts and derives the tool displacement from the forces produced by the interaction of the cutting teeth and the workpiece at each simulation time step. The simulation parameters used are detailed in Table 1. The parameter values are constant throughout each cutting operation, and the parameters varied across the samples in the produced dataset are chip width and spindle speed in ranges from 4e-3 to 5e-3 and 3000 to 4000 respectively. The generated signals represent the displacement of the cutting tool during the third revolution of the cutting tool, sampled at a rate proportional to the spindle speed so that all signals are of the same length.

Table 1. Milling time domain simulation parameters

Parameter	Value
Feed rate f	10.2
Spindle speed ω	3000 to 4000
Number of teeth N_t	3
Chip width b	4e-3 to 5e-3
Steps per revolution	256
Start angle of cut ϕ_s	126.9
Exit angle of cut ϕ_e	180
Process dependent coefficient K_s	2250e6
Force angle β	75
x Direction dynamics parameter k_x	9e6
x Direction dynamics parameter ζ_x	0.02
y Direction dynamics parameter k_y	1e7
y Direction dynamics parameter ζ_y	0.01
Number of revolutions (data recorded for third revolution only)	3

2.2 Model Architecture

The proposed digital twin is based on the generative adversarial network (GAN) model conceived in 2014 [5]. The authors combined two neural networks within a zero-sum game. One network, the discriminator is rewarded for high accuracy of classification of data samples as either real or fake. The other network, the generator, is rewarded for generation of fake samples that are classified by the discriminator as real. Therefore, the generator approximates the true data distribution through the training process. The approach was extended in multiple directions, including but not limited to research on various neural network architectures for the generator and the discriminator (e.g., Deep Convolutional GAN [13], BigGAN [2], StackGAN [19], WaveGAN [4], SeqGAN [18], Bayesian GAN [14]) reviews of the GAN training approaches and the networks' loss functions (notably, the application of Earth Mover distance as the loss metric in Wasserstein GAN [1], its extension with gradient penalty in WGAN-GP [6] and progressive GAN growing [9]),experiments with conditioning the GAN by additional inputs or outputs, as proposed in Conditional GAN [11], InfoGAN [3] and ss-InfoGAN [16].

The developed neural network architecture is inspired by StyleGAN [10], an image generation model based on two-dimensional deep convolutional discriminator and generator networks. Elements of the StyleGAN are repurposed for the 1D case of a time domain signal, excluding the noise inputs, as the variation of outputs of the target model is deterministic with respect to the input process parameters. The architecture is enhanced with the substitution of the random input latent vector for continuous labels C: the machining process parameters, chip width and spindle speed. The process parameters are used as inputs to the generator and as outputs of the discriminator, i.e. the discriminator learns to not only identify synthetic data samples, but also to estimate the labels associated with a given time-series. The architecture includes a non-linear mapping network M that projects latent inputs into disentangled latent space, approximated by a multi-layer feedforward neural network. The styles $S = M(C)$ produced from the input labels C by the mapping network subsequently control the modulation of outputs of the convolutional layers within the synthesis network F of the generator (see Fig. 1).

The GAN loss function is based on Wasserstein GAN with gradient penalty (WGAN-GP) [6]. WGAN-GP losses for the generator and the discriminator are

$$\begin{aligned} L_G^{wgan\text{-}gp} &= -\mathop{\mathbb{E}}_{\tilde{x}\sim\mathbb{P}_g}[D(\tilde{x})], \\ L_D^{wgan\text{-}gp} &= \mathop{\mathbb{E}}_{\tilde{x}\sim\mathbb{P}_g}[D(\tilde{x})] - \mathop{\mathbb{E}}_{x\sim\mathbb{P}_r}[D(x)] + \lambda_{gp}L^{gp} \end{aligned} \tag{1}$$

respectively, where

$$L^{gp} = \mathop{\mathbb{E}}_{\tilde{x}\sim\mathbb{P}_{\tilde{x}}}[(||\nabla_{\tilde{x}}D(\tilde{x})||_2 - 1)^2] \tag{2}$$

is the gradient penalty and λ_{gp} is its scaling hyperparameter. The loss functions are adjusted to accommodate the inclusion of machining process parameters in the networks architecture by addition of terms that penalise inaccurate label predictions. This is similar to the approach followed by the authors of InfoGAN [3], with the following difference. The accuracy of label predictions for training data L_D^{info} impacts only the discriminator, while the accuracy of the predictions for fake data samples L_G^{info} is taken into account only by the generator. The loss terms are

$$\begin{aligned} L_G^{info} &= \sqrt{\frac{\sum_{j=1}^{n}(c_{f,j} - c_{t,j})^2}{n}}, \\ L_D^{info} &= \sqrt{\frac{\sum_{j=1}^{n}(c_{r,j} - c_{t,j})^2}{n}}, \end{aligned} \tag{3}$$

where $c_{f,j}$ is a value of parameter j predicted by the discriminator based on a fake signal, $c_{r,j}$ is a value predicted from a real signal, and $c_{t,j}$ are the true parameter values. On one hand, the generator is thus incentivised to encode the

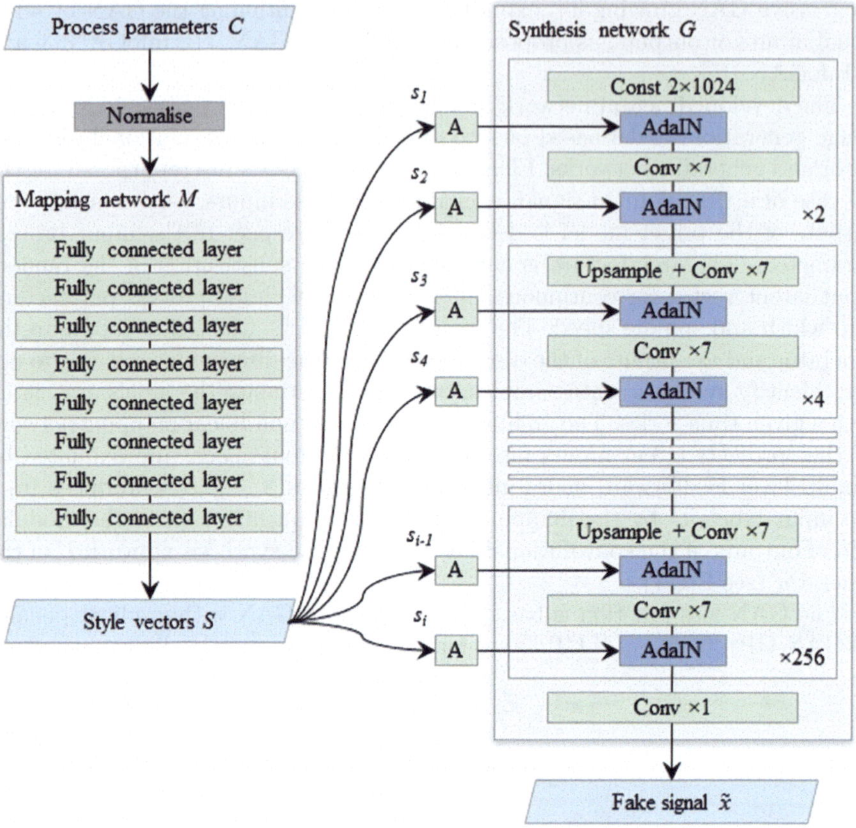

Fig. 1. Architecture of the generator F. "A" denotes learned affine transformations of style components s_i; "AdaIN" - adaptive instance normalisation [8], outputs of which are modulated by the transformed style components.

label information in an identifiable way within the synthesised samples. On the other hand, the discriminator learns the relationship between labels and samples only on the real data, thus preserving the non-cooperative nature of the minimax game between the generator and the discriminator. The total loss functions for the generator L_G and the discriminator L_D are therefore:

$$
\begin{aligned}
L_G &= L_G^{wgan\text{-}gp} + \lambda_{info} L_G^{info}, \\
L_D &= L_D^{wgan\text{-}gp} + \lambda_{info} L_D^{info},
\end{aligned} \tag{4}
$$

where λ_{info} is the scaling factor for the label prediction accuracy error loss.

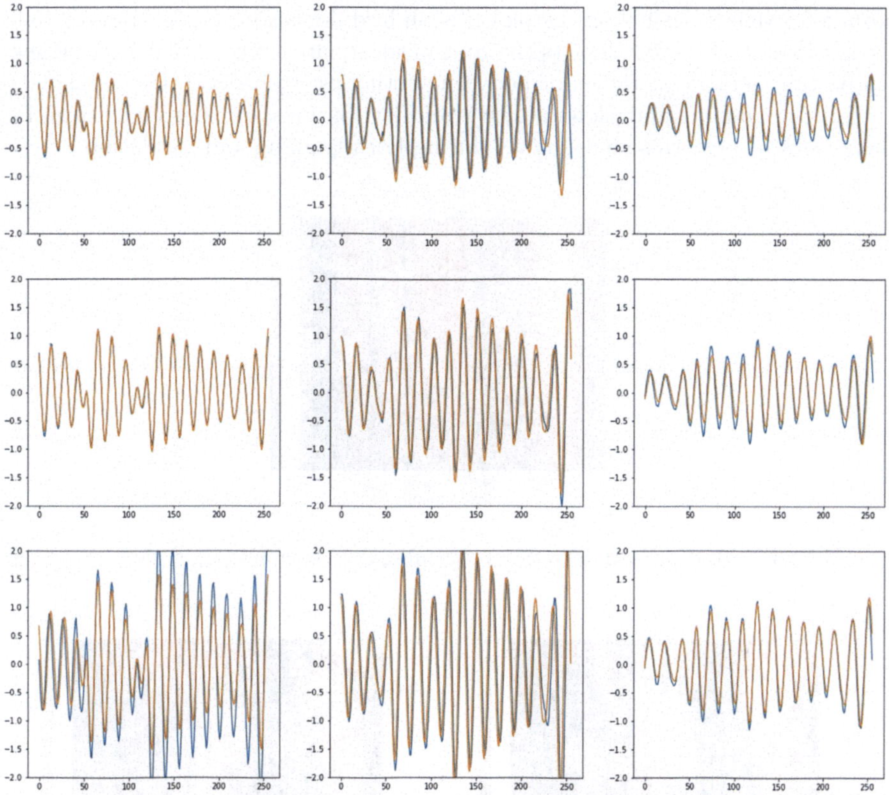

Fig. 2. Comparison of generated time-series samples (blue) and validation data samples (yellow). X axis represents time steps, Y axis - displacement magnitude in log scale.

3 Experimental Results

The paper shows that the generator successfully learns to capture the relationship between the process parameters and the time domain signal and performs well both on training and validation data. Figure 2 depicts several samples of generated time-series against the signals from training data produced using the same process parameters.

3.1 Visualisation of Generator Performance

The generative performance of the neural network is investigated via analysis of metrics mapped across machining process parameter values, chip width and spindle speed. This is visualised by calculating the inspected metric for a range of process parameter pairs and plotting the values on a two-dimensional figure with spindle speed varied across the X axis and chip width across the Y axis. The training data exhibits high variability, especially across the spindle speed parameter values, visible on the plot of standard deviations of the training data signals (Fig. 3). Figure 4 depicts the root mean square error (RMSE) of the generated time-series (i.e. the error between synthetics signals and dataset signals) on training and on validation data. RMSE distributions are nearly identical, i.e. the generator performs equivalently during both training and validation.

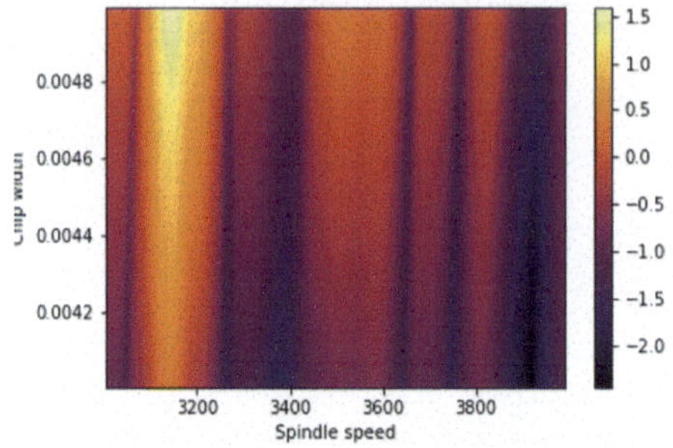

Fig. 3. Standard deviation of training data samples (log scale).

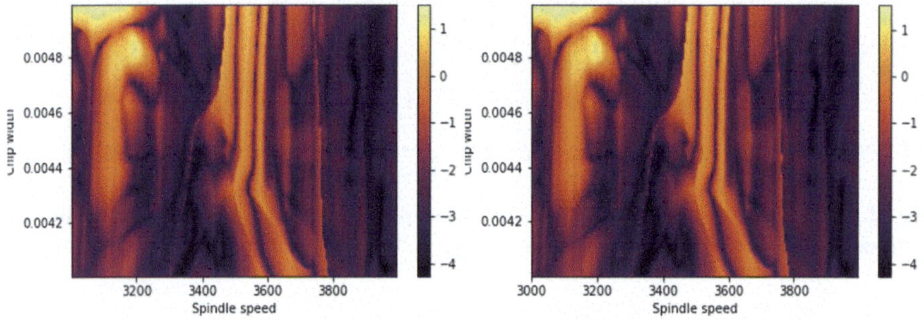

Fig. 4. RMSE values in log scale for generated time-series across various process parameter values for training data (left) and validation data (right). Equivalence of accuracy on both indicates low over-fitting.

In contrast to the high accuracy of the generator in the areas of the parameter space characterised by low dispersion in the training data, the generative performance is suboptimal in some regions of high training data variance. Closer inspection of a region between 3500 and 3600 spindle speed reveals that the generator experiences local mode collapse (for an example refer to Fig. 5). The troughs visible on the RMSE map in this region represent a parameter space where the generator successfully learnt the modes of the target signal, while the three peaks between and to the sides along the X axis from these narrow bands of high accuracy are indicative of the dropped modes. An inspection of the dynamics of change of the training data signals compared to the change of the synthesised signals reveals that whereas the training data signals change shape

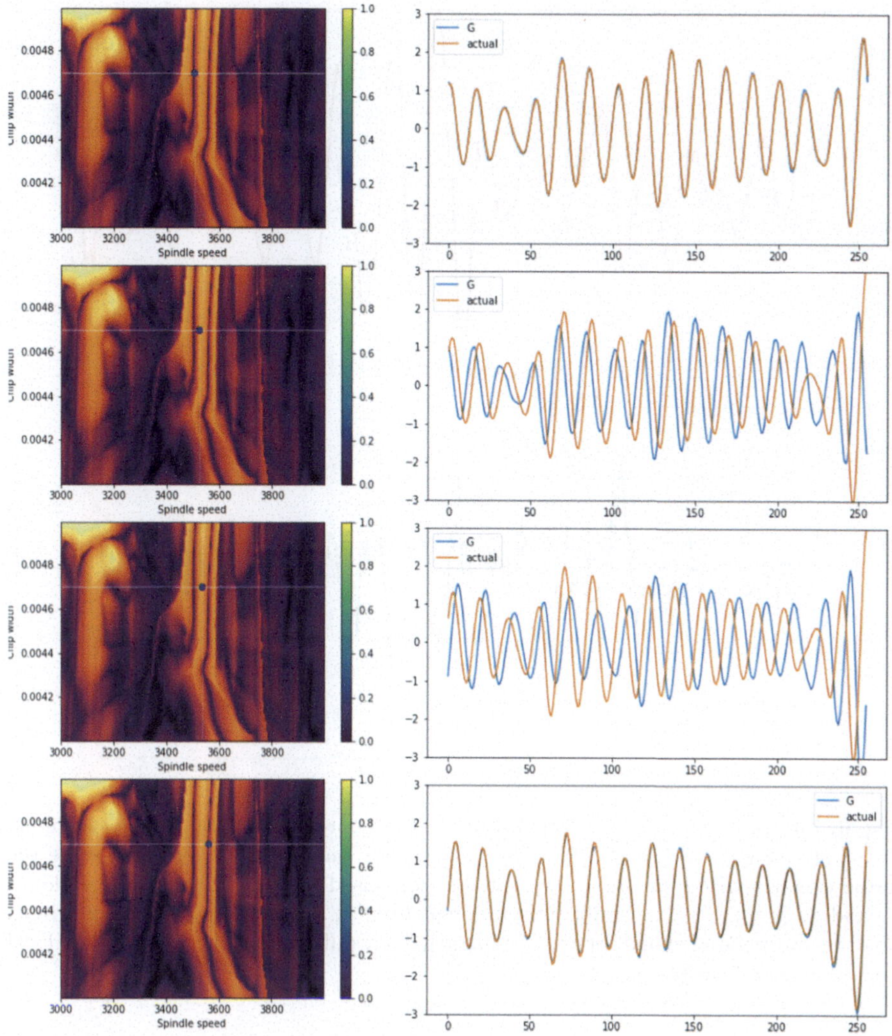

Fig. 5. Example of a path in labels space where the transition between the signal modes is smooth in the training data, but abrupt in the signals produced by the generator. The blue dot on the RMSE maps (left) indicates the parameter values used to compare the two signals (right), real signal in yellow and generated signal in blue. The differences between the fake signals along the labels transition paths shown on the two top figures and the two bottom figures are much lower than for the real signal. The opposite is true for the transition captured by the two middle figures.

linearly with the change in spindle speed, the generated signals remain constant for most of the inspected parameter space and sharply switch to the next mode near the peak on the RMSE map.

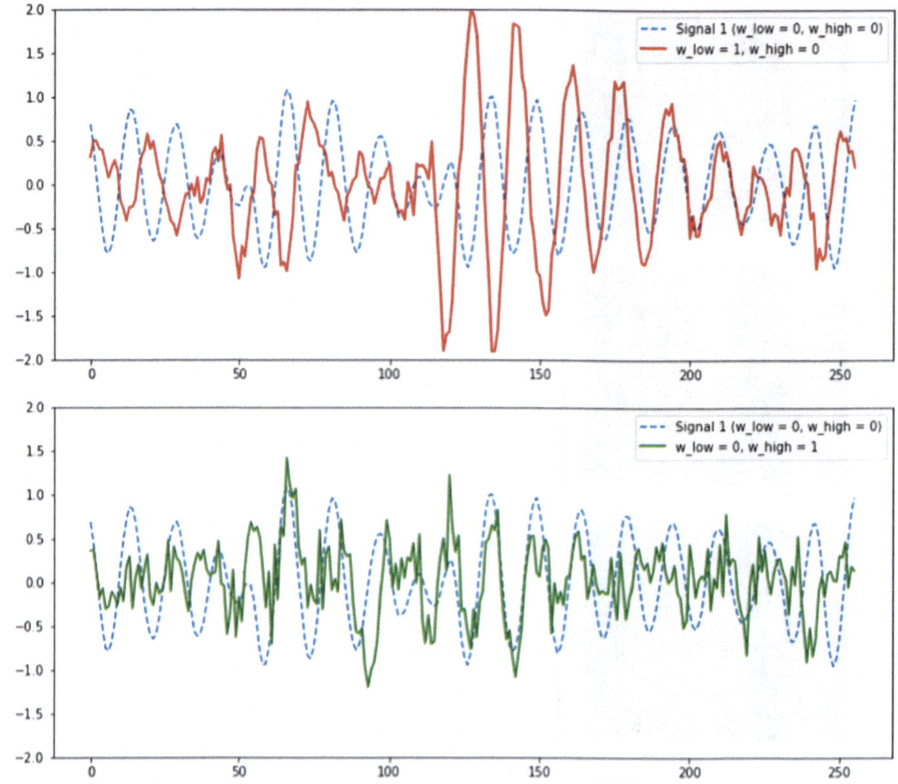

Fig. 6. Interpolated signal $\tilde{x}_3$ comparison with a source signals $\tilde{x}_1$ (top two figures) and $\tilde{x}_2$ (bottom two figures). The blue dashed line on the first figure represents the initial signal $\tilde{x}_1$. Red line, an interpolated signal based on $s_{1..5}$ from signal 2 style set S_2 and $s_{6..16}$ from S_1, is significantly different from $\tilde{x}_1$ in its phase and modes. Green line, an interpolated signal for $w_{1..5} = 0, w_{6..16} = 1$, differs from the source in its local high-frequency features.

3.2 Interpolation Analysis

The style-based neural network architecture enables inspection of the influence of the disentangled input parameter vectors s_i at the different layers i of the synthesis network $G(S)$ within GAN, where $S = \{s_i\} = M(C)$ is a set of style vectors produced by the mapping network of the generator $M()$ from the input label vectors C. This is performed by analysing the changes in the generated signals arising from alteration of the disentangled inputs. For two different sets of styles $S_1 = \{s_{1,i}\}$ and $S_2 = \{s_{2,i}\}$ and the respective generated signals $\tilde{x}_1 = G(S_1)$ and $\tilde{x}_2 = G(S_2)$, an interpolated styles set S_3 is produced as a set of affine combinations of elements of S_1 and S_2: $S_3 = \{s_{3,i}\} = \{s_{1,i} * w_i + s_{2,i} * (1 - w_i)\}$. Thus, at each style level i the style component of S_3 is the weighted sum of the components of S_1 and S_2 at this level, with the weight $w_i = 0$ indicating that only the component of the first style set is used and $w_i = 1$ implying that only the second style is applied at this level. The interpolated signal is acquired from the interpolated style set by feeding the styles into the synthesis network, $\tilde{x}_3 = G(S_3)$.

The variation of the generated signals produced as a result of gradual changes to one or several style components reveals the features that the style components at the respective levels control. By performing a linear interpolation between $s_{1,i}$ and $s_{2,i}$ for each $i = k$ while keeping $s_{3,i} = s_{1,i}$ for each $i \neq k$, we observe that the generator model style layers can be classified into two groups: low-level styles s_1 to s_5 and high-level styles s_6 to s_{16}. The low-level styles significantly affect the low-frequency features of the output signal like its phase and general shape. The high-level styles impact the high-frequency detail of the generated output. Figure 6 visualises the end points of this interpolation: an initial signal $\tilde{x}_1$, its interpolation towards $\tilde{x}_2$ in low-level styles only and in high-level styles only.

4 Conclusion

To the best of authors' knowledge this work is the first attempt to develop a generative model of a machining process using GANs. The neural network architecture at the base of the proposed model is computationally cheap at inference time. This and the generative nature of GAN enable the development of a machining digital twin component that digitally recreates the underlying physical process in real-time. The architecture described in the paper allows a significant degree of control over the generator via input process parameters, thus enhancing the flexibility of the model and opening the potential for exploratory analysis of the modelled process. The shown success of GAN in recreating the machining vibration is an important step towards widespread implementation of data-driven simulation models in Industry 4.0, which could find important applications in monitoring and predictive analytics within manufacturing.

The analysis of the interaction between the inputs and the per-layer style components within the trained GAN model shows the distinct parts of the model that separately control the high- and the low-level features of the generated signal. The accuracy of developed model is analysed, revealing certain conditions under which the generator fails to learn the correct signal mode distribution. Investigation of the conditions under which the proposed model performance is suboptimal would be the likely next research steps. The conditions of suboptimal model behaviour can be investigated via analysis of the activations output by the convolutional layers of the generator. Furthermore, the convolutional kernels learned by the neural network could be analysed to identify possible similarities with filter models used in expert-based signal processing. Both the activations and the kernels could be analysed relationship with the style modulation components could be additionally explored via the interpolation analysis described in the paper.

As a real world implementation would likely be limited in terms of available data, an investigation of the model's capability with sparse data or unobservable factors is an important step in its verification. Categorisation of the continuous labels used to condition the model could make the dataset more closely represent data likely to be encountered on a shop-floor. Other next steps in this research direction would include evaluation of alternative neural network architectures and validation of the proposed model on real manufacturing data, as well as broadening the scope of the digital twin with inclusion of multiple data sources and modelled processes.

Acknowledgments. Professor Ashutosh Tiwari acknowledges the support of the Royal Academy of Engineering under the Research Chairs and Senior Research Fellowships scheme (RCSRF1718\5\41).

References

1. Arjovsky, M., Chintala, S., Bottou, L.: Wasserstein GAN (2017). http://arxiv.org/abs/1701.07875
2. Brock, A., Donahue, J., Simonyan, K.: Large scale GAN training for high fidelity natural image synthesis (2018). http://arxiv.org/abs/1809.11096
3. Chen, X., Duan, Y., Houthooft, R., Schulman, J., Sutskever, I., Abbeel, P.: InfoGAN: interpretable representation learning by information maximizing generative adversarial nets (2016). http://arxiv.org/abs/1606.03657
4. Donahue, C., McAuley, J., Puckette, M.: Adversarial audio synthesis (2018). http://arxiv.org/abs/1802.04208
5. Goodfellow, I.J., Pouget-Abadie, J., Mirza, M., Xu, B., Warde-Farley, D., Ozair, S., Courville, A., Bengio, Y.: Generative adversarial networks (2014). http://arxiv.org/abs/1406.2661
6. Gulrajani, I., Ahmed, F., Arjovsky, M., Dumoulin, V., Courville, A.: Improved training of Wasserstein GANs (2017). http://arxiv.org/abs/1704.00028
7. Henning, K., Wolfgang, W., Johannes, H.: Recommendations for implementing the strategic initiative INDUSTRIE 4.0. Technical Report, April (2013)
8. Huang, X., Belongie, S.: Arbitrary style transfer in real-time with adaptive instance normalization (2017). http://arxiv.org/abs/1703.06868
9. Karras, T., Aila, T., Laine, S., Lehtinen, J.: Progressive growing of GANs for improved quality, stability, and variation (2017). http://arxiv.org/abs/1710.10196
10. Karras, T., Laine, S., Aila, T.: A style-based generator architecture for generative adversarial networks (2018). http://arxiv.org/abs/1812.04948
11. Mirza, M., Osindero, S.: Conditional generative adversarial nets (2014). http://arxiv.org/abs/1411.1784
12. Niggemann, O., Biswas, G., Kinnebrew, J.S., Khorasgani, H., Volgmann, S., Bunte, A.: Data-driven monitoring of cyber-physical systems leveraging on big data and the internet-of-things for diagnosis and control. CEUR Workshop Proc. **1507**, 185–192 (2015)
13. Radford, A., Metz, L., Chintala, S.: Unsupervised representation learning with deep convolutional generative adversarial networks (2015). http://arxiv.org/abs/1511.06434
14. Saatchi, Y., Wilson, A.G.: Bayesian GAN (2017). http://arxiv.org/abs/1705.09558
15. Schmitz, T.L., Smith, K.S.: Machining Dynamics. Springer, Cham (2019). https://doi.org/10.1007/978-3-319-93707-6

16. Spurr, A., Aksan, E., Hilliges, O.: Guiding InfoGAN with semi-supervision. In: Ceci, M., Hollmén, J., Todorovski, L., Vens, C., Džeroski, S. (eds.) Machine Learning and Knowledge Discovery in Databases, Lecture Notes in Computer Science, pp. 119–134. Springer, Cham (2017)
17. Tao, F., Cheng, J., Qi, Q., Zhang, M., Zhang, H., Sui, F.: Digital twin-driven product design, manufacturing and service with big data. Int. J. Adv. Manuf. Technol. **94**(9–12), 3563–3576 (2018)
18. Yu, L., Zhang, W., Wang, J., Yu, Y.: SeqGAN: sequence generative adversarial nets with policy gradient (2016). https://doi.org/10.1001/jamainternmed.2016.8245
19. Zhang, H., Xu, T., Li, H.: StackGAN: text to photo-realistic image synthesis with stacked generative adversarial networks. In: 2017 IEEE International Conference on Computer Vision (ICCV), vol. 2017-Octob, pp. 5908–5916. IEEE (2017)

λ-DNNs and Their Implementation in Aerodynamic and Conjugate Heat Transfer Optimization

Marina Kontou(✉), Dimitrios Kapsoulis, Ioannis Baklagis, and Kyriakos Giannakoglou

Parallel CFD & Optimization Unit, School of Mechanical Engineering, National Technical University of Athens, Athens, Greece
kgianna@mail.ntua.gr

Abstract. A fully-connected Deep Neural Network (DNN) architecture, to be referred to as λ-DNN, used to predict 2D/3D scalar fields is presented. In aerodynamics, the λ-DNN is firstly trained on fields computed using a Computational Fluid Dynamics (CFD) software. Then, it can be incorporated into engineering processes in various ways. One possibility is to use them in optimization problems solved by stochastic population-based methods, in which the λ-DNN may act as the surrogate evaluation model, replacing calls to the CFD tool. Another possibility is in multi-disciplinary problems, to replicate the numerical solver for any of the disciplines. This small list of possible usages is not exhaustive and, of course, different usages can be combined. The input to each DNN contains information to identify the geometrical shape and case-related data, nodal coordinates and, in multi-disciplinary problems, interfacing data connecting solvers for different disciplines on adjacent domains. In this paper, the λ-DNN is firstly used in the aerodynamic shape optimization of a wing using evolutionary algorithms, in which it replicates the CFD solver. Then, it is used in a conjugate heat transfer problem dealing with a solid domain in contact with a flow within a duct. In this problem, the λ-DNN acts as a surrogate to the solver of the heat conduction equation on the solid domain, by interfacing with a CFD solver of the fluid domain.

Keywords: Deep Neural Networks · Flow prediction · Computational Fluid Dynamics · Conjugate heat transfer · Evolutionary optimization of aerodynamic shapes · Multi-disciplinary optimization

1 Introduction

In shape optimization, in one or more disciplines, a number of different designs must be evaluated in order to reach optimal solutions. This number increases when a stochastic optimization method is used so as to avoid being trapped into a local minimum. In multi-disciplinary optimization, such as a Conjugate

L. Iliadis et al. (Eds.): EANN 2020, INNS 2, pp. 202–214, 2020.
https://doi.org/10.1007/978-3-030-48791-1_15

Heat Transfer (CHT) one, the analysis of any configuration requires the iterative solution of the flow equations over the fluid domain and the heat conduction PDE over the adjacent solid domain; during the iterative solution, the two domain solvers communicate at their interface by exchanging heat flux and temperature distributions. The repetitive calls to the two solvers make the cost of a CHT analysis high enough. As industrial requirements become more demanding, not only the number of evaluations needed to reach the optimal solution but, also, the cost per evaluation must be kept as low as possible. This is the main purpose of this paper and the main reason for developing the proposed λ-DNN.

Deep Neural Networks (DNNs) [6] are known to effectively replicate complex tasks by recognizing their core features. As such, in view of the previous discussion, DNNs should learn how to predict the outcome of simulation codes solving PDEs modeling physical phenomena or only the integral quantities needed to evaluate the quality of a configuration, as it may suffice in most optimization problems. In a CHT or any other multi-disciplinary problem, a good idea is to make them replicate the solver corresponding, for instance, to one of the involved disciplines. This might be good enough to shorten the wall clock time of such a simulation. For instance, in an optimization loop, the expected gain from such an algorithm must be evaluated by considering the cost for performing runs to collect the necessary training patterns and that for training the DNN together with the expected reduction in the cost of the optimization loop involving DNNs. This paper demonstrates the efficiency of the proposed optimization techniques based on the newly developed DNNs.

The proposed DNN, which will be referred to as the λ-DNN, Fig. 1, is a Fully-Connected Neural Network (FCNN), compact and with a relatively small number of trainable parameters. This is described in detail in Sect. 2.1.

It is not the first time DNNs are used for predicting flow fields. Convolutional Neural Networks (CNNs), which consist of convolutional layers with local connections between neurons of successive layers, have been used to predict aerodynamic flow fields in unseen flow conditions and geometries, [4]. U-Networks have been used for the prediction of incompressible laminar flows, [5]. They consist of an encoder which compresses the information with successive convolutional layers and a decoder which decompresses it with deconvolution layers and yields the output. In [9], a hybrid DNN, formed by CNN, convolutional Long Short Term Memory network (ConvLSTM) and decoding-CNN (D-CNN), is used for the prediction of unsteady flows.

In this paper, the λ-DNN architecture is applied in the aerodynamic shape optimization of a wing and that of a fluid and a solid domain in a CHT problem, using evolutionary algorithms occasionally assisted by on-line trained metamodels (Radial Basis Function, RBF) networks. The λ-DNN is capable of predicting physical quantities (flow fields in CFD, temperature distributions in CHT) on any type of computational grids (structured or unstructured), since grid connectivity is not required. The λ-DNN requires a small number of training fields and has a low computational cost (compared to [4,5]), ensuring acceptable accuracy.

2 Methods and Tools

2.1 The Proposed λ-DNN

A DNN consists of many layers of neurons, with weights and biases being the network parameters to be computed during the training phase. During this phase, a cost function expressed as the root-mean-squared (RMS) of the differences between the network outputs and the known/archived responses is minimized. To this end, the back-propagation algorithm, [15], using closed-form expressions for the derivatives of the cost function with respect to the network parameters, is used.

The λ-DNN is exclusively formed by fully-connected layers. For better data handling, its architecture consists of two separated branches (Fig. 1), one for each type of input. Each branch first passes through fully-connected layers and then connects to the main branch which further processes signals through its own fully-connected layers and concludes to the network output(s). In the cases presented below, there are two different kinds of inputs, one refers to the mesh (nodal coordinates) and the other to parameterization or physical quantities. The different branches allow separate processing of input data of different nature. This leads to extraction of different features for each branch, before merging them to produce the final output.

The Rectified Linear Unit (ReLU) activation function [8] is used in all but the last layer which uses the sigmoid function, for the one-discipline case, and the Hyberbolic Tangent function (tanh) for the two-discipline one. The pre- and post-processing of the set of training patterns and all DNN phases (construction, training and testing) have been implemented in Python 3.6 [14] linked with TensorFlow [1] and run on both GPUs and CPUs.

The λ-DNN is applied according to two different modes. The first is based on a node-to-node logic, meaning that the network predicts only one output, namely the flow variable at each grid node, while the second processes the whole grid at once and the output of a λ-DNN run is a whole field. The difference between the two modes lies on whether grid connectivity is taken into account; the former is independent of the grid connectivity while the latter is not.

2.2 Computational Tools for Aerodynamic and CHT Analyses

For the numerical solution of CHT problems, [2,12], coupled and decoupled solution schemes are in use. In the coupled approach, PDEs on different domains are simultaneously solved while, in the decoupled approach, each discipline is solved separately and provides boundary conditions for the others by exchanging information along their interface. In either approach, proper solvers' interfacing guarantees heat flux conservation and equal temperatures over the fluid-solid interface. Herein, the decoupled approach is used. The procedure is computationally expensive as it requires many iterative cycles (CHT cycles), with calls to the CFD solver (for the fluid domain) and the Heat Conduction one (for the solid domain). Each domain is solved separately and the interaction of the

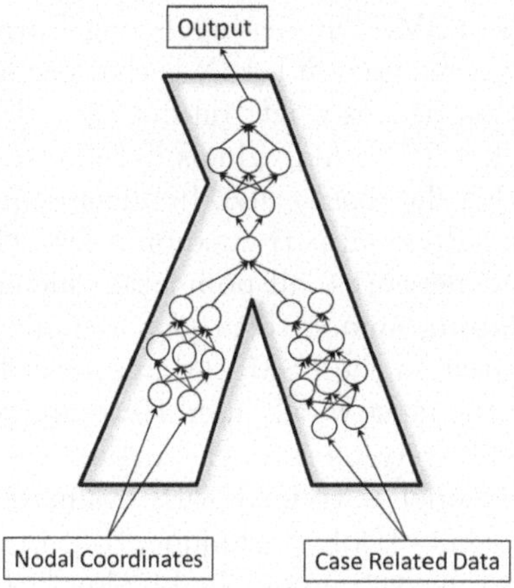

Fig. 1. The proposed λ-DNN architecture. The DNN is named after its shape that looks like the Greek letter λ. For visualization reasons, each circle/layer comprises a number of neurons/layers. The number of inputs/outputs and that of fully-connected layers vary among the cases.

solvers is taking place at their interface, so a DNN trained on the contribution of the one solver to the interface can be very helpful. By doing so, the cost of one solver will be significantly reduced, together with the overall cost of the CHT evaluation. More details about this implementation and the offered gains will be provided in Sect. 4, where the corresponding case is described.

Regarding the analysis of fluid flows, an in-house Reynolds-Averaged Navier-Stokes equations' solver, [3,10], coupled with a Heat Conduction equations' solver is used. The governing equations are discretized using the finite volume technique. The CFD code solves incompressible and compressible flows; herein, all cases are studied with the compressible variant. Fluid and solid domain solvers fully exploit the CUDA programming environment and run on a GPU cluster. CFD/CHT evaluations and DNN training were performed on NVIDIA K20 or K40 GPUs.

2.3 EA-Based Optimization, Without or with Metamodels

For the EA-based optimizations presented in Sects. 3 and 4, the optimization platform EASY, [7], developed by the Parallel CFD & Optimization Unit of the National Technical University of Athens is used. Real encoding of the design variables, with 5% mutation probability and simulated binary crossover with 90% probability are used. To reduce the cost of the EA-based optimization, EASY optionally employs on-line trained metamodels (RBF networks) and this is performed in a rather unique way compared to other similar tools. The role of the metamodel(s) is to replace calls to the problem-specific method (PSM; herein, either a CFD or a CHT solver) by approximating the objective function(s) value(s) at negligible cost, after training them on data collected for individuals already evaluated on the PSM. The distinguishing feature of the Metamodel-Assisted EA (MAEA) implemented in EASY is that the RBF networks' training occurs during the evolution (this is what "on-line" stands for). The use of metamodels starts after the first T^{MM} individuals have been evaluated on the PSM and recorded in the MAEA database (DB). In all subsequent generations, a different RBF network per individual is trained on a few selected neighboring DB entries. Using these RBF networks, all population members are pre-evaluated and only the most promising among them (λ_e; a small user-defined value per generation) are re-evaluated on the PSM, [11] and recorded in the DB.

This is contrasted to the most widely used EAs supported by off-line trained metamodels, which usually rely on a single metamodel, valid over the whole search space. This metamodel is trained with evaluated individuals resulting from a Design of Experiments (DoE) technique, [13]. In such an algorithm, the EA–based search relies exclusively upon the previously (off-line) trained metamodel. The "optimal" solution(s) is/are re-evaluated on the PSM and the process goes on by re-training the metamodel on the updated DB and performing a new EA-based search until a termination criterion be met.

In this paper, in the sake of pluralism, both on- and off-line metamodels are used within EASY. The λ-DNN is used as off-line metamodel, replacing the CFD tool. The λ-DNN is updated if, upon convergence of the EA-based search using the same λ-DNN, the re-evaluation of the "optimal" solution (quotes denote the outcome of an optimization in which the evaluation tool is a surrogate model) on the CFD asks for better accuracy. In the CHT problem, the evaluation s/w combines an accurate tool (CFD solver) for the fluid domain and the λ-DNN for the solid domain. This optimization also uses on-line trained metamodels (a MAEA with RBF networks, implemented as described above).

3 Case I: Aerodynamic Shape Optimization

The first application is concerned with the use of the λ-DNN in the prediction and the aerodynamic shape optimization of a transonic wing. The geometry of [16] is the reference wing. The flow is inviscid with free-stream Mach number and flow angles equal to $M_\infty = 0.8395$, $a_{\infty,pitch} = 3.06^o$ and $a_{\infty,yaw} = 0^o$. The wing shape is encapsulated within a $6 \times 3 \times 3$ volumetric NURBS (trivariate Non-Uniform Rational B-Splines) control grid. A knot vector and a degree per parametric direction are needed to complete the parameterization. The morphing used in this case is graphically presented (as a 2D example, though) in Case II. 12, out of the 54 control points (CPS), are allowed to move in the chordwise and the normal-to-the-planform directions within ±20% of their reference coordinate values, resulting to $12 \times 2 = 24$ design variables in total. In this case, the parameterization is used not only for generating training patterns but, also, as an input to the DNN to identify different wing shapes. An unstructured 3D CFD grid of $\sim 1.33 \times 10^6$ nodes generated around the reference geometry and adapted to all changed shapes is used. A single run of the CFD software takes ~2min on a K20 GPU.

Both a λ-DNN and an FCNN are used. The first branch of the λ-DNN consists of four fully-connected layers with $128, 256, 256, 128$ neurons each; the second branch consists of three fully-connected layers with $128, 256, 128$ neurons each. After their merging, another three fully-connected layers with $128, 256, 128$ neurons each lead to the final output. For comparison reasons the number of neurons and layers in the λ-DNN and the FCNN are kept the same. The FCNN consists of seven layers with $256, 512, 512, 256, 256, 512, 256$ neurons, respectively. The 200 wings are used for training the λ-DNN and the FCNN by randomly changing the position of the pre-defined CPs of the morphing box. In this case, a node-to-node procedure is followed.

The networks are trained on the $M \simeq 27000$ surface nodes of each CFD grid, thus the total number of training patterns is 200×27000. The input data to the networks are the 24 coordinates of the free-to-move control points along with the (x, y, z) coordinates of any surface node, i.e. 27 inputs in total, and the output is a single pressure value at this surface node. The first branch of the λ-DNN processes the coordinates of the control points, while the second one the (x, y, z) coordinates.

In this case, the training cost is ∼1.2 h for both networks. Before proceeding with the shape optimization, the prediction quality of the DNNs on two new wings generated by displacing the control points within the aforementioned bounds, and not seen by the DNNs before, is checked. Predictions of pressure (p_{DNN}) using the trained DNNs are compared with CFD evaluations (p_{CFD}) using the Mean Absolute Percentage Error ($MAPE_p$) indicator per wing, given by:

$$MAPE_p = \frac{1}{M} \sum_{i=1}^{M} \left| \frac{p_{i,CFD} - p_{i,DNN}}{p_{i,CFD}} \right| \tag{1}$$

The average $MAPE_p$ computed on the two new wings is equal to 0.81% for the λ-DNN and 3.83% for the FCNN; and this demonstrates the superiority of the proposed network type.

Then, two EA-based shape optimizations, for maximum wing lift (L), are performed. During the first one, the λ-DNN assists the EAs to reduce the total number of calls to the expensive CFD s/w, by acting as an off-line trained surrogate (Run_1). The λ-DNN predicts the pressure field on the surface of each new wing presented to it which, through integration, computes the lift force. A CFD run on the "optimal" solution is performed only at the end of the EA-based cycle. The second one is a MAEA (with on-line trained RBF networks, $T^{MM} = 40$ and $\lambda_e = 3$) optimization relying upon the CFD code instead of the λ-DNN (Run_2). A comparison between Run_1 and Run_2 is made. Both are configured with 10 parents and 20 offspring, i.e. they are (10,20) EAs or MAEAs. This is a well performing set-up of the optimization method in this case which was kept the same in both cases, in the sake of fair comparison.

For either run, a total budget of 250 CFD evaluations ("time-units") is a priori defined. For Run_1, this budget corresponds to: 200 time-units to form the DB, 33 to train the network and only 17 for running the optimization, spent, in particular, for the necessary CFD re-evaluations. Run_1 resulted to a wing geometry having a lift that is by 2.9% higher than the solution of Run_2. We conclude that the usage of the λ-DNN improves the efficiency of the EA-based search even more than the (already very fast) MAEA. In Fig. 2, the convergence histories of the two optimizations are illustrated. To quantify the gain with respect to the original shape, L is always dimensionalized by the reference wing L value.

In Fig. 3, the pressure field for the optimal geometry is shown for the solutions of Run_1 and Run_2. For the former, two pressure fields are presented, that evaluated by the CFD and that predicted by the λ-DNN. The pressure fields differ between Run_1 and Run_2, since the two optimizations resulted in different wing shapes. For the optimized wing of Run_1, the pressure prediction of the λ-DNN (Fig. 3, right) is so close to the CFD solution (Fig. 3, middle), and this demonstrates the reliability of the proposed network.

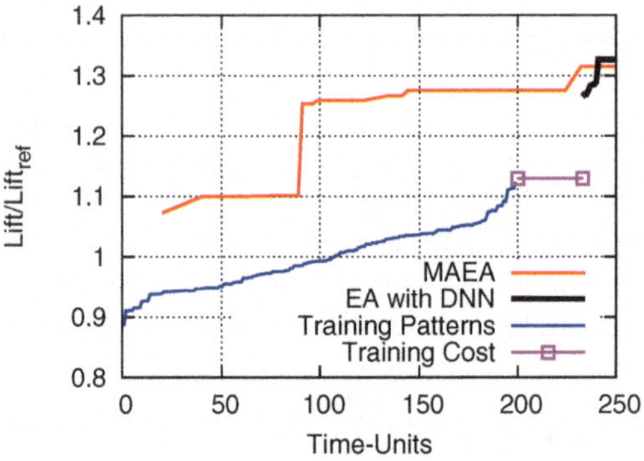

Fig. 2. Case I: Convergence History of the EA relying on the λ-DNN (Run_1) and the MAEA (based on on-line trained RBF networks) (Run_2). The blue line corresponds to the 200 training patterns plotted in ascending order, the pink line represents the training cost, while the black line represents the EA relying on the λ-DNN; all three of them stand for Run_1.

4 Case II: CHT Shape Optimization

Here, the λ-DNN is used in the CHT optimization of a fluid duct adjacent to a solid domain, to replace the heat conduction equation solver on the solid domain. The same CFD code for the fluid domain (this time solving the Reynolds-Averaged Navier-Stokes equations with the Spalart-Allmaras turbulence model, [17]) is used. In the absence of the λ-DNN, the CFD code interacts with a solver for the conduction equation over the solid domain. The same morphing technique (adapted to 2D cases) is used. The high temperature solid domain is cooled by fluid of lower temperature (T) flowing within the S-bend duct. The two domains are solved in a decoupled manner, by interchanging the computed heat flux (from the fluid to the solid) and temperature (in the opposite direction) distributions over the fluid-solid interface (FSI).

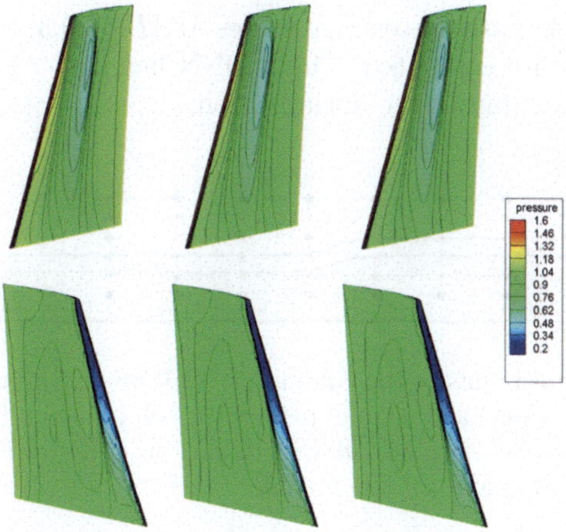

Fig. 3. Case I: Pressure Fields on the surface of the transonic wing. Left: Optimized solution of Run_2. Middle: Optimized solution of Run_1, evaluated by CFD. Right: Optimized solution of Run_1, re-evaluated by the λ-DNN.

For the fluid domain, the flow has inlet total pressure $p_{t,inlet} = 105$ kPa, inlet total temperature $T_{t,inlet} = 300$ K, outlet static pressure $p_{outlet} = 100$ kPa. For the solid domain, a constant temperature of $T = 500$ K is imposed along its bottom boundary, while the rest non-FSI nodes are considered adiabatic. The geometry is parameterized using a 8×6 volumetric NURBS control grid, Fig. 4. 24 CPs are allowed to move within ±10% of their reference coordinate values in either direction, resulting to $24 \times 2 = 48$ design variables in the optimization problem. In this 2D case, the parameterization is common for both the fluid and the solid domain but it is not used as input (information) to the DNN. A mono-block structured grid of ~330000 nodes is used to discretize both domains, where $M = 240000$ of them correspond to the solid domain. A single run of the CHT solver takes ~20min on a K40 GPU.

The database for training the λ-DNN is built by evaluating 180 geometries by randomly moving the CPs. As in the previous case, a λ-DNN and an FCNN are used. The two branches of the λ-DNN consist of one layer each with 512 neurons. The two branches merge to a single layer of 20 neurons that leads to the final output. The network architecture is selected after a trial-and-error procedure. The FCNN consists of two layers with 1024 and 512 neurons each.

The input data are the (x, y) coordinates and the heat fluxes at the 600 FSI nodes, i.e. 1800 inputs in total. At the λ-DNN, the first branch processes the (x, y) coordinates, while the other the heat fluxes. The output is the temperature (T) field on the entire solid domain; grid connectivity and number of nodes remain the same for all the geometries. It is important to notice that, in contrast to the previous case where a node-to-node procedure was followed, here, the nodal T values over the entire solid domain are simultaneously predicted. Two new geometries, not seen by the DNNs before, are used to validate the λ-DNN and the FCNN. In this case the average values $MAPE_T$ 0.3% for the λ-DNN and 0.8% for the FCNN are computed. The λ-DNN has better prediction accuracy and, thus, this is used during the optimization.

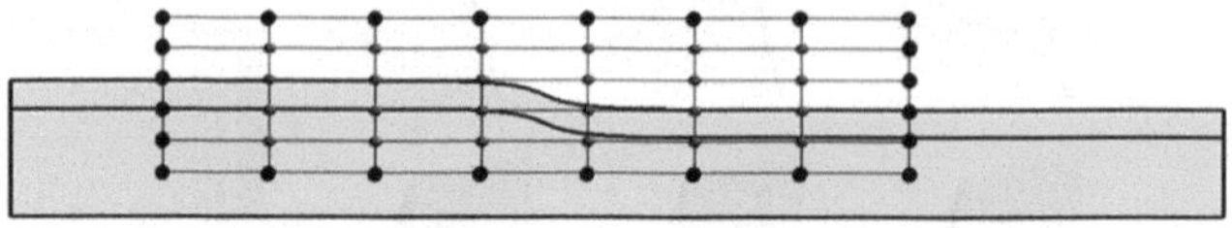

Fig. 4. Case II: Control Points of the volumetric NURBS, morphing box, parameterizing the S-bend duct (upper) and a small part of the solid domain (lower). Black points are kept fixed, whereas red ones are allowed to vary in either direction, morphing the enclosed parts of the fluid and solid domains.

Three MAEA-based optimizations are performed with 10 parents and 20 offspring, supported by on-line trained RBF networks with $T^{MM}=40$ and $\lambda_e=3$.

The first two optimizations aim at minimizing the mass-averaged total pressure losses between the inlet (I) and the outlet (O) of the S-bend duct, i.e. they are dealing with an objective defined only in the fluid domain,

$$F_1 = \frac{\int_{S_I} p_t \rho v_n dS + \int_{S_O} p_t \rho v_n dS}{\int_{S_I} \rho v_n dS} \tag{2}$$

ρ, v_n stand for the density and the normal (directed outwards) to the boundary velocity component.

The first optimization (Run_1) uses the λ-DNN as surrogate to the solid domain solver, while the second one (Run_2) is based exclusively on the solution of the governing PDEs. A total budget of 250 CHT evaluations ("time-units"; one time-unit is the cost per evaluation in Run_2) is decided for both of them. For Run_1, this budget corresponds to 30 time-units to form the database, 24 for training the network and 196 for the optimization, since an evaluation on the (CFD and λ-DNN) tool costs about 0.76 time-units. Then, Run_2 is performed. Figure 5 presents the convergence histories of the MAEAs and the resulting optimal geometry; a reduction in $F_1 \sim 8.6\%$, compared to the initial/reference geometry, is obtained in both Run_1 and Run_2. F_1 is normalized by the value of the same quantity in the reference geometry. The optimal solution of Run_1 is re-evaluated on the exact CHT solver; the λ-DNN error is less than 0.008% verifying the network accuracy.

Then, a two-objective optimization, by adding a second target defined over the solid domain, is performed. The second objective function is the percentage of the area of the solid domain over which T exceeds a threshold value, scaled by the excess temperature, namely

$$F_2 = \frac{1}{\Omega_s} \int_{\Omega_S} (T - T_{thres}) d\Omega \tag{3}$$

F_2 should be minimized. The $T = 500\,\text{K}$ value along the bottom boundary of the solid domain is the highest temperature over the domain. The value of the $T_{thres} = 450\,\text{K}$ is defined in order to minimize the area of the domain which exceeds this threshold value. In whatever follows, F_1 and F_2 are presented in a non-dimensional form; they are both divided by the corresponding values of the reference solution (the one presented in Fig. 4).

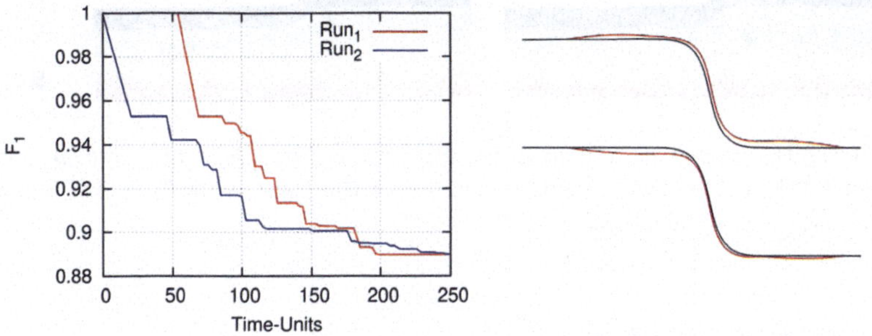

Fig. 5. Case II: Left: Convergence histories of the MAEA-based optimizations for Run_1 (Fluid-(λ-DNN)) and Run_2 (Fluid-Solid). Right: The initial (black) and the optimal (red) geometries (x and y axes not in scale).

The new optimization (Run_3) uses the λ-DNN as the surrogate to the solid domain solver. The total budget is still 250 CHT evaluations distributed as for Run_1. In Fig. 6, the front of non-dominated solutions resulted from Run_3 is presented. The members of the front are re-evaluated with the exact CHT solver to verify the network accuracy. The re-evaluated members remain non-dominated and the errors in F_1 and F_2 are ~0.008% and ~0.09%, respectively.

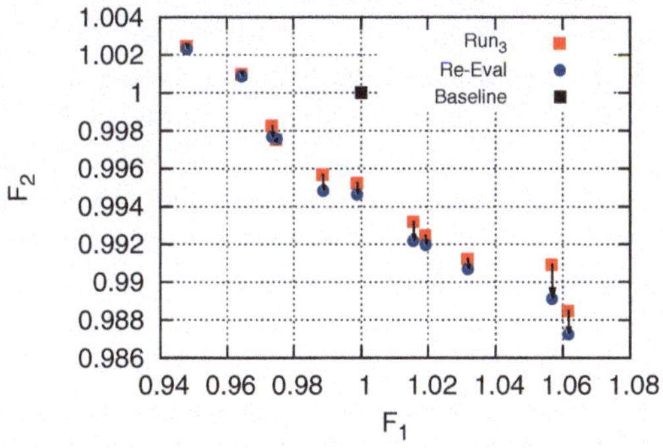

Fig. 6. Case II: Front of non-dominated solutions computed from Run_3 (red squares), plotted along with the baseline geometry (black square). The front members are re-evaluated on the exact CHT solver resulting to a new non-dominated front (blue circles). The computed "optimal" members on the front remain non-dominated after the re-evaluation using the computational mechanics s/w.

The T field from Run_3 and its re-evaluation as well as the prediction error are shown for the member of the front with $F_1 = 0.975$ and $F_2 = 0.997$ in Figs. 7 and 8, respectively. As shown in Figs. 6, 7 and 8, the accuracy of the λ-DNN is high enough to sufficiently replicate the heat conduction equation solver on the solid domain during an optimization and reduce its overall cost.

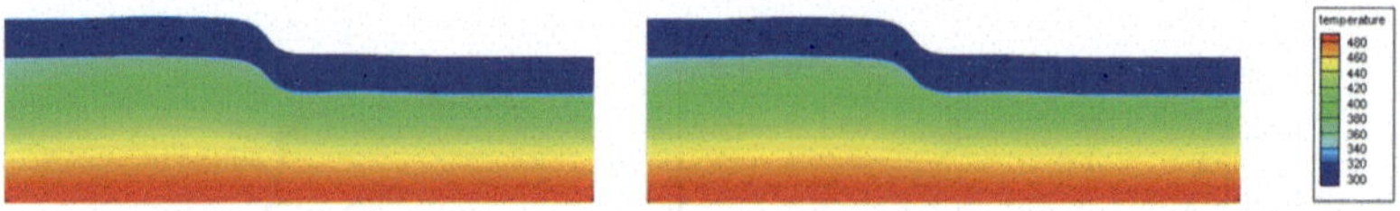

Fig. 7. Case II: Temperature field as resulted from Run_3 (left) and re-evaluated with the exact CHT solver (right) for the member of the front with $F_1 = 0.975$ and $F_2 = 0.997$ (x and y axes not in scale).

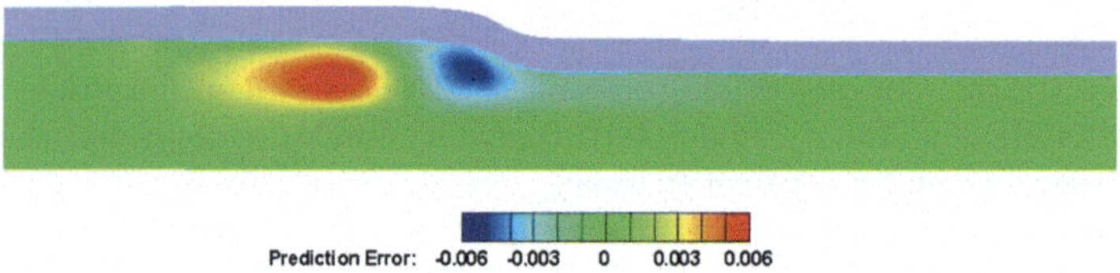

Fig. 8. Case II: Prediction error of the solid domain temperature field for the member of the front with $F_1 = 0.975$ and $F_2 = 0.997$.

5 Conclusions

This paper presented a new DNN architecture, called λ-DNN, which can be used in single- and multi-disciplinary optimization. The λ-DNN is used to predict CFD and CHT results in the form of entire flow fields or temperature distributions, so as to replace expensive runs of CFD/CHT solvers in design/optimization processes. The proposed method has been demonstrated in a 3D one-discipline and a 2D two-discipline case. The DNN yields very good predictions of fields. Inputs are presented to two different branches for better and separate processing of the given input data and, then, these two branches meet at a single one that gives the required output. The λ-DNN manages to reduce the training cost and number of patterns required. The high prediction accuracy of the proposed λ-DNN was demonstrated in a wing flow problem and a solid domain adjacent to a S-bend duct as a surrogate to the heat conduction solver. Regarding the one-discipline case optimization, the trained λ-DNN is used as metamodel during an EA-based optimization and improves the search performance with results comparable with those provided by the MAEA. Regarding the two-discipline case, the λ-DNN is used instead of the Heat Conduction solver during a MAEA optimization. Therefore, the proposed λ-DNN is shown to be capable of replacing the CFD and CHT solvers in expensive (analysis and optimization) processes. Future work includes the use of the λ-DNN in 3D real-world one- and two- discipline applications, such as aeroelastic shape optimization.

Acknowledgments. This work has been supported by the Greek Research and Technology Network (GRNET) High Performance Computing Services, through the TurboNN and CGT-DNN projects.

References

1. Abadi, M., Agarwal, A., Barham, P.: TensorFlow: Large-scale machine learning on heterogeneous systems (2015). http://tensorflow.org/, software available from tensorflow.org
2. Andrei, L., Andreini, A., Facchini, B., Winchler, L.: A decoupled CHT procedure: application and validation on a gas turbine vane with different cooling configurations. In: 68th Conference of the Italian Thermal Machines Engineering Association (2013)
3. Asouti, V., Trompoukis, X., Kampolis, I., Giannakoglou, K.: Unsteady CFD computations using vertex-centered finite volumes for unstructured grids on graphics processing units. Int. J. Numer. Methods Fluids **67**(2), 232–246 (2011)
4. Bhatnagar, S., Afshar, Y., Pan, S., Duraisamy, K., Kaushik, S.: Prediction of aerodynamic flow fields using convolutioanl neural networks. Comput. Mech. **64**, 525–545 (2019)
5. Chen, J., Viquerat, J., Hachem, E.: U-net architectures for fast prediction of incompressible laminar flows (2019)
6. Deng, L., Yu, D.: Deep learning: methods and applications. Found. Trends Signal Process. **7**(3–4), 1–199 (2014)
7. Giannakoglou, K.: The EASY (Evolutionary Algorithms SYstem) software (2008). http://velos0.ltt.mech.ntua.gr/EASY
8. Goodfellow, I., Bengio, Y., Courville, A.: Deep Learning. The MIT Press, Cambridge (2016)
9. Han, R., Wang, Y., Zhang, Y., Chen, G.: A new prediction method of unsteady wake flow by the hybrid deep neural network (2019)
10. Kampolis, I., Trompoukis, X., Asouti, V., Giannakoglou, K.: CFD-based analysis and two-level aerodynamic optimization on graphics processing units. Comput. Methods Appl. Mech. Eng. **199**(9–12), 712–722 (2010)
11. Karakasis, M., Giotis, A., Giannakoglou, K.: Inexact information aided, low-cost, distributed genetic algorithms for aerodynamic shape optimization. Int. J. Numer. Methods Fluids **43**(10–11), 1149–1166 (2003)
12. Moretti, R., Errera, M.P., Couaillier, V., Feyel, F.: Stability, convergence and optimization of interface treatments in weak and strong thermal fluid-structure interaction. Int. J. Therm. Sci. **126**, 23–37 (2017)
13. Myers, R., Montgomery, D.: Response Surface Methodology Process and Product Optimization Using Designed Experiments, 2nd edn. Wiley, New York (2002)
14. Rossum, G.: Python tutorial. Technical Report CS-R9526 (1995)
15. Rumelhart, D., Hinton, G., Williams, R.: Learning representations by back-propagating errors. Nature **323**(6088), 533–536 (1986)

16. Schmitt, V., Charpin, F.: Pressure distributions on the ONERA M6 wing at transonic mach numbers, experimental data base for computer program assessment. Technical report, AGARD 138 (1979)
17. Spalart, P., Allmaras, S.: A one-equation turbulence model for aerodynamic flows. La Rech. Aerosp. **1**, 5–21 (1994)

Symbols in Engineering Drawings (SiED): An Imbalanced Dataset Benchmarked by Convolutional Neural Networks

Eyad Elyan(✉), Carlos Francisco Moreno-García, and Pamela Johnston

The Robert Gordon University, Garthdee Road, Aberdeen, UK
{e.elyan,c.moreno-garcia,p.johnston2}@rgu.ac.uk

Abstract. Engineering drawings are common across different domains such as Oil & Gas, construction, mechanical and other domains. Automatic processing and analysis of these drawings is a challenging task. This is partly due to the complexity of these documents and also due to the lack of dataset availability in the public domain that can help push the research in this area. In this paper, we present a multiclass imbalanced dataset for the research community made of 2432 instances of engineering symbols. These symbols were extracted from a collection of complex engineering drawings known as Piping and Instrumentation Diagram (P&ID). By providing such dataset to the research community, we anticipate that this will help attract more attention to an important, yet overlooked industrial problem, and will also advance the research in such important and timely topics. We discuss the datasets characteristics in details, and we also show how Convolutional Neural Networks (CNNs) perform on such extremely imbalanced datasets. Finally, conclusions and future directions are discussed.

Keywords: CNN · Multiclass · Classification · Imbalanced dataset · Engineering drawings · P&ID

1 Introduction

Engineering drawings are known to be one of the most complex types of documents to process and analyse. They are widely used in different industries such as construction and city planning (i.e. floor plan diagrams [2]), Oil & Gas (i.e. P&IDs [9]), Mechanical Engineering [33], AutoCAD Drawing Exchange Format (DXF) [13] and others. Interpreting these drawings requires highly skilled people, and in some cases long hours of work. Processing and analysing these drawings is becoming increasingly important. This is partly due to the urgent need to improve business practices such as inventory, asset management, risk analysis, safety checks and other types of applications, and also due to the recent advancements in the domain of machine vision and image understanding. Deep Learning

L. Iliadis et al. (Eds.): EANN 2020, INNS 2, pp. 215–224, 2020.
https://doi.org/10.1007/978-3-030-48791-1_16

(DL) [15], in particular, had significantly improved the performance by orders of magnitude in many domains such as the Gaming and AI [17], Natural Language Processing [36], Health [12], Cyber Security [28], and others.

The concept of Convolutional Neural Networks (CNNs) [16] has made significant progress in recent years in many image-related tasks. It has been successfully applied to several fields such as hand-written digit recognition [22], image classification [20, 30], face recognition & biometrics [27], amongst others. Before CNNs, improvements in image classification, segmentation, and object detection were marginal and incremental. CNNs revolutionised this field. For example, Deep Face [31], which is a face recognition system that was first proposed by Facebook in 2014, achieved an accuracy of 97.35%, beating the then state-of-the-art, by 27%.

Despite extensive progress in the field of image processing and analysis, very little progress has been made in the area of analysing complex engineering drawings, and extracting information from these diagrams is still considered a challenging problem [5]. Consider for example the case of the Piping and Instrumentation Diagram (P&ID), which is a schematic engineering drawing, commonly used in the Oil and Gas industry [9, 24]. This type of diagram, as can be seen in Fig. 1, is made of symbols, connectivity information (lines, dashed lines, combinations of lines), text, and other graphical elements.

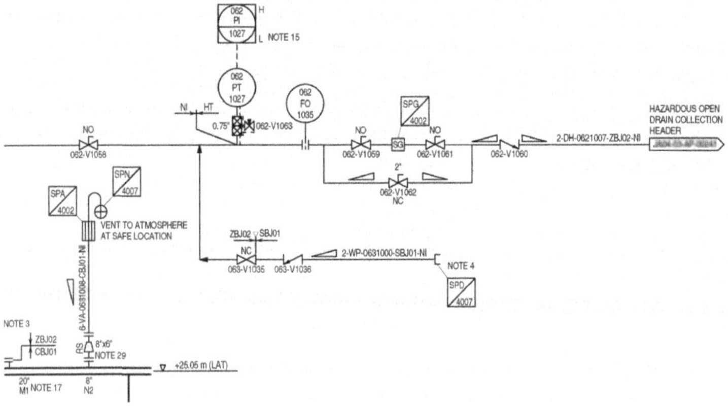

Fig. 1. A typical example of elements within a P&ID diagram

Identification of the symbols within this kind of diagram would appear to be an ideal problem which could be easily solved by convolutional neural networks. However, a recent review on the subject [7] showed that publicly available datasets are not common in this area, with research commonly applied to small, proprietary datasets. To take full advantage of the recent advances in machine vision, and to facilitate reproducible experiments, a sizeable, labelled dataset in the public domain is required.

Several factors make processing and analysing engineering drawings a challenging tasks. First, the quality of the images/scanned documents is sometimes of a standard which requires the application of various image-enhancements methods. Second, the nature of these diagrams, where various types of elements might be overlapping (i.e. a text overlaid on a symbol), in addition to possible data annotations and other graphic elements makes accurate localisation of individual elements more challenging. It is difficult to isolate one particular symbol from its neighbours. Another inherent problem is the imbalanced distribution of various symbols within these drawings. Handling all related challenges is beyond the scope of this paper. The reader is referred to [24] for more detailed description about the inherent characteristics and challenges of these types of drawings.

In this paper, we present a new multiclass dataset of symbols extracted from engineering drawings to the research community. Realistically reflecting the problem, this dataset is subject to some class-imbalance. The remaining parts of this paper are organised as follows: In Sect. 2 we discuss relevant literature to the digitisation of engineering drawings and class imbalance. In Sect. 3 we present our methods which includes detailed discussion of the dataset, and our approach for classifying engineering symbols. Benchmarking experiments and results are presented in Sect. 4, and finally, conclusions and future directions are discussed in Sect. 5.

2 Related Work

Attempts to process and analyse symbolic drawings date back to at least the early 90's. These include: analysis of musical notes [6]; processing mechanical drawings [19]; and optical character recognition (OCR)[21,23,26]. In recent years, digitising engineering drawings has become increasingly important as they are widely used in different domains [2,9,13,33], however, literature is still limited. To the best of our knowledge, there is no large, publicly available dataset to facilitate the advantages of modern, data-hungry CNNs. A recent review [7] detailed the whole process of digitisation and contextualisation of the three main shapes contained in engineering drawings (i.e. text, lines and symbols). The authors identified that, typically, symbols are located within the drawing either in a *specific* or a *holistic* way. In *specific* localisation, the system has a predefined symbol description/template, and an algorithm recursively looks for such symbol. In contrast, *holistic* methods require differentiation of the three shapes to then be able to split the drawing into layers. One of the most widely-used frameworks in this regard is text-graphics separation [32], which is a family of algorithms which distinguish text from lines and symbols based on properties such as height-to-width radio, stroke, amongst others. CNNs could be applied to both of these, given sufficient labelled data.

One type of engineering drawings, namely P&IDs, has attracted more research attention in recent years. Typical examples, presented in [9,18,25], aimed at detecting and recognising symbols within these diagrams. It can be argued however, that most of the existing literature followed a traditional image processing approach [14], which requires feature extraction [8], feature representation [37], and classification to determine the class of objects (i.e. symbols, digits, ...) [1].

Most recently in [9], authors presented a first step towards creating a symbol repository for engineering drawings. A total of 1187 symbols split into 37 different classes was compiled. The repository was then processed by means of class decomposition [10,11], resulting in a total of 57 sub-classes. Classification accuracy was calculated using three different classification frameworks: Random Forests (RF), Support Vector Machine (SVM) and a CNN. Class decomposition demonstrated a slight improvement in classification results for SVM and CNN, with a more considerable improvement in RF.

Overall, there is a growing interest in the research community in digitising and analysing engineering drawings. Yet, the lack of public domain datasets is considered as one of the main challenges to push the research boundaries in this area. In addition to this, the class-imbalance problem could also be considered as another challenge, in particular when certain types of symbols either dominate, or rarely appear in the dataset. Class-imbalance is common across different domains, and not only limited to engineering drawings [34,35]. Handling this problem is often done by means of data resampling, where majority classes are undersampled to reduce their dominance, or minority classes are oversampled [35]. In addition to this, Generative Adversarial Neural Networks [15] were successfully applied recently to augment an imbalanced dataset and improve learning algorithm performance [3,4].

3 Methodology

This section presents our novel dataset of Symbols in Engineering Drawings (SiED). First we give a brief description of how this dataset was constructed. This is followed by a detailed description of dataset and class distribution. Finally, a brief discussion related to the classification method used to benchmark this dataset is presented.

3.1 Data Extraction

A collection of P&ID sheets was provided by an industrial partner. Following the work in [25], a thresholding method was first applied to reduce noise. Areas of interest were then identified interactively to discard boundaries, text and annotation outside the border of each drawing. A traditional machine-vision approach was then used to extract a set of symbols. A set of heuristic-based methods were developed and applied sequentially to localise symbols within each P&ID drawing. Figure 2 shows a random selection of typical symbols that appear in P&IDs.

The methods proved to be stable enough to provide a list of extracted and well-defined symbols. However, a key limitation of such heuristic-based methods is that they require extensive feature engineering and require fine-tuning and customisation to generalise to unseen symbols or different types of diagrams [7].

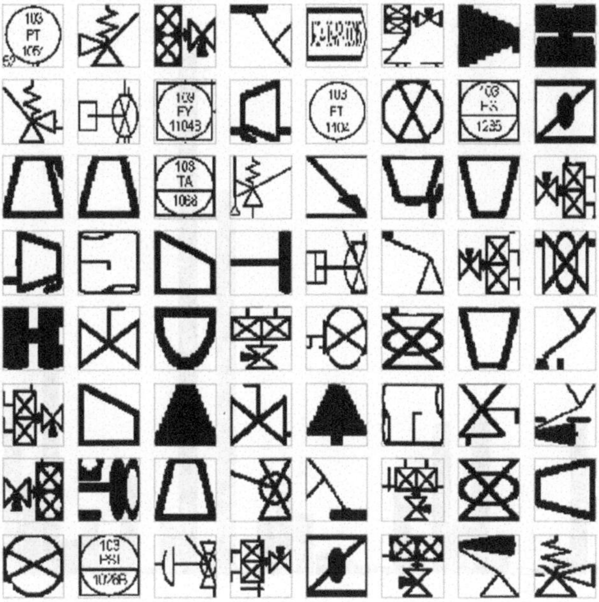

Fig. 2. A random selection of typical symbols that appear in P&IDs

3.2 Dataset

Using the method presented above, a series of P&IDs have been processed and analysed. This resulted in a collection of symbols that represent different types of equipment within the drawings. In total, a dataset of 2432 instances representing 39 different type of symbols were compiled. All symbols have been scaled to a standard size of 100×100 pixels. The dataset provides rich source of information to evaluate various supervised machine learning algorithms. However, and as can be seen in Fig. 3, the dataset is hugely imbalanced. Some symbols, such as sensors, dominate the dataset, while others appear only once or are vastly underrepresented.

The imbalance between symbols is huge in some cases. For example symbols of type *sensor* appears 392 times in the dataset, while symbols such as *Barred Tee* and *Ultrasonic Flow Meter* appear only once. Similarly, *Reducer* appears in the dataset 285 times, while *Control Valve Angle Choke* only once.

Interestingly, eight types of symbols populate more than 64% of the dataset. These are: Sensor, Reducer, Arrowhead, Valve Ball, DB&BBV, Valve Check, Continuity Label and DB&BPV. At the same time, 18 symbols populate together less than 6% of the whole dataset. These are: Valve Slab Gate, Control Valve Globe, Flange + Triangle, Control, Exit to Atmosphere, Rupture Disc, ESDV Valve Slab Gate, Box, ESDV Valve Butterfly, Temporary Strainer, Control Valve, Valve Gate Through Conduit, Deluge, Vessel, Line Blindspacer, Control Valve Angle Choke, Barred Tee and Ultrasonic Flow Meter. In other words, the dataset is hugely imbalanced.

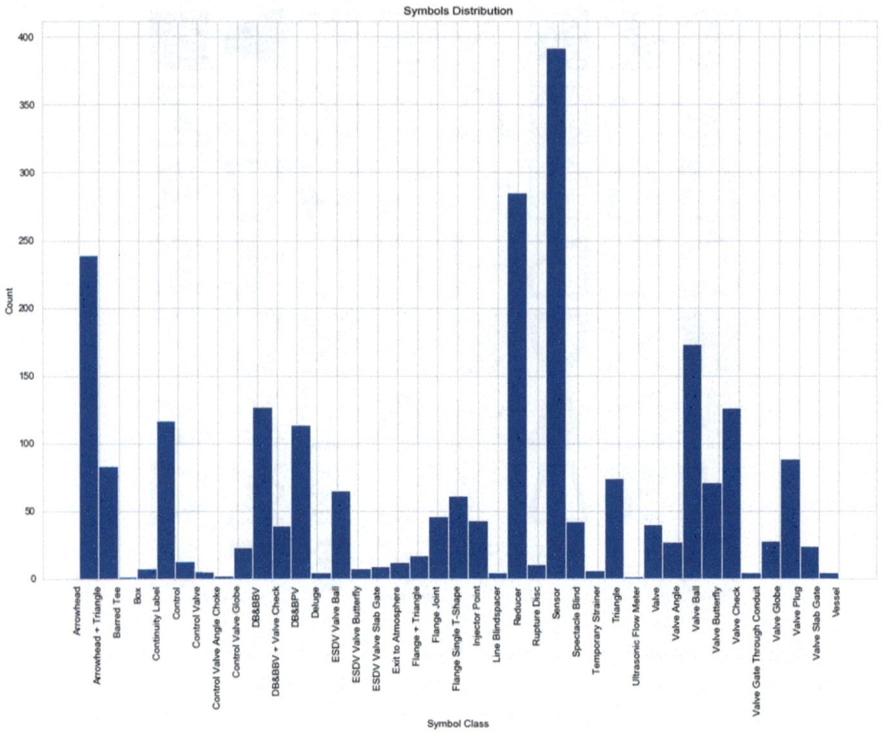

Fig. 3. Class distribution in the dataset

3.3 Classification Method

To provide base-line results on this imbalanced dataset of symbols, we use CNNs. CNNs [16] have made significant progress in recent years in many image-related tasks and in particular in image classification [20,30].

The network architecture used in this paper consists of an input layer of 100×100 of the raw pixel values of the symbol and 32 filters (3×3). Then a 2×2 max pooling layer. Then, two convolutional layers followed by a 2×2 max pooling layer. This structure is then repeated twice with two convolutional layers, with 64 filters of size (3×3) followed by a max pooling layer. Finally, a fully-connected layer composed of two hidden layers and an output layer of 39 (number of classes) units with softmax activation function. All convolutional layers in the network used *ReLU* activations. Dropout [29] was used in the in the fully connected layer with rates 0.1.

4 Experiments and Results

A series of experiments were carried out to establish the validity and stability of the proposed CNN architecture.

Table 1. Performance across different symbols in the dataset

Symbol	Precision	Recall	F1-score	Symbol	Precision	Recall	F1-score
Control Valve	0.00	0.00	0.00	Control	1.00	1.00	1.00
Flange + Triangle	0.00	0.00	0.00	DB& BBV	1.00	1.00	1.00
Line Blindspacer	0.00	0.00	0.00	DB& BBV + Valve Check	1.00	0.90	0.95
Valve Gate Through Conduit	0.00	0.00	0.00	DB& BPV	1.00	0.95	0.98
Rupture Disc	0.33	1.00	0.50	Deluge	1.00	1.00	1.00
Valve Angle	0.33	1.00	0.50	ESDV Valve Ball	1.00	0.92	0.96
Valve Slab Gate	0.50	1.00	0.67	ESDV Valve Slab Gate	1.00	0.50	0.67
Valve Globe	0.57	1.00	0.73	Exit to Atmosphere	1.00	1.00	1.00
ESDV Valve Butterfly	0.67	1.00	0.80	Flange Single T-Shape	1.00	0.93	0.96
Control Valve Globe	0.80	0.57	0.67	Injector Point	1.00	0.62	0.77
Valve	0.80	1.00	0.89	Reducer	1.00	1.00	1.00
Flange Joint	0.85	1.00	0.92	Sensor	1.00	0.98	0.99
Arrowhead + Triangle	0.90	1.00	0.95	Spectacle Blind	1.00	1.00	1.00
Triangle	0.94	0.84	0.89	Valve Ball	1.00	0.97	0.99
Arrowhead	1.00	0.96	0.98	Valve Butterfly	1.00	1.00	1.00
Box	1.00	1.00	1.00	Valve Check	1.00	0.93	0.96
Continuity Label	1.00	1.00	1.00	Valve Plug	1.00	0.89	0.94

4.1 Set up

The dataset was split into disjoint training, validation and testing sets. First, the dataset was split into training and testing sets where 80% of the data was used for training and the remaining 20% for testing. The training set was then split into training and validation sets with ratios of 90% and 10% of the remaining training set respectively. The CNN model was trained with a batch size of 64 for 25 epochs. These parameters were set empirically.

4.2 Results and Discussion

On the training set, an accuracy of 99.8%, with only 2 symbols incorrectly classified was recorded. On the test set, results were slightly lower, with accuracy of 95.3%. In other words 23 symbols were incorrectly identified. Table 1 provides more details about performance across the different symbols and using three different metrics: Precision, Recall, and F1-Score.

A closer look at the results, shows as expected that some of the minority class instances went completely undetected. For example, for the control valve symbols which has only five instances in the whole dataset, the corresponding F1-score is zero. Such score can also be seen in Table 1 for the symbols the *'Flange + Triangle'* (17 instances in the whole dataset), the *'Line Blindspacer'* (4 instances only), *'Valve Gate Through Conduit'* with only 4 instances in the whole dataset. Conversely, well represented symbols in the dataset were correctly classified with relatively high precision and recall. For example, the *'Reducer'* F1-score is 1. Notice that 285 instances of reducers are present in the dataset. A similar performance can be observed for other majority class instances such as *'Sensor'* (392 instances), *'Valve Ball'* (173 instances in the dataset), and others.

These results are consistent with the literature and showed clearly that the learning algorithm tend to be biased toward majority class-instances. Despite this, it can be said that CNN performed extremely well on the testing set with an overall accuracy reaching 95.3%, and an average precision, recall, and F1-score of 0.785, 0.822, and 0.784 respectively across all symbols in the dataset.

5 Conclusions

In this paper, we presented a new multiclass imbalanced dataset for the research community. The dataset represents a collection of symbols extracted from P&IDs. Despite the importance of processing and analysing engineering drawings, no such dataset exists in the public domain. We anticipate that donating this dataset to the research community will help researchers in the domain of machine learning and in particular imbalanced-class classification, and also research in the machine vision domain who are interested in processing and analysing engineering drawings. Future work will focus on handling this multi-class imbalanced problem, where advanced methods such as GANs and other data augmentation techniques might be utilised to improve the learning performance.

References

1. Ablameyko, S.V., Uchida, S.: Recognition of engineering drawing entities: review of approaches. Int. J. Image Graph. **07**(04), 709–733 (2007)
2. Ahmed, S., Liwicki, M., Weber, M., Dengel, A.: Automatic room detection and room labeling from architectural floor plans. In: 2012 10th IAPR International Workshop on Document Analysis Systems, pp. 339–343, March 2012

3. Ali-Gombe, A., Elyan, E., Jayne, C.: Multiple fake classes GAN for data augmentation in face image dataset. In: 2019 International Joint Conference on Neural Networks (IJCNN), pp. 1–8, July 2019
4. Ali-Gombe, A., Elyan, E.: Mfc-gan: class-imbalanced dataset classification using multiple fake class generative adversarial network. Neurocomputing **361**, 212–221 (2019)
5. Arroyo, E., Fay, A., Chioua, M., Hoernicke, M.: Integrating plant and process information as a basis for automated plant diagnosis tasks. In: Proceedings of the 2014 IEEE Emerging Technology and Factory Automation (ETFA), pp. 1–8, September 2014
6. Blostein, D.: General Diagram-Recognition Methodologies. In: Proceedings of the 1st International Conference on Graphics Recognition (GREC 1995), pp. 200–212 (1995)
7. Moreno-García, C.F., Elyan, E., Jayne, C.: New trends on digitisation of complex engineering drawings. Neural Computing and Applications, June 2018
8. Chhabra, A.K.: Graphics Recognition Algorithms and Systems. In: Proceedings of the 2nd International Conference on Graphics Recognition (GREC 1997), pp. 244–252 (1997)
9. Elyan, E., Moreno-Garcia, C.F., Jayne, C.: Symbols classification in engineering drawings. In: 2018 International Joint Conference on Neural Networks (IJCNN), pp. 1–8, July 2018
10. Eyad Elyan and Mohamed Medhat Gaber: A fine-grained random forests using class decomposition: an application to medical diagnosis. Neural Comput. Appl. **27**(8), 2279–2288 (2016)
11. Eyad Elyan and Mohamed Medhat Gaber: A genetic algorithm approach to optimising random forests applied to class engineered data. Inf. Sci. **384**, 220–234 (2017)
12. Esteva, A., Robicquet, A., Ramsundar, B., Kuleshov, V., DePristo, M., Chou, K., Cui, C., Corrado, G., Thrun, S., Dean, J.: A guide to deep learning in healthcare. Nat. Med. **25**(1), 24–29 (2019)
13. Goh, K.N., Mohd. Shukri, S.R., Manao, R.B.H.: Automatic assessment for engineering drawing. In: Zaman, H.B., Robinson, P., Olivier, P., Shih, T.K., Velastin, S. (eds.) Advances in Visual Informatics, pp. 497–507. Springer, Cham (2013)
14. Gonzalez, R.C., Woods, R.E.: Digital Image Processing. Prentice Hall, Upper Saddle River (2008)
15. Goodfellow, I., Bengio, Y., Courville, A.: Deep Learning. MIT Press, 2016. http://www.deeplearningbook.org
16. Jiuxiang, G., Wang, Z., Kuen, J., Ma, L., Shahroudy, A., Shuai, B., Liu, T., Wang, X., Wang, G., Cai, J., Chen, T.: Recent advances in convolutional neural networks. Pattern Recogn. **77**, 354–377 (2018)
17. Holcomb, S.D., Porter, W.K., Ault, S.V., Mao, G., Wang, J.: Overview on deepmind and its alphago zero AI. In: Proceedings of the 2018 International Conference on Big Data and Education, ICBDE 2018, pp. 67–71. ACM, New York (2018)
18. Howie, C., Kunz, J., Binford, T., Chen, T., Law, K.H.: Computer interpretation of process and instrumentation drawings. Adv. Eng. Softw. **29**(7), 563–570 (1998)
19. Kanungo, T., Haralick, R.M., Dori, D.: Understanding engineering drawings: a survey. In: Proceedings of the 1st International Conference on Graphics Recognition (GREC 1995), pp. 119–130 (1995)
20. Krizhevsky, A., Sutskever, I., Hinton, G.E.: Imagenet classification with deep convolutional neural networks. Commun. ACM **60**(6), 84–90 (2017)

21. Kulkarni, C.R., Barbadekar, A.B.: Text detection and recognition: a review. Int. Res. J. Eng. Technol. (IRJET) **4**(6), 179–185 (2017)
22. Lecun, Y., Bottou, L., Bengio, Y., Haffner, P.: Gradient-based learning applied to document recognition. Proc. IEEE **86**(11), 2278–2324 (1998)
23. Lu, Y.: Machine printed character segmentation - an overview. Pattern Recogn. **28**(1), 67–80 (1995)
24. Moreno-Garcia, C.F., Elyan, E.: Digitisation of assets from the oil gas industry: challenges and opportunities. In: 2019 International Conference on Document Analysis and Recognition Workshops (ICDARW), vol. 7, pp. 2–5, September 2019
25. Moreno-García, C.F., Elyan, E., Jayne, C.: Heuristics-based detection to improve text / graphics segmentation in complex engineering drawings. Eng. Appl. Neural Netw., volume CCIS **744**, 87–98 (2017)
26. Mori, S., Suen, C.Y., Yamamoto, K.: Historical review of ocr research and development. Proc. IEEE **80**(7), 1029–1058 (1992)
27. Park, U., Jain, A.K.: Face matching and retrieval using soft biometrics. IEEE Trans. Inf. Forens. Secur. **5**(3), 406–415 (2010)
28. Shone, N., Ngoc, T.N., Phai, V.D., Shi, Q.: A deep learning approach to network intrusion detection. IEEE Trans. Emerg. Topics Comput. Intell. **2**(1), 41–50 (2018)
29. Srivastava, N., Hinton, G., Krizhevsky, A., Sutskever, I., Salakhutdinov, R.: Dropout: a simple way to prevent neural networks from overfitting. J. Mach. Learn. Res. **15**, 1929–1958 (2014)
30. Szegedy, C., Liu, W., Jia, Y., Sermanet, P., Reed, S., Anguelov, D., Erhan, D., Vanhoucke, V., Rabinovich, A.: Going deeper with convolutions. In: 2015 IEEE Conference on Computer Vision and Pattern Recognition (CVPR), pp. 1–9, June 2015
31. Taigman, Y., Yang, M., Ranzato, M., Wolf, L.: Deepface: closing the gap to human-level performance in face verification. In: 2014 IEEE Conference on Computer Vision and Pattern Recognition, pp. 1701–1708, June 2014
32. Tombre, K., Tabbone, S., Lamiroy, B., Dosch, P.: Text/Graphics separation revisited. Document Anal. Syst. **2423**, 200–211 (2002)
33. Vaxiviere, P., Tombre, K.: Celesstin: CAD conversion of mechanical drawings. Computer **25**(7), 46–54 (1992)
34. Vuttipittayamongkol, P., Elyan, E.: Neighbourhood-based undersampling approach for handling imbalanced and overlapped data. Inf. Sci. **509**, 47–70 (2020)
35. Vuttipittayamongkol, P., Elyan, E., Petrovski, A., Jayne, C.: Overlap-based undersampling for improving imbalanced data classification. In: Yin, H., Camacho, D., Novais, P., Tallon-Ballesteros, A. (eds.) Intelligent Data Engineering and Automated Learning, pp. 689–697. Springer, Cham (2018)
36. Yang, Z., Yang, D., Dyer, C., He, X., Smola, A., Hovy, E.: Hierarchical attention networks for document classification. In: Proceedings of the 2016 Conference of the North American Chapter of the Association for Computational Linguistics: Human Language Technologies, pp. 1480–1489. Association for Computational Linguistics, San Diego, June 2016
37. Zhang, D., Lu, G.: Review of shape representation and description techniques. Pattern Recogn. **37**(1), 1–19 (2004)

Deep Learning/Image Processing-Classification

A Novel Spatial-Spectral Framework for the Classification of Hyperspectral Satellite Imagery

Shriya T. P. Gupta(✉) and Sanjay K. Sahay

Department of Computer Science and Information Systems, BITS Pilani Goa Campus, Goa, India
shriyatp99@gmail.com, ssahay@goa.bits-pilani.ac.in

Abstract. Hyperspectral satellite imagery is now widely being used for accurate disaster prediction and terrain feature classification. However, in such classification tasks, most of the present approaches use only the spectral information contained in the images. Therefore, in this paper, we present a novel framework that takes into account both the spectral and spatial information contained in the data for land cover classification. For this purpose, we use the Gaussian Maximum Likelihood (GML) and Convolutional Neural Network (CNN) methods for the pixel-wise spectral classification and then, using segmentation maps generated by the Watershed algorithm, we incorporate the spatial contextual information into our model with a modified majority vote technique. The experimental analyses on two benchmark datasets demonstrate that our proposed methodology performs better than the earlier approaches by achieving an accuracy of 99.52% and 98.31% on the Pavia University and the Indian Pines datasets respectively. Additionally, our GML based approach, a non-deep learning algorithm, shows comparable performance to the state-of-the-art deep learning techniques, which indicates the importance of the proposed approach for performing a computationally efficient classification of hyperspectral imagery.

Keywords: Neural networks · Hyperspectral imaging · Machine learning · Land cover classification · Spatial segmentation

1 Introduction

Hyperspectral satellite imaging collects high resolution images within contiguous spectral bands across a wide range of the electromagnetic spectrum. Its primary aim is to obtain the spectrum of each pixel in the image of a scene, with the goal of identifying materials or discovering objects. In general, hyperspectral satellite images are captured through an imaging spectrometer in narrow bands of 10–20 nm with up to thousands of bands. On the contrary, multispectral images have 3–10 bands and are captured using a remote sensing radiometer. Such remotely

L. Iliadis et al. (Eds.): EANN 2020, INNS 2, pp. 227–239, 2020.
https://doi.org/10.1007/978-3-030-48791-1_17

sensed satellite images, either air-borne or space-borne, cover large areas of the earth's surface with rich spectral information and hence can be used for the robust classification of land cover with a good accuracy.

Recently, machine learning and deep learning techniques have shown promising results for various classification problems in the fields of natural language processing, computer vision, speech recognition, etc. [1]. Thus, we investigate both, GML, a machine learning technique as well as CNN, a popular deep learning approach. In conventional pixel-wise classification techniques, the algorithms independently process each and every pixel without using the neighboring spatial information. However, to minimize the uncertainty in the data, one can exploit the spatially adjacent pixels, which have more or less similar spectral features. Therefore, in this paper, we develop a novel spatial-spectral algorithm for the robust classification of land cover. Experimental results show that our model is suitable for the classification of images with large spatial structures especially when the spectral responses of different classes are dissimilar. Hence, our proposed approach works well for the task of hyperspectral image classification and it can also be adapted to other domains that are similar to terrain feature classification.

The rest of this paper is organized as follows: Sect. 2 covers the related work and in Sect. 3, we give a brief outline of the classification and segmentation methods. Section 4 describes the datasets used and the detail of our approach is given in Sect. 5. In Sect. 6, we discuss our experimental results and finally, Sect. 7 contains the conclusion and future directions.

2 Related Work

Spectral imaging techniques are now widely being used for solving land cover classification problems. In this context, Ahmad et al. [2] have shown that if there exists a distinct separation between the classes in the decision space, as seen in the case of land cover classification tasks, the use of a GML classifier provides a good accuracy. Further, Ablin et al. [3] reported that classifying an unknown pixel can be done efficiently by the maximum likelihood classifier, as it quantitatively evaluates both the variance and co-variance of the spectral response pattern for each class.

In 2018, Khan et al. [4] discussed in detail the recent research in classification techniques used for hyperspectral satellite imagery. In their paper, they state that most of the current research efforts and studies follow the standard pattern recognition paradigm, which is based on the construction of complex handcrafted features. In contrast to the approaches discussed by Khan et al. [4], LeCun et al. [5] proposed the deep learning based classification methods which use hierarchically constructed high-level features in an automated way. In the context of deep learning based satellite image classification, Makantasis et al. [6] used a combination of CNN for feature extraction along with a multi layer perceptron for classification and achieved an accuracy of up to 98.88% on the Indian Pines dataset. Similarly, Audebert et al. [7] used 3D CNNs for the classification of Indian Pines and Pavia University datasets, and obtained accuracies of 96.87% and 96.71% respectively. An alternate approach of using Recurrent Neural Networks (RNN) was proposed by Ma et al. [8]. Their RNN based model achieved an accuracy of 96.20% on the Pavia University dataset which indicates the superiority of CNNs over RNNs for image classification tasks.

Later, many authors combined the aforementioned pixel-wise classification algorithms with different segmentation approaches to enhance the efficiency of the spectral classification. For instance, Tarabalka et al. [9] studied the use of Watershed segmentation methodologies for spatial-spectral classification of hyperspectral images. They also described the various plausible approaches to combine it with a pixel-wise classifier, viz. they used a SVM classifier with Watershed segmentation and reported an accuracy of 90.64% on the Indian Pines image and 95.21% on the University of Pavia dataset. Furthermore, some authors have explored the use of Markov Random Fields (MRF) to incorporate the spatial information contained in the data. For example, Qing et al. [10] used an MRF-based loopy belief propagation technique and obtained an accuracy of 98.5% on the Indian Pines dataset.

Hence, we consider these approaches as the baselines for our work and in our proposed model, we further improve the classification accuracy as well as the computational efficiency using both, GML, a machine learning technique as well as CNN, a deep learning approach for pixel wise classification. To the best of our knowledge, land cover classification has rarely been done by using the watershed segmentation algorithm with the above-mentioned spectral classifiers.

3 Preliminaries

In this section, we briefly explain the GML and CNN models used for the pixel-wise classification as well as the Watershed algorithm used to generate the segmentation maps.

3.1 Gaussian Maximum Likelihood

The Gaussian Maximum Likelihood classifier is a supervised classification method derived from the Naive-Bayes theorem. It classifies each unidentified pixel θ by using the probability density functions to compute the likelihood of a given pixel belonging to a particular category C. The GML algorithm evaluates the probability values for each class as follows:

$$P(C|\theta) = P(C)\frac{P(\theta|C)}{P(\theta)} \tag{1}$$

Here, the pixel is assigned to the most likely class based on the highest probability value or it is labelled as 'unknown' if the probability values are below an analytically defined threshold. As the GML is a pixel by pixel classification method, it does not take into account the contextual information about neighboring classes while labeling a pixel. Also, it is assumed that the distribution of the cloud of points forming a particular class is Gaussian. Here, the mean vector and the co-variance matrix can be used to entirely describe the distribution of the response pattern for each category.

3.2 Convolutional Neural Network

A Convolutional Neural Network is comparatively more accurate than a traditional machine learning algorithm mainly because a CNN learns the filters automatically while the features of a traditional algorithm are hand-engineered. Here, we briefly describe the working of a CNN with hyperspectral image data as the input and the detailed description of its usage in our model is presented in Sect. 5. Since a hyperspectral image is composed of L spectral layers, the input image can be represented as X = $[x_1, x_2, ..., x_L]$ where x_i is a matrix of pixels corresponding to the layer i. The first convolutional layer consists of n_1 filters of kernel size $f_1 \times f_1$ and it is employed to extract the features of the input image as follows:

$$F_1(X) = \theta_1(u_1) \tag{2}$$

where θ_1 denotes the activation function of the entire layer. Here $u_1 = \sum_{l=1}^{L} x_l * w_l + b_1$, where w_l represents the weights of the filter acting on the input hyperspectral data, $*$ represents the convolution operation, and b_1 is an n_1-dimensional vector which represents the bias of the entire layer. Also, each element of this vector is associated with every filter and the output is composed of n_1 feature maps corresponding to the n_1 filters.

3.3 Watershed Transformation

The Watershed transformation is a powerful mathematical technique for geomorphological image segmentation. It considers a 2D one-band image as a topographic structure wherein the value of a pixel stands for its elevation. In order to associate each basin with a minima, the Watershed lines divide the entire image into catchment basins. This segmentation method requires the user to define seeds, which are pixels belonging unambiguously to a region. The Watershed transformation is usually applied to the gradient function of the image. The gradient defines the transitions between regions, so that it has high values on the borders between objects and minima in the homogeneous regions. If the crest lines in the gradient image correspond to the edges of image objects, then the Watershed transformation successfully partitions the entire image into meaningful regions. Hence, it is very well suited for hyperspectral satellite image segmentation where the main aim is to segment the imagery into distinct geographical regions.

4 Datasets and Pre-processing

In this section we describe the two publicly available benchmark datasets (Indian Pines [11] and Pavia University [12]) and the preprocessing that has been used for our experimental analysis.

4.1 Indian Pines

The Indian Pines dataset consists of 145×145 pixels and 224 spectral reflectance bands and was gathered by the 220-band Airborne Visible / Infrared Imaging Spectrometer (AVIRIS) sensor over the Indian Pines test site in North-western Indiana. The ground truth corresponding to this dataset is designated into sixteen classes which is not entirely mutually exclusive and consists of two-thirds agriculture and one-third forest or other natural perennial vegetation. Along with this, there are two dual lane highways, a rail line, low density housing, and some smaller roads.

4.2 Pavia University

The Pavia University dataset was acquired by the 103-band Reflective Optics System Imaging Spectrometer (ROSIS) sensor during a flight campaign over Pavia, northern Italy with dimensions of 610×610 pixels and 103 spectral bands. However, some of the samples contain no information. Hence, they are discarded in our experimental analysis and are depicted using broad black strips. The geometric resolution of this image is 1.3 m and the corresponding ground truth differentiates among all the nine classes.

4.3 Pre-processing

For the empirical analysis, the preprocessing steps of the Indian Pines and the Pavia dataset are same for both the approaches (GML and CNN). First, we over sample the weak classes in order to make the hyperspectral images more balanced. The pixel values are then standardized by subtracting the mean and scaling them to unit variance. Next, we apply Principal Component Analysis (PCA) to the input data in order to transform the original high-dimensional data into a low-dimensional space by extracting the key features and then padding it with zeros. Then, we save the preprocessed data for the experimental analysis.

5 Methodology

This section describes our approach in detail which includes the pixel-wise classification techniques, the segmentation method, and the modified majority vote algorithm.

5.1 Spatial-Spectral Classifier

An overall architecture of the CNN used in our work is shown in Fig. 1. It comprises of two 2D convolutional layers with the first layer having C_1 filters of size $f_1 = 3$, second layer having $C_2 = 3 \times C_1$ filters of size $f_2 = 3$, and followed by a flatten layer. Here, the parameter C_1 corresponds to the number of principle components that preserve at least 99.9% of the initial information

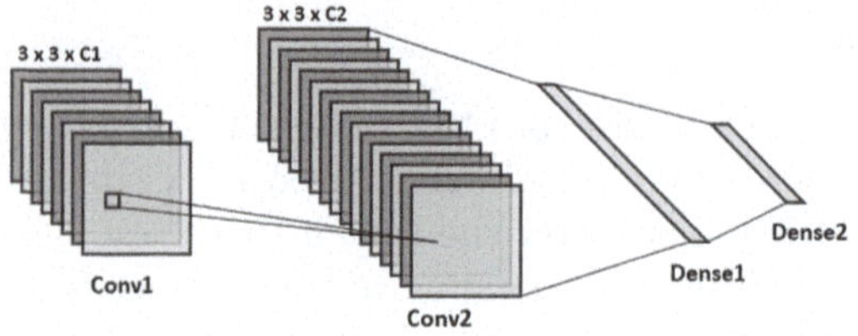

Fig. 1. An overall architecture of the CNN

contained in the original datasets after applying PCA. The size of the filter is determined empirically which dictates the number of neighbors of each pixel that has been taken into consideration during the classification. The convolution layer is composed of a set of separate filters and each filter is independently convolved with the image to obtain the corresponding feature maps as described in Sect. 3.2. In contrast to the conventional CNNs, we do not use a max pooling layer after the convolution layer, since there is no need to account for the translation and scale invariance. Next, we use two regular densely connected neural network layers in our model. The first dense layer has 120 units with a dropout of 0.5 and the second layer is the last layer of the network. It has as many units as the number of classes and in this layer, we use a softmax algorithm to produce the final outputs.

The second pixel-wise classification scheme that we used is the GML algorithm as outlined in Sect. 3.1, and in our analysis, the GML classification technique differs significantly from the CNN method. The GML algorithm performs the classification in a pixel by pixel fashion which preserves their individual values. On the contrary, the convolution operation in the CNN technique averages out individual values using adjacent pixels that lie within the dimensions of an applied filter.

(a) (b) (c)

Fig. 2. (a) Overlaps (b) Distances and the (c) Separated objects for Indian Pines data

Next, we generate a segmentation map of the image using the Watershed algorithm as detailed in Sect. 3.3. In our model, local maxima of the distance map to the background are used as seeds. These maxima are chosen as markers in order to segment the entire image into regions and the flooding of catchment basins from such markers separates the areas along a Watershed line. The segmentation maps obtained using the Watershed algorithm are shown in Fig. 2

(a) (b) (c)

Fig. 3. (a) Overlaps (b) Distances and the (c) Separated objects for the Pavia dataset

and Fig. 3 for the Indian Pines and the Pavia University datasets respectively. For images where the pixels are not uniformly distributed across the classes, the Watershed algorithm typically produces over segmented maps, and so in our case, the image is over segmented. However, the problem is alleviated when we combine the segmentation map with the pixel-wise classification results.

Algorithm 1: Our majority vote approach.

```
uni_labels = unique values (labels in segmentation map)
final_map = 0
for i in uni_labels do
    arr ← []
    height ← height of segmentation map
    width ← width of segmentation map
    for j = 0 to j = height do
        for k = 0 to k = width do
            find all pixels in the segmentation map having label i
            append their pixel-wise classification labels to arr
        end for
    end for
    max_freq_label ← most frequent label in arr
    for j = 0 to j = height do
        for k = 0 to k = width do
            find all pixels in the segmentation map having label i
            assign max_freq_label as the label for these pixels in the final_map
        end for
    end for
end for
return final_map
```

Finally, we combined the outputs of the pixel-wise classification algorithms with the segmentation maps using a modified majority vote technique (Algorithm 1), wherein for each region of the segmentation map, all the pixels are assigned to the most frequent class. However, in our proposed approach, the majority vote is performed with an adaptive neighborhood instead of a fixed neighborhood and for every pixel, the region it belongs to is defined by the segmentation map. Then, we use this region as its neighborhood for the vote on the spectral classification.

6 Experimental Results

First, we test our proposed models, GML with Watershed (GML-W) and CNN with Watershed (CNN-W), on the Indian Pines and the Pavia University datasets. Then, we compare the performance of our hybrid models with the traditional GML and CNN algorithms on the same datasets. For this purpose, we split the datasets in the ratio of 3:1 for the training and testing data respectively.

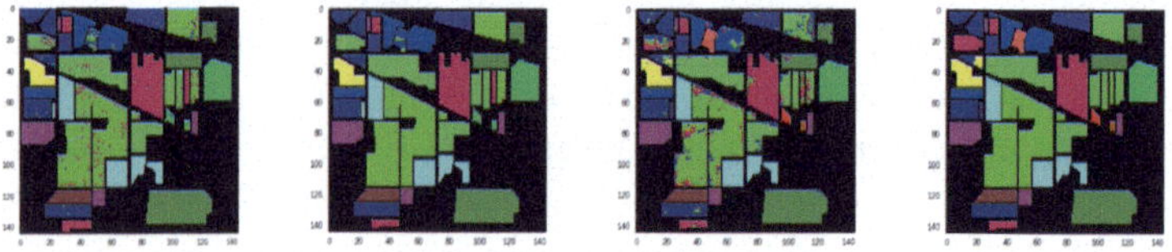

(a) (b) (c) (d)

Fig. 4. Results of (a) GML (b) GML-W (c) CNN and (d) CNN-W on Indian Pines data

The results obtained by the traditional GML and the proposed GML-W algorithms are shown in Fig. 4(a) and Fig. 4(b) respectively. For the Indian Pines dataset, the GML gives an accuracy of 97.46% and the GML-W provides an accuracy of 98.31%. Next, we experimented with the CNN classifier and the obtained results are shown in Fig. 4(c) and Fig. 4(d). In terms of accuracies, the CNN and CNN-W models give results of 87.08% and 97.7% respectively. As is evident from the results, the use of the spatial-spectral classifier led to a significant improvement with an increase of 10.6% in the overall accuracy. Additionally, from a visual observation, the classification maps obtained by the spatial-spectral classification are seen to be much less noisy than the ones obtained by the pixel-wise classification.

The detailed results obtained for each category, viz. GML, CNN, GML-W, and CNN-W on the Indian Pines dataset is shown in Table 1. From the results, it is evident that incorporating the spatial information with the traditional pixel-wise classification algorithm improves the accuracies considerably. This is due to the fact that most of the classes in the image represent large crop fields, and the segmentation step makes these regions of fields homogeneous, thereby improving the classification results. The accuracies of almost all classes are significantly improved, except for some small classes like Oats and Stone-Steel Towers which are incorrectly assimilated into neighboring regions. However, the GML algorithm fails to correctly identify the regions of Corn-notill, Hay-windrowed, and Soybean-notill as the number of pixels in the training set is almost a hundred

Table 1. Accuracies (%) for Indian Pines dataset

Category	GML	GML-W	CNN	CNN-W
Alfalfa	100.0	100.0	100.0	100.0
Corn-notill	0.00	100.0	80.11	0.00
Corn-mintill	94.74	82.35	89.90	100.0
Corn	97.83	88.19	96.61	93.37
Grass-pasture	100	100.0	95.04	100.0
Grass-trees	99.79	96.89	98.90	96.89
Grass-pasture-mowed	99.72	100.0	100.0	100.0
Hay-windrowed	0.00	100.0	100.0	0.00
Oats	100.0	100.0	100.0	100.0
Soybean-notill	0.00	100.0	88.06	0.00
Soybean-mintill	99.48	99.48	72.14	99.48
Soybean-clean	90.59	98.20	87.83	98.28
Wheat	99.32	100.0	100.0	100.0
Woods	100.0	100.0	98.41	100.0
Buildings-Grass-Trees	99.60	99.20	93.81	99.84
Stone-Steel-Towers	98.96	87.56	100.0	87.04
Average accuracy	93.80	96.99	80.10	91.76
Overall accuracy	97.46	98.31	87.08	97.7

times lesser than other regions, which leads to the misclassification of the pixels into neighboring categories.

A similar analysis of the Pavia University dataset has been done by splitting the data in the ratio of 3:1 for training and testing. First, using the GML classifier, we were able to obtain an accuracy of 99.03% which was later on improved to 99.52% using our proposed hybrid classifier and the results are shown in Fig. 5(a) and Fig. 5(b), respectively. Next, we carried out the pixel-wise classification using a deep learning based CNN model and obtained an accuracy of 97.39%. We further improved the performance by $\sim 2\%$ using our proposed approach which led to an overall accuracy of 99.44%. Figure 5(c) and Fig. 5(d)

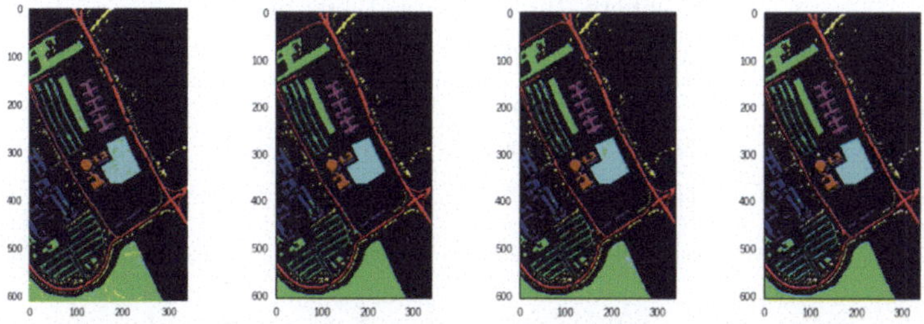

(a) (b) (c) (d)

Fig. 5. Results of (a) GML (b) GML-W (c) CNN and (d) CNN-W on the Pavia dataset

represent the results obtained before and after combining with the Watershed transformation respectively.

Table 2. Accuracies (%) for the Pavia university dataset

Category	GML	GML-W	CNN	CNN-W
Asphalt	100.0	100.0	98.13	100.0
Meadows	95.02	98.02	98.62	97.49
Gravel	94.98	96.02	89.33	96.02
Trees	92.42	96.56	99.73	91.47
Painted metal sheets	99.18	99.18	100.0	99.18
Bare soil	100.0	100.0	98.96	100.0
Bitumen	94.96	100.0	99.39	100.0
Self-blocking bricks	96.76	100.0	93.81	100.0
Shadows	92.85	99.10	100.0	98.66
Average accuracy	96.24	98.76	97.55	98.09
Overall accuracy	99.03	99.52	97.39	99.44

Furthermore, we did a detailed analysis of our models for the Pavia University dataset and the category wise results for the nine classes are summarized in Table 2. From the analysis, we observed that the spatial-spectral algorithm using GML gives the best overall accuracy (99.52%). The variations in the accuracies for different regions depends largely on the area of that particular region. For instance, a comparatively bigger structure belonging to the painted metal sheets class in the center of the image is mostly represented by one region, which leads to a significant improvement on combining it with the segmentation map. On the contrary, regions like the asphalt and bitumen are spread across a large number of regions.

Table 3. Comparison of the overall accuracies of our methods

Classifiers	Indian Pines	Pavia Scene
GML	97.46%	99.03%
GML-W	98.31%	99.52%
CNN	87.08%	97.39%
CNN-W	97.7%	99.44%

A summary of the overall results obtained on the two datasets are given in Table 3. Our experimental results show that the GML based approach outperforms the CNN based approach for both the datasets. This is because the

GML performs the classification on a pixel by pixel basis and hence it precisely assigns most of the pixels to their correct classes. However, the CNN technique averages out individual pixel values during the convolution step and so it classifies many of the pixels into neighboring regions which leads to lower accuracies. Our technique also proved to be better than the traditional classifiers of GML and CNN, which gave accuracies of 99.03% and 97.39% respectively. As for the Indian Pines dataset, our proposed approach led to a significant improvement of 10.6% over the traditional CNN based classification approach. In addition to this, our method performed considerably better than the conventional GML classifier with an overall accuracy of 98.31% on the Indian Pines dataset.

Table 4. Comparison with existing deep learning based methods

Classifiers	Indian Pines	Pavia Scene
3D CNN [13]	99.07%	99.39%
CNN-MRF [14]	99.27%	99.55%
Ours (GML-W)	98.31%	99.52%

In order to have a more detailed analysis, we compare our approach to the existing deep learning based methods in Table 4. As seen from the empirical results on the Pavia university scene, our GML based spatial-spectral methodology, without any kind of deep learning aspects has an accuracy of 99.52%, which is better than the performance of 99.39% achieved by the 3D CNN based spectral classification technique proposed by Li et al. [13]. Our method's performance is also comparable to the state-of-the-art deep learning based technique of CNN-MRF given by Cao et al. [14] that has an accuracy of 99.55%, even though our approach does not require any sort of expensive training or learning procedures. However, our method achieves an accuracy of 98.31% on the Indian Pines dataset which is lesser than the accuracy of 99.27% given by the existing deep learning method because our approach is more suitable for images where the distribution of pixels amongst the different classes is comparatively uniform.

7 Conclusion

In this paper, we present a novel spatial-spectral methodology for the classification of land cover using hyperspectral satellite image data. The proposed approach combines the results of a pixel-wise spectral classification and segmentation maps of the Watershed algorithm, by performing a majority vote on the initial classification output using adaptive neighborhoods defined by the segmentation map. We investigated GML, a machine learning technique as well as CNN, a popular deep learning approach for the pixel-wise image classification, and found that by incorporating the spatial information with the spectral data, the overall classification map contains more homogeneous regions, as compared to only pixel-wise classification of the hyperspectral images. The empirical analyses indicate that our approach performs better than the results discussed in Sect. 2 for the spatial-spectral classification of hyperspectral images, with an overall accuracy of 99.52% on the Pavia University dataset and up to 98.31% on the Indian Pines dataset. Experimental results also demonstrate that our proposed GML based framework - without any kind of expensive training or learning procedures, achieves comparable performance to the state-of-the-art deep learning based methods and is hence a computationally efficient alternative for the classification of hyperspectral image data.

In order to further improve the overall classification, different feature extraction methods need to be investigated so as to find the most effective features for segmentation. Also, our proposed approaches should be verified on multispectral satellite image data to analyze their robustness and in this direction, work is in progress.

References

1. Shrestha, A., Mahmood, A.: Review of deep learning algorithms and architectures. IEEE Access **7**, 53040–53065 (2019)
2. Ahmad, A., Quegan, S.: Analysis of maximum likelihood classification on multispectral data. Appl. Math. Sci. **6**(129), 6425–6436 (2012)
3. Ablin, R., Sulochana, C.H.: A survey of hyperspectral image classification in remote sensing. Int. J. Adv. Res. Comput. Commun. Eng. **2**(8), 2986–3000 (2013)
4. Khan, M.J., Khan, H.S., Yousaf, A., Khurshid, K., Abbas, A.: Modern trends in hyperspectral image analysis: a review. IEEE Access **6**, 14118–14129 (2018)
5. LeCun, Y., Bengio, Y., Hinton, G.: Deep learning. Nature **521**(7553), 436 (2015)
6. Makantasis, K., Karantzalos, K., Doulamis, A., Doulamis, N.: Deep supervised learning for hyperspectral data classification through convolutional neural networks. In: 2015 IEEE International Geoscience and Remote Sensing Symposium (IGARSS), pp. 4959–4962. IEEE (2015)
7. Audebert, N., Le Saux, B., Lefèvre, S.: Deep learning for classification of hyperspectral data: a comparative review. IEEE Geosci. Remote Sens. Mag. **7**(2), 159–173 (2019)
8. Ma, A., Filippi, A.M., Wang, Z., Yin, Z.: Hyperspectral image classification using similarity measurements-based deep recurrent neural networks. Remote Sens. **11**(2), 194 (2019)
9. Tarabalka, Y., Benediktsson, J.A., Chanussot, J.: Spectral-spatial classification of hyperspectral imagery based on partitional clustering techniques. IEEE Trans. Geosci. Remote Sens. **47**(8), 2973–2987 (2009)
10. Qing, C., Ruan, J., Xu, X., Ren, J., Zabalza, J.: Spatial-spectral classification of hyperspectral images: a deep learning framework with markov random fields based modelling. IET Image Process. **13**(2), 235–245 (2018)
11. Landgrebe, D., Biehl, K.: Aviris nw indiana's indian pines data set (1992). https://engineering.purdue.edu/~biehl/MultiSpec/hyperspectral.html
12. Gamba, P.: Pavia university scene (2001). http://www.ehu.eus/ccwintco/index.php/

13. Li, Y., Zhang, H., Shen, Q.: Spectral-spatial classification of hyperspectral imagery with 3D convolutional neural network. Remote Sens. **9**(1), 67 (2017)
14. Cao, X., Zhou, F., Xu, L., Meng, D., Xu, Z., Paisley, J.: Hyperspectral image classification with markov random fields and a convolutional neural network. IEEE Trans. Image Process. **27**(5), 2354–2367 (2018)

Detection of Shocking Images as One-Class Classification Using Convolutional and Siamese Neural Networks

Pavel Gulyaev(✉) and Andrey Filchenkov

ITMO University, Kronverkskiy Pr. 49, 197101 St. Petersburg, Russia
paw.gulyaev@yandex.ru, afilchenkov@corp.ifmo.ru

Abstract. Not safe for work content automatic detection is a serious challenge for social media due to overwhelming growth of uploaded images, gifs and videos. This paper focuses on shocking images automatic detection by convolutional neural networks. It was considered that the correct recognition of the shocking class is more important than the non-shocking one. Binary classification by a convolutional network that training during operation has been used as a baseline solution. However, this solution has two drawbacks: the network highlights incorrect features of non-shocking images (infinite class) and tends to forget rare subclasses of shocking images, which is unacceptable. To eliminate the first drawback, we approach this problem as a one-class classification with having in mind that a "non-shocking" image can be defined only via contradiction with a shocking one. This method is based on using sparse autoencoders build on top of a pretrained convolutional neural network and is not trained during operation. To eliminate the second drawback, we memorized vectors of images that were incorrectly classified during operation. A trained siamese network during the prediction is used to search for similar images in the database. In the case of an incorrect prediction by the combined model, vectors of images are added to the database and the siamese network is trained on them. This method allows you to minimize the number of errors in rare subclasses identified only during the operation phase of the model.

Keywords: Image recognition · One-class classification · Siamese network

1 Introduction

The amount of information uploaded by users to social media instantly grows, and this information flow becomes more and more difficult to control in terms of preventing uploading of socially unacceptable content, which may be not safe for work (NSFW) or even not safe for life (NSFL).

NSFW content contains nudity, intense sexuality, profanity, violence/gore or other disturbing subject matter, which usually are seen inappropriate if accesses in a public or formal environment including a workplace or school.

L. Iliadis et al. (Eds.): EANN 2020, INNS 2, pp. 240–250, 2020.
https://doi.org/10.1007/978-3-030-48791-1_18

Not safe for life content is a subclass of NSFW-content refers to subject matter that might not be in the interest of a person to view regardless of location and potential coviewers for being horrifying, disgusting, offensive, or even mentally disturbing to the viewer.

Many works are devoted to detecting possible negative effect of NSFW content present and availability for a wide audience [1, 3, 4, 9].

Existing works on the shock image detection, which will be discussed in detail in Sect. 3, has two main drawbacks. The first problem encountered by the developers of the shock image recognition system is the lack of a specific definition of shock-content. To overcome this drawback, we decided to narrow the concept of shock content to images of real cruelty over people, blood, mutilations, etc.

The second problem is related to solving shocking content detection as a binary classification task. These days, social networks and search engines prefer to block shock-content on user complaints and train a binary classification model using these complaints, which is later used for blocking similar images. This approach has the following weaknesses:

A model needs many diverse non-shocking content and a large number of complaints to learn, requiring thus a large number of users getting acquainted with shocking materials before reporting.

A model shows unpredictable behavior for objects that are different from those in the training sample. It can support its decision based on features of non-shocking content, which is incorrect, because 1) the number of classes of non-shocking images is infinite, and 2) the presence of features of a non-shocking image should not reduce the significance of the features of the shocking image (for example, the presence of a nice cat in an image should not prevent the system from detecting a severely torn mouse in the same photo).

The network quickly forgets or does not learn at all rare subclasses of shocking images, such as, for instance, brain worms.

To overcome these limitations, we will reduce the problem to the one-class classification task. A one-class classification, unlike a binary one, occurs in the conditions of impossibility to collect a sufficiently large number of objects of one of the classes, or the impossibility of unambiguous representation of one of the classes [6].

In this task, shocking images are contrasted with all other existing images, because it is impossible to correctly define the class of "non-shocking images".

This helps to eliminate the listed weakness of binary classification:

1. There is no need for many non-shocking images.
2. A model learns only features of shocking content. If an image is dissimilar to any of the shocking images in the training sample, it is classified as non-shocking.
3. The amount of data for training is smaller, therefore the relative number of representatives of rare subclasses is larger, hence the model is easier to learn from them.

When developing a one-class classifier of shock images, we took into account the heterogeneity and a large number of subclasses of this class of images.

The rest of the paper has the following structure. In Sect. 2, we review and discuss related papers. We present the methods and technique we use in Sect. 3. Empirical study of their performance is presented in Sect. 4 and discussed in Sect. 5. Section 6 concludes.

2 Related Work

In one of the first papers on the recognition of cruelty in images [13], the images used as training data were collected by sending relevant queries to Google. Despite the good results presented in the article (90.1 $\pm$ 1.5% accuracy), such inaccurate data collecting led to the results presented in Fig. 1. In addition, the approach used by the authors (bag of words using various selected features) did not consider the relationship of different parts of an image, which is critically important in cruelty recognition.

Fig. 1. Images classified by the system [13] as cruel.

In another paper [8], the authors recognized images from horror movies using the concept of image context, which was an important innovation. However, the context and the "awfulness"‘ of an image were determined solely using color features, which was inefficient for recognizing shock images.

Finally, in the work using pretrained convolutional networks [14], the problem of accounting for the interaction of different image segments was solved, but it had drawbacks: the use of binary classification and careless (semi-automatic) data collection. Binary classification leads to the uncertainty of the network, as already discussed in the introduction.

3 Learning Methods

3.1 One-Class Classification

Convolutional Autoencoders. Autoencoders perform a data-specific lossy coding learned automatically from training data [2]. One-class classification is performed by a convolutional autoencoder (CAE) learned using images of a given class (shock-content), which would receive a smaller error for recovering images of this class in comparison with error of restoring any other random images submitted to the input. Setting the boundary of the recovery error will result into a classifier, which will detect shocking image in case of a smaller recovery error and a non-shocking image otherwise.

Ordinary and Sparse Autoencoders. We trained both types of autoencoders [2, 10] to encode the values of the last layer of a pretrained convolutional neural network (CNN). In this case, the last layer was trained from scratch and was added on top of the layers of pretrained networks. First, we used an idea similar to the one from the CAE approach: the recovery error for the learning class is significantly less than the recovery error for the remaining values.

However, using only recovery error is just a single feature, so we decided to add values of autoencoder internal representation vector as new features, increasing thus their number from 1 to 2001.

One-class support vector machine (OCSVM). OCSVM is another approach we can use on top of a CNN. We use a one-class support vector machine [11] on the values of the last layer vectors of the CNNs pretrained on ImageNet images. There was no significant difference in the quality of the CNNs performance.

We found out when learning these networks that replacement of a loss function softmax to hinge loss function gives a significant increase in quality for OCSVM. This can be explained by the fact that the estimates given by the softmax function are non-normalized logarithmic probabilities of the class, which can easily be transformed into class probabilities. When training a network, changing the evaluation of one class affects the ratings of all other classes. In this work, we try to isolate the characteristics of a certain class, estimating random images should not affect the estimates of shocking images. To do this, we replace the used loss function: from binary cross-entropy to hinge and change the activation function of last layer from softmax to tanh (because binary hinge loss function should be used with labels in interval $\{-1, +1\}$).

3.2 Siamese Network

Siamese network is a class of neural network architectures that contain two or more subnetworks (CNN) that share all their parameters and weights [7]. They are used in tasks that involve finding similarity or a relationship between two comparable objects. A set of pairs of such objects labelled with values of their proximity are used as training data. The architecture of Siamese networks used in this work is shown in the Fig. 2.

It consists of three components:

1. *Feature extraction* is pretrained CNNs that do not update their parameters during training. In this paper, we use Inception3 [12] (Inc3), ResNet50 [5] (RN50) and ResNet50 + fused [15] (RN50f) CNNs as feature extraction components.
2. *Distance* is a measure of vectors dissimilarity. In this paper, we use the cosine distance, the Manhattan distance and the Euclidean distance.
3. *Classifier* is a classifier that determines the similarity $(0; 1)$ of input objects on an integrated vector. In this paper, this role is performed by SVM, Random Forest, XGBoost and Feedforward Neural Network (FNN).

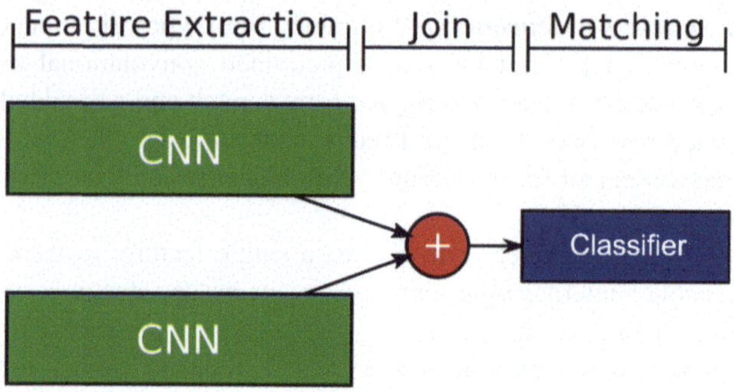

Fig. 2. General architecture for all siamese networks used in this work.

In this work, siamese network learns to determine how similar the pairs of images are to each other and helps to consider the presence of very rare subclasses of shocking images. During the exploitation of the system, after the classification by the one-class classifier, an image is checked for similarity to a limited number of images poorly recognized by the network and the one-class classifier. If the image is similar to one of the representatives of the rare subclasses, then the final answer is the class to which the subclass belongs, otherwise—the prediction of the one-class classifier. In case of detection of incorrect classification by a one-class classifier and the absence of similar images in the base of rare subclasses, a new subclass is created and additional training of the siamese network starts: similar images are generated by data augmentation methods, and not similar images are taken randomly from opposite class; new image proximity pairs and sampled old pairs become a learning sample. Since the siamese network is designed to solve one-shot learning problems, two images of the same subclass are enough for it to remember a new subclass.

4 Empirical Study

4.1 Dataset

The problem of the methods described in the Introduction is an inaccurate semiautomatic data collection. Often on pages with materials about accidents, as well as in the search for relevant requests, in addition to images of the deaths and injuries themselves, there are photos of rescuers, landscape, etc. which is not a shock-content. These images were selected manually.

The collection of data took into account the presence of contextual shock (for example, worms inside a human body or python, which completely swallowed a person). We manually collected:

1. 2500 shocking images;
2. 5150 non-shocking images (random pictures from the Internet);
3. 115 "border"' shocking images divided into 14 subclasses that were incorrectly classified by the model [14];

4. 50 "border"' non-shocking images divided into 5 subclasses that were incorrectly classified by the model [14].

The breakdown into the training, validation and test sets was stratified: the image of each class and each boundary subclass was represented proportionally in three sets. For the validation set, 20% of all images were used. For test, 20% of the remaining sample was used. Thus, the ratio of classes was used: 64%:16%:20% (train:test:validation). For the training of a pre-trained convolutional network and siamese networks, images of all classes are used. To train auto-encoders and a one class SVM, only shocking and "border"' shocking images are used. To test all models, both shocking and non-shocking images are used.

We compare the models with respect to their accuracy, precision and recall in classifying shocking and non-shocking images. Additionally, we compare recall and precision measures for "border" shock and non-shock images separately.

4.2 Baseline Model

As a baseline solution, we used the binary classification with modern convolutional networks ImageNet v3, ResNet50 and the implementation of ResNet50 with Fused-layers. We used threshold movement to increase the recall of recognizing shock images and see how other metrics change. The probabilities of the classes were weighed in accordance with the cost matrix of the classes. The cost of misclassification of shocking images as non-shocking consistently increased until the overall quality of the model did not start to fall precipitously, or metrics ceased to change. The results of the work are presented in Table 1.

Table 1. Results of the basic models.

CNN	Accuracy	Shock Precision	Shock Recall	Border Precision	Border Recall	Precision	Recall
Inception3	0.936	0.882	0.906	0.792	0.790	0.942	0.937
ResNet50	0.949	0.927	0.915	0.792	0.801	0.949	0.949
ResNet50 Fused	**0.957**	**0.946**	0.918	**0.807**	**0.813**	**0.956**	**0.956**
Inception3 with moving threshold	0.861	0.709	0.962	0.740	0.433	0.891	0.861
ResNet50 with moving threshold	0.883	0.736	0.993	0.788	0.432	0.912	0.883
ResNet50 Fused with moving threshold	0.898	0.763	**0.988**	0.802	0.504	0.919	0.897

4.3 Results of One-Class Classification

Convolutional Autoencoders. Several CAEs with different sizes and activation functions were built and trained:

1. Six-layer CAE with ReLu at the inner layers and at the output.
2. Six-layer CAE with tanh at the inner layers and at the output.
3. Six-layer CAE with tanh at the inner layers and ReLu at the output.
4. Eight-layer CAE with tanh at the inner layers and ReLu at the output.
5. A thirty-two-layer CAE using VGG-16 as an encoder.
6. A thirty-two-layer CAE using pre-engineered VGG-16 as an encoder.

The best recovery error was shown by the eight-layer autoencoder, but the recovery threshold could not be found: recovery errors for both classes are uniformly distributed across the sample. As a result, the model gives 0.528 accuracy on the validation set, with precision equals to 0.598 and recall equals to 0.525, which is which is very close to random selection. There are some factors that should be taken into consideration in the analysis of reasons for failure, including short network training time and too broad definition of a class of shocking images for such small sample. This conclusion is because when CAE work with the subclass "cut hands" (a small sample of 150 images containing cut hands), the six-layer CAE showed a 0.86 accuracy on validation after the threshold was selected with F1-score. Photos of the cut hands are very similar to each other and can clearly be combined into one subclass of images. An example of the work is shown in Fig. 3, the recovery errors of different classes differ by an order of magnitude.

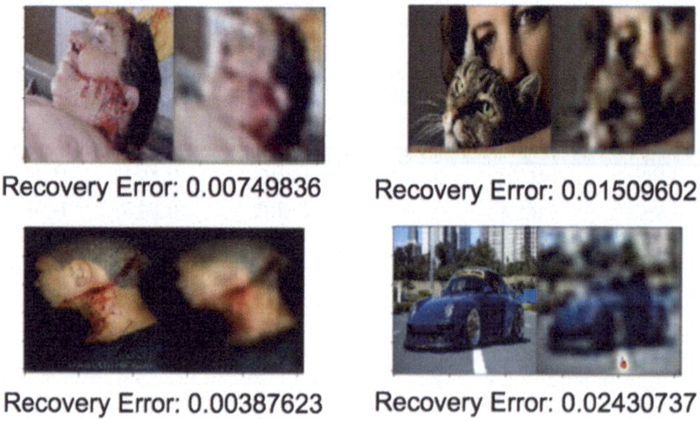

Fig. 3. Original image and image recovered by an eight-layer convolutional autoencoder.

OCSVM. The models were trained only on shocking images without considering the boundary shock, because this increases the efficiency of the model. The model is primitive enough and cannot handle with boundary images well enough.

The main parameters for tuning were the type of kernel (linear, rbf, polynomial) and ν that sets an upper bound on the fraction of outliers (training examples regarded out-of-class) and sets a lower bound on the number of training examples used as support vectors. Results are shown in Table 2.

Table 2. OCSVM-model classification results.

Pretrained CNN/loss	Accuracy	Shock Precision	Shock Recall	Border Precision	Border Recall	Precision	Recall
Inceptionv3 cross-entropy	0.846	0.683	0.944	0.632	0.365	0.880	0.846
Inceptionv3 hinge	0.908	0.787	**0.979**	0.732	0.614	0.923	0.908
ResNet50 cross-entropy	0.852	0.696	0.945	0.637	0.370	0.883	0.885
ResNet50 hinge	0.917	0.825	0.941	**0.745**	**0.628**	0.923	0.917
ResNet50 Fused cross-entropy	0.862	0.715	0.956	0.645	0.377	0.891	0.861
ResNet50 Fused hinge	**0.924**	**0.843**	0.953	0.744	0.625	**0.932**	**0.921**

Autoencoders. Stacked autoencoder can store a large amount of information in its internal representation and improve the basic solution with respect to all metrics, as it presented in Table 3.

Table 3. Autoencoder-model classification results.

Autoencoder	Accuracy	Shock Precision	Shock Recall	Border Precision	Border Recall	Precision	Recall
SAE	0.920	0.821	**0.962**	0.826	0.650	0.929	0.920
SAE + internal representation	**0.973**	**0.973**	0.942	**0.885**	**0.887**	**0.974**	**0.973**
AE	0.896	0.772	**0.962**	0.797	0.521	0.912	0.896
AE + internal representation	0.927	0.968	0.8	0.661	0.702	0.930	0.927

As it can be seen, SAE using internal representation showed the best performance.

4.4 Siamese Networks

Siamese Network Training. As a result of all experiments, feed-forward network proved to be the best classifier, so the Table shows only the results of the work of the best models using other classifiers (for comparison). As it can be seen from Table 4, siamese network that has Resnet50Fused as the feature extractor, the Euclidean distance, and feedforward neural network as classifier was the best.

Table 4. Comparison of siamese networks.

Feature extractor	Distance	Classifier	Accuracy	Precision	Recall
ResNet50	Euclidean	SVM	0.801	0.807	0.807
ResNet50	Euclidean	RF	0.792	0.794	0.793
ResNet50	Manhattan	XGBoost	0.898	0.902	0.908
Inception v3	Manhattan	FNN	0.900	0.904	0.906
ResNet50	Manhattan	FNN	0.905	0.909	0.909
ResNet50 Fused	Manhattan	FNN	0.909	0.911	0.912
Inception v3	Euclidean	FNN	0.912	0.919	0.920
ResNet50	Euclidean	FNN	0.918	0.923	0.924
ResNet50 Fused	Euclidean	FNN	**0.924**	**0.929**	**0.931**
Inception v3	Cosine	FNN	0.878	0.881	0.885
ResNet50	Cosine	FNN	0.881	0.884	0.897
ResNet50 Fused	Cosine	FNN	0.885	0.892	0.895

After finding the best siamese network, we combined it with the best one-class classifier. Results are presented in Table 5.

Table 5. The results of the best reviewed models.

Model	Accuracy	Shock Precision	Shock Recall	Border Precision	Border Recall	Precision	Recall
Baseline	0.957	0.946	0.918	0.807	0.813	0.956	0.956
SAE + internal representation	0.973	0.973	0.942	0.885	0.887	0.974	0.973
SAE + internal representation + siamese neural network	**0.985**	**0.979**	**0.977**	**0.940**	**0.939**	**0.986**	**0.986**

As it can be seen, the proposed solution significantly outperforms the baseline, and usage of siamese networks help to achieve the highest result.

5 Discussion

The empirical study presented in Sect. 5 reveals that the best result is a model that uses a CNN resnet50 fused as feature extractor for autoencoder and siamese network, SVM trained on stacked autoencoder internal representation and recovery error as one-class classifier and siamese network with the Euclidean distance and feed-forward neural network as classifier. It is quite obvious that simpler models such as the normal autoencoder or one-class SVM showed the worst results, because they could not allocate sufficient information for good classification. The reason for the unsuccessful application of the convolutional auto-encoder is most likely that it was not pretrained but was trained from scratch on a small diverse set of data. The resulting pipeline is presented on Fig. 4.

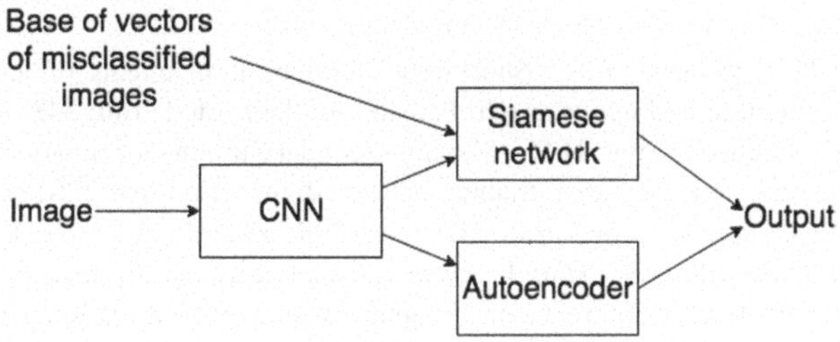

Fig. 4. Architecture of the best solution.

6 Conclusion

In this paper, we suggest a new method for shocking image detection. It includes using one-class classifiers for learning representation solely of shocking images, and siamese network for handling with different and rare subclasses of shocking images.

For method evaluation, we use manually collected dataset that contains 2500 shocking images, 5150 random non-shocking images, as well as 115 “border” shocking images divided into 14 subclasses and 50 “border” non-shocking images divided into 5 subclasses, which were tricky for the best-known model.

We used several methods of one-class classification, namely CAE, AE and SAE with pretrained CNN, OCSVM with pretrained CNN. Due to the class of shock images contains a lot of very dissimilar subclasses, it was necessary to get the maximum amount of information about the data during the training, which was performed with the help of information stored in the internal representation of the sparse autoencoder.

As a result, SAE recovery error combined with vector of inner representation of images showed the best result.

The achieved results are improved by using siamese networks, which remember images-representatives of especially rare subclasses. We tested several siamese network architectures resulting in the best model being the siamese network with ResNet50 + Fused network for extracting image feature vectors, Euclidean distance for combining feature vectors and FNN as a classifier.

In the future, we are going to more intently consider the possibilities of using the siamese network as an assistant to the main classifier. We plan to investigate whether the use of the Siamese network will reduce the number of errors of the classifier training in the process of operation (algorithm of online machine learning).

Acknowledgments. This work was financially supported by the Government of the Russian Federation (Grant 08-08). The authors would like to thank Aleksey Artamonov for his constructive comments and suggestions.

References

1. Anderson, C.A., Berkowitz, L., Donnerstein, E., Huesmann, L.R., Johnson, J., Linz, D.: The influence of media violence on youth. Psychol. Sci. Public Interest **4**, 81–110 (2003)
2. Bourlard, H., Kamp, Y.: Auto-association by multilayer perceptrons and singular value decomposition. Biol. Cybern. **59**(4–5), 291–294 (1988)
3. Bushman, B.J., Huesmann, L.R.: Short-term and long-term effects of violent media on aggression in children and adults. Arch. Pediatr. Adolesc. Med. **160**, 348–352 (2006)
4. Dubberley, S., Griffin, E., Bal, H.M.: Making secondary trauma a primary issue: a study of eyewitness media and vicarious trauma on the digital frontline (2015). http://eyewitnessmediahub.com/uploads/browser/files/Trauma%20Report.pdf. Accessed 15 Jan 2020
5. He, K., Zhang, X., Ren, S., Sun, J.: Deep residual learning for image recognition. In: Proceedings of the IEEE Conference on Computer Vision and Pattern Recognition, pp. 770–778 (2016)
6. Khan, S.S., Madden, M.G.: A survey of recent trends in one class classification. In: Irish Conference on Artificial Intelligence and Cognitive Science, pp. 188–197. Springer, Heidelberg (2009)
7. Koch, G., Zemel, R., Salakhutdinov, R.: Siamese neural networks for one-shot image recognition. In ICML Deep Learning Workshop, vol. 2 (2015)
8. Li, B., Xiong, W., Wu, O., Hu, W., Maybank, S., Yan, S.: Horror image recognition based on context-aware multi-instance learning. IEEE Trans. Image Process. **24**(12), 5193–5205 (2015)
9. Luxton, D.D., June, J.D., Fairall, J.M.: Social media and suicide: a public health perspective. Am. J. Public Health **102**(S2), S195–S200 (2012)
10. Poultney, C., Chopra, S., Cun, Y.L.: Efficient learning of sparse representations with an energy-based model. In: Advances in neural information processing systems, pp. 1137–1144 (2007)
11. Schlkopf, B., Williamson, R.C., Smola, A.J., Shawe-Taylor, J., Platt, J.C.: Support vector method for novelty detection. In: Advances in Neural Information Processing Systems, pp. 582–588 (2000)
12. Szegedy, C., Vanhoucke, V., Ioffe, S., Shlens, J., Wojna, Z.: Rethinking the Inception architecture for computer vision. In: Proceedings of the IEEE Conference on Computer Vision and Pattern Recognition, pp. 2818–2826 (2016)
13. Wang, D., Zhang, Z., Wang, W., Wang, L., Tan, T.: Baseline results for violence detection in still images. In: IEEE Ninth International Conference on Advanced Video and Signal-Based Surveillance, pp. 54–57 (2012)
14. Zampoglou, M., Papadopoulos, S., Kompatsiaris, Y., Spangenberg, J. A WebBased Service for Disturbing Image Detection. In: *International Conference on Multimedia Modeling*, pp. 438–441, Springer, Cham (2017)
15. Zheng, L., Zhao, Y., Wang, S., Wang, J., Tian, Q.: Good practice in CNN feature transfer (2016). arXiv preprint arXiv:1604.00133

Factors Affecting Accuracy of Convolutional Neural Network Using VGG-16

Jyoti Rawat(✉), Doina Logofătu(✉), and Sruthi Chiramel(✉)

Department of Computer Science and Engineering,
Frankfurt University of Applied Sciences, 60318 Frankfurt a.M., Germany
{rawat,chiramel}@stud.fra-uas.de, logofatu@fb2.fra-uas.de

Abstract. In this paper, performance evaluation of image data-set using 2-layer Convolutional Neural Network Architecture and transfer learning method, is studied on Fashion MNIST dataset. Fashion MNIST is a dataset of images consisting 70000 28×28 gray-scale images, associated with label of 10 classes. The area of research of this paper in transfer learning is limited to pre-trained neural network VGG-16. The accuracy and respective losses are evaluated using the two mentioned methods. The work under this paper is inspired by widely famous Image-net Large Scale Visual Recognition Challenge, although due to constraint on time, resources, a smaller data set i.e. Fashion MNIST is taken for the study. The work is dependent on Keras Functional API and Tensor Flow. With the accuracy 88.24% and loss 29.02 as per CNN model, the model can be utilised by online clothing stores to classify their articles under right category.

Keywords: Deep learning · ConvNet · Learning rate · Image classification · VGGNet · Dense layer · Neural Networks · Machine Learning · Algorithm Optimisaton · Transfer learning

1 Introduction

Image classification is one of the core task in Computer Vision which has always enjoyed limelight. We have taken into account 70000 Grayscale images of size 28×28. Images are treated as a 2-D matrix by Convolutional Neural Network(CNN). Depending on pixel i.e. intensity of color at a particular point, a numeric integer on the scale of 0–255 is assigned. The numeric values in pixel are uniformly changed from zero (black pixels) to 255 (white pixels). The grid of matrix changes with factors like light, occlusion, viewpoint, deformation etc. but somehow overall grid represents the same picture. Hence, a model should be robust enough to overcome such limitations. A CNN uses multiple linear classifiers within it to classify images on their respective class labels. Class label is assigned to the image on the basis of maximum probability attained.

L. Iliadis et al. (Eds.): EANN 2020, INNS 2, pp. 251–260, 2020.
https://doi.org/10.1007/978-3-030-48791-1_19

The approach used in Neural Networks is called parametric approach as it is driven by the parameters obtained on different layers during the course of training. In real time, almost all small and big firms are extensively using Image Classifiers, made up of different learning algorithms.

As training of a CNN with large datasets can exhaust a significant amount of time, concept of transfer learning can be used as a saviour. It is defined as a situation where what has been learned in one setting is exploited to improve generalization in another setting [18]. It enables CNN to utilise its learning (features, weights) and generalize it on another similar problems. The smaller datasets give a better result on a pre-trained neural network. VGG-16 is a CNN proposed by Simonyan and Zisserman from the University of Oxford in the paper "Very Deep Convolutional Networks for Large Scale Image Recognition". The model was fed on ImageNet, which is a dataset of over 14 million images belonging to 1000 classes. It achieved an accuracy of 92.7%, which was among top-5 test accuracy. VGG-16 was trained on NVIDA Titan Black GPU's for couple of weeks.

Fig. 1. MNIST dataset

2 Problem Description

Image Classification is a well known supervised learning problem, which defines a set of target classes and train a model to recognize them using training data. Training data comprises of images and labels associated with them. A model is required to learn features of training images and provides a good accuracy on test data. In a parametric approach, a test image (28×28 here) is converted into $28 \times 28 \times 1$ (1 as the images are gray-scale, in case of coloured images 3 is used to represent each of RGB channel) matrix, which is a representation of array consisting 784 elements. The array is convoluted with predefined weights generating scores i.e. probabilities for each class label. Class label with highest probability is assigned as the "correct" label of image. The more accuracy we get, better is the model. Figure 2 shows an image from data set, the label of the image is Sneaker in parenthesis. After passing the image from a classifier model the prediction should also be maximum for 'Sneaker class'. In the figure, 100% shows the probability obtained by the 'Class Sneaker' which is represented by a full length green bar. The aim of Image Classification problem is to classify images to their 'correct classes'. One of the approach to solve such problems is neural networks, where model gains features and information from training data and based on its knowledge, classifies the new data.

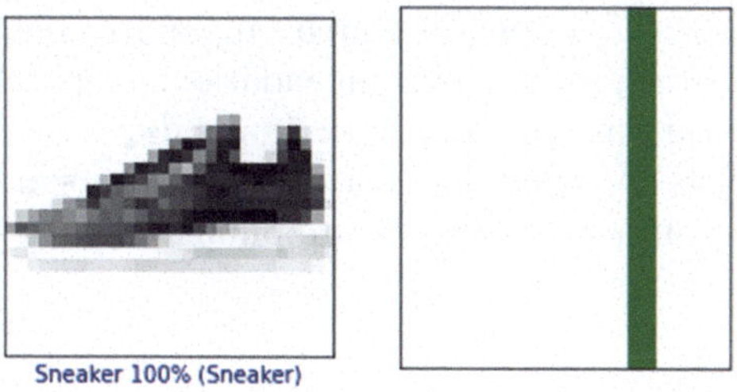

Fig. 2. Graphic representation of the problem

A neural network is made of neurons arranged in layers. Input (Image matrices: X) are fed to each and every neuron and convoluted with weights (w) of the next layer results in activation functions (a). Mathematically,

$$a_1^{(2)} = g(\Theta_{10}^{(1)} x_0 + \Theta_{11}^{(1)} x_1 + \Theta_{12}^{(1)} x_2 + \Theta_{13}^{(1)} x_3)$$
$$a_2^{(2)} = g(\Theta_{20}^{(1)} x_0 + \Theta_{21}^{(1)} x_1 + \Theta_{22}^{(1)} x_2 + \Theta_{23}^{(1)} x_3)$$
$$a_3^{(2)} = g(\Theta_{30}^{(1)} x_0 + \Theta_{31}^{(1)} x_1 + \Theta_{32}^{(1)} x_2 + \Theta_{33}^{(1)} x_3)$$
$$output = h_\Theta(x) = a_1^3 = g(\Theta_{10}^{(2)} x_0 + \Theta_{11}^{(2)} x_1 + \Theta_{12}^{(2)} x_2 + \Theta_{13}^{(2)} x_3)$$

${a_i}^{(j)}$ = activation unit i in layer j
$\Theta^{(j)}$ = matrix of weights controlling function mapping from layer j to j+1
$g(\Theta)$ = Sigmoid function

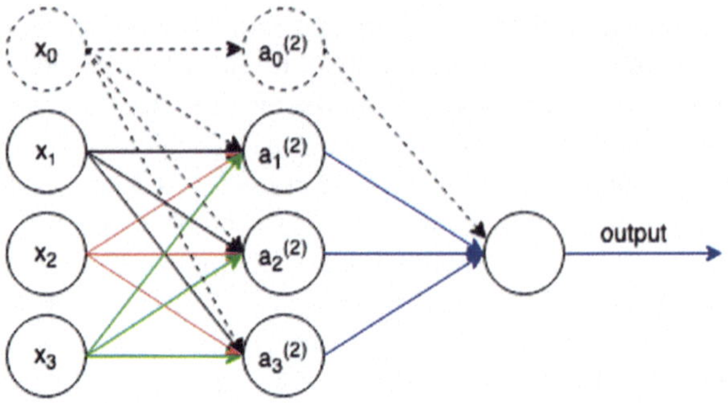

Fig. 3. Neural network

3 Related Research

Deep learning techniques are famous among the fashion related business on their e-commerce websites such as apparel search, apparel recognition, apparel classification and automatic product recommendation. Apparel classification is a complex task due to various apparel properties, and categorisation in the depth of categorisation. CNNs are a popular choice of researchers in this area. There are various models based on neural network are published with trustworthy results [11].

3.1 ALEXNet(2012)

The paper, titled "ImageNet Classification with Deep Convolutional Networks", has been referenced a total of 6,184 times and is widely regarded as one of the most core source of publications in the field. It contains eight learned layers—five convolutional and three fully-connected. It used Relu non Linear function, as deep convolutional network with ReLu function trains several times faster than their tanh units. The model was trained on two GTX 580 GPU connected in parallel. The two-GPU net takes slightly less time to train than the one-GPU net. The output of the last fully-connected layer is fed to a 1000-way softmax which produces a distribution over the 1000 class labels. The first convolutional layer filters the $224 \times 224 \times 3$ input image with 96 kernels of size $11 \times 11 \times 3$ with a stride of 4 pixels. It achieves top-1 and top-5test set error rates of 37.5% and 17.0%. In 2012, the improvised version attained top-1 and top-5 error rates on this dataset are 67.4% and 40.9%, with an additional, sixth convolutional layer over the last pooling layer [8].

3.2 ZF Net(2013)

In the paper titled "Visualizing and Understanding Convolutional Neural Networks", Zeiler and Fergus begin by discussing the idea due to the accessibility of large training sets and increased computational power with the usage of GPUs, the topic came into limelight. It requires a careful initialization and does not give any information about the unit's in-variances. A large set of N labeled images x,y, where label y_i is a discrete variable indicating the true class. A cross-entropy loss function, suitable for image classification, is used to compare $\hat{y}$ and y_i. The parameters of the network (filters in the convolutional layers, weight matrices in the fully connected layers and biases) are trained by back-propagating the derivative of the loss with respect to the parameters throughout the network, and updating the parameters via stochastic gradient descent. The visualization technique used was a multi-layered De-convolutional Network (de-convnet), as proposed by (Zeiler et al. [9]), to project the feature activations back to the input pixel space. It used an architecture of 8 layer convnet model.

3.3 VGGNet(2014)

The use of only 3×3 sized filters is quite different from AlexNet's 11×11 filters in the first layer and ZF Net's 7×7 filters. The combination of two 3×3 convolution layers has an effective receptive field of 5×5. This in turn simulates a larger filter while keeping the benefits of smaller filter sizes. One of the benefits is a decrease in the number of parameters. Also we can use two ReLU layers instead of one with the combination of two 3×3. 3 convolutional layers back to back have an effective receptive field of 7×7. As input volumes at each layer decreases in terms of spatial (result of the convolution and pool layers), the depth of the volumes increase due to the increased number of filters as network goes to interiors. However, the number of filters doubles after each maxpool layer. This adds up the idea of shrinking spatial dimensions, but growing depth.

4 Implementation Details

We evaluate the performance of Fashion MNIST on a 2 layer CNN trained from scratch and on a model which uses pre-trained weights of VGG-16.

Figure 4 depicts handling of data during the course of work.

- Understand dataset
- Pre-process Data
- Visualize Data
- Build a Model
- Train and Test Data

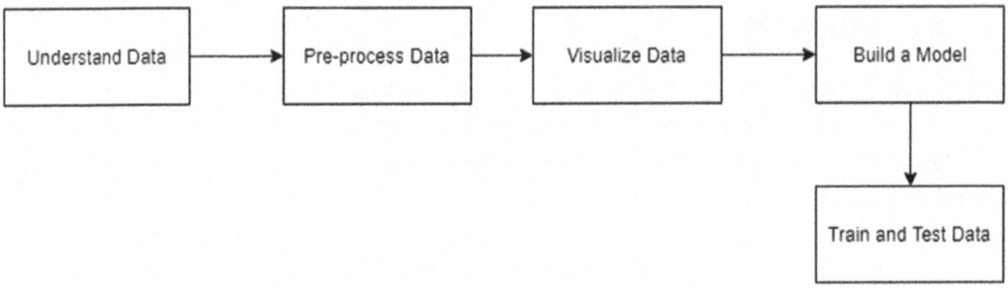

Fig. 4. Data processing flow

4.1 Understand and Pre-process Data

Fashion MNIST consists of 70000 28*28 grayscale images. Out of which 60000 images are in training set along with their class labels. Rest of 10000 images are in test data set. Data set is directly accessed from Keras library of python. There are ten class labels: Tshirt/top, Trouser, Pullover, Dress, Coat, Sandal, Shirt, Sneaker, Bag, Ankle Boot. Data has been shuffled 5 times to include randomness in the values. The large scale image has been pre-processed first before undergoing through convolution. The images are flattened to 1- D array and the pixel values ranging from 0–255 are normalised between 0,1.

4.2 Model Building

A model is the sequence of the layers, which generates predictions by finding patterns in the data. The model used here comprises of input layer, that converts 2D array of 28*28 into 1D array to get computed in further layers, dense layer which is a fully connected node (i.e. each input neuron is connected to each output neuron) and output layer that has 10 outputs as data set has 10 class labels. The non linear function used is ReLu in the hidden layer and softmax in the output layer. Softmax function will predict the labels in the form of probabilities. ADAM optimiser is used to combat with loss function of data-sets and optimisation of the model. This 2-layer neural network model uses back-propagation technique to find the best suitable weights for the datasets.

The model provides the accuracy of 87.8% with loss of 0.27. Predictions can be viewed in the Fig. 5, where green bar shows the right predictions and red bar shows the wrong predictions. In the pictures with multiple bars, the bar with highest probability is considered as the right label. The other bars with less probabilities show that the test image might be similar to the templates of those other probabilities. The graphs shown in Fig. 6 and Fig. 7 shows that accuracy is increasing from 82% to 87% on test images as epochs are increasing and in the same way losses occurred are decreasing from 0.50 to 0.24 with number of epochs.

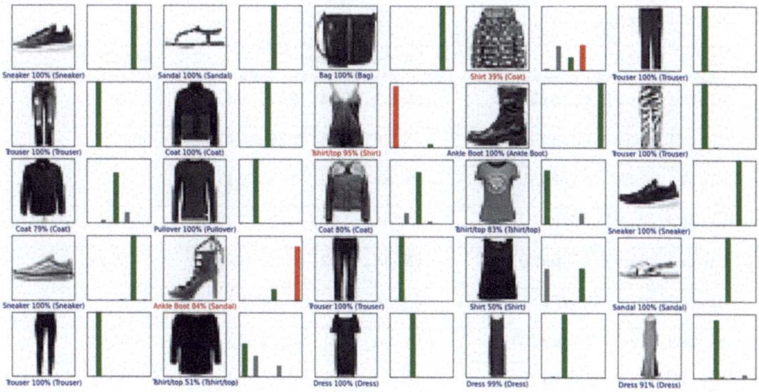

Fig. 5. Prediction on test images

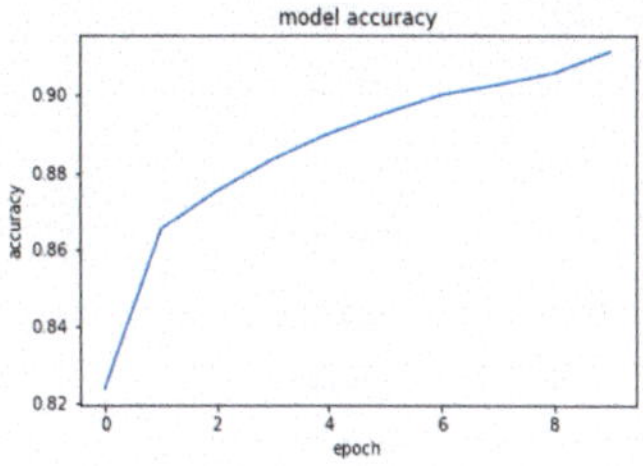

Fig. 6. Accuracy graph

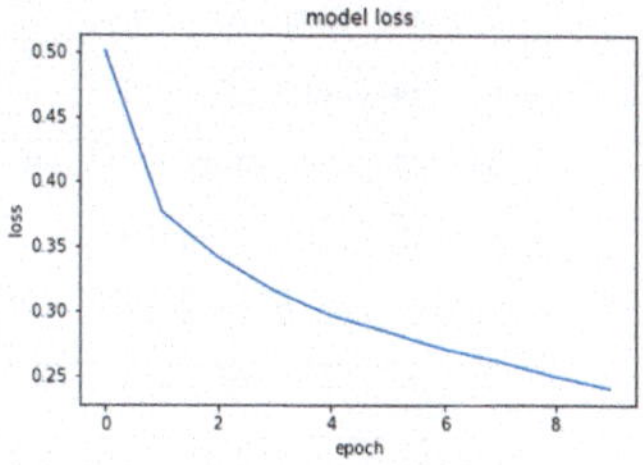

Fig. 7. Loss graph

4.3 Transfer Learning Using VGG-16

The Neural Information Processing Systems (NIPS) 1995 workshop Learning to Learn: Knowledge Consolidation and Transfer in Inductive Systems is believed to have provided the initial motivation for research in this field. Transfer Learning is different from traditional learning as traditional learning is isolated and occurs purely based on specific tasks, datasets and training separate isolated models on them, on the contrary, transfer learning can leverage (features, weights etc.) from previously trained models for training newer models. As mentioned there are various transfer learning models available. VGG-16, is considered as it has 92.7% accuracy top-5 test accuracy in ImageNet, which is a dataset of over 14 million images belonging to 1000 classes [7].

```
Model: "sequential_1"
_________________________________________________________________
Layer (type)                 Output Shape              Param #
=================================================================
block1_conv1 (Conv2D)        (None, 224, 224, 64)      1792
_________________________________________________________________
block1_conv2 (Conv2D)        (None, 224, 224, 64)      36928
_________________________________________________________________
block1_pool (MaxPooling2D)   (None, 112, 112, 64)      0
_________________________________________________________________
block2_conv1 (Conv2D)        (None, 112, 112, 128)     73856
_________________________________________________________________
block2_conv2 (Conv2D)        (None, 112, 112, 128)     147584
_________________________________________________________________
block2_pool (MaxPooling2D)   (None, 56, 56, 128)       0
_________________________________________________________________
block3_conv1 (Conv2D)        (None, 56, 56, 256)       295168
_________________________________________________________________
block3_conv2 (Conv2D)        (None, 56, 56, 256)       590080
_________________________________________________________________
block3_conv3 (Conv2D)        (None, 56, 56, 256)       590080
_________________________________________________________________
block3_pool (MaxPooling2D)   (None, 28, 28, 256)       0
_________________________________________________________________
block4_conv1 (Conv2D)        (None, 28, 28, 512)       1180160
_________________________________________________________________
block4_conv2 (Conv2D)        (None, 28, 28, 512)       2359808
_________________________________________________________________
block4_conv3 (Conv2D)        (None, 28, 28, 512)       2359808
_________________________________________________________________
block4_pool (MaxPooling2D)   (None, 14, 14, 512)       0
_________________________________________________________________
block5_conv1 (Conv2D)        (None, 14, 14, 512)       2359808
_________________________________________________________________
block5_conv2 (Conv2D)        (None, 14, 14, 512)       2359808
_________________________________________________________________
block5_conv3 (Conv2D)        (None, 14, 14, 512)       2359808
_________________________________________________________________
block5_pool (MaxPooling2D)   (None, 7, 7, 512)         0
_________________________________________________________________
flatten (Flatten)            (None, 25088)             0
_________________________________________________________________
fc1 (Dense)                  (None, 4096)              102764544
_________________________________________________________________
fc2 (Dense)                  (None, 4096)              16781312
_________________________________________________________________
dense_1 (Dense)              (None, 10)                40970
=================================================================
Total params: 134,301,514
Trainable params: 40,970
Non-trainable params: 134,260,544
_________________________________________________________________
```

VGG-16 has 16 layers comprised of Convolutional layers, Max Pooling layers, Activation layers, Fully connected layers. There are 13 convolutional layers, 5 Max Pooling layers and 3 Dense layers which sums up to 21 layers but only 16 weight layers. Convolution layer 1 has number of filters as 64 while Convolution layer 2 has 128 filters, Convolution layer 3 has 256 filters while Convolution layer 4 and Convolution layer 5 has 512 filters.

Input layer works on 224*224 size of images hence our dataset images of 28*28 needs to be reshaped. In order to avoid over-fitting of data and optimize results without any biasing training data is split between test data and validation set i.e. 2000 images in validation set and 80000 images in testing set along with their labels. The data is distributed randomly in order to preserve the randomness of dataset. For cross validation, data is further split in batches within training, testing and validation data randomly. For training data and testing data batch size is chosen to be 10, for validation data, batch size is chosen to be 4. VGG-16's output layer has 1000 labels originally (as it was trained on ImageNet dataset which has 1000 class labels), it is modified to 10 output class labels. To compare the results on same grounds, Adam optimizer and categorical crossentropy is used for optimization and evaluation of loss (as used in 3 layer CNN). The model provides an accuracy of 94% with 0.19 loss, which is significantly better than training a convolutional neural network from scratch.

5 Results and Discussion

The better results are obtained, retraining an already trained data, however chances of over-fitting are fairly high in retraining the same model. An accuracy of 90% is achieved after re-training 2 layer CNN model on the same time, however it violates the concept of Machine Learning, as the basic idea in Machine Learning is to have better predictions on new data than on old data.

Model	Accuracy	Loss
2 Layer CNN	87%	0.27
VGG-16	94%	0.19

Better results can be achieved by increasing number of hidden layers of neural network as here we have used only 1 hidden layer. Learning rate used in VGG-16 model is 0.0001. We evaluated accuracy and loss values on different learning rates ranges from 0.001 to 0.0001. There was not a significant difference among values which can used by online stores. A very low learning rate progresses the training slowly as convergence is slow. On the other hand, if learning rate (generally represented by α), cost function may not decrease on every iteration and may not converge. Learning rate is one of the hyper parameters for this model.

6 Conclusion

We have evaluated performance of a 2 layer neural network and predefined VGG-16 on an imgeset comprised of 70000 gray-scale images having 10 output labels. The scope of future work can be focused on different factors like:

- Increasing number of layers in CNN model.
- Evaluation of performances can be played around on different sizes of epochs, batch sizes, filter kernels of hidden layers, activation functions used.
- Tweaking more than one layer(not just output layer).

References

1. Simonyan, K., Zisserman, A.: Very deep convolutional networks for large scale. In: Conference ICLR (2015)
2. He, K., Zhang, X., Ren, S., Sun, J.: Deep residual learning for image recognition. In: Computer Vision and Pattern Recognition (2015)
3. Szegedy, C., Vanhoucke, V., Ioffe, S., Shlens, J., Wojna, Z.: Rethinking the inception architecture for computer vision. In: Computer Vision and Pattern Recognition (2015)
4. Kryvobokov, M., Wilhelmsson, M.: Analysing location attributes with a hedonic model for apartment prices in donetsk, Ukraine. Int. J. Strateg. Property Manag. **11**(3), 157–178 (2007)
5. Qi, X., Liao, R., Jia, J., Fidler, S., Urtasun, R.: 3D graph neural networks for RGBD semantic segmentation. In: IEEE International Conference on Computer Vision (ICCV) (2017)
6. Behera, A., Gidney, A.G., Wharton, Z., Robinson, D.P., Quinn, K.: A CNN model for head pose recognition using wholes and regions. In: 2019 14th IEEE International Conference on Automatic Face & Gesture Recognition (2019)
7. Russakovsky, O.: ImageNet large scale visual recognition challenge. Int. J. Comput. Vis. **115**, 211–252 (2014). ISSN 1573-1405
8. Krizhevsky, A., Sutskever, I., Hinton, G.: Large, deep convolutional neural network (2012)
9. Zeiler, M.D., Fergus, R.: Visualizing and understanding convolutional neural networks (2013)
10. Goodfellow, I., Bengio, Y., Courville, A.: Deep Learning. MIT Press, Cambridge (2016). http://www.deeplearningbook.org
11. Seo, Y., Shin, K.S.: Hierarchical convolutional neural networks for fashion image classification. Exp. Syst. Appl. **116**, 328–339 (2019). ISSN 0957-4174

Image Recoloring of Art Paintings for the Color Blind Guided by Semantic Segmentation

Stamatis Chatzistamatis(✉), Anastasios Rigos, and George E. Tsekouras

Department of Cultural Technology and Communication, University of the Aegean, University Hill, 81100 Mytilene, Lesvos Island, Greece
{stami,a.rigos}@aegean.gr, gtsek@ct.aegean.gr

Abstract. This paper introduces a semantic-segmentation guided image recoloring approach of digitized art paintings to enhance the color perception of color- blind people that suffer from protanopia and deuteranopia. Semantic segmentation using transfer learning between natural images and art paintings is applied to extract annotated color information. By using a standard technique, the annotated colors are transformed to simulate the effects of protanopia and deuteranopia. Then, a specialized objective function is minimized to recolor only the colors that are significantly different from the respective simulated ones, because these colors are perceived as confusing by the color blind. The effectiveness of the proposed method is demonstrated through its comparison with other algorithms in several experimental cases.

Keywords: Color vision deficiency · Digitized art paintings · Image recoloring · Semantic segmentation · Deep network

1 Introduction

The human color vision system generates the color perception by using three types of photoreceptor cells, called cones, to perform photon absorption: the L-cones, the M-cones, and the S-cones. The L-cones correspond to the red color, the M-cones to the green color, and the S-cones to the blue color. Malfunction of one or more photoreceptors results in color vision deficiency (CVD), also called color blindness, which consists of three types: the monochromacy, the dichromacy, and the anomalous trichromacy [16, 17, 20]. The most challenging CVD is the dichromacy, which embraces three categories [5, 16, 20]: (a) protanopia caused by the absence of L-cones, (b) deuteranopia caused by the absence of M-cones, and (c) tritanopia caused by the absence of S-cones. The protanopes and deuteranopes cannot distinguish between red and green, while the tritanopes between blue and yellow.

People with strong CVDs face difficulties in daily life, where problematic color perception becomes annoying or even critical (e.g. road signs), making their accessibility in colored content a challenge. Regarding this issue, the accessibility of

L. Iliadis et al. (Eds.): EANN 2020, INNS 2, pp. 261–273, 2020.
https://doi.org/10.1007/978-3-030-48791-1_20

color-blind people in cultural content, such as art paintings, has been acknowledged as an important demand by worldwide organizations dealing with the CVDs and cultural organizations such as museums, as well [7, 10, 12]. Many color-blind people are at a disadvantage when choosing to study or enjoy art paintings because they can only discern a confusing set of objects and colors.

So far, a wide variety of image recoloring methods has been proposed to enhance the color perception of the color-blind [16]. Hassan and Paramersan [5] set up the image recoloring in the XYZ color space utilizing three steps namely, color normalization, angular color rotation, and color un-normalization. Huang et al. [8] performed the color enhancement by extracting key colors and determining an optimal mapping to maintain the contrast between pairs of those colors. In [9], special requirements were quantified by minimizing an objective function in the CIE Lab space. Rani and Rajeev [14] assisted deuteranopic viewers by enhancing the contrast between adjacent shades.

Although too much effort has been put on the recoloring of natural images, there are relatively few works that consider the case study of digitized art painting images. Due to the complexity of such kind of images, maintaining a color natural appearance of the recolored image is a very challenging problem [1, 18]. The requirement of color naturalness focuses on minimizing the perceptual difference between the colors in the original image and the respective modified colors in the recolored image [16].

In this paper, we introduce a novel approach that attempts to meet the requirement of naturalness, regarding the protanopia and deuteranopia CVDs. A transfer learning based semantic image segmentation algorithm is implemented to extract annotated color information of the original image. The semantic segmentation is implemented by introducing a framework for transferring learning from a Mask RCNN network [3, 15], trained on available large collections of labeled natural images, to the context of art paintings. Then, the colors identified above are transformed to simulate the corresponding color blind perception [20]. The above information is further processed by a specialized objective function, which is minimized to obtain the recolored art painting.

The material is organized as follows. Section 2 describes the proposed algorithm in detail. Section 3 illustrates the simulation results and the respective analysis. Finally, the paper concludes in Sect. 4.

2 The Proposed Recoloring Method

The flowsheet of the algorithm is illustrated in Fig. 1. Given an RGB color $\boldsymbol{C} = (C_R\ C_G\ C_B)^T$, with $C_R, C_G, C_B \in [0, 255]$, its simulation to protanopia or deuteranopia is denoted as $\boldsymbol{C}_D = (C_{R,D}\ C_{G,D}\ C_{B,D})^T$, where subscript D describes the protanopia or deuteranopia.

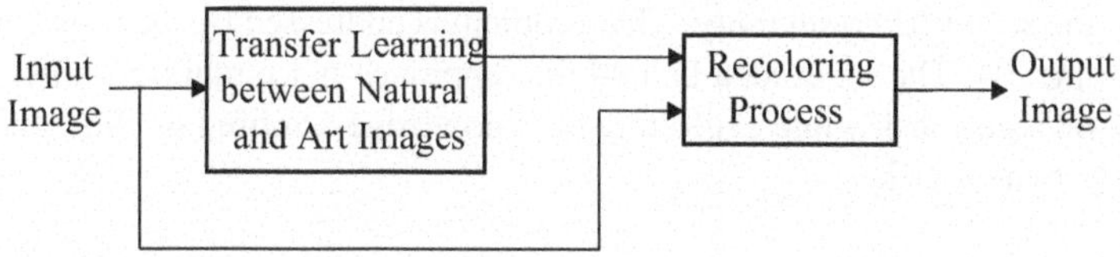

Fig. 1. The basic algorithmic steps of the recoloring process.

The vector $\boldsymbol{C}_D$ is calculated by matrix transformations that involve the XYZ and LMS color spaces, where the transformations are functionally represented $\boldsymbol{C}_D = f_D(\boldsymbol{C})$. For a detailed description of the color simulation procedure, the interested reader is referred to [20].

2.1 Semantic Segmentation Using Transfer Learning Between Natural and Art Digitized Paintings

R-CNN [3] is one of the first deep learning networks inspired by AlexNet [11] and it uses segments of that network with minor changes. Network's functionality is improved using the Selective Search [19] technique to perform object recognition in the image instead of classifying the whole image as one object. After identifying the regions of interest (RoIs) with bounding boxes, a processed version of AlexNet is used to classify the object. At the last level of the network, a support vector machine (SVM) categorizes the object into a class. However, after executing the network's training process, one more step takes place to optimize the rectangular boundaries, which is considered a simple regression problem. In a nutshell, it gets as input the bounding boxes of the objects and improves them. The main drawback of the R-CNN is the utilization of many feed-forward iterations ($\sim$2 K) of AlexNet for each RoI, and separately trains the three subsequent models: (a) CNN for extracting image features, (b) SVM, and (c) a simple regression model to improve the bounding boxes.

Fast R-CNN [2] was implemented to solve these problems and accelerate the R-CNN. It performs only one feed-forward pass of the CNN throughout the image and then pools on every bounding box (named Region of Interest Pooling - RoIPool). Then, it integrates all the aforementioned three models on a common network, where the regression takes place in parallel with the classification which is carried out by Softmax classifier instead of the SVM, taking as an input the result of the RoIPool layer. The next improved network is the Faster R-CNN which uses a Region Proposal Network (RPN) to accomplish the tasks of the Selective Search algorithm. The latest suggestion based on R-CNN is the Mask R-CNN which is the Faster R-CNN [15] with the exception that instead of bounding boxes it detects the real contours (i.e. masks) of the objects in the image. To achieve this, a parallel branch of the network is responsible for classifying the pixels into objects. Each mask is classified into two classes using binary regression rather than Softmax.

The above-mentioned deep learning algorithms were able to achieve very good results on classification problems after trained on large datasets. The lack of available training data in many domains such as medical images and art images is a well-known problem in the scientific community. That problem is addressed by the transfer learning mechanism [4, 21]. The main idea behind that approach is to train a machine learning framework on a new task while exploiting the knowledge acquired by the framework in a previously related task.

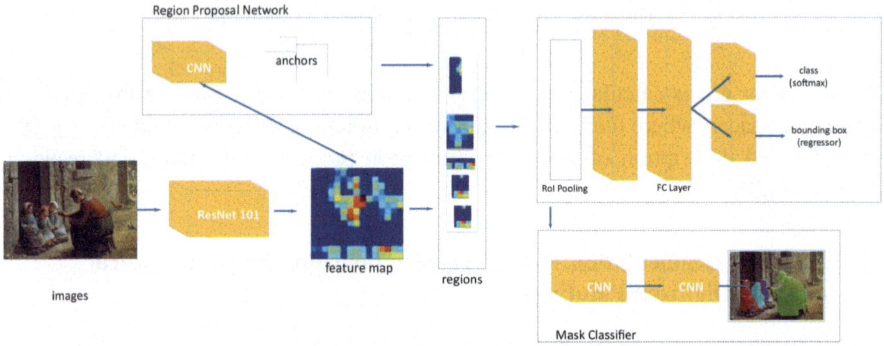

Fig. 2. The basic structure of the transfer learning based semantic segmentation scheme.

The flowsheet of the network used in this paper is depicted in Fig. 2. We use Matterport's[1] implementation of Mask-RCNN for training nine classes of art paintings images with seventy-five annotated images in each class. Firstly, data preprocessing is carried out in terms of image augmentation. The key point is to follow a set process of taking in existing images from our training dataset and apply some image transformation operations to them. Specifically, regarding each image, a horizontal flip is performed, the image is randomly cropped to a scale between 0.9 and 1 times the original dimension, a Gaussian blur with random standard deviation is applied, the contrast is adjusted, the brightness is adjusted, and a series of random affine transformations are also applied so each image has dimensions 500×500. The nine trained classes are: person, boat, bird, horse, bowl, chair, table, vase and fruit.

The ResNet101 architecture [6] is used as a backbone model to extract relevant features from the input image. Instead of using the pre-trained weights for MS COCO[2], we initialize the weights of our backbone model using weights pre-trained on Imagenet[3]. The backbone model serves as a feature extractor, where the early layers detect low-level features (edges and corners), and later layers successively detect higher-level features (person, boat, etc.). To fine-tune the model pre-trained on Imagenet, we train only the model heads and the layers from ResNet101 level 4 and up for the remaining epochs, because we reuse the weights of the model learned to extract features from natural images. The image is converted from a tensor of shape (500, 500, 3) to a feature map of shape (32, 32, 2048). The extracted feature map is then fed into a Region

[1] https://github.com/matterport/Mask_RCNN.

[2] http://cocodataset.org/.

[3] http://www.image-net.org/.

Proposal Network (RPN) [15]. The RPN scans regions of the feature map with sliding bounding boxes, trying to determine regions that contain objects. For each box, called anchor, the RPN assigns an anchor class (i.e. possible object, not an object or neutral). A proposal layer then picks the anchors most likely to contain an object and refine the anchor box to fit the object more closely, obtaining the RoIs. For each region that contains an object selected by the RoI classifier, the model generates 28 × 28 masks.

2.2 Image Recoloring

The chosen color space is the RGB space. Let us denote the input image as $\boldsymbol{I} = [\boldsymbol{p}_{ij}]\ (1 \le i \le N;\ 1 \le j \le K)$ where $\boldsymbol{p}_{ij}$ symbolizes the RGB color vector of the (i, j) image pixel, and $N \times K$ is the image size. The pixels of the input image are divided into two disjoint sets namely, T_V and T_U. The set T_V includes all pixels that belong to the objects identified by the semantic segmentation algorithm, while the set T_U includes the rest of the pixels. Next, we form the set $S_V = \left\{\boldsymbol{C}_{V,1}, \boldsymbol{C}_{V,2}, \ldots, \boldsymbol{C}_{V,|S_V|}\right\}$ that includes the distinct colors of T_V, and the set $S_U = \left\{\boldsymbol{C}_{U,1}, \boldsymbol{C}_{U,2}, \ldots, \boldsymbol{C}_{U,|S_U|}\right\}$ that includes the distinct colors of T_U, where $|\bullet|$ stands for the set cardinality. Colors in S_V are transformed to simulate the dichromacy effect, $\boldsymbol{C}_{k,D} = f_D(\boldsymbol{C}_k)\ (k = 1, 2, \ldots, |S_V|)$. By appropriately choosing $\phi > 1$ (trial and error), if for some k it holds $\left\|\boldsymbol{C}_k - \boldsymbol{C}_{k,D}\right\| < \phi$ the colors $\boldsymbol{C}_k$ and $\boldsymbol{C}_{k,D}$ are similar, meaning that dichromats do not confuse the color $\boldsymbol{C}_k$. Therefore, this color must remain intact. All colors of S_V satisfying the above condition are transferred to the set S_U. This updating mechanism reads as

$$\forall \boldsymbol{C}_k \in S_V : \ \left\|\boldsymbol{C}_k - \boldsymbol{C}_{k,D}\right\| < \phi \ \rightarrow \ S_V = S_V - \{\boldsymbol{C}_k\} \wedge S_U = S_U \cup \{\boldsymbol{C}_k\}. \quad (1)$$

After the end of the updating process, colors belonging to the set S_U will remain intact, whereas the colors belonging to the set S_V will be appropriately modified to enhance their perception by the color blind.

Next, the fuzzy c-means is used to divide the elements of S_V in n_1 clusters with centers $\boldsymbol{V} = \{\boldsymbol{v}_1, \boldsymbol{v}_2, \ldots, \boldsymbol{v}_{n_1}\}$, and the elements of S_U in n_2 clusters with centers $\boldsymbol{U} = \{\boldsymbol{\upsilon}_1, \boldsymbol{\upsilon}_2, \ldots, \boldsymbol{\upsilon}_{n_2}\}$. The cluster centers are called *key colors*. The target is to obtain a recoloring set $\boldsymbol{V}_{rec} = \left\{\boldsymbol{v}_{rec,1}, \boldsymbol{v}_{rec,2} \ldots, \boldsymbol{v}_{rec,n_1}\right\}$ of the set $\boldsymbol{V}$.

The error vector between the key color $\boldsymbol{v}_i$ and its simulation $f_D(\boldsymbol{v}_i)$ is: $\boldsymbol{er}_i = \boldsymbol{v}_i - f_D(\boldsymbol{v}_i)\ (i = 1, 2, \ldots, n_1)$. Then, the recoloring process of $\boldsymbol{v}_i$ is [1, 18].

$$\boldsymbol{v}_{rec,i} = \boldsymbol{v}_i + \boldsymbol{M}_{D,i}\,\boldsymbol{er}_i \quad (2)$$

$$\text{with} \qquad \boldsymbol{M}_{D,i} = \begin{bmatrix} \alpha & \mu_{D,i,3} & 0 \\ \mu_{D,i,1} & \beta & 0 \\ \mu_{D,i,2} & \mu_{D,i,4} & 1 \end{bmatrix} \quad (3)$$

In the case of protanopia, $\alpha \in [-1, 0]$, $\beta = 1$, and $\mu_{D,i,3} = \mu_{D,i,4} = 0$ are prefixed, while $\mu_{D,i,1}$ and $\mu_{D,i,2}$ are adjustable positive parameters. In the case of deuteranopia,

$\alpha = 1, \beta \in [-1, 0]$ and $\mu_{D,i,1} = \mu_{D,i,2} = 0$ are prefixed, while $\mu_{D,i,3}$, $\mu_{D,i,4}$ are adjustable positive parameters. Considering protanopia, the implementation of (2) along with the respective matrix in (3) leads to a reduction of the Red in favor of G and B, obtaining less saturated red/oranges and more saturated greens, increasing the contrast and therefore, decreasing color confusion of a protanope viewer. In the case of deuteranopia, the above process leads to the reduction of green in favor of red and blue colors obtaining similar results. In both cases, the color confusion is alleviated.

Given two key colors $\boldsymbol{v}_i \in \boldsymbol{V}$ and $\boldsymbol{\upsilon}_i \in \boldsymbol{U}$, their distance is $\left\|\boldsymbol{v}_i - \boldsymbol{\upsilon}_j\right\|$. After transforming the key color $\boldsymbol{v}_i$ into $\boldsymbol{v}_{rec,i}$, the distance between $\boldsymbol{v}_{rec,i}$ and $\boldsymbol{\upsilon}_i$ as seen by a dichromat is $\left\|f_D(\boldsymbol{v}_{rec,i}) - f_D(\boldsymbol{\upsilon}_j)\right\|$. The objective is to keep the above distances as similar as possible so that the dichromat will be able to perceive the differences between colors in a similar way as the normal color vision viewer. Thus, summing over all pairs.

$$E_1 = \frac{1}{n_1 n_2} \sum_{i=1}^{n_1} \sum_{j=1}^{n_2} \left| \left\|\boldsymbol{v}_i - \boldsymbol{\upsilon}_j\right\| - \left\|f(\boldsymbol{v}_{rec,i}) - f(\boldsymbol{\upsilon}_j)\right\| \right| \tag{4}$$

Following the same approach for all color pairs in the set $\boldsymbol{V}$ we arrive at

$$E_2 = \frac{1}{n_1^2} \sum_{i=1}^{n_1} \sum_{j=1}^{n_1} \left| \left\|\boldsymbol{v}_i - \boldsymbol{v}_j\right\| - \left\|f(\boldsymbol{v}_{rec,i}) - f(\boldsymbol{v}_{rec,j})\right\| \right|. \tag{5}$$

It can be easily seen that minimizing E_1 and E_2 enhances the contrast between the objects identified by the semantic segmentation when compared each other and when compared with the rest of the image regions. To further preserve the naturalness the $\boldsymbol{v}_{rec,i}$ must be as close to $\boldsymbol{v}_i$ as possible. To do so, we use the next error function.

$$E_3 = \frac{1}{n_1} \sum_{i=1}^{n_1} \left\|\boldsymbol{v}_i - \boldsymbol{v}_{rec,i}\right\| \tag{6}$$

The overall objective function reads as

$$E = E_1 + E_2 + \gamma E_3 \tag{7}$$

where γ is a regularization factor that takes positive values and is used to obtain a counterbalance between the distinct parts of the function E.

The function E is optimized with respect to the parameters $\mu_{D,i,1}$, $\mu_{D,i,2}$ for protanopia, and $\mu_{D,i,3}$, $\mu_{D,i,4}$ for deuteranopia. In each case, the total number of adjusted parameters is $2n_1$. To perform the minimization, we employ the well-known differential evolution (DE) algorithm [13]. The DE comprises three evolving learning phases: the mutation, crossover and selection. There are two parameters that must be defined namely, the $F_{FR} \in (0, \ 1]$ that controls the rate at which the population evolves, and the $C_{FR} \in [0, \ 1]$ that controls the fraction of the parameter values copied from one generation to the next. A detailed description of DE is provided in [13].

The above procedure obtains the matrices $\boldsymbol{M}_{D,i}$ $(i = 1, 2, \ldots, n_1)$ that minimize the function E. Each matrix corresponds to one key color of the set $\boldsymbol{V}$. The recoloring process of the image pixels $\boldsymbol{p}_{ij}$ $(1 \le i \le N; \ 1 \le j \le K)$ is described next. If $\boldsymbol{p}_{ij} \in S_V$ then this pixel must be modified. The methodology of Vienot et al. [20] is applied to obtain the simulated color $f_D(\boldsymbol{p}_{ij})$ and calculate the corresponding error vector using Eq. (1): $\boldsymbol{er}_{ij} = \boldsymbol{p}_{ij} - f_D(\boldsymbol{p}_{ij})$. The closest key color to $\boldsymbol{p}_{ij}$ is denoted as $\boldsymbol{v}_{\ell_0}$ and defined as: $\left\|\boldsymbol{p}_{ij} - \boldsymbol{v}_{\ell_0}\right\| = \min_{1 \le \ell \le n_1} \left\{\left\|\boldsymbol{p}_{ij} - \boldsymbol{v}_{\ell}\right\|\right\}$, with $\boldsymbol{v}_{\ell_0} \in \boldsymbol{V}$. Then, the recoloring of $\boldsymbol{p}_{ij}$ is carried out in terms of Eq. (2).

$$\boldsymbol{p}_{rec,ij} = \boldsymbol{p}_{ij} + \boldsymbol{M}_{D,\ell_0}\,\boldsymbol{er}_{ij} \tag{8}$$

Finally, all pixels of the input image with colors belonging to the set S_V are appropriately recolored, while the rest are kept intact. The impact of this effect is that the number of elaborated pixels reduces and therefore, the naturalness of the recolored image increases because the number of modified pixels is kept to a minimum.

3 Simulation Experiments

In this section, six art paintings are used to perform several experiments for protanopia and deuteranopia. The paintings are presented in Fig. 3. The proposed method is compared to two recoloring algorithms. The first was developed by Huang et al. in [8] and concerns both protanopia and deuteranopia. The second was developed by Rani and Rajeev in [14] and concerns only the deuteranopia. The performance index to conduct the comparison is the naturalness index [9].

$$J = \frac{1}{NK}\sum_{i=1}^{N}\sum_{j=1}^{K}\left\|\boldsymbol{p}_{ij} - \boldsymbol{p}_{rec,ij}\right\| \tag{9}$$

For our experiments we set $\phi = 11$, meaning that all color combinations belonging to sphere with radius 11 are consider similar to the color located at the center of that sphere. An odd number is selected to achieve uniformity in R, G, and B axis. The numbers of key colors for the sets $\boldsymbol{V}$ and $\boldsymbol{U}$ are $n_1 = n_2 = 12$. Thus, in total there are 24 key color. Based on trial and error approach, in the case of protanopia we select $\alpha = -0.5$, and in the case of deuteranopia $\beta = -0.5$. The domain of values for the adjustable parameters $\mu_{D,i,1}$, $\mu_{D,i,2}$, $\mu_{D,i,3}$, and $\mu_{D,i,4}$ is the interval [0, 1].

Fig. 3. (a) Painting 1 (by Terence Clarke), (b) painting 2 (by Stratis Axiotis), (c) painting 3 (by Ektor Doukas), (d) painting 4 (by Raphael), (e) painting 5 (by William Redmore Bigg), and (f) painting 6 (by Angeliki Leousi-Karatza).

Fig. 4. Semantic segmentation results for the first three paintings of Fig. 3.

For the differential evolution the parameters are: $F_{FR} = 0.8$, $C_{FR} = 0.9$, the population size is equal to 50, and the maximum number of iterations $t_{\max} = 100$. As far as the parameter setting of the other two methods is concerned, it is the same as reported in the respective references.

The results of the transfer learning-based semantic segmentation for the first three paintings are illustrated in Fig. 4. It can be easily seen that the obtained object recognition is sufficiently accurate.

Fig. 5. Results on painting 3 (protanopia): (a) recolored (proposed method), (b) recolored as seen by a protanope (proposed method), (c) recolored (method of Huang et al. [8]), (d) recolored as seen by a protanope (method of Huang et al. [8]).

Fig. 6. Results on painting 4 (protanopia): (a) recolored (proposed method), (b) recolored as seen by a protanope (proposed method), (c) recolored (method of Huang et al. [8]), (d) recolored as seen by a protanope (method of Huang et al. [8]).

Fig. 7. Results on paintings 1 and 5 (deuteranopia): (a) and (b) recolored (proposed method), (c) and (d) recolored as seen by a deuteranope (proposed method), (e) and (f) recolored (method of Rani and Rajeev [14]), (g) and (h) recolored as seen by a deuteranope (method of Rani and Rajeev [14]).

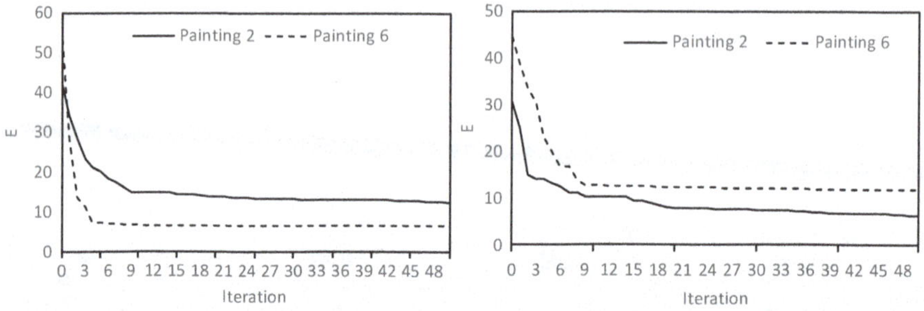

Fig. 8. Dynamic behavior of the objective function E during the application of the DE algorithm for the paintings 2 and 6 in the cases of protanopia (left figure) and deuteranopia (right figure).

Figures 5 and 6 visualize the recolored and the corresponding protanope simulations for paintings 3 and 4, as they are obtained by the proposed algorithm and the method in [8]. Note that the recolored paintings obtained by our approach use colors that are more similar to the respective colors of the original paintings reported in Fig. 3.

The same visual characteristics are observed in Fig. 7, where the proposed method is compared with the recoloring algorithm developed in [14], regarding the case of deuteranopia for the paintings 1 and 5.

Figure 8 depicts the minimization of E as a function of the iteration during the DE implementation for the paintings 2 and 6.

Table 1. Values of the naturalness index (J) obtained by the three algorithms for the six images regarding the cases of protanopia and deuteranopia (best values for each case are in bold fonts).

Paintings	Protanopia		Deuteranopia		
	Proposed	Huang et al. [8]	Proposed	Huang et al. [8]	Rani and Rajeev [14]
1	**3.7168**	12.3482	**8.7589**	13.8699	87.8429
2	**9.0473**	9.8727	**5.0898**	5.1581	25.8787
3	**7.4945**	20.0707	5.8445	**2.1712**	77.3267
4	**5.5553**	23.8336	9.3129	**3.3042**	83.9168
5	**3.9349**	14.6587	**18.5893**	63.8226	90.4925
6	**1.9294**	22.8655	**8.0602**	9.3072	89.9749

Quantitative comparative results in terms of the naturalness index given in Eq. (9) are reported in Table 1. The results of this table are quite convincing since, apart from two experimental cases in deuteranopia (paintings 3 and 4), the proposed algorithm significantly outperforms the other two algorithms. The main conclusion extracted from this table is that the naturalness index is sufficiently minimized by the proposed recoloring approach, yielding colors that are not curious for a normal color vision viewer, while maintaining an aesthetic result for the dichromat viewers, also. This fact is supported by both the visual and quantitative results.

4 Conclusions

The problem investigated in this paper was the recoloring of digitized art paintings in order to improve the color perception of dichromat viewers that suffer from protanopia or deuteranopia. Initially, a transfer learning based semantic segmentation mechanism was applied to extract meaningful color information. The colors of the objects recognized by the deep network were simulated to match the way a dichromat perceives them. Based on the above information, the pixels of the input image were divided into two sets. The first set included colors that must be recolored, whereas the second one included colors that remained intact. This process reduces the number of modified pixels yielding a recolored image that retains its natural appearance. Then, a specially designed objective function was minimized using differential evolution. The optimization parameters are elements of a matrix transformation involved in the recoloring process. The structure of the objective function favored the selection of colors that keep similar the color differences in the original and the dichromat simulation of the recolored image. The method was tested in several experimental cases. The simulation results indicated that the proposed methodology can naturally modify the original colors enhancing the perception of color blind viewers.

Future efforts could extend the present algorithm by developing more sophisticated learning approaches and effective color transformations in order to enhance the protanopia, deuteranopia, and tritanopia effects and the color adaptation procedures, as well.

Acknowledgments. This research is co-financed by Greece and the European Union (European Social Fund-ESF) through the Operational Programme "Human Resources Development, Education and Lifelong Learning 2014–2020" in the context of the project "Color perception enhancement in digitized art paintings for people with Color Vision Deficiency" (MIS 5047115).

References

1. Doliotis, P., Tsekouras, G.E., Anagnostopoulos, C.N., Athitsos, V.: Intelligent modification of colors in digitized paintings for enhancing the visual perception of color-blind viewers. In: The Proceedings of the 5th International Conference on Artificial Intelligence Applications and Innovations, pp. 293–301 (2009)
2. Girshick, R.: Fast R-CNN. In: The Proceedings of the 2015 IEEE International Conference on Computer Vision (ICCV), Santiago, Chile, pp. 1440–1448 (2015)
3. Girshick, R., Donahue, J., Darrell, T., Malik, J.: Rich feature hierarchies for accurate object detection and semantic segmentation. In: The Proceedings of the 2014 IEEE Conference on Computer Vision and Pattern Recognition (CVPR), Columbus, OH, USA, pp. 580–587 (2014)
4. Gonthier, N., Gousseau, Y., Ladja, S., Bonfait, O.: Weakly supervised object detection in artworks. In: The Proceedings of the 2018 European Conference on Computer Vision (ECCV 2018), Munich, Germany, pp. 692–709 (2018)
5. Hassan, M.F., Paramesran, R.: Naturalness preserving image recoloring method for people with red–green deficiency. Sig. Process. Image Commun. **57**, 126–133 (2017)
6. He, K., Zhang, X., Ren, S., Sun, J.: Deep residual learning for image recognition. In: The Proceedings of the 2016 IEEE Conference on Computer Vision and Pattern Recognition (CVPR), Las Vegas, NV, USA, pp. 770–778 (2016)
7. Ho, G.W.: Color, vision, and art: teaching, learning, and making art with color blind awareness. M.Sc. thesis, University of Florida (2014)
8. Huang, J-B., Chen, C.S., Jen, T.S., Wang, S.J.: Image recolorization for the color blind. In: The Proceedings of the 2009 IEEE International Conference on Acoustics, Speech and Signal Processing (ICASSP 2009), pp. 1161–1164 (2009)
9. Huang, J.-B., Tseng, Y.-C., Wu, S.-I., Wang, S.-J.: Information preserving color transformation for protanopia and deuteranopia. IEEE Signal Process. Lett. **14**(10), 711–714 (2007)
10. Johnston-Feller, R.: Color Science in the Examination Museum Objects. The Getty Conservation Institute, Los Angeles (2001)
11. Krizhevsky, A., Sutskever, I., Hinton, G.E.: ImageNet classification with deep convolutional neural networks. Commun. ACM **60**(6), 84–90 (2017)
12. Marmor, M.F., Lanthony, P.: The dilemma of color deficiency and art. Surv. Ophthalmol. **45** (5), 407–414 (2001)
13. Price, K.V., Storn, R.M., Lampinen, J.A.: Differential Evolution: A Practical Approach to Global Optimization. Springer, Berlin (2005)

14. Rani, S.S., Rajeev, R.: Colour transformation for deuteranopic viewers. Int. J. Control Theor. Appl. **9**(10), 4527–4535 (2016)
15. Ren, S., He, K., Girshick, R., Sun, J.: Faster R-CNN: towards real-time object detection with region proposal networks. IEEE Trans. Pattern Anal. Mach. Intell. **39**(6), 1137–1149 (2017)
16. Ribeiro, M., Gomes, A.J.P.: Recoloring algorithms for colorblind people: a survey. ACM Comput. Surv. **52**(4), 72:1–72:37 (2019)
17. Stockman, A., Sharpe, L.T.: The spectral sensitivities of the middle- and long-wavelength-sensitive cones derived from measurements in observers of known genotype. Vision. Res. **40**, 1711–1737 (2000)
18. Tsekouras, G.E., Chatzistamatis, S., Anagnostopoulos, C.N., Makris, D.: Color adaptation for protanopia using differential evolution-based fuzzy clustering: a case study in digitized paintings. In: The Poceedings of the 2018 IEEE Conference on Evolving and Adaptive Intelligent Systems (EAIS 2018), Rhodes Island, Greece (2018)
19. Uijlings, J.R.R., van de Sande, K.E.A., Gevers, T., Smeulders, A.W.M.: Selective search for object recognition. Int. J. Comput. Vision **104**, 154–171 (2013)
20. Vienot, F., Brettel, H., Mollon, J.: Digital video colourmaps for checking the legibility of displays by dichromats. Color Res. Appl. **24**(4), 243–252 (1999)
21. Yin, R., Monson, E., Honig, E., Daubechies, I., Maggioni, M.: Object recognition in art drawings: transfer of a neural network. In: The Proceedings of the 2016 IEEE International Conference on Acoustics, Speech and Signal Processing (ICASSP), Shanghai, China (2016)

Large-Scale Geospatial Data Analysis: Geographic Object-Based Scene Classification in Remote Sensing Images by GIS and Deep Residual Learning

Konstantinos Demertzis[1], Lazaros Iliadis[1(✉)], and Elias Pimenidis[2]

[1] School of Engineering, Democritus University of Thrace, 67100 Xanthi, PC, Greece
kdemertz@fmenr.duth.gr, liliadis@civil.duth.gr
[2] University of the West of England Bristol, FET-Computer Science and Creative Technologies, Bristol, UK
Elias.Pimenidis@uwe.ac.uk

Abstract. Recent advances in optical sensor technologies and Geoinformatics, can support very large scale high definition, used for multispectral and panchromatic images. This capability allows the use of remote sensing for the observation of complex earth ecosystems. Application areas include, sustainability of biodiversity, precision agriculture, land, crops and parasites management. Moreover, it supports advanced quantitative studies of biophysical and biogeochemical cycles, in costal or inland waters. The requirement for precise and effective scene classification, can significantly contribute towards the development of new types of decision support systems. This offers considerable advantages to business, science and engineering. This research paper proposes a novel and effective approach based on geographic *object-based* scene classification in remote sensing images. More specifically, it introduces an important upgrade of the well-known *Residual Neural Network* (*ResNet*) architecture. The omission of some layers in the early stages of training, achieves an effective simplification of the network, by eliminating the "*Vanishing Gradient Problem*" (VGP) which causes efficiency limitations in other "*Deep Learning*" (DEL) architectures. The use of the *Softmax* activation function instead of the *Sigmoid* in the last layer, is the most important innovation of the proposed system. The *ResNet* has been trained using the novel *AdaBound* algorithm that employs dynamic bounds on the employed learning rates. The result is the employment of a smooth transition of the stochastic gradient descent, tackling the noise dispersed points of misclassification with great precision. This is something that other spectral classification methods cannot handle. The proposed algorithm was successfully tested, in scene identification from remote sensing images. This confirms that it could be further used in advanced level processes for *Large-Scale Geospatial Data Analysis*, such as cross-border classification, recognition and monitoring of certain patterns and multi-sensor data fusion.

Keywords: Geospatial Data · GIS · Remote Sensing · Scene Classification · Residual Neural Networks · Vanishing Gradient Problem

L. Iliadis et al. (Eds.): EANN 2020, INNS 2, pp. 274–291, 2020.
https://doi.org/10.1007/978-3-030-48791-1_21

1 Introduction

1.1 Scene Classification and Machine Learning

The rapid advances of digital and communication technologies combined with recent developments in optical sensor technologies have resulted in major changes in the way that we monitor land. This is due to the availability of many different systems that offer high spectral image analysis of the earth's surface (e.g. Multispectral, Hyperspectral [1], Panchromatic and Synthetic Aperture Radar) [2]. Despite such advances, the effective comprehension of the semantic content of such images is still a major challenge and a significant research topic. More specifically, scene classification, aims to achieve automatic semantic tagging of each remote sensing object. This process is content-based and it is one of the most critical problems in *Geoinformatics*. It is very important in a wide range of applications such as, the design and the management of land resources, the applications of precision agriculture, the monitoring of complex ecosystems, the sustainable management of biodiversity and the recording of nature destruction and traffic control.

The past few decades have seen the development of various methods of *Scene Classification* (SCC) based on remote sensing. The early SCC methods were primarily based on low level features or heuristics, which focused on colour, texture, and shape. It is worth mentioning Color Histogram (CH), Histogram of Oriented Gradients (HOG), Local Binary Pattern (LBP), Scale Invariant Feature Transform (SIFT) and Gabor filters Grey Level Co-occurrence Matrix (GLCM) [3]. These methods perform well with images of uniform texture, but their ability to identify more complex scenes is poor. The design of features by humans, affects the effectiveness of the above models considerably. On the other hand, methods based on middle level features, can produce a holistic representation of a scene, which is developed through local visual features such as SIFT, CH, or LBP of local image patches. The deployment of a system capable to develop middle level features, starts with the extraction of the local features of the image, and continues with the codification that can lead to an intermediate representation. The most well-known and widely used model for classifying images of middle level is the *Bag of Visual Words* (BoVW) due to its simplicity and effectiveness [5]. Despite having evolved through considerable improvements in the effectiveness of classification, the techniques based on BoVW have not seen further development and utilisation due to their limitations in representing scenes of high resolution.

Deep Learning (DL) is a branch of computational intelligence that utilises a series of algorithms in attempting to model data of high levels of abstraction. This is achieved by using a multilevel processing architecture, based on consecutive linear and non-linear transformations. It is part of the group of learning techniques that exploit data representations to explain and extract optimal results. In the case of image classification they can produce spatial information such as, edges, shapes and relevant chromatic regions.

Deep Learning Architectures use distributed representation whose main hypothesis is that the observed data are extracted from the interaction of factors grouped in levels.

DL adds the assumption that these levels of factors are either the result of abstraction or synthesis of various scales, depending on their volume and size. Such architectures explore the idea of a hierarchical decomposition of the factors from a high to a low level, with the more abstract concepts drawn from the lowest levels. Thus, they are hierarchically distributed according to levels of abstraction, creating the conditions for selecting the most suitable features of the learning process.

Using the above processes, DL architectures and more specifically Deep Neural Networks (DNN), have achieved impressive performance in many remote sensing applications such as, the accurate representation of features in image classification, the identification of objects and their semantic segmentation. DNN, simulate processes of human vision. Multiple operational levels and intermediate representations are created from image capture in the human eye's retina caused by the reaction of muscles. Such process relies in the transformation of every intermediary unit of input representation into a representation at a higher level. The features at higher level are more generic and less changeable, while those of lower level support the classification of inputs. Their effectiveness can be interpreted based on the *Universal Approximation Theorem* which refers to the potential of a neural structure to approximate continuous functions and the Probabilistic Inference which assumes the activation of non-linearity as a cumulative distribution function [5].

In DNN, every hidden layer trains a discreet group of features resulting from the output of the previous layer. The functioning of such a network allows for the analysis of the most complex features as they recompose and decompose from layer to layer. Such a feature is called a hierarchy. As the decomposition of information increases the complexity of the system hierarchically, it offers the ability to process high level data through non-linear functions. Such networks are suitable for the discovery of non-structured data, for revealing latent structures in unlabelled data and the handling of other problematic structures. Even miniscule similarities or anomalies that these might entail can be identified.

Despite all their important functionality and their advantages, the gradients of the loss function approximate zero, when layers that use activation functions are added neural network architectures. This may cause considerable difficulties in the training of the network, almost to the point of not being capable of training at all, depending on the number of hidden layers that are added. The above is a major vulnerability of deep learning neural networks, called *Vanishing Gradient Problem* (VGP) [6].

2 Theoretical Background

2.1 Facing the Vanishing Gradient Problem

In *Machine Learning* the VGP problem pauses a problem in the constriction of neural networks with gradient-based learning methods and backpropagation. In such methods, each of the weights receives, at each iteration, an analogue update with the partial derivative of the error function in relation to the weight it currently uses. In some cases though, the gradient is insignificantly low effectively preventing the weight to change its value. In the worst case, this could prevent the neural network in completing its training [7]. The following Eq. 1, corresponds to a sigmoid activation function (SGA).

$$S(a) = \frac{1}{1+e^{-a}} \tag{1}$$

It compresses and projects a large range of inputs to a relative small vector space e.g. [0, 1]. Thus, a large change of the input to the sigmoid activation function, corresponds to a small change in its output. Thus the partial derivative becomes extremely small. It is worth noting that when the inputs to the SGA increase, i.e. when |x| increases or decreases, the partial derivative moves towards zero. The above properties of the sigmoid activation function are ideal for the representation of probabilities and classification procedures. However, both the Sigmoid and the Tangent Hyperbolic (TanH) activation functions, have decreased in popularity recently due to the VGP problem [7].

Let us assume a neural network (NN) with 4 hidden layers with a single neuron at each layer. In the above NN the activity of each neuron depends on the activity of that in the previous layer. More specifically the activity of each neuron depends on that of the previous, multiplied by a given weight. This value is propagated via an activation function (the input is a case of special exemption from the above rule). The margin of error J at the end of the network shows the total error of the system. The backpropagation process is executed to modify the weights via *Gradient Descent* in such a way as to minimise the value of J. To calculate the first weight derivative, the chain rule to backpropagate is used as follows:

$$\frac{\partial error}{\partial w_1} = \frac{\partial error}{\partial output} * \frac{\partial output}{\partial hidden_2} * \frac{\partial hidden_2}{\partial hidden_1} * \frac{\partial hidden_1}{\partial w_1} \tag{2}$$

Subsequently the derivatives are used repetitively until the lowest point has been reached using gradient descent following a specific Learning Rate. The first derivative is used for the activation of the second hidden layer as it is given below. This is performed using the sigmoid activation function (from the output to $hidden_2$) based on the equations below:

$$z_1 = hidden_2 * w_3 \tag{3}$$

$$\frac{\partial output}{\partial hidden_2} = \frac{\partial Sigmoid(z_1)}{\partial z_1} w_3 \tag{4}$$

Similarly the second derivative is used for the propagation from the $hidden_2$ to the $hidden_1$ layer:

$$z_2 = hidden_1 * w_2 \tag{5}$$

$$\frac{\partial hidden_2}{\partial hidden_1} = \frac{\partial Sigmoid(z_2)}{\partial z_2} w_2 \tag{6}$$

In both cases the propagated values contain the derivatives of the sigmoid activation function. This can collectively be expressed as follows:

$$\frac{\partial output}{\partial hidden_2}\frac{\partial hidden_2}{\partial hidden_1} = \frac{\partial Sigmoid(z_1)}{\partial z_1} w_3 * \frac{\partial Sigmoid(z_2)}{\partial z_2} w_2 \tag{7}$$

Both the values of the Sigmoid (z_1) and Sigmoid (z_2), are less than 0.25. The weights w_1, w_2, w_3, are initialised by the Gauss method so that they can have a mean value equal to 0 and standard deviation equal to 1. Therefore every $\|w_i\|$ is smaller than 1. Thus for the calculation of the derivatives we multiply numbers that are less than 1 and 0.25. Given that two numbers in the range [0, 1] are multiplied, the result will always be a smaller value, e.g. 1/3*1/3 = 1/9. Thus, multiplying such small numbers many times, results in a gradient that is so small that will force the network to stop the learning process. The various terms used in such a multiplication is shown in (8) below:

$$\frac{\partial output}{\partial hidden_2}\frac{\partial hidden_2}{\partial hidden_1} = \overset{<1/4}{\frac{\partial Sigmoid(z_1)}{\partial z_1}} \overset{<1}{w_3} * \overset{<1/4}{\frac{\partial Sigmoid(z_2)}{\partial z_2}} \overset{<1}{w_2} \tag{8}$$

In networks with a small number of layers, employing Sigmoid activation functions is not considered a major problem, whereas in multi-layered architectures it could cause major disruption to the normal and effective training of the network.

Totally, four types of solutions for the VGP problem have been proposed in the literature [8]:

a) Methods that do not use gradients such as *Simulated Annealing*, *Multi-Grid Random Search* and *Random Weight Guessing*. Generally the Global Search Methods (GSM) work well in the case of simple problems with long term dependencies. Simple problems can be resolved with networks that use only a few parameters and do not require complex calculations. Such solutions are characterized as *Flat Minima* situations where the network is attempting to solve the problem using a simple architecture. The weights' interconnection levels, are included in a very specific vector space with the error being almost constant. This can only cover a small range of problems, therefore the use of *Flat Minima* is not recommended as a general solution.
b) Methods that enforce higher gradients. Higher gradients can be reinforced by using optimization methods. These are considered time consuming and computationally costly. Furthermore, they appear to have problems in learning to store accurate information, related to the real value of classification.
c) Methods that operate on higher levels. They employ the *Rectified Linear Unit* (ReLU) activation functions that do not yield small derivatives:

$$ReLU(x) = max(0, x) \quad \text{or} \quad ReLU(x) = \begin{cases} 0\, if\, x < 0 \\ x\, if\, x \geq 0 \end{cases} \tag{9}$$

In some cases though, the ReLU neurons can be forced to situations in which they become inactive for all inputs. In such cases, none of the gradients backpropagate via the neuron, resulting in the neuron being stuck in an interminable inactive condition and effectively dies. This category also includes methods that attempt to solve the problem by following an intuitive process, via the use of high level parameters, such as metadata. These cases also fail in yielding solid and generalizing solutions.

d) Methods that use special architectures. The most important solutions for the VGP problem have been proposed via the use of ResNets [9]. This addresses the stagnation of multiple layer levels even when the size of the network exceeds the 150 layers.

3 The Employed Residual Neural Networks

ResNets, are brain inspired. They are utilizing "skip connections-shortcuts", in order to jump over some layers. They operate similarly to the Convolutional Neural Networks (CNN), however in ResNets the input is provided sequentially at the exit of the hidden layers, if they are in a certain distance from each other.

In the majority of neural networks, one layer feeds the very next one. In a ResNet that consists of several blocks, every single layer feeds the successive one, but at the same time it provides input to a layer which is located 2 maybe 3 positions far (it skips the order as in Fig. 1). Many linearly interconnected Residual Blocks (REB) constitute a Residual Neural Network. The values of REB parameters are determined based on the network's structure. They aim at modelling a high level of abstraction of the incoming samples, using multiple stacked non-linear transformations. Their architecture assumes the following characteristics, namely: *Local Receptive Fields* (LRF), *Weight Sharing* (WS), *Spatial Subsampling* (SpaSu), *Feature Combination* (FC) [10].

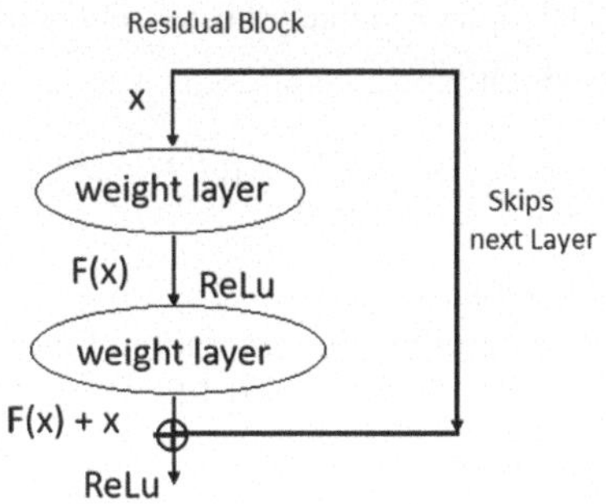

Fig. 1. Image of a Residual Block. Several of them are forming a Residual Neural Net

Essentially, ResNet architecture consists of a set of levels that are characterized by different functionality. They can be configured through their parameters and hyperparameters. The purpose is to convert an input volume into an output one, through a differential function. Interconnection based on the *Residual Block* parameter, determines the overall architecture of the network. The levels of neurons commonly used fall into the following basic categories, namely: *Convolutional Layers* (CL), *Fully Connected Layer* (FCL), *Pooling Layers* (PL), *Dropout Layer* (DRL), *Feed-Forward Layer* (FFL). After any level architecture and sequence, all of the top-level neurons are input to an FFL array or any similar forward-current array [10]. The *Loss Function* (LF) aims to attribute the classification error, which is the difference between the prediction output and the known desired output during the training process.

As noted above, the substantial difference between CNNs and ResNets is the sequential addition of the input to the output of the hidden layers, provided that the hidden layers are at certain distance apart. The Residual Block consists of a set of CLs defined by architectural standardization (usually 2). The input vector x of the Block is stored in a local buffer and after passing all levels of the Block, it is added to the output of F(x) + x. The increased output is presented as input to the next *Residual Block* and so on [10]. In the case of single skips we can use the notation l-2 to l. More specifically, let $W^{l-1,l}$ be the weight vector for connection weights from layer l-1 to l and let $W^{l-2,l}$ be the weight vector for weights from layer l-2 to l. Thus, the forward propagation through the use of the activation function would be the following [9]:

$$a^l = g\left(W^{l-1,l} \cdot a^{l-1} + \beta^l + W^{l-2,l} \cdot a^{l-2}\right) = g\left(Z^l + W^{l-2,l} \cdot a^{l-2}\right) \quad (10)$$

Where, a^l is the output of neurons in layer *l*, *g* is the activation function for layer *l*, $W^{l-1,l}$ is the weight matrix for neurons between layer *l-1* and *l*. Also, $W^{l-2,l}$ is the weight matrix for neurons between layer *l-2* to *l* and

$$Z^l = W^{l-1,l} \cdot a^{l-1} + \beta^l. \quad (11)$$

ResNets, are inspired by the function of pyramidal cells in the cerebral cortex of the brain, where forward skips take place in many layers. This forward propagation process is expressed by the following equation:

$$a^l = g\left(Z^l + \sum\nolimits_{k=2}^{K} W^{l-k,l} \cdot a^{l-k}\right) \quad (12)$$

where k-1 is the number of skips.

In backward propagation through the activation function, the *Normal Path* is described by Eq. 13 and the *Skip Paths* by Eq. 14:

$$\Delta w^{l-1,l} = -\eta \frac{\partial E^l}{\partial w^{l-1,l}} = -\eta \alpha^{l-1} \cdot \delta^l \quad (13)$$

$$\Delta w^{l-2,l} = -\eta \frac{\partial E^l}{\partial w^{l-2,l}} = -\eta \alpha^{l-2} \cdot \delta^l \quad (14)$$

Where η is the learning rate, δ^l is the error signal of neurons at layer l and α^l is the activation of neurons at layer l. For the case of a ResNet using forward propagation, the above equations are transformed as follows:

$$\Delta w^{l-k,l} = -\eta \frac{\partial E^l}{\partial w^{l-k,l}} = -\eta \alpha^{l-k} \cdot \delta^l \tag{15}$$

This residual connection does not go through activation functions that "squash" the derivatives, resulting in a higher overall derivative of the block.

4 Literature Review

Inspired by the success of deep learning in the field of computer vision, several related studies have been conducted suggesting various DL architectures for the analysis of ultrasonic data, which have admittedly provided new impetus to this field. The authors of [11] use a hybrid method which combines stacked *Autoencoder*, *Principle Component Analysis* (PCA), and *Logistic Regression* to perform hyperspectral data classification. Tao et al. [12] use a sparse stacked *Autoencoder* to efficiently represent features from unmarked spatial data, and then learned features are fed into a linear SVM for hyperspectral data classification. Various 1D [13] and 2D [14] CNN architectures have been proposed from time to time to encode spectral and spatial information. The latest and most sophisticated proposal concerns 3D CNN [15] in which the third dimension refers to the time axis resulting in a spatio-temporal architecture in the spectral classification. In 3D CNNs, the convolution functions are spatial-spectral, whereas in 2D CNNs, they are spatial only. Compared to 1D and 2D CNNs, 3D CNNs can better spectral information thanks to 3D convolution functions.

Trying to exploit the particularities and advantages of unsupervised learning, the authors [16] propose an unsupervised CNN architecture to perform learning of spectral-spatial features. This is performed by using sparse learning to estimate the network's weights in a greedy layer-wise fashion instead of an end-to-end approach. The algorithm is rooted on sparse representations and enforces both population and lifetime sparsity of the extracted features, simultaneously. They successfully illustrate the expressive power of the extracted representations in several scenarios: classification of aerial scenes, as well as land-use classification in very high resolution or land-cover classification from multi- and hyperspectral images [4].

The proposed algorithm clearly outperforms PCA. The results have shown that single-layer CNNs can extract powerful discriminative features only when the receptive field accounts for neighboring pixels. They are preferred when the classification requires high resolution and detailed results. However, Deep architectures significantly outperform single-layer variants, capturing increasing levels of abstraction and complexity throughout the feature hierarchy.

In [17] authors propose a Deep Recurrent Neural Network model with a new activation function (*parametric rectified Tanh – PRetanh*). The proposed activation function makes it possible to use fairly high learning rates without the risk of divergence during the training procedure. Moreover, a modified gated recurrent unit, which uses PRetanh for hidden representation, is adopted to construct the recurrent layer in the network to efficiently process hyperspectral data and reduce the total number of parameters.

All of the above architectures have major malfunctions and are hampered by the VGP problem, which generally disrupts deep approaches. He et al. [9] tried to overcome this problem by employing the idea of very deep networks by proposing the 152-layers ResNet, which allowed CNNs to grow much deeper without suffering the problem of vanishing/exploding gradients. The authors provide an in-depth analysis about the degradation problem, i.e., simply increasing the number of layers in plain networks results in higher training and test errors.

It is suggested that it is easier to optimize the residual mapping in the ResNet than to optimize the original, unreferenced mapping in the conventional CNNs. In essence, instead of learning a direct map from low-quality inputs to high-quality outputs, the CNN is tasked with learning the residual, i.e., the difference between the low and high-quality signals, which typically represents missing high-frequency information, at least for the case of super-resolution. To allow networks to capture and extract features from multiple scale, skip connections between different layers have also been considered and are now part of state-of-the-art approaches.

The authors of [18], are proposing a novel network architecture, which is a fully Convolutional/Deconvolutional network, for unsupervised spectral–spatial feature learning of hyperspectral images, which is able to be trained in an end-to-end manner. Specifically, the proposed architecture, is based on the so-called *encoder–decoder* paradigm. The input 3-D hyperspectral patch is first transformed into a typically lower dimensional space via a convolutional sub-network (encoder). Then it is expanded to reproduce the initial data by a *de-convolutional sub-network* (decoder).

However, during the experiments, we have found out, that such a network is not easy to be optimized. Although the proposed network has not been explicitly designed for the task of object detection, we have observed that the target object can be localized by the activated or suppressed pixels in some specific learned feature maps of the first residual block. This makes it possible to achieve the unsupervised object detection in hyperspectral images. Experimental results also demonstrate that the features learned by the proposed unsupervised network can be used for the hyperspectral image classification task, and the obtained classification results are competitive compared with the other supervised approaches.

5 The Introduced Methodology

The methodology that is introduced by this research paper, is based on the Convolutional/Deconvolutional (CN/DC) Network architecture that has been used by Mou et al. [18]. The above authors have proposed a fully CN/DC network approach, in which the desired output is the input data itself. Specifically, the introduced model, consists of two parts as its name typically states, namely the Convolutional and Deconvolutional subsystem. The first subsystem corresponds to an encoder that transforms the input characteristics xi into an abstract representation of intermediate features hi.

The corresponding Deconvolutional subset, plays the role of the decoder that reproduces in the original xi input data, the encrypted, intermediate hi features. Essentially the CN/DC network with Residual Learning is a modular network architecture that stacks residual blocks. Similar to Convolutional blocks, a Residual block consists of several Convolutional layers that have the same feature map size and the same number of filters. Their function performs the following calculation.

$$\phi_n = g(\varphi_n) + F(\varphi_n; \Theta_n) \tag{16}$$

$$\varphi_{n+1} = f(\phi_n) \tag{17}$$

Where φ_n refers to feature maps, Θ_n to a collection of weights associated with residual block, F is a residual function and f is the activation function. The corresponding function g, is fixed to an identity mapping:

$$g(\varphi_n) = \varphi_n \tag{18}$$

If *f* is a linear activation function and $\varphi_{(n+1)} = \varphi_n$, the output for the nth residual block is calculated by Eqs. (16) and (17) so that:

$$\varphi_{n+1} = \varphi_n + F(\varphi_n; \Theta_n) \tag{19}$$

The following Eq. 20 is recursively produced:

$$\varphi_{n+2} = \varphi_{n+1} + F(\varphi_{n+1}; \Theta_{n+1}) = \varphi_n + F(\varphi_n; \Theta_n) + F(\varphi_{n+1}; \Theta_{n+1}) \tag{20}$$

The recurrence formula below, is obtained for any shallower block *n* and any deeper block *L*.

$$\varphi_L = \varphi_n + \sum\nolimits_{i-n}^{L-1} F(\varphi_i; \Theta_i) \tag{21}$$

The way residual learning helps in the effective training of the deep network in question, is found in the rules of backpropagation, where E stands for the loss function:

$$\frac{\partial E}{\partial \varphi_n} = \frac{\partial E}{\partial \varphi_L}\frac{\partial \varphi_L}{\partial \varphi_n} = \frac{\partial E}{\partial \varphi_L}\left(1 + \frac{\partial}{\partial \varphi_n}\sum\nolimits_{i=1}^{L-1} F(\varphi_i; \Theta_i)\right) \tag{22}$$

In this way, the classification information of a layer in the network does not disappear even when the trainable weights are arbitrarily small, which is the key to make the training in the deep network possible. Also, in order to be able to successfully complete the processes performed by the Convolutional/Deconvolutional subsystems, the need for a pooling layer is imperative. However, the pooling layer leads to a reduced resolution of feature maps. This recreates the original input data to Deconvolutional, through an Unpooling process, in order to separate the feature maps, that is, to increase their spatial range, as opposed to the concentration applied by the Convolutional web.

It should be noted that using *Max-Pooling* indices the system is able to record the position of the maximum value in each local concentration area while concentrating in the Convolutional sub-net. Recently, an advanced version of the *max* and *argmax* functions was presented [19]. It can receive not only the maximum value in the field of indicators of a maximum concentration layer, but the corresponding index of this value as well [19]. Specifically, these two functions can be calculated as follows:

$$\mu = \sum\nolimits_{v} z(i,j) \frac{exp(az(i,j))}{\sum\nolimits_{v} exp(az(i,j))} \approx max_{v} z(i,j) \tag{23}$$

$$\mu = \sum\nolimits_{v} [i,j]^{T} \frac{exp(az(i,j))}{\sum\nolimits_{v} exp(az(i,j))} \approx argmax_{v} z(i,j) \tag{24}$$

It is a fact, that with the use of the *max* and *argmax* functions, the *max-poling* indices can be obtained in any pooling layer. Then, by performing interpolation in the *Unpooling* layers of the *Deconvolutional* sub-network, the interconnected values which are transferred by the *max-pooling* indices can be successfully handled. The use of *max-pooling* indices allows for a more accurate display of location information and allows feature maps to record detailed information about input features.

6 The Geographic Object-Based Scene Classification Algorithm

This research paper suggests an important modification that upgrades the ResNet architecture discussed above, which employs the Softmax activation function, instead of the Sigmoid at its last level. According to the introduced novel approach, the fully Residual Network is trained using the novel AdaBound algorithm that employs dynamic bounds on their learning rates. It achieves a smooth transition to the stochastic Gradient Descent, which accurately addresses the noisy scattered misspellings that other spectral classification methods cannot handle. As it has already been said, the following Softmax activation function which maps the non-normalized output of a neural network to a probability distribution over predicted output classes, was used instead of the Sigmoid, in the last CL [10]:

$$\sigma(z)_i = \frac{e^{z_i}}{\sum_{j=1}^{k} e^{z_j}}, \quad i = 1, \ldots, k \quad z = (z_1, \ldots, z_k) \in R^k \tag{25}$$

Where, zj is every element of the input vector z, $\sigma(z)$ is the output vector and the sum of its components $\sigma(z)_i$ is equal to 1.

The choice of the *Softmax* was based on the fact that it performs better on multi-classification problems, like the one under consideration. On the other hand, the *Sigmoid* is suitable on binary classification tasks. In the case of *Softmax*, the sum of probabilities is equal to 1 whereas in Sigmoid it does not have to be equal to 1. Finally for the *Softmax*, the highest value has the highest probability, whereas in the *Sigmoid*, the highest value has a high probability but not the highest. The fully residual network was trained using the novel *AdaBound* algorithm [20] that employs dynamic bounds on their learning rates. It achieves a smooth transition to stochastic gradient descent. The following algorithm 1, (in the form of pseudocode) presents the *AdaBound* function [20]:

Algorithm 1. AdaBound

Input: $x_1 \in F$, initial step size $\alpha, \{\beta_{1t}\}_{t=1}^{T}, \beta_2$ lower bound function η_l, upper bound function η_u

1: Set $m_0 = 0, u_0 = 0$
2: **for** $t = 1$ **to T do**
3: $g_t = \nabla f_t(x_t)$
4: $m_t = \beta_{1t} m_{t-1} + (1 - \beta_{1t}) g_t$
5: $u_t = \beta_2 u_{t-1} + (1 - \beta_2) g_t^2$ and $V_t = diag(u_t)$
6: $\hat{\eta}_t = Clip\left(\frac{a}{\sqrt{V_t}}, \eta_l(t), \eta_u(t)\right)$ and $\eta_t = \frac{\hat{\eta}_t}{\sqrt{t}}$
7: $x_{t+1} = \prod_{f, diag(\eta_t^{-1})}(x_t - \eta_t \cdot m_t)$
8: **end for**

Compared with other approaches, the *AdaBound* method has two advantages. First, there exists a fixed turning point to distinguish, in the simple ADAM algorithm and the SGD is uncertain. So the *Adabound* addresses this problem with a continuous transforming procedure rather than a "hard" switch. Second, the *AdaBound* introduces an extra hyperparameter to decide the switching time, which is not very easy to fine-tune. In general, the use of the *AdaBound* algorithm has a high convergence speed compared to stochastic gradient descent models and it exceeds the poor generalization ability of adaptive approaches. Moreover, it has dynamic limits on the learning rate, in order to achieve the highest accuracy for the dataset under consideration [20].

7 The Data Experiments and Results

The dataset used in this research, includes images taken from the Reflective Optics System Imaging Spectrometer (ROSIS) covering the Engineering School at the University of Pavia [21]. The available training samples belong to nine categories that are mainly related to land cover items. Each image is 610 × 340 pixels with a resolution of 1.3 m per pixel. Ultrasound imaging consists of 115 spectral channels ranging from 430 to 860 nm of which only 103 were used in the work as 12 were removed due to noise.

For the network configuration, we leverage convolutional filters with a very small receptive field of 3 × 3. In addition, the convolutional stride is fixed to 1 pixel; the spatial padding is also 1 pixel. Max-pooling is performed over 3 × 3 pixel windows with stride 3. All the convolutional layers are using ReLU as an activation function except for the last layer that uses Softmax. The fully residual network was trained using the novel AdaBound algorithm [9] and all the suggested default parameters were used for all the following experiments. Once the training of the residual network is complete, we can start to fine-tune the network for hyperspectral data classification. We have made use of stochastic gradient descent with a fairly low learning rate equal to 0.0001.

The following criteria were used to evaluate the performance of the geographic object-based scene classification algorithms in remote sensing images [22]:

a) Overall Accuracy (OA): This metric represents the number of samples that are classified correctly, divided by the number of test samples. b) Average Accuracy (AA): This index shows the average accuracy of the classifications of all categories. c) Kappa coefficient: This is a statistical measurement that provides information on the level of agreement between the truth map and the final classification map. It takes into account the percentage of agreement which could be expected only chance. In general, it is considered to be a more robust index than a simple percent agreement calculation, since k takes into account the agreement occurring by chance.

In addition, in order to evaluate the importance of the classification accuracy derived from different approaches, a McNemar statistical test is performed [23]:

$$z_{12} = \frac{f_{12} - f_{21}}{\sqrt{f_{12} + f_{21}}} \tag{26}$$

Where f_{ij} is the number of correctly classified samples in the ith classification and of the incorrectly classified in the jth classification. The McNemar's test is based on the standardized normal test statistic and therefore, the null hypothesis, which is "*no significant difference*," is rejected at the widely used $p = 0.05(|z| > 1.96)$ level of significance. This assessment test, determines the significance of the differences between the classification accuracy values obtained by the proposed model, versus the accuracy values obtained by other examined approaches.

To validate the effectiveness of the proposed architecture, the method is compared with the most widely used supervised deep learning models which are summarized as follows:

a. 1-D CNN: The 1-D CNN network architecture was designed as in [24] and includes an input layer, a convolutional layer, a max-pooling layer, a fully connected layer, and an output layer. The number of convolutional filters is 20, the length of each filter is 11 and the pooling size 3. Finally, 100 hidden units are contained in the fully connected layer.
b. 2-D CNN: The 2-D CNN architecture was designed as in [15]. It contains three convolutional layers equipped with 4 × 4, 5 × 5 and 4 × 4 convolutional filters, respectively. The 2-D CNN architecture was designed as in [15]. It contains three convolutional layers equipped with 4 × 4, 5 × 5 and 4 × 4 convolutional filters, respectively.
c. The Convolutional layers - except for the latter - are followed by max-pooling layers. In addition, the numbers of convolutional filters for CL are 32, 64 and 128, respectively.
d. Simple Convolutional/Deconvolutional network: The simple Convolutional/ Deconvolutional network with simple convolutional blocks and the Unpooling function are applied in the cases of [25,26].

e. Residual Convolutional/Deconvolutional network: It is an architecture using residual blocks and a more precise Unpooling function, as presented in [18].

***Optimized Residual Convolutional/Deconvolutional* (ORCD) network**

It is the improved version of the above architecture which was presented in this research paper. It differs in the fact that it uses the *Softmax* activation function in the last convolutional layer and that its fully residual network is trained using the novel AdaBound algorithm. This is achieved by employing dynamic bounds on the learning rates, which results in a smooth transition to stochastic gradient descent. This method shows great efficacy while maintaining advantageous properties of adaptive learning, such as rapid initial progress and hyperparameter insensitivity. Note that, we have used the standard types of training and testing samples in order make the proposed approach fully comparable with other classifiers in the literature.

The ORCD network was trained using the *AdaBound* algorithm, and all the suggested default parameters were used for all the following experiments. The number of Convolutional filters (CF), increases towards deeper layers of the convolutional sub-networks: There were 64 CF in the first residual block, 128 in the following block, and 256 in the last one. This rule is turned over for the *Deconvolutional sub-network*. All of the convolutional layers are with ReLU as activation function except the last layer that uses the *Softmax*.

All weight matrices in the network and the bias vectors are initialized with a uniform distribution, and their values are initialized in the range [−0.1, 0.1]. The number of the unlabeled data samples of the Pavia University that were used for training the network is 10000. These unlabeled samples are randomly selected from the whole set of images.

In the *Optimized Residual Convolutional/Deconvolutional* network, the hyperspectral data are normalized in the closed interval [0, 1]. Then, all of the weights are updated during the training procedure. Once the training of the network is completed, the *fine-tuning* process for hyperspectral data classification follows. The *stochastic gradient descent* with a fairly low learning rate of 0.0001 has been employed, for the fine tuning of the network. During this process, a percentage equal to 10% of both hyperspectral data sets, has been randomly selected as the validation set.

That is, during fine-tuning, 90% of the dataset has been used for learning and the remaining 10% of the available data samples served as the validation set, to perform tuning of the *hyper-parameters*, such as the numbers of convolutional filters in the convolutional layers. All of the test samples were used to evaluate the final performance of the learned *spectral–spatial feature representations* and the *fine-tuned network* was used to perform the classification.

The following Table 1 shows the classification maps using the *Pavia University* data set and the comparison of the accuracies between the classifiers *1-D CNN, 2-D CNN, Simple Convolutional/Deconvolutional Network (Simple C/D N), Residual C/D N* and the proposed *Optimized R C/D N*.

Trying to evaluate the above algorithms based on the obtained results, it is easy to conclude that the proposed ORCD *Network* outperforms the competing Deep Learning approaches for the *OA, AA*, and *Kappa* evaluation indices.

Table 1. Comparison of the accuracies between the classifiers

Class No	Class Name	1D CNN	2D CNN	Simple C/D N	Residual C/D N	Optimized R C/D N*
1	Asphalt	83.73	69.25	82.81	78.99	**86.59**
2	Meadows	65.70	93.39	97.11	**97.16**	97.01
3	Gravel	67.03	63.13	60.31	61.46	**69.97**
4	Trees	94.03	94.39	95.59	**95.76**	94.91
5	Metal Sheets	99.41	**100**	97.55	97.77	98.83
6	Bare Soil	**96.30**	49.06	59.38	59.46	69.87
7	Bitumen	**93.83**	72.26	78.42	79.50	86.49
8	Bricks	93.56	94.32	96.50	96.82	**96.85**
9	Shadows	**99.79**	93.77	92.29	92.40	97.71
OA	–	79.28	82.66	87.82	87.39	**90.51**
AA	–	88.15	81.06	84.44	84.37	**88.69**
Kappa	–	0.7423	0.7688	0.8363	0.8308	**0.8482**
Significance	–	31.362	31.464	23.178	22.232	21.871

The proposed method produces extremely accurate results without repeated problems of undetermined cause, because all of the features in the considered dataset are handled very efficiently. In addition, one of the key advantages gained from the results is the high reliability, resulting from the high kappa values (maximum reliability if $k \geq 0.81$). This can be considered as the result of data processing that allows the most reliable relevant data for the forthcoming forecasts. The above Table 1, also provides information on the results of the *McNemar* test to assess the significance of the difference between the classification accuracy of the proposed network and the other approaches considered. The results of the *McNemar* test, have proven that there exist statistically significant differences among the results obtained by the employed methods. More specifically, the differences between the 1D and 2D CNN with the rest of them are quite high, whereas there are minor but significant differences between the Optimized R C/D N (our proposed approach) and the Residual.

8 Discussion - Conclusions

This research proposes an innovative and highly effective geographic object-based scene classification system in remote sensing images, using an innovative Residual Neural Network (ResNet) architecture. This approach eliminates VGP as it is using Softmax activation function instead of Sigmoid on the last layer of the network. The fully residual network was trained using the novel AdaBound algorithm that employs dynamic bounds on their learning rates. It achieves a smooth transition to stochastic gradient descent, and it precisely addresses the noisy scattering points of misclassification that other spectral classification methods cannot handle properly.

Its implementation is based on the optimal use and combination for the first time in the literature, of two highly efficient and fast learning processes (Softmax activation function and AdaBound algorithm), which create an integrated intelligent system.

This network also remarkably implements a Large-Scale Geospatial Data Analysis approach that attempts to balance latency, throughput, and fault-tolerance using ResNet while simultaneously exploiting learning processes optimally and as efficiently as possible. The reliability of the proposed network has been successfully tested in the recognition of scenes from remote sensing photographs, which suggests that it can be used in higher level Geospatial Data Analysis processes. Such cases are the classification, the recognition and monitoring of specific standards, and the fusion of multisensor data.

Suggestions for the evolution and future improvements of this network should focus on further optimizing the parameters of the algorithms used in ResNet architecture. This will be done in order to achieve an even more efficient, more accurate and faster categorization process using a heuristic approach [27] or customization of the algorithm with the use of Spiking Neural Networks [28]. It would also be important to study the extension of this system by implementing the Lamda architecture [29] in an environment of parallel and distributed big data analysis systems (Hadoop). Finally, an additional target that could be considered in the direction of future expansion concerns the operation of the network by methods of self-improvement [30] and redefinition of its parameters in meta-learning. This can fully automate the geographic object-based scene classification process in remote sensing images.

References

1. Plaza, A., Plaza, J., Paz, A., Sanchez, S.: Parallel hyperspectral image and signal processing. IEEE Sign. Process. Mag. **28**, 119–126 (2011)
2. Hubert, M.J., Carole, E.: Airborne SAR-efficient signal processing for very high resolution. Proc. IEEE **101**, 784–797 (2013)
3. Zhang, W., Tang, P., Zhao, L.: Remote sensing image scene classification using CNN-CapsNet. Remote Sens. MDPI **11**(5), 494 (2019). https://doi.org/10.3390/rs11050494
4. Yang, Y., Newsam, S.: Bag-of-visual-words and spatial extensions for land-use classification. In: Proceedings of the 18th SIGSPATIAL International Conference on Advances in Geographic Information Systems, San Jose, CA, USA, pp. 270–279 (2010)
5. Penatti, O.A., Nogueira, K., dos Santos, J. A.: Do deep features generalize from everyday objects to remote sensing and aerial scenes domains? In: Proceedings of the IEEE Conference on Computer Vision and Pattern Recognition Workshops, Boston, MA, USA, pp. 44–51 (2015)
6. Schmidhuber, J.: Deep learning in neural networks: an overview. Neu. Netw. **61**, 85–117 (2015)
7. Hochreiter, S., Bengio, Y., Frasconi, P., Schmidhuber, J.: Gradient Flow in Recurrent Nets: The Difficulty Of Learning Long-term Dependencies. IEEE Press, New York (2001)
8. Kolen, J.F., Kremer, S.C.: Gradient flow in recurrent nets: the difficulty of learning long-term dependencies. In: A Field Guide to Dynamical Recurrent Networks, pp. 237–243. IEEE, (2001)

9. He, K., Zhang, X., Ren, S., Sun, J.: Deep residual learning for image recognition (2015). arXiv:1512.03385
10. Goodfellow, I., Bengio, Y., Courville, A.: Deep Learning. MIT Press, Cambridge (2016)
11. Chen, Y., Lin, Z., Zhao, X., Wang, G., Gu, Y.: Deep learning-based classification of hyperspectral data. IEEE J. Appl. Earth Obs. Remote Sens. **7**(6), 2094–2107 (2014)
12. Tao, C., Pan, H., Li, Y., Zou, Z.: Unsupervised spectral-spatial feature learning with stacked sparse autoencoder for hyperspectral imagery classification. IEEE Explore Geosci. Remote Sens. **8**(6), 2381–2392 (2015)
13. Kussul, N., Lavreniuk, M., Skakun, S., Shelestov, A.: Deep learning classification of land cover and crop types using remote sensing data. IEEE Explore Geosci. Remote Sens. **14**(5), 778–782 (2017)
14. Makantasis, K., Karantzalos, K., Doulamis, A., Doulamis, N.: Deep supervised learning for hyperspectral data classification through convolutional neural networks. In: Geoscience & Remote Sensing (2015)
15. Chen, Y., Jiang, H., Li, C., Jia, X., Ghamisi, P.: Deep feature extraction and classification of hyperspectral images based on CNN. IEEE Trans. Geosci. Remote Sens. **54**(10), 6232–6251 (2016)
16. Romero, A., Gatta, C., Camps-Valls, G.: Unsupervised deep feature extraction for remote sensing image classification. IEEE Trans. Geosci. Remote Sens. **54**(3), 1349–1362 (2016)
17. Mou, L., Ghamisi, P., Zhu, X.: Deep recurrent neural networks for hyperspectral image classification. IEEE Trans. Geosci. Remote Sens. **55**(7), 3639–3655 (2017)
18. Mou, L., Ghamisi, P., Zhu, X.: Unsupervised spectral-spatial feature learning via deep residual conv–deconv network for hyperspectral image classification. IEEE Trans. Geosci. Remote Sens. **56**(1), 391–406 (2018)
19. Glorot X., Bengio Y.: Understanding the difficulty of training deep feedforward neural networks. In: Proceedings International Conference Artificial Intelligence Statistics, pp. 249–256 (2010)
20. Luo, L., Xiong, Y., Liu, Y., Sun, X.: Adaptive gradient methods with dynamic bound of learning rate (2019). arXiv:1902.09843
21. Grana, M., Veganzons, M.A., Ayerdi, B.: Hyperspectral remote sensing scenes (2020). http://www.ehu.eus/ccwintco/index.php/Hyperspectral_Remote_Sensing_Scenes. Grupo De Inteligencia, Computacional
22. Fawcett, T.: An introduction to ROC analysis. Pattern Recogn. Lett. **27**, 861–874 (2006)
23. Agresti, A.: Categorical Data Analysis, p. 413. Wiley, Hoboken (2002). ISBN 978-0-471-36093-3
24. Hu, W., Huang, Y., Wei, L., Zhang, F., Li, H.: Deep convolutional neural networks for hyperspectral image classification. J. Sens. S.I. Deep Learn. Remote Sens. Image Underst., art. no. 258619 (2015)
25. Dosovitskiy, A., Springenberg, J. T., Brox, T.: Learning to generate chairs, tables and cars with convolutional networks. In: Proceedings IEEE Conference Computer Vision Pattern Recognition, pp. 1538–1546 (2015)
26. Dosovitskiy, A., Fischer, P., Springenberg, J.T., Riedmiller, M., Brox, T.: Discriminative unsupervised feature learning with exemplar convolutional neural networks. IEEE Trans. Pattern Anal. Mach. Intell. **38**(9), 1734–1747 (2016)
27. Demertzis, K., Iliadis, L.: Adaptive elitist differential evolution extreme learning machines on big data: intelligent recognition of invasive species. In: Proceedings of the INNS Conference Advances in Big Data, Advances in Intelligent Systems and Computing, vol. 529. Springer, Heidelberg (2016)

28. Demertzis, K., Iliadis, L., Anezakis, V.: A deep spiking machine-hearing system for the case of invasive fish species. In: Proceedings IEEE-SMC Innovations in Intelligent Systems & Applications (INISTA), pp. 23–28 (2017)
29. Demertzis, K., Tziritas, N., Kikiras, P., Sanchez, S.L., Iliadis, L.: The next generation cognitive security operations center: adaptive analytic lambda architecture for efficient defense against adversarial attacks. Big Data Cogn. Comput. **3**, 6 (2019). https://doi.org/10.3390/bdcc3010006
30. Demertzis, K., Iliadis, L.S., Anezakis, V.D.: Extreme deep learning in biosecurity: the case of machine hearing for marine species identification. J. Inf. Telecommun., 1–19 (2018). Taylor & Francis

Semantic Segmentation of Vineyard Images Using Convolutional Neural Networks

Theofanis Kalampokas, Konstantinos Tziridis, Alexandros Nikolaou, Eleni Vrochidou, George A. Papakostas(✉), Theodore Pachidis, and Vassilis G. Kaburlasos

Human-Machines Interaction Laboratory (HUMAIN-Lab), International Hellenic University, Agios Loukas 65404, Kavala, Greece
{theokala, kenaaske, alexniko, evrochid, gpapak, pated, vgkabs}@teiemt.gr

Abstract. This paper aims to study the segmentation demands of vineyard images using Convolutional Neural Networks (CNNs). To this end, eleven CNN models able to provide semantic segmented images are examined as part of the sensing subsystem of an autonomous agricultural robot. The task is challenging due to the similar color between grapes, leaves and image's background. Moreover, the lack of controlled lighting conditions results in varying color representation of grapes and leaves. The studied CNN model architectures combine three different feature learning sub-networks, with five meta-architectures for segmentation purposes. Investigation on three different datasets consisting of vineyard images of grape clusters and leaves, provided segmentation results, by mean pixel intersection over union (IU) performance index, of up to 87.89% for grape clusters and 83.45% for leaves, for the case of ResNet50_FRRN and MobileNetV2_PSPNet model, respectively. Comparative results reveal the efficacy of CNNs to separate grape clusters and leaves from image's background. Thus, the proposed models can be used for in-field applications for real-time localization of grapes and leaves, towards automation of harvest, green harvest and defoliation agricultural activities by an autonomous robot.

Keywords: Semantic segmentation · Convolutional neural network · Computer vision · Deep learning · Precision agriculture · Harvesting robot

1 Introduction

Robotics are entering the agricultural fields in slow but persistent way [1]. Most researches are testing agricultural robotics, namely *Agrobots*, in controlled environments such as greenhouses, while little has been done in real-field applications [2, 3]. This work investigates the segmentation task of grapes clusters and leaves, based on CNNs, to be integrated into an agrobot for in-field grape harvesting tasks. Convolutional neural networks (CNNs) are a class of deep neural networks for visual imagery analysis, mainly for object recognition and classification [4, 5]. Over many benchmark datasets, CNNs have demonstrated their capability to advance the state-of-the-art

L. Iliadis et al. (Eds.): EANN 2020, INNS 2, pp. 292–303, 2020.
https://doi.org/10.1007/978-3-030-48791-1_22

accuracies of object recognition [6, 7]. The capacity of a CNN can be controlled by varying their depth and breadth, estimating the stationary characteristics of images and the locality of pixel dependencies [8]. Visual object recognition is a basic task in remote sensing that finds among others, application in agriculture [3, 9], with our special interest focused on *viniculture*.

Convolutional neural networks have been applied to viticulture [10–16]. In [11] a benchmark hyperspectral dataset of grape images is employed to test a five-layer CNN for object identification. Hyperspectral images of grapes are used in [13], with a deep CNN, which extracts spectral-spatial information of hyperspectral images using a limited number of samples. Also in [16], hyperspectral images of grapes are tested with a CNN architecture to predict class-related results. In [10], an automated image-based workflow is developed quantifying inflorescences and single flowers images of grapevines. Image regions depicting inflorescences are identified and localized by segmenting the images into classes using a Fully Convolutional Network (FCN). Morphological and color features of grapes are used in [12] for ripeness estimation with a CNN. In a recent work [14] satellite image data is used to identify a vineyard, integrating the Continuous Wavelet Transform (CWT) and a CNN. A CNN is used to estimate vineyard grape yield in [15], by measuring the weight of grapes on a vine from an image with relatively good accuracy.

In this work, the recent advances in handling uncertainties during a segmentation task in vineyard images, using CNNs are investigated. More specifically, eleven CNN deep pixel-to-pixel architectures are applied in three sets of RGB images of red grapes, white grapes and a mixture of both kinds of grapes. The proposed architectures are derived from combining three different types of feature learning sub-networks with five different types of classification sub-networks.

This work examines and adopts existing methods on plant phenotyping using visual imaging and furthers the capabilities of in-field image classification. The modular design of the proposed models points out new combinations of segmentation architectures that fit the problem under study, i.e. grape and leaves segmentation. Thus, it paves the way forward for an autonomous robot to discriminate grapes and leaves on the spot, towards automating agricultural tasks such as harvest, green harvest and defoliation.

The rest of the paper is structured as follows. In Sect. 2 the image datasets and the examined CNN models are presented. Results are discussed in Sect. 3. Section 4 concludes by summarizing the contribution of this work and future research directions.

2 Materials and Methods

This section summarizes the main materials used to execute the proposed study as well as briefly describes the applied methods.

2.1 Image Datasets

Three datasets are used to evaluate the CNN models under investigation; dataset 1 consists of 274 images of white grapes and leaves, dataset 2 consists of 259 images of red grapes and leaves and dataset 3 is derived by combining dataset 1 and 2. Images of dataset 1 are captured by an RGB high resolution Samsung Mirrorless camera (NX500), while images of dataset 2 are captured by a USB 3.0 high resolution Thorlabs camera (DCC3240C) with lens C-MOUNT 12 mm (MVL12M23). All images are taken from three vineyards of well-known North Greek wine producers as part of a national research program [17] and are available to the public upon request. Two different types of cameras are used to test the performance of the models for the different equipment of the research program, since two RGB cameras will be mounted on the harvesting robot; one on the vehicle and one on the robotic arm that will approach the grape clusters to complete the agricultural tasks. Moreover, images of different quality comprise each dataset. The different quality of datasets is intentional, in order to test the performance of the networks under varying conditions and point out the most robust among them. In-field applications are characterized by unstable and varying conditions resulting in a lack of consistency in capturing the images to be used. In our case, for example, one of the cameras will be mounted on the moving, i.e. non-stable, robotic arm of the ground harvesting vehicle. This will lead to images of different characteristics i.e. varying illuminations, different viewing angles etc. These characteristics are the difficulties and challenges that the Agrobot will encounter in the real-field application, and therefore need to be explored. The original datasets are augmented in order to generate sufficient number of images for training the CNN models, as described in the next section. All the captured images have been annotated (ground truth) in order the pixels to belong to one of 3 classes, namely grapes, leaves and background. Ground truth images are constructed using the LabelMe annotation tool [18]. The details of each dataset are summarized below.

Dataset 1. Dataset 1 consists of 274 images of white grapes, augmented to 1370. The initial dataset contains 1064 white grape clusters and 1192 leaves. Dataset 1 consists of images of single isolated grape clusters, without any overlapping.

Dataset 2. Dataset 2 consists of 259 images of red grapes, augmented to 1295. The initial dataset contains 1282 red grape clusters and 1264 leaves. Dataset 2 consists of images of many and overlapping grape clusters or with dense leave coverage.

Dataset 3. Dataset 3 is the merge of datasets 1 and 2 (2665 augmented images).

2.2 Data Augmentation

The most common method to reduce overfitting on image data is to artificially augment the dataset using label-preserving transformations [19, 20]. Traditional transformations consist of using a combination of affine transformations to manipulate the training data. We employ four distinct forms of data augmentation that allow transformed images to be produced from the original images with minimum computations; flip, rotate, shift and shearing. For each input image, four duplicated images, 60% transformed compared to the original, are generated. Original image and duplicates are fed into the CNN models. Thus, for a dataset of N images size, the final size of the augmented dataset is 5N (N + 4N).

2.3 Examined Models

Convolutional neural networks are trainable multistage architectures [21]. The input and output of each stage are sets of arrays. At the output, each array represents a feature extended at all locations on the input. Typically, each stage is composed of three layers; a filter-bank layer, a non-linearity layer and a feature pooling layer [4]. The 3-layer stages that form the feature learning network, are followed by a classification module, as shown in Fig. 1. In this work, three feature learning networks are combined with five classification convents, where it is possible, by forming eleven models that are evaluated for the problem under study; optimal in-field localization of grape clusters and leaves by a harvesting robot.

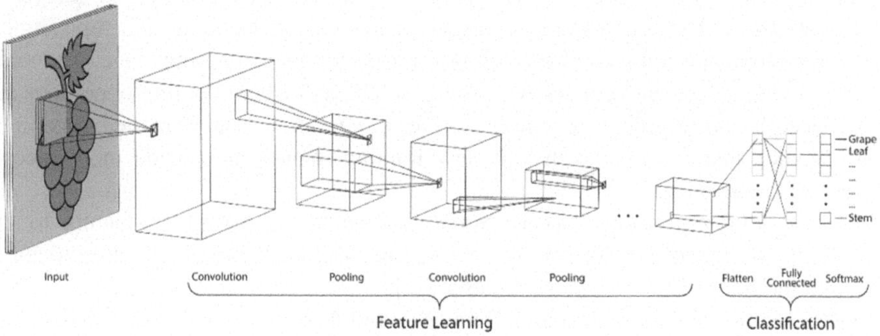

Fig. 1. Typical structure of a CNN.

Feature Learning Networks. In a typical CNN architecture, initial layers deal with feature learning (Fig. 1). First layer includes a set of independent filters that are randomly initialized. At this point, the network learns from the data and detects low-level features such as edges are curves. An activation function is also applied to the feature maps to increase non-linearity in the network. The pooling layer reduces the spatial size of input representation, the number of parameters and thus, the overall required computations. Herein, three CNN architectures are examined, the *VGG16*, the *ResNet50* and *MobilNetV2*.

- VGG16 is a very deep convolutional neural network with 16 layers for large-scale image classification [22].
- ResNet50 is a very deep 50-layer convolutional neural network. ResNets can handle more layers by having lower complexity than VGG networks [23].
- MobileNetV2 introduces a new CNN layer, the inverted residual and linear bottleneck layer, enabling high accuracies in mobile and embedded vision applications [24], with lower complexity.

Classification Convents. The last layer of the typical CNN architecture comprised a fully connected classification scheme, namely a meta-architecture (Fig. 1). Artificial Neural Networks (ANN) are added to combine the image features into attributes.

Backpropagation minimizes the errors and weights are adjusted to optimize the models' performance. In this work five meta-architectures able to provide class label for each input image's pixel and thus performing semantic segmentation of the vineyard images, are examined, as listed below.

- *FPN.* The Feature Pyramid Network [25] creates a feature pyramid that has strong semantics at all scales. The main idea relies on an architecture that combines low-resolution, semantically strong features with high-resolution, semantically weak features via a top-down pathway and lateral connections.
- *FCN8.* In a Fully Connected Network [5] the fully connected layers for the image classification are replaced by multiple convolutional layers and decoder layers, forming two phases; the feature extraction phase and the decoder phase, resulting into a classification model that assigns a class label in each pixel of the image.
- *U-Net.* The U-Net architecture represents a method of decoding, that up-samples features by using transposed convolution for each down-sampling stage. The main idea is to increase the network with successive layers where pooling operations are replaced by up-sampling operations. U-Net is a modified and extended version of FCN such that it works with very few training images and yields more precise segmentations [26].
- *PSPNet.* Pyramid Scene Parsing Network extends the pixel-level-feature to the specially designed global pyramid pooling one. The local and global clues together make the final prediction more reliable [27].
- *FRRN.* Full-Resolution Residual Network exhibits strong localization and recognition performance. A multi-scale context is combined with pixel-level accuracy by using two processing streams within FRRN; one that carries information at the full image resolution and one that undergoes a sequence of pooling operation. The two streams are coupled at the full image resolution using residuals [28].

3 Results and Discussion

Eleven CNN based semantic segmentation models, derived by combining the above mentioned feature learning sub-networks and classification met-architectures, were evaluated with dataset 1, 2 and 3. The experimental results of the conducted study, along with the experimental setup are summarized in this section.

3.1 Experimental Setup

To evaluate the examined models, the labeled datasets are divided into training and testing sets. For all datasets, the testing set consists of 20 images while the rest of the images are used for training. For all experiments, categorical weighted cross entropy Loss is used [29]. ADADELTA optimizer learning rate [30] is set to 1.0. ADADELTA is selected due to its capability to dynamically adapt the learning rate during the training process. Batch size is 12 for all models. All models are trained for 200 epochs. All methods were implemented in Python 3.7 using TensorFlow and Keras, on a computer equipped with Nvidia RTX 2070 GPU.

3.2 Results

Results are reported for the three datasets under study. The performance of each model is evaluated by the mean intersection over union (IU) on the testing set for the three classes of each dataset (Tables 1, 2 and 3) and their average. Moreover, Loss, F1-score and average IU for all models during training in each dataset (Tables 4, 5 and 6), are also presented.

The experimental results regarding the testing set are summarized in Tables 1, 2 and 3. The best performance network for dataset 1 is MobileNetV2_PSPNet, which achieves IU of 87.79% and 83.45%, for grapes and leaves, respectively. The best average performance for all classes is achieved by the same network, which reaches a state-of-the art average IU 88.21%.

Table 1. IU (%) on the testing set for dataset 1.

CNN models	IU grapes	IU leaves	IU background	Average IU
VGG16_FPN	83.09	72.90	89.60	81.86
VGG16_FCN8	81.47	63.58	87.90	77.65
VGG16_U-Net	81.96	65.47	88.26	78.56
VGG16_PSPNet	86.00	78.83	91.98	85.60
ResNet50_FPN	78.90	66.94	87.26	77.70
ResNet50_U-Net	80.57	67.29	87.73	78.53
ResNet50_PSPNet	82.01	71.36	89.35	80.90
ResNet50_FRRN	79.10	70.07	85.80	78.32
MobileNetV2_FPN	87.07	78.62	92.29	85.99
MobileNetV2_U-Net	86.76	78.63	92.22	85.87
MobileNetV2_PSPNet	**87.79**	**83.45**	**93.4**	**88.21**

Table 2. IU (%) on the testing set for dataset 2.

CNN models	IU grapes	IU leaves	IU background	Average IU
VGG16_FPN	67.15	56.99	77.33	67.15
VGG16_FCN8	65.42	52.04	73.80	63.73
VGG16_U-Net	66.08	57.17	77.13	66.79
VGG16_PSPNet	68.35	57.40	76.62	67.45
ResNet50_FPN	64.56	53.28	75.92	64.58
ResNet50_U-Net	66.84	56.34	76.12	66.43
ResNet50_PSPNet	57.42	44.17	73.43	58.34
ResNet50_FRRN	**79.51**	59.04	72.69	**70.41**
MobileNetV2_FPN	65.85	**59.27**	76.52	67.21
MobileNetV2_U-Net	68.91	58.11	**77.44**	68.15
MobileNetV2_PSPNet	64.10	54.74	74.79	64.54

Table 3. IU (%) on the testing set for dataset 3.

CNN models	IU grapes	IU leaves	IU background	Average IU
VGG16_FPN	71.32	61.09	79.41	70.60
VGG16_FCN8	71.08	58.89	78.35	69.44
VGG16_U-Net	68.40	55.83	78.46	67.56
VGG16_PSPNet	68.07	61.24	80.51	69.94
ResNet50_FPN	68.07	54.41	77.89	66.79
ResNet50_U-Net	69.14	54.34	78.04	67.17
ResNet50_PSPNet	70.07	58.45	80.04	69.52
ResNet50_FRRN	**87.89**	62.19	**89.77**	**79.95**
MobileNetV2_FPN	75.76	**64.12**	82.83	74.23
MobileNetV2_U-Net	75.88	64.10	83.75	74.57
MobileNetV2_PSPNet	74.04	64.37	83.07	73.82

For dataset 2, the best performance is achieved by combinations ResNet50_FRRN (IU 79.51%), MobileNetV2_FPN (IU 59.27%) for grapes and leaves segmentation respectively, while for all classes an IU 77.44% is reached by MobileNetV2_U-Net. For dataset 3, the models ResNet50_FRRN (IU 87.89%), MobileNetV2_FPN (IU 64.12%) shown the best accuracy for grapes and leaves segmentation, respectively, with the former being the best performed model on average (IU 79.95%).

Table 4, 5 and 6 summarize the models' performance in terms of Loss, F1-score and IU on the training set for each dataset. For dataset 1, best scores are achieved by MobileNetV2_U-Net, providing 0.039 Loss, 97.47% F1-score and 95.09% IU. For dataset 2, VGG16_FPN model (0.065 Loss, 96.15% F1-score and 92.69% IU) shown the best performance.

Table 4. Loss, F1-score and IU on the training set for dataset 1.

CNN models	Loss	F1-score (%)	Average IU (%)
VGG16_FPN	0.087	95	90.66
VGG16_FCN8	0.125	92.13	91.13
VGG16_U-Net	0.088	95.02	90.60
VGG16_PSPNet	0.114	93.60	88.09
ResNet50_FPN	0.117	92.14	84.12
ResNet50_U-Net	0.095	93.18	89.57
ResNet50_PSPNet	0.189	90.64	83.08
ResNet50_FRRN	0.176	80.56	89.63
MobileNetV2_FPN	0.039	97.59	95.33
MobileNetV2_U-Net	**0.039**	**97.47**	**95.09**
MobileNetV2_PSPNet	0.079	95.35	91.20

Table 5. Loss, F1-score and IU on the training set for dataset 2.

CNN models	Loss	F1-score (%)	Average IU (%)
VGG16_FPN	**0.065**	**96.15**	**92.69**
VGG16_FCN8	0.270	92.11	89.41
VGG16_U-Net	0.069	95.80	92.06
VGG16_PSPNet	0.114	93.31	87.96
ResNet50_FPN	0.071	95.80	92.04
ResNet50_U-Net	0.077	95.39	91.33
ResNet50_PSPNet	0.150	91.80	85.15
ResNet50_FRRN	0.089	95.40	86.17
MobileNetV2_FPN	0.102	94.14	89.12
MobileNetV2_U-Net	0.103	93.88	88.70
MobileNetV2_PSPNet	0.199	89.80	81.82

Table 6. Loss, F1-score and IU on the training set for dataset 3.

CNN models	Loss	F1-score (%)	Average IU (%)
VGG16_FPN	0.143	93.44	91.61
VGG16_FCN8	0.291	88.67	87.30
VGG16_U-Net	0.141	92.91	86.89
VGG16_PSPNet	0.189	90.64	83.08
ResNet50_FPN	0.168	91.53	84.59
ResNet50_U-Net	0.153	92.27	85.80
ResNet50_PSPNet	0.103	94.48	89.64
ResNet50_FRRN	0.379	**96.73**	**92.56**
MobileNetV2_FPN	**0.100**	94.16	89.11
MobileNetV2_U-Net	0.079	95.20	90.96
MobileNetV2_PSPNet	0.151	91.95	85.31

For dataset 3, lower Loss (0.100) was achieved by MobileNetV2_FPN, while the best F1-score (96.73%) and IU 92.56% reached by ResNet50_FRRN model. From the Table 1, 2, 3, 4, 5 and 6, it is obvious that the performance of the models is higher for dataset 1, then dataset 2. This is attributed to the different quality of the images between datasets 1 and 2.

From the overall experimental results, it seems that in most cases models based on MobileNetV2 network reach comparatively high or higher performances. More specific U-Net, PSPNet and FRRN meta-architectures with MobileNetV2 and ResNet50 achieved the biggest scores in general, for both grapes and leaves classes. However, the highest performance (average IU) is achieved with MobileNetV2_PSPNet (88.21%). This can be attributed to the fact that PSPNet needs image resolution divisible by 48, e.g. 192 × 192, 240 × 240, 288 × 288 etc. In our case, all networks were trained with image size of 224 × 224, while the nearest permissible resolution to that, that is 240 × 240, was used

Fig. 2. Qualitative results from the testing (a) dataset 1 with MobilNetV2_PSPNet model, (b) dataset 2 with ResNet50_FRRN model and (c), (d) dataset 3 with ResNet50_FRRN model. From left to right: input RGB image, ground truth image and segmented image.

for the PSPNet. As it comes to the restriction of the 224 × 224 resolution for the rest of the models, this is due to the fact that our datasets consist of an insufficient number of photos to train the models from the beginning, so pretrained models, that required image size of 224 × 224, where used. When comparing the examined networks in terms of computational time, all models need 26–32 s average time per epoch, while the three combinations with MobileNetV2 need less time; 14–21 s average time per epoch. This is due to the light weighted architecture of MobileNetV2. Time is crucial when it comes to real-time applications, especially in our case, where the optimal model is intended to run on a Jetson TX2 for in-field segmentation by a harvesting robot. Figure 2 displays the image of each dataset from the testing dataset with the best segmented performance in terms of average IU, as reported in Tables 1, 2 and 3, alongside the corresponding ground truth image and the segmented final image.

4 Conclusions

In this paper, the task of semantic segmentation of vineyard images using convolutional neural networks was studied. For this purpose, a modular design framework that enables the creative combination of three different feature learning sub-networks and five meta-architectures was applied. In total, eleven different models were evaluated to three datasets with vineyard images and they compared to each other in terms of segmentation accuracy. The applied benchmarking framework provides researchers and practitioners with a means to evaluate design choices for their task in the frame of viniculture, and more particularly for grape and leaves segmentation. The latter segmentation task is the first step for the development of an autonomous robot able to discriminate grapes and leaves on the spot, towards automating agricultural tasks such as harvest, green harvest and defoliation. Future work includes training and testing the networks using more in-field images captured from the mounted cameras of the Agrobot.

Acknowledgment. This research has been co-financed by the European Union and Greek national funds through the Operational Program Competitiveness, Entrepreneurship and Innovation, under the call RESEARCH – CREATE – INNOVATE (project code: T1EDK-00300).

References

1. Xue, J., Zhang, L., Grift, T.E.: Variable field-of-view machine vision based row guidance of an agricultural robot. Comput. Electron. Agric. **84**, 85–91 (2012). https://doi.org/10.1016/j.compag.2012.02.009
2. Søgaard, H.T., Lund, I.: Application accuracy of a machine vision-controlled robotic micro-dosing system. Biosyst. Eng. **96**, 315–322 (2007). https://doi.org/10.1016/j.biosystemseng.2006.11.009
3. Mavridou, E., Vrochidou, E., Papakostas, G.A., Pachidis, T., Kaburlasos, V.G.: Machine vision systems in precision agriculture for crop farming. J. Imaging **5**, 89 (2019). https://doi.org/10.3390/jimaging5120089
4. LeCun, Y., Kavukcuoglu, K., Farabet, C.: Convolutional networks and applications in vision. In: Proceedings of 2010 IEEE International Symposium on Circuits and Systems, pp. 253–256. IEEE (2010). https://doi.org/10.1109/ISCAS.2010.5537907
5. Long, J., Shelhamer, E., Darrell, T.: Fully convolutional networks for semantic segmentation. In: 2015 IEEE Conference on Computer Vision and Pattern Recognition (CVPR), pp. 3431–3440. IEEE (2015). https://doi.org/10.1109/CVPR.2015.7298965

6. Chatfield, K., Simonyan, K., Vedaldi, A., Zisserman, A.: Return of the devil in the details: delving deep into convolutional nets. In: Proceedings of the British Machine Vision Conference 2014, pp. 6.1–6.12. British Machine Vision Association (2014). https://doi.org/10.5244/C.28.6
7. Szegedy, C., Wei Liu, Yangqing Jia, Sermanet, P., Reed, S., Anguelov, D., Erhan, D., Vanhoucke, V., Rabinovich, A.: Going deeper with convolutions. In: 2015 IEEE Conference on Computer Vision and Pattern Recognition (CVPR), pp. 1–9. IEEE (2015). https://doi.org/10.1109/CVPR.2015.7298594
8. Krizhevsky, A., Sutskever, I., Hinton, G.E.: ImageNet classification with deep convolutional neural networks. Commun. ACM **60**, 84–90 (2017). https://doi.org/10.1145/3065386
9. Badeka, E., Kalabokas, T., Tziridis, K., Nicolaou, A., Vrochidou, E., Mavridou, E., Papakostas, G.A., Pachidis, T.: Grapes visual segmentation for harvesting robots using local texture descriptors. In: 12th International Conference on Computer Vision Systems (ICVS 2019), pp. 98–109 (2019). https://doi.org/10.1007/978-3-030-34995-0_9
10. Rudolph, R., Herzog, K., Töpfer, R., Steinhage, V.: Efficient identification, localization and quantification of grapevine inflorescences and flowers in unprepared field images using fully convolutional networks. Vitis J. Grapevine Res. **58**(3), 95–104 (2019). https://doi.org/10.5073/vitis.2019.58.95-104
11. Mei, S., Ji, J., Bi, Q., Hou, J., Du, Q., Li, W.: Integrating spectral and spatial information into deep convolutional neural networks for hyperspectral classification. In: 2016 IEEE International Geoscience and Remote Sensing Symposium (IGARSS), pp. 5067–5070. IEEE (2016). https://doi.org/10.1109/IGARSS.2016.7730321
12. Kangune, K., Kulkarni, V., Kosamkar, P.: Grapes ripeness estimation using convolutional neural network and support vector machine. In: 2019 Global Conference for Advancement in Technology (GCAT), pp. 1–5. IEEE (2019). https://doi.org/10.1109/GCAT47503.2019.8978341
13. . Li, N., Wang, C., Zhao, H., Gong, X., Wang, D.: A novel deep convolutional neural network for spectral-spatial classification of hyperspectral data. Int. Arch. Photogramm. Remote Sens. Spat. Inf. Sci. ISPRS Arch. **42**, 897–900 (2018). https://doi.org/10.5194/isprs-archives-XLII-3-897-2018
14. Zhao, L., Li, Q., Zhang, Y., Wang, H., Du, X.: Integrating the continuous wavelet transform and a convolutional neural network to identify vineyard using time series satellite images. Remote Sens. **11**, 2641 (2019). https://doi.org/10.3390/rs11222641
15. Monga, T.: Estimating vineyard grape yield from images. In: Lecture Notes in Computer Science (Lecture Notes in Artificial Intelligence and Lecture Notes in Bioinformatics), pp. 339–343 (2018). https://doi.org/10.1007/978-3-319-89656-4_37
16. Yu, S., Jia, S., Xu, C.: Convolutional neural networks for hyperspectral image classification. Neurocomputing **219**, 88–98 (2017). https://doi.org/10.1016/j.neucom.2016.09.010
17. Personalized Optimal Grape Harvest by Autonomous Robot (POGHAR). http://evtar.eu/
18. Russell, B.C., Torralba, A., Murphy, K.P., Freeman, W.T.: Labelme: a database and web-based tool for image annotation. Int. J. Comput. Vis. **77**, 157–173 (2008). https://doi.org/10.1007/s11263-007-0090-8
19. Wong, S.C., Gatt, A., Stamatescu, V., McDonnell, M.D.: Understanding data augmentation for classification: when to warp? In: 2016 International Conference on Digital Image Computing: Techniques and Applications (DICTA), pp. 1–6. IEEE (2016). https://doi.org/10.1109/DICTA.2016.7797091
20. Mikolajczyk, A., Grochowski, M.: Data augmentation for improving deep learning in image classification problem. In: 2018 International Interdisciplinary Ph.D. Workshop (IIPhDW), pp. 117–122. IEEE (2018). https://doi.org/10.1109/IIPHDW.2018.8388338

21. Gatys, L.A., Ecker, A.S., Bethge, M.: Image style transfer using convolutional neural networks. In: 2016 IEEE Conference on Computer Vision and Pattern Recognition (CVPR), pp. 2414–2423. IEEE (2016). https://doi.org/10.1109/CVPR.2016.265
22. Simonyan, K., Zisserman, A.: Very Deep Convolutional Networks for Large-Scale Image Recognition. In: 3rd International Conference Learning Representations, ICLR 2015, Conference Track Proceedings (2014)
23. He, K., Zhang, X., Ren, S., Sun, J.: Deep residual learning for image recognition. In: 2016 IEEE Conference on Computer Vision and Pattern Recognition (CVPR), pp. 770–778. IEEE (2016). https://doi.org/10.1109/CVPR.2016.90
24. Sandler, M., Howard, A., Zhu, M., Zhmoginov, A., Chen, L.-C.: Mobilenetv2: inverted residuals and linear bottlenecks. In: 2018 IEEE/CVF Conference on Computer Vision and Pattern Recognition, pp. 4510–4520. IEEE (2018). https://doi.org/10.1109/CVPR.2018.00474
25. Lin, T.-Y., Dollar, P., Girshick, R., He, K., Hariharan, B., Belongie, S.: Feature pyramid networks for object detection. In: 2017 IEEE Conference on Computer Vision and Pattern Recognition (CVPR), pp. 936–944. IEEE (2017). https://doi.org/10.1109/CVPR.2017.106
26. Ronneberger, O., Fischer, P., Brox, T.: U-Net: convolutional networks for biomedical image segmentation. In: Lecture Notes in Computer Science (Lecture Notes in Artificial Intelligence and Lecture Notes in Bioinformatics), pp. 234–241 (2015). https://doi.org/10.1007/978-3-319-24574-4_28
27. Zhao, H., Shi, J., Qi, X., Wang, X., Jia, J.: Pyramid scene parsing network. In: 2017 IEEE Conference on Computer Vision and Pattern Recognition (CVPR), pp. 6230–6239. IEEE (2017). https://doi.org/10.1109/CVPR.2017.660
28. Pohlen, T., Hermans, A., Mathias, M., Leibe, B.: Full-resolution residual networks for semantic segmentation in street scenes. In: 2017 IEEE Conference on Computer Vision and Pattern Recognition (CVPR), pp. 3309–3318. IEEE (2017). https://doi.org/10.1109/CVPR.2017.353
29. Siam, M., Gamal, M., Abdel-Razek, M., Yogamani, S., Jagersand, M.: RTseg: real-time semantic segmentation comparative study. In: 2018 25th IEEE International Conference on Image Processing (ICIP), pp. 1603–1607. IEEE (2018). https://doi.org/10.1109/ICIP.2018.8451495
30. Zeiler, M.D.: ADADELTA: an adaptive learning rate method (2012)

Towards a Reliable Face Recognition System

Adamu Ali-Gombe[1(✉)], Eyad Elyan[1], and Johan Zwiegelaar[2]

[1] Robert Gordon University, Aberdeen, UK
{a.ali-gombe,e.elyan}@rgu.ac.uk
[2] Mintra Group, Oslo, Norway
johan.zwiegelaar@mintragroup.com
https://www.rgu.ac.uk, https://www.mintragroup.com

Abstract. Face Recognition (FR) is an important area in computer vision with many applications such as security and automated border controls. The recent advancements in this domain have pushed the performance of models to human-level accuracy. However, the varying conditions in the real-world expose more challenges for their adoption. In this paper, we investigate the performance of these models. We analyze the performance of a cross-section of face detection and recognition models. Experiments were carried out without any preprocessing on three state-of-the-art face detection methods namely HOG, YOLO and MTCNN, and three recognition models namely, VGGface2, FaceNet and Arcface. Our results indicated that there is a significant reliance by these methods on preprocessing for optimum performance.

Keywords: Face detection · Face recognition · Deep learning · YOLO

1 Introduction

Face detection and recognition have numerous real-world applications such as person identification and tracking. The real-world environment is typically unconstrained and has been the attention of the computer vision community for some time now. Despite exceeding human performances on test data, FR models hardly meet the requirements in the real-world [28]. Thus, preprocessing steps such as pose augmentation and illumination normalization continue to be crucial especially in mismatched conditions [16]. However, extra preprocessing steps could add delays to real-time recognition.

Majority of the established deep learning face recognition systems consist of three modules namely, a detector module, a pre-processing module and a recognition module [17,19,23]. Established detections model such as Viola and Jones [25], Bob [3] and fiducial detectors [23] are employed to localize the

Supported by InnovateUK, Mintra Group and Robert Gordon University.

L. Iliadis et al. (Eds.): EANN 2020, INNS 2, pp. 304–316, 2020.
https://doi.org/10.1007/978-3-030-48791-1_23

required face area before a recognition model is used. This makes the process reliant on the accuracy of the detection model. The stand-out face recognition models that reported close to or better than human performances are Deepface [17], DeepID [21], VGGFace [5], SpereFace [15], ArcFace [7], CosFace [26] and FaceNet [23].

Although some of the results reported are close to perfect, it was discovered when testing is done at scale, these models' performances degrade considerably [11]. Moreover, these tests were carried out in controlled environments and most of these datasets were carefully curated. Furthermore, the bias in data collection such as ethnicity and race creates skewed model performances [1,2,30]. Again, recognition across wide age gaps is still challenging even for state-of-the-art models with near-perfect results. Other challenges include disguise or individual appearance and variations such as beard, facial expression, and others. Pictorial conditions such as illumination, pose, occlusion due to dressing (wearing a cap or eyeglasses), image quality, etc. [16] and Face spoofing [4] are all considered challenging problems to state-of-the-art FR systems.

In this paper, we perform face detection and recognition using state-of-art models and demonstrate that despite the great successes, challenges still exist in deploying these models in the real-world. Our experiments highlight these challenges and we show that without preprocessing and post-processing such as alignment, illumination normalization and frontalization, models under-performs below the reported results.

The rest of the paper is organised as follows. In Sect. 2, related literature is reviewed and discussed. Section 3 presents the methods used in this work. Section 4 discusses in details experimental set-up and the datasets used. Findings are discussed in Sect. 5. Finally, we conclude and suggest future directions in Sect. 6.

2 Related Works

2.1 Face Detection

While face detection can be achieved using a general detection framework such as Histogram of Oriented Gradients (HOG) [6], You Look Only Once (YOLO) [18], Single Shot Detector (SSD) [14], Region Convolution Neural Network (R-CNN) [9], Max Margin Object Detection (MMOD) [12]; there are specialized face detection frameworks like Multi-Task Cascade CNN (MTCNN) [31], retina face [8] and Face Attention Networks (FAN) [27] built specifically for this purpose. Both categories have merits and the choice of a detector will depend on the application or nature of the data available. That said, specialized detectors benefit from the inclusion of ad-hoc detection pipelines with little to no overhead such as facial landmark detection that could be beneficial in post-processing. Face detection techniques such as HOG, Haar cascade are considered traditional machine learning approaches. Recent face detection techniques such as YOLO, use deep learning model or a Convolutional Neural Network (CNN) as the backbone model. The shift in trend is that fact that traditional approaches require features to be extracted before a machine learning classifier such as an SVM could be trained. Thus, features engineering reduces the generalization of these approaches. Whereas deep learning approaches learn features directly from pixel values over many training iterations thereby, generalizing better to unseen samples.

Haar cascades method [25] is one of the early successes in face detection systems and remains a popular choice. This method introduces the concept of integral images which is calculated based on region neighborhood. Similarly, HOG divides the image into cells with discrete angular bins of gradient orientations. Both are effective and fast but are affected by pose and occlusion or partial face view. These techniques are best suited for frontal faces with fewer pose effects.

Cascade CNN [13] are quite efficient in detecting faces with high visual variation such as pose and facial expressions. This approach performs detection in three different stages at different scales. A combined six CNN are used with three CNNs to determine face candidates and the other three CNNs are for bounding box calibration. Multi-Task Cascade CNN (MTCNN) is an extension of cascade CNN. While both use a cascade of CNNs, MTCNN is much faster and more accurate than the former. RetinaFace [8] added a self-supervised signal using 3D dense face regression alongside identity classification, face and facial landmark regression. According to the authors, the intuition is that since mask prediction in Mask-RCNN improved localization, then additional supervisory signal will be just as important in face localization. RetinaFace is a one-stage detector i.e faces are detected in a single go with no branches or sub-networks. Face Attention Network (FAN) [27] adds attention mechanism using a RetinaNet structure with a novel anchor assignment strategy.

Apart from generalizing better, deep learning methods enhance performances through preprocesses such as augmentation, random cropping, hard mining of samples, negative detection and others. Günther *et al.* [10] observed that on open-set detection challenge using UCCS dataset, both TinyFaces, Cascade CNN, YOLO, LBF and LgfNet performed well on face detection. The models were able to detect at least 33000 of the 36153 labeled test faces. However, the authors observed this was at the expense of high false detections. Generally, there is a trade-off between speed and accuracy when choosing a detector. Deep learning-based detectors are more accurate but are slower than traditional approaches such as HOG, but traditional approaches are less accurate. The difference in prediction time could be negligible when experimenting with few images or locally but when providing services at scale or remotely, this may be a factor to consider.

2.2 Face Recognition

Face recognition is achieved using a machine learning model by training on either engineered features or raw pixel values. A face recognition model learns an embedding function that brings together similar identities closer in the embedding space irrespective of the image conditions. Deep models in FR share a lot of commonalities and mostly use standards CNNs (such as ResNet, VGG, SENet) as their backbone. Regardless of the model used, deep learning approaches use a classifier [5] on identification task or a distance metric when verification is the task [19].

DeepFace recognition [23] presented an improved recognition approach using 3D face alignment and frontalization technique. The facial alignment was guided by 6 fiducial points and refined by a Support Vector Regressor (SVR). DeepFace achieved identification task using a softmax and the learned model was used as a Siamese network with a chi-squared (χ^2) distance metric as the objective in a verification task. An extension of DeepFace was presented in DeepFace2 [24] which extend the process with bootstrapping (semantic bootstrapping). similarly, VGGface [5] and VGGface2 [17] were trained using softmax.

Deep IDentity features (DeepID) [21] learned identity-related features in a multi-class identification task using multiple CNNs (60). DeepID features are 160-D each and were combined with features from other networks ($160 \times 2 \times 60$). Faces were detected using fiducial detectors and the CNNs were trained on multiple face region crops. DeepID features were found to generalize well to face verification even to unseen faces. This was extended to DeepID2 [20] and DeepID2+ [22] with better network architecture, bigger hidden representations and supervision in convolution layers.

FaceNet [19] used triplet loss with Euclidean distance to train an inception model in image recognition. The approach implemented a triplet batch of two matching pairs and a non-matching sample. To choose the right pairs, FaceNet developed a novel negative exemplar mining of the most difficult triplets during training. In the Euclidean space, identical faces were held at smaller margins while different faces were pushed apart. FaceNet turned out to be highly invariant to illumination and pose on test images.

Arcface [7] utilizes an additive angular margin in obtaining highly discriminative features in face recognition. Essentially, this approaches uses centers which are determined by employing the weights of the last fully connected layer and the embedding after normalization. Extensive experiments were performed on many public datasets and the results obtained showed better performances than other existing approaches. Closely related to this are Sphereface [15] and Cosface [26].

The recent deep models use similar backbones and what differentiates them most is the training protocol. Some employ a different training function such as a softmax or additive angular margin loss or even a distance measure. All these approaches present compelling evidence on the choices made. These choices in some literature show some dependency on the task, for instance, FaceNet employed a triplet loss on their verification task which is quite logical. However, VGGface2 was trained using softmax but the model also showed comparable results on verification when the model was used as a face features and a face similarity is evaluated.

3 Methods

Three detector models considered in this paper, these are; YOLO, MTCNN and HOG. The choice of these is to compare the performance of a general-purpose detector, a specialized detector, and a mix of deep learning model and traditional machine learning models. Three face recognition models were considered namely: VGG2faces, Arcface and Facenet, All of which are deep models. Thus, this gives us a cross-section of loss flavors that is; a VGG2face trained using softmax, an Arcface model trained using additive angular margin and a Facenet trained on triplet loss.

The first detector considered is HOG. HOG is a general detector and relies on image structure to perform detection. HOG first divides the images into local regions/grids and evaluate the gradient and orientation of pixels within these regions. Then a histogram is generated from each region. Gradients are changes in intensities along the x and y directions both of which are evaluated to be the magnitude at that pixel. The orientation is the gradients angle. An image histogram is then generated from each region/grid using these two values. Gradient normalization is usually applied to minimize the effect of illumination in the process. Equations 1, 2, 3, 4 shows how the total gradient and orientation angle is calculated.

$$g_{x_i} = x_{(i+1)} - x_{(i-1)} \tag{1}$$

$$g_{y_i} = y_{(i+1)} - y_{(i-1)} \tag{2}$$

$$G = \sqrt{g_{x_i}^2 + g_{y_i}^2} \tag{3}$$

$$\phi = \arctan(g_{y_i}/g_{x_i}) \tag{4}$$

The second detector is YOLO which uses a CNN backbone and detect/ classify objects in a single pass. This feature improves the speed of detection in real-time application. YOLO performs detection by subdividing an image into grid cells. Each grid cell outputs a bounding box, a confidence score and a class. The confidence is a measure of how accurate the model thinks an object exists within the cell. The bounding box is center of the object with width and height relative to the entire image. The cumulative loss is calculated as shown in Eq. 5.

$$
\begin{aligned}
L = \lambda_{coord} \sum_{i=0}^{s^2} \sum_{j=0}^{B} l_{ij}^{obj} [(x_i - \hat{x}_i)^2 + (y_i - \hat{y}_i)^2] \\
+\lambda_{coord} \sum_{i=0}^{s^2} \sum_{j=0}^{B} l_{ij}^{obj} [(\sqrt{w_i} - \sqrt{\hat{w}_i})^2 + (\sqrt{h_i} - \sqrt{\hat{h}_i})^2] \\
+ \sum_{i=0}^{s^2} \sum_{j=0}^{B} l_{ij}^{obj} (C_i - \hat{C}_i)^2 \\
+\lambda_{noobj} \sum_{i=0}^{s^2} \sum_{j=0}^{B} l_{ij}^{noobj} (C_i - \hat{C}_i)^2 \\
+ \sum_{i=0}^{s^2} l_i^{obj} \sum_{c \in classes} (p_i(c) - \hat{p}_i(c))^2
\end{aligned}
\tag{5}
$$

Where l_i^{obj} denotes the presence of object in cell i, l_{ij}^{obj} the jth bounding box in cell i, C is a set of classes with $p(c)$ probability, B is the set of bounding boxes, S^2 is the grids and x, y, w, h are coordinates.

Our final detector is MTCNN. This method employs online hard mining of samples to improve detection. These samples are positive face samples, negative face samples and partial faces. Detection is achieved in three-stages with three different CNNs from a coarse to fine-grained detection (P-Net, R-Net and O-Net). The first stage, P-Net, proposes candidate faces which are graded using bounding box regression and Non-Maxima Suppression (NMS) to get the high likely face candidates. The second stage is used to isolate false candidates through NMS and bounding box regression. The final stage applies supervision in learning the correct face regions. The supervision signal is a face classification and the overall loss is the sum of the Eqs. 6 and 7.

$$L_i^{det} = -(y_i^{det} \log(p_i) + 1 - y_i^{det}(1 - \log(p_i))) \tag{6}$$

$$l_i^{box} = ||\hat{y}_i^{box} - y_i^{box}||_2^2 \tag{7}$$

where y_i are ground truths and $p_i, \hat{y}$ are the network outputs.

3.1 Face Recognition

Different loss functions are employed in this domain that captures the similarities between image pairs or sometimes the popular probabilistic based softmax functions. The basic idea in these losses is somewhat similar but newer losses provide better parameter handling and samples combination [28]. Losses may be task-dependent, that is whether the target is an open-set or a closed-set recognition.

VGGface2 relies on a simple softmax classifier to train a ResNet for face identification task. Because of the size of the network and dataset, VGGFace learns to separate samples of different identities and brings closet samples from the same identity in the embedding space.

FaceNet uses a triplet loss to achieve face verification. The triplet loss function makes use of an anchor image x^a, positive image x^p and a negative image x^n. The loss maximizes the distance between the anchor and a negative image while minimizing the distance between the anchor and the positive sample. However, the models require the right anchor, positive, negative batch combinations for best performance. Equation 8 shows how the triplet loss is evaluated.

$$L = ||f(x_i^a) - f(x_i^p)||_2^2 + \alpha < ||f(x_i^a) - f(x_i^n)||_2^2 \tag{8}$$

Where α is a margin hyper-parameter.

Arcface uses an additive angular margin to penalizes the loss based on a geodesic distance between samples in a hyper-sphere using an arc-cosine function. This is an extension of angular softmax. Angular softmax (A-softmax) [26] adds a constraint in the hypersphere to learn better discriminative features in face recognition. A-softmax is more efficient than traditional softmax because it adopts a different decision boundary for each class. Equation 9 shows how the additive angular margin is calculated.

$$L_{arcface} = -\frac{1}{N}\sum_{i=1}^{N} \log \frac{e^{s(\cos(\theta_{y_i}+m))}}{e^{s(\cos(\theta_{y_i}+m))} + \sum_{i=i,j\neq y_i}^{n} e^{s\cos\theta_j}} \tag{9}$$

Where s is the scale of the embedding and m is the margin (kept at 0.5).

4 Experiment

4.1 Datasets

Experiments were carried on two datasets namely, Wider face [29] & VGG2 [5]. Wider face is a popular benchmark for face detection in an uncontrolled environment. It contains faces with high variations in scale, pose, occlusion and illumination. The choice of the dataset is because it captures all the ideal scenarios for a face detection task in the wild. Wider face contains 32,203 images with 393,703 labeled faces. The dataset is split into a train, validation and a test set (40-10-50 split). The train set was used to train detectors and the validation set was kept as a hold out for evaluation. Results were reported on the validation set because we do not have access to the test set ground truth.

VGG2 Dataset is a large scale face recognition dataset with about 3.3 m images. Images are taken in a more controlled environment but some pictures contain multiple faces, occlusion and varying light conditions. VGG2 has many samples per identity. The dataset is split across 8631 identities in the training set and 500 identities in the test set. Both of these sets are disjoint, making the dataset ideal for facial verification task. For our recognition task, the test set is kept as a hold-out for evaluation.

4.2 Experimental Set-Up

The detector models (HOG, MTCNN, YOLO) were trained using wider face dataset. Our HOG detector is based on the implementation in Dlib library, details can be found here[1]. Wider Face annotations were converted to XML using a python script. For MTCNN, we used a pre-trained model available at[2] which was also trained on wider face. YOLO version 3 model was trained on Wider Face following the protocol specified in[3]. Annotations were first converted to YOLO standards then, new filters and anchor boxes were evaluated before training. We used a batch size of 64 and subdivision of 16, and training was stopped when the loss remained unchanged for many iterations. In all experiments, no further pre-processing was applied to data apart from augmentation and sampling/mining techniques peculiar to the models. The models were evaluated on the test set on the number of correctly detected faces and a positive detection is considered if the IOU is over 0.4.

The recognition models (Arcface, VGGFace and FaceNet) were trained on VGG2 dataset. Prior to training, the face area was cropped out from the images using the bounding box information provided. All models were trained using a ResNet-50 backbone. The Arcface model was obtained from the authors official GitHub repository[4]. No age prediction or LFW dataset verification was employed during training. We only used a validation set for verification after 2000 batches. The training was terminated when the error rate was less than zero when the validation and training accuracies are almost the same. We trained FaceNet model using the Arcface repository but changed the loss function to a triplet loss and all other settings remain thesame. We used a pre-trained VGGface model from[5] which was trained on thesame dataset and ResNet-50 model. These models were evaluated on face crops from the test data with no further facial alignment or augmentation done. This is to give us a better understanding of the actual performance or effect of the approaches used in training the models.

Testing was carried out by generating image pairs from the test set. Using ten folds, a total of 100k pairs were generated with 50% negative matches in the pairs. The models were evaluated by measuring the True Accept Rate (TAR), False Accept Rate (FAR) and False Reject Rate (FRR). These metrics were calculated using Eqs. 10, 11 and 12. At test time, the models were used to extract facial embeddings from pairs. A correct match is measured using cosine similarity between these facial embeddings. A threshold of 0.5 was chosen and all faces with similarity less than or equal to the threshold are considered a match. The threshold value was chosen from repeated experimentation.

$$TAR = \frac{matches}{samplesize} \tag{10}$$

[1] https://github.com/davisking/dlib.
[2] https://pypi.org/project/mtcnn/.
[3] https://github.com/pjreddie/darknet.
[4] https://github.com/deepinsight/insightface.
[5] https://github.com/WeidiXie/Keras-VGGFace2-ResNet50.

$$FAR = \frac{falseacceptance}{samplesize} \quad (11)$$

$$FRR = \frac{falserejections}{samplesize} \quad (12)$$

5 Discussion

Table 1 shows the detection performances from each model. HOG detection had the lowest false detection rate of 1.32% with YOLO and MTCNN at 8.95% and 5.04% respectively. This is not surprising given the number of detected samples. HOG detector struggled to detect face because of the varying image conditions in the dataset. As seen in Fig. 1, HOG detector is affected significantly by scale, pose and occlusion.

YOLO is a general detector but shows robustness in this challenging domain. YOLO performed significantly better than HOG. From the sample detection in Fig. 1, we can see that Partial face view or partial occlusion do not affect YOLO. However, it struggles with considerable occlusion. Also, it had the worst false detection rate among the models. This may indicate that it sometimes finds it difficult to distinguish the background from faces. YOLO re-scale images in training and this is meant to improve detection of smaller objects. But we discovered that some small and blurry faces were also missed.

MTCNN detected more faces than the other detectors in this experiment. It also had a low false detection rate which demonstrates the benefits of training on negative samples. The model is also not affected by scale or partial occlusion. However, we observed that there were instances when partial faces were missed.

Generally, all the models show good IOU on the detected faces. The high average IOU returned by these models suggest reliability in these challenging circumstances. That said, none of the detectors achieved over 50% detection with IOU threshold of over 0.4.

Table 1. Face detection performances

Model	Ground truth	Detected faces	False detections	Average IOU
HOG	39708	5774	76	0.69
YOLO	39708	14846	1328	0.62
MTCNN	39708	17047	860	0.73

Table 2. Face recognition performances

Model	TAR	FAR	FRR
VGGface2	86.27	0.15	13.58
FaceNet	84.97	0.13	14.90
Arcface	88.13	1.25	10.62

(a) HOG

(b) YOLO

(c) MTCNN

Fig. 1. Sample face detection output from the three detection models

Tables 2 shows the performances of the face recognition models. All models had a very low false acceptance rate. This points to the facts that there was a clear separation of dissimilar samples by the models in the embedding space. However, the number of false rejections is significantly high. This is could be associated with the varying image conditions in the dataset used. We observed that some of the false rejection were due to pose angle and partial faces.

In this experiment, both VGGface2 and Arcface generated better embeddings than FaceNet. This shows that the two models trained using variants of softmax produced better facial features that the model trained on triplets. But this was at the expense of a slightly higher false acceptance rate. That said, the performances were generally below expectations and demonstrate the reliance of these model of preprocessing to achieve optimum performances.

Furthermore, one may argue that the metric or threshold value chosen could have played a part. However, when face alignment was introduced as a preprocessing step in a different experiment, the TAR increased by almost 9% across board. Thus, there is little connection between the threshold or metric and the performance. And this indicates that preprocessing continue to be significant in face recognition models.

6 Conclusion

In this paper, we analyze the performances of established face detection and recognition models. Experiments were conducted to compare models trained on a common dataset and the same recognition task. The performances of these models were evaluated using different metrics and the results indicated that optimum performance can be obtained only when extra preprocessing steps are carried out. These techniques are domain-specific and may create an overhead on the overall system and this may hinder their uses in real-time applications. This work opens a new research direction on the need for methods that rely less on preprocessing for optimum performances.

References

1. Ali-Gombe, A., Elyan, E.: MFC-GAN: class-imbalanced dataset classification using multiple fake class generative adversarial network. Neurocomputing **361**, 212–221 (2019)
2. Ali-Gombe, A., Elyan, E., Jayne, C.: Multiple fake classes GAN for data augmentation in face image dataset. In: 2019 International Joint Conference on Neural Networks (IJCNN)
3. Anjos, A., El-Shafey, L., Wallace, R., Günther, M., McCool, C., Marcel, S.: Bob: a free signal processing and machine learning toolbox for researchers. In: Proceedings of the 20th ACM International Conference on Multimedia. ACM (2012)
4. Boulkenafet, Z., Komulainen, J., Hadid, A.: Face spoofing detection using colour texture analysis. IEEE Trans. Inf. Forensics Secur. **11**, 1818–1830 (2016)
5. Cao, Q., Shen, L., Xie, W., Parkhi, O.M., Zisserman, A.: VGGFace2: a dataset for recognising faces across pose and age. In: 13th IEEE International Conference on Automatic Face and Gesture Recognition (FG 2018) (2018)

6. Dalal, N., Triggs, B.: Histograms of oriented gradients for human detection. In: IEEE Computer Society Conference on Computer Vision & Pattern Recognition (2005)
7. Deng, J., Guo, J., Xue, N., Zafeiriou, S.: ArcFace: additive angular margin loss for deep face recognition. In: Proceedings of the IEEE Conference on CVPR (2019)
8. Deng, J., Guo, J., Zhou, Y., Yu, J., Kotsia, I., Zafeiriou, S.: RetinaFace: single-stage dense face localisation in the wild. arXiv preprint arXiv:1905.00641 (2019)
9. Girshick, R., Donahue, J., Darrell, T., Malik, J.: Region-based convolutional networks for accurate object detection and segmentation. IEEE Trans. Pattern Anal. Mach. Intell. **38**, 142–158 (2015)
10. Günther, M., et al.: Unconstrained face detection and open-set face recognition challenge. In: IEEE International Joint Conference on Biometrics (IJCB) (2017)
11. Kemelmacher-Shlizerman, I., Seitz, S.M., Miller, D., Brossard, E.: The MegaFace benchmark: 1 million faces for recognition at scale. In: Proceedings of the IEEE Conference on Computer Vision and Pattern Recognition (2016)
12. King, D.E.: Max-margin object detection. arXiv preprint arXiv:1502.00046 (2015)
13. Li, H., Lin, Z., Shen, X., Brandt, J., Hua, G.: A convolutional neural network cascade for face detection. In: Proceedings of the IEEE Conference on Computer Vision and Pattern Recognition (2015)
14. Liu, W., Anguelov, D., Erhan, D., Szegedy, C., Reed, S., Fu, C.Y., Berg, A.C.: SSD: Single shot multibox detector. In: European Conference on Computer Vision (2016)
15. Liu, W., Wen, Y., Yu, Z., Li, M., Raj, B., Song, L.: SphereFace: deep hypersphere embedding for face recognition. In: Proceedings of the IEEE Conference on Computer Vision and Pattern Recognition (2017)
16. Mehdipour Ghazi, M., Kemal Ekenel, H.: A comprehensive analysis of deep learning based representation for face recognition. In: Proceedings of the IEEE Conference on Computer Vision and Pattern Recognition Workshops, pp. 34–41 (2016)
17. Parkhi, O.M., Vedaldi, A., Zisserman, A., et al.: Deep face recognition. In: BMVC, vol. 1, p. 6 (2015)
18. Redmon, J., Divvala, S., Girshick, R., Farhadi, A.: You only look once: unified, real-time object detection. In: Proceedings of the IEEE Conference on Computer Vision and Pattern Recognition (2016)
19. Schroff, F., Kalenichenko, D., Philbin, J.: Facenet: a unified embedding for face recognition and clustering. In: Proceedings of the IEEE Conference on Computer Vision and Pattern Recognition, pp. 815–823 (2015)
20. Sun, Y., Chen, Y., Wang, X., Tang, X.: Deep learning face representation by joint identification-verification. In: Advances in Neural Information Processing Systems, pp. 1988–1996 (2014)
21. Sun, Y., Wang, X., Tang, X.: Deep learning face representation from predicting 10,000 classes. In: Proceedings of the IEEE Conference on Computer Vision and Pattern Recognition, pp. 1891–1898 (2014)
22. Sun, Y., Wang, X., Tang, X.: Deeply learned face representations are sparse, selective, and robust. In: Proceedings of the IEEE Conference on Computer Vision and Pattern Recognition, pp. 2892–2900 (2015)
23. Taigman, Y., Yang, M., Ranzato, M., Wolf, L.: DeepFace: closing the gap to human-level performance in face verification. In: Proceedings of the IEEE Conference on Computer Vision and Pattern Recognition, pp. 1701–1708 (2014)
24. Taigman, Y., Yang, M., Ranzato, M., Wolf, L.: Web-scale training for face identification. In: Proceedings of the IEEE Conference on CVPR (2015)

25. Viola, P., Jones, M.J.: Robust real-time face detection. Int. J. Comput. Vis. **57**(2), 137–154 (2004)
26. Wang, H., Wang, Y., Zhou, Z., Ji, X., Gong, D., Zhou, J., Li, Z., Liu, W.: CosFace: large margin cosine loss for deep face recognition. In: Proceedings of the IEEE Conference on Computer Vision and Pattern Recognition (2018)
27. Wang, J., Yuan, Y., Yu, G.: Face attention network: an effective face detector for the occluded faces. arXiv preprint arXiv:1711.07246 (2017)
28. Wang, M., Deng, W.: Deep face recognition: a survey. arXiv:1804.06655 (2018)
29. Yang, S., Luo, P., Loy, C.C., Tang, X.: Wider face: a face detection benchmark. In: IEEE Conference on Computer Vision and Pattern Recognition (CVPR) (2016)
30. Zeng, Y., Lu, E., Sun, Y., Tian, R.: Responsible facial recognition and beyond. arXiv preprint arXiv:1909.12935 (2019)
31. Zhang, K., Zhang, Z., Li, Z., Qiao, Y.: Joint face detection and alignment using multitask cascaded convolutional networks. IEEE Signal Process. Lett. **23**, 1499–1503 (2016)

Machine Learning in Medical Systems and Applications

Automated Screening of Patients for Dietician Referral

Kamran Soomro and Elias Pimenidis(✉)

Computer Science Research Centre, University of the West of England, Bristol, UK
{kamran.soomro,elias.pimenidis}@uwe.ac.uk

Abstract. Critical Care Units (CCU) in a hospital treat the severely sick patients that need constant monitoring and close medical attention. Feeding patients, enteral feeding in particular, is a critical and continuous process. Monitoring patients, managing their feeding and referring to a dietician is a key factor in CCUs. Screening patients for referral to a dietician in a CCU is an error-prone and complicated task. One of the main challenges in this regard is that the data needed to screen patients is scattered among many different variables and textual forms. The number of patients being treated in the CCU is also a significant problem since it becomes difficult for the staff to keep track of the needs of all patients. Therefore, an automated screening tool can support effectively the feeding process and contribute considerably towards improving the quality and consistency of patient care. In this paper we present early stages of a project that aims at using machine learning techniques to help CCU consultants to automatically screen patients for dietician referral.

Keywords: Automated patient screening · CCU screening · Dietician referral · Patient data processing

1 Introduction

This paper presents the early stages of a project that aims at using Artificial Intelligence to analyse data collected in the critical care units (or intensive care units) of a National Health Service (NHS) hospital in the UK. Critical Care Units (CCUs) are where the sickest patients are admitted and where large amounts of detailed clinical data are collected (usually hourly) for the duration of the patient's stay. Most CCUs, have moved from paper to clinical information systems to capture data from the patients' monitor, ventilator and other equipment into an extensive database. Currently, CCUs are not using these systems and data to their advantage, with much of the captured data left unanalysed. In an era of limited NHS resources, these digital resources have the potential to both optimise patient outcomes and make systems more efficient and effective.

Supported by the University of the West of England, Bristol.

L. Iliadis et al. (Eds.): EANN 2020, INNS 2, pp. 319–325, 2020.
https://doi.org/10.1007/978-3-030-48791-1_24

Data analysis and machine learning systems have been used widely in CCUs, primarily to automate processes where problems are well known and fully defined, and there the deliverables to efficiency and accuracy achieved are well within the expected levels [1,7].

CCUs aim to optimise the patients' survival, clinical outcomes and to reduce harm caused by therapies. All CCUs have recognised targets to improve outcomes, such as maintaining an optimal sedation level, maintaining lung volumes delivered by the ventilator within a specific range and delivering a minimum amount of nutrition to patients whilst they are critically ill. Yet, these targets are often not achieved. This study aims to use these common targets to assess the feasibility of using this clinical data routinely collected can be used to improve the achievement of these targets.

The aim of this project is to determine how routine clinical data collected in CCUs can be used to optimise patient outcomes by augmenting clinician decision making and altering clinician behaviour to optimise patient clinical outcomes.

This study will focus on optimising three common clinical targets: sedation level, mechanical ventilation and enteral nutrition in patients of all ages requiring intensive care. These interventions have been selected because they can be defined regardless of age; and are known to be poorly met in practice [8,9]. Data produced by the clinical information system at the CCUs has been studied to determine its quality and suitability for exposure to advanced analysis techniques. Data has been filtered and cleaned to develop a suitable experimental repository that is compatible with further analysis techniques. The data will be mined to reveal potential associations that will enhance the detail, quality and significance of the information that could be passed on to the clinicians at the CCUs.

1.1 Aims and Project Plan

The collected data has been formatted in a way that allows for it to be uniform, easily stored and accessed in an efficient way. The formatting and cleaning of the data will allow for the results of processing to return outputs that are consistent in the nature and format of the output, can be interpreted consistently over the same organisational criteria, guaranteeing that outcomes are compatible throughout time. This phase will determine which of the data elements produced by the clinical information system will be useful for further processing and suitable for delivering coherent outcomes. All patient data has been anonymised in accordance to the ethics of the NHS in the UK and in accordance to the UK Data Protection Act which encompasses the GDPR.

Data will be stored in repositories that are only accessible to the members of the team of this project. The processing at this initial stage will involve data mining techniques that will aim to reveal hidden associations within the data. These will be explored as to being consistent over time, i.e. the same types of associations confirmed over different data batches. The analysis will also explore the logic of the associations revealed as to whether these are relevant to the aims of the clinicians, i.e. whether the extracted context in the data associations is suitable to support decision making in the target areas that have been identified for this project. These conclusions will allow, the members of the project team working on the analysis of the data, to carefully select among the data produced those elements that will support meaningful further processing. Thus, the volume of data that will be utilised for the next stage of the research will be those reduced to those data that will contribute directly to meeting the aims of this project, by processing via advanced Artificial Intelligence techniques.

For the next phase of the work, different machine learning techniques and algorithms will be utilised. The aim here will be to process the data items selected in the previous phase of the analysis to allow the work team and the participating clinicians to assess the efficiency and effectiveness of these techniques and algorithms. The data that has been cleaned, prepared and formatted at the initial phase will be split into training and test sections, with the formal used to train the machine learning algorithms and the latter to attempt to reproduce known results. The accuracy and efficiency, of the algorithms that will be exposed to this experimental data, will be assessed by the project team. Decisions as to the usefulness of each of the techniques explored will be made; if deemed necessary, the clinicians will provide additional patient case data to assist resolving the suitability of these techniques. On completion of this phase of processing and testing, results and conclusions will be reviewed by the project team to assess their usefulness and the potential of expanding this research further to a full scale system. Such a system will be engaged to process data in real time and aim to support decisions made by the clinicians, by drawing away the complexity of processing rich and voluminous data and providing the benefits of data associations that will support faster and more accurate decision making the CCU clinicians.

One of the most urgent needs in any CCU is that of screening and managing a patient's enteral feeding [4]. There could be complications in a patient's health that could lead to a reaction to feeding at any time during the day. These would in turn lead to decisions in changing the patient's feeding patterns, stopping feeding temporarily, or referring the patient to a dietician for further assessment. Screening is complicated due to the sources and types of data that have to be considered at very frequent intervals, the number of nursing staff available to do so and the impact it could have on the overall treatment of the patient. This has been identified as a first priority in this project.

2 The Problem

After consultation with CCU consultants, one of the problems identified to be targeted within this project is the screening of patients for referral to dieticians. The main problem in this regard is that there are numerous factors to consider. These include:

1) Patient Body Mass Index less than $18.5\,kg/m^2$.
2) Patient received little or no nutrition for 5 days or more.

3) Patient has been admitted in critical care ≥3 days and receiving enteral tube feeding as per protocol.
4) Patient received Jejunal tube feeding.
5) Patient received renal replacement therapy (intermittent or continuous) 3 days or more.
6) Patient has liver disease.
7) Patient has Pancreatitis.
8) Patient has Chyle leak.
9) Patient has significant short bowel resections and/or high output ileostomy.
10) Pressure has ulcer category 2 or above.
11) Health professionals have concerns regarding nutrition.

Determining whether a patient needs referral to a dietician requires subjective assessment by the clinicians based on these factors. The issue is further complicated by the fact that this information is not directly recorded. It either needs to be inferred from various attributes recorded in the patient history or from the text-based patient history. For example, whether a patient has liver disease or not is not directly recorded anywhere. A consultant can look at an attribute such as the patient's Albumin or Bilirubin levels and determine that the patient has liver problems, though this would still not indicate if the problems are chronic or acute [3]. That aspect is only recorded in the patient history.

The aforementioned complications present significant challenges in the automation of the nutritional screening process. Therefore, the first challenge in developing such a system is to synthesise the variables that can be fed into an appropriate learning algorithm. Different approaches could be adopted for this purpose. For example, for determining the presence of liver disease, one approach could be to perform a fuzzy word match to search the patient history for text related to liver disease. This text could then be analysing using natural language processing to determine if the patient has acute or chronic liver disease. Another approach could be to analyse the patient's Albumin and Bilirubin levels within the algorithm and determine if there are indications of liver disease. However, this approach has the potential pitfall that it analysing such measurements usually requires expert knowledge.

3 The Data

The CCU data is recorded in a Microsoft SQL Server database using a metamodel specifically developed to store the information. Each patient is afforded a *PatientID* upon first encounter with the NHS. Thereafter, each patient visit is recorded as a separate *encounter* with a unique *EncounterID*. This helps to keep track of each unique visit by the patient to the NHS, which may be spread out over time and for different healthcare issues. The NHS database contains a predefined list of *interventions* that may be applied to patients, identified by a unique *InterventionID*. Each intervention further has different *attributes* that can be recorded, each with its own *AttributeIDs*. For example, two sample interventions along with their attributes are shown in Fig. 1.

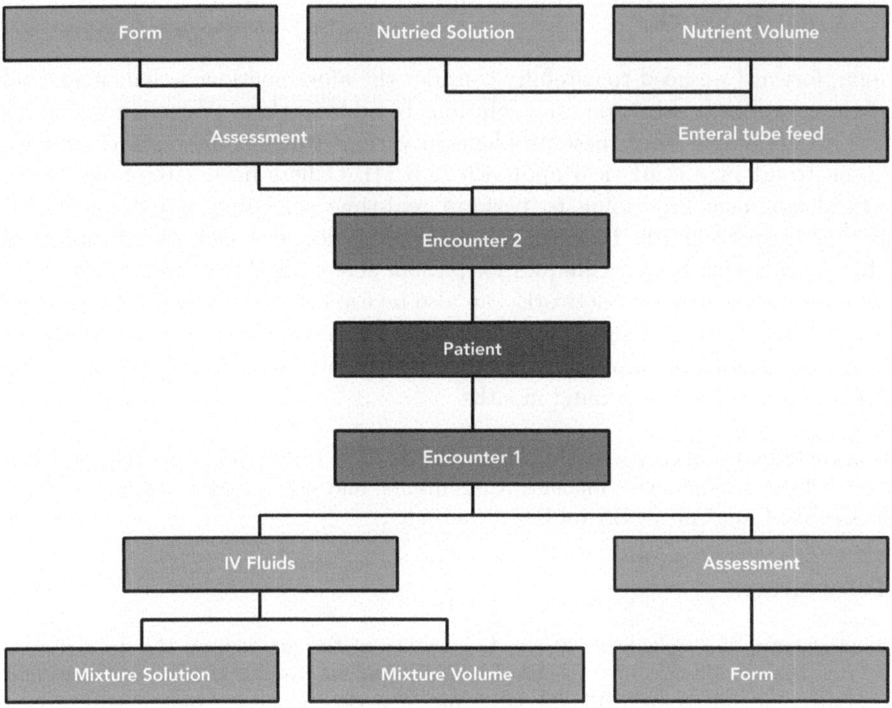

Fig. 1. Simplified NHS data model.

In total the database comprises about 250 GB consisting of data of approximately 5,000 patients. Each *encounter* also has a free-form text field associated with it that contains the CCU consultant's notes about the patient. Furthermore, various patient measurements are also recorded such as weight, height, age, initial diagnosis etc. Some patient attributes such as height and weight are recorded only upon admission and/or discharge and additionally as needed. Other attributes, such as blood pressure, heart rate etc are automatically recorded more frequently by the monitoring equipment on the beds. The exact frequency can be set by the CCU consultants such as half hourly, hourly, daily etc. For the purposes of this project, the complexity arises from the fact that much of the information is recorded in the free-form text fields and is not directly recorded anywhere. For example, to determine whether a patient has received little or no nutrition over the past 5 days, we face the same challenge as with determining if the patient has liver disease. We could either aggregate the nutritional intake information recorded in the database, or use natural language processing techniques to extract the same information from the free-form text field. For the former, there are additional issues such as classifying the nutrition as too little or sufficient. Another issue is that the nutritional intake information is not recorded as a single intervention, but in many different interventions. Careful study and foresight is required to accurately extract the necessary information.

4 Future Work

Going forward we need to carefully consider the aforementioned challenges, and devise appropriate strategies and solutions to address them. Various researchers have attempted to solve these problems in various ways. Some researchers have chosen to adopt a statistical approach [2,6,11]. Others have attempted to use natural language processing to perform real-time screening of patients based on their history [5,10]. However, there appears to be a lack of utilisation of other machine-learning techniques for patient screening. We propose that other techniques such as neural networks can also be used to effectively screen patients for dietician referral. A significant challenge in this regard would be synthesis of the required data for input into the learning algorithm. These aspects will be explored further in the coming months.

Acknowledgements. We would like to acknowledge the support and help provided by Dr Chris McWilliams, Clinicians, Consultants, and other clinical researchers from the Critical Care Unit at Bristol Royal Infirmary.

References

1. Ghassemi, M., Celi, L.A., Stone, D.J.: State of the art review: the data revolution in critical care. In: Vincent, J.L. (ed.) Annual Update in Intensive Care and Emergency Medicine 2015, vol. 2015, pp. 573–586. Springer, Cham (2015)
2. González, C., García-Berrocal, B., Pérez, M., Navajo, J.A., Herraez, O., González-Buitrago, J.M.: Laboratory screening of connective tissue diseases by a new automated ENA screening assay (EliA Symphony) in clinically defined patients. Clinica Chim. Acta **359**(1–2), 109–114 (2005). https://doi.org/10.1016/j.cccn.2005.03.042
3. Hall, P., Cash, J.: What is the real function of the liver 'function' tests? Ulster Med. J. **81**(1), 30–36 (2012)
4. Hansen, C.C., Dissanaike, S.: Nutrition in the intensive care unit. Southwest Respir. Crit. Care Chron. **3**(10), 10–16 (2015). https://pulmonarychronicles.com/index.php/pulmonarychronicles/article/view/195
5. He, Q., Veldkamp, B.P., Glas, C.A.W., de Vries, T.: Automated assessment of patients' self-narratives for posttraumatic stress disorder screening using natural language processing and text mining. Assessment **24**(2), 157–172 (2017). https://doi.org/10.1177/1073191115602551
6. Jeong, S., Yang, H., Hwang, H.: Evaluation of an automated connective tissue disease screening assay in Korean patients with systemic rheumatic diseases. PLOS ONE **12**(3), e0173597 (2017). https://doi.org/10.1371/journal.pone.0173597
7. Lovejoy, C.A., Buch, V., Maruthappu, M.: Artificial intelligence in the intensive care unit. Crit. Care **23**(1), 7 (2019). https://doi.org/10.1186/s13054-018-2301-9
8. Mehta, N.M., Bechard, L.J., Cahill, N., Wang, M., Day, A., Duggan, C.P., Heyland, D.K.: Nutritional practices and their relationship to clinical outcomes in critically ill children–an international multicenter cohort study. Crit. Care Med. **40**(7), 2204–2211 (2012). https://doi.org/10.1097/CCM.0b013e31824e18a8
9. Nassar, A.P., Zampieri, F.G., Salluh, J.I., Bozza, F.A., Machado, F.R., Guimarães, H.P., Damiani, L.P., Cavalcanti, A.B.: Organizational factors associated with target sedation on the first 48 h of mechanical ventilation: an analysis of checklist-ICU database. Crit. Care **23**(1), 34 (2019). https://doi.org/10.1186/s13054-019-2323-y

10. Ni, Y., Bermudez, M., Kennebeck, S., Liddy-Hicks, S., Dexheimer, J.: A real-time automated patient screening system for clinical trials eligibility in an emergency department: design and evaluation. JMIR Med. Inf. **7**(3), e14185 (2019). https://doi.org/10.2196/14185
11. Valentine, N.A., Alhawassi, T.M., Roberts, G.W., Vora, P.P., Stranks, S.N., Doogue, M.P.: Detecting undiagnosed diabetes using glycated haemoglobin: an automated screening test in hospitalised patients. Med. J. Aust. **194**(4), 160–164 (2011). https://doi.org/10.5694/j.1326-5377.2011.tb03762.x

Drug2vec: A Drug Embedding Method with Drug-Drug Interaction as the Context

Pengfei Liu, Xubin Zheng, Man-Hon Wong, and Kwong-Sak Leung(✉)

The Chinese University of Hong Kong, Shatin, Hong Kong SAR, China
{pfliu,xbzheng,mhwong,ksleung}@cse.cuhk.edu.hk

Abstract. The combinatorial pharmacological effects of drugs are influenced by the complex interactions among them. When the patient is allergic to some drugs, the combination of drugs have to be changed. Based on that, we put forward a linear-algebra-equation query task. In this paper, we propose a model called Drug2vec that approximates the relationship among drugs and can solve the linear-algebra-equation query task. For example, we can find drugs with the following relationship: *drug A + drug B = drug C*. Drug2vec applies a three-layer neural network, which firstly projects a drug into an embedded space and then retrieves another drug that interacts with it. Experimental results show that Drug2vec can approximate the relationship among drugs to linear equations, and the drugs that fit a linear equation have connections with respect to their structures. We also propose a metric called AUE (area under the enrichment curve) to evaluate the performance of our model. Drug2vec can predict drug-drug interactions with high accuracy, and the AUE can be 0.96 in the normal test. The AUE score of Drug2vec can be greatly increased with linear modification in the blind test.

Keywords: Deep learning · Drug-drug interaction · Drug discovery

1 Introduction

Drug combinatorial therapy plays an important role in modern medical healthcare as it can provide more comprehensive treatment for patients. In many cases, patients are treated with multiple medicines at the same time. Some patients may be allergic to some drugs and the drug combination should be replaced. Hence, it is important to search for new drug combinatorial treatment and provide suggestions for physician. Analyzing drug-drug interaction (DDI) via *in vivo* and *in vitro* methods are accurate and reliable, however, they are also relatively expensive, time consuming and even involves moral considerations [14]. On the other

P. Liu, X. Zheng—Both authors contributed equally to the work.

L. Iliadis et al. (Eds.): EANN 2020, INNS 2, pp. 326–337, 2020.
https://doi.org/10.1007/978-3-030-48791-1_25

hand, estimating drug-drug interaction *in silico* is much more convenient, expeditious and economical. Therefore, we come up with a task called linear-algebra-equation query in drug-drug interaction analysis via computational method.

In this paper, we proposed a model called Drug2vec that can estimate the drug-drug interaction. It can be applied to do linear-algebra-equation query and to predict drug-drug interaction. Linear-algebra-equation query is a task that finds a set of drugs that have relationship described by a linear algebra equation. For example, we want to find *drug A, B, C* that meet the requirement represent by an equation: $drug\ A + drug\ B = drug\ D$. The query relation among drugs is presented as a linear algebra equation. That is why we call it linear-algebra-equation query.

Our model is inspired by the Word2vec model in natural language processing (NLP)[5]. Word2vec is a three-layer neural network with only one hidden layer. It breaks long sentences into word pairs within local contexts. Then a one-hot representation of the word pairs is projected to a lower-dimensional vector in a smaller embedded space. This vector is called embedded vector. Word2vec model is of critical importance in NLP as it simplifies the relationship among words.

Drug2vec has the same structure as word2vec, in which there is only one hidden layer and no activation or pooling function is applied. The context for Drug2vec is defined as the DDI network. Similar to what word2vec achieves in NLP, Drug2vec can represent drugs as vectors and approximate the relationships among drugs to simple linear algebra equations. The new representative vectors can also be applied to predict DDI with high accuracy. However, when dealing with a new drug that has never met before, the model does not perform well. In that case, we apply linear repair method in our model to make the whole model more robust.

In this paper, Drug2vec is implemented using Pytorch (version 1.00) which is a widely used package in deep learning. All the codes and data are available online: https://github.com/Lowpassfilter/Drug2vec.

The rest of this paper is arranged as follows: the related works in DDI analysis are given in Sect. 2, and the linear-algebra-equation task and the details of Drug2vec model are discussed in Sect. 3. Section 4 is about the evaluation method for Drug2vec, and the experimental results and discussion are given in Sect. 5. In the end, we draw a conclusion of this work in Sect. 6.

2 Related Works

The field of computer-aided drug-drug interaction (DDI) analysis has been explored for a few years. The most effective methods developed in the recent year can be classified as matrix factorization (MF) approach or neural network approach. For example, in [12] the authors applied a semi-non-negative matrix factorization for DDI prediction. The values in the low-ranked decomposed matrix are restricted to be non-negative to provide better understandability. Deep learning is known for its ability to comprehend relationship among high dimensional data. It is quite suitable for understanding the complex interaction among drugs. [7] built an 8 layers fully connected neural network for DDI and drug-food interactions. The authors also conducted experiments on Drugbank and gave detailed statistics for this database. [15] designed a position aware multi-task deep neural network and outperformed the state of the art in DDI Extraction Challenge 2013.

The word2vec technique in natural language processing (NLP) gradually shows its power in cheminformatics and bioinformatics in the recent years. [1] proposed ProtVec to represent the amino-acid sequences and applied it to do protein family classification. [10] and [8] applied word2vec to find the adverse drug reactions from Twitter data or medical records. Later on Mol2vec was introduced in [2] to learn vector representations of the molecular substructures. The compounds encoded vectors were then combined with supervised machine learning methods to predict compound properties. In [3] FP2VEC was proposed to obtain the embedding vector of compounds for their quantitative structure-activity relationship (QSAR) model in order to predict properties of chemical compounds. [13] introduced IVS2vec and dense fully connected neural network (DFCNN) to predict whether a molecule can bind the potential targets or not.

Despite the success of applying word2vec, there are still works that have not done yet. Firstly, the word2vec focuses on representing the complex relationships among words, but till now, the applications in bioinformatics are only focus on classification tasks. We believe that the word2vec can do more. We came up with an idea to represent the complex relationship among drugs and furthermore to deal with the linear-algebra-equation query task. Secondly, the word2vec has not been applied for DDI analysis. Therefore, in this paper, we define a linear-algebra-equation query task and then propose the Drug2vec model, a derivative of word2vec for this task and DDI analysis.

3 Drug2vec

The idea behind Drug2vec is inspired by the word2vec technique in natural language processing (NLP) area. In this section, the linear-algebra-equation query is firstly defined and then the word2vec is briefly introduced. After that, the Drug2vec is explained in details including how it works and how to solve the linear-algebra-equation query task. However, there is limitation of the neural network in the model. Therefore, we include the matrix factorization (MF) in our Drug2vec model for the so-called blind test.

3.1 Linear-Algebra-Equation Query

In drug therapy, some patients may be allergic to some drugs. In that situation, the doctor have to find other drugs that have the similar pharmacological effect. If combinatorial therapy is applied, the situation may become more complicated, because the doctor may have to use another combination of different drugs. For example, omeprazole, clarithromycin and amoxicillin are used to treat the helicobacter pylori. Sometimes the patient may be allergic to amoxicillin and then this drug combination have to be changed.

For replacing one drug, if we describe it in a linear algebra equation, it would be:

$$DrugA = DrugB \tag{1}$$

If it is a combination of drugs, it can also be described in linear algebra equation. For example,

$$DrugA + DrugB = DrugC \tag{2}$$

Generally speaking, we can describe the relationships among drugs via linear algebra equation. As mentioned above, in some real-world situations, we may want to find out which drugs have that kind of relationship described as specific linear algebra equations. Therefore, we come up with a task that is finding drugs interaction or combination given the relationship described in linear algebra equations. It is like searching for records that meet the relationship requirements. Therefore, we name it linear-algebra-equation query.

3.2 Drug2vec Architecture

Although word2vec is initially invented to handle sequential data, it can be modified and applied in approximating the DDI. The definition of context is the key in word2vec. It chops the long word sequences into short overlapped segments and extracts the local relationship among words in each segment. A similar concept of context can be defined for DDI and an example is showed in Fig. 1 (a).

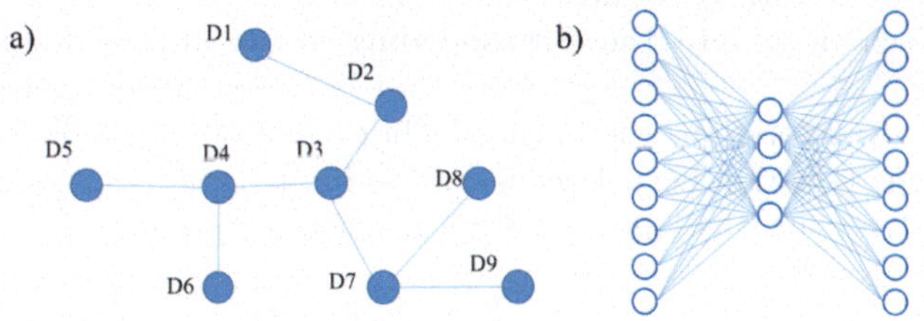

Fig. 1. (a) an example context for the drug-drug interaction network (b) network architecture for Drug2vec method

In DDI networks, the context for each drug within a radius of n can be defined as drugs that can be reached with no more than n steps from it. For example, in Fig. 1 (a), the context for $D2$ with radius 2 is $D1$, $D3$, $D4$, $D7$. For every drug in the context, it composes a drug pair with the central drug. All those drug pairs are used to train the model Drug2vec.

The goal of Drug2vec is to approximate the relationships among drugs and to represent them using linear algebra equations so that we can use it to trace the drugs with relationships described in linear algebra equations. We apply a three-layer neural network to capture the linear relationship. The network structure of Drug2vec is showed in Fig. 1 (b). The first layer is the input layer, where the number of neurons equals the total number of drugs. A drug is represented as a one-hot vector in the input layer. The length of the vector equals to the number of drugs. For each drug, only the value that refer to the drug is 1 while all the other values equal to 0. In Fig. 1 (a), *D*2 is represented as [0, 1, 0, 0, 0, 0, 0, 0, 0]. The middle layer, also called the hidden layer, is the embedding vector space. A drug's one-hot vector is projected to this space, the dimension of which is number of neurons in the hidden layer. The vector obtained in this layer is called the embedded vector or encoded vector. The output layer is of the same size as the input layer. Each neuron in the output layer corresponds to a drug. The output is a one-hot vector in which different indexes representing different drugs. The value corresponding to the drug that have interactions with the input drug is expected to be 1. All the other values equal to 0.

In order to ensure strict linear property of the model, non-linear operations are not used in the network, such as pooling, normalization, or activation function like sigmoid and ReLU [6]. It is important to ensure the network has strict linear relations. Otherwise, it cannot fit the linear algebra relationship very well.

3.3 Drug2vec for Linear-Algebra-Equation Query

The procedures to tackle the linear-algebra-equation query via Drug2vec are described as follows.

- Drug2vec is trained using all the drug pairs to learn to encode a drug into a vector while preserving the relationship between different drugs. The three-layer neural network is obtained that fits the training data most.
- Encode each drug into the corresponding vector in the hidden layer of Drug2vec.
- Fit encoded vectors into the linear algebra equation and look for the drugs that suit the equation best. Because of the limited computational power, we test Drug2vec with the following 3 linear algebra equations:

$$\text{linear relationships} = \begin{cases} A = B \\ A + B = C \\ A + B = C + D \end{cases} \tag{3}$$

We choose the drugs combination with the least L2 loss as the best fitting drugs. As for (3), the L2 loss functions are:

$$\begin{aligned} L2\ Loss_1 &= (f(A) - f(B))^2 \\ L2\ Loss_2 &= (f(A) + f(B) - f(C))^2 \\ L2\ Loss_3 &= (f(A) + f(B) - f(C) - f(D))^2 \end{aligned} \tag{4}$$

where $f(.)$ represent the encoding of the drug.

3.4 Drug2vec for Predicting Drug-Drug Interaction

Drug2vec can also be applied to predict the interactions between drugs. For each drug, the output of the three-layer neural network is a vector that has the same length as the number of drugs. The values in the vector are expected to be approximately 1 at the positions of the interactive drugs, and close to 0 at the positions representing the non-interactive drugs.

In new drug discovery, researchers may produce drugs that have never been seen before. In that case, the neural network may not work well, because the neuron of the drug has never been active during the training process. The three layer neural network can be explained in a more mathematical way as shown in Fig. 2 (a). Suppose the one-hot vector for drug is $d = \{s_1, s_2, ..., s_n\} \subset R^n$, where $s_i \in 0, 1$ and n is the number of drugs. For a drug interaction pair (d_i, d_j), the neural network is actually looking for two matrix $U \subset R^{n \times m}$ and $V \subset R^{m \times n}$, so that $d_i UV = d_j$, where m is the size of the embedded space. The input d_i is a one-shot vector that represents a drug. The linear transformation between the input layer and the hidden layer can be regard as a matrix U. The ith row in the trained matrix U should actually be the embedded vector for drug i. The matrix V represents the transformation between encoded vector of the drug and the output d_j. If the drugs never appear in the training stage, the corresponding rows in U never get trained and keep the initial random values. Then the outputs for the unseen drugs is meaningless. In that situation, the neural network architecture does not work well. Hence, Drug2vec model includes the linear repair method to approximate the untrained rows in U.

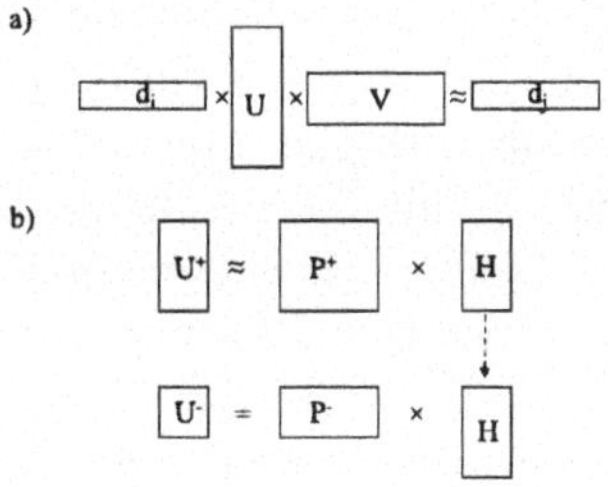

Fig. 2. Drug2vec can be interpreted in a matrix operation view, so that a linear repair method can be defined for the blind test. (a) a matrix perspective to understand Drug2vec (b) an illustration of linear repair method for the blind test

The idea of linear repair method is shown in Fig. 2 (b). Suppose the rows corresponding to the training drugs in U compose a new matrix U^+, and the rows corresponding to the new drugs compose another new matrix U^-. We introduce the feature matrix for training drugs denoted as P^+, and the feature matrix for new drugs denoted as P^-. Using linear regression, a matrix H can be obtained to transfer P^+ to U^+ with the minimal loss shown below:

$$\left\| U^+ - HP^+ \right\|_2 \tag{5}$$

H can also be applied to transfer P^- into a new matrix U^* which is an approximation to U^-:

$$U^* = HP^- \tag{6}$$

When facing a new drug, Drug2vec applies the approximate matrix U^* to repair U of the neural network model. More specifically, the U^- in U is replaced by U^*.

4 Evaluation

There are two objectives of the Drug2vec model. One is to solve the linear-algebra-equation query task, the other is to predict a drug-drug interaction. Therefore, two groups of experiments are conducted to test the performance of Drug2vec.

For the linear-algebra-equation query, Drug2vec is applied to retrieve drugs among the dataset that have the relationship shown as 3 linear-algebra-equation in 3. Then the structure of the drugs is displayed to see whether the drugs retrieved by Drug2vec meet the requirement.

To predict drug-drug interaction, the output of Drug2vec is not a number indicating the probability of the interaction between two drugs. It is a vector whose nearest neighbors indicate interactive drugs. Because there are still interactions among drugs unknown, we cannot decide whether it has interaction if we find the nearest neighboring drug not marked as interactive in the dataset. In that case, we had better evaluate the ability of the model to find existing interaction regardless of the false positive. Moreover, having interaction or not depends on the Euclidean distance from the output vector to the one-hot vector representing a drug. If the output vector is close to a drug, then the drug will be regard as having interaction with the input drug in Drug2vec model. If we choose the closest 20% drugs as interactive drugs, the result will be different from choosing the top 5%. Therefore, it is not applicable to use the metrics in classification to measure the prediction ability in Drug2vec, such as AUROC or AUPR.

To evaluate Drug2vec quantitatively, we define a new metric called area under the enrichment curve (AUE), which is similar to AUROC. The horizontal axis in the enrichment curve is the percentage of the nearest drugs that are predicted as interactive with the input drug. The vertical axis represents the percentage of the testing drugs whose interactive drugs are found. The area under the enrichment curve (AUE) measures how well Drug2vec can find the interactive drugs in a given searching range. The enrichment curve looks similar to the receiver operating curve which starts from the bottom left corner to top right corner. However, the meaning is different. The AUE focuses more on the ability of finding the interaction within the nearest neighborhood of the output vector.

When testing the prediction accuracy of Drug2vec, there are two different settings, which are the normal test and the blind test. In the normal test, drugs can exist in the training and testing set at the same time, and the AUE score can be directly used to measure the performance of Drug2vec. In the blind test, drugs are divided into a big set and a small set. The interactions within the big set are used as training set, and the interactions across the two sets are used as testing set. In the blind test, a drug cannot exist in training and testing set at the same time. The blind test is to simulate the ability of predicting interactions for a new drug. In that situation, the linear repair method is included to enhance the prediction ability of Drug2vec.

5 Experimental Result

5.1 Dataset and Prepossessing

Drugs and their interaction information are downloaded from Drugbank [11], and are prepossessed based on the method reported in [12]. Initially, 2329 drugs are downloaded from Drugbank. 603 of them are selected and the drugs with incomplete information are abandoned. After that, those drugs without the off-label side effects in OFF-SIDES [9], or without chemical structures are further removed. The final drug interaction network contains 568 drugs and 21,351 interactions among them. Among these interactions, 16,757 of them are enhancive DDIs and are regarded as the enhancive network in this paper. On the other hand, 4594 of them are degressive DDIs and are regarded as the degressive network in this paper. If the type of DDIs is not considered, the 21,351 DDIs are regarded as the binary network. Then the context of each drug can be obtained and moreover the pair drugs can be used for training the Drug2vec. From the view of graphics, the enhancive network consists of 2 disconnected components and the degressive network consists of 27 disconnected components which is more fragmental.

The canonical SMILES, drug structure images of the 568 drugs are downloaded from PubChem [4], a comprehensive public online database for molecules. Drugbank provides drug names and drug CIDs that can be retrieved from PubChem. While the names and CIDs of some drugs provided in Drugbank are not consistent in PubChem. On that occasion, CIDs are used with a higher priority. Besides, each drug has an 881-dimensional structural feature vector and a 9149-dimensional OFFSIDES feature vector.

5.2 Result of Linear-Algebra Equation Query

Drug2vec is tested to show its capacity to retrieve drugs for linear-algebra-equation query. Drug2vec is trained on the complete set of the drug pairs for 100 epochs. Then, the one-hot representations of the 568 drugs are put into Drug2vec and their embedded vectors in the hidden layers are saved. After that, these 568 embedded vectors of drugs are fed into three linear-algebra-equation queries in 3 respectively. The most suitable combinations of drugs that meet the linear-algebra-equation requirement are retrieved using L2 loss shown in 4. The structures of the best drug combinations are shown in Fig. 3.

Figure 3 (a) is the result for equation $A = B$. It can be seen that when structures of the retrieved drugs are extremely similar to each other with only

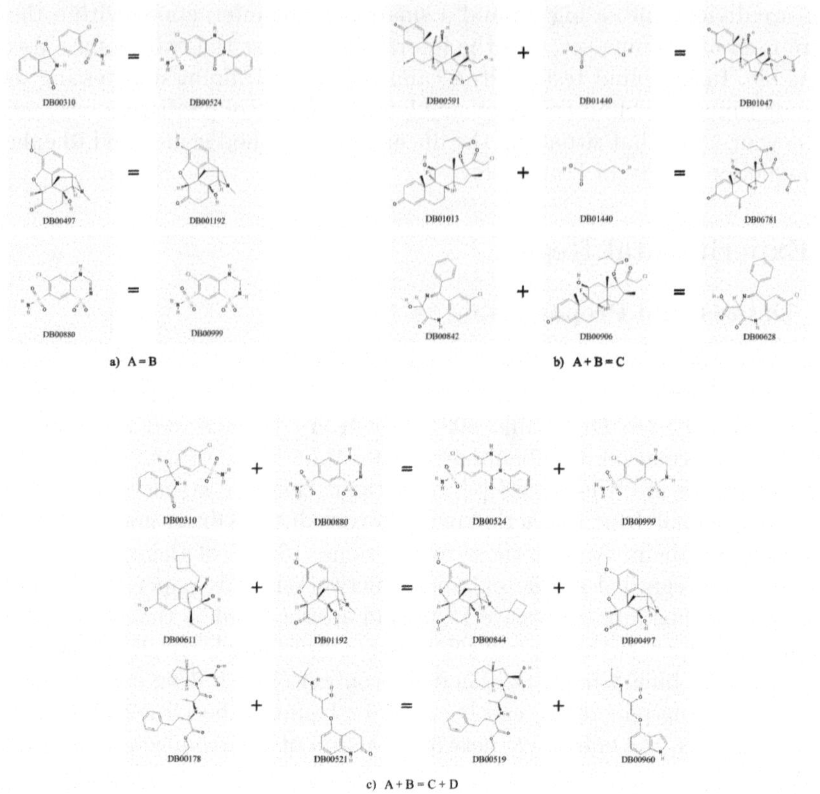

Fig. 3. Samples of the best drug combinations retrieved by Drug2vec for three linear-algebra-equation queries: (a) $A = B$, (b) $A + B = C$, (c) $A + B = C + D$. The structure of the drugs are downloaded from Pubchem, and the number at the bottom of each drug is their corresponding drug IDs in DrugBank.

one atom different. For example, the carbon "C" in drug with ID DB00310 is replaced by nitrogen "N" in DB00524. The drug with ID DB00999 is with one more hydrogen "H" than DB00880. The drugs DB00497 and DB01192 are exactly similar.

Figure 3 (b) shows the result for equation $A + B = C$. It can be seen that relationship among these drug can be interpreted as "transferring the aldehyde (-CHO) from one drug to another". In Fig. 3 (b), drug DB01440 (gamma-Hydroxybutyric acid) appear in the top two drug combinations for this linear-algebra-equation query. Its aldehyde is transferred to an existing drug and form another drugs. Same thing happens in the third example, where the aldehyde from drug DB00906 is added to DB00842 to form drug DB00628.

Figure 3 (c) is the result for equation $A + B = C + D$. This equation quite resembles the combination of the first equation $A = C$ and $B = D$. In the third combination in Fig. 3 (c), drug DB00178 is similar to DB00519, while drug DB0

0521 is akin to DB00960. Thus, drug DB00178 plus drug DB00521 is similar to drug DB00960 plus drug DB00519.

5.3 Performance of Predicting Drug-Drug Interaction

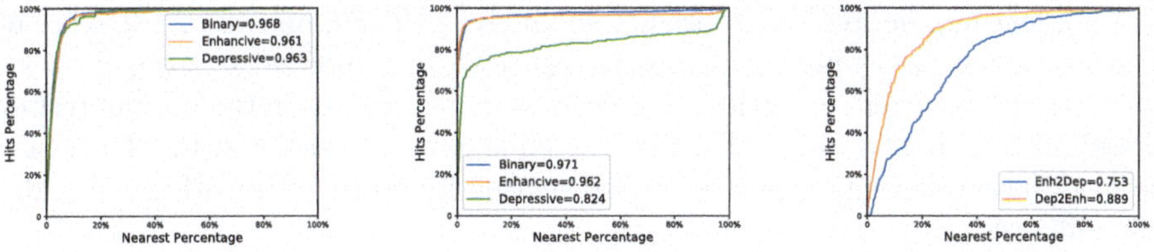

(a) Normal test (b) Blind test (c) Cross test

Fig. 4. Enrichment curves of Drug2vec in (a) Normal test, (b) Blind test and (c) Cross test. The horizontal line is the percentage of drugs that predicted to be connected with the input drug, and the vertical line is the percentage of input drugs whose neighboring drugs are found.

For drug-drug interaction (DDI) prediction, the normal test and the blind test are conducted for three DDI networks, binary network, enhancive network and depressive network. Besides, the cross test is proposed here to see whether the knowledge learnt by Drug2vec can be transferred. In the cross test, Drug2vec is trained on the enhancive network and testing on the depressive network, and vice versa. The cross test is designed to check whether the knowledge that Drug2vec learned from one network can transfer to another network.

In the normal test, 90% of the DDIs are randomly chosen as the training set and 10% are left as the testing set. Drug2vec is trained on the training set for several rounds and tested on the testing set. The performance on the testing set is used to evaluate the model. The number of rounds is chosen manually and is less than 10 for most experiments. The performance in the normal test for the three networks is showed in Fig. 4 (a), in which the AUE score is 0.968 for the binary network, 0.961 for the enhancive network, and 0.963 for the depressive network. This result shows that Drug2vec performs consistently well in DDI prediction in the normal test.

In the blind test, 90% of drugs are randomly selected and the DDIs within these drugs are used as the training set. The DDI pairs between those drugs and the remaining 10% drugs are used for testing. In the blind test, linear repair are included. From Fig. 4 (b) we can see that Drug2vec can achieve relatively high performance in the blind test for the binary network and the enhancive network. But for the depressive network, the AUE score is 0.824, which is less than in the normal test. Moreover, experiments are also conducted to test the performance of Drug2vec with linear repair and without linear repair. The result is shown in Table 1. As we expect, without linear repair the AUE score is just around 0.5.

The reason is discussed before that the parameters associated with testing drugs in the neural network have never been trained. Using linear repair will fix the problem.

In the cross test, the training set and the testing set are chosen based on the type of DDIs. Firstly, Drug2vec is trained on the enhancive network and tested on the degressive network. Then, Drug2vec is trained and tested in the other way round. The result of the cross test is shown in Fig. 4 (c). The AUE score of learning depressive to predict enhancive is 0.889, and the AUE score of learning enhancive to predict depressive is 0.753. The knowledge of one network can partially transfer to another. The score is not so high as in the normal test or the blind test. It is probably because the enhancive network and the depressive network have different properties. So estimating from one to the other is a really difficult task.

Table 1. Linear repair AUE for the blind test.

Blind type	Without linear repair	With linear repair
Binary	0.51 ± 0.02	0.971 ± 0.03
Positive	0.51 ± 0.02	0.969 ± 0.04
Negative	0.51 ± 0.02	0.824 ± 0.03

6 Conclusions

In this paper, we put forward a linear-algebra-equation query task and then propose a model Drug2vec to solve it. Drug2vec can simplify the relationship among drugs using drug-drug interaction as the context. Drug2vec embeds the one-hot representation of a drug into a low-dimensional vector. The embedded vector of drug can approximate the linear-algebra relationship of drug. After that, the embedded vector is restored to the interactive drug. Hence, Drug2vec can also be applied for predicting drug-drug interaction.

The experimental results show that Drug2vec can retrieve drugs with relationship described by linear-algebra equations. Furthermore, Drug2vec is able to find the interactive drugs for a given drug with high accuracy. The AUE score can be around 0.96.

Acknowledgement. The authors sincerely thank Prof. Shi from the Northwestern Polytechnical University to share their drugs date to us, which accelerated the production of this paper.

References

1. Asgari, E., Mofrad, M.R.: Continuous distributed representation of biological sequences for deep proteomics and genomics. PloS one **10**(11), e0141287 (2015)

2. Jaeger, S., Fulle, S., Turk, S.: Mol2vec: unsupervised machine learning approach with chemical intuition. J. Chem. Inf. Model. **58**(1), 27–35 (2018)
3. Jeon, W., Kim, D.: FP2VEC: a new molecular featurizer for learning molecular properties. Bioinformatics **35**, 4979–4985 (2019)
4. Kim, S., Thiessen, P.A., Bolton, E.E., Chen, J., Fu, G., Gindulyte, A., Han, L., He, J., He, S., Shoemaker, B.A., et al.: Pubchem substance and compound databases. Nucleic Acids Res. **44**(D1), D1202–D1213 (2015)
5. Mikolov, T., Sutskever, I., Chen, K., Corrado, G.S., Dean, J.: Distributed representations of words and phrases and their compositionality. In: Advances in Neural Information Processing Systems, pp. 3111–3119 (2013)
6. Ramachandran, P., Zoph, B., Le, Q.V.: Searching for activation functions. arXiv preprint arXiv:1710.05941 (2017)
7. Ryu, J.Y., Kim, H.U., Lee, S.Y.: Deep learning improves prediction of drug-drug and drug-food interactions. Proc. Nat. Acad. Sci. **115**(18), E4304–E4311 (2018)
8. Tafti, A.P., Badger, J., LaRose, E., Shirzadi, E., Mahnke, A., Mayer, J., Ye, Z., Page, D., Peissig, P.: Adverse drug event discovery using biomedical literature: a big data neural network adventure. JMIR Med. Inform. **5**(4), e51 (2017)
9. Tatonetti, N.P., Patrick, P.Y., Daneshjou, R., Altman, R.B.: Data-driven prediction of drug effects and interactions. Sci. Transl. Med. **4**(125), 12ra31–12ra31 (2012)
10. Wang, C., Singh, O., Dai, H., Jonnagaddala, J., Jue, T.R., Iqbal, U., Su, E., Abdul, S.S., Li, J.: NTTMUNSW system for adverse drug reactions extraction in Twitter data. In: Proceedings of the Social Media Mining Shared Task Workshop at the Pacific Symposium on Biocomputing, pp. 4–8 (2016)
11. Wishart, D.S., Feunang, Y.D., Guo, A.C., Lo, E.J., Marcu, A., Grant, J.R., Sajed, T., Johnson, D., Li, C., Sayeeda, Z., et al.: Drugbank 5.0: a major update to the drugbank database for 2018. Nucleic Acids Res. **46**(D1), D1074–D1082 (2017)
12. Yu, H., Mao, K.T., Shi, J.Y., Huang, H., Chen, Z., Dong, K., Yiu, S.M.: Predicting and understanding comprehensive drug-drug interactions via semi-nonnegative matrix factorization. BMC Syst. Biol. **12**(1), 14 (2018)
13. Zhang, H., Liao, L., Cai, Y., Hu, Y., Wang, H.: IVS2vec: a tool of inverse virtual screening based on word2vec and deep learning techniques. Methods **166**, 57–65 (2019)
14. Zhang, P., Wang, F., Hu, J., Sorrentino, R.: Label propagation prediction of drug-drug interactions based on clinical side effects. Sci. Rep. **5**, 12339 (2015)
15. Zhou, D., Miao, L., He, Y.: Position-aware deep multi-task learning for drug-drug interaction extraction. Artif. Intell. Med. **87**, 1–8 (2018)

Feature Selection with Artificial Bee Colony Algorithms for Classifying Parkinson's Diseases

Rafet Durgut[1], Yusuf Yargı Baydilli[1], and Mehmet Emin Aydin[2(✉)]

[1] Department of Computing Engineering, Karabuk University, Karabuk, Turkey
{rafetdurgut,yusufbaydilli}@karabuk.edu.tr
[2] Department of Computer Science and Creative Technologies, UWE Bristol, Bristol, UK
mehmet.aydin@uwe.ac.uk

Abstract. Parkinson's is a brain disease that affects the quality of human life significantly with very slow progresses. It is known that early diagnosis is of great importance to arrange relevant and efficient treatments. Data analytics and particularly predictive approaches such as machine learning techniques can be efficiently used for earlier diagonosis. As a typical big data problem, the number of features in the collected data of Parkinson's symptoms per case matters crucially. It is known that the higher the number of features considered the more complexities incur in the handling algorithms. This leads to the dimensionality problem of datasets, which requires optimisation to overcome the trade-off between complexity and accuracy. In this study, artificial bee colony-based feature selection methods are employed in order to select the most prominent features for successful Parkinson's Disease classification over the datasets. The optimised set of features were used in training and testing *k nearest neigbourhood* algorithm, and then verifed with *support vector machine* algorithm over the public dataset. This study demonstrates that binary versions of artificial bee colony algorithms can be significanlty successful in feature selection in comparison to the relevant literature.

Keywords: Parkinson's disease classification · Speech analysis · Feature selection · Artificial bee colony

1 Introduction

According to a report published in 2015, 6.2 million people globally suffer from Parkinson's Disease (PD), and about 177 thousand of these cases have resulted in death [1]. Although the main reasons leading to the emergence of PD are not fully known and there is no known cure, it is possible to apply some treatments to improve the symptoms observed in the patient [2]. In this way, it is aimed that the patient lives its remaining life with a relatively higher standard. From

L. Iliadis et al. (Eds.): EANN 2020, INNS 2, pp. 338–351, 2020.
https://doi.org/10.1007/978-3-030-48791-1_26

this point of view, early diagnosis of the disease is very important. The fact that the disease has a neurodegenerative structure, that is, targets motor reflexes, negatively affecting the patient's movement and mental activities, makes it possible to diagnose the disease through the tests carried out [3]. One of these tests is "speech analysis". Findings such as phonetic and speech disorders observed in PD patients, even, the onset of some deformations before the PD clinically diagnosed, reveal that this test is highly effective for early diagnosis [4]. Besides, this test is very simple and cheap. So, it provides that PD can be diagnosed by medical personnel as soon as possible [5].

In the first of the studies that developed a Computer-aided Diagnosis (CAD) model with the results obtained from these tests, Little et al. [5] tried to detect the dysphonia that occurred in Parkinson's patients through the phonations obtained from 31 patients. The authors who trained Support Vector Machine (SVM) using the uncorrelated features in the dataset, stated that they achieved 91.4% classification success. As of this date, many researchers have carried out studies to select the most suitable features in the related dataset and to increase the classification success by using different machine learning algorithms [6]. For example, Das [7] used Artificial Neural Networks (ANN) and raise the classification success rate to 92.9%. Li et al. [9] used SVM and fuzzy-based non-linear method and reported their classification success as 93.47%. In their studies, Chen et al. [10] performed feature selection and achieved 96.47% classification accuracy with the hybrid extreme learning machine. On the other hand, Zuo et al. [11] achieved 97.47% success rate using fuzzy k-Nearest Neighbor (k-NN) method improved with Particle Swarm Optimization (PSO). Finally, Gük [12] was able to increase the classification score to 98.46% by using rotation-forest ensemble k-NN.

Since speech analysis has an important place in the classification of PD, Sakar et al. [13] have brought a new dataset to the literature. The authors who examined 40 subjects (20 Parkinson's patients, 20 normal) in their study, took samples of words and sentences as well as the vowel letter 'a'. At the end of the study, they reported that vowel samples had more distinctive features than word and sentence samples. They trained a SVM using the features extracted from the samples and achieved 77.5% classification success as a result. In the other studies performed on this dataset; while Zhang et al. [14] employed ensemble learning with the multi-edit-nearest-neighbor algorithm, Abrol et al. [15] used the kernel sparse greedy algorithm. Abrol et al. was able to increase classification success up to 99.4%.

As seen in the literature, the studies mostly propose hybrid feature selection and machine learning approaches for higher success in classifications in expense of various aspects. It is observed that the high success rates achieved by the researchers seem proportional to the cross-validation methods used (e.g. Leave-one-out CV or 10-fold CV), which imples that different samples from the same cases are used for both training and validation purposes. Obviously, this is a tricky approach that has potiantial to undermine the real success level with respect to generalisation of the learning approaches [16]. In addition, the datasets used in the studies underconsideration contain samples from a small number of cases and need wider range os samples from larger dataset highly accurate early diagnosis of PD. Sakar et al. [17] have created a dataset consisting of 252 cases for this purpose. The dataset covers a wide range of features including the basic features, many additional discriminative features extracted from the audio signals using various techniques. The corresponding study reports a wideer use of feature selection and machine learning techniques to hit the performance of 86% by SVM over 50 efficiently selected features.

The motivation of this study is to enhance the efficency and performance of classifiers, particularly *k nearest heighbourhood (k-NN)* via efficent feature selection using the varients of one of the prominent and recent swarm intelligence approaches; *artificial bee colony (ABC)* algorithms. This is due to the attractive performance of binary versions of ABC in the recent publications. At the end of the study, the classification success was observed with competetive results and verified with SVM, too.

The rest of the paper is organised as follows: Sect. 2 reviews and introduces feature selection while Sect. 3 overviews the original and binary versions of ABC algorithm. The experimental results are provided and discussed with relevant works in Sect. 4 and 5, respectfully, while the study is concluded in Sect. 6.

2 Feature Selection

Feature selection is one very prominant areas of data analysis and machine learning, which plays crutial role in the success of the approches with respect ot algorithmic complexity and the accuracy of the results. Big data studies emerge to particularly take care this very issue in data analysis due to the fact that the size of data tables, particularly the number of columns/attributes, hugely matters in processing. However, each attribute in a dataset may not promise significant contribution to classification success. It is a fact that excessive number of features enlarges the problem size and, subsequently, causes higher complexity on machine learning algorithms that tackle the provided classification problems. On the contrary, reduced number of features ends up with underfitting and lower accuracy in results. Hence, feature selection turns in a crutial optimisation problem in which the complexity is minimised without compromising accuracy once the most relevant and impactful features are optimally selected. This helps chose a sub-set of all features, which provide a stable classification on the test data [18].

One of the methods used in feature selection is to develop a search strategy in the features in the dataset. In this way, it is aimed to raise the classification success to the highest possible point by selecting sub-sets from the features pool. Since brute-force searching will result in serious time and computational complexity, researchers develop strategies continuously to speed up this process through heuristic methods [19,20]. In this study, ABC-based search strategy was implemented in 756 features of the dataset. The fitness value of each solution was calculated by the k-NN algorithm. The validation of the training phase was provided by the LOSOCV method as seen in Fig. 1.

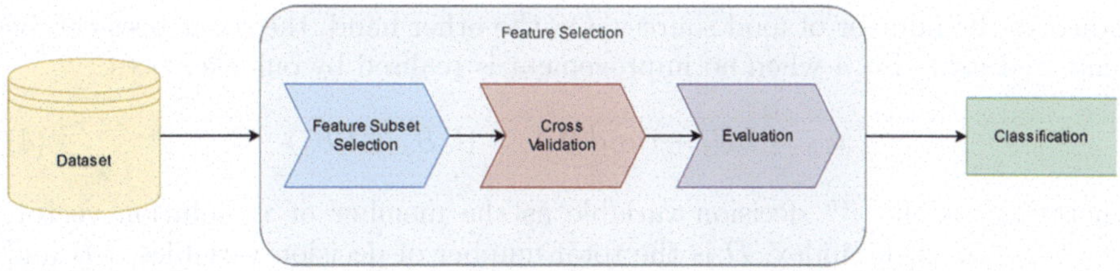

Fig. 1. Flowchart of the feature selection and classification process

3 Artificial Bee Colony (ABC) Algorithms for Feature Selection

The artificial bee colony (ABC) algorithm is one of recently developed swarm intelligence approaches inspired of food search behaviors of the honey bee swarms. The original algorithm has been developed by Karaboğa [21], which imitates the collective behaviour of honey bees within their hives. The algorithm implies use of two types of bees within the hive; employed and onlooker bees. These social insects fulfil collective behaviour in three different phases as modeled into this approach, where first phase imposes each employed bee to improve its own food source, while the second phase involves each onlooker bee to look for improving the quality of its own food source. In the final phase, an exploration is initiated for new food sources by onlooker bees, subsequently transorfmed into scout bees, if non-adequate improvement is achieved. Further investigations and enhamncements for functional optimisation problems are reported in [8].

The conceptualisation of the ABC algorithm translates the natural processes and activities into algorithmic components and functionalities, where "food source" is translated into a "feasible solution" denoted with $\mathbf{x}_i$, while "nectar amount" is recognised as the fitness of a solution denoted by $F(\mathbf{x}_i)$ as given in Eq. 1.

$$F(\mathbf{x}_i) = \begin{cases} \frac{1}{1+f(\mathbf{x}_i)} & f(\mathbf{x}_i) \geq 0 \\ 1 + |f(\mathbf{x}_i)| & \text{otherwise} \end{cases} \tag{1}$$

The probability of a particular food source to be selected through the process of ABC algorithm is calculated with Eq. 2, while a neighbouring solution such as $\mathbf{x}_n = \mathbf{x}_i + \mathbf{v}_i$ generated using Eq. 3

$$p(\mathbf{x}_i) = \frac{F(\mathbf{x}_i)}{\sum_{j=1}^{N} F(\mathbf{x}_j)} \tag{2}$$

$$\mathbf{v}_i = \mathbf{x}_i + \phi_i(\mathbf{x}_i - \mathbf{x}_n) \tag{3}$$

where $\mathbf{x}_i, \mathbf{x}_n, \mathbf{v}_i$ in the equations refer to the current solution, neighbor solution and candidate solution, respectively. ϕ_i is a randomly generated number in the scale of $[-1, 1]$. $i = 1, 2 \ldots, N$ indicates the index of the food source, where N

indicates the number of food sources. On the other hand, the scout bees can be genereted using Eq. 4 when no improvement is realised by onlooker bees.

$$x_{i,j} = LB_j + rand(0,1) \times (UB_j - LB_j) \tag{4}$$

where, $x_{i,j}$ is the jth decision variable as the member of $\mathbf{x}_i$ solution vector; $j = 1, 2, .., D$ is the index, D is the total number of decision variables, LB and UB are the upper and lower boundary values defined for the decision variable.

Feature selection is a binary optimization problem, but, the ordinary ABC algorithm is developed for the continuous domains. The ABC version for solving binary problems is suggested in [22], where Eq. 3 and Eq. 4 are replaced with Eq. 5, based on Bernoulli process, as given below.

$$x_{i,j} = \begin{cases} 0 & rand < 0.5 \\ 1 & \text{otherwise} \end{cases} \tag{5}$$

The following four methods are different variants of developed ABC for binary optimization problems and used for feature selection purposes as reported below.

A. BinABC (ABCv1) Algorithm has been proposed by Kiran et al. [23] imposing Eq. 6 to replace Eq. 3 in which XOR logical operator is used to produce neighbour solutions noting that the variables provided in Eq. 3 as in vector form while are in Eq. 6 as scalar form. The parameter of ϑ is used as the logical NOT operator with which neighbour generation is applied alongside a pre-set threshold value (e.g. 0.5), if the resulted vaule is to be taken or its complement as the output value.

$$v_{i,j} = x_{i,j} \oplus \vartheta(x_{i,j} \oplus x_{n,j}) \tag{6}$$

Table 1. XOR based neighborhood operation.

Current solution ($x_{i,j}$)	Neighbor solution ($x_{n,j}$)	XOR operation ($x_{i,j} \oplus x_{n,j}$)	State 1 ($\vartheta < 0.5$)	State 2 ($\vartheta \geq 0.5$)	State 1 ($v_{i,j}$)	State 2 ($v_{i,j}$)
0	0	0	1	0	1	0
0	1	1	0	1	0	1
1	0	1	0	1	1	0
1	1	0	1	0	0	1

As the procedure can be seen in Table 1, XOR operator is applied to current,$x_{i,j}$, and neighbor, $x_{i,j}$, solutions, then the output value is negated if $\vartheta < 0.5$, kept as is, otherwise. Afterwards, XOR is re-applied to the current solution, $x_{i,j}$ and the output value filtered with ϑ for the final output value, $v_{i,j}$.

B. DisABC (ABCv2) Algorithm is proposed by Kashan et al. [24] which uses a similarity measure calculated by Eq. 7 in which the similarity of the bits in two compared solutions plays the key role. A dissimilarity measure, which names the algorithm, is subsequently calculated for this version of the algorithm in order to be used for neighbour solution generation. As the approach imposes, a new solution, was generated by Eq. 4 previously for non-binary problems, is now replaced with Eq. 7, which calculates Jaccard's similarity constant together with Eq. 8.

$$sim(x_i, x_j) = \frac{M_{11}}{M_{01} + M_{10} + M_{11}} \tag{7}$$

$$dissim(x_i, x_j) = 1 - sim(x_i, x_j) \tag{8}$$

where M_{11} is the number of 1 bits in both x_i and x_n at the same positions, while M_{01} and M_{10} are determined, accordingly. Eq. 9 declares that the dissimilarity of the current solution with the neighbour-to-be is an approximate of the dissimilarity of two existing solutions, x_i and x_j, normalised with ϕ while Eq. 10 presents a minimisation model with a number of constraints, which imples that the new solution to-be, v_i, is expected to satisfy the constraints and let the objective function be minimum.

$$dissim(v_i, x_i) \approx \phi \times dissim(x_i, x_j) \tag{9}$$

$$\min \; |dissim(v_i, x_i) - \phi \times dissim(x_i, x_j)| \tag{10}$$

Subject to:

$$M_{11} + M_{01} = n_1$$

$$M_{10} \leq n_0$$

$$\{M_{10}, M_{11}, M_{01}\} \geq 0 \text{ and } \in \mathbb{Z}$$

where ϕ is a random positive value, n_1 and n_0 represent the number of bits with a value of 1 and 0 in the current solution, x_i. The aim in here is to determine the closest possible minimum value according to the difference between the candidate solution and the current solution. Detailed information and examples can be found in [24].

C. Improved BinABC (ABCv3) ABC algorithm updates the value of only one decision variable among D number of decision variables per iteration, while various other swarm intelligence algorithms propose updating multiple variables within the complete vector of decision variables. Obviously, there is a trade-off between exploration and exploitation balance to handle while attemting the updates.

This binary version of the ABC, as discussed in [26], attempts to balance exploration and exploitation with an exponantially calculated rate, d_t as in Eq. 11.

$$d_t = rand(0, \alpha) + e^{-(\frac{t}{t_{max}}) \times 0.1 \times D} + 1 \tag{11}$$

where, the α is randomly determined perturbation number, D is the problem dimension, number of decison variables, and t and t_{max} indicate the current and maximum number of iterations, respectively. It is worthwhile to note that d_t will decrease with growing t, which means that the exploration is higher in earlier iterations while exploitation gets stronger in later iterations. That is believed to help keep the balance explained above.

The neighbourhood operator in Eq. 6 proposed by Kıran et al. [23] is revised to be used in this version due to the fact that ϑ is originally setup with 0.5 in Eq. 6 as the exploitation factor. This pre-set fixed threshold weakens the exploitation as it involves a more random process. Eq. 12 proposes a new way to determine ϑ. This rule allocates 0 to ϑ if the new solution is worse, otherwise, it is updated depending on the iteration.

$$\vartheta = \begin{cases} Q_{max} - (\frac{Q_{max} - Q_{min}}{t_{max}}) \times t & F(x_n) < F(x_i) \\ 0 & \text{otherwise} \end{cases} \tag{12}$$

where Q_{max} and Q_{min} represent the upper and lower limits of the defined range, respectively [25].

D. NBABC (ABCv4) In this binary ABC (NBABC) version that proposed by Santana et al. [26], it is ensured the influencing of the specified number of decision variables during the implementation of the neighborhood operator. Trough the *max_dim* parameter in the algorithm, the maximum number of dimension values is determined in each iteration. The pseudo code of the neighborhood operator is as follows:

Algorithm 1: NBABC Algorithm

Input: $\mathbf{x}_i$
Select $\boldsymbol{x}_j$ *where* $i \neq j$ `/* A new Food Source */`
Set *The number of selected dimensions* ($max\_dim \times D$)
Select *random dimensions for the food source* (***Dims***)
Foreach $d \in Dims$ **do**
    if $x_{i,d} = x_{j,d}$ **then**
        $v_{i,d} = x_{i,d}$
    end
    else
        $v_{i,d} = x_{j,d}$
    end
Return v_i

4 Experimental Results

The following experimental study has been fulfilled to test the algorithms underconsideration for feature selection purposes. The dataset created by Sakar et al. [17] has been widely used. This dataset contains samples from 188 Parkinson's patients and 64 healthy cases. While constructing the dataset, the voice of patients for the vowel 'a' was recorded 3 times from each case, hence, $252 \times 3 = 756$ audio signals were obtained. In addition to the baseline features of audio signals, feature extraction was made through many techniques (e.g. Time Frequency Measures, Mel Frequency Cepstral Coefficients, Wavelet Transform Based Features, Vocal Fold Features, Tunable Q-Factor Wavelet Transform Based Features). Thus, they were able to create a dataset including a total of 754 feature vectors.

The algorithmic hyper parameters considered through out of these experimentations have been tabulated in Table 2 per algorithm.

Table 2. Control parameters of algorithms

	ABCv1	ABCv2	ABCv3	ABCv4
Population Size	20	20	20	20
Max number of Function Evaluation	1000	1000	1000	1000
max_dim	-	-	-	0.1
ϕ_{max}/Q_{max}	-	0.9	0.3	-
ϕ_{min}/Q_{min}	-	0.1	0.1	-
Limit	100	100	100	100

Table 3 shows the success metrics on each feature category. Since the Bandwidth features in the dataset are few, all methods achieved the best results. When the algorithms run using the TQWT features that have the highest number of features, ABCv2, ABCv3 and ABCv4 showed the best performance according to calculated mean and maximum success values. Although ABCv2 performed the best on the Wavelet Transform features according to the mean results, ABCv3 and ABCv4 achieved the maximum success value. For MFCC features, ABCv4 algorithm achieved the highest scores for both mean and maximum results. Finally, ABCv2 performed better than other methods for Baseline and Vocal Fold features.

From this part of the study, it can be concluded that the MFCC features contain the most qualified features to distinguish between classes. Therefore, all four algorithms showed the best performance on these features. Another important point is that although the number of these features is 84, the algorithms have achieved the highest results with an average of 40.

In the second stage of the study, classification was performed with SVM using the features selected for k-NN algorithm. That was to verify how robust was ABC-based feature selection. As can be seen from Table 4, the features selected

Table 3. Feature selection with k-NN results.

		Baseline (26 Features)			Bandwidth (8 Features)			Vocal Fold (22 Features)			MFCC (84 Features)			WT Applied to F0 (182 Features)			TQWT (432 Features)		
		ACC	**F1**	**MCC**	**ACC**	**F1**	**MCC**	**ACC**	**F1**	**MCC**	**ACC**	**F1**	**MCC**	**ACC**	**F1**	**MCC**	**ACC**	**F1**	**MCC**
ABCv1	*Mean*	0.79	0.87	0.39	**0.77**	**0.86**	**0.30**	0.80	0.88	0.41	0.85	0.90	0.56	0.77	0.85	0.31	0.84	0.90	0.55
	Max	0.83	0.89	0.49	**0.77**	**0.86**	**0.30**	0.81	0.89	0.45	0.87	0.92	0.63	0.79	0.87	0.37	0.86	0.91	0.59
ABCv2	*Mean*	**0.82**	**0.89**	**0.48**	**0.77**	**0.86**	**0.30**	**0.82**	**0.89**	**0.46**	0.85	0.91	0.58	**0.79**	**0.87**	**0.37**	**0.85**	**0.91**	**0.58**
	Max	0.83	0.89	0.49	**0.77**	**0.86**	**0.30**	0.83	0.89	0.49	0.86	0.91	0.61	0.79	0.87	0.39	0.86	0.91	0.61
ABCv3	*Mean*	0.80	0.87	0.40	**0.77**	**0.86**	**0.30**	0.80	0.88	0.41	0.85	0.91	0.58	0.78	0.86	0.34	**0.85**	**0.91**	**0.58**
	Max	0.83	0.89	0.49	**0.77**	**0.86**	**0.30**	0.82	0.89	0.48	0.87	0.92	0.62	0.80	0.88	0.42	0.86	0.91	0.60
ABCv4	*Mean*	0.80	0.88	0.42	**0.77**	**0.86**	**0.30**	0.81	0.88	0.44	**0.86**	**0.91**	**0.59**	0.78	0.86	0.36	**0.85**	**0.91**	**0.59**
	Max	0.83	0.89	0.49	**0.77**	**0.86**	**0.30**	0.82	0.89	0.48	0.87	0.92	0.64	0.80	0.87	0.40	0.87	0.92	0.63

Table 4. SVM results for selected features

		Baseline (26 Features)			Bandwidth (8 Features)			Vocal Fold (22 Features)			MFCC (84 Features)			WT Applied to F0 (182 Features)			TQWT (432 Features)		
		ACC	**F1**	**MCC**	**ACC**	**F1**	**MCC**	**ACC**	**F1**	**MCC**	**ACC**	**F1**	**MCC**	**ACC**	**F1**	**MCC**	**ACC**	**F1**	**MCC**
ABCv1	*Mean*	0.79	0.87	0.35	**0.77**	**0.86**	**0.29**	0.76	0.86	0.27	0.82	0.89	0.50	0.76	0.86	0.24	0.82	0.89	0.49
	Max	0.82	0.89	0.46	**0.77**	**0.86**	**0.29**	0.78	0.87	0.34	0.85	0.91	0.59	0.77	0.86	0.29	0.85	0.90	0.56
ABCv2	*Mean*	0.76	0.85	0.28	**0.77**	**0.86**	**0.29**	0.73	0.83	0.18	**0.84**	**0.90**	**0.54**	**0.77**	**0.86**	**0.25**	**0.83**	**0.89**	**0.51**
	Max	0.76	0.85	0.28	**0.77**	**0.86**	**0.29**	0.73	0.83	0.18	0.84	0.90	0.54	0.77	0.86	0.25	0.83	0.89	0.51
ABCv3	*Mean*	**0.79**	**0.87**	**0.37**	**0.77**	**0.86**	**0.29**	0.76	0.85	0.26	0.83	0.89	0.51	0.76	0.86	0.24	0.82	0.89	0.48
	Max	0.83	0.90	0.51	**0.77**	**0.86**	**0.29**	0.79	0.87	0.38	0.88	0.92	0.66	0.78	0.87	0.32	0.84	0.90	0.55
ABCv4	*Mean*	0.79	0.87	0.36	**0.77**	**0.86**	**0.29**	**0.77**	**0.86**	**0.30**	0.83	0.89	0.52	0.76	0.86	0.24	0.82	0.89	0.48
	Max	0.82	0.89	0.48	**0.77**	**0.86**	**0.29**	0.79	0.87	0.36	0.86	0.91	0.60	0.77	0.86	0.29	0.84	0.90	0.55

by ABCv3 algorithm gave the best results according to the maximum success criteria. However, according to the mean success criteria, ABCv2 and ABCv4 were able to compete with ABCv3.

The fact that SVM algorithm, which is trained with 35 features selected by ABCv3 algorithm, produces higher results compared to k-NN, shows that SVM algorithm is a more successful classification algorithm than k-NN. On the other hand, it can be concluded that the features selected by the binary ABC algorithms create a reasonable and fair benchmark environment for classification algorithms. Moreover, it is possible to achieve higher successes by using SVM instead of k-NN while calculating fitness values in the feature selection stage of ABC algorithms.

5 Related Works and Discussions

Since the dataset used in this study has been made public, several studies have been carried out to improve the classification successes. For example, Altay and Atlas [27] used two different evolutionary algorithms in their work. Badem et al. [28] employed ABC algorithm for feature selection. Tuncer and Dogan [29] performed feature extraction with Singular Value Decomposition (SVD) and feature selection with Neighborhood Component Analysis (NCA). In the classification phase, they used SVM. Castro et al. [30] provided classification with ANN. Finally, Tuncer et al. [31] extracted features from the dataset using minimum average maximum tree and SVD, and then performed classification with k-NN. It was observed that some of their results remian better in accuracy than our score. However, with closer look into the details, it was seen that the 10-fold CV method was used during the training and validation phase. But, as mentioned in the work by Sakar et al. [17], using this kind of cross-validation cannot provide generalization for all subjects and causes in biased results. Therefore, it is found unfair to make a comparison between the results in [31] and our study's. For this reason, our results are evaluated with the results obtained in the original study, namely the study using LOSOCV (Leave-One-Subject-Out Cross Validation). The relevant comparison is as in Table 5 below.

Table 5. Comparison of the results with the original study

	Feature selection algorithm	# of features	Classification algorithm	Acc. (mean)	Acc. (max)
Sakar et al	mRMR	50	SVM	-	0.84
This study	ABCv$	39	k-NN	0.86	0.87
	ABCv5	35	SVM	0.83	0.88

In general, it is observed that the MFCC features in the Parkinson dataset are the best definitive and the most discriminative features for classification. In this respect, it can be concluded that the MFCC features will provide more stable and successful results in more comprehensive Parkinson datasets to be created in the future. However, as seen in the original study, the classification success rate achieved using only MFCC features remained at the level of 0.84. This leads to the question of whether or not more successful results can be obtained through feature selection algorithms.

In their study, Sakar et al. [17] stated that the highest score was obtained with an SVM trained with 50 features selected from all features (756). However, as can be seen in Table 5, when evaluated on the basis of mean values, it can be observed that the NBABC (ABCv4) algorithm can achieve more successful results with less features (0.86). When the algorithms were evaluated in terms of the maximum success rate, all algorithms except disABC (ABCv2) produced the highest accuracy value (0.87). Moreover, if SVM is trained with the selected features, it has been observed that the success rates can be increased a little more. Accordingly, improved binABC (ABCv3) algorithm obtained the highest success value (0.88). As a result, it can be said that thanks to the feature selection to be applied in Parkinson datasets, higher successes can be achieved and binary ABC methods are highly capable in this task.

6 Conclusions

The datasets of Parkinson's sympthoms collated provide great support to study data-driven computational approaches if they are helpful in diagnosis of the disease. The dimensionality problem of such datasets has to be eased before devicing automatic methods to help medical staff. One of the collated datasets are of sound samples they receive from patients through signal processing techniques to apply speech analysis, which help understand any anomlies detected. Machine learning techniques are prominantly used in predictive analysis of the data for diagnosis purposes. However, the dimansionality problem matters and the number of features has to be studied and optimsed accordingly.

In this study, the variants of binary ABC algorithms have been studied for feature selection and dimensionality problem of the datasets underconsideration, which includes 756 features. In the first stage of the study, feature selection was made using four different binary ABC algorithms, and the success values of the selected features were evaluated with the k-NN algorithm. In the second stage of the study, SVMs were trained with the selected features and it was seen that the selected features could increase the classification success compared to the original study. Thus, it has been shown that effective results can be achieved in PD classification by the methods used in the study.

References

1. Wang, H., et al.: Global, regional, and national life expectancy, all-cause mortality, and cause-specific mortality for 249 causes of death, 1980–2015: a systematic analysis for the Global Burden of Disease Study 2015. Lancet **388**(10053), 1459–1544 (2016)

2. Oertel, W.H.: Recent advances in treating Parkinson's disease. F1000Research, 6 Mar 2017
3. Massano, J., Bhatia, K.P.: Clinical approach to Parkinson's disease: features, diagnosis, and principles of management. Cold Spring Harb. Perspect. Med. **2**(6), a008870 (2012)
4. Little, M.A., McSharry, P.E., Roberts, S.J., Costello, D.A., Moroz, I.M.: Exploiting nonlinear recurrence and fractal scaling properties for voice disorder detection. BioMed. Eng. OnLine **6**(1), 1–19 (2007)
5. Little, M.A., McSharry, P.E., Hunter, E.J., Spielman, J., Ramig, L.O.: Suitability of dysphonia measurements for telemonitoring of Parkinson's disease. IEEE Trans. Biomed. Eng. **56**(4), 1015–1022 (2009)
6. Cai, Z., et al.: An intelligent Parkinson's disease diagnostic system based on a chaotic bacterial foraging optimization enhanced fuzzy KNN approach. Comput. Math. Methods Med. **1–24**, 2018 (2018)
7. Das, R.: A comparison of multiple classification methods for diagnosis of Parkinson's disease. Expert Syst. Appl. **37**(2), 1568–1572 (2010)
8. Düğnci, M., Aydin, M.E.: A honeybees-inspired heuristic algorithm for numerical optimisation. Neural Comput. Appl. 1-15 (2019)
9. Li, D.C., Liu, C.W., Hu, S.C.: A fuzzy-based data transformation for feature extraction to increase classification performance with small medical data sets. Artif. Intell. Med. **52**(1), 45–52 (2011)
10. Chen, H.L., Wang, G., Ma, C., Cai, Z.N., Liu, W.B., Wang, S.J.: An efficient hybrid kernel extreme learning machine approach for early diagnosis of Parkinson's disease. Neurocomputing **184**, 131–144 (2016)
11. Zuo, W.L., Wang, Z.Y., Liu, T., Chen, H.L.: Effective detection of Parkinson's disease using an adaptive fuzzy k-nearest neighbor approach. Biomed. Signal Process. Control **8**(4), 364–373 (2013)
12. Gük, M.: An ensemble of k-nearest neighbours algorithm for detection of Parkinson's disease. Int. J. Syst. Sci. **46**(6), 1108–1112 (2015)
13. Sakar, B.E., et al.: Collection and analysis of a Parkinson speech dataset with multiple types of sound recordings. IEEE J. Biomed. Health Inf. **17**(4), 828–834 (2013)
14. Zhang, H.-H., et al.: Classification of Parkinson's disease utilizing multi-edit nearest-neighbor and ensemble learning algorithms with speech samples. BioMed. Eng. OnLine **15**(1), 122 (2016)
15. Abrol, V., Sharma, P., Sao, A.K.: Greedy dictionary learning for kernel sparse representation based classifier. Pattern Recogn. Lett. **78**, 64–69 (2016)
16. Refaeilzadeh, P., Tang, L., Liu, H.: Cross-validation. In: Encyclopedia of Database Systems, pp. 532–538, Springer, Berlin (2009)
17. Sakar, C.O., et al.: A comparative analysis of speech signal processing algorithms for Parkinson's disease classification and the use of the tunable Q-factor wavelet transform. Appl. Soft Comput. **74**, 255–263 (2019)
18. Cai, J., Luo, J., Wang, S., Yang, S.: Feature selection in machine learning: a new perspective. Neurocomputing **300**, 70–79 (2018)
19. Yusta, S.C.: Different metaheuristic strategies to solve the feature selection problem. Pattern Recogn. Lett. **30**(5), 525–534 (2009)
20. Nguyen, B.H., Xue, B., Zhang, M.: A survey on swarm intelligence approaches to feature selection in data mining. Swarm Evol. Comput. **54**, 100663 (2020)
21. Karaboga, D., Basturk, B.: A powerful and efficient algorithm for numerical function optimization: artificial bee colony (ABC) algorithm. J. Glob. Optim. **39**(3), 459–471 (2007)

22. Karaboga, D., Gorkemli, B., Ozturk, C., Karaboga, N.: A comprehensive survey: artificial bee colony (ABC) algorithm and applications. Artif. Intell. Rev. **42**(1), 21–57 (2014)
23. Kiran, M.S., Gunduz, M.: XOR-based artificial bee colony algorithm for binary optimization. Turk. J. Electr. Eng. Comput. Sci. **21**, 2307–2328 (2013)
24. Kashan, M.H., Nahavandi, N., Kashan, A.H.: DisABC: A new artificial bee colony algorithm for binary optimization. Appl. Soft Comput. **12**(1), 342–352 (2012)
25. Durgut, R.: Improved binary artificial bee colony algorithm. arXiv preprint arXiv:2003.11641
26. Santana, C.J., Macedo, M., Siqueira, H., Gokhale, A., Bastos-Filho, C.J.A.: A novel binary artificial bee colony algorithm. Future Gener. Comput. Syst. **98**, 180–196 (2019)
27. Altay, E. V., Alatas, B. : Multi-objective association analysis of Parkinson disease with intelligent optimization algorithms. In: Proceedings of the 1st International Informatics and Software Engineering Conference (UBMYK), pp. 1–6, Ankara, Turkey (2019)
28. Badem, H., Turkusagi, D., Caliskan, A., Çil, Z.A.: Feature selection based on artificial bee colony for Parkinson disease diagnosis. In: Medical Technologies Congress (TIPTEKNO), İzmir. Turkey **2019**, 1–4 (2019)
29. Tuncer, T., Dogan, S.: A novel octopus based Parkinson's disease and gender recognition method using vowels. Appl. Acoust. **155**, 75–83 (2019)
30. Castro, C., Vargas-Viveros, E., Sanchez, A., Gutierrez-Lopez, E., Flores, D.L.: Parkinson's disease classification using artificial neural networks. In: VIII Latin American Conference on Biomedical Engineering and XLII National Conference on Biomedical Engineering, Cancun, Mexico, pp. 1060–1065 (2020)
31. Tuncer, T., Dogan, S., Acharya, U.R.: Automated detection of Parkinson's disease using minimum average maximum tree and singular value decomposition method with vowels. Biocybern. Biomed. Eng. **40**(1), 211–220 (2020)

Medical Knowledge-Based Deep Learning Framework for Disease Prediction on Unstructured Radiology Free-Text Reports Under Low Data Condition

Shashank Shetty[1(✉)], V. S. Ananthanarayana[1], and Ajit Mahale[2]

[1] Department of Information Technology, National Institute of Technology Karnataka, Mangalore, India
shashankshetty06@gmail.com, anvs@nitk.ac.in

[2] Department of Radiology, Kasturba Medical College, MAHE, Mangalore, Karnataka, India
ajit.mahale@manipal.edu
http://nitk.edu.in/

Abstract. There has been increasing popularity in medical text mining due to its vast applications in the field of disease prediction and clinical Recommendation systems. Radiology reports possess rich information depicting radiologists investigations on the health conditions of the patients in associated radiology images. However, radiology reports exist in a free-text unstructured format consisting of valuable information for disease prediction. This information cannot be easily retrieved and utilized for prediction without suitable text mining techniques. The medical dataset available in the current procedure is small, domain-specific and restricted to the institution. However, data is one of the critical factors to power Machine Learning (ML) and Deep Learning (DL) models. To overcome the above challenge of predicting disease in the low data condition, we present a practical Deep Learning framework that combines a Knowledge Base (KB) with the Deep Learning for accurate text mining and predicting the lung diseases from the unstructured radiology free-text reports. We adopt Glove word embeddings with the KB trained on large corpus for effective text modelling. Further, we incorporate Convolutional Neural Network-based Discriminative Dimensionality Reduction (CNN-DDR) to obtain the most discriminative feature vector. Finally, a fully connected Deep Neural Network (DNN) is leveraged as the prediction model to detect the diseases. We applied the proposed framework to predict the lung diseases on radiology reports from both publicly available Indiana University (IU) dataset [6] and data collected from the private hospital. We benchmark the performance of the proposed framework, which outperforms against the standard ML Techniques.

Keywords: Clinical recommendation systems · Deep learning · Disease prediction · Knowledge base · Unstructured text mining

L. Iliadis et al. (Eds.): EANN 2020, INNS 2, pp. 352–364, 2020.
https://doi.org/10.1007/978-3-030-48791-1_27

1 Introduction

Radiology is an essential medical discipline and central to modern healthcare, that provides comprehensive insights for disease detection, staging and treatment planning through medical imaging such as Chest X-Ray (CXR) and Computed Tomography (CT). Medical radiology reports are the processed data prepared by the radiologist from the raw images comprising of valuable prognostic informations that are yet to be investigated for predictive analytics applications like disease predictions. The radiologist or critical care physicians classify and predict the diseases from the report manually. Automating the process when there is more number of patients with higher risk will assist the clinicians with lesser experience to input their observations and obtain the predicted outcome. However, the diagnostic report exists in the unstructured free-text format making it inaccessible and challenging for automatic analysis. Radiology report comprises of finding section outlining the detailed medical examination containing both regular and irregular features, an impression section signifying the concluding remarks containing key observations and other sections like details of patients and indications. Out of these sections, the finding section is considered as an essential module, due to the coverage of major details of the organs, detection of any abnormalities and possible diseases. Other than the common NLP challenges, some of the significant challenges faced in radiology text report mining are: detection or identification of findings (normal or abnormal) and lack of publicly available medical datasets.

The unstructured radiology free-text report classification can be divided into two categories: Rule-based methods [7,10] and conventional ML-based methods [4,15]. The Rule-based approaches typically rely on traditional pattern matching with the pre-defined medical terms determined by radiologists or general medical terminologies extracted from the standard healthcare ontologies such as SNOMED CT[1]. The main disadvantage of rule-based approaches is the effectiveness of the system rely on the accuracy of the pre-defined patterns or the medical keywords. The ML-based techniques classify reports based on the medical features learned from the labelled reports [4,15]. Currently, the DL techniques have given promising results in the general text classification tasks such as sentimental analysis and relation extractions from the free-text [9,12]. The success of DL techniques in various applications has inspired us to apply it on clinical decision making by predicting diseases from radiology reports.

Word Embedding technique such as Global Vector (GloVe) [14] map every word to the dense and real-valued vector space that captures its meaning and syntactic properties of the words in raw corpus. Generally, the bigger the size of the corpora, superior is the quality of the learned word embeddings. But, there is a need for more time and considerable resources to train the larger corpora [13]. Thus, various groups and labs have released their learned word embeddings trained on the massive corpora [14]. Traditionally, word embeddings are determined at the word level from the medical corpus of unlabelled unstructured text

[1] http://www.snomed.org/.

considering only the implicit semantics of the words, neglecting the valuable information accessible in domain-specific medical resources [4]. Recently, few studies have implied that incorporating domain knowledge, or KB with the text corpus can benefit the improvement of word embeddings quality [3]. We use the embeddings trained on massive medical corpora as a medical Knowledge-base to enrich the effectiveness of word embeddings learnt from the radiology medical corpus. By leveraging Knowledge-base, the rare medical words can be acquired, projecting the word embeddings in more discriminative direction, strengthening the salient information and decreasing the noise. Due to the insufficient benchmark studies on publicly accessible data [4,7,10,15], there is a need to establish a best prediction techniques on radiology reports. Hence, we have leveraged the publicly available corpus: IU dataset as well as real-time data and benchmarked the results against the standard ML Techniques. In this research, we address the challenge of low data situation in the medical radiology report dataset by adapting the medical KB at the text feature extraction stage. We present an intelligent medical knowledge-based framework for disease classification and prediction on Unstructured Radiology Reports under Low data Conditions.

1.1 Motivations and Contributions

Most of the existing Clinical Decision Support or recommendation Systems utilizes only numerical or structured data. However, there is limited work on unstructured data like radiology free-text reports that as a good source of information for the prediction of diseases. Medical cohorts available in current practice is small, domain-specific and are limited to the medical institutes causing "low data situation" effecting the performance of DL models. Henceforth, motivation of this research work is to handle the unstructured radiology report in the low data situation and predict the disease outcomes. The main contribution of this research work is summarized as follows:

- We point out the significance of incorporating Knowledge-based Medical Text modelling with CNN-DDR and DNN for classifying and predicting diseases in Radiology Reports in low data environment.
- We carry out comprehensive analysis on two medical datasets (i.e., publicly available IU dataset and real-time corpus collected from the private medical institute) to illustrate the competency and rationality of the proposed DL Framework and benchmarked against the standard ML Techniques. To the best of our knowledge, this is the first work leveraging radiology data collected from Indian Private Hospital.
- We examine the effectiveness of incorporating Knowledge-base in enhancing the performance of the overall framework.

2 Proposed Methodology

The proposed Knowledge-based Deep Learning framework for Disease prediction from the unstructured radiology reports is shown in Fig. 1. As an overview,

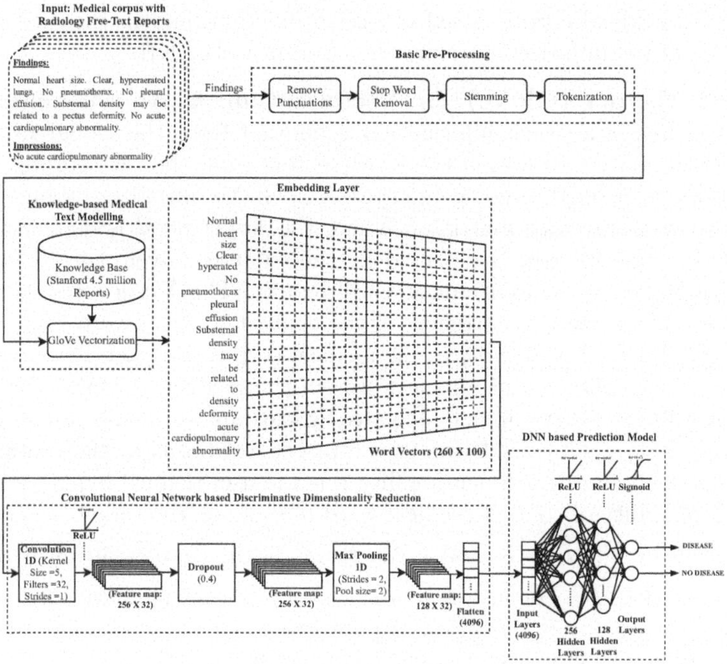

Fig. 1. Medical Knowledge-based Deep Learning Framework

the radiology findings are pre-processed to obtain the essential latent medical concepts. The word embeddings are learnt from the medical words by applying customized knowledge-based Medical Text modelling. Dense word embeddings obtained are mapped to the medical words from the findings in the Embedding Layer. Most Discriminative features are extracted by reducing the dimension using the CNN-DDR. Finally, the flattened discriminative features are fed to the DNN for predicting the disease outcome.

2.1 Basic Pre-processing

The radiology findings are extracted from the medical corpus and these findings are passed through a series of NLP tasks such as removing punctuation's; stop words to retain only essential medical words and filter insignificant words and symbols. Stemming helps in clearing away the suffixes and retains only the root word. During the Tokenization phase, the medical findings are divided into smaller units called tokens. Next, the tokens are processed through Knowledge-based Medical Text modelling phase to obtain the latent medical information.

2.2 Knowledge-Based Medical Text Modelling (KB-MTM)

In the proposed model, the word embeddings are jointly learnt from both the medical corpus and the KB. Firstly, we will revisit the GloVe that creates the base for the medical corpus-based objective function, and in the next section, we will derive the improved objective function from the KB.

i. Global Vectors (GloVe) for Vectorization: GloVe [14] word embedding model uses statistical information generated from the global word-word co-occurrence matrix to obtain the word vectors from the text corpus. In particular, given a medical radiology Corpus MC, GloVe initializes by building the Word-word co-occurrence matrix X, where the *target word* is depicted by the row and the *context word* is depicted by the column. Given a medical corpus with n words, the co-occurence matrix will be nxn. The X_{ij} denotes the tabular entries, that is the total occurrences of the context medical word $\tilde{mw}_j$ appears in the target medical word mw_i in the medical corpus MC. Let V represent the Vocabulary, the collection of all the words in the medical corpora. For a given medical word mw_i, GloVe model instigates by learning word embeddings or word vectors mv_i, $\tilde{mv}_i \in \mathbb{R}^d$ considering it as a target word mw_i or the context word $\tilde{mw}_i$ respectively and the dimensionality d is the user defined hyper-parameter.

The probability of context medical word $\tilde{mw}_j$ given the target medical word mw_i is given by $P(j|i) = X_{ij} \big/ X_i$. Where, X_i is the total occurrence of target word mw_i in the MC. For instance, $mv_i^T \cdot \tilde{mv}_i$ gives the similarity between the two medical words mw_i and $\tilde{mw}_j$. We have to learn the medical word vectors that are true to the global word-word co-occurrence matrix given by,

$$mv_i^T \cdot \tilde{mv}_j = logP(j|i) = log(X_{ij}) - log(X_i) \tag{1}$$

Similarly $X_{ij} = X_{ji}$,

$$mv_j^T \cdot \tilde{mv}_i = logP(i|j) = log(X_{ij}) - log(X_j) \tag{2}$$

Adding Eq. (1) and Eq. (2). Since, $mv_i^T \cdot \tilde{mv}_j = mv_j^T \cdot \tilde{mv}_i$, we get

$$2mv_i^T \cdot \tilde{mv}_j = 2log(X_{ij}) - log(X_i) - log(X_j) \tag{3}$$

In the Eq. (3), the left hand side are the learnable parameters and the right hand side are the counts learnt from the medical corpus. Since $log(X_i)$ and $log(X_j)$ rely only on the medical words mw_i and $\tilde{mw}_j$, we consider them as the biases particular to the medical word that will be learned.

$$mv_i^T \cdot \tilde{mv}_j = log(X_{ij}) - b_i - b_j \tag{4}$$

$$mv_i^T \cdot \tilde{mv}_j + b_i + b_j = log(X_{ij}) \tag{5}$$

Where, b_i and b_j are the scalar biased real-valued terms associated with mw_i and $\tilde{mw}_j$ respectively. The objective function of the GloVe Embedding method minimizes the weighed least square errors with weighting function f:

$$J_{MC} = \sum_{i,j=1}^{V} f(X_{ij})(R^{MC} + b_i + \tilde{b_j} - log(X_{ij}))^2 \tag{6}$$

Here, $R^{MC} = mv_i^T \cdot \tilde{mv_j}$, is the scalar vaiue obtained by the inner dot product between the transpose of target word vector mv_i and the context word vector $\tilde{mv_j}$ from *MC*. The $f(X_{ij})$ is the weighting function that allocates lower weights for frequent co-occurrences to prevent from skewing of objective function due to over-emphasizing of most common word pairs and is given by:

$$f(m) = \begin{cases} (\frac{m}{m_{max}})^{\alpha} & \text{if } m < m_{max} \\ 1 & \text{otherwise} \end{cases} \tag{7}$$

As per [14], the effectiveness of the model relies on the cutoff. So, m_{max} is set to 100 and α to 3/4. The objective function defined from the medical corpus in Eq. (6) aim to learn the co-occurrence between the two medical words mw_i and $\tilde{mw_j}$ by minimizing the squared difference between the inner dot product and the logarithm of the co-occurences between the medical words in the matrix X.

ii. Integrating Medical Knowledge Base to GloVe: GloVe is the word embeddings technique that learns only from the corpus and does not use any existing KB's. Henceforth, failing to learn embeddings from the rare words and faces a significant challenge in capturing the semantics, which is essential in medical text mining. Likewise, the medical dataset available will be domain-specific restricted to private medical institute and small in number, causing a considerable challenge to learn word embeddings due to the smaller vocabulary size. To deal with this issue, we incorporate learnt word embeddings as a KB during the text modelling of the medical corpus. Given a Medical Knowledge Base *MKB*, we derive the objective function J_{MKB} that considers the semantic relation R(mw_i, $\tilde{mw_j}$) between the corresponding target and context medical words mw_i and $\tilde{mw_j}$ respectively. We use learnt word embeddings trained on 4.5 million Stanford reports [17] as a concrete case for KB in this experiment. There are no rigid rules to use any specific KB. However we can utilize any KB that derives meaningful connection between the medical words.

Let $R^{MKB} = kv_i^T \cdot \tilde{kv_j}$ be the scalar vaiue obtained by the inner dot product between the transpose of target word knowledge vector kv_i and the context word knowledge vector $\tilde{kv_j}$ from MKB corresponding to the words mw_i and $\tilde{mw_j}$ in the *MC*. The Medical Knowledge-based objective function can be described as follows:

$$J_{MKB} = \sum_{i,j=1}^{V} f(X_{ij})(R^{MKB} + b_i + \tilde{b_j} - log(X_{ij}))^2 \tag{8}$$

Where, b_i and b_j are the scalar biased real-valued terms associated with mw_i and $\tilde{mw_i}$ respectively. The Medical Knowledge-based objective function defined by Eq. (8) learns the co-occurrence between the two medical words mw_i and $\tilde{mw_j}$ by minimizing the squared difference between the inner dot product of knowldege vectors derived from the *MKB* and the logarithm of the co-occurences between the words mw_i and $\tilde{mw_j}$ in the matrix X.

iii. Embedding Layer: The Embedding layer is loaded with the pre-trained word embedding weights obtained from the huge corpus and the word embeddings for each medical words in the training medical corpus is learned.

The medical findings are of different length and are padded to have the same length. Matrix Multiplication of one hot vector of each word in a vocabulary and Embedding Weight Matrix returns the corresponding matrix of the medical words in a given corpus as the output of Embedding Layer (i.e., hidden layer). Here, Embedding weight Matrix is treated as a look-up table, where the hidden layer output can be obtained by look-up operation with the encoded integer of the medical word. The complete pre-trained medical KB is loaded as a dictionary of 260 padded words to produce the embedding matrix of word vectors with output dimension 100. The algorithm for proposed KB-MTM is mentioned in the Sect. A.

2.3 Convolutional Neural Network Based Discriminative Dimentionality Reduction (CNN-DDR)

We have proposed CNN-DDR technique with the objective of reducing the storage and computational costs, by learning from the high dimensional embeddings into low dimensional representation, such that the most discriminative features are retained. The architecture employed for CNN-DDR is a modified version of CNN architecture [5]. Let $mx_i \in \mathbb{R}^d$ denote i-th medical word in the sentence (i.e., findings) of d-dimensional word vector. Here, we consider 100 dimension word vectors for each medical word (i.e., $d = 100$). The medical sentence (i.e., findings from the radiology report) of length k (i.e., $k = 260$) with padding when required is represented as: $mx_{1:k} = mx_1 \oplus mx_2 \oplus ... \oplus mx_k$. Here, $\oplus$ represent the concatenation operator. Let the concatenation of the medical words $mx_i, mx_{i+1}, ..., mx_{i+j}$ be represented as $mx_{i:i+j}$. Let $W \in \mathbb{R}^{pd}$ be the filter involved in convolution operation applied to the window of p medical words to generate the Discriminative features. We leverage 32 filters of window size 5 (i.e., $p = 5$). For instance, from the window of medical words $mx_{i:i+p-1}$, the new discriminative medical feature mc_i is produced and is represented by $mc_i = f(W \cdot mx_{i:i+p-1} + b)$., where b is a bias term, $b \in \mathbb{R}$.

Rectified Linear Unit (ReLU) [1] activation function, f with filter W is employed on each available window of medical words $\{mx_{1:p}, mx_{2:p+1}, ..., mx_{k-p+1:k}\}$ to generate the feature map, $mc = [mc_1, mc_2, ..., mc_{k-p+1}]$, here $mc \in \mathbb{R}^{k-p+1}$. Later, we apply dropout mechanism [9] after the first layer of convolution operation for regularization and addressing overfitting problem. Dropout mechanism is utilized to avoid co-adaptation at the Hidden layer by randomly dropping out a few units at the time of the training process. Let $z = [\tilde{mc}_1, \tilde{mc}_2, ..., \tilde{mc}_n]$ be the penultimate layer and n be the number of filters. Let y be the output of forward propagation in the CNN and is represented by $y = W \cdot z + b$. When the dropout operation is applied at the penultimate layer, $y = W \cdot (z \otimes \delta_i) + b$, where $\delta_i \in \mathbb{R}^n$ is the Bernoulli random variables that drops the ith neuron with the probability (p_i) of being 1 and $\otimes$ denote the element-wise multiplication operator. Regularizing the convolution layer with the dropout probability gives the maximum robustness to the overfitting. For our experiment, based on a grid search approach [2], dropout probability of 0.4 is applied after the first hidden layer to restrain the model from overfitting.

Let $\tilde{y} = [\tilde{y_1}, \tilde{y_2}, ..., \tilde{y}_L]$, where $L = k-p+1$ be the feature map generated from the Dropout Layer. Max-pooling [5] is used to down sample the input features by reducing the dimensionality of the feature map. The main aim is to learn the most discriminative features with the maximum value for every feature map. Max-pooling produces the discriminative feature map $y^{'}$ by applying the strides s and pooling window size pw on the feature map $\tilde{y}$. Let $||$ be the customized concatenation operation and Max-pooling operation is applied to every possible windows on the feature map $\tilde{y}$ to produce, $y^{'} = ||_{i=1,i=i+s}^{L-pw+1} max\{\tilde{y}_{i:i+pw-1}\}$, where $y^{'} \in \mathbb{R}^n$. For instance in our case, we have applied pool window size, *pw=2* and strides, *s=2* on feature map of length, *L=256*. Initially, i will be equal to 1 and incremented with the number of strides till it reaches *L-pw+1*. The discriminative feature map obtained is $y^{'}_{1:128} = max\{\tilde{y}_{1:2}\} \oplus max\{\tilde{y}_{3:4}\} \oplus ... \oplus max\{\tilde{y}_{255:256}\}$. The feature maps obtained from the max-pooling layer containing discriminative features is flattened into channel dimension and is given as the input to the prediction model.

2.4 DNN Based Prediction Model

DNN [9] is applied in the proposed framework for predicting the disease exists or not in the Radiology report. DNN is typically a multi-layer neural network, influenced by a biological neural network consisting of a collection of connected modules named neurons. DNN's comprises of multiple such connected units between the input and output layers. The flattened discriminative features $y^{'} \in \mathbb{R}^n$ obtained from the CNN-DDR module is given as the input to fully connected four layered DNN for predicting whether disease exists or not in the radiology reports. The basic operation performed by DNN on the flattened discriminative features are forward propagation or inference represented as,

$$y^{'}_{i+1} = h(W_i \cdot y'_i + b_i), \tag{9}$$

where $W_{i=0,1,2}$ are the weight arrays and $b_{i=0,1,2}$ are the bias of the DNN Layers. Here, *h()* is the non-linear function applied on every element of the feature vector. Non-linear function, ReLU is applied at the penultimate layers and the Sigmoid operation for the binary classification at the output layers. For our experiment, based on a grid search approach [2], dropout probability of 0.2 is applied after the first hidden layer to restrain the model from overfitting.

3 Experimental Results and Evaluation

3.1 Datasets and Cohort Selection

Thorough investigation was conducted on two medical datasets: medical expert labelled publicly accessible radiology cohort of IU Dataset [6] and real-time data collected from KMC Hospital (Mangalore, India) (Ethics approval was granted by the Institutional Ethics Committee (IEC), Kasturba Medical College (KMC),

Mangalore to leverage the de-identified data for the research purpose). The radiology reports collected are de-identified and categorized as either "normal" (i.e., cases with no acute abnormality or any active diseases) or "abnormal" (i.e., cases with acute pulmonary abnormalities such as Cardiomegaly, Pulmonary atelectasis, Pleural effusion, Opacity/lung base, Calcified granuloma, etc.). IU dataset [6] is the manually labelled publicly available dataset consisting of de-identified clinical radiology images paired up with the diagnostic reports. Most of the existing works on IU dataset are cross-modal retrieval (i.e., report generation) from images [11,16]. The dataset is unseen in terms of radiology report classification and disease prediction. We selected 3638 radiology reports comprising of *Findings* and reports with missing *findings* are removed. The Medical Subject Heading (MeSH) indexing is leveraged to find the ground truth annotation and based on the MeSH terms, the reports are categorized into two classes "normal" and "abnormal". The final annotated data is manually validated by an experienced radiologist to verify the correctness of the annotations. Table 1 depicts the summary statistics of both the datasets.

Table 1. Cohort statistics: Radiology reports from two Institutions

Characteristic	IU dataset	KMC dataset
Total # of Radiology Reports	3996	502
Total # of Final Cohort selected	3638	502
Total # of Sentences	11541	3649
Total # of Words	91171	17198
Total # of Vocabulary	1568	393
Total # of Training set	3274	452
Total # of test set	364	50
% of Normal cases	38%	52%
% of Abnormal cases	62%	48%

3.2 Benchmarking the Proposed Prediction Model Against the State-of-the-Art Machine Learning Techniques

In order to comprehensively validate the proposed Medical knowledge-based Deep Learning framework, we leverage various traditional ML techniques such as Support Vector Machine (SVM), K-Nearest Neighbour (KNN), Random Forest (RF), Logistic Regression (LR) and AdaBoost classifier (AB) [8]. For our experiment, we have used the NVIDIA Tesla M40 server with 24 GB GPU, 3 TB Hard disk, 128 GB RAM and Ubuntu server Operating System. The radiology corpora are divided into training and test set. The Medical Knowledge-based Deep Learning model was trained for 100 epochs and 10-fold stratified cross-validation is applied to examine the proposed model. The findings extracted from the report are preprocessed and padded with the input size of 260. The proposed KB-MTM is applied to the free-text to obtain the word vectors of size $260 \times 100 = 26000$. The CNN-DDR is utilized to produce the most discriminative medical features of size 4096. Further, the DNN based prediction model is employed on the low dimensional features extracted from CNN-DDR to detect the pathology present on the reports. Also, these KB features were tested on traditional ML techniques for validation. The grid search technique [2] is used to choose the optimal hyperparameters for fine-tuning of the model parameter setting. Empirically, the classical ANN with one hidden layer was tested, and it did not perform well compared to the DNN with two hidden layers. We implemented the proposed model using a well-known deep learning framework, Tensorflow [9]. The following are the hyperparameters set for CNN-DDR and DNN model: Kernel Size:5, filter size:32, strides:1, dropout probability: 0.4, pool size:2 and learning rate: 0.001. We have also utilized Adam optimizer and binary cross-entropy as the loss function. The benchmark results are presented in Table 2 for IU and KMC Hospital dataset. The performance and the quality of the disease prediction were examined with the following five metrics: accuracy, precision, recall, F1 score and Matthews correlation coefficient (MCC) [8]. The proposed model with KB achieves high precision signifies that most cases belonging to the "abnormal" class are detected, which is the main objective of our disease prediction model. We have measured the F1-Score and MCC, which are also an essential evaluation metrics in our experiment, as our data exhibit class imbalance problem (i.e., In IU dataset, the pathology or abnormal class are in more significant number compared to the normal class; refer Table 1). The proposed model with KB has the staggering improvement in F1-Score and MCC for IU dataset. The higher value of F1-Score and MCC of the proposed Knowledge-based Deep Learning model on both dataset signifies that even if there was a class imbalance, the model was able to accurately classify. It is observed that RF with KB has produced good results after the proposed model for KMC dataset. It is due to the ensemble of decision trees generated by RF on the feature vectors obtained from KB-MTM is more discriminative for predicting disease compared to DNN without KB. However, the proposed DNN with KB features outperforms RF with KB features and other traditional ML models in terms of performance for both the dataset.

3.3 Effect of Knowledge-Based Medical Text Modelling

We have also examined the effect of customized KB-MTM compared with the Glove word embedding, as shown in Fig. 2a and Fig. 2b respectively. There is a significant increase of 3% and 2% in terms of accuracy, precision, recall, F1 score and around 7% and 3% improvement in MCC for IU dataset and KMC dataset respectively. The results depict that incorporating KB with the word-embedding models significantly increases the performance of the disease prediction due to the knowledge gained from the word embeddings trained on the large corpora.

Table 2. Benchmarking the proposed DNN model with and without KB against the State-of-the-Art ML Model for IU and KMC Hospital Dataset

Models	Indiana University Dataset					KMC Hospital Dataset				
	Acc.	Pre.	Recall	F-Sc.	MCC	Acc.	Pre.	Recall	F-Sc.	MCC
SVM	73.75%	0.732	0.737	0.597	0.415	76.16%	0.786	0.762	0.797	0.529
KNN	77.16%	0.780	0.772	0.705	0.521	88.88%	0.892	0.889	0.895	0.777
RF	86.36%	0.873	0.864	0.787	0.708	93.53%	0.942	0.935	0.937	0.873
LR	79.74%	0.795	0.797	0.704	0.555	88.88%	0.892	0.889	0.896	0.777
GB	76.55%	0.779	0.766	0.591	0.482	88.28%	0.889	0.883	0.891	0.765
DNN-KB *(Proposed)*	**87.27%**	**0.874**	**0.873**	**0.813**	**0.723**	**92.53%**	**0.927**	**0.925**	**0.929**	**0.850**
DNN+KB *(Proposed)*	**90.40%**	**0.908**	**0.904**	**0.858**	**0.794**	**94.13%**	**0.947**	**0.941**	**0.944**	**0.883**

Note: Acc.=Accuracy, Pre.=Precision, F-Sc.=F1-Score, DNN-KB=DNN without KB, DNN+KB=DNN with KB

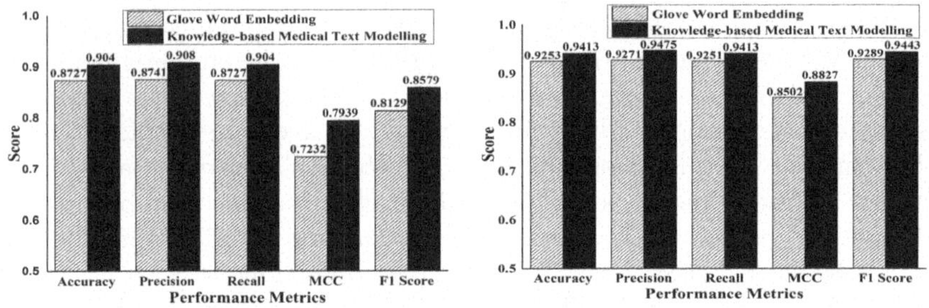

(a) Indiana university dataset (b) KMC Hospital dataset

Fig. 2. Effectiveness of proposed KB-MTM compared to the GloVe Embeddings

4 Conclusion and Future Work

As an outline, we have proposed the Medical Knowledge-based Deep Learning framework for predicting the lung diseases from the radiology reports at low data condition. We have found that there is no adequate literature for comparing the prediction techniques on radiology reports. Hence, we have benchmarked our results in comparison with the Standard ML Techniques on publicly available IU dataset and real-time collected dataset from the KMC Hospital. To the best of our knowledge, this is the first work on the disease prediction from the radiology reports collected from Indian private Hospital. To overcome the issue of handling the scarce data situation in the prediction models, the KB-MTM is proposed to incorporate the trained word embeddings from the large medical corpora. It is observed that integrating knowledge-base trained on a large corpus of radiology reports has increased the performance of the proposed prediction model. When we benchmark against the standard ML techniques, our proposed Medical Knowledge-based Deep Learning framework outperforms by 4–17% and 1–18% in terms of accuracy on IU and KMC Hospital dataset, respectively.

In future work, we would like to explore the DL architecture for enhancing the disease prediction accuracy. We would further like to analyze the multi-class classification of abnormal classes to group of pathologies.

Acknowledgement. We thank the Department of Information Technology, NITK Surathkal for providing resources for this research. We are grateful to KMC Hospital, Mangalore for granting access to the de-identified radiology reports for this research (*Ref. IEC KMC MLR 01-2020/80 dated 15.01.2020*).

A Appendix

Algorithm 1: Knowledge-based Medical Text Modelling

Input: *Medical-Knowledge-Base:* Pre-Trained Word embeddings on 4.5 million Stanford Radiology Report, *Medical-Corpus:* Unstructured Radiology Reports
Output: A Text Model trained on Unstructured Radiology Report Corpus with Word Embedding Representation
initialization;
Function `Clean`(S):
  Remove the Punctuation from S.
  Remove Stopwords from S.
  Stemming operation is applied on S to remove suffix.
  return S;
End Function
Function `Tokenize`(*Medical-Corpus*):
  for *each findings* $f_i \in$ *Medical-Corpus* **do**
    Cleaned-Findings $\longleftarrow$ *Clean*(f_i);
    tokens $\longleftarrow$ *Cleaned-Findings* are split into tokens;
  end
  return *tokens*;
End Function
Function `Convert-Word-to-Embeddings`(*Medical-Corpus*):
  - *Tokenized-Docs* $\longleftarrow$ *Tokenize*(*Medical-Corpus*)
  - Let $v_1, v_2, \ldots, v_n$ be the Unique medical words (i.e., Vocabulary) obtained from the $Tokenized - Docs$.
  - Generate one hot vector $hv_{i:n}$ for each word in a Vocabulary $v_{i:n}$.
  - Let k be the input length of each $Tokenized - Docs$ (Pad the documents if necessary.
  - Generate the knowledge-based word embeddings.
    • The co-occurrence between the two medical words are learnt by the objective function defined in the Eq. (8) using Stochastic Gradient Descent by minimizing the kv_i, $\tilde{kv_j}$, b_i and $\tilde{b_j}$ from the large corpus (refer Eq. (8) for term details).
    • Load the *Medical-Knowledge-Base* as the Embedding Weight Matrix with d-dimension word knowledge vectors $kv^1_{i:d}, kv^2_{i:d}, \ldots, kv^k_{i:d} = kv^{j:k}_{i:d}$, (where, $i = 1, 2, \ldots, d$) for all the medical words k.
  - The corresponding matrix is obtained by matrix multiplication (denoted by $\times$) between one hot vector of each word in a vocabulary and Embedding Weight Matrix through Embedding Layer with input size k and the output dimension d is,
  $\tilde{kv}^{j:k}_{i:d} \longleftarrow hv_{i:n} \times kv^{j:k}_{i:d}$
  return Word Vectors $\tilde{kv}^{j:k}_{i:d}$ of size $k \times d$
End Function

References

1. Agarap, A.F.: Deep learning using rectified linear units (relu). CoRR abs/1803.08375, March 2018
2. Bergstra, J., Bengio, Y.: Random search for hyper-parameter optimization. J. Mach. Learn. Res. **13**, 281–305 (2012)

3. Cao, Y., Huang, L., Ji, H., Chen, X., Li, J.: Bridge text and knowledge by learning multi-prototype entity mention embedding, pp. 1623–1633. ACL (2017)
4. Castro, S., Tseytlin, E., Medvedeva, O., Mitchell, K., Visweswaran, S., Bekhuis, T., Jacobson, R.: Automated annotation and classification of BI-RADS assessment from radiology reports. J. Biomed. Inform. **69**, 177–187 (2017)
5. Collobert, R., Weston, J., Bottou, L., Karlen, M., Kavukcuoglu, K., Kuksa, P.P.: Natural language processing (almost) from scratch. CoRR (2011)
6. Demner-Fushman, D., Kohli, M.D., Rosenman, M.B., Shooshan, S.E., Rodriguez, L., Antani, S.K., Thoma, G.R., McDonald, C.J.: Preparing a collection of radiology examinations for distribution and retrieval. JAMIA **23**(2), 304–10 (2016)
7. Dutta, S., Long, W.J., Brown, D.F., Reisner, A.T.: Automated detection using natural language processing of radiologists recommendations for additional imaging of incidental findings. Ann. Emerg. Med. **62**(2), 162–169 (2013)
8. Flach, P.: Machine Learning: The Art and Science of Algorithms That Make Sense of Data. Cambridge University Press, Cambridge (2012)
9. Goodfellow, I., Bengio, Y., Courville, A.: Deep Learning. The MIT Press, Cambridge (2016)
10. Hassanpour, S., Bay, G., Langlotz, C.: Characterization of change and significance for clinical findings in radiology reports through natural language processing. J. Digit. Imaging **30**, 314–322 (2017)
11. Liu, G., Hsu, T.H., McDermott, M.B.A., Boag, W., Weng, W., Szolovits, P., Ghassemi, M.: Clinically accurate chest x-ray report generation. CoRR (2019)
12. Santos, I., Nedjah, N., Mourelle, L.: Sentiment analysis using convolutional neural network with fastText embeddings, pp. 1–5, November 2017. https://doi.org/10.1109/LA-CCI.2017.8285683
13. Patel, K., Patel, D., Golakiya, M., Bhattacharyya, P., Birari, N.: Adapting pre-trained word embeddings for use in medical coding, pp. 302–306. ACL (2017)
14. Pennington, J., Socher, R., Manning, C.: Glove: Global vectors for word representation, pp. 1532–1543. Association for Computational Linguistics, October 2014
15. Trivedi, H., Mesterhazy, J., Laguna, B., Vu, T., Sohn, J.: Automatic determination of the need for intravenous contrast in musculoskeletal MRI examinations using IBM Watson's natural language processing algorithm. J. Digit. Imaging **31**(2), 245–251 (2017)
16. Xue, Y., Xu, T., Rodney Long, L., Xue, Z., Antani, S., Thoma, G.R., Huang, X.: Multimodal recurrent model with attention for automated radiology report generation, pp. 457–466. Springer International Publishing, Cham (2018)
17. Zhang, Y., Ding, D.Y., Qian, T., Manning, C.D., Langlotz, C.P.: Learning to summarize radiology findings. CoRR (2018)

Multidataset Incremental Training for Optic Disc Segmentation

Javier Civit-Masot[1(✉)], Antonis Billis[2], MJ Dominguez-Morales[1], Saturnino Vicente-Diaz[1], and Anton Civit[1]

[1] Escuela Superior de Ingenieria Informatica, University of Seville, Seville, Spain
{jcivit,mdominguez,satur,civit}@atc.us.es
[2] Lab of Medical Physics, Aristotle University of Thessaloniky, Thessaloniky, Greece
ampillis@med.auth.gr

Abstract. When convolutional neural networks are applied to image segmentation results depend greatly on the data sets used to train the networks. Cloud providers support multi GPU and TPU virtual machines making the idea of cloud-based segmentation as service attractive. In this paper we study the problem of building a segmentation service, where images would come from different acquisition instruments, by training a generalized U-Net with images from a single or several datasets. We also study the possibility of training with a single instrument and perform quick retrains when more data is available. As our example we perform segmentation of Optic Disc in fundus images which is useful for glaucoma diagnosis. We use two publicly available data sets (RIM-One V3, DRISHTI) for individual, mixed or incremental training. We show that multidataset or incremental training can produce results that are similar to those published by researchers who use the same dataset for both training and validation.

Keywords: Deep learning · Eye fundus image segmentation · Multiple dataset training · Incremental training · Glaucoma

1 Introduction

Glaucoma is a disabling decease that can lead to blindness in about 2 to 5% of the cases and sight impairment in 10% of the cases [19]. Although Loss of vision can occur even with the best treatment, correct therapy and follow-up will stabilize the majority of patients with glaucoma.

The key to detection and management of glaucoma is understanding how to examine the optic disc (OD) [4]. The OD is an oval 'plughole' down which the retinal nerve fibres descend through a sheet known as the lamina cribrosa. The retinal nerve fibres are then bundled together to form the optic nerve. The optic cup (OC) is the white, cup-like area in the center of the optic disc. The tissue between the border of the cup and the disc is the neuroretinal rim. This tissue

L. Iliadis et al. (Eds.): EANN 2020, INNS 2, pp. 365–376, 2020.
https://doi.org/10.1007/978-3-030-48791-1_28

consists mainly of nerve fibers with some glial cells and is usually pink. Most normal discs are more vertically oval and their cup more horizontally oval. A typical retina fundus image is shown in Fig. 1.

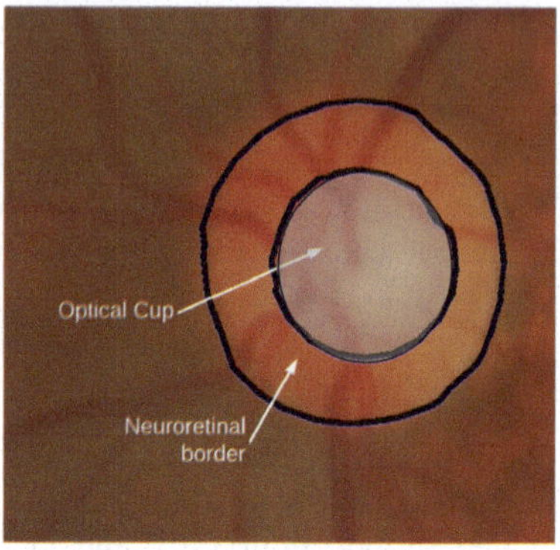

Fig. 1. Optic disc and cup

Several indicators are used to aid the diagnosis of glaucoma from fundus eye images. The cup to disc ratio (CDR) [18] which is the rate between the diameters of the optic disc and cup is the most widely used. In the mean CDRs of the glaucoma and normal eyes were 0.65 ± 0.13 and 0.39 ± 0.15, respectively allowing CDR to be used as a diagnostic aid. Another diagnostic approach is based on the rule based on the shape of the neuroretinal RIM. According to this rule in normal eyes, the thickness of the neuroretinal rim along the cardinal meridians of the OD decreases in the order inferior (I) > superior (S) > nasal (N) > temporal (T) [9]. In any case accurate OC/OD segmentation is required to be able to apply these techniques. This segmentation is an error prone process even for expert ophthalmologists specially in typical work overloaded scenarios.

Thus machine learning (ML) approaches are attractive for fundus image segmentation. Segmentation methodologies are based in three possible approaches [24]: Form matching based on random forests, support vector machines or K-means [14]; techniques based on transformations and active contours [3] oe Deep learning-based methods [1,21,22,26].

There are two scenarios for using image segmentation tools in a clinical set up. In the first one the tool is marketed by the provider of the image acquisition instrument. In this case we can train using images captured with the instrument linked to the tool. In a second scenario the segmentation is implemented as a service and has to be able to segment images from different clinics acquired with different instruments. Some approaches have been proposed for combined dataset training e.g. [5], however, they have not been applied, to medical image segmentation. Some previous works [1,21] have used different data sets but they train and test with each set independently. In [8] authors use several datasets but training is always performed with a combined dataset and, thus, it does not show the influence of performing single or multidataset training.

The objective of this paper is to study the problems that we would face to implement fundus segmentation as a service. For this purpose we will first find a suitable architecture for fundus image segmentation. Then we will train the system using a single data set and use it to predict over images from that set and images acquired with other instruments. After this we will use a mixed training dataset combining images from the different datasets, train our net with it and use it to make predictions on the different testing datasets. Finally we will study the realistic approach for clinical practice, i.e., to train with what is available and later do retraining when more data becomes available.

2 Materials and Methods

Implementation. Selection of Architectures for Segmentation. U-Net is a widely used fully convolutional neural network introduced in [20]. It has been widely used in image segmentation applications including several works related to ophthalmologic images including OD segmentation [21], retinal vessel segmentation [16] and diabetic retinopathy diagnosis [2]. In this work tools were developed to generalize U-Net models to allow rapid implementation in cloud-based GPU and TPU [10] architectures. We use a Keras [7] Tensorflow 2.1 implementation on the Google Collaboratory Python notebook environment.

In this section we will establish a methodology to select a generalized U-Net that correctly segments the OD. For this purpose we will train using combined datasets leaving the comparison of this approach with other alternatives for later sections.

Our networks are optimized versions of the U-Net proposed in [21]. Among the modifications are the use of a different image generator that produces the larger image batches for TPU training by means of static and dynamic data augmentation [27]. Also, to be able to modify our U-Net structure without recoding, we use a highly parameterizable U-Net recursive model. With this model we can change the depth and width of the net, the possibility of batch normalization, the use of upsampling or transpose convolution and the width ratio between successive layers known as increment ratio (IR). IR [13] is widely used as an effective pruning method.

We select network with the smallest IR and, thus, the one with less trainable parameters when two networks produce similar results. Although we train and make predictions in the web pruning improves time and reduces operating costs. The reduction of the initial network width and its depth are alternatives that we also explore.

We use 96 image batches for both training and testing, and train for 15 epoch using 100 training steps and 30 test steps per time. We use an Adam optimization algorithm with a learning rate of 0.0008. These values have proven suitable for TPU and GPU based training and provide good results with training times of less than 30 min for the TPU implementation.

Regarding the data sets, we use the publicly available RIM-ONE v3 and DRISHTI fundus image data sets. RIM ONE-v3 [12], form the MIAG group at the University of La Laguna (Spain), consists of 159 images labeled by expert ophthalmologists for OD/OC. DRISHTI-GS [23], from Aravind Eye Hospital, Madurai (India), consists of 101 images also labeled for OC/OD. In Fig. 2 we can see that the images that come from both data sets have very different characteristics.

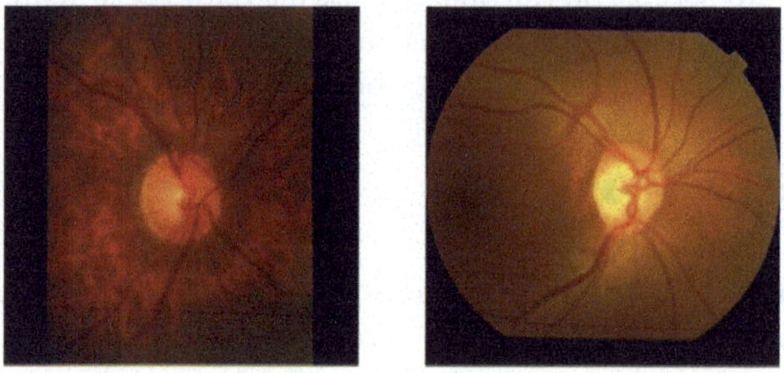

Fig. 2. Images RIM ONE (left) and DRISHTI (right) datasets

Figure 3 shows the used segmentation methodology. We start by trimming and resizing the images in the data sets by removing a 10% border on all edges of the image to reduce the black borders. After this, we resize the images to 128×128 pixels and perform a limited clip contrast histogram equalization. After, we split the data sets. For each set, we use 75% of the images for training and 25% for validation. Next, we perform, for each data set, static data augmentation by creating images with modified brightness and different contrast parameters. Later, we merge the data from the different sets. In the merging process, we perform data replication and random combustion to provide longer vectors as input for our dynamic image generators. Image generators [6] increase the data by performing random rotations, moving, zooming and flipping over the images of the extended merged data set.

Dice coefficient [11] is used to estimate the similarity between the correct and predicted disc. This figure of merit, also known as F1 score, is widely used and allows us to compare our results with those from other works. Dice coefficient is defined as:

$$DC = \frac{2TP}{2TP + FP + FN} \tag{1}$$

In this equation TP indicates true positives, FP false positives, and FN false negatives.

2.1 Instrument Based Versus Cloud-Based Segmentation

To show the results obtained when training with data from a single instrument or when training as a service, we will first train the system using a single data set and use it to predict images from other sets. After this we will use last section's mixed data set to train our network and use it to make the same predictions. In this section we use a generalized 6-layer U-Net which had good results in the previous section. It has only 40 channels in the first layer and the layer IR is 1.1. Given that we also resize the images in the sets to 128×128, the number of trainable parameters is less than 1 million.

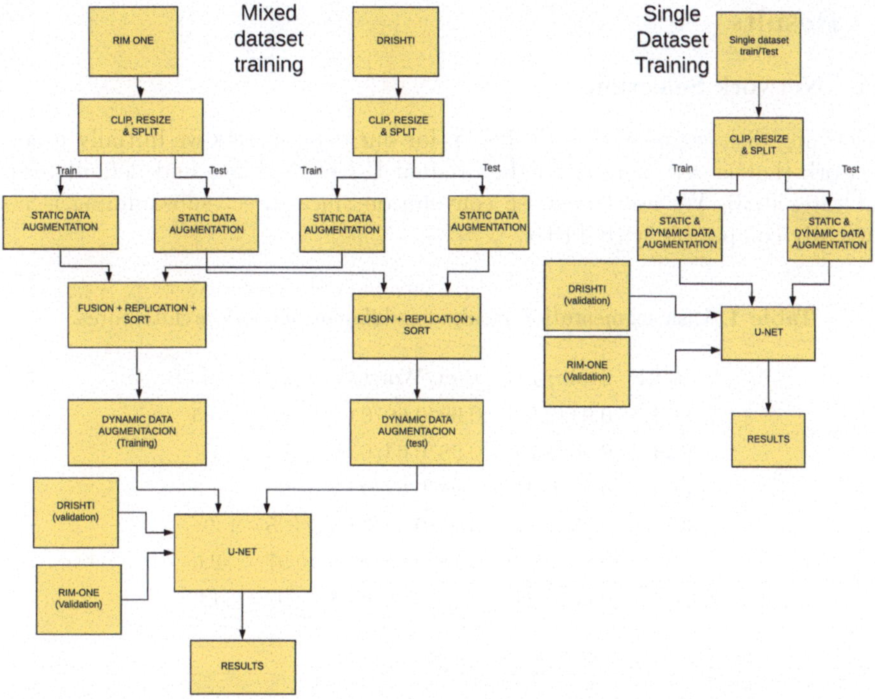

Fig. 3. Segmentation methodology

2.2 Study of the Viability of Incremental Learning

An interesting alternative, essential to implement cloud services, is to train initially with the available data and later modify the weights incrementally as we have data from new instruments. In this section, we will first train the system using a single data set and make predictions as stated above. Subsequently we will perform a short retraining (3 epochs) using images from the other data set and study the influence on the results. Thus, we test the feasibility of an incremental training using the resources and networks that we would deploy to implement a web service for segmentation of fundus images. This methodology is different from that used in other papers (e.g., [1,21,22,26]), where data from a single source are used for both training and testing.

We compare our work with those works that use deep learning for OD segmentation and use the DRISHTI or RIM-ONE data set. Zilly et al. [26] use a light three-layer CNN including sophisticated pre and postprocessing and apply it independently to both data sets. Sevastopolsky [21] uses a very light U-Net and provides results for RIM ONE. Al-Bander [1] uses a heavily modified, dense U-Net and provides results for both data sets. Shankaranarayana [22] uses a residual U-Net and provides results for RIM ONE.

3 Results

3.1 Network Selection

Regarding disk segmentation (Table 1), for our experiments we initially used a network that is very similar to the original U-Net: 5 stages and default dropout rates (0.3). We use transpose convolution since direct subsampling is not currently compatible with TPUs.

Table 1. Disk segmentation results for different network architectures.

D/W/IR	Train/Test	Best/Worst/Std.	RRP	MTP
5/32/1.5	0.94/0.91	0.99/0.69/0.07	95	3.5
5/40/1.2	0.90/0.79	0.98/0.64/0.09	95	1.1
6/40/1.3	0.95/0.91	0.98/0.64/0.09	96	3.3
6/40/1.1	0.95/0.91	0.97/0.59/0.09	95	.9
7/40/1.2	0.95/0.92	0.98/0.61/0.11	97	2.6
7/64/1.3	0.96/0.94	0.99/0.62/0.08	97	14

Table 1 shows Dice coefficients for train and for test sets for various evaluated U-Net alternatives. The first row of the table defines the main parameters of the architecture, that is, the network depth (D), the number of filters in the first layer (W), and the IR. As an example, 6/40/1.1 means that we use a generalized 6-layer U-Net with 40 channels in the first layer and an IR of 1.1. This network is shown in Fig. 4.

In addition to this base case we provide data for pruned networks where we try to obtain the same or greater performance with a smaller number of parameters. To achieve this goal, we decrease the IR while increasing the number of filters in the first layer, the depth of the network or both. The MTP column in Table 1 shows the millions of trainable parameters in the network. For each network architecture, we provide the mean Dice coefficient for the training and test sets, the Dice coefficient for the best and worst predicted images in the test set and the Dice standard deviation over the test set.

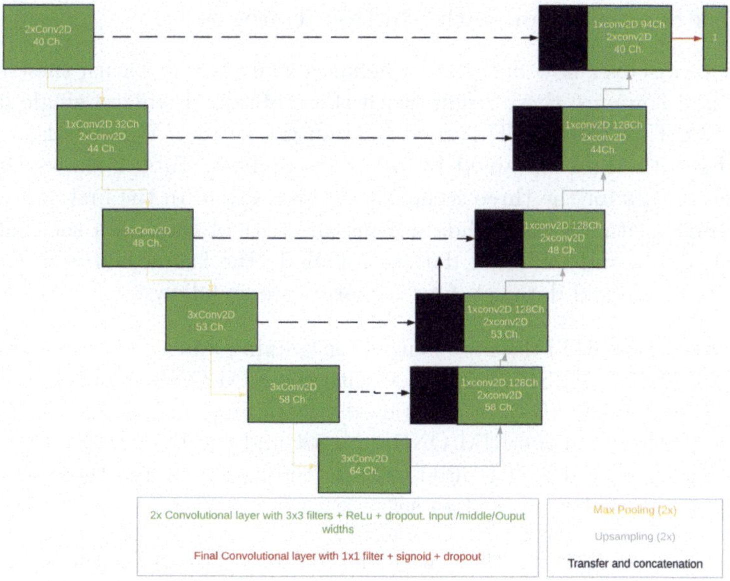

Fig. 4. Generalized 6 layer 6/40/1.1 U-Net architecture

Real disk shapes are not circular, but are approximately elliptical. In general, the ratio of the horizontal cup and disc diameters is larger than that of the diameters in the horizontal direction [17], however, in most of the works on the subject including all those mentioned in Table 2 the CDR is calculated using the mean diameters of the OC and OD. Although there are several possible interpretations of the average diameter, they have small differences with the real fundus images. In this paper we consider that the average radius of the OD is the square root of its area divided by π. We define a new parameter (Radio Ratio-RRP parameter) that is very useful for estimating the accuracy of the CDR. This parameter is defined as the percentage of test images for which the predicted disk radius has less than 10% error compared to the average radius of the ground truth. As an example, for the deepest network in the table, for 97% of the images our estimate of the radius has an error below 10% (RRP = 97).

We can see that deep networks with few parameters such as 6/40/1.1, which has less than 1M trainable parameters, achieve good results for disk segmentation. In this specific case, it achieves a RRP of 95. We will use this architecture for all the experiments in the rest of this paper. As a reference, we include in the Table 1 a very wide and deep network (7/64/1.3) with more than 14 million parameters. Although the performance of this network is better than in any other case, the small improvement does not justify the additional complexity of the network.

3.2 Disk Segmentation with Multiple Datasets

We want to discover how our system behaves when training with the combined data set and compare these results with those obtained when a single data set (i.e. RIM ONE or DRISHTI) is used to train the system. We will also compare the results with those obtained by other researchers. Table 2 shows Disk segmentation results for the three scenarios in this section. In the first two we train using a single data set and validate using the part of that data set that is not used for training and the other data set, while in the last scenario we train and validate with a mixed data set. Our scenarios are as follows:

- 75% of the DRISHTI data set is used for training and validation is done first with the rest of DRISHTI and then with the RIM ONE data set.
- 75% of the RIM ONE data set is used for training and validation is carried out with the rest of the RIM ONE data set and the DRISHTI data set.
- 75% of a mixed data set is used to train the networks and then we validate with the rest of the mixed data set.

We can see in Table 2 that, with our 6-layer network in the scenarios in which we train with a single data set the results when testing with images of that data set are good with Dice coefficients greater than 0.98 (DRISHTI) and 0.96 (RIM1). However, when we validate these networks with the other set, the results are below 0.66 or even 0.50 in some cases. In the third scenario in which we train with a mixed data set, we get results that are more similar when we test with images that come from both data sets. In this case, we obtain a Dice of 0.96 for the DRISHTI test subset and 0.87 for the RIM ONE subset.

Table 2. Multiple/single set dice coefficients.

Author	DRI	RIM
Zilly et al. [26]	0.97	-
Al-Bander [1]	0.95	0.90
Sevastopolsky [21]	-	0.94
Shankaranarayana et al. [22]	-	0.98
Drishti trained	0.98	0.50
RIM trained	0.66	0.97
Multi-dataset	0.96	0.87

In Table 2 we also results of previously referenced works which have trained and tested with each data set independently. Thus, they are related to our first two scenarios but they never test a network trained with one data set with images from another. Although we use networks with a small number of parameters, when we train with a single set we obtain results similar to those obtained by other papers. When training with DRISHTI, we obtained a Dice value of 0.98.

This value is slightly higher than 0.97 [26]. In the RIM ONE trained case, we get a dice value of 0.97 which compares well with 0.98 [1].

The most significant results in the Table 2 come from what can't be obtained in other studies, i.e., when we train with a dataset and predict using data from another source. In this case, we always get poor prediction results. This demonstrates that it is not feasible to create a service using training data captured with a single acquisition device. We also see in Table 2 that when you train with a combined data set, the network produces good results for both data sets, although not as good as when the training and prediction sets are part of the same set of data.

Regarding the clinically significant RRP parameter (Table 3), in the first two scenarios almost all radios for the test data are predicted with less than 10% error when compared to the segmentation done by ophthalmologists. However, the prediction for the other data set is much worse and, in some cases, we never get errors below 10%. This situation improves significantly when we train with a mixed data set.

Table 3. Radio ratio parameter.

	DRI	RIM
Drishti trained	100	38
RIM ONE trained	62	100
Multi-dataset	100	82

3.3 Incremental Training Results

We want to find out how our system behaves, when training with one set and then retraining lightly with some data from the other, and see if the results similar to those obtained when a single set of data is used (i.e. RIM ONE or DRISHTI) to train the system. Table 4 shows the results of disk segmentation for our two cases. On the first train, we use only DRISHTI data and validate using remaining of that data set and RIM ONE. In the second scenario, we make a brief retrain (3 epochs) using RIM ONE and the data set. Our scenarios are defined as follows:

- 75% of DRISHTI is used for training and validation is carried out first with the rest DRISHTI and then with the complete RIM ONE.
- 75% of RIM ONE is used to retrain the network and then we validate with the test part of both sets.

We can see in Table 4 that when we train with DRISHTI the tests with images from that same data set obtain very good Dice values. Specifically, we obtain an average Dice of 0.98 (DRISHTI) but only 0.64 (RIM1). The situation is worse than it seems as in the worst case for some RIM images the segmentation does not produce any pixels.

Table 4. Segmentation dice with retraining

Author	DRI	RIM
Zilly et al. [26]	0.97	-
Al-Bander [1]	0.95	0.90
Sevastopolsky [21]	-	0.94
Shankaranarayana et al. [22]	-	0.98
Drishti trained	0.98	0.64
RIM retrained	0.89	0.80

When we retrain the network with the other data set, the Dice values are 0.89 (DRISHTI) and 0.80 (RIM). For the worst case, we get a Dice of 0.69. Therefore, we can see that with a light retraining, the network can quickly learn the specific characteristics of the second data set. In Table 4 we include results of the other papers analyzed before. When we train with a single set of data, we obtain results for that set that are similar to those obtained by other papers. When training with the DRISHTI data set, we obtained a dice value of 0.98 for OD segmentation. This value is slightly above 0.97 [26]. As in the previous section the most significant results in Table 4 come from what is not available from other studies. The results obtained when we do a quick retraining show that, in this case, we get good prediction results for all test images.

4 Conclusions

We have been able to demonstrate that through the use of data from different data sets, adequate image preprocessing and significant data augmentation, we have been able to perform disk segmentation obtaining results with a performance similar to those obtained by other authors who use a single set for training and testing.

The use of a generalized configurable U-net recursive model allows us to easily train and test any U-Net configuration without having to make any changes to the code. This allows great flexibility for testing different architectures. We have tested networks with 4 to 7 layers, from 32 to 92 input channels, and with IR from 1.1 to 2.0. The number of parameters has varied from 0.9 to 44 million. Several U-Net architectures have been proven suitable for disk segmentation.

We have shown that by performing a rapid retraining with data from a new data set, and by preprocessing images and performing data augmentation, we can implement disk segmentation with performance equivalent to that reported by researchers using a single set for both training and testing.

4.1 Future Work

There are many possibilities to expand this work in the future. Among other possible topics, it would be interesting to implement modifications to always produce disc shapes that are acceptable to ophthalmologists. The automation of architecture configuration parameters and the use of other CNN architectures in parallel for the direct detection of glaucoma.

This work shows the importance of retraining by adding new sources to the segmentation system. In a real clinical service scenario, we would have to start training the network with the initially available data and retrain it when new images become available. The possibility of improving the network architecture by including residual blocks [25] or the combination of these blocks and a conventional U-Net [15] has proven effective in several segmentation applications and could potentially improve the performance of our process. The robustness of these networks when analyzing images from many different instruments remains an open problem for the future.

References

1. Al-Bander, B., Williams, B., Al-Nuaimy, W., Al-Taee, M., Pratt, H., Zheng, Y.: Dense fully convolutional segmentation of the optic disc and cup in colour fundus for glaucoma diagnosis. Symmetry **10**(4), 87 (2018)
2. Aujih, A., Izhar, L., Mériaudeau, F., Shapiai, M.I.: Analysis of retinal vessel segmentation with deep learning and its effect on diabetic retinopathy classification. In: 2018 International Conference on Intelligent and Advanced System (ICIAS), pp. 1–6. IEEE (2018)
3. Bhat, S.H., Kumar, P.: Segmentation of optic disc by localized active contour model in retinal fundus image. In: Smart Innovations in Communication and Computational Sciences, pp. 35–44. Springer (2019)
4. Bourne, R.R.: The optic nerve head in glaucoma. Community Eye Health **19**(59), 44 (2006)
5. Choi, Y., Choi, M., Kim, M., Ha, J.W., Kim, S., Choo, J.: Stargan: Unified generative adversarial networks for multi-domain image-to-image translation. In: Proceedings of the IEEE Conference on Computer Vision and Pattern Recognition, pp. 8789–8797 (2018)
6. Chollet, F.: Building powerful image classification models using very little data. Keras Blog (2016)
7. Chollet, F.: Deep Learning with Python, 1st edn. Manning Publications Co., Greenwich (2017)
8. Civit-Masot, J., Luna-Perejón, F., Vicente-Díaz, S., Rodríguez Corral, J.M., Civit, A.: TPU cloud-based generalized U-net for eye fundus image segmentation. IEEE Access **7**, 142379–142387 (2019). https://doi.org/10.1109/ACCESS.2019.2944692
9. Das, P., Nirmala, S., Medhi, J.P.: Diagnosis of glaucoma using CDR and NRR area in retina images. Netw. Model. Anal. Health Inform. Bioinform. **5**(1), 3 (2016)
10. Dean, J., Patterson, D., Young, C.: A new golden age in computer architecture: empowering the machine-learning revolution. IEEE Micro **38**(2), 21–29 (2018)
11. Dice, L.R.: Measures of the amount of ecologic association between species. Ecology **26**(3), 297–302 (1945)
12. Fumero, F., Alayón, S., Sanchez, J.L., Sigut, J., Gonzalez-Hernandez, M.: Rim-one: an open retinal image database for optic nerve evaluation. In: 2011 24th International Symposium on Computer-Based Medical Systems (CBMS), pp. 1–6. IEEE (2011)

13. Howard, A.G., Zhu, M., Chen, B., Kalenichenko, D., Wang, W., Weyand, T., Andreetto, M., Adam, H.: Mobilenets: Efficient convolutional neural networks for mobile vision applications. arXiv preprint arXiv:1704.04861 (2017)
14. Kim, S.J., Cho, K.J., Oh, S.: Development of machine learning models for diagnosis of glaucoma. PLoS One **12**(5), e0177726 (2017)
15. Kim, S., Bae, W., Masuda, K., Chung, C., Hwang, D.: Fine-grain segmentation of the intervertebral discs from MR spine images using deep convolutional neural networks: BSU-Net. Appl. Sci. **8**(9), 1656 (2018)
16. Lian, S., Li, L., Lian, G., Xiao, X., Luo, Z., Li, S.: A global and local enhanced residual u-net for accurate retinal vessel segmentation. IEEE/ACM Trans. Comput. Biol. Bioinform. (2019)
17. Lingam, C.L., Mansberger, S., Miglior, S., Paranhos, A., Pasquale, L.R., Susanna Jr., R., Wang, N.: 4. risk factors (ocular). Diagnosis of Primary Open Angle Glaucoma: WGA consensus series-10, vol. 10, p. 127 (2017)
18. MacIver, S., MacDonald, D., Prokopich, C.L.: Screening, diagnosis, and management of open angle glaucoma. Can. J. Optom. **79**(1), 5–71 (2017)
19. Quigley, H.A., Broman, A.T.: The number of people with glaucoma worldwide in 2010 and 2020. Br. J. Ophthalmol. **90**(3), 262–267 (2006)
20. Ronneberger, O., Fischer, P., Brox, T.: U-net: convolutional networks for biomedical image segmentation. In: International Conference on Medical Image Computing and Computer-Assisted Intervention, pp. 234–241. Springer (2015)
21. Sevastopolsky, A.: Optic disc and cup segmentation methods for glaucoma detection with modification of U-net convolutional neural network. Pattern Recogn. Image Anal. **27**(3), 618–624 (2017)
22. Shankaranarayana, S.M., Ram, K., Mitra, K., Sivaprakasam, M.: Joint optic disc and cup segmentation using fully convolutional and adversarial networks. In: Fetal, Infant and Ophthalmic Medical Image Analysis, OMIA 2017, pp. 168–176. Springer International Publishing (2017)
23. Sivaswamy, J., Krishnadas, S., Joshi, G.D., Jain, M., Tabish, A.U.S.: Drishti-GS: retinal image dataset for Optic Nerve Head (ONH) segmentation. In: 2014 IEEE 11th International Symposium on Biomedical Imaging (ISBI), pp. 53–56. IEEE (2014)
24. Thakur, N., Juneja, M.: Survey on segmentation and classification approaches of optic cup and optic disc for diagnosis of glaucoma. Biomed. Signal Process. Control **42**, 162–189 (2018)
25. Xiuqin, P., Zhang, Q., Zhang, H., Li, S.: A fundus retinal vessels segmentation scheme based on the improved deep learning U-net model. IEEE Access **7**, 122634–122643 (2019). https://doi.org/10.1109/ACCESS.2019.2935138
26. Zilly, J., Buhmann, J.M., Mahapatra, D.: Glaucoma detection using entropy sampling and ensemble learning for automatic optic cup and disc segmentation. Comput. Med. Imaging Graph. **55**, 28–41 (2017)
27. Zoph, B., Cubuk, E.D., Ghiasi, G., Lin, T.Y., Shlens, J., Le, Q.V.: Learning data augmentation strategies for object detection. arXiv preprint arXiv:1906.11172 (2019)

On Image Prefiltering for Skin Lesion Characterization Utilizing Deep Transfer Learning

K. Delibasis[1](✉), S. V. Georgakopoulos[1], S. K. Tasoulis[1], I. Maglogiannis[2], and V. P. Plagianakos[1]

[1] Department of Computer Science and Biomedical Informatics, University of Thessaly, Papassiopoulou 2-4, Lamia 35100, Greece
{kdelimpasis,spirosgeorg,stasoulis,vpp}@uth.gr

[2] Department of Digital Systems, University of Piraeus, Grigoriou Lampraki 126, Piraeus 18532, Greece
imaglo@unipi.gr

Abstract. Skin cancer is one of the most diagnosed cancers according to the World Health Organization and one of the most malignant. Unfortunately, still the available annotated data are in most cases not enough to successfully train deep learning algorithms that would allow highly accurate predictions. In this paper, we propose the utilization of transfer learning to fine-tune the parameters at the very last layers of a pre-trained a deep learning neural network. We expect that a limited number of skin lesion images is enough to affect significantly the later data-specific layers. Furthermore, we propose a pre-process step for skin lesion images that segments and crops the lesion, whereas smooths the effect of image masking, thus enhancing the network's classification capabilities. The reported results are very promising, since the overall accuracy, as well as the accuracy of individual class classification improved in 7 out of the 8 classes, suggesting future developments in medical diagnosis through pre-trained deep learning models and specialized image prefiltering.

Keywords: Convolutional Neural Networks (CNN) · Skin Lesion Classification · Cancer detection · Image pre-processing

1 Introduction and Related Work

Skin cancer is one of the most frequently diagnosed cancers according to the World Health Organization [1] and one of the most malignant. There are many types of skin carcinomas, with "melanoma" having the highest rate of mortality [16], while "basal cell carcinoma" being the most common skin cancer with lower mortality. Trained machine learning computational tools capable of discriminating between normal skin images and images of skin cancer is crucial.

L. Iliadis et al. (Eds.): EANN 2020, INNS 2, pp. 377–388, 2020.
https://doi.org/10.1007/978-3-030-48791-1_29

The task of further discriminating types of cancer can be much more challenging but still of great importance, since different types of cancer are characterized by significantly different mortality rates.

In the literature, there have also been unsupervised methods able to provide such discrimination in their pattern findings [19], [2] indicating class separability to some degree. His prior knowledge justifies the use of supervised methods that are able to achieve much higher accuracy in similar complexity tasks [13]. The most recent advances in supervised approaches use Convolutional Neural Networks variants for both segmentation and classification of skin images.

The utilization of filtertering is widely adopted by supervised methods aiming to extract appropriate features for training a classifier [14]. Even in the case of state-of-the-art supervised methods such as the Convolutional Neural Networks (CNNs) that are able to construct the most relevant features for each problem, the use of global image filters significantly improves CNN performance in some cases [7]. A common use of filters on CNN is when artifacts occur within an image [8]. In particular, pre-processing of dermoscopy images for lesion classification is very common. In [15] the authors proposed a method for detecting the lesion type, where a pre-process stage for removing the hairs from the skin and the lesion is performed. Next the deep transfer learning approach is used to fine-tune the pre-trained model Alexnet [9] using dermoscopy images. Deep transfer learning is a recent popular approach used in medical imaging where knowledge is transferred from pre-trained models using large-scale data into new models [18].

However, recent findings [7] show that CNN models trained to classify general purpose images can achieve higher classification performance when compared with pre-trained models on medical domain problems. In [10] the authors examined the transfer learning approach for skin cancer classification employing several state-of-the-art architectures (VGG-16, ResNet50, ResNet101, Inception-v3) trained on the popular ImageNet dataset. It was shown that the fine-tuned VGG-16 model outperformed the rest of the CNNs under comparison.

In this work, we deal with the problem of classifying dermoscopy images into different skin cancer types. Our aim is to investigate the effect of prior lesion segmentation on the classification performance of a CNN and to derive an optimal way of incorporating the segmentation information into the image dataset without inducing artifacts that may affect the features learn by the CNN. More specifically, it is expected that, since the segmentation is a masking operation, it produces strong edges at the lesion border, which represent irrelevant information that may deteriorate the performance of the CNN classifier. However, if the mask-generated edges are filtered-out from the image dataset, the clipping and segmentation process should preclude irrelevant image information and consequently increase the achieved classification accuracy. To this end, we propose a pre-process filtering method that minimizes the artificial edges after lesion segmentation. Then, we use the deep transfer learning methodology where a deep learning model is fine-tuned by the aforementioned images. Comparative results confirm the superiority of including image segmentation and clipping in conjunction with the image filtering to suppress the segmentation-related edges.

2 Methodology

Motivated by [7], the proposed methodology is based on fine-tuning a pre-trained CNN model. More precisely, we evaluate a model, is trained using the well-established ImageNet dataset that consists of real world images, and subsequently fine tune it with dermoscopy images, which have been segmented and prepossessed using the proposed approach, to remove the background of the lesion.

The preprocessing step consists of two main parts. In the first part the segmentation of the lesion from the background skin takes place, while in the second part we proceed to the filtering of the edges induced by the aforementioned lesionsegmentation. In Fig. 1 the workflow of the proposed methodology is presented. More precisely, the original input dermoscopy image is segmented through a trained CNN [12] producing a binary mask. The resulting segmentation mask is applied on the original dermoscopy image, filtering-out the background, while retaining the lesion. However the lesion boundary edges introduced through this procedure are expected to prevent the efficient training of the CNN. To avoid this side effect, we filter the images by filling the zero-valued pixels of segmented image appropriate image values of the lesion edges. In the final step, the pre-processed images are used to fine-tune the pre-trained CNN model towards real-world object classification.

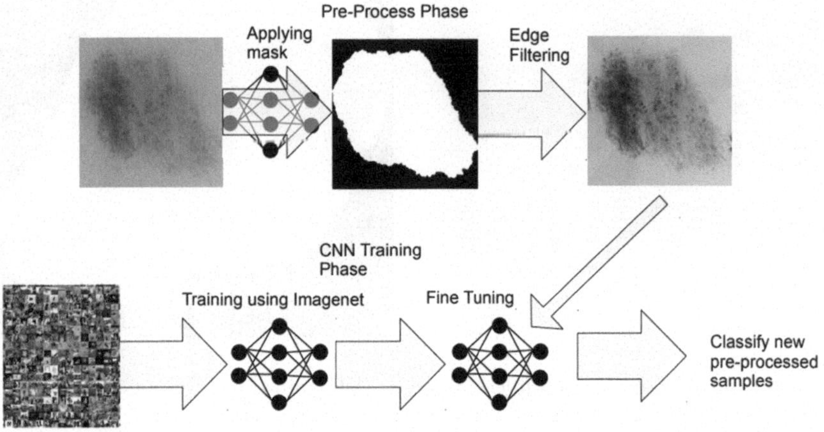

Fig. 1. An overview of the proposed approach

2.1 Image Preprocessing

Lesion Segmentation

Lesion segmentation in a dermosopy image involves the separation of the skin lesion from the surrounding skin and the creation of the corresponding binary masks. Several methodologies are reported in the literature concerning lesion segmentation [11].

The preprocessing phase of the proposed workflow creates such binary skin lesion masks. In this study the methodology based on adaptive thresholding published in [12] was utilized. Nevertheless, the proposed methodology can exploit any other similar algorithm.

Image Cropping, Masking and Filtering

After lesion segmentation, cropping is performed to extract the image patch that will be input to the CNN. Since the CNN requires input of standard dimensions, the original image patch is cropped as a square, masked using the segmentation result and rescaled to the desired dimensions, using the standard bicubic interpolation. It is however reasonable to assume that the strong edge introduced by binary masking can induce irrelevant features during the deep learning process, thus deteriorate the performance of the CNN (Fig. 2). In order to test this assumption and improve the classification accuracy, we propose a special preprocessing of the input image mask that retains the image information, whereas minimizing the artificial edges due to cropping and masking.

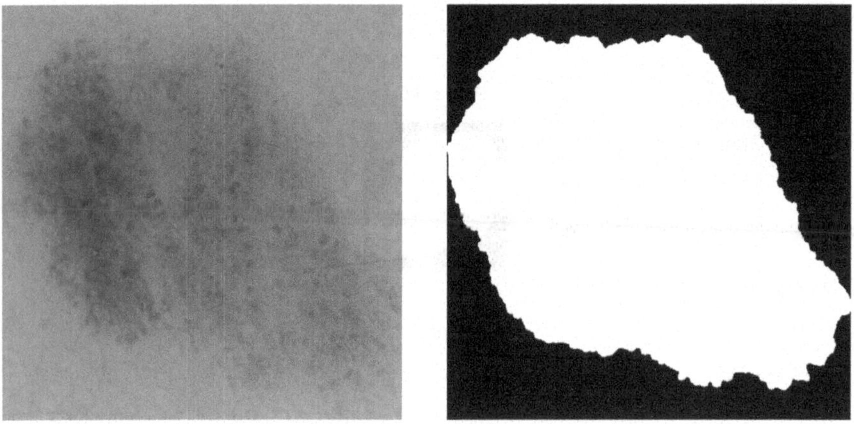

Fig. 2. A typical example of cropped image, I_c (left) and the corresponding segmented image, B_c (right)

Let I be the original RGB dermoscopy image that is decomposed into its three color channels and B_c the square binary segmented image, cropped round the detected lesion. The following steps are applied to each masked and cropped color channel I_c. Let us also denote by g_σ the 2-dimensional Gaussian kernel with standard deviation equal to σ. The proposed pre-processing algorithm is described in the following steps.

$$J_l = J * g_\sigma$$

A typical example of J and J_l is shown in Fig. 3

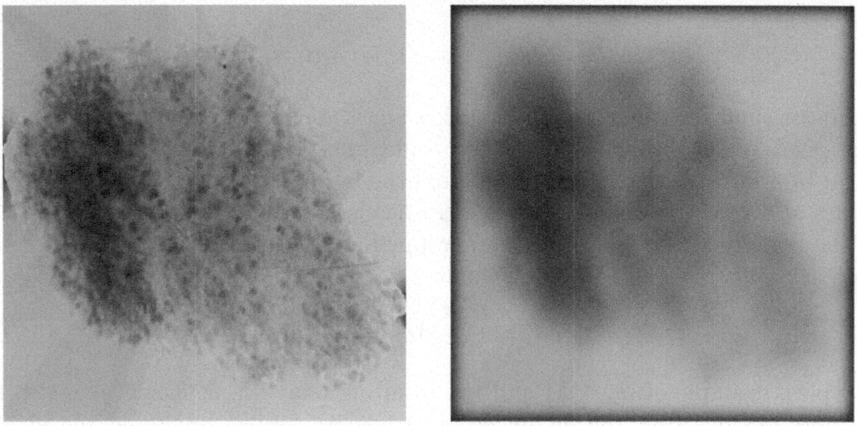

Fig. 3. Typical examples of the images of step 3 of the preprocessing algorithm. The J image in the left, the blurred image J_l in the right.

Step 1. The masked and cropped image is convolved with g_σ to produce a smoother version: $I_g = I_c * g_\sigma$

Step 2. The Distance Transform is applied to B_c, yielding for each zero-valued pixel in B_c the distance from the nearest non-zero (boundary) pixel, as well as the coordinates of the nearest pixel $(p_{i,j}, q_{i,j})$.

Step 3. An intermediate image is generated as following,

$$J(i,j) = \begin{cases} I_c(i,j) & B_c(i,j) > 0 \\ I_g(p_{i,j}, q_{i,j}) & B_c(i,j) = 0 \end{cases}$$

According to its definition, this image is identical to I_c at the non-zero pixels of the B_c, whereas the rest of its pixels hold the value of the nearest boundary pixel of the smoothed, cropped image I_g. As it can be visually observed, this image (J) is prone to radial edges, thus the preceding convolution with the Gaussian is employed to smoothing of the boundary values and smear the radial edges. Please note that this smoothing is applied to the boundary values that are replicated in the zero-valued pixels of the Bc image and does not affect the pixels inside the lesion (where $B_c > 0$). Furthermore, the aforementioned image

J is also convolved with a Gaussian kernel to blur the radial edges. In this case also, the blurring is applied on the zero valued pixels of the B_c without affecting the useful image part. The following equation it is utilized:

Step 4. The final image is composed by the pixels of Ic that have non-zero values in Bc and the blurred pixels of J1 that have zero values in Bc. In order to avoid a sharp image value change at the border, an image mask M is constructed as following:

$$M = max(d_{max} - DT(B_c), 0)\frac{1}{d_{max}}$$

It can be confirmed that by its definition, mask M has a value of 1 at the non-zero pixels of B_c, zero value at the zero-valued pixels of B_c that lie at a distance equal to or greater than d_{max} pixels from the border of B_c and linearly varying values at the rest of the pixels (the zero pixels of Bc that lie closer than d_{max} to the border of B_c). Then the final cropped and masked image, which will be used as input to the CNN, is defined as:

$$I_p = (1 - M)J + I_c$$

A typical example of mask M and the resulting image I_p is shown in Fig. 4. It becomes obvious that the finally cropped image contains unaltered the pixels of the lesion, whereas the masked-out pixels are smoothed, without noticeable transition at the lesion contour that may interfere with the image features that are automatically generated by the CNN. The above steps are repeated for all three color channels and the RGB smoothed cropped image is finally constructed.

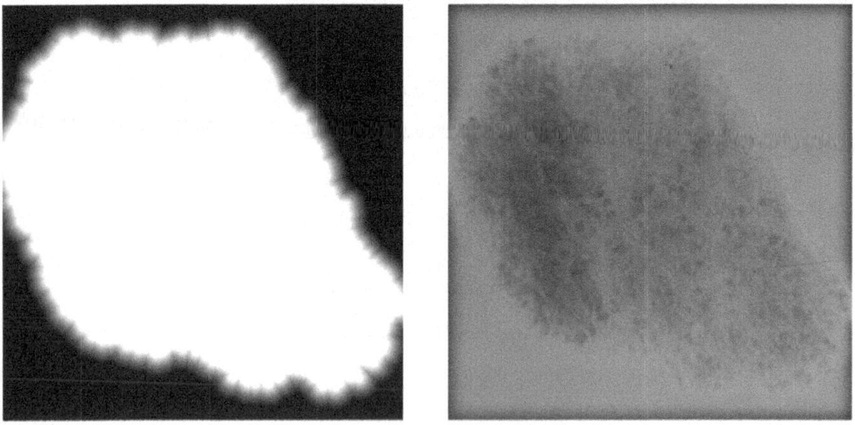

Fig. 4. A typical example of the image mask M (left) and the final cropped and masked image, after the application of filtering (right).

2.2 Convolutional Neural Networks Fine-Tuning

The processed dermoscopy images can be fed to a CNN for training. However, most medical image datasets are highly unbalanced with some classes, being dominant with respect to the number of samples they contain. Even the use of dataset augmentation techniques do not allow for proper CNN-training from scratch.

We deal with this problem leveraging knowledge from an already trained network in order to fine-tune the model and achieve highly accurate results. This technique usually referred to as transfer learning, is based on the assumption that the knowledge of a model which is capable of solving a problem in a specific domain can be used as a baseline for a model to solve an image classification problem in another domain. Adopting this strategy we select the well-established architecture VGG-16 [17] trained on the ImageNet dataset [6] as baseline to our model. The VGG-16 consisted of 13 convolutional layers, two fully-connected layers and one output layer with 1000 neurons equal to the number of classes of the ImageNet dataset. For the task at hand, the number of the classes is significantly lower, therefore the output layer is replaced by 9 neurons, according to the number of lesion types found in our dataset.

Next, we fine-tune the aforementioned pre-trained VGG-16 model by adapting its baseline knowledge to the medical domain of interest and finally classify the lesions. Since the CNN have internal structures which tend to learn generic features on their first layers such as color blobs, Gabor filters etc [21]; we choose to keep all the kernel weights of the convolutional layers that contain generic purpose information. As such, fine-tuning is performed only for the weights of the fully-connected layers and the output layer. We use a small learning rate parameter value equal to 0.001 for fine-tuning, since the pre-trained weights are expected to be more relevant than the randomly initialized weights and thus they need to adapt smoothly. Finally, we use the Stochastic Gradient Descent algorithm for the training [3] for 100 epochs with input batch size equal to 64 images. The dermoscopy images are resized to 224×224 as required by the VGG-16 architecture.

3 Experimental Results

We begin our experimental analysis by describing the specification of the dataset used for evaluation. Then we proceed by examining the various aspects of the proposed methodology. For this purpose we employ the original fine-tuned VGG-16 model along with both the original dermoscopy images and the images that have been preprocessed removing the background skin from the lesion.

3.1 Dataset Description and Image Classification Experiments

The dataset evaluated in this work is the train dataset, obtained from the International Skin Imaging Collaboration (ISIC) [20], [5] 2019 dataset, which contains

25.331 clinical dermoscopy images of skin lesions, of eight (8) different malignant and benign classes, along with their labels. The image classes labeled in this dataset and their population is given in Table 1.

Table 1. The number of samples per class (lesion type) of ISIC dataset.

Lesion	Number of samples
Melanoma	4522
Melanocytic nevus	12875
Basal cell carcinoma	3323
Actinic keratosis	867
Benign keratosis	2624
Dermatofibroma	239
Vascular lesion	253
Squamous cell carcinoma	628

As described above, the VGG deep learning model, pre-trained on the Imagenet dataset is subjected to transfer learning, under three experiments that are performed and compared in terms of classification accuracy, using the available dermoscopy image dataset, processed as following:

1. The original images of the dataset are used for training and testing.
2. The original images of the dataset are masked and clipped.
3. The original images are masked, clipped and finally processed using the filter described in Sect. 2.

3.2 Evaluation and Results

This section is devoted to the evaluation of the effectiveness of the preprocessing methodology on dermoscopy images for training a CNN through transfer learning against using the original images or the images for which the background skin has been simply masked-out. For this purpose, the described CNN model, VGG-16, has been fine-tuned separately using all three variations of input images through the process described in the previous Subsect. 3.1.

The evaluation of image classification is performed by 10-fold cross validation, applied to each class separately, due to increased class asymmetry. For the same reason, the performance of the different CNN models is evaluated using the accuracy measure along with the balanced accuracy [4], which is the mean accuracy of the model for each individual category of lesion.

In a baseline examination, the training of a CNN from scratch using augmentation techniques achieves mean accuracy below 60%. In contrast, as shown in Table 2 all aforementioned versions that utilize transfer learning as it is described

Table 2. The accuracy and the balance accuracy of the examined methods using cross validation 10-fold.

	Proposed method (masked, clipped and filtered images)	Original images	Segmented and Clipped images
Accuracy	**85.3%**	82%	76.1%
Ballanced accuracy	**73.6%**	70.8%	61.6%

Table 3. The classification accuracy of the different image processing methods for each lesion using the VGG-16 with transfer learning.

	Proposed method (masked, clipped and filtered images)	Original images	Segmented and Clipped images
Melanoma	**77%**	70%	63%
Melanocytic nevus	**94%**	91%	89%
Basal cell carcinoma	**87%**	83%	73%
Actinic keratosis	**62%**	59%	48%
Benign keratosis	**68%**	66%	53%
Dermatofibroma	**59%**	56%	38%
Vascular lesion	**78%**	77%	73%
Squamous cell carcinoma	59%	**61%**	50

Table 4. The Recall and Precision measures of 10-fold cross validation of the proposed method.

	Proposed method (masked, clipped and filtered images)	
	Precision	Recall
Melanoma	87%	82%
Melanocytic nevus	90%	94%
Basal cell carcinoma	82%	86%
Actinic keratosis	64%	68%
Benign keratosis	76%	70%
Dermatofibroma	74%	61%
Vascular lesion	96%	80%
Squamous cell carcinoma	78%	59%

in Sect. 2, perform significantly better. In more detail, Table 3 reports the accuracy and balanced accuracy of the three described techniques. As shown, the proposed method achieves the most accurate classification with respect to both metrics. Interestingly, we observe that the usage of the segmented images for training the CNN model provide lower classification accuracy than using the original images. This behavior indicates that the strong edges resulting from the lesion segmentation have an adverse effect on the performance of the CNN. It may be assumed that the CNN model tends to learn the shape of the lesion, instead of extracting the useful image features, which are related to the discrimination of the lesions. Furthermore, we conclude that the skin beyond the lesion does not contribute to classification, probably due to the irrelevant information it contains such as hairs etc. The proposed image pocessing approach seems to bypass this drawback by managing to remove the original human skin, while adding a blurring effect to minimize side effects of this procedure. In Table 4 is presented the recall and precision measures of the proposed methodology for each lesion.

4 Conclusion

This study utilized an extensive, multi-class image dermoscopy dataset to evaluate the effect of transfer learning and special image preprocessing on the classification accuracy achieved by a well-established deep learning model (VGG-16). Results show that transfer learning is essential for increasing the accuracy to acceptable levels, even in this case of a dataset with relatively high population of images (more than 25.000). The inclusion of lesion segmentation alone is not beneficial for the classification task, since the resulting accuracy deteriorated, probably due to the artificial boundary edges that are introduced during the masking process. Finally, the design of an elaborate image pre-processing filter that leaves intact the lesion pixel values and fills the rest of the mask pixels with appropriate values that smooth the boundary effect, proved beneficial, since it increased the overall 10-fold classification accuracy from 70.8% to 73.6%. Furthermore, it increased the accuracy of 7 out of the 8 lesion classes. The remaining class "squamous cell carcinoma" showed a marginal reduction of classification accuracy from 61% to 59%. More importantly, the accuracy for the classification of melanoma (the class of the highest malignancy) showed significant increase from 70% to 77%.

Acknowledgment. This project has received funding from the Hellenic Foundation for Research and Innovation (HFRI) and the General Secretariat for Research and Technology (GSRT), under grant agreement No 1901. We gratefully acknowledge the support of NVIDIA Corporation with the donation of the Titan X Pascal GPU used for this research.

References

1. https://www.who.int/uv/faq/skincancer/en/index1.html
2. Abbas, Q., Fondón, I., Rashid, M.: Unsupervised skin lesions borderdetection via two-dimensional image analysis. Comput. Methods Prog. Biomed. **104**(3), e1–e15 (2011). https://doi.org/10.1016/j.cmpb.2010.06.016
3. Bottou, L.: On-line learning and stochastic approximations. In: In On-line Learning in Neural Networks, pp. 9–42. Cambridge University Press, Cambridge (1998)
4. Brodersen, K.H., Ong, C.S., Stephan, K.E., Buhmann, J.M.: The balanced accuracy and its posterior distribution. In: 2010 20th International Conference on Pattern Recognition, pp. 3121–3124 (2010)
5. Codella, N.C.F., Gutman, D., Celebi, M.E., Helba, B., Marchetti, M.A., Dusza, S.W., Kalloo, A., Liopyris, K., Mishra, N., Kittler, H., Halpern, A.: Skin lesion analysis toward melanoma detection: a challenge at the 2017 international symposium on biomedical imaging (isbi), hosted by the international skin imaging collaboration (isic) (2017)
6. Deng, J., Dong, W., Socher, R., Li, L.J., Li, K., Fei-Fei, L.: ImageNet: a large-scale hierarchical image database. In: CVPR09 (2009)
7. Georgakopoulos, S.V., Kottari, K., Delibasis, K., Plagianakos, V.P., Maglogiannis, I.: Improving the performance of convolutional neural networkfor skin image classification using the response of image analysis filters. Neural Comput. Appl. **31**(6), 1805–1822 (2019). https://doi.org/10.1007/s00521-018-3711-y
8. Jafari, M.H., Nasr-Esfahani, E., Karimi, N., Soroushmehr, S.M.R., Samavi, S., Najarian, K.: Extraction of skin lesions from non-dermoscopic images using deep learning (2016). arXiv: 1609.02374
9. Krizhevsky, A., Sutskever, I., Hinton, G.E.: Imagenet classification with deep convolutional neural networks. In: Pereira, F., Burges, C.J.C., Bottou, L., Weinberger, K.Q. (eds.) Advances in Neural Information Processing Systems, vol. 25, pp. 1097–1105. Curran Associates Inc., New York (2012)
10. Li, Y., Shen, L.: Skin lesion analysis towards melanoma detection using deep learning network. Sensors **18**(2), 556 (2018). https://www.mdpi.com/1424-8220/18/2/556
11. Maglogiannis, I., Doukas, C.N.: Overview of advanced computer vision systems for skin lesions characterization. IEEE Trans. Inf. Technol. Biomed. **13**(5), 721–733 (2009)
12. Maglogiannis, I., Zafiropoulos, E., Kyranoudis, C.: Intelligent segmentation and classification of pigmented skin lesions in dermatological images. In: Antoniou, G., Potamias, G., Spyropoulos, C., Plexousakis, D. (eds.) Advances in Artificial Intelligence, pp. 214–223. Springer, Heidelberg (2006)
13. Mhaske, H.R., Phalke, D.A.: Melanoma skin cancer detection and classification based on supervised and unsupervised learning. In: 2013 International Conference on Circuits, Controls and Communications (CCUBE), pp. 1–5 (2013)
14. Oliveira, R., Filho, M., Papa, J., Pereira, A., Manuel, J., Tavares, J.: Computational methods for the image segmentation of pigmented skin lesions: a review. Comput. Methods Programs Biomed. **131**, 127–141 (2016)
15. Salido, J.A., Ruiz, C.: Using deep learning for melanoma detection in dermoscopy images. Int. J. Mach. Learn. Comput. **8**, 61–68 (2018). https://doi.org/10.18178/ijmlc.2018.8.1.664
16. Siegel, R.L., Miller, K.D., Fedewa, S.A., Ahnen, D.J., Meester, R.G.S., Barzi, A., Jemal, A.: Colorectal cancer statistics, 2017. CA: Cancer J. Clin. **67**(3), 177–193 (2017)

17. Simonyan, K., Zisserman, A.: Very deep convolutional networks for large-scale image recognition. In: International Conference on Learning Representations (2015)
18. Talo, M., Baloglu, U.B., Yıldırım, Ö., Acharya, U.R.: Application of deep transfer learning for automated brain abnormality classification using mr images. Cogn. Syst. Res. **54**, 176–188 (2019)
19. Tasoulis, S.K., Doukas, C.N., Maglogiannis, I., Plagianakos, V.P.: Skin lesions characterisation utilising clustering algorithms. In: Konstantopoulos, S., Perantonis, S., Karkaletsis, V., Spyropoulos, C.D., Vouros, G. (eds.) Artificial Intelligence: Theories, Models and Applications, pp. 243–253. Springer, Heidelberg (2010)
20. Tschandl, P., Rosendahl, C., Kittler, H.: The ham10000 dataset: a large collection of multi-source dermatoscopic images of common pigmented skin lesions. Sci. Data **5**, 180161 (2018)
21. Yosinski, J., Clune, J., Bengio, Y., Lipson, H.: How transferable are features in deep neural networks? In: Advance in Neural Information Processing System, vol. 27, pp. 3320–3328 (2014)

Identification of Eyelid Basal Cell Carcinoma Using Artificial Neural Networks

Evagelos Georgios Chatzopoulos[1], George Anastassopoulos[2,3], Efstathios Detorakis[4], and Adam Adamopoulos[1](✉)

[1] Laboratory of Medical Physics, Department of Medicine, Democritus University of Thrace, Komotini, Greece
tsohoulis@gmail.com, adam@med.duth.gr
[2] Laboratory of Medical Informatics, Department of Medicine, Democritus University of Thrace, Komotini, Greece
anasta@med.duth.gr
[3] Department of Electrical and Computer Engineering, University of Patras, Patras, Greece
[4] Clinic of Ophthalmology, Department of Medicine, University of Crete, Heraklion, Greece
detorakis@gmail.com

Abstract. First results of the classification of the eyelid Basal Cell Carcinoma using Artificial Neural Networks are presented. Full, or half-face photographs of healthy subjects and patients suffering from eyelid Basal Cell Carcinoma were used to train and validate Artificial Neural Networks for the purpose of pattern recognition, identification and classification. The efficiency of the algorithm was tested using various training methods and it was evaluated using the accuracy score, that is, the ration of the number of the correctly classified cases over the total number of cases under examination. With respect to the accuracy, the proposed algorithm reached up to 100% performance. The algorithm is accompanied by a specifically designed and developed user friendly Graphical User Interface.

Keywords: Eyelid Basal Cell Carcinoma · Pattern recognition · Artificial Neural Networks

1 Introduction

Basal Cell Carcinoma (BCC) is defined as a slowly growing, locally expanding, malignant epidermal tumor [1–3]. It is the most common type of skin cancer as over 70% of cases are related to it. In fact, 90% of BCC concern the head and neck area, while 10% of cases occur in the eyelid, which confirms the relationship between BCC and sun exposure [4–7]. Effective treatment of BCC in the ophthalmic region is achieved by a variety of methods and depends on both the characteristics of the BCC and the patient himself. Depending on the size, the topographic location of the tumor, the age and the general health condition of the patient, there is a wide variety of approaches aimed at correcting the eyelid deficit [8–13]. Of course, to understand the

L. Iliadis et al. (Eds.): EANN 2020, INNS 2, pp. 389–396, 2020.
https://doi.org/10.1007/978-3-030-48791-1_30

functional anatomy of the peripheral region, it is essential to understand the principles of repairing the eyelids. Appropriate treatment may consists of either surgical resection of the tumor or repair of the lesion through nonsurgical procedures, using state-of-the-art technologies such as subtractive cryotherapy and photodynamic therapy. In addition, it is possible to use modern pharmaceutical preparations such as imikumimod 5% cream, as well as the use of multiple interventions to repair eyelid defects [14–16].

In order to select the most appropriate therapeutic technique, it is necessary to classify the tumors into specific categories according to their characteristics and through clinical control of the patient. Balancing tumor removal techniques, combined with functionality of the surgical site and cosmetic repair of the lesion, make the therapeutic approach applied successful. While there are a variety of invasive and non-invasive techniques to repair BCC in the eyelid, the choice of a more appropriate method that will lead to treatment is a complicated process. Due to the fact that there are so many types of BCC, identification and classification are difficult tasks and depend on many factors. For this reason, as in many areas of medicine for diagnostic support [17–21], in the present work it was developed an Artificial Intelligence (AI) system that can distinguish cases of BCC in order to support physicians in decision making and to confirm or assist timely and valid diagnosis. The proposed AI system is based on Artificial Neural Networks (ANN), a method that, along with fuzzy systems, as well as, evolutionary optimization algorithms can be utilized for face identification, detection and recognition [22–28].

The purpose of this work is to develop an intelligent pattern recognition system for identifying eyelid BCC from a patient's full or half-face photograph. To accomplish this task, ANN were constructed and trained to identify and classify face photographs of normal subjects and photographs of eyelid BCC patients. To gain user-friendliness the developed algorithms are executed under a specially designed Graphical User Interface (GUI). The performance of the developed ANN were evaluated with respect to their classification accuracy score. The obtained results indicated that AI systems based on ANN can favorably be utilized for eyelid BCC identification and classification.

2 Material and Methods

The material used for the present work consisted of full or half-face photographs of normal subjects and eyelid BCC patients. Image files were saved in raw, jpeg and tiff format. The preprocessing procedure consisted of two steps. At the first step a special function script was developed and utilized in order to convert all photographs to the same size varying in the range of 200 × 200 pixels up to 1000 × 1000 pixels. At the second step images were turned from RGB format to grayscale for purpose of the faster execution of thc learning algorithm, without missing any vital information. Representative examples of images of a normal and two pathological cases are shown in Fig. 1.

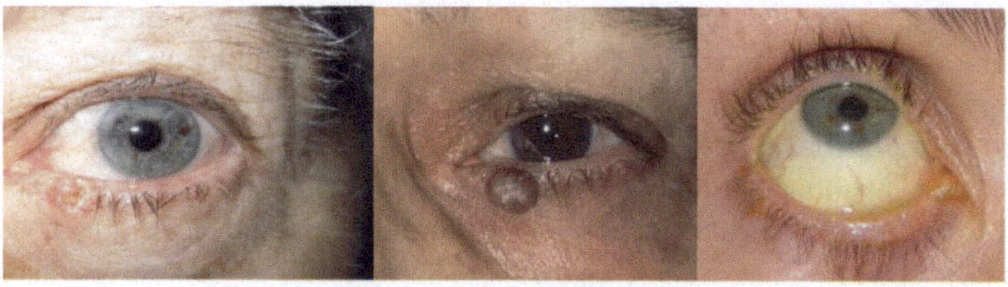

Fig. 1. Photograph of a normal subject eyelid (left) and two eyelid BCC cases (middle and right).

The overall purpose of this study was to develop a pattern recognition algorithm that would detect, identify and classify the presence of eyelid BCC in a patient's face photograph with the use of ANN. For purpose of convenience a suitable GUI was developed which allows the user either to train ANN by selecting a large set of images from the patients' database, or, to pick and upload a specific image and request from the system to identify and classify it, by providing an answer to the question of whether it corresponds to an eyelid BCC case or not. The ANN algorithms and the GUI were developed using the Matlab programming environment [29].

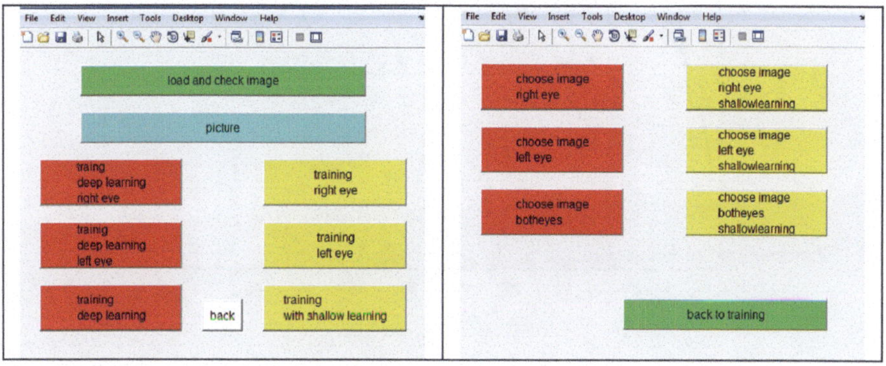

Scr. 1. Screenshots of GUI at the ANN training procedure (left) and at the specific case image selection procedure (right).

During the ANN training procedure, three options were provided: (i) right-eye training, (ii) left-eye training, and (iii) both-eye training. In the first two cases the algorithm uploads the corresponding images (right-eye or left-eye respectively) from the patients' database. In the last case the image was splitted in a right and a left part, each one containing the corresponding eye and then the right-eye training algorithm or the left-eye training algorithm was invoked, depending on the eye of interest. Screenshots of the GUI training procedure representation and the image selection of the specific case under consideration are shown in Scr. 1. Parameters that define the architecture of the ANN, namely, number of neural layers, number of neurons per layers, as well as the functional parameters of the ANN like percentage of training, testing and validation subsets over the total set of samples, training methods, number of training epochs and termination conditions, were user defined, through selections provided by the GUI.

As it was mentioned in the previous section, the performance of the ANN was evaluated in terms of the accuracy of classification. By denoting as TP, FP, TN and FN the number of cases that were classified by the algorithms as true positive, false positive, true negative and false negative respectively, the *accuracy* (*ACC*) of the classification method is given by the expression:

$$ACC = \frac{TP + TN}{TP + TN + FP + FN} \quad (1)$$

i.e., ACC is the ratio of the number of correctly classified cases over the total number of cases. Accuracy-Loss diagrams were generated during the training procedure of the ANN.

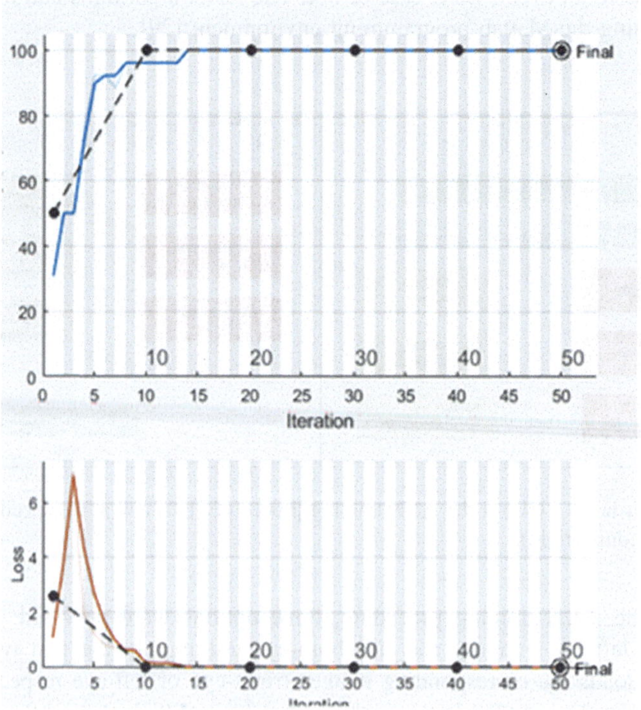

Scr. 2. Accuracy diagram and Loss diagram using the SGDM training method for the training (solid lines) and the validation procedure (dotted lined).

3 Results

Numerous computer experiments were conducted using the proposed algorithms in order to evaluate their performance and efficiency. Screenshot of the obtained Accuracy-Loss diagrams obtained by training the ANN using the Stochastic Gradient Descent with Momentum optimizer (SGDM) in the training method [30, 31] are shown in Scr. 2, where the ANN managed to reach accuracy up to 100% and to zero classification error. The corresponding results that were obtained using the Root Mean Square Propagation optimizer (RMSProp) in the training method [32] are shown in Scr. 3, where again the ANN succeeded to achieve accuracy up to 100% and zero error.

In Scr. 4, the representative results are presented with respect to the classification of a specific case by a trained ANN. These classification results refer to a full-face photograph of a normal subject and the right eye of a eyelid BCC patient that were selected to be identified and classified by the algorithm using SGDM. The algorithm at a first step splitted the full-face photograph of the normal subject to a right and a left part and subsequently examined if either the right or the left eyelid is pathological, concluding to a true negative answer for both eyelids. On the other hand, the case of the right eye of the eyelid BCC patient was classified as true positive by the algorithm.

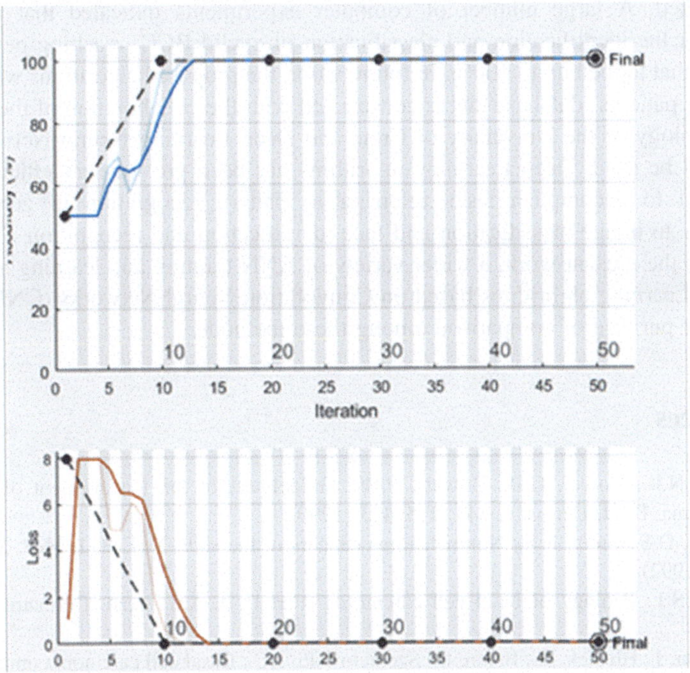

Scr. 3. Accuracy diagram and Loss diagram using the RMSProp training method for the training (solid lines) and the validation procedure (dotted lined).

Scr. 4. Left and middle: true negative classification of a full-face photograph of a normal subject (splitted in right and left part by the algorithm during preprocessing). Right: true positive classification of the right half-face photograph of an eyelid BCC patient.

4 Discussion

In this work, the first results of an intelligent pattern recognition algorithm for the identification and classification of eyelid BCC were presented. AI classification algorithms were developed based on ANN and were applied on face photographs of normal subjects and eyelid BCC patients. The algorithms were executed under a specially designed user-friendly GUI. To our knowledge it is the first time that such a task is accomplished. A large number of computer experiments indicated that ANN can account for the identification and classification of eyelid BCC, reaching performance efficiency that topped up to 100%. In future work, the proposed algorithms will be used on a larger patients' database that is constructed with the collaboration of the Clinic of Ophthalmology of the University of Crete and Deep Learning Neural Network algorithms will be used. Deep Learning algorithms has been proven very efficient in the recent past to accomplish tasks referring to pattern recognition in general, and specifically to image classification and face identification and recognition [33–35]. In addition to the present work, a wider variety of ANN training and learning algorithms and Deep Learning algorithms based on Convolution Neural Networks (CNN) will be utilized for purpose of comparison among these methods.

References

1. Telfer, N.R., Colver, G.B., Bowers, P.W.: Guidelines for the management of basal cell carcinoma. Br. J. Dermatol. **141**, 415–423 (1999)
2. Preston, D.S., Stern, R.S.: Nonmelanoma cancers of the skin. N. Eng. J. Med. **327**, 1649–1662 (1992)
3. Miller, S.J.: Biology of basal cell carcinoma (Part I). J. Am. Acad. Dermatol. **24**, 1–13 (1991)
4. Salomon, J., Bieniek, A., Baran, E., Szepietowski, J.C.: Basal cell carcinoma on the eyelids: own experience. Dermatol. Surg. **24**, 1–13 (1991)
5. Goldberg, D.P.: Assessment and surgical treatment of basal cell skin cancer. Clin. Plast. Surg. **24**, 673–686 (1997)
6. Duong, H.Q., Copeland, R.: Basal cell carcinoma, eyelid. Emedicine (2001)

7. Green, A.: Changing patterns in incidence of non-melanoma skin cancer. Epithelial Cell Biol. **1**, 47–51 (1992)
8. Allali, J., D'Hermies, F., Renard, G.: Basal cell carcinomas of the eyelids. Ophthalmologica **219**, 57–71 (2005)
9. Gaughan, L.J., Bergeron, J.R., Mullins, J.F.: Giant basal cell epithelioma developing in acute burn site. Arch. Dermatol. **99**(5), 594–595 (1969)
10. Margolis, M.H.: Superficial multicentric basal cell epithelioma arising in thermal burn scar. Arch. Dermatol. **102**(4), 474–476 (1970)
11. Anderson, N.P., Anderson, H.E.: Development of basal cell epithelioma as a consequence of radiodermatitis. AMA Arch. Dermatol. Syphilol. **63**(5), 586–596 (1951)
12. Gilbody, J.S., Aitken, J., Green, A.: What causes basal cell carcinoma to be the commonest cancer? Aust. J. Public Health **18**, 218–221 (1994)
13. Gilde, K.: Malignant tumors of the skin. Orv. Hetil. **147**(48), 2321–2330 (2006)
14. Schulze, H.J., Cribier, B., Requena, L.: Imiquimod 5% cream for the treatment of superficial basal cell carcinoma: results from a randomized vehicle-controlled phase III study in Europe. Br. J. Dermatol. **152**(5), 939–947 (2005)
15. Warren, R.C.; Nerad, J.A.: Micrographic (Mohs') surgery in the management of periocular basal cell epitheliomas. Arch. Ophthalmol. **108**(6), 845–850 (1990)
16. Lindgren, G., Larko, O.: Long-term follow-up of cryosurgery of basal cell carcinoma of the eyelid. J. Am. Acad. Dermatol. **36**, 742–746 (1997)
17. Mantzaris, D., Anastassopoulos, G., Adamopoulos, A.: Genetic algorithm pruning of probabilistic neural networks in medical disease estimation. Neural Netw. **24**(8), 831–835 (2011)
18. Stephanakis, I.M., Iliou, T., Anastassopoulos, G.: Mutual information algorithms for optimal attribute selection in data driven partitions of databases. Evolving Systems (2018). https://doi.org/10.1007/s12530-018-9237-9
19. Stephanakis, I.M., Anastassopoulos, G.C.: A multiplicative multilinear model for inter-camera prediction in free view 3D systems. J. Eng. Intell. Syst. **21**(2/3), 193–207 (2013)
20. Stephanakis, I.M., Anastassopoulos, G.C., Iliadis, L.: A self-organizing feature map (SOFM) model based on aggregate-ordering of local color vectors according to block similarity measures. Neurocomput. J. **107**, 97–107 (2013)
21. Stephanakis, I.M., Iliou, T., Anastassopoulos, G.: Information feature selection: using local attribute selections to represent connected distributions in complex datasets. In: Boracchi, G., Iliadis, L., Jayne, C., Likas, A. (eds.) Engineering Applications of Neural Networks. EANN 2017, Communications in Computer and Information Science, vol. 744, pp. 441–450. Springer, Cham (2017)
22. Vaillant, R., Monrocq, C., Le Cun, Y.: Original approach for the localisation of objects in images. IEE Proc. Vis. Image Sign. Process. **141**(4), 245–250 (1994)
23. Le Cun, Y., Bottou, L., Bengio, Y., Haffner, P.: Gradient-based learning applied to document recognition. Proc. IEEE **86**(11), 2278–2324 (1998)
24. Owley, H., Baluja, S., Kanade, T.: Neural network-based face detection. IEEE Trans. Pattern Anal. Mach. Intell. **20**(1), 23–38 (1998)
25. Hjelmas, E., Low, B.K.: Face detection: a survey. Comput. Vis. Image Underst. **83**(3), 236–274 (2001)
26. Zhao, W., Chellappa, R., Phillips, P.J., Rosenfeld, A.: Face recognition: a literature survey. ACM Comput. Surv. (CSUR) **35**(4), 399–458 (2003)
27. Tolba, A.S., El-Baz, A.H., El-Harby, A.A.: Face recognition: a literature review. Int. J. Sign. Process. **2**(2), 88–103 (2006)
28. Zhang C., Zhang, Z.: A survey of recent advances in face detection. Technical report, Microsoft Research (2010)

29. Matlab homepage. https://www.mathworks.com/products/matlab.html
30. Qian, N.: On the momentum term in gradient descent learning algorithms. Neural Netw. **12**(1), 145–151 (1999)
31. Sutskever, I., Martens, J., Dahl, G.E., Hinton, G.E.: On the importance of initialization and momentum in deep learning. In: ICML, vol. 3, no. 28, pp. 1139-1147 (2013)
32. Wilson, A.C., Roelofs, R., Stern, M., Srebro, N., Recht, B.: The marginal value of adaptive gradient methods in machine learning. In: Bengio, S., Wallach, H., Larochelle, H., Grauman, K., Cesa-Bianchi, N., Garnett, R. (eds.) 31st Conference on Neural Information Processing Systems (NIPS 2017), Long Beach, CA, USA (2017)
33. Krizhevsky, A., Sutskever, I., Hinton, G.E. Imagenet classification with deep convolutional neural networks. In: Advances in neural information processing systems, pp. 1097–1105 (2012)
34. Russakovsky, O., Deng, J., Su, H., Krause, J., Satheesh, S., Ma, S., Huang, Z., Karpathy, A., Khosla, A., Bernstein, M., Berg, A., Fe-Fei, L.: Imagenet large scale visual recognition challenge. Int. J. Comput. Vis. **115**(3), 1–42 (2014)
35. Bengio, Y., Goodfellow, I.J., Courville, A.: Deep Learning. MIT Press, Cambridge (2015)

Fuzzy Logic Modeling

Application of Algorithmic Fuzzy Implications on Climatic Data

Stefanos Makariadis, Georgios Souliotis, and Basil K. Papadopoulos(✉)

Department of Civil Engineering Section of Mathematics and Informatics, Democritus University of Thrace, 67100 Kimeria, Greece
{smakaria,gsouliot,papadob}@civil.duth.gr

Abstract. In this paper we present a new Fuzzy Implication Generator via Fuzzy Negations which was generated via conical sections, in combination with the well-known Fuzzy Conjunction T-norm = min. Among these implications we choose the most appropriate one, after comparing them with the empiristic implication, which was created with the help of real temperature and humidity data from the Hellenic Meteorological Service. The use of the empiristic implication is based on real data and also it reduces the volume of the data but without cancelling them. Finally, the pseudo-code, which was used in the programming part of the paper, uses the new Fuzzy Implication Generator and approaches the empiristic implication satisfactorily which is our final goal.

Keywords: Fuzzy implication · Empiristic implication · Fuzzy negation via conical sections

1 Introduction

The Theory of Fuzzy Implications and Fuzzy Negations plays an important role in many applications of fuzzy logic, such as approximate reasoning, formal methods of proof, inference systems, decision support systems (cf [2] and [5]). Recognizing the above important role of Fuzzy Implications and Fuzzy Negations, we tried to construct Fuzzy implications from Fuzzy negations, so that we could change the implication with one parameter, thus giving an algorithmic procedure of the "if...... then......" rule. The tools for this construction, namely a fuzzy implication generator, were mainly the conclusions of (cf [11]) and in particular the following formula 1

$$N(x) = \sqrt{(a^2-1)x^2+1} + ax, \quad x \in [0,1], \quad a \leq 0. \tag{1}$$

producing fuzzy negations via conical sections and Corollary 2.5.31. (see [1]). The combination of these two through the fuzzy conjunction T-norm = min gave us an algorithmic procedure for the evaluation of the best implication with respect to the problem data. For the evaluation of the best implication we used

L. Iliadis et al. (Eds.): EANN 2020, INNS 2, pp. 399–409, 2020.
https://doi.org/10.1007/978-3-030-48791-1_31

the empiristic implication (see [8]) as a comparison measurement. The empiristic implication does not satisfy any of the properties of the fuzzy implications and has no specific formula, meaning it is not a function. However, the choice of this particular implication was not random as it was based on its ability to be directly calculated by the empirical data without being affected by the amount of the data.

The paper follows the following structure: The section Preliminaries presents the theoretical background of the paper, such as the definitions of the Fuzzy Implications, Fuzzy Negations and Triangular norms. The section Main Results shows the implication which is constructed by a strong fuzzy negation and a t-norm with $T_M(x,y) = \min\{x,y\}$. Next, the empiristic implication and the algorithm for its calculation are presented. The data used are real, such as the average monthly temperature and the average monthly relative humidity, two of the most important climatic variables in meteorology (see [4]). Furthermore, the algorithmic process for finding the best fuzzy implication among the empiristic implication, the three known implications from the literature (Kleen-Dienes, Lukasiewicz, Reichenbach) (see [1]) and the constructed parametric implication is analysed. The calculation of the implications with the use of data was done in the Matlab programming environment. We present the documentation of the Matlab code which was used to calculate the implications.

2 Preliminaries

The following short theoretical background is important in order to understand this paper.

2.1 Fuzzy Implication

In the literature we can find several different definitions of fuzzy implications. In this paper we will use the following one, which is equivalent to the definition proposed by Kitainik [6], (see also [3] and [1]).

Definition 1. *A function* $I : [0,1]x[0,1] \to [0,1]$ *is called a fuzzy implication if for all* $x, x_1, x_2, y, y_1, y_2 \in [0,1]$ *the following conditions are satisfied:*
(*I1*) $x_1 \leq x_2$ *then* $I(x_1, y) \geq I(x_2, y)$, *i.e,* $I(\cdot, y)$ *is decreasing,*
(*I2*) $y_1 \leq y_2$ *then* $I(x, y_1) \leq I(x, y_2)$, *i.e.,* $I(x, \cdot)$ *is increasing,*
(*I3*) $I(0,0) = 1$
(*I4*) $I(1,1) = 1$
(*I5*) $I(1,0) = 0$

Example 1. *Some examples of Fuzzy Implications are given below:*
Kleene-Dienes: $I_{KD}(x,y) = \max\{1-x, y\}$
Lukasiewicz: $I_{LK}(x,y) = \min\{1, 1-x+y\}$
Reichenbach: $I_{RC}(x,y) = 1 - x + x \cdot y$

2.2 Fuzzy Negations

The following definitions and examples can be found [1,3,9], and [10].

Definition 2. *A function* $N : (0,1) \to [0,1]$ *is called a Fuzzy negation if*
$(N1)$ $N(0) = 1, \ N(1) = 0$
$(N2)$ N *is decreasing*

Definition 3. *A fuzzy negation N is called strict if, in addition,*
(N3) N is strictly decreasing,
(N4) N is continuous,
A fuzzy negation N is called strong if the following property is met,
$(N5)$ $N(N(x)) = x, \ x \in [0,1]$

Example 2. *Examples of Fuzzy Negations are given below.*
$N_K(x) = 1 - x^2$, *strict*
$N_R(x) = 1 - \sqrt{x}$, *strict*
$N^\lambda(x) = \frac{1-x}{1+\lambda x}$, $\lambda \in (-1, +\infty)$ *strong Sugeno class*
$N^W(x) = (1 - x^w)^{\frac{1}{w}}$, $w \in (0, +\infty)$ *strong Yager class*

Remark 1. The paper [11] proves a new family of strong fuzzy negations, which is produced by conical sections and is given from the Eq. (1), which will play a key role in building the algorithmic procedure we propose in the section Main Results.

2.3 Triangular Norms (Conjunctions)

The Triangular norms were introduced by Menger [9] and were later reconstructed by Schweizer and Sklar [10] in the form they have today. In essence, they are a generalization of the classical binary conjunction ($\wedge$) into a fuzzy intersection. The following definition can be found in the monograph by Klement et. al [7], (see also [1]).

Definition 4. *A function* $T : [0,1]^2 \to [0,1]$ *is called triangular norms shortly t- norm, if it satisfies, for all* $x, y \in [0,1]$, *the following conditions:*
$(T1)$ $T(x,y) = T(y,x)$ *(commutativity)*
$(T2)$ $T(x, T(y,z)) = T(T(x,y), z)$
$(T3)$ *if* $y \leq z$, *then* $T(x,y) \leq T(x,z)$ *(monotonicity)*
$(T4)$ $T(x,1) = x$ *(boundary condition)*

Table 1 lists a few of the common t-norms.

In the paper we will use the most basic of all t-norms, which is the minimum

$$T_M(x,y) = \min\{x,y\} \tag{2}$$

Table 1. Table basic t-norms

Minimum	$T_M(x,y) = \min\{x,y\}$
Algebraic product	$T_p(x,y) = x \cdot y$
Lukasiewicz	$T_{LK}(x,y) = \max(x+y-1,0)$
Active product	$T_D(x,y) = \begin{cases} 0 & x,y \in [0,1) \\ min(x,y) & otherwise \end{cases}$
Nilpotent minimum	$T_{nM}(x,y) = \begin{cases} 0 & x+y \leq 1 \\ min(x,y) & otherwise \end{cases}$

3 Main Results

3.1 Construction of Fuzzy Implications via Strong Negations

The main purpose of this work is to create a two plays function that satisfies Definition 1, utilizing the temperature and humidity data given by the Hellenic National Meteorological Service. That is, the construction of an implication that gives the degree of truth of the two variables, the temperature and the humidity. To achieve this, the two variables are normalized with the help of fuzzy sets. In this way the temperature gets values of [0, 1] and the humidity gets values of [0, 1], which is the degree of truth of the two variables. For example, if the temperature between $[21°, 31°]$ degrees is considered high, then it has a degree of truth 1. And similarly if the humidity between [40%, 50%] is considered low, then it has a degree of truth of 0.7. Our goal is to construct an implication that gives the degree of truth, as does the statement below:

"If the temperature is high, then the humidity is low."

To what degree of truth can we respond to this statement?

This is our intention, that is, to find an implication that is close enough to the correlation of the two variables, the temperature and the humidity, as are shown in our data. But to find such an implication there must be a comparison measure, that is, we want from our data to ensure the degree of truth of the temperature and the humidity pair as they are given. The comparison measure in the present work is the empiristic implication that uses all the data in order to produce a table in which in the first row and the first column there will be the data grouped into classes and in each cell there will be the corresponding degree of truth of the data. Then, we compare each of the Kleen-Dienes, Lukasiewicz, Reichenbach (see [1]) and the parametric implications which will be generated, with the empiristic one, using the square error of the difference of the aforementioned implication tables from the empiristic implication table.

The smallest square error will give the best implication.

In book [1], and in particular in Corollary (2.5.31), the implication generated by a strong fuzzy negation and a t-norm is examined and the formula

$$I(x,y) = N(T(x,N(y)), \quad x,y \in [0,1] \tag{3}$$

is proposed. Using the above implication (3) (see 3) with t-norm (2) (see 2) and the formula (1) (see 1) with parameter α and after the appropriate calculations, the following equation occurs.

$$I(x,y) = \sqrt{(a^2-1).\left(\min\left(x, \sqrt{(a^2-1)\,y^2+1}+ay\right)\right)^2+1} + a.\min\left(x, \sqrt{(a^2-1)\,y^2+1}+ay\right), y \in [0,1], a \leq 0 \quad \text{(equation a)}$$

The above implication of (equation a), which is a new generator fuzzy implications, is important because it has the parameter α which helps us to use the implication on our data and at the same time examine for which value of α we have the best approach. Hence, an algorithmic process of finding a better implication is created which will play an important role in the course of the paper.

3.2 Empiristic Implication

In order to be able to estimate which of the proposed implications approaches the pairs (Temperature, humidity) of the Hellenic Meteorological Service, we need to have a comparison measurement. In this paper we use the empiristic implication as a measure see [8]. The empiristic implication will be presented while explaining the steps of the algorithm, based on our data, which derive from the Hellenic Meteorological Service and are the average monthly temperature and the average monthly humidity of the last five years from the 13 regions of Greece (see Fig. 1, Fig. 2).

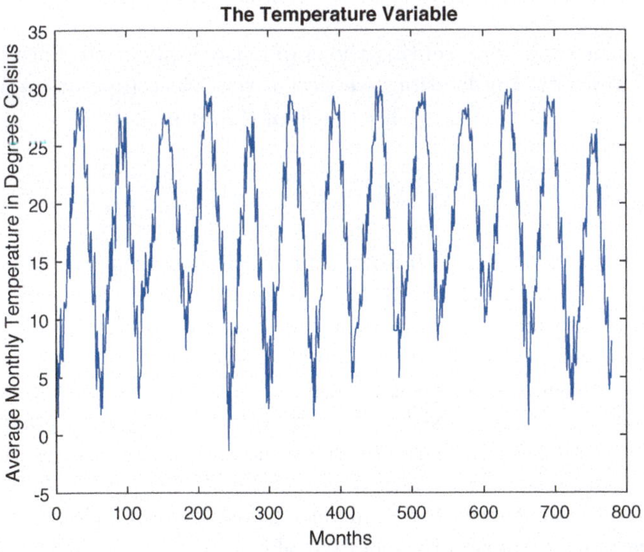

Fig. 1. Temperature variable

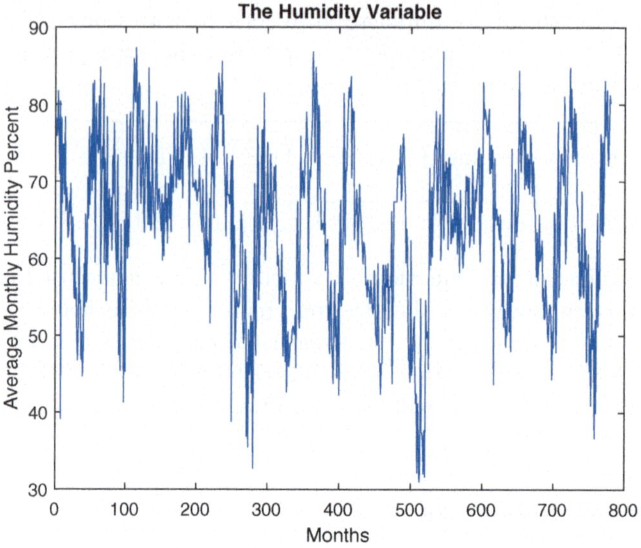

Fig. 2. The humidity variable

Our goal is to find which implication approaches best our data dependence (temperature and humidity), giving us as a result the degree of the true coexistence of the two corresponding values. For example, we would like to see the degree of truth of the statement:

if the temperature is 20 °C then the humidity is 60%

First, we find the table representing the empiristic implication. For the construction of the empiristic implication, we divide the 780 temperature and relative humidity data into 11 classes with the use of the Sturges type

$$c = 1 + \log_2 n \overset{n=780}{\Leftrightarrow} c = 1 + \log_2(780) \Leftrightarrow c = 1 + \frac{\log(780)}{\log(2)} \Leftrightarrow c = 10.6 \tag{4}$$

after first placing them in ascending order. Each class has its median as a representative. This is how we create the empiristic implication table, which has the medians of the humidity classes in the first row while the medians of the temperature classes are in the first column. Each cell of the table is divided by the sum of the column in which it belongs. In this way, we have in each cell the degree of the truth of the coexistence of the values of the corresponding column and row of the cell (see Table 2). Then we normalize the temperature and the humidity medians. Next, we check first whether the three known implications (Kleen-Dienes, Lukasiewicz, Reichenbach) (see [1]) approach the table above. Then, we examine the norm of each of the above implications with the empirical implication. The results are as follows.

Table 2. Table of the empiristic implication

0.0282	0	0.0141	0.0423	0.0282	0.0563	0.1127	0.1127	0.1831	0.1972	0.2286
0.0141	0	0.0141	0.0704	0.0563	0.0845	0.1972	0.0704	0.1268	0.2113	0.1571
0	0	0	0.0563	0.0423	0.1127	0.0986	0.1408	0.1127	0.1408	0.3000
0	0.0141	0.0423	0.0563	0.0704	0.1408	0.0986	0.1408	0.1831	0.1690	0.0857
0.0141	0.0423	0.0845	0.0423	0.1268	0.0986	0.0845	0.1549	0.1268	0.1127	0.1143
0.0423	0.0282	0.1408	0.0845	0.1972	0.0563	0.0423	0.1690	0.0563	0.1127	0.0714
0.0563	0.0563	0.1268	0.1268	0.1268	0.1690	0.1127	0.0845	0.0704	0.0423	0.0286
0.0845	0.1268	0.1831	0.1972	0.0845	0.0986	0.0845	0.0423	0.0704	0.0141	0.0143
0.1127	0.2254	0.1408	0.1127	0.1127	0.1268	0.0845	0.0282	0.0563	0	0
0.2676	0.1690	0.1549	0.1549	0.0704	0.0423	0.0704	0.0563	0.0141	0	0
0.3803	0.3380	0.0986	0.0563	0.0845	0.0141	0.0141	0	0	0	0

The Results of the Norms. The squared error of the two implications (empiristic and Kleen-Dienes) gives the result is 6.2465.

The squared error of the two implications (empiristic and Kleen-Dienes) gives the result is 8.7386.

The squared error of the two implications (empiristic and Kleen-Dienes) gives the result is 7.4448.

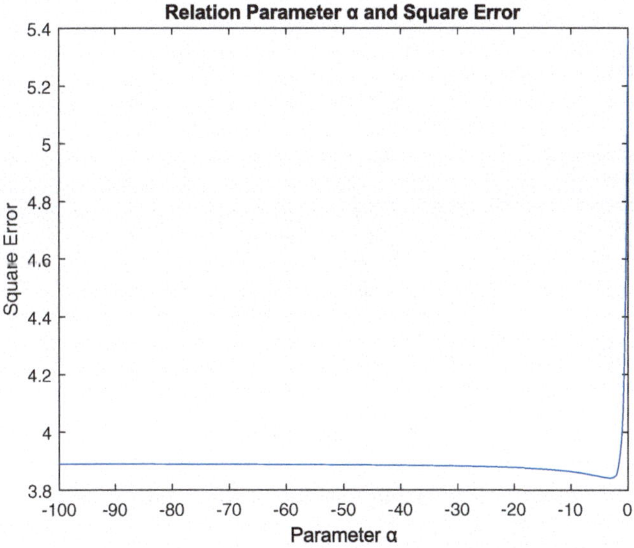

Fig. 3. Relation parameter α and square error.

After the examination of the three implications is completed, we proceed to find the best parameter $a \leq 0$ that we have from the (equation a). We have the best approach for the value $\alpha = -3$ and with a very good approach the squared error of the two implications (empiristic and Kleen-Dienes) gives the result is 3.8425 (see Fig. 3).

Remark 2. To achieve our goal, that is, to approach the empiristic implication table, we used 3 linguistic variables (low, medium and high) for temperature and humidity respectively.
$[a, b, c, d] = [-1.33 \ -1.33 \ 7 \ 12]$ is low temperature
$[a, b, c, d] = [10 \ 13 \ 15 \ 18]$ is medium temperature
$[a, b, c, d] = [16 \ 21 \ 30.21 \ 30.21]$ is high temperature
$[a, b, c, d] = [31.01 \ 31.01 \ 40 \ 45]$ is low humidity
$[a, b, c, d] = [43 \ 50 \ 60 \ 65]$ is medium humidity
$[a, b, c, d] = [64 \ 75 \ 87.39 \ 87.39]$ is high humidity
(see Fig. 4, Fig. 5). Also, to avoid the property of the implication I (0,1) = 1, which reinforces the falsehood, we tried to obtain the values of $x \neq 0$.

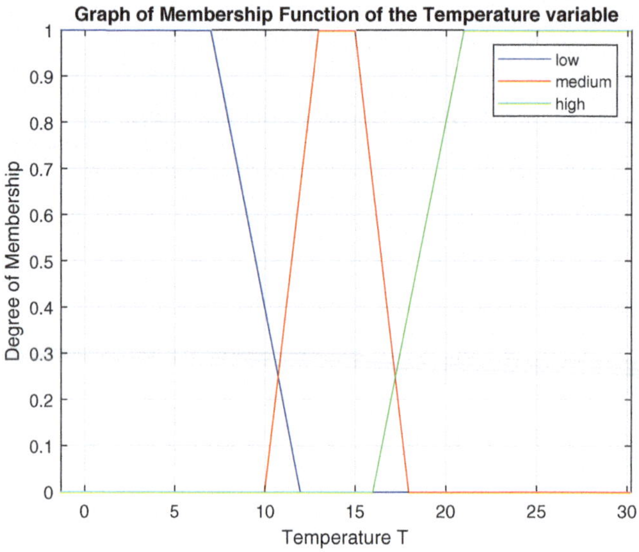

Fig. 4. Membership function of the temperature.

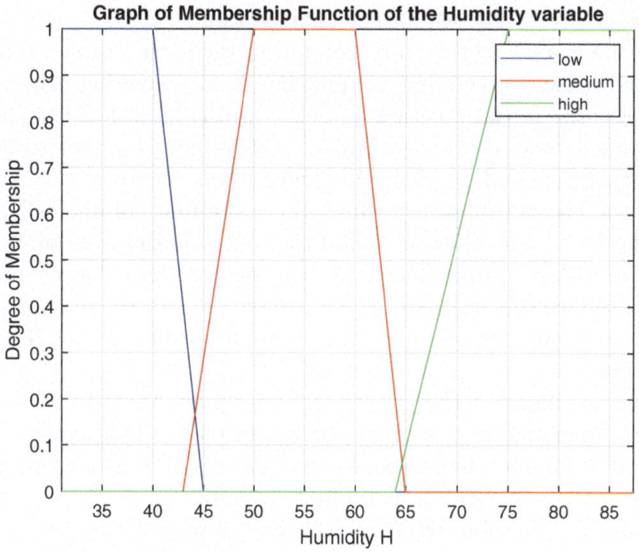

Fig. 5. Membership function of the humidity.

3.3 The Documentation of the Matlab Code

The data are in the file Data.xlsx. Our application includes a case study, which uses real climatic data (average monthly temperature and average monthly relative humidity) of the last five years 2015–2019 from the 13 regions of Greece for the 12 months of each year and evaluates the empiristic implication, with fuzzy implications we created. The application was implemented in Matlab R2018b and includes the steps:

1. We load the data onto the program, which creates two 780 × 1 tables. The lines in the tables are the 780 observations and the columns in the tables are the temperature and relative humidity variables. Temperature, Humidity.
2. We find the minimum and maximum values of the columns that make up the range of the variables.
3. We have the original table with the first column is X and the second is Y.
4. We add to this table a column which is the increment number in order not to miss the original pairs (xi, yi). The column we add is the third one.
5. Later, we create a different table for X together with its increment number and a different one for Y. Then, we have the initial position for each X and Y so we sort in ascending order according to the values. We notice that in the first column we have X and Y in ascending order and in the second column their position in the original data.
6. We normalize using trapezoidal membership functions
7. We apply the Sturges rule: (see 4) in order to divide the sorted data columns in classes.

8. Next, we create 11 classes for each sorted table.
9. We add the classes to the third column in the sorted tables. The format of the sorted tables is: the first column has X in ascending order, the second column has the initial position and the third column has the class.
10. Then, we sort the above two tables by increment number to get the data back to their original position along with their classes.
11. We put the above tables in a table where the first column is X, the second is the class of X, the third is Y and the fourth is the class of Y.
12. We create a Zero Table. The table will be a column larger and a column smaller to place the medians.
13. Finally, we create the table we want without adding values to the first row and column.
14. We create medians for the classes of X and place them in the Final Table.
15. We create medians for the classes of Y and place them in the Final Table.
16. The Final Table has the medians of the classes of Y as its first row and the medians of the classes of X as its first column.
17. We create a new table who has the first row and the first column with medians.
18. We form the rest of the table by calling the function of parametric implication.
19. The table imp1 is the table of the empiristic implication.
20. We will check three well-known implications with the data we have.
21. The first is Kleen-Dienes (see Examples1.)
22. Table A is an 11×1 column table containing the temperature medians.
23. Table B is a 1×11 row table containing the humidity medians.
24. Table A1 is an 11×1 column table containing the nondimensionalized values of the temperature medians.
25. Table B1 is a 1×11 row table containing the nondimensionalized values of humidity medians.
26. The final table of Kleen-Dienes implication is imp2 and the control of the norm of the two implications (empiristic and Kleen-Dienes) is nor1 = norm (imp1-imp2).
27. The second implication is Lukasiewicz (see Examples1.)
28. The final table of the Lukasiewicz implication is imp3 and the control of the norm of the two implications (empiristic and Lukasiewicz) is nor2 = norm (imp1-imp3).
29. The third implication is Reichenbach (see Examples1.)
30. The final table of Reichenbach's implication is imp4 and the control of the norm of the two implications (empiristic and Reichenbach) is nor3 = norm (imp1-imp4).
31. The final table of Parametric's implication is OtherTable and the control of the norm of the two implications (empiristic and Parametric) is nor4 = norm (imp1-OtherTable).

4 Conclusions

It is now evident that the type of the strong fuzzy negations that are generated via conical sections, combined with the fuzzy conjunction (T-norm = min), give us a robust algorithmic process of finding the more appropriate fuzzy implication. So we see that a purely mathematical process and even a geometric one is a powerful tool when it is well supported to achieve approximate reasoning. In addition, a thorough and careful study of the data in the correct order will greatly reduce the computational complexity. Our future research on the applications of fuzzy implications will continue with the aim of achieving better results of the convergence of the empiristic implication and the implications the strong fuzzy negations that are generated via conical sections.

Acknowledgements. We would like to thank the Hellenic National Meteorological Service for the quick reply to our request for the concession of the climatic data of the last five years, in order to be used in the present paper (see [4]).

References

1. Baczynski, M., Jayaram, B.: Fuzzy Implications. Springer-Verlag, Heidelberg (2008). https://doi.org/10.1007/978-3-540-69082-5_1
2. Fodor, J.C.: Contrapositive symmetry of fuzzy implications. Fuzzy Sets Syst. **69**, 141–156 (1995)
3. Fodor, J.C., Roubens, M.: Fuzzy preference Modelling and Multicriteria Decision Support. Kluwer, Dordrecht (1994)
4. Hellenic National Meteorological Service. http://www.hnms.gr/emy/el/climatology/climatology_month
5. Jenei, S.: A new approach for interpolation and extrapolation of compact fuzzy quantities. The one dimensional case. In: Klement, E.P., Stout, L.N. (eds.) Proceedings of the 21th Linz Seminar on Fuzzy Set Theory, Linz, Austria, pp. 13–18 (2000)
6. Kitainik, L.: Fuzzy Decision Procedures with Binary Relations. Kluwer, Dordrecht (1993)
7. Klement, E.P., Mesiar, R., Pap, E.: Triangular Norms. Kluwer, Dordrecht (2000)
8. Mattas, K., Papadopoulos, B.: Fuzzy empiristic implication, a new approach. In: Mattas, K., Papadopoulos, B. (eds.) Modern Discrete Mathematics and Analysis, SOIA. Springer Optimization and Its Applications, vol. 131, pp. 317–331 (2018)
9. Menger, K.: Statistical metrics. Proc. Nat. Acad. Sci. USA **28**, 535–537 (1942)
10. Schweizer, B., Sklar, A.: Probabilistic Metric Spaces. North-Holland, New York (1983)
11. Souliotis, G., Papadopoulos, B.: An algorithm for producing fuzzy negations via conical sections. Algorithms **12**(5), 89 (2019). https://doi.org/10.3390/a12050089

Fuzzy Logic Application to Searchable Cryptography

Hassan B. Kazemian[1(✉)] and Yang Ma[2]

[1] School of Computing and Digital Media, London Metropolitan University, London, UK
h.kazemian@londonmet.ac.uk
[2] Underwriters Laboratories, UK Security Lab, Basingstoke, UK
Yang.Ma@ul.com

Abstract. Public Key Encryption with Keyword Search (PEKS) allows users to search encrypted files by a specific keyword without compromising the original data security. Almost all current PEKS schemes enable users to search exact keyword only instead of imprecise keyword (such as "latest", "biggest", etc.). Therefore, if the keyword is fuzzy, these PEKS schemes will be terminated and then report errors. Besides, some PEKS schemes are not secure mainly because they are vulnerable to Off-line Keyword Guessing Attack (OKGA). This research paper incorporates with Mamdani Fuzzy Inference System to PEKS for supporting Fuzzy Keyword Search. Secondly, the proposed scheme is proved to be semantic secure under the random oracle models so that it is able to resist OKGA. In addition, the new scheme allows users to search multiple keywords and therefore, it could be applied to the general public networks.

Keywords: Public Key Encryption with Keyword Search (PEKS) · Off-line Keyword Guessing Attack (OKGA) · Mamdani Fuzzy Inference System

1 Introduction

The rising popularity of cloud computing attracts companies and individuals to upload their data into the online trusted servers (i.e. cloud servers). It brings about substantial merits, such as saving local memory and reducing maintenance fee, etc. How to keep data security becomes an intractable problem. Interestingly, Public Key Encryption with Keyword Search (PEKS) protects information security and data transmission security.

Boneh et al. [1] defined the first PEKS scheme in 2004 which requires a secure channel (i.e. Secure Sockets Layer) between the server and the receiver. But building a secure channel is much expensive and unrealistic in some cases. Besides, Byun et al. [3] pointed out that the first PEKS was compromising from Off-line Keyword Guessing Attack (OKGA). In 2008, Baek et al. [2] proposed a new PEKS scheme to remove the secure channel from the first PEKS system.

L. Iliadis et al. (Eds.): EANN 2020, INNS 2, pp. 410–422, 2020.
https://doi.org/10.1007/978-3-030-48791-1_32

But, Yau et al. [4] also found that Baek et al.'s PEKS suffers OKGA. Tang et al. [5] introduced a new PEKS scheme resisting OKGA, but the encryption algorithm is complex. Soon later, Rhee et al. [6] defined the concept of Trapdoor Indistinguishability to PEKS (called dPEKS) for preventing OKGA. However, dPEKS scheme is able to search single keyword only instead of multiple keywords so that it may not be applied to the general public networks. Meanwhile, Baek et al.'s proposed MPEKS [2] scheme to solve multiple keywords search problem. However, MPEKS also needs a secure channel. Later on, Wang et al. [7] came up with a Secure Channel Free MPEKS system to remove the secure channel and support multiple keywords search, but it suffers OKGA. Recently, PEKS witnesses a dramatic development and becomes much security and functionalities.

In practice, several keywords are distilled to represent the whole document instead of one keyword only. Besides, the user may type imprecise keyword for searching, such as "latest", "biggest", etc. Due to PEKS ciphertext may contain fuzzy keyword leading to system errors, therefore, Mamdani Fuzzy Inference method could be perfectly applied to PEKS scheme in order to solve fuzzy keyword search problem. In 1973, Lotifi Zadeh's [8] came up with new fuzzy algorithms to analyse complex systems and decision processes. Later, Ebrahim Mamdani [9] revisited Lotifi's approach and then proposed an inference system to control a steam engine and boiler combination based on linguistic rules from human knowledge. However, Mamdani-style inference is not computationally efficient, Michio Sugeno [10] proposed a new fuzzy inference using a single spike (a singleton) as the rule consequent. Recently, Fuzzy sets theory has been applied successfully in many areas. Singh et al. [11] pointed out fuzzy systems could applied to classification, modelling control problems. Lermontov et al. [12] analysed water quality using fuzzy set. Meanwhile, Marchini et al. [13] proposed a framework for fuzzy indices of environmental conditions.

This paper formally defines a new PEKS scheme named *Public Key Encryption with Multi-keywords Search using Mamdani System (m-PEMKS)* and then presents a concrete construction of it. Besides, m-PEMKS is proved to be semantic secure under random oracle models so that it could resist OKGA. In addition, the proposed scheme incorporates with Mamdani System to solve fuzzy keyword search problem, which is the first paper combining Fuzzy Logic and PEKS.

2 Methodology

2.1 Bilinear Pairings

Let G_1 be an additive cyclic group and G_T be a multiplicative cyclic group. g is a generator of G_1 and a prime number p is the order of G_1. Suppose a and b are the elements in Z_p. A bilinear pairing can be regarded as a map $e : G_1 \times G_1 \rightarrow G_T$, which has the following properties:

i. Bilinear: $e(aU, bV) = e(U, V)^{ab}$ for all $U, V \in G_1$ and $a, b \in Z_p$.
ii. Computable: $e(U, V) \in G_T$ is computable in a polynomial time algorithm, for any $U, V \in G_1$.
iii. Non-degenerate: $e(U, V) \neq 1$.

2.2 The Bilinear Diffie-Hellman (BDH) Assumption

Given g, xg, yg, zg as input (where $x, y, z \in Z_p$), compute $e(g,g)^{xyz} \in G_T$. An algorithm A has an advantage ε in solving BDH assumption in G_1, if $Pr[A(g, xg, yg, zg) = e(g,g)^{xyz}] \geq \varepsilon$. It is shown that BDH assumption holds in G_1 if no t time algorithm has an advantage at least ε in solving BDH assumption in G_1.

2.3 The 1-Bilinear Diffie-Hellman Inversion (1-BDHI) Assumption

Given g, xg as input (where $x \in Z_p$), compute $e(g,g)^{\frac{1}{x}}$. An algorithm A has an advantage in solving 1-BDHI assumption in G_1, if $Pr[A(g, xg) = e(g,g)^{\frac{1}{x}}] \geq \varepsilon$. It is shown that 1-BDHI assumption holds in G_1 if no t time algorithm has an advantage at least ε in solving 1-BDHI assumption in G_1.

2.4 Fuzzy Rule Based Model

The fuzzy rule based model has four steps as follows:

1. *Fuzzification of the input variables:* The aim of this step is transforming crisp inputs into fuzzy inputs by the membership functions.
2. *Rules evaluation:* The fuzzified inputs are applied to the antecedents of the fuzzy rules and then apply "AND" operation to these rule antecedents.
3. *Aggregation of the rule outputs:* The membership functions of all rule consequents previously clipped or scaled are combined into a single fuzzy set.
4. *Defuzzification:* The defuzzification method, center of gravity (COG), is utilized to transform fuzzy outputs into crisp outputs.

3 Public Key Encryption with Multi-keywords Search Using Mamdani System

Let sender, server and receiver be three parties in PEKS scheme. The sender is a party who runs PEKS algorithm to create a Searchable ciphertext. Besides, the receiver is a party who executes Trapdoor algorithm to create a Trapdoor query. Once the server receives the encrypted messages from the sender and the receiver, it will run Test algorithm to estimate whether two ciphertexts contain the same keyword or not, and replies to the receiver in the end.

3.1 Formal Definition of m-PEMKS

The proposed scheme has eight Probabilistic Polynomial Time algorithms:

1. $KeyGen_{Param-PEMKS}(1^{\varsigma})$: Input 1^{ς} for generating a common parameter cp.
2. $KeyGen_{Param-RSA}(k)$: Input k for generating a global parameter gp.
3. $KeyGen_{Server-PEMKS}(cp)$: Input cp and then produce a public and private PEMKS key pair $(pk_{Ser-PEMKS}, sk_{Ser-PEMKS})$ of the server.

4. $KeyGen_{Server-RSA}(gp)$: Input gp and then produce a public and private RSA key pair $(pk_{Ser-RSA}, sk_{Ser-RSA})$ of the server.
5. $KeyGen_{Receiver-PEMKS}(cp)$: Input cp and then produce a public and private PEMKS key pair $(pk_{Rec-PEMKS}, sk_{Rec-PEMKS})$ of the receiver.
6. $Encryption(pk_{Ser-PEMKS}, pk_{Rec-PEMKS}, pk_{Ser-RSA}, W)$: A searchable encryption $E = (E_1, E_2) = \text{SCF-PEMKS}(pk_{Ser-PEMKS}, pk_{Rec-PEMKS}, W_{part1}) \| \text{RSA}(pk_{Ser-RSA}, W_{part2})$ is created, where $W = (W_{part1}, W_{part2}) = [(w_1, w_2, ..., w_n); w_{n+1}]$.
7. $Request(pk_{Ser-PEMKS}, sk_{Rec-PEMKS}, pk_{Ser-RSA}, W)$: A trapdoor request $R = (R_1, R_2) = \text{Trapdoor}(pk_{Ser-PEMKS}, sk_{Rec-PEMKS}, W_{part1}) \| \text{RSA}(pk_{Ser-RSA}, W_{part2})$ is created, where $W = (W_{part1}, W_{part2}) = [(w_1, w_2, ..., w_m); w_{fuzzy}]$.
8. $Test(E, R, sk_{Ser-PEMKS}, sk_{Ser-RSA})$: Test algorithm contains two parts: Exact Match and Fuzzy Match.

For Exact Match: Input the server's PEMKS private key $sk_{Ser-PEMKS}$, an encryption $E_1 = \text{SCF-PEMKS}(pk_{Ser-PEMKS}, pk_{Rec-PEMKS}, W_{part1})$ and a request $R_1 = \text{Trapdoor}(pk_{Ser-PEMKS}, sk_{Rec-PEMKS}, W^*_{part1})$. If $W^*_{part1} \in W_{part1}$, the system will go to Fuzzy Match. Otherwise, the system will terminate.

For Fuzzy Match: Input the server's RSA private key $sk_{Ser-RSA}$, an encryption $E_2 = \text{RSA}(pk_{Ser-RSA}, W_{part2})$ and a request $R_2 = \text{RSA}(pk_{Ser-RSA}, W^*_{part2})$. Then, the server decrypts E_2 and R_2 to obtain W_{part2} and W^*_{part2}. Let W^*_{part2} and W_{part2} be the conclusion and the condition of the rules in Mamdani system. Next, the encrypted file is filtered by Mamdani system and the server will reply to the receiver in the end.

3.2 The Concrete Construction of m-PEMKS

The details of m-PEMKS are listed in the following (Fig. 1):

1. $KeyGen_{Param-PEMKS}(1^{\varsigma})$: Let G_1 be an additive cyclic group and G_T be a multiplicative cyclic group. g is a random generator of G_1 whose order is a prime number p. A bilinear pairing is a map $e : G_1 \times G_1 \to G_T$. Let $H : \{0,1\}^{\circ} \to G_1$ and $H^* : G_T \to \{0,1\}^{\bullet}$ be two specific hash functions. This algorithm returns the common parameter $cp = \{g, p, G_1, G_T, e, H, H^*\}$.
2. $KeyGen_{Param-RSA}(K)$: Randomly select prime numbers u and v (where $u \neq v$) and calculate $L = u \times v$ and $\phi(L) = (u-1) \times (v-1)$.
3. $KeyGen_{Server-PEMKS}(cp)$: The server randomly chooses $a \in Z_p$ and then computes $A = aP$. Besides, the server chooses $B \in G_1$ uniformly at random. Therefore, the server's PEMKS public key is $pk_{Ser-PEMKS} = (cp, A, B)$ and the PEMKS private key is $sk_{Ser-PEMKS} = (cp, a)$.
4. $KeyGen_{Server-RSA}(gp)$: The server randomly selects $x \in Z_q$, where $gcd(\phi(L), x) = 1$ and $1 < x < \phi(L)$. Next, the server calculates y by $y \equiv x^{-1}(mod\phi(L))$. Therefore, the server's RSA public key is $pk_{Ser-RSA} = (x, L)$ and the private key is $sk_{Ser-RSA} = (y, L)$.

5. $KeyGen_{Receiver-PEMKS}(cp)$: The receiver randomly chooses $c \in Z_p$ and then computes $C = cP$. Therefore, the receiver's PEMKS public key is $pk_{Rec-PEMKS} = (cp, C)$ and the PEMKS private key is $sk_{Rec} = (cp, c)$.
6. $Encryption(pk_{Ser-PEMKS}, pk_{Rec-PEMKS}, pk_{Ser-RSA}, W)$: The sender randomly chooses $t \in Z_p$ and a keyword-vector $W{=}(W_{part1}, W_{part2}){=}[(w_1, w_2, ..., w_n); w_{n+1}]$. The sender then computes a searchable encryption $E = (E_1, E_2) = [(M, N_1, N_2, ..., N_n); N_{n+1}] = [(tA, H^*(D_1), H^*(D_2), ..., H^*(D_n)); (w_{n+1})^x mod\, L]$, where $D_1 = e(H(w_1), C)^t$,$D_2 = e(H(w_2), C)^t$,...,$D_n = e(H(w_n), C)^t$.
7. $Request(pk_{Ser-PEMKS}, sk_{Rec-PEMKS}, pk_{Ser-RSA}, W)$: The receiver randomly chooses $t^* \in Z_p$ and a keyword-vector $W{=}(W_{part1}, W_{part2}){=} [(w_1, w_2,..., w_m); w_{fuzzy}]$. The receiver then computes $R = (R_1, R_2) = [(Z, T_1, T_2, ..., T_m), T_{fuzzy}] = [(e(A, t^*B), cH(w_1) \oplus e(A, B)^{t^*+c}, cH(w_2) \oplus e(A, B)^{t^*+c}, ..., cH(w_{m-1}) \oplus e(A, B)^{t^*+c}); (w_{fuzzy})^x mod\, L]$.
8. $Test(E, R, sk_{Ser-PEMKS}, sk_{Ser-RSA})$: For $i \in \{1, 2, ..., n\}$ and $j \in \{1, 2, ..., m\}$, where $j \leq i$.

(i) *For Exact Match*: Firstly, the server calculates
$T_{w_1} = T_1 \oplus Z \bullet e(aB, C) = cH(w_1^*), ...,$
$T_{w_j} = T_j \oplus Z \bullet e(aB, C) = cH(w_j^*), ...,$
$T_{w_m} = T_m \oplus Z \bullet e(aB, C) = cH(w_m^*)$
Then, the server checks whether $H^*[e(T_{w_j}, \frac{M}{a})] = N_i$ or not. If "yes", the system will go to Fuzzy Match. Otherwise, the system will terminate.

(ii) *For Fuzzy Match*: The server decrypts w_{n+1} and w_{fuzzy} from $\{[(w_{n+1})^x mod\, L]^y mod\, L\}$ and $\{[(w_{fuzzy})^x mod\, L]^y mod\, L\}$. Let w_{fuzzy} and w_{n+1} be the conclusion and condition of the rules in Mamdani system.

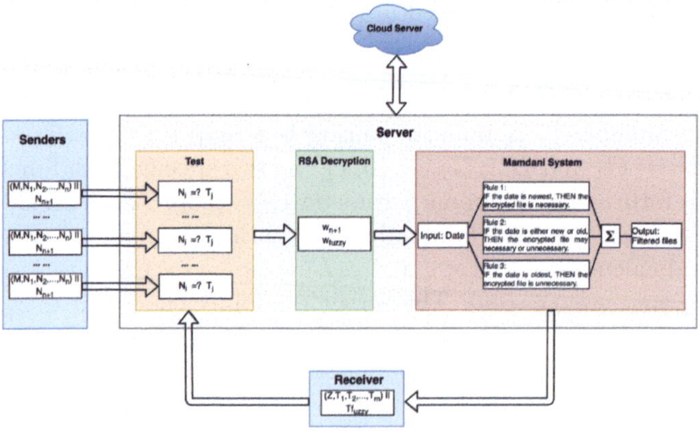

Fig. 1. The concrete construction of m-PEMKS

Without loss of generality, suppose w_{fuzzy} is the keyword "latest" while w_{n+1} stands for a set of "DATE". Therefore, three rules can be defined in the following:
Rule1: IF DATE is oldest, THEN the encrypted file is unnecessary.
Rule2: IF DATE is newest, THEN the encrypted file is necessary.
Rule3: IF DATE is either new or old, THEN the encrypted file may necessary or may unnecessary.

3.3 The Correctness of m-PEMKS

For Exact Match: for $i \in \{1, 2, ..., n\}$ and $j \in \{1, 2, ..., m\}$, the proposed scheme is completely correct in the following:
Firstly,
$T_{w_j} = T_j \oplus Z \bullet e(aB, C) = cH(w_j^*) \oplus e(A, B)^{t^*+c} \oplus e(A, t^*B) \bullet e(aB, cP) = cH(w_j^*) \oplus e(A, B)^{t^*+c} \oplus e(A, B)^{t^*} \bullet e(A, B)^c = cH(w_j^*) \oplus e(A, B)^{t^*+c} \oplus e(A, B)^{t^*+c} = cH(w_j^*)$
Then,
$H^*[e(T_{w_j}, \frac{M}{a})] = H^*[e(cH(w_j^*), \frac{tA}{a})] = H^*[e(cH(w_j^*), tP)] = H^*[e(H(w_j^*), C)^t] = N_i$

For Fuzzy Match: this algorithm is still correct due to the properties of Mamdani Fuzzy Inference System.

3.4 The Security Analysis of m-PEMKS

The proposed scheme contains two cryptographic algorithms: PEKS and RSA. The security of proposed scheme mainly relies on Ciphertext Indistinguishability of Chosen Plaintext Attack (IND-CPA) and Trapdoor Indistinguishability of Chosen Plaintext Attack (Trapdoor-IND-CPA).

IND-CPA security is that a malicious server (**Game1**) could not decide which PEMKS ciphertext contains which encrypted keyword, if it has not received the Trapdoor containing the given keyword. Besides, if a malicious receiver (**Game2**) that has not obtained the server's PEMKS private key cannot check whether PEMKS ciphertext and Trapdoor have the same keyword, even if he/she intercepts all Trapdoors for any specific keyword. For **Trapdoor-IND-CPA** security, it is an outside attacker excluding the server and the receiver (**Game3**) cannot differentiate any difference between Trapdoors containing the same keyword. To conclude, the proposed scheme satisfies Ciphertext Indistinguishability and Trapdoor Indistinguishability against a Chosen Plaintext Attack (CPA).

Theorem 1. The m-PEMKS above is IND-CPA secure against CPA in Game1 under the random oracle model assuming that BDH assumption is intractable.

Game 1: **A** is supposed to be a malicious server.

Proof: Suppose that **E** has $(g, p, G_1, G_T, e, xg, yg, zg)$ as an input of BDH assumption whose running time is bounded by T. **E**'s aim is to calculate a BDH key $e(g, g)^{xyz}$ of xg, yg and zg using **A**'s IND-CPA. Besides, **A** asks for at most h and h^* times for the queries of H and H^* hash functions.

Setup Simulation
E firstly sets $C = xg$ and randomly selects $a \in Z_p$ and then calculates $A = ag$. **E** also picks up $B \in G_1$ uniformly at random. After that, **A** obtains the common parameter $(g, p, G_1, G_T, e, H, H^*)$, the server's PEMKS public key (cp, A, B) and PEMKS private key (cp, a) and the receiver's PEMKS public key (cp, C). Besides, **E** chooses two hash functions H and H^* in the following:

- **A** can query a keyword w_i to H function at any time. To respond, **E** searches *H_List* for a tuple $(w_i, F_i, f_i, \theta_i)$ and the *H_List* is empty in original. If the tuple exists, **A** will receive $H(w_i) = F_i$ as a response. Otherwise, **E** does the following steps:

i. **E** picks up a coin θ_i uniformly at random and then calculates $Pr[\theta_i = 0] = \frac{1}{h+1}$.
ii. **E** selects $f_i \in Z_p$ uniformly at random. If $\theta_i = 0$, **E** will calculate $F_i = yg + f_i g$. If $\theta_i = 1$, **E** will calculate $F_i = f_i g$.
iii. **E** returns F_i as an answer to **A** and adds $(w_i, F_i, f_i, \theta_i)$ into *H_List*.

- **A** queries D_i to H^* function at any time. Then, **E** searches *H^*_List* for a tuple (D_i, N_i). If the tuple exists, **A** will receive N_i as a response. Otherwise, **E** selects $N_i \in \{0, 1\}^\bullet$ uniformly at random and then returns it to **A** and also adds (D_i, N_i) into *H^*_List*.

Phase 1–1 Simulation (Trapdoor queries)
A issues a query for the trapdoor corresponding to the keyword-vector $W_l = (w_{l1}^*, w_{l2}^*, ..., w_{lm}^*)$. To respond, **E** executes the following steps:

- **E** randomly selects $i' \in \{1, 2, ..., m\}$
- **E** runs the above algorithms for simulating H function to create a tuple $(w_{li'}, F_{li'}, f_{li'}, \theta_{li'})$. If $\theta_{li'} = 0$, **E** will output "Suspend" and terminate the system. Otherwise, **E** conducts the following:

- **E** selects $t^* \in Z_p$ and then computes $T_1 = f_{l1}C \oplus e(A, B)^{t^*+x} = f_{l1}xg \oplus e(A, B)^{t^*+x} = xF_{l1} \oplus e(A, B)^{t^*+x} = xH(w_{l1}) \oplus e(A, B)^{t^*+x}$, $T_2 = xH(w_{l2}) \oplus e(A, B)^{t^*+x}$,...,$T_m - xH(w_{lm})$ and $Z = e(A, t^*B)$. Therefore, $T_W = (Z, T_1, T_2, ..., T_m)$.

Challenge Simulation
A sends $W_0 = (w_{01}, w_{02}, ..., w_{0n})$ and $W_1 = (w_{11}, w_{12}, ..., w_{1n})$ to **E**. Once **E** receives the target keyword-vector pair, he/she does the following:

- **E** randomly selects $i \in \{1, 2, ..., n\}$.
- **E** runs the above algorithms for simulating H function to obtain two vectors of tuples $(W_{0i}^*, F_{0i}^*, f_{0i}^*, \theta_{0i}^*)$ and $(W_{1i}^*, F_{1i}^*, f_{1i}^*, \theta_{1i}^*)$. If θ_{0i}^* and θ_{1i}^* are equal to 1, **E** will output "Suspend" and terminate the system. Otherwise, **E** runs the above algorithms for simulating H function at $2(n-1)$ times to obtain two vectors of tuples $((w_{01}^*, F_{01}^*, f_{01}^*, \theta_{01}^*), ..., (w_{0i-1}^*, F_{0i-1}^*, f_{0i-1}^*, \theta_{0i-1}^*), (w_{0i+1}^*, F_{0i+1}^*, f_{0i+1}^*, \theta_{0i+1}^*), ..., (w_{0n}^*, F_{0n}^*, f_{0n}^*, \theta_{0n}^*))$ and $((w_{11}^*, F_{11}^*, f_{11}^*, \theta_{11}^*), ..., (w_{1i-1}^*, F_{1i-1}^*, f_{1i-1}^*, \theta_{1i-1}^*), (w_{1i+1}^*, F_{1i+1}^*, f_{1i+1}^*, \theta_{1i+1}^*), ..., (w_{1n}^*, F_{1n}^*, f_{1n}^*, \theta_{1n}^*))$. If θ_{0i}^* and θ_{1i}^* are equal to 0 for all $i = 0, ..., i-1, i+1, ..., n$, **E** will output "Suspend" and terminate the system. Otherwise, **E** does the following:
- **E** chooses $\beta \in \{0, 1\}$ uniformly at random.
- **E** chooses $N_i \in \{0, 1\}^{\bullet}$ uniformly at random and creates a target SCF-PEMKS

Ciphertext $S^* = (M^*, N_1^*, N_2^*, ..., N_n^*) = (zA, H^*[J_1], H^*[J_2], ..., H^*[J_n])$ So, $S^* = (M^*, N_1^*, ..., N_{i-1}^*, N_{i+1}^*, ..., N_n^*) = (zA, H^*[e(H(w_{\beta_1}), C)^z], ..., H^*[e(H(w_{\beta_{i-1}}), C)^z], H^*[e(H(w_{\beta_1+1}), C)^z], ..., H^*[e(H(w_{\beta_n}), C)^z])$
Note that $J_i = e(H(w_{\beta_i}), C)^z = e(yg + f_{\beta_i} g, xg)^z = e(yg, xg)^z \bullet e(f_{\beta_i} g, xg)^z = e(g, g)^{xyz} \bullet e(zg, xg)^{f_{\beta i}}$
Note also that $e(f_{\gamma_i} g, xg)^z = e(f_{\gamma_i} g, C)^z = e(H(w_{\gamma_i}), C)^z$

Phase 1–2 Simulation (Trapdoor queries)
A can continue to ask **E** for Trapdoor queries for the keyword-vector W_i. **E** answers to **A** as in Phase 1–1, as long as $w_i \notin W_0, W_1$.
Guess
A outputs the guess $\beta^* \in \{0, 1\}$. Then, **E** selects d in the list for H^* function and returns $\frac{d_{\beta_i^*}}{e(zg, xg)^{f_{\beta_i^*}}}$ as its guess for BDH key.

Analysis of Game 1. Let *Event1* and *Event2* be events that **E** does not suspend during Phase 1–1 and Phase 1–2 (Trapdoor queries) and **E** does not suspend during Challenge Simulation respectively. Therefore, the probability of *Event1* happening is at least $[(1 - \frac{1}{h+1})^m]^h \geq \frac{1}{e^m}$. Besides, the probability of *Event2* happening is at least $(1 - \frac{1}{h+1})^{2(n-1)}\{1 - (1 - \frac{1}{h+1})^2\} \geq (\frac{1}{h+1}) \bullet (\frac{h}{h+1})^{2(n-1)}$. In addition, let $Hybrid_r$ for $r \in \{1, 2, ..., n\}$ be an *event* that the attacker **A** can successfully guess the keyword of the left part of a "hybrid" PEMKS Ciphertext formed with r, coordinates from W_β followed by $(n-r)$ coordinates from $W_{1-\beta}$. Consequently, $Pr[Event3] = 2\Sigma_{k=1}^n (Pr[Hybrid_r] - Pr[Hybrid_{r-1}]) = 2(Pr[Hybrid_r] - Pr[Hybrid_0]) = 2\varepsilon$. However, the probability that **A** requests a query for either $H^*(e(H(W_{0i}^*), C)^z)$ or $H^*(e(H(W_{1i}^*), C)^z)$ is at least 2ε, so the probability that **A** issues a query for $H^*(e(H(W_i^*), C)^z)$ is at least ε. In total, **E**'s success probability ε^* is $(\frac{h}{h+1})^{2(n-1)} \bullet \frac{\varepsilon}{e^m (h+1) h^*}$, which is negligible.

Theorem 2. The m-PEMKS above is IND-CPA secure against CPA in Game2 under the random oracle model assuming that 1-BDHI assumption is intractable.

Game 2: **A** is supposed to be a malicious receiver.

Proof: Suppose that **E** has (g, p, G_1, G_T, e, xg) as an input of 1-BDHI assumption whose running time is bounded by T. **E**'s aim is to calculate a 1-BDHI key $e(g,g)^{\frac{1}{x}}$ of xg using **A**'s IND-CPA. Besides, **A** asks for at most h and h^* times for the queries of H and H^* hash functions.

Setup Simulation
E firstly sets $A = xg$ and $B \in G_1$. **E** also selects $c \in Z_p$ uniformly at random and calculates $C = cP$. Then, **A** obtains the common parameter $(g, p, G_1, G_T, e, H, H^*)$, the server's PEMKS public key (cp, A, B), the receiver's PEMKS public key (cp, C) and PEMKS private key (cp, c). Besides, **E** chooses two hash functions H and H^* in the following:

- **A** can query a keyword w_i to H function at any time. To respond, **E** selects $f_i \in Z_p$ uniformly at random and then calculates $F_i = f_i g$ and finally returns F_i as a response to **A**.
- **A** can query D_i to H^* function at any time. Then, **E** searches H^*_List for a tuple (D_i, N_i). If the tuple exists, **A** will receive N_i as a response. Otherwise, **E** selects $N_i \in \{0,1\}^\bullet$ uniformly at random and then sends it to **A**. **E** also adds (D_i, N_i) into H^*_List.

Challenge Simulation
A sends $(W_{0i}^*, F_{0i}^*, f_{0i}^*, \theta_{0i}^*)$ and $(W_{1i}^*, F_{1i}^*, f_{1i}^*, \theta_{1i}^*)$ to **E**, where $W_0^* = (w_{01}, w_{02}, ..., w_{0n})$ and $W_1^* = (w_{11}, w_{12}, ..., w_{1n})$. **E** randomly chooses $\beta \in \{0,1\}$ and $N_i \in \{0,1\}^\bullet$. Then, **E** creates a target PEMKS Ciphertext $S^* = (M^*, N_1^*, N_2^*, ..., N_n^*) = (\psi xg, H^*[J_1], H^*[J_2], ..., H^*[J_n])$
So, $S^* = (M^*, N_1^*, N_2^*, ..., N_n^*) = (\psi xg, H^*(e(H(w_{\beta_1}), C)^\psi), H^*(e(H(w_{\beta_2}), C)^\psi), ..., H^*(e(H(w_{\beta_n}), C)^\psi))$
Notice that $e(H(w_{\beta_i^*}), C)^\psi) = e(f_i g, cg)^\psi = e(g,g)^{\psi \cdot f_i c}$.

Guess
A outputs the guess $\beta^* \in \{0,1\}$. Then, **E** returns $\psi = \frac{1}{x \cdot f_i c}$ as the guess for 1-BDHI key.

Analysis of Game 2. Let *Event4* and *Event5* be events that **E** does not suspend during Challenge Simulation and **A** does not issue a query for either one of $H^*(e(H(W_{0i}^*), C)^\psi)$ or $H^*(e(H(W_{1i}^*), C)^\psi)$ respectively. So, the probability of *Event4* happening is equal to 1. Besides, according to Bayes's rule and the definition above, the probability of *Event5* happening is at least 2ε and therefore, the probability that **A** issues a query for $H^*(e(H(W_i^*), C)^\psi)$ is at least ε. Therefore, $e(H(W_j^*), C)^\psi = e(g,g)^{\psi \cdot f_i c}$ will appear in H*_List. Due to **A** asks for at most h^* times H^* hash function queries, the probability that **E** selects the correct answer is at least $\frac{1}{h^*}$. In total, E's success probability ε^* is $\frac{\varepsilon}{h^*}$, which is negligible.

Theorem 3. The m-PEMKS above is Trapdoor-IND-CPA secure against CPA in Game3 under the random oracle model assuming that BDH assumption is intractable.

Game 3: **A** is supposed to be an outside attacker excluding the server and the receiver.

Proof: Suppose that **E** has $(g, p, G_1, G_T, e, xg, yg, zg)$ as an input of BDH assumption whose running time is bounded by T. **E**'s aim is to calculate a BDH key $e(g, g)^{xyz}$ of xg, yg and zg using **A**'s Trapdoor-IND-CPA. Besides, **A** asks for at most h and h^* times for the queries of H and H^* hash functions.

Setup Simulation
E firstly sets $A = xg, B = yg$, $C = zg$ and returns (cp, A, B) as the server's PEMKS public key and (cp, C) as the receiver's PEMKS public key. **E** also chooses two H and H^* hash functions at random.
Phase 3–1 Simulation (Trapdoor queries)
A issues a query for the trapdoor corresponding the keyword-vector W_i, where $i \in \{1, 2, ..., m\}$. To respond, **E** chooses $t^* \in Z_p$ uniformly at random. Then, **E** computes $T_1 = zH(w_{i1}) \oplus e(yg, xg)^{t^*+z}, T_2 = zH(w_{i2}) \oplus e(yg, xg)^{t^*+z}, ..., T_m = zH(w_{im}) \oplus e(yg, xg)^{t^*+z}$ and $Z = e(t^* yg, xg)$. So $T_W = (Z, T_1, T_2, ..., T_m)$. Finally, **E** returns T_W to **A**.
Challenge Simulation
A sends (W_0^*, W_1^*) to **E**, where $W_0^* = (w_{01}, w_{02}, ..., w_{0m})$, $W_1^* = (w_{11}, w_{12}, ..., w_{1m})$. **E** creates the challenge Trapdoor request as follows:
E randomly selects a bit $\beta \in \{0, 1\}$. Therefore, $T_1 = zH(w_{\beta_1^*}) \oplus e(yg, xg)^{t^*+z} = zH(w_{\beta_1^*}) \oplus e(g, g)^{xyz} \bullet e(g, g)^{xyt^*}, T_2 = zH(w_{\beta_2^*}) \oplus e(g, g)^{xyz} \bullet e(g, g)^{xyt^*}, ..., T_m = zH(w_{\beta_m^*}) \oplus e(g, g)^{xyz} \bullet e(g, g)^{xyt^*}$, $R = e(t^* yg, xg)$.
Phase 3–2 Simulation (Trapdoor queries)
A can continue to ask Trapdoor queries for the keyword-vector W_i. While, **E** answers to **A** as in Phase 3–1, as long as $W_i \neq W_0, W_1$.
Guess
A outputs the guess $\beta^* \in \{0, 1\}$. If $\beta = \beta^*$, **E** outputs "yes", otherwise, **E** outputs "no".

Analysis of Game 3. Due to **A** is a malicious outside attacker, he/she cannot distinguish any difference between two Trapdoors even though these two Trapdoors have the same keyword. The reason is that **E** randomly chooses $t^* \in Z_p$ and t^* changes every time leading to $T_i = cH(w_{\beta i}) \oplus e(A, B)^{t^*+c}$ changes every time. Even if two Trapdoors have the same keyword, the results are still different because of t^*. Therefore, the key part of Trapdoor Indistinguishability in this proposed scheme is the confidentiality of $e(A, B)^{t^*+c}$.

Suppose the attacker **A** obtains the value of $e(A, B)^{t^*+c}$, he/she can distinguish whether two Trapdoors have the same keyword. The reason is that the attacker **A** only calculates one extra XOR operation as $T_i = cH(w_{\beta i}) \oplus e(A, B)^{t^*+c} \oplus e(A, B)^{t^*+c} = cH(w_{\beta i})$. Therefore, the attack **A** can distinguish that $T_{w_{0i}} = cH(w_{0i})$ and $T_{w_{1i}} = cH(w_{1i})$ are equal as long as $w_{0i} = w_{1i}$. Consequently, the attack A could distinguish two Trapdoors T_{W_0} and T_{W_1}. However, according to Challenge Simulation in Game3, it is easy to acquire $e(A, B)^{t^*+c} = e(g, g)^{xyz} \bullet e(g, g)^{xyt^*}$, which satisfies BDH assumption. Hence, the attacker **A** cannot calculate the value of $e(A, B)^{t^*+c}$ and therefore, it cannot compute $T_i = cH(w_{\beta i}) \oplus e(A, B)^{t^*+c}$.

4 The Performance of m-PEMKS

The proposed system is implemented by JAVA, which requires two libraries in the following: JPBC library [14] and jFuzzyLogic library [15,16].

The proposed scheme applies the Single Input Single Output (SISO) Mamdani Fuzzy Inference System. The is because of the properties of Artificial Intelligence and Cryptography. Artificial Intelligence explores and analyses the data for discovering the relationships between the different data sets. On the contrary, the purpose of cryptography is hiding as much as possible information. Besides, the input value of Mamdani system is plaintext. Therefore, if m-PEMKS applies Two or More Input Single Out (T/MISO) Mamdani Fuzzy Inference System, sufficient data will be exposed to the public networks and therefore, crackers are able to launch attacks to recover more information. Figure 2 shows the membership functions for an example of searching "latest" financial reports and Fig. 3 shows the assessed value for each input. More specially, three senders upload the financial reports with different dates to the server by m-PEMKS system. Once the server receives them, it will run *Test* algorithm incorporating with SISO Mamdani Fuzzy Inference System to filter the "latest" reports. By Fig. 3, it can be seen that the first report partly belongs to the old and acceptable financial report while the second report belongs to the acceptable financial report. However, the third report completely belongs to the "latest" financial report.

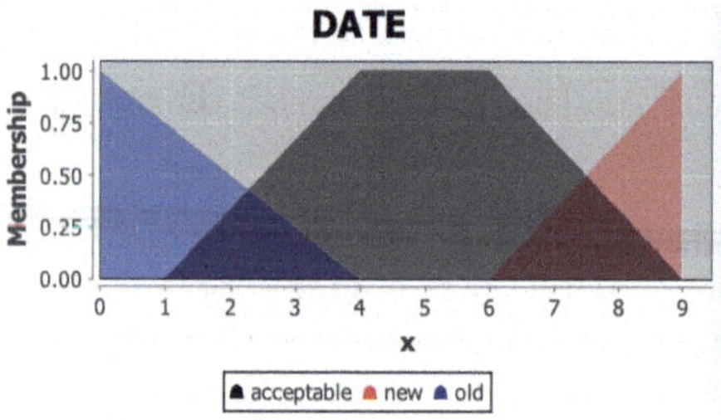

Fig. 2. Membership functions for an example of searching "latest" financial reports

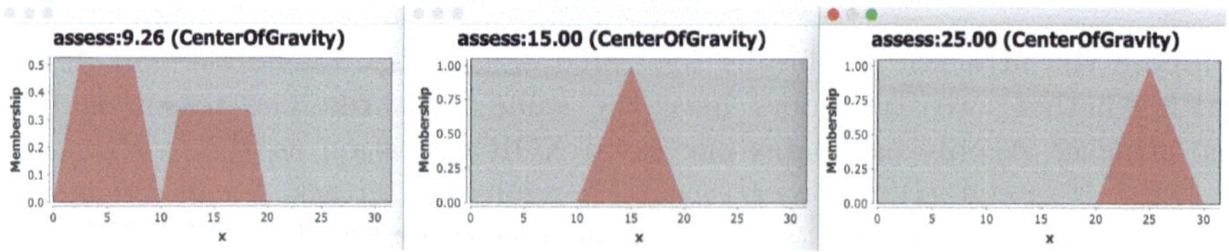

Fig. 3. Assessed values for an example of searching "latest" financial reports

5 Conclusion

In this paper, a novel and a robust *Public Key Encryption with Multiple Keywords Search using Mamdani System(m-PEMKS)* scheme is presented. The new scheme is proved to be semantic secure in the random oracle models under BDH and 1-BDHI assumptions and also satisfies the properties of Ciphertext Indistinguishability and Trapdoor Indistinguishability and therefore, it is able to resist Off-line Keyword Guessing Attack. Furthermore, Single Input Single Output Mamdani technique is applied to m-PEMKS so that it has the ability to solve fuzzy and imprecise keywords, such as "latest" and "tallest", etc., as described in the paper.

References

1. Boneh, D., Di Crescenzo, G., Ostrovsky, R., Persiano, G.: Public key encryption with keyword search. In: Advances in Cryptology - EUROCRYPT, pp. 506–522 (2004)
2. Baek, J., Safavi-Naini, R., Susilo, W.: Public key encryption with keyword search revisited. In: Computational Science and its Applications? ICCSA 2008, pp. 1249–1259 (2008)
3. Byun, J., Rhee, H., Park, H., Lee, D.: Off-line keyword guessing attacks on recent keyword search schemes over encrypted data. Lecture Notes in Computer Science, pp. 75–83 (2006)
4. Yau, W., Heng, S., Goi, B.: Off-line keyword guessing attacks on recent public key encryption with keyword search schemes. Lecture Notes in Computer Science, pp. 100–105 (2008)
5. Tang, Q., Chen, L.: Public-key encryption with registered keyword search. In: Public Key Infrastructures, Services and Applications, pp. 163–178 (2010)
6. Rhee, H., Park, J., Susilo, W., Lee, D.: Trapdoor security in a searchable public-key encryption scheme with a designated tester. J. Syst. Softw. **83**(5), 763–771 (2010)
7. Wang, T., Au, M., Wu, W.: An efficient secure channel free searchable encryption scheme with multiple keywords. In: Network and System Security, vol. 9955, pp. 251–265 (2016)
8. Zadeh, L.: Outline of a new approach to the analysis of complex systems and decision processes. IEEE Trans. Syst. Man Cybern SMC **3**(1), 28–44 (1973)
9. Mamdani, E.H., Assilian, S.: An experiment in linguistic synthesis with a fuzzy logic controller. Int. J. Man-Mach. Stud. **7**(1), 1–13 (1975)
10. Takagi, T., Sugeno, M.: Fuzzy identification of systems and its applications to modeling and control. IEEE Trans. Syst. Man Cybern. **15**, 116–132 (1985)
11. Singh, J., Singh, N., Sharma, J.K.: Fuzzy modeling and identification of intelligent control for refrigeration compressor. J. Sci. Ind. Res. **65**, 22–30 (2006)
12. Lermontov, A., Yokoyama, L., Lermontov, M., Machado, M.A.S.: River quality analysis using fuzzy water quality index: Ribeira do Iguape river watershed, Brazil. Ecol. Indic. **9**, 1188–1197 (2009)
13. Marchini, A., Facchinetti, T., Mistri, M.: F-IND: a framework to design fuzzy indices of environmental conditions. Ecol. Indic. **9**, 485–496 (2009)
14. De Caro, A., Iovino, V.: JPBC: Java pairing based cryptography. In: 2011 IEEE Symposium on Computers and Communications (ISCC) (2011)

15. Cingolani, P., Alcalá-Fdez, J.: jFuzzyLogic: a Java library to design fuzzy logic controllers according to the standard for fuzzy control programming. Int. J. Comput. Intell. Syst. **6**(Supplement 1), 61–75 (2013)
16. Cingolani, P., Alcala-Fdez, J.: jFuzzyLogic: a robust and flexible Fuzzy-Logic inference system language implementation. In: 2012 IEEE International Conference on Fuzzy Systems (FUZZ-IEEE). IEEE (2012)

Personal Car Driver Black Box: A Wearable System for Data Log and Prediction Based on EVOS Paradigms

Mario Malcangi(✉)

Computer Science Department, Università degli Studi di Milano, Milan, Italy
malcangi@di.unimi.it

Abstract. Car driver's performance is affected by physiologic behavior, causing automotive accidents. A system that predicts incoming behaviors is proposed considering vital signs as data to infer by Evolving Systems (EVOS) paradigms and several behaviors as prediction targets. A black-box like approach is proposed. It implements data loging of the vital signs and it applies an evolving prediction paradigm. Long term data log enables post-event analysis and data set building for supervised learning for the prediction paradigms.

Keywords: EFuNN · Behavior's onset · Wearable systems · EVOS · Car driver's performance · Vital signs

1 Introduction

Several physiologic behaviors affect the car driver's performance and are the cause of automotive accidents: drosiness, fatigue, alcohol abuse, drug abuse, hyperarousal. [1]. The main investigation topic has concerned sleep onset prediction [2, 3], but effective solutions to this issue need to consider all the physiologic behavior and the vital signs that concur to affect the car driver's performance. Heart rate (HR) and its variability (HRV) are the primary vital signs correlated to driver behavior because they are under the control of the Autonomic Nervous System (ANS) that consists of two main divisions: the sympathetic (SNS) and the parasympathetic (PNS).

PNS controls the homeostasis and body's rest-and-digest response. SNS controls the body's fight-or-flight response. SNS and PNS execute antagonist control of body's functions: e.g. PNS decreases the HR and SNS increases HR. That is, when a subject is falling asleep or relaxed PNS is active and SNS is inactive, when the subject is awake or fatigued SNS is active and PNS is inactive [2, 3].

Because HR and HRV reflects the ANS activity, by measuring the HR and HRV vital signs is possible to know which one, PNS or SNS, is active, that is, if the subject is asleep or awake (fatigued or relaxed). The transition between PNS and SNS activity is when happens the behavior onset. The switching between PNS and SNS activity could be detected measuring the power spectrum density (PSD) of the HRV time-series sequences: SNS modulates HRV's low frequencies (0.04–0.15 Hz) and PNS modulates HRV's high frequencies (0.18–0.4 Hz) [6].

L. Iliadis et al. (Eds.): EANN 2020, INNS 2, pp. 423–431, 2020.
https://doi.org/10.1007/978-3-030-48791-1_33

ANS also controls other physiologic body functions, such as respiration, contraction of muscles, release of adrenaline so that other vital signs could be measured to predict the subject's physiologic behavior: e.g. bio-impedance, temperature, muscle's activity. Measuring vital signs and executing prediction on such measurements can lead to develop a system that predicts subject's behavior and do him aware about incoming unwanted physiologic status such as sleep onset or loss of attention when he is involved in critical activities (e.g. car driving).

A variety of technologies have been investigated to the purpose of maintaining alertness in car driving activity, most of them with limited success [4]. A popular approach to the issue consists in measuring and predicting from movements mainly related to arms (actigraphy) [5]. This is hardcomputing-based and do not measure other physiologic parameters.

In our investigation we had an holistic approach combining the measurement of most of the vital signs in a softcomputing-based paradigm for prediction in evolving mode and online.

1.1 EVOS Paradigms

Prediction from physical data like vital signs is a challenge because the fuzzy nature of such data. Evolving brain-inspired paradigms demonstrated to perform well when applied to real data [7]. Best performing and optimal paradigms are the Evolving Fuzzy Neural Networks (EFuNNs) and Evolving Spiking Neural Networks (ESNNs).

EFuNN [8] is an implementation of the Evolving Connectionist Systems (ECOSs), a class of neural networks that combine the adaptive/evolving learning capability of neural networks with the approximate reasoning and linguistic feature representation of fuzzy logic.

ECOSs, because based on local learning, is characterized by:

- Fast learning
- Real-time adaptation
- Evolving
- Spatio-temporal representation.

These peculiarities fits well the wearable system-oriented applications.

ESNNs are further development of ECOSs where the neuron's model is the biological neuron and its synapses, the spiking neuron [9]. This assumes that the information is represented as trains of spikes over time. The spiking neuron accumulates input information (spikes) and emits at its axon a spike when a threshold exceeded.

ESNNs are brain-inspired neural networks that are characterized by:

- Fast learning
- Real-time adaptation
- Evolving
- Spatio-temporal representation.

These fits well the requirements of the wearable system-oriented applications.

1.2 Wearable Technologies and Vital Signs Measurements

Vital signs measurement when became common practice as uninvasive wearable technology was released by electronic industries [10]. After a first generation of wearable electronics was released for sport performance monitoring (chest belts), a second generation made available wrist wearable (watch-like) and finger wearable sensors-based on photodetecting technology that enabled the deployment of uninvasive applications in medical and consumer fields [11].

Photodetector sensing is an optimal alternative to electrodes-based bioelectric measurements (ECG). Photodetectors are a Light Emitting Diodes (LEDs) technology combined with PhotoDiode (PD) technology that enable to record the Heart Rate (HR) by the PhotoPlethysmoGram (PPG). PPG method is uninvasive and reliable because the sensor don't require electrical coupling with the person's body (skin) requiring the application of conductive gel or pasta for optimal conductivity.

Another important wearable technology advancement was been the AnalogFront-End (AFE) deployment on a Chip Scale Package (CSP), a less than 1 mm × 1 mm × 0.1 mm thin package developed by Analog Devices Inc. (ADI), and CSP deployment of a 32-bit microcomputer developed by (Freescale, NXP). These technologies enable complex tasks such as ultra-small and noisy signal amplification and processing with very low-power consumption (nanoWatt).

The availability of RadioFrequency (RF) communication such as a sub-1 GHz RF Transceiver ultra-low power (under 10 nA), CSP packaged, developed by Microsemi Corp. completed the wearable technology's mosaic.

The last step in this wearable technology innovation was system integration in System-on-Chip (SoC) scale devices that deploy all the required technologies (sensing, signal processing, communication) in a small device that can be hosted in a small wearable case like a watch or a bracelet [12].

Bluetooth Low Energy (BLE) was also available at very small integration scale and available for the development of the personal wireless area network and targeted to wearable device's connectivity in medical and fitness applications.

2 System Framework

The proposed Personal Car Driver Black Box is a wearable system consisting of an analog subsystem (sensors and amplifiers), of a mixed-signal subsystem (Analog to Digital Converters (ADCs)) and of a digital subsystem (Microcontroller Unit (MCU), an embedded memory (eM), a wireless communication) (Fig. 1).

The analog subsystem consists of a set of uninvasive sensors such as metal surface contact electrodes, photosensors, thermistor, inertial sensors (accelerometer, gyroscope), connected to an analog-front-end (AFE) for signal conditioning (amplification, filtering, impedance adaptation).

The vital signs captured and conditioned by the analog subsystem are then applied to the mixed-signal subsystem (ADC) to be sampled and quantized as data streams.

The data streams are processed by the digital subsystem that runs the learning and prediction paradigm, and are stored on a nonvolatile memory (NVM).

All the subsystems consist of state of the art wearable ultra-embedded microelectronics (ultra-low power, ultra-small, ultra-low cost). All the electronics is packaged in a watch-like case, so the noninvasiveness's requirement was accomplished.

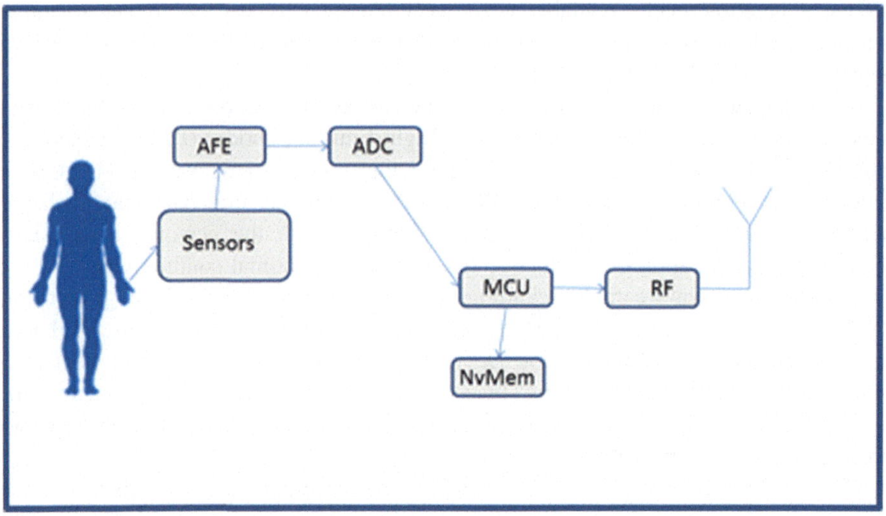

Fig. 1. Personal Car Driver Black Box system architecture

3 Prediction Paradigm

The reference prediction paradigm is the Evolving Fuzzy Neural Network (EFuNN). EFuNN's peculiarities such as adaptability to new data of unknown distribution, avoiding of catastrophic forgetting, fast adaptation (one step-learning), linguistically meaningful information representation and online learning concur to accomplish the prediction requirements for a personal behavior prediction system based on vital signs measurements.

EFuNN is a predictive paradigm that belongs to the Evolving Connectionist Systems (ECOSs), a class of modular connectionist-based systems that evolve continuously their structure and functionality, self-organizing, adapting interactively from incoming data.

EFuNN is a five layers Feed-Forward Artificial Neural Network (ANN) (Fig. 2) that implements fuzzy rules and a fuzzy logic inference engine in connectionist mode by four layer of connections. This architecture enables the EFuNN to infer by rules and to learn by data.

The first layer inputs the crisp data. The second layer encodes the membership functions that fuzzify the crisp data from the first layer. The third layer encodes the fuzzy rules that connect the inputs to the outputs. The fourth layer implements the defuzzification of the output data. The fifth layer is the final output (crisp) (Fig. 2).

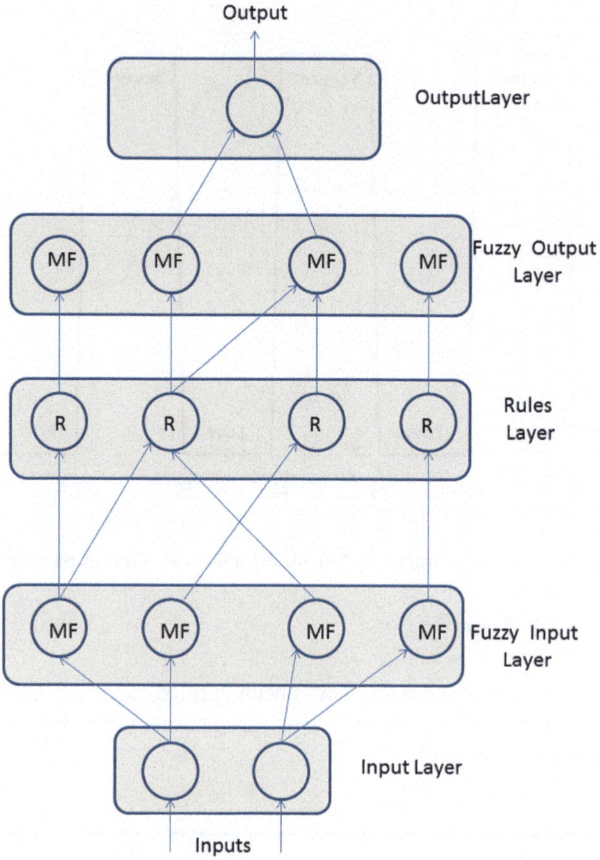

Fig. 2. EFuNN five layers feed forward ANN architecture.

4 Data Set

To train and test the EFuNN a dataset was collected by sensors data measuring vital signs (Heart rate, movements). The dataset consists of values of heart rate and movement at time (t − n) as input variables, with the fatigue level at the moment (t) as an output variable (label).

To train and test the EFuNN the simulation environment NEUCOM [13] was been used that requires a set of patterns of labeled data such as:

$H_1\ M_1\ H_2\ M_2\ H_3\ M_3\ H_4\ M_4\ H_5\ M_5\ H_6\ M_6 \ldots H_j\ M_j \ldots H_N\ M_N\ L_n$
H_j : i-th amplitude of the i-th sample of the n-th HR measure
M_j : j-th amplitude of the j-th sample of the n-th Movement measure
L_n : n-th label associated to the n-th sequence.

The dataset was built by collecting the HR and movement measurements of a driver, labeling two fatigue behavioral conditions: (low, severe) (Fig. 3) [14].

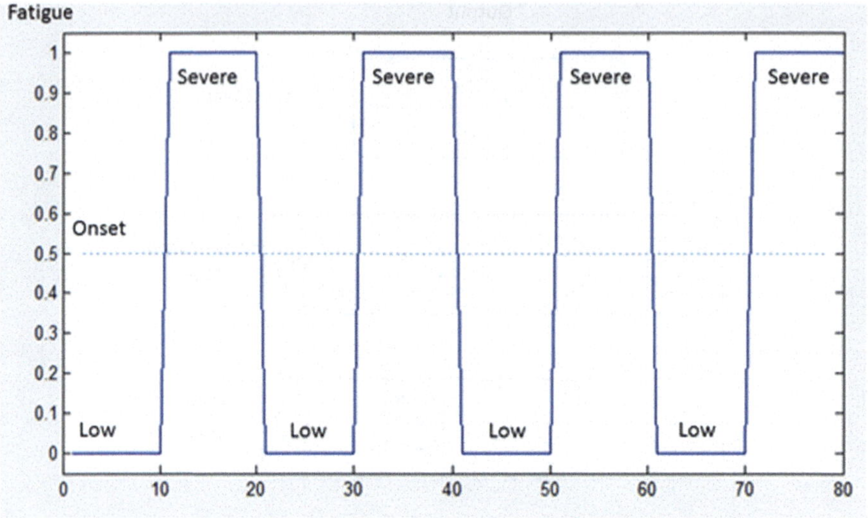

Fig. 3. Dataset to train and test the EFuNN's prediction paradigm.

5 Training and Test

To train the EFuNN the fatigue dataset was been applied to the NEUCOM simulation environment by splitting randomly it in two sub-datasets (80% for training purpose, 20% for test purpose) (Fig. 4).

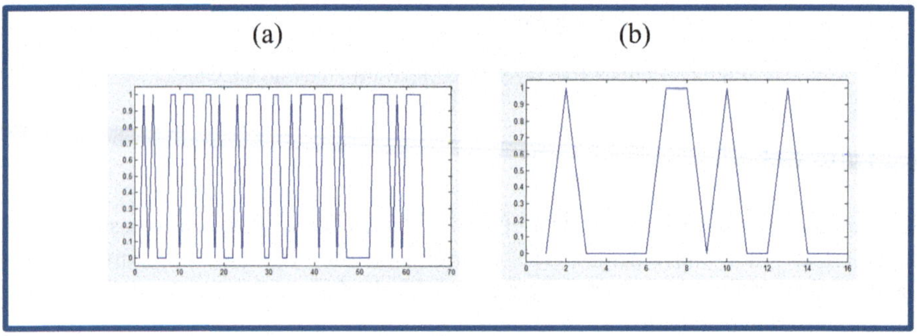

Fig. 4. Dataset to train and test the EFuNN's prediction paradigm. (a) Train: random split (80%), (b) Test: random split (20%).

After training the EFuNN's setup is as follow with three membership functions (triangular):

Sensitivity Threshold: 0.9
Error Threshold: 0.1
Number of Membership Functions: 3

Learning rate for: W1: 0.1
Learning Rate for W2: 0.1
Pruning: On
Node age: 60
Aggregation: On

At the end of training a set of six rules resulted. Follows the Rule 4:

if
[Var 1] –> (MF 1) @ 0.000 & (MF 2) @ 0.091 & (MF 3) @ 0.909
[Var 2] –> (MF 1) @ 0.000 & (MF 2) @ 0.091 & (MF 3) @ 0.909
[Var 3] –> (MF 1) @ 0.000 & (MF 2) @ 0.100 & (MF 3) @ 0.900
[Var 4] –> (MF 1) @ 0.000 & (MF 2) @ 0.091 & (MF 3) @ 0.909
then Output for (MF 1) @ 0.000 Output for (MF 2) @ 0.091 Output for (MF 3) @ 0.909

After training was executed (Fig. 5) the prediction capabilities of the EFuNN was tested by 20% dataset (Fig. 6). The test confirmed the EFuNN capability to predict the fatigue onset from HR and movements measurements captured by the wearable device (Fig. 6 and Fig. 7).

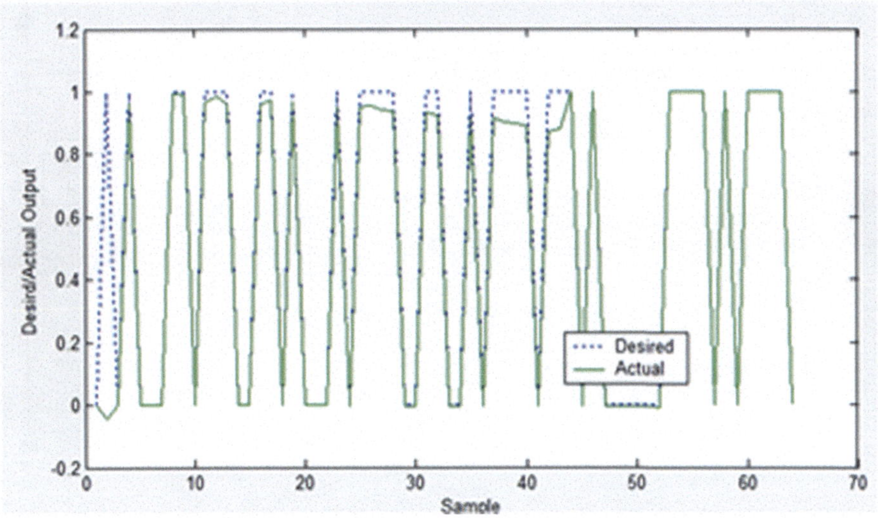

Fig. 5. EFuNN's train with the 80% random splitted dataset

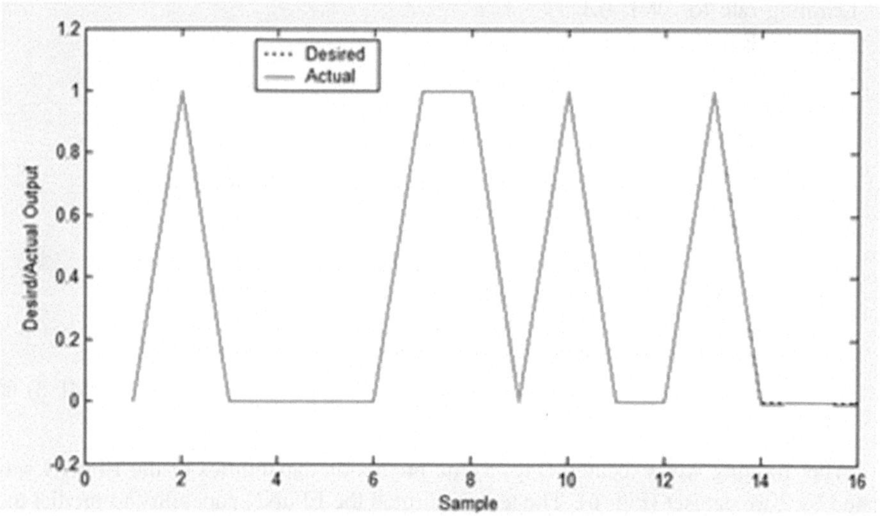

Fig. 6. EFuNN's test after test with 20% random splitted dataset.

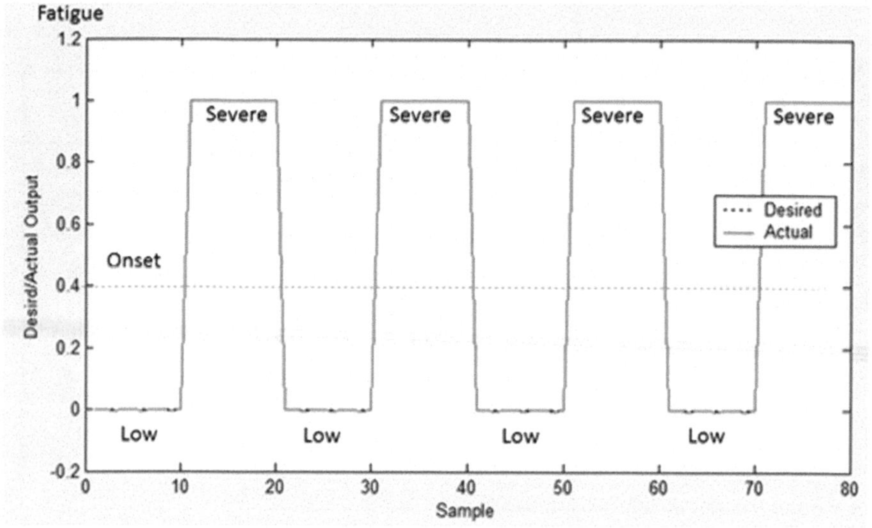

Fig. 7. EFuNN's after test with full dataset

6 Conclusion and Discussion

The modeling and the tests executed on different behavioral status of the car driver confirmed that the method could be applied to several risky behavioral condition to warn the driver about his ability to continue to drive (safe/risky). Because several vital signs measurements concur to assess the driver condition, a data fusion strategy need to be investigated, considering it one of the capabilities embedded in the EFuNN paradigm.

Another topic to be elaborated on is the continuous data gathering targeted to post event analysis and dataset building (black box mode).

References

1. NHTSA: Drowsy driving. Published by NHTSA's National Center for Statistics and Analysis. 1200 New Jersey Avenue SE, Washington, DC 20590 (2011)
2. Malcangi, M., Smirne, S.: Fuzzy-logic inference for early detection of sleep onset. Neural Comput. Appl. **27**, 41–50 (2015)
3. Dorfman, G.F., Baharav, A., Cahan, C., Akselrod, S.: Early detection of falling asleep at the wheel: a heart rate variability approach. Comput. Cardiol. **35**, 1109–1112 (2008)
4. Stutts, J.C.: Sleep Deprivation Countermeasures. National Academy Press, Wascinton D.C. (2000)
5. Straczkiewicz, M., Urbanek, J.K., Crainiceanu, C.M., Harezlak, J.: Automatic car driving detection using raw accelerometry data. Physiol. Meas. **37**(10), 1757–1769 (2016)
6. Quintana, S.D., Heathers, J.A.J.: Considerations in the assessment of heart rate variability in behavioral research. Front. Psychol. **5**, 805 (2014)
7. Malcangi, M.: Applying evolutionary methods for early prediction of sleep onset. Neural Comput. Appl. **27**, 1165–1173 (2016). https://doi.org/10.1007/s00521-015-1928-6
8. Kasabov, N.: Evolving fuzzy neural network – algorithms, applications and biological motivation. In: Yamakawa, T., Matsumoto, G. (eds.) Methodologies for Conception, Design and Application of the Soft Computing. World Computing, pp. 271–274 (1998)
9. Kasabov, N.: Time-Space, Spiking Neural Networks and Brain-Inspired Artificial Intelligence. Springer Series on Neurosystems. Springer, Berlin (2019)
10. Broeders, J.H.: Wearable electronic devices monitor vital signs activity level and more. Analog Dialog (December 2014)
11. Palhmi, J., Broeders, J.H.: Optical integration without compromises (1995). https://www.analog.com/en/technical-articles/optical-integration-without-compromises.html
12. Broeders, J.H.: The sensors behind the GEN II wearable device, Technical Article, https://www.analog.com/media/en/technical-documentation/tech-articles/the-sensors-behind-the-GEN-II-wearable-device.pdf
13. https://Kedri.aut.nz/areas-of-expertise/data-mining-and-support/neucom
14. Sahayadhas, A., Sundaraj, K., Murugappan, M.: Detecting driver drowsiness based on sensors: a review. Sensors **12**, 16937–16953 (2012)

Learning/Clustering

Instance Weighted Clustering: Local Outlier Factor and K-Means

Paul Moggridge(✉), Na Helian, Yi Sun, Mariana Lilley, and Vito Veneziano

The University of Hertfordshire, Hatfield, UK
p.moggridge@herts.ac.uk

Abstract. Clustering is an established unsupervised learning method. Substantial research has been carried out in the area of feature weighting, as well instance selection for clustering. Some work has paid attention to instance weighted clustering algorithms using various instance weighting metrics based on distance information, geometric information and entropy information. However, little research has made use of instance density information to weight instances. In this paper we use density to define instance weights. We propose two novel instance weighted clustering algorithms based on Local Outlier Factor and compare them against plain k-means and traditional instance selection.

Keywords: Machine learning · Unsupervised learning · Instance weighting

1 Introduction

In the area of Data Mining, clustering is one type of unsupervised learning that involves finding groups of similar instances in data. Arguably the most popular clustering algorithm is k-means [11]. This algorithm partitions instances into a given number of clusters k. K-means iteratively assigns instances to clusters based on their distance to the centroids of the clusters, the centroids' positions are then recalculated to be the means of instances in their respective clusters.

Instance selection is a well established technique. It is often used for removing instances that are outliers. Feature weighting (also referred to as "attribute weighting") is an ongoing area of research. In Feature weighting the features of a dataset are weighted based on their various metrics typically related to how much they enhance the accuracy of the main data mining activity. Inspired by instance selection and feature weighting, Instance weighting assigns a weight to each of the instances in a dataset. Considering outliers for example, from a statistics' perspective, outlierness is a scale rather a boolean property, so it makes sense to use weighting rather than selection in response.

Thanks you to Innovate UK for your support.

L. Iliadis et al. (Eds.): EANN 2020, INNS 2, pp. 435–446, 2020.
https://doi.org/10.1007/978-3-030-48791-1_34

Hawkins defines an outlier as "an observation which deviates so much from the other observations as to arouse suspicions that it was generated by a different mechanism" [9]. Outlier accommodation is enabling algorithms to accommodate outliers, it is the opposite of outlier diagnosis, where outliers are identified and removed before processing. Instance Weighting can provide a way for clustering algorithms to accommodate outliers, by adjusting how much to learn from outlying instances. This is important since clustering algorithms, such as k-means can be adversely effected by the presence of outliers in a dataset. Whilst it is true that some types and severities of outlier should be fully discarded, some types and severities of outliers may be best partially retained for the clustering process to learn from. This is especially important when the total number of instances is low.

This paper is structured as follows. Section 2 presents the related work. Section 3 describes our two novel instance weighted clustering algorithms. Section 4 is the methodology, experimental results and discussion of our findings. Finally, Sect. 5 draws conclusions from our findings and presents our recommendations for future work.

2 Related Work

Nock and Neilsen's [12] research is inspired by boosting algorithms (from supervised learning) and k harmonic means clustering [15]. They are the first to formalise a boosting based approach, their solution penalises bad clustering accuracy by updating the instance weights. Their algorithm gives more weight to data points that are not well modelled. Their approach could be described as a statistics based approach. Their paper investigates, for which scenarios, instance weighting improves the accuracy of clustering and if instance weighting can reduce initialisation sensitivity. They investigate applying instance weighting on multiple algorithms including k-means, fuzzy k-means, harmonic k-means and Exception Maximisation and prove the applicability of instance weighting to a range of algorithms. Their research shows that instance weighting could speed up the clustering algorithms. They highlight the growing attention around weighted iterative clustering algorithms in unsupervised learning. In our research we have applied a simpler method, but used a density based technique. We also investigate the benefit of instance weighting and how instance weighting can address the presence of outliers in a dataset.

Sample Weighted Clustering by Jian Yu et al. weights instances using a probability distribution derived from an information theory approach [14]. They point out that there is little research on sample (another name of instance) weighted clustering compared to feature weighted clustering. Like our work they investigate the benefit instance weighting for datasets with outliers wrapping the popular k-means algorithm. They highlight that just one outlier can adversely effect the clustering output of k-means, fuzzy c-means and expectation maximisation. Their information theory based approach produces promising results which are robust to outliers across a variety of datasets. They also found their weighting also made their algorithm less sensitive to initialisation.

Lei Gu's research uses geometric based weighting that also takes local neighbour information into account [7]. Their approach uses two weighting schemes per cluster. One scheme for points close to the center of the clusters and another scheme for ambiguous points near the clusters boundaries. Their algorithm outperforms Jain Yu et al.'s algorithm (described in the previous paragraph) for accuracy. Lei Gu's research also considers non image segmentation based clustering problems.

Hammerly and Elkan's research [8] investigates the k harmonic mean algorithm [15]. They found that it produces better accuracy than k-means and show that having a non-constant (iterative) weight function is also useful. They point out many wrapper based solutions have been proposed, such as random restart, optimising the initialisation and optimising k-selection around clustering, but less research has been put into wrappers which iteratively effect the clustering. Hammerly and Elkan point out the benefit of wrapper methods is that they can often be simultaneously applied.

In Adaptive Nonparametric Clustering by Efimov et al. [6] the weightings are assigned to both the instances and features w_{ij} rather than just w_i (instance weighting) or just w_j (feature weighting). The idea of their algorithm is to look for structures in the clustering, for example, slopes away from local homogeneity. Their approach has several strengths, their algorithm supports manifold clustering and is robust against outliers. Another useful property of their algorithm is the lack of a tunable parameter, which many algorithms has. Their paper does not attempt generalise or suggest the possibility of applying their method as a wrapper method.

Jain provides an overview of clustering discussing the key issues in designing clustering algorithms, and points out some of the emerging and useful research directions [10]. Jain's paper outlines six problems/research areas, one of which is "A fundamental issue related to clustering is its stability or consistency. A good clustering principle should result in a data partitioning that is stable with respect to perturbations in the data. We need to develop clustering methods that lead to stable solutions". This is the problem our research considers solving through instance weighting. Their review paper also points out challenges related semi-supervised clustering (however, we are not considering semi-supervised clustering in this paper), one challenge in the area of semi-supervised clustering is "how to provide the side information". Instance weighting is one possible solution to this problem, our algorithm could be adapted to work in a hybrid mode. Also, with regard to semi-supervised learning it is highlighted that it is desirable to have approach which avoids changing clustering existing algorithms, and instead wrap around them.

Instance weighting is an established technique but there is much less research compared feature weighting. For instance, in recent and comprehensive literature, for example, Data Clutering [1] instance weighting is not mentioned. However, instance weighting is a promising technique and can provide several enhancements to several existing clustering algorithms. Instance weighting is also an increasingly important technique, on the popular dataset website UCI

[5], the average size of the datasets in terms of instances is increasing. Instance weighting like ours makes clustering more robust leading towards an increasingly automated knowledge discovery process by reducing the requirement for preprocessing of data.

Some work has paid attention to instance weighted clustering algorithms using various instance weighting metrics based on distance information, geometric information and entropy information. However, little research has made use of instance density information to weight instances. In this paper we use density to define instance weights, develops clustering methods that lead to stable solutions by using instance density information to weight instances.

2.1 Local Outlier Factor

Local Outlier Factor (LOF) is an outlier detection algorithm which provides a measure of outlierness. LOF works by comparing the density of an instance to that of its neighbours [3]. Equations (1), (2) and (3)[1] show how to calculate the LOF of a point A. A represents the point we are calculating the local density of. k represents the number of neighbours to consider. $k-distance$ is the distance from a given point to its kth furthest point. $N_K(A)$ is the set of k nearest neighbours to A.

$$reachability - distance_k(A, B) = \max\{k - distance(B), d(A, B)\} \tag{1}$$

$$\mathrm{lrd}_k(A) := 1/\left(\frac{\sum_{B \in N_k(A)} \text{reachability-distance}_k(A, B)}{|N_k(A)|}\right) \tag{2}$$

$$\mathrm{LOF}_k(A) := \frac{\sum_{B \in N_k(A)} \frac{\mathrm{lrd}(B)}{\mathrm{lrd}(A)}}{|N_k(A)|} = \frac{\sum_{B \in N_k(A)} \mathrm{lrd}(B)}{|N_k(A)|} / \mathrm{lrd}(A) \tag{3}$$

Consider the example dataset in Fig. 1 (left), the data point at location $(5, 5)$ labelled a is moderately outlying. *k-distance* is the distance to the kth furthest point, so if $k = 3$, then k^{th} nearest neighbour of a would be the point at location $(1, 1)$ labelled b. If point a is within the k neighbours of point b (See Fig. 1 (right)) the $reachability - distance_k(a, b)$ will be the $k - distance$ of b, the distance to the kth further point $(2, 1)$ from b. Otherwise, it will be the real distance of a and b. So in Fig. 1 it is **not** within the k neighbours of point b so in this case it is the real distance between a and b.

To get the lrd (local reachability density) for the point a, we will first calculate the reachability distance of a to all its k nearest neighbours and take the average of that number. The lrd is then simply the inverse of that average. Since a is not the third nearest point to b see Fig. 1 (right), the reachability distance in this case is always the actual distance. A value greater than one indicates a lower density (thus the instance is outlier). A value one indicates similar density to neighbours. Less than one indicates a higher density. So low density becomes a high LOF score highlighting a instance as an outlier.

[1] https://en.wikipedia.org/wiki/Local_outlier_factor.

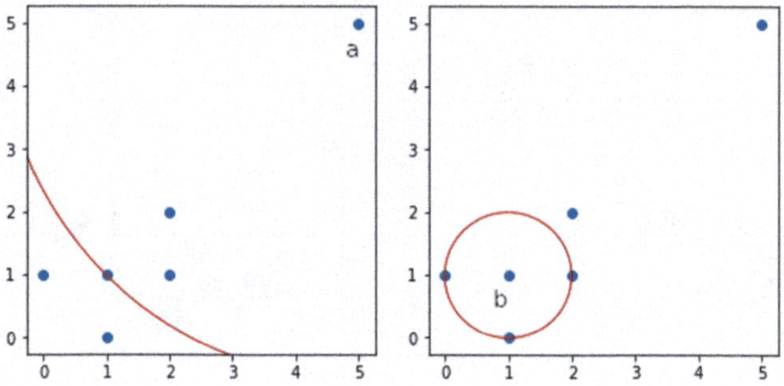

Fig. 1. Calculating the reachability distance.

One of properties that makes LOF ideal is that the LOF algorithm can work on datasets with clusters of different densities and instance count. As long as the number of k neighbours is below the number of instances in the smallest cluster. This is advantageous since it places little restriction on the dataset to which the weighted clustering algorithm can be applied to. However, one possible drawback to the LOF algorithm is its time complexity of $O(n^2)$, where n is the data size. However, there is existing work speeding up LOF using GPU acceleration [2].

3 Proposed Methods

We have proposed two novel algorithms based on k-means, Local Outlier Factor Instance Weighted K-Means (LOFIWKM) and Iterative Local Outlier Factor Instance Weighted K-Means (ILOFIWKM). LOFIWKM calculates the weights over the **whole dataset once upon initialisation**, whereas ILOFIWKM calculates the weights **for each cluster upon each iteration**. The weights generated by executing the LOF algorithm are used when calculating means for the positions of the new centroids in the k-means algorithm. In Fig. 3 the weights are represented by black circles, where the smaller the circle the higher the weight.

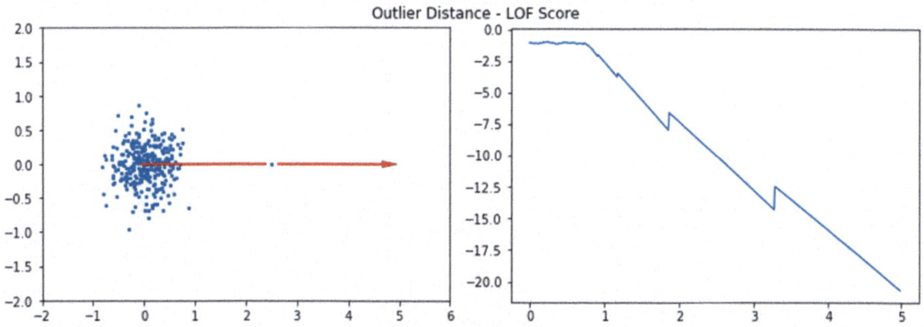

Fig. 2. Demonstrating the LOF scores.

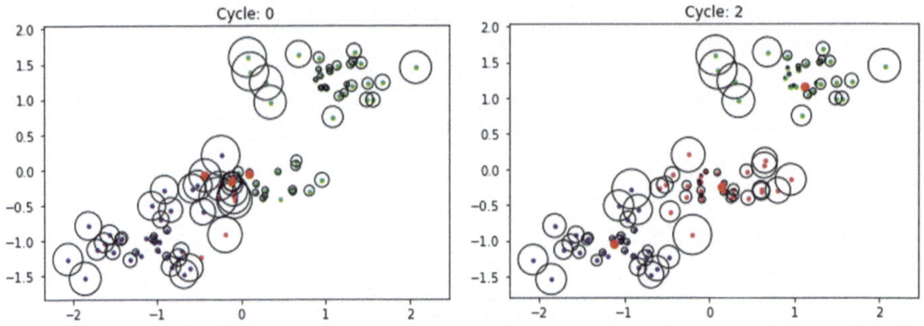

Fig. 3. The I LOF IW K-Means showing different how weights change as the algorithm executes.

More formally, LOFIWKM, starts by calculates the LOF score of every instance considering the whole dataset. Taking the whole dataset into consideration, we highlight outliers relative to the whole dataset. Then as per k-means, centroids are initialised. However, our algorithm uses a weighted random initialisation based on LOF scores and instance positions. Then as per k-means, instances are assigned to the centroids they are closest to. Then as per k-means, the algorithm iterates until converged (there is no more reassignments of instance between clusters) or a max allowed iterations is met. Then, the algorithm calculates the new positions of the centroids based on its' instances, taking a weighted average using normalised LOF scores as weights to moderate the impact of the instance positions on the mean. Then as per k-means instances are assigned the new centroid they are nearest to. Figure 1 shows a formal description of the algorithm where, Dataset of instances = D_i, $D = \{D_1, D_2 \ldots D_i\ D_N\}$. LOF Scores for each instance in the dataset = LOF_i, $LOF = \{LOF_1, LOF_2, \ldots LOF_i, LOF_N\}$. Clusters corresponding the K value entered = C_k, $C = \{C_1, C_2 \ldots C_k, C_K\}$ a centroid has a position and collection of instances. The number of iterations/k-means cycles = c.

ILOFIWKM operates the same as LOFIWKM upto the end of iteration step. Then the algorithm LOF score of every instance running the LOF algorithm per cluster and normalising the LOF scores per cluster. Figure 2 shows a formal description of the algorithm.

Algorithm 1. LOFIWKM

```
Calculate LOF for D
for all w in LOF do
    Assign (w − min(LOF)) / (max(LOF) − min(LOF)) to w*
end for
Assign LOF* to LOF
Use LOF weighted random to select K positions from D assign to C
for all i in D do
    Assign i to k according to min(dist(i, C))
end for
Assign 0 to c
while C not converged or c ≤ c^max do
    for all k in C do
        Assign (Σ_{k_N}^{k_0} i·w) / (Σ_{k_N}^{k_0} w) to k
    end for
    for all i in D do
        Assign i to k where min(dist(i, C))
    end for
    Assign c + 1 to c
end while
```

4 Experimentation

The purpose of the proposed algorithms is to improve k-means ability to handle outliers. Two variables, count of outliers and range of outliers are experimented with, furthermore the two new algorithms were compared against plain k-means. All experiments are repeated 175 times as the algorithms and the synthetic dataset generation are both stochastic. The outliers are generated using a uniform distribution over a given range, and appended to the dataset. Both synthetic and real world datasets are experimented on. All datasets used included their ground truths and this was used assess clustering accuracy using ARI (Adjusted Random Index). The ARI computes a similarity measure between clusterings by considering all pairs of instances and counting pairs that are assigned in the same or different clusters in the predicted and true clusterings.

The experiments use the scikit-learn libraries where possible [13] to speed development and aid repeatability. Most notably scikit-learn's LOF implementation was used for calculating the measures of outlyingness. Furthermore, scikit-learn's Blobs Dataset Generator, Standard Scaler, PCA and Adjusted Random Index were utilised. For the k-means algorithm, our own python implementation was used and updated to create the novel algorithms. This ensures that the only difference between k-means and our instance weighted k-means algorithms was changes described in this paper.

For each run of the experiments the dataset was regenerated. The synthetic blob datasets (noise = 0.3) are generated with 90 instances, 2 features and 3 clusters of equal sizes. For the outlier count various amounts of outliers were tested: 5, 10, 15, 20, 25. For the outlier range experiment, various ranges were tested: 20, 40, 60, 80, 100, the (dataset with outliers spans a range of 10 in either axis) (Fig. 4).

Algorithm 2. ILOFIWKM

Calculate LOF for D
for all w in LOF **do**
  Assign $\frac{w-min(LOF)}{max(LOF)-min(LOF)}$ **to** w^*
end for
Use LOF weighted random to select K positions from D assign **to** C
for all i in D **do**
  Assign i **to** k according to $\min(dist(i, C))$
end for
Assign 0 **to** c
while C **not** converged **or** $c \leq c^{max}$ **do**
  for all k in C **do**
    Assign $\frac{\Sigma_{k_N}^{k_0} i \cdot w}{\Sigma_{k_N}^{k_0} w}$ **to** k
  end for
  for all i in D **do**
    Assign i **to** k where $\min(dist(i, C))$
  end for
  for all C **do**
    Partially recalculate LOF for i in k
    for all w in k **do**
      Assign $\frac{w-min(LOF)}{max(LOF)-min(LOF)}$ **to** w^*
    end for
  end for
  Assign $c + 1$ **to** c
end while

Also experiments are conducted on a real world dataset containing 210 instances, 7 features and 3 clusters the measurements are of damaged wheat kernels of 3 different varieties [4]. The dataset was obtained via the UCI Machine Learning Repository [5] (Fig. 5).

4.1 Outlier Count and Range Synthetic Dataset Results

Figure 6 shows positive results for density based instance weighted clustering. The instance weighted algorithms were able to achieve better clustering accuracy

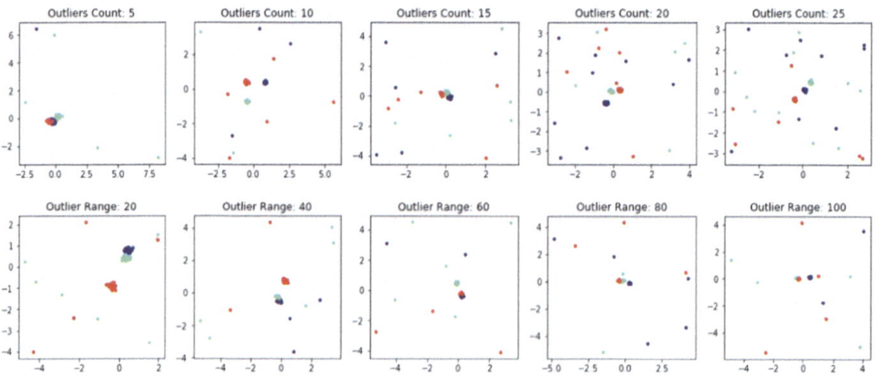

Fig. 4. A sample of the blobs datasets.

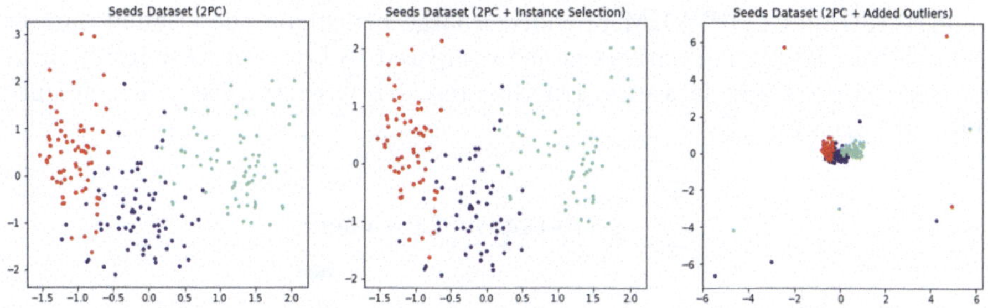

Fig. 5. The seeds datasets.

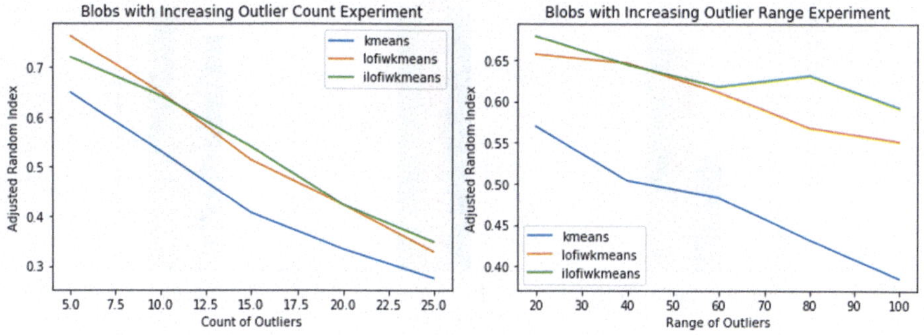

Fig. 6. Adjusted Random Index scores for the blobs datasets

than k-means. In Fig. 6 on the left, the impact of increasing the count outliers can be seen. In Fig. 6 on the right, the impact of creating increasingly distance outliers is shown. The accuracy of k-means quickly deteriorates as the outliers get distant. The LOFIWKM and ILOFIWKM algorithms are not as strongly effected by the presence of increasing distant outliers. Across both experiments, a minimal gain can be seen in using the iterative version, ILOFIWKM.

4.2 Real World Dataset Results

In Fig. 7 instance weighting is compared with instance selection. The three groups of columns show different conditions of the dataset. Left shows the results with dataset having additional synthetic outliers added. Center shows the results of the algorithms having the outliers removed (i.e. Instance Selection). The outliers were removed using the LOF algorithm with the same neighbours count as in LOFIWKM algorithms (neighbours = 5). The outlier contamination value was set to 0.1 to remove the most outlying 10% of the dataset. Finally right shows results for the original dataset. We can compare instance weighting to instance selection by comparing the right group's LOFIWKM result to the central group's k-means result. It can be seen that instance weighting slightly outperformed instance selection in ARI score, however only slightly. It can also been seen that

ILOFIWKM and LOFIWKM provided a large benefit on the original dataset and the with additional outliers added compared to k-means. Our results mirror tests on the seeds dataset in Lei Gu's research were weighting also enhance clustering accuracy [7].

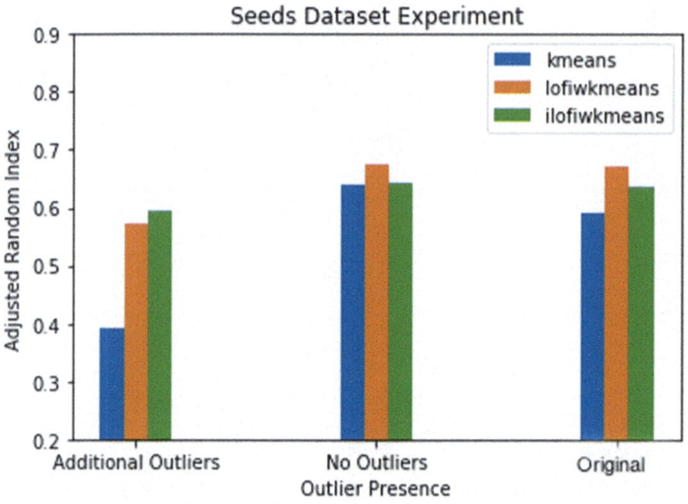

Fig. 7. Adjusted Random Index scores for the seeds dataset

5 Conclusion and Future Work

In conclusion, this paper has shown that instance weighting can help mitigate the effect of outliers on both a synthetic and a real world dataset.

In this paper we only investigated k-means which has a hard membership function and the LOF algorithm. However, there is likely more useful combinations to be found. Hammerly and Elkan found that varying weights did improve the performance of hard membership function algorithms (i.e. k-means) [8]. However, Nock and Neilsen's research confirmed instance weighting to be more advantageous for clustering algorithms with soft membership functions such as fuzzy k-means [12]. A future work of this paper should be to investigate soft membership function algorithms.

Our modifications were made to a basic version of the k-means algorithm. However, it would be possible to combine the LOF instance weighting with a version of k-means which has more optimisations or is being used in conjunction with wrapper functions. Furthermore, with instance weighting there is potential to simultaneously apply multiple instance weights which could prove to increase robustness or accuracy.

The time complexity LOFIWKM is equivalent to LOF instance selection $O(n^2)$ plus k-means $O(n)$, however ILOFIWKM is significantly more costly taking the complexity of k-means plus the execution of the LOF algorithm per cluster (for each clusters instances), further experimentation may prove that ILOFIWKM may be not suitable for large datasets, without optimisation of the LOF algorithm, such as, the research by Alshawabkeh et al. [2].

Future work also includes testing the algorithms with a more thorough outlier generation process. In this paper we added instances from a uniform distribution, centred on the dataset. This had two disadvantages, firstly this method possibly does not highlight one of the advantages of instance weighting. Instance weighting has the potential to retain some of the information an outlier presents, since the "outliers" are uniformly random these benefits are negated. Secondarily, it is possible that when generating the "outliers" that a proportion of fall within a normal range and end up not being outliers.

Currently our algorithm requires parameter selection of k clusters and the size of the LOF neighbourhood. Other algorithms [7, 14] require some parameter selection with the exception of the state of the art [6]. It would be clearly better to not require the parameter selection and it does seem possible to automate the selection of these parameters.

References

1. Aggarwal, C.C., Reddy, C.K.: Data Clustering: Algorithms and Applications, 1st edn. Chapman Hall CRC, Boca Raton (2013)
2. Alshawabkeh, M., Jang, B., Kaeli, D.: Accelerating the local outlier factor algorithm on a GPU for intrusion detection systems. In: Proceedings of the 3rd Workshop on General-Purpose Computation on Graphics Processing Units, pp. 104–110 (2010)
3. Breunig, M.M., Kriegel, H.P., Ng, R.T., Sander, J.: LOF: identifying density-based local outliers. In: ACM Sigmod Record, vol. 29, pp. 93–104. ACM (2000)
4. Charytanowicz, M., Niewczas, J., Kulczycki, P., Kowalski, P.A., Łukasik, S., Żak, S.: Complete gradient clustering algorithm for features analysis of x-ray images. In: Information Technologies in Biomedicine, pp. 15–24. Springer (2010)
5. Dua, D., Graff, C.: UCI machine learning repository (2017). http://archive.ics.uci.edu/ml
6. Efimov, K., Adamyan, L., Spokoiny, V.: Adaptive nonparametric clustering. IEEE Trans. Inf. Theory **65**(8), 4875–4892 (2019)
7. Gu, L.: A novel sample weighting k-means clustering algorithm based on angles information. In: 2016 International Joint Conference on Neural Networks (IJCNN), pp. 3697–3702. IEEE (2016)
8. Hamerly, G., Elkan, C.: Alternatives to the k-means algorithm that find better clusterings. In: Proceedings of the Eleventh International Conference on Information and Knowledge Management, pp. 600–607 (2002)
9. Hawkins, D.M.: Identification of outliers, vol. 11. Springer (1980)
10. Jain, A.K.: Data clustering: 50 years beyond k-means. Pattern Recogn. Lett. **31**(8), 651–666 (2010)
11. Lloyd, S.: Least squares quantization in PCM. IEEE Trans. Inf. Theory **28**(2), 129–137 (1982)

12. Nock, R., Nielsen, F.: On weighting clustering. IEEE Trans. Pattern Anal. Mach. Intell. **28**(8), 1223–1235 (2006)
13. Pedregosa, F., Varoquaux, G., Gramfort, A., Michel, V., Thirion, B., Grisel, O., Blondel, M., Prettenhofer, P., Weiss, R., Dubourg, V., Vanderplas, J., Passos, A., Cournapeau, D., Brucher, M., Perrot, M., Duchesnay, E.: Scikit-learn: machine learning in python. J. Mach. Learn. Res. **12**, 2825–2830 (2011)
14. Yu, J., Yang, M.S., Lee, E.S.: Sample-weighted clustering methods. Comput. Math. Appl. **62**(5), 2200–2208 (2011)
15. Zhang, B.: Generalized k-harmonic means. Hewlett-Packard Laboratories Technical Report (2000)

Detecting Pattern Efficiently with Don't Cares

Hayam Alamro[1,2(✉)] and Costas Iliopoulos[1]

[1] Department of Informatics, King's College London, London, UK
{hayam.alamro,costas.iliopoulos}@kcl.ac.uk
[2] Department of Information Systems, Princess Nourah Bint Abdulrahman University, Riyadh, Kingdom of Saudi Arabia

Abstract. In this paper, we introduce our efficient simple method which can locate all occurrences of pattern P of k subpatterns with "don't cares" of length m in text S of length n. Our algorithm employs advanced data structure and the *Kangaroo* method, which can be applied to selected suffixes of the *suffix tree* of S to answer subsequent queries in $O(k)$ time using a predefined computational method to find all occurrences of pattern P with "don't cares" in text S in a fast and effective manner.

Keywords: Pattern · Don't cares · Detect

1 Introduction

Pattern matching is the problem of string matching which is to find the location(s) of a given word, the pattern within another one, the text [15,16]. The classical pattern matching problem is to find all the occurrences of a given pattern P of length m in a text S of length n, both being sequences of characters drawn from a finite character set Σ. This problem is interesting as a fundamental computer science problem and is a basic need of many applications, such as text retrieval, music retrieval, computational biology, data mining, network security, among many others. Solutions to the pattern matching in strings can be roughly classified into two categories, window shifts and automaton, and text indexing [14]. In the first one, the pattern is examined using a window shift where the window slides along the text from left to right according to the window rules of each algorithm, such that the found location is reported after a whole match with the corresponding pattern. The algorithms that are adopted this approach are *Brute-force* algorithm, *Karp-Rabin* algorithm [25] and *Boyer-Moore* algorithm [6] which works on skipping a large portion of the text while searching a pattern, which helps in speeding up the searching process. The *KMP* is the first linear-time pattern matching algorithm, which stores the information of matching to prevent a backward shift to improve the search time with the help of the failure function [26]. Also, the *Aho-Corasick* algorithm [1], which is

L. Iliadis et al. (Eds.): EANN 2020, INNS 2, pp. 447–459, 2020.
https://doi.org/10.1007/978-3-030-48791-1_35

an improved version of the *KMP* algorithm and based on the automaton approach, preprocesses the keywords (dictionary strings) then search for the keywords simultaneously which runs in time proportional to the sum of the lengths of the keywords. At the multi-pattern matching level, Commentz-Walter [13] presented an algorithm which is a combination of the Boyer-Moore and Aho-Corasick, and Wu-Manber [36] also uses the idea of Boyer-Moore in addition to building three tables (SHIFT, HASH, and PREFIX) to determine how many characters should be skipped and which pattern is a candidate for the match. The other pattern matching solutions involve building an index for a text such that the occurrences of a query pattern can be reported, where the data structure contains all the suffixes of the text. *Suffix tree* and *Suffix array* are data structures for text indexing, linear space, and hold the compact representation of the text suffixes. Recently, classical string indexing problems are extended to address the patterns with more complicated forms, such as don't cares characters, gaps and errors to meet many applications needs in reality. A *don't care* character means that this position of the pattern can match any character in the text and is denoted with '*'. Don't care is also called wildcard [5] or gap [32]. A Suffix tree is an efficient data structure as it stores the suffixes of a given string in linear space and time, and is useful in various applications concerning string matching like finding longest common prefix, repeated substrings and antiperiods of a string. The majority of applications that use complex patterns like don't cares characters, focus on non-indexing data structure where the text is not preprocessed in advance, while few of them adopted this approach as we will see in the next section. Hence, in this paper, we propose an algorithm that is simple and efficient in terms of using text indexing data structure without using additional data structures. The algorithm is based on preprocessing the text using a suffix tree without using a generalization suffix tree, and instead, it applies the Kangaroo method which is enabled by a predefined computational method. The contributions of this paper as follows:

1. To innovate an efficient and simple approach that can locate all occurrences of a given pattern P of length m in a text S of length n, where pattern P is defined over the alphabet $\Sigma \cup \{*\}$ and text S is sequences of characters drawn from a finite character set Σ.
2. To achieve the following specific contribution: propose an efficient algorithm which relies on constructing the *suffix tree* T for the text S without using a generalization *suffix tree* concept of $(P+S)$, instead, it applies the *Kangaroo* method on selected suffixes of the *suffix tree* of S using a predefined computational method to find all occurrences of pattern P in a fast and effective manner.

The rest of the paper as follows. In Sect. 2, the related work about pattern matching with don't cares is described. In Sect. 3, we introduce background concepts and definitions, and formally define the problem we address. In Sect. 4, we detailed our approach in detecting pattern with "don't cares" and present our algorithm. In Sect. 5, we conclude.

2 Related Work

Pattern matching has been generalized to searching in the presence of errors, e.g. Hamming distance [4,20,28], edit distance [11,28,33]. These variations of the original problem are known as approximate pattern matching. Fischer and Paterson [19] introduced the solution for the pattern matching with don't cares based on Fast Fourier Transform (FFT) and presented the algorithm that runs in $O(n \log m \log |\Sigma|)$ time. Subsequently, Indyk [23] gave a randomized algorithm which removed the dependency on the alphabet and involved convolution, running in time $O(n \log n)$. Afterward, Kalai [24] presented a slightly faster and simpler randomised algorithm as it uses a single simple convolution based on the simple randomized fingerprinting algorithm of Karp and Rabin [25] and runs in $O(n \log m)$. Finally, Cole and Hariharan in [12], solved the long lasting open problem of removing the dependency on $|\Sigma|$ in the algorithm and presented a deterministic $O(n \log m)$ time algorithm which also used convolution. Chen et al. [7] presented SAIL algorithm that conducts two phases (forward and backward) to return each matching substring of P in T in $O(n + klmg)$ time complexity, where k is the frequency of P's last character occurring in T, l is a user defined maximum length for each matching substring, and g is the maximum difference between the user defined maximum length and the minimum number of wildcard characters between two consecutive letters in P. Pinter [31] on the other hand avoided the use of convolution and used the Aho-Corasick algorithm [1] to solve the problem. The running time of Pinter's algorithm is $O(n+m+\alpha)$, where α is the total number of occurrences of the component subpatterns. However, Pinter's technique cannot be used to index the text. Furthermore, Cole and Lewenstein [10] also presented an algorithm to solve this problem considering a centroid path decomposition on tree T. The algorithm in [10] first prepossesses the text in $O(n \log Kn + n \log |\Sigma|)$ time to build a data structure of size $O(n \log Kn)$ which answers subsequent queries in time $O(2K \log \log n + m + |occ(P)|)$. Here K is the number of don't cares in the pattern and $occ(P)$ denotes the set of occurrences of the pattern in the text. Philip et al. [5] used the ART decomposition introduced by [3] to decompose the tree into a single top tree and a number bottom trees, and used the LCP data structure by [10] to report the occurrences of P in T. Rahman et al. [32] presented an algorithm where they prepossess the text in optimal $O(n)$ time and can answer subsequent queries in $O(m + \alpha \log \log n)$ time. Thereafter, Iliopoulos and Rahman [22] presented algorithms for pattern matching which can solve the problem of pattern matching with don't cares in $O(n + m + \alpha)$ time, where α is the total number of occurrences of the component subpatterns. Lam et al. [27] make use of [22] to find a set of candidate positions in T which are a superset of all matches of P in T, then the algorithm verifies whether each of them is real or not. Clifford and Porat [9] presented a filtering based algorithm for the k mismatch pattern with don't care symbols in either pattern P or text T and bounded with k mismatch and runs in $(nm^{1/3}k^{1/3}\log^{2/3} m)$. Subsequently, Clifford et al. [8] presented two solutions for pattern matching with don't cares and bounded with k mismatches. The first solution uses a randomized algorithm that works in $(n(k + \ logm \log k) \log n)$ time, and the second solution uses a deterministic algorithm which runs in $(nkpoly \log m)$ time and based on k selectors to find k mismatch problem with don't cares. Nicolae and Rajasekaran [30] gave two algorithms for pattern matching with k mismatches and don't cares in the pattern. The first one runs in $O(n\sqrt{(q+k)\log m})$ time, and the second one runs in $O(\sqrt[3]{qk\log^2 m}+n\sqrt{k\log m})$ time. Finally, Liu et al. [29] proposed two suffix tree-based algorithm (MMST-S and MMST-L) to solve variable length wildcards, according to the length of exact characters in a pattern. The algorithms involve three phases: the first phase includes constructing the suffix tree, the second phase for preprocessing the multipattern by sorting them which requires to split the exact characters into groups and gaps and then classified them according to the alphabetical order of each character in MMST-S and according to the last exact characters' group in MMST-L approach, finally, they are solved using the proposed algorithms. Most relevant to our work is the work of Iliopoulos and Rahman [22] as the algorithm based on text indexing approach by building a suffix array for the text T, then, it works on dividing the pattern P into l groups of sub-patterns, where each sub-pattern P_i is a string over the alphabet Σ and $1 \leq i \leq l-1$. For each sub-pattern, there is parameter k_i which indicates the number of don't cares characters between P_i and P_{i+1}. The algorithm in [22] computes the occurrences of $occ(P_i)$ using $SA(T)$ and for each occurrence position ($r \in occ(P_i)$), the algorithm uses two arrays (*val* and *permitted*) which computes the accumulated length of each sub-pattern P_i in *val* array first, then uses that array in *permitted* array to check each candidate position is an occurrence position for the pattern P. This is done, after comparing the result of the checking with the total number of the subpatterns each time a new candidate position is tested, which requires the algorithm to test all the subpatterns of P to decide whether it has an occurrence in the text or not. However, comparing to our work, this paper focuses on innovating simple, less complicated and efficient algorithm that can exactly locate all occurrences of a given pattern P of length m with don't cares characters in a text S of length n based on selected suffixes of the *suffix tree* of S using a predefined simple equation to enable the *Kangaroo* method without using additional data structures. Furthermore, the test for each P comes logically coherent and sequential such that the test starts from the first subpattern of P, then it moves to the next subpattern as long as the previous test was successful, otherwise, it stops testing the remaining subpatterns of P to save the time of the algorithm and report that pattern does not exist.

3 Background and Problem Definition

3.1 Background

String and Substring. Let $S = S[1,n]$ be a string of length $|S| = n$ over an alphabet Σ of size $|\Sigma| = \sigma$. The empty string ε is the string of length 0. For $1 \leq i \leq j \leq n$, $S[i]$ denotes the ith symbol of S, and $S[i \ldots j]$ the contiguous sequence of symbols (called *factor* or *substring*) $S[i]S[i+1]\ldots S[j]$. A substring

$S[i \ldots j]$ is a suffix of S if $j = n$ and it is a prefix of S if $i = 1$. A string p is a *repeat* of $S \iff p$ has at least two occurrences in S. In addition p is said to be *right-maximal* in $S \iff$ there exist two positions $i < j$ such that $S[i, i + |p| - 1] = S[j, j + |p| - 1] = p$ and either $j + |p| = n + 1$ or $S[i, i + |p|] \neq S[j, j + |p|]$ [15,21].

Suffix Tree. The *suffix tree* T for a string S of length n over the alphabet Σ is a rooted directed compacted trie built on the set of suffixes of S. The suffix tree has n leaves and its internal nodes have at least two children whiles its edges are labelled with substrings of S. The labels of all outgoing edges from a given node start with a different character. All leaves of the suffix tree are labelled with an integer i, where $i \in \{1 \ldots n\}$ and the concatenation of the labels on the edges from the root to the leaf gives us the suffix of S which starts at position i. The nodes of the (non-compacted) trie which have branching nodes and leaves of the tree are called *explicit nodes*, while the others are called *implicit nodes*. The occurrence of a substring P in S is represented on T by either an explicit node or implicit node and called the *locus* of P. The *suffix tree* T can be constructed in $O(n)$ time and space. In order to have one-to-one correspondence between the suffixes of S and the leaves of T, a character $\$ \notin \Sigma$ is added to the end of the label edge for each suffix i to ensure that no suffix is a prefix of another suffix. To each node α in T is also associated an interval of leaves $[i..j]$, where $[i..j]$ is the set of labels of the leaves that have α as an ancestor (or the interval $[i..i]$ if α is a leaf labelled by i). The intervals associated with the children of α (if α is an internal node) form a partition of the interval associated with α (the intervals are disjoints sub-intervals of $[i..j]$ and their union equals $[i..j]$). For any internal node α in the *suffix tree* T, the concatenation of all edge labels in the path from the root to the node α is denoted by $\bar{\alpha}$ and the string depth of a node α is denoted by $|\bar{\alpha}|$ [2,17,21].

Definition 1. *The Lowest Common Ancestor (LCA) of two nodes u and v in a tree T is defined as the deepest node in T that is an ancestor of both u and v. This node, denote it by α, lies on all root to u and on all root to v path [18].*

Pattern Matching. In what follows, we assume that we are given a text S of length n and a pattern P of length m. The classical matching problem consists in locating all occurrences of P in S, that is, all possible i such that for all $j \in [1, m]$, $S[i + j - 1] = P[j]$. This problem has been extended by introducing "don't care" character as follows:

Definition 2. *A don't care character, denoted by '$*$' is a character such that $* \notin \Sigma$ and matches any character $\sigma \in \Sigma$ for all $\sigma \in \Sigma$ [22].*

3.2 Problem Definition

Given a text S over the alphabet Σ and a pattern P over the alphabet $\Sigma \cup \{*\}$. The problem is to find all the occurrences of P in S.

Example 1. Consider that we have the following text S over the alphabet Σ and a pattern of actions P over the alphabet $\Sigma \cup \{*\}$:

$S = ABXABGCABGCAFFBYBGAFABGCAFFBY$
$P = AB * CA * *BY$

As we note from the example, '$*$' can match any action in S, therefore the pattern of actions P has two occurrences in S at positions 7 and 20. Note that indexing the text starts from 0. Before describing our proposed solution, we will start by stating some useful lemmas.

Lemma 1. *Two sub-strings* $S[i, i+d-1]$ *and* $S[j, j+d-1]$ *are equal* $\Longleftrightarrow$ *they have the same locus in the suffix tree of* S *[2].*

Example 2. Consider the sequence S in example 1, and the pattern $P = ABGCAFFBY$. The pattern P has two occurrences in S at positions 7 and 20 ($S[7, 15], S[20, 28]$) and have the same locus on the suffix tree (Fig. 1) at suffixes 7 and 20.

Lemma 2. *If* X *is a subsequence of sequence* S*, then* X *is the deepest non leaf node from the root node, and* X *must be the longest common subsequence or the longest repeat subsequence [29].*

Example 3. As shown in Fig. 1, the subsequence $X = AB$ is the deepest non leaf node from the root node, and the longest common subsequence of length 2 for the suffixes $(0, 7, 20, 3)$. This also means that the subsequence X occurred 4 times in S.

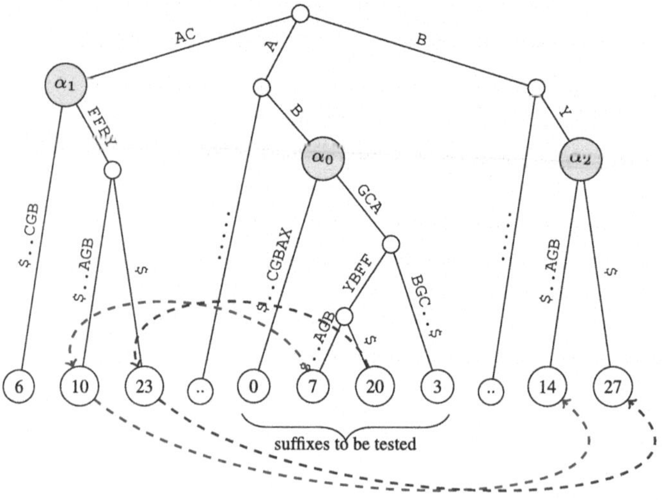

Fig. 1. Sub-tree of the suffix tree of the text S (see Example 1) and illustration of locating occurrences of the pattern $P = AB * CA * *BY$ in S using our method. The occurrences of pattern P in S are at (7 and 20).

Table 1. P_α array of pattern $P = AB * CA * *BY$

j	$\bar{\alpha}_j$	$\lvert\bar{\alpha}_j\rvert$	δ_j
0	AB	2	1
1	CA	2	2
2	BY	2	0

4 Detecting Pattern with "Don't Cares"

In a pattern with "don't cares" characters problem, we are given a string S of length n over the alphabet Σ and a pattern P of length m over the alphabet $\Sigma \cup \{*\}$ and have to find all occurrences of P in S efficiently. This problem can be solved using the *suffix tree* of S and *Kangaroo method* to find all occurrences of P with its sub-patterns in S. To find a pattern P with "don't cares" characters, it will be useful to define a pattern P having "don't cares" characters as follows:

Definition 3. *A pattern P with "don't cares" characters is a pattern consists of k subpatterns, where each subpattern P_j is a string over the alphabet $\Sigma \cup \{*\}$. For each $0 \leq j \leq k-1$, we have a pair $(|\bar{\alpha}_j|, \delta_j)$, where $|\bar{\alpha}_j|$ is the letters string length starting at position 0 at P_j and $\in \Sigma$, and δ_j is the "don't cares characters" length followed $|\bar{\alpha}_j|$ at P_j.*

For example: suppose we have $P = AB * CA * *BY$. We divide P into P_k sub-patterns as follows:

$$\text{AB}^*\text{CA}^{**}\text{BY} = P_0P_1P_2 = (|\bar{\alpha}_0|, \delta_0)(|\bar{\alpha}_1|, \delta_1)(|\bar{\alpha}_2|, \delta_2) = (2,1)(2,2)(2,0)$$

4.1 Kangaroo Method

Kangaroo approach is commonly used in string pattern matching with at most k mismatches. The *Kangaroo* method is usually used with a generalization *suffix tree* of $(P + T)$ and works on matching strings by using LCA (Lowest Common Ancestor) query on the *suffix tree*. More precisely, to match pattern P with text T_i with at most k mismatches, the LCP (Longest Common Prefix) between P and T_i is found by using LCA query in the suffix tree between the nodes representing P and T_i. The LCP ends either at the first mismatch between P and T_i at position q of P or one of the strings terminates. The first mismatch can be skipped using a *Kangaroo* jump in $O(1)$ time. To allow for another mismatch, another *Kangaroo* jump should be done from the suffix $q+1$ of P and suffix $i+q-1$ of T on the *suffix tree*. We continue on doing *Kangaroo* jumps until we hit the maximum number of mismatches in $O(k)$ time or one of the strings terminates [37]. Our algorithm uses a new simple and efficient approach such that it relies on constructing a suffix tree T for the text S only without using the generalization concept of $(P + T)$, and instead, the algorithm applies the *Kangaroo* jumps on chosen suffixes of the *suffix tree* using a predefined computational method to find all occurrences of the pattern P with "don't cares" in S, in a fast and effective manner.

4.2 Detecting Pattern with "Don't Cares"

The proposed algorithm starts by preprocessing the *suffix tree* T of text S and decomposing pattern P into k subpatterns $(P_0 \ldots P_{k-1})$ such that each subpattern consists of a pair $(|\bar{\alpha}_j|, \delta_j)$, where $|\bar{\alpha}_j|$ represents the letters string length of P_j over the alphabet Σ, δ_j represents the '*' length at P_j and k is the number of subpatterns, (see Algorithm 1 Step 2). The algorithm also, constructs an array P_α

of length k at the preprocessing phase which retains the letters of each subpattern P_j that corresponds to the label $\bar{\alpha}_j$ on the *suffix tree*, the label length $|\bar{\alpha}_j|$, the '*' length δ_j and indexed with a value of j, (see Table 1 for illustration). The algorithm proceeds into k phases. At the first phase, the algorithm traces the *suffix tree* T of S starting from the root to find the locus of the first subpattern α_0 of the label $P_\alpha[0,0]$, which is of length $|\bar{\alpha}_0|$. If the locus α_0 is found, the algorithm locates its associated suffixes interval $[i_s, i_e]$ such that α_0 is its ancestor and represents the longest common prefix for those suffixes (lemma 2), see (Steps 4–8). The associated suffixes interval $[i_s, i_e]$ represents the possible suffixes that the pattern P with "don't cares" characters occurs at one or more of them. To check the occurrence of pattern P, the remaining subpatterns $(P_1 \dots P_{k-1})$ of P should be found on the tree. To do so, for each $l \in [i_s, i_e]$, the algorithm applies the *Kangaroo* method (Steps 10–11) such that it starts from the suffix l and find the next suffix d of the subpattern P_1 by adding the suffix number l to the label length $|\bar{\alpha}_0|$ and "don't cares" length δ_0 on the tree as follows:

$$l + |\bar{\alpha}_0| + \delta_0 = d$$

Next, the algorithm jumps to the suffix d, where $d \in [1 \dots n]$ suffixes of the tree and a query runs at this suffix starting from the root of T to test the label existence of the next subpattern $P_\alpha[1,0]$ where its locus is α_1 and of length $|\bar{\alpha}_1|$. If the returned result of the query is true, then a second *Kangaroo* jump should be done at the suffix (d) to go to the next suffix $(d+1)$ to test the next subpattern P_{j+1} by adding the suffix number d to the label length of the previous subpattern $|\bar{\alpha}_j|$ and "don't cares" length δ_j on the tree as follows (Steps 16–29):

$$d + |\bar{\alpha}_j| + \delta_j = d + 1$$

The algorithm will continue to do this procedure until it achieves the query of the last subpattern P_{k-1} and an occurrence is reported at l (Steps 30–33). At any phase the algorithm fails in testing l such that the query returns false, the algorithm stops testing l (Steps 26–27) and proceeds to test the next l in the suffixes interval $[i_s, i_e]$ which saves the time of the algorithm and can find all occurrences of the pattern P in a faster and effective way. Figure 1 illustrates our algorithm in finding the occurrence(s) of pattern P on the suffix tree of text S (which is given in Example 1). At this example, the algorithm divides pattern P into 3 subpatterns and builds the *suffix tree* of S as a preliminary stage. Then, starts with the first subpattern P_0 to find its locus on the *suffix tree* which is denoted by α_0 and represents the label at $P_\alpha[0,0]$. Afterwards, it locates its associated suffixes subset where "*AB*" is its ancestor which are $[0,7,20,3]$. Then, for each $l \in [0,7,20,3]$, the algorithm conducts a testing for the occurrence of pattern P using the equation in (Algorithm 1 Step 19) where it calculates the next suffix that the algorithm should jump to test the next subpattern existence. This can be done by adding the length of $|\bar{\alpha}_{j-1}|$ and δ_{j-1} to the current suffix being tested. At our example, pattern P has two occurrences at suffix 7 (which its *Kangaroo* jumps illustrated using blue dotted curve) and at suffix 20 (which its *Kangaroo* jumps illustrated using violet dotted curve) but has no occurrence at suffixes 0 and 3. For further clarification, at suffix 7, the algorithm computes the next suffix d to jump which is 10 $(7 + 2 + 1)$, and it inquiries the occurrence of the subpattern $P_\alpha[1, 0]$ at suffix 10 which is found at locus α_1. Next, a second jump should be done to the next suffix $d+1$ which is 14 $(10+2+2)$ and a second query at this suffix runs to test the existence of $P_\alpha[2, 0]$ where the returned result is true and the locus is α_2. At the end, an occurrence of the pattern P is reported at the current suffix l being tested which is 7. The efficiency of our algorithm lies on testing only subset of the suffixes of the suffix tree T of S. In addition to, testing only the alphabetic part of each subpattern without caring of "don't cares" symbols, which shortens the search process and thus reduces the search time. Furthermore, the test for each pattern P in terms of its subpatterns is conducting sequentially such that the pattern test starts from the first subpattern of P, then it moves to the next subpattern as long as the previous test was successful, otherwise, it does not require completion of the remaining subpatterns, which improves the search efficiency. We have thus obtained the following theorems.

Algorithm 1. Detect Pattern P with Don't Cares in text S

Input: Text string S, Pattern P with Don't Cares
Output: $P\_occ[]$: all suffixes where P has an occurrence in S

```
procedure LOCATE PATTERN P WITH DON'T CARES IN TEXT S
▷ Phase 0: (Preprocessing)
    - Build Suffix Tree T of S
    - Decompose pattern P into sub-patterns (P_0 ... P_{k-1}), where each P_j = (|ᾱ_j|, δ_j) and 0 ≤ j ≤ k − 1,
      k = no. of sub-patterns
    - Build an array P_α indexed j = (0 ... k − 1), where P_α[j, 0] = ᾱ_j, P_α[j, 1] = |ᾱ_j| and P_α[j, 2] = δ_j
▷ Phase 1: (Find Occ (P_0))
  Start from the root T
  Find the locus α_0 of P_α[0, 0]
  if (found) then
      Locate the associated suffixes interval [i_s, i_e] where the locus α_0 is its ancestor
      occ ← 0
      // Find all occurrences of P in S
       for each l ∈ [i_s, i_e]
       go to Phase 2
   else                                                              ▷ P is not found
       exit matching
   end if
▷ Phase 2: (Find Occ (P_1 ... P_{k-1}))
   j ← 1
   d_0 ← l
   while (j ≤ k − 1) do
       d_1 ← d_0 + |ᾱ_{j-1}| + δ_{j-1}               ▷ d_1 ← d_0 + P_α[j − 1, 1] + P_α[j − 1, 2]
       go to suffix (d_1)                                          ▷ Kangaroo jump
       Start from the root T
       Find the locus α_j of P_α[j, 0]
       if (found) then
           j ← j + 1
           d_0 ← d_1
       else
           exit                          ▷ there is no occurrence for pattern P at suffix l
       end if
   end while
   if (j = k) then
       P_occ[occ] ← l                          ▷ there is an occurrence at suffix l
       occ ← occ + 1
   end if
end procedure
```

Theorem 1. *Given a text S over the alphabet Σ of length n and a pattern P over the alphabet $\Sigma \cup \{*\}$ of length m, we can compute the occurrence of P in S in $O(n+m+k)$ time complexity, where k is the total number of the subpatterns of P.* □

Proof. Let us analyse the time complexity of Algorithm 1. *Phase* 0, is the preprocessing stage which consists of constructing the suffix tree of sequence S of length n in $O(n)$ linear time and space using linear algorithm [35], decomposing pattern P of length m into k subpatterns in $O(m)$ time, and then storing them in an indexed two dimensional array P_α of length k which requires $3k$ space as each subpattern is split into ($|\bar{\alpha}|$ and δ) with $\bar{\alpha}$. Given that, the time requires to access an index array is $O(1)$ time, and the time requires to answer the lowest common ancestor (LCA) on the suffix tree is $O(1)$ time [34], we analyse the rest of the algorithm as follows. At *Phase* 1, after the algorithm finds the locus of the first subpattern P_0 of P of length $|\bar{\alpha_0}|$, it uses the (for) loop to test l selected suffixes of the suffix tree in $O(l)$ time. For each l tested, *Phase* 2 should be implemented to find the occurrences of remaining subpatterns $(P_1 \dots P_{k-1})$. Here, we have three possibilities. **Case 1**, the pattern P is exist in the text and therefore the (while) loop will be executed $(k-1)$ times which is the case for finding the pattern in the text. Knowing that $(k-1)$ kangaroo jumps should be executed at this case, where at each kangaroo jump, the algorithm runs the LCA query at the current suffix that it moved to in total $O(k-1)$ time. Therefore, the time required for this case is $O(k-1)$. **Case 2**, when only the first q subpatterns are found, the algorithm will exit the while loop after testing subpattern $(q+1)$ which means that there is no occurrence for the pattern P in S. Therefore, the time required for this case is $O(q)$. **Case 3**, When only the first subpattern P_0 is located at phase 1, but there is no occurrence for the remaining $(k-1)$ subpatterns. At this case, the (while) loop will be executed only once at phase 2, and the time is $O(1)$ which is considered as an efficient time for the execution time when the pattern is not part of the text, and the algorithm requires no completion on testing the remaining of subpatterns which saves the time of the algorithm. Therefore, the time required for this case is $O(1)$ time. Since we are interested in the degree of the function $f(n)$ for the algorithm which is related to the execution time of the statements inside the (for) loop, we will ignore l. Hence, the time complexity of Algorithm 1 is $O(n+m+k)$ for the **Case 1**, $O(n+m+q)$ for the **Case 2** and $O(n+m)$ for the **Case 3**. □

According to Theorem 1, we can conclude our next theorem to find all occurrences of pattern P with "don't cares" in text S as follows.

Theorem 2. *Given a text S over the alphabet Σ of length n and a pattern P over the alphabet $\Sigma \cup \{*\}$ of length m, we can compute all occurrences of P in S in $O(n+m+k+occ(P))$ time complexity, where k is the total number of the subpatterns of P and $occ(P)$ is the total number of occurrences of P in S.* □

5 Conclusion

We have introduced our simple and efficient method which can find all the occurrences of pattern P with "don't cares" in text S. This problem is interesting as a fundamental computer science problem and is a basic need for many applications which are concerned with the occurrence of the subsequence of the original pattern sequence. In response, we designed our algorithm using linear space and time data structure with help of the *Kangaroo* method such that be able to test only selected suffixes of the *suffix tree* of S in a fast and effective way. Comparing to the work in [22] and to the others described in the related work, our algorithm adopted the logical sequential approach for testing each pattern P such that the test starts from the first subpattern of P, then it moves to the next subpattern as long as the previous test was successful which saves the time of the algorithm and speeds up the locating process. The interesting issues that will be studied in our future work are, improving our work to detect patterns with "don't cares" and errors from the text, and detecting patterns from a text contains "don't cares" characters, while maintaining our goal of the algorithm simplicity and efficiency.

References

1. Aho, A.V., Corasick, M.J.: Efficient string matching: an aid to bibliographic search. Commun. ACM **18**(6), 333–340 (1975)
2. Alamro, H., Badkobeh, G., Belazzougui, D., Iliopoulos, C.S., Puglisi, S.J.: Computing the antiperiod (s) of a string. In: 30th Annual Symposium on Combinatorial Pattern Matching (CPM 2019). Schloss Dagstuhl-Leibniz-Zentrum fuer Informatik (2019)
3. Alstrup, S., Husfeldt, T., Rauhe, T.: Marked ancestor problems. In: Proceedings 39th Annual Symposium on Foundations of Computer Science (Cat. no. 98CB36280), pp. 534–543. IEEE (1998)
4. Amir, A., Lewenstein, M., Porat, E.: Faster algorithms for string matching with k mismatches. J. Algorithms **50**(2), 257–275 (2004)
5. Bille, P., Gørtz, I.L., Vildhøj, H.W., Vind, S.: String indexing for patterns with wildcards. Theory Comput. Syst. **55**(1), 41–60 (2014)
6. Boyer, R.S., Moore, J.S.: A fast string searching algorithm. Commun. ACM **20**(10), 762–772 (1977). https://doi.org/10.1145/359842.359859
7. Chen, G., Wu, X., Zhu, X., Arslan, A.N., He, Y.: Efficient string matching with wildcards and length constraints. Knowl. Inf. Syst. **10**(4), 399–419 (2006)
8. Clifford, R., Efremenko, K., Porat, E., Rothschild, A.: Pattern matching with don't cares and few errors. J. Comput. Syst. Sci. **76**(2), 115–124 (2010)
9. Clifford, R., Porat, E.: A filtering algorithm for k-mismatch with don't cares. In: International Symposium on String Processing and Information Retrieval, pp. 130–136. Springer (2007)
10. Cole, R., Gottlieb, L.A., Lewenstein, M.: Dictionary matching and indexing with errors and don't cares. In: Proceedings of the Thirty-Sixth Annual ACM Symposium on Theory of Computing, pp. 91–100 (2004)
11. Cole, R., Hariharan, R.: Approximate string matching: a simpler faster algorithm. SIAM J. Comput. **31**(6), 1761–1782 (2002)

12. Cole, R., Hariharan, R.: Verifying candidate matches in sparse and wildcard matching. In: Proceedings of the Thirty-Fourth Annual ACM Symposium on Theory of Computing, pp. 592–601 (2002)
13. Commentz-Walter, B.: A string matching algorithm fast on the average. In: International Colloquium on Automata, Languages, and Programming, pp. 118–132. Springer (1979)
14. Crochemore, M., Hancart, C.: Pattern matching in strings. In: Mikhail, J.A. (ed.) Algorithms and Theory of Computation Handbook, pp. 11.1–11.28. CRC Press (1998). https://hal-upec-upem.archives-ouvertes.fr/hal-00620790
15. Crochemore, M., Hancart, C., Lecroq, T.: Algorithms on Strings. Cambridge University Press, Cambridge (2007)
16. Crochemore, M., Perrin, D.: Pattern matching in strings. In: Image Analysis and Processing II, pp. 67–79. Springer (1988)
17. Farach, M.: Optimal suffix tree construction with large alphabets. In: Proceedings 38th Annual Symposium on Foundations of Computer Science, pp. 137–143. IEEE (1997)
18. Fischer, J., Huson, D.H.: New common ancestor problems in trees and directed acyclic graphs. Inf. Process. Lett. **110**(8–9), 331–335 (2010)
19. Fischer, M.J., Paterson, M.S.: String-matching and other products. Tech. rep. Massachusetts Institute of Technology, Cambridge Project MAC (1974)
20. Galil, Z., Giancarlo, R.: Improved string matching with k mismatches. ACM SIGACT News **17**(4), 52–54 (1986)
21. Gusfield, D.: Algorithms on stings, trees, and sequences: computer science and computational biology. ACM SIGACT News **28**(4), 41–60 (1997)
22. Iliopoulos, C.S., Rahman, M.S.: Pattern matching algorithms with don't cares. In: Proceedings of 33rd SOFSEM, pp. 116–126 (2007)
23. Indyk, P.: Faster algorithms for string matching problems: matching the convolution bound. In: Proceedings 39th Annual Symposium on Foundations of Computer Science (Cat. no. 98CB36280), pp. 166–173. IEEE (1998)
24. Kalai, A.T.: Efficient pattern-matching with don't cares. In: SODA 2002 Proceedings of the Thirteenth Annual ACM-SIAM Symposium on Discrete Algorithms, pp. 655–656. ACM Press (January 2002). https://www.microsoft.com/en-us/research/publication/efficient-pattern-matching-dont-cares/
25. Karp, R.M., Rabin, M.O.: Efficient randomized pattern-matching algorithms. IBM J. Res. Dev. **31**(2), 249–260 (1987)
26. Knuth, D.E., Morris Jr., J.H., Pratt, V.R.: Fast pattern matching in strings. SIAM J. Comput. **6**(2), 323–350 (1977)
27. Lam, T.W., Sung, W.K., Tam, S.L., Yiu, S.M.: Space efficient indexes for string matching with don't cares. In: International Symposium on Algorithms and Computation, pp. 846–857. Springer (2007)
28. Landau, G.M., Vishkin, U.: Fast parallel and serial approximate string matching. J. Algorithms **10**(2), 157–169 (1989)
29. Liu, N., Xie, F., Wu, X.: Multi-pattern matching with variable-length wildcards using suffix tree. Pattern Anal. Appl. **21**(4), 1151–1165 (2018)
30. Nicolae, M., Rajasekaran, S.: On pattern matching with k mismatches and few don't cares. Inf. Process. Lett. **118**, 78–82 (2017)
31. Pinter, R.Y.: Efficient string matching with don't-care patterns. In: Combinatorial Algorithms on Words, pp. 11–29. Springer (1985)
32. Rahman, M.S., Iliopoulos, C.S., Lee, I., Mohamed, M., Smyth, W.F.: Finding patterns with variable length gaps or don't cares. In: International Computing and Combinatorics Conference, pp. 146–155. Springer (2006)

33. Sahinalp, S.C., Vishkin, U.: Efficient approximate and dynamic matching of patterns using a labeling paradigm. In: Proceedings of 37th Conference on Foundations of Computer Science, pp. 320–328. IEEE (1996)
34. Sung, W.K.: Algorithms in Bioinformatics: A Practical Introduction. CRC Press, Boca Raton (2009)
35. Ukkonen, E.: On-line construction of suffix trees. Algorithmica **14**(3), 249–260 (1995)
36. Wu, S., Manber, U., et al.: A fast algorithm for multi-pattern searching. University of Arizona, Department of Computer Science (1994)
37. Ziviani, N., Baeza-Yates, R.: String processing and information retrieval. In: 14th International Symposium, SPIRE 2007 Santiago, Chile, October 29–31, 2007 Proceedings, vol. 4726. Springer (2007)

Eye Movement Data Analysis

Olga Georgieva[1(✉)], Nadejda Bocheva[2], Bilyana Genova[2], and Miroslava Stefanova[2]

[1] Faculty of Mathematics and Informatics, Sofia University "St. Kliment Ohridski", 5 James Bourchier Blvd., 1164 Sofia, Bulgaria
o.georgieva@fmi.uni-sofia.bg

[2] Institute of Neurobiology, Bulgarian Academy of Sciences, 1113 Sofia, Bulgaria
nadya@percept.bas.bg

Abstract. The aim of the present study is to investigate the separation abilities of three statistical parameters for grouping participants in the visual-motor experiment by their age and gender. These parameters represent different characteristics of the decision-making process and were determined by applying the hierarchical drift diffusion model to the response time and accuracy of the experimental data [1]. The objective function cluster analysis was applied to explore distinct data spaces formed by the parameters' data. The ability for grouping is assessed and interpreted according to the differences in the subjects' capabilities to perform the visuo-motor task. The study compares the conclusions based by drift-diffusion model using Bayesian parameter estimation with those based on the cluster analysis in terms of ability to distinguish the performance of different age groups. The investigation of gender effects are uniquely investigated by cluster analysis technique.

Keywords: Decision making · Visuo-motor task · Cluster analysis · Fuzzy clustering

1 Introduction

A significant part of the brain studies concerns the revealing existing dependencies of the biosignal parameters. The common implementation base of these purposes is the new generation of communication devices as well as the new information technologies. The problem of research is to investigate and apply an appropriate algorithm for data processing enabling information retrieval in order to bring significant information about the existing dependencies of the brain activity [10, 12].

The potential of the unsupervised learning algorithms as cluster analysis could be considered as possible alternative for biosignal discrimination. These methods are powerful in dealing with complex and uncertain information. They find groups within the data and thus conclude about existing relations and features among them. Different brain states have been benefited by this approach as a basis for theoretical and experimental evidence for a scientific forecast of the human condition [10, 11].

L. Iliadis et al. (Eds.): EANN 2020, INNS 2, pp. 460–470, 2020.
https://doi.org/10.1007/978-3-030-48791-1_36

The process of human decision making involves a multitude of processes - from coding stimulus information to organizing a response based on the decision choice. A successful approach to separate the contribution of these processes is the drift diffusion model [5–9]. The model is applicable for two-choice decision tasks and assumes that the decision is reached by sequential accumulation of evidence in support of the two decision choices. It combines the information about the accuracy and the speed of performance and decomposes the processes not related to the decision in a separate parameter (t-c) that describes the time needed to code the stimulus information and prepare the response. The model assumes that the evidence in support of the two possible choices accumulates in time and this process is noisy. The speed of evidence accumulation depends on the task difficulty and is characterized by a parameter labelled drift rate (v-c). An additional parameter (a-c) describes the balance between the accuracy and speed of the response representing the decision boundary between the two choices – if this boundary is large, more time is needed to make a choice, however, the probability of accidental errors diminishes. If there is no imbalance in stimulus presentation or a bias in selecting one choice more often, the starting point of evidence accumulation is at the middle of the boundary between the two choices. However, all main parameters of the model have variability due to instability to keep a constant criterion in the decision process, the random variations in evidence accumulation from trial to trial and the variability in the non-decision processes.

A Python toolbox named Hierarchical Drift Diffusion Model (HDDM) [13] applies the drift-diffusion model by using Bayesian parameter estimation. It is flexible, allows estimation of both individual and group parameters, tolerates missing values and requires less data to estimate model parameters. However, coding mixed-effects models with the toolbox is a challenge. In certain cases, it is quite difficult to evaluate the interaction of between-subject factors. More complex models are also time-consuming.

In this study we try to evaluate whether, based on the parameters evaluated by HDDM, it is possible to estimate the contribution of other between-subject factors, not included in the analysis and to obtain additional information about different characteristics of the stimulus conditions or experimental groups. The first part of the study compares the conclusions based on the hypothesis testing in the HDDM with those based on the application of a methodology by clustering algorithm about the informativeness of different experimental conditions and respective parameters of the drift diffusion model. The assessment focuses the ability to distinguish the performance of different age groups. The last study part extracts information about gender effects and their interaction with age that were not assessed by the HDDM.

2 Data Description

Data from four types of visual experiments have been examined. Three types of movements and one static condition were used. The stimuli were the so-called glass patterns. They are generated by repeating the initial dot pattern after being transformed by a certain rule e.g. all points are offset or rotated at a certain angle or offset from the center of the set. In this way a pattern is formed in which each point is paired with another. In our experiments, the points were offset from a given center, but it was displaced from the mid-point of the image in a horizontal direction. The pairs of dots are relatively close together (at a distance of 60 pixels = 2 cm) and rotated in such a way that if connected with a line, most lines would intersect at the displaced center of the pattern. Out of 25 pairs of points (50 points in total) 18 pointed to the center of the pattern, and 7 pairs were randomly oriented (this is called coherence of 72%). This description corresponds to the static condition in the experiments.

The other conditions used are combined, flicker and motion. In all of them the lifetime of the dots was three frames (100 ms). In the flicker condition, one-third of the pairs are re-generated elsewhere on every frame keeping their initial orientation. This gives the impression of movement, but it is not related to the orientation of the pairs. In the combined condition, the pairs move in the direction of their orientation, so that those pointing to the center of the set move away from it and the others (7) move in a random direction. Again, each frame updates the position of one-third of the pairs. In motion condition, there are no pairs, and 18×2 (36) points in the pattern move away from a common center, while the remaining 7×2 (14) move randomly.

Data of 35 observers participating in the four experiments were collected. The subjects are classified in three age groups: 12 young (19 to 34 years, median = 23 years); 11 middle aged (36 to 52 years, median = 44 years); 12 old (57 to 84 years, median = 72) having a parity representation of both sexes in each group. Each pattern was presented to each participant 20 times in random order. Each condition was performed on a separate day. The task of the participants was to determine whether the center of the patterns was to the left or to the right of the screen. They had to make a saccade to the perceived pattern center and to press a mouse button according to their decision.

3 Methodology

The present study aims to analyze the capabilities to extract information based on statistical parameters, which represent the relationship between the accuracy of the response and the response time when examining data from eye saccade movements in the visuo-motor task. The problem needs to explore different spaces formed by these data in order to answer which parameters best define the difference between the age groups, as well as to assess the impact of the gender on their performance abilities.

For this search the raw data of the four experiments were processed to calculate the statistical characteristics related to decisions in a two-choice task determined by applying the HDDM to the response time and accuracy of the experimental task [1]. These parameters represent different properties of the decision-making process:

A) Time data not related to decision making processes, t-c. It represents the time needed for coding the stimulus information and for organizing motor response.
B) Boundary between the two alternatives, a-c in decision. This parameter represents the individual willingness for higher accuracy or faster speed.
C) Rate of accumulation of evidence about the two alternatives, v-c.

Two types of data spaces could be organized to reveal different information:

1. The separation abilities of each parameter: t-c, a-c and v-c, could be investigated by processing the corresponding four-dimensional space formed by each parameter data obtained via all four experiments.
2. The distinguishing ability of each experiment namely static, combined, flicker and motion, could be discovered by processing the corresponding three-dimensional data space formed by the data of the parameters t-c, a-c and v-c obtained for the respective experiment.

Our understanding is that clustering based on the parameters data characterizes the decision-making process, whereas clustering by movement types - performance accuracy related to the task difficulty. Exploring the structure of these spaces by determining significant data groups we would be able to detect the influence of the separate characteristics of the calculated parameters as well as the condition - combined, motion, flicker, static on separating the contribution of the age and gender on the decision process. Due to the lack of a reference model, studies of these data spaces can be carried out using unsupervised learning methods as cluster analysis. For each formed data space the research procedure follows several steps:

a) Data clustering;
b) Evaluation of clustering quality to find the optimal number of clusters;
c) Comparative analysis of the obtained grouping;
d) Visualization and interpretation of the results.

According to the preliminary investigations the data do not present clear structure due to the complexity of the visuo-motor factors' dependencies. In this situation, an effective solution could be found by methods of objective function clustering. These are methods based on optimization of clustering criterion for desirable separation. The clusters are described by their center, which is a point in the data space that is most representative for the cluster in probabilistic sense. Further, we apply fuzzy clustering technique as a good opportunity to deal with uncertainty of the spaces. Its advantage is that it assesses belonging, as well as the degree of belonging to the distinct clusters.

Fuzzy-C-Means* (*FCM*) *Algorithm

Fuzzy clustering technique is particularly successful in partitioning not well separated data groups with vague and uncertain boundaries. Every point of the data space belongs to the clusters with degree of membership, which is a value between 0 and 1. If the data is close to the cluster center, the membership degree is closer to one. FCM is an objective function-based algorithm with clustering criteria J that minimizes the following sum [4]:

$$J = \sum_{i=1}^{c} \sum_{k=1}^{N} u_{ik}^{m} \|x_k - v_i\|^2, \tag{1}$$

where u_{ik} denotes the membership degree of the data point x_k, $k = 1, \ldots, N$, to the i-th cluster center v_i, $i = 1, \ldots, c$. Here N is the number of data in the data space and c is the number of clusters. The coefficient $m \in [1, \infty)$ determines how much clusters may overlap and its default value is $m = 2$. As we don't have a preliminary knowledge about the shape and orientation of the searched clusters, Euclidean distance is incorporated as a data distance measure of (1).

Quality of Clustering
Several indexes are calculated to evaluate the quality of clustering:

1) Average within cluster distance (AWCD) value estimates the data distances to the cluster center in the clusters. Minimum value is preferred, however the "knee" principle is applied to determine the best clustering for a given data space.

$$\mathrm{AWCD} = \frac{1}{c}\sum_{i=1}^{c} \frac{\sum_{k=1}^{N} u_{ik}^{m} u \|x_k - v_i\|^{m}}{\sum_{k=1}^{N} u_{ik}^{m}} \tag{2}$$

2) Average partition density (APD) assesses the density of the clusters. An index measures the fuzziness of the partition but without considering the data set itself. Good partitions are indicated by large values of APD.

$$APD = \frac{1}{c}\sum_{i=1}^{c} \frac{S_i}{\sum_{k=1}^{N} u_{ik}}, \tag{3}$$

where $S_i = \sum_{k=1}^{N} u_{ik}$ for every point k that $(x_k - v_i)(x_k - v_i)^T < 1$.

3) The cluster volume, V_i, $i = 1,.., c$, is calculated by a sum of the memberships values that form the cluster. Maximum value indicates better clustering.

The AWCD, APD and V_i indexes are parameters that evaluate the quality of the obtained data grouping itself, but not the classification capabilities of the obtained grouping. In order to assess the extent to which the obtained clusters cover actually existing groups in data in terms to the age and gender, it is necessary to account for the degrees of affiliation of the subject data to each cluster presented. As all data belong to all clusters in order to evaluate the subject affiliation the maximum degree of membership is taken to determine the affiliation to a particular cluster.

4 Results and Analysis

Results of FCM application to the four-dimensional data spaces of each experimental parameter: t-c, a-c, v-c, are considered.

4.1 Age Grouping Assessment

The obtained values for AWCD and APD indexes allow to set appropriate data separation among division in 2, 3, 4 and 5 clusters as well as to compare the three studied data spaces t-c, a-c, v-c (Table 1). Best clustering in terms of group compactness, which means better informativeness, is identified in space t-c as the APD index takes highest values, followed by space v-c. The least informative is the space a-c. This result means that the parameter that could best distinguishes the age of the participants in a decision making task is the time needed for coding the stimulus information and for organizing motor response. The parameters that are directly involved in making a decision like the rate of evidence accumulation or the boundary between the two choices are less informative for this task.

The results of AWCD enable to set the proper number of clusters. However, this answer is not straightforward. By applying the knee method to all data spaces we found that most representative is clustering in 3 and 4 clusters. Bearing in mind the number of data, division in more than five clusters does not give reliable information.

Table 1. Clustering indexes results of the distinct parameters

Index \c	2	3	4	5
t-c data space				
AWCD	0,279133	0,179799	0,129162	0,053895
APD	0,887900	0,886915	0,910591	0,913007
a-c data space				
AWCD	0,710794	0,489768	0,377499	0,261670
APD	0,638586	0,766424	0,769378	0,779237
v-c data space				
AWCD	0,555400	0,351397	0,270981	0,217894
APD	0,752245	0,855247	0,827687	0,851103

Further consideration of t-c data space division as most informative one could reveal more existing dependences. Thus, when dividing into three clusters, the interpretability of the results is directly referred to the three studied age subjects groups, whereas at c = 4 three significant clusters and one of outliers could be discussed.

The coordinates of the cluster centers give us some more inside information about the obtained grouping (Table 2). For separation in three clusters, c = 3, the first cluster comprises most of the young and part of the middle aged adults, the second cluster includes part of the elderly people and the third - most of the elderly and part of the middle aged subjects. This division is not able to recognize the middle aged persons, whereas the two others – young and old, are well defined. The division in four clusters, c = 4, identifies well the young and old people as the first cluster comprises only young people and the fourth cluster includes only elderly people. The second cluster is formed mostly by middle aged; the third one is mostly formed by old subjects.

Table 2. Cluster centers of t-c parameter data clustering grouped into 3 and 4 clusters

c	Combined	Flicker	Motion	Static	c	Combined	Flicker	Motion	Static
1	0,3219	0,3314	0,3340	0,3264	1	0,2786	0,2589	0,2479	0,2534
2	0,9736	1,0641	1,3208	0,6849	2	0,3993	0,4169	0,4737	0,4298
3	0,5477	0,5353	0,5965	0,5439	3	0,5865	0,5795	0,6284	0,5729
	–	–	–	–	4	0,9609	1,0519	1,3070	0,7344

It could be summarized that the middle aged group is difficult to distinguish, especially when separation is in three clusters. The elderly group is more scattered than the young one in both clustering (Fig. 1). According to the cluster centers values, the dynamic conditions better distinguish participants then the static one. In particular, best one is motion condition, where no form information (e.g., orientation grouping) is presented. This implies that the absence of form information (no orientation grouping) in the visual motion task allows better separation of the age groups.

In order to assess the extent to which the obtained clusters cover actually existing data groups formed by the age and gender, it is necessary to account for the degrees of membership of each person's data to each cluster obtained. The maximum degree of membership determines the affiliation with a particular cluster. The affiliation of participants from different age groups to a cluster for each of the studied spaces in 4 clusters is presented in Figs. 1, 2 and 3, where young subjects' data are in pink, in green are data of the middle group and in blue – elderly subjects. Each examined person is represented by a line connecting it to the center of a cluster. The length of the line corresponds to the degree of membership to that cluster.

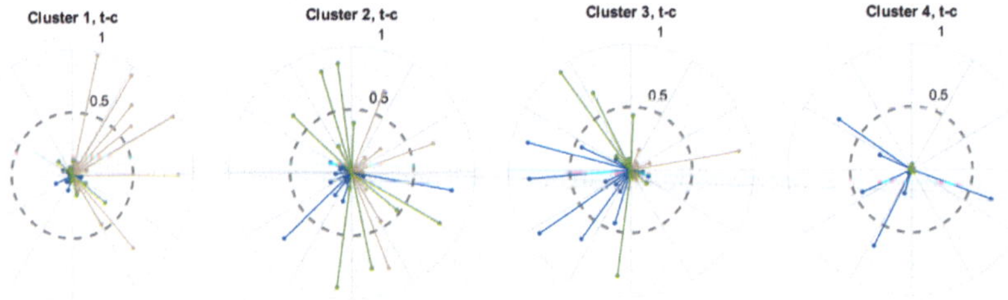

Fig. 1. Clustering in 4 clusters based on t-c: time unrelated to the decision-making process.

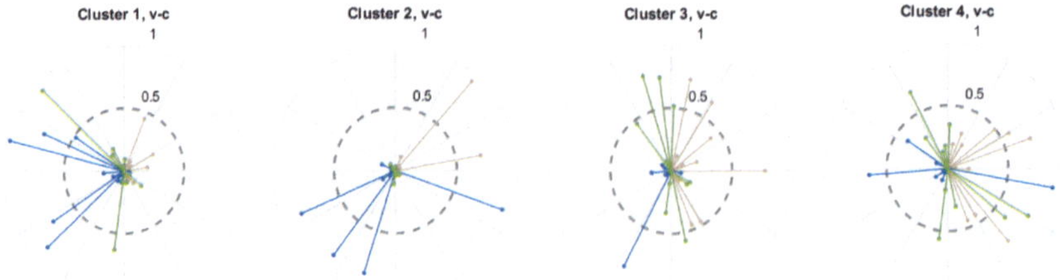

Fig. 2. Clustering in 4 clusters via v-c: rate of information accumulation for the two alternatives.

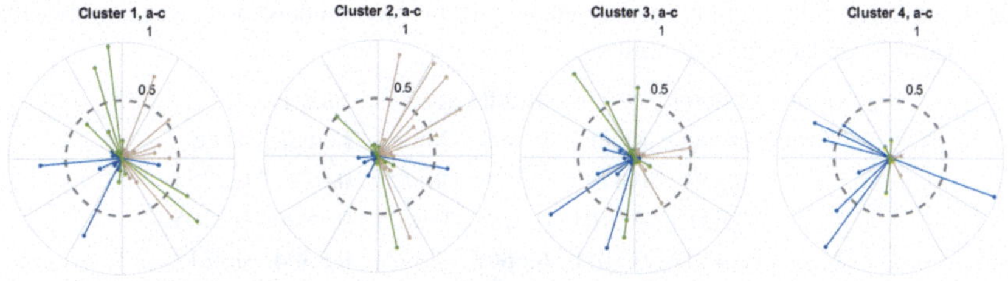

Fig. 3. Clustering in 4 clusters based on a-c: the boundary between the two alternatives

The results of three-dimensional spaces organized for the data of the different conditions of the experiments are less informative and will not be presented here.

4.2 Gender Grouping Assessment

The assessment of the gender differentiation of the subjects participated in the visual experiments can be done by the grouping of the four-dimensional space. For this purpose, the volume of clusters, V_i, $i = 1, c$ formed from the data for the two genders are compared. The respective relative volume values are calculated in order to account for the different number of female and male participants in each group.

Relative value of the cluster volumes of t-c data set separation shows that males are more represented in the clusters of young people and part of the middle-aged, whereas women predominantly form the cluster of elderly. The bold values at Table 3 present the highest volume for each gender for separation in 3 and 4 clusters, respectively.

Table 3. Relative values of the cluster volumes for the two genders of t-c data clustering

	c = 3			c = 4	
Cluster	Female	Male	Cluster	Female	Male
1	0,3019	**0,5844**	1	0,1598	0,3268
2	0,1544	0,0834	2	0,3178	**0,4033**
3	**0,5438**	0,3322	3	**0,3855**	0,2110
			4	0,1369	0,0589

By the same method the two genders are distinguished for each group separately (Table 4). Again, female are less likely to form the group of young people, while male are strongly represented in it: 0,559 vs. 0,8799 for division into 3 clusters and 0,3645 vs. 0,6945 for division into 4 clusters. Conversely, women more strongly form the elderly group, whereas male are less represented. These results are visible at Fig. 4a and b. The interaction between age and gender obtained here for a task of decision making based on dynamic visual information is in agreement with previous data analysis on motion direction discrimination [2].

Table 4. Relative volumes of clusters calculated for the two genders in t-c space; a) division in three clusters; b) division in four clusters

a)	Young		Middle aged		Elderly	
Cluster	Female	Male	Female	Male	Female	Male
1	**0,559**	**0,8799**	0,3104	**0,5859**	0,079	0,2384
2	0,0213	0,0191	0,0291	0,0211	0,3906	0,2105
3	0,4197	0,1011	**0,6605**	0,3931	**0,5304**	**0,5511**
b)	Young		Middle aged		Elderly	
Cluster	Female	Male	Female	Male	Female	Male
1	**0,3645**	**0,6957**	0,1048	0,0969	0,0443	0,0881
2	0,3223	0,2507	**0,4896**	**0,6369**	0,109	**0,3866**
3	0,2614	0,0444	0,3853	0,2572	**0,4891**	0,3669
4	0,0118	0,0092	0,0204	0,0091	0,3576	0,1585

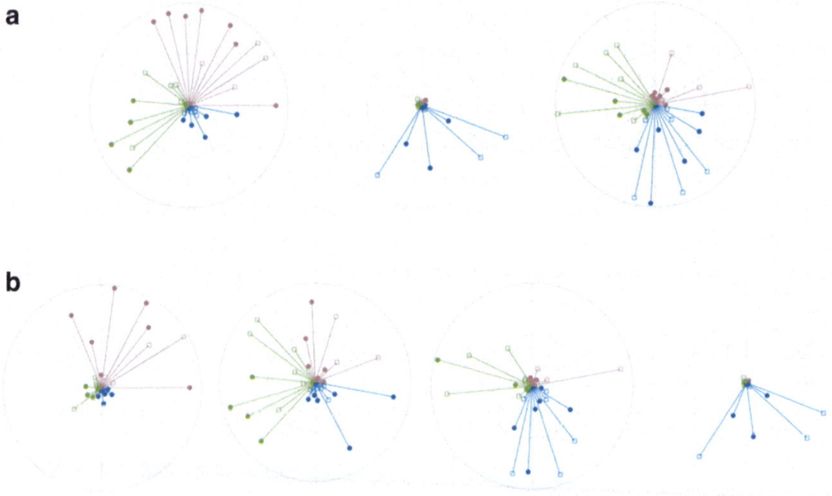

Fig. 4. a. Gender distribution for division into 3 clusters of t-c groups of young (pink), middle aged (green) and elderly (blue); female - empty square, male - filled circles. b. Gender distribution for division into 4 clusters of t-c groups of young (pink), middle aged (green) and elderly (blue); female - empty square, male - filled circles.

5 Conclusion

The results shown can be used to account for existing dependencies in the age and gender to deal with the visual decision making task. The accuracy of the responses for different types of stimuli and reaction time are accounted for. The results of separating the age groups based on the values of the parameters of the drift diffusion model are in agreement with the conclusions based on the probability to distinguish the three age groups in the different tasks obtained by the HDDM [1]. In our experimental condition the non-decision time provides better separation of the age groups than any other parameter. In single experiments Ratcliff and colleagues found that the boundary separation and the non-decision time distinguish most the young and the old participants [9]. They showed that the non-decision time is the parameter that correlates most between the different studies with the same participants. This result may imply that the non-decision time is the most stable individual characteristic of the participants in the two-choice decision tasks.

Our findings suggest that the differences in the experimental conditions in a common task significantly affect various aspects of the process of decision making and allow separating the participants in the experiments by some individual characteristics in the space of the HDDM parameters. The correspondence of the conclusions based on the HDDM and the clustering data of our study validates the possibility to complement the analysis of the subjects' performance in two-choice decision tasks by method based on fuzzy clustering analysis. The application of this approach provides additional information based on the cluster separation. It implies that in a visual task where the location of the pattern center could be determined by form cues (orientation), motion cues (direction of motion) or by their combination, the dynamic conditions provide better separation of the age groups. These conclusions are in agreement with the knowledge that static information is predominantly processed by the ventral pathway in the brain and dynamic information by the dorsal pathway [3]. The first pathway is slower and involves the recognition of images as the final stage of information processing, while the dorsal pathway is associated with determining the location of objects, their spatial location and their movement.

Our results also imply that between-factors not studied by HDDM can be evaluated based on the individual values of the parameters extracted from the model application. Clustering methodology is successful to the gender estimation obtaining results similar to our previous findings. This possibility allows the simplification of model coding and estimation by HDDM. Improvement of the interpretability of the clustering results is also expected by processing of the raw data recorded by the eye tracker.

Acknowledgement. This work was supported by the National Science Fund under Grant DN02/3/2016 "Modelling of voluntary saccadic eye movements during decision making" and by the Science Fund of Sofia University "St. Kliment Ohridski" under project no. 80-10-61/13.04.2020.

References

1. Bocheva, N., Genova, B., Stefanova, M.: Drift diffusion modeling of response time in heading estimation based on motion and form cues. Int. J. Biol. Biomed. Eng. **12**, 75–83 (2018)
2. Bocheva, N., Georgieva, O., Stefanova, M.: Data analysis of age-related changes in visual motion perception. In: ICAART, no. 1, pp. 556–561 (2011)
3. Goodale, M.A., Milner, A.D.: Separate visual pathways for perception and action. Trends Neurosci. **15**, 20–25 (1992)
4. Bezdek, J.C.: Pattern Recognition with Fuzzy Objective Function Algorithms. Plenum Press, NY (1981)

5. Ratcliff, R., Smith, P., Brown, S., MacKoon, G.: Diffusion decision model: current issues and history. Trends Cogn. Sci. **20**(4), 260–281 (2016)
6. Ratcliff, R., Smith, P.: Perceptual discrimination in static and dynamic noise: the temporal relation between perceptual encoding and decision-making. J. Exp. Psychol. Gen. **139**(1), 70–94 (2010)
7. Ratcliff, R.: A diffusion model account of response time and accuracy in a brightness discrimination task: fitting real data and failing to fit fake but plausible dat. Psychon. Bull. Rev. **9**, 278–291 (2002)
8. Ratcliff, R., MacKoon, G.: The diffusion decision model: theory and data for two-choice decision tasks. Neural Comput. **20**(4), 873–922 (2008)
9. Ratcliff, R., Thapar, A., MacKoon, G.: Aging and individual differences in rapid two-choice decisions. Psychon. Bull. Rev. **13**(4), 626–635 (2006)
10. Viswanathan, M., Whangbo, T.K., Yang, Y.K.: Data mining in ubiquitous healthcare. In: Kimito, F. (ed.) New Fundamental Technologies in Data Mining. InTech (2011). http://www.intechopen.com/books/newfundamentaltechnologies-in-data-mining/data-mining-inubiquitoushealthcare. ISBN:978-953-307-547-1
11. Di, W., Zhu, D.: Study on brainfag based on EEG signal analysis. In: Proceedings of ETP International Conference on Future Computer and Communication, pp. 134–137 (June 2009)
12. Calvo, R.A., D'Mello, S.K.: Affect detection: an interdisciplinary review of models, methods, and their applications. IEEE Trans. Affect Comput. **1**(1), 18–37 (2010)
13. Wiecki, T.V., Sofer, I., Frank, M.J.: HDDM: hierarchical Bayesian estimation of the drift-diffusion model in Python. Front. Neuroinform. **7**, 1–10 (2013)

Machine Learning for Neuro/Biological Modeling

Computational Complexity of Kabsch and Quaternion Based Algorithms for Molecular Superimposition in Computational Chemistry

Rafael Dolezal[1,2(✉)], Katerina Fronckova[3], Ayca Kirimtat[1], and Ondrej Krejcar[1]

[1] Faculty of Informatics and Management, Center for Basic and Applied Research, University of Hradec Kralove, Rokitanskeho 62, 50003 Hradec Kralove, Czech Republic
rafael.dolezal@uhk.cz
[2] Biomedical Research Center, University Hospital Hradec Kralove, Sokolska 581, 500 05 Hradec Kralove, Czech Republic
[3] Department of Informatics and Quantitative Methods, University of Hradec Kralove, Rokitanskeho 62, 50003 Hradec Kralove, Czech Republic

Abstract. This work deals with the analysis of Kabsch and quaternion algorithms, which may be used for 3D superimposition of molecules by rigid roto-translation in computational chemistry and biology. Both algorithms, which are very important for *in silico* drug design, were studied from the point of view of their non-trivial mathematical structure. Their computational complexity was investigated by a superimposition of various random pseudo-molecules with 2 – 100,000 atoms in Matlab. It was found that both proposed algorithm implementations exhibit the same asymptotic time computational complexity of $O(n)$, with the quaternion algorithm involving a higher number of floating-point operations (FLOPs) and showing lower computational performance in terms of serial CPU time.

Keywords: Molecular superimposition · Computational complexity · Kabsch algorithm · Quaternions · Drug design

1 Introduction

Over the last few decades, rational approaches in computational chemistry, computational biology, bioinformatics, chemoinformatics and drug research have increasingly applied various algorithms, which can predict, under certain conditions, structures of chemical substances with the desired biological activity before they are synthesized and biologically tested on living organisms [1, 2]. This gradually leads to a qualitative departure from outdated drug development methods based on trial-and-error heuristic approaches towards cheaper, faster and more efficient ways of drug design using modern biomedical technologies. The impact of these applied information technologies is evidenced mainly by more than 200 drugs that have been successfully introduced

L. Iliadis et al. (Eds.): EANN 2020, INNS 2, pp. 473–486, 2020.
https://doi.org/10.1007/978-3-030-48791-1_37

into clinical trials with significant help of so-called computer-aided drug design (CADD) methods [3]. However, CADD methods are not widespread globally and their potential is not fully realized at present. On the other, CADD methods still present a challenge for computer scientists, since the required high accuracy in the desired predictions may be satisfied only by extremely demanding calculations.

From the vast number of different CADD methods (e.g. pharmacophore analysis, structure-activity relationships, molecular docking, molecular metadynamics, Free energy perturbation, core hopping, virtual screening, *ab initio* calculations), we will select and focus on a crucial problem of efficient superimposing two chemical molecules in a three-dimensional Euclidean space [4]. The superimposition of two molecules is an important computational operation performed, for example, to assess similarity of the electron density of chemical structures, to create a reference Cartesian system for molecular interaction fields in 3D structure-biological activity analyses (3D QSAR), or to quantify conformational changes of molecules in molecular dynamics studies [5, 6]. In a certain variation, the problem of the best superimposition of two structures is also encountered in bioinformatics, where it has a related principle of searching for similarities between text strings that represent the genetic code as a sequence of nucleic acids.

We will focus, in this work, on the presentation of the computational part of the roto-translation of molecules in the context of computational chemistry. The aim of this work will, thus, be to outline present techniques to superimpose two molecules that differ in a particular way (e.g. by the constitution, configuration, conformation, position and rotation in 3D space). We will try to define and interpret the problem from the point of view of theoretical computer science. This part will be followed by an overview of possible program implementations that superimpose two molecules and by an experimental analysis of their computational complexity in Matlab 2018. Although molecular superimposition has been to some extent reported in the literature, this work clearly proves and explains that the Kabsch algorithm is better for implementation in bioinformatics tasks than the quaternion based superimposition algorithm.

2 Problem Definition

At first, we introduce the problem of optimal superimposition of two molecules A and B by defining each molecule as a separate, rigid object in three-dimensional space. We will characterize each molecule in a simplified way as a point group in 3D space using Cartesian coordinates of all n atoms. We will use a matrix notation, where chemical symbols of the elements (Z, consisting of one or two characters) are in the first column and the Cartesian coordinates x, y and z, expressed in units Å (10^{-10} m) in the next three columns. We call this matrix molecular identity matrix **I** (1).

$$\mathbf{I} = \begin{bmatrix} Z_1 & x_1 & y_1 & z_1 \\ \vdots & \vdots & \vdots & \vdots \\ Z_n & x_n & y_n & z_n \end{bmatrix} \quad (1)$$

The simplest case of superimposing two identical molecules can be solved as a problem of minimizing the distances of the same atoms in their identity matrices $\mathbf{I_A}$ and $\mathbf{I_B}$ (Fig. 1). If two different molecules are to be superimposed, it is necessary to specify additional superimposition rules for two molecules in mathematical terms. For instance, it is possible to superimpose only some important atoms or groups of atoms in molecules (e.g. pharmacophores) or to add a factor that favors the closest superimposition of the atoms that are most chemically similar (e.g. bioisosteric groups, atoms in the same group of elements). In the special case of constitutional isomers (e.g. 1,4-dichlorobenzene and 1,3-dichlorobenzene, Fig. 1, right part), we can also use the same algorithm as in the case of the superimposition of identical molecules roto-translated in 3D space which minimizes Euclidian distances between the corresponding chemical elements in the identity matrices $\mathbf{I_A}$ and $\mathbf{I_B}$. In the case of "very" different molecules, it is therefore necessary to introduce similarity or priority criteria for matching atoms, but this is evidently an arbitrary condition that opens door to various solutions.

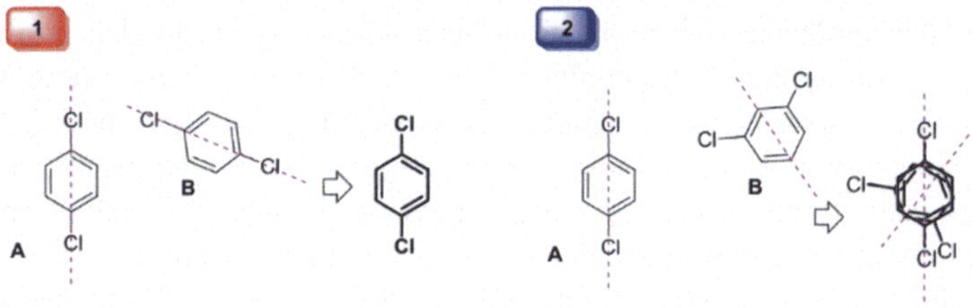

Fig. 1. A symbolic superimposition of two molecules in 2D space, which may be identical (1) or different (2).

Thus, the problem of superimposing two molecules is to minimize the distances of the same or similar atoms in the two molecules. In the case of superimposing so-called conformational isomers or proteins, root-mean-square distance (RMSD) is used to evaluate the achieved superimposition. When comparing conformers A and B, i.e. two molecules with the same identity and connectivity, the calculation of RMSD is given by Eq. (2):

$$\mathrm{RMSD} = \sqrt{\frac{1}{n}\sum\nolimits_{i=1}^{n} \left(x_i^A - x_i^B\right)^2 + \left(y_i^A - y_i^B\right)^2 + \left(z_i^A - z_i^B\right)^2} \quad (2)$$

where x_i, y_i and z_i represent coordinates of the same atoms in the identity matrices $\mathbf{I}$ of molecules A and B. The RMSD function in this definition can only be used to characterize a pair of the same molecules in a different conformations. For instance, RMSD can be utilized to compare results of X-ray analysis and molecular docking simulation of a drug-receptor complex. When calculating RMSD for two conformers, distances between two corresponding atoms in the identity matrices $\mathbf{I_A}$ and $\mathbf{I_B}$ are simply evaluated. In the case of two different molecules, RMSD could be alternatively calculated from all intermolecular atom pair distances. In such a case, the asymptotic time calculation complexity of the RMSD calculation has a value of $O(n \times m)$.

In practice, several simplifying rules can be applied to achieve lower complexity of RMSD calculations, because this measure should be simple in order to be utilized in superimposing algorithms as an objective function which should be minimized. Then the optimal superimposing algorithm can be selected for massive calculations with millions of molecules.

3 State of the Art

3D molecular superimposition currently plays an important role in studies of energetic, physical-chemical, and biological properties of chemical substances (e.g. small molecule drugs, proteins, nucleic acids). The basic difficulty in superimposing molecules is that there are many ways to superimpose molecules. This makes the problem inherently very complex, especially if the conformational flexibility is allowed. In practice, therefore, various heuristic approaches or sampling techniques are used to perform molecular superimposition.

In principle, molecular superimposition techniques can be divided into two basic categories: 1) comparing dimensionless atoms or groups of atoms (e.g. functional groups or pharmacophores); 2) comparing atoms or groups of atoms having a volume. From a computational point of view, the least squares methods, genetic algorithms, Monte Carlo algorithms, brute force algorithms or simulated annealing are used in practice to superimpose two molecules [7]. From a chemical point of view, superimposition methods can be divided into those that consider the simple qualitative identity of dimensionless atoms and those that are derived from maximizing the electron density overlap between two molecules [8]. In addition, various approximate superimposition algorithms that are inaccurate but very fast are used in practice (e.g. algorithms for projecting chemical structures into a symmetric icosahedron, maximization of molecular surface overlap). Other algorithms are based on the insertion of elastic bonds between similar atoms of the ordered molecules and subsequent geometrical minimizing the potential energy of the system thus defined. However, many of these algorithms are implemented in commercial programs for computational chemistry and revealing their structure or determining their asymptotic time complexity is quite demanding due to the unavailability of the program source codes [9].

Mathematically, the problem of superimposing two molecules is commonly solved by orthogonal rotation of one molecule, with RMSD being an objective function that needs to be minimized. In the case of protein alignment, RMSD is calculated only for alpha carbons of the same amino acids. Several least squares algorithms have been proposed to find a rotation that minimizes RMSD [10]. The most effective superimposition methods require finding the eigenvectors of a matrix of squares of interatomic distances (e.g. Kabsch method, Diamond method) [11, 12]. Currently, superimposing techniques are still evolving and turn out to be more computationally efficient than older matrix-based methods. For example, a quick and easy iterative Newton-Raphson (NR) superimposition method that determines the eigenvalues of the quadratic molecular distance matrix from its characteristic polynomial may be mentioned [13].

Based on the NR method, a quaternion based algorithm was lately proposed which seems to be very efficient and less complex in comparison to the Diamond algorithm [14]. Quaternion algorithms are utilized for example in molecular docking software to superimpose various molecules.

In the study, we will focus on two types of superimposing algorithms, namely on the Kabsch algorithm which uses 3 × 3 rotation matrices and on the quaternion method which applies 4 × 4 rotation matrices. We will try to briefly describe their computational complexity and compare them experimentally in Matlab. Up to our best knowledge, performance and scalability testing of both algorithms has not been published yet.

4 Methodology and Proposed Solutions

4.1 Formal Definition of Superimposition

Let us have two vectors $\pi = \{p_1, p_2, \ldots, p_n\}$ and $\rho = \{r_1, r_2, \ldots, r_n\}$, which denote two point groups with one-to-one correspondence. Each component p_i and r_i has three sub-components: $(p_i(x), p_i(y), p_i(z))$, $(r_i(x), r_i(y), r_i(z))$. Assuming that the vectors π and ρ have properties of a rigid body, the superimposition problem can be defined as finding the optimal rotation matrix $\boldsymbol{R}$ and the translation vector t so that the following holds (3):

$$RMSD = \sqrt[2]{\frac{e}{n}}; e = \min|\mathbf{R}\pi + t - \rho|^2 = \min \sum_{i=1}^{n} |\mathbf{R}p_i + t - r_i|^2. \quad (3)$$

The task defined in this way belongs to the problems of finding the least squares. It can be shown that the optimization of translation vector t is independent of rotation (4–6):

$$\frac{\partial e}{\partial t} = \frac{\partial}{\partial t} \sum_{i=1}^{n} |\mathbf{R}p_i + t - r_i|^2 = \sum_{i=1}^{n} 2\frac{\partial(\mathbf{R}p_i + t - r_i)}{\partial t}(\mathbf{R}p_i + t - r_i) = 0, \quad (4)$$

$$\frac{\partial e}{\partial t} = \sum_{i=1}^{n} (\mathbf{R}p_i + t - r_i) = 0 \rightarrow t = \frac{\sum_{i=1}^{n} r_i}{n} - \mathbf{R}\frac{\sum_{i=1}^{n} p_i}{n}, \quad (5)$$

$$t = centroid(\pi) - \mathbf{R}centroid(\rho). \quad (6)$$

Importantly, the rotation of a centroid point is identity. It follows that after moving both vectors π and ρ to their centroids, the optimal superimposition can be simply found by rotating the vectors (7):

$$e = \min \sum_{i=1}^{n} |\mathbf{R}p_i' - r_i'|^2, \text{ where } p_i' = p_i - \frac{\sum_{i=1}^{n} p_i}{n} \text{ and } r_i' = r_i - \frac{\sum_{i=1}^{n} r_i}{n}. \quad (7)$$

4.2 Kabsch Algorithm

In this subsection, our implementation of Kabsch algorithm is described. This algorithm was designed to minimize RMSD for two molecular systems A and B with defined atom one-to-one correspondence, which optimizes the rotation matrix **R** (8).

$$RMSD = \sqrt[2]{\frac{e}{n}}; e = \min\|\mathbf{I_B R} - \mathbf{I_A}\|^2. \tag{8}$$

The Kabsch algorithm can be separated into three main steps:

1. translation of the geometric center of molecule A (e.g. centroid) into the geometric center of molecule B,
2. calculation of the covariance matrix,
3. calculation of the optimal rotation matrix **R**.

Translation of molecule A requires the calculation of the geometric centers of molecules A and B. The calculation can be characterized by a simple algorithm whose time complexity is given by the number of atoms n in a given molecule, respectively in the corresponding identity matrix **I**, as $O(n)$.

```
function mid = ctrd(I,n) % I is an identity matrix
mid = [0, 0, 0];
for (int i = 1; i <= n; i++) {
   mid (1,1) = mid (1,1) + I(i,2);
   mid (1,2) = mid (1,2) + I(i,3);
   mid (1,3) = mid (1,3) + I(i,4);}
mid = mid./n;
```

The translation itself is accomplished by determining the translation vector t, which is subtracted from the coordinates of the mobile molecule B. Again, it is a calculation with time complexity of $O(n)$, which is dependent only on the number of atoms n in molecules A and B.

```
mid1 = ctrd(I_A,n); % I_A is the identity matrix of A
mid2 = ctrd (I_B,n);
t = mid2 - mid1,
function C = shift (I_B, n, t)
for (int i = 1; i <= n; i++) {
   I_B(i,2) = I_B(i,2) - t(1,1);
   I_B(i,3) = I_B(i,3) - t(1,2);
   I_B(i,4) = I_B(i,4) - t(1,3);}
C = sqrt(sum(t.*t)); % returning the magnitude of t
```

Calculating the covariance matrix **H** from the identity matrix of molecule A ($\mathbf{I_A}$) and the shifted molecule B ($\mathbf{I_B}$) is a mathematical operation that involves transposition and multiplication of the matrices ($\mathbf{H} = \mathbf{A^T B}$). Summing up the transposition and the product into one algorithm, this calculation shows an asymptotic time complexity of $O(n)$. At this point, the algorithm assumes that the matrices $\mathbf{I_A}$ and $\mathbf{I_B}$ contain the same number of n corresponding atoms (i.e. unmatched atoms have to be excluded from the calculation).

```
function H = covariance (I_A, I_B, n)
H = zeros(3,3);
for (int i = 2; i <= 4; i++) {
   for (int j = 2; j <= 4; j++) {
      for (int k = 1; k <=n; k++) {
      H(i-1,j-1) = H(i-1,j-1) + I_A(k,i)*I_B(k,j);}}}
```

However, it should be recalled here that iterative multiplication of square matrices that is performed in the covariance calculation has generally time computational complexity of $O(n^3)$ due to three nested `for` loops, as seen in the above algorithm. However, in the above multiplication of matrices $n \times 3$, the asymptotic time complexity in the big O notation is only proportional to n. Regarding multiplication of matrices of different dimensions, there are currently algorithms the time complexity of which is proportional to n with an exponent between 2 and 3 (e.g. Strassen or CW-like algorithms).

The last step of the Kabsch algorithm is the calculation of the optimal rotation matrix **R**. This matrix can be calculated according to the following mathematical formula (9):

$$\mathbf{H} = \mathbf{USV}^{\mathrm{T}}, d = \det\left(\mathbf{VU}^{\mathrm{T}}\right), \mathbf{R} = \mathbf{V}\begin{pmatrix} 1 & 0 & 0 \\ 0 & 1 & 0 \\ 0 & 0 & d \end{pmatrix}\mathbf{U}^{\mathrm{T}}. \tag{9}$$

Since the covariance matrix **H** has a dimension of 3×3 in this case, the calculation of the rotational matrix **R** by singular value decomposition (SVD), determinant calculation and matrix multiplication have a constant time complexity of $O(1)$. However, if the matrix **H** were generally of $m \times n$ dimensions, the asymptotic time complexity of the SVD calculation would be of $O(m^2n + mn^2)$ and the calculation of the determinant by the Bareiss algorithm of $O(n^3)$.

Importantly, the most complicated operation in superimposition of two molecules is calculation of the covariance matrix **H**, which is essentially based on matrix multiplication. Another question, however, is how effective the Kabsch algorithm is, for example, in achieving minimum RMSD.

4.3 Quaternion Algorithm

The quaternion algorithm is based on the same problem definition of superimposition as the Kabsch algorithm (see Eq. (8)). If we expand the Eq. (8), we get the relation (10), in which the center, linear and negative term causes a change in distance as a function of rotation. The other two quadratic terms are constant.

$$e = \min\|\mathbf{I_B R} - \mathbf{I_A}\|^2 = \sum_{i=1}^{n} \|\mathbf{R}(b_i)\|^2 - 2\sum_{i=1}^{n} \mathbf{R}(b_i) \cdot a_i + \sum_{i=1}^{n} \|a_i\|^2. \tag{10}$$

The middle, non-quadratic term can be expressed using quaternion notation (11):

$$\sum_{i=1}^{n} \mathbf{R}(b_i) \cdot a_i = \sum_{i=1}^{n} q a_i q^* \cdot b_i = \sum_{i=1}^{n} (q a_i) \cdot (b_i q). \tag{11}$$

The quaternion can be expressed as a four-component vector $q = (q_0, q_1, q_2, q_3)^T$ or it can be expanded to a quaternion matrix **Q** with dimensions 4 × 4 (12):

$$\mathbf{Q} = \begin{pmatrix} q_0 & -q_1 & -q_2 & -q_3 \\ q_1 & q_0 & -q_3 & q_2 \\ q_2 & q_3 & q_0 & -q_1 \\ q_3 & -q_2 & q_1 & q_0 \end{pmatrix}. \tag{12}$$

Using the quaternion matrix form (12), the coordinate part of identity matrices for molecules A (e.g. **A**) and B (e.g. **B**) may be expressed as quaternions, whose first components will be zeros (13):

$$\mathbf{A_i} = \begin{pmatrix} 0 & -a_{i,x} & -a_{i,y} & -a_{i,z} \\ a_{i,x} & 0 & -a_{i,z} & a_{i,y} \\ a_{i,y} & a_{i,z} & 0 & -a_{i,x} \\ a_{i,z} & -a_{i,y} & a_{i,x} & 0 \end{pmatrix}, \mathbf{B_i} = \begin{pmatrix} 0 & -b_{i,x} & -b_{i,y} & -b_{i,z} \\ b_{i,x} & 0 & -b_{i,z} & b_{i,y} \\ b_{i,y} & b_{i,z} & 0 & -b_{i,x} \\ b_{i,z} & -b_{i,y} & b_{i,x} & 0 \end{pmatrix}. \tag{13}$$

By means of the quaternion definitions of molecules **A** and **B**, the rotation of the molecular system can be expressed as (14):

$$\sum_{i=1}^{n} (\mathbf{A_i q}) \cdot (\mathbf{B_i q}) = \sum_{i=1}^{n} \mathbf{q^T A_i^T B_i q} = \mathbf{q^T} \left(\sum_{i=1}^{n} \mathbf{A_i^T B_i} \right) \mathbf{q}. \tag{14}$$

When we define these equations: $\mathbf{N_i} = \mathbf{A_i^T B_i}, \mathbf{N} = \sum_{i=1}^{n} \mathbf{N_i}$, then we get the following relationship (15):

$$\mathbf{Nq} = \lambda \mathbf{q}, \tag{15}$$

where **N** is a symmetric matrix and its elements $\mathbf{N_i}$ are equal to (16):

$$\mathbf{N_i} = \begin{pmatrix} a_{x_i}b_{x_i} + a_{y_i}b_{y_i} + a_{z_i}b_{z_i} & a_{z_i}b_{y_i} - a_{y_i}b_{z_i} & a_{x_i}b_{z_i} - a_{z_i}b_{x_i} & a_{y_i}b_{x_i} - a_{x_i}b_{y_i} \\ a_{z_i}b_{y_i} - a_{y_i}b_{z_i} & a_{x_i}b_{x_i} - a_{y_i}b_{y_i} - a_{z_i}b_{z_i} & a_{y_i}b_{x_i} + a_{x_i}b_{y_i} & a_{x_i}b_{z_i} + a_{z_i}b_{x_i} \\ a_{x_i}b_{z_i} - a_{z_i}b_{x_i} & a_{y_i}b_{x_i} + a_{x_i}b_{y_i} & -a_{x_i}b_{x_i} + a_{y_i}b_{y_i} - a_{z_i}b_{z_i} & a_{z_i}b_{y_i} - a_{y_i}b_{z_i} \\ a_{y_i}b_{x_i} - a_{x_i}b_{y_i} & a_{x_i}b_{z_i} + a_{z_i}b_{x_i} & a_{z_i}b_{y_i} + a_{y_i}b_{z_i} & -a_{x_i}b_{x_i} - a_{y_i}b_{y_i} + a_{z_i}b_{z_i} \end{pmatrix}. \tag{16}$$

To simplify the calculation, let's define the paired products of the coordinates S_{xy} in A and B molecules using summations (17):

$$S_{xy} = \sum_{i=1}^{n} a_{x_i} b_{y_i}. \tag{17}$$

Subsequently, we can express the total matrix **N** by summations S (18):

$$\mathbf{N} = \begin{pmatrix} S_{xx}+S_{yy}+S_{zz} & S_{zy}-S_{yz} & S_{xz}-S_{zx} & S_{yx}-S_{xy} \\ S_{zy}-S_{yz} & S_{xx}-S_{yy}-S_{zz} & S_{yx}+S_{xy} & S_{xz}+S_{zx} \\ S_{xz}-S_{zx} & S_{yx}+S_{xy} & -S_{xx}+S_{yy}-S_{zz} & S_{zy}-S_{yz} \\ S_{yx}-S_{xy} & S_{xz}+S_{zx} & S_{zy}+S_{yz} & -S_{xx}-S_{yy}+S_{zz} \end{pmatrix}. \quad (18)$$

If we diagonalize the matrix **N**, we obtain eigenvectors $\mathbf{v_i}$ and eigenvalues λ_i for which this holds (19):

$$\begin{aligned} \mathbf{q} &= \sum_{i=1}^{4} \alpha_i v_i; \mathbf{Nq} = \sum_{i=1}^{4} \alpha_i \lambda_i v_i; \mathbf{q}^{\mathbf{T}}\mathbf{Nq} = \sum_{i=1}^{4} \alpha_i \lambda_i \mathbf{q}^{\mathbf{T}} v_i \\ &= \sum_{i=1}^{4} \alpha_i \lambda_i \left(\sum_{j=1}^{4} \alpha_j v_j^T \right) v_i. \end{aligned} \quad (19)$$

The eigenvector, which has the maximum eigenvalue (i.e. the maximum because we require the relationship (11) to have the maximum value and, due to its negative sign, to cause the lowest decrease in RMSD), represents quaternion elements that provide the most advantageous rotation minimizing RMSD. The characteristic polynomial of the matrix **N**, whose roots represent eigenvalues, can be expressed as follows (20–21):

$$\det|\mathbf{N} - \lambda \mathbf{I}| = p_0\lambda^4 + p_1\lambda^3 + p_2\lambda^2 + p_3\lambda + p_4 = 0, \quad (20)$$

$$(\lambda - e_1)(\lambda - e_2)(\lambda - e_3)(\lambda - e_4) = 0. \quad (21)$$

The roots of a characteristic polynomial can be obtained e.g. by the Ferrari method (22–25):

$$e_{1,2} = -\frac{p_1}{4p_0} - S \pm \frac{1}{2}\sqrt{-4S^2 - 2\alpha + \frac{\omega}{S}},\ e_{3,4} = -\frac{p_1}{4p_0} + S \pm \frac{1}{2}\sqrt{-4S^2 - 2\alpha + \frac{\omega}{S}}, \quad (22)$$

$$\alpha = \frac{8p_0p_2 - 3p_1^2}{8p_0^2}, \omega = \frac{p_1^3 - 4p_0p_1p_2 + 8p_0^2p_4}{8p_0^3},\ S = \frac{1}{2}\sqrt{-\frac{2}{3}\alpha + \frac{1}{3p_0}\left(Q + \frac{\Delta_0}{Q}\right)}, \quad (23)$$

$$Q = \sqrt[3]{\frac{\Delta_1 + \sqrt[2]{\Delta_1^2 - 4\Delta_0^3}}{2}},\ \Delta_0 = p_2^2 - 3p_1p_3 + 12p_0p_4, \quad (24)$$

$$\Delta_1 = 2p_2 - 9p_1p_2p_3 + 27p_1^2p_4 + 27p_0p_3^2 - 72p_0p_2p_4 \quad (25)$$

When we define the relationships between the characteristic polynomial parameters and the elements of the matrix **N**, the following relationships hold (26–29):

$$p_0 = 1, p_1 = 0, \tag{26}$$

$$p_2 = -2\left((S_{xx})^2 + (S_{xy})^2 + (S_{xz})^2 + (S_{yx})^2 + (S_{yy})^2 + (S_{yz})^2 + (S_{zx})^2 + (S_{zy})^2 + (S_{zz})^2\right), \tag{27}$$

$$p_3 = -8\left(S_{xx}S_{yy}S_{zz} + S_{yz}S_{zx}S_{xy} + S_{xy}S_{yx}S_{xz}\right), \tag{28}$$

$$\begin{aligned} p_4 = & \left((S_{xy})^2 + (S_{xz})^2 - (S_{yx})^2 - (S_{zx})^2\right)^2 + \left[-(S_{xx})^2 + (S_{yy})^2 + (S_{zz})^2 + (S_{yz})^2\right. \\ & \left.+ (S_{zy})^2 - 2(S_{yy}S_{zz} - S_{yz}S_{zy})\right] \times \left[-(S_{xx})^2 + (S_{yy})^2 + (S_{zz})^2 + (S_{yz})^2 + (S_{zy})^2 + 2(S_{yy}S_{zz} - S_{yz}S_{zy})\right] \\ & + \left[-(S_{xz} + S_{zx})(S_{yz} - S_{zy}) + (S_{xy} - S_{yx})(S_{xx} - S_{yy} - S_{zz})\right] \times \left[-(S_{xz} - S_{zx})(S_{yz} + S_{zy})\right. \\ & \left.+ (S_{xy} - S_{yx})(S_{xx} - S_{yy} + S_{zz})\right] + \left[-(S_{xz} + S_{zx})(S_{yz} + S_{zy})\right. \\ & \left.- (S_{xy} + S_{yx})(S_{xx} + S_{yy} - S_{zz})\right] \times \left[-(S_{xz} - S_{zx})(S_{yz} - S_{zy}) - (S_{xy} + S_{yx})(S_{xx} + S_{yy} + S_{zz})\right] \\ & + \left[(S_{xy} + S_{yx})(S_{yz} + S_{zy})\right. \\ & \left.+ (S_{xy} + S_{zx})(S_{xx} - S_{yy} + S_{zz})\right] \times \left[-(S_{xy} - S_{yx})(S_{yz} - S_{zy})\right. \\ & \left.- (S_{xz} + S_{zx})(S_{xx} + S_{yy} + S_{zz})\right] + \left[(S_{xy} + S_{yx})(S_{yz} + S_{zy})\right. \\ & \left.+ (S_{xz} + S_{zx})(S_{xx} - S_{yy} - S_{zz})\right] \times \left[-(S_{xy} - S_{yx})(S_{yz} - S_{zy}) + (S_{xz} + S_{zx})(S_{xx} + S_{yy} - S_{zz})\right]. \end{aligned} \tag{29}$$

The above equations represent a non-trivial mathematical way for finding the optimal rotational matrix **R** using quaternion calculus. If we look at these calculations from the informatics point of view, we can draw the following conclusions:

- The translation of the centers of molecules is the same in the quaternion algorithm as in the Kabsch algorithm,
- the most computationally intensive is finding a quaternion that maximizes expression (11),
- once the highest eigenvalue of the matrix **N** λ_{max} is found, the optimal quaternion can be found as eigenvector by solving the equation (e.g. by the Gaussian method) (30):

$$(\mathbf{N} - \lambda_{max}\mathbf{I})\mathbf{v} = 0. \tag{30}$$

Let us take a closer look at the time complexity of the steps involved in finding the optimal quaternion to minimize RMSD of two molecules by rotation. The expression (17) can be calculated by the following simple algorithm:

```
Sxy = 0;
for (int i = 1; i <= n, i++) {
   Sxy = Sxy + I_A(i,2)*I_B(i,3); }% I_A, I_B - identity matrices
```

The algorithm for calculating S_{ij} has an asymptotic time complexity of $O(n)$. However, S_{ij} has to be calculated for all variations from the set of x, y, z coordinates for molecules A and B, which are 3^2, (see (19)). Even though the above formula seems to be complicated, the complete quaternion rotation still retains the asymptotic time complexity of $O(n)$.

Similarly, all operations in (19–21) involve a constant number of algebraic operations and therefore they have an asymptotic time complexity equal to constant, that is, $O(1)$. It would be possible to prove that the Gaussian method for calculating eigenvectors of the matrix **N** also exhibits the asymptotic time complexity of $O(1)$. If we compare the Kabsch and quaternion algorithms, it follows that both algorithms have the same time complexity. However, it is obvious that the Kabsch algorithm includes fewer floating-point operations (FLOPs).

5 Results and Discussion

In this study, both the Kabsch and quaternion algorithms were implemented and tested to evaluate their computational complexity in Matlab 2018. Taking into account Matlab's publicly available M codes, custom algorithms for the Kabsch and quaternion based superimposition were developed which estimated the relationship between the time necessary to superimpose two molecules containing 2 – 100,000 randomly positioned atoms. During the tests, calculation wall-time and RMSD values were monitored. The following simple script for Matlab was designed for the tests:

```
function []=test (n) % n is the maximal number of atoms to test
for i=2:n
    A = rand (3,i); % generation of random pseudo-molecule
    B = rand (3,i);
    tic; % start of time measurement
    lrmsd_1(i-1) = kabsch(A,B); % evaluation of RMSD
    time(i-1)=toc; % stop of time measurement
    tic;
    lrmsd_2(i-1) = quaternion (A,B); % evaluation of RMSD
    time_b(i-1)=toc;
end
a = subplot(2,1,1);
plot(2:n,time,2:n,time_b);
legend(a, {'Kabsch','Quaternion'});
b = subplot(2,1,2);
plot(lrms_1,lrms_2);
legend(b, {'Kabsch vs. Quaternion'});
```

The calculations confirmed that when the number of atoms in molecules got increased from 2 to 10, the computational wall-time required by the quaternion algorithm was higher compared to that of the Kabsch algorithm (Fig. 2). Higher time demands of the quaternion algorithm indicate that this method involves a higher number of FLOPs. Regarding the resulting RMSD value, both algorithms give exactly the same results (e.g. $R^2 = 1$) when testing molecules with 2 to 10 atoms.

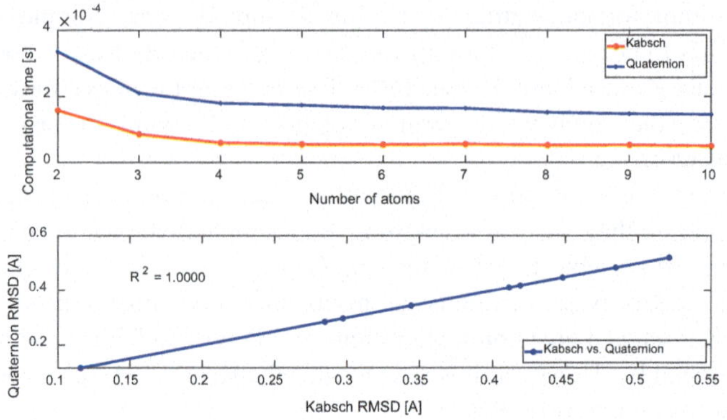

Fig. 2. Computational time to superimpose two molecules with random configuration of 2 - 10 atoms and the resulting RMSD by Kabsch and quaternion algorithms.

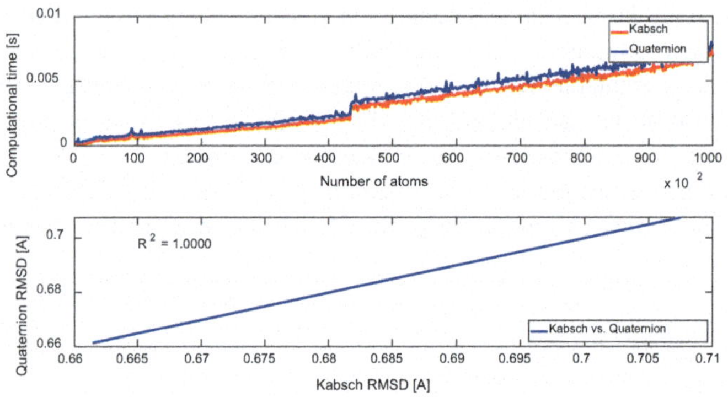

Fig. 3. Computational time to superimpose two molecules with random configuration of 2 – 100,000 atoms and the resulting RMSD by Kabsch and quaternion algorithms.

Testing computational time complexity for molecules with randomly generated 2 - 100,000 atoms proved that both algorithms have linear time complexity of *O(n)*, with the quaternion algorithm being more time consuming (Fig. 3). The RMSD values by both algorithms are exactly the same for molecules with up to 100,000 atoms.

A comparison of the Kabsch and quaternion algorithms shows that both have the same asymptotic time complexity of *O(n)*. The most demanding step in the Kabsch algorithm is the computation of the covariance matrix, in the case of the quaternion algorithm, it is the computation of the elements of the matrix **N**. Calculating diagonal matrices and determinants has a constant asymptotic complexity of *O(1)*, because they perform these operations on matrices of constant sizes.

However, in terms of the number of FLOPs, the two algorithms differ as the Kabsch algorithm comprises fewer FLOPs than the quaternion algorithm does. This result is clearly evident from the computational time testing, in which the quaternion algorithm requires constantly increased computational time to superimpose two molecules in comparison with the Kabsch algorithm. This is related to the fact that the Kabsch algorithm uses 3×3 rotation matrices, whereas the quaternion algorithm is loaded by calculating a 4×4 matrix **N**. Overall, the quaternion algorithm appears to be less advantageous for molecule superimposition, which opposes the proposition by Popov [15].

6 Conclusions

The objective of this work is to briefly introduce the problem of rigid superimposing two molecules by roto-translation so that the molecule atoms get as close as possible to each other and the resulting RMSD has the lowest value. The analyzed Kabsch and quaternion algorithms for superimposition differ mainly in the methodology and in the number of mathematical steps performed. Importantly, it was found by analysis of the mathematical principles of the algorithms and confirmed by computer simulations in Matlab that both algorithms have the same, trivial asymptotic time complexity of $O(n)$. Nonetheless, application of the Kabsch algorithm should be prioritized for application in computational chemistry and biology, because it is less computationally demanding.

Acknowledgements. The work was supported by the Ministry of Education, Youth and Sports of Czech Republic (project ERDF no. CZ.02.1.01/0.0/0.0/18_069/0010054).

References

1. Dolezal, R., Ramalho, T., Franca, T.C., Kuca, K.: Parallel Flexible Molecular Docking in Computational Chemistry on High Performance Computing Clusters. In: Núñez, M., Nguyen. (eds.), LNCS, vol. 9330, pp. 418–427. Springer, Heidelberg (2015)
2. Bajorath, J.: Integration of virtual and high-throughput screening. Nat. Rev. Drug Discov. **1**, 882–894 (2002)
3. Kubinyi, H.: Success stories of computer-aided design. In: Computer Applications in Pharmaceutical Research and Development, pp. 377–724. Wiley, New Jersey (2006)
4. Veselovsky, A.V., Ivanov, A.S.: Strategy of computer-aided drug design. Curr. Drug Targets Infect. Disord. **3**, 33–40 (2003)
5. Taminau, J., Thijs, G., De Winter, H.: Pharao. J. Mol. Graph. Model. **27**, 161–169 (2008)
6. Tosco, P., Balle, T., Shiri, F.: Open3DALIGN. J. Com. Aid. Mol. Des. **25**, 777–783 (2011)
7. Taylor, W.R., May, A.C., Brown, N.P., Aszodi, A.: Protein structure: geometry, topology and classification. Reg. Prog. Phys. **64**, 517–590 (2001)
8. Carbó, R., Leyda, L., Arnau, M.: How similar is a molecule to another? Int. J. Quant. Chem. **17**, 1185–1189 (1980)
9. Sierk, M.L., Pearson, W.R.: Sensitivity and selectivity in protein structure comparison. Protein Sci. **13**, 773–785 (2004)
10. McLachlan, A.: Rapid comparison of protein structures. Acta Cryst. **38A**, 871–873 (1982)
11. Diamond, R.: A note on the rotational superposition problem. Acta Cryst. **44A**, 211–216 (1998)

12. Kabsch, W.: A discussion of the solution for the best rotation to relate two sets of vectors. Acta Cryst. **34A**, 827–828 (1978)
13. Ypma, T.: Historical development of the Newton-Raphson method. SIAM Rev. **37**, 531–551 (1995)
14. Theobald, D.L.: Rapid calculation of RMSDs using a quaternion-based characteristic polynomial. Acta Cryst. **61A**, 478–480 (2005)
15. Popov, P., Grudinin, S.: Rapid determination of RMSDs corresponding to macromolecular rigid body motions. J. Comput. Chem. **35**, 950–956 (2014)

Electronic Equivalent of Consciousness with Elementary Mental Process Model

Leonard Bernau(✉), Filip Paulu, and Jan Voves

FEE in Prague, Czech Technical University in Prague, Prague, Czechia
{polnirob,paulufil,voves}@fel.cvut.cz

Abstract. We present a project to design of the simplified model of thinking located in a little-explored field between neurobiology and psychology. While neurobiology in the incredibly complex microscopic system is dedicated to the structures and signals at the molecular level and the psychology is committed at the opposite extreme with highly sophisticated, they are very abstract and, therefore, difficult to grasp these wholes. There is a vast space between these two extremes. From the perspective of the inherent observers, it is investigable without overcoming the complexity of both points of interest. The primary goal of this research is to construct a multi-layer analog configuration space, the Electronic Equivalent of Consciousness (ECC), wherein the signals have the same properties (bioelectrical) as in the human brain.

Keywords: Neural network · Neurobiology · Electronics · Reticular formation · Neurohumoral process

1 Introduction

To create insight into the issue, it will follow the mental process in human from his point of view, as a human sees from his own subjective perspective. Thus creating an analogy subsequently usable for technological applications. our deepest pe A newborn baby is a highly plastic neural network (NN) defined by the 11 essential sensory inputs which are following: vision [17], hearing [37], smell [23], touch, heat, cold, pain [7], proprioception [39], vestibular sensor [18], interoreceptors [26] and taste [25]. All input signals are transformed via receptor systems into a bioelectric signal of a similar amplitude, which propagates across the NN at an average speed of 15–30 m/s [11,27], forming a signal object within the organic spatial structure where signals interfere with each other. The result of the harmonious constructive interference of these signals is a system of reflex actions that control the physiological functions of the body. They create an eleven-dimensional configuration space, formed by sensory inputs in the superposition, and they develop the mental activity. For the simplified model, we

Faculty of Electrical Engeneering, Czech Technical University in Prague, Czechia.

L. Iliadis et al. (Eds.): EANN 2020, INNS 2, pp. 487–496, 2020.
https://doi.org/10.1007/978-3-030-48791-1_38

consider only optical VISUAL (V) and verbal AUDIO (A) signals. The anatomical region of this signal object with two parameters (A, V) in the human body is the reticular formation located in the extended spinal cord [24]. In the course of further development of the NN, a newborn encounters incoming signals A and V, which repeatedly assign the oral formulation A to each optical V signal and vice versa.

2 Introduction

To create insight into the issue, it will follow the mental process in human from his point of view, thus creating an analogy subsequently usable for technological applications. A newborn baby is a highly plastic neural network (NN) defined by the 11 essential sensory inputs which are following: vision [17], hearing [37], smell [23], touch, heat, cold, pain [7], proprioception [39], vestibular sensor [18], interoreceptors [26] and taste [25]. All input signals are transformed via receptor systems into a bioelectric signal of a similar amplitude, which propagates across the NN at an average speed of 15–30 m/s [11,27], forming a signal object within the organic spatial structure where signals interfere with each other. The result of the harmonious constructive interference of these signals is a system of reflex actions that control the physiological functions of the body. They create an eleven-dimensional configuration space, formed by sensory inputs in the superposition, and they develop the mental activity. For the simplified model, we consider only optical VISUAL (V) and verbal AUDIO (A) signals. The anatomical region of this signal object with two parameters (A, V) in the human body is the reticular formation located in the extended spinal cord [24]. In the course of further development of the NN, a newborn encounters incoming signals A and V, which repeatedly assign the oral formulation A to each optical V signal and vicc versa.

An example of this process could be the mother's face in the visual field of the newborn (V), which is repeatedly interfered with the word the mother (A) [13,32]. This creates the AUDIO/VISUAL COMPLEX (AV), where the NN is gradually learned to assign a verbal (A) signal to the optical signal (V) of each person, object, situation and the phenomenon to verbal signal (A) and vice versa. When a particular AV complex is implemented into the NN, the NN completes the second component of AUDIO mother to mother face VISUAL and conversely. The gradual learning of the individual AV complexes arises in the NN with the 11- dimensional harmonic matrix of all acquired AV complexes and their interactions – the complex information (CI). The CI is a fundamental determining mechanism modifying the initially thoughtful responses to a superset of all relationships and interactions between all other implemented AV complexes. This superset is called, for this model, the cognitive resonance (CR). The continuous increase of the complexity of the CR develops the phenomenon of self-awareness and germination.

3 Hypotesis of Redundancy

Ongoing mental processes in the configuration space, nature creates an evolutionary extension of the original sensorimotor system to predict future events, which increases the ability to adapt to changing external conditions to improve survival chances. The complexity of human neurobiology is very redundant for the mental process because it is the consequence of all the demands which nature has for the human systems, as is described in [2,5]. The model of selective attention, the Intersensory Redundancy Hypothesis (IRH) [3,4], to explain how and under what conditions attention and perceptual processing are promoted to different aspects of events (amodal versus modality specific). Intersensory redundancy refers to the temporally synchronous and spatially collocated occurrence of the same information (e.g. rate, rhythm, duration, intensity shifts) across two or more senses. According to the IRH, intersensory redundancy is highly salient, it directs selective attention to the amodal aspects of events that are redundantly specified across the senses at the expense of nonredundantly specified information within the same event, particularly during early development.

The human bodies have to maintain homeostasis [22], neurohumoral regulation [14], obtain food, use movement, reproduce, grow up, control the immune system [28], breath. The fundamental principles based on our mental processes are significantly elementary. Therefore the construction of a device for creating a simulation of the simplified human conscious model does not have too extreme complexity.

4 Project Description

The primary goal of this research is to construct a multi-layer electronic analog configuration space wherein the incoming optical signals, in the first layer, form an input matrix which shifts the message of each point towards to the next layer at an average speed 15–30 m/s [11,27]. The distribution speed of signals between layers is 15–30 m/s [11,27]. By this method, a three-dimensional dynamic visual record of the current situation (V) (the analogy of short-term memory) is created. In parallel with the active optical 3D matrix, in individual layers, the acoustic signal is assigned for each point of the matrix separately, and their frequencies and amplitudes are partially summed. Thus each particular matrix point gets a unique dynamic address summed from the VISUAL for a pixel and the current AUDIO for the moment defined by each layer. Matrix points of all layers are created by AV complexes, which represent the input data for the superior NNs for further processing, as shown in Fig. 1.

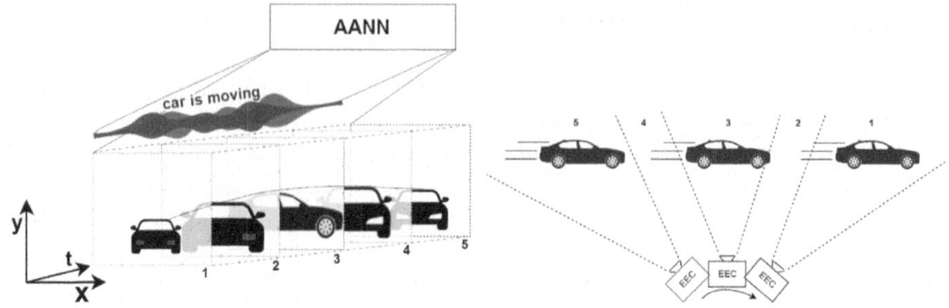

Fig. 1. Top: The schema of the situational processor, bottom: the situational model

4.1 Electronic Equivalent of Consciousness (EEC)

The EEC design does not replicate the human NN, but simulates the perception of spatial events over time, according to the subjective perception of the observer. The EEC creates a simplified dynamic model of a particular situation for the hierarchically superior networks. Figure 2 shows a functional block schema of the EEC. The optical input signal is connected to the first EEC layer (AVout) as a pixel array and proceeds at a speed of 15–30 m/s to the other layers [11,27]. Each point (pixel) of the layers is summed with an adjusted acoustic signal to the same amplitude. A spatial signal object is created, the situational processor, which contains the flow of each situation (complex information). The input optical signal in the layers is shifted in the space towards the rear (to the past), and for each point is summed the acoustic signal separately. A time delay of the visual flow (VISUAL) is created if the signals and their layering are slowed in the EEC structure. In the time delay, the visual flow (VISUAL) is associated with the acoustic signal of a verbal formulation. The result is the spatial signal object (complex information) where each situation is layered by a specific word formulation plus the accompanying AUDIO situation.

The configuration space, which simulates the situation as perceived in the user's consciousness, is created. Each point (pixel) in each layer is an input for the superior Analog Artificial Neural Networks audio and visual (AANN_A and AANN_V), which are learned by subtracting the dynamic variation of the whole situation from the AV complex. The AANN_V subtracts a dynamic variation of the acoustic signal (AUDIO) from the AVout complex and proposes to the next situation process AVin its own design of the Vin (VISUAL). AANN_A subtracts the dynamic visual signal variation (VISUAL) from the AVout complex and proposes to the next situation process AVin its design of the Ain (AUDIO). The AVin situation processor creates another AVcomplex which forms the simulation (model) of the observer imagination.

The Artificial Analog Neural Network decision ($\text{AANN}_{Decision}$), the highest hierarchically superior Analog Artificial Neural Network, performs the corrections comparisons (weight adjustment) in the AANNA and AANNV. The $\text{AANN}_{Decision}$ is a simulation of the decision-making process. In the learning

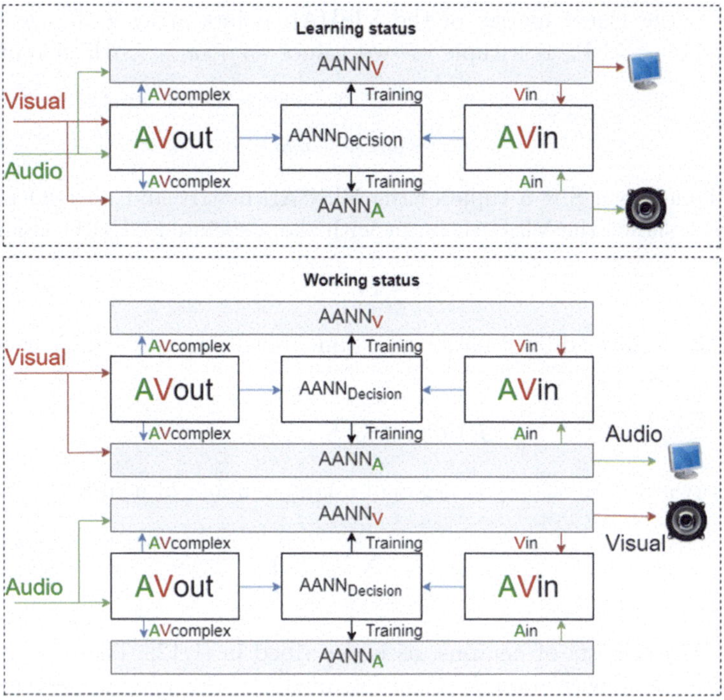

Fig. 2. Learning and working status block schema of the EEC.

status, the input of the AVout is an AUDIO signal simultaneously with the VISUAL signal. The $AANN_{Decision}$ includes the external signal for the network configuration, where the correction is performed between inputs of the AVout and the outputs AANNV and AANNA. In the working status, the AANN network performs the corrections automatically. The output of the learned device is a verbal formulation or an acoustic expression if the input is a visual signal of a particular situation. Verbal communication, which is the input of the learned device produces a visual representation of the output.

The VISUAL point P_v is a tuple of three values where first is the luminance (cd/m^2), second the chrominance and third the saturation.

$$P_v = (v_{imunance} + v_{chrominance} + v_{saturation}) \tag{1}$$

The VISUAL screen is defined by

$$V = \begin{pmatrix} a_{1,1} & \cdots & a_{1,n} \\ \vdots & \ddots & \vdots \\ a_{m,1} & \cdots & a_{m,n} \end{pmatrix} = (a_{i,j}) \in P_v^{m \times n} \tag{2}$$

where V is the visual matrix of the VISUAL points array with size m × n. The AUDIO point P_a is a tuple of two values a_{left}, a_{right}, which represent 2 microphones.

$$P_a = (a_{left}, a_{right}) \tag{3}$$

The Timescreen S is a tuple of the VISUAL matrix and AUDIO point. In the Fig. 1 is shown the VISUAL input with the associated AUDIO input.

$$S = (V, P_a) \tag{4}$$

The EEC is formed by situations per time units. S_0 has speed 15–30 m/s [11, 27].

$$EEC = (S_0, S, ..., S_t) \tag{5}$$

The forward promotion y consists of a large number of neurons.

$$y = s\left(\sum_{i=1}^{n} w_i x_i\right) \tag{6}$$

The (NN) consists of neurons, as is described in [1,12]. There is y outputs of neuron, s is an activation function (sigmoid), w_i are weights (synapsis) and x_i are inputs of the neuron. These weights determine how the NN works. In the multilevel NN are outputs the inputs of the next layer.

The ($AANN_{Decision}$) decides the accurate of the imagination (AV_{inside}) and the output is the ERROR (E). Classical NN learns step by step according to the formula:

$$w_{t+1} = w_t - \eta \frac{\partial E}{\partial w_t} \tag{7}$$

where w_{t+1} - he weight in the time t + 1 time unit. The most widespread method of training the NN is backpropagation with gradient descendent, where each weight is updated by partial derivation of Error by the weight itself (8),

$$w_t = w_{t_0} - \eta \int_{t_0}^{t} \frac{\partial E}{\partial w_t} d\tau \tag{8}$$

where w_t = the weight in the time t and η shapes the learning rate [8].

The NNs are trained from continuous signal because the sampling of the signals causes loss of pieces of informations, and Von Neumann Bottleneck [33–35].

4.2 Possible Technological Realization

The selection of suitable technology is governed mainly by the price per mm2 of the proposed chip and by technology performance. One of the main criteria of nanotechnologies for the EEC development is the deacceleration of signals propagation in the material to 15–30 m/s [11,27].

One of the most widely used technologies for analog circuits is CMOS architecture. However, the individual pixels (neurons) are not physically separated from the others. The solution for manufacturing physical separation of the structure on the chip is to place the sensitive part (neuron) and electronic circuits on the same wafer. Silicon On Insulator (SOI) technology seems to be an ideal solution for this application [10]. The analog delay structures are included in SOI technology. The Buried Oxide (BOX) layer isolates the CMOS electronics implemented on a thin, low resistivity, epitaxial silicon layer from a thick, high resistivity handle wafer. The sensitive element (neuron) is integrated into the handle wafer, as illustrated in Fig. 3.

In contrast to other SOI technologies, the thick film SOI provides a double-well structure to shield the thin gate transistors from the BOX layer. The chosen technological process allows applying high bias voltages (up to 200 V), which are used to deplete the substrate partially and to fabricate devices with higher resistivity. At this time, there is no backside processing. Thus, the HV is applied from the top side using an ohmic contact. The pixel electronics are processed on a 3.5 μm thin epitaxial layer separated from the handle wafer by a 1 μm thin BOX layer. The electronics circuit of each pixel is located in an insulating substrate, which is surrounded by Deep Trench Insulation (DTI) [6].

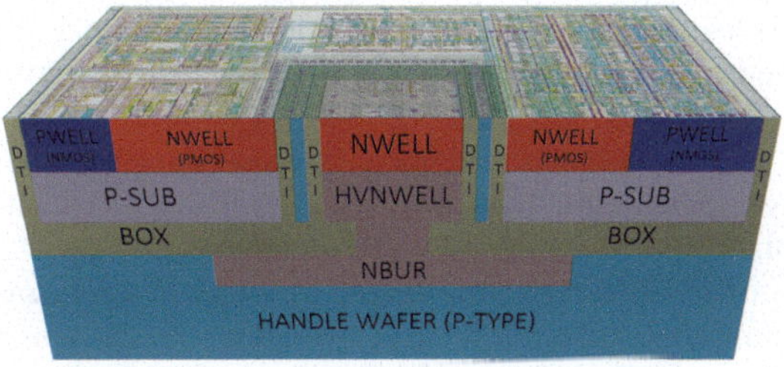

Fig. 3. Cross section of the SOI CMOS technology. The sensitive part of a pixel (neuron) is in the middle separated from electronics by DTI. The pixel is separated from the other by the DTI [6].

5 Conclusion

Although the artificial intelligence (AI) is an excessively evolving field with a partial performance, which dramatically exceeds our abilities (chess, voice recognition, faces), its real cognitive abilities are confronted with fundamental limits. The AI is currently unable to understand humor, read between the lines, and has no hint of self-awareness. The reason is that the mathematical models and systems of the current AI have no question of consciousness in their structure.

It is precisely the question of the inclusion of consciousness into the fundamental innovations of the AI field. The AI which is described in this paper is applicable in medicine [15], economy [20], sociology [40], education and music [19], music composition [38], emotional computation [36], philosophy [31] and many other research areas. The simplified model of human thinking and the ensuing development of its electronics equivalent (EEC) might be able to bring new technological applications. Many articles deal with the problem of sensorimotor transformation [9,21,30], however, the innovative approach of this project corresponds to questions of the perception and the consciousness of humans [29] and animals [16].

Acknowledgments. Research described in the paper was supported by the Czech Technical University grant SGS20/176/OHK3/3T/133 and Nadace Science 21 foundation.

References

1. Almási, A.D., Woźniak, S., Cristea, V., Leblebici, Y., Engbersen, T.: Review of advances in neural networks: neural design technology stack. Neurocomputing **174**, 31–41 (2016)
2. Aylett, M., Turk, A.: The smooth signal redundancy hypothesis: a functional explanation for relationships between redundancy, prosodic prominence, and duration in spontaneous speech. Lang. Speech **47**(1), 31–56 (2004)
3. Bahrick, L., Lickliter, R.: Intersensory redundancy guides attentional selectivity and perceptual learning in infancy. Dev. Psychol. **36**(2), 190–201 (2000). https://doi.org/10.1037//0012-1649.36.2.190
4. Bahrick, L., Lickliter, R.: Intersensory redundancy guides early perceptual and cognitive development. In: Kail, R.V. (ed.) Advances in Child Development and Behavior, vol. 30, pp. 153–187. Elsevier, Boston (2002)
5. Bahrick, L.E., Lickliter, R., Castellanos, I., Todd, J.T.: Intrasensory redundancy facilitates infant detection of tempo: extending predictions of the intersensory redundancy hypothesis. Infancy **20**(4), 377–404 (2015). https://doi.org/10.1111/infa.12081. https://onlinelibrary.wiley.com/doi/abs/10.1111/infa.12081
6. Benka, T., Havranek, M., Hejtmanek, M., Jakovenko, J., Janoska, Z., Marcisovska, M., Marcisovsky, M., Neue, G., Tomasek, L., Vrba, V.: Characterization of pixel sensor designed in 180 nm SOI CMOS technology. J. Instrum. **13**(1), C01025–C01025 (2018)
7. Cabibihan, J., Joshi, D., Srinivasa, Y.M., Chan, M.A., Muruganantham, A.: Illusory sense of human touch from a warm and soft artificial hand. IEEE Trans. Neural Syst. Rehabil. Eng. **23**(3), 517–527 (2015). https://doi.org/10.1109/TNSRE.2014.2360533
8. Chandra, B., Sharma, R.K.: Deep learning with adaptive learning rate using laplacian score. Expert Syst. Appl. **63**, 1–7 (2016). https://doi.org/10.1016/j.eswa.2016.05.022. http://www.sciencedirect.com/science/article/pii/S0957417416302470
9. Crochet, S., Lee, S.H., Petersen, C.C.: Neural circuits for goal-directed sensorimotor transformations. Trends Neurosci. **42**(1), 66–77 (2019). https://doi.org/10.1016/j.tins.2018.08.011. http://www.sciencedirect.com/science/article/pii/S0166223618302364

10. Dovhij, V., Holota, V., Kogut, I.: Architecture development and elements simulation of analytical microsystem-on-chip with "silicon-on-insulator" structures. In: 2016 13th International Conference on Modern Problems of Radio Engineering, Telecommunications and Computer Science (TCSET), pp. 368–372 (2016)
11. Drukarch, B., Holland, H.A., Velichkov, M., Geurts, J.J.G., Voorn, P., Glas, G., de Regt, H.W.: Thinking about the nerve impulse: a critical analysis of the electricity-centered conception of nerve excitability. Prog. Neurobiol. **169**, 172–185 (2018)
12. Duan, S., Hu, X., Dong, Z., Wang, L., Mazumder, P.: Memristor-based cellular nonlinear/neural network: design, analysis, and applications. IEEE Trans. Neural Netw. Learn. Syst. **26**(6), 1202–1213 (2014)
13. Futagi, Y.: Eye-hand-mouth coordination in the human newborn. Pediatr. Neurol. **75**, 43–47 (2017)
14. Golovin, M.S., Balioz, N.V., Krivoschekov, S.G., Aizman, R.I.: Integration of functional, psychophysiological, and biochemical processes in athletes after audiovisual stimulation. Hum. Physiol. **44**(1), 54–59 (2018)
15. Graham, S.A., Depp, C.A.: Artificial intelligence and risk prediction in geriatric mental health: what happens next? Int. Psychogeriatr. **31**(7), 921–923 (2019). https://doi.org/10.1017/S1041610219000954
16. Helmbrecht, T.O., dal Maschio, M., Donovan, J.C., Koutsouli, S., Baier, H.: Topography of a visuomotor transformation. Neuron **100**(6), 1429–1445.e4 (2018)
17. Hickey, C., Peelen, M.: Neural mechanisms of incentive salience in naturalistic human vision. Neuron **85**(3), 512–518 (2015). https://doi.org/10.1016/j.neuron.2014.12.049. http://www.sciencedirect.com/science/article/pii/S0896627314011581
18. Hitier, M., Sato, G., Zhang, Y.F., Zheng, Y., Besnard, S., Smith, P.F., Curthoys, I.S.: Anatomy and surgical approach of rat's vestibular sensors and nerves. J. Neurosci. Methods **270**, 1–8 (2016)
19. Holland, S.: Artificial intelligence, education and music: the use of artificial intelligence to encourage and facilitate music composition by novices (1989)
20. Huang, M.H., Rust, R., Maksimovic, V.: The feeling economy: managing in the next generation of artificial intelligence (AI). Calif. Manag. Rev. **61**(4), 43–65 (2019). https://doi.org/10.1177/0008125619863436
21. Huda, R., Goard, M.J., Pho, G.N., Sur, M.: Neural mechanisms of sensorimotor transformation and action selection. Eur. J. Neurosci. **49**(8), 1055–1060 (2019)
22. Iurlaro, M., von Meyenn, F., Reik, W.: Dna methylation homeostasis in human and mouse development. Curr. Opin. Genet. Dev. **43**, 101–109 (2017)
23. Jacobs, L.F.: Of space and smell: the strange evolution of the human nose. In: HRI 2017: Proceedings of the 2017 ACM/IEEE International Conference on Human-Robot Interaction, pp. 350–351. Association for Computing Machinery, New York (2017)
24. Jang, S.H., Kwon, H.G.: The ascending reticular activating system from pontine reticular formation to the hypothalamus in the human brain: a diffusion tensor imaging study. Neurosci. Lett. **590**, 58–61 (2015)
25. Ji, M., Su, X., Su, X., Chen, Y., Huang, W., Zhang, J., Gao, Z., Li, C., Lu, X.: Identification of novel compounds for human bitter taste receptors. Chem. Biol. Drug Des. **84**(1), 63–74 (2014)
26. Lazovic, B., Zlatkovic Svenda, M., Durmic, T., Stajic, Z., Duric, V., Zugic, V.: The regulation role of carotid body peripheral chemoreceptors in physiological and pathophysiological conditions. Med. pregl. **69**(11–12), 385–390 (2016)
27. Lima, P.M., Ford, N.J., Lumb, P.M.: Computational methods for a mathematical model of propagation of nerve impulses in myelinated axons. Appl. Numer. Math. **85**, 38–53 (2014)

28. Liston, A., Carr, E., Linterman, M.: Series: lifetime immunity shaping variation in the human immune system. Trends Immunol. **37**(10), 637–646 (2016)
29. Manson, G., Blouin, J., Kumawat, A., Crainic, V., Tremblay, L.: Rapid online corrections for upper limb reaches to perturbed somatosensory targets: evidence for non-visual sensorimotor transformation processes. Exp. Brain Res. **237**(3), 839–853 (2019)
30. Mayrhofer, J.M., El-Boustani, S., Foustoukos, G., Auffret, M., Tamura, K., Petersen, C.C.H.: Distinct contributions of whisker sensory cortex and tongue-jaw motor cortex in a goal-directed sensorimotor transformation. Neuron **103**(6), 1034–1043.e5 (2019)
31. McCarthy, J.: What has ai in common with philosophy? In: IJCAI, pp. 2041–2044 (1995)
32. Orioli, G., Bremner, A.J., Farroni, T.: Multisensory perception of looming and receding objects in human newborns. Curr. Biol. **28**(22), R1294–R1295 (2018)
33. Pham, H.L.: Characterisations of von neumann algebras. J. Math. Anal. Appl. **454**(2), 542–556 (2017)
34. Saini, S., Singh, P.: Von neumann stability of modified loop quantum cosmologies. Class. Quantum Gravity **36**(10), 105010 (2019)
35. Sebastian, A., Le Gallo, M., Eleftheriou, E.: Computational phase-change memory: beyond von neumann computing. J. Phys. D-Appl. Phys. **52**(44), 443002 (2019)
36. Sood, S.O.: Emotional computation in artificial intelligence education. In: AAAI (2008)
37. Sottek, R., Genuit, K.: Models of signal processing in human hearing. AEU - Int. J. Electron. Commun. **59**(3), 157–165 (2005). https://doi.org/10.1016/j.aeue.2005.03.016. http://www.sciencedirect.com/science/article/pii/S1434841105000701
38. Sterne, J., Razlogova, E.: Machine learning in context, or learning from LANDR: artificial intelligence and the platformization of music masterin. Soc. Media + Soc. **5**(2), 2056305119847525 (2019). https://doi.org/10.1177/2056305119847525
39. Tuthill, J.C., Azim, E.: Proprioception. Curr. Biol. **28**(5), R194–R203 (2018). https://doi.org/10.1016/j.cub.2018.01.064. http://www.sciencedirect.com/science/article/pii/S0960982218300976
40. Wu, W., Guo, Z., Zhou, X., Wu, H., Zhang, X., Lian, R., Wang, H.: Proactive human-machine conversation with explicit conversation goals (2019)

Metalearning-Non Linear Engineering Modelling

A Metalearning Study for Robust Nonlinear Regression

Jan Kalina(✉) and Petra Vidnerová

The Czech Academy of Sciences, Institute of Computer Science,
Pod Vodárenskou věží 2, 182 07 Praha 8, Czech Republic
kalina@cs.cas.cz, petra@cs.cas.cz

Abstract. Metalearning is a methodology aiming at recommending the most suitable algorithm (or method) from several alternatives for a particular dataset. Its classification rule is learned over an available training database of datasets. It gradually penetrates to various applications in computer science and has also the potential to recommend the most suitable statistical estimator for a given dataset. We consider the nonlinear regression model. While there are some robust alternatives to the traditional (and very non-robust) nonlinear least squares available, it is not theoretically known which estimator performs the best for a particular dataset. In this work, we perform a metalearning study performed over 721 datasets predicting the best nonlinear regression estimator for an independent dataset. The estimators considered here include standard nonlinear least squares as well as its robust alternatives with a high breakdown point. On the whole, the presented study brings new arguments in favor of the nonlinear least weighted squares estimator, which is based on the idea to assign implicit weights to individual observations based on outlyingness of their residuals.

Keywords: Metalearning · Nonlinear regression · Robustness

1 Introduction

The aim of regression modeling is to explain a continuous response variable based on one or more independent variables (regressors), where the latter may be continuous and/or discrete, and thus to predict the response for individual fixed values of the regressors. Parametric estimators in the standard nonlinear regression model with a known regression function will considered in this paper.

Numerous estimation techniques for the nonlinear regression have established and successfully applied in economics, engineering, biomedicine etc. The most traditional tool here, i.e. the nonlinear least squares estimator, is well known to be too vulnerable to the presence of outlying measurements (outliers) in the data [19]. Therefore, robust alternatives to the least squares principle are highly

The work is supported by the projects 19-05704S (J. Kalina) and 18-23827S (P. Vidnerová) of the Czech Science Foundation.

L. Iliadis et al. (Eds.): EANN 2020, INNS 2, pp. 499–510, 2020.
https://doi.org/10.1007/978-3-030-48791-1_39

desirable for the nonlinear regression model [2,17]. The concept of breakdown point as a measure of robustness suitable for nonlinear regression estimators was developed in [21]. Metalearning is a machine learning approach aiming at recommending the most suitable algorithm (or method) from several alternatives for a particular dataset. In the current paper, metalearning will be in the context of nonlinear regression with the aim to predict the best method for particular datasets not contained in the training database containing 721 datasets. Recommending a suitable estimator is even more important for the nonlinear regression for several reasons, namely due to the higher complexity of the model. Complications of nonlinear regression models namely include their bias, sensitivity to model specification, unknown properties for small sample sizes etc.

Section 2 of the paper recalls various estimators for the nonlinear regression model. Section 3 describes our metalearning study and its results are presented in Sect. 4. Finally, Sect. 5 concludes the paper.

2 Robust Estimation in Nonlinear Regression

Let us consider the nonlinear regression model

$$Y_i = f(\beta_1 X_{i1}, \ldots, \beta_p X_{ip}) + e_i, \quad i = 1, \ldots, n, \tag{1}$$

where f is a given continuous nonlinear function, $Y_1, \ldots, Y_n$ is a continuous response, and $(X_{i1}, \ldots, X_{ip})^T$ is the vector of regressors (independent variables) available for the i-th observation. We use the notation $e_1, \ldots, e_n$ for random errors and X for the matrix with elements X_{ij}, where $i = 1, \ldots, n$ and $j = 1, \ldots, p$. The task is to estimate the parameters $\beta = (\beta_1, \ldots, \beta_p)^T$. We stress here that the function f is specified. The most commonly used method for this estimation task is nonlinear least squares (NLS) estimator of β. Thus, the task is different from nonlinear regression tasks with an unknown f, which is a common situation in machine learning; in such a situation, multilayer perceptrons or support vector regression (SVR) [6] would be the commonly used tools for estimating the unknown nonlinear trend.

The NLS estimator is known to be vulnerable to the presence of outliers in the data [2,17]. Therefore, we recall several of its potential robust alternatives in this section, which are natural generalizations of robust estimators known in linear regression [7]. All of them will be used later in the metalearning study of Sect. 3.

2.1 Nonlinear Least Trimmed Squares

The nonlinear least trimmed squares (NLTS) estimator represents one of robust methods with a high breakdown point [21] and also an extension of the popular least trimmed squares from linear regression [16]. We denote by $\mathbb{R}$ the set of real numbers. Denoting the residual for any (fixed) $b = (b_1, \ldots, b_p)^T \in \mathbb{R}^p$ as

$$u_i(b) = Y_i - f(b_1 X_{i1}, \ldots, b_p X_{ip}), \quad i = 1, \ldots, n, \tag{2}$$

squared residuals will be arranged in ascending order as

$$u^2_{(1)}(b) \le u^2_{(2)}(b) \le \dots \le u^2_{(n)}(b). \tag{3}$$

The user must specify a suitable value of the trimming constant h ($n/2 \le h \le n$). Then, the NLTS estimator b_{NLTS} of β is obtained as

$$\arg\min_{b \in \mathbb{R}^p} \sum_{i=1}^{h} u^2_{(i)}(b). \tag{4}$$

While it may be profitable to choose h to reflect the true percentage of contaminated data, we use here the very popular choice $h = \lfloor 3n/4 \rfloor$, where $\lfloor x \rfloor$ denotes the integer part of $x \in \mathbb{R}$ [7].

2.2 Nonlinear Least Weighted Squares

The nonlinear least weighted squares (NLWS) estimator represents an extension of the least weighted squares estimator from the linear regression [9,22,23] and at the same time a weighted analogy of the NLTS estimator. Let us assume the magnitudes $w_1, \dots, w_n$ of nonnegative weights to be given. The NLWS estimator of the parameters in (1) is defined as

$$\arg\min_{b \in \mathbb{R}^p} \sum_{i=1}^{n} w_i u^2_{(i)}(b), \tag{5}$$

where the argument of the minimum is computed over all possible values of $b = (b_1, \dots, b_p)^T$ and squared residuals are arranged as in (3).

The choice of weights has a determining influence on properties of the estimator [13]. If zero weights are assigned to outlying observations, then the estimator is ensured to be highly robust in terms of the breakdown point. The main reason for such robustness of the NLWS estimator is the implicitly weighted construction of the estimator itself, just like for the LWS estimator in the linear regression. Various weighting schemes will be described in Sect. 2.4. The NLWS algorithm may be computed by means of a generalization of the FAST-LTS algorithm of [18].

2.3 Nonlinear Regression Median

Regression quantiles represent a natural generalization of sample quantiles to the linear regression model. Their parameter $\alpha \in (0,1)$, which corresponds to dividing the disturbances to $\alpha \cdot 100\%$ values below the regression quantile and the remaining $(1-\alpha) \cdot 100\%$ values above the regression quantile. In general, regression quantiles represent an important tool of regression methodology, which is popular in economic applications. A natural extension of regression quantiles to nonlinear regression was investigated already in [15], while the most important special case remains to be the nonlinear regression median (NRM) with $\alpha = 1/2$.

2.4 Estimators Used in the Computation

We use the following seven available estimators, which will be denoted as estimators 1, ..., 7. For each of the choices for the NLWS, we require a standard normalization of weights to $\sum_{i=1}^{n} w_i = 1$.

1. Nonlinear least squares (NLS).
2. Nonlinear regression median (NRM).
3. NLTS with h equal to $\lfloor 3n/4 \rfloor$.
4. NLWS with data-dependent adaptive weights of [4].
5. NLWS with linear weights
$$w_i = \frac{2(n+1-i)}{n(n+1)}, \quad i = 1, \ldots, n. \tag{6}$$
6. NLWS with trimmed linear weights
$$w_i = \frac{h-i+1}{h} I[i \leq h], \quad i = 1, \ldots, n, \tag{7}$$
where $I[.]$ denotes an indicator function and h equals again to $\lfloor 3n/4 \rfloor$.
7. NLWS with weights generated by the (strictly decreasing) logistic function
$$w_i = \left(1 + \exp\left\{\frac{i-n-1}{n}\right\}\right)^{-1}, \quad i = 1, \ldots, n. \tag{8}$$

2.5 Computational Complexity

The NLTS and NLWS estimators are computed (as already mentioned) by means of an adaptation of the FAST-LTS algorithm [18], which includes a selected number J of initial choices of p observations out of their total number n. Further, iterations are performed to permute the observations to order them according to the outlyingness of their residuals from the estimated trend. The computational complexity of the algorithm heavily depends on the choice of J. We believe this is the reason why the FAST-LTS has not been, to the best of our knowledge, analyzed in the literature in terms of computational complexity as a function of n and p. While the approximate computational complexity in terms of n and of the number of variables p is very difficult to evaluate here, it is mainly the repeated evaluation of the iterative part of the algorithm, which influences the complexity.

In addition, we are not aware of any study of computational aspects of the NLTS and NLWS estimators. There seem no recommendations for the choice of J. For the LTS in the linear regression model, $J = 500$ is advocated in the original paper [18]. However, it is clear that a larger J will be necessary in the nonlinear situation. The choice $J = 10\,000$ was proposed in [9], however without studying the effect of reducing J to smaller values. Therefore, we decided to use $J = 10\,000$ here for both the NLTS and NLWS, even at the price of high computational demands, while improving the speed was the main aim of our work. This gives a very high probability that the algorithm gives a reasonable approximation to the true value of the robust estimate.

Concerning the nonlinear regression median, its available algorithm based on the interior point method [15] stands on principles close to the algorithm for regression quantiles, which has been proven reliable in the linear regression model [14].

2.6 Illustration of Robust Nonlinear Regression

We randomly generate 70 observations following the Gompertz curve model

$$Y_i = \beta_1 + \beta_2 \exp\{\beta_3 + e^{\beta_4 X_i}\} + e_i, \quad i = 1, \ldots, n, \tag{9}$$

to illustrate the performance of the NLWS estimator with $\beta = (2, 1.5, -1, -1)^T$. The Gompertz growth curve is known as a model suitable e.g. for modeling of economic growth or as a consumption curve. The random error are generated as independent identically distributed random variables following the normal distribution $\mathsf{N}(0, \sigma^2)$ with $\sigma = 0.05$. Figure 1 (left) contains the plot of the response depending on the single regressor. To study the performance of various estimators under contamination, we performed an additional contamination by outliers as shown in Fig. 1 (right). Particularly, values in 10 observations with index $i = 10k$ for $k \in \{1, 2, \ldots, 7\}$ are increased by 1.

We used several estimates of regression parameters of the model (9) based on the simulated data set and the results are presented in Table 1. We are especially interested in implicitly weighted methods with a high breakdown point here. For raw (non-contaminated) data, all estimates are close to the true values of the parameters, while the NLS seems to be the most accurate estimate here. For contaminated data, the NLS estimates are heavily influenced by the contamination, but they are resistant for the other estimates, i.e. they are changed only slightly. From the practical point of view, using (any) robust method is more suitable compared to the non-robust NLS estimate. Such results reveal shows the added value of the robust approach in the nonlinear model in a unique way, because asymptotic interrelations of robust estimators (studied in [8] for the linear model) are not available for the nonlinear model.

Table 1. Estimated values of the vector of parameters $\beta = (2, 1.5, -1, -1)^T$ for raw and contaminated data of Sect. 2.6.

	Raw data				Contam. data			
	b_0	b_1	b_0	b_1	b_0	b_1	b_0	b_1
NLS	2.00	1.52	−0.98	−0.99	2.07	1.65	−0.97	−0.82
NLTS ($h = \lfloor 3n/4 \rfloor$)	1.98	1.55	−0.97	−0.94	1.98	1.57	−0.97	−0.90
NLWS (7)	1.97	1.55	−0.95	−0.93	2.01	1.56	−0.96	−0.92

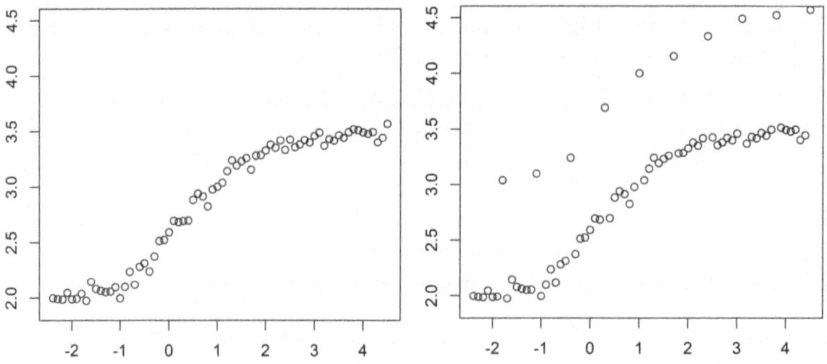

Fig. 1. Dataset from Sect. 2.6. Left: raw data. Right: contaminated data.

3 Description of the Metalearning Study

Metalearning is a computational approach allowing to exploit information from previously observed datasets and to extend them to new datasets [3]. It is popular for algorithm selection for optimization or classification tasks [20], although it may be also exploited for recommending the most suitable statistical estimator in regression context. In this paper, we describe our metalearning study with the aim to compare various nonlinear regression estimators. The study allows us also to detect the most relevant criteria for determining the most suitable weights for the NLWS.

In the primary learning part of the task, various nonlinear regression estimators are fitted for each of the given datasets and the best estimator is found using either the prediction mean square error or its robust version, described in Sect. 3.2. The subsequent secondary learning part has the aim to learn a classification rule allowing to predict the best regression method for a new dataset not present in the training database. Its input data are only selected features of individual datasets together with the result of the primary learning, which typically has the form of the index of the best method for each of the training datasets. In general, the user of metalearning must specify a list of essential components (parameters). We will now describe our choices for the primary and secondary parts of the metalearning task.

3.1 Data Acquisition

We work with the database of about 2000 real publicly available datasets available at the website [1]. The datasets come originally from various packages of R statistical software. The datasets come from different applications domains, e.g. there are datasets concerning economics, sociology, biomedicine, engineering etc.; a homogeneity of the datasets in terms of the domain application would be beneficial, but could be hardly acquired under our fully automatic process of downloading the datasets. On the other hand, such data acquisition ensures a desirable heterogeneity (diversity) of the datasets from the point of view of their statistical properties. To explain this, let us consider the skewness of residuals of the NLS estimator, considered as one of the features below in Sect. 3.4. If these residuals are heavily skewed and thus not likely to be considered as Gaussian, a highly robust estimator is more likely to be more suitable than the NLS. Thus, diverse statistical properties of the datasets is beneficial for the metalearning, because it allows to recommend the most suitable estimator correctly also for datasets with extreme characteristics.

First, we implemented an automated procedure for downloading each dataset and pre-processing the data from the internet. With the requirement to work with a large number of datasets effectively, the linux command line was used for an automatic manipulation with the datasets and particularly the command *wget* allowed us to download all the files in a CSV format. Then, the transformed datasets were loaded to Python. All the remaining manipulations and computations were implemented in Python, which gradually becomes a popular tool among data scientists thanks to numerous available packages for a more comfortable programming. The datasets were prepared to a format suitable for metalearning by means of a script exploiting packages Pandas and NumPy of Python. Each dataset is stored in a CVS file and is accompanied by a text description about the task of the analysis, number of observations and variables, and a link to a text description in a corresponding package of R software.

The sizes of the datasets were reduced in order to reduce the computational complexity of the datasets. Also this improves the homogeneity of the datasets (from the point of view of their sizes), which is desirable, as some of the features used below in Sect. 3.4 depend on the size of the dataset. To be specific, features in the form of p-values of hypothesis tests do not only depend on the violation of the null hypothesis, but also heavily depend on the size of the considered dataset, as the powers of these tests converge to 1 with an increasing size of the datasets. The reduction of their sizes is performed in the following way. If the number of observations in a particular dataset exceeded 100, we generated a random variable (say m) generated from the uniform distribution over the set $\{50,\ldots,100\}$. Then, m observations were randomly selected from the dataset and retained, ignoring all remaining ones. In this way, sample sizes of individual datasets are diverse.

All observations with at least one missing value were omitted. While various automatic tools for perform imputation of missing values are available in R software, these would increase the computational costs even further, as the missing values appear in most of the datasets. Thus, we prefered reducing the sizes of the datasets, as explained in the previous paragraph.

Further, we performed an automatically detection of categorical variables. One of the remaining (i.e. continuous) variables was randomly chosen to be the response. Categorical variables such with 3 or more categories were omitted for the purpose of computational complexity. Binary variables were replaced by a single dummy variables, interpreted as indicators of the first group. We do not however keep all the variables. If a dataset contains more than 9 variables, some randomly chosen ones are omitted to have finally 9 variables; if there are binary regressors, these are omitted preferably. We consider the intercept in each of the datasets, i.e. a column with all ones was included to each dataset. Thus, the number of regressors (apart from intercept) is always between 1 and 9.

3.2 Data Pre-processing

In some of the datasets, regressors happen to be more or less multicollinear. We do not perform any special treatment, as prediction (rather than testing) in nonlinear regression is known not to suffer from multicollinearity. The computation of robust estimators of Sect. 3.3 seems resistant to multicollinearity as well. Nevertheless, to be sure, we computed each of the estimators for each of the datasets and if some warnings were reported, we omitted the whole dataset from the study. If the dataset after all these steps contains less than 20 observations or no regressor, it is omitted. Thus, the total number of datasets was reduced to the final number of 721. This is about 36% of the initial number of datasets in [1], which are to a large extent small and contain many missing values. The data acquisition and pre-processing often belongs to the most demanding tasks in applied machine learning problem and also in our study consumed most of the time and effort.

The response $Y_1, \ldots, Y_n$ was transformed to contain values between 0 and 1 by the commonly used transform

$$Y_i \longmapsto \frac{Y_i - \min_i Y_i}{\max_i Y_i - \min_i Y_i}, \quad i = 1, \ldots, n. \tag{10}$$

In the same way, all continuous regressors were transformed. Such transforms do not influence the prediction ability of the regression estimators, because all regression methods of this study are scale- and regression-equivariant, but do influence the features computed from each dataset. This is beneficial, as the original measurements differ greatly among datasets, as they also come from different fields and applications. On the whole, the fully automatic pre-processing has some disadvantages (e.g. the need for a random selection of the response), but a manual approach would not be feasible with this metalearning study, which is extraordinarily large (cf. [3,20]).

3.3 Primary Learning

In each of the 721 datasets, we consider the nonlinear model

$$Y_i = \beta_0 + \sum_{j=1}^{p} \beta_j X_{ij} + \sum_{j=1}^{p} \beta_{p+j}(X_{ij} - \bar{X}_j)^2 + e_i, \quad i = 1, \ldots, n, \tag{11}$$

with the total number of $2p+1$ regressors (which depend on the original p regressors), where the variables are centered using the mean of the j-th variable $\bar{X}_j$ (for $j = 1, \ldots, p$) for the sake of numerical stability.

For the prediction measure, we use the (prediction) mean square error (MSE), which represents the most standard choice. We find the best method for each dataset using MSE in a leave-one-out cross validation, which represents a standard attempt for an independent validation. In addition, two possible robust alternatives are the trimmed mean square error (TMSE) and weighted mean square error (WMSE). To define them, we denote prediction errors as $r_1, \ldots, r_n$ and consider their ordered squared values $r^2_{(1)} \leq \cdots \leq r^2_{(n)}$. The user chooses h as integer between $n/2$ and h, and some non-negative weights $w_1, \ldots, w_n$. The robust error measures are defined as

$$TMSE = \frac{1}{h}\sum_{i=1}^{h} r^2_{(i)} \quad \text{and} \quad WMSE = \sum_{i=1}^{n} w_i r^2_{(i)}, \tag{12}$$

while we use the particular choices $h = \lfloor 3n/4 \rfloor$ for TMSE and trimmed linear weights (7) for WMSE.

3.4 Secondary Learning

The output of the primary learning is used in the form of the factor variable (index, indicator) of the best method for each of the datasets together with a list of features computed for each dataset. In the nonlinear model, we must consider the features for the metalearning rather carefully. For example, there is no meaningful analogue of the coefficient of determination in the nonlinear model. Other features must be evaluated for the NLS fit. Thus we came to selecting the following set of 9 features.

(A). The number of observations n,
(B). The number of regressors p (excluding the intercept),
(C). The ratio n/p,
(D). Condition number of the matrix $(X^T X)^{-1}$,
(E). P-value of the Shapiro-Wilk test of normality of NLS residuals,
(F). Skewness of residuals of the NLS,
(G). Kurtosis of residuals of the NLS,
(F). P-value of White's test of heteroscedasticity based on NLS residuals,
(I). P-value of the Wald test of linearity, i.e. of $H_0 : \beta_{p+1} = \cdots = \beta_{2p} = 0$ in (11), based on NLS estimates of β.

For the subsequent metalearning task, which is a task of classification to 7 groups (i.e. finding the best among the 7 estimators of Sect. 2.4), we exploit various classification methods including support vector machines (SVM), a classification tree, k-nearest neighbors, and a multilayer perceptron with one hidden layer. We use also several other less known methods including a regularized version of linear discriminant analysis (LDA) denoted as SCRDA of [5], or a robust version of LDA denoted as linear MWCD classification [10].

4 Results

We used the R software for all the computations including necessary libraries (robustbase, quantreg, rda) for specific tasks such as robust estimation and classification. Our metalearning codes (for a preliminary version of the study) are presented on the website [11]. Using MSE in a leave-one-out cross validation study, the NLWS turns out to be the best estimator. The NLS yields the minimal prediction error for 23% of the datasets, the NRM for 20%, the NLTS in 26% and any of the versions of the NLWS in the remaining 31% of datasets. If TMSE is used, the NLWS becomes most successful for 35% and the NLTS for 39% of datasets. If WMSE is used, the NLWS becomes the best for 45% and the NLTS for 34% of datasets. In terms of these percentages, all the four choices of weights for the NLWS turn out to be roughly equally successful for any choice of the error measure.

Within the subsequent metalearning task, we computed various classifiers, while default settings of parameters was used for those computed using the R software. Hyperparameters for SVM or neural networks were estimated in a standard leave-one-out cross validation. The results are presented in Table 2 evaluated as the classification accuracy, i.e. ratio of correctly classified cases (datasets). The SVM classifier turns out to yield the best performance. The best result is obtained for the SVM with a Gaussian kernel for the TMSE; in this situation, the best regression method is found correctly in 71% of datasets. Because there are as many as 7 classes, the overall prediction ability is not very high. The most useful criteria for the choice of weights for the NLWS turn out to be heteroscedasticity and normality of the NLS residuals, which correspond to our intuition, because their heavy violation requires a strongly robust approach.

Table 2. Results of metalearning evaluated as the classification accuracy in a leave-one-out cross validation study. Three different prediction error measures are compared.

Classification method	Classification accuracy		
	MSE	TMSE	WMSE
Classification tree	0.35	0.45	0.47
k-nearest neighbor ($k = 3$)	0.56	0.61	0.64
LDA	0.60	0.68	0.65
SCRDA	0.60	0.68	0.66
Linear MWCD-classification	0.60	0.68	0.66
Multilayer perceptron	0.56	0.66	0.66
Logistic regression	0.56	0.67	0.69
SVM (linear)	0.60	0.69	0.70
SVM (Gaussian kernel)	0.64	0.71	0.70

5 Conclusions

In this paper, a metalearning study for finding the most suitable nonlinear regression estimator is presented. To our knowledge, this is the first metalearning study for nonlinear regression. The metalearning study presented here has the aim to construct a classification rule allowing to predict the most suitable nonlinear regression estimator for a particular dataset. For this purpose, we work with 721 real publicly available datasets. The NLWS seems to yield the best result for the majority of the datasets, while no weighting scheme is uniformly optimal over all datasets.

The results obtained here and presented in Table 1 are evaluated across all datasets, i.e. from various domains of applications (economy, sociology, biomedicine, engineering etc.). Concerning the analysis of a single dataset, the benefits of robust approaches (compared to the classical NLS) are also revealed here, i.e. the paper indicates the necessity of a robust approach for analyzing a dataset contaminated by more or less severe outliers. The NLTS and the nonlinear regression median have a weaker performance due to a low efficiency. Thus, the concept of efficiency (and not only the robustness) also seems to play a prominent role in the nonlinear regression modeling of real data. While the NLTS estimator has been already considered already in [4], the more novel NLWS estimator seems more promising as it has the ability to combine global and local robustness with efficiency. Robust prediction measures, and especially TMSE, are superior to the standard MSE.

The resulting metalearning is relatively successful in recommending the most suitable nonlinear regression estimator, even in spite of the difficulty of the secondary learning into as many as 7 groups. The results go far beyond those of [12], where only 30 datasets were considered.

As future research, we intend to work on the robustification of the whole metalearning process, which would bring very practical consequences to metalearning. Investigating computational aspects of the NLTS and NLWS estimators seem as a major open problem. After it becomes possible to reduce computational demands by improving the algorithm for their computation, our future aim remains to be a sophisticated (and computationally demanding) imputation of missing values. After the study being finalized, we also plan to make the database of 721 datasets to be made available in the github repository.

Acknowledgment. The authors would like to thank Aleš Neoral for help.

References

1. Arel-Bundock, V.: Website of datasets. https://vincentarelbundock.github.io/Rdatasets/datasets.html. Accessed 10 Sep 2019
2. Baldauf, M., Silva, J.M.C.S.: On the use of robust regression in econometrics. Econ. Let. **114**, 124–127 (2012)
3. Brazdil, P., Giraud-Carrier, C., Soares, C., Vilalta, E.: Metalearning: Applications to Data Mining. Springer, Berlin (2009)
4. Čížek, P.: Semiparametrically weighted robust estimation of regression models. Comput. Stat. Data An. **55**, 774–788 (2011)
5. Guo, Y., Hastie, T., Tibshirani, R.: Regularized discriminant analysis and its application in microarrays. Biostatistics **8**, 86–100 (2007)

6. Hastie, T., Tibshirani, R., Friedman, J.: The Elements of Statistical Learning. Springer, New York (2001)
7. Jurečková, J., Picek, J., Schindler, M.: Robust Statistical Methods with R, 2nd edn. CRC Press, Boca Raton (2019)
8. Jurečková, J., Sen, P.K., Picek, J.: Methodology in Robust and Nonparametric Statistics. CRC Press, Boca Raton (2013)
9. Kalina, J.: Highly robust methods in data mining. Serb. J. Manag. **8**, 9–24 (2013)
10. Kalina, J.: A robust pre-processing of BeadChip microarray images. Biocybern. Biomed. Eng. **38**, 556–563 (2018)
11. Kalina, J.: Metalearning for robust regression. https://github.com/jankalinaUI/Metalearning-for-robust-regression. Accessed 20 Oct 2019
12. Kalina, J., Peštová, B.: Robust regression estimators: a comparison of prediction performance. In: Proceedings of the 35th International Conference Mathematical Methods in Economics MME 2017, pp. 307–312. University of Hradec Králové, Hradec Králové (2017)
13. Kalina, J., Schlenker, A.: A robust supervised variable selection for noisy high-dimensional data. BioMed Res. Int. **2015**, 1–10 (2015). Article 320385
14. Koenker, R.: Quantile Regression. Cabridge University Press, Cambridge (2005)
15. Koenker, R., Park, B.J.: An interior point algorithm for nonlinear quantile regression. J. Econometrics **71**, 265–283 (1996)
16. Mount, D.M., Netanyahu, N.S., Piatko, C.D., Silverman, R., Wu, A.Y.: On the least trimmed squares estimator. Algorithmica **69**, 148–183 (2014)
17. Riazoshams, H., Midi, H.B., Sharipov, O.S.: The performance of robust two-stage estimator in nonlinear regression with autocorrelated error. Commun. Stat. Simulat. **39**, 1251–1268 (2010)
18. Rousseeuw, P.J., van Driessen, K.: Computing LTS regression for large datasets. Data Min. Knowl. Disc. **12**, 29–45 (2006)
19. Seber, G.A.F., Wild, C.J.: Nonlinear Regression. Wiley, New York (2003)
20. Smith-Miles, K., Baatar, D., Wreford, B., Lewis, R.: Towards objective measures of algorithm performance across instance space. Comput. Oper. Res. **45**, 12–24 (2014)
21. Stromberg, A.J., Ruppert, D.: Breakdown in nonlinear regression. J. Am. Stat. Assoc. **87**, 991–997 (1992)
22. Víšek, J.Á.: Robust error-term-scale estimate. In: Antoch, J., Hušková, M., Sen, P.K. (eds.) Nonparametrics and Robustness in Modern Statistical Inference and Time Series Analysis: A Festschrift in Honor of Professor Jana Jurečková. IMS Collections, **7**, pp. 254–267 (2010)
23. Víšek, J.Á.: Consistency of the least weighted squares under heteroscedasticity. Kybernetika **47**, 179–206 (2011)

An ASP-Based Approach for Phase Balancing in Power Electrical Systems

Theofanis Aravanis[1,2(✉)], Andreas Petratos[3], and Georgia Douklia[4]

[1] Department of Business Administration, School of Economics & Business, University of Patras, Patras, Greece
taravanis@upatras.gr
[2] Department of Mechanical Engineering, School of Engineering, University of the Peloponnese, Patras, Greece
[3] Elikonos 10, 263 31 Patras, Greece
andreas.petratos89@gmail.com
[4] Department of Mathematics, School of Natural Sciences, University of Patras, Patras, Greece
doukliageo10@gmail.com

Abstract. Unbalanced electrical loads on feeders of power electrical systems can cause serious problems, including power losses, significantly lower power quality, damaging of electrical equipment, and tripping of protective devices. Nevertheless, the problem of balancing such systems—which essentially is equivalent to the problem of integer partitioning—has proven to be NP-complete. Against this background, in this article, an algorithm based on the powerful, declarative framework of Answer Set Programming (ASP) is provided, that efficiently attacks practical instances of the phase-balancing problem. To the best of our knowledge, this is the first attempt of approaching this significant engineering problem by means of the ASP paradigm. The whole study indicates that the examined problem is of great interest from an algorithmic viewpoint, as well as an engineering application that highlights ASP's modelling methodology.

Keywords: Answer Set Programming · Power electrical systems · Phase-balancing problem · Energy distribution

1 Introduction

Modern power electrical systems demand high efficiency, robustness, and high-quality power supply for the consumers' sensitive electrical loads [3,12].

A typical three-phase 4-wire power system is depicted in Fig. 1. A three-phase alternating current (AC) source, connected as a wye (Y), feeds a three-phase wye (Y) connected, *linear* load.[1] Each (complex) impedance Z_a, Z_b and Z_c represents

[1] The current of a linear electrical load (e.g., resistor, motor, capacitor) is, at any time, *linearly proportional* to its voltage.

L. Iliadis et al. (Eds.): EANN 2020, INNS 2, pp. 511–520, 2020.
https://doi.org/10.1007/978-3-030-48791-1_40

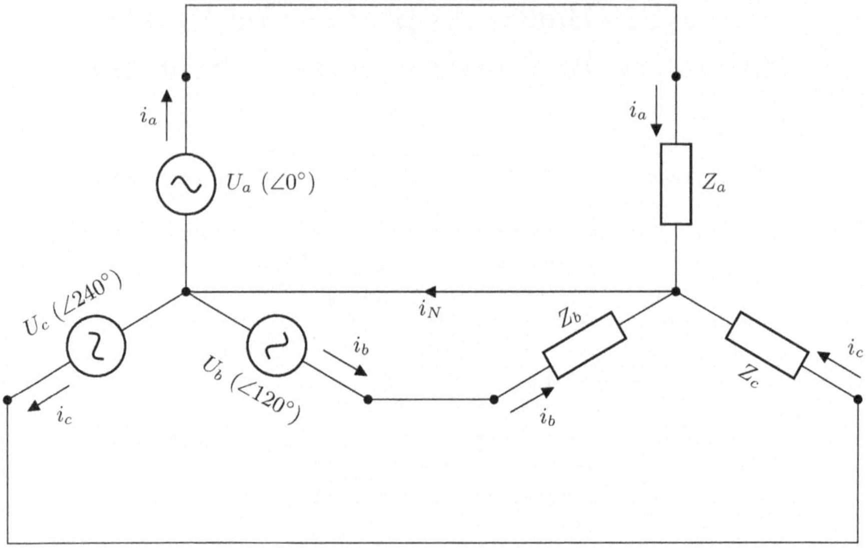

Fig. 1. A typical three-phase 4-wire power electrical system.

a single or, sometimes, a *cluster* of single-phase loads. Kirchhoff's Law enforces that the sum total of the phase currents i_a, i_b, i_c is equal to the current i_N of the neutral line; i.e., $i_a + i_b + i_c = i_N$.

For reasons that will become apparent in what follows, the ideal case is where the load is fully *balanced* (or *symmetric*), that is, $Z_a = Z_b = Z_c$, and the current i_N in the neutral line is zero (since $i_a + i_b + i_c = 0$). Nevertheless, achieving balance is not always an easy task, as the impedance of each phase is *changing frequently* over time (for instance, due to single-phase load variations), and the system drifts into *unbalance*; thus, $i_a + i_b + i_c \neq 0$. The goal of the network administrator is, therefore, to effectively distribute the loads in the first place, so that the minimum possible degree of unbalance to be achieved.

Unbalanced electrical loads of power electrical systems can cause numerous undesirable circumstances, including power losses, significantly lower power quality, damaging of electrical equipment, and tripping of protective devices [16].

The problem of phase balancing of feeders becomes even more demanding whenever a single-phase-to-ground fault has been occurred, and a *single-pole tripping* situation is ongoing, as depicted in Fig. 2. In this case, for as long as the faulted phase is out of service, and the total electrical load is served by the remaining two healthy phases, the feeder becomes significantly unbalanced. Given that faults of power electrical systems are predominantly single-phase-to-ground faults, the single-pole tripping situation is a quite often phenomenon [9].

In power systems where single-phase distribution transformers are utilized—a common practice in USA and Canada—the problem of phase balancing concerns HV/MV power transformers as well, since each single-phase distribution

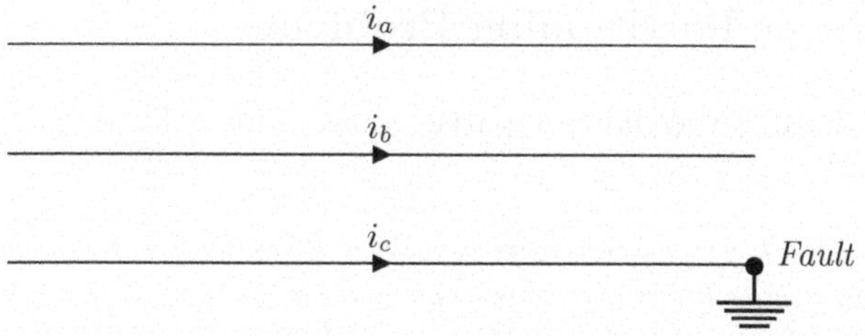

Fig. 2. A single-phase-to-ground fault in a three-phase power transmission line; only currents i_a and i_b reach the load, as i_c flows to the ground due to the fault.

transformer acts as a single-phase load for the HV/MV power transformers.[2] Therefore, a failure of the former can cause the unbalanced loading of the latter.

Against this background, an algorithm based on the powerful paradigm of *Answer Set Programming* (ASP) is provided in this article, that efficiently attacks practical instances of the phase-balancing problem. ASP is a modelling tool oriented towards difficult declaratively-specified search problems [7,8]. Despite the fact that it is a rather new programming framework, it has already successfully implemented to a plethora of real-world applications, including applications in science and humanities, industrial applications, data management and Artificial Intelligence [2].

Although there has been work made concerning phase balancing—the interested reader may, indicatively, refer to [10,13,16,17]—to the best of our knowledge, this is the first attempt of attacking this interesting search problem by means of ASP. As a matter of fact, this work constitutes a first step of our work-in-project according to which standard optimization problems in electrical engineering are addressed employing declarative problem-solving tools. It is noteworthy, lastly, that, as the phase-balancing problem is strongly related to power losses, the proposed algorithm is a useful tool for efficient energy management in any type of power transmission system, such as in *smart grids* [15]; see [14] for a study on phase balancing in a distribution smart grid.

For ease of presentation, throughout this work, we shall assume that each phase is compensated so that all three phases have the *same power factor*; i.e., $\texttt{arg}(Z_a) = \texttt{arg}(Z_b) = \texttt{arg}(Z_c)$.[3] For details on the structure and operation of power electrical systems, the interested reader is referred to [4,12].

The remainder of this paper is structured as follows: The next section introduces the problem of three-way integer partitioning, which, as it turns out, is equivalent to the phase-balancing problem. Section 3 presents the basic syntax and semantics of the ASP language, Sect. 4 introduces the alluded ASP-based algorithm, whereas, Sect. 5 conducts a brief experimental case study evaluating the proposed algorithm. The last two sections are devoted to a brief discussion and some concluding remarks.

[2] HV and MV stand for High-Voltage and Medium-Voltage, respectively.

[3] For a (non-zero) complex number z, $\texttt{arg}(z)$ denotes the argument of z.

2 The Integer Partitioning Problem

The problem of three-way integer partitioning is formally described as follows [11]:

> *Given a multiset of positive integers, the three-way integer partitioning problem is to divide them into three subsets, so that the sum of the numbers in each subset are as nearly equal as possible.*[4]

The integer partitioning problem has been shown to be NP-complete [5].

It turns out that the problem of three-way integer partitioning is *equivalent* to the three-phase-balancing problem, where each positive integer represents the *apparent power* of a load, and the three subsets correspond to the three phases of the feeder. Notice that, as $\texttt{arg}(Z_a) = \texttt{arg}(Z_b) = \texttt{arg}(Z_c)$, it is indifferent whether the apparent power, the impedance or the current of each load is utilized as the entity under partition.

Before presenting our ASP-based algorithm that addresses the phase-balancing problem, in the next section we introduce the basic syntax and semantics of the ASP language.

3 Answer Set Programming in a Nutshell

Answer Set Programming (alias, ASP) is a *declarative* problem-solving framework, that constitutes an easy and powerful modelling tool for *Knowledge Representation and Reasoning* applications (mainly, for solving NP-hard search problems) [7,8]. ASP's expressive power allows for a transparent and natural representation of the basic characteristics of the underlying problem.

The basic idea of ASP is to express a problem in a formal way, so that the *stable models* of its representation (alias, the *answer sets*) correspond to the solutions of the original problem. From a representational viewpoint, the *closed-world assumption* is adopted; that is, considering propositions as false, unless proved otherwise. In this sense, ASP can effectively capture *non-monotonicity*, a crucial feature for a wide range of applications.

In the rest of this section, we shall briefly review a subset of ASP's language that is sufficient for the purpose of this article, mainly borrowed from [1]; for more technical details on ASP, the reader is referred to [6].

3.1 Syntax

Definition 1 (Predicate Atom). *A predicate atom (or simply predicate) is denoted by $p(t_1, \ldots, t_n)$, where p is a predicate name, $t_1, \ldots, t_n$ are terms (constants or variables)—i.e., the arguments of predicate atoms—and the non-negative integer n is the arity of the predicate atom.*

---

[4] Recall that a multiset is a special type of set that allows for multiple instances for each of its elements.

Definition 2 (Conditional Atom). *A conditional atom is denoted by* $a_0 : a_1, \ldots, a_n$*, where every* a_i *for* $0 \leqslant i \leqslant n$ *is a predicate atom,* $a_1, \ldots, a_n$ *is the condition, and ':' resembles mathematical set notation.*

The purpose of ':' is to govern the instantiation of the "head literal" a_0, through the ones of $a_1, \ldots, a_n$. When a conditional atom is in the body of a rule, it expands conjunctively, whereas, when it is in the head of a rule, it expands disjunctively. If $n = 0$, we get a regular predicate atom, and denote it by a_0.

Definition 3 (ASP Logic Program). *An ASP logic program is a finite set of rules of the form:*

$$h_1; \ldots; h_m \leftarrow b_1, \ldots, b_n.$$

In the *head* of the rule, every h_j (for $1 \leqslant j \leqslant m$) is a predicate atom. In the *body* of the rule, every b_i (for $1 \leqslant i \leqslant n$) is a *literal* of the form a, $\texttt{not}\ a$, or $\neg a$, where a is a predicate atom, and the connectives '`not`' and '$\neg$' denote *default* and *classical* negation, respectively. Operators ';' and ',' express disjunctive and conjunctive connectives, respectively.

The rule is called *integrity constraint* if $m = 0$ (i.e., filters solution candidates, meaning that the literals in its body must *not jointly satisfied*), and *fact* if $m = 1$ and $n = 0$. In this latter case, the '$\leftarrow$' sign is usually omitted.

3.2 Semantics

Let $\mathbf{P}$ be an ASP logic program. The set of all constants that occur in $\mathbf{P}$ is called *Herbrand universe* of $\mathbf{P}$. The set of all predicate atoms constructible combining predicate names appearing in $\mathbf{P}$, with elements of the Herbrand universe of $\mathbf{P}$, is called *Herbrand base* of $\mathbf{P}$. A (Herbrand) *interpretation* $\mathcal{I}$ for $\mathbf{P}$ is a subset of the Herbrand base of $\mathbf{P}$ that contains all atoms interpreted as true by $\mathcal{I}$.

A rule is *ground* if it contains no variables. The *grounding* $\mathbf{P}^g$ of $\mathbf{P}$ is the set of all ground rules obtained by replacing all variables in each rule of $\mathbf{P}$ by all combinations of constants in the Herbrand universe. Given that an ASP logic program $\mathbf{P}$ with variables can be regarded as an abbreviation for $\mathbf{P}^g$, we henceforth concentrate on the propositional case.

Let $\mathcal{I}$ be an interpretation of $\mathbf{P}$. For a variable-free predicate atom a, $\mathcal{I} \models a$ iff $a \in \mathcal{I}$. For a default negated literal $\texttt{not}\ a$, $\mathcal{I} \models \texttt{not}\ a$ iff $\mathcal{I} \not\models a$, and for a classically negated literal $\neg a$, $\mathcal{I} \models \neg a$ iff $\neg a \in \mathcal{I}$.

A rule of $\mathbf{P}$ is satisfied by $\mathcal{I}$ if, for some h_j of the rule, $\mathcal{I} \models h_j$ whenever $\mathcal{I} \models b_i$, for all b_i of the rule. In this sense, an ASP logic program $\mathbf{P}$ is satisfied by $\mathcal{I}$ iff all rules of $\mathbf{P}$ are satisfied by $\mathcal{I}$.

Definition 4 (Model). *An interpretation* $\mathcal{I}$ *that satisfies an ASP logic program* $\mathbf{P}$ *is called a model of* $\mathbf{P}$*. A model of an ASP logic program* $\mathbf{P}$ *is a minimal model of* $\mathbf{P}$ *iff no proper subset of it satisfies* $\mathbf{P}$*.*

Those rules for which $\mathcal{I} \models b_i$, for all b_i, constitute the *reduct* $\mathbf{P}^{\mathcal{I}}$ of $\mathbf{P}$, with respect to $\mathcal{I}$.

Definition 5 (Answer Set—Stable Model). *An interpretation $\mathcal{I}$ is an answer set or stable model of an ASP logic program* $\mathbf{P}$ *iff $\mathcal{I}$ is a minimal model of the reduct* $\mathbf{P}^{\mathcal{I}}$.

4 The ASP-Based Algorithm

This section is devoted to the presentation of the alluded ASP-based algorithm that minimizes the degree of unbalance on feeders. The approach that the algorithm follows is the automated generation of *optimal* solutions for the declaratively-specified phase-balancing (search) problem. The source code of the program is presented subsequently in Listing 1, whereas, the predicates used are explained in Table 1.

```
1  phase(a).  phase(b).  phase(c).

2  l(1,25).  l(2,10).  ...  l(n,30).

3  { line(F,l(N,W)) } :- phase(F), l(N,W).
4  :- line(F1,l(N,_)), line(F2,l(N,_)), F1 != F2.
5  :- not line(_,l(N,W)), l(N,W).
6  :- not line(F,_), phase(F).

7  line_load(F,S) :- phase(F), S = #sum{ P,N : line(F,l(N,P)) }.
8  balanced(S/3) :- S = #sum{ P,N : l(N,P) }.
9  error(F,|P-S|) :- phase(F), balanced(P), line_load(F,S).
10 total_error(S/3) :- S = #sum{ P,F : error(F,P) }.

11 #minimize { S : total_error(S) }.

12 #show line/2.  #show line_load/2.  #show total_error/1.
```

Listing 1. The ASP-based algorithm for the three-phase-balancing problem.

Some comments on the source code are in order. First of all, observe that a logic program consists of statements, all of which are terminated by a period '`.`'. Moreover, the connective '`:-`' can be read as '*if*'.

The algorithm takes as input the power S_i of each load i (for $1 \leqslant i \leqslant n$). Note that a cluster of loads can be, also, regarded as a single load.

Line 1 sets (in the form of facts) the three phases of the system, whereas, line 2 sets the available electrical loads, along with their power consumption (the number of phases and the power consumption of loads are indicative). Note that ASP's language supports only integer numbers (written as sequences of the digits $0 \ldots 9$), however, for all practical purposes of the examined application, the (potential) loss in precision is insignificant. Moreover, the load range can be set between 1 and 100, and larger loads range can be scaled accordingly to this range.

Table 1. Explanation of the predicates appearing in Listing 1.

Predicate name	Explanation
`phase/1`	Phase (a or b or c)
`l/2`	Number (i) and power (S_i) of an electrical load
`line/2`	Phase on which an electrical load is connected
`line_load/2`	Total power that each phase supplies
`balanced/1`	Balanced power (S_{bal})
`error/2`	Power error for each phase (ϵ_a or ϵ_b or ϵ_c)
`total_error/1`	Total power error (ϵ)

Line 3 generates solution candidates, by means of a *choice rule*. The idea of a choice rule is to express choices over subsets of atoms. Any subset of its head atoms can be included in an answer set, provided the body literals are satisfied.[5] Hence, in each solution candidate, arbitrary connections of each load to some phase(s) are made.

Line 4 is an integrity constraint which ensures that a load cannot be connected, simultaneously, to two distinct phases. In the same manner, line 5 ensures that every load is connected to at least one phase, and line 6 excludes phases without load. We note here that, unlike a variable name, whose recurrences within a rule refer to the same variable, the token '_' (not followed by any letter) stands for an anonymous variable that does not recur anywhere; one can view this as if a new variable name is invented on each occurrence of '_'.

Line 7 calculates the total power that each phase supplies. Line 8 calculates what we shall call *balanced power*. Balanced power, denoted S_{bal}, is the power of each phase when the three-phase load is perfectly balanced, and is calculated by the sum of the power of all electrical loads, divided by 3. In symbols:

$$S_{bal} = \frac{\sum_{i=1}^{n} S_i}{3} \tag{1}$$

Line 9 calculates the *power error* ϵ_x (where x stands for a phase a, b or c) for each one of the three phases; that is, the absolute value of the difference between S_{bal} and the total power that each phase supplies. Line 10 calculates the *total power error* ϵ; that is, the mean value of the errors of each phase. In symbols:

$$\epsilon = \frac{\epsilon_a + \epsilon_b + \epsilon_c}{3} \tag{2}$$

Line 11 is a minimization statement which generates the answer set with the minimum value of total power error ϵ. Lastly, line 12 indicates that only atoms over the predicates `line/2`, `line_load/2` and `total_error/1` ought to be printed.

[5] For instance, the logic program $\mathbf{P} = \{$ `a, {b} :- a` $\}$ has two answer sets; i.e., `{a}` and `{a,b}`.

Table 2. Computation time for indicative load distributions; the electrical loads are separated by semi-colons.

Loads distributions (kVA)	Total load (kVA)	Time (ms)
1; 5; 7; 10; 4; 8; 4; 1; 2; 3	45	410
11; 3; 3; 6; 5; 4; 7; 2; 1; 1	43	449
2; 4; 1; 10; 1; 4; 3; 2; 8; 13	48	550
6; 3; 9; 1; 5; 4; 3; 2; 1; 1	35	310
2; 4; 1; 2; 1; 5; 3; 7; 2; 14	41	406

5 Experimental Case Study

In order to test the performance of the proposed algorithm, indicative instances of the phase-balancing problem shall be considered in this section. The electrical system under investigation is assumed to be the electricity distribution network of Greece. The typical feeder of this network is a pole-mounted three-phase transformer, with the following technical characteristics: 50 kVA, 20/0.4 kV, Dyn1, 4%.

We consider 10 electrical loads (or cluster of loads). The computation time for indicative (random) load distributions of the electrical system is presented in Table 2. All computations were performed on an Intel© Core™ i5-2410M CPU @ 2.30 GHz machine, with 4 GB RAM available, using Clingo (version 4.5.4).[6]

The results obtained by Clingo for the first electrical load distribution are reported subsequently.

```
line(a,l(4,10))  line(a,l(5,4))

line(b,l(1,1))   line(b,l(3,7))   line(b,l(6,8))

line(c,l(2,5))   line(c,l(7,4))
line(c,l(8,1))   line(c,l(9,2))   line(c,l(10,3))

line_load(a,14)  line_load(b,16)  line_load(c,15)

total_error(0)
```

It is evident from Table 2 that the algorithm performs excellent for all practical instances of the problem; the time required to find the optimal solution for every considered scenario is in the order of *milliseconds* (ms). As it may be expected, its performance depends, not only on the total number of loads, but also on the loads distribution. In any case, if quality is what primarily matters, then lower performance can be tolerated, whereas, if protection is the main factor under consideration, then high performance seems to be imperative.

[6] https://potassco.org/clingo.

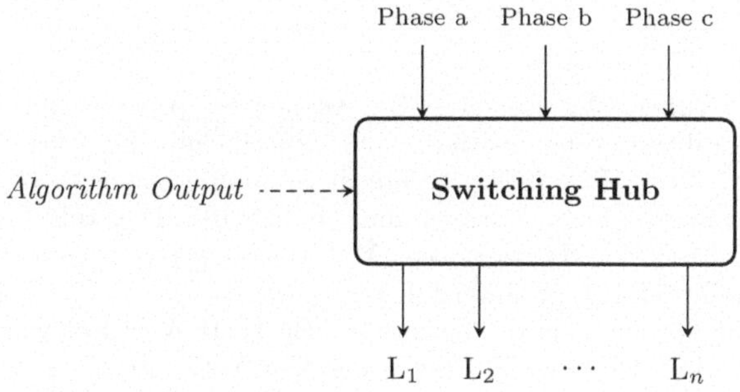

Fig. 3. The switching hub of the system. The hub implements the proper hard-wiring, so that each phase a, b or c of the feeder feeds the appropriate electrical load L_i (with $1 \leqslant i \leqslant n$), according to the output of Listing 1.

6 Discussion

In order for the results of the algorithm of Listing 1 to be practically implemented, a hardware installation in the form of *switching hub* is necessary, so that the appropriate connections between the three phases of the feeder and the available (clusters of) electrical loads to be employed (see Fig. 1). Such switching hub is depicted in Fig. 3, where the three phases of the feeder enter the hub which, given the output of the proposed algorithm, implements the proper hard-wiring so that each phase feeds the appropriate electrical load L_i (with $1 \leqslant i \leqslant n$).

7 Conclusion

In this article, we provided an ASP-based algorithm that efficiently attacks practical instances of the phase-balancing problem, a well-known NP-complete problem of power electrical systems. This is an interesting search problem from an algorithmic viewpoint, as well as an electrical-engineering application that highlights ASP's modelling methodology. The proposed algorithm aims to contribute to the development of a robust method for phase balancing in high-quality modern power electrical systems, given that unbalanced feeders may lead to a plethora of undesirable and harmful circumstances.

Following a line of research according to which standard optimization problems in electrical engineering are addressed by means of declarative problem-solving tools, future work is to be devoted to the study of the electricity cost-minimization problem with the aid of ASP.

Acknowledgements. The authors are grateful to the two anonymous reviewers for their valuable comments on this work.

References

1. Brenton, C., Faber, W., Batsakis, S.: Answer set programming for qualitative spatio-temporal reasoning: methods and experiments. In: Carro, M., King, A., Saeedloei, N., Vos, M.D. (eds.) Technical Communications of the 32nd International Conference on Logic Programming, ICLP 2016. Dagstuhl Publishing (2016)
2. Brewka, G., Eiter, T., Truszczyński, M.: Answer set programming at a glance. Commun. ACM **54**(12), 93–103 (2011)
3. Dugan, R., McGranaghan, M., Santoso, S., Beaty, H.W.: Electrical Power Systems Quality, 3rd edn. McGraw-Hill Education, New York (2012)
4. El-Hawary, M.E.: Electrical Energy Systems. CRC Press, Boca Raton (2018)
5. Garey, M.R., Johnson, D.S.: Computers and Intractability: A Guide to the Theory of NP-Completeness. W. H. Freeman, New York (1979)
6. Gebser, M., Kaminski, R., Kaufmann, B., Lindauer, M., Ostrowski, M., Romero, J., Schaub, T., Thiele, S.: Potassco User Guide, 2nd edn. University of Potsdam, Potassco (2017)
7. Gebser, M., Kaminski, R., Kaufmann, B., Schaub, T.: Answer Set Solving in Practice. Synthesis Lectures on Artificial Intelligence and Machine Learning. Morgan & Claypool Publishers, San Rafael (2012)
8. Gelfond, M.: Answer sets. In: van Harmelen, F., Lifschitz, V., Porter, B. (eds.) Handbook of Knowledge Representation, pp. 285–316. Elsevier Science, Amsterdam (2008)
9. Godoy, E., Celaya, A., Altuve, H.J., Fischer, N., Guzmán, A.: Tutorial on single-pole tripping and reclosing. In: Proceedings of the 39th Annual Western Protective Relay Conference (2012)
10. Gupta, N., Swarnkar, A., Niazi, K.R.: A novel strategy for phase balancing in three-phase four-wire distribution systems. In: 2011 IEEE Power and Energy Society General Meeting (2011)
11. Korf, R.E.: A complete anytime algorithm for number partitioning. Artif. Intell. **106**, 181–203 (1998)
12. Kothari, D.P., Nagrath, I.J.: Modern Power System Analysis, 4th edn. Tata McGraw Hill, New York (2011)
13. Lin, C.H., Chen, C.S., Chuang, H.J., Ho, C.Y.: Heuristic rule-based phase balancing of distribution systems by considering customer load patterns. IEEE Trans. Power Syst. **20**, 709–716 (2005)
14. Mansouri, K., Hamed, M.B., Sbita, L., Dhaoui, M.: Three-phase balancing in a LV distribution smart-grids using electrical load flow variation: "L.F.B.M.". In: Proceedings of the 16th International Conference on Sciences and Techniques of Automatic Control and Computer Engineering, STA 2015, pp. 427–431 (2015)
15. Momoh, J.A.: Smart Grid: Fundamentals of Design and Analysis, 1st edn. Wiley-IEEE Press, Hoboken (2012)
16. Wang, K., Skiena, S., Robertazzi, T.G.: Phase balancing algorithms. Electr. Power Syst. Res. **96**, 218–224 (2013)
17. Wang, W., Yu, N.: Phase balancing in power distribution network with data center. ACM SIGMETRICS Perform. Eval. Rev. **45**, 64–69 (2017)

Neural Networks Algorithmic Foundations

A New Lyapunov Analysis of Robust Stability of Neural Networks with Discrete Time Delays

Sabri Arik(✉)

Department of Computer Engineering, Faculty of Engineering, Istanbul University-Cerrahpasa, 34320 Avcilar, Istanbul, Turkey
ariks@istanbul.edu.tr

Abstract. This paper studies the global asymptotic robust stability of dynamical neural networks with discrete time delays under parameter uncertainties. By utilising the Lyapunov stability and Homeomorphic mapping theorems, a new sufficient condition is presented for the existence, uniqueness and global robust asymptotic stability of this class of neural systems with respect to the Lipschitz continuous activation functions. The proposed stability criterion is derived by employing a new type of Lyapunov functional and it unifies some of the key robust stability results obtained in the past literature.

Keywords: Delayed neural networks · Robust stability analysis · Homeomorphic mapping · Lyapunov functionals

1 Introduction

In the past years, dynamical neural networks have been successfully employed to solve real world engineering problems such as combinatorial optimization, image processing, pattern recognition, and associative memories. These applications usually require that the employed neural network must possess unique and globally asymptotically stable equilibrium points. Therefore, it is of great interest to carrying out the stability analysis of dynamical neural networks. Another important issue regarding stability of neural systems is the problem of time delays due to the finite switching speed of amplifiers during the neuronal signal transmission, which can have negative impact on the dynamical behaviours of the system. On the other hand, when electronically implementing neural systems, some external disturbances may cause undesired deviations in the values of the network parameters. Therefore, in order to conduct a complete and proper stability analysis of neural systems, the time delays and parameter uncertainties must be adequately introduced into the mathematical models of neural networks. This leads us to study the robust stability of neural networks in the presence of time delays. Recently, many papers have proposed various robust stability

L. Iliadis et al. (Eds.): EANN 2020, INNS 2, pp. 523–534, 2020.
https://doi.org/10.1007/978-3-030-48791-1_41

results for different types of delayed neural networks [1–20]. In this paper, by employing the Lyapunov stability and Homeomorphic mapping theorems, a new sufficient condition is obtained for the existence, uniqueness and global robust asymptotic stability of neural systems involving discrete time delays with respect to the Lipschitz continuous activation functions.

Notations: Let $v = (v_1, v_2, ..., v_n)^T$ be real vector and $Q = (q_{ij})_{n\times n}$ be a real matrix. $|v|$ will denote $|v| = (|v_1|, |v_2|, ..., |v_n|)^T$ and $|Q|$ will denote $|Q| = (|q_{ij}|)_{n\times n}$. If $P = (p_{ij})_{n\times n}$ and $Q = (q_{ij})_{n\times n}$ are two real matrices, then, $P \preceq Q$ will imply that $p_{ij} \leq q_{ij}, i, j = 1, 2, ..., n$. The three commonly used vector norms for v and matrix norms for Q are as follows:

$$||v||_1 = \sum_{i=1}^{n} |v_i|, \ ||v||_2 = \sqrt{\sum_{i=1}^{n} v_i^2}, \ ||v||_\infty = \max_{1\leq i\leq n} |v_i|$$

$$||Q||_1 = \max_{1\leq i\leq n} \sum_{j=1}^{n} |q_{ji}|, ||Q||_2 = [\lambda_{\max}(Q^TQ)]^{1/2}, ||Q||_\infty = \max_{1\leq i\leq n} \sum_{j=1}^{n} |q_{ij}|$$

This paper will consider the following neural network model with discrete time delays:

$$\frac{dx_i(t)}{dt} = -c_ix_i(t) + \sum_{j=1}^{n} a_{ij}f_j(x_j(t)) + \sum_{j=1}^{n} b_{ij}f_j(x_j(t-\tau_j)) + u_i, i = 1, 2, ..., n \quad (1)$$

where n is the number of the neurons, $x_i(t)$ denotes the state of the neuron i at time t, $f_i(\cdot)$ denote activation functions, a_{ij} and b_{ij} denote the strengths of connectivity between neurons j and i at time t and $t - \tau_j$, respectively; τ_j represents the time delay required in transmitting a signal from the neuron j to the neuron i, u_i is the constant input to the neuron i, the positive constant c_i is the charging rate for the neuron i.

The matrix-vector form of (1) is as follows:

$$\dot{x}(t) = -Cx(t) + Af(x(t)) + Bf(x(t-\tau)) + u \quad (2)$$

where $x(t) = (x_1(t), x_2(t), ..., x_n(t))^T$, $A = (a_{ij})_{n\times n}$, $B = (b_{ij})_{n\times n}$, $C = diag$ (c_i), $u = (u_1, u_2, ..., u_n)^T$, $f(x(t)) = (f_1(x_1(t)), f_2(x_2(t)), ..., f_n(x_n(t)))^T$ and $f(x(t-\tau)) = (f_1(x_1(t-\tau_1)), f_2(x_2(t-\tau_2)), ..., f_n(x_n(t-\tau_n)))^T$.

In order to study the stability of dynamical neural networks, we first require to define properties of the activation functions. In the current paper, the activation functions f_i will be choosen to be Lipschitz continuous. Lipschitz activation functions satisfy the following condition:

$$|f_i(x) - f_i(y)| \leq \ell_i|x - y|, \ i = 1, 2, \cdots, n, \quad \forall x, y \in R, x \neq y. \quad (3)$$

where ℓ_i are the Lipschitz constants.

When studying the robust stability of neural systems, it is customary to assume that the system matrices $A = (a_{ij})$, $B = (b_{ij})$ and $C = diag(c_i > 0)$ are defined in the following intervals:

$$\begin{aligned} C_I &:= \{C : 0 \prec \underline{C} \preceq C \preceq \overline{C}, i.e., 0 < \underline{c}_i \leq c_i \leq \overline{c}_i\} \\ A_I &:= \{A = (a_{ij}) : \underline{A} \preceq A \preceq \overline{A}, i.e., \underline{a}_{ij} \leq a_{ij} \leq \overline{a}_{ij}\} \\ B_I &:= \{B = (b_{ij}) : \underline{B} \preceq B \preceq \overline{B}, i.e., \underline{b}_{ij} \leq b_{ij} \leq \overline{b}_{ij}\} \end{aligned} \quad (4)$$

Note that (4) implies that the system matrices $A = (a_{ij})$, $B = (b_{ij})$ and $C = diag(c_i > 0)$ have the bounded norms. Therefore, in this paper, we will assume that the norms of the matrices $A = (a_{ij})$, $B = (b_{ij})$ and $C = diag(c_i > 0)$ are bounded. In other words, the matrices $A = (a_{ij})$, $B = (b_{ij})$ and $C = diag(c_i > 0)$ may have different upper bound norms. In the following, we unify the previous literature results which define various upper bound norms for the matrices intervalized in the form given in (4).

Lemma 1: Assume that the matrices A and B in (2) are defined within the intervals given by (4). Define $A^* = \frac{1}{2}(\overline{A} + \underline{A})$, $A_* = \frac{1}{2}(\overline{A} - \underline{A})$, $\hat{A} = (\hat{a}_{ij})_{n \times n}$ with $\hat{a}_{ij} = max\{|\underline{a}_{ij}|, |\overline{a}_{ij}|\}$, $B^* = \frac{1}{2}(\overline{B} + \underline{B})$, $B_* = \frac{1}{2}(\overline{B} - \underline{B})$, $\hat{B} = (\hat{b}_{ij})_{n \times n}$ with $\hat{b}_{ij} = max\{|\underline{b}_{ij}|, |\overline{b}_{ij}|\}$. Let

$$\begin{aligned} \sigma_1(A) &= \sqrt{\| |A^{*T} A^*| + 2|A^{*T}|A_* + A_*^T A_* \|_2} \\ \sigma_2(A) &= \|A^*\|_2 + \|A_*\|_2 \\ \sigma_3(A) &= \sqrt{\|A^*\|_2^2 + \|A_*\|_2^2 + 2\|A_*^T |A^*|\|_2} \\ \sigma_4(A) &= \|\hat{A}\|_2 \end{aligned}$$

and

$$\begin{aligned} \sigma_1(B) &= \sqrt{\| |B^{*T} B^*| + 2|B^{*T}|B_* + B_*^T B_* \|_2} \\ \sigma_2(B) &= \|B^*\|_2 + \|B_*\|_2 \\ \sigma_3(B) &= \sqrt{\|B^*\|_2^2 + \|B_*\|_2^2 + 2\|B_*^T |B^*|\|_2} \\ \sigma_4(B) &= \|\hat{B}\|_2 \end{aligned}$$

Then, the following conditions are satisfied:

$$\|A\|_2 \leq \sigma_m(A) = min\{\sigma_1(A), \sigma_2(A), \sigma_3(A), \sigma_4(A)\} \quad (5)$$

and

$$\|B\|_2 \leq \sigma_m(B) = min\{\sigma_1(B), \sigma_2(B), \sigma_3(B), \sigma_4(B)\} \quad (6)$$

We note here that the conditions $\|A\|_2 \leq \sigma_1(A)$, $\|A\|_2 \leq \sigma_2(A)$, $\|A\|_2 \leq \sigma_3(A)$ and $\|A\|_2 \leq \sigma_4(A)$ have been obtained in the references [1–3] and [4], respectively.

The following well known result provides an important toll for the analysis of the existence and uniqueness equilibrium point for nonlinear systems:

Lemma 6 [5]: If a map $H(x) \in C^0$ satisfies the conditions $H(x) \neq H(y)$ for all $x \neq y$ and $||H(x)||\rightarrow\infty$ as $||x||\rightarrow\infty$, then, $H(x)$ is homeomorphism of R^n.

2 Existence and Uniqueness Analysis of Equilibrium Point

In this section, we will present a new sufficient condition that ensures the existence and uniqueness of the equilibrium point of the neural network model (1).

Theorem 1: For the neural system defined by (1), let the activation functions $f_i(\cdot)$ satisfy (3) and the network matrices A, B and C satisfy (4). Then, the neural network model (1) has a unique equilibrium point for each u, if the following condition holds:

$$\Upsilon = \frac{c_m^2}{\ell_M^2} - \sigma_m^2(A) - \sigma_m^2(B) - 2||\hat{A}^T\hat{B}||_2 > 0$$

where $c_m = min\{\underline{c}_i\}$, $\ell_M = max\{\ell_i\}$, $\sigma_m(A) = min\{\sigma_1(A), \sigma_2(A), \sigma_3(A), \sigma_4(A)\}$ and $\sigma_m(B) = min\{\sigma_1(B), \sigma_2(B), \sigma_3(B), \sigma_4(B)\}$, $\hat{A} = (\hat{a}_{ij})_{n\times n}$ with $\hat{a}_{ij} = max\{|\underline{a}_{ij}|, |\overline{a}_{ij}|\}$ and $\hat{B} = (\hat{b}_{ij})_{n\times n}$ with $\hat{b}_{ij} = max\{|\underline{b}_{ij}|, |\overline{b}_{ij}|\}$.

Proof: In order to prove the existence and uniqueness of the equilibrium point, we will make use of the result of Lemma 6. For the neural network model (1), we can define the following associated map:

$$H(x) = -Cx + Af(x) + Bf(x) + u \tag{7}$$

$H(x) = 0$ implies that

$$-Cx + Af(x) + Bf(x) + u = 0$$

which is exactly the equilibrium equation of system (1). Therefore, every solution of $H(x) = 0$ is an equilibrium point of (1) since $H(x) = 0$ is equivalent to $\dot{x} = 0$. Therefore, the fact that $H(x)$ is homeomorphism of R^n will directly imply the the proof of Theorem 1. We will now show that the condition given Theorem 1 ensures that $H(x)$ is homeomorphism of R^n. Let $x \in R^n$ and $y \in R^n$ be two vectors such that $x \neq y$. Then, for $H(x)$ defined by (7), we can write

$$H(x) - H(y) = -C(x - y) + A(f(x) - f(y)) + B(f(x) - f(y)) \tag{8}$$

For the activation functions belonging to class $\mathcal{K}$, $x \neq y$ implies two distinct cases: $x \neq y$ and $f(x) - f(y) = 0$, or $x \neq y$ and $f(x) - f(y) \neq 0$. In the case of $x \neq y$ and $f(x) - f(y) = 0$, (8) takes the form

$$H(x) - H(y) = -C(x - y)$$

Since C is a positive diagonal matrix, $x - y \neq 0$ directly implies that $H(x) \neq H(y)$. Now consider the case where $x - y \neq 0$ and $f(x) - f(y) \neq 0$. In this case, from (8), we can derive the following

$$\begin{aligned}
&[2C(x-y) + H(x) - H(y)]^T[H(x) - H(y)] \\
&= [C(x-y) + A(f(x) - f(y)) + B(f(x) - f(y))]^T \\
&\quad \times[-C(x-y) + A(f(x) - f(y)) + B(f(x) - f(y))] \\
&= (x-y)^T C^2 (x-y) + (f(x) - f(y))^T A^T A(f(x) - f(y)) \\
&\quad +(f(x) - f(y))^T B^T B(f(x) - f(y)) + 2(f(x) - f(y))^T A^T B(f(x) - f(y)) \\
&\leq -c_m^2\|x-y\|_2^2 + \|A\|_2^2\|f(x) - f(y)\|_2^2 + \|B\|_2^2\|f(x) - f(y)\|_2^2 \\
&\quad +2|f(x) - f(y)|^T|A^T||B||f(x) - f(y)|
\end{aligned} \tag{9}$$

From Lemma 1, we know that $\|A\|_2^2 \leq \sigma_m^2(A)$ and $\|B\|_2^2 \leq \sigma_m^2(B)$. Thus, (9) satisfies

$$\begin{aligned}
&[2C(x-y) + H(x) - H(y)]^T[H(x) - H(y)] \\
&\leq -c_m^2\|x-y\|_2^2 + \sigma_m^2(A)\|f(x) - f(y)\|_2^2 + \sigma_m^2(B)\|f(x) - f(y)\|_2^2 \\
&\quad +2|f(x) - f(y)|^T|A^T||B||f(x) - f(y)|
\end{aligned} \tag{10}$$

Since $|A| \preceq \hat{A}$ and $|B| \preceq \hat{B}$, we can write the following inequality

$$\begin{aligned}
|f(x) - f(y)|^T|A^T||B||f(x) - f(y)| &\leq |f(x) - f(y)|^T|\hat{A}^T||\hat{B}||f(x) - f(y)| \\
&\leq \|\hat{A}^T\hat{B}\|_2\|f(x) - f(y)\|_2^2
\end{aligned} \tag{11}$$

Using (11) in (10) leads to

$$\begin{aligned}
&[2C(x-y) + H(x) - H(y)]^T[II(x) - H(y)] \\
&\leq -c_m^2\|x-y\|_2^2 + \sigma_m^2(A)\|f(x) - f(y)\|_2^2 + \sigma_m^2(B)\|f(x) - f(y)\|_2^2 \\
&\quad +2\|\hat{A}^T\hat{B}\|_2\|f(x) - f(y)\|_2^2
\end{aligned} \tag{12}$$

In the light of (3), we can write $\|f(x) - f(y)\|_2^2 \leq \ell_M^2\|x-y\|_2^2$. Hence, (12) takes the form:

$$\begin{aligned}
&[2C(x-y) + H(x) - H(y)]^T[H(x) - H(y)] \\
&\leq -c_m^2\|x-y\|_2^2 + \ell_M^2\sigma_m^2(A)\|x-y\|_2^2 + \ell_M^2\sigma_m^2(B)\|x-y\|_2^2 \\
&\quad +2\ell_M^2\|\hat{A}^T\hat{B}\|_2\|x-y\|_2^2 \\
&= -\ell_M^2\Upsilon\|x-y\|_2^2
\end{aligned} \tag{13}$$

(13) can be written as

$$\begin{aligned}
&2(x-y)^T C(H(x) - H(y)) + (H(x)) - H(y))^T(H(x) - H(y)) \\
&\leq -\ell_M^2\Upsilon\|x-y\|_2^2
\end{aligned} \tag{14}$$

Since the term $(H(x)) - H(y))^T(H(x) - H(y)) \geq 0$, it follows from (14) that

$$2(x-y)^T C(H(x) - H(y)) \leq -\ell_M^2\Upsilon\|x-y\|_2^2 \tag{15}$$

Since $\Upsilon > 0$, for $x - y \neq 0$, (15) implies that

$$2(x-y)^T C(H(x) - H(y)) < 0 \tag{16}$$

It can be directly concluded from (16) that $H(x) \neq H(y)$ for all $x \neq y$.

Letting $y = 0$ in (15) leads to

$$2x^T C(H(x) - H(0)) \leq -\ell_M^2 \Upsilon \|x\|_2^2 \tag{17}$$

Taking the absolute value of both sides of (17) yields:

$$2|x^T C(H(x) - H(0))| \geq \ell_M^2 \Upsilon \|x\|_2^2 \tag{18}$$

Form (18), the following can be written

$$2\|C\|_\infty \|x\|_\infty \|H(x) - H(0)\|_1 \geq \ell_M^2 \Upsilon \|x\|_2^2 \tag{19}$$

Since $\|x\|_\infty \leq \|x\|_2$ and $\|H(x) - H(0)\|_1 \leq \|H(x)\|_1 + \|H(0)\|_1$, we obtain from (19) that

$$\|H(x)\|_1 \geq \frac{\ell_M^2 \Upsilon \|x\|_2}{2\|C\|_\infty} - \|H(0)\|_1 \tag{20}$$

Since, $\|C\|_\infty$ and $\|H(0)\|_1$ are real finite values, it directly follows from (20) that $\|H(x)\| \to \infty$ as $\|x\| \to \infty$. Thus, the proof of Theorem 1 is complete.

3 Stability Analysis of Equilibrium Point

In this section, it will be shown that the condition obtained in Theorems 1 for the existence and uniqueness of the equilibrium point also implies the asymptotic stability of equilibrium point of neural system (1). Let x^* denote the equilibrium point of neural network model (1). By using the transformation $z_i(\cdot) = x_i(\cdot) - x_i^*,\ i = 1, 2, ..., n$, system (1) can be put into the following form:

$$\dot{z}_i(t) = -c_i z_i(t) + \sum_{j=1}^{n} a_{ij} g_j(z_j(t)) + \sum_{j=1}^{n} b_{ij} g_j(z_j(t - \tau_j)) \tag{21}$$

where $g_i(z_i(t)) = f_i(z_i(t) + x_i^*) - f_i(x_i^*), \forall i$. Note that neural system (21) inherits the assumption given by (3), namely,

$$|g_i(z_i(t))| \leq \ell_i |z_i(t)|, \ \forall i. \tag{22}$$

The stability of the origin of the transformed system (21) is equivalent to the stability of the equilibrium point x^* of (1). Therefore, we will establish the stability of the origin of system (21) instead of considering the stability of the equilibrium point of system (1).

System (21) can be written in the form:

$$\dot{z}(t) = -Cz(t) + Ag(z(t)) + Bg(z(t - \tau)) \tag{23}$$

with $z(t) = (z_1(t), z_2(t), ..., z_n(t))^T$, $g(z(t)) = (g_1(z_1(t)), g_2(z_2(t)), ..., g_n(z_n(t)))^T$ and $g(z(t - \tau)) = (g_1(z_1(t - \tau_1)), g_2(z_2(t - \tau_2)), ..., g_n(z_n(t - \tau_n)))^T$.

We can now proceed with the following result:

Theorem 2: For the neural system defined by (21), let the activation functions $g_i(\cdot)$ satisfy (22) and the network matrices A, B and C satisfy (4). Then, the origin of neural network model (21) is globally asymptotically stable, if the following condition holds:

$$\Upsilon = \frac{c_m^2}{\ell_M^2} - \sigma_m^2(A) - \sigma_m^2(B) - 2\|\hat{A}^T\hat{B}\|_2 > 0$$

where $c_m = min\{\underline{c}_i\}$, $\ell_M = max\{\ell_i\}$, $\sigma_m(A) = min\{\sigma_1(A), \sigma_2(A), \sigma_3(A), \sigma_4(A)\}$ and $\sigma_m(B) = min\{\sigma_1(B), \sigma_2(B), \sigma_3(B), \sigma_4(B)\}$, $\hat{A} = (\hat{a}_{ij})_{n\times n}$ with $\hat{a}_{ij} = max\{|\underline{a}_{ij}|, |\overline{a}_{ij}|\}$ and $\hat{B} = (\hat{b}_{ij})_{n\times n}$ with $\hat{b}_{ij} = max\{|\underline{b}_{ij}|, |\overline{b}_{ij}|\}$.

Proof: We employ the following Lyapunov functional [21]:

$$V(z(t)) = \sum_{i=1}^{n} c_i z_i^2(t) + \sum_{i=1}^{n} \int_{t-\tau_i}^{t} \dot{z}_i^2(s)ds + \alpha \sum_{i=1}^{n} \int_{t-\tau_i}^{t} g_i^2(z_i(s))ds$$
$$+ \beta \sum_{i=1}^{n} \int_{t-\tau_i}^{t} z_i^2(s)ds$$

where α and β are some positive constant whose values will be obtained in what follows. The time derivative of the functional along the trajectories of system (23) is obtained as follows

$$\dot{V}(z(t)) = \sum_{i=1}^{n} 2c_i z_i(t)\dot{z}_i(t) + \sum_{i=1}^{n} \dot{z}_i^2(t) - \sum_{i=1}^{n} \dot{z}_i^2(t-\tau_i)$$
$$+\alpha \sum_{i=1}^{n} g_i^2(z_i(t)) - \alpha \sum_{i=1}^{n} g_i^2(z_i(t-\tau_i)) + \beta \sum_{i=1}^{n} z_i^2(t) - \beta \sum_{i=1}^{n} z_i^2(t-\tau_i)$$
$$= \sum_{i=1}^{n} (2c_i z_i(t) + \dot{z}_i(t))\dot{z}_i(t) - \sum_{i=1}^{n} \dot{z}_i^2(t-\tau_i)$$
$$+\alpha \sum_{i=1}^{n} g_i^2(z_i(t)) - \alpha \sum_{i=1}^{n} g_i^2(z_i(t-\tau_i)) + \beta \sum_{i=1}^{n} z_i^2(t) - \beta \sum_{i=1}^{n} z_i^2(t-\tau_i)$$
$$= \sum_{i=1}^{n} [(c_i z_i(t) + \sum_{j=1}^{n} a_{ij} g_j(z_j(t)) + \sum_{j=1}^{n} b_{ij} g_j(z_j(t-\tau_j)))$$
$$\times(-c_i z_i(t) + \sum_{j=1}^{n} a_{ij} g_j(z_j(t)) + \sum_{j=1}^{n} b_{ij} g_j(z_j(t-\tau_j))))]$$
$$-\sum_{i=1}^{n} \dot{z}_i^2(t-\tau_i) + \alpha \sum_{i=1}^{n} g_i^2(z_i(t)) - \alpha \sum_{i=1}^{n} g_i^2(z_i(t-\tau_i))$$

$$+\beta\sum_{i=1}^{n}z_i^2(t)-\beta\sum_{i=1}^{n}z_i^2(t-\tau_i)$$

$$\leq\sum_{i=1}^{n}[(c_iz_i(t)+\sum_{j=1}^{n}a_{ij}g_j(z_j(t))+\sum_{j=1}^{n}b_{ij}g_j(z_j(t-\tau_j)))$$

$$\times(-c_iz_i(t)+\sum_{j=1}^{n}a_{ij}g_j(z_j(t))+\sum_{j=1}^{n}b_{ij}g_j(z_j(t-\tau_j)))]$$

$$+\alpha\sum_{i=1}^{n}g_i^2(z_i(t))-\alpha\sum_{i=1}^{n}g_i^2(z_i(t-\tau_i))+\beta\sum_{i=1}^{n}z_i^2(t)-\beta\sum_{i=1}^{n}z_i^2(t-\tau_i)$$

$$=\sum_{i=1}^{n}[-c_i^2z_i^2(t)+(\sum_{j=1}^{n}a_{ij}g_j(z_j(t)))(\sum_{j=1}^{n}a_{ij}g_j(z_j(t)))$$

$$+(\sum_{j=1}^{n}b_{ij}g_j(z_j(t-\tau_j))))(\sum_{j=1}^{n}b_{ij}g_j(z_j(t-\tau_j))))$$

$$+2(\sum_{j=1}^{n}a_{ij}g_j(z_j(t)))(\sum_{j=1}^{n}b_{ij}g_j(z_j(t-\tau_j))))]$$

$$+\alpha\sum_{i=1}^{n}g_i^2(z_i(t))-\alpha\sum_{i=1}^{n}g_i^2(z_i(t-\tau_i))+\beta\sum_{i=1}^{n}z_i^2(t)-\beta\sum_{i=1}^{n}z_i^2(t-\tau_i)$$

$$=-\sum_{i=1}^{n}c_i^2z_i^2(t)+\sum_{i=1}^{n}(\sum_{j=1}^{n}a_{ij}g_j(z_j(t)))(\sum_{j=1}^{n}a_{ij}g_j(z_j(t)))$$

$$+\sum_{i=1}^{n}(\sum_{j=1}^{n}b_{ij}g_j(z_j(t-\tau_j))))(\sum_{j=1}^{n}b_{ij}g_j(z_j(t-\tau_j))))$$

$$+2\sum_{i=1}^{n}(\sum_{j=1}^{n}a_{ij}g_j(z_j(t)))(\sum_{j=1}^{n}b_{ij}g_j(z_j(t-\tau_j))))+\alpha\sum_{i=1}^{n}g_i^2(z_i(t))$$

$$-\alpha\sum_{i=1}^{n}g_i^2(z_i(t-\tau_i))+\beta\sum_{i=1}^{n}z_i^2(t)-\beta\sum_{i=1}^{n}z_i^2(t-\tau_i) \tag{24}$$

(24) can be written as

$$\begin{aligned}\dot{V}(z(t))&\leq -z^T(t)C^2z(t)+g^T(z(t))A^TAg(z(t))\\&+g^T(z(t-\tau))B^TBg(z(t-\tau))+2g^T(z(t))A^TBg(z(t-\tau))\\&+\alpha g^T(z(t))g(z(t)-\alpha g^T(z(t-\tau))g(z(t-\tau))\\&\leq -z^T(t)C^2z(t)+g^T(z(t))A^TAg(z(t))\\&+g^T(z(t-\tau))B^TBg(z(t-\tau))+2|g^T(z(t))||A^T||B||g(z(t-\tau))|\\&+\alpha g^T(z(t))g(z(t)-\alpha g^T(z(t-\tau))g(z(t-\tau))\\&+\beta z^T(t)z(t)-\beta z^T(t-\tau)z(t-\tau)\end{aligned} \tag{25}$$

Since $|A| \preceq \hat{A}$ and $|B| \preceq \hat{B}$, (25) can be written in the form:

$$\begin{aligned}\dot{V}(z(t)) &\leq -z^T(t)C^2z(t) + g^T(z(t))A^TAg(z(t)) \\ &\quad +g^T(z(t-\tau))B^TBg(z(t-\tau)) + 2|g^T(z(t))|\hat{A}^T\hat{B}|g(z(t-\tau))| \\ &\quad +\alpha g^T(z(t))g(z(t) - \alpha g^T(z(t-\tau))g(z(t-\tau)) \\ &\leq -c_m^2\|z(t)\|_2^2 + \|A\|_2^2\|g(z(t))\|_2^2 + \|B\|_2^2\|g(z(t-\tau))\|_2^2 \\ &\quad +2\|\hat{A}^T\hat{B}\|_2\|g(z(t))\|_2\|g(z(t-\tau))\|_2 \\ &\quad +\alpha g^T(z(t))g(z(t) - \alpha g^T(z(t-\tau))g(z(t-\tau)) \\ &\quad +\beta z^T(t)z(t) - \beta z^T(t-\tau)z(t-\tau) \end{aligned} \tag{26}$$

Since $\|A\|_2 \leq \sigma_m(A)$ and $\|B\|_2 \leq \sigma_m(B)$, (26) leads to

$$\begin{aligned}\dot{V}(z(t)) &\leq -c_m^2\|z(t)\|_2^2 + \sigma_m^2(A)\|g(z(t))\|_2^2 + \sigma_m^2(B)\|g(z(t-\tau))\|_2^2 \\ &\quad +\|\hat{A}^T\hat{B}\|_2(\|g(z(t))\|_2^2 + \|g(z(t-\tau))\|_2^2) \\ &\quad +\alpha g^T(z(t))g(z(t) - \alpha g^T(z(t-\tau))g(z(t-\tau)) \\ &= -c_m^2\|z(t)\|_2^2 + \sigma_m^2(A)\|g(z(t))\|_2^2 + \sigma_m^2(B)\|g(z(t-\tau))\|_2^2 \\ &\quad +\|\hat{A}^T\hat{B}\|_2\|g(z(t))\|_2^2 + \|\hat{A}^T\hat{B}\|_2\|g(z(t-\tau))\|_2^2 \\ &\quad -\alpha\|g^T(z(t-\tau))\|_2^2 \\ &\quad +\beta z^T(t)z(t) - \beta z^T(t-\tau)z(t-\tau) \end{aligned} \tag{27}$$

If we choose $\alpha = \sigma_m^2(B) + \|\hat{A}^T\hat{B}\|_2$, then (27) takes the form

$$\begin{aligned}\dot{V}(z(t)) &= -c_m^2\|z(t)\|_2^2 + \sigma_m^2(A)\|g(z(t))\|_2^2 + \|\hat{A}^T\hat{B}\|_2\|g(z(t))\|_2^2 \\ &\quad +(\sigma_m^2(B) + \|\hat{A}^T\hat{B}\|_2)\|g^T(z(t))\|_2^2 \\ &= -c_m^2\|z(t)\|_2^2 + \sigma_m^2(A)\|g(z(t))\|_2^2 + \sigma_m^2(B)\|g(z(t))\|_2^2 \\ &\quad +2\|\hat{A}^T\hat{B}\|_2\|g(z(t))\|_2^2 + \beta\|z(t)\|_2^2 \end{aligned} \tag{28}$$

In the light of (22), we can write $\|g(z(t))\|_2^2 \leq \ell_M^2\|z(t)\|_2^2$. Hence, (28) becomes:

$$\begin{aligned}\dot{V}(z(t)) &\leq (-c_m^2 + (\sigma_m^2(A) + \sigma_m^2(B) + 2\|\hat{A}^T\hat{B}\|_2)\ell_M^2)\|z(t)\|_2^2 + \beta\|z(t)\|_2^2 \\ &= -\ell_M^2(\frac{c_m^2}{\ell_M^2} - \sigma_m^2(A) - \sigma_m^2(B) - 2\|\hat{A}^T\hat{B}\|_2)\|z(t)\|_2^2 + \beta\|z(t)\|_2^2 \\ &= -\ell_M^2\Upsilon\|z(t)\|_2^2 + \beta\|z(t)\|_2^2 = -(\ell_M^2\Upsilon - \beta)\|z(t)\|_2^2 \end{aligned} \tag{29}$$

It can be seen from (29) that, if $\beta < \ell_M^2\Upsilon$, then $\dot{V}(z(t)) < 0$ for all $z(t) \neq 0$. Let $z(t) = 0$. In this case, from (26), we have

$$\dot{V}(z(t)) \leq \|B\|_2^2\|g(z(t-\tau))\|_2^2 - \alpha\|g(z(t-\tau))\|_2^2 - \beta\|z(t-\tau)\|_2^2 \tag{30}$$

Since $\alpha > \|B\|_2^2$, it follows from (30) that

$$\dot{V}(z(t)) \leq -\beta\|z(t-\tau)\|_2^2 \tag{31}$$

(31) implies that $\dot{V}(z(t))$ is negative definite for all $z(t-\tau) \neq 0$. Let $z(t) = 0$ and $z(t-\tau) = 0$ in which case $\dot{z}(t) = 0$, implying that

$$\dot{V}(z(t)) = -\sum_{i=1}^{n} \dot{z}_i^2(t-\tau_i) = -\dot{z}^T(t-\tau)\dot{z}(t-\tau) \quad (32)$$

(32) implies that $\dot{V}(z(t)) < 0$ for all $\dot{z}(t-\tau) \neq 0$. Hence, we observe that $\dot{V}(z(t)) = 0$ if and only if $z(t) = z(t-\tau) = \dot{z}(t) = \dot{z}(t-\tau) = 0$, otherwise $\dot{V}(z(t)) < 0$. In addition, $V(z(t))$ is radially unbounded since $V(z(t)) \to \infty$ as $\|z(t)\| \to \infty$. Thus, the origin of (21) is globally asymptotically robust stable.

4 A Numerical Example and Comparisons

In this section, a numerical example is given to make a comparison between the result of this paper and the previous literature results. We first unify the robust stability results obtained in [1–4] and [6–8] in the following theorem:

Theorem 3: For system (21), let the activation functions $g_i(\cdot)$ satisfy (22) and the network matrices A, B and C satisfy (4). Then, the origin of (21) is globally asymptotically stable, if the following condition holds:

$$\Delta = \frac{c_m}{\ell_M} - \sigma_m(A) - \sigma_m(B) > 0$$

where $c_m = min\{\underline{c}_i\}$, $\ell_M = max\{\ell_i\}$, $\sigma_m(A) = min\{\sigma_1(A), \sigma_2(A), \sigma_3(A), \sigma_4(A)\}$ and $\sigma_m(B) = min\{\sigma_1(B), \sigma_2(B), \sigma_3(B), \sigma_4(B)\}$.

$$\underline{A} = \begin{bmatrix} -1 & -1 & -1 & -1 \\ -1 & -1 & -1 & -1 \\ -1 & -1 & -1 & -1 \\ 1 & -1 & -1 & 1 \end{bmatrix}, \overline{A} = \begin{bmatrix} 1 & 1 & 1 & 1 \\ 1 & 1 & 1 & 1 \\ 1 & 1 & 1 & 1 \\ 1 & 1 & 1 & 1 \end{bmatrix}, \underline{B} = \begin{bmatrix} -3 & -3 & -3 & -3 \\ -3 & -3 & -3 & -3 \\ -2 & -2 & -2 & -2 \\ -2 & -2 & -2 & -2 \end{bmatrix}, \overline{B} = \begin{bmatrix} 3 & 3 & 3 & 3 \\ 3 & 3 & 3 & 3 \\ 2 & 2 & 2 & 2 \\ 2 & 2 & 2 & 2 \end{bmatrix},$$

$$\underline{c}_1 = \underline{c}_2 = \underline{c}_3 = \underline{c}_4 = c_m, \quad \ell_1 = \ell_2 = \ell_3 = \ell_4 = 1$$

We obtain the following matrices:

$$A^* = B^* = \begin{bmatrix} 0 & 0 & 0 & 0 \\ 0 & 0 & 0 & 0 \\ 0 & 0 & 0 & 0 \\ 0 & 0 & 0 & 0 \end{bmatrix}, A_* = \hat{A} = \begin{bmatrix} 1 & 1 & 1 & 1 \\ 1 & 1 & 1 & 1 \\ 1 & 1 & 1 & 1 \\ 1 & 1 & 1 & 1 \end{bmatrix}, B_* = \hat{B} = \begin{bmatrix} 3 & 3 & 3 & 3 \\ 3 & 3 & 3 & 3 \\ 2 & 2 & 2 & 2 \\ 2 & 2 & 2 & 2 \end{bmatrix}$$

We have $\|\hat{A}^T\hat{B}\|_2 = 40$, $\sigma_1(A) = \sigma_2(A) = \sigma_3(A) = \sigma_4(A) = 4$ and $\sigma_m(A) = 4$, $\sigma_1(B) = \sigma_2(B) = \sigma_3(B) = \sigma_4(B) = 10.198$ and $\sigma_m(B) = 10.198$.

Applying the result of Theorem 3 to this example yields

$$\Delta = \frac{c_m}{\ell_M} - \sigma_m(A) - \sigma_m(B) = c_m - 14.198 > 0$$

from which the robust stability condition is obtained as $c_m > 14.198$. When applying the result of Theorem 3 to this example, we get that

$$\Upsilon = \frac{c_m^2}{\ell_M^2} - \sigma_m^2(A) - \sigma_m^2(B) - 2\|\hat{A}^T\hat{B}\|_2 = c_m^2 - 16 - 104 - 80 = c_m^2 - 200 > 0$$

from which the robust stability condition is obtained as $c_m > 14.140$. Thus, for the parameters of this example, Theorem 2 yields a weaker robust stability condition than the robust stability condition stated in Theorem 3.

5 Conclusion

This paper has studied the global asymptotic robust stability of delayed neural networks with the uncertain system matrices having the bounded norms and presented a novel sufficient condition for the existence, uniqueness and global asymptotic stability of the equilibrium point with respect to the Lipschitz activation functions. By giving a numerical example, the proposed result has been shown to be a new sufficient condition when compared with previously reported corresponding robust stability results.

Acknowledgements. This study was funded by Scientific Research Projects Coordination Unit of Istanbul University-Cerrahpasa. Project numbers: BYP-2020-34652

References

1. Faydasicok, O., Arik, S.: A new upper bound for the norm of interval matrices with application to robust stability analysis of delayed neural networks. Neural Netw. **44**, 64–71 (2013)
2. Cao, J., Huang, D.S., Qu, Y.: Global robust stability of delayed recurrent neural networks. Chaos, SolitonsFractals **23**(1), 221–229 (2005)
3. Ensari, T., Arik, S.: New results for robust stability of dynamical neural networks with discrete time delays. Expert Syst. Appl. **37**, 5925–5930 (2010)
4. Singh, V.: Global robust stability of delayed neural networks: Estimating upper limit of norm of delayed connection weight matrix. Chaos, Solitons Fractals **32**, 259–263 (2007)
5. Forti, M., Tesi, A.: New conditions for global stability of neural networks with applications to linear and quadratic programming problems. IEEE Trans. Circuits Syst. I: Regul. Pap. **42**, 354–365 (1995)
6. Ozcan, N., Arik, S.: Global robust stability analysis of neural networks with multiple time delays. IEEE Trans. Circuits Syst. I: Regul. Pap. **53**, 166–176 (2006)
7. Yucel, E., Arik, S.: Novel results for global robust stability of delayed neural networks. Chaos, Solitons Fractals **39**, 1604–1614 (2009)
8. Samli, R., Yucel, E.: Global robust stability analysis of uncertain neural networks with time varying delays. Neurocomputing **167**, 371–377 (2015)
9. Shao, J.L., Huang, T.Z., Zhou, S.: Some improved criteria for global robust exponential stability of neural networks with time-varying delays. Commun. Nonlinear Sci. Numer. Simul. **15**, 3782–3794 (2010)

10. Qi, H.: New sufficient conditions for global robust stability of delayed neural networks. IEEE Trans. Circuits Syst. I: Regul. Pap. **54**(5), 1131–1141 (2007)
11. Qiu, J., Zhang, J., Wang, J., Xia, Y., Shi, P.: A new global robust stability criteria for uncertain neural networks with fast time-varying delays. Chaos, Solitons Fractals **37**(2), 360–368 (2008)
12. Kwon, O.M., Park, J.H., Lee, S.M., Cha, E.J.: Analysis on delay-dependent stability for neural networks with time-varying delays. Neurocomputing **103**, 114–120 (2013)
13. Zhang, H., Wang, Z., Liu, D.: Robust stability analysis for interval Cohen-Grossberg neural networks with unknown time-varying delays. IEEE Trans. Neural Netw. **19**(11), 1942–1955 (2008)
14. Zhu, Q., Cao, J.: Robust exponential stability of Markovian jump impulsive stochastic Cohen-Grossberg neural networks with mixed time delays. IEEE Trans. Neural Netw. **21**(8), 1314–1325 (2010)
15. Huang, H., Feng, G., Cao, J.: Robust state estimation for uncertain neural networks with time-varying delay. IEEE Trans. Neural Netw. **19**(8), 1329–1339 (2008)
16. Huang, T., Li, C., Duan, S., Starzyk, J.A.: Robust exponential stability of uncertain delayed neural networks with stochastic perturbation and impulse effects. IEEE Trans. Neural Netw. Learn. Syst. **23**(6), 866–875 (2012)
17. Zhang, H., Wang, Z., Liu, D.: Global asymptotic stability and robust stability of a class of Cohen-Rossberg neural networks with mixed delays. IEEE Trans. Circuits Syst. I: Regul. Pap. **56**(3), 616–629 (2009)
18. Hu, S., Wang, J.: Global robust stability of a class of discrete-time interval neural networks. IEEE Trans. Circuits Syst. I: Regul. Pap. **53**(1), 129–138 (2006)
19. Wu, Z.G., Shi, P., Su, H., Chu, J.: Passivity analysis for discrete-time stochastic Markovian jump neural networks with mixed time delays. IEEE Trans. Neural Netw. **22**(10), 1566–1575 (2011)
20. Zhang, H., Liu, Z., Huang, G.B.: Novel delay-dependent robust stability analysis for switched neutral-type neural networks with time-varying delays via SC technique. IEEE Trans. Syst. Man, Cybern. Part B: (Cybern.) **40**(6), 1480–1491 (2012)
21. Arik, S.: An analysis of stability of neutral-type neural systems with constant time delays. J. Franklin Inst. **351**(11), 4949–4959 (2014)

Generalized Entropy Loss Function in Neural Network: Variable's Importance and Sensitivity Analysis

Krzysztof Gajowniczek(✉) and Tomasz Ząbkowski

Warsaw University of Life Sciences,
Nowoursynowska 159, 02-776 Warsaw, Poland
{krzysztof_gajowniczek, tomasz_zabkowski}@ssgw.edu.pl

Abstract. Artificial neural networks are powerful tools for data analysis and are particularly suitable for modelling relationships between variables for best prediction of an outcome. A large number of error functions have been proposed in the literature to achieve a better predictive power of a neural network. Only a few works employ Tsallis statistics, although the method itself has been successfully applied in other machine learning techniques. This paper undertakes the effort to examine various characteristics of the q-generalized function based on Tsallis entropy as an alternative loss measure in neural networks. To achieve this goal, we will explore various methods that can be used to interpret supervised neural network models. These methods can be used to visualize the model using the neural network interpretation diagram, assess the importance of variables by disaggregating the model's weights (Olden's and Garson's algorithms) and perform a sensitivity analysis of model responses to input variables (Lek's profile).

Keywords: Generalized entropy · Neural networks · Sensitivity analysis · Variable's importance

1 Introduction

Artificial intelligence (AI) methods, especially those based on machine learning methods, are rapidly becoming essential for the analysis of complex data. Artificial neural networks (ANNs) are highly parametrized, non-linear models with sets of processing units called neurons that can be used to approximate the relationship between the input and the output signals of a complex system [1]. They have been extensively and successfully applied in areas such as pattern recognition, signal processing, and system control in a number of real-world problems including engineering, medicine, or business [2–4].

In general, neural networks must determine the required mapping of input to output variables to solve a given problem during iterative training process. The main goal of the training is to find the correct weights values between the inputs and the outputs of the layers that minimize some predefined loss function (also called error measure) [5]. For the successful application it is important to train the network with a loss function

L. Iliadis et al. (Eds.): EANN 2020, INNS 2, pp. 535–545, 2020.
https://doi.org/10.1007/978-3-030-48791-1_42

that reflects the objective of the problem. For instance, the mean square error (MSE) is the most commonly used function, however it is not necessarily the best function for classification tasks. Consequently, a number of alternative loss functions have been investigated, and for the classification tasks the cross entropy loss function is considered as more appropriate [6].

In this article we make an effort to investigate an extension of the cross entropy loss function, which is a q-generalized loss function based on Tsallis statistics [7]. We will explore the properties of the proposed loss function and measure the performance of the neural network by assessing the variables' importance through a sensitivity analysis of response variable to changes in the input variables.

Although ANNs can be seen as powerful predictive tools compared to more conventional models such as linear or logistic regression, they are also criticized as 'black boxes', because ANN based models are hard to interpret and it is difficult to determine which features are most important for the problem and how they are related to the modelled phenomenon. To address this weakness, we will present several methods that will help broad audience to understand various aspects of the final neural network model'outcome. For this purpose a Garson and Olden algorithms will be used to assess the importance of each input variable and the Lek's profile will be used to evaluate the effects of input variables by returning a plot of model predictions across the range of values for each variable [1, 8].

In particular, using artificially simulated data with the known underlying structure, we aim to answer the following research questions:

- What is the effect of the q-parameter in the proposed loss function on the various properties of the neural network?
- To what extent is it possible to analyse various characteristics of the neural network?

The remainder of this paper is organized as follows: Sect. 2 provides an overview of the similar research problems as well as the theoretical frameworks of the generalized entropy and artificial neural networks. In Sect. 3, the research framework was outlined, including the details of numerical implementation, artificial dataset and model performance measures. Section 4 outlines the experiments and presents the discussion of the results. The paper ends with concluding remarks in Sect. 5.

2 Theoretical Background

2.1 Artificial Neural Networks

Artificial neural networks are a set of algorithms created to mimic the human brain, that are designed to recognize patterns. They interpret input data through a kind of machine perception, labelling or clustering raw input. The patterns they recognize are numerical, contained in vectors, into which all real-world data, be it images, sound, text or time series, must be translated [9]. Usually ANNs are composed of several layers (e.g. multilayer perceptron; MLP) [10]. The layers are made of nodes. A node is just a place where computation happens, loosely patterned on a neuron in the human brain, which fires when it encounters sufficient stimuli. A node combines input from the data with a set of coefficients, or weights, that either amplify or dampen that input, thereby assigning significance to inputs with regard to the task the algorithm is trying to learn. These input-weight products are summed and then the sum is passed through a node's so-called activation function, to determine whether and to what extent that signal should progress further through the network to affect the ultimate outcome [11].

In general, artificial neural network (MLP) with a one hidden layer consisting of J hidden neurons and p input neurons (neurons from each layer activated by the logistic function f) estimates the following function:

$$ANN = f\left(w_0 + \sum\nolimits_{j=1}^{J} w_j f\left(w_{0j} + \sum\nolimits_{i=1}^{p} w_{ij} x_i\right)\right), \tag{1}$$

where w_0 stands for the bias synaptic weight of the output neuron, w_{0j} stands for the bias synaptic weight of the j-th hidden neuron, x_i stands for the i input feature, w_j stands for the weight corresponding to the synapse starting at the j-th hidden neuron and leading to the output neuron and w_{ij} stands for the weight of the i-th neuron from the input layer to the j neuron from the hidden layer [6].

ANNs are matched to data by learning algorithms during the iterative training process by the use of a given output, which is compared to the predicted output and the adjustment of all parameters. The parameters of ANNs are their weights. A common learning algorithm is the resilient backpropagation algorithm [12] that modifies neural network weights to find a local minimum (in ideal case a global minimum) of some predefined loss function E, which is, in this article, the function defined in the Eqs. 3 and 4.

2.2 Generalized Entropy

Information entropy introduced by Shannon [13] is the average rate at which information is produced by a stochastic source of data (or equivalently unpredictability of a particular event/state). The value of the entropy depends on two parameters: (1) disorder (uncertainty) and it is maximum when the probability of every possible states are equal; (2) number of possible events.

Standard Shannon entropy assumes a compromise contributions from the main mass of the distribution and the tail. To control both parameters, a generalization was proposed by Tsallis [7], defined as:

$$H_{T_q} = \frac{1}{q-1}\left(1 - \sum\nolimits_{i=1}^{n} t_i^q\right), \tag{2}$$

where t_i is the probability of occurrence of an event x_i being an element of a random variable X that can take values $x_1, \ldots, x_n$, and q is the adjustable generalization parameter. Using this generalized entropy with $q > 1$, high probability events contribute to the entropy value more than these with low probability. Therefore, the higher the value of q, the greater is the share of highly probable events in the final result.

ANNs require loss function that accepts target variable and its predicted value. To estimate this loss the Kullback-Leibler (K-L) divergence measuring distance between two distributions can be used. Generally K-L divergence measures the inefficiency of assuming that the distribution is $\{y_i\}$, when the true distribution is $\{t_i\}$. For the same reason, the mutual entropy of Tsallis is a generalization of K-L entropy, the latter being only a limiting case of the former for $q \to 1$. The mutual entropy of Tsallis refers to two probability distributions $\{t_i\}$ and $\{y_i\}$, $(i = 1, \ldots, n)$, over the same alphabet, and is defined as [5]:

$$H_{T_q}(t||y) = \frac{1}{1-q}\left(1 - \sum\nolimits_{i=1}^{n} t_i^q y_i^{1-q}\right). \tag{3}$$

The loss function being minimized during the training should accept input data, output data and the parameter vector. Based on these, a given loss function returns both the current loss and its gradients. For this reason, the loss function that implements Tsallis mutual entropy is defined as follows [5]:

$$E(t, y, q) = \frac{1}{1-q}\left(1 - t^q y^{1-q} - (1-t)^q (1-y)^{1-q}\right), \tag{4}$$

where (as previously) t and y stand for the true value and output of a given neural network respectively. Moreover q stands for the current value of the q-parameter and the gradient of the loss function defined as:

$$\frac{\partial}{\partial y} E(t, y, q) = (-(y-1)y)^{-q} (y^q (1-t)^q - (1-y)^q t^q), \tag{5}$$

is required for any gradient-based optimization algorithms.

2.3 Related Works on Variable's Importance

Machine learning systems are increasingly capable of solving many complex problems in many disciplines. Unfortunately, these systems remain characteristically opaque as these are difficult to look inside so the underlying relations between the input variables and the output cannot be easily captured.

In the last decades, several methods have been proposed to measure the importance of input variables, which basically apply some changes into input values and checks what happens to the output. In some methods called pruning, the approach is to eliminate irrelevant input e.g. [14–16], where the most significant input variables are determined first and, then these which are below a threshold are excluded from the neural network. This minimizes redundancy and allows to limit the size of the network.

There are some methods, as opposite to pruning methods, which aim to capture the relative contribution or the contribution profile of the input factors. For instance partial derivatives method by Dimopoulos et al. [17], which consists in calculating the partial derivatives of the output with respect to each input variable.

Some approaches are called 'weights' methods as these apply a computation using the connection weights. For example, Garson [18] proposed a method of partitioning the ANN connection weights in order to determine the relative importance of each input variable within the network. The same idea has been modified and applied by Goh [19]. In the case of a single layer of hidden units, the equation is:

$$Q_{ik} = \frac{\sum_{j=1}^{J} \left| w_{ij} v_{jk} \right| / \sum_{r=1}^{p} \left| w_{rj} \right|}{\sum_{i=1}^{p} \sum_{j=1}^{J} \left(\left| w_{ij} v_{jk} \right| / \sum_{r=1}^{p} \left| w_{rj} \right| \right)}, \tag{6}$$

where w_{ij} is the connection weight between the input i-th neuron and the j-th hidden neuron, v_{jk} is the connection weight between the j-th hidden neuron and the k-th output neuron, and $\sum_{r=1}^{p} \left| w_{rj} \right|$ is the sum of the connection weights between the p input neurons (features) and the j-th hidden neuron. Q_{ik} represents the percentage of influence of the input variable on the output. In order to avoid the counteracting influence due to positive and negatives values, all connection weights were given their absolute values in the modified Garson algorithm.

Similarly, the Olden's algorithm [20], which, in comparison to the Garson's method, uses the product of the raw connection weights between each input and the output neuron and sums the product across all hidden neurons. An advantage of this approach is that relative contributions of each connection weight are maintained in terms of both, magnitude and sign, as compared to Garson's algorithm which considers only the absolute magnitude.

An alternative approach to assess the relationship of variables in the neural network is Lek's profile method [21]. The profile method is fundamentally different from Garson's, Olden's algorithms or pruning methods, as it is to assess the behaviour of target across different values of the input variables [8].

The Lek's profile method evaluates the effects of each input feature by returning a model forecast graph across the range of values for this variable. The remaining features are kept constant when assessing the effects of each input variable. This method provides two options for setting fixed values of other invaluable features. The first option holds invaluable features at different quantiles such as minimum, 20th percentile, median or maximum. The second option clusters the invaluable features according to their natural grouping defined by data. Covariance among the variables may present unlikely scenarios if all invaluable features are kept at the same level. In other words high values for one features may be unlikely with high values for other features. This approach holds invaluable features at means defined by natural clusters in the data using k-means clustering algorithm.

The relationship between an outcome and the predictor may vary, taking into account the context of other variables (i.e. the presence of interactions) and sensitivities may vary at different points in the surface, taking into account the ability of the model to describe non-linear relationships [1]. Basically, this method generates a partial derivative of the response for each investigated feature and can provide insight into these complex relationships described by the model. Unfortunately, the Lek's profile is only applicable to models with continuous features.

This paper intends to deal with the problem of variables' importance ranking applicable to the neural networks that use generalized entropy loss functions. Specifically, Olden's and Garson's algorithms were tested followed by sensitivity analysis using Lek's profile as those are supposed to be helpful based on the literature review.

3 Research Framework and Settings

3.1 Artificial Dataset

To assess any statistical method it is desirable to carry out an appropriate simulation analysis which may give results where the true signal is known in advance. A good simulation system should test several different aspects of classification problems such as linear and nonlinear features, non-informative features and correlation among the features. The dataset simulation was prepared according to the process described by Gajowniczek et al. [5]. Based on this aforementioned framework in the current article the simulation system (*twoClassSim* function from the *caret* package [22]) models a logarithmic binary event (Bernoulli random target variable) as a function of real signals using additive sets of a few different types. The final set consists of the following features:

- Factor1 and Factor2 which are truly important features;
- Linear having linear relationship with the target variable;
- Nonlinear adding some fluctuation to the log-odds;
- Noise which is non-informative for the target variable.

The entire dataset consist of 10,000 observations while the class imbalance ratio for binary classification task is set at approx. 50–50%. Moreover, all aforementioned variables were normalized to the range [0,1].

3.2 Numerical Implementation

All numerical experiments presented below were prepared using R programming language [23] installed on Ubuntu 18.04 operating system on a personal computer equipped with Intel Core i7-9750H2.6 GHz processor (12 threads) and 32 GB of RAM. As stated previously the dataset was prepared using the *caret* package. Each ANN was built using *neuralnet* package [24] which allows for flexible settings through custom-choice of loss function (see Eq. 4 and 5). Each time the ANN had 5 input neurons (equal to the number of the investigated features), 4 hidden neurons and one output neuron. All neurons were activated by the logistic function and the maximum steps for the training of the ANN was set at 10,000 iterations. Since usually the standard Shannon entropy is used as a loss function (q equals 1), to investigate the influence of the q-parameter on the ANN's structure, we set this parameter at 0.000001 (due to the numerical issues in calculating Eq. 4 from now on we will use the abbreviation 0), 1.000001 (abbreviation 1; approximately equals Shannon entropy) and 2. Finally, to prepare the variable's importance plots and Lek's profiles we used the *NeuralNetTools* package [8].

4 Numerical Experiment

The weights connecting neurons in ANN are partially analogous to the coefficients in the generalized linear model. The combined impact of the weights on model forecasts represents the relative importance of the predictors in their relationship to the output variable. However, there are a number of weights that combine one predictor with the output in the ANN. The large number of adjustable weights in ANN makes it very flexible in modelling non-linear effects, but imposes challenges for the interpretation.

To overcome this issue one can calculate the importance of each predictor using Olden's and Garson's algorithms (please see Fig. 1). The Garson's method suggests that Factor2 (left part of the figure) has the strongest relationship with the output variable (followed by Factor1 and NonLinear), similar to a strong positive association shown with the Olden's method (right part of the figure). For both methods all features are ranked in the same order.

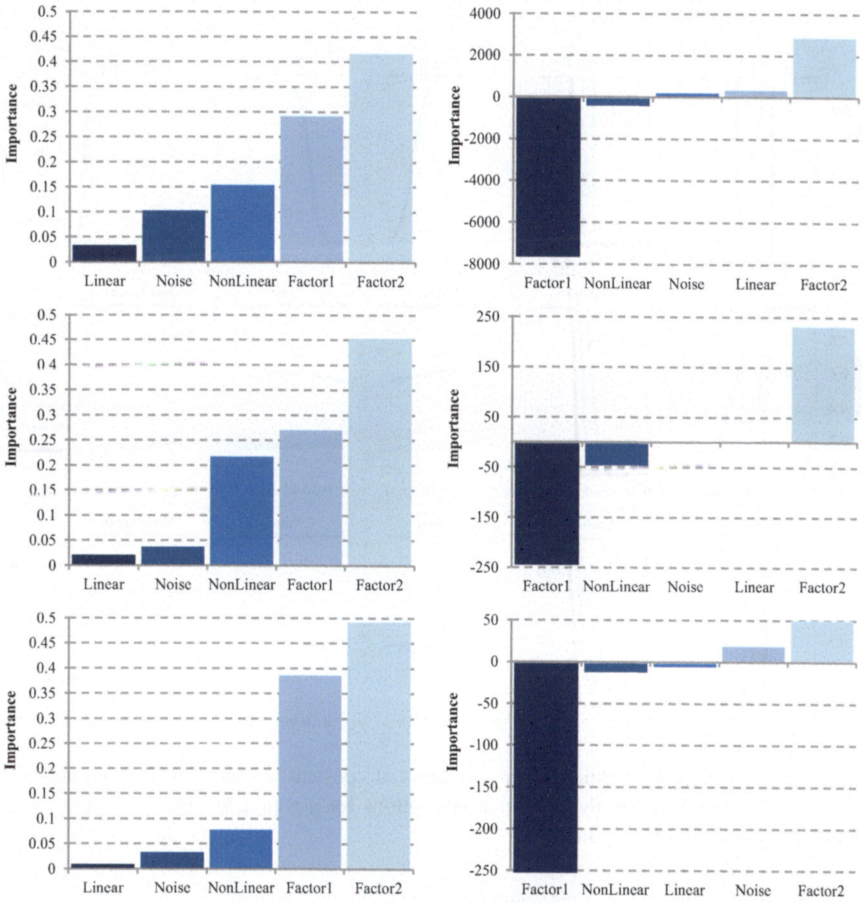

Fig. 1. Importance of each predictor using Garson's (left part) and Olden's (right part) for q-parameter set at 0 (upper part), 1 (middle part) and 2 (bottom part).

When analysing vertically the left part of the Fig. 1 it can be seen that q-parameter changes affect the validity of features. The relative importance of the most important feature (Factor2) increases from 0.42 (q equals 0 for the upper part of the figure) even up to 0.50 (q equals 2 for the bottom part of the figure). Simultaneously, the relative importance of other less important features (Linear and Noise) decreases even to 0.01-0.03. In total, the overall importance of the two most important features (which are truly relevant) becomes bigger and clearer from the initial value of about 0.71 even up to 0.89.

Right part of the Fig. 1 reveals that some features have positive and some negative impact on the target variable. Factor1 which is the second most important feature based on the Garson's method has very strong negative influence on the outcome variable based on the Olden's method. When using this method one can notice that when q-parameter increases from 0 to 2 the range/diversity of the relative importance flattens from the range 2500–(-7500) to the range 50–(-300). One more time the joint importance of Factor1 and Factor2 becomes bigger.

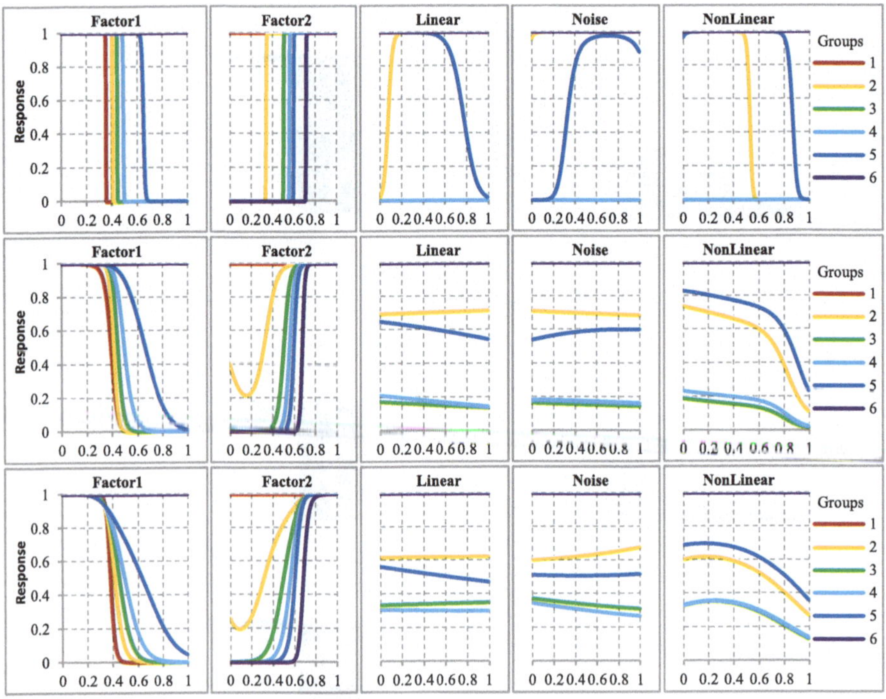

Fig. 2. Lek's profiles by holding other predictors at constant values of their minimum, 20th, 40th, 60th, 80th quantiles and the maximum algorithms for q-parameter set at 0 (upper part), 1 (middle part) and 2 (bottom part).

The results in Fig. 2 present Lek's profiles by holding other predictors at six different constant values i.e. their minimum (red colour), 20th, 40th, 60th, 80th quantiles (orange, green, cyan, and blue colours, respectively) and the maximum (purple colour). The horizontal axes present the whole range of each feature (as provided in Sect. 3.1 all the features were normalized) while the vertical axes show values of the response variable. Let's take first look on the most important variables presented in the upper part of the figure (q set at 0). The Olden's algorithm revealed that Factor1 and Factor2 have negative and positive influence on the target, respectively.

The Lek's profile shows the same relationship i.e. when the values of the Factor1 (x-axis) are increasing then the values of the outcome are decreasing from 1 to 0. This happens for the Factor1 values approx. between 0.3 and 0.7. In opposite, the behaviour of Factor2 is almost the same but has inverse relationship. In general, for both features the change is rapid i.e. all lines are almost vertical. For other three variables it can be seen that when other remaining variables are set at their minimums (group 1) or their 60th percentiles (group 4) there is no impact on the target variable (straight horizontal lines). On the other hand, the change is observed for group 5 (80th percentile; Noise) or for group 2 and 5 (20th and 80th percentiles; Linear and NonLinear).

When q-parameter is set at 1 or 2 (middle and bottom part of the Fig. 2) the influence on the outcome changes its behaviour and shape. Firstly, for Factor1 and Factor2 the change is not so rapid as previously i.e. curves are smoothed at the ends and are slightly tilted. Secondly, other three features lose their influence on the target and become almost horizontal.

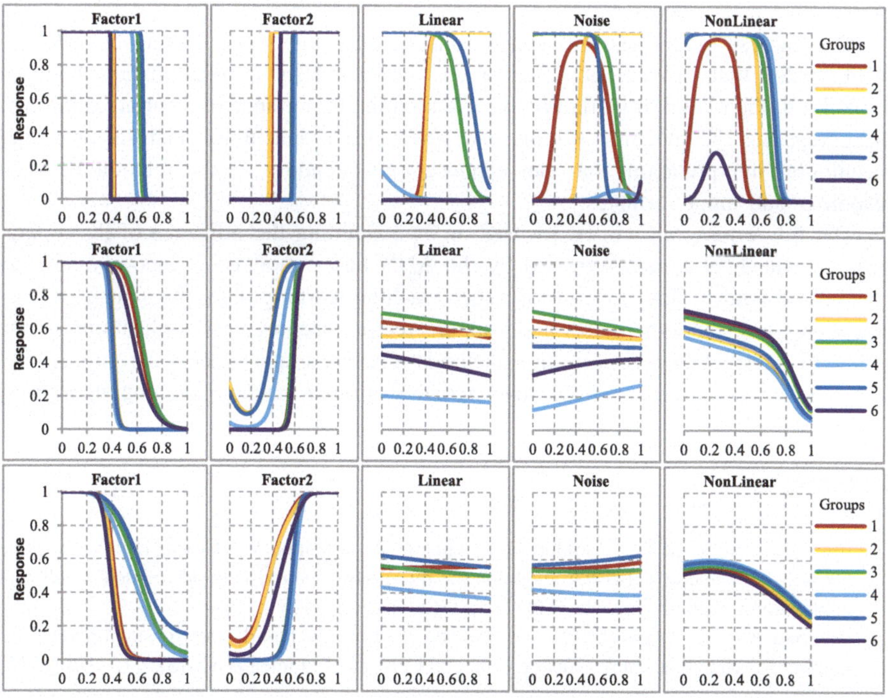

Fig. 3. Lek's profiles by holding other predictors at constant values at means defined by k-means algorithm for q-parameter set at 0 (upper part), 1 (middle part) and 2 (bottom part).

Results in Fig. 3 present Lek's profiles by holding other predictors at six different constant values (their means) defined by natural clusters in the data using k-means clustering algorithm.

The first difference is for Factor1 and Factor2 (upper part of the figure when q is set at 0). This time all curves changed their shapes (previously group 6 remained constant). This observation is also valid for three other features. Profile for the Linear confirms that this feature has straight influence on the outcome, i.e. target becomes either 0 or 1 after the change. Profiles for the Noise and for the NonLinear confirm that these features have variable impact on the outcome, especially for the group 1 and 6 which theoretically define the lowest and the biggest averages from the data.

Finally, with increased q-parameter to 1 or 2, in comparison to the Fig. 2, the similar behaviour can be observed. However, this time all curves for all features are squeezed next to each other more than before.

5 Conclusions

In this work, we have presented non-standard loss function based on the generalized (Tsallis) entropy measure and the methods to evaluate variable importance (Garson's, Olden's) and conduct a sensitivity analysis based on Lek's profiles. With our analysis we confirmed that the q-parameter within proposed loss function has an impact on different properties of the neural network, including variables importance and sensitivity of the neural network.

The analysis addresses the typical concern that supervised neural networks are black boxes that provide no information about underlying relationships between variables in the model. Importantly, we assessed the importance of a variables through disaggregating the model's weights and performed a sensitivity analysis providing meaningful interpretations that can enhance understanding of the relation between responses and input variables.

The future research will be focused on 1) examining the influence of the q-parameter on the final results provided by the ANN based models; 2) incorporating the generalized entropy loss function in other machine learning algorithms such as classification trees, random forests and support vector machines; 3) applications of the proposed interpretation/visualization methods (Garson's and Olden's algorithms, and Lek's profiles) to analyse various characteristics of other machine learning algorithms.

References

1. Zhang, Z., Beck, M.W., Winkler, D.A., Huang, B., Sibanda, W., Goyal, H.: Opening the black box of neural networks: methods for interpreting neural network models in clinical applications. Ann. Transl. Med. **6**(11), 216 (2018)
2. Gajowniczek, K., Orłowski, A., Ząbkowski, T.: Entropy based trees to support decision making for customer churn management. Acta Physica Polonica A **129**(5), 971–979 (2016)

3. Gajowniczek, K., Karpio, K., Łukasiewicz, P., Orłowski, A., Ząbkowski, T.: Q-entropy approach to selecting high income households. Acta Physica Polonica A **127**(3a), A38–A44 (2015)
4. Nafkha, R., Gajowniczek, K., Ząbkowski, T.: Do customers choose proper tariff? empirical analysis based on polish data using unsupervised techniques. Energies **11**(3), 514 (2018)
5. Gajowniczek, K., Orłowski, A., Ząbkowski, T.: Simulation study on the application of the generalized entropy concept in artificial neural networks. Entropy **20**(4), 249 (2018)
6. Golik, P., Doetsch, P., Ney, H.: Cross-entropy vs squared error training: a theoretical and experimental comparison. In: Proceedings of the 14th Annual Conference of the International Speech Communication Association "Interspeech-2013", Lyon, France, pp. 1756–1760 (2013)
7. Tsallis, C.: Introduction to Nonextensive Statistical Mechanics. Springer, New York (2009)
8. Beck, M.W.: NeuralNetTools: visualization and analysis tools for neural networks. J. Stat. Softw. **85**(11), 1–20 (2018)
9. Liu, W., Wang, Z., Liu, X., Zeng, N., Liu, Y., Alsaadi, F.E.: A survey of deep neural network architectures and their applications. Neurocomputing **234**, 11–26 (2017)
10. Gajowniczek, K., Ząbkowski, T.: Short term electricity forecasting based on user behavior from individual smart meter data. J. Intell. Fuzzy Syst. **30**(1), 223–234 (2016)
11. Rumelhart, D.E., Hinton, G.E., Williams, R.J.: Learning representations by BackPropagating errors. Nature **323**(6088), 533–536 (1986)
12. Riedmiller, M.: Rprop – Description and Implementation Details; Technical Report. University of Karlsruhe, Germany (1994)
13. Shannon, C.E.: A mathematical theory of communication. Bell Syst. Tech. J. **27**, 623–666 (1948)
14. Zurada, J.M., Malinowski, A., Cloete, I.: Sensitivity analysis for minimization of input data dimension for feedforward neural network. In: IEEE International Symposium on circuits and Systems, ISCAS1994, vol. 6. IEE Press, London (1994)
15. Engelbrecht, A.P., Cloete, I., Zurada, J.M.: Determining the significance of input parameters using sensitivity analysis. From natural to artificial neural computation, Springer, Malaga-Torremolinos (1995)
16. Kim, S.H., Yoon, C., Kim, B.J.: Structural monitoring system based on sensitivity analysis and a neural network. Comput.-Aided Civil Infrastruct. Eng. **155**, 309–318 (2000)
17. Dimopoulos, Y., Bourret, P., Lek, S.: Use of some sensitivity criteria for choosing networks with good generalization ability. Neural Process. Lett. **2**, 1–4 (1995)
18. Garson, G.D.: Interpreting neural network connection weights. Artif. Intell. Exp. **6**, 46–51 (1991)
19. Goh, A.T.C.: Back-propagation neural networks for modeling complex systems. Artif. Intell. Eng. **9**, 143–151 (1995)
20. Olden, J.D., Joy, M.K., Death, R.G.: An accurate comparison of methods for quantifying variable importance in artificial neural networks using simulated data. Ecol. Model. **178**(3–4), 389–397 (2004)
21. Lek, S., Delacoste, M., Baran, P., Dimopoulos, I., Lauga, J., Aulagnier, S.: Application of neural networks to modelling nonlinear relationships in ecology. Ecol. Model. **90**(1), 39–52 (1996)
22. Kuhn, M.: Building predictive models in R using the caret package. J. Stat. Softw. **28**(5), 1–26 (2008)
23. The R Development Core Team. R: A Language and Environment for Statistical Computing; R Foundation for Statistical Computing: Vienna, Austria (2014)
24. Fritsch, S., Guenther, F.: Neuralnet: training of neural networks. R Package Version 1.33.2016. https://CRAN.R-project.org/package=neuralnet. Accessed 10 Jan 2020

Robust Multilayer Perceptrons: Robust Loss Functions and Their Derivatives

Jan Kalina and Petra Vidnerová(✉)

The Czech Academy of Sciences, Institute of Computer Science,
Pod Vodárenskou věží 2, 182 07 Praha 8, Czech Republic
{kalina,petra}@cs.cas.cz

Abstract. Common types of artificial neural networks have been well known to suffer from the presence of outlying measurements (outliers) in the data. However, there are only a few available robust alternatives for training common form of neural networks. In this work, we investigate robust fitting of multilayer perceptrons, i.e. alternative approaches to the most common type of feedforward neural networks. Particularly, we consider robust neural networks based on the robust loss function of the least trimmed squares, for which we express formulas for derivatives of the loss functions. Some formulas, which are however incorrect, have been already available. Further, we consider a very recently proposed multilayer perceptron based on the loss function of the least weighted squares, which appears a promising highly robust approach. We also derive the derivatives of the loss functions, which are to the best of our knowledge a novel contribution of this paper. The derivatives may find applications in implementations of the robust neural networks, if a (gradient-based) backpropagation algorithm is used.

Keywords: Neural networks · Loss functions · Robust regression

1 Introduction

Neural networks represent a wide class of habitually used tools for the task of nonlinear regression. Numerous applications of estimation in nonlinear regression in various fields are nowadays solved by neural networks. Thus, they represent important exploratory tools of modern data analysis [15], particularly of exploratory data analysis (see e.g. [7]). However, the most commonly used methods for training regression neural networks based on the least squares criterion are biased under contaminated data [18] as well as vulnerable to adversarial examples.

Under the presence of outlying measurements (outliers) in the data, training multilayer perceptrons is known to be unreliable (biased). Such their nonrobustness, caused by their minimization of the sum of squared residuals (see [11]

The research was financially supported by the projects GA19-05704S (J. Kalina) and GA18-23827S (P. Vidnerová) of the Czech Science Foundation.

L. Iliadis et al. (Eds.): EANN 2020, INNS 2, pp. 546–557, 2020.
https://doi.org/10.1007/978-3-030-48791-1_43

for discussion), becomes even more severe for data with a very large number of regressors [3]. Therefore, researchers have recently become increasingly interested in proposing alternative robust (resistant) methods for training of multilayer perceptrons [2]. So far, only a few robust approaches for training for MLPs have been introduced and even smaller attention has been paid to a robustification of radial basis function (RBF) networks. Approaches replacing the common sum of squared residuals by a robust loss considered the loss functions corresponding to the median [1], least trimmed absolute value (LTA) estimator [17], or least trimmed squares (LTS) estimator [2,18]. The last two estimators were proposed for the model of the so-called contaminated normal distribution, assuming the residuals to come from a mixture of normally distributed errors with outliers, typically assumed to be normally distributed as well but with a (possibly much) larger variance than the majority of the data points. Other robust loss functions within multilayer perceptrons were examined in [13]. A different robust approach to neural networks based on finding the least outlying subset of observations but exploiting the standard loss minimizing the sum of least squares of residuals was proposed in [11], where also some other previous attempts for robustification of neural networks are cited. All these robust approaches were also verified to be meaningful in numerical experiments. Robust approaches to fitting neural networks were investigated also in the context of clustering (unsupervised learning), based on replacing means of clusters by other centroids (e.g. medoids [4]).

Here, we use the idea to replace the common loss function of multilayer perceptron by a robust version. On the whole, we consider here three particular loss functions for multilayer perceptrons, corresponding to

- Least squares (i.e. the most common form of the loss for multilayer perceptrons),
- Least trimmed squares (see Sect. 2),
- Least weighted squares (see Sect. 2).

As the main contribution, partial derivatives of the loss function with respect to each of the parameters are evaluated here for robust multilayer perceptrons. These are very useful, because the backpropagation algorithm for computing the robust neural networks requires them. We derive the derivatives for a particular architecture of the multilayer perceptron, while they can be extended in a straightforward way to more complex multilayer perceptrons. Nevertheless, we point out that the derivatives are difficult to find in the literature even for a standard multilayer perceptron with a loss based on minimizing the least squares criterion. Available robust estimators for linear regression and for the location model are recalled in Sect. 2 of this paper. Section 3 presents derivatives of standard as well as robust loss functions for a multilayer perceptron with one hidden layer. Section 4 concludes the paper.

2 Linear Model and Robust Estimation

This section recalls robust estimates in linear regression model (and the location model, which is its special case), which will serve as inspiration for the robust versions of neural networks studied later in Sect. 3. The standard linear regression model

$$Y_i = \beta_0 + \beta_1 X_{i1} + \cdots + \beta_p X_{ip} + e_i, \quad i = 1, \ldots, n, \tag{1}$$

considers n observations, for which a continuous response is explained by p regressors (independent variables, features) under the presence of random errors $e_1, \ldots, e_n$. The presence of the intercept β_0 in the model can be interpreted as the presence of a vector of ones in the design matrix X containing the elements X_{ij}. As the most common least squares estimator of $\beta = (\beta_0, \beta_1, \ldots, \beta_p)^T$ in (1) is vulnerable to the presence of outliers in the data, various robust alternatives have been proposed [8].

Robust statisticians have proposed a variety of estimation tools, which are resistant to the presence of outliers in the data. Such estimators are considered *highly* robust with respect to outliers, which have a high value of the breakdown point. We can say that the breakdown point, which represents a fundamental concept of robust statistics [8], is a measure of robustness of a statistical estimator of an unknown parameter. Formally, the finite-sample breakdown point evaluates the minimal fraction of data that can drive an estimator beyond all bounds when set to arbitrary values. Keeping in mind the high robustness, we decide for replacing the sum of squared residuals by loss functions of the least trimmed squares and least weighted squares estimators, which are known to yield reliable and resistant results over real data [10].

The least trimmed squares (LTS) estimator [16] represents a very popular regression estimator with a high breakdown point (cf. [8]). Consistency of the LTS and other properties were derived in [19]. Formally, the LTS estimate of β is obtained as

$$\arg\min_{b \in \mathbb{R}^{p+1}} \frac{1}{h} \sum_{i=1}^{h} u_{(i)}^2(b), \tag{2}$$

where the user must choose a fixed h fulfilling $n/2 \leq h < n$; here, $u_i(b)$ is a residual corresponding to the i-th observation for a given b, and we consider squared values arranged in ascending order denoted as $u_{(1)}^2(b) \leq \cdots \leq u_{(n)}^2(b)$. The LTS estimator may attain a high robustness but cannot achieve a high efficiency [19].

The least weighted squares (LWS) estimator [20] for the model (1), motivated by the idea to down-weight potential outliers, remains much less known compared to the LTS, although it has more appealing statistical properties. The definition of the LWS exploits the concept of weight function, which is defined as a function $\psi : [0, 1] \to [0, 1]$ under technical assumptions. The LWS estimator with a given ψ, which is able to much exceed the LTS in terms of efficiency, is defined as

$$\arg\min_{b \in \mathbb{R}^{p+1}} \sum_{k=1}^{n} \psi\left(\frac{k - 1/2}{n}\right) u_{(i)}^2(b). \tag{3}$$

We may refer to [20] and references cited therein for properties of the LWS; it may achieve a high breakdown point (with properly selected weights), robustness to heteroscedasticity, and efficiency for non-contaminated samples. The performance of the LWS on real data (see [9] and references cited therein) can be described as excellent. We also need to consider the location model, which is a special case of (1), in the form

$$Y_i = \mu + e_i, \quad i = 1, \ldots, n \tag{4}$$

with a location parameter $\mu \in \mathbb{R}$. The LTS and LWS estimators are meaningful (and successful [9]) also under (4), while the LWS estimator in (4) inherits the appealing properties from (1).

3 Theoretical Results

This section presents partial derivatives of three loss functions for a particular architecture of a multilayer perceptron, i.e. assuming a single hidden layer. Their usefulness is discussed in Sect. 4.

3.1 Model and Notation

We assume that a continuous response variable $Y_i \in \mathbb{R}$ and a vector of regressors (independent variables) $X_i = (X_{i1}, \ldots, X_{ip})^T \in \mathbb{R}^p$ are available for the total number of n observations. The regression modeling in the nonlinear model

$$Y_i = \varphi(X_i) + e_i, \quad i = 1, \ldots, n, \tag{5}$$

with an unknown function φ and random errors $e_1, \ldots, e_n$ will be performed using a multilayer perceptron (MLP) with a single hidden layer, which contains N hidden neurons.

The MLP estimates the response Y_i of the i-th observation by

$$\hat{Y}_i = \hat{Y}_i(c, \gamma, \omega) = g\left(\sum_{k=1}^{N} \gamma_k f\left(\sum_{j=1}^{p} \omega_{kj} X_{ij} + \omega_{k0}\right) + \gamma_0\right) + c, \quad i = 1, \ldots, n, \tag{6}$$

where f and g must be specified (possibly nonlinear) functions. The formula (6) for computing the fitted values of the response considers two layers only however can be generalized for more layers easily. We use here a notation following [6], although other more or less different versions of notation may be used in this context as well. If g is an identity function, then of course $\gamma_0 + c$ represents a single parameter (intercept).

We estimate parameters c, $\gamma = (\gamma_0, \gamma_1, \ldots, \gamma_N)^T$, and

$$\omega = (\omega_{10}, \ldots, \omega_{N0}, \omega_{11}, \ldots, \omega_{N1}, \ldots, \omega_{1p}, \ldots, \omega_{Np})^T \tag{7}$$

of (6) exploiting a (rather complicated) nonlinear optimization of a certain (selected) loss function. To simplify the notation, we further denote

$$\tau_i = \sum_{k=1}^{N} \gamma_k f\left(\sum_{j=1}^{p} \omega_{kj} X_{ij} + \omega_{k0}\right) + \gamma_0, \quad i = 1, \ldots, n. \tag{8}$$

In the rest of the paper, we require that the derivatives of f and g exist. Under such (rather common) assumption, these derivatives will be denoted as f' and g', respectively. Although it is common in regression tasks to choose g in (6) as an identity function, which simplifies the computational efforts, we retain the general notation g here. Independently on the choice of the loss function we will use the notation $u_i = Y_i - \hat{Y}_i$ for residuals of the multilayer perceptron for $i = 1, \ldots, n$.

3.2 Derivatives of Fitted Values

As a preparatory result for further computations, we now derive independently on the choice of the loss function

$$\frac{\partial \hat{Y}_i}{\partial c}(c, \gamma, \omega) = 1, \quad i = 1, \ldots, n, \tag{9}$$

$$\frac{\partial \hat{Y}_i}{\partial \gamma_0}(c, \gamma, \omega) = g'(\tau_i), \quad i = 1, \ldots, n, \tag{10}$$

$$\frac{\partial \hat{Y}_i}{\partial \gamma_a}(c, \gamma, \omega) = g'(\tau_i) f\left(\sum_{j=1}^{p} \omega_{aj} X_{ij} + \omega_{a0}\right), \quad i = 1, \ldots, n, \quad a = 1, \ldots, N, \tag{11}$$

$$\frac{\partial \hat{Y}_i}{\partial \omega_{a0}}(c, \gamma, \omega) = \gamma_a g'(\tau_i) f'\left(\sum_{j=1}^{p} \omega_{aj} X_{ij} + \omega_{a0}\right), \quad i = 1, \ldots, n, \quad a = 1, \ldots, N, \tag{12}$$

and

$$\frac{\partial \hat{Y}_i}{\partial \omega_{ab}}(c, \gamma, \omega) = \gamma_a X_{ib} g'(\tau_i) f'\left(\sum_{j=1}^{p} \omega_{aj} X_{ij} + \omega_{a0}\right), \tag{13}$$

where $i = 1, \ldots, n$, $a = 1, \ldots, N$, and $b = 1, \ldots, p$.

These partial derivatives of (6) were derived by a repeatedly used chain rule for computing derivatives of a composite function. They are expressed as functions, i.e. depending on their parameters c, γ, and ω. Of course, computations with real data (e.g. within the neural network training) require to use estimated versions of these derivatives, which can be easily obtained by replacing c, γ, and ω by their estimates. We would like to point out that such estimates are always available within the backpropagation algorithm, because its user is required to specify initial estimates of these parameters. These partial derivatives appear in derivatives of the loss function, which will be now expressed for three different versions of the loss function, namely for the standard one based on least squares and for two robust alternatives.

3.3 Multilayer Perceptron with a Standard Loss

The most commonly used loss for multilayer perceptrons will be denoted as

$$\xi_1 = \xi_1(c, \gamma, \omega) = \frac{1}{n} \sum_{i=1}^{n} u_i^2, \tag{14}$$

which is known as the mean square error (MSE), corresponding to the least squares estimator in a location model. To estimate all parameters of (6), the common optimization criterion has the form

$$\arg \min_{c,\gamma,\omega} \xi_1(c, \gamma, \omega), \tag{15}$$

which is commonly solved by backpropagation. To derive the explicit expressions for partial derivatives, which are formulated below as a lemma, we will exploit the facts that e.g. it holds for $a = 1, \ldots, N$ that

$$\frac{\partial \xi_1}{\partial \gamma_a} = \frac{\partial}{\partial \gamma_a} \sum_{i=1}^{n} \left(Y_i - \hat{Y}_i\right)^2 = \sum_{i=1}^{n} \frac{\partial}{\partial \gamma_a} \left(Y_i - \hat{Y}_i\right)^2 = -2 \sum_{i=1}^{n} \left(Y_i - \hat{Y}_i\right) \frac{\partial \hat{Y}_i}{\partial \gamma_a}. \tag{16}$$

Lemma 1. *Under the notation of Sect. 3.1, it holds that*

(a)

$$\frac{\partial \xi_1}{\partial c}(c, \gamma, \omega) = -\frac{2}{n} \sum_{i=1}^{n} u_i, \tag{17}$$

(b)

$$\frac{\partial \xi_1}{\partial \gamma_0}(c, \gamma, \omega) = -\frac{2}{n} \sum_{i=1}^{n} u_i g'(\tau_i), \tag{18}$$

(c)

$$\frac{\partial \xi_1}{\partial \gamma_a}(c, \gamma, \omega) = -\frac{2}{n} \sum_{i=1}^{n} u_i g'(\tau_i) f \left(\sum_{j=1}^{p} \omega_{aj} X_{ij} + \omega_{a0} \right), \tag{19}$$

where $a = 1, \ldots, N$,

(d)

$$\frac{\partial \xi_1}{\partial \omega_{a0}}(c, \gamma, \omega) = -\frac{2}{n} \sum_{i=1}^{n} u_i \gamma_a g'(\tau_i) f' \left(\sum_{j=1}^{p} \omega_{aj} X_{ij} + \omega_{a0} \right), \tag{20}$$

where $a = 1, \ldots, N$,

(e)

$$\frac{\partial \xi_1}{\partial \omega_{ab}}(c, \gamma, \omega) = -\frac{2}{n} \sum_{i=1}^{n} u_i \gamma_a X_{ib} g'(\tau_i) f' \left(\sum_{j=1}^{p} \omega_{aj} X_{ij} + \omega_{a0} \right), \tag{21}$$

where $a = 1, \ldots, N$ and $b = 1, \ldots, p$.

It is rather surprising that we are not aware of the results of Lemma 1 being available anywhere in the literature. The formulas do not appear in standard textbooks (e.g. [6]), and texts on this topic available on the internet usually contain serious mistakes. Concerning the computations of the derivatives, Lemma 1 formulates them as depending on c, γ and ω, while the derivatives for numerical data can be estimated by using estimates of c, γ and ω, respectively.

3.4 LTS-loss in Linear Regression

The loss function of the LTS estimator in (1) is defined as

$$\xi_2 = \xi_2(\beta) = \frac{1}{h}\sum_{i=1}^{h} u_{(i)}^2. \tag{22}$$

To express its derivatives, we may recall the following result given on p. 7 of [19] stating that

$$\frac{\partial \xi_2}{\partial \beta}(\beta) = -\frac{2}{n}\sum_{i=1}^{n}\left[u_i(\beta)X_i \mathbb{1}[u_i^2(\beta) \le u_{(h)}^2(\beta)]\right] \tag{23}$$

almost everywhere, where $u_i(\beta) = Y_i - X_i^T\beta$ for each i are residuals and $\mathbb{1}$ denotes an indicator function. The expression (23) contains $p+1$ particular derivatives for individual elements of β. In (23), the i-th squared residual is compared with the h-th largest *squared* residual. To conclude, the LTS estimator b_{LTS} in (1) can be computed (using now our notation) as the solution of the set of equations

$$\sum_{i=1}^{n} u_i(b)X_i \mathbb{1}[u_i^2(b) \le u_{(h)}^2(b)] = 0, \tag{24}$$

where b is the $p+1$-dimensional variable.

3.5 Multilayer Perceptron with an LTS-loss

An MLP with the loss function corresponding to the LTS estimator was considered already in [17], where however the derivatives of the loss function are in our opinion incorrect. The same formulas were repeated in [18]. However, we must be much more careful in deriving the derivatives, which turn out to be have more complex formulas. Let us first consider the loss

$$\xi_2 = \xi_2(c,\gamma,\omega) = \frac{1}{h}\sum_{i=1}^{h} u_{(i)}^2, \tag{25}$$

where h is a specified constant fulfilling $n/2 \le h < n$. The loss corresponds to the LTS estimator and thus we introduce the notation LTS-MLP for the (robust) multilayer perceptron with parameters estimated by the criterion

$$\arg\min_{c,\gamma,\omega} \xi_2(c,\gamma,\omega). \tag{26}$$

The derivatives of ξ_2 will be derived in an analogous way to the approach of Sect. 3.4.

Lemma 2. *We use the notation of Sect. 3.1. To avoid confusion, let us denote the residuals of the LTS-MLP as* $\tilde{u} = \tilde{u}_i(c, \gamma, \omega)$ *for* $i = 1, \ldots, n$, *to stress that they are functions of* c, γ *and* ω. *Let us further denote* $\tilde{u}^2_{(1)} \leq \cdots \leq \tilde{u}^2_{(n)}$. *It holds that*

(a)

$$\frac{\partial \xi_2}{\partial c}(c, \gamma, \omega) = -\frac{2}{h} \sum_{i=1}^{n} \tilde{u}_i \mathbb{1}[\tilde{u}_i^2 \leq \tilde{u}^2_{(h)}], \tag{27}$$

(b)

$$\frac{\partial \xi_2}{\partial \gamma_0}(c, \gamma, \omega) = -\frac{2}{h} \sum_{i=1}^{n} \tilde{u}_i \mathbb{1}[\tilde{u}_i^2 \leq \tilde{u}^2_{(h)}] g'(\tau_i), \tag{28}$$

(c)

$$\frac{\partial \xi_2}{\partial \gamma_a}(c, \gamma, \omega) = -\frac{2}{h} \sum_{i=1}^{n} \tilde{u}_i \mathbb{1}[\tilde{u}_i^2 \leq \tilde{u}^2_{(h)})] g'(\tau_i) f \left(\sum_{j=1}^{p} \omega_{aj} X_{ij} + \omega_{a0} \right), \tag{29}$$

where $a = 1, \ldots, N$,

(d)

$$\frac{\partial \xi_2}{\partial \omega_{a0}}(c, \gamma, \omega) = -\frac{2}{h} \sum_{i=1}^{n} \tilde{u}_i \mathbb{1}[\tilde{u}_i^2 \leq \tilde{u}^2_{(h)}] \gamma_a g'(\tau_i) f' \left(\sum_{j=1}^{p} \omega_{aj} X_{ij} + \omega_{a0} \right), \tag{30}$$

where $a = 1, \ldots, N$,

(e)

$$\frac{\partial \xi_2}{\partial \omega_{ab}}(c, \gamma, \omega) = -\frac{2}{h} \sum_{i=1}^{n} \tilde{u}_i \mathbb{1}[\tilde{u}_i^2 \leq \tilde{u}^2_{(h)}] \gamma_a X_{ib} g'(\tau_i) f' \left(\sum_{j=1}^{p} \omega_{aj} X_{ij} + \omega_{a0} \right), \tag{31}$$

where $a = 1, \ldots, N$ *and* $b = 1, \ldots, p$.

3.6 LWS-Loss in Linear Regression

Let us now consider the model (1) with the loss corresponding to an LWS estimator. The loss

$$\xi_3(\beta) = \sum_{i=1}^{n} \psi \left(\frac{i - 1/2}{n} \right) u^2_{(i)} \tag{32}$$

exploits a specified weight function ψ. Equivalently, we may express

$$\xi_3(\beta) = \sum_{i=1}^{n} w_i u^2_{(i)}, \tag{33}$$

where the weights are generated by ψ under a natural requirement $\sum_{i=1}^{n} w_i = 1$. The LWS estimator is defined by

$$\arg\min_{\beta} \xi_3(\beta). \tag{34}$$

The set of derivatives of the loss function in (1) has the form

$$\frac{\partial \xi_3}{\partial \beta} = -2 \sum_{i=1}^{n} X_i u_i \psi \left(\hat{F}^{(n)} \left(|u_i(\beta)| \right) \right), \tag{35}$$

where $\hat{F}^{(n)}$ denotes the empirical distribution function

$$\hat{F}^{(n)}(r) = \frac{1}{n} \sum_{j=1}^{n} \mathbb{1}[|u_j(\beta)| < r], \quad r \in \mathbb{R}; \tag{36}$$

a detailed proof was given on p. 183 of [20]. The special case for (4) again considers $X_i \equiv 1$ for each i. Let us consider the empirical distribution function

$$\hat{F}(r, b) = \frac{1}{n} \sum_{j=1}^{n} \mathbb{1}[|u_j(b)| < r], \quad r \in \mathbb{R}. \tag{37}$$

The LWS estimator b_{LWS} in (1) can be obtained as the solution of

$$\sum_{i=1}^{n} u_i(b) X_i \psi \left(\hat{F} \left(|u_i(b)|, b \right) \right) = 0, \tag{38}$$

which is a set of normal equations with the variable $b \in \mathbb{R}^{p+1}$. Here, $|u_i(b)|$ for each i plays the role of the threshold r from (37).

3.7 Multilayer Perceptron with An-LWS Loss

We introduce the notation LWS-MLP for the (robust) multilayer perceptron based on the robust loss function corresponding to the LWS estimator. Let us consider the loss

$$\xi_3(c, \gamma, \omega) = \sum_{i=1}^{n} \psi \left(\frac{i - 1/2}{n} \right) u_{(i)}^2, \tag{39}$$

formulated using a specified weight function ψ. The loss can be equivalently expressed as

$$\xi_3 = \xi_3(c, \gamma, \omega) = \sum_{i=1}^{n} w_i u_{(i)}^2, \tag{40}$$

if the weights are generated by ψ and again fulfil $\sum_{i=1}^{n} w_i = 1$. The loss corresponds to an LWS estimator and therefore we introduce the notation LWS-MLP for the (robust) multilayer perceptron with parameters given by

$$\arg\min_{c,\gamma,\omega} \xi_3(c, \gamma, \omega). \tag{41}$$

Our deriving the derivatives of ξ_3 is analogous to the reasoning of Sect. 3.6.

Lemma 3. *We use the notation of Sect. 3.1. Residuals of the multilayer perceptron will be denoted as $\tilde{u}_i = \tilde{u}_i(c, \gamma, \omega)$ and the corresponding empirical distribution function as*

$$\hat{F}(r) = \frac{1}{n} \sum_{i=1}^{n} \mathbb{1}[|\tilde{u}_i| < r], \quad r \in \mathbb{R}. \tag{42}$$

It holds that

(a)

$$\frac{\partial \xi_3}{\partial c}(c, \gamma, \omega) = -2 \sum_{i=1}^{n} \tilde{u}_i \psi\left(\hat{F}^{(n)}(|\tilde{u}_i|)\right), \tag{43}$$

(b)

$$\frac{\partial \xi_3}{\partial \gamma_0}(c, \gamma, \omega) = -2 \sum_{i=1}^{n} \tilde{u}_i \psi\left(\hat{F}^{(n)}(|\tilde{u}_i|)\right) g'(\tau_i), \tag{44}$$

(c)

$$\frac{\partial \xi_3}{\partial \gamma_a}(c, \gamma, \omega) = -2 \sum_{i=1}^{n} \tilde{u}_i \psi\left(\hat{F}^{(n)}(|\tilde{u}_i|)\right) g'(\tau_i) f\left(\sum_{j=1}^{p} \omega_{aj} X_{ij} + \omega_{a0}\right), \tag{45}$$

where $a = 1, \ldots, N$,

(d)

$$\frac{\partial \xi_3}{\partial \omega_{a0}}(c, \gamma, \omega) = -2 \sum_{i=1}^{n} \tilde{u}_i \gamma_a \psi\left(\hat{F}^{(n)}(|\tilde{u}_i|)\right) g'(\tau_i) f'\left(\sum_{j=1}^{p} \omega_{aj} X_{ij} + \omega_{a0}\right), \tag{46}$$

where $a = 1, \ldots, N$,

(e)

$$\frac{\partial \xi_3}{\partial \omega_{ab}}(c, \gamma, \omega) = -2 \sum_{i=1}^{n} \tilde{u}_i \gamma_a X_{ib} \psi\left(\hat{F}^{(n)}(|\tilde{u}_i|)\right) g'(\tau_i) f'\left(\sum_{j=1}^{p} \omega_{aj} X_{ij} + \omega_{a0}\right), \tag{47}$$

where $a = 1, \ldots, N, \quad b = 1, \ldots, p$.

3.8 Applications

Several datasets were analyzed by the presented robust neural networks (LTS-MLP and LWS-MLP) in [12]. In all datasets, which are contaminated by outliers, a robust mean square error was better (i.e. smaller) for all the robust MLPs than that of a plain MLP. This is true especially for simple artificial data and also the Boston housing dataset [5] and the Auto MPG dataset [5]. For the Boston housing dataset, some real estates in the very center of Boston are outlying, as they are small but extremely overpriced compared to those in the suburbs of the city. For the Auto MPG, we found those cars to be outlying for the model, which have a high weight and a high consumption. Other outliers can be identified as cars with a low weight, as there appears only a small percentage of them; such findings are in accordance with those of [14].

4 Conclusions

Standard training of neural networks, including their most common types, is vulnerable to the presence of outliers in the data and thus it is important to consider robustified versions instead. Due to a lack of reliable approaches, robustness in neural networks with respect to outliers remains a perspective topic in machine learning with a high potential to provide interesting applications in the analysis of contaminated data. In this paper, we focus on robust versions of multilayer perceptrons, i.e. alternative training techniques for the most common type of artificial neural networks. We propose an original robust multilayer perceptron based on the LWS loss.

We derive here derivatives of the loss functions based on the LTS and LWS estimates for a particular (rather simple) architecture of a multilayer perceptron. Our presenting this compact overview of derivatives needed for any available gradient-based optimization technique is motivated by an apparent mistake in the derivatives for a similar (although different) robust multilayer perceptron based on the LTA estimator in [18]. The main motivation for our deriving the derivatives is however their usefulness within the backpropagation algorithm, allowing to compute the robust neural networks. This paper does not however investigate any convergence issues of the proposed robust multilayer perceptron; to the best of our knowledge, convergence is not available for any other type of versions of neural networks, which are proposed as robust to the presence of outliers in the data. Implementing the LTS-MLP and LWS-MLP using the presented results is straightforward. Derivatives for more complex multilayer perceptrons, i.e. for networks with a larger number of hidden layers, can be obtained in an analogous way only with additional using the chain rule for computing derivatives.

While the presented results represent a theoretical foundation for our future research, there seems at the same time a gap of systematic comparisons of various different robust versions of neural networks over both real and simulated data. Such comparisons are intended to be a topic for our future work, because a statistical interpretation of the results of robust neural networks remains crucial.

Acknowledgments. The authors would like to thank David Coufal and Jiří Tumpach for discussion.

References

1. Aladag, C.H., Egrioglu, E., Yolcu, U.: Robust multilayer neural network based on median neuron model. Neural Comput. Appl. **24**, 945–956 (2014)

2. Beliakov, G., Kelarev, A., Yearwood, J.: Derivative-free optimization and neural networks for robust regression. Optimization **61**, 1467–1490 (2012)
3. Cisse, M., Bojanowski, P., Grave, E., Dauphin, Y., Usunier, N.: Parseval networks: improving robustness to adversarial examples. In: Proceedings of the 34th International Conference on Machine Learning ICML 2017, pp. 854–863 (2017)
4. D'Urso, P., Leski, J.M.: Fuzzy c-ordered medoids clustering for interval-valued data. Pattern Recogn. **58**, 49–67 (2016)
5. Frank, A., Asuncion, A.: UCI Machine Learning Repository. University of California, Irvine (2010). http://archive.ics.uci.edu/ml/
6. Haykin, S.O.: Neural Networks and Learning Machines: A Comprehensive Foundation, 2nd edn. Prentice Hall, Upper Saddle River (2009)
7. Henderson, D.J., Parmeter, C.F.: Applied Nonparametric Econometrics. Cambridge University Press, New York (2015)
8. Jurečková, J., Picek, J., Schindler, M.: Robust Statistical Methods with R, 2nd edn. Chapman & Hall/CRC, Boca Raton (2019)
9. Kalina, J.: A robust pre-processing of BeadChip microarray images. Biocybern. Biomed. Eng. **38**, 556–563 (2018)
10. Kalina, J., Schlenker, A.: A robust supervised variable selection for noisy high-dimensional data. BioMed Res. Int. **2015**, 1–10 (2015). Article no. 320385
11. Kalina, J., Vidnerová, P.: Robust training of radial basis function neural networks. In: Proceedings 18th International Conference ICAISC 2019. Lecture Notes in Computer Science, vol. 11508, pp. 113–124 (2019)
12. Kalina, J., Vidnerová, P.: On robust training of regression neural networks. In: Proceedings 5th International Workshop on Functional and Operatorial Statistics IWFOS (2020, accepted)
13. Kordos, M., Rusiecki, A.: Reducing noise impact on MLP training-techniques and algorithms to provide noise-robustness in MLP network training. Soft. Comput. **20**, 46–65 (2016)
14. Paulheim, H., Meusel, R.: A decomposition of the outlier detection problem into a set of supervised learning problems. Mach. Learn. **100**, 509–531 (2015)
15. Racine, J., Su, L., Ullah, A.: The Oxford Handbook of Applied Nonparametric and Semiparametric Econometrics and Statistics. Oxford University Press, Oxford (2014)
16. Rousseeuw, P.J., Van Driessen, K.: Computing LTS regression for large data sets. Data Min. Knowl. Disc. **12**, 29–45 (2006)
17. Rusiecki, A.: Robust learning algorithm based on LTA estimator. Neurocomputing **120**, 624–632 (2013)
18. Rusiecki, A., Kordos, M., Kamiński, T., Greń, K.: Training neural networks on noisy data. Lect. Notes Artif. Intell. **8467**, 131–142 (2014)
19. Víšek, J.Á.: The least trimmed squares. Part I: consistency. Kybernetika **42**, 1–36 (2006)
20. Víšek, J.Á.: Consistency of the least weighted squares under heteroscedasticity. Kybernetika **47**, 179–206 (2011)

Stability Analysis of Neutral-Type Hopfield Neural Networks with Multiple Delays

Ozlem Faydasicok(✉)

Department of Mathematics, Faculty of Science, Istanbul University, Istanbul, Turkey
kozlem@istanbul.edu.tr

Abstract. The main aim of this paper is to study the stability problem for neutral-type Hopfield neural networks possessing multiple time delays in the states of the neurons and multiple neutral delays in time derivative of states of the neurons. By using a suitable Lyapunov functional, a novel sufficient stability condition is obtained for global asymptotic stability of neutral-type neural networks with multiple delays. The derived stability criterion can be expressed in terms of the parameters of the neural network model which totally relies on some simple relationships established between the network parameters and it is completely independent of time delays and neutral delays. Hence, this new global asymptotic stability condition can be easily tested and verified by using some algebraic mathematical properties. We will also make a comparison between the result of this paper and previously published corresponding results. This comparison will indicate the advantages of our proposed stability condition over the previously reported stability conditions. Since obtaining stability conditions for neutral type neural networks with multiple delays is a difficult task to achieve due to the insufficient mathematical methods and techniques, the result given in this paper can be considered an important and alternative result for this class of neutral type neural systems.

Keywords: Neutral systems · Delayed neural networks · Stability analysis · Lyapunov functionals

1 Introduction

In recent years, various classes of neural networks have been studied by many researches to solve some important engineering problems such as optimization, signal processing, control problems, pattern recognition and associative memories [1–6]. In most of these applications, the designed neural networks are required be stable as the processed information is represented by the stable states of the neurons. Therefore, it is of great importance to carry out a proper stability analysis of dynamical behaviors of neural networks. On the other hand, when

L. Iliadis et al. (Eds.): EANN 2020, INNS 2, pp. 558–568, 2020.
https://doi.org/10.1007/978-3-030-48791-1_44

electronically implementing neural networks, due to the finite switching speed of amplifiers and the communication times among the neurons cause time delays, which can turn a stable neural network into an unstable neural network. These time delay parameters can effect the dynamical behaviours of neural networks. Hence, when analyzing the stability properties of dynamical neural networks, it is needed to consider the effect of the time delays on the dynamics of the designed neural network model. On the other hand, in order to evaluate the exact effect of time delays, the delays must also be introduced into the time derivatives of the states of the neurons. The neural networks having delays in both the states and the time derivative of the states are called neutral-type neural networks. This type of neural networks has been widely used to solve many engineering problems. Therefore, the stability of the class of neutral type neural networks has been studied by many researchers and a variety of important stability results have been proposed [7–32]. This paper will consider the neutral-type Hopfield neural networks involving multiple time delays in the states of the neurons and multiple neutral delays in time derivatives of the states of the neurons described by the following sets of differential equations:

$$\begin{aligned}\dot{x}_i(t) = -c_i x_i(t) + \sum_{j=1}^{n} a_{ij} f_j(x_j(t)) + \sum_{j=1}^{n} b_{ij} f_j(x_j(t-\tau_{ij})) + u_i \\ + \sum_{j=1}^{n} e_{ij} \dot{x}_j(t-\zeta_{ij}), \quad i = 1, \cdots, n. \end{aligned} \tag{1}$$

where x_i represents the state of the ith neuron, c_i are some positive constants, the constant parameters a_{ij} and b_{ij} represent the strengths of the neuron interconnections. τ_{ij} $(1 \leq i,j \leq n)$ are the time delays and ζ_{ij} $(1 \leq i,j \leq n)$ are the neutral delays. The constants e_{ij} are coefficients of the time derivative of the delayed states. The $f_j(\cdot)$ represent the nonlinear neuron activation functions, and the constants u_i are some external inputs. In neural system (1), if we let $\tau = max\{\tau_{ij}\}$, $\zeta = max\{\zeta_{ij}\}$, $1 \leq i,j \leq n$, and $\delta = max\{\tau, \zeta\}$, then, the initial conditions of neural network model (1) are given by: $x_i(t) = \varphi_i(t)$ and $\dot{x}_i(t) = \vartheta_i(t) \in C([-\delta, 0], R)$, where $C([-\delta, 0], R)$ represents the set of all continuous functions from $[-\delta, 0]$ to R.

In the stability analysis of neutral network model defined by (1), it is important to first determine the characteristics of activation functions $f_i(x)$. In general, these activation functions are assumed to satisfied the following conditions:

$$|f_i(x) - f_i(y)| \leq \ell_i |x - y|, \; i = 1, 2, \cdots, n, \quad \forall x, y \in R, x \neq y. \tag{2}$$

where ℓ_i are the Lipschitz constants.

2 Stability Analysis

This section is devoted to determining the criterion that establishes global stability of neutral-type delayed neural system described by (1). For the sake of simplicity of the proofs, the equilibrium points $x^* = (x_1^*, x_2^*, ..., x_n^*)^T$ possessed by (1) will be transferred to the origin. By defining $z(t) = x(t) - x^*$, we can deduce the following neutral-type neural system

$$\dot{z}_i(t) = -c_i z_i(t) + \sum_{j=1}^{n} a_{ij} g_j(z_j(t)) + \sum_{j=1}^{n} b_{ij} g_j(z_j(t-\tau_{ij})) + \sum_{j=1}^{n} e_{ij} \dot{z}_j(t-\zeta_{ij}), \ \forall i \quad (3)$$

where $g_i(z_i(t)) = f_i(z_i(t)+x_i^*) - f_i(x_i^*), \forall i$. Note that neutral-type neural system (3) inherits the assumption given by (2), namely,

$$|g_i(z_i(t))| \leq \ell_i |z_i(t)|, \ \forall i. \quad (4)$$

It can now be proceeded further with the following theorem:

Theorem 1: For neutral-type neural system (3), let the activation functions satisfy (4). Then, the origin of neutral-type Hopfield neural network model (3) is globally asymptotically stable if there exist positive constants $p_1, p_2, ..., p_n$ and a positive constant $0 < \kappa < 1$ such that

$$\xi_i = p_i \frac{c_i}{\ell_i} - \sum_{j=1}^{n} p_j (|a_{ji}| + |b_{ji}|) > 0, \ \forall i$$

and

$$\eta_{ji} = \frac{\kappa}{n} p_i - p_j |e_{ji}| > 0, \ \forall i, j.$$

Then, the origin of system (3) is globally asymptotically stable.

Proof: We will construct the following positive definite Lyapunov functional

$$\begin{aligned} V(t) = & \sum_{i=1}^{n} p_i \Big(1 - \kappa sgn(z_i(t)) sgn(\dot{z}_i(t))\Big) sgn(z_i(t)) z_i(t) \\ & + \frac{1}{n}\kappa \sum_{i=1}^{n}\sum_{j=1}^{n} p_j \int_{t-\zeta_{ij}}^{t} |\dot{z}_j(s)| ds + \sum_{i=1}^{n}\sum_{j=1}^{n} p_i \int_{t-\tau_{ij}}^{t} |b_{ij}||g_j(z_j(s))| ds \\ & + \epsilon \sum_{i=1}^{n}\sum_{j=1}^{n} \int_{t-\tau_{ij}}^{t} |z_j(s)| ds \end{aligned} \quad (5)$$

where ϵ is a positive constant whose value will be obtained in what follows. The time derivative of $V(t)$ can be obtained as follows:

$$\begin{aligned}\dot{V}(t) &= \sum_{i=1}^{n} p_i\Big(1-\kappa sgn(z_i(t))sgn(\dot{z}_i(t))\Big)sgn(z_i(t))\dot{z}_i(t)\\&+\frac{1}{n}\kappa\sum_{i=1}^{n}\sum_{j=1}^{n}p_j|\dot{z}_j(t)|-\frac{1}{n}\kappa\sum_{i=1}^{n}\sum_{j=1}^{n}p_j|\dot{z}_j(t-\zeta_{ij})|\\&+\sum_{i=1}^{n}\sum_{j=1}^{n}p_i|b_{ij}||g_j(z_j(t))|-\sum_{i=1}^{n}\sum_{j=1}^{n}p_i|b_{ij}||g_j(z_j(t-\tau_{ij}))|\\&+\epsilon\sum_{i=1}^{n}\sum_{j=1}^{n}|z_j(t)|-\epsilon\sum_{i=1}^{n}\sum_{j=1}^{n}|z_j(t-\tau_{ij})|\end{aligned}\tag{6}$$

Since

$$\begin{aligned}&p_i\Big(1-\kappa sgn(z_i(t))sgn(\dot{z}_i(t))\Big)sgn(z_i(t))\dot{z}_i(t)\\&=p_i\Big(sgn(z_i(t))-\kappa\Big(sgn(z_i(t))\Big)^2sgn(\dot{z}_i(t))\Big)\dot{z}_i(t)\\&=p_isgn(z_i(t))\dot{z}_i(t)-p_i\kappa\Big(sgn(z_i(t))\Big)^2sgn(\dot{z}_i(t))\dot{z}_i(t)\end{aligned}\tag{7}$$

and

$$\begin{aligned}\frac{1}{n}\kappa\sum_{i=1}^{n}\sum_{j=1}^{n}p_j|\dot{z}_j(t)|&=\frac{1}{n}\kappa\sum_{i=1}^{n}\sum_{j=1}^{n}p_i|\dot{z}_i(t)|=\kappa\sum_{i=1}^{n}p_i|\dot{z}_i(t)|\\&=\kappa\sum_{i=1}^{n}p_isgn(\dot{z}_i(t))\dot{z}_i(t)\end{aligned}\tag{8}$$

Using (7) and (8) in (6) results in

$$\begin{aligned}\dot{V}(t) &= \sum_{i=1}^{n}p_isgn(z_i(t))\dot{z}_i(t)-\sum_{i=1}^{n}p_i\kappa\Big(sgn(z_i(t))\Big)^2sgn(\dot{z}_i(t))\dot{z}_i(t)\\&+\sum_{i=1}^{n}p_i\kappa sgn(\dot{z}_i(t))\dot{z}_i(t)-\frac{1}{n}\kappa\sum_{i=1}^{n}\sum_{j=1}^{n}p_j|\dot{z}_j(t-\zeta_{ij})|\\&+\sum_{i=1}^{n}\sum_{j=1}^{n}p_i|b_{ij}||g_j(z_j(t))|-\sum_{i=1}^{n}\sum_{j=1}^{n}p_i|b_{ij}||g_j(z_j(t-\tau_{ij}))|\\&+\epsilon\sum_{i=1}^{n}\sum_{j=1}^{n}|z_j(t)|-\epsilon\sum_{i=1}^{n}\sum_{j=1}^{n}|z_j(t-\tau_{ij})|\end{aligned}\tag{9}$$

Let

$$\begin{aligned}\upsilon_i(t)&=p_isgn(z_i(t))\dot{z}_i(t)-p_i\kappa\Big(sgn(z_i(t))\Big)^2sgn(\dot{z}_i(t))\dot{z}_i(t)\\&\quad+p_i\kappa sgn(\dot{z}_i(t))\dot{z}_i(t),\ \ i=1,2,\cdots,n\end{aligned}$$

Then, (9) can be written as

$$\dot{V}(t) = \sum_{i=1}^{n} \upsilon_i(t) - \frac{1}{n}\kappa \sum_{i=1}^{n}\sum_{j=1}^{n} p_j|\dot{z}_j(t-\zeta_{ij})| + \sum_{i=1}^{n}\sum_{j=1}^{n} p_i|b_{ij}||g_j(z_j(t))|$$
$$-\sum_{i=1}^{n}\sum_{j=1}^{n} p_i|b_{ij}||g_j(z_j(t-\tau_{ij}))| + \epsilon \sum_{i=1}^{n}\sum_{j=1}^{n}(|z_j(t)| - |z_j(t-\tau_{ij})|) \quad (10)$$

If $z_i(t) \neq 0$, then, $\Big(sgn(z_i(t))\Big)^2 = 1$. In this case, we obtain

$$\begin{aligned}
\upsilon_i(t) &= p_i sgn(z_i(t))\dot{z}_i(t) \\
&= -p_i sgn(z_i(t))c_i z_i(t) + \sum_{j=1}^{n} p_i sgn(z_i(t))a_{ij}g_j(z_j(t)) \\
&\quad + \sum_{j=1}^{n} p_i sgn(z_i(t))b_{ij}g_j(z_j(t-\tau_{ij})) + \sum_{j=1}^{n} p_i sgn(z_i(t))e_{ij}\dot{z}_j(t-\zeta_{ij}) \\
&\leq -p_i c_i|z_i(t)| + \sum_{j=1}^{n} p_i|a_{ij}||g_j(z_j(t))| \\
&\quad + \sum_{j=1}^{n} p_i|b_{ij}||g_j(z_j(t-\tau_{ij}))| + \sum_{j=1}^{n} p_i|e_{ij}||\dot{z}_j(t-\zeta_{ij})|
\end{aligned}$$

If $z_i(t) = 0$, then, $sgn(z_i(t)) = 0$. In this case, we obtain

$$\upsilon_i(t) = p_i\kappa sgn(\dot{z}_i(t))\dot{z}_i(t)$$

Since $\kappa < 1$, we get

$$\begin{aligned}
\upsilon_i(t) &\leq p_i sgn(\dot{z}_i(t))\dot{z}_i(t) \\
&= -p_i sgn(\dot{z}_i(t))c_i z_i(t) + \sum_{j=1}^{n} p_i sgn(\dot{z}_i(t))a_{ij}g_j(z_j(t)) \\
&\quad + \sum_{j=1}^{n} p_i sgn(\dot{z}_i(t))b_{ij}g_j(z_j(t-\tau_{ij})) + \sum_{j=1}^{n} p_i sgn(\dot{z}_i(t))e_{ij}\dot{z}_j(t-\zeta_{ij}) \\
&\leq -p_i c_i|z_i(t)| + \sum_{j=1}^{n} p_i|a_{ij}||g_j(z_j(t))| \\
&\quad + \sum_{j=1}^{n} p_i|b_{ij}||g_j(z_j(t-\tau_{ij}))| + \sum_{j=1}^{n} p_i|e_{ij}||\dot{z}_j(t-\zeta_{ij})|
\end{aligned}$$

Thus, for all $z_i(t) \in R$, the following holds:

$$\upsilon_i(t) \leq -p_i c_i |z_i(t)| + \sum_{j=1}^{n} p_i |a_{ij}||g_j(z_j(t))| + \sum_{j=1}^{n} p_i |b_{ij}||g_j(z_j(t-\tau_{ij}))| + \sum_{j=1}^{n} p_i |e_{ij}||\dot{z}_j(t-\zeta_{ij})| \tag{11}$$

Hence, using (11) in (10) yields

$$\begin{aligned}\dot{V}(t) \leq &-\sum_{i=1}^{n} p_i c_i |z_i(t)| + \sum_{i=1}^{n}\sum_{j=1}^{n} p_i |a_{ij}||g_j(z_j(t))| + \sum_{i=1}^{n}\sum_{j=1}^{n} p_i |b_{ij}||g_j(z_j(t-\tau_{ij}))| \\ &+ \sum_{i=1}^{n}\sum_{j=1}^{n} p_i |e_{ij}||\dot{z}_j(t-\zeta_{ij})| - \frac{1}{n}\kappa \sum_{i=1}^{n}\sum_{j=1}^{n} p_j |\dot{z}_j(t-\zeta_{ij})| \\ &+ \sum_{i=1}^{n}\sum_{j=1}^{n} p_i |b_{ij}||g_j(z_j(t))| - \sum_{i=1}^{n}\sum_{j=1}^{n} p_i |b_{ij}||g_j(z_j(t-\tau_{ij}))| \\ &+ \epsilon \sum_{i=1}^{n}\sum_{j=1}^{n} |z_j(t)| - \epsilon \sum_{i=1}^{n}\sum_{j=1}^{n} |z_j(t-\tau_{ij})| \end{aligned} \tag{12}$$

(12) can be rewritten in the form:

$$\begin{aligned}\dot{V}(t) \leq &-\sum_{i=1}^{n} p_i c_i |z_i(t)| + \sum_{i=1}^{n}\sum_{j=1}^{n} p_i |a_{ij}||g_j(z_j(t))| + \sum_{i=1}^{n}\sum_{j=1}^{n} p_i |b_{ij}||g_j(z_j(t))| \\ &+ \sum_{i=1}^{n}\sum_{j=1}^{n} p_i |e_{ij}||\dot{z}_j(t-\zeta_{ij})| - \frac{1}{n}\kappa \sum_{i=1}^{n}\sum_{j=1}^{n} p_j |\dot{z}_j(t-\zeta_{ij})| + \epsilon \sum_{i=1}^{n}\sum_{j=1}^{n} |z_j(t)| \\ = &-\sum_{i=1}^{n} p_i c_i |z_i(t)| + \sum_{i=1}^{n}\sum_{j=1}^{n} p_j |a_{ji}||g_i(z_i(t))| + \sum_{i=1}^{n}\sum_{j=1}^{n} p_j |b_{ji}||g_i(z_i(t))| \\ &+ \sum_{i=1}^{n}\sum_{j=1}^{n} p_i |e_{ij}||\dot{z}_j(t-\zeta_{ij})| - \frac{1}{n}\kappa \sum_{i=1}^{n}\sum_{j=1}^{n} p_j |\dot{z}_j(t-\zeta_{ij})| + n\epsilon \sum_{i=1}^{n} |z_i(t)| \end{aligned} \tag{13}$$

Under the assumption given by (4), we can write (13) as follows:

$$\begin{aligned}\dot{V}(t) \leq &-\sum_{i=1}^{n} p_i c_i |z_i(t)| + \sum_{i=1}^{n}\sum_{j=1}^{n} \ell_i p_j |a_{ji}||z_i(t)| + \sum_{i=1}^{n}\sum_{j=1}^{n} \ell_i p_j |b_{ji}||z_i(t)| \\ &+ \sum_{i=1}^{n}\sum_{j=1}^{n} p_i |e_{ij}||\dot{z}_j(t-\zeta_{ij})| - \frac{1}{n}\kappa \sum_{i=1}^{n}\sum_{j=1}^{n} p_j |\dot{z}_j(t-\zeta_{ij})| + n\epsilon \sum_{i=1}^{n} |z_i(t)| \\ = &-\sum_{i=1}^{n} (p_i c_i - \ell_i \sum_{j=1}^{n} p_j(|a_{ji}| + |b_{ji}|))|z_i(t)| \\ &- \sum_{i=1}^{n}\sum_{j=1}^{n} (\frac{\kappa}{n} p_i - p_j|e_{ji}|)|\dot{z}_i(t-\zeta_{ji})| + n\epsilon \sum_{i=1}^{n} |z_i(t)| \\ = &-\sum_{i=1}^{n} \xi_i |z_i(t)| - \sum_{i=1}^{n}\sum_{j=1}^{n} \eta_{ji} |\dot{z}_i(t-\zeta_{ji})| + n\epsilon \sum_{i=1}^{n} |z_i(t)| \end{aligned} \tag{14}$$

Since $\eta_{ji} > 0, \forall i, j$, (14) satisfies:

$$\begin{aligned}\dot{V}(t) &\leq -\sum_{i=1}^{n} \xi_i |z_i(t)| + n\epsilon \sum_{i=1}^{n} |z_i(t)| \leq -\sum_{i=1}^{n} \xi_m |z_i(t)| + n\epsilon \sum_{i=1}^{n} |z_i(t)| \\ &= -\xi_m ||z(t)||_1 + n\epsilon ||z(t)||_1 \\ &= -(\xi_m - n\epsilon)||z(t)||_1 \end{aligned} \tag{15}$$

where $\xi_m = min\{\xi_i\} > 0,\ i = 1, 2, \cdots, n$. Clearly, the choice $0 < \epsilon < \frac{\xi_m}{n}$ directly implies from (15) that

$$\dot{V}(t) < 0, \forall z(t) \neq 0$$

Now, we consider the case where $z(t) = 0$. In this case, (14) satisfies:

$$\dot{V}(t) \leq -\sum_{i=1}^{n}\sum_{j=1}^{n} \eta_{ji} |\dot{z}_i(t-\zeta_{ji})| \tag{16}$$

Clearly, since $\eta_{ji} > 0$, if $\dot{z}_i(t-\zeta_{ji}) \neq 0$ for any pairs of i and j, then, from (16) we get that $\dot{V}(t) < 0$.

Now, we consider the case where $z(t) = 0$ and $z_i(t-\zeta_{ji}) = 0$ In this case, (12) satisfies:

$$\dot{V}(t) \leq -\epsilon \sum_{i=1}^{n}\sum_{j=1}^{n} |z_j(t-\tau_{ij})|$$

Clearly, since $\epsilon > 0$, if $z_j(t-\tau_{ij}) \neq 0$ for any pairs of i and j, then, $\dot{V}(t) < 0$. Let $z(t) = 0$, (for $z(t) = 0$, we have $g(z(t)) = 0$), $\dot{z}_i(t-\zeta_{ji}) = 0$, $\forall i, j$, and $z_j(t-\tau_{ij}) = 0$, ($z_j(t-\tau_{ij}) = 0$ implies that $g_j(z_j(t-\tau_{ij})) = 0$). In this case, $\dot{z}_i(t) = 0$, $\forall i$ and $\dot{V}(t) = 0$. Hence, $\dot{V}(t) = 0$ holds iff $z(t) = 0$, $g(z(t)) = 0$),

$\dot{z}_i(t-\zeta_{ji}) = 0, \forall i,j, z_j(t-\tau_{ij}) = 0, g_j(z_j(t-\tau_{ij})) = 0$) and $\dot{z}_i(t) = 0, \forall i$. Clearly, $\dot{V}(t) < 0$ except for the origin. Hence, origin $z(t) = 0$ of (3) is asymptotically stable. It is easy to observe that the Lyapunov function employed to carry out the stability analysis is radially unbounded, ($V(t) \to \infty$ as $||z(t)|| \to \infty$), and therefore, $z(t) = 0$ is globally asymptotically stable. Q.E. D.

3 Comparisons

In this section, we will compare our results with the previous key stability results obtained in the literature. In order to make a precise comparison, we need to express these previously derived results for the stability of neutral-type Hopfield neural network model (1):

Theorem 2 [31]**:** For the neutral-type neural network model (3), assume that the activation functions satisfy (4). Let α be a positive constant with $0 < \alpha < 1$. Then, the origin of neutral-type Hopfield neural network model (3) is globally asymptotically stable if there exist positive constants $p_1, p_2, ..., p_n$ such that

$$\omega_i = p_i\frac{c_i}{\ell_i} - \frac{1+\alpha}{1-\alpha}\sum_{j=1}^{n} p_j(|a_{ji}| + |b_{ji}|) > 0, \ \forall i$$

and

$$\varepsilon_{ji} = \frac{\alpha}{n}p_i - (1+\alpha)p_j|e_{ji}| > 0, \ i,j = 1,2,...,n.$$

Theorem 3 [32]**:** For the neutral-type neural network model (3), assume that the activation functions satisfy (4) and $\zeta_{ij} = \zeta_j, \forall i,j$. Then, the origin of neutral-type Hopfield neural network model (3) is globally asymptotically stable if there exist positive constants $p_1, p_2, ..., p_n$ such that

$$\rho_i = p_i\frac{c_i}{\ell_i} - \sum_{j=1}^{n} p_j(|a_{ji}| + |b_{ji}|) > 0, \ \forall i$$

and

$$\mu_i = p_i\alpha - \sum_{j=1}^{n} p_j|e_{ji}| > 0, \ \forall i$$

In Theorem 2, since $0 < \alpha < 1$, the term $\frac{1+\alpha}{1-\alpha} > 1$, the conditions given by ξ_i in Theorem 1 improves the conditions given by ω_i in Theorem 2. It should also be noted that, if we choose $\kappa = \alpha$, then the conditions given by ε_{ji} in Theorem 2 are always less than the conditions given by η_{ji} in Theorem 1 since $0 < \alpha < 1$. Therefore, the results of Theorem 1 generalize the results of Theorem 2.

When the results of Theorems 1 and 3 are examined, it can be seen that the results of these two theorems are very similar. However, Theorem 1 considers the multiple neutral delays and Theorem 3 considers the discrete neutral delays in the neural network model (1). Therefore, the results of Theorem 1 can be considered as the generalizations of the results of Theorem 3 as Theorem 1 involves the stability results for a more general class of neutral-type neural network model.

4 Conclusions

The main aim of this study was to carry out an investigation into stability problem for the class of neutral-type Hopfield neural networks involving multiple time delays in states and multiple neutral delays in time derivative of states. By using a suitable Lyapunov functional, a new sufficient condition has been proposed for global asymptotic stability of neutral-type neural network of this class. The proposed stability condition is independently of time delay and neutral delay parameters, and it is totally stated in terms of the system matrices and network parameters. Thus, this new stability condition can be validated by only examining the some algebraic equations that are related to the system parameters and matrices of this neutral-type neural network. We have also compared the result of this paper with the previously reported key stability results for the neutral-type neural network with multiple delays. This comparison has demonstrated the main advantages of our results over the past literature results. Since stability analysis of the class of neutral-type neural networks considered in this paper has not been studied because of the difficulty of employing the proper and efficient mathematical techniques and methods to investigate the stability analysis of such neutral-type neural systems, the stability criterion obtained in this paper can be considered as one of important stability results for neutral-type Hopfield neural networks with multiple time and multiple neutral delays.

References

1. Chua, L.O., Yang, L.: Cellular neural networks: applications. IEEE Trans. Circ. Syst. Part-I **35**, 1273–1290 (1988)
2. Cohen, M., Grossberg, S.: Absolute stability of global pattern formation and parallel memory storage by competitive neural networks. IEEE Trans. Syst. Man Cybern. **13**(5), 815–826 (1983)
3. Hopfield, J.: Neural networks and physical systems with emergent collective computational abilities. Proc. Nat. Acad. Sci. **79**, 2554–2558 (1982)
4. Tong, S.C., Li, Y.M., Zhang, H.G.: Adaptive neural network decentralized backstepping output-feedback control for nonlinear large-scale systems with time delays. IEEE Trans. Neural Netw. **22**(7), 1073–1086 (2011)
5. Galicki, M., Witte, H., Dorschel, J., Eiselt, M., Griessbach, G.: Common optimization of adaptive preprocessing units and a neural network during the learning period. Application in EEG pattern recognition. Neural Netw. **10**, 1153–1163 (1997)
6. Kosko, B.: Bi-directional associative memories. IEEE Trans. Syst. Man Cybern. **18**, 49–60 (1988)
7. Niculescu, S.I.: Delay Effects on Stability: A Robust Control Approach. Springer, Berlin (2001)
8. Kolmanovskii, V.B., Nosov, V.R.: Stability of Functional Differential Equations. Academic Press, London (1986)
9. Kuang, Y.: Delay Differential Equations with Applications in Population Dynamics. Academic Press, Boston (1993)

10. Samidurai, S., Marshal, A., Balachandran, R.K.: Global exponential stability of neutral-type impulsive neural networks with discrete and distributed delays. Nonlinear Anal. Hybrid Syst. **4**(1), 103–112 (2010)
11. Shi, K., Zhu, H., Zhong, S., Zeng, Y., Zhang, Y.: New stability analysis for neutral type neural networks with discrete and distributed delays using a multiple integral approac. J. Franklin Inst. **352**(1), 155–176 (2015)
12. Liu, P.L.: Further improvement on delay-dependent robust stability criteria for neutral-type recurrent neural networks with time-varying delays. ISA Trans. **55**, 92–99 (2015)
13. Lee, S.M., Kwon, O.M., Park, J.H.: A novel delay-dependent criterion for delayed neural networks of neutral type. Phys. Lett. A **374**(17–18), 1843–1848 (2010)
14. Chen, H., Zhang, Y., Hu, P.: Novel delay-dependent robust stability criteria for neutral stochastic delayed neural networks. Neurocomputing **73**(13–15), 2554–25561 (2010)
15. Zhang, Z., Liu, K., Yang, Y.: New LMI-based condition on global asymptotic stability concerning BAM neural networks of neutral type. Neurocomputing **81**(1), 24–32 (2012)
16. Lakshmanan, S., Park, J.H., Jung, H.Y., Kwon, O.M., Rakkiyappan, R.: A delay partitioning approach to delay-dependent stability analysis for neutral type neural networks with discrete and distributed delays. Neurocomputing **111**, 81–89 (2013)
17. Dharani, S., Rakkiyappan, R., Cao, J.: New delay-dependent stability criteria for switched Hopfield neural networks of neutral type with additive time-varying delay components. Neurocomputing **151**, 827–834 (2015)
18. Shi, K., Zhong, S., Zhu, H., Liu, X., Zeng, Y.: New delay-dependent stability criteria for neutral-type neural networks with mixed random time-varying delays. Neurocomputing **168**, 896–907 (2015)
19. Zhang, G., Wang, T., Li, T., Fei, S.: Multiple integral Lyapunov approach to mixed-delay-dependent stability of neutral neural networks. Neurocomputing **275**, 1782–1792 (2018)
20. Liu, P.L.: Improved delay-dependent stability of neutral type neural networks with distributed delays. ISA Trans. **52**(6), 717–724 (2013)
21. Liao, X., Liu, Y., Wang, H., Huang, T.: Exponential estimates and exponential stability for neutral-type neural networks with multiple delays. Neurocomputing **149**(3), 868–883 (2015)
22. Jian, J., Wang, B.: Stability analysis in Lagrange sense for a class of BAM neural networks of neutral type with multiple time-varying delays. Neurocomputing **149**, 930–939 (2015)
23. Arik, S.: An analysis of stability of neutral-type neural systems with constant time delays. J. Franklin Inst. **351**(11), 4949–4959 (2014)
24. Lien, C.H., Yu, K.W., Lin, Y.F., Chung, Y.J., Chung, L.Y.: Global exponential stability for uncertain delayed neural networks of neutral type with mixed time delays. IEEE Trans. Syst. Man Cybern. Part B Cybern. **38**(3), 709–720 (2008)
25. Yang, Y., Liang, T., Xu, X.: Almost sure exponential stability of stochastic Cohen-Grossberg neural networks with continuous distributed delays of neutral type. Optik Int. J. Light Electron. Opt. **126**(23), 4628–4635 (2015)
26. Samli, R., Arik, S.: New results for global stability of a class of neutral-type neural systems with time delays. Appl. Math. Comput. **210**(2), 564–570 (2009)
27. Orman, Z.: New sufficient conditions for global stability of neutral-type neural networks with time delays. Neurocomputing **97**, 141–148 (2012)

28. Cheng, C.J., Liao, T.L., Yan, J.J., Hwang, C.C.: Globally asymptotic stability of a class of neutral-type neural networks with delays. IEEE Trans. Syst. Man Cybern. Part B Cybern. **36**(5), 1191–1195 (2008)
29. Akca, H., Covachev, V., Covacheva, Z.: Global asymptotic stability of Cohen-Grossberg neural networks of neutral type. J. Math. Sci. **205**(6), 719–732 (2015)
30. Ozcan, N.: New conditions for global stability of neutral-type delayed Cohen-Grossberg neural networks. Neural Netw. **106**, 1–7 (2018)
31. Arik, S.: New criteria for stability of neutral-type neural networks with multiple time delays. IEEE Trans. Neural Netw. Learn. Syst. (2019). https://doi.org/10.1109/TNNLS.2019.2920672
32. Arik, S.: A modified Lyapunov functional with application to stability of neutral-type neural networks with time delays. J. Franklin Inst. **356**, 276–291 (2019)

Reduction of Variables and Generation of Functions Through Nearest Neighbor Relations in Threshold Networks

Naohiro Ishii[1(✉)], Kazunori Iwata[2], Kazuya Odagiri[3], Toyoshiro Nakashima[3], and Tokuro Matsuo[1]

[1] Advanced Institute of Industrial Technology, Tokyo, Japan
nishii@acm.org, tokuro@aiit.ac.jp
[2] Aichi University, Nagoya, Japan
kazunori@vega.aichi-u.ac.jp
[3] Sugiyama Jyogakuen University, Nagoya, Japan
{kodagiri,nakasima}@sugiyama-u.ac.jp

Abstract. Reduction of data variables is an important issue and it is needed for the processing of higher dimensional data in the application domains and AI, in which threshold neural networks are extensively used. We develop a reduction of data variables and classification method based on the nearest neighbor relations for threshold networks. First, the nearest neighbor relations are shown to be useful for the generation of threshold functions and Chow parameters. Second, the extended application of the nearest neighbor relations is developed for the reduction of variables based on convex cones. The edges of convex cones are compared for the reduction of variables. Further, hyperplanes with reduced variables are obtained on the convex cones for data classification.

Keywords: Nearest neighbor relation · Generation of Chow parameters · Reduction of variables · Degenerate convex cones

1 Introduction

By Pawlak's rough set theory [1], a reduct is a minimal subset of features, which has the discernibility power as using the entire features, which shows the dimensionality reduction of features. Skowlon [2, 3] developed the reduct derivation by using the Boolean reasoning for the discernibility of data, which is a computationally complex task using all the data. A new consistent method for the generation of reduced variables and their classification in threshold networks is expected from the point of the efficient processing of data. In this paper, we have developed a method of reduction of data variables and it's classification based on the nearest neighbor relations [8]. First, it is shown that the nearest neighbor relations are useful for the generation of threshold functions and Chow parameters [5, 6]. Next, the extended application of the nearest neighbor relations is developed for the reduction of variables [9–11]. Then, the degenerate convex cones and their operations using nearest neighbor relation, are developed. The dependent relations and algebraic operations of the edges on the

L. Iliadis et al. (Eds.): EANN 2020, INNS 2, pp. 569–578, 2020.
https://doi.org/10.1007/978-3-030-48791-1_45

degenerate convex cones in the linear subspaces are derived for the reduction of variables. Finally, the hyperplanes using the reduced variables is derived based on the convex cones of nearest neighbor relations.

2 Nearest Neighbor Relations in Threshold Function

The nearest neighbor relation is also applicable to the generation of threshold functions. The function f is characterized by the hyperplane $WX - \theta$ with the weight vector $W(= (w_1, w_2, \ldots, w_n))$ and threshold θ. The X is a vertex of the cube 2^n. In the following, the threshold function is assumed to be positive and canonical threshold function, in which the Boolean variables hold the partial order [5].

Definition 1. The nearest neighbor relation (X_i, X_j) on the threshold function f is defined to be vertices satisfying the following equation,

$$\{(X_i, X_j) : f(X_i) \neq f(X_j) \wedge |X_i - X_j| \leq \delta(= 1)\}, \tag{1}$$

where $\delta = 1$ shows one bit difference between X_i and X_j in the Hamming distance (also in the Euclidean distance).

Definition 2. The boundary vertex X is defined to be the vertex which satisfies

$$|WX - \theta| \leq |WY - \theta| \quad \text{for the} \quad X(\neq Y \in 2^n) \tag{2}$$

Theorem 3. The boundary vertex X becomes an element of nearest neighbor relation in the threshold function.

Corollary 4. The boundary vertex X generates a pair of nearest neighbor relation in the threshold function.

2.1 Logical Operation for Nearest Neighbor Relation

Generation of threshold function is performed as follows. As an example, the three dimensional vertices are shown in the cube in Fig. 1. As true valued vertices, (101), (110) and (111) are given in the black circle, ●, which belongs to +1 class. As false valued vertices, (000), (010), (100), (001), and (011) are given in the circle, O, which belongs to 0 class. In Fig. 1, the true vertex (101) has nearest neighbor relations as {(101), (001)} and {(101), (100)}. Then, the directed arrow vector indicates the nearest neighbor relation as $\overrightarrow{\{(101), (001)\}}$ Two directed arrow vectors, $\overrightarrow{\{(101), (001)\}}$ and $\overrightarrow{\{(101), (100)\}}$ generate one plane in the Boolean AND operation in Fig. 2. The $\overrightarrow{\{(101), (100)\}}$ has x_3 variable, while, $\overrightarrow{\{(101), (001)\}}$ has x_1 variable. By the AND operation x_1 and x_3, the Boolean product $x_1 \cdot x_3$ is generated. Similarly, the Boolean product $x_1 \cdot x_2$ is generated. Since these two planes are orthogonal, the threshold function $x_1 \cdot x_3 + x_1 \cdot x_2$ is obtained by OR connecting two perpendicular planes.

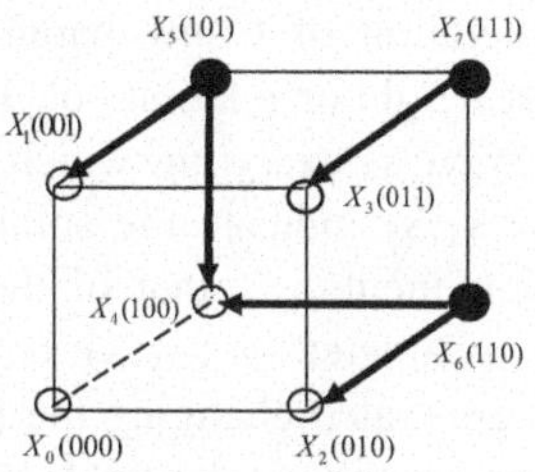

Fig. 1. Directed arrows for nearest neighbor relations

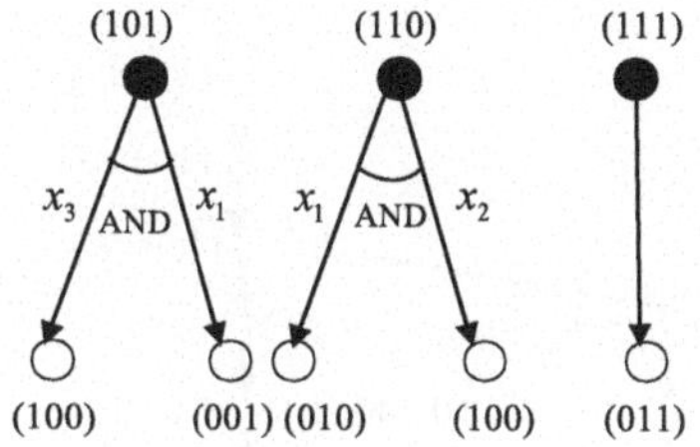

Fig. 2. Boolean AND operations for nearest neighbor relations

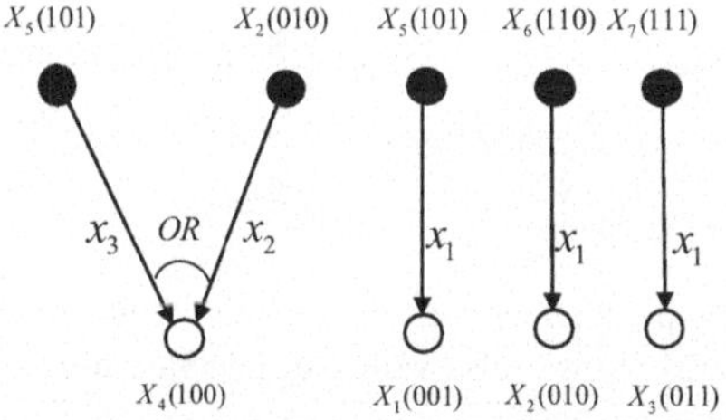

Fig. 3. Boolean OR operation for nearest neighbor relations

Similarly, another logical operation OR is developed as shown in Fig. 3, which also realizes the threshold function $x_1 \cdot x_2 + x_1 \cdot x_3$.

Theorem 5. Nearest neighbor relations in the threshold function are minimal information for generating the given threshold function in the Boolean logical form.

2.2 Iterative Generation of Chow Parameters of Threshold Functions Activated Through Nearest Neighbor Relations

The hyperplane is based on the independent true and false vertices, which are derived from the linear inequality equations of inputs [4, 5]. These independent true and false inputs become boundary vertices, which also make respective nearest neighbor relations in Theorem 5.

In Fig. 4, the iterative generation of Chow parameters with 5 variables [6] is performed based on the nearest neighbor relations of threshold functions. The Chow parameter shows 6 tuples $[m : s_1, s_2, s_3, s_4, s_5]$, in which m shows the summed number of true vertices, while s_1, s_2, s_3, s_4, s_5 indicate the summed number of the first component, that of the second component, ..., that of the fifth component of the true vertices [6]. From the Chow parameter $[m : s_1, s_2, s_3, s_4, s_5] = [6 : 11111]$, the new Chow parameter $[7 : 22111]$ is generated changing the false boundary vertex (11000) to the true vertex in the nearest neighbor relation $\{(10000), (11000)\}$. The iterative generation of Chow parameters is performed through the small change of weights of the boundary vertex.

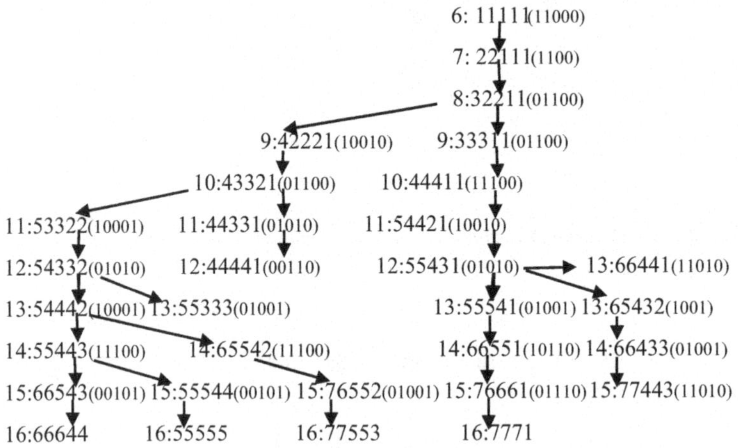

Fig. 4. Generation of Chow parameters with 5 variables of threshold functions through nearest neighbor relations. Parenthesis shows false vertex to generate next Chow parameter.

3 Extension to Threshold Networks Based on Nearest Neighbor Relations

A nearest neighbor relation with minimal distance is introduced here for the extension to threshold networks.

Definition 6. A nearest neighbor relation with minimal distance is a set of pair of instances, which are described in

$$\{(x_i, x_j) : d(x_i) \neq d(x_j) \wedge |x_i - x_j| \leq \delta\}, \tag{3}$$

where $|x_i - x_j|$ shows the distance between x_i and x_j. Further, $d(x_i)$ is a decision function and δ is the minimal distance. Then, x_i and x_j in the Eq. (3) are called to be in the x_j nearest neighbor relation with minimal distance δ.

3.1 Reduction of Variables Based on Convex Cones

An example of the decision table is shown in Table 1. The left side data in the column in Table 1 as shown in, $\{x_1, x_2, x_3, \ldots, x_7\}$ is a set of instances, while the data $\{a, b, c, d\}$ on the upper row, shows the set of attributes of the instance.

Table 1. Decision table of data example (instances)

Attribute	a	b	c	d	Class
x_1	1	0	2	1	+1
x_2	1	0	2	0	+1
x_3	2	2	0	0	−1
x_4	1	2	2	1	−1
x_5	2	1	0	1	−1
x_6	2	1	1	0	+1
x_7	2	1	2	1	−1

In Fig. 5, linearly separated classifications are shown for the data in Table 1. As the first step, one hyperplane A_1 divides the instances of data $\{x_3, x_5, x_7, x_4\}$ shown with $\times$ from those of $\{x_2, x_6\}$ shown with •. But, it misclassifies the instance $\{x_1\}$ with • from $\{x_3, x_5, x_7, x_4, x_1\}$ with $\times$. As the second step, another hyperplane A_2 divides the instance $\{x_1\}$ with • from $\{x_3, x_5, x_7, x_4\}$ with $\times$. In the linearly separated sub spaces, the divided instances are represented by the system of the linear inequality equations. Processing steps for the reduction of variables are classified to the following two steps, which are shown in circles ① and ② in Fig. 6.

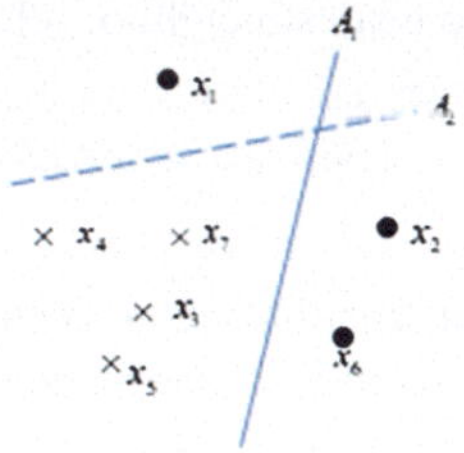

Fig. 5. Piecewise linear separated classification for data in Table 1

Step ① Variables of Nearest Neighbor Relations
Each approximated reduct based on the convex cone is generated based on the nearest neighbor relation, in the step, ① in Fig. 6. The obtained convex cone plays for the reduction of variables in steps ②.

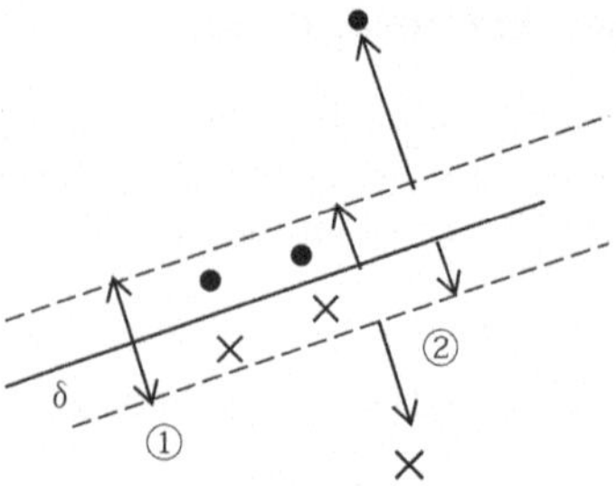

Fig. 6. Processing steps based on hyperplane derived from nearest neighbor relation

Step ② Removal of Variables Using Nearest Neighbor Relations
The convex cones based on the nearest neighbor relations are transformed to the reduced ones for the reduction of variables. Dependent relations and edge processing between the convex cones are applied for the complete reducts, which show the reduction of variables in the step ② in Fig. 6. In the next section, the reduction of variables on the convex cones is shown in the next Sect. 3.2, step (3.2.1) and step (3.2.2).

3.2 Dependent Relations on Degenerate Convex Cones, Step (3.2.1)

Independent vectors of nearest neighbor relations, which consist of the degenerate convex in the affine subspaces, are useful for the operations of dimensional reduction. Independent vectors are derived in the subspaces [4, 7] as follows.

$$\vec{X}'_3 = X'_3 - X'_6,\ \vec{X}'_5 = X'_5 - X'_6 \text{ and } \vec{X}'_7 = X'_7 - X'_6 \tag{4}$$

In the Eq. (4) vectors $\vec{X}'_3$, $\vec{X}'_5$ and $\vec{X}'_7$ are independent. The set of reduced variables $\{b, c\}$ is preserved from $\vec{X}'_3$ of the nearest neighbor relation $\{X_3, X_6\}$. Similarly, the set of reduced variables $\{c, d\}$ is preserved from $\vec{X}'_5$ or $\vec{X}'_7$ of the nearest neighbor relation $\{X_5, X_6\}$ or $\{X_7, X_6\}$, respectively. Thus, the reduced variables $\{b, c, d\}$ are preserved as shown in Fig. 7.

Theorem 7. If a linear dependent equation of the vector value holds on the degenerate convex of the nearest neighbor relations, the corresponding Boolean term to the vector value is removed by the absorption of Boolean terms of the nearest neighbor relations.

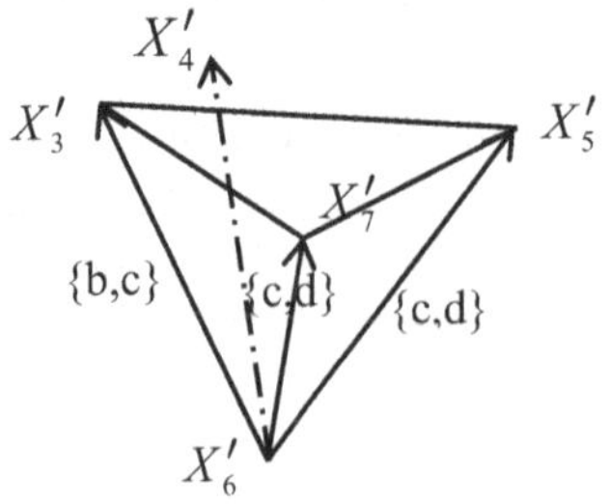

Fig. 7. Degenerate convex cone generated by X'_3, X'_5, X'_7 and X'_6

3.3 Chaining of Edges Between Degenerate Convex Cones, Step (3.2.2)

We can construct two degenerate convex cones as shown in Fig. 8. The upper de degenerate convex cone (solid line) is made of the nearest neighbor relations which is from different classes data, while the lower one (dotted line) is made of the same class data.

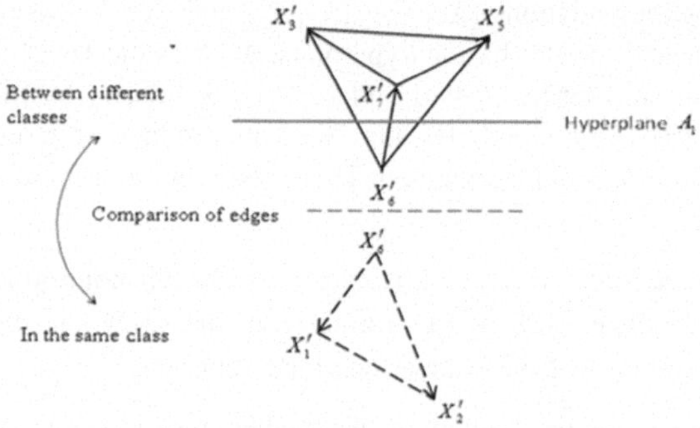

Fig. 8. Comparison of edges on degenerate convex cones in the subspaces

The data difference equations except the nearest neighbor relations are shown in (5)

$$(X_i' - X_j')_k \neq 0 \text{ for } i = 3,\ 4,\ 5,\ j = 1,\ 2 \text{ and } k = b,\ c,\ d \tag{5}$$

If the Eq. (5) hold for both $k = b$ and $k = c$, the element (x_i, x_j), is removed by the equality equation of $(X_i = X_j)_{k=b,k=c}$, since it is absorbed from the nearest neighbor relation $\{b, c\}$. Similarly, if the Eqs. (5) holds for both $k = c$ and $k = d$, the element (x_i, x_j) is removed, since it is absorbed from the nearest neighbor relation $\{c, d\}$. The left side of the Eqs. (5) is replaced to the following equation using the nearest neighbor relation in Fig. 8.

$$(X_i' - X_j')_k = (X_i' - X_6')_k - (X_j' - X_6')_k \tag{6}$$

From the Eq. (5), the Eq. (6) becomes

$$(X_i' - X_6')_k \neq (X_j' - X_6')_k \tag{7}$$

Theorem 8. The element (x_i, x_j) with Boolean variables are removed by the nearest relations with reference data X_ξ', where X_ξ' is in the class $\{j\}(\neq \{i\})$, if the following equations hold

$$(X_i' - X_\xi')_k \neq (X_j' - X_\xi')_k \tag{8}$$

for $i \in \{i\}, j \in \{j\}$, i and j are in the different class and k is components in X_l'.

By Theorem 8, an example of $X'_{\xi} = X'_6$ and $(X'_3 - X'_2)$, which are in the case of $i = 3,\ j = 2$, is developed as follows,

$$(X'_3 - X'_2) = (X'_3 - X'_6) - (X'_2 - X'_6) \quad (9)$$

As the final results in this section, by Theorem 8, all the elements (x_i, x_j) are removed by the nearest neighbor relations (X_3, X_6), (X_5, X_6) and (X_7, X_6) using the hyperplane A_1. Thus, the reduced variables by the hyperplane A_1, become $\{b, c\}$ and $\{c, d\}$, which derive the Boolean sum terms $(b + c)$ and $(c + d)$. Similarly, by the hyperplane A_2, reduced variable (b) is obtained. By the Boolean product of terms of A_1 and A_2, $b \cdot (b + c) \cdot (c + d) = bc + bd$ is obtained. Then, complete reducts of reduced variables become $\{bc,\ bd\}$.

Corollary 9. The element (x_i, x_j) with Boolean variables is not removed, if the Eq. (8) holds. Then, the Boolean sum of the variables in the (x_i, x_j) is multiplied to other Boolean sum of variables of the nearest neighbor relations.

Theorem 10. Dimensionality reduction of variables for reducts is realized by convex cones on the nearest neighbor relations, which are generated by the linear subspaces.

4 Hyperplanes of Reduced Variables for Threshold Network

By using this reduct $\{bc\}$, a classification of the reduced variables is performed as shown in Fig. 9. In Fig. 9, three hyperplanes, $H_{1\{bc\}}, H_{2\{bc\}}, H_{3\{bc\}}$ are shown. The hyperplane A_1 in Fig. 5 is shown, which is also in the degenerated convex in Fig. 8.

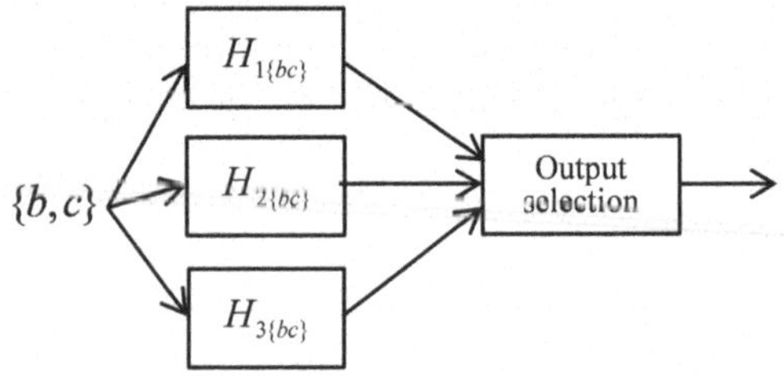

Fig. 9. Hyperplanes generated on convex cones with nearest neighbor relations

All the correct classifications of the classes are carried out by majority voting using these three hyperplanes with reduced variables, $H_{1\{bc\}}$, $H_{2\{bc\}}$, $H_{3\{bc\}}$ in Fig. 9. Then, all the instances are classified, correctly. Combining these three hyperplanes with reduced variables, correct classification is performed using the majority selection. The comparison of the classification accuracy is shown in Fig. 10.

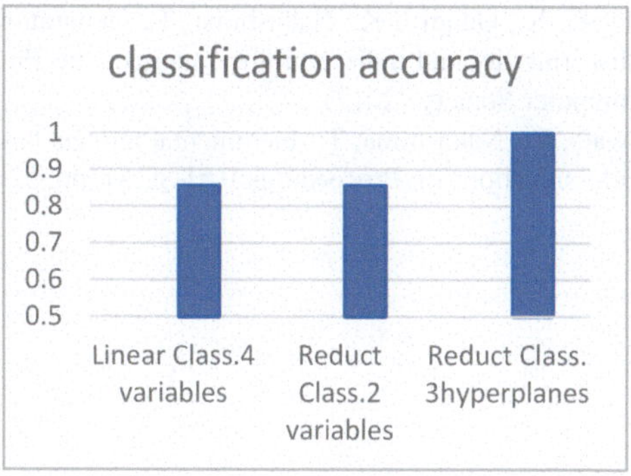

Fig. 10. Comparison of classification accuracy of reduced variables

5 Conclusion

In this paper, the reduction of data variables and it's classification through the nearest neighbor relations are proposed. First, it is shown that the nearest neighbor relations are useful for the generation of threshold functions and the Chow parameters. Next, the extended application of the nearest neighbor relations is proposed for the reduction of variables based on convex cones. Then, the dependent relations and the algebraic operations of edges on the degenerate convex cones are carried out in the linear subspaces. Further, hyperplanes with reduced variables are obtained on the same degenerate convex cones for data classification.

References

1. Pawlak, Z.: Rough sets. Int. J. Comput. Inf. Sci. **11**, 341–356 (1982)
2. Skowron, A., Polkowski, L.: The discernibility matrices and functions in information systems. In: Intelligent Decision Support-Handbook of Application and Advances of Rough Sets Systems, vol. 11, pp. 331–362. Kluwer Academic Publisher, Dordrech (1992)
3. Skowron, A., Polkowski, L.: Decision algorithms, a survey of rough set theoretic methods. Fundam. Inform. **30**(3-4), 345–358 (1997)
4. Fan, K.: On systems of linear inequalities. In: Kuhn, H.W., Tucker, A.W. (eds.) Linear Inequalities and Related Systems, pp. 99–156. Princeton University Press, Princeton (1966)
5. Hu, S.T.: Threshold Logic. University of California Press, California (1965)
6. Chow, C.K.: On the characterization of threshold functions. In: Switching Circuit Theory and Logical Design, vol. S-134, pp. 34–38. IEEE Special Publication (1961)
7. Prenowitz, W., Jantosciak, J.: Join Geometries - A Theory of Convex Sets and Linear Geometry. Springer, Cham (2013)
8. Ishii, N., Torii, I., Iwata, K., Odagiri, K., Nakashima, T.: Generation and nonlinear mapping of reducts-nearest neighbor classification. In: Advances in Combining Intelligent Methods, pp. 93–108. Springer (2017)
9. Ishii, N., Torii, I., Iwata, K., Odagiri, K., Nakashima, T.: Generation of reducts based on nearest neighbor relations and boolean reasoning. In: HAIS 2017, LNCS, vol. 10334, pp. 391–401. Springer (2017)

10. Ishii, N., Torii, I., Iwata, K., Odagiri, K., Nakashima, T.: Generation of reducts and thresh old function using discernibility and indiscernibility matrices. In: Proceedings ACIS-SERA, pp. 55–61. IEEE Computer Society (2017)
11. Ishii, N., Torii, I., Iwata, K., Nakashima, T.: Incremental reducts based on nearest neighbor relations and linear classification. In: Proceedings IIAI-SCAI, pp. 528–533. IEEE Computer Society (2019)

Optimization/Machine Learning

A Comparative Study on Bayesian Optimization

Lam Gia Thuan[1] and Doina Logofatu[2](✉)

[1] Vietnamese-German University, Le Lai Street, Binh Duong New City, Binh Duong Province, Vietnam
cs2014_thuan.lg@student.vgu.edu.vn

[2] Nibelungenplatz 1, 60318 Frankfurt am Main, Hessen, Germany

Abstract. Well-known as an effective algorithm for optimizing expensive black-box functions, the popularity of Bayesian Optimization has surged in recent years alongside with the rise of machine learning thanks to its role as the most important algorithm for hyperparameter optimization. Many have used it, few would comprehend, since behind this powerful technique is a plethora of complex mathematical concepts most computer scientists and machine learning practitioners could barely familiarize themselves with. Even its simplest and most traditional building block - Gaussian Process - alone would involve enough advanced multivariate probability that can fill hundreds of pages. This work reviews this powerful algorithm and its traditional components such as Gaussian Process and Upper Confidence Bound in an alternative way by presenting a fresh intuition and filtering the complications of mathematics. Our paper will serve well as a functional reference for applied computer scientists who seek for a quick understanding of the subject to apply the tool more effectively.

Keywords: Bayesian Optimization · Gaussian Process · Upper Confidence Bound · Hyperparameter optimization · Expensive black-box functions

1 Introduction

1.1 What Is Bayesian Optimization?

Life always involves choices, each may bring forth certain up- and downsides. A normal person would be fine with making a random decision, but for big companies, especially those specialized in mass manufacturing, a slightly better or worse decision could generate an additional revenue or loss in millions. That inspired the birth of optimization algorithms that could optimize the decision-making process and search for a choice that maximizes the overall beneficial gain

---

Supported by the Frankfurt University of Applied Sciences.

L. Iliadis et al. (Eds.): EANN 2020, INNS 2, pp. 581–592, 2020.
https://doi.org/10.1007/978-3-030-48791-1_46

as much as possible. Bayesian Optimization [12] is one such algorithm with certain characteristics that distinguish itself from the vast majority of alternatives such as quick convergence, no derivative required and combinable with other well-studied techniques. In its most generic form, the goal of this technique can be represented as in (1).

$$x^* = \underset{x \in X}{\operatorname{argmax}}(f(x)), \tag{1}$$

where f can be not only a non-differentiable function but also an extremely costly one implying that it may take a significant amount of resources such as time or money to evaluate.

1.2 Why Bayesian Optimization?

Optimization is an old and on-going research topic for decades with countless known solutions, many of which have demonstrated state-of-the-art performance in numerous scenarios such as genetic algorithm [9], ant colony optimization [6], particle swarm optimization [19], gradient descent [23] or Newton-Quasi method [13], L-BFGS-B [8] and much more. That leads to the question as for why Bayesian Optimization should be given special attention. The answer lies in its role as the most effective method for optimizing hyperparameters of machine learning algorithms.

The past decade has witnessed an incredible growth of machine learning and data science. Their influence on human lives has been pervasive more than never before and every bit of improvement on machine learning may have an enormous impact on every part of our society since they are everywhere. Machine learning algorithms can, however, rarely work out-of-the-box, but they must undergo a sequence of steps as illustrated in Fig. 1 to fully unleash their ability and hyperparameter optimization is one indispensable part.

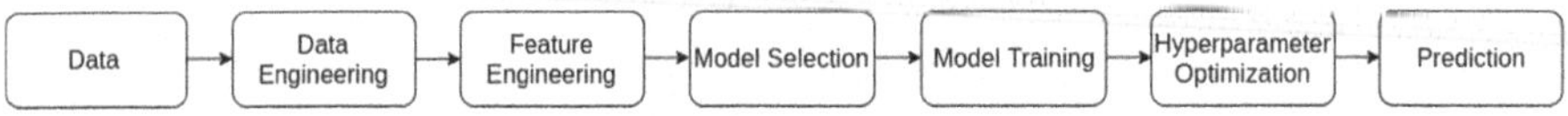

Fig. 1. A simplified workflow for machine learning

This step is, nonetheless, not something just any optimization algorithm can apply for the following reasons:

1. **Expensive.** Machine learning tasks are closely coupled with data. In this era of big data, machine learning rarely involves small number of training examples, which makes the process extremely costly. Population-based optimization techniques such as evolutionary algorithms, ant colony optimization or particle swarm optimization usually require a huge number of computations and hence are unsuitable for this task.

2. **Derivative-free.** A training algorithm is usually perceived as derivative-free and even if a derivative exists, formulating its analytic form is a demanding task. That disqualifies various gradient-based techniques such as Newton-Quasi method, L-BFGS-B or Gradient Descent. Albeit numerical methods [4] provide a painless alternative to compute the derivative (if exists), it is again too costly to be practical.

These problems, however, align perfectly with Bayesian Optimization's advantages. First, it is known for quick convergence in a small number of evaluations and hence reducing the need to evaluate the costly objective function too often. Secondly, it is known to work for any black-box derivative-free function. Optimization algorithms are numerous, but those with such properties are few, and Bayesian Optimization algorithm is the most important solution out of these few especially in hyperparameter optimization as it is the foundation of many techniques such as the recent Bayesian Optimization and Hyperband (BOHB) [7] which is just another variant. In addition, it is also the chosen technique utilized by various machine learning platforms such as Google Cloud, Amazon Web Services and Microsoft Azure [16]. That is why such an important algorithm deserves special attention.

1.3 Why This Review?

This powerful technique has been embedded in a variety of machine learning framework, and using them requires no knowledge of how Bayesian Optimization works. That is, nevertheless, not favorable against the research and development of optimization algorithms for machine learning. Furthermore, behind this powerful technique are complex mathematical concepts that are beyond the reach of the majority of applied computer and data scientists. Understanding this fact led us to the creation of this work to provide a more comprehensible and insightful guide to researchers who wish to learn more about this method, either for future research or just to apply it more effectively. After finishing this paper, researchers should have a vivid picture of how this algorithm works without worrying much of its internal implementation, which is impossible to achieve with the current publications in this area.

1.4 Organization

This work would begin by introducing the simplest-by-nature algorithm for optimization: Random Search. After that is a connection to the target Bayesian Optimization by minimal improvements. To aid the readers in acquiring the general idea easier, we also provide an example of *The Girlfriend and Flowers* to support our explanation. Last, but not least, will come a brief intuitive explanation for its most important building blocks: Gaussian Process as a probabilistic model and Upper Confidence Bound as an acquisition function. These concepts will, unfortunately, require a general understanding of basic probability including Gaussian (normal) distribution. Nonetheless, readers are only required to know the surface of these concepts like what it is about and need not to worry about its advanced properties, which is insignificant compared to the required knowledge in all classical literature in existence about this topic.

2 Bayesian Optimization - An Insightful Intuition

2.1 Random Search

In search of the best decision, the best method would be to try all possibilities and decide on the best after gathering all results. That method is, unfortunately, impractical for problems with infinite solution space. For example when searching for a flower a girl likes most, it is infeasible to buy all flowers in the world and ask for her opinion for all of them. Assuming that the budget is sufficient, it may still take her a lifetime just to analyze each and every kind of flower in existence. Alternatively, picking a few random types of flower and offer the one she likes most would be a more reasonable approach. That is the idea behind random search. In the view of a computer scientist, a random search algorithm would look like Algorithm 1.

Algorithm 1. Random Search

1: $x^* \in \emptyset, y^* \leftarrow -\infty$
2: **for** $i \in \{1, 2 \ldots N\}$ **do**
3:     Generate a random x
4:     $y \leftarrow f(x)$
5:     **if** $y^* < y$ **then**
6:         $x^* \leftarrow x$
7:         $y^* \leftarrow y$
8:     **end if**
9: **end for**
10: Output (x^*, y^*)

Algorithm 1 illustrates how a random search algorithm can be implemented where N in line 2 represents our budget such as the number of flowers that can be bought for testing. Line 3 says that we just consider a random solution such as picking a random flower. Line 4 indicates that we are testing the current solution by, for example, asking the girl how much she likes it. It is worth noting that process f is treated as an expensive black-box function in this paper. For example, it will take time to invite the girl on a date, a sufficient amount of money to book a place in a 5-star restaurant and a great amount of effort asking for her opinion. The whole procedure is, as described, extremely costly and non-differentiable. Steps 5–7 compare and optimize the current solution x^* - the currently best flower - and y^* - her opinion on it, which is a common block in all optimization algorithms. After repeating it as much as our budget N is allowed, step 10 concludes our algorithm. How can this simple, popular and intuitive algorithm be related to the advanced and efficient Bayesian Optimization?

2.2 Improved Random Search and Bayesian Optimization

As mentioned, since our objective function f is very costly, its evaluation should be prioritized for *special candidates* instead of random solutions. The question is how these special candidates can be found? What will happen if your obedient sister is already the best friend of the girl you like and they have shared a good amount of time together shopping and going out?

If that is the case, they may share the same hobbies, hence a flower your sister loves may also be your girlfriend's favorite, and asking your sister is much easier or you may already know it yourself as a good brother. So the process is as follows: 1) Ask for the best flower your sister likes, 2) show it to your girlfriend and ask for her opinion, and 3) tell your sister the new information to help her improve her knowledge. In the language of a computer scientist, the process is as the one described in Algorithm 2.

Algorithm 2. Bayesian Optimization

1: Make g from initial (x, y)
2: $x^* \in \emptyset, y^* \leftarrow -\infty$
3: **for** $i \in \{1, 2 \ldots N\}$ **do**
4: $\quad x' \leftarrow \underset{x \in \mathcal{X}}{\operatorname{argmax}}(g(x))$
5: $\quad y \leftarrow f(x')$
6: $\quad$ **if** $y^* < y$ **then**
7: $\quad\quad x^* \leftarrow x'$
8: $\quad\quad y^* \leftarrow y$
9: $\quad$ **end if**
10: $\quad$ Update g with (x', y)
11: **end for**
12: Output (x^*, y^*)

As can be seen in Algorithm 2, from a random search algorithm that can be written from scratch by any computer science student in a couple of minutes to the advanced and extremely hard to understand, let alone implementing, Bayesian Optimization, the outlines differ by only 3 minor modifications in line 1, line 4 and line 10.

Line 1 means that we should not immediately focus on our expensive-to-handle target, and should search for a third-party helper which is inexpensive, such as asking the sister instead of the girlfriend. Line 4 says that instead of trying a random solution, asking the third-party helper for the best is more reasonable. For example, it is easier to ask your sister what her best flower is. Last, but not least, line 10 indicates that after the new information is acquired, it should be transferred to the third-party helper to improve its own reliability and performance. For instance, if the sister knows that the girlfriend does not like her choice, she may come up with a better plan next time. Those simple steps are the essence of Bayesian Optimization. After this section, readers should have the general idea of how Bayesian Optimization works. All classical publications in existence would start off differently by jumping right into the concept of Gaussian Process which may require hundreds of pages of literature to explain [17].

Further subsections will give an intuitive description of Gaussian Process which is known as a *surrogate* or *probabilistic model*, and Upper Confidence Bound - another building block of Bayesian Optimization named *acquisition function*. These concepts are important to implement the function g mentioned in Algorithm 2. Functionally, g is expected to possess the following qualities: a) cheap to evaluate, b) suitable for derivative-free black-box function, and c) commensurate to f, implying that if $g(x)$ is high, $f(x)$ is likely to be high and vice versa. After countless studies, it has been discovered that such a g function could be realized by composing 2 different function as shown in (2) where $\mathcal{A}$ is called an acquisition function such as Upper Confidence Bound and $\mathcal{S}$ is a surrogate or probabilistic model such as Gaussian Process. After such a function g is acquired, all known optimization techniques can be applied with no restrictions as it has been free of all special characteristics of a machine learning problem (Bayesian Optimization's most popular application).

$$g(x) = \mathcal{A} \circ \mathcal{S}(x) = \mathcal{A}(\mathcal{S}(x)) \tag{2}$$

2.3 Extending Bayesian Optimization

The simple design of Bayesian Optimization gives it the flexibility to evolve. By mutating $\mathcal{A}$ and $\mathcal{S}$ with appropriate acquisition functions and surrogate models, respectively, a variety of new algorithms could be born with their own interesting properties. Hence Bayesian Optimization acts more like a framework rather than an individual algorithm. Studies on this topic has existed since the last century with various results on what could integrate well with the Bayesian Optimization framework.

For surrogate models, the traditional and probably the first candidate is Gaussian Process [17] which implies that its resulting distributions will be Gaussian (normal distributions) [20]. This method has demonstrated state-of-the-art performance in various machine learning applications where the input vector is consisted of only real numeric features $x = (x_1, x_2 \cdots x_n)$ where $x_i \in \mathbb{R}$, which is in most of the cases, and hence still enjoys high popularity even after decades of presence. Recently, research on this topic has involved other types of distributions including the inverse Wishart [15] and Student-t distribution [11], and gave birth to a promising alternative called Student-t Process [18], but they are not yet as popular as the traditional model. Last, but not least, another lesser known model worth mentioning is Random Forests [1] - a well-known machine learning model which has also proven to work well as a surrogate for data with categorical features.

In the area of acquisition functions, the traditional methods still remain relevant. They include, but not restrict to, Upper Confidence Bound (UCB) [5], Expected Improvement (EI) [2], Knowledge Gradient (KG) [22], Entropy Search (ES) [10] and Probability of Improvement (PI) [21]. Nevertheless, most applications would employ EI and UCB by default for their superior performance.

In this paper, only Gaussian Process and UCB will be considered. The former has been known as the de facto standard for Bayesian Optimization, whilst for the latter, it is the simplest of all, which works well and is free from the burden of probability (at least for using it).

3 Gaussian Process

3.1 An Intuitive Explanation

Probably the best-known companion to Bayesian Optimization, a Gaussian Process (GP) is mathematically defined as a *probability distribution over all possible functions.* This popular definition of Gaussian Process is, however, far beyond the comprehensible realm of most applied engineers with a novice understanding of probability. Alternatively, a Gaussian Process could be regarded as *a collection of points* (x, y) and *all the functions (lines) going through ALL these points.* An intuitive example of a Gaussian Process in the 2-dimensional space could be visualized in Fig. 2. As can be seen in Fig. 2a, all functions - just lines in space - controlled by a Gaussian Process intersect at a certain number of points. There may be infinitely many such functions, but most of them are contained in the shaded area in Fig. 2b.

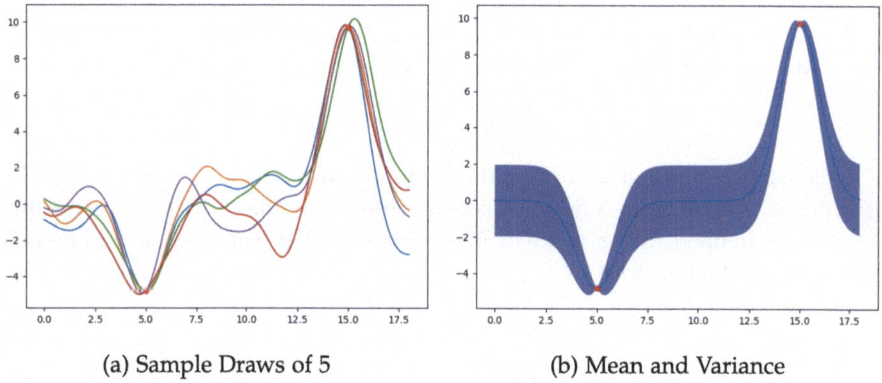

Fig. 2. A sample Gaussian Process of 2 points

What exactly are these lines? It is known that each function may be represented by a line. Our target function f is also a line in the multi-dimensional space. A Gaussian process is a tool that allows governance over an infinite number of lines with some common properties, one of which is to go through a fixed set of points. These points are the real observations we acquired from lines 4–5 in Algorithm 2. Since all the lines controlled by our Gaussian process going through the same points of our target function, they are believed to behave similarly to f. By updating the Gaussian process with new information as said in line 10 of

Algorithm 2, it means adding a newly found observation (point) to our Gaussian process as visualized in Fig. 3. As can be seen, the shaded area has become thinner, implying that the number of possible target functions has been reduced significantly and they have all been closer to our target, implying that even if our choice is wrong, it is still acceptable as it is close enough.

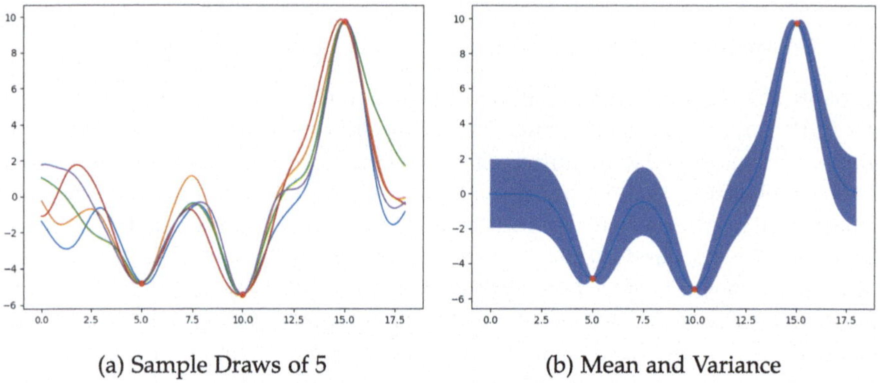

Fig. 3. A sample Gaussian Process of 3 points

As shown in (2), a Gaussian process acts like a normal mathematical function as shown in (3) known as a probabilistic model.

$$y = f(x) \tag{3}$$

In essence, compared to a normal function, a probabilistic model $\mathcal{S}$ differ by returning a probabilistic object called distribution, or more precisely a normal distribution defined by its mean μ and variance σ^2 in the case of a Gaussian process as illustrated in (4).

$$\mathcal{N}(\mu, \sigma^2) = \mathcal{S}(x) \tag{4}$$

Why is $\mathcal{S}(x)$ a distribution? Figure 4 explains why evaluating a function at a candidate solution x can return a distribution by drawing a vertical line at that location. As already known, a Gaussian process is a collection of lines, and all the lines belonging to our Gaussian process will intersect with the vertical line at an infinite number of locations. Their intersection values will form a distribution, which is assumed to be normal.

To summarize, a Gaussian distribution is a powerful mathematical tool that allows us to govern over an infinite number of possible candidate target functions which are expected to be similar to our original target function. A Gaussian process can be treated as a mathematical function which can be evaluated for a given solution x and can return some output which is, unfortunately, a distribution defined by its mean and variance. However, the pair (μ, σ^2) is like quality

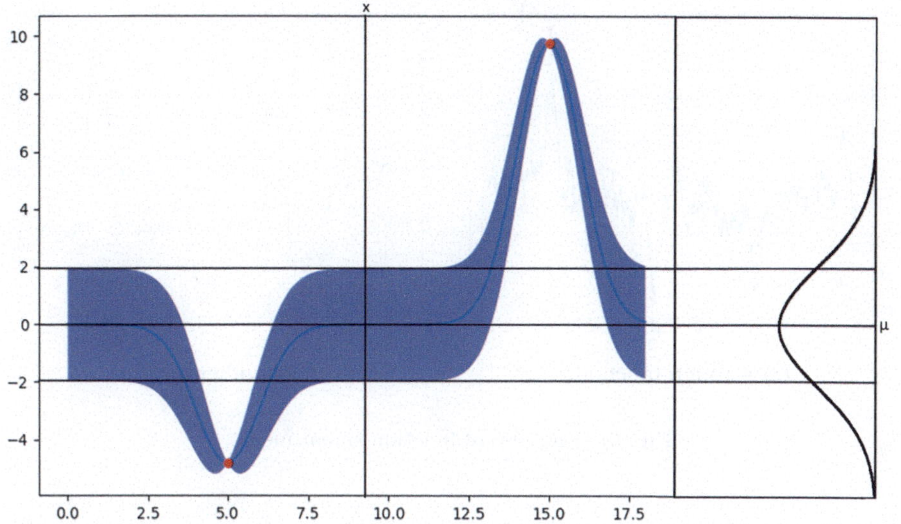

Fig. 4. Gaussian Process - evaluation as a normal distribution

and quantity which cannot be optimized simultaneously, and hence it requires another so-called acquisition function to summarize into a single numeric value that can be used for optimization problem.

3.2 Kernel for Gaussian Process

The previous subsection has provided sufficient information on what a Gaussian process is, but for those who wish to further explore it, it is insufficient. A Gaussian process could also be treated as a machine learning model, implying that it also needs training before being usable with the data being the observation points which we have known. What exactly needs to be trained? As previously know, a Gaussian process contains an infinite number of lines, but as shown in Fig. 2 and 3, it is far from enough to cover all possible lines in space, which implied that only some specific type of line can be considered for a Gaussian process. The one controlling that is called a *kernel* which is at the same time the component that needs to be trained. Exactly how the selection of lines is conducted is beyond the scope of this review. Alternatively, an insightful example can be given. As can be seen in Fig. 3a, all the line functions are very *smooth*. In case the term 'smooth' is confusing, let's take a look at a few *rough* (not so smooth) functions in Fig. 5 for comparison.

At this point, readers should have acquired a feeling of smoothness for a function, but mathematically, smoothness is measured by to what extent a function can be differentiated. The reason why functions in Fig. 3a are so smooth is because its kernel uses the radial basis function (RBF) whose analytic form is represented in (5) where x and x' are some multidimensional vectors of the same number of dimensions.

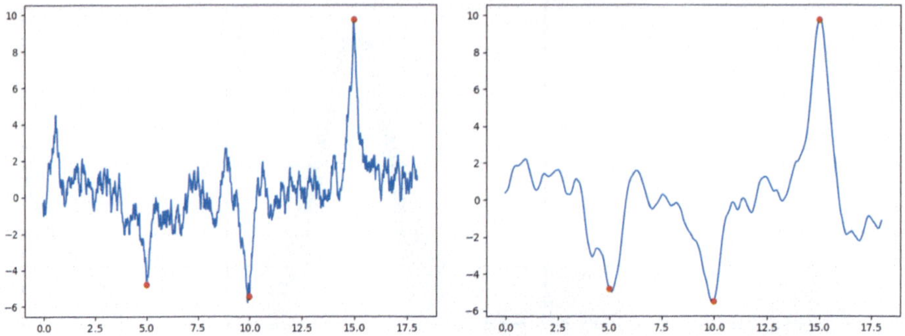

(a) A rough function

(b) A smoother function

Fig. 5. Examples of function smoothness

$$k(x, x') = -\exp \frac{\|x - x'\|^2}{2\sigma^2} \tag{5}$$

As you may know, a function of type e^x is infinitely differentiable and hence its representative lines are extremely smooth. By mutating the kernel function with others, such as the Matern covariance function [14], the lines can be very rough as in Fig. 5a. This is but one example to show a criterion for filtering the target functions. The most important gain after reading this subsection is to understand what a kernel does for a Gaussian process.

3.3 Upper Confidence Bound

As known from the previous subsection, a probabilistic model such as Gaussian process will evaluate to a pair (μ, σ^2) defining a normal distribution which can not be directly used in an optimization problem. That is why an acquisition function comes in handy as it can summarize the information from the given distribution into a single numeric value suitable for maximizing or minimizing. One popular method for this task is Upper Confidence Bound, which works by balancing the trade-off between exploitation and exploration.

The pair (μ, σ^2) could be viewed as quality and quantity. If the mean is high, that means the overall fitness of all lines contained by the Gaussian process is high. As for the variance, high variance means that the shaded area is wider and that there are more possible functions implying that the probability that one of them is our target function is also higher. The Upper Confidence Bound theorem says that the best choice is one with high mean (exploitation) and high variance (exploration) and the 2 terms must be balanced by a third parameter called the confidence band β. The full form of the Upper Confidence Bound function is presented in (6). As can be deduced, the result will be just a single numeric value.

$$\mathcal{A}(\mu, \sigma^2) = \mu + \beta^{1/2}\sigma \tag{6}$$

How can it work? The answer to this question may require unnecessary mathematical knowledge which is against the purpose of this article, which is why to assure the readers that this formula works, it is worth pointing out that the same strategy has been applied in various applications, especially games and artificial intelligence, and has gained state-of-the-art performance in many of them. Most recent was the birth of the AlphaGo program by Google which was famous for defeating the human champion in Go [3] by employing a similar strategy in a slightly different form. In fact, this method is known to provide top performance for Bayesian Optimization, on par with Expected Improvement - the most popular technique in use - but much simpler to implement.

4 Conclusion and Future Work

This paper reviews the popular Bayesian Optimization algorithm and its popular building blocks from a fresh perspective of an applied computer or data scientist without the hassles of advanced mathematics such as multivariate probability. Beginning with the story of *The Girlfriend and Flowers* and the basic Random Search algorithm, we have presented the general idea of Bayesian Optimization in the most comprehensible way without analyzing the complex concept of Gaussian Process as in all articles in existence. After that comes intuitive explanations for Gaussian Process and Upper Confidence Bound with most focus on what they are. Our paper aims to provide researchers in this area a quick and functional reference to gain a general understanding of the subject without the need to read hundreds of pages in classical publications.

Albeit our paper emphasizes the importance of intuition, the value of mathematics is undeniable, especially for those who wish to completely explore the depth of this algorithm. To promote further research and development for this technique rather than its use only as a black box optimization method, we are working towards a short but comprehensible mathematics manual for all mentioned concepts which will complement, but not replace, this work.

References

1. Bajer, L., Pitra, Z., Holeňa, M.: Benchmarking Gaussian processes and random forests surrogate models on the BBOB noiseless testbed. In: Proceedings of the Companion Publication of the 2015 Annual Conference Genetic Evolutionary Computation, pp. 1143–1150 (2015)
2. Benassi, R., Bect, J., Vazquez, E.: Robust Gaussian process-based global optimization using a fully Bayesian expected improvement criterion. In: International Conference on Learning and Intelligent Optimization, pp. 176–190. Springer (2011)
3. Chang, H.S., Fu, M.C., Hu, J., Marcus, S.I.: Google deep mind's AlphaGo. OR/MS Today **43**(5), 24–29 (2016)

4. Chapra, S.C., Canale, R.P., et al.: Numerical Methods for Engineers. McGraw-Hill Higher Education, Boston (2010)
5. Contal, E., Buffoni, D., Robicquet, A., Vayatis, N.: Parallel Gaussian process optimization with upper confidence bound and pure exploration. In: Joint European Conference on Machine Learning and Knowledge Discovery in Databases, pp. 225–240. Springer (2013)
6. Dorigo, M., Blum, C.: Ant colony optimization theory: a survey. Theor. Comput. Sci. **344**(2–3), 243–278 (2005)
7. Falkner, S., Klein, A., Hutter, F.: BOHB: robust and efficient hyperparameter optimization at scale. arXiv preprint arXiv:1807.01774 (2018)
8. Fei, Y., Rong, G., Wang, B., Wang, W.: Parallel L-BFGS-B algorithm on GPU. Comput. Graph. **40**, 1–9 (2014)
9. Harik, G.R., Lobo, F.G., Goldberg, D.E.: The compact genetic algorithm. IEEE Trans. Evol. Comput. **3**(4), 287–297 (1999)
10. Hernández-Lobato, D., Hernandez-Lobato, J., Shah, A., Adams, R.: Predictive entropy search for multi-objective Bayesian optimization. In: International Conference on Machine Learning, pp. 1492–1501 (2016)
11. Ismail, M.E., et al.: Bessel functions and the infinite divisibility of the student t-distribution. Ann. Probab. **5**(4), 582–585 (1977)
12. Lizotte, D.J.: Practical Bayesian optimization. University of Alberta (2008)
13. Martınez, J.M.: Practical quasi-Newton methods for solving nonlinear systems. J. Comput. Appl. Math. **124**(1–2), 97–121 (2000)
14. Minasny, B., McBratney, A.B.: The Matérn function as a general model for soil variograms. Geoderma **128**(3–4), 192–207 (2005)
15. Nydick, S.W.: The Wishart and inverse Wishart distributions. J. Stat. **6**, 1–19 (2012)
16. Ranjit, M.P., Ganapathy, G., Sridhar, K., Arumugham, V.: Efficient deep learning hyperparameter tuning using cloud infrastructure: intelligent distributed hyperparameter tuning with Bayesian optimization in the cloud. In: 2019 IEEE 12th International Conference on Cloud Computing (CLOUD), pp. 520–522. IEEE (2019)
17. Rasmussen, C.E.: Gaussian processes in machine learning. In: Summer School on Machine Learning, pp. 63–71. Springer (2003)
18. Shah, A., Wilson, A., Ghahramani, Z.: Student-t processes as alternatives to Gaussian processes. In: Artificial Intelligence and Statistics, pp. 877–885 (2014)
19. Shi, Y., Eberhart, R.C.: Empirical study of particle swarm optimization. In: Proceedings of the 1999 Congress on Evolutionary Computation-CEC 1999 (Cat. No. 99TH8406), vol. 3, pp. 1945–1950. IEEE (1999)
20. Tong, Y.L.: The Multivariate Normal Distribution. Springer Science & Business Media, New York (2012)
21. Viana, F., Haftka, R.: Surrogate-based optimization with parallel simulations using the probability of improvement. In: 13th AIAA/ISSMO Multidisciplinary Analysis Optimization Conference, p. 9392 (2010)
22. Wu, J., Poloczek, M., Wilson, A.G., Frazier, P.: Bayesian optimization with gradients. In: Advances in Neural Information Processing Systems, pp. 5267–5278 (2017)
23. Zinkevich, M., Weimer, M., Li, L., Smola, A.J.: Parallelized stochastic gradient descent. In: Advances in Neural Information Processing Systems, pp. 2595–2603 (2010)

A Genetic Programming Method for Scale-Invariant Texture Classification

Haythem Ghazouani[1,2], Walid Barhoumi[1,2(✉)], and Yosra Antit[1]

[1] Institut Supérieur d'Informatique, Research Team on Intelligent Systems in Imaging and Artificial Vision (SIIVA), LR16ES06 Laboratoire de recherche en Informatique, Modélisation et Traitement de l'Information et de la Connaissance (LIMTIC), Université de Tunis El Manar, Ariana, Tunisia
haythem.ghazouani@enicar.u-carthage.tn, yosra.antit@gmail.com

[2] Ecole Nationale d'Ingénieurs de Carthage, Université de Carthage, Tunis-Carthage, Tunisia
walid.barhoumi@enicarthage.rnu.tn

Abstract. Texture offers an effective characterization of image shape and orientation. Thus, a predominant task is to detect and extract texture features that discriminate accurately images within different semantic classes. The challenge resides in making these features invariant to several changes, such as affine transformation and viewpoint change, in order to ensure their robustness. Besides, the training phase requires a large number of images. To deal with these issues, Genetic Programming (GP) is adopted in this work with the intention of classifying precisely texture images using some training images per class. In fact, in order to automatically generate a descriptor that is invariant to illumination, rotation and scale; the proposed method combines GP with the scale extraction technique involved by SIFT. The performance of the proposed method is validated on five challenging datasets of non-scaled as well as scaled texture images. Results show that the method is robust not only to scale but also to rotation, while achieving significant performance compared to the state of the art methods.

Keywords: Texture · Genetic programming · Scale invariance · SIFT · Image classification

1 Introduction

Texture is an important characteristic in the field of image analysis compared to both shape and color primitives. It has been used in different areas of research in computer vision, pattern recognition and content-based image retrieval. Texture can be recognized either by touch or by vision. Indeed, the toughness level and the impression can give an important information about the texture type and this is known as "tactile texture". Nevertheless, human can distinguish between textures not only by the touch, but it exists another form which is the "visual texture". It is a variation of the intensity of a surface that affects human vision.

L. Iliadis et al. (Eds.): EANN 2020, INNS 2, pp. 593–604, 2020.
https://doi.org/10.1007/978-3-030-48791-1_47

The visual texture can be noticeable without the need of the tactile texture. In order to represent the perception of the texture and to promote an automatic processing of the information that represents the texture, the analysis process aims to produce numerical features that represents the texture. To deal with this issue, three steps are commonly involved: (1) keypoint detection (2) feature detection and (3) feature extraction. The first step runs through the whole image and decides whether the current pixel is a keypoint or not. Various methods have been used to achieve this task, such as Hessian and Harris corner detection, Sobel Operator, Laplacian of Gaussian (LoG) for corner detection, Canny and Harris for edge detection, grey-level blobs and Principal Curvature-Based Region detector (PCBR) for blobs detection [12,16]. The second step consists to extract informative features, what means going from raw pixel values to another set of values in a lower dimension using mainly statistical measures (*e.g.* mean, variance, histogram...). This step aims to extract the important information while reducing the irrelevant ones. The last step is the feature extraction. It is the same process as the previous one with some changes in the input data, which are the extracted features from the previous step. The main goal is to reproduce a better set of features in order to improve the performance of the model. The difficulty resides in using an important number of images for training the model due to the increase in the complexity while detecting a reliable set of features. Indeed, training a model to perform the classification task is highly relying on the number of the training images and the quality of the extracted features. In this work, we propose to adopt the Genetic Programming (GP) within the task of supervised image classification, using a relatively small training set of textured images, while being invariant to illumination, rotation and scale. The main contribution of this work resides in constructing an efficient descriptor that preserves the rotation change while being invariant to several scale and illumination changes. Besides, the proposed method allows to reduce remarkably the computational cost of the training process.

The rest of this paper is structured as follows. A brief review about the related work is presented in Sect. 2. The proposed method is discussed in Sect. 3. The experimental design and the obtained results are described in Sect. 4. A conclusion and some ideas for future work are discussed in Sect. 5.

2 Related Work

In this section, classical texture classification methods are briefly discussed, before detailing a very well-known GP-based method that we adopted. Most research on texture classification focuses on feature extraction, since more powerful and highly discriminative features generally yield higher classification accuracies regardless the used classifier [14]. Indeed, descriptors must be invariant to many classes of transformations in order to ensure that changes in lighting conditions and camera parameters, notably scale change, do not induce large changes in feature description [2,6]. Classical descriptors can be divided into two groups: "dense" descriptors and "sparse" ones. Dense descriptors (*e.g.* Local

Binary Patterns (LBP)...) discriminate between the model and the background. However, sparse descriptors (*e.g.* Scale Invariant Feature Transform (SIFT) [9], Speeded-up Robust Filter (SURF) [4]...) are known by their robustness to variations in viewpoints and scales. In order to deal with invariance against the scale change, many methods are based on extracting a scale invariant feature from a selection of interest area in the image [7,11]. Differently, some methods are based on logpolar transforms [15]. Furthermore, the fractal dimension and the Gabor filters proved to be scale invariant feature descriptors. To overcome scale variation, other methods generate a set of multi-scale representations from training images. Nevertheless, existing texture descriptors have multiple limitations. First, they require a domain expert to identify specific keypoints in an image. Second, the difficulty to find such a descriptor increases while the number of classes increases, and the final results rely on the preselected keypoints. Third, these descriptors are convoluted and some of them rely only on detecting a specific type of keypoints. Generally, the choice of keypoints is crucial for the quality of the descriptor and automating their detection would be much better than extracting them in a way that can be subjective. In addition, automation can be configured to reduce the search in a specific set of keypoints to ensure robustness to rotation and scale changes. An effective tool for the automation of keypoint extraction is Genetic Programming (GP), which has been evolving rapidly, and new techniques have been constantly proposed in order to tackle image changes within the texture classification framework. For instance, GP-criptor has been proposed [3] for the attention of manipulating an illumination-invariant descriptor. Al-Sahaf [1] extended this work and designed the GP-criptor^{ri} to handle image with rotation changes. The method incorporates automatically the illumination and rotation invariant descriptors while using only two instances, and it operates on raw pixel values like the previous method. Therefore, there is no human intervention to determine a set of predefined features. It is inspired by the LBP descriptor and uses specific operators in order to handle rotation changes. In the proposed method, we adapt the GP technique for the automatic extraction of keypoints. However, instead of making random sampling of the image, we select a specific set of keypoints. We use the first step of the SIFT algorithm to select only scale invariant keypoints. The reduction of the search space leads automatically to a reduction of the training computational cost without decreasing the classification accuracy, as will be shown in the results.

3 Proposed Method

The proposed Evolutionary Texture Classification Algorithm (ETCA) is an extension of the GP-criptor^{ri} technique, what guarantees the invariance against rotation and illumination changes. Besides, since features are defined according to only some SIFT-based keypoints, ETCA is also invariant against scale change, while being computationally efficient. In fact, in order to generate the descriptor, two main processes have to be performed (Fig. 1). First, the generation of SIFT features is performed on the input image in order to detect keypoints that form the GP process input. Then, the GP-based texture descriptor is generated.

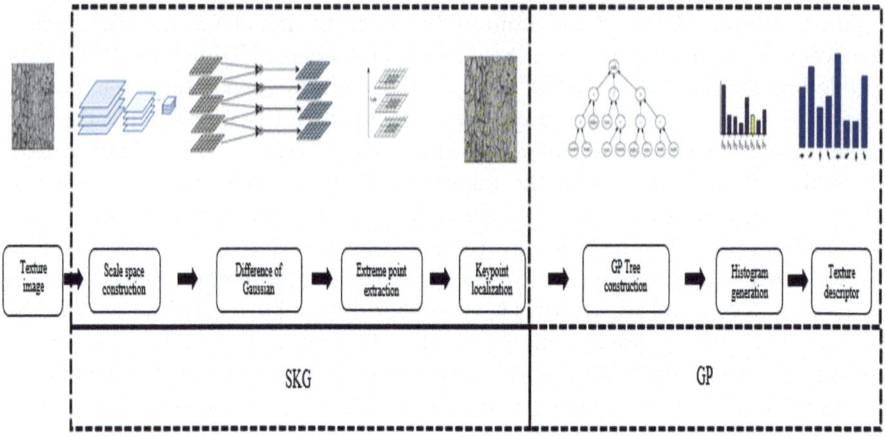

Fig. 1. Flowchart of the proposed method for scale-invariant texture classification.

3.1 First Step: SIFT Keypoint Generation (SKG)

Gaussian pyramids are firstly created from the input images by smoothing and subsampling them in various repetitions. Each image is processed with multiple Gaussian filters to generate a scale for each filter. Each set of scales is called octave, and the algorithm moves to the next octave by down-scaling the image of a factor 2 while generating another set of Gaussian blurred images. The algorithm continues until reaching a predefined threshold. From the set of octaves we can build the scale-space S which applies a smooth filter on the octave with multiple Gaussian filters of different values in order to create various scale of the image. Secondly, in order to detect stable keypoints locations in each scale-space, the difference of Gaussian is used to locate scale-space extrema. Then, keypoints are selected from local minima or maxima. In fact, each pixel $(x,\ y)$ is compared with its $3 \times 3 \times 3$ neighborhood σ; eight neighbor in the same scale and nine neighbors up and down scale. If the selected pixel represents an extremum, then it is a potential SIFT interest point. Finally, the keypoint localization step aims to localize for each interest point what is the best scale location (x, y, σ). Having a large number of keypoints, the goal is to eliminate those that cause noise due to low contrast or poor localized pixel on an edge. The edge should not be detected as a keypoint because it has a high maximal curvature and low minimal curvature. In contrast, a corner represents a keypoint since it has a high maximal and minimal curvature. This work relies not only on detecting those potential SIFT keypoints but also their neighborhoods, which offer a rich additional information. Hence, the $LBP_{8,1}$ is used to deal with invariance against rotation change and illumination variation. It detects image keypoints and generates a histogram that corresponds to the distribution of these keypoints.

3.2 Second Step: GP-Criptor^{ri} Loop

The input of the second step is the set of scale-invariant keypoints for each image. This allows to minimize the computation cost by using only potential keypoints instead of running through all the image pixel by pixel. Thus, a small number of input images is sufficient for the training, without needing human intervention. In the following paragraphs, we detail the representation of individuals as well as the fitness function. Then, we show the step of building histograms from the individual programs. Finally, we describe how the elected individuals generate the descriptors to be fed to the classifier. It is very important to begin by explaining the structure of the individuals (also referred to as "programs") of our GP process. In fact, each program corresponds to a tree of functions (Fig. 2), such that a quality fitness measure is assigned to it. These fitness values are then used to select the best parents for reproduction using crossover and mutation operators. Once the offspring programs are generated, children and parents compete for survival based on an environmental selection mechanism. Thus, the GP parent population is updated with the best programs. By running the GP for a certain number of generations, GP programs are optimized automatically thanks to the intelligent sampling of the search space. At the end of the run, the parent population programs define the descriptors for texture classification.

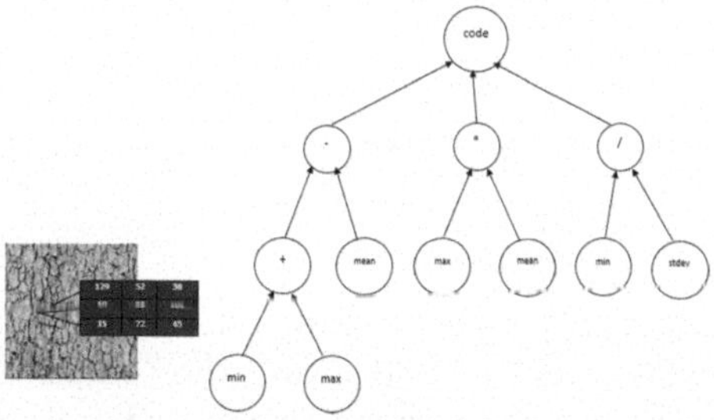

Fig. 2. Tree representation of an evolved program.

More specifically, a program is a tree made up by a root node, some internal nodes, and some leaf nodes (Fig. 2). The leaf nodes are scalar values, and the others are functions that could be arithmetic operators or complex loop structures. The terminal set can be categorized into four nodes of different type: min($\vec{x}$), max($\vec{x}$), mean($\vec{x}$) and stdev($\vec{x}$) which return minimum, maximum, mean and standard deviation values of a given vector $\vec{x}$, respectively. These four functions give always the same value even if the vector elements change orders, what is useful when dealing with rotation changes. The function set is composed by the code node and four arithmetic operators (+, −, *, /). The whole program is constructed to automatically detect the main keypoints in an image and extract a feature vector from it. To do so, we pursue five steps. Firstly, the system examines the leaf nodes and calculates its corresponding arithmetic function.

Secondly, the resulting values are communicated to the parent node. Thirdly, the parent node, which is the internal node, evaluates and returns the corresponding results to the parent node until it is the code node. Fourthly, the code node returns a binary code. Finally, the generated binary code is converted into decimal and fed into its position in a histogram which is incremented by 1. As in the GP-criptor^{ri}, we use a knowledge base D, which contains a set of feature vectors. D is a set that is thereafter used to train the classifier. Indeed, the two instances that are used during the mutative process are fed to the evolved descriptor to generate the knowledge base. To measure the performance of each program, accuracy cannot be used in this case. In fact, the number of instances is very low (only two instances), what can increase the probability of over-fitting. Instead of this, we adopt the fitness presented in [3] and described by (1):

$$fitness = 1 - (\frac{1}{1 + \exp^{-5(D_b - D_w)}}), \tag{1}$$

where, D_b is the average distance of between-class instances (2) and D_w is the average distance of within-class instances (3).

$$D_b = \frac{1}{z(z-m)} \sum_{\substack{u^\alpha, v^\beta \in S_{tr} \\ \forall \vec{u} \in u^\alpha \\ \forall \vec{v} \in v^\beta}} X^2(\vec{u}, \vec{v}), \qquad \alpha, \beta \in \{1, 2, \ldots, C\}, \alpha \neq \beta \tag{2}$$

$$D_w = \frac{1}{z(m-1)} \sum_{\substack{u^\alpha, v^\alpha \in S_{tr} \\ \forall \vec{u} \in u^\alpha \\ \forall \vec{v} \in v^\alpha}} X^2(\vec{u}, \vec{v}), \qquad \alpha \in \{1, 2, \ldots, C\} \tag{3}$$

$S_{tr} = \{(\vec{x_i}, y_i),\ i \in \{1, \ldots, z\}\}$ is the training set, where $\vec{x_i}$ ($\in \mathbb{R}+$) is the feature vector and y_i is the class label. C and m are the total number of classes and the number of instances per class, respectively, and z is the total number of instances in the training set ($=C.m$), and x^α is the set of all instances of the αth class in S_{tr}. The widely used $X^2(\cdot, \cdot)$ function measures the distance between two normalized vectors of the same length as follows:

$$X^2(\vec{u}, \vec{v}) = \frac{1}{2} \sum_i \frac{(u_i - v_i)^2}{(u_i + v_i)}, \tag{4}$$

where, u_i and v_i are the ith element in the $\vec{u}$ and $\vec{v}$ vectors, respectively. Since X^2 returns values in [0, 1] and the fitness function returns values in [0.27, 0.73], the factor 5 is used in order to scale the output interval to be in [0, 1]. If the denominator of Eq. 4 is equal to 0, the function returns 0 in order to prevent the division per zero. Thus, the fitness measure (Eq. 1) returns 0 in the best scenario and 1 in the worst scenario. After the computation of the best fitness function of each keypoint, the best keypoints are fed into the knowledge base. The main difference between the GP-criptor^{ri} and ETCA is the input of the terminal set. The leaf nodes of an individual, in GP-criptor^{ri}, compute statistics of the pixel values of the sliding window, whereas ETCA takes statistics of the coordinates values of the sliding window of the generated keypoints from the scale space analysis process. The idea behind this is to enhance the program to take a set of pre-generated keypoints that are invariant to scale and fed them to the GP-criptor^{ri} program at the leaves' nodes. This permits particularly to reduce the computational time, since that instead of using a sliding window of a generated image that is invariant to scale, we use only the significant keypoints processed from the previous step. In fact, the sliding window is represented by only the selected keypoints. Furthermore, in order to understand how the descriptor is designed, it is very important to show how the program constructs the histogram from the selected keypoints. Indeed, each tree constructs a feature vector which is the binary code developed from the root node. The set of the feature vectors defines the histogram of the input instance. Indeed, the proposed method treats only the keypoints extracted by SIFT while using a sliding window. Then, for each keypoint, the ETCA performs six main steps: (1) the values of the current pixel are fed into the leaf nodes of the program tree, (2) minimum, maximum, mean and standard deviation values of the current window are computed, (3) resulting values are fed into the terminal nodes of the individual, (4) internal (non-terminal) nodes, apart from the root node, are evaluated starting from those near the leaves by applying the corresponding operator to the list of arguments, (5) the root node returns a binary code by converting each of its arguments to 0 if it is negative and to 1 otherwise, and here comes the role of the $LBP_{8,1}$ that works as a thresholding parameter (the central pixel represents the threshold), (6) the generated binary code is converted to decimal, and the corresponding bin of the feature vector (histogram) is incremented by 1. It is worth noting that the length of the generated code depends on the number of the children of the code node, which is equal to 2^n, where n is the number of the code node children.

To summarize briefly, the proposed method offers a descriptor that is invariant to scale, rotation and illumination using small number of instances. In fact, ETCA combines arithmetic operators and first-order statistics in order to form a model that takes an image as input and generates a feature vector in various steps as previously mentioned. The generated codes (histograms) are thereafter fed into a classifier to predict the class label. An important task is how to select and discriminate between the training instances in order to classify them regarding to the small number of images used in the training phase. Instead of using the accuracy to measure the fitness function that will be used to detect as much representative keypoints as possible, it reliably separates the distances of different classes further apart and keeps the distances between instances of the same class as close to each other as possible.

4 Experimental Study

Realized experiments are highlighted and discussed in this section. The discussion includes datasets, performance metrics, parameter settings and the results. The experiments have been executed on a PC with Windows 10 with

Table 1. A summary of the benchmark image classification datasets.

Dataset	Classes	Instances	Changes			Dimensions	
			Illum.	Rotation	Scale	Width	Height
KTH-TIPS [10]	10	810	✓	x	✓	200	200
UIUC [8]	25	1000	✓	✓	✓	640	480
MINC [5]	23	2500	✓	✓	✓	192	192
OUTEXTC10 [13]	24	4320	✓	✓	x	128	128
OUTEXTC00 [13]	24	4800	✓	x	x	128	128

Intel®$Core^{TM}$ i7-7500U CPU @ 2.70 GHz and 8G of memory. It is worth noting that the measured time in our experiments is the CPU time and not the wall-clock time.

4.1 Datasets and Evaluation Protocol

ETCA is evaluated on five challenging datasets widely used for texture classification assessment. The total number of instances in each dataset is equally divided between the training set and the test set. The instances of all texture datasets are grey-scale images. These five image datasets vary in number of classes (binary and multi-class), size of instances (from 128×128 to 640×480 pixels) and various texture applications (foliage classification, hair classification, brick, wall...). Thus, since the methods investigated in this work are evaluated using a set of carefully chosen benchmarks for image classification of varying difficulty, these methods can be used not only in the domain of image classification but also to perform other tasks such as image segmentation and content-based image retrieval. The datasets vary in domain (texture and object classification), illumination, scale, point of view, rotation, size of instances (images), number of classes and number of instances per class (Table 1). The datasets mentioned in Table 1 are primarily sorted in ascending order based on the total number of classes and then sorted by the total number of instances. As performance metrics, the classification accuracy is used as a fitness measure to indicate the performance of each individual to differentiate between instances of various classes. It is defined as the ratio between the number of correctly classified instances and the total number of instances. In the case of small number of instances (less than 10 instances), the use of accuracy is insufficient because the system can easily capture features that are good enough to discriminate between the training instances, but not sufficient to classify the unseen data. Thus, we rely also on the fitness function as defined in Eq. 1. Furthermore, in order to compute the required time to evolve a descriptor by the proposed method, the CPU time is measured for each evolutionary run from the beginning of generating the initial population until it reaches the stopping criterion.

Table 2. Parameter settings of the genetic process.

Parameter	Value	Parameter	Value
Crossover rate	*0.80*	Generations	*50*
Mutation rate	*0.20*	Population size	*200*
Elitism	*Keep the best*	Initial population	*Ramped half-and-half*
Tree min depth	*2*	Selection type	*Tournament*
Tree max depth	*10*	Tournament size	*7*

Table 3. The average time required to evolve a descriptor by ETCA.

Dataset	KTH-TIPS	MINC	UIUC	OutexTC00	OutexTC10
Time (hour)	4	4.9	4.8	1.4	1.1

4.2 Experimental Setup and Results

The parameter settings of ETCA are summarized in Table 2. The ramped half-and-half method is used to generate the initial GP population. Since we use a small number of instances, the task of dealing with the input images is an expensive task, so the population size is set to 200 individuals. A tournament of a size 7 is used to maintain the population diversity. The crossover probability is set to 0.80 and the mutation probability is set to 0.20. We notice that only the best mechanism in kept to prevent the evolutionary process from degrading. The tree depth of an evolved program is between 2 and 10 levels in order to avoid code bloating. To end with, the evolving process stops when the fitness value is very close to 0 ($<10^{-6}$), or the maximum number of generations is attempt (=50). It is known that the multi-scale space should cover a sufficient range of scales. It is worth noting that the size of the images is small (=128×128 in OutexTC00 and OutexTC10) and with the down-sampling process the image size will be much smaller, so we suppose that the down-sampling rate is greater than 1/10, what results to sub-images of a size larger than 20×20. Furthermore, we recorded the average time required to evolve an image descriptor on the different datasets (Table 3). It is clear that ETCA needs shorter time to evolve a descriptor on the OutexTC10 dataset compared to the time needed for the other datasets. This is expected mainly because this dataset has minimum size and number of instances. It has also cropped texture with different scales unlike the MINC dataset which has background with the texture. The UIUC dataset requires more time than the other datasets, given that it has bigger size instances.

Table 4 shows the results of applying seven relevant classification techniques using the generated features by ETCA as well as the ones of the baseline methods. Using the studied classification techniques, ETCA achieves comparable or better performance in most of the cases. This is the case with OutexTC00 and OutexTC10 datasets. However, the accuracy level degrades for MINC and UIUC datasets, as compared with the other datasets. Overall, ETCA has achieved

Table 4. The average accuracy (%) of seven classifiers using five image descriptors on five challenging standard datasets (best values are in bold).

	SIFT		SURF		DIF		$GPcript^{ri}$		ETCA	
	Training	Test	Training	Test	Training	Test	Training	Test	Training	Test
KTH-TIPS										
1-NN	100	52.4	100	64.8	22.5	17.4	95.1	40.9	100	**93.6**
Adaboost	100	78.4	93.05	45.2	11.1	9.0	52.1	48.9	100	**92.9**
SVM	96.4	90.4	98.1	53.9	15.3	14.7	100	31.0	100	**93.4**
NB	81.8	56.1	76.9	54.9	12.1	11.1	98.3	39.3	100	**91.3**
NB-Tree	93.8	50	93.8	53.0	12.2	12.3	100	34.5	100	**90.8**
NNge	92.4	90.1	93.1	53.0	15.9	15.7	97.8	45.1	100	**90.9**
K*	100	32.7	100	43.2	14.0	14.0	97.8	35.1	100	**93.1**
OutexTC00										
1-NN	100	65.1	100	73.2	25.2	17.4	100	87.7	100	**95.0**
Adaboost	100	72.4	70.1	45.1	11.6	9.0	60.2	57.1	100	**94.0**
SVM	93.1	70.7	65.7	35.2	16.2	14.7	85.1	73.9	100	**95.0**
NB	78.9	44.1	43.6	61.1	13.2	11.1	80.0	72.0	100	**93.2**
NB-Tree	89.3	64.1	88.2	44.7	15.1	12.3	95.0	79.9	100	**94.0**
NNge	70.4	33.1	100	77.9	16.2	15.7	100	85.4	100	**90.1**
K*	60.1	45.5	100	45.1	14.0	14.0	100	87.6	100	**95.2**
OutexTC10										
1-NN	90.5	45.1	80.0	33.1	15.1	8.2	100	86.8	100	**87.5**
Adaboost	80.8	32.1	60.4	22.1	10.2	6.6	70.0	51.2	100	**82.2**
SVM	70.1	15.0	55.5	15.2	10.5	7.4	90.0	72.2	100	**80.5**
NB	33.6	22.3	60.1	50.9	12.0	7.5	80.5	70.5	97.3	**81.5**
NB-Tree	20.1	9.5	20.0	10.1	12.0	7.7	100	**87.1**	100	**87.1**
NNge	20.0	11.2	15.2	7.6	12.0	9.4	100	85.6	100	**88.1**
K*	50.0	44.1	12.3	6.9	10.0	7.4	100	86.2	100	**87.1**
UIUC										
1-NN	100	**93.7**	100	72.1	54.1	32.5	85.0	33.1	100	85.8
Adaboost	80.1	54.4	75.0	66.1	33.2	8.9	77.1	25.9	100	**74.0**
SVM	93.2	65.4	83.4	71.8	12.1	7.9	56.2	23.3	100	**72.0**
NB	92.9	84.3	89.4	**72.5**	10.9	6.8	40.5	12.7	100	70.1
NB-Tree	96.4	70.9	53.3	48.4	33.5	10.9	36.7	15.1	100	**75.0**
NNge	71.1	66.3	93.4	**77.9**	12.1	7.4	28.5	18.1	98.3	70.0
K*	100	89.8	100	72.1	45.8	22.9	46.1	21.6	100	**75.0**
MINC										
1-NN	100	52.4	100	64.8	55.4	25.2	21.1	10.1	100	**72.0**
Adaboost	95.0	66.0	80.4	44.1	75.8	66.1	33.1	12.5	100	**74.0**
SVM	85.1	45.2	50.2	21.3	44.8	20.0	35.6	12.1	100	**75.0**
NB	81.8	56.1	76.9	54.9	25.1	9.4	40.1	25.3	100	**73.0**
NB-Tree	93.8	50.0	93.8	53.0	10.1	5.4	20.5	11.1	100	**77.0**
NNge	71.1	66.3	93.4	**77.9**	12.1	7.4	19.2	11.0	96.9	70.0
K*	100	32.7	100	43.2	33.1	10.1	23.4	10.1	100	**75.0**

the best performance among all the baseline methods with almost all the classifiers. Indeed, for the KTH-TIPS dataset the proposed method has achieved 93.6% as accuracy using 1-NN. KTH-TIPS provides images with variations in scale as well as variations in pose and illumination. In particular, ETCA shows better performance regarding SIFT and GP-criptor^{ri}. The latter one achieves only 41% average accuracy, since it does not handle scale change. Likewise, ETCA has achieved the overall best performance, which is 95.0%, on the OutexTC00 dataset, using the classifiers 1-NN, SVM and K*. This dataset is characterized by its extensive viewpoint and illumination changes, but it does not have scale and rotation changes. ETCA shows better performance to handle these changes in comparison to the GP-criptor^{ri}. Furthermore, in order to validate invariance against rotation change without considering scale change, the studied methods have been validated on the OutexTC10 dataset. The results show that the proposed method achieves the best performance accuracy, which is 88.1% using the NNge classifier. This confirms that our method is able to handle rotated and non rotated images with and without scale changes. Similarly, results on the UIUCTex dataset show that the proposed method records 95.00% accuracy using the 1-NN classifier and has the overall best performance among the compared methods (*e.g.* best SIFT accuracy is 89.8% using the K* classifier). This dataset is very challenging due to its high intra-class variation and to the presence of many deformations (illumination, viewpoint, rotation and scale). For the MINC-2500 dataset, SURF achieves the best accuracy which is 77.9% using the NNge classifier. Proposed method has achieved comparable performance accuracy which is 77.00% using the NB-Tree classifier. This confirms that ETCA can handle all kind of deformation at once. The overall (for all the classifiers) average accuracy for this dataset is about 77% for ETCA and about 50% for SURF.

5 Conclusion

This work is devoted to introducing a genetic programming method to elaborate optimal texture image descriptor for scale-invariant texture classification. Features are extracted using the SIFT technique in order to have potential keypoints with a significant neighborhood distance that captures keypoints at different levels (zoom) and fed them to a tree representation. Proposed method has the potential of classifying not only texture images but also real-world images. Moreover, ETCA does not require domain expert to detect a set of keypoints, since it detects these keypoints automatically and it does not require any domain knowledge. The main contribution of this work is to automatically evolve a descriptor generated from genetic programming based on a scale invariant set of keypoints extracted in a pretreatment step. The evaluation shows that the method is effective to evolve a descriptor that is invariant against illumination, rotation and scale changes, with no need to human intervention. Indeed, the application area and the obtained results demonstrate that using ETCA may result in data-driven elaboration of an optimal filter image descriptor for subsequent solution of the image classification task. As future work, genetic programming could be also adapted to generate a combination of textural and edge description of the texture, while preserving rotation and scale invariance.

References

1. Al-Sahaf, H., Al-Sahaf, A., Xue, B., Johnston, M., Zhang, M.: Automatically evolving rotationinvariant texture image descriptors by genetic programming. IEEE Trans. Evol. Comput. **21**(1), 83–101 (2017)
2. Al-Sahaf, H., Zhang, M., Johnston, M.: Genetic programming for multiclass texture classification using a small number of instances. In: Proceedings of the 10th International Conference on Simulated Evolution and Learning, pp. 335–346 (2014)
3. Al-Sahaf, H., Zhang, M., Johnston, M., Verma, B.: Image descriptor: a genetic programming approach to multiclass texture classification. In: Evolutionary Computation (CEC), pp. 2460–2467 (2015)
4. Bay, H., Tuytelaars, T., Gool, L.V.: SURF: speeded up robust features. In: Computer Vision-ECCV 2006, vol. 3951, no. 1, pp. 404–417 (2006)
5. Bell, S., Upchurch, P., Snavely, N., Bala, K.: Material recognition in the wild with the materials in context database. In: Computer Vision and Pattern Recognition (CVPR) (2015)
6. Giveki, D., Karami, M.: Scene classification using a new radial basis function classifier and integrated SIFT–LBP features. Pattern Anal. Appl. 1–14 (2020). https://doi.org/10.1007/s10044-020-00868-7
7. Kokkinos, I., Yuille, A.: Scale invariance without scale selection. In: IEEE Conference on Computer Vision and Pattern Recognition, pp. 1–8 (2008)
8. Lazebnik, S., Schmid, C., Ponce, J.: A sparse texture representation using local affine region. IEEE Trans. Pattern Anal. Mach. Intell. **27**, 1265–1278 (2005)
9. Lowe, D.: Distinctive image features from scale-invariant keypoints. Comput. Vision **60**(2), 91–110 (2004)
10. Mallikarjuna, P., Targhi, A., Fritz, M., Hayman, E., Caputo, B., Eklundh, J.O.: Thc KTH TIPS database, July 2004
11. Mellor, M., Hong, M., Brady, M.: Locally rotation contrast and scale invariant descriptors for texture analysis. Trans. Pattern Anal. Mach. Intell. **30**(1), 52–61 (2008)
12. Mikolajczyk, K., Schmid, C.: A performance evaluation of local descriptors. IEEE Trans. Pattern Anal. Mach. Intell. **27**(10), 1615–1630 (2005)
13. Ojala, T., Maenpaa, T., Pietikainen, M., Viertola, J., Kyllonen, J., Huovinen, S.: Outex - new framework for empirical evaluation of texture analysis algorithms. In: Object Recognition Supported by user Interaction for Service Robots, vol. 1, pp. 701–706 (2002)
14. Roy, S.K., Ghosh, D.K., Dubey, S.R., Bhattacharyya, S., Chaudhuri, B.B.: Unconstrained texture classification using efficient jet texton learning. Appl. Soft Comput. **86**, 105910 (2020)
15. Sun, X., Wang, J., Kong, F.M.L.: Scale invariant texture classification via sparse representation. Neurocomputing **112**(1), 338–348 (2013)
16. Venkataramana, M., Sreenivasa, E., Satyanarayana, C., Anuradha, A.: A review of recent texture classification: methods. IOSR J. Comput. Eng. (IOSR-JCE) **14**(1), 54–60 (2013)

A Monetary Policy Strategy Based on Genetic Algorithms and Neural Networks

Talitha F. Speranza[1(✉)], Ricardo Tanscheit[2], and Marley M. B. R. Vellasco[2]

[1] Barcelona Graduate School of Economics, 08005 Barcelona, Spain
talitha.speranza@barcelonagse.eu

[2] Pontifical Catholic University of Rio de Janeiro, Rio de Janeiro 22451-900, Brazil
{ricardo,marley}@ele.puc-rio.br

Abstract. We propose a novel monetary policy strategy in an attempt to provide an auxiliary tool to central banks, whose main predictive models are still from the Dynamic Stochastic General Equilibrium (DSGE) family, which has some flaws. We derive an objective function from three empirical relationships that have long been established in the economic literature and we seek to minimise the value of this function by choosing the interest rate via a genetic algorithm. Since the function is forward looking, we use a neural network to predict values of unemployment and inflation. Using data from Brazil, simulation results suggest that had the Brazilian central bank applied our strategy, and all other economic conditions remained equal, inflation could have been lower for 62.48% of the time. Predicted unemployment, however, was lower only for 39.69% of covered periods, as it faces a trade-off with inflation.

Keywords: Neural networks · Monetary policy · Genetic algorithms

1 Introduction

Monetary authorities around the world conduct policy in order to stabilise inflation and mitigate its deleterious effects. Some of them also take unemployment explicitly into account, trying to minimise the trade-off between this variable and inflation. Whether this is the case or not, the policy instrument is the short-term interest rate almost everywhere and Dynamic Stochastic General Equilibrium (DSGE) models are the favourite choice of central bankers to help them setting the interest rate, despite these models' flaws. Efforts to subdue the shortcomings have been insufficient: to this date, there is an ongoing demand for building a new framework to support monetary policy.

We aim at filling this gap and apply our strategy to the case of Brazil. In contrast with the traditional approach, we do not build a model affected by *ad hoc* assumptions, identification issues, and questionable policy prescriptions. Rather,

Supported by Pontifical Catholic University of Rio de Janeiro.

L. Iliadis et al. (Eds.): EANN 2020, INNS 2, pp. 605–616, 2020.
https://doi.org/10.1007/978-3-030-48791-1_48

in a novel approach, we use a genetic algorithm and a neural network, seeking to minimise an objective function that depends on the interest rate through future inflation and future unemployment. We derive this objective function from three empirical relationships observed in a wide range of countries and periods.

Since the objective function is prospective, it is necessary to estimate future unemployment and inflation for every potential solution (i.e. series of interest rates) generated by the genetic algorithm. Predictions are computed by a multilayer perceptron, whose inputs are the attempted series of interest rates and a large set of covariates. Our results suggest that had the Brazilian central bank applied our strategy, and all other economic conditions remained equal, inflation could have been lower for 62.48% of the time. Predicted unemployment, however, was lower only for 39.69% of covered periods, as it faces a trade-off with inflation.

Given the importance of inflation and unemployment for any given country, and in particular for Brazil, where inflation has been historically high and unemployment is currently a major concern, this work's contribution intends to be of a practical nature above all. Nonetheless, it also adds to the literature on machine learning applied to monetary policy. There are few papers relating both subjects and, to the best of our knowledge, this is only the second study trying to create a novel interest rate rule based on machine learning. Unlike this previous study, which automatises a central bank's behaviour, ours suggests that our framework could be of help in lowering inflation.

The remainder of this article is organised as follows. The Sect. 2 is devoted to a very brief literature review. Section 3 describes our proposed model and lists the time series we used. Section 4 discusses the results and shows how the model can be used in practice. Section 5 concludes the article.

2 Background

2.1 Failure of DSGE Models

Before the 2008 financial crisis, the DSGE framework was standard, but the crisis was a disruption in the financial sector only comparable to that of 1929 and no economist could see it coming. Their models were evidently flawed. Problems have been recognised by several researchers: (i) assumptions are unrealistic and most conclusions were not empirically confirmed [1], (ii) policy implications are unconvincing [4], and (iii) there are more parameters to estimate than equations and all estimation methods are prone to cherry-picking [10]. The most promising proposed alternative to DSGEs, agent-based models, are also subjected to this last issue.

2.2 Macroeconomic Relationships

Our model stems from economic relationships that are observed across almost all countries and at most periods for which historical data is available. In the next subsections, we briefly discuss the literature on these relationships and their empirical validity, besides describing the correlations themselves.

Okun's Law: This law implies an empirical and negative relationship between the unemployment rate and the gross domestic product (GDP)[1] growth rate. Evidence that it holds for most countries is available [2]. Its general form is:

$$u - \bar{u} = F(y - \bar{y}) + \kappa \tag{1}$$

where u is the unemployment rate, $\bar{u}$ is the natural[2] unemployment rate, y is the GDP growth rate, κ is a random shock, $\bar{y}$ is the natural GDP growth rate and F is a function such that $\frac{\partial F(y-\bar{y})}{\partial(y-\bar{y})} < 0$.

Phillips Curve: The Phillips Curve, in its modern form, is an inverse relationship between expected inflation and unemployment. Strong empirical evidence across countries can be easily found [8]. The curve is stated as follows:

$$\pi = E_t[\pi] + H(u - \bar{u}) \tag{2}$$

where π is the inflation rate and ϵ is a stochastic variable. H is assumed to be a function such that $\frac{\partial H((u-\bar{u})}{\partial(u-\bar{u})} < 0$.

Liquidity Effects: Interest rates established by central banks impact a country's total production, albeit not immediately, but over time. Higher interest rates gradually decrease GDP growth, as empirically demonstrated by [6]. This relationship, the so-called liquidity effects, is shown below:

$$y_t = G^L(i) \equiv G(i_{t-d}, i_{t-d-1}, ..., i_L) \tag{3}$$

where i is the interest rate, d is an integer representing the distance of the first lag, L is the number of lags on i, and G is a function such that $\frac{\partial G(i)}{\partial i} < 0$.

2.3 Machine Learning Applied to Monetary Policy

Literature relating machine learning to monetary economics is rather scarce. Some recent applications can be found in [5,11]. The only study that is closely related to ours is [9], in which the authors proposed a new model for inflation targeting based on fuzzy control techniques. However, the fuzzy rules merely automate the Czech Central Bank's actual strategy, instead of pursuing a method for improving its performance.

---

[1] A country's total production of final goods and services.

[2] The word *natural* refers to the value of a given country's economic variable when production of goods and services is operating at full capacity, i.e. production would not increase with more resources.

3 Developing the Framework

The method we propose to minimise future inflation and unemployment consists of three steps. First, from three empirical relationships, we derive an objective function that depends on current and past interest rates (in Brazil, the SELIC rate[3]) through future inflation and future unemployment rates. Then the genetic algorithm generates potential solutions to the central bank's problem. Finally, using these potential solutions, a neural network predicts future inflation and unemployment rates. These two are necessary to evaluate the objective function for each potential solution and then pick the best among them. If the number of generations has reached a maximum, the procedure stops and the solution is considered to be the one for which the objective function value is the lowest. Otherwise, the genetic algorithm generates new potential solutions from the ones that were previously picked.

3.1 Overview

We now detail the procedure a little longer. For clarity, the whole process is illustrated in Fig. 1. The starting box (the upper pink one) states that there is an objective function $O(.)$ that we need to minimise by choosing an interest rate series $\{i_t\}_{t=1}^{T}$. We derived $O(.)$ from the three empirical relationships that were explained and justified in Sect. 2.2, and it has the following form:

$$O(.) = \sum_{t=1}^{T} R^t \cdot E_t[\pi_{t+17}] \cdot E_t[u_{t+17}] \cdot E_t[\pi_{t+34}] \cdot E_t[u_{t+34}] \tag{4}$$

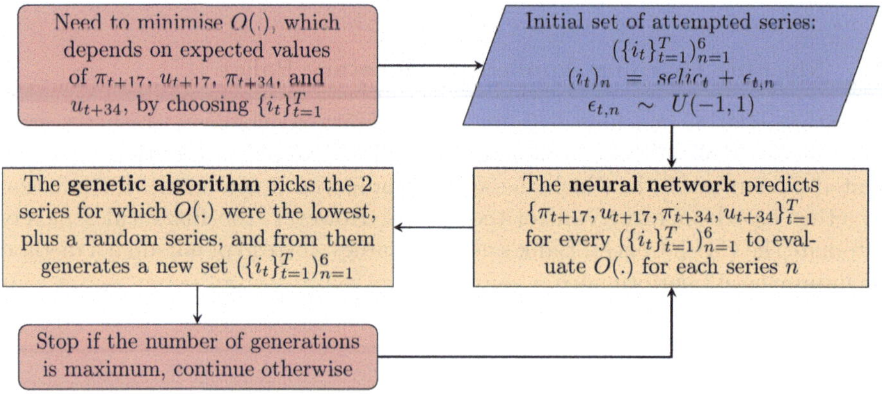

Fig. 1. Detailed overview of the framework

[3] From portuguese, *Sistema Especial de Liquidação e Custódia*, which stands for Special Clearance and Escrow System. It is the base interest rate in Brazil.

Hence our objective function is a discounted sum of Cobb-Douglas value functions[4] $V(.) = E_t[\pi_{t+17}] \cdot E_t[u_{t+17}] \cdot E_t[\pi_{t+34}] \cdot E_t[u_{t+34}]$ where the discount factor is $R \in [0, 1]$, i.e. inflation and unemployment have more weight in periods that are closer to the current one (since the central bank is more concerned about recent periods). The arguments of $V(.)$ are the expected inflation and unemployment seventeen weeks (four months) ahead, as well as inflation and unemployment thirty four weeks (eight months) ahead, and these four variables are actually functions of the interest rate at time t. This means that we need to minimise $O(.)$ by choosing a whole series $\{i_t\}_{t=1}^{T}$.

Any choice of how far is the future (in our notation, it means how big is d) is good as any other, so here we defined that $\pi = \pi_{t+17}$ and $u = u_{t+17}$[5], i.e. both inflation and unemployment four months ahead. Moreover, we add π_{t+34} and u_{t+34} to the value function with two purposes: (i) increase the precision of the estimates, and (ii) account for mid-term inflation and unemployment.

Since $O(.)$ is forward looking, we need to calculate expected values for future inflation and unemployment. We do so by using a neural network, specified in Sect. 3.4. As depicted in the blue box in Fig. 1, the neural network initially predicts values for six series: the original SELIC series and five other series generated from this series by adding a draw from a random uniform distribution to each of its elements, five different times. Afterwards, as shown by the loop in Fig. 1, the network is fed by the genetic algorithm, which generates a new set of six series in its attempt to minimise $O(.)$.

3.2 Data

Time series were all extracted from the Central Bank of Brazil (CBB) website, with the exception of unemployment. In this case, the National Continuous Household Sample Survey (PNADC[6]) was used. A complete list of these series, their frequencies and precise sources is shown in Table 1. Note that most series are originally monthly ones, but if we had kept this frequency, there would have been too few data points to train the neural network. Since there are also daily series, we decided to work with weekly data[7]. Values for monthly data were repeated for all weeks of a given month, while data for daily series were collapsed in weekly averages. As a result, we obtained 728 observations ($T \equiv 728$) per series, stretching from the 48th week of year 2001 to the 34th week of 2016.

[4] This family of functions, i.e. $z = x_1^{a1} \cdot x_2^{a2} \cdot \ldots \cdot x_n^{a_n}$, possesses a number of important properties which have made it widely useful in the analysis of economic theories.

[5] We tried several other horizons, but this one delivered the best results.

[6] From portuguese, *Pesquisa Nacional por Amostra de Domicílios Contínua*, which translates into Continuous National Household Sample Survey.

[7] Although real world unemployment and inflation vary weekly, for these variables we dispose only of aggregate data from the end of each month. Therefore, the best approximation for a week of a given month is the value reported for the end of that same month. Some available data is daily and can be used to enhance this approximation through a forecasting model, which is part of what we are doing here.

Table 1. Time series used in this study

Description	Frequency	Source
International reserves (US$ millions)	Daily	CBB
Net public sector debt (%GDP)	Monthly	CBB
Public sector borrowing requirements (%GDP)	Monthly	CBB
United States official interest rates (%p.y.)	Monthly	FED[a]
Net current account (US$ millions)	Monthly	CBB
Net capital account (US$ millions)	Monthly	CBB
Exchange rate US$	Daily	CBB
National consumer price index (in 12 months)	Monthly	IBGE[b]
SELIC target (%p.y.)	Daily	CBB
SELIC in annual terms (basis 252, %p.y.)	Daily	CBB
GDP accumulated in the last 12 months (current R$ millions)	Monthly	CBB
Unemployment rate (PNADC, chained backwards)	Monthly	IBGE/FGV[c]

[a] Federal Reserve System
[b] Brazilian Institute of Geography and Statistics
[c] Fundação Getulio Vargas

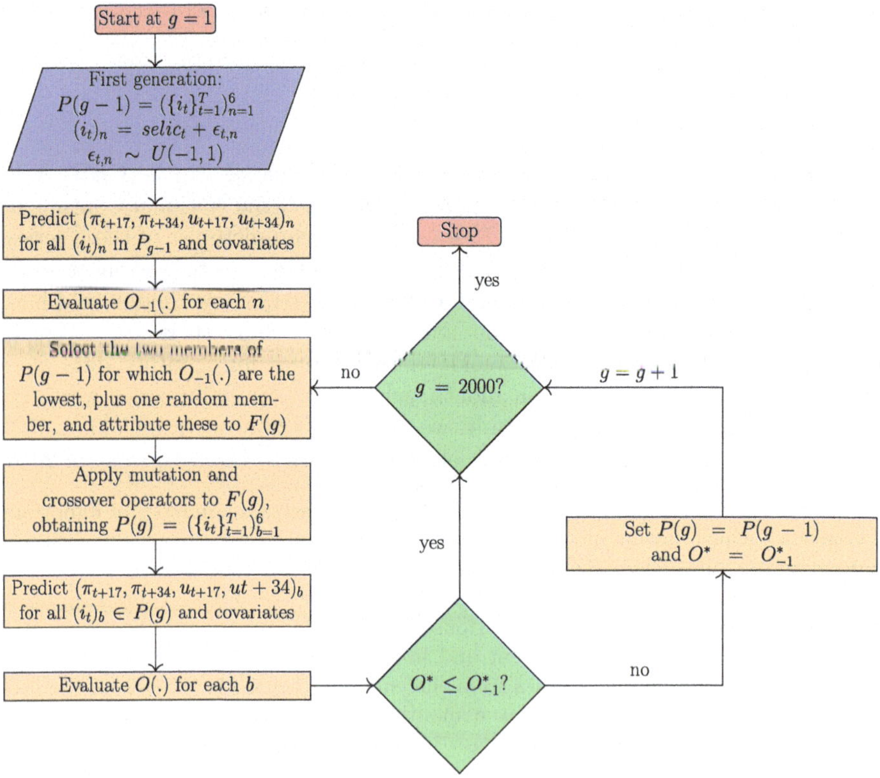

Fig. 2. Genetic algorithm flowchart

3.3 Genetic Algorithm

The algorithm we use to minimise Eq. 4 by choosing the whole SELIC time series is illustrated in Fig. 2 and works as follows. An individual (chromosome) is denoted by $\{i_t\}_{t=1}^{T}$. Naturally, a gene is considered to be an observation of the series. There are 728 observations for each series, but there is no need to find 728 values. In fact, the CBB chooses the SELIC every seven weeks so, since our data is weekly, an individual actually has $N \equiv T/7 = 728/7 = 104$ genes.

The first generation population, $P(g = 0)$, is composed of six individuals: the actual (original) SELIC rate and five other individuals generated from the actual SELIC series by adding an stochastic component, namely, a uniform random variable. We denote this set by $P(g = 0) = (\{i_t\}_{t=1}^{T})_{n=1}^{6}$, where $n \in [1, 6]$ indexes the individuals, so $(i_t)_n$ represents a gene t from individual n.

We then are able to evaluate the objective function $O(.)$ for each one of the six initial individuals. The weekly discount rate (parameter R in $O(.)$) we use is 0.0012. Thus, $(1 + R)^{52} \approx 6.5$, which is the mean annual SELIC interest rate over the period covered by the data. Using the base interest rate as a discount rate is standard in economic literature.

Next, we pick the two individuals for which $O(.)$ are the lowest and a random individual, the three survivors of the current generation. We apply crossover and mutation operations to these survivors to obtain six new individuals (by combining all possible pairs of survivors when crossing over), the candidate members of the new generation. If the lowest value $O^*(.)$ of the objective function among all members of the new generation is lower than the lowest value for the previous generation, $O^*_{-1}(.)$, we substitute the new generation for the old one. If not, we discard the new generation and apply the operators to the old one again, restarting the cycle. The algorithm stops after two thousand generations, the reason being explained in Sect. 4.2.

Crossover operation is standard: new individuals are generated from $N/2$ random genes from two parents, using a one-point cut in each chromosome (individual). As for mutation, a percentage of the total number of genes is randomly picked to be replaced by a random value. The percentage of mutated genes decays with generations: it starts at 7% and is reduced by a factor of 1.001 until it reaches the lower bound of 3%.

3.4 Neural Network Regression

Every week, the central bank will estimate future unemployment and inflation for each $i_t \in \{i_t\}_{t=1}^{T}$ for all attempted solutions, in order to evaluate the objective function 4, as part of the algorithm defined in Sect. 3.3. We use a multilayer perceptron (MLP) for this purpose.

The inputs of the MLP are seven lags of the following variables: unemployment rate, inflation rate, base interest rate (SELIC), effective interest rate[8], net government debt, government deficit, net current account, net capital account,

[8] This rate is slightly different from the SELIC, since it is determined by the market.

GDP, exchange rate with respect to US dollars, and United States official interest rate. Additionally, there are four outputs: unemployment in seventeen weeks (four months ahead), inflation in seventeen weeks, unemployment in thirty four weeks (eight months ahead), and inflation in thirty four weeks. All values are normalised to increase convergence speed.

The reason why we chose a window of size eight is that the CBB makes its decision about the base interest rate every seven weeks. Therefore, we assume it considers current variables as well as their values on each of the seven previous weeks. As for the variables themselves, they have long been established in economic literature to have predictive power over inflation and unemployment. We use a subset of variables that figure in the classical paper by James Stock and Mark Watson [12], which focus on forecasting inflation, and in a more recent work by Regis Barnichon and Paula Garda [3], about predicting unemployment.

4 Simulations

4.1 Neural Network's Predictions

We have tested a large range of parameters using a grid search to find the most appropriate configuration for the MLP. Choice was based on a 10-fold nested cross-validation procedure (also known as double cross validation), performed over 80% of randomly picked observations in our total sample, further split into random training (70% of the sub-sample) and validation (remaining 30% of the sub-sample) sets, both in external and internal loops. The other 20% of total observations have been used as a final testing set, again to avoid training bias.

The mean root mean square error (RMSE) over the 10 outer folds was of 0.104 and the best configuration turned out to be the following: (i) the activation function is the hyperbolic tangent (HTAN); (ii) there are four hidden layers with five neurons each; (iii) the solving method is the limited-memory Broyden–Fletcher–Goldfarb–Shanno (BFGS) algorithm. The RMSE of this network is of 0.095 for the training set and of 0.149 for the testing set, so the fact that the preferred configuration for the MLP does not suffer from overfitting seems warranted.

The other options for the activation function were the rectified linear unit function (RELU) and the logistic sigmoid function (LSIG), while the other possibilities for the solving method were the standard stochastic gradient descent (SGD) and the adaptive moment estimator (ADAM). The whole set of parameters used in the grid search are shown in Table 2.

4.2 Genetic Algorithm Evolution

Testing a range of parameters for the genetic algorithm was a challenge, since each battery of 1000 generations took approximately five hours[9] to run when the

[9] The machine in which we ran the algorithm has the following specifications: processor Intel(R) Core(TM) i7-4700MQ, CPU 2.40 GHz; memory 16 gb; operating system Ubuntu 18.04.2 LTS.

Table 2. Set of parameters used in the grid search

Parameter	Values
Number of neurons per hidden layer	3 to 5
Number of hidden layers	2 or 4
Solving algorithm	ADAM, SGD, or BFGS
Activation function	RELU, HTAN, or LSIG

least number of survivors per generation (2) was set. When we added one more survivor, the running time almost doubled: eight hours per 1000 generations. With four survivors per generation the running time got prohibitive and we simply interrupted the algorithm. A similar running time hike happened when we increased the initial population from six to greater numbers. The full set of tested values for parameters are presented in Table 3.

Table 3. Set of parameter values that were tested for the genetic algorithm. Preferred values are highlighted in blue.

Operator/Property	Parameter	Values
Mutation	Rate	0.03, 0.04, 0.06, 0.07, or [0.03, 0.07]
	Decay	1.001 or 1.0005
	Type	Random choice or random sum
Crossover	Type	One point
Survivors	Number	2, 3, or 4
Initial population	Number	6, 12, or 18

Other values were rejected on the basis of convergence speed. Fixed mutation rates reduced convergence speed, and the same was observed if the mutation rate was allowed to decrease from 7% to 3% at a rate of 1.0005, or if the mutation operator was adding to the chosen genes a random draw from a standard normal distribution (random sum) and not substituting random draws from a set of predetermined values for these genes (random choice).

Most of the evolution happened before 250 generations and convergence seems to have been achieved around the 1600th generation. We tested for 4000 generations and there were no significant changes, i.e. the best individual improved only by a few hundreds, but these 2000 extra generations had a large cost in terms of time (10 h, due to nested loops inside the crossover operator).

4.3 Results

We now evaluate our strategy's performance. First, we compare the original SELIC series with the one generated by the genetic algorithm (the best individual after 2000 generations). Both are depicted in Fig. 3. We can see that, according to the strategy, the SELIC rate should in general have been lower. This is specially true in the two extremes of the period covered by our model.

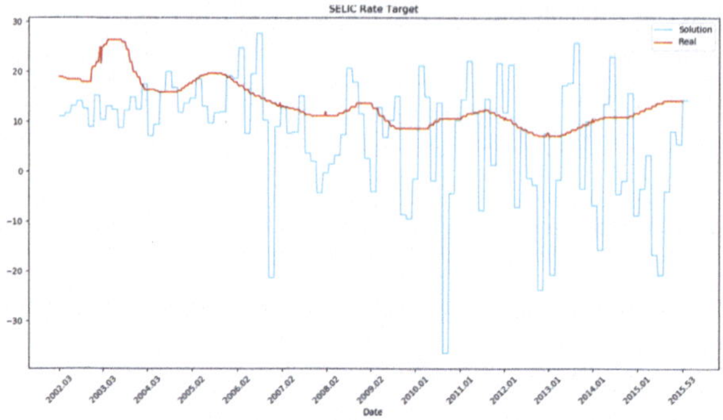

Fig. 3. SELIC target: actual series versus solution generated by the genetic algorithm

Moreover, it is clear that the generated SELIC series is significantly less persistent than the original series, albeit remaining in a shorter interval. Low persistence might pose a problem. According to several authors, for monetary policy to work, agents must be able to understand the central bank behaviour in order to adjust their expectations and make the decisions that, ultimately, policy-makers expect them to [7].

In agreement with this view, the central bank must have credibility and be able to commit to a certain smooth path for the target interest rate. If the SELIC frequently suffers large shocks, agents may not be able to believe in central bank's commitment, even if the institution anticipates these changes to the public. The policy would possibly be seen as discretionary, leading to negative effects on the economy. To avoid these possible deleterious effects, we smoothed the SELIC series, calculating its 12-month moving average (MA). As we note in Fig. 4, results now seem much less likely to cause the problems discussed above.

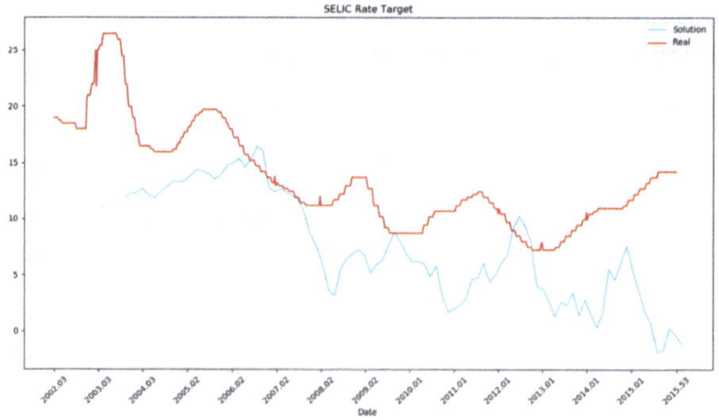

Fig. 4. SELIC target: actual series versus 12-month MA solution. First values were lost when calculating the MA.

We use the neural network to predict the values of unemployment and inflation for the MA version of our solution and compare it to actual inflation and unemployment. Inflation, for both horizons, was quite frequently lower when predicted by our solution as compared to what was observed under CBB actual policy decisions, while the same cannot be said about the unemployment rate. Table 4 summarises these results. On average, predicted inflation was lower than actual inflation for 62.48% of the time. Predicted unemployment, however, was lower only for 39.69% of weeks. This result might seem undesirable, but we need to stress, as we did in Sect. 2.2, that there is a trade-off between the expected inflation and the unemployment rate, so in fact we have achieved a reasonable outcome. It is possible, then, that the objective function has another minimum, where the predicted unemployment rate would be lower for most of the periods, as opposed to the predicted inflation.

Table 4. Descriptive statistics of genetic algorithm solution as compared to actual CBB solution

	Lower (%)	Relative volatility	Relative persistence
Inflation 4 mo	58.6	−0.07	−0.059
Unemployment 4 mo	45.27	−0.24	0.005
Inflation 8 mo	66.36	−0.08	−0.063
Unemployment 8 mo	34.11	−0.45	−0.009
SELIC	94.88	0.11	0.001

As a rule, predicted inflation and unemployment rate were less volatile than actual inflation and unemployment. This means that both variables remained bounded in a smaller interval, i.e. our strategy reduced the variance of both variables for the two horizons. This, of course, is a desirable feature of prospective inflation and unemployment, as it implies less uncertainty in the economy.

In spite of that, jumps were more frequent, with persistence, as estimated by AR(1) coefficient, being lower in all cases but the 4-months ahead unemployment and the SELIC. The MA version of the SELIC series generated by our strategy is, in its turn, lower than the actual SELIC for 94.88% of the time, which is a positive outcome in general, since lower interest rates is commonly associated with higher economic growth. In addition, using the same criteria as before, the MA of the SELIC series found by our algorithm is relatively more volatile, albeit almost as persistent as the CBB SELIC, meaning that we achieved our goal overall.

5 Conclusion

This paper presented in detail a novel tool to back the decision-making process of central banks. Our framework was based on well-established empirical evidence.

The first step was to obtain an objective function for the central bank, which we derived from three empirical relationships: Okun's Law, the Phillips Curve, and liquidity effects. Then we designed a genetic algorithm to minimise this objective function by choosing a time series of interest rates. Since the function is forward looking, we used a tuned multilayer perceptron to predict future values of unemployment and inflation.

The best individual was less persistent than the actual series set by the CBB. Thus we smoothed the series to avoid unfavourable economic results that could stem from low persistence. Compared to the original SELIC rate series, our solution was shown to be less volatile and lower 94.88% of the time, which is most likely positive from an economic standpoint. Besides, it implied lower values for inflation 62.48% of covered periods. Predicted unemployment, however, was lower only at 39.69% of the time, as it faces a trade-off with inflation.

References

1. Akerlof, G.A.: The missing motivation in macroeconomics. Am. Econ. Rev. **97**(1), 5–36 (2007)
2. Ball, L. et al.: Does one law fit all? Cross-country evidence on Okun's Law. In: documento presentado en el IMF-OCP Workshop on Global Labour Markets, Paris, vol. 1 (2016)
3. Barnichon, R., Garda, P.: Forecasting unemployment across countries: the ins and outs. Eur. Econ. Rev. **84**, 165–183 (2016)
4. Blanchard, O.: On the future of macroeconomic models. Oxford Rev. Econ. Policy **34**(1–2), 43–54 (2018)
5. Chakraborty, C., Joseph, A.: Machine learning at central banks. Bank of England working papers 674. Bank of England, September 2017
6. Christiano, L.J., Eichenbaum, M.: Liquidity effects, monetary policy, and the business cycle. J. Money Credit Bank. **27**(4), 1113–1136 (1995)
7. Clarida, R., Gali, J., Gertler, M.: The science of monetary policy: a new Keynesian perspective. J. Econ. Lit. **37**(4), 1661–1707 (1999)
8. Coibion, O., Gorodnichenko, Y., Ulate, M.: Is Inflation just around the corner? The Phillips curve and global inflationary pressures. In: AEA Papers and Proceedings, vol. 109, pp. 465–469 (2019)
9. Kukal, J., Van Quang, T.: A monetary policy rule based on fuzzy control in an inflation targeting framework. Prague Econ. Pap. **23**, 290–314 (2014)
10. Romer, P.: The trouble with macroeconomics. New York University, Technical report, Stern School of Business (2016)
11. Röonnqvist, S., Sarlin, P.: Bank distress in the news: describing events through deep learning. Neurocomputing **264**, 57–70 (2017)
12. Stock, J.H., Watson, M.W.: Forecasting inflation. J. Monet. Econ. **44**(2), 293–335 (1999)

Author Index

L. Iliadis et al. (Eds.): EANN 2020, INNS 2, pp. 617–619, 2020.
https://doi.org/10.1007/978-3-030-48791-1

The manufacturer's authorised representative in the EU is Springer Nature Customer Service Centre GmbH, Europaplatz 3, 69115 Heidelberg, Germany. If you have any concerns regarding our products, please contact ProductSafety@springernature.com

Printed and bound by CPI Group (UK) Ltd, Croydon, CR0 4YY
05/10/2026
02228122-0019